CENSUS OF INDIA 1911

CENSUS OF INDIA, 1911

VOLUME - I

INDIA

PART II - TABLES

E. A. GAIT

GYAN

Published by

Gyan Publishing House
5, Ansari Road
Daryaganj, New Delhi-110002
Phone: 011-47034999, 9811692060
E-mail: books@gyanbooks.com

Distribution Network
gyanbooks.com
India, USA, Canada, UK, Australia

ISBN: 978-81-212-7127-1 (Set) 23 Vols. In 41 Bindings

ISBN: 978-81-212-7505-7 (PB) Vol. I, Pt. II

First Published, 1913

2nd Impression 2024

Printed at: Gyan Press, Delhi.

CENSUS OF INDIA 1911

CENSUS OF INDIA, 1911
Volume I

INDIA

Part II.—TABLES

AGENTS FOR THE SALE OF BOOKS

PUBLISHED BY THE

Superintendent of Government Printing, India, Calcutta.

IN THE UNITED KINGDOM.

Bernard Quaritch, 11, Grafton Street, New Bond Street, London, W.

Constable & Co., 10, Orange St., Leicester Square, London, W.C.

H. S. King & Co., 65, Cornhill, and 9, Pall Mall, London.

P. S. King & Son, 2 & 4, Great Smith St., Westminster, London, S.W.

Kegan Paul, Trench, Trubner & Co., 68—74, Carter Lane, E.C.

Grindlay & Co., 54, Parliament Street, London, S.W.

T. Fisher Unwin, 1, Adelphi Terrace, London, W.C.

W. Thacker & Co., 2, Creed Lane, London, E.C.

Luzac & Co., 46, Great Russell Street, London, W.C.

Deighton, Bell & Co., Cambridge.

B. H. Blackwell, 50 and 51, Broad Street, Oxford.

Oliver & Boyd, Tweeddale Court, Edinburgh.

E. Ponsonby, Ld., 116, Grafton Street, Dublin.

ON THE CONTINENT.

R. Friedlander & Sohn, Berlin W. N. Carlstrasse, 11.

Otto Harrassowitz, Leipzig, Germany.

Karl W. Hiersemann, Leipzig, Germany.

Martinus Nijhoff, The Hague, Holland.

Ernest Leroux, 28, Rue Bonaparte, Paris, France.

IN INDIA AND CEYLON.

Thacker, Spink & Co., Calcutta and Simla.

Newman & Co., Calcutta.

R. Cambray & Co., Calcutta.

S. K. Lahiri & Co., Calcutta.

B. Banerjee & Co., Calcutta.

Rai M. C. Sircar Bahadur & Sons, 75-1-1, Harrison Road, Calcutta.

The Calcutta School Book and Useful Literature Society, 309, Bowbazar Street, Calcutta.

Butterworth & Co. (India), Ld., Calcutta.

The Weldon Library, 18—5, Chowringhee, Calcutta.

Thacker & Co., Ld., Bombay.

A. J. Combridge & Co., Bombay.

D. B. Taraporevala, Sons & Co., Bombay.

Gopal Narayan & Co., Bombay.

Radhabai Atmaram Sagoon, Bombay.

Sundar Pandurang, Bombay.

Ram Chandra Govind & Son, Bombay.

V. Kalyanarama Iyer & Co., Madras.

G. A. Natesan & Co., Madras.

Higginbotham & Co., Madras.

S. Murthy & Co., Madras.

Thompson & Co., Madras.

Temple & Co., Madras.

Combridge & Co., Madras.

P. R. Rama Iyer & Co., Madras.

N. B. Mathur, Superintendent, Nazir Kanun Hind Press, Allahabad.

Superintendent, American Baptist Mission Press, Rangoon.

A. Chand & Co., Lahore.

Rai Sahib M. Gulab Singh and Sons, Mufid-i-Am Press, Lahore and Calcutta.

Babu S. C. Talukdar, Proprietor, Students & Co., Cooch Behar.

A. M. and J. Ferguson, Colombo, Ceylon.

CENSUS OF INDIA, 1911
VOLUME I

INDIA

PART II.—TABLES

BY

E. A. GAIT, C.S.I., C.I.E., I.C.S.,
FELLOW OF THE ROYAL STATISTICAL SOCIETY

CALCUTTA
SUPERINTENDENT GOVERNMENT PRINTING, INDIA
1913

CONTENTS.

IMPERIAL TABLES.

SPECIAL TABLES FOR CITIES.

LIST OF ERRATA.

Page 120, against total under Sikkim State, *for* 4,286 *read* 42,861.

Page 125, second row, column 4 against New Zealand, under Born in Australasia, *for* 3 *read* 43.

Page 171, column 1, under Bihar and Orissa, *for* Teli and Til *read* Teli and Tili.

Page 253, column 26, under United Provinces of Agra and Oudh, *for* SHAKH *read* SHEIKH.

Page 314, columns 458 and 459 against serial number 14, *for* 9 and 1,59 ,085 *read* 1,779 and 1,591,085 respectively.

TABLE I.—Area, Houses

Province, State or Agency.	Area in square miles.	Towns.	Villages.	Occupied Houses. Total.	Occupied Houses. In towns.	Occupied Houses. In villages.
1	2	3	4	5	6	7
INDIA.	**1,802,657**	**2,153**	**720,342**	**63,710,179**	**6,037,456**	**57,672,723**
Provinces.	**1,093,074**	**1,452**	**537,357**	**49,140,947**	**4,409,121**	**44,731,826**
1. Ajmer-Merwara	2,711	5	743	122,832	37,712	85,120
2. Andamans and Nicobars	3,143	...	224	3,669	...	3,669
3. Assam	53,015	20	27,875	1,468,429	30,457	1,437,972
4. Baluchistan	54,228	6	1,564	84,689	12,671	72,018
5. Bengal	78,699	119	119,732	8,631,502	546,551	8,084,951
6. Bihar and Orissa	83,181	70	87,675	6,660,315	265,521	6,394,794
Bihar	*42,361*	*48*	*47,249*	*4,558,481*	*200,239*	*4,358,242*
Orissa	*13,743*	*8*	*15,667*	*1,051,496*	*38,098*	*1,013,398*
Chota Nagpur	*27,077*	*14*	*24,759*	*1,050,338*	*27,184*	*1,023,154*
7. Bombay (*Presidency*)	123,059	200	26,056	3,890,927	602,876	3,288,051
Bombay	*75,993*	*172*	*21,087*	*3,211,050*	*500,882*	*2,710,168*
Sind	*46,986*	*25*	*4,969*	*674,400*	*96,517*	*577,883*
Aden	*80*	*3*	...	*5,477*	*5,477*	...
8. Burma	230,839	63	37,678	2,471,597	212,869	2,258,728
9. Central Provinces and Berar	99,823	112	39,005	2,858,302	260,151	2,598,151
Central Provinces	*82,057*	*65*	*33,156*	*2,203,068*	*177,602*	*2,025,466*
Berar	*17,766*	*47*	*5,849*	*655,234*	*82,549*	*572,685*
10. Coorg	1,582	2	498	33,747	2,185	31,562
11. Madras	142,330	279	53,835	7,829,410	856,114	6,973,296
12. North-West Frontier Province (*Districts and Administered Territories*)	13,418	19	3,033	435,161	57,471	377,690
13. Punjab	99,779	139	33,421	4,454,236	467,731	3,986,505
14. United Provinces of Agra and Oudh	107,267	418	106,023	10,196,131	1,056,812	9,139,319
Agra	*83,109*	*344*	*81,706*	*7,469,203*	*863,459*	*6,605,744*
Oudh	*24,158*	*74*	*24,317*	*2,726,928*	*193,353*	*2,533,575*
States and Agencies.	**709,583**	**701**	**182,985**	**14,569,232**	**1,628,335**	**12,940,897**
15. Assam State (Manipur)	8,456	1	1,477	69,491	15,322	54,169
16. Baluchistan States	80,410	3	2,120	83,978	2,235	81,743
17. Baroda State	8,182	41	3,054	506,297	112,678	393,619
18. Bengal States	5,393	5	3,513	158,446	5,137	153,309
19. Bihar and Orissa States	28,648	6	20,274	781,889	8,814	773,075
20. Bombay States	63,864	132	14,619	1,625,667	272,747	1,352,920
21. Central India Agency	77,367	77	33,023	2,039,955	210,991	1,828,964
22. Central Provinces States	31,174	5	8,663	388,571	8,580	379,991
23. Hyderabad State	82,698	85	20,151	2,713,845	291,441	2,422,404
24. Kashmir State	84,432	61	8,865	553,124	61,886	491,238
25. Madras States	10,549	21	4,736	913,519	61,008	852,511
26. Mysore State	29,475	91	16,740	1,158,004	133,850	1,024,154
27. N.-W. F. Province (*Agencies and Tribal areas*)	25,500	...	...	...	...	...
28. Punjab States	36,551	35	10,979	950,779	84,409	866,370
29. Rajputana Agency	128,987	133	32,271	2,438,346	337,125	2,101,221
30. Sikkim State	2,818	...	315	16,733	...	16,733
31. United Provinces States	5,079	5	2,185	170,588	22,112	148,476

AND POPULATION.

POPULATION.									Serial No.
PERSONS.			MALES.			FEMALES.			
Total.	Urban.	Rural.	Total.	Urban.	Rural.	Total.	Urban.	Rural.	
8	9	10	11	12	13	14	15	16	
315,156,396	**29,748,228**	**285,408,168**	**161,338,935**	**16,108,304**	**145,230,631**	**153,817,461**	**13,639,924**	**140,177,537**	
244,267,542	22,817,715	221,449,827	124,873,691	12,525,830	112,347,861	119,393,851	10,291,885	109,101,966	
501,395	140,394	361,001	266,198	77,177	189,021	235,197	63,217	171,980	1
26,459	...	26,459	19,570	...	19,570	6,889	...	6,889	2
6,713,635	136,668	6,576,967	3,467,621	83,500	3,384,121	3,246,014	53,168	3,192,846	3
414,412	49,609	364,803	239,181	37,660	201,521	175,231	11,949	163,282	4
45,483,077	2,945,622	42,537,455	23,365,225	1,805,560	21,559,665	22,117,852	1,140,062	20,977,790	5
34,490,084	1,285,752	33,204,332	16,859,929	666,006	16,193,923	17,630,155	619,746	17,010,409	6
23,752,969	*963,217*	*22,789,752*	*11,606,482*	*496,889*	*11,109,548*	*12,146,587*	*466,328*	*11,680,209*	
5,131,753	*177,178*	*4,954,575*	*2,476,284*	*93,397*	*2,382,887*	*2,655,469*	*83,781*	*2,571,688*	
5,605,862	*145,857*	*5,460,005*	*2,777,213*	*75,720*	*2,701,493*	*2,828,149*	*69,637*	*2,758,512*	
19,672,642	3,738,571	15,934,071	10,245,847	2,094,891	8,150,956	9,426,795	1,643,680	7,783,115	7
16,113,042	*3,240,500*	*12,872,542*	*8,275,233*	*1,808,520*	*6,466,713*	*7,837,809*	*1,431,980*	*6,405,829*	
3,513,435	*451,906*	*3,061,529*	*1,939,324*	*255,081*	*1,684,248*	*1,574,111*	*196,825*	*1,377,286*	
46,165	*46,165*	...	*31,290*	*31,290*	...	*14,875*	*14,875*	...	
12,115,217	1,127,975	10,987,242	6,183,494	680,760	5,502,734	5,931,723	447,215	5,484,508	8
13,916,308	1,176,225	12,740,083	6,930,392	610,417	6,319,975	6,985,916	565,808	6,420,108	9
10,859,146	*806,431*	*10,052,715*	*5,379,778*	*418,090*	*4,961,658*	*5,479,368*	*388,341*	*5,091,027*	
3,057,162	*369,794*	*2,687,368*	*1,550,614*	*192,327*	*1,358,287*	*1,506,548*	*177,467*	*1,329,081*	
174,976	9,981	164,995	97,279	5,897	91,382	77,697	4,084	73,613	10
41,405,404	4,892,626	36,512,778	20,382,955	2,413,517	17,969,438	21,022,449	2,479,109	18,543,340	11
2,196,933	291,714	1,905,219	1,182,102	179,449	1,002,653	1,014,831	112,265	902,566	12
19,974,956	2,211,964	17,762,992	10,992,067	1,273,147	9,718,920	8,982,889	938,817	8,044,072	[illegible]
47,182,044	4,810,614	42,371,430	24,641,831	2,597,849	22,043,982	22,540,213	2,212,765	20,327,448	
34,624,040	*3,967,520*	*30,656,520*	*18,157,131*	*2,142,613*	*16,014,518*	*16,466,909*	*1,824,907*	*14,642,002*	
12,558,004	*843,094*	*11,714,910*	*6,484,700*	*455,236*	*6,029,464*	*6,073,304*	*387,858*	*5,685,446*	
70,888,854	6,930,513	63,958,341	36,465,244	3,582,474	32,882,770	34,423,610	3,348,039	31,075,571	
346,222	74,650	271,572	170,666	36,393	134,273	175,556	38,257	137,299	15
420,291	9,950	410,341	227,238	5,368	221,870	193,053	4,582	188,471	16
2,032,798	405,017	1,627,781	1,053,935	209,455	846,480	976,863	195,562	781,301	17
822,565	22,625	799,940	438,368	14,505	423,863	384,197	8,120	376,077	18
3,945,209	37,201	3,906,008	1,955,125	18,697	1,936,428	1,990,084	18,504	1,971,580	19
7,411,675	1,166,657	6,245,018	3,765,401	584,387	3,181,014	3,646,274	582,270	3,064,004	20
9,356,980	786,114	8,570,866	4,801,459	412,859	4,388,600	4,555,521	373,255	4,182,266	21
2,117,002	36,824	2,080,178	1,053,630	17,958	1,035,672	1,063,372	18,866	1,044,506	22
13,374,676	1,295,305	12,079,371	6,797,118	660,940	6,136,178	6,577,558	634,365	5,943,193	23
3,158,126	300,879	2,857,247	1,674,367	167,028	1,507,339	1,483,759	133,851	1,349,908	24
4,811,841	348,892	4,462,949	2,411,758	178,012	2,233,746	2,400,083	170,880	2,229,203	25
5,806,193	658,329	5,147,864	2,934,621	338,996	2,595,625	2,871,572	319,333	2,552,239	26
1,622,094	...	1,622,094	864,876	...	864,876	757,218	...	757,218	27
4,212,794	355,318	3,857,476	2,322,908	202,166	2,120,742	1,889,886	153,152	1,736,734	28
10,530,432	1,343,095	9,187,337	5,515,275	688,936	4,826,339	5,015,157	654,159	4,360,998	29
87,920	...	87,920	45,059	...	45,059	42,861	...	42,861	30
832,036	89,657	742,379	481,440	46,774	384,666	400,596	42,883	357,718	31

DETAILS FOR PRINCIPAL STATES IN AGENCIES AND PROVINCIAL GROUPS.

Name of State and Province.	Area in square miles.	Towns and villages.	Occupied houses.	Population. Persons.	Males.	Females.
1	2	3	4	5	6	7
BALUCHISTAN STATES—						
Kalat	73,278	1,826	71,387	359,086	194,598	164,488
BENGAL STATES—						
Cooch Behar	1,307	1,201	113,801	592,952	316,548	276,404
BIHAR AND ORISSA STATES—						
Mayurbhanj	4,243	3,850	135,606	729,218	362,570	366,648
BOMBAY STATES—						
Cutch	7,616	948	125,044	513,429	252,453	260,976
Kathiawar	20,911	4,269	463,947	2,496,057	1,271,497	1,224,560
Kolhapur	3,217	1,069	179,181	833,441	424,435	409,006
Mahikantha Agency	3,124	1,853	107,264	412,631	208,922	203,709
Palanpur Agency	6,393	1,199	121,165	515,092	267,099	247,093
Rewakantha Agency	4,936	2,543	137,311	665,099	340,376	324,723
Southern Maratha Jagirs	3,036	615	121,740	616,139	313,500	305,639
CENTRAL INDIA AGENCY—						
Bhopal	6,902	2,991	168,629	730,383	370,560	359,823
Gwalior	25,133	10,404	661,339	3,102,279	1,630,327	1,471,952
Indore	9,506	3,736	236,061	1,007,856	517,501	490,355
Orchha	2,079	764	73,322	330,032	168,633	161,399
Rewah	13,000	5,407	304,839	1,514,843	752,297	762,546
CENTRAL PROVINCES STATES—						
Bastar	13,062	2,475	75,616	433,310	218,015	215,295
Surguja	6,055	1,598	76,567	428,703	217,749	210,954
MADRAS STATES—						
Cochin	1,361	282	163,296	918,110	457,342	460,768
Pudukkottai	1,178	432	76,573	411,886	196,566	215,320
Travancore	7,594	3,966	663,153	3,428,975	1,731,363	1,697,612
PUNJAB STATES—						
Bahawalpur	15,000	1,010	163,939	780,641	430,254	350,387
Patiala	5,412	3,524	335,531	1,407,659	792,540	615,119
RAJPUTANA AGENCY—						
Alwar	3,141	1,772	176,494	791,688	413,659	378,029
Bikaner	23,315	2,186	152,773	700,983	371,489	329,494
Bharatpur	1,982	1,292	134,268	558,785	302,254	256,531
Jaipur	15,579	5,803	598,333	2,636,647	1,385,750	1,250,897
Kotah	5,684	2,558	157,136	639,089	330,324	308,765
Marwar	34,963	4,093	461,303	2,057,553	1,075,269	982,284
Mewar	12,756	7,306	322,140	1,293,776	670,750	623,026
Tonk	2,553	1,278	71,548	303,181	156,390	146,791
UNITED PROVINCES STATES—						
Rampur	899	1,003	125,062	531,217	282,978	248,239
Tehri-Garhwal	4,180	1,187	45,506	300,819	148,462	152,357

AREAS UNDER BRITISH ADMINISTRATION IN CERTAIN NATIVE STATES.

Tract.	Area in square miles.	Population. Persons.	Males.	Females.
1	2	3	4	5
Total	**71·43**	**343,519**	**186,079**	**157,440**
Central India	31·84	86,712	49,400	37,312
Cantonments and Military Stations — *Mhow Cantonment*	*6·00*	*29,820*	*17,723*	*12,097*
Nimach „	*4·00*	*12,318*	*6,741*	*5,577*
Nowgong „	*7·50*	*9,421*	*5,454*	*3,967*
Agar Station	*1·00*	*3,487*	*1,981*	*1,506*
Guna „	*2·00*	*5,099*	*2,768*	*2,331*
Sehore „	*2·00*	*7,741*	*4,156*	*3,585*
Civil Stations — *Manpur (British Pargana)*	*6·70*	*6,609*	*3,445*	*3,164*
Other areas	*2·64*	*12,217*	*7,132*	*5,085*
Mysore (Civil and Military Station, Bangalore)	13·54	100,834	51,752	49,082
Baroda (Baroda Cantonment)	1·00	3,478	2,274	1,204
Hyderabad	21·23	143,414	76,958	66,456
Residency Bazars	*·53*	*17,971*	*9,504*	*8,467*
Secunderabad, including Bolarum Cantonment	*17·17*	*113,490*	*60,755*	*52,735*
Aurangabad Cantonment	*3·53*	*11,953*	*6,699*	*5,254*
Rajputana	3·82	9,081	5,095	3,986
Mewar — *Kherwara Cantonment*	*1·00*	*2,016*	*1,295*	*721*
Kotra „	*1·00*	*746*	*461*	*285*
Sirohi — *Erinpura Cantonment*	*1·00*	*3,033*	*1,856*	*1,177*
Mount Abu	*·59*	*3,286*	*2,083*	*1,203*

Note.—The district of Anjengo which forms an enclave of the Travancore State has been omitted from this statement as it is administered as part of the Madras Presidency and its statistics are included in the Census Tables of that Province.

TABLE II.

Variation in Population since 1872.

1. The population returned at previous censuses has been corrected, as far as possible, in order to allow for subsequent interprovincial transfers. Manipur, which was treated as British territory in 1901, has now been entered under the head States and Agencies. The tribal areas in the North-West Frontier Province have also been shown under the latter head. Sikkim, which in 1901 was classed under Bengal States, is now shown separately. In four cases the figures differ from those now given in the local reports—the Kashmir Superintendent has included in his figures for 1891 the present population of the Frontier Ilaqas which were not then enumerated; in Burma, though the total population of 1891 agrees, there is a small discrepancy in the details by sex, due to the adjustments made locally to allow for internal changes of jurisdiction; in the North-West Frontier Province a discrepancy of ten occurs in the sex details of the 1881 population; and the Rajputana Table includes 167,850 persons enumerated in 1881 in three parganas of the Tonk State who were omitted from the Imperial Tables for that census. These parganas are here treated as enumerated for the first time in 1891, *vide* paragraph 3 below.

2. In some cases the figures entered for 1872 refer to censuses taken in other years, *viz.*, Ajmer-Merwara 1876; Berar, 1867; Coorg, Madras and Mysore, 1871; Punjab, 1868; Oudh, 1869; Cochin and Travancore, 1875.

3. The areas newly enumerated at each census with their population are noted below:—

1911. Unadministered area (the Sema and eastern Angami villages) in the Naga Hills (39,586), in Assam; Makran (71,942), Western Sinjrani country (1,620) and Kharan (22,663) in Baluchistan; Unadministered area in Pakokku Hill Tracts (9,123), West Manglun (18,562) and Kokang (25,604) in Burma; Agencies and Tribal areas, except Malakand, Kurram and Shirani country, (1,604,265) in the North-West Frontier Province.
Total 1,793,365.

1901. Native Tribes (8,393) in the Andamans; South Lushai (26,129) and Manipur (284,465) in Assam; Baluchistan, except Makran, Western Sinjrani country and Kharan, (810,746); Shan States and part of Upper Burma (1,237,749); Malakand (Dir, Swat and Chitral) 8,128, Kurram (54,257) and Shirani country (12,371) in the North-West Frontier Province; the Bhils of Mewar, Kushalgarh and Dungarpur and the Grassias of Sirohi (estimated at 229,839) in Rajputana. *Total 2,672,077.*

1891. North Lushai (43,634) in Assam; Upper Burma, excluding Shan States, (2,946,933); Burma Frontier population (116,493); Biloch Trans-Frontier area (5,934) in the Punjab; Kashmir (2,543,952); Chhabra, Pirawa and Sironj parganas (181,135) of the Tonk State, detached districts of Nandwas and Gangapur situated in Mewar (18,118), and the Bhils of Banswara and Partabgarh (estimated at 48,315) in Rajputana; Sikkim (30,458). *Deduct* population in 1881 of the Manipur State (221,070). The schedules of the 1891 census were destroyed in the disturbances which took place in March 1891 before the results had been tabulated. *Net Total 5,713,902.*

1881. Convict Settlement of Port Blair (14,628); Manipur (221,070) in Assam; Central India Agency (9,261,907); Hyderabad State (9,845,594); Punjab States (3,861,683); Rajputana Agency (9,934,199). *Total 33,139,081.*

4. On pages 9 and 10 details are given of the variation in the population of certain States which are not shown separately in the body of the Table.

5. The figures for Madras States include those for Cochin and Travancore, which are given separately on page 10.

TABLE II—VARIATION IN

PROVINCE, STATE OR AGENCY.	PERSONS.					
	1911.	1901.	1891.	1881.	1872.	1911.
1	2	3	4	5	6	7
INDIA . . .	**315,156,396**	**294,361,056**	**287,314,671**	**253,896,330**	**206,162,360**	**161,338,935**
Provinces . . .	**244,267.542**	**231,605,940**	**221,240,836**	**198,882,817**	**185,163,435**	**124,873,691**
1. Ajmer-Merwara . . .	501,395	476,912	542,358	460,722	396,331	266,198
2. Andamans and Nicobars . .	26,459	24,649	15,609	14,628	...	19,570
3. Assam	6,713,635	5,841,878	5,477,302	4,907,792	4,150,769	3,467,621
4. Baluchistan	414,412	382,106	...	...	...	239,181
5. Bengal	45,483,077	42,141,477	39,089,632	36,316,728	34,119,465	23,365,225
6. Bihar and Orissa . . .	34,490,084	33,242,783	32,876,557	30,988,320	26,486,482	16,859,929
Bihar	*23,752,969*	*23,360,212*	*23,581,538*	*22,418,367*	*19,735,627*	*11,606,432*
Orissa	*5,131,753*	*4,982,142*	*4,666,227*	*4,343,964*	*3,603,156*	*2,476,284*
Chota Nagpur	*5,605,362*	*4,900,429*	*4,628,792*	*4,225,989*	*3,147,699*	*2,777,213*
7. Bombay (*Presidency*) . .	19,672,642	18,559,650	18,878,471	16,494,538	16,301,362	10,245,847
Bombay	*16,113,042*	*15,304,766*	*15,959,292*	*14,042,621*	*14,075,508*	*8,275,233*
Sind	*3,513,435*	*3,210,910*	*2,875,100*	*2,417,057*	*2,206,565*	*1,939,324*
Aden	*46,165*	*43,974*	*44,079*	*34,860*	*19,289*	*31,290*
8. Burma	12,115,217	10,490,624	7,722,053	3,736,771	2,747,148	6,183,494
9. Central Provinces and Berar .	13,916,308	11,971,452	13,048,972	11,943,363	9,951,268	6,930,392
Central Provinces . .	*10,859,146*	*9,217,436*	*10,151,481*	*9,270,690*	*7,723,614*	*5,379,778*
Berar	*3,057,162*	*2,754,016*	*2,897,491*	*2,672,673*	*2,227,654*	*1,550,614*
10. Coorg	174,976	180,607	173,055	178,302	168,312	97,279
11. Madras	41,405,404	38,229,654	35,644,428	30,841,154	31,280,622	20,382,955
12. North-West Frontier Province (*Districts and Administered Territories*).	2,196,933	2,041,534	1,857,519	1,575,943	} 17,609,672	1,182,102
13. Punjab	19,974,956	20,330,337	19,009,368	17,274,597		10,992,067
14. United Provinces of Agra and Oudh	47,182,044	47,692,277	46,905,512	44,149,959	42,002,004	21,641,831
Agra	*34,624,040*	*34,859,109*	*34,254,588*	*32,762,127*	*30,780,961*	*18,157,131*
Oudh	*12,558,004*	*12,833,168*	*12,650,924*	*11,387,832*	*11,221,043*	*6,484,700*
States and Agencies .	**70,888,854**	**62,755,116**	**66,073,835**	**55,013,513**	**20,998,925**	**36,465,244**
15. Assam State (Manipur) . .	346,222	284,465	...	221,070	...	170,666
16. Baluchistan States . . .	420,291	428,640	...	...	...	227,238
17. Baroda State	2,032,798	1,952,692	2,415,396	2,182,158	1,997,598	1,055,935
18. Bengal States	822,565	740,299	716,310	698,261	567,827	438,368
19. Bihar and Orissa States . .	3,945,209	3,314,474	3,028,018	2,410,611	1,728,900	1,955,125
20. Bombay States	7,411,675	6,908,559	8,061,950	6,937,893	6,797,970	3,765,401
21. Central India Agency . .	9,356,980	8,497,805	10,136,408	9,261,907	...	4,801,459
22. Central Provinces States . .	2,117,002	1,631,140	1,712,562	1,387,294	928,116	1,053,630
23. Hyderabad State . . .	13,374,676	11,141,142	11,537,040	9,845,594	...	6,797,118
24. Kashmir State	3,158,126	2,905,578	2,543,952	...	...	1,674,367
25. Madras States	4,811,841	4,188,086	3,700,622	3,344,849	3,289,392	2,411,758
26. Mysore State . . .	5,806,193	5,539,399	4,943,604	4,186,188	5,055,402	2,934,621
27. N.-W. F. Province (*Agencies and Tribal areas*).	1,622,094	83,962	...	...	...	864,876
28. Punjab States	4,212,794	4,424,398	4,263,280	3,861,683	...	2,322,908
29. Rajputana Agency . . .	10,530,432	9,853,366	12,171,749	9,984,255	...	5,515,275
30. Sikkim State	87,920	59,014	30,458	...	...	45,059
31. United Provinces States .	832,036	802,097	792,491	741,750	638,720	431,440

Population since 1872.

Males.				Females.					Serial No.
1901.	1891.	1881.	1872.	1911.	1901.	1891.	1881.	1872.	
8	9	10	11	12	13	14	15	16	
149,951,824	**146,769,629**	**129,949,290**	**106,055,545**	**153,817,461**	**144,409,232**	**140,545,042**	**123,947,040**	**100,106,815**	
117,653,127	112,574,217	101,839,222	95,297,739	119,393,851	113,952,813	108,666,619	97,543,595	89,865,696	
251,026	288,325	248,844	212,265	235,197	225,886	254,033	211,878	184,066	1
18,695	13,375	12,640	...	6,889	5,954	2,234	1,988	...	2
3,004,060	2,819,936	2,516,885	2,133,774	3,246,014	2,887,818	2,657,366	2,390,907	2,016,995	3
219,523	...	...	...	175,231	162,583	...	...	...	4
21,488,265	19,797,757	18,204,014	17,112,208	22,117,852	20,653,212	19,291,875	18,112,714	17,007,257	5
16,202,658	16,074,525	15,277,614	13,169,462	17,630,155	17,040,125	16,802,032	15,710,706	13,317,020	6
11,363,784	*11,505,657*	*11,039,721*	*9,797,483*	*12,146,537*	*11,996,428*	*12,075,881*	*11,378,646*	*9,938,144*	
2,429,608	*2,291,095*	*2,144,324*	*1,780,730*	*2,655,469*	*2,552,534*	*2,375,132*	*2,199,640*	*1,822,426*	
2,409,266	*2,277,773*	*2,093,569*	*1,591,249*	*2,828,149*	*2,491,163*	*2,351,019*	*2,132,420*	*1,556,450*	
9,583,456	9,782,420	8,523,239	8,530,038	9,426,795	8,976,194	9,096,051	7,971,299	7,771,324	7
7,791,136	*8,181,083*	*7,181,903*	*7,292,303*	*7,837,809*	*7,513,630*	*7,778,209*	*6,860,718*	*6,783,205*	
1,761,790	*1,570,423*	*1,318,601*	*1,226,062*	*1,574,111*	*1,449,120*	*1,304,677*	*1,098,456*	*980,503*	
30,530	*30,914*	*22,735*	*11,673*	*14,875*	*13,444*	*13,165*	*12,125*	*7,616*	
5,342,033	3,942,548	1,991,005	1,435,518	5,931,723	5,148,591	3,779,505	1,745,766	1,311,630	8
5,926,357	6,573,559	6,056,311	5,082,986	6,985,916	6,045,095	6,475,413	5,887,052	4,868,282	9
4,532,057	*5,081,733*	*4,675,819*	*3,930,804*	*5,479,368*	*4,685,379*	*5,069,748*	*4,594,871*	*3,792,810*	
1,394,300	*1,491,826*	*1,380,492*	*1,152,182*	*1,506,548*	*1,359,716*	*1,405,665*	*1,292,181*	*1,075,472*	
100,258	95,907	100,439	94,454	77,697	80,349	77,148	77,863	73,858	10
18,851,329	17,626,390	15,264,417	15,696,347	21,022,449	19,378,325	18,018,038	15,576,737	15,534,275	11
1,105,709	1,007,653	866,343	9,594,386	1,014,831	935,825	849,866	709,600	8,015,286	12
10,942,682	10,248,341	9,343,758		8,982,889	9,387,655	8,761,027	7,930,839		13
24,617,076	24,303,481	22,933,713	22,236,301	22,540,213	23,075,201	22,602,031	21,216,246	19,765,703	14
18,048,870	*17,812,680*	*17,082,009*	*16,413,381*	*16,466,909*	*16,810,239*	*16,441,908*	*15,680,118*	*14,367,580*	
6,568,206	*6,490,801*	*5,851,704*	*5,822,920*	*6,073,304*	*6,264,962*	*6,160,123*	*5,536,128*	*5,398,123*	
32,298,697	34,195,412	28,610,068	10,757,806	34,423,610	30,456,419	31,878,423	26,403,445	10,241,119	
139,682	...	109,557	...	175,556	144,833	...	111,513	...	15
225,997	...	...	...	193,053	202,643	...	...	..	16
1,008,634	1,252,983	1,138,139	1,056,662	976,863	944,058	1,162,413	1,044,019	940,936	17
393,877	374,053	363,136	296,847	384,197	346,422	342,257	335,125	270,980	18
1,653,592	1,525,643	1,224,568	873,788	1,990,084	1,660,882	1,502,375	1,186,043	850,112	19
3,512,956	4,131,686	3,570,518	3,551,557	3,646,274	3,395,603	3,950,264	3,367,375	3,246,413	20
4,361,136	5,298,602	4,882,823	...	4,555,521	4,136,669	4,837,801	4,379,084	...	21
811,970	862,501	700,892	469,874	1,063,372	819,170	850,061	686,402	458,242	22
5,673,629	5,873,129	5,002,137	...	6,577,558	5,467,513	5,663,911	4,843,457	...	23
1,542,057	1,353,229	...	...	1,483,759	1,363,521	1,190,723	...	...	24
2,098,048	1,853,976	1,662,540	1,635,006	2,400,083	2,090,038	1,846,646	1,682,309	1,654,386	25
2,797,024	2,483,451	2,085,842	2,535,924	2,871,572	2,742,375	2,460,153	2,100,346	2,519,478	26
53,608	...	...	...	757,218	30,354	...	...	...	27
2,409,809	2,324,091	2,112,303	...	1,889,886	2,014,589	1,939,189	1,749,380	...	28
5,171,519	6,436,856	5,372,914	...	5,015,157	4,681,847	5,734,893	4,561,341	...	29
30,795	15,742	...	...	42,861	28,219	14,716	...	...	30
414,414	409,470	384,699	338,148	400,596	387,683	383,021	357,051	300,572	31

TABLE II.—Variation in Population since 1872—*concluded.*

Province, State or Agency.	Variation—Increase (+), Decrease (—). 1901 to 1911.	1891 to 1901.	1881 to 1891.	1872 to 1881.	Net variation in period 1872 to 1911. Increase (+). Decrease (—).
1	17	18	19	20	21
INDIA	**+20,795,340**	**+7,046,385**	**+33,418,341**	**+47,783,970**	**+108,994,036**
Provinces.	**+12,661,602**	**+10,365,104**	**+22,358,019**	**+13,719,382**	**+59,104,107**
1. Ajmer-Merwara	+24,483	—65,446	+81,636	+64,391	+105,064
2. Andamans and Nicobars	+1,810	+9,040	+981	...	...
3. Assam	+871,757	+364,576	+569,510	+757,023	+2,562,866
4. Baluchistan	+32,306	...	...	...	...
5. Bengal	+3,341,600	+3,051,845	+2,772,904	+2,197,263	+11,363,612
6. Bihar and Orissa	+1,247,301	+366,226	+1,888,237	+4,501,838	+8,003,602
Bihar	*+392,757*	*—221,326*	*+1,163,171*	*+2,682,740*	*+4,017,342*
Orissa	*+149,611*	*+315,915*	*+322,263*	*+740,808*	*+1,528,597*
Chota Nagpur	*+704,933*	*+271,637*	*+402,803*	*+1,078,290*	*+2,457,663*
7. Bombay (*Presidency*)*	+1,112,992	—318,821	+2,383,933	+193,176	+3,371,280
Bombay	*+808,276*	*—654,526*	*+1,916,671*	*—32,887*	*+2,037,534*
Sind	*+302,525*	*+335,810*	*+458,043*	*+210,492*	*+1,306,870*
Aden	*+2,191*	*—105*	*+9,219*	*+15,571*	*+26,876*
8. Burma	+1,624,593	+2,768,571	+3,985,282	+989,623	+9,368,069
9. Central Provinces and Berar	+1,944,856	—1,077,520	+1,105,609	+1,992,095	+3,965,040
Central Provinces	*+1,641,710*	*—934,045*	*+880,791*	*+1,547,076*	*+3,135,532*
Berar	*+303,146*	*—143,475*	*+224,818*	*+445,019*	*+829,508*
10. Coorg	—5,631	+7,552	—5,247	+9,990	+6,664
11. Madras	+3,175,750	+2,585,226	+4,803,274	—389,468	+10,174,782
12. North-West Frontier Province (*Districts and Administered Territories*).	+155,399	+184,015	+281,576	+1,240,868 (12 and 13 together)	+4,562,217 (12 and 13 together)
13. Punjab	—355,381	+1,320,969	+1,734,771		
14. United Provinces of Agra and Oudh	—510,233	+786,765	+2,755,553	+2,147,955	+5,180,040
Agra	*—235,069*	*+604,521*	*+1,492,461*	*+1,981,166*	*+3,843,079*
Oudh	*—275,164*	*+182,244*	*+1,263,092*	*+166,789*	*+1,336,961*
States and Agencies	**+8,133,738**	**—3,318,719**	**+11,060,322**	**+34,014,588**	**+49,889,929**
15. Assam State (Manipur)	+61,757	...	...	...	...
16. Baluchistan States	—8,349	...	...	...	...
17. Baroda State	+80,106	—462,704	+233,238	+184,560	+35,200
18. Bengal States	+82,266	+23,989	+18,049	+130,434	+254,738
19. Bihar and Orissa States	+630,735	+286,456	+617,407	+686,711	+2,221,309
20. Bombay States	+503,116	—1,173,391	+1,144,057	+139,923	+613,705
21. Central India Agency	+859,175	—1,638,598	+874,496	...	...
22. Central Provinces States	+485,862	—81,422	+325,268	+459,178	+1,188,886
23. Hyderabad State	+2,233,534	—395,898	+1,691,446	...	...
24. Kashmir State	+252,548	+361,626	...	...	...
25. Madras States	+623,755	+487,464	+355,773	+55,457	+1,522,449
26. Mysore State	+266,794	+595,795	+757,416	—869,214	+750,791
27. N.-W. F. Province (*Agencies and Tribal areas*)	+1,538,132	...	...	...	...
28. Punjab States	—211,604	+161,118	+401,597	...	...
29. Rajputana Agency	+677,066	—2,818,383	+2,237,494	...	...
30. Sikkim State	+28,906	+28,556	...	...	...
31. United Provinces States	+29,939	+9,606	+50,741	+103,030	+193,316

Details of Variation in the Population of the Principal States.

Name of State and Province.	Persons.					Males.					Females.					Variation: Increase (+), Decrease (—).				Net Variation in Period 1872 to 1911, Increase (+), Decrease (—).
	1911.	1901.	1891.	1881.	1872.	1911.	1901.	1891.	1881.	1872.	1911.	1901.	1891.	1881.	1872.	1901 to 1911.	1891 to 1901.	1881 to 1891.	1872 to 1881.	
1	2	3	4	5	6	7	8	9	10	11	12	13	14	15	16	17	18	19	20	21
BALUCHISTAN STATES—																				
Kalat	359,086	372,531	..	..	..	194,598	196,279	..	..	..	164,488	176,252	..	..	..	— 13,445	..	..	..	..
BENGAL STATES—																				
Cooch Behar	592,952	566,974	578,868	602,624	532,565	316,548	301,382	302,457	311,678	278,585	276,404	265,592	276,411	290,946	253,980	+ 25,978	— 11,894	— 23,756	+ 70,059	+ 60,387
BIHAR AND ORISSA STATES—																				
Mayurbhanj	729,218	610,383	532,238	385,737	258,680	362,570	303,266	265,880	194,827	129,543	366,648	307,117	266,358	190,910	129,137	+ 118,835	+ 78,145	+ 146,501	+ 127,057	+ 470,538
BOMBAY STATES—																				
Cutch	513,429	488,022	558,415	512,084	488,507	252,453	244,643	278,441	260,251	255,084	260,976	243,379	279,974	251,833	233,423	+ 25,407	— 70,393	+ 46,331	+ 23,577	+ 24,922
Kathiawar	2,496,057	2,329,196	2,752,404	2,343,899	2,318,642	1,271,497	1,187,901	1,416,633	1,218,803	1,224,467	1,224,560	1,141,295	1,335,771	1,125,096	1,094,175	+ 166,861	— 423,208	+ 408,505	+ 25,257	+ 177,415
Kolhapur	833,441	910,011	913,131	800,189	804,103	424,435	460,874	467,572	410,647	410,482	409,006	449,137	445,559	389,542	393,621	— 76,570	— 3,120	+ 112,942	— 3,914	+ 29,338
Mahi Kantha Agency	412,631	361,545	581,568	517,485	447,056	208,922	182,368	296,646	266,566	238,648	203,709	179,177	284,922	250,919	208,408	+ 51,086	— 220,023	+ 64,083	+ 70,429	— 34,425
Palanpur Agency	515,092	467,271	645,526	576,478	508,526	267,999	242,697	335,587	301,550	267,801	247,093	224,574	309,939	274,928	240,725	+ 47,821	— 178,255	+ 69,048	+ 67,952	+ 6,566
Rewakantha Agency	665,099	479,065	733,506	549,892	512,569	340,376	245,205	376,146	283,445	273,555	324,723	233,860	357,360	266,447	239,014	+ 186,034	— 254,441	+ 183,614	+ 37,323	+ 152,530
Southern Maratha Jagirs	618,139	626,084	639,270	523,753	610,434	312,500	315,148	320,531	260,136	310,680	305,639	310,936	318,739	263,617	299,754	— 7,945	— 13,186	+ 115,517	— 86,681	+ 7,705
CENTRAL INDIA AGENCY—																				
Bhopal	730,383	667,350	952,486	954,901	..	370,560	333,932	491,885	498,643	..	359,823	333,418	460,601	456,258	..	+ 63,033	— 285,136	— 2,415	..	..
Gwalior	3,102,279	2,949,596	3,394,718	3,008,163	..	1,630,327	1,547,496	1,812,673	1,626,770	..	1,471,952	1,402,100	1,582,045	1,381,393	..	+ 152,683	— 445,122	+ 386,555	..	..
Indore	1,007,856	853,012	1,099,990	1,054,237	..	517,501	438,709	578,042	559,616	..	490,355	414,303	521,948	494,621	..	+ 154,844	— 246,978	+ 45,753	..	..
Orchha	330,032	321,678	333,020	311,514	..	168,633	165,747	172,980	162,611	..	161,399	155,931	160,031	148,903	..	+ 8,354	— 11,342	+ 21,506	..	..
Rewah	1,514,843	1,326,802	1,507,669	1,305,124	..	752,297	659,240	758,049	654,182	..	762,546	667,562	749,620	650,942	..	+ 188,041	— 180,867	+ 202,545	..	..

Details of Variation in the Population of the Principal States—*concluded.*

Name of State and Province.	Persons.					Males.					Females.					Variation. Increase (+), Decrease (—).				Net Variation in Period 1872 to 1911. Increase (+), Decrease (—).
	1911.	1901.	1891.	1881.	1872.	1911.	1901.	1891.	1881.	1872.	1911.	1901.	1891.	1881.	1872.	1901 to 1911.	1891 to 1901.	1881 to 1891.	1872 to 1881.	
1	2	3	4	5	6	7	8	9	10	11	12	13	14	15	16	17	18	19	20	21
Central Provinces States—																				
Bastar	433,310	306,501	310,884	196,248	78,856	218,015	155,683	159,656	103,046	40,745	215,295	150,818	151,228	93,202	38,111	+ 126,809	— 4,383	+ 114,636	+ 117,392	+ 354,454
Surguja	428,703	351,011	324,552	270,311	182,831	217,749	177,961	165,294	137,389	91,291	210,954	173,050	159,258	132,922	91,540	+ 77,692	+ 26,459	+ 54,241	+ 87,480	+ 245,872
Madras States—																				
Cochin	918,110	812,025	722,906	600,278	601,114	457,342	405,200	361,904	301,815	302,373	460,768	406,825	361,002	298,463	298,741	+ 106,085	+ 89,119	+ 122,628	— 836	+ 316,996
Pudukkottai	411,886	380,440	373,096	302,127	316,695	196,566	180,794	177,912	142,810	151,929	215,320	199,646	195,184	159,317	164,766	+ 31,446	+ 7,344	+ 70,969	— 14,568	+ 95,191
Travancore	3,428,975	2,952,157	2,557,736	2,401,158	2,311,379	1,731,363	1,490,165	1,290,415	1,197,134	1,149,927	1,697,612	1,461,992	1,267,321	1,204,024	1,161,452	+ 476,818	+ 394,421	+ 156,578	+ 89,779	+ 1,117,596
Punjab States—																				
Bahawalpur	780,641	720,877	650,042	573,494	..	430,254	395,684	355,153	314,395	..	350,387	325,193	294,889	259,099	..	+ 59,764	+ 70,835	+ 76,548	..	..
Patiala	1,407,659	1,596,692	1,583,521	1,467,433	..	792,540	877,197	871,467	806,984	..	615,119	719,495	712,054	660,449	..	— 189,033	+ 13,171	+ 116,088	..	..
Rajputana Agency—																				
Alwar	791,688	828,487	767,786	682,926	..	413,659	431,035	403,898	360,384	..	378,029	397,452	363,888	322,542	..	— 36,799	+ 60,701	+ 84,860	..	..
Bharatpur	558,785	626,665	640,303	645,540	..	302,254	335,156	347,830	350,475	..	256,531	291,509	292,473	295,065	..	— 67,880	— 13,638	— 5,237	..	..
Bikaner	700,983	584,755	832,065	509,077	..	371,489	306,462	440,114	293,684	..	329,494	278,293	391,951	215,393	..	+ 116,228	— 247,310	+ 322,988	..	..
Jaipur	2,636,647	2,658,666	2,823,966	2,527,142	..	1,385,750	1,405,458	1,505,765	1,365,194	..	1,250,897	1,253,208	1,318,201	1,161,948	..	— 22,019	— 165,300	+ 296,824	..	..
Kotah	639,089	544,879	718,771	707,402	..	330,324	280,912	375,210	371,255	..	308,765	263,967	343,561	336,147	..	+ 94,210	— 173,892	+ 11,369	..	..
Marwar	2,057,553	1,935,565	2,528,178	1,757,618	..	1,075,269	1,015,531	1,329,478	973,065	..	982,284	920,034	1,198,700	784,553	..	+ 121,988	— 592,613	+ 770,560	..	..
Mewar	1,293,776	1,030,212	1,728,697	1,443,144	..	670,750	537,913	904,288	772,685	..	623,026	492,299	824,409	670,459	..	+ 263,564	— 698,485	+ 285,553	..	..
Tonk	303,181	273,267	380,069	170,179	..	156,390	140,928	200,097	88,256	..	146,791	132,339	179,972	81,923	..	+ 29,914	— 106,802	+ 209,890	..	..
United Provinces States—																				
Rampur	531,217	533,212	551,249	541,914	507,004	282,978	280,987	291,092	282,359	266,814	248,239	252,225	260,157	259,555	240,190	— 1,995	— 18,037	+ 9,335	+ 34,910	+ 24,213
Tehri-Garhwal	300,819	268,885	241,242	199,836	131,716	148,462	133,427	118,378	102,340	71,334	152,357	135,458	122,864	97,496	60,382	+ 31,934	+ 27,643	+ 41,406	+ 68,120	+ 169,103

TABLE III.

Towns and Villages Classified by Population.

1. The population here dealt with falls short of that in Table I by 1,622,094 persons in the Agencies and tribal areas of the North-West Frontier Province, where statistics of the number of villages are not available.

2. In this Table, as in Tables I, IV and V, a cantonment adjoining a municipality has been treated as an integral part of it.

3. In the districts in which a revenue and cadastral survey has been carried out, the mauza or survey village has been taken as the census village. Elsewhere it is the residential village, or group of houses bearing a separate name, small outlying hamlets being ordinarily treated as part of the main residential villages to which they appertain.

4. Travellers enumerated in encampments, boats and trains, etc., have, as a rule, been shown separately in this Table, whereas in Tables IV and V they have been included in the population of the town in which the place of enumeration is situated.

5. The figures for Madras States include those for Cochin and Travancore, which are as follows :—

Class of Towns and Villages.	Cochin.		Travancore.	
	Number.	Population.	Number.	Population.
Total	**282**	**918,110**	**3,966**	**3,428,975**
Under 500	9	2,573	1,867	894,687
500—1,000	24	18,480	951	689,894
1,000—2,000	78	117,272	789	1,098,952
2,000—5,000	130	412,645	328	910,394
5,000—10,000	30	208,541	22	130,451
10,000—20,000	8	92,709	6	85,488
20,000—50,000	3	68,277	2	55,548
50,000—100,000	...	...	1	63,561
100,000 and over	...	...	...	...
Encampments, Boat and Railway Population unclassed.	...	2,613	...	...

TABLE III.—Towns and Villages

Province, State or Agency.	Total number of inhabited Towns and Villages.	Population.	Under 500.		500—1,000.		1,000—2,000.	
			Number.	Population.	Number.	Population.	Number.	Population.
1	2	3	4	5	6	7	8	9
INDIA.	**722,495**	**313,534,302**	**552,109**	**102,030,197**	**107,545**	**74,644,948**	**45,843**	**62,262,892**
Provinces.	538,809	244,267,542	403,983	75,756,865	84,444	58,671,877	36,726	49,901,649
1. Ajmer-Merwara	748	501,395	521	113,025	139	96,144	56	74,658
2. Andamans and Nicobars	224	26,459	210	14,871	12	8,472	1	1,048
3. Assam	27,895	6,713,635	24,658	3,667,903	2,424	1,647,368	654	882,006
4. Baluchistan	1,570	414,412	1,366	176,862	143	96,019	49	68,[illegible]41
5. Bengal	119,851	45,483,077	95,915	17,473,513	15,801	10,897,271	6,134	8,278,424
6. Bihar and Orissa	87,745	34,490,084	69,016	12,919,855	11,921	8,226,708	4,979	6,790,274
Bihar	*47,297*	*23,752,969*	*33,426*	*6,745,679*	*8,240*	*5,739,154*	*3,974*	*5,462,614*
Orissa	*15,675*	*5,131,753*	*12,786*	*2,330,109*	*2,093*	*1,432,493*	*692*	*922,409*
Chota Nagpur	*24,773*	*5,605,362*	*22,804*	*3,844,067*	*1,588*	*1,055,061*	*313*	*405,251*
7. Bombay (*Presidency*)	26,256	19,672,642	15,264	3,766,484	6,497	4,577,798	3,270	4,441,812
Bombay	*21,259*	*16,113,042*	*12,522*	*3,102,971*	*5,147*	*3,620,289*	*2,541*	*3,456,288*
Sind	*4,994*	*3,513,435*	*2,742*	*663,513*	*1,350*	*957,509*	*728*	*984,225*
Aden	*3*	*46,165*	...	...	...	...	*1*	*1,299*
8. Burma	37,741	12,115,217	30,446	4,278,120	5,229	3,606,645	1,714	2,260,306
9. Central Provinces and Berar	39,117	13,916,308	31,960	6,391,120	5,339	3,590,470	1,350	1,790,200
Central Provinces	*33,221*	*10,859,146*	*27,898*	*5,502,364*	*4,116*	*2,743,305*	*922*	*1,202,428*
Berar	*5,896*	*3,057,162*	*4,062*	*883,756*	*1,223*	*847,165*	*428*	*587,772*
10. Coorg	495	174,976	373	67,847	98	67,011	19	23,900
11. Madras	54,114	41,405,404	31,741	5,530,787	10,131	7,285,082	7,947	11,087,248
12. North-West Frontier Province (*Districts and Administered Territories*).	3,052	2,196,933	1,902	401,919	604	424,922	334	463,319
13. Punjab	33,560	19,974,956	21,599	4,909,841	7,477	5,253,617	3,333	4,495,659
14. United Provinces of Agra and Oudh.	106,441	47,182,044	78,992	16,044,718	18,629	12,894,350	6,896	9,243,954
Agra	*82,050*	*34,624,040*	*62,871*	*12,178,932*	*12,884*	*8,893,287*	*4,849*	*6,518,110*
Oudh	*24,391*	*12,558,004*	*16,121*	*3,865,786*	*5,745*	*4,001,063*	*2,047*	*2,725,844*
States and Agencies.	183,686	69,266,760	148,126	26,273,332	23,101	15,973,071	9,117	12,361,243
15. Assam State (Manipur)	1,478	346,222	1,353	168,206	102	68,672	19	25,379
16. Baluchistan States	2,123	420,291	1,932	238,955	139	93,639	41	55,527
17. Baroda State	3,095	2,032,798	1,921	432,439	709	489,338	325	435,960
18. Bengal States	3,518	822,565	3,071	352,050	285	196,471	135	180,802
19. Bihar and Orissa States	20,280	3,945,209	18,955	2,844,522	1,085	717,495	205	262,748
20. Bombay States	14,751	7,411,675	10,727	2,214,863	2,588	1,794,358	999	1,351,824
21. Central India Agency	33,100	9,356,980	29,007	4,778,466	2,895	2,001,070	907	1,221,362
22. Central Provinces States	8,668	2,117,002	7,778	1,415,127	760	495,169	114	140,319
23. Hyderabad State	20,236	13,374,676	11,684	2,945,668	5,220	3,687,144	2,511	3,409,391
24. Kashmir State	8,926	3,158,126	7,268	1,394,906	1,182	820,636	382	514,092
25. Madras States	4,757	4,811,841	2,080	446,894	1,119	810,865	986	1,375,340
26. Mysore State	16,831	5,806,193	13,999	2,750,791	2,099	1,423,128	574	773,902
27. Punjab States	11,014	4,212,794	8,715	1,841,786	1,338	92[illegible],028	720	985,804
28. Rajputana Agency	32,404	10,530,432	27,472	4,419,741	3,326	2,262,552	1,129	1,539,432
29. Sikkim State	315	87,920	285	64,625	27	19,579	3	3,716
30. United Provinces States	2,190	832,036	1,879	464,293	227	153,897	67	85,645

CLASSIFIED BY POPULATION.

2,000—5,000.		5,000—10,000.		10,000—20,000.		20,000—50,000.		50,000—100,000.		100,000 and over.		Encampments, Boat and Railway Population unclassed.	Serial No.
Number.	Population.	Number.	Population.	Number	Population.	Number.	Population.	Number.	Population.	Number.	Population.		
10	11	12	13	14	15	16	17	18	19	20	21	22	
14,643	**41,282,411**	**1,616**	**10,652,043**	**485**	**6,651,606**	**179**	**5,463,259**	**45**	**2,978,075**	**30**	**7,045,292**	**523,579**	
11,829	33,377,494	1,250	8,171,755	376	5,205,034	140	4,253,919	35	2,275,627	26	6,185,555	467,767	
27	76,990	2	11,131	...	...	2	42,761	1	85,471	...	...	1,215	1
1	2,068	...	...	...	...	...	...	...	...	...	...	...	2
143	374,950	11	65,680	5	65,117	...	...	...	...	...	...	10,611	3
10	30,278	1	6,597	...	...	1	33,922	...	...	...	...	1,893	4
1,758	4,858,299	162	1,084,422	48	674,185	28	795,269	2	104,181	3	1,177,965	139,528	5
1,677	4,695,185	108	674,161	26	345,642	14	467,367	3	188,317	1	135,747	46,828	6
1,527	*4,291,578*	*97*	*601,194*	*20*	*259,320*	*10*	*354,696*	*2*	*136,272*	*1*	*135,747*	*26,715*	
94	*251,917*	*3*	*17,930*	*4*	*58,846*	*2*	*59,269*	*1*	*52,045*	...	...	*6,735*	
56	*151,690*	*8*	*55,037*	*2*	*27,476*	*2*	*53,402*	...	...	...	...	*13,378*	
1,010	2,925,032	145	954,210	46	637,692	15	457,050	4	236,008	5	1,621,849	54,707	7
866	*2,542,703*	*124*	*812,169*	*40*	*566,153*	*13*	*396,107*	*2*	*122,785*	*4*	*1,469,946*	*23,631*	
144	*382,329*	*20*	*134,051*	*6*	*71,539*	*1*	*24,067*	*2*	*113,223*	*1*	*151,903*	*31,076*	
...	...	*1*	*7,990*	...	...	*1*	*36,876*	...	...	...	...	...	
284	748,012	43	292,573	16	213,948	6	172,021	1	57,582	2	421,647	64,363	8
354	1,043,751	64	411,979	22	301,002	6	185,720	...	...	2	202,066	...	9
227	*633,716*	*88*	*246,879*	*14*	*202,764*	*4*	*125,624*	...	...	*2*	*202,066*	...	
127	*410,035*	*26*	*165,100*	*8*	*98,238*	*2*	*60,096*	...	...	...	...	...	
4	9,949	1	6,269	...	...	...	...	...	...	...	...	...	10
3,718	10,671,268	408	2,680,722	120	1,647,240	38	1,208,099	8	480,385	3	772,309	42,264	11
183	541,890	21	133,392	4	49,532	3	83,282	1	97,707	...	...	970	12
1,000	2,814,396	116	749,251	26	371,170	10	274,642	6	448,964	3	611,928	45,488	13
1,660	4,585,426	168	1,101,368	63	899,506	17	533,786	9	577,012	7	1,242,024	59,900	14
1,236	*3,431,710*	*133*	*870,352*	*48*	*685,814*	*15*	*485,559*	*8*	*522,815*	*6*	*983,060*	*54,401*	
424	*1,153,716*	*35*	*231,016*	*15*	*213,692*	*2*	*48,227*	*1*	*54,197*	*1*	*258,964*	*5,499*	
2,814	7,904,917	366	2,480,288	109	1,446,572	39	1,209,340	10	702,448	4	859,737	55,812	
3	9,315	...	...	...	...	...	...	1	74,650		...	...	15
10	26,559	1	5,007	...	...	...	...	...	...	...	...	604	16
114	322,314	16	111,766	8	112,797	1	28,339	1	99,345	...	...	...	17
22	52,864	4	28,916	1	10,841	...	...	...	...	...	...	621	18
30	87,215	5	33,071	...	...	...	...	...	...	...	...	158	19
351	1,015,478	54	378,909	21	292,944	10	297,499	1	60,694	...	...	5,106	20
234	647,299	39	277,542	11	155,334	6	215,125	1	55,953	...	...	4,829	21
11	29,563	4	24,845	1	11,979	...	...	...	...	...	...	...	22
730	1,998,624	68	465,683	18	233,877	4	128,000	...	...	1	500,623	5,666	23
84	201,195	8	57,169	...	...	1	31,726	...	...	1	121,552	15,850	24
496	1,430,449	55	353,247	14	178,197	6	150,675	1	63,561	...	...	2,613	25
131	375,009	22	144,265	2	23,182	1	48,552	2	159,186	1	100,703	7,475	26
206	581,963	24	160,939	8	108,659	3	92,198	...	...	...	...	2,417	27
378	1,089,106	64	423,815	25	318,762	7	217,226	2	114,924	1	136,859	7,985	28
...	...	...	...	...	...	...	...	...	...	...	...	..	29
14	37,464	2	15,114	...	...	...	...	1	74,135			1,488	30

TABLE IV.

Towns Classified by Population with Variation since 1872.

1. For the purpose of this Table a town was defined as including every municipality of whatever size, every cantonment, all civil lines not included in municipal limits, and every other collection of houses permanently inhabited by not less than 5,000 persons, which is of an urban character though not under municipal government. The numerical test, however, was not always strictly applied; some places with less than 5,000 inhabitants were, for special reasons, treated as towns, while others with a larger population were omitted. Some places treated as towns in 1901 have now been excluded, and others have been newly included. The net result of these changes on the urban population is shown on page 22.

2. The towns are grouped in six classes. The first class consists of towns with a population of 100,000 and over, the second with from 50,000 to 100,000, the third from 20,000 to 50,000, the fourth from 10,000 to 20,000, the fifth from 5,000 to 10,000, and the sixth under 5,000. In the first three classes the towns, other than the three Presidency towns which come first, are arranged alphabetically in each class; in the last three only the number of towns and their aggregate population are given.

3. This Table takes in five censuses and gives the net variation for the period 1872—1911 as well as for each intervening decade. As mentioned in paragraph 2 to the explanatory note to Table II, the figures entered for 1872 refer in some cases to censuses taken in other years. Where the first census took place in 1881 columns 8, 12 and 13 are blank. It has been found impossible to ascertain the former population of many of the places now treated as towns for the first time. There are also certain towns where the total population has been ascertained but the distribution by sex cannot be given, so that the population does not agree with the figures in the sex columns.

4. In some towns such as Nagpur, Gaya and Indore, where plague was prevalent at the time of the census, many of the inhabitants were absent from their homes, and the population shown in this Table is far less than it would otherwise have been. The population of some of these towns, according to the returns of a fresh census taken after the epidemic had subsided, is noted below :—

Province.	Town.	Persons.	Males.	Females.
Bihar and Orissa	Gaya	70,423	38,717	31,706
Central Provinces	Nagpur	134,008	70,441	63,567
United Provinces	Cawnpore	195,498	115,243	80,255
	Mirzapur	55,304	28,171	27,133
	Fyzabad-*cum*-Ajodhya	62,446	36,024	26,422
Central India	Indore	68,733	37,910	30,823
	Lashkar	60,921	32,241	28,680

5. The following figures show the population of certain hill stations according to a census taken during the season of 1910 in the United Provinces and of 1911 in Bengal and the Punjab :—

Province.	Town.	Persons.	Males.	Females.
Bengal	Darjeeling (including Jalapahar and Lebong)	24,696	15,416	9,280
Punjab	Simla (including Jutogh Cantonment)	37,895	28,459	9,436
	Dalhousie	7,592	5,826	1,766
	Murree	16,934	12,999	3,935
United Provinces	Naini Tal	18,027	13,260	4,767
	Ranikhet	9,672	7,679	1,993
	Almora	2,222	1,673	549
	Mussoorie	17,420	12,869	4,551
	Landour	3,518	2,623	895
	Chakrata	5,646	4,926	720
	Lansdowne	5,316	4,335	981

TABLE IV.—Towns Classified by

Serial No.	Town.	Province, State or Agency.	District or State.	Population. 1911.	1901.	1891.	1881.	1872.
	1	2	3	4	5	6	7	8
	INDIA.	**2,153 Towns**		**29,748,228**	**29,183,528**	**27,254,611**	**23,935,382**	**18,082,484**
	Class I (100,000 and over)		**30 Towns**	**7,075,782**	**6,634,749**	**6,179,480**	**5,295,097**	**4,321,917**
1	CALCUTTA AND FORT *	......	......	896,067	847,796	682,305	612,307	633,009
2	BOMBAY	......	......	979,445	776,006	821,764	773,196	644,405
3	MADRAS AND CANTONMENT	......	......	518,660	509,346	452,518	405,848	397,552
4	Agra and Cantonment	United Provinces	Agra	185,449	188,022	168,662	160,203	149,008
5	Ahmadabad and Cantonment	Bombay	Ahmadabad	216,777	185,889	148,412	127,621	110,872
6	Allahabad and Cantonment	United Provinces	Allahabad	171,697	172,032	175,246	160,118	143,693
7	Amritsar and Cantonment	Punjab	Amritsar	152,756	162,429	136,766	151,896	135,813
8	Bangalore Civil and Military Station †	Mysore	Bangalore	100,834	89,599	100,081	93,540	81,810
9	Bareilly and Cantonment	United Provinces	Bareilly	129,462	133,167	122,837	115,138	104,553
10	Benares and Cantonment	United Provinces	Benares	203,804	213,079	223,375	218,573	178,300
11	Cawnpore and Cantonment	United Provinces	Cawnpore	178,557	202,797	194,048	155,369	125,877
12	Dacca	Bengal	Dacca	108,551	89,733	81,585	78,369	68,595
13	Delhi and Cantonment	Punjab	Delhi	232,837	208,575	192,579	173,393	154,417
14	Howrah	Bengal	Howrah	179,006	157,594	116,606	90,813	84,069
15	Hyderabad and Cantonment	Hyderabad	Hyderabad	500,623	448,466	415,039	367,417	...
16	Jaipur	Rajputana	Jaipur	137,098	160,167	158,787	142,578	...
17	Jubbulpore and Cantonment	C. P. and Berar	Jubbulpore	100,651	90,533	84,682	75,023	55,460
18	Karachi and Cantonment	Bombay	Karachi	151,903	116,663	105,199	73,560	56,753
19	Lahore and Cantonment	Punjab	Lahore	228,687	202,964	176,854	157,287	125,413
20	Lucknow and Cantonment	United Provinces	Lucknow	259,798	264,049	273,028	261,303	284,779
21	Madura	Madras	Madura	134,130	105,984	87,428	73,807	51,987
22	Mandalay and Cantonment	Burma	Mandalay	138,299	183,816	188,815	...	...
23	Meerut and Cantonment	United Provinces	Meerut	116,227	118,129	119,399	99,565	81,386
24	Nagpur	C. P. and Berar	Nagpur	101,415	127,734	117,014	98,299	84,441
25	Patna	Bihar and Orissa	Patna	136,153	134,785	165,192	170,654	158,900
26	Poona and Cantonment	Bombay	Poona	158,856	153,320	161,390	129,751	118,886
27	Rangoon and Cantonment	Burma	Rangoon	293,316	245,430	182,080	134,176	98,745
28	Srinagar and Cantonment	Kashmir	Kashmir South	126,344	122,618	118,960	...	...
29	Surat and Cantonment	Bombay	Surat	114,868	119,306	109,229	109,844	107,855
30	Trichinopoly and Cantonment	Madras	Trichinopoly	123,512	104,721	90,609	84,449	76,530
	Class II (50,000—100,000)		**45 Towns**	**3,010,281**	**2,930,565**	**2,710,259**	**2,411,470**	**1,856,297**
1	Ajmer	Ajmer-Merwara	Ajmer	86,222	73,839	68,843	48,735	35,111
2	Ambala and Cantonment	Punjab	Ambala	80,131	78,638	79,294	67,463	50,649
3	Bangalore City	Mysore	Bangalore	88,651	69,447	80,285	62,317	60,703
4	Baroda and Cantonment	Baroda	Baroda	99,345	103,790	116,420	106,512	116,274
5	Bhagalpur	Bihar and Orissa	Bhagalpur	74,349	75,760	69,106	68,238	65,377
6	Bhatpara	Bengal	24-Parganas	50,414	21,540	14,135	10,299	11,283
7	Bhavnagar	Bombay	Kathiawar	60,694	56,442	57,653	47,793	35,971
8	Bhopal	Central India	Bhopal	56,204	77,023	70,338	55,402	...
9	Bikaner	Rajputana	Bikaner	55,826	53,075	50,513	33,154	...
10	Calicut and Cantonment	Madras	Malabar	78,417	76,981	66,078	57,085	47,962
11	Cocanada	Madras	Godavari	54,110	48,096	40,553	28,856	17,839
12	Conjeeveram	Madras	Chingleput	53,864	46,164	42,549	37,275	37,327
.3	Cuddalore	Madras	South Arcot	56,574	52,216	47,355	43,545	40,290
	Cuttack	Bihar and Orissa	Cuttack	52,528	51,364	47,186	42,656	42,667
	Darbhanga	Bihar and Orissa	Darbhanga	62,628	66,244	73,561	65,955	53,744
16	Farrukhabad-*cum*-Fatehgarh and Cantonment.	United Provinces	Farrukhabad	59,647	67,338	78,032	79,761	79,204
17	Ferozepore and Cantonment	Punjab	Ferozepore	50,836	49,341	50,437	39,570	36,453
18	Fyzabad-*cum*-Ajodhya and Cantonment	United Provinces	Fyzabad	54,655	71,179	74,806	67,652	35,817
19	Gorakhpur	United Provinces	Gorakhpur	56,892	64,148	63,620	59,908	51,117
20	Hubli	Bombay	Dharwar	61,440	60,214	52,595	36,677	37,961
21	Hyderabad and Cantonment	Bombay	Hyderabad	75,952	69,378	58,048	48,153	43,088
22	Imphal	Assam	Manipur	74,650	72,234	...	...	...
23	Jhansi and Cantonment	United Provinces	Jhansi	70,208	55,724	53,779	32,967	30,000
24	Jodhpur (Major)	Rajputana	Marwar	59,262	60,437	61,759	57,211	...
25	Jullundur and Cantonment	Punjab	Jullundur	69,318	67,735	66,202	52,119	62,039
26	Koil—Aligarh	United Provinces	Aligarh	64,825	70,434	61,485	62,443	58,539
27	Kumbakonam	Madras	Tanjore	64,647	59,673	54,307	50,098	44,444
28	Manicktola	Bengal	24-Parganas	53,767	32,387	28,161	48,125	53,992
29	Moradabad	United Provinces	Moradabad	81,168	75,128	72,921	69,352	62,417
30	Moulmein	Burma	Amherst	57,582	58,446	55,785	53,107	46,472
31	Multan and Cantonment	Punjab	Multan	99,243	87,394	74,562	68,674	54,652
32	Muttra and Cantonment	United Provinces	Muttra	58,183	60,042	61,195	57,724	59,281
33	Mysore City	Mysore	Mysore	71,306	68,111	74,048	60,292	57,815
34	Negapatam	Madras	Tanjore	60,168	57,190	59,221	53,855	48,525
35	Peshawar and Cantonment	N.-W. F. Province	Peshawar	97,935	95,147	84,191	79,982	...
36	Rampur and Cantonment	United Provinces	Rampur	74,316	78,758	76,733	74,250	...
37	Rawalpindi and Cantonment	Punjab	Rawalpindi	86,483	87,688	73,795	52,975	28,586
38	Saharanpur	United Provinces	Saharanpur	62,850	66,254	63,194	59,194	43,844
39	Salem	Madras	Salem	59,153	70,621	67,710	50,667	50,012
40	Shahjahanpur	United Provinces	Shahjahanpur	71,778	76,458	78,522	77,404	72,136
41	Shikarpur	Bombay	Sukkur	53,944	49,491	42,004	42,496	38,107
42	Sholapur	Bombay	Sholapur	61,345	75,288	61,915	59,890	53,403
43	Sialkot and Cantonment	Punjab	Sialkot	64,869	57,956	55,087	45,762	41,121
44	Tanjore	Madras	Tanjore	60,341	57,870	54,390	54,745	52,175
45	Trivandrum and Cantonment	Madras	Travancore	63,561	57,882	27,887	41,173	...
	Class III (20,000—50,000)		**181 Towns**	**5,545,820**	**5,473,989**	**5,099,770**	**4,470,995**	**3,338,490**
1	Aden and Cantonment	Bombay	Aden	36,876	35,790	34,966	34,711	19,289
2	Adoni	Madras	Bellary	31,645	30,416	26,243	22,441	22,723
3	Ahmadnagar and Cantonment	Bombay	Ahmadnagar	42,940	42,032	41,689	37,492	37,240
4	Akola	C. P. and Berar	Akola	25,826	29,289	21,470	16,614	14,606
5	Akyab	Burma	Akyab	37,893	35,680	37,938	33,989	19,230
6	Alleppey	Madras	Travancore	25,665	24,918	22,768	25,754	...
7	Alwar	Rajputana	Alwar	41,305	56,771	51,427	49,867	...
8	Amraoti	C. P. and Berar	Amraoti	34,270	34,216	39,946	23,550	23,410
9	Amroha	United Provinces	Moradabad	42,410	41,071	36,108	37,040	35,768
10	Anakapalle	Madras	Vizagapatam	20,625	18,539	17,010	13,341	13,044

* The above figures for Calcutta exclude the population of Cossipore-Chitpur, Manicktola and Garden Reach. These places have a separate municipal the Hooghly. If the first-mentioned Municipalities be added, the population

† Bangalore city and Bangalore Civil and Military Station are structurally a single unit, but for the purpose of the census they have been treated

Population with Variation since 1872.

Variation. Increase (+) or Decrease (—) 1901 to 1911.	1891 to 1901.	1881 to 1891.	1872 to 1881.	Variation in period 1872 to 1911. Increase (+), Decrease (—).	Males. 1911.	1901.	1891.	Females. 1911.	1901.	1891.	Serial No.
9	10	11	12	13	14	15	16	17	18	19	
+ 564,700	+ 1,928,917	+ 3,319,229	+ 5,852,898	+ 11,665,744	16,108,304	15,423,261	14,418,029	13,639,924	13,686,668	12,783,548	
+ 441,033	+ 464,269	+ 875,383	+ 973,180	+ 2,753,865	4,135,392	3,757,771	3,478,972	2,940,390	2,876,978	2,692,408	
+ 48,271	+ 165,491	+ 69,998	— 20,702	+ 263,058	607,674	562,596	447,162	288,393	285,200	235,143	1
+ 203,439	— 45,758	+ 48,568	+ 128,791	+ 335,040	640,288	479,786	518,093	339,157	296,220	303,671	2
+ 9,314	+ 56,828	+ 46,670	+ 8,296	+ 121,108	266,465	256,730	225,817	252,195	252,616	226,701	3
— 2,573	+ 19,360	+ 8,459	+ 11,195	+ 36,441	101,335	99,903	90,923	84,114	88,119	77,739	4
+ 30,888	+ 37,477	+ 20,791	+ 7,949	+ 97,105	117,303	97,343	76,630	99,475	88,546	71,782	5
— 335	— 3,214	+ 15,128	+ 16,425	+ 28,004	96,208	91,762	94,784	75,489	80,270	80,463	6
— 9,673	+ 25,663	— 15,130	+ 16,083	+ 16,948	88,879	93,199	78,786	63,877	69,230	57,980	7
+ 11,235	— 10,462	+ 6,541	+ 11,730	+ 19,024	51,752	45,122	50,189	40,083	44,477	49,892	8
— 3,705	+ 10,330	+ 7,609	+ 10,585	+ 24,909	70,601	70,933	65,424	58,861	62,234	57,413	9
— 9,275	— 10,296	+ 4,802	+ 40,273	+ 25,504	105,815	110,782	117,135	97,989	102,297	106,240	10
— 24,240	+ 8,749	+ 38,679	+ 29,492	+ 52,680	103,316	114,573	109,827	75,241	88,224	84,231	11
+ 18,818	+ 8,148	+ 3,216	+ 9,774	+ 39,956	63,091	49,871	44,795	45,460	39,862	36,790	12
+ 24,262	+ 15,996	+ 19,186	+ 18,976	+ 78,420	133,864	114,815	105,677	98,973	93,760	86,902	13
+ 21,412	+ 40,988	+ 25,793	+ 6,744	+ 94,937	114,566	99,904	70,477	64,440	57,690	46,129	14
+ 52,157	+ 33,427	+ 47,632	...	...	258,454	232,295	216,324	242,169	216,171	196,715	15
— 23,069	+ 1,380	+ 16,209	...	...	70,846	83,854	84,024	66,252	76,313	74,763	16
+ 10,118	+ 5,851	+ 8,659	+ 20,554	+ 45,183	56,035	46,989	45,045	44,616	43,544	39,637	17
+ 35,240	+ 11,464	+ 31,639	+ 16,807	+ 95,150	90,233	68,386	63,486	61,670	48,277	42,713	18
+ 25,723	+ 26,110	+ 19,567	+ 31,874	+ 103,274	143,249	119,906	104,710	85,438	83,968	72,144	19
— 4,251	— 8,979	+ 11,725	— 23,476	— 24,981	144,785	140,759	145,848	115,013	123,290	127,180	20
+ 28,146	+ 18,556	+ 13,621	+ 21,820	+ 82,143	67,001	52,667	43,880	67,039	53,317	43,548	21
— 45,517	— 4,909	...	...	...	69,718	93,583	93,503	68,581	90,233	96,312	22
— 1,903	— 1,261	+ 19,825	+ 18,179	+ 34,841	66,286	65,568	68,016	40,941	52,561	51,374	23
— 26,319	+ 10,720	+ 18,715	+ 13,858	+ 16,974	53,696	66,255	60,640	47,719	61,479	56,374	24
+ 1,368	— 30,407	— 5,463	+ 11,764	— 22,747	70,841	67,038	82,006	65,312	67,747	83,184	25
+ 5,536	— 8,070	+ 31,639	+ 10,865	+ 39,970	85,319	80,065	87,097	73,537	73,255	74,293	26
+ 47,886	+ 63,350	+ 47,904	+ 35,431	+ 194,571	208,111	174,587	125,898	85,205	70,843	56,183	27
+ 3,726	+ 3,658	...	...	...	68,378	65,542	62,720	57,966	57,076	56,240	28
— 4,438	+ 10,077	— 615	+ 1,989	+ 7,013	59,674	61,653	66,074	55,234	57,653	53,155	29
+ 18,791	+ 14,112	+ 6,160	+ 7,919	+ 46,982	61,560	51,215	44,080	61,953	53,506	46,529	30
+ 79,716	+ 220,306	+ 298,789	+ 555,173	+ 1,153,984	1,634,234	1,556,358	1,452,238	1,376,947	1,374,297	1,258,021	
+ 12,383	+ 4,906	+ 20,106	+ 13,624	+ 51,111	47,354	39,467	37,985	38,868	34,372	30,858	1
+ 1,493	— 656	+ 11,831	+ 16,814	+ 20,482	49,204	45,729	47,511	30,927	32,909	31,783	2
+ 19,204	— 10,838	+ 17,068	+ 1,614	+ 27,948	45,997	35,964	40,873	42,654	33,483	39,412	3
— 4,445	— 12,630	+ 9,906	— 9,763	— 16,929	53,616	56,009	63,671	45,729	47,781	53,549	4
— 1,411	+ 6,634	+ 868	+ 2,861	+ 8,973	39,947	39,729	34,708	34,402	36,031	34,398	5
+ 28,874	+ 7,405	+ 3,896	— 1,044	+ 30,131	34,739	13,978	9,173	15,675	7,562	4,962	6
+ 4,252	— 1,211	+ 9,861	+ 11,921	+ 24,833	31,869	29,745	31,116	28,825	26,697	26,537	7
— 20,819	+ 6,685	+ 14,936	...	...	29,043	39,177	36,891	27,161	37,846	33,447	8
+ 2,751	+ 2,562	+ 17,359	...	...	28,275	26,709	24,979	27,551	26,366	25,534	9
+ 1,436	+ 10,903	+ 8,993	+ 9,123	+ 30,455	40,680	39,986	34,507	37,737	36,995	31,571	10
+ 6,014	+ 7,543	+ 11,697	+ 11,017	+ 36,271	26,629	23,504	20,828	27,481	24,502	20,225	11
+ 7,700	+ 3,616	+ 5,273	— 52	+ 16,537	26,451	22,533	20,615	27,413	23,631	21,933	12
+ 4,368	+ 4,661	+ 3,810	+ 3,255	+ 16,284	28,012	25,738	23,197	28,562	26,478	24,158	13
+ 1,164	+ 4,178	+ 4,530	— 11	+ 9,861	28,504	27,693	25,235	24,024	23,672	21,951	14
— 3,616	— 7,317	+ 7,606	+ 12,211	+ 8,884	31,274	32,907	38,267	31,364	33,337	36,294	15
— 7,691	— 10,694	— 1,729	+ 557	— 19,557	33,144	34,873	41,140	27,503	32,465	36,802	16
+ 1,495	— 1,006	+ 10,867	+ 3,117	+ 14,383	31,459	30,311	30,622	19,377	19,030	19,815	17
— 16,524	— 3,627	+ 7,154	+ 31,835	+ 18,838	31,078	38,829	41,515	23,577	33,360	33,291	18
— 7,256	+ 528	+ 3,712	+ 8,791	+ 5,775	31,236	32,598	32,675	25,656	31,560	30,945	19
+ 1,226	+ 7,619	+ 15,918	— 1,284	+ 23,479	31,577	30,865	26,818	29,863	29,349	25,777	20
+ 6,574	+ 11,330	+ 9,896	+ 5,065	+ 32,864	41,883	37,275	30,632	34,070	33,103	27,416	21
+ 2,416	...	...	...	...	36,303	35,487	..	38,257	36,747	...	22
+ 14,484	+ 1,945	+ 20,722	+ 2,987	+ 40,206	38,323	29,778	30,986	31,885	25,946	22,793	23
— 1,175	— 1,322	+ 4,548	...	...	29,351	30,043	31,663	29,911	30,394	30,096	24
+ 1,583	+ 1,533	+ 14,083	— 9,920	+ 7,279	39,816	37,209	37,471	29,503	30,436	28,731	25
— 5,609	+ 8,949	— 958	+ 3,904	+ 6,286	36,265	38,095	32,843	28,560	33,339	28,642	26
+ 4,974	+ 5,366	+ 4,209	+ 6,654	+ 20,208	31,327	28,650	26,471	33,320	31,023	27,836	27
+ 21,380	+ 4,226	— 19,964	— 5,867	— 225	31,735	19,142	16,418	22,032	13,245	11,743	28
+ 6,040	+ 2,207	+ 3,569	+ 6,935	+ 18,751	43,381	38,517	37,249	37,787	36,611	35,673	29
— 864	+ 2,661	+ 2,678	+ 6,635	+ 11,110	35,130	36,690	34,252	22,453	21,756	21,533	30
+ 11,849	+ 12,832	+ 5,888	+ 14,022	+ 44,591	56,280	49,328	41,963	42,963	38,066	32,609	31
— 1,859	— 1,153	+ 3,471	— 1,557	— 1,098	32,133	32,118	33,284	26,050	27,924	27,911	32
+ 3,195	— 5,937	+ 13,756	+ 2,477	+ 13,491	36,112	34,328	36,601	35,194	33,783	37,357	33
+ 2,978	— 2,031	+ 5,366	+ 5,330	+ 11,643	29,905	26,540	27,041	30,173	30,650	32,180	34
+ 2,788	+ 10,956	+ 4,209	...	...	59,680	57,526	51,264	38,255	37,621	32,927	35
— 4,443	+ 2,025	+ 2,483	...	...	38,833	40,271	40,660	35,483	38,487	36,073	36
— 1,206	+ 13,893	+ 20,820	+ 24,389	+ 57,897	57,451	57,519	51,043	29,032	30,169	22,753	37
— 3,404	+ 3,060	+ 4,000	+ 15,350	+ 19,006	35,416	35,602	34,266	27,434	30,563	28,928	38
— 11,468	+ 2,911	+ 17,043	+ 655	+ 9,141	29,232	34,337	32,860	29,921	36,284	34,850	39
— 4,680	— 2,064	+ 1,118	+ 5,268	— 358	36,780	38,175	39,109	34,989	38,283	39,353	40
+ 4,453	+ 7,487	— 402	+ 4,389	+ 15,837	28,532	25,735	21,154	25,412	23,756	20,850	41
— 13,943	+ 13,373	+ 2,026	+ 6,487	+ 7,943	31,801	38,163	31,734	29,454	37,125	30,181	42
+ 6,918	+ 2,860	+ 9,325	+ 4,641	+ 23,746	38,130	31,614	31,456	26,739	26,342	23,631	43
+ 2,471	+ 3,480	— 355	+ 2,570	+ 8,166	28,777	27,611	25,945	31,564	30,259	28,445	44
+ 5,679	+ 29,995	— 13,286	...	...	32,293	29,903	14,707	31,269	27,890	13,180	45
+ 71,831	+ 374,219	+ 628,775	+ 1,132,565	+ 2,207,330	2,976,399	2,882,101	2,689,173	2,569,421	2,591,888	2,410,597	
+ 1,086	+ 932	+ 257	+ 15,422	+ 17,567	25,845	26,632	25,741	11,031	10,158	9,227	1
+ 1,229	+ 4,173	+ 3,802	— 282	+ 8,922	16,080	15,468	13,252	15,565	14,948	12,091	2
+ 908	+ 343	+ 4,197	+ 252	+ 5,700	23,378	21,683	22,073	19,562	20,340	19,616	3
— 3,463	+ 7,819	+ 4,856	+ 2,008	+ 11,220	14,006	16,038	11,814	11,820	12,351	9,656	4
+ 2,213	— 2,258	+ 3,949	+ 14,759	+ 18,663	29,509	27,581	29,208	8,384	8,099	8,730	5
+ 747	+ 2,150	— 2,966	...	..	13,370	12,748	11,286	12,295	12,170	11,492	6
— 15,466	+ 5,344	+ 1,560	...	...	22,264	29,574	27,764	19,051	27,197	23,668	7
+ 54	+ 5,270	+ 5,396	+ 140	+ 10,860	18,147	18,295	15,833	16,123	15,921	13,113	8
+ 1,339	+ 4,968	— 937	+ 1,272	+ 6,642	20,550	19,585	17,297	21,860	21,486	18,806	9
+ 2,086	+ 1,529	+ 3,069	+ 297	+ 7,581	10,165	9,023	8,489	10,460	9,516	8,521	10

administration, but for all practical purposes they form an integral part of Calcutta. So also does Howrah except that it lies on the opposite bank of
of Calcutta rises to 1,043,307. If Howrah also be included, it comes to 1,222,313.
as separate places.

TABLE IV.—Towns Classified by

Serial No.	Town.	Province, State or Agency.	District or State.	Population 1911.	1901.	1891.	1881.	1872.
	1	2	3	4	5	6	7	8
	Class III (20,000—50,000) *—contd.*							
11	Arrah	Bihar and Orissa	Shahabad	38,549	46,170	46,905	42,998	39,386
12	Aruppukkottai	Madras	Ramnad	26,681	23,633	12,673	10,831	10,729
13	Asansol	Bengal	Burdwan	21,910	14,906	...	...	...
14	Aurangabad and Cantonment	Hyderabad	Aurangabad	34,902	36,837	33,887	30,219	
15	Bahraich	United Provinces	Bahraich	26,907	27,304	24,046	21,998	18,086
16	Baidyabati	Bengal	Hooghly	20,516	17,174	16,380	14,477	13,382
17	Balasore	Bihar and Orissa	Balasore	21,362	20,880	20,775	20,265	18,263
18	Bally	Bengal	Howrah	22,394	18,662	16,700	14,818	13,715
19	Banda	United Provinces	Banda	21,061	22,565	23,071	28,974	27,746
20	Bandra	Bombay	Thana	24,286	22,075	16,317	14,987	7,327
21	Bankura	Bengal	Bankura	23,453	20,737	16,743	18,747	15,070
22	Baranagar	Bengal	24-Parganas	25,895	25,432	23,556	19,729	...
23	Barisal	Bengal	Backergunge	22,473	18,078	15,462	13,186	12,501
24	Bassein	Burma	Bassein	37,081	31,864	30,177	28,147	20,688
25	Batala	Punjab	Gurdaspur	26,430	27,365	27,223	24,281	27,280
26	Beawar	Ajmer-Merwara	Merwara	22,800	21,928	20,978	15,829	13,308
27	Belgaum and Cantonment	Bombay	Belgaum	42,623	36,878	40,737	32,697	30,813
28	Bellary and Cantonment	Madras	Bellary	34,956	58,247	59,467	53,460	51,766
29	Berhampore	Bengal	Murshidabad	26,143	24,397	23,515	23,605	27,110
30	Berhampur	Madras	Ganjam	31,456	25,729	25,653	23,599	21,670
31	Bettiah	Bihar and Orissa	Champaran	25,793	24,696	22,780	21,263	13,726
32	Bezwada	Madras	Kistna	32,867	24,224	20,741	9,336	8,036
33	Bhadreswar	Bengal	Hooghly	24,353	15,150	9,639	9,241	7,417
34	Bharatpur	Rajputana	Bharatpur	33,918	43,601	67,555	66,163	...
35	Bhiwani	Punjab	Hissar	31,100	35,917	35,487	33,762	32,254
36	Bhuj and Cantonment	Bombay	Cutch	21,570	26,362	25,421	22,308	25,020
37	Bihar	Bihar and Orissa	Patna	35,151	45,063	47,723	48,968	44,295
38	Bijapur	Bombay	Bijapur	27,615	23,811	16,759	11,434	12,938
39	Bishnupur	Bengal	Bankura	20,478	19,090	18,190	18,863	17,426
40	Bodinayakkanur	Madras	Madura	20,183	22,209	17,570	14,759	13,154
41	Brahmanbaria	Bengal	Tippera	22,295	19,915	18,006	17,438	15,372
42	Broach	Bombay	Broach	43,403	42,896	40,168	37,281	36,932
43	Budaun	United Provinces	Budaun	39,230	30,031	35,372	33,680	33,322
44	Burdwan	Bengal	Burdwan	35,921	35,022	34,477	34,080	32,321
45	Burhanpur	C. P. and Berar	Nimar	22,777	33,341	32,252	30,017	29,303
46	Cambay	Bombay	Cambay	29,096	31,780	31,390	36,007	33,700
47	Cannanore and Cantonment	Madras	Malabar	28,957	27,811	27,418	26,386	31,070
48	Chandausi	United Provinces	Moradabad	22,255	25,711	28,111	27,521	23,686
49	Chapra	Bihar and Orissa	Saran	42,373	45,901	57,352	51,670	46,287
50	Chidambaram	Madras	South Arcot	21,327	19,909	18,640	19,837	15,519
51	Chittagong	Bengal	Chittagong	28,766	23,140	24,069	20,969	18,790
52	Cochin	Madras	Malabar	20,023	19,274	17,601	15,698	13,840
53	Coimbatore	Madras	Coimbatore	47,007	53,080	46,383	38,967	35,310
54	Comilla	Bengal	Tippera	22,692	19,169	14,680	13,372	12,948
55	Cossipore-Chitpur	Bengal	24-Parganas	48,178	40,750	31,423	26,294	25,369
56	Dehra and Cantonment	United Provinces	Dehra Dun	38,610	28,095	25,684	18,959	7,316
57	Dera Ismail Khan and Cantonment	N.-W. F. Province	Dera Ismail Khan	35,131	31,737	26,884	22,164	...
58	Dharwar	Bombay	Dharwar	30,280	31,279	32,841	26,520	27,136
59	Dhoraji	Bombay	Kathiawar	24,116	24,815	20,406	16,121	15,562
60	Dhulia	Bombay	Khandesh West	30,900	24,726	21,880	18,440	12,489
61	Dinapore and Cantonment	Bihar and Orissa	Patna	31,025	33,699	44,419	37,893	42,084
62	Dindigul	Madras	Madura	25,052	25,182	20,203	14,182	12,866
63	Ellore	Madras	Kistna	37,819	33,521	29,382	25,092	25,487
64	Ernakulam	Madras	Cochin	21,195	21,901	17,870	15,467	14,038
65	Etawah	United Provinces	Etawah	45,350	42,570	38,793	34,721	30,549
66	Gadag	Bombay	Dharwar	30,429	30,652	23,699	17,001	19,036
67	Garden Reach	Bengal	24-Parganas	45,295	28,211	27,924	12,456	9,258
68	Gaya	Bihar and Orissa	Gaya	49,921	71,288	80,383	76,415	66,843
69	Ghazipur	United Provinces	Ghazipur	23,165	39,429	44,970	43,232	38,853
70	Godhra	Bombay	Panch Mahals	22,144	20,915	14,691	13,343	10,635
71	Gudiyattam	Madras	North Arcot	23,390	21,335	18,747	10,641	10,804
72	Gujranwala	Punjab	Gujranwala	20,472	29,224	26,785	22,884	19,371
73	Gulbarga	Hyderabad	Gulbarga	32,437	29,228	28,200	[illegible]	...
74	Guntur	Madras	Guntur	40,529	30,833	23,359	19,646	18,033
75	Hanamkonda	Hyderabad	Warangal	35,637	20,661	24,764	...	...
76	Hardwar Union	United Provinces	Saharanpur	28,682	25,597	29,125	28,106	21,555
77	Hathras	United Provinces	Aligarh	37,854	42,578	39,181	34,932	23,589
78	Henzada	Burma	Henzada	25,052	24,756	19,762	16,724	15,307
79	Hooghly-Chinsura	Bengal	Hooghly	28,916	20,383	33,060	31,177	34,761
80	Indore	Central India	Indore	44,947	86,686	82,984	75,401	...
81	Jamalpur	Bengal	Mymensingh	21,109	17,965	15,388	14,727	14,312
82	Jamalpur	Bihar and Orissa	Monghyr	20,526	13,929	18,089	13,213	10,453
83	Jammu and Cantonment	Kashmir	Jammu	31,726	35,672	34,084	...	...
84	Jamnagar	Bombay	Kathiawar	44,887	53,844	48,530	39,068	34,744
85	Jaunpur	United Provinces	Jaunpur	30,473	42,771	42,819	42,845	23,327
86	Jhang-Maghiana	Punjab	Jhang	25,914	24,383	23,290	21,629	20,613
87	Jodhpur (Minor)	Rajputana	Marwar	20,494	18,672	18,646	6,118	...
88	Junagarh	Bombay	Kathiawar	35,413	34,251	31,640	24,679	30,025
89	Karnal	Punjab	Karnal	21,961	23,559	21,963	24,183	[illegible]
90	Kasur	Punjab	Lahore	24,783	22,022	20,290	17,336	16,581
91	Khandwa	C. P. and Berar	Nimar	21,604	19,401	15,589	15,142	14,119
92	Khurja	United Provinces	Bulandshahr	27,387	29,277	26,349	27,190	26,856
93	Kohat and Cantonment	N.-W. F. Province	Kohat	22,654	30,762	27,003	18,179	...
94	Kolar Gold Fields	Mysore	Kolar	48,635	38,204	7,085	...	...
95	Kolhapur and Cantonment	Bombay	Kolhapur	48,122	54,373	45,815	38,500	37,663
96	Kotah	Rajputana	Kotah	32,753	33,657	38,620	40,270	...
97	Krishnagar	Bengal	Nadia	23,475	24,547	25,500	27,477	36,750
98	Kulasekarapatnam	Madras	Tinnevelly	21,812	19,898	15,024	14,972	11,552
99	Kurnool	Madras	Kurnool	26,040	25,376	24,376	20,329	25,579
100	Lashkar	Central India	Gwalior	46,952	89,154	104,083	88,066	...
101	Ludhiana	Punjab	Ludhiana	44,170	48,649	46,334	44,163	39,983
102	Malerkotla	Punjab	Malerkotla	23,880	21,122	21,754	20,621	...
103	Malvan	Bombay	Ratnagiri	22,080	19,626	17,063	18,588	13,965
104	Mandvi	Bombay	Cutch	24,235	24,683	38,155	35,980	35,986
105	Mangalore	Madras	South Canara	48,412	44,108	40,922	32,099	29,712

POPULATION WITH VARIATION SINCE 1872—*continued.*

VARIATION. Increase (+) or Decrease (—)				Variation in period 1872 to 1911.	MALES.			FEMALES.			Serial No.
1901 to 1911.	1891 to 1901.	1881 to 1891.	1872 to 1881.	Increase (+). Decrease (—).	1911.	1901.	1891.	1911.	1901.	1891.	
9	10	11	12	13	14	15	16	17	18	19	
— 7,621	— 735	+ 3,907	+ 3,612	— 837	19,965	23,019	23,426	18,504	24,151	23,479	11
+ 3,946	+ 10,960	+ 1,843	+ 103	+ 15,952	13,998	11,551	6,131	13,893	12,063	8,542	12
+ 7,013	...	...	...	...	12,496	8,400	...	9,433	6,606	...	13
— 1,935	+ 3,950	+ 3,668	...	...	17,992	19,005	17,186	16,910	17,833	16,701	14
— 397	+ 3,358	+ 3,048	+ 3,012	+ 7,921	14,327	14,275	13,703	12,680	13,029	11,344	15
+ 3,343	— 1,206	+ 3,903	+ 1,145	+ 7,164	11,792	9,839	9,995	8,734	7,315	8,385	16
+ 483	+ 105	+ 510	+ 2,002	+ 3,099	11,223	10,886	10,550	10,139	9,994	10,235	17
+ 3,732	+ 1,062	+ 1,885	+ 1,100	+ 8,679	14,317	11,383	9,515	8,177	7,279	7,185	18
— 1,504	— 506	— 5,903	+ 1,228	— 6,685	10,543	11,068	11,444	10,518	11,497	11,627	19
+ 2,211	+ 3,758	+ 3,330	+ 7,780	+ 17,059	13,250	12,079	9,877	11,036	9,996	8,440	20
+ 3,718	+ 1,994	— 4	+ 2,768	+ 7,474	12,159	10,532	9,782	11,297	10,205	9,461	21
+ 463	+ 2,876	+ 3,837	...	...	14,092	14,748	13,080	10,913	10,684	9,476	22
+ 2,495	+ 3,495	+ 2,296	+ 685	+ 9,972	15,498	13,250	10,384	6,985	5,728	5,098	23
+ 5,217	+ 1,687	+ 2,030	+ 7,459	+ 16,393	24,246	20,422	19,013	12,835	11,442	11,164	24
— 935	+ 142	+ 2,943	— 2,909	— 850	14,180	14,037	14,065	13,250	13,328	13,158	25
+ 873	+ 950	+ 5,149	+ 3,521	+ 10,492	12,328	11,146	11,446	10,472	10,782	9,532	26
+ 5,745	— 3,859	+ 8,040	— 5,815	+ 4,111	23,097	19,627	22,137	19,526	17,251	18,600	27
— 23,291	— 1,320	+ 6,007	+ 1,694	— 16,810	18,474	29,690	30,244	16,483	28,548	30,223	28
+ 1,746	+ 882	— 90	— 3,505	— 967	14,302	13,003	12,260	11,841	11,394	11,255	29
+ 5,727	+ 76	+ 2,054	+ 1,929	+ 9,786	15,331	12,103	12,337	16,125	13,826	13,256	30
+ 1,007	+ 1,916	+ 1,517	+ 7,537	+ 12,067	13,096	12,341	11,799	13,897	12,355	10,981	31
+ 8,643	+ 3,483	+ 11,405	+ 1,310	+ 24,841	17,026	12,449	11,404	15,841	11,775	9,387	32
+ 9,203	+ 5,511	+ 398	+ 1,824	+ 16,936	15,862	9,376	5,229	8,401	5,774	4,410	33
— 9,683	— 33,954	+ 1,802	...	...	18,903	23,703	37,339	15,115	19,896	30,216	34
— 4,817	+ 430	+ 1,725	+ 1,508	— 1,154	16,240	16,388	18,203	14,851	17,529	17,285	35
— 4,783	+ 941	+ 3,113	— 2,712	— 3,441	10,556	13,494	13,423	11,023	13,868	11,908	36
— 9,912	— 2,660	— 1,245	+ 4,673	— 9,144	16,996	21,338	22,917	18,156	23,725	24,806	37
+ 3,804	+ 7,053	+ 5,335	— 1,514	+ 14,677	14,345	13,025	8,530	13,270	11,786	8,229	38
+ 1,388	+ 900	— 673	+ 1,427	+ 3,043	10,025	9,205	8,824	10,453	9,885	9,366	39
— 2,026	+ 4,639	+ 3,811	+ 1,605	+ 7,039	9,671	10,770	8,440	10,512	11,430	9,124	40
+ 2,380	+ 1,909	+ 568	+ 2,066	+ 6,923	11,671	10,317	9,224	10,624	9,598	8,783	41
+ 507	+ 2,728	+ 2,887	+ 349	+ 6,471	23,630	22,198	20,700	20,773	20,698	19,378	42
— 801	+ 3,659	+ 1,692	+ 358	+ 4,906	20,048	19,788	17,187	18,182	19,263	18,185	43
+ 899	+ 546	+ 397	+ 1,759	+ 3,600	20,527	19,413	18,537	15,394	15,609	15,950	44
— 10,564	+ 1,089	+ 2,336	+ 714	— 6,526	11,624	16,793	16,533	11,153	16,549	15,720	45
— 3,682	+ 390	— 4,617	+ 2,398	— 5,611	13,858	15,654	15,273	14,240	16,126	16,117	46
+ 1,146	+ 393	+ 1,082	— 4,684	— 2,113	14,241	13,711	13,273	14,716	14,100	14,145	47
— 3,456	— 2,400	+ 590	+ 3,835	— 1,481	12,367	13,509	15,048	9,888	12,203	13,063	48
— 3,528	— 11,451	+ 5,682	+ 5,383	— 3,914	21,601	22,361	26,743	20,772	23,540	28,609	49
+ 1,418	+ 1,269	— 1,197	+ 4,318	+ 5,806	10,279	9,631	9,079	11,048	10,278	9,561	50
+ 6,626	— 1,929	+ 3,100	+ 2,189	+ 9,986	18,779	13,701	14,254	9,967	8,439	9,815	51
+ 749	+ 1,673	+ 1,903	+ 1,858	+ 6,183	10,764	10,335	9,379	9,259	8,939	8,222	52
— 6,073	+ 6,697	+ 7,416	+ 3,657	+ 11,697	23,399	25,913	23,238	23,608	27,167	24,145	53
+ 3,533	+ 4,489	+ 1,308	+ 424	+ 9,744	13,706	11,573	8,580	8,986	7,596	6,100	54
+ 7,428	+ 9,327	+ 5,129	+ 925	+ 22,809	30,793	26,189	19,424	17,385	14,561	11,090	55
+ 10,515	+ 2,411	+ 6,725	+ 11,643	+ 31,294	24,470	16,869	16,019	14,140	11,236	9,065	56
+ 3,394	+ 4,853	+ 4,720	...	...	21,844	18,526	16,314	13,287	13,211	10,570	57
— 990	— 1,562	+ 6,321	— 616	+ 3,153	15,528	16,014	16,749	14,761	15,265	16,092	58
— 699	+ 4,409	+ 4,285	+ 559	+ 8,554	10,950	11,619	9,547	13,166	13,196	10,859	59
+ 6,074	+ 2,846	+ 3,431	+ 5,960	+ 18,311	16,231	13,075	11,578	14,569	11,651	10,302	60
— 2,674	— 10,720	+ 6,536	— 4,191	— 11,059	15,788	16,594	21,803	15,237	17,105	22,526	61
— 130	+ 4,979	+ 6,021	+ 1,317	+ 12,187	12,720	12,628	10,027	12,332	12,554	10,176	62
+ 4,298	+ 4,139	+ 4,200	— 395	+ 12,332	18,303	16,289	14,287	19,517	17,232	15,095	63
— 706	+ 4,031	+ 2,403	+ 1,429	+ 7,157	11,944	12,205	9,520	9,351	9,606	8,341	64
+ 2,780	+ 3,777	+ 4,072	+ 4,172	+ 14,801	24,249	22,496	20,337	21,101	20,074	18,456	65
— 223	+ 6,753	+ 6,898	— 2,034	+ 11,304	15,570	15,506	13,107	14,859	15,146	11,792	66
+ 17,064	+ 287	+ 15,468	+ 3,196	+ 36,037	27,665	16,928	16,595	17,630	11,283	11,329	67
— 31,367	— 9,085	+ 3,968	+ 9,572	— 16,922	26,310	36,553	40,893	23,611	34,735	39,400	68
— 17,264	— 5,541	+ 1,738	+ 4,379	— 16,688	13,005	19,667	23,077	10,160	19,762	21,803	69
+ 1,229	+ 6,224	+ 1,340	+ 2,707	+ 11,509	11,599	10,780	7,286	10,545	10,135	7,405	70
+ 2,055	+ 2,598	+ 8,106	— 163	+ 12,596	11,386	10,263	9,226	12,004	11,072	9,521	71
+ 246	+ 2,439	+ 3,901	+ 3,513	+ 10,101	16,271	15,524	14,489	13,201	13,700	12,296	72
+ 3,209	+ 1,028	+ 5,366	...	...	16,849	15,274	14,747	15,688	13,954	13,453	73
+ 9,696	+ 7,474	+ 3,713	+ 1,613	+ 22,406	20,826	15,628	11,753	19,703	15,205	11,606	74
+ 14,966	— 4,103	...	...	...	18,324	10,861	12,803	17,308	9,800	11,962	75
+ 3,085	— 3,528	+ 1,019	+ 6,551	+ 7,127	16,824	14,459	17,886	12,058	11,139	11,239	76
— 4,724	+ 3,397	+ 4,249	+ 11,843	+ 14,265	21,360	23,096	21,066	16,494	19,482	18,115	77
+ 296	+ 4,994	+ 3,038	+ 1,417	+ 9,745	14,009	13,257	10,640	11,043	11,409	9,122	78
— 467	— 3,677	+ 1,883	— 3,584	— 5,845	15,817	15,377	17,018	18,099	14,006	16,043	79
— 41,739	+ 3,702	+ 7,583	...	...	24,793	46,164	46,328	20,155	40,622	36,656	80
+ 3,144	+ 2,577	+ 661	+ 415	+ 6,797	11,728	9,713	8,192	9,381	8,252	7,196	81
+ 6,597	— 4,160	+ 4,876	+ 2,760	+ 10,073	10,881	7,506	9,547	9,645	6,333	8,543	82
— 3,946	+ 1,598	...	...	...	19,362	21,872	22,196	13,364	13,800	11,888	83
— 8,957	+ 5,314	+ 8,863	+ 4,924	+ 10,143	22,025	26,759	24,460	22,862	27,085	34,070	84
— 12,398	— 48	— 26	+ 19,518	+ 7,146	15,868	21,271	21,494	14,685	21,500	21,325	85
+ 1,632	+ 1,092	+ 1,661	+ 1,116	+ 5,401	13,212	13,477	13,170	12,702	11,905	11,120	86
+ 1,822	+ 26	+ 12,528	...	...	12,487	11,459	11,664	8,007	7,213	6,962	87
+ 1,163	+ 2,611	+ 6,961	+ 4,654	+ 15,388	18,565	17,849	16,710	16,848	16,408	14,930	88
— 1,598	+ 1,596	— 1,170	— 5,874	— 7,046	11,959	12,613	12,311	10,002	10,946	9,752	89
+ 2,761	+ 1,732	+ 2,954	+ 785	+ 8,233	13,769	11,756	10,596	11,014	10,264	9,694	90
+ 2,208	+ 3,812	+ 447	+ 1,023	+ 7,485	11,511	10,388	8,302	10,098	9,013	7,287	91
— 1,890	+ 2,928	— 841	+ 332	+ 529	14,540	15,364	13,594	12,838	14,013	12,755	92
— 8,106	+ 3,759	+ 8,824	...	...	14,429	22,492	30,043	8,225	8,270	6,961	93
+ 10,431	+ 31,119	...	...	...	27,960	23,493	4,703	20,675	15,712	2,383	94
— 6,251	+ 8,688	+ 7,316	+ 936	+ 10,459	25,437	27,854	23,393	22,685	26,519	22,432	95
— 904	— 4,963	— 1,650	...	...	16,949	17,588	20,008	15,804	16,069	18,617	96
— 1,072	— 953	— 1,977	+ 727	— 3,275	11,767	12,353	12,444	11,708	12,294	13,066	97
+ 1,914	+ 3,974	+ 953	+ 3,420	+ 10,260	9,525	8,391	7,026	12,287	11,507	8,898	98
+ 664	+ 1,000	+ 4,047	— 5,250	+ 461	12,766	12,404	11,671	13,274	12,912	12,705	99
— 43,203	— 14,939	+ 16,017	...	...	24,345	45,696	54,553	22,707	43,268	49,530	100
— 4,479	+ 2,315	+ 2,171	+ 4,180	+ 4,187	25,517	26,839	25,506	18,653	21,830	20,828	101
+ 3,758	— 682	+ 1,133	...	...	13,538	10,815	10,963	10,343	10,307	10,701	102
+ 2,454	+ 2,573	+ 1,488	+ 1,610	+ 8,125	10,327	9,368	7,843	11,753	10,288	9,310	103
— 448	— 13,473	+ 2,175	— 8	— 11,753	11,139	12,326	18,407	12,907	12,457	19,748	104
+ 4,304	+ 3,186	+ 5,698	+ 2,387	+ 18,700	25,129	22,501	21,357	23,283	21,607	19,565	105

TABLE IV.—Towns Classified by

Serial No.	Town.	Province, State or Agency.	District or State.	POPULATION. 1911.	1901.	1891.	1881.	1872.
	1	2	3	4	5	6	7	8
	Class III (20,000—50,000)—*concld.*							
106	Mannargudi	Madras	Tanjore	21,306	20,449	20,395	19,409	17,703
107	Masulipatam	Madras	Kistna	42,123	39,507	38,809	35,056	36,188
108	Mattancheri	Madras	Cochin	23,508	20,061	17,254	14,634	13,775
109	Mayavaram	Madras	Tanjore	27,121	24,276	23,765	23,044	21,165
110	Mhow Cantonment	Central India	Indore	29,820	36,039	31,773	27,227	...
111	Midnapore	Bengal	Midnapore	32,740	33,140	32,264	33,560	31,491
112	Miraj	Bombay	S. M. Jagirs	21,168	18,425	26,060	20,616	22,630
113	Mirzapur	United Provinces	Mirzapur	32,332	66,071	69,602	70,621	65,774
114	Monghyr	Bihar and Orissa	Monghyr	46,913	35,890	57,077	55,372	59,698
115	Muzaffarnagar	United Provinces	Muzaffarnagar	23,611	23,444	18,166	15,080	10,793
116	Muzaffarpur	Bihar and Orissa	Muzaffarpur	43,668	45,617	40,192	42,460	38,341
117	Nadiad	Bombay	Kaira	27,145	31,435	29,048	28,304	24,551
118	Nagercoil	Madras	Travancore	29,883	25,782	11,187	16,534	...
119	Narayanganj	Bengal	Dacca	27,876	24,472	17,715	12,508	11,377
120	Narnaul	Punjab	Patiala	21,350	19,489	21,159	20,052	...
121	Nasik	Bombay	Nasik	33,463	21,490	24,429	23,786	23,436
122	Nasirabad Cantonment	Ajmer-Merwara	Ajmer	20,241	22,494	21,710	21,320	20,097
123	Nawabganj	Bengal	Malda	23,322	17,016	...	...	...
124	Nellore	Madras	Nellore	33,246	32,040	29,336	27,505	29,922
125	Nowshera and Cantonment	N.-W. F. Province	Peshawar	25,406	9,518	6,885	5,473	...
126	Pakokku	Burma	Pakokku	20,010	19,456	19,972	...	...
127	Palamcottah	Madras	Tinnevelly	44,909	39,545	18,686	17,964	17,945
128	Palghat	Madras	Malabar	44,319	44,177	39,481	36,330	30,752
129	Pandharpur	Bombay	Sholapur	28,550	32,405	19,954	16,910	16,275
130	Panipat	Punjab	Karnal	26,342	26,914	27,547	25,022	25,276
131	Patan	Baroda	Baroda	28,339	31,402	32,646	32,712	31,523
132	Patiala	Punjab	Patiala	46,974	53,545	55,856	53,629	...
133	Pilibhit	United Provinces	Pilibhit	31,554	33,490	33,799	29,721	29,840
134	Porbandar	Bombay	Kathiawar	24,821	24,620	18,805	14,570	14,563
135	Prome	Burma	Prome	26,911	27,375	30,022	28,813	31,157
136	Pudukkottai	Madras	Pudukkottai	26,850	20,347	16,885	15,381	13,979
137	Puri	Bihar and Orissa	Puri	30,686	49,334	28,794	22,095	22,695
138	Purulia	Bihar and Orissa	Manbhum	20,886	17,291	12,128	9,306	5,696
139	Quetta and Cantonment	Baluchistan	Quetta-Pishin	33,922	24,584	18,802	...	...
140	Raichur	Hyderabad	Raichur	25,084	22,165	23,174	15,367	...
141	Raipur	C. P. and Berar	Raipur	35,335	32,114	23,759	24,948	19,116
142	Rajahmundry	Madras	Godavari	48,417	36,408	28,397	24,555	19,738
143	Rajapalaiyam	Madras	Ramnad	28,412	25,360	13,301	12,031	10,894
144	Rajkot	Bombay	Kathiawar	26,413	27,159	21,564	15,139	11,979
145	Rampur Boalia	Bengal	Rajshahi	23,406	21,589	21,407	19,228	22,291
146	Ranchi	Bihar and Orissa	Ranchi	32,094	25,970	20,306	18,443	12,086
147	Ratlam	Central India	Ratlam	27,957	36,321	29,822	31,066	...
148	Rewah	Central India	Rewah	26,247	24,608	23,626	22,016	...
149	Rewari	Punjab	Gurgaon	24,780	27,295	27,934	23,972	24,608
150	Rohtak	Punjab	Rohtak	20,361	20,323	16,702	15,609	16,153
151	Sambhal	United Provinces	Moradabad	45,276	42,838	40,153	37,983	49,626
152	Santipur	Bengal	Nadia	26,703	26,898	30,437	29,687	28,635
153	Sasaram	Bihar and Orissa	Shahabad	23,097	23,644	22,713	21,818	21,023
154	Saugor and Cantonment	C. P. and Berar	Saugor	45,908	42,330	44,674	44,416	45,655
155	Sembiem	Madras	Chingleput	21,325	17,567	14,276	11,901	9,956
156	Serampur	Bengal	Hooghly	49,594	44,451	35,952	25,559	24,440
157	Sikar	Rajputana	Jaipur	22,317	21,523	19,897	17,739	...
158	Sirajganj	Bengal	Pabna	24,777	23,114	23,287	21,037	21,048
159	Sitapur	United Provinces	Sitapur	21,678	22,557	21,380	18,544	5,780
160	South Barrackpore and Cantonment	Bengal	24-Parganas	27,605	19,307	35,647	30,317	30,393
161	South Suburbs	Bengal	24-Parganas	31,533	26,374	30,967	26,378	...
162	Srirangam	Madras	Trichinopoly	24,799	23,039	21,632	19,773	11,271
163	Srivilliputtur	Madras	Ramnad	29,066	26,383	21,448	18,256	16,087
164	Sukkur	Bombay	Sukkur	35,294	31,316	29,303	27,389	13,818
165	Tavoy	Burma	Tavoy	25,074	22,371	15,099	13,372	14,469
166	Tellicherry	Madras	Malabar	29,258	27,883	27,196	26,410	20,504
167	Tinnevelly	Madras	Tinnevelly	44,805	40,469	24,768	23,221	21,044
168	Tiruchendur	Madras	Tinnevelly	25,531	26,056	8,266	7,582	7,051
169	Tiruvannamalai	Madras	North Arcot	21,244	17,069	12,155	9,592	9,312
170	Titagarh	Bengal	24-Parganas	45,171	16,065	...	...	...
171	Tonk	Rajputana	Tonk	33,864	38,759	45,944	40,726	...
172	Trichur	Madras	Cochin	23,574	15,585	12,945	10,822	11,109
173	Tuticorin	Madras	Tinnevelly	40,185	28,048	25,107	16,281	10,565
174	Udaipur	Rajputana	Mewar	33,229	45,976	46,693	38,214	...
175	Ujjain	Central India	Gwalior	39,295	39,892	34,691	32,033	...
176	Vaniyambadi	Madras	North Arcot	20,406	12,005	15,838	15,436	8,627
177	Vellore	Madras	North Arcot	49,746	43,537	44,925	37,491	38,022
178	Viramgam	Bombay	Ahmadabad	20,769	18,952	23,209	18,990	19,661
179	Virudupatti	Madras	Ramnad	21,355	16,837	14,075	9,506	5,169
180	Vizagapatam	Madras	Vizagapatam	43,413	40,892	34,487	30,291	32,191
181	Vizianagram	Madras	Vizagapatam	37,550	37,270	30,881	22,577	20,169
	Class IV (10,000—20,000)	**442 Towns**		**6,163,954**	**5,975,180**	**5,410,063**	**4,942,072**	**3,634,373**
	Class V (5,000—10,000)	**848 Towns**		**5,944,503**	**5,993,471**	**5,762,965**	**5,029,457**	**3,567,272**
	Class VI (under 5,000)	**607 Towns**		**2,007,868**	**2,175,574**	**2,101,054**	**1,886,291**	**1,344,065**

Note.—The figures in columns 15 and 18, 16 and 19 against Classes IV, V and VI do not work up to the total shown in columns 5 and 6 respectively

POPULATION WITH VARIATION SINCE 1872—*concluded.*

Variation, Increase (+) or Decrease (−): 1901 to 1911.	1891 to 1901.	1881 to 1891.	1872 to 1881.	Variation in period 1872 to 1911. Increase (+), Decrease (−).	Males: 1911.	1901.	1891.	Females: 1911.	1901.	1891.	Serial No.
9	10	11	12	13	14	15	16	17	18	19	
+ 949	+ 54	+ 966	+ 1,706	+ 3,695	10,554	9,961	9,708	10,843	10,488	10,889	106
+ 3,616	+ 698	+ 3,753	− 1,132	+ 6,935	20,536	19,087	16,601	21,587	20,440	20,308	107
+ 3,447	+ 2,807	+ 3,620	+ 859	+ 9,733	12,625	10,687	9,028	10,863	9,374	8,296	108
+ 2,845	+ 811	+ 721	+ 1,879	+ 5,956	13,264	11,745	11,584	13,857	12,581	12,231	109
− 6,219	+ 4,306	+ 4,546	...	...	17,723	20,766	18,300	12,097	15,251	13,473	110
− 400	+ 878	− 1,296	+ 2,089	+ 1,349	17,577	17,641	16,253	15,163	15,408	16,011	111
+ 2,743	− 7,636	+ 5,444	− 1,904	− 1,352	10,747	9,350	13,106	10,481	9,066	12,955	112
− 33,739	− 3,531	− 1,019	+ 14,947	− 23,443	16,661	33,857	34,693	15,471	33,214	34,020	113
+ 11,033	− 31,197	+ 1,705	− 4,336	− 12,745	24,053	17,673	27,166	22,960	19,307	29,869	114
+ 367	+ 5,278	+ 3,066	+ 4,297	+ 13,018	13,973	13,640	10,997	9,638	9,804	7,169	115
− 1,949	− 3,575	+ 6,732	+ 4,219	+ 5,427	23,636	24,465	27,166	19,832	21,153	22,027	116
− 4,290	+ 2,367	+ 744	+ 3,753	+ 2,594	14,364	16,664	15,043	12,781	14,771	14,006	117
+ 4,101	+ 14,595	− 5,347	...	...	14,553	12,520	8,335	15,330	13,262	5,453	118
+ 3,404	+ 6,757	+ 5,307	+ 1,131	+ 16,499	16,738	17,068	12,116	9,138	7,404	5,899	119
+ 1,951	− 1,670	+ 1,107	...	...	10,985	9,464	10,413	10,365	10,023	10,746	120
+ 11,978	− 2,939	+ 603	+ 1,390	+ 11,037	16,897	10,869	12,540	16,566	10,631	11,889	121
− 2,253	+ 794	+ 390	+ 1,223	+ 144	11,296	11,893	11,285	9,943	10,603	10,425	122
+ 6,306	...	...	...	...	11,123	9,266	...	12,200	8,750	...	123
+ 1,206	+ 2,704	+ 1,831	− 2,417	+ 3,334	16,180	15,507	14,310	17,066	16,538	15,036	124
+ 15,990	+ 2,633	+ 1,412	...	...	16,839	7,196	5,185	6,669	3,320	1,700	125
+ 554	− 516	...	...	...	9,658	9,123	9,390	10,353	10,333	10,593	126
+ 5,364	+ 30,859	+ 722	+ 19	+ 26,964	21,231	18,398	8,945	23,679	21,157	9,841	127
+ 142	+ 4,696	+ 3,143	+ 5,687	+ 13,567	21,776	21,673	19,128	22,543	23,504	20,353	128
− 3,855	+ 12,451	+ 3,044	+ 635	+ 12,275	14,591	17,097	9,890	13,959	15,306	10,064	129
− 573	− 633	+ 2,525	− 254	+ 1,066	13,554	13,516	14,312	13,788	13,306	13,236	130
− 3,063	− 1,244	− 66	+ 1,169	− 3,184	13,904	15,690	15,724	14,435	15,713	16,923	131
− 6,871	− 2,311	+ 2,227	...	...	26,663	31,494	34,129	18,311	22,051	21,726	132
− 1,996	− 309	+ 4,078	− 119	+ 1,714	16,817	17,278	17,236	14,737	16,313	16,564	133
+ 201	+ 5,615	+ 4,235	+ 7	+ 10,258	12,673	12,753	9,410	12,149	11,667	9,396	134
− 464	− 2,047	+ 1,309	− 2,344	− 4,246	14,385	14,057	15,533	12,586	13,336	14,490	135
+ 6,503	+ 3,462	+ 1,501	+ 1,406	+ 12,873	13,106	9,949	8,090	13,743	10,398	8,796	136
− 9,646	+ 20,540	+ 6,699	− 600	+ 16,991	22,905	25,932	15,930	16,781	23,402	12,964	137
+ 3,595	+ 5,163	+ 2,823	+ 3,600	+ 15,190	11,377	9,335	6,540	9,579	7,956	5,570	138
+ 9,338	+ 5,792	...	...	...	25,289	19,161	15,815	6,653	5,433	3,069	139
+ 2,869	− 1,009	+ 7,787	...	...	12,651	9,982	11,836	12,353	12,183	11,338	140
+ 3,221	+ 9,355	− 1,189	+ 5,832	+ 16,319	18,038	16,573	11,983	17,297	15,541	11,776	141
+ 12,009	+ 8,011	+ 3,812	+ 4,817	+ 29,679	23,761	17,779	13,934	24,656	18,039	14,453	142
+ 3,053	+ 12,059	+ 1,390	+ 1,137	+ 17,528	14,108	12,639	6,607	14,301	12,731	6,694	143
− 747	+ 5,595	+ 6,425	+ 3,160	+ 14,433	13,267	14,021	11,300	13,145	13,138	10,264	144
+ 1,817	+ 182	+ 2,179	− 3,063	+ 1,115	13,057	11,590	11,751	10,349	9,999	9,656	145
+ 7,034	+ 5,654	+ 1,863	+ 6,357	+ 20,908	16,078	13,287	10,798	16,016	13,683	9,508	146
− 8,364	+ 6,499	− 1,244	...	...	14,340	18,519	15,322	13,617	17,603	14,500	147
+ 1,639	+ 983	+ 1,610	...	...	14,346	12,202	12,155	11,909	12,406	11,471	148
− 3,515	− 659	+ 3,963	− 531	+ 277	12,685	13,990	14,432	11,896	13,356	13,503	149
+ 38	+ 3,621	+ 1,008	+ 1,546	+ 6,208	11,035	10,724	8,626	9,336	9,599	8,076	150
+ 2,436	+ 3,685	+ 2,190	− 11,663	− 4,350	23,234	21,386	20,151	22,043	21,453	20,003	151
− 196	− 3,539	+ 750	+ 1,052	− 1,933	12,196	12,514	14,000	14,517	14,384	16,437	152
− 547	+ 981	+ 895	+ 706	+ 2,074	10,483	10,382	9,769	12,614	12,962	12,944	153
+ 3,678	− 2,344	+ 258	− 1,259	+ 253	24,330	21,981	23,735	21,578	20,349	20,949	154
+ 3,788	+ 3,291	+ 3,375	+ 1,943	+ 11,367	11,000	8,876	7,246	10,325	6,691	7,030	155
+ 5,143	+ 8,499	+ 10,393	+ 1,119	+ 25,154	30,303	26,931	20,200	19,231	17,530	15,753	156
+ 794	+ 1,626	+ 2,166	...	...	11,604	11,373	10,624	10,813	10,150	9,273	157
+ 1,063	− 153	+ 2,230	− 11	+ 3,729	13,236	12,560	13,090	11,541	10,534	10,177	158
− 979	+ 1,177	+ 2,836	+ 13,764	+ 15,708	12,859	12,621	12,704	9,219	9,736	8,676	159
+ 8,296	− 16,340	+ 5,330	− 6,075	− 8,787	17,132	11,249	20,370	10,473	8,056	15,277	160
+ 5,159	− 4,593	+ 4,569	...	...	17,683	14,171	16,630	13,850	12,208	14,328	161
+ 1,760	+ 1,407	+ 1,859	+ 8,502	+ 13,528	11,683	10,943	10,238	13,116	12,006	11,394	162
+ 3,684	+ 4,934	+ 3,193	+ 3,189	+ 12,909	14,331	12,897	10,448	14,735	13,468	11,000	163
+ 3,978	+ 3,014	+ 1,913	+ 14,071	+ 21,076	21,009	18,469	18,315	14,225	12,947	10,987	164
+ 2,708	+ 7,273	+ 1,727	− 1,097	+ 10,605	12,573	10,904	7,166	12,501	11,467	7,933	165
+ 1,375	+ 687	+ 786	+ 5,906	+ 8,754	14,275	13,657	13,408	14,983	14,226	13,793	166
+ 6,396	+ 15,701	+ 1,547	+ 2,177	+ 23,761	21,346	19,053	11,789	23,559	21,417	13,009	167
− 535	+ 17,790	+ 694	+ 531	+ 18,480	16,136	16,953	4,378	9,395	9,103	2,886	168
+ 4,175	+ 4,914	+ 2,563	+ 280	+ 11,932	10,621	8,416	5,976	10,623	8,653	6,179	169
+ 29,106	...	...	...	...	31,225	11,461	...	13,946	4,604	...	170
− 4,896	− 7,186	+ 5,218	...	...	16,637	18,985	23,203	17,027	19,774	23,741	171
+ 7,989	+ 2,640	+ 3,123	− 287	+ 12,465	12,089	7,932	6,502	11,485	7,053	6,353	172
+ 12,187	+ 2,941	+ 8,836	+ 6,716	+ 20,620	20,820	13,953	13,713	19,865	14,095	11,394	173
− 12,747	− 717	+ 6,479	...	...	17,460	23,453	24,873	15,709	22,533	21,620	174
− 597	+ 5,201	+ 1,759	...	...	20,864	20,829	19,302	18,431	19,063	16,300	175
+ 8,401	− 3,833	+ 412	+ 6,799	+ 11,779	9,205	5,467	6,968	11,201	6,536	8,850	176
+ 6,209	− 1,386	+ 7,484	− 581	+ 11,724	23,831	20,514	21,785	25,915	28,023	23,640	177
+ 1,817	− 4,257	+ 4,219	− 671	+ 1,108	10,355	9,332	11,506	10,414	9,620	11,613	178
+ 4,518	+ 2,762	+ 4,569	+ 4,387	+ 16,186	10,710	8,093	6,547	10,645	8,744	7,538	179
+ 2,531	+ 6,406	+ 4,196	− 1,900	+ 11,222	21,465	20,034	16,702	21,946	20,858	17,785	180
+ 280	+ 6,389	+ 6,304	+ 2,409	+ 17,381	17,907	17,817	14,883	19,053	19,453	15,990	181
+ 188,774	+ 565,117	+ 567,991	+ 1,297,699	+ 2,589,581	3,221,481	3,064,191	2,796,735	2,942,593	2,909,871	2,614,298	
− 48,968	+ 229,496	+ 733,598	+ 1,442,085	+ 2,357,131	3,077,287	3,035,627	2,915,623	2,967,216	2,909,899	2,891,076	
− 167,696	+ 74,599	+ 214,763	+ 542,256	+ 663,852	1,063,561	1,127,213	1,067,188	944,327	1,049,834	1,007,118	

as sex details of the population of certain towns in the United Provinces and Central Provinces and Berar are not available.

Statement showing the net variation during the decade 1901-11, in the places treated as towns at both censuses.

Province, State or Agency.	Places treated as towns in 1901 but now omitted.		Places now treated as towns which were not so treated in 1901.		Net variation in decade 1901-11, due to differences in the list of towns.	Variation in aggregate population of places which were treated as towns at both censuses.
	Number.	Aggregate population in 1901.	Number.	Aggregate population in 1911.		
1	2	3	4	5	6	7
INDIA	**199**	**725,496**	**204**	**1,090,666**	**+ 365,170**	**+ 117,309**
Ajmer-Merwara	...	...	1	5,205	+ 5,205	+ 9,875
Assam	...	...	2	4,045	+ 4,045	+ 20,111
Baluchistan	...	...	3	9,950	+ 9,950	+ 9,576
Bengal	...	...	2	27,255	+ 27,255	+ 341,834
Bihar and Orissa	6	21,243	6	30,472	+ 9,229	− 36,575
Bombay	11	48,324	10	36,366	− 11,958	+ 124,946
Burma	3	12,691	14	99,964	+ 87,273	+ 46,469
Central Provinces and Berar	7	18,929	11	58,125	+ 39,196	− 105,916
Coorg	3	4,234	...	...	− 4,234	− 1,034
Madras	1	4,397	46	378,427	+ 374,030	+ 249,921
North-West Frontier Province	2	10,975	1	20,256	+ 9,281	+ 12,528
Punjab	64	260,979	12	77,811	− 183,168	− 38,923
United Provinces of Agra and Oudh	48	187,402	12	72,943	− 114,459	− 360,477
Baroda State	7	33,848	2	4,727	− 29,121	− 34,712
Central India Agency	7	30,530	7	32,547	+ 2,017	− 175,309
Cochin State	...	...	2	9,934	+ 9,934	+ 12,540
Hyderabad State	2	10,823	9	56,985	+ 46,162	+ 106,927
Kashmir State	...	...	59	142,809	+ 142,809	− 220
Mysore State	37	77,633	...	...	− 77,633	+ 13,859
Rajputana Agency	1	3,488	3	11,007	+ 7,519	− 96,528
Travancore State	...	...	2	11,838	+ 11,838	+ 16,417

Note 1.—The figures in this statement include the States attached to each Province, but those for Madras exclude Cochin and Travancore.

Note 2.—In a few cases towns have been subdivided since 1901, *e.g.*, Halisahar in Bengal has been separated from Naihati and given its own municipal administration. Such changes have not been taken into account in this statement.

TABLE V.

Towns arranged Territorially with Population by Religion.

1. This Table shows the territorial distribution of the urban population by religion.

2. As in Table IV, the towns are grouped into six classes according to their population. Those in the first three classes are entered separately in alphabetical order. Those in the last three are not shown in detail: only the total number of towns in each class is given with their aggregate population.

3. The figures for Madras States include those for Cochin and Travancore, which are given separately on page 36.

4. The Column "Others" includes the following :—

Province, State or Agency.	Religion.	Persons.	Males.	Females.
1	2	3	4	5
Total	......	42,200	24,466	17,734
Ajmer-Merwara	Arya	836	495	341
Assam	Confucian	1	1	...
	Brahmo	170	94	76
Baluchistan	Brahmo	38	19	19
	Arya	532	335	197
	No Religion	1	1	...
Bengal	Confucian	1,055	904	151
	Brahmo	2,505	1,263	1,242
	Arya	9	5	4
Bihar and Orissa	Brahmo	418	223	195
	Arya	1,064	569	495
	Kumbhipatia	31	19	12
	Birsait	6	4	2
Bombay	Brahmo	110	58	52
	Hindu-Muhammadan	79	51	28
	Unspecified	17	10	7
Burma	Confucian	71	57	14
	Agnostic and Secularist	35	19	16
Central Provinces and Berar	Brahmo	23	10	13
	Arya	512	303	209
Madras	Confucian	21	21	...
	Brahmo	371	216	155
	Atheist	14	7	7
United Provinces of Agra and Oudh	Brahmo	41	24	17
	Arya	30,564	17,694	12,870
Baroda State	Brahmo	6	4	2
	Arya	275	190	85
Bengal States	Brahmo	46	24	22
Bombay States	Hindu-Muhammadan	1,440	750	690
Central India Agency	Brahmo	9	6	3
	Arya	77	50	27
Hyderabad State	Brahmo	36	18	18
	Arya	109	55	54
Kashmir State	Brahmo	1	...	1
	Arya	391	250	141
Mysore State	Brahmo	65	31	34
Rajputana Agency	Brahmo	71	37	34
	Arya	1,032	585	447
United Provinces States	Arya	118	64	54

NOTE.—In Bengal details by religion are not available for 640 persons (males 458, females 182) in a place classed as a town after the statistics had been compiled.

TABLE V.—Towns arranged Territorially

Serial No.	Town.	District or State.	Population. Persons.	Population. Males.	Population. Females.	Hindu. Males.	Hindu. Females.	Sikh. Males.	Sikh. Females.	Jain. Males.	Jain. Females.
	1	2	3	4	5	6	7	8	9	10	11
	INDIA	**2,153 Towns**	**29,748,228**	**16,108,304**	**13,639,924**	**10,358,164**	**8,820,068**	**132,802**	**71,331**	**194,741**	**174,437**
	Provinces	1,452 Towns	22,817,715	12,525,830	10,291,885	8,003,285	6,620,354	103,363	53,343	92,747	69,703
	Ajmer-Merwara	5 Towns	140,394	77,177	63,217	46,560	38,636	774	130	3,060	2,677
	Class II.—Ajmer	**Ajmer**	**86,222**	**47,354**	**38,868**	**27,187**	**22,021**	**61**	**26**	**1,440**	**1,252**
	Class III	**2 Towns**	**43,041**	**23,626**	**19,415**	**14,626**	**12,728**	**627**	**75**	**1,387**	**1,248**
1	Beawar	Merwara	22,800	12,328	10,472	8,397	7,136	1	...	1,236	1,130
2	Nasirabad Cantonment	Ajmer	20,241	11,298	8,943	6,229	5,592	626	75	151	118
	Class V	**2 Towns**	**11,131**	**6,197**	**4,934**	**4,747**	**3,887**	**86**	**29**	**233**	**177**
	Assam	20 Towns	136,668	83,500	53,168	54,782	32,116	85	18	471	87
	Class IV	**5 Towns**	**65,879**	**38,371**	**27,508**	**25,286**	**16,444**	**65**	**14**	**110**	**29**
	Class V	**9 Towns**	**55,096**	**34,908**	**20,188**	**23,375**	**12,748**	**20**	**4**	**289**	**52**
	Class VI	**6 Towns**	**15,693**	**10,221**	**5,472**	**6,121**	**2,924**	...	...	**72**	**6**
	Baluchistan	6 Towns	49,609	37,660	11,949	12,782	4,455	2,898	712	8	1
	Class III.—Quetta and Cantonment	**Quetta-Pishin**	**33,922**	**25,269**	**8,653**	**8,439**	**3,226**	**1,413**	**442**	**8**	**1**
	Class V—Sibi	**Sibi**	**6,597**	**4,900**	**1,697**	**2,092**	**582**	**344**	**93**	...	...
	Class VI	**4 Towns**	**9,090**	**7,491**	**1,599**	**2,251**	**647**	**1,141**	**177**	...	...
	Bengal	119 Towns	2,945,622	1,805,560	1,140,062	1,214,838	764,414	1,145	236	2,663	1,011
	Class I	**3 Towns**	**1,183,624**	**785,331**	**398,293**	**525,722**	**271,534**	**793**	**172**	**1,358**	**444**
1	Calcutta and Fort	Calcutta	896,067	607,674	288,393	404,528	200,325	769	163	1,353	444
2	Dacca	Dacca	108,551	63,091	45,460	36,249	23,745	11	5	...	...
3	Howrah	Howrah	179,006	114,566	64,440	84,945	47,464	13	4	5	...
	Class II	**2 Towns**	**104,181**	**66,474**	**37,707**	**42,912**	**24,137**	**19**	**7**	**9**	**6**
4	Bhatpara	24-Parganas	50,414	34,739	15,675	23,115	11,013	...	...	9	6
5	Manicktola	24-Parganas	53,767	31,735	22,032	19,797	13,124	19	7	...	...
	Class III	**28 Towns**	**796,998**	**466,082**	**330,916**	**311,293**	**217,416**	**284**	**44**	**214**	**33**
6	Asansol	Burdwan	21,919	12,486	9,433	8,033	5,809	...	...	5	6
7	Baidyabati	Hooghly	20,516	11,792	8,724	10,178	8,040	5	...	...	...
8	Bally	Howrah	22,394	14,217	8,177	11,241	8,823	...	...	5	1
9	Bankura	Bankura	23,453	12,156	11,297	11,439	10,704	...	...	...	1
10	Baranagar	24-Parganas	25,895	14,982	10,913	11,287	8,604	...	...	...	1
11	Barisal	Backergunge	22,473	15,488	6,985	8,861	3,753	...	...	...	...
12	Berhampore	Murshidabad	26,143	14,302	11,841	11,714	9,810	...	...	7	2
13	Bhadreswar	Hooghly	24,353	15,862	8,491	11,253	6,700	...	...	...	...
14	Bishnupur	Bankura	20,478	10,025	10,453	9,685	10,063	...	...	...	...
15	Brahmanbaria	Tippera	22,295	11,671	10,624	7,358	6,585	...	...	...	...
16	Burdwan	Burdwan	35,921	20,527	15,394	15,364	11,167	3	1	...	...
17	Chittagong	Chittagong	28,766	18,779	9,987	8,874	2,631	...	...	3	...
18	Comilla	Tippera	22,692	13,706	8,986	6,773	3,302	...	...	..	...
19	Cossipore-Chitpur	24-Parganas	48,178	30,793	17,385	22,142	12,290	21	1	12	4
20	Garden Reach	24-Parganas	45,295	27,665	17,630	14,022	7,264	...	...	...	...
21	Hooghly-Chinsura	Hooghly	28,916	15,817	13,099	13,080	11,204	1	...	2	...
22	Jamalpur	Mymensingh	21,109	11,728	9,381	4,015	2,565	...	...	4	...
23	Krishnagar	Nadia	23,475	11,767	11,708	7,993	7,825	...	...	...	...
24	Midnapore	Midnapore	32,740	17,577	15,163	13,503	11,284	2	...	3	2
25	Narayanganj	Dacca	27,876	18,738	9,138	10,306	4,227	1	...	6	...
26	Nawabganj	Malda	23,322	11,122	12,200	3,453	3,269	...	...	3	...
27	Rampur Boalia	Rajshahi	23,406	13,067	10,349	7,417	6,564	...	...	18	8
28	Santipur	Nadia	26,703	12,186	14,517	8,291	9,663	...	..	...	...
29	Serampur	Hooghly	49,594	30,363	19,231	23,379	16,083	3	...	...	...
30	Sirajganj	Pabna	24,777	13,336	11,541	5,595	3,907	...	...	146	9
31	South Barrackpore and Cantonment	24-Parganas	27,605	17,132	10,473	11,537	6,868	246	42	...	...
32	South Suburbs	24-Parganas	31,533	17,683	13,850	13,229	10,901	...	...	...	...
33	Titagarh	24-Parganas	45,171	31,225	13,946	21,271	10,492	...	...	...	...
	Class IV	**39 Towns**	**570,052**	**326,662**	**243,390**	**218,823**	**158,225**	**35**	**10**	**870**	**476**
	Class V	**33 Towns**	**244,584**	**135,669**	**108,915**	**99,436**	**79,825**	**14**	**3**	**103**	**46**
	Class VI	**14 Towns**	**46,183**	**25,342**	**20,841**	**16,652**	**13,277**	...	...	**109**	**6**
	Bihar and Orissa	70 Towns	1,285,752	666,006	619,746	503,760	453,981	594	612	887	792
	Class I—Patna	**Patna**	**136,153**	**70,841**	**65,312**	**58,666**	**47,102**	**38**	**1**	**29**	**38**
	Class II	**3 Towns**	**189,505**	**99,725**	**89,780**	**75,340**	**64,097**	...	...	**84**	**96**
1	Bhagalpur	Bhagalpur	74,349	39,947	34,402	29,145	23,666	...	...	60	67
2	Cuttack	Cuttack	52,528	28,504	24,024	23,344	18,257	...	...	22	26
3	Darbhanga	Darbhanga	62,628	31,274	31,354	22,851	22,174	...	...	2	3

WITH POPULATION BY RELIGION.

DISTRIBUTION BY RELIGION.														
BUDDHIST.		ZOROASTRIAN.		MUSALMAN.		CHRISTIAN.		JEW.		ANIMISTIC.		OTHERS.		Serial No.
Males.	Females.	Males.	Females.	Males.	Females.	Males.	Females.	Males.	Females.	Males.	Females.	Males.	Females.	
12	13	14	15	16	17	18	19	20	21	22	23	24	25	
355,832	353,391	44,369	42,199	4,461,371	3,750,613	464,888	361,401	9,340	8,678	61,873	39,890	24,924	17,916	
354,613	352,324	39,580	36,475	3,473,105	2,821,914	379,397	285,628	8,675	8,034	48,205	27,806	22,860	16,304	
...	...	133	128	23,066	19,355	2,920	1,819	14	13	155	118	495	341	
...	...	94	87	16,635	14,019	1,459	1,132	12	13	52	49	414	269	
...	...	38	41	5,345	4,515	1,419	667	2	...	102	69	80	72	
...	...	6	10	2,417	1,030	196	208	...	..	8	5	67	58	1
...	...	32	31	2,928	2,585	1,223	464	2	...	94	64	13	14	2
...	...	1	...	1,086	821	42	20	...	...	1	...	1	...	
127	75	...	.	22,809	15,742	1,709	1,692	1	...	3,421	3,362	95	76	
116	67	.	...	8,800	6,672	1,341	1,346	...	...	2,602	2,892	51	44	
8	8	...	...	10,534	6,867	309	312	1	...	333	167	39	30	
3	...	..	...	3,475	2,203	59	34	...	...	486	303	5	2	
7	7	90	72	17,777	5,358	3,713	1,106	30	22	...	...	355	216	
6	6	75	59	11,512	3,741	3,514	990	27	20	...	...	275	168	
..	...	14	13	2,328	920	83	65	2	2	...	..	37	22	
1	1	1	...	3,937	697	116	51	1	...	...	...	43	26	
6,643	4,775	360	205	537,861	338,422	34,091	26,885	965	999	3,464	1,536	2,630	1,579	
1,958	526	308	187	228,006	104,883	24,227	18,428	942	991	210	63	1,807	1,065	
1,837	506	293	174	173,785	67,603	22,472	17,079	933	986	39	17	1,665	897	1
67	18	1	...	20,119	21,176	518	380	6	2	12	1	108	133	2
54	2	14	13	28,102	15,905	1,237	969	3	3	159	45	34	35	3
7	...	...	...	23,150	13,472	277	82	...	...	100	3	...	...	
7	...	...	..	11,350	4,616	158	37	...	...	100	3	...	...	4
...	...	...	...	11,800	8,850	119	45	..	...	...	...	...	...	5
593	107	20	8	146,545	107,794	5,406	4,643	12	6	1,517	693	204	182	
...	...	...	...	3,471	2,787	974	831	...	...	3	...	...	...	6
...	...	...	...	1,567	676	2	3	...	...	40	5	...	1	7
...	...	9	...	2,477	1,044	188	136	...	...	287	169	10	4	8
...	...	...	...	530	426	171	165	...	...	16	...	..	1	9
...	...	...	...	3,508	2,104	83	95	...	...	5	6	9	14	10
6	...	...	...	6,123	2,320	453	376	...	...	1	...	44	27	11
5	...	...	...	2,420	1,873	135	153	1	1	15	1	5	1	12
17	...	...	...	4,464	1,775	60	12	...	...	68	4	...	...	13
...	...	...	...	334	388	6	3	...	...	...	...	...	...	14
1	1	...	...	4,286	4,009	26	29	...	...	...	...	...	...	15
...	...	...	...	5,053	4,105	101	120	1	...	2	1	3	...	16
401	78	5	...	8,941	6,743	480	475	7	5	22	6	46	49	17
17	21	...	...	6,837	5,584	59	49	...	...	...	...	20	30	18
8	1	1	...	8,294	4,743	283	326	1	...	11	...	20	20	19
105	4	1	1	13,404	10,303	129	58	...	...	...	...	4	1	20
4	1	...	...	2,660	1,700	42	89	...	...	10	...	9	6	21
2	...	...	...	7,692	6,812	7	3	...	...	4	..	4	1	22
...	...	...	...	3,345	3,334	429	540	...	...	..	...	...	..	23
..	...	..	...	3,417	3,220	262	263	...	...	378	383	12	11	24
2	...	1	...	8,307	4,836	111	72	...	...	..	.	4	3	25
...	...	...	...	7,666	8,931	...	...	...	...	...	...	...	...	26
5	...	...	...	5,582	4,743	23	33	2	...	10	1	...	..	27
...	...	...	...	3,888	4,848	...	..	...	...	...	.	7	6	28
9	...	1	...	6,388	2,955	237	128	...	...	346	65	.	...	29
...	..	...	...	7,472	7,008	22	20	...	...	...	..	1	2	30
2	...	...	...	4,597	3,062	738	466	...	...	10	15	...	...	31
...	...	...	...	3,932	2,749	260	171	...	...	256	24	6	5	32
9	1	2	7	9,800	3,414	119	19	...	...	24	13	...	...	33
2,633	2,139	28	10	98,906	79,049	3,836	2,719	8	1	1,053	466	576	395	
551	501	4	...	33,723	27,212	1,230	996	3	1	566	297	39	34	
901	1,502	...	...	7,637	6,022	21	17	...	...	18	14	4	3	
23	5	15	8	145,256	149,889	9,883	9,455	10	14	4,763	4,286	815	704	
2	...	...	...	18,372	17,664	243	457	...	...	...	...	71	50	
2	...	...	...	23,017	24,020	1,173	1,479	2	2	20	4	87	82	
2	...	...	...	10,287	10,426	296	214	2	2	20	4	35	23	1
...	...	...	...	4,302	4,539	791	1,149	...	...	...	...	45	53	2
..	...	...	...	8,328	9,055	86	116	...	...	...	..	7	6	3

TABLE V.—Towns arranged Territorially

Serial No.	Town.	District or State.	Population. Persons.	Population. Males.	Population. Females.	Distribution by Religion. Hindu. Males.	Hindu. Females.	Sikh. Males.	Sikh. Females.	Jain. Males.	Jain. Females.
	1	2	3	4	5	6	7	8	9	10	11
	Bihar and Orissa —*concld.*										
	Class III	**14 Towns**	**471,944**	**245,481**	**226,463**	**182,706**	**160,969**	**526**	**594**	**312**	**339**
4	Arrah	Shahabad	38,540	19,955	18,594	14,803	13,088	3	1	158	206
5	Balasore	Balasore	21,332	11,323	10,139	8,906	7,739	...	...	...	...
6	Bettiah	Champaran	25,793	13,006	12,697	8,665	7,646	...	...	...	...
7	Bihar	Patna	35,151	16,095	18,156	11,145	11,273	...	...	5	4
8	Chapra	Saran	43,373	21,601	20,772	16,505	15,330	...	...	34	45
9	Dinapore and Cant.	Patna	31,025	15,788	15,237	11,351	11,343	...	...	...	...
10	Gaya	Gaya	49,921	26,310	23,611	19,846	17,574	3	1	58	39
11	Jamalpur	Monghyr	20,526	10,881	9,645	8,273	7,306	23	17	25	18
12	Monghyr	Monghyr	46,913	24,053	22,900	18,287	17,172	...	...	...	...
13	Muzaffarpur	Muzaffarpur	43,668	23,836	10,832	17,404	13,471	...	...	...	...
14	Puri	Puri	39,686	22,905	16,781	22,740	16,603	...	...	...	...
15	Purulia	Manbhum	20,886	11,377	9,509	9,409	7,743	1	...	1	...
16	Ranchi	Ranchi	32,994	16,078	16,016	9,438	6,262	1	...	20	23
17	Sasaram	Shahabad	23,097	10,483	12,614	5,844	6,431	406	575	11	4
	Class IV	**20 Towns**	**274,514**	**141,012**	**133,502**	**111,032**	**103,688**	**4**	**5**	**146**	**164**
	Class V	**25 Towns**	**183,012**	**93,498**	**89,514**	**70,035**	**66,479**	**26**	**12**	**273**	**183**
	Class VI	**7 Towns**	**30,624**	**15,449**	**15,175**	**12,567**	**12,246**	...	...	**43**	**32**
	Bombay (*including Sind and Aden.*)	**200 Towns**	**3,738,571**	**2,094,891**	**1,643,680**	**1,440,320**	**1,147,661**	**1,680**	**503**	**46,533**	**31,879**
	Class I	**5 Towns**	**1,621,849**	**992,776**	**629,073**	**668,845**	**419,130**	**291**	**104**	**27,658**	**15,478**
1	Ahmadabad and Cant.	Ahmadabad	216,777	117,302	99,475	82,912	69,202	5	3	8,334	7,753
2	Bombay	Bombay	979,445	640,288	339,157	436,521	227,521	93	14	15,395	5,065
3	Karachi and Cant.	Karachi	151,903	90,233	61,670	41,069	25,132	189	84	434	213
4	Poona and Cantonment	Poona	158,856	85,310	73,537	66,030	59,098	4	3	1,347	690
5	Surat and Cantonment	Surat	114,868	59,634	55,234	42,313	38,177	...	...	2,148	1,758
	Class II	**4 Towns**	**252,681**	**133,882**	**118,799**	**88,222**	**81,100**	**280**	**111**	**957**	**711**
6	Hubli	Dharwar	61,440	31,577	29,863	20,265	19,257	15	1	597	426
7	Hyderabad and Cant.	Hyderabad	75,952	41,882	34,070	26,559	23,134	149	59	4	3
8	Shikarpur	Sukkur	53,944	28,532	25,412	18,072	17,009	115	51	...	...
9	Sholapur	Sholapur	61,345	31,891	29,454	23,306	21,610	1	...	356	283
	Class III	**16 Towns**	**498,706**	**269,076**	**229,630**	**172,659**	**156,307**	**345**	**130**	**4,841**	**4,195**
10	Aden and Cantonment	Aden	36,876	25,845	11,031	1,498	472	17	3	188	47
11	Ahmadnagar and Cant.	Ahmadnagar	42,940	23,378	19,563	16,678	14,760	...	...	676	573
12	Bandra	Thana	24,286	13,250	11,036	6,870	5,208	...	...	101	33
13	Belgaum and Cant.	Belgaum	42,623	23,097	19,526	15,104	13,287	19	27	750	710
14	Bijapur	Bijapur	27,615	14,345	13,270	10,163	9,289	...	...	169	79
15	Broach	Broach	43,403	22,630	20,773	13,580	12,147	...	...	358	318
16	Dharwar	Dharwar	30,289	15,528	14,761	11,401	10,624	...	...	148	113
17	Dhulia	Khandesh West	30,800	16,231	14,560	11,857	10,614	...	...	334	247
18	Gadag	Dharwar	30,429	15,570	14,859	11,403	10,980	...	...	173	76
19	Godhra	Panch Mahals	22,144	11,599	10,545	5,643	4,531	...	...	318	312
20	Malvan	Ratnagiri	22,080	10,327	11,753	9,531	10,960	...	...	23	21
21	Nadiad	Kaira	27,145	14,364	12,781	11,814	10,536	...	...	91	80
22	Nasik	Nasik	33,463	16,897	16,566	14,077	14,007	...	...	126	104
23	Pandharpur	Sholapur	28,550	14,591	13,959	13,598	12,943	...	...	319	336
24	Sukkur	Sukkur	35,294	21,069	14,225	12,387	9,005	309	100	2	1
25	Viramgam	Ahmadabad	20,769	10,355	10,414	7,057	6,948	...	...	1,067	1,155
	Class IV	**45 Towns**	**626,643**	**324,715**	**301,928**	**234,618**	**219,867**	**645**	**83**	**4,542**	**3,536**
	Class V	**84 Towns**	**572,224**	**288,977**	**283,247**	**214,273**	**211,220**	**105**	**70**	**7,194**	**6,741**
	Class VI	**46 Towns**	**166,468**	**85,465**	**81,003**	**61,703**	**59,917**	**14**	**5**	**1,341**	**1,218**
	Burma	**63 Towns**	**1,127,975**	**680,760**	**447,215**	**169,412**	**38,189**	**4,191**	**1,000**	**348**	**78**
	Class I	**2 Towns**	**431,615**	**277,829**	**153,786**	**94,297**	**21,937**	**1,667**	**325**	**260**	**38**
1	Mandalay and Cant.	Mandalay	138,299	69,718	68,581	5,269	2,615	572	157	2	...
2	Rangoon and Cant.	Rangoon	293,316	208,111	85,205	89,028	19,322	1,095	168	258	38
	Class II—Moulmein	**Amherst**	**57,582**	**35,130**	**22,452**	**11,761**	**3,403**	**4**	...	**22**	**14**
	Class III	**6 Towns**	**172,021**	**104,380**	**67,641**	**20,920**	**2,460**	**63**	**18**	**12**	**5**
3	Akyab	Akyab	37,893	20,500	8,384	8,333	288	33	4	9	5
4	Bassein	Bassein	37,081	24,246	12,835	7,633	1,033	...	...	3	...
5	Henzada	Henzada	25,052	14,009	11,043	2,360	414	3	...	...	...
6	Pakokku	Pakokku	20,010	9,658	10,352	205	78	20	13	...	...
7	Prome	Prome	26,911	14,385	12,526	1,919	600	7	1	...	...
8	Tavoy	Tavoy	25,074	12,573	12,501	471	47	...	...	...	...
	Class IV	**16 Towns**	**213,957**	**124,514**	**89,443**	**25,202**	**6,319**	**549**	**183**	**40**	**17**
	Class V	**32 Towns**	**229,708**	**125,946**	**103,762**	**15,712**	**3,721**	**1,547**	**300**	**14**	**4**
	Class VI	**6 Towns**	**23,092**	**12,961**	**10,131**	**1,590**	**349**	**361**	**165**	...	...
	Central Provinces and Berar.	**112 Towns**	**1,176,225**	**610,417**	**565,808**	**468,472**	**439,250**	**1,354**	**268**	**9,330**	**8,598**
	Class I	**2 Towns**	**202,066**	**109,731**	**92,335**	**79,521**	**69,522**	**632**	**113**	**1,074**	**916**
1	Jubbulpore and Cant.	Jubbulpore	100,651	56,035	44,616	37,334	31,568	538	64	730	644
2	Nagpur	Nagpur	101,415	53,696	47,719	42,187	37,954	94	49	364	270

WITH POPULATION BY RELIGION—*continued.*

DISTRIBUTION BY RELIGION.														
BUDDHIST.		ZOROASTRIAN.		MUSALMAN.		CHRISTIAN.		JEW.		ANIMISTIC.		OTHERS.		Serial No.
Males.	Females.	Males.	Females.	Males.	Females.	Males.	Females.	Males.	Females.	Males.	Females.	Males.	Females.	
12	13	14	15	16	17	18	19	20	21	22	23	24	25	
12	5	5	6	53,868	57,421	6,165	5,543	...	...	1,395	1,137	496	449	
...	...	...	...	4,044	5,257	44	41	...	...	...	...	3	3	4
...	...	...	...	1,963	2,100	324	285	...	...	9	...	21	15	5
...	...	...	...	3,777	4,218	654	833	...	...	...	...	...	...	6
...	...	...	...	5,844	6,875	1	4	...	...	...	...	...	...	7
...	...	...	...	4,896	5,310	76	87	...	...	...	...	...	...	8
6	4	...	...	3,411	3,577	843	191	...	...	...	...	183	126	9
...	...	...	...	6,236	6,862	159	131	...	...	...	...	2	...	10
...	...	...	...	2,036	1,857	517	442	...	...	...	...	8	5	11
3	1	5	6	5,414	5,310	126	120	...	...	...	...	226	258	12
				6,103	6,062	331	292	...	...	...	...	...	...	13
...	...	...	...	36	93	113	80	...	...	...	...	7	5	14
2	...	...	...	1,412	1,260	340	351	...	...	213	154	1	1	15
...	...	...	...	3,677	4,034	2,634	2,678	...	...	1,173	963	47	36	16
...	...	...	...	4,119	5,606	13	8	...	...	...	...	...	...	17
...	...	2	...	28,487	29,188	852	726	1	2	404	325	84	64	
7	...	8	2	18,755	18,781	1,396	1,190	7	10	2,917	2,798	74	59	
...	...	...	...	2,757	2,815	54	60	...	...	27	22	1	...	
458	209	36,776	34,523	477,303	370,268	79,362	47,121	6,970	6,410	5,370	5,019	119	87	
[illegible]	176	[illegible]	29,976	209,464	134,636	50,292	25,379	4,281	3,911	283	225	71	58	
...	...	744	682	24,249	21,033	722	502	128	130	201	166	7	5	1
425	168	26,764	24,167	118,984	60,362	38,583	18,772	3,505	3,092	4	2	14	9	2
3	16	1,121	1,044	41,632	32,443	5,479	2,457	278	257	...	...	28	24	3
1	7	1,139	1,039	11,185	8,867	5,218	3,379	370	432	29	25	6	7	4
...	...	3,404	3,054	13,414	11,931	290	269	...	...	49	32	16	13	5
...	...	[illegible]	237	41,415	34,796	2,696	1,800	23	25	...	...	20	19	
...	...	73	60	9,307	9,070	1,283	1,029	17	20	...	...	...	...	6
...	...	43	37	14,206	10,617	805	196	6	5	...	...	20	19	7
...	...	1	1	10,326	8,257	18	4	...	...	...	...	...	...	8
...	...	152	139	7,496	6,852	500	571	...	...	...	...	...	...	9
13	6	2,215	2,279	71,861	54,518	13,183	8,438	1,934	1,770	2,801	1,977	24	10	
9	...	263	114	19,717	8,344	2,281	326	1,873	1,724	1	1	...	...	10
3	4	98	101	2,618	3,003	2,290	1,112	12	5	6	8	...	...	11
...	...	644	674	2,021	1,860	3,603	3,448	8	9	...	...	...	...	12
...	...	76	68	4,717	4,082	2,418	1,351	13	6	...	...	...	...	13
...	...	10	11	3,930	3,819	73	71	...	1	...	...	...	...	14
...	...	853	1,096	6,353	5,842	194	107	...	...	1,269	1,253	24	10	15
...	...	15	14	3,549	3,652	392	339	20	19	3	...	...	...	16
...	...	40	23	3,557	3,214	61	84	...	...	382	387	...	...	17
...	...	30	18	3,363	3,267	610	514	2	4	...	...	...	...	18
...	...	76	69	5,158	5,272	73	39	1	1	331	321	...	...	19
...	...	4	...	261	214	508	552	...	...	...	...	...	...	20
...	...	21	21	2,194	2,044	241	108	...	...	3	2	...	...	21
1	2	35	19	2,341	2,168	313	265	5	1	1	2	...	...	22
		6	1	655	658	12	29	...	...	...	...	...	...	23
...	...	35	39	8,246	5,007	90	73	...	...	...	...	...	...	24
...	...	20	16	2,181	2,272	25	20	...	...	5	3	...	...	25
13	26	1,586	1,585	73,154	68,258	8,885	6,552	336	293	1,732	1,608	4	...	
...	...	356	286	61,424	59,449	4,421	4,389	306	313	898	788	...	...	
3	1	188	160	20,985	18,611	685	572	90	98	456	421	...	...	
346,749	346,840	174	95	110,039	37,868	28,148	18,951	526	440	21,097	3,724	76	30	
103,824	102,876	147	75	53,802	15,795	16,215	10,874	412	369	7,133	1,468	72	27	
51,687	57,546	26	...	8,696	6,267	2,238	1,807	31	...	1,197	187	...	...	1
52,137	45,330	121	75	45,106	9,528	13,977	9,067	381	369	5,936	1,281	72	27	2
18,289	13,685	3	1	6,663	3,420	1,563	1,492	30	20	1,755	417	...	...	
58,671	58,442	14	10	20,476	4,970	2,114	1,458	42	24	2,068	254			
8,790	6,074	...	...	13,730	1,801	350	158	19	7	345	47	...	...	3
11,517	9,368	13	10	3,000	1,522	587	610	14	13	490	59	...	...	4
9,978	9,879	...	...	934	417	400	300	6	4	319	29	...	...	5
8,808	9,977	...	...	294	172	91	88	...	...	155	29	...	...	6
10,638	11,063	2	...	1,149	550	196	199	...	...	484	74	...	...	7
10,965	11,861	...	...	679	469	190	108	3	...	275	16	...	...	8
74,844	71,761	5	5	14,687	7,032	5,354	3,280	40	26	4,387	837	4	3	
86,860	91,855	5	4	12,277	5,354	2,753	1,798	...	...	5,369	727	...	...	
8,410	8,219	...	...	2,134	1,297	149	79	2	1	385	21	...	...	
7	5	941	607	111,468	102,488	12,534	8,446	76	45	5,922	5,879	313	222	
4	...	386	277	20,681	16,940	6,507	3,763	30	22	821	739	75	45	
2	...	65	51	12,827	10,205	4,340	1,961	7	1	118	77	75	45	1
2	...	321	226	7,854	6,735	2,158	1,802	23	21	703	662	...	...	2

TABLE V.—Towns arranged Territorially

Serial No.	Town.	District or State.	Population. Persons.	Population. Males.	Population. Females.	Distribution by Religion. Hindu. Males.	Hindu. Females.	Sikh. Males.	Sikh. Females.	Jain. Males.	Jain. Females.
	1	2	3	4	5	6	7	8	9	10	11
	Central Provinces and Berar—*concld.*										
	Class III	**6 Towns**	**185,720**	**97,656**	**88,064**	**69,681**	**63,015**	**575**	**77**	**1,596**	**1,356**
3	Akola	Akola	25,826	14,006	11,820	10,285	8,606	...	...	133	94
4	Amraoti	Amraoti	34,270	18,147	16,123	13,860	12,155	7	...	344	322
5	Burhanpur	Nimar	22,777	11,624	11,153	6,119	6,025	...	...	35	26
6	Khandwa	Nimar	21,604	11,511	10,093	7,310	6,338	...	...	207	159
7	Raipur	Raipur	35,335	18,038	17,297	14,421	13,775	8	13	209	179
8	Saugor and Cantonment	Saugor	45,906	24,330	21,576	17,677	16,116	560	64	668	576
	Class IV	**22 Towns**	**301,002**	**154,864**	**146,138**	**118,962**	**112,757**	**66**	**47**	**2,541**	**2,374**
	Class V	**64 Towns**	**411,979**	**206,932**	**203,047**	**168,535**	**164,465**	**42**	**15**	**3,490**	**3,330**
	Class VI	**18 Towns**	**75,458**	**39,234**	**36,224**	**31,793**	**29,551**	**39**	**16**	**629**	**624**
	Coorg	**2 Towns**	**9,981**	**5,897**	**4,084**	**3,704**	**2,512**	...	...	**27**	**38**
	Class V—Mercara	**Coorg**	**6,269**	**3,692**	**2,577**	**2,649**	**1,740**	...	...	**1**	...
	Class VI—Virarajendrapet	**Coorg**	**3,712**	**2,205**	**1,507**	**1,055**	**772**	...	...	**26**	**38**
	Madras	**279 Towns**	**4,892,626**	**2,413,517**	**2,479,109**	**1,960,062**	**2,004,911**	**5**	**2**	**1,880**	**989**
	Class I	**3 Towns**	**776,302**	**395,116**	**381,186**	**317,580**	**306,610**	...	...	**730**	**268**
1	Madras and Cantonment	Madras	518,660	266,465	252,195	213,731	202,179	...	...	699	255
2	Madura	Madura	134,130	67,091	67,039	58,924	58,875	...	...	4	...
3	Trichinopoly and Cant.	Trichinopoly	123,512	61,560	61,952	44,925	45,556	...	...	27	13
	Class II	**8 Towns**	**487,274**	**241,103**	**246,171**	**200,133**	**204,564**	...	...	**251**	**228**
4	Calicut and Cantonment	Malabar	78,417	40,680	37,737	23,585	20,945	...	...	21	27
5	Cocanada	Godavari	54,110	26,629	27,481	24,756	25,596	...	...	2	1
6	Conjeeveram	Chingleput	53,864	26,451	27,413	25,416	26,448	...	...	56	56
7	Cuddalore	South Arcot	56,574	28,012	28,562	25,702	26,420	...	...	32	23
8	Kumbakonam	Tanjore	64,647	31,327	33,320	29,196	31,100	...	...	30	36
9	Negapatam	Tanjore	60,168	29,995	30,173	21,513	20,197	...	...	18	...
10	Salem	Salem	59,153	29,282	29,021	26,238	26,905	...	...	...	...
11	Tanjore	Tanjore	60,341	28,777	31,564	24,727	26,953	...	...	95	85
	Class III	**39 Towns**	**1,237,469**	**613,204**	**624,265**	**478,223**	**483,873**	**5**	**2**	**302**	**141**
12	Adoni	Bellary	31,645	16,080	15,565	9,970	9,565	...	...	65	19
13	Anakapalle	Vizagapatam	20,625	10,165	10,460	10,060	10,347	...	...	...	...
14	Aruppukkottai	Ramnad	26,681	12,988	13,693	12,306	12,940	...	...	...	...
15	Bellary and Cantonment	Bellary	34,956	18,474	16,482	10,363	9,301	...	...	6	...
16	Berhampur	Ganjam	31,456	15,331	16,125	14,405	15,316	...	...	...	...
17	Bezwada	Kistna	32,867	17,026	15,841	14,251	13,360	...	...	...	...
18	Bodinayakkanur	Madura	20,183	9,671	10,512	8,810	9,634	...	...	...	...
19	Cannanore and Cant.	Malabar	28,957	14,241	14,716	5,835	6,004	...	...	...	...
20	Chidambaram	South Arcot	21,327	10,279	11,048	9,554	10,285	...	...	3	1
21	Cochin	Malabar	20,023	10,764	9,259	2,553	2,129	...	...	...	...
22	Coimbatore	Coimbatore	47,007	23,390	23,608	10,686	19,853	...	...	...	...
23	Dindigul	Madura	25,062	13,720	12,332	9,689	9,276	...	...	...	...
24	Ellore	Kistna	37,819	18,302	19,517	16,112	17,303	...	...	...	...
25	Gudiyattam	North Arcot	23,390	11,386	12,004	9,343	9,735	...	...	...	...
26	Guntur	Guntur	40,529	20,826	19,703	15,143	14,414	...	...	41	...
27	Kulasekarapatnam	Tinnevelly	21,812	9,535	12,287	5,181	5,731	...	...	...	...
28	Kurnool	Kurnool	26,040	12,766	13,274	6,300	5,492	...	...	43	6
29	Mangalore	South Canara	46,412	25,129	23,283	13,072	12,555	...	...	25	5
30	Mannargudi	Tanjore	21,308	10,556	10,842	9,906	10,190	...	...	60	86
31	Masulipatam	Kistna	42,123	20,536	21,567	17,686	18,525	...	...	...	...
32	Mayavaram	Tanjore	27,121	13,264	13,857	12,553	12,941	...	...	...	..
33	Nellore	Nellore	33,246	16,180	17,066	11,002	11,646	...	...	...	.
34	Palamcottah	Tinnevelly	44,909	21,281	23,678	12,851	14,074	...	...	...	...
35	Palghat	Malabar	44,319	21,776	22,543	17,765	18,451	...	...	2	3
36	Rajahmundry	Godavari	48,417	23,761	24,656	22,206	23,005	...	...	24	2
37	Rajapalaiyam	Ramnad	28,412	14,108	14,304	13,501	13,593	...	...	...	...
38	Sembiem	Chingleput	21,325	11,000	10,325	9,831	9,276	...	...	9	9
39	Srirangam	Trichinopoly	24,799	11,683	13,116	11,603	13,031	...	...	...	...
40	Srivilliputtur	Ramnad	29,066	14,331	14,735	13,557	13,804	...	...	...	...
41	Tellicherry	Malabar	29,258	14,275	14,983	7,900	8,070	...	...	...	
42	Tinnevelly	Tinnevelly	44,805	21,246	23,550	18,516	20,346	...	...	...	...
43	Tiruchendur	Tinnevelly	25,531	16,136	9,395	14,840	8,091	...	...	...	...
44	Tiruvannamalai	North Arcot	21,244	10,621	10,623	9,128	9,253	...	...	8	11
45	Tuticorin	Tinnevelly	40,185	20,320	19,865	14,224	13,653	...	...	...	...
46	Vaniyambadi	North Arcot	20,403	9,205	11,201	4,507	5,041	...	...	...	...
47	Vellore	North Arcot	49,745	23,831	25,015	17,367	18,068	5	2	...	...
48	Virudupatti	Ramnad	21,355	10,710	10,045	9,946	9,707	...	...	...	...
49	Vizagapatam	Vizagapatam	43,413	21,465	21,948	19,001	19,646	...	...	8	...
50	Vizianagram	Vizagapatam	37,550	17,897	19,653	16,561	18,231	...	...	...	...
	Class IV	**165 Towns**	**1,488,071**	**729,468**	**759,603**	**599,946**	**628,243**	...	...	**349**	**172**
	Class V	**113 Towns**	**861,221**	**418,706**	**442,515**	**342,991**	**359,843**	...	...	**211**	**134**
	Class VI	**11 Towns**	**50,349**	**24,920**	**25,429**	**21,189**	**21,778**	...	...	**46**	**46**
	North-West Frontier Province.	**19 Towns**	**291,714**	**179,449**	**112,265**	**40,682**	**24,089**	**12,023**	**4,662**	**1**	**2**
	Class II—Peshawar and Cantonment	**Peshawar**	**97,935**	**59,680**	**38,255**	**10,406**	**5,920**	**3,455**	**1,571**	**1**	**2**

WITH POPULATION BY RELIGION—*continued.*

DISTRIBUTION BY RELIGION.														
BUDDHIST.		ZOROASTRIAN.		MUSALMAN.		CHRISTIAN.		JEW.		ANIMISTIC.		OTHERS.		Serial No.
Males.	Females.	Males.	Females.	Males.	Females.	Males.	Females.	Males.	Females.	Males.	Females.	Males.	Females.	
12	13	14	15	16	17	18	19	20	21	22	23	24	25	
1	..	161	92	24,217	22,221	1,130	1,051	19	16	217	181	59	55	
...	...	65	29	3,305	2,933	143	95	...	...	71	60	4	3	3
...	...	14	12	3,855	3,581	50	43	9	3	8	7	...	..	4
...	...	5	1	5,454	5,000	11	11	...	...	...	...	...	...	5
1	...	47	33	3,587	3,225	336	322	7	12	5	3	2	1	6
...	...	27	17	2,962	2,926	278	278	...	...	127	106	6	3	7
...	...	3	...	5,054	4,466	312	303	3	1	6	5	47	48	8
2	5	237	141	27,477	26,365	3,273	2,224	9	...	2,197	2,144	120	81	
...	...	141	96	32,911	31,399	1,303	1,200	7	2	2,444	2,559	59	41	
...	...	16	1	6,182	5,563	321	208	11	5	243	256	...	...	
...	...	12	14	1,683	1,025	463	495	...	...	8	..	...		
...	...	12	14	764	548	260	275	...	...	6	...	...	...	
...	...	...	...	919	477	203	220	...	...	2	...	...	...	
393	237	222	230	327,429	346,551	119,243	122,121	34	24	4,005	3,882	244	162	
326	213	91	80	44,680	41,147	31,628	32,811	13	6	...	...	68	51	
323	209	66	80	30,994	28,185	20,584	21,230	10	6	...	...	68	51	1
...	...	4	...	5,416	5,170	2,743	2,994	...	...	...	...	...	..	2
3	4	21	...	8,280	7,792	8,301	8,587	3	...	...	...	...	...	3
37	2	37	30	29,937	30,559	10,638	10,762	...	...	...	...	70	26	
1	...	26	24	15,592	14,300	2,442	2,423	...	..	...	...	13	9	4
...	...	11	6	1,388	1,254	437	607	...	...	...	...	35	17	5
1	...	...	...	906	840	70	69	..	...	...	...	...	...	6
16	...	...	...	1,197	1,164	1,065	955	...	...	...	...	...	..	7
...	...	...	...	1,382	1,376	719	908	...	...	...	...	...	...	8
18	3	...	...	5,386	7,326	3,044	2,648	...	...	..	...	21	..	9
1	...	...	...	2,439	2,413	554	604	...	...	..	.	...	...	10
...	...	...	...	1,647	1,878	2,307	2,648	...	...	...	...	1	...	11
19	3	57	53	92,446	95,865	40,446	42,529	21	18	1,582	1,642	103	79	
...	...	...	...	5,050	5,913	80	60	...	...	...	...	...	...	12
...	...	...	...	101	110	4	3	...	...	...	...	...	...	13
...	...	...	...	475	544	207	209	.	...	...	...	...	...	14
...	3	...	...	6,344	5,827	1,762	1,353	...	...	...	...	...	...	15
...	...	...	...	603	527	323	283	...	...	...	...	...	...	16
...	...	9	6	2,284	2,052	482	423	...	...	...	...	...	...	17
...	...	...	...	659	703	202	175	...	...	...	.	...	...	18
2	...	9	10	6,608	6,776	1,796	1,926	1	...	...	.	...	...	19
...	...	...	..	669	708	53	54	...	...	...	..	...	...	20
4	...	...	...	2,973	1,984	5,216	5,130	19	16	...	...	...	...	21
...	...	...	...	1,967	1,816	1,744	1,040	...	...	...	..	...	...	22
2	...	...	...	1,153	1,089	1,876	1,967	...	...	. .	...	...	...	23
...	...	1	4	1,028	1,906	241	245	...	...	...	...	...	...	24
...	...	...	...	2,007	2,232	37	37	...	...	.	...	...	...	25
...	...	10	2	4,661	4,361	964	921	...	...	8	5	...	...	26
...	...	...	...	1,970	3,778	2,374	2,788	...	.	...	...	...	...	27
...	...	2	3	6,140	6,536	281	237	...	.	...	...	...	..	28
...	..	6	10	3,097	2,621	7,352	8,023	...	...	...	...	77	69	29
...	...	...	...	308	320	273	237	...	...	...	...	...	..	30
...	...	...	...	2,382	2,403	468	570	...	...	...	...	...	..	31
...	...	...	...	279	314	432	603	..	...	..	..	...	...	32
...	...	...	...	3,041	3,050	504	731	...	...	1,573	1,637	...	...	33
...	...	...	...	6,660	7,899	1,719	1,705	...	...	..	..	1	...	34
...	...	...	...	3,355	3,403	633	684	1	2	..	:		..	35
...	...	...	...	1,100	1,032	431	617	...	...	...	.	...	...	36
...	...	...	...	469	547	138	164	...	..	.	..	...	...	37
...	...	9	5	444	377	708	658	...	..	.			...	38
...	...	...	...	26	30	54	55	.	...	..	.		...	39
...	...	...	...	265	260	499	561	.	.	..			...	40
...	...	.	...	5,520	6,067	839	844	.	..	...		7	2	41
...	...	...	...	2,285	2,786	431	423	..	...	..		14	2	42
...	...	...	...	160	23	1,136	1,281	...	...	.	.	...	...	43
...	...	...	..	1,354	1,212	131	147	...	...	..	..		...	44
9	1	2	2	1,268	1,086	4,797	5,123	...	...	..	...		...	45
...	...	...	...	4,604	6,130	34	30		...	...	...		...	46
..	...	..	...	5,854	6,247	601	692		...	..	...	4	6	47
...	...	...	...	505	727	257	211	.	...	...	..			48
2	.	9	11	1,343	1,214	1,011	1,077	..		1	...	..		49
...	...	...	...	1,009	1,106	327	316	...	..	..	..	.	.	50
10	17	20	38	98,573	109,580	20,458	20,463	...	..	1,119	1,087	2	3	
1	2	17	29	59,743	67,256	14,444	14,096	...	..	1,296	1,152	1	3	
...	...	...	...	2,050	2,144	1,629	1,460	...	...	6	1	...	...	
...	...	40	8	121,374	82,368	5,324	1,127	5	9	...	..		...	
...	..	40	7	42,963	30,235	2,813	519	...	1	...	.	...	...	

TABLE V.—Towns arranged Territorially

Serial No.	Town.	District or State.	Population. Persons.	Population. Males.	Population. Females.	Distribution by Religion. Hindu. Males.	Hindu. Females.	Sikh. Males.	Sikh. Females.	Jain. Males.	Jain. Females.
	1	2	3	4	5	6	7	8	9	10	11
	N.-W. F. Province—*concld.*										
	Class III	**3 Towns**	**83,283**	**53,102**	**30,181**	**13,774**	**8,260**	**3,947**	**885**	...	...
1	Dera Ismail Khan and Cantonment	Dera Ismail Khan	35,131	21,844	13,287	6,658	5,058	1,103	228	...	...
2	Kohat and Cantonment	Kohat	22,654	14,429	8,225	3,365	1,485	1,271	422	...	...
3	Nowshera and Cant.	Peshawar	25,498	16,829	8,669	3,751	1,717	1,573	235	...	...
	Class IV	**4 Towns**	**49,532**	**30,992**	**18,540**	**10,310**	**6,011**	**2,470**	**1,056**	...	...
	Class V	**6 Towns**	**46,641**	**26,654**	**19,987**	**3,916**	**2,660**	**1,630**	**881**	...	...
	Class VI	**5 Towns**	**14,323**	**9,021**	**5,302**	**1,774**	**1,238**	**521**	**269**	...	...
	Punjab	**139 Towns**	**2,211,964**	**1,273,147**	**938,817**	**515,030**	**371,457**	**73,105**	**43,625**	**11,368**	**9,772**
	Class I	**3 Towns**	**614,280**	**365,992**	**248,288**	**156,131**	**101,591**	**22,577**	**12,596**	**2,662**	**1,988**
1	Amritsar and Cant.	Amritsar	152,756	88,870	63,877	34,667	24,053	11,706	8,651	371	281
2	Delhi and Cantonment	Delhi	232,837	133,864	98,973	71,010	50,725	1,764	175	2,008	1,523
3	Lahore and Cantonment	Lahore	228,687	143,249	85,438	50,454	26,813	9,107	3,770	283	184
	Class II	**6 Towns**	**450,880**	**272,340**	**178,540**	**98,159**	**67,822**	**17,028**	**7,706**	**2,428**	**2,107**
4	Ambala and Cantonment	Ambala	80,131	49,204	30,927	22,671	15,521	2,592	800	535	422
5	Ferozepore and Cant.	Ferozepore	50,836	31,459	19,377	13,174	8,368	1,913	1,038	253	226
6	Jullundur and Cant.	Jullundur	69,318	39,816	29,502	13,386	9,997	2,413	723	220	218
7	Multan and Cant.	Multan	99,243	56,280	42,963	21,583	16,750	1,712	947	188	200
8	Rawalpindi and Cant.	Rawalpindi	86,483	57,451	29,032	18,237	10,869	5,385	2,921	524	430
9	Sialkot and Cantonment	Sialkot	64,869	38,130	26,739	9,109	6,308	3,013	1,277	708	602
	Class III	**10 Towns**	**275,313**	**148,631**	**126,682**	**63,450**	**53,252**	**4,398**	**2,832**	**2,209**	**2,025**
10	Batala	Gurdaspur	26,430	14,180	13,250	4,536	3,867	393	294	...	...
11	Bhiwani	Hissar	31,100	16,249	14,851	13,305	12,298	9	4	164	172
12	Gujranwala	Gujranwala	29,472	16,271	13,201	4,791	3,756	1,810	1,390	395	318
13	Jhang-Maghiana	Jhang	25,914	13,212	12,702	6,056	6,339	427	369	4	...
14	Karnal	Karnal	21,961	11,959	10,002	6,929	5,843	100	30	90	92
15	Kasur	Lahore	24,783	13,769	11,014	3,194	2,097	412	219	88	81
16	Ludhiana	Ludhiana	44,170	25,517	18,653	8,493	5,586	1,188	406	346	312
17	Panipat	Karnal	26,342	13,554	12,788	3,563	3,144	5	1	339	355
18	Rewari	Gurgaon	24,780	12,885	11,895	6,808	6,066	15	2	330	310
19	Rohtak	Rohtak	20,361	11,035	9,326	5,685	4,256	40	27	453	385
	Class IV	**22 Towns**	**323,496**	**183,386**	**140,110**	**77,514**	**54,368**	**8,089**	**4,105**	**1,620**	**1,547**
	Class V	**59 Towns**	**408,843**	**224,159**	**184,684**	**84,224**	**67,931**	**15,980**	**12,823**	**2,112**	**1,796**
	Class VI	**39 Towns**	**139,152**	**78,639**	**60,513**	**35,552**	**26,493**	**5,033**	**3,563**	**337**	**307**
	United Provinces	**418 Towns**	**4,810,614**	**2,597,849**	**2,212,765**	**1,572,881**	**1,298,683**	**5,509**	**1,575**	**16,171**	**13,779**
	Class I	**7 Towns**	**1,244,994**	**688,346**	**556,648**	**425,448**	**340,005**	**2,571**	**625**	**3,027**	**2,436**
1	Agra and Cantonment	Agra	185,449	101,335	84,114	64,296	52,475	75	39	1,546	1,251
2	Allahabad and Cant.	Allahabad	171,697	96,208	75,489	63,340	49,628	842	157	153	146
3	Bareilly and Cantonment	Bareilly	129,462	70,601	58,861	34,532	27,401	95	46	2	...
4	Benares and Cantonment	Benares	203,804	105,815	97,989	75,105	60,403	282	64	141	103
5	Cawnpore and Cant.	Cawnpore	178,557	103,316	75,241	72,670	52,510	338	63	218	147
6	Lucknow and Cant.	Lucknow	259,798	144,785	115,013	81,970	63,125	815	205	283	234
7	Meerut and Cantonment	Meerut	116,227	66,286	40,941	33,545	25,373	124	51	684	555
	Class II	**9 Towns**	**580,206**	**316,765**	**263,441**	**183,827**	**148,171**	**1,251**	**292**	**1,555**	**1,252**
8	Farrukhabad-*cum*-Fatehgarh and Cant.	Farrukhabad	59,647	32,144	27,503	22,100	18,545	7	17	71	48
9	Fyzabad-*cum*-Ajodhya and Cantonment.	Fyzabad	54,655	31,078	23,577	21,514	16,690	195	55	13	10
10	Gorakhpur	Gorakhpur	56,892	31,236	25,656	20,881	16,346	9	1	25	27
11	Jhansi and Cantonment	Jhansi	70,208	38,323	31,885	26,593	23,288	811	112	200	167
12	Koil-Aligarh	Aligarh	64,825	36,265	28,560	19,755	15,256	33	7	228	150
13	Moradabad	Moradabad	81,168	43,381	37,787	16,724	13,216	18	6	141	117
14	Muttra and Cantonment	Muttra	58,183	32,133	26,050	24,547	20,271	10	3	116	58
15	Saharanpur	Saharanpur	62,850	35,416	27,434	14,818	10,232	153	75	759	673
16	Shahjahanpur	Shahjahanpur	71,778	36,780	34,989	16,892	14,327	15	16	2	2
	Class III	**17 Towns**	**535,935**	**290,124**	**245,811**	**168,226**	**132,757**	**556**	**295**	**1,694**	**1,426**
17	Amroha	Moradabad	42,410	20,550	21,860	5,703	5,302	4	2	16	53
18	Bahraich	Bahraich	26,907	14,227	12,680	6,802	5,453	25	14	40	31
19	Banda	Banda	21,061	10,543	10,518	7,593	7,327	5	3	99	110
20	Budaun	Budaun	38,230	20,048	18,182	7,984	6,213	5	5	...	...
21	Chandausi	Moradabad	22,255	12,367	9,888	8,306	6,557	5	3	13	7
22	Dehra and Cantonment	Dehra Dun	38,610	24,470	14,140	16,218	9,116	400	111	78	58
23	Etawah	Etawah	45,350	24,249	21,101	15,458	13,096	4	7	476	406
24	Ghazipur	Ghazipur	22,165	12,005	10,160	8,412	6,637	...	...	1	...
25	Hardwar Union	Saharanpur	28,682	16,624	12,058	12,259	8,477	37	10	38	26
26	Hathras	Aligarh	37,854	21,360	16,404	17,563	13,637	...	...	316	250
27	Jaunpur	Jaunpur	30,473	15,888	14,585	9,135	8,025	9	7	3	3
28	Khurja	Bulandshahr	27,387	14,549	12,838	7,816	6,660	7	4	106	111
29	Mirzapur	Mirzapur	32,332	16,861	15,471	12,956	12,050	2	...	30	32
30	Muzaffarnagar	Muzaffarnagar	23,811	13,973	9,838	7,603	5,192	26	14	421	306
31	Pilibhit	Pilibhit	31,554	16,817	14,737	9,440	7,436	3	3	1	...
32	Sambhal	Moradabad	45,276	23,234	22,042	7,131	6,489	...	...	24	19
33	Sitapur	Sitapur	21,578	12,359	9,219	7,757	5,092	24	13	25	5
	Class IV	**65 Towns**	**911,612**	**484,356**	**427,256**	**278,590**	**234,444**	**627**	**258**	**3,119**	**2,737**
	Class V	**139 Towns**	**944,937**	**501,270**	**443,667**	**306,326**	**257,640**	**151**	**82**	**3,922**	**3,299**
	Class VI	**181 Towns**	**592,930**	**316,988**	**275,942**	**216,484**	**185,666**	**353**	**113**	**2,854**	**2,629**

WITH POPULATION BY RELIGION—*continued.*

DISTRIBUTION BY RELIGION.														
BUDDHIST.		ZOROASTRIAN.		MUSALMAN.		CHRISTIAN.		JEW.		ANIMISTIC.		OTHERS.		Serial No.
Males.	Females.	Males.	Females.	Males.	Females.	Males.	Females.	Males.	Females.	Males.	Females.	Males.	Females.	
12	13	14	15	16	17	18	19	20	21	22	23	24	25	
...	...	...	1	**33,257**	**20,609**	**2,119**	**418**	**5**	**8**	...	...	...	...	
...	...	...	...	13,856	7,00 3	227	98	...	...	...	...	...	...	1
...	...	...	...	9,684	6,246	104	64	5	8	...	...	...	...	2
...	...	...	1	9,717	6,460	1,786	256	...	...	...	—	...	...	3
...	...	...	...	**17,429**	**11,366**	**283**	**107**	...	...	...	...	...	...	
...	...	...	...	**21,648**	**16,397**	**60**	**49**	...	...	...	...	...	...	
...	...	...	...	**6,677**	**3,761**	**49**	**34**	...	...	...	...	...	...	
92	74	356	240	639,540	498,182	33,638	15,431	18	36	...	...	...	...	
64	**64**	**191**	**129**	**176,669**	**126,959**	**7,691**	**4,948**	**7**	**13**	...	...	...	...	
...	...	26	22	41,469	30,362	620	508	... 3	...	...	...	...	...	1
...	...	44	30	57,277	45,190	1,756	1,317		4	...	...	...	...	2
64	64	121	77	77,903	51,398	5,313	3,123	4	9	...	...	...	...	3
6	**4**	**118**	**80**	**136,412**	**96,518**	**18,183**	**4,287**	**6**	**16**	...		...	...	
...	...	22	9	18,426	13,215	4,958	960	...	...	...	...	...	...	4
...	...	11	5	14,120	9,289	1,968	451	...	...	...	...	...	...	5
...	...	11	7	22,614	18,280	1,172	268	...	...	...	...	...	...	6
...	...	30	28	31,161	24,525	1,606	409	1	5	...	...	...	...	7
6	4	31	27	27,285	13,393	5,978	1,368	5	11	...	...	...	...	8
...	...	13	4	22,806	17,807	2,461	741	...	...	...	...	...	...	9
...	...	**4**	**2**	**77,526**	**67,561**	**1,044**	**990**	...	...	...	...	...	...	
...	...	...	...	9,206	8,047	46	42	...	...	...	...	...	...	10
...	...	1	1	2,750	2,344	20	32	...	...	...	...	...	...	11
...	...	...	...	8,931	7,467	344	270	...	...	...	...	...	...	12
...	...	...	...	6,720	5,987	5	7	...	...	...	...	...	...	13
...	...	...	...	4,747	3,920	93	117	...	...	...	...	...	...	14
...	...	2	1	10,026	8,562	47	54	...	...	...	...	...	...	15
...	...	...	...	15,213	11,984	277	275	...	...	...	...	...	...	16
...	...	...	...	9,599	9,266	48	22	...	...	...	...	...	...	17
...	...	1	...	5,519	5,391	122	126	...	...	...	...	...	...	18
...	...	...	...	4,815	4,613	42	45	...	...	...	...	...	...	19
20	**6**	**21**	**9**	**93,948**	**77,779**	**2,169**	**2,289**	**5**	**7**	...	...	...	...	
...	...	**13**	**11**	**119,795**	**100,607**	**2,035**	**1,514**	...	...	...	...	...	...	
2	...	**9**	**9**	**35,190**	**28,738**	**2,516**	**1,403**	...	...	...	...	...	...	
114	97	461	345	937,500	854,398	47,169	30,979	26	22	...	...	17,718	12,887	
24	**19**	**264**	**158**	**229,620**	**198,400**	**23,322**	**12,437**	**19**	**15**	...	...	**4,051**	**2,553**	
...	...	37	22	31,264	27,787	3,226	2,067	5	2	...	...	796	481	1
10	6	59	27	27,536	22,549	3,948	2,782	1	1	...	...	319	103	2
3	...	14	7	32,135	29,748	3,124	1,080	...	...	...	...	606	579	3
...	...	2	2	29,363	27,373	606	797	5	3	...	...	219	154	4
...	...	38	22	26,564	20,359	3,069	1,860	1	2	...	...	401	278	5
11	13	101	67	55,240	48,338	5,831	2,691	7	7	...	...	527	333	6
...	...	13	11	27,401	22,246	3,426	1,170	...	...	...	...	1,008	535	7
7	**5**	**142**	**149**	**120,804**	**107,651**	**7,064**	**4,302**	**6**	**5**	...	...	**2,109**	**1,614**	
5	2	...	...	9,333	8,376	343	273	...	...	...	...	283	242	8
2	3	3	4	7,881	6,360	1,362	397	2	3	...	...	106	55	9
...	...	...	2	9,711	8,780	457	407	4	2	...	...	149	91	10
...	...	122	135	8,609	7,308	1,930	845	...	...	...	...	55	30	11
...	...	2	...	15,600	13,589	206	309	...	...	...	...	261	189	12
...	...	8	7	25,011	23,042	788	775	...	...	...	...	691	624	13
...	...	...	...	6,267	5,100	995	473	...	...	...	...	198	145	14
...	...	4	...	18,756	15,870	716	471	...	...	...	...	210	113	15
...	...	3	1	19,546	20,226	177	292	...	...	...	...	154	125	16
...	...	**19**	**8**	**112,894**	**106,211**	**3,113**	**2,668**	**1**	**2**	...	...	**3,621**	**2,534**	
...	...	...	...	14,538	16,274	67	53	...	...	...	...	222	176	17
...	...	...	...	7,290	7,107	31	35	1	1	...	...	29	25	18
...	...	...	...	2,716	2,978	40	37	...	...	...	...	81	63	19
...	...	...	...	11,405	11,300	263	303	...	...	...	...	385	352	20
...	...	7	1	3,737	3,164	84	77	...	...	...	...	125	70	21
...	...	...	1	6,057	3,806	1,364	884	...	...	...	...	355	164	22
...	...	3	1	7,424	6,060	59	55	...	1	...	...	825	567	23
...	...	...	...	3,468	3,415	79	83	...	...	...	...	45	26	24
...	...	2	...	4,167	3,445	24	15	...	...	...	...	97	76	25
...	...	...	...	3,090	2,291	291	257	...	...	...	...	100	65	26
...	...	...	...	6,659	6,471	16	31	...	...	...	...	66	40	27
...	...	3	2	6,220	5,835	103	109	...	...	...	...	294	118	28
...	...	2	1	3,720	3,256	101	90	...	...	...	...	41	33	29
...	...	2	2	5,716	4,203	32	31	...	...	...	...	173	90	30
...	...	...	...	7,062	7,014	134	133	...	...	...		177	151	31
...	...	...	...	15,344	14,880	265	240	...		...		470	414	32
...	...	...	...	4,272	3,804	145	223	...	...		...	136	82	33
15	**8**	**9**	**4**	**193,116**	**182,260**	**5,563**	**5,074**	.	...	...	..	**3,311**	**2,471**	
...	**1**	**22**	**24**	**187,890**	**175,994**	**5,870**	**4,125**	...	...	...	..	**3,089**	**2,502**	
68	**64**	**5**	**2**	**93,176**	**83,882**	**2,531**	**2,373**	...	...	...		**1,537**	**1,213**	

TABLE V.—Towns arranged Territorially

Serial No.	Town.	District or State.	Population.			Distribution by Religion.					
						Hindu.		Sikh.		Jain.	
			Persons.	Males.	Females.	Males.	Females.	Males.	Females.	Males.	Females.
	1	2	3	4	5	6	7	8	9	10	11
	States and Agencies.	701 Towns	6,930,513	3,582,474	3,348,039	2,354,879	2,199,714	29,439	17,988	101,994	104,734
	Assam State Class II—(Imphal).	Manipur	74,650	36,393	38,257	34,262	36,806	5	2	101	6
	Baluchistan States	3 Towns	9,950	5,368	4,582	548	384	75	36	...	...
	Class V—Mastung	Kalat	5,007	2,775	2,232	181	135	...	...	...	...
	Class VI.	2 Towns	4,943	2,593	2,350	367	249	75	36	..	...
	Baroda State	41 Towns	405,017	209,455	195,562	160,579	147,207	15	1	8,383	8,496
	Class II—Baroda and Cantonment.	Baroda	99,345	53,616	45,729	42,103	36,115	12	1	1,153	1,055
	Class III—Patan	Baroda	28,339	13,904	14,435	10,133	10,257	...	...	1,513	1,820
	Class IV.	8 Towns	112,797	56,181	56,616	41,836	40,902	2	...	1,894	1,916
	Class V	16 Towns	111,766	58,035	53,731	45,697	41,735	...	...	2,786	2,764
	Class VI.	15 Towns	52,770	27,719	25,051	20,810	18,198	1	...	1,037	941
	Bengal States	5 Towns	22,625	14,505	8,120	11,539	6,362	4	...	188	14
	Class IV—Cooch Behar	Cooch Behar	10,841	6,852	3,989	5,240	2,890	..	...	126	6
	Class V—Agartala	Hill Tippera	6,831	4,176	2,655	3,565	2,382	4	...	2	...
	Class VI.	3 Towns	4,953	3,477	1,476	2,734	1,090	...	...	60	8
	Bihar and Orissa States.	6 Towns	37,201	18,697	18,504	17,813	17,603	...	...	10	15
	Class V	5 Towns	33,071	16,698	16,373	15,832	15,493	...	...	10	15
	Class VI—Binka	Sonpur	4,130	1,999	2,131	1,981	2,110	...	...	...	...
	Bombay States	132 Towns	1,166,657	584,387	582,270	403,292	390,782	39	19	38,603	39,887
	Class II.—Bhavnagar	Kathiawar	60,694	31,869	28,825	23,456	20,951	...	...	2,489	2,492
	Class III	10 Towns	298,851	149,315	149,536	96,091	93,801	3	2	8,784	9,228
1	Bhuj and Cantonment	Cutch	21,579	10,556	11,023	6,175	6,311	...	...	582	671
2	Cambay	Cambay	28,098	13,858	14,240	9,598	9,404	...	...	1,340	1,458
3	Dhoraji	Kathiawar	24,116	10,950	13,166	4,929	4,700	...	...	634	668
4	Jamnagar	Kathiawar	44,887	22,025	22,832	12,071	13,107	...	...	1,783	1,802
5	Junagarh	Kathiawar	35,413	18,565	16,848	9,809	8,767	...	...	492	516
6	Kolhapur and Cant.	Kolhapur	48,122	25,437	22,685	22,122	19,611	...	...	741	605
7	Mandvi	Cutch	24,295	11,238	12,007	5,434	6,319	...	...	1,075	1,170
8	Miraj	S. M. Jagirs	21,168	10,747	10,421	8,043	7,781	...	...	274	250
9	Porbandar	Kathiawar	24,821	12,672	12,140	9,328	8,422	3	2	551	550
10	Rajkot	Kathiawar	26,412	13,267	13,145	9,683	9,379	...	...	1,412	1,436
	Class IV	21 Towns	289,678	144,058	145,620	88,965	87,001	36	17	13,241	14,152
	Class V	45 Towns	324,118	161,528	162,590	113,878	111,742	...	...	8,873	9,611
	Class VI	55 Towns	193,316	97,617	95,699	78,962	77,287	...	...	5,216	5,004
	Central India Agency.	77 Towns	786,114	412,859	373,255	286,940	259,073	759	317	10,949	10,007
	Class II—Bhopal	Bhopal	56,204	29,043	27,161	11,566	10,459	125	96	314	330
	Class III	6 Towns	215,218	116,212	99,006	80,305	68,296	150	88	3,180	2,854
1	Indore	Indore	44,917	24,792	20,155	17,536	14,127	134	77	515	400
2	Lashkar	Gwalior	46,932	24,245	22,707	18,263	17,109	8	7	109	138
3	Mhow Cantonment	Indore	20,820	17,728	12,097	10,087	7,292	1	2	155	150
4	Ratlam	Ratlam	27,957	14,340	13,617	8,285	7,904	...	...	1,915	1,800
5	Rewah	Rewah	26,247	14,248	11,909	11,700	9,205	7	2	34	31
6	Ujjain	Gwalior	39,295	20,864	18,431	14,425	12,509	...	...	392	335
	Class IV.	11 Towns	155,334	81,213	74,121	56,629	51,627	32	7	2,113	1,839
	Class V	39 Towns	279,547	145,576	133,971	106,798	96,252	264	96	4,472	4,133
	Class VI.	20 Towns	79,811	40,815	38,996	31,642	30,439	188	30	870	851
	Central Provinces States.	5 Towns	36,824	17,958	18,866	15,140	15,924	11	4	270	192
	Class IV—Rajnandgaon.	Nandgaon	11,979	6,041	5,938	5,024	4,990	...	...	215	136
	Class V	4 Towns	24,845	11,917	12,928	10,116	10,934	11	4	55	56
	Hyderabad State	85 Towns	1,295,305	660,940	634,365	421,649	404,958	1,509	1,085	2,009	1,808
	Class I—Hyderabad and Cantonment.	Hyderabad	500,623	258,454	242,169	135,638	126,493	644	334	223	156
	Class III	4 Towns	128,000	65,846	62,154	42,703	40,631	152	147	131	98
1	Aurangabad and Cant.	Aurangabad	34,902	17,992	16,910	9,960	9,287	57	41	43	36
2	Gulbarga	Gulbarga	32,437	16,849	15,588	9,002	8,187	3	1	77	52
3	Hanamkonda	Warangal	35,627	18,324	17,303	14,163	13,490	92	105	2	2
4	Raichur	Raichur	25,034	12,681	12,353	9,578	9,667	...	...	9	7

WITH POPULATION BY RELIGION—*continued.*

DISTRIBUTION BY RELIGION.															
Buddhist.		Zoroastrian.		Musalman.		Christian.		Jew.		Animistic.		Others.		
Males.	Females.	Males.	Females.	Males.	Females.	Males.	Females.	Males.	Females.	Males.	Females.	Males.	Females.	Serial No.
12	13	14	15	16	17	18	19	20	21	22	23	24	25	
1,219	1,067	4,789	5,724	988,266	928,699	85,491	75,773	665	644	13,668	12,084	2,064	1,612	
1	...	...	...	1,277	665	39	25	...	...	706	733	...	...	
1	...	...	...	4,737	4,160	7	2	...	...	...	...	...	...	
...	...	...	...	2,591	2,095	3	2	...	...	..	...	...	...	
1	...	...	...	2,146	2,065	4	..	...	...	...	...	...	...	
...	...	2,627	3,730	34,579	33,486	976	578	21	16	2,081	1,961	194	87	
...	...	319	242	9,250	7,956	522	226	7	10	119	90	131	44	
...	...	...	...	2,250	2,353	5	4	...	...	...	...	3	1	
...	...	1,663	2,612	10,496	10,955	62	34	13	6	183	168	32	23	
...	...	554	787	8,167	7,669	325	283	..	...	479	474	27	19	
...	...	91	89	4,416	4,553	62	31	1	...	1,300	1,239	1	...	
21	11	...	...	2,672	1,685	57	26	...	...	...	...	24	22	
2	9	...	...	1,426	1,053	39	11	...	...	...	...	19	20	
19	2	...	...	568	263	13	6	...	...	...	...	5	2	
...	...	...	...	678	369	5	9	...	...	...	...	...	...	
...	...	...	...	585	597	40	54	...	...	249	235	...	...	
...	...	...	...	567	576	40	54		...	249	235	...	...	
...	...	...	...	18	21	...	...	...	...	...	...	...	...	
1	...	659	677	137,539	147,052	1,819	1,543	88	78	1,597	1,542	750	690	
...	...	166	163	5,625	5,147	131	72	2	...	...	...	...	...	
1	...	191	202	41,547	45,613	574	582	9	6	...	...	115	102	
...	...	34	33	3,741	4,002	17	4	...	...	...	...	7	2	1
...	...	44	77	2,058	3,283	18	19	...	...	...	...	4	6	2
...	...	3	...	5,380	17,702	...	...	...	...	...	...	...	...	3
...	...	35	43	7,181	7,883	54	27	1	...	...	...	...	...	4
...	...	18	10	8,209	7,543	37	12	...	...	...	...	...	...	5
...	...	12	6	2,341	2,076	221	387	...	...	...	...	...	...	6
1	...	5	3	4,585	5,412	38	2	1	...	...	...	99	91	7
...	...	5	4	2,277	2,277	148	109	...	...	...	...	...	...	8
...	...	32	23	2,723	3,040	35	12	...	...	...	...	...	...	9
...	...	3	3	2,153	2,306	6	10	7	6	...	...	5	3	10
...	...	95	90	40,359	43,152	193	86	13	10	1,123	1,079	33	33	
...	...	173	196	37,341	40,434	769	710	26	20	187	202	281	275	
...	...	34	26	12,667	12,706	152	93	38	42	287	261	321	280	
...	...	581	561	106,384	99,109	5,210	2,479	28	23	1,952	1,656	56	30	
...	...	36	28	16,859	16,146	127	91	3	3	13	8	...	...	
...	...	303	282	28,976	26,152	3,126	1,196	20	16	145	109	7	13	
...	...	14	7	6,484	5,469	86	71	...	...	23	4	...	...	1
...	...	35	27	5,659	5,264	72	64	...	...	37	33	2	5	2
...	...	209	218	4,533	3,587	2,707	825	17	12	10	7	4	4	3
...	...	33	27	3,844	3,631	193	185	3	4	68	62	1	4	4
...	...	...	...	2,405	2,758	3	3	...	...	...	...	...	...	5
...	...	13	3	5,961	5,443	66	48	...	...	7	3	...	...	6
...	...	90	100	21,218	19,907	777	338	3	3	346	297	5	3	
...	...	138	146	31,386	29,338	1,106	799	2	1	1,364	1,192	44	14	
...	...	14	5	7,943	7,566	74	55	..	...	84	50	...	...	
2	...	15	7	1,838	1,925	184	199	...	...	498	615	...	...	
...	...	10	7	652	630	58	86	...	...	82	89	...	..	
2	...	5	...	1,186	1,295	126	113	...	...	416	526	...	...	
8	12	641	548	222,522	216,616	11,970	8,828	8	4	551	434	73	72	
6	7	443	365	111,770	106,126	9,623	6,617	8	4	38	3	61	64	
2	5	92	75	22,016	20,505	746	692	...	...	2	1	..	...	
2	5	61	54	7,464	7,063	414	423	...	...	1	1	..	...	1
...	...	12	7	7,703	7,296	52	45	...	...	...	...	...	...	2
...	...	13	14	3,922	3,582	131	110	...	...	1	...	...	...	3
...	...	6	...	2,037	2,565	151	114	...	...	...	...	...	...	4

TABLE V.—Towns arranged Territorially

Serial No.	Town.	District or State.	Population.			Distribution by Religion.					
						Hindu.		Sikh.		Jain.	
			Persons.	Males.	Females.	Males.	Females.	Males.	Females.	Males.	Females.
	1	2	3	4	5	6	7	8	9	10	11
	Hyderabad State—*concld.*										
	Class IV	**18 Towns**	239,543	123,759	115,784	85,381	78,563	512	434	967	934
	Class V	**58 Towns**	411,209	205,184	206,025	152,190	153,123	201	170	688	620
	Class VI	**4 Towns**	15,930	7,697	8,233	5,728	6,148	...	...	...	...
	Kashmir State	61 Towns	300,879	167,028	133,851	50,722	37,313	1,741	1,266	183	154
	Class I—Srinagar and Cantonment.	**Kashmir South**	126,344	68,378	57,966	15,696	13,043	316	170	..	.
	Class III—Jammu and Cantonment.	**Jammu**	31,726	19,362	12,364	12,032	7,746	414	281	181	153
	Class V	**7 Towns**	51,671	28,468	23,203	6,451	4,956	437	383	...	...
	Class VI	**52 Towns**	91,138	50,820	40,318	16,543	11,568	574	432	2	1
	Madras States (*including Cochin and Travancore*).	21 Towns	348,892	178,012	170,880	117,625	113,476	...	...	90	49
	Class II—Trivandrum and Cantonment.	**Travancore**	63,561	32,292	31,269	26,180	25,166	...	...	...	...
	Class III	**6 Towns**	150,675	77,689	72,986	48,389	45,508	...	...	90	49
1	Alleppey	Travancore	25,665	13,370	12,295	6,676	5,956	...	...	8	3
2	Ernakulam	Cochin	21,195	11,944	9,251	6,521	4,644	...	...	1	...
3	Mattancheri	Cochin	23,508	12,625	10,583	5,926	4,090	...	...	81	46
4	Nagercoil	Travancore	29,883	14,553	15,330	10,996	11,483	...	...	...	...
5	Pudukkottai	Pudukkottai	26,850	13,108	13,742	11,922	12,625	...	...	...	...
6	Trichur	Cochin	23,574	12,089	11,485	6,346	5,901	...	...	...	...
	Class IV	**5 Towns**	75,313	38,310	37,003	23,516	23,074	...	...	...	...
	Class V	**6 Towns**	45,540	22,516	23,024	14,485	14,937	...	...	..	...
	Class VI	**3 Towns**	13,803	7,205	6,598	5,055	4,791	...	...	...	...
	Mysore State	91 Towns	658,329	338,996	319,333	255,509	244,650	223	40	2,040	1,496
	Class I—Bangalore Civil and Military Station.	**Bangalore**	100,834	51,752	49,082	28,660	27,886	202	31	207	113
	Class II	**2 Towns**	159,957	82,109	77,848	65,655	62,903	14	5	432	332
1	Bangalore City	Bangalore	88,651	45,997	42,654	37,472	35,160	...	...	248	198
2	Mysore City	Mysore	71,306	36,112	35,194	28,183	27,743	14	5	184	134
	Class III—Kolar Gold Fields.	**Kolar**	48,635	27,960	20,675	20,209	15,186	3	...	...	...
	Class IV	**2 Towns**	23,192	11,874	11,318	8,952	8,671	4	4	77	30
	Class V	**20 Towns**	134,027	67,526	66,501	52,432	52,176	...	...	453	394
	Class VI	**65 Towns**	191,684	97,775	93,909	79,601	77,828	...	...	871	697
	Punjab States	35 Towns	355,318	202,166	153,152	86,265	64,746	24,614	15,000	2,059	1,564
	Class III	**3 Towns**	92,204	53,186	39,018	21,819	16,277	5,909	2,749	1,049	708
1	Malerkotla	Malerkotla	23,880	13,538	10,342	3,455	2,346	604	551	756	468
2	Narnaul	Patiala	21,350	10,985	10,365	6,630	5,791	21	5	142	122
3	Patiala	Patiala	46,974	28,663	18,311	11,734	8,140	5,284	2,193	151	98
	Class IV	**8 Towns**	108,659	63,033	45,626	24,885	17,610	7,960	4,798	367	316
	Class V	**18 Towns**	131,049	73,208	57,841	33,917	26,043	9,211	6,230	557	452
	Class VI	**6 Towns**	23,406	12,739	10,667	5,644	4,816	1,534	1,223	86	88
	Rajputana Agency	133 Towns	1,343,095	688,936	654,159	482,146	451,078	443	218	37,010	40,967
	Class I—Jaipur	**Jaipur**	137,098	70,846	66,252	46,962	44,508	60	58	3,863	3,640
	Class II	**2 Towns**	115,088	57,626	57,462	40,064	40,070	147	33	3,697	4,277
1	Bikaner	Bikaner	55,826	28,275	27,551	20,522	19,949	141	27	1,610	2,200
2	Jodhpur (Major)	Marwar	59,262	29,351	29,911	19,542	20,121	6	6	2,087	2,077
	Class III	**7 Towns**	217,880	116,294	101,586	74,678	63,279	49	44	4,114	3,737
3	Alwar	Alwar	41,305	22,254	19,051	15,711	13,533	7	8	289	190
4	Bharatpur	Bharatpur	33,918	18,803	15,115	12,734	10,014	19	17	298	239
5	Jodhpur (Minor)	Marwar	20,404	12,487	8,007	10,088	6,277	7	3	223	208
6	Kotah	Kotah	32,753	16,940	15,804	11,389	10,447	13	10	517	450
7	Sikar	Jaipur	22,317	11,504	10,813	6,716	5,963	3	4	384	454
8	Tonk	Tonk	33,834	16,837	17,027	7,560	7,310	...	3	520	489
9	Udaipur	Mewar	33,229	17,460	15,700	10,401	9,736	1	...	1,883	1,689
	Class IV	**24 Towns**	319,860	160,770	159,090	112,087	108,690	96	55	7,971	9,885
	Class V	**59 Towns**	397,958	203,248	194,710	152,115	142,839	20	12	11,272	12,754
	Class VI	**40 Towns**	155,211	80,152	75,059	56,240	51,092	71	16	6,093	6,674
	United Provinces States.	5 Towns	89,657	46,774	42,883	10,850	9,352	1	...	99	79
	Class II—Rampur and Cantonment.	**Rampur**	74,316	38,833	35,483	8,111	6,818	1	...	72	61
	Class V—Shahabad	**Rampur**	5,622	2,924	2 698	848	777	..	..	...	...
	Class VI	**3 Towns**	9,719	5,017	4,702	1,891	1.737		..	27	18

WITH POPULATION BY RELIGION—*concluded.*

DISTRIBUTION BY RELIGION.

Buddhist.		Zoroastrian.		Musalman.		Christian.		Jew.		Animistic.		Others.		Serial No.
Males.	Females.	Males.	Females.	Males.	Females.	Males.	Females.	Males.	Females.	Males.	Females.	Males.	Females.	
12	13	14	15	16	17	18	19	20	21	22	23	24	25	
...	...	80	74	35,791	34,903	731	612	...	...	290	259	7	5	
...	...	26	34	50,993	51,013	851	891	...	...	221	171	5	3	
...	...	...	...	1,952	2,069	17	16	...	...	..	...	...	...	
852	797	22	9	112,933	93,958	325	212	...	...	...	...	250	142	
...	...	20	6	52,271	44,670	51	60	...	...	...	...	24	17	
...	...	2	3	6,552	4,066	94	70	...	...	...	...	87	45	
1	...	...	...	21,337	17,746	137	57	...	...	...	...	105	61	
851	797	...	...	32,773	27,476	43	25	...	...	...	...	34	19	
...	...	3	2	18,496	17,283	41,310	39,577	488	493	...	...	...	...	
...	...	...	...	2,475	2,173	3,626	3,926	11	4	...	...	...	...	
...	...	3	2	9,750	9,268	19,014	17,684	443	475	...	...	...	...	
...	...	...	...	3,299	3,370	3,387	2,966	...	...	...	...	...	...	1
...	...	...	...	613	335	4,561	4,032	248	240	...	...	...	...	2
...	...	...	...	3,002	2,791	3,330	2,913	194	234	...	...	...	...	3
...	...	...	...	1,391	1,534	2,166	2,313	...	...	...	...	...	...	4
...	...	...	...	769	755	417	362	...	...	...	...	...	...	5
...	...	3	2	586	483	5,153	5,108	1	1	...	...	...	...	6
...	...	...	...	3,961	3,679	10,781	10,236	32	14	...	...	...	...	
...	...	...	...	1,662	1,642	6,369	6,445	...	...	...	..	...	...	
...	...	...	..	628	521	1,520	1,286	2	...	...	...	...	...	
331	247	54	46	58,058	50,938	21,409	20,621	18	18	1,323	1,243	31	34	
39	33	29	17	12,159	10,627	10,257	10,173	17	17	172	175	10	10	
6	1	16	25	12,522	10,890	3,049	3,341	...	...	395	327	20	24	
...	...	...	...	5,826	4,761	2,043	2,105	...	...	389	316	19	24	1
6	1	16	25	6,696	6,129	1,006	1,146	...	...	6	11	1		2
268	200	..	...	2,282	821	5,194	4,466	...	...	4	2	...	...	
15	11	2	...	2,342	2,134	415	400	...	...	67	68	..	...	
...	...	2	...	13,132	12,507	1,237	1,222	...	...	270	272	...	...	
3	2	5	4	15,621	13,959	1,257	1,019	1	1	415	399	1	...	
...	...	17	7	88,779	71,459	432	376	...	...	...	...	...	...	
...	...	10	3	24,294	19,165	105	116	...	...	...	..	...	...	
...	...	...	...	8,720	6,946	3	11	...	..	...	...	..	...	1
...	...	...	...	4,192	4,447			..	...	..	..	.	...	2
...	...	10	3	11,382	7,772	102	105	...	...	...	..	...	...	3
..	...	7	4	29,675	22,797	139	161	...	...	..	...	...	...	
...	...	...	...	29,347	24,963	176	153	..	...	...		...	...	
...	...	...	...	5,463	4,534	12	6	..	...	...	...	...	...	
2	...	170	137	162,251	156,504	1,569	1,097	14	12	4,709	3,665	622	481	
...	...	10	9	19,773	17,891	139	103	...	...	...	..	39	43	
...	...	2	3	13,534	12,975	109	66	...	...	7	4	66	34	
...	...	1	3	5,887	5,312	87	40	...	...	..	...	27	11	1
...	...	1	...	7,647	7,663	22	17	...	...	7	4	39	23	2
1	...	51	43	35,478	33,206	509	437	2	...	1,204	670	208	170	
...	...	2	1	6,207	5,277	33	29	...	...	1	...	4	4	3
...	...	3	4	5,328	4,540	271	223	..	...	...	...	100	78	4
...	...	37	28	1,963	1,316	96	95	1	...	17	52	65	59	5
1	...	...	...	4,942	4,801	33	46	1	...	18	13	36	28	6
...	...	2	2	4,397	4,391	1	...	...	...	...	...	1	...	7
...	...	..	...	8,720	9,218	6	6	...	...	1	1	1	...	8
...	...	7	8	3,931	3,663	69	38	...	...	1,167	684	1	1	9
...	...	13	9	40,210	40,143	84	68	...	...	180	150	129	90	
...	...	68	44	37,557	37,230	374	287	5	4	1,708	1,440	129	100	
1	...	26	29	15,699	15,059	354	136	7	8	1,610	1,401	51	44	
...	...	...	...	35,616	33,242	144	156	...	...	...	...	64	54	
...	...	...	...	30,523	28,477	80	88	...	...	...	...	46	39	
...	...	...	...	2,031	1,873	45	48	...	..	..	...	...	...	
...	...	...	...	2,062	2,892	19	20	...	...	...	...	13	15	

Details of Towns in Cochin and Travancore.

Town.	Number of Towns.	Population.			Distribution by Religion.											
					Hindu.		Jain.		Zoroastrian.		Musalman.		Christian.		Jew.	
		Persons.	Males.	Females.	Males.	Females.	Males.	Females.	Males.	Females.	Males.	Females.	Males.	Females.	Males.	Females.
1	2	3	4	5	6	7	8	9	10	11	12	13	14	15	16	17
Cochin State	9 Towns	109,952	57,236	52,716	33,237	30,260	82	46	3	2	5,541	4,796	17,930	17,137	443	475
Class III	3 Towns	68,277	36,658	31,619	18,795	15,444	82	46	3	2	4,291	3,609	13,044	12,043	443	475
Ernakulam	....	21,195	11,944	9,251	6,521	4,644	1	..	..	..	613	335	4,561	4,032	248	240
Mattancheri	....	23,508	12,625	10,883	5,928	4,999	81	46	..	..	3,092	2,791	3,330	2,813	194	234
Trichur	....	23,574	12,089	11,485	6,346	5,801	..	..	3	2	586	483	5,153	5,198	1	1
Class V	4 Towns	31,741	15,476	16,265	10,079	10,626	..	..	..	..	1,046	1,036	4,351	4,603	..	..
Class VI	2 Towns	9,934	5,102	4,832	4,363	4,190	..	..	..	..	204	151	535	491	..	..
Travancore State	11 Towns	212,090	107,668	104,422	72,466	70,591	8	3	..	..	12,186	11,732	22,963	22,078	45	18
Class II—Trivandrum and Cantonment.	1 Town	63,561	32,292	31,269	26,180	25,166	..	..	..	..	2,475	2,173	3,626	3,926	11	4
Class III	2 Towns	55,548	27,923	27,625	17,672	17,439	8	3	..	..	4,690	4,904	5,553	5,279	..	..
Alleppey	....	25,665	13,370	12,295	6,676	5,956	8	3	..	..	3,299	3,370	3,387	2,966	..	..
Nagercoil	....	29,883	14,553	15,330	10,996	11,483	..	..	..	..	1,391	1,534	2,166	2,313	..	..
Class IV	5 Towns	75,913	38,310	37,603	23,516	23,674	..	..	..	..	3,981	3,679	10,781	10,236	32	14
Class V	2 Towns	13,799	7,040	6,759	4,406	4,311	..	..	..	..	616	606	2,018	1,842	..	..
Class VI—Alwaye	1 Town	3,869	2,103	1,766	692	601	..	..	..	..	424	370	985	795	2	..

TABLE VI.

The Population by Religion.

1. The total population shown in this Table is less than that shown in Table I owing to the omission of 1,608,556 persons (males 852,235, females 756,321) in the North-West Frontier Province who were not enumerated by religion.

2. The general arrangement is the same as in the corresponding Table of the last census. Vedic Theists (Arya Samaj) and Eclectic Theists (Brahmo Samaj) are included in the general total of Hindus, but are also shown separately. The term Animistic denotes the primitive forms of belief which are found among the jungle tribes, Mundas, Santals, Bhils, etc. There is no name for these beliefs in any Indian vernacular, and in practice it is very difficult to draw the line between Animism and Hinduism. The question has been discussed in the Report Volume. Here it must suffice to say that all persons who said they were Hindus, Musalmans or Christians, etc., were recorded as such. Those who did not profess to belong to any recognized religion were entered under the name of their caste or tribe. In the course of tabulation all such persons were treated as Hindus if they belonged to a recognized Hindu caste, however low it might be. Those who belonged to jungle tribes outside the caste system, *e.g.*, Bhils, Khonds, Garos, Todas, etc., were classed as Animists.

3. The figures for Hindu, Musalman and Sikh include the following persons whose caste was shown in the religion column :—

Included in Hindu—156 Barrars, 201 Bawarias, 15 Bhangis, 17 Chamars, 8 Chuhras, 252 Dhais, 181 Gaggars, 60 Gandhilas, 1 Jogi Kampatta, 3 Ramles, 5,989 Sansis, 6 Udasis and 12 Zind Kalianis in the Punjab; 15 Chamars, 2,046 Mehtars and 6 Purbias in the North-West Frontier Province; 968 Chuhras and 18 Sansis in Baluchistan; 2 Sansis and 1 Megh in Kashmir.

Included in Musalman—15 Rabs in the Punjab and 84 Chuhras in Kashmir.

Included in Sikh—4 Mazhabis in the Punjab.

4. In addition to the Aryas shown in column 11 there were 63 Sikh Aryas (males 28, females 35) in the Punjab who have been included in column 17.

5. The head "Minor Religions and Religion not returned" includes the following :—

Province or State.	Religion.	Population.		Province or State.	Religion.	Population.	
		Males.	Females.			Males.	Females.
Andamans and Nicobars	Confucian	21	...	Bombay—*contd.*	Unspecified	57	40
Assam	"	1	...	Burma	Confucian	57	14
"	Atheist (Chinese)	1	...	"	Secularist, Rationalist and Agnostic.	27	18
Baluchistan	No religion	1	...	Madras	Atheist and Agnostic	7	7
Bengal	Confucian	907	151	"	Confucian	21	...
Bihar and Orissa	Kumbhipatia (*Alekh or Mahima*).	273	176	Bihar and Orissa States	Kumbhipatia (*Alekh or Mahima*).	198	108
"	Birsait	11	4	Bombay States	Hindu-Muhammadan	16,145	16,294
Bombay	Hindu-Muhammadan	269	268	"	Unspecified	9	7

6. The figures for Madras States include those for Cochin and Travancore, which are as follows :—

Religion.	Cochin.			Travancore.		
	Persons.	Males.	Females.	Persons.	Males.	Females.
Total	**918,110**	**457,342**	**460,768**	**3,428,975**	**1,731,363**	**1,697,612**
Total Hindu	615,710	304,003	311,707	2,283,617	1,145,511	1,137,106
Hindu (Brahmanic)	*615,708*	*304,002*	*311,706*	*2,283,617*	*1,145,511*	*1,137,106*
Hindu (Brahmo)	*2*	*1*	*1*	......	......	......
Jain	129	83	46	11	8	3
Buddhist	......	......	......	16	15	1
Zoroastrian (*Parsi*)	5	3	2	......	......	......
Musalman	63,822	32,707	31,115	226,617	116,488	110,129
Christian	233,092	117,848	115,244	903,868	461,165	442,703
Jew	1,175	571	604	73	53	20
Animistic	4,177	2,127	2,050	15,773	8,123	7,650

TABLE VI.—The

Province, State or Agency.	A.—Population.			B.—Total Hindu.		
	Persons.	Males.	Females.	Persons.	Males.	Females.
1	2	3	4	5	6	7
INDIA.	**313,547,840**	**160,486,700**	**153,061,140**	**217,586,892**	**110,866,131**	**106,720,761**
Provinces.	**244,267,542**	**124,873,691**	**119,393,851**	**163,621,431**	**83,239,957**	**80,381,474**
1. Ajmer-Merwara	501,395	266,198	235,197	389,436	205,380	184,056
2. Andamans and Nicobars	26,459	19,570	6,889	9,527	7,979	1,548
3. Assam	6,713,635	3,467,621	3,246,014	3,637,828	1,898,701	1,739,127
4. Baluchistan	414,412	239,181	175,231	26,488	18,926	7,562
5. Bengal	45,483,077	23,365,225	22,117,852	20,380,720	10,547,218	9,833,502
6. Bihar and Orissa	34,490,084	16,859,929	17,630,155	28,365,235	13,888,893	14,476,342
Bihar	*23,752,969*	*11,606,432*	*12,146,537*	*19,716,498*	*9,656,909*	*10,059,589*
Orissa	*5,131,753*	*2,476,284*	*2,655,469*	*4,903,592*	*2,366,478*	*2,537,114*
Chota Nagpur	*5,605,362*	*2,777,213*	*2,828,149*	*3,745,145*	*1,865,506*	*1,879,639*
7. Bombay (*Presidency*)	19,672,642	10,245,847	9,426,795	14,922,965	7,660,552	7,262,413
Bombay	*16,113,042*	*8,275,233*	*7,837,809*	*14,083,033*	*7,194,626*	*6,888,407*
Sind	*3,513,435*	*1,939,324*	*1,574,111*	*837,887*	*464,366*	*373,521*
Aden	*46,165*	*31,290*	*14,875*	*2,045*	*1,560*	*485*
8. Burma	12,115,217	6,183,494	5,931,723	389,679	312,650	77,029
9. Central Provinces and Berar	13,916,308	6,930,392	6,985,916	11,497,460	5,732,491	5,764,969
Central Provinces	*10,859,146*	*5,379,778*	*5,479,368*	*8,829,312*	*4,380,070*	*4,449,242*
Berar	*3,057,162*	*1,550,614*	*1,506,548*	*2,668,148*	*1,352,421*	*1,315,727*
10. Coorg	174,976	97,279	77,697	138,922	76,822	62,100
11. Madras	41,405,404	20,382,955	21,022,449	36,806.978	18,109,158	18,697,820
12. North-West Frontier Province (*Districts and Administered Territories*)	2,196,933	1,182,102	1,014,831	119,942	71,397	48,545
13. Punjab	19,974,956	10,992,067	8,982,889	6,682,818	3,686,923	2,995,895
14. United Provinces of Agra and Oudh	47,182,044	24,641,831	22,540,213	40,253,433	21,022,867	19,230,566
Agra	*34,624,040*	*18,157,131*	*16,466,909*	*29,415,490*	*15,419,804*	*13,995,686*
Oudh	*12,558,004*	*6,484,700*	*6,073,304*	*10,837,943*	*5,603,063*	*5,234,880*
States and Agencies.	**69,280,298**	**35,613,009**	**33,667,289**	**53,965,461**	**27,626,174**	**26,339,287**
15. Assam State (Manipur)	346,222	170,666	175,556	201,369	99,264	102,105
16. Baluchistan States	420,291	227,238	193,053	11,838	6,538	5,300
17. Baroda State	2,032,798	1,055,935	976,863	1,697,750	884,859	812,891
18. Bengal States	822,565	438,368	384,197	567,637	302,529	265,108
19. Bihar and Orissa States	3,945,209	1,955,125	1,990,084	3,388,453	1,678,240	1,710,213
20. Bombay States	7,411,675	3,765,401	3,646,274	6,055,051	3,081,722	2,973,329
21. Central India Agency	9,356,980	4,801,459	4,555,521	8,262,786	4,241,790	4,020,996
22. Central Provinces States	2,117,002	1,053,630	1,063,372	1,311,420	650,825	660,595
23. Hyderabad State	13,374,676	6,797,118	6,577,558	11,626,355	5,897,266	5,729,089
24. Kashmir State	3,158,126	1,674,367	1,483,759	690,390	372,682	317,708
25. Madras States	4,811,841	2,411,758	2,400,083	3,321,757	1,652,660	1,669,097
26. Mysore State	5,806,193	2,934,621	2,871,572	5,340,973	2,689,882	2,651,091
27. N.-W. F. Province (*Agencies and Tribal areas*)	13,538	12,641	897	2,686	2,335	351
28. Punjab States	4,212,794	2,322,908	1,889,886	2,090,803	1,134,108	956,695
29. Rajputana Agency	10,530,432	5,515,275	5,015,157	8,753,919	4,601,244	4,152,675
30. Sikkim State	87,920	45,059	42,861	58,675	30,035	28,640
31. United Provinces States	832,036	431,440	400,596	583,599	300,195	283,404

POPULATION BY RELIGION.

I.—INDO-ARYAN.												
(a) HINDU (*Brahmanic*).			(b) HINDU (*Arya*).			(c) HINDU (*Brahmo*).			C.—SIKH.			Serial No.
Persons.	Males.	Females.	Persons.	Males.	Females.	Persons.	Males.	Females.	Persons.	Males.	Females.	
8	9	10	11	12	13	14	15	16	17	18	19	
217,337,943	**110,725,612**	**106,612,331**	**243,445**	**137,580**	**105,865**	**5,504**	**2,939**	**2,565**	**3,014,466**	**1,734,797**	**1,279,669**	
163,381,380	83,104,588	80,276,792	234,841	132,583	102,258	5,210	2,786	2,424	2,171,908	1,251,256	920,652	
388,552	204,856	183,696	884	524	360	...	...	...	922	783	139	1
9,467	7,927	1,540	60	52	8	...	...	...	455	419	36	2
3,637,400	1,898,460	1,738,940	...	...	...	428	241	187	750	470	280	3
25,764	18,470	7,294	674	431	243	50	25	25	5,290	4,393	897	4
20,377,793	10,545,714	9,832,079	20	10	10	2,907	1,494	1,413	2,217	1,771	446	5
28,360,589	13,886,520	14,474,069	4,085	2,066	2,019	561	307	254	2,177	1,110	1,067	6
19,712,260	*9,654,753*	*10,057,507*	*4,013*	*2,026*	*1,987*	*225*	*130*	*95*	*1,865*	*920*	*945*	
4,903,379	*2,366,369*	*2,537,010*	*1*	*1*	...	*212*	*108*	*104*	*37*	*22*	*15*	
3,744,950	*1,865,398*	*1,879,552*	*71*	*39*	*32*	*124*	*69*	*55*	*275*	*168*	*107*	
14,922,311	7,660,148	7,262,163	523	331	192	131	73	58	11,887	7,171	4,716	7
14,082,841	*7,194,515*	*6,888,326*	*164*	*94*	*70*	*28*	*17*	*11*	*701*	*581*	*120*	
837,426	*464,074*	*373,352*	*358*	*236*	*122*	*103*	*56*	*47*	*11,166*	*6,573*	*4,593*	
2,044	*1,559*	*485*	*1*	*1*	...	...	...	...	*20*	*17*	*3*	
389,679	312,650	77,029	...	...	...	..	...	...	6,693	5,527	1,166	8
11,496,486	5,731,936	5,764,550	944	538	406	30	17	13	2,201	1,730	471	9
8,828,377	*4,379,540*	*4,448,837*	*906*	*514*	*392*	*29*	*16*	*13*	*1,997*	*1,626*	*371*	
2,668,109	*1,352,396*	*1,315,713*	*38*	*24*	*14*	*1*	*1*	...	*204*	*104*	*100*	
138,922	76,822	62,100	...	...	...	...	...	...	...	...	...	10
36,806,604	18,108,939	18,697,665	...	...	...	374	219	155	7	5	2	11
119,942	71,397	48,545	...	...	...	...	...	...	30,345	19,967	10,378	12
6,585,633	3,631,108	2,954,525	96,497	55,429	41,068	688	386	302	2,093,804	1,197,922	895,882	13
40,122,238	20,949,641	19,172,597	131,154	73,202	57,952	41	24	17	15,160	9,988	5,172	14
29,289,754	*15,349,789*	*13,939,965*	*125,707*	*70,000*	*55,707*	*29*	*15*	*14*	*12,618*	*8,267*	*4,351*	
10,832,484	*5,599,852*	*5,232,632*	*5,447*	*3,202*	*2,245*	*12*	*9*	*3*	*2,542*	*1,721*	*821*	
53,956,563	27,621,024	26,335,539	8,604	4,997	3,607	294	153	141	842,558	483,541	359,017	
201,369	99,264	102,105	...	...	...	...	...	...	7	5	2	15
11,838	6,538	5,300	...	...	...	...	...	...	3,100	1,624	1,476	16
1,697,146	884,474	812,672	598	381	217	6	4	2	90	59	31	17
567,586	302,503	265,083	...	...	...	51	26	25	4	4	...	18
3,388,429	1,678,229	1,710,200	...	...	...	24	11	13	51	34	17	19
6,054,992	3,081,688	2,973,304	55	32	23	4	2	2	1,191	644	547	20
8,262,638	4,241,694	4,020,944	139	90	49	9	6	3	1,384	953	431	21
1,311,388	650,807	660,581	30	16	14	2	2	...	136	72	64	22
11,626,146	5,897,158	5,728,988	173	90	83	36	18	18	4,726	2,643	2,083	23
689,342	372,089	317,253	1,047	593	454	1	...	1	31,553	17,038	14,515	24
3,321,755	1,652,659	1,669,096	...	...	..	2	1	1	...	...	...	25
5,340,908	2,689,851	2,651,057	...	...	...	65	31	34	293	242	51	26
2,686	2,335	351	...	...	...	...	...	...	1,114	1,050	64	27
2,086,505	1,131,599	954 906	4,286	2,499	1,787	12	10	2	789,925	453,673	336,252	28
8,752,045	4,600,170	4,151,875	1,792	1,032	760	82	42	40	8,958	5,489	3,469	29
58,675	30,035	28,640	...	..	...	...	..	...	...	...	..	30
563,115	299,931	263,184	484	264	220	...	...	...	26	11	15	31

TABLE VI.—THE

Province, State or Agency.	I.—INDO-ARYAN—concld.					
	D.—Jain.			E.—Buddhist.		
	Persons.	Males.	Females.	Persons.	Males.	Females.
1	20	21	22	23	24	25
INDIA.	**1,248,182**	**643,553**	**604,629**	**10,721.453**	**5,286,275**	**5,435,178**
Provinces.	458,578	250,704	207,874	10,644,409	5,247,177	5,397,232
1. Ajmer-Merwara	20,302	10,809	9,493	...	...	...
2. Andamans and Nicobars	...	...	...	1,597	1,584	13
3. Assam	2,398	2,032	366	10,506	6,199	4,307
4. Baluchistan	10	9	1	14	7	7
5. Bengal	6,206	4,816	1,390	240,854	122,212	118,642
6. Bihar and Orissa	4,440	2,575	1,865	496	295	201
Bihar	*3,092*	*1,854*	*1,238*	*35*	*30*	*5*
Orissa	*158*	*82*	*76*	*438*	*245*	*193*
Chota Nagpur	*1,190*	*639*	*551*	*23*	*20*	*3*
7. Bombay (*Presidency*)	212,309	117,519	94,790	691	478	213
Bombay	*210,725*	*116,525*	*94,200*	*660*	*463*	*197*
Sind	*1,349*	*806*	*543*	*21*	*5*	*16*
Aden	*235*	*188*	*47*	*10*	*10*	...
8. Burma	495	416	79	10,384,579	5,113,459	5,271,120
9. Central Provinces and Berar	70,258	36,109	34,149	9	8	1
Central Provinces	*51,358*	*26,434*	*24,924*	*9*	*8*	*1*
Berar	*18,900*	*9,675*	*9,225*	...	...	...
10. Coorg	97	45	52	...	...	...
11. Madras	26,995	14,158	12,837	693	429	264
12. North-West Frontier Province (*Districts and Administered Territories*)	4	2	2	...	...	...
13. Punjab	39,637	21,319	18,318	4,190	2,062	2,128
14. United Provinces of Agra and Oudh	75,427	40,895	34,532	780	444	336
Agra	*73,710*	*39,950*	*33,760*	*749*	*429*	*320*
Oudh	*1,717*	*945*	*772*	*31*	*15*	*16*
States and Agencies.	789,604	392,849	396,755	77,044	39,098	37,946
15. Assam State (Manipur)	110	104	6	7	5	2
16. Baluchistan States	...	...	...	2	2	...
17. Baroda State	43,462	21,875	21,587	...	...	...
18. Bengal States	576	519	57	6,012	3,176	2,836
19. Bihar and Orissa States	189	128	61	1,431	759	672
20. Bombay States	277,643	137,132	140,511	1	1	...
21. Central India Agency	87,471	45,711	41,760	...	...	...
22. Central Provinces States	1,159	671	488	...	...	...
23. Hyderabad State	21,026	11,032	9,994	20	8	12
24. Kashmir State	345	191	154	36,512	18,281	18,231
25. Madras States	150	99	51	20	15	5
26. Mysore State	17,630	9,392	8,238	622	354	268
27. N.-W. F. Province (*Agencies and Tribal areas*)	...	...	...	...	...	...
28. Punjab States	7,138	3,961	3,177	3,500	1,665	1,835
29. Rajputana Agency	332,397	161,856	170,541	2	2	...
30 Sikkim State	...	...	...	28,915	14,830	14,085
31. United Provinces States	308	178	130	...	...	...

POPULATION BY RELIGION—*continued.*

II.—IRANIAN.			III.—SEMITIC.						
F.—ZOROASTRIAN—(*Parsi*).			G.—MUSALMAN.			H.—CHRISTIAN.			Serial No.
Persons.	Males.	Females.	Persons.	Males.	Females.	Persons.	Males.	Females.	
26	27	28	29	30	31	32	33	34	
100,096	**51,123**	**48,973**	**66,647,299**	**34,738,342**	**31,908,957**	**3,876,203**	**2,010,729**	**1,865,474**	
86,155	44,541	41,614	57,423,889	29,881,399	27,542,490	2,492,284	1,301,555	1,190,729	
262	134	128	81,035	43,833	37,202	5,432	3,258	2,174	1
...	...	...	4,580	4,080	500	566	384	182	2
5	5	...	1,866,528	977,463	909,065	66,480	33,548	32,882	3
166	93	73	377,356	211,828	165,528	5,030	3,892	1,138	4
610	402	208	23,989,719	12,245,542	11,744,177	129,518	70,127	59,391	5
35	25	10	3,666,861	1,766,496	1,900,365	229,825	114,009	115,816	6
23	*15*	*8*	*3,216,670*	*1,541,570*	*1,675,100*	*22,076*	*11,360*	*10,716*	
...	...	...	*117,589*	*55,762*	*61,827*	*8,007*	*3,804*	*4,203*	
12	*10*	*2*	*332,602*	*169,164*	*163,438*	*199,742*	*98,845*	*100,897*	
80,980	41,470	39,510	4,024,485	2,190,195	1,834,290	233,246	134,480	98,766	7
78,185	*39,943*	*38,242*	*1,347,548*	*711,927*	*635,621*	*219,621*	*124,455*	*95,166*	
2,411	*1,259*	*1,152*	*2,639,929*	*1,453,351*	*1,186,578*	*10,911*	*7,658*	*3,253*	
384	*268*	*116*	*37,008*	*24,917*	*12,091*	*2,714*	*2,367*	*347*	
300	195	105	420,777	271,428	149,349	210,061	111,033	99,048	8
1,728	1,031	697	564,909	292,047	272,862	34,697	19,731	14,966	9
1,197	*710*	*487*	*326,244*	*168,594*	*157,650*	*31,874*	*18,210*	*13,664*	
531	*321*	*210*	*238,665*	*123,453*	*115,212*	*2,823*	*1,521*	*1,302*	
34	16	18	13,143	8,397	4,746	3,553	1,986	1,567	10
488	249	239	2,740,408	1,351,119	1,389,289	1,191,266	586,836	604,430	11
49	41	8	2,039,994	1,085,276	954,718	6,585	5,414	1,171	12
626	376	250	10,955,721	5,967,408	4,988,313	198,106	116,039	82,067	13
872	504	368	6,658,373	3,466,287	3,192,086	177,949	100,818	77,131	14
689	*394*	*295*	*4,957,686*	*2,596,958*	*2,360,728*	*163,069*	*91,311*	*71,758*	
183	*110*	*73*	*1,700,687*	*869,329*	*831,358*	*14,880*	*9,507*	*5,373*	
13,941	6,582	7,359	9,223,410	4,856,943	4,366,467	1,383,919	709,174	674,745	
...	...	...	14,504	7,505	6,999	132	84	48	15
4	3	1	405,292	219,022	186,270	55	49	6	16
7,955	3,420	4,535	160,887	82,986	77,901	7,203	3,855	3,348	17
1	1	...	247,509	131,673	115,836	228	133	95	18
...	...	...	16,577	9,160	7,417	38,440	19,177	19,263	19
2,585	1,333	1,252	877,431	445,640	431,791	12,411	6,307	6,104	20
1,330	689	641	511,200	266,494	244,706	9,358	6,170	3,188	21
29	21	8	20,120	10,180	9,940	38,704	19,477	19,227	22
1,529	822	707	1,380,990	706,821	674,169	54,296	29,495	24,801	23
31	22	9	2,398,320	1,265,535	1,132,785	975	618	357	24
6	4	2	314,498	160,692	153,806	1,154,209	587,412	566,797	25
101	55	46	314,494	165,824	148,670	59,844	31,853	27,991	26
...	...	...	9,605	9,146	459	133	110	23	27
27	20	7	1,319,756	728,535	591,221	1,645	946	699	28
342	191	151	985,825	517,560	468,265	4,256	2,409	1,847	29
1	1	...	44	38	6	285	155	130	30
...	...	...	246,358	130,132	116,226	1,745	924	821	31

TABLE VI.—The Population by Religion—*concluded.*

Province, State or Agency.	III.—Semitic—*concld.* I.—Jew. Persons.	Males.	Females.	IV.—Primitive. J.—Animistic. Persons.	Males.	Females.	V.—Miscellaneous. K.—Minor Religions and Religion not returned. Persons.	Males.	Females.
1	35	36	37	38	39	40	41	42	43
INDIA.	**20,980**	**10,813**	**10,167**	**10,295,168**	**5,126,932**	**5,168,236**	**37,101**	**18,005**	**19,096**
Provinces.	18,524	9,561	8,963	7,348,024	3,645,888	3,702,136	2,340	1,653	687
1. Ajmer-Merwara	27	14	13	3,979	1,987	1,992	...	...	...
2. Andamans and Nicobars	2	2	...	9,711	5,101	4,610	21	21	...
3. Assam	1	1	...	1,109,187	549,200	559,987	2	2	..
4. Baluchistan	57	32	25	...	...	...	1	1	...
5. Bengal	1,993	982	1,011	730,182	371,248	358,934	1,058	907	151
6. Bihar and Orissa	25	11	14	2,220,526	1,086,231	1,134,295	464	284	180
Bihar	*24*	*10*	*14*	*792,686*	*393,764*	*398,922*	...	...	...
Orissa	...	...	...	*101,483*	*49,618*	*51,865*	*449*	*273*	*176*
Chota Nagpur	*1*	*1*	...	*1,326,357*	*642,849*	*683,508*	*15*	*11*	*4*
7. Bombay (*Presidency*)	15,081	7,792	7,289	170,355	85,864	84,491	643	326	317
Bombay	*10,739*	*5,519*	*5,220*	*161,484*	*81,017*	*80,467*	*346*	*177*	*169*
Sind	*595*	*311*	*284*	*8,869*	*4,846*	*4,023*	*297*	*149*	*148*
Aden	*3,747*	*1,962*	*1,785*	*2*	*1*	*1*	...	...	...
8. Burma	1,024	559	465	701,473	368,143	333,330	116	84	32
9. Central Provinces and Berar	125	78	47	1,744,921	847,167	897,754	...	..	...
Central Provinces	*95*	*54*	*41*	*1,617,060*	*784,072*	*832,988*	...	...	...
Berar	*30*	*24*	*6*	*127,861*	*63,095*	*64,766*	...	...	...
10. Coorg	...	...	...	19,227	10,013	9,214	...	...	...
11. Madras	71	39	32	638,463	320,934	317,529	35	28	7
12. North-West Frontier Province (*Districts and Administered Territories*)	14	5	9	...	...	...	...	...	...
13. Punjab	54	18	36	...	...	...	...	...	...
14. United Provinces of Agra and Oudh	50	28	22	...	...	...	...	...	...
Agra	*29*	*18*	*11*	...	...	..	...	..	...
Oudh	*21*	*10*	*11*	...	...	...	...	...	...
States and Agencies.	2,456	1,252	1,204	2,947,144	1,481,044	1,466,100	34,761	16,352	18,409
15. Assam State (Manipur)	...	...	...	130,093	63,699	66,394	...	...	...
16. Baluchistan States	...	...	...	...	...	...	...	..	...
17. Baroda State	40	23	17	115,411	58,858	56,553	...	...	...
18. Bengal States	...	...	...	598	333	265	...	...	...
19. Bihar and Orissa States	...	...	...	499,762	247,429	252,333	306	198	108
20. Bombay States	1,028	527	501	149,879	75,941	73,938	34,455	16,154	18,301
21. Central India Agency	57	34	23	483,394	239,618	243,776	...	...	...
22. Central Provinces States	...	...	...	745,434	372,384	373,050	...	...	...
23. Hyderabad State	12	8	4	285,722	149,023	136,699	...	...	...
24. Kashmir State	...	...	...	...	...	...	...	...	...
25. Madras States	1,248	624	624	19,953	10,252	9,701	...	...	...
26. Mysore State	40	20	20	72,196	36,999	35,197	...	...	...
27. N.-W. F. Province (*Agencies and Tribal areas*)	...	...	...	...	...	.	...	...	...
28. Punjab States	...	...	...	...	...	...	...	...	...
29 Rajputana Agency	31	16	15	444,702	226,508	218,194	...	...	...
30. Sikkim State	...	...	...	...	...	...	...	...	...
31. United Provinces States	...	...	...	...	...	...	...	...	...

TABLE VII.

Age, Sex and Civil Condition by Religions.

1. The age shown in this Table represents the number of years completed and not the current year of age. Divorced persons have been entered as "Widowed." Persons recognized by custom as married have been shown as such, even though they have not gone through any formal ceremony.

2. The Table is divided into two parts. Part I contains the statistics for the total population of India and for each religion. Part II contains the statistics for the total population and three (numerically) most important religions of the main Provinces and States.

3. The population here dealt with falls short of that in Table I by 2,512,703 persons enumerated in tracts where age and civil condition were not recorded, as noted below :—

	Persons.	Males.	Females.
Included in Tables I and VI.	*904,147*	*485,378*	*418,769*
Andamans and Nicobars	1,692	818	874
Baluchistan	352,218	190,583	161,635
Burma	76,134	38,023	38,111
Baluchistan States	419,478	226,565	192,913
Kashmir State	54,625	29,389	25,236
Included in Table I, but not included in Table VI.			
North-West Frontier Province	1,608,556	852,235	756,321
Total	2,512,703	1,337,613	1,175,090

4. The distribution by religion of the 904,147 persons omitted from this Table but included in Table VI is as follows :—

Hindu	17,548	9,992	7,556
Arya	1	1	..
Sikh	3,371	1,823	1,548
Buddhist	225	133	92
Musalman	805,371	434,733	370,638
Christian	7	5	2
Animistic	77,624	38,691	38,933

A further difference between the number of Hindus, Aryas and Brahmos as shown in this Table and in Table VI is due to the fact that in the Punjab the figures for Aryas (Total 100,783, males 57,928, females 42,855) and Brahmos (Total 700, males 396, females 304) were amalgamated with those for Hindus.

5. Jews, who were shown separately in Table VI, have here been included in "Minor and Unspecified."

6. The figures for Madras States in Part II include those for Cochin and Travancore.

TABLE VII.—Age, Sex and Civil Condition.

Age and Religion.	Population.			Unmarried.		Married.		Widowed.	
	Persons.	Males.	Females.	Males.	Females.	Males.	Females.	Males.	Females.
1	2	3	4	5	6	7	8	9	10
ALL RELIGIONS	**312,643,693**	**160,001,322**	**152,642,371**	**78,384,686**	**52,516,947**	**72,906,881**	**73,704,162**	**8,709,755**	**26,421,262**
0—1 . .	10,249,031	5,120,053	5,128,078	5,110,357	5,113,852	10,164	13,212	432	1,014
1—2 . .	5,255,438	2,575,202	2,680,236	2,565,054	2,661,627	9,675	17,753	473	856
2—3 . .	8,891,266	4,337,666	4,553,600	4,310,469	4,502,006	26,153	49,787	1,044	1,807
3—4 . .	9,733,059	4,712,328	5,020,731	4,669,647	4,928,410	40,879	87,568	1,802	4,753
4—5 . .	8,982,501	4,490,036	4,492,465	4,422,472	4,349,087	64,647	134,105	2,917	9,273
Total 0—5 .	*43,111,295*	*21,236,185*	*21,875,110*	*21,077,999*	*21,554,982*	*151,518*	*302,425*	*6,668*	*17,703*
5—10 . .	43,244,659	22,131,817	21,112,842	21,286,142	18,798,794	810,577	2,219,778	35,098	94,270
10—15 . .	38,863,282	16,640,581	15,222,701	16,145,450	8,444,235	2,408,136	6,555,424	91,995	223,042
15—20 . .	26,181,473	13,567,760	12,613,713	9,025,628	2,059,855	4,364,438	10,087,024	177,694	466,834
20—25 . .	27,341,920	13,154,601	14,187,319	4,988,314	622,134	7,785,484	12,663,431	380,803	901,754
25—30 . .	28,213,629	14,335,940	13,882,689	2,593,244	309,648	11,116,064	12,183,406	626,632	1,389,635
30—35 . .	25,998,912	13,258,251	12,740,661	1,236,403	221,237	11,235,008	10,356,841	786,840	2,162,583
35—40 . .	18,431,102	9,946,860	8,484,242	587,642	116,698	8,646,547	6,285,143	712,671	2,082,406
40—45 . .	19,767,976	10,140,739	9,627,237	519,378	127,005	8,597,795	5,767,258	1,023,566	3,732,974
45—50 . .	11,244,547	6,082,167	5,162,380	250,496	56,915	5,077,517	2,697,341	754,154	2,408,124
50—55 . .	13,675,701	6,917,004	6,758,697	278,585	72,293	5,441,486	2,403,716	1,196,983	4,282,688
55—60 . .	5,322,126	2,824,725	2,497,401	104,317	29,247	2,151,792	846,650	568,616	1,621,504
60—65 . .	8,761,214	4,111,465	4,649,749	151,244	48,937	2,854,405	821,969	1,105,816	3,778,843
65—70 . .	2,473,336	1,324,871	1,150,465	43,425	14,977	931,802	215,206	349,644	920,282
70 and over	5,004,909	2,328,086	2,676,823	96,316	39,849	1,339,215	298,399	892,555	2,338,575
Age Unspecified.	612	270	342	153	146	97	151	20	45
HINDU . .	**217,421,878**	**110,773,944**	**106,647,934**	**52,076,487**	**33,875,130**	**52,283,045**	**52,753,753**	**6,414,412**	**20,019,051**
0—1 . .	6,984,318	3,485,172	3,499,146	3,475,806	3,486,484	8,995	11,796	371	866
1—2 . .	3,579,169	1,749,675	1,829,494	1,740,571	1,812,564	8,692	16,175	412	755
2—3 . .	6,001,082	2,922,985	3,078,097	2,898,357	3,031,593	23,724	44,940	904	1,564
3—4 . .	6,556,222	3,161,516	3,394,706	3,123,614	3,312,232	36,317	78,487	1,585	3,987
4—5 . .	6,002,487	2,997,974	3,004,513	2,937,744	2,876,569	57,675	120,341	2,555	7,603
Total 0—5 .	*29,123,278*	*14,317,322*	*14,805,956*	*14,176,092*	*14,519,442*	*135,403*	*271,739*	*5,827*	*14,775*
5—10 . .	29,006,667	14,804,500	14,202,167	14,059,551	12,255,658	714,358	1,868,924	30,591	77,585
10—15 . .	23,245,466	12,753,469	10,491,997	10,645,412	5,192,855	2,030,380	5,117,635	77,677	181,507
15—20 . .	18,017,663	9,429,880	8,587,783	5,903,546	1,045,748	3,386,602	7,179,069	139,732	362,966
20—25 . .	19,229,425	9,262,382	9,967,043	3,290,428	302,132	5,691,581	8,962,898	280,373	702,013
25—30 . .	19,821,457	10,061,045	9,760,412	1,712,386	160,273	7,895,706	8,528,294	452,951	1,071,845
30—35 . .	18,452,334	9,334,164	9,118,170	843,538	125,514	7,919,526	7,321,054	571,100	1,671,602
35—40 . .	13,057,230	6,967,340	6,089,890	413,080	64,693	6,031,071	4,437,188	523,189	1,588,009
40—45 . .	14,262,097	7,259,106	7,002,991	375,183	74,406	6,116,182	4,069,239	767,741	2,859,346
45—50 . .	8,060,762	4,318,517	3,742,245	181,354	30,851	3,569,570	1,887,058	567,593	1,824,336
50—55 . .	9,895,336	4,946,388	4,948,948	204,787	40,834	3,838,668	1,663,171	902,933	3,244,943
55—60 . .	3,824,262	2,008,462	1,815,800	75,464	14,012	1,503,893	576,723	429,105	1,225,065
60—65 . .	6,322,057	2,908,786	3,413,871	106,393	25,268	1,987,028	544,947	815,365	2,848,656
65—70 . .	1,685,389	854,050	831,339	28,072	5,876	574,434	137,806	251,544	687,657
70 and over	3,417,462	1,548,272	1,869,190	61,053	17,505	888,548	187,958	598,671	1,663,727
Age Unspecified.	393	261	132	148	63	98	50	20	19
ARYA . .	**142,661**	**79,651**	**63,010**	**37,030**	**20,296**	**35,690**	**31,869**	**6,931**	**10,845**
0—1 . .	4,833	2,568	2,265	2,566	2,262	2	3	..	..
1—2 . .	1,765	906	859	904	857	1	2	1	..
2—3 . .	3,040	1,569	1,471	1,562	1,460	7	9	..	2
3—4 . .	3,197	1,580	1,617	1,574	1,601	4	12	2	4
4—5 . .	3,131	1,685	1,446	1,666	1,428	18	18	1	..
Total 0—5 .	*15,966*	*8,308*	*7,658*	*8,272*	*7,608*	*32*	*44*	*4*	*6*
5—10 . .	17,174	9,444	7,730	9,240	7,422	194	276	10	32
10—15 . .	16,906	10,057	6,849	8,620	4,206	1,383	2,569	45	74
15—20 . .	14,241	8,277	5,964	4,309	540	3,784	5,181	184	243
20—25 . .	14,542	7,908	6,634	2,259	157	5,254	5,975	395	502
25—30 . .	13,060	7,413	5,647	1,367	137	5,576	4,922	470	588
30—35 . .	11,425	6,469	4,956	911	65	4,914	4,090	644	801
35—40 . .	8,772	5,224	3,548	547	37	4,032	2,718	645	793
40—45 . .	8,750	4,796	3,954	512	42	3,448	2,510	836	1,402
45—50 . .	5,798	3,427	2,371	305	20	2,405	1,384	717	967
50—55 . .	6,191	3,226	2,965	295	23	2,014	1,136	917	1,806
55—60 . .	2,916	1,725	1,191	111	11	1,112	424	502	756
60—65 . .	3,677	1,798	1,879	162	14	901	404	735	1,461
65—70 . .	1,129	615	514	39	3	310	110	266	401
70 and over	2,114	964	1,150	72	11	331	126	561	1,012
BRAHMO .	**4,804**	**2,543**	**2,261**	**1,512**	**1,196**	**911**	**825**	**190**	**240**
0—1 . .	152	78	74	78	74	..	..	..	..
1—2 . .	75	39	36	39	36	..	..	..	..
2—3 . .	111	51	60	51	60	..	..	..	..
3—4 . .	137	77	60	77	60	..	..	..	..
4—5 . .	122	70	52	70	51	..	1	..	..
Total 0—5	*597*	*315*	*282*	*315*	*281*	..	*1*	..	..
5—10 .	539	299	340	297	334	2	5	..	1
10—15 . .	613	313	300	309	283	4	13	..	4
15—20 . .	532	248	284	235	176	13	100	..	8
20—25 .	481	238	243	188	62	44	162	6	19
25—30 . .	401	190	211	90	40	93	154	7	17
30—35 . .	362	210	152	33	8	172	123	5	21
35—40 . .	320	193	127	13	7	164	95	16	25
40—45 . .	268	171	97	14	2	134	68	23	27
45—50 . .	164	102	62	6	1	83	32	13	29
50—55 . .	161	90	71	4	1	75	46	11	24
55—60 . .	90	62	28	3	1	53	15	6	12
60—65 . .	94	59	35	3	..	40	4	16	31
65—70 . .	38	25	13	..	..	18	6	7	7
70 and over .	44	28	16	2	..	16	1	10	15

Part I.—General Table—India.

Age and Religion.	Population.			Unmarried.		Married.		Widowed.	
	Persons.	Males.	Females.	Males.	Females.	Males.	Females.	Males.	Females.
1	2	3	4	5	6	7	8	9	10
SIKH	**3,011,095**	**1,732,974**	**1,278,121**	**936,621**	**454,035**	**630,102**	**632,224**	**166,251**	**191,862**
0—1	121,650	64,549	57,101	64,541	57,095	7	6	1	..
1—2	49,225	26,330	22,895	26,327	22,891	3	4	..	..
2—3	71,924	39,134	32,790	39,116	32,769	16	20	2	1
3—4	77,958	41,827	36,131	41,804	36,101	23	30	..	..
4—5	74,856	41,829	33,027	41,786	32,982	39	40	4	5
Total 0—5	*395,613*	*213,669*	*181,944*	*213,574*	*181,838*	*88*	*100*	*7*	*6*
5—10	382,564	215,855	166,709	213,250	160,922	2,306	5,290	299	497
10—15	327,527	203,114	124,413	186,077	87,393	15,665	36,103	1,372	917
15—20	269,334	169,208	100,126	121,537	16,970	44,270	80,985	3,401	2,171
20—25	271,252	157,446	113,806	73,767	2,573	76,320	106,533	7,359	4,700
25—30	270,809	154,120	116,689	45,815	1,251	95,759	107,169	12,546	8,269
30—35	231,026	127,694	103,332	24,502	756	88,655	89,997	14,537	12,579
35—40	160,452	92,179	68,273	13,617	547	65,422	55,727	13,140	11,999
40—45	183,068	98,461	84,607	12,669	497	68,882	59,202	16,910	24,908
45—50	120,051	69,944	50,107	7,698	253	47,274	31,837	14,972	18,017
50—55	146,781	83,781	63,000	8,796	284	52,595	29,540	22,390	33,176
55—60	59,652	36,174	23,478	3,564	115	21,269	10,678	11,341	12,685
60—65	86,008	44,598	41,410	5,423	263	19,196	11,267	19,979	29,880
65—70	42,956	31,553	11,403	1,770	79	21,935	3,114	7,848	8,210
70 and over	64,002	35,178	28,824	3,962	294	10,466	4,682	20,750	23,848
JAIN	**1,248,182**	**643,553**	**604,629**	**317,197**	**181,705**	**268,938**	**269,627**	**57,418**	**153,297**
0—1	39,663	19,944	19,719	19,887	19,623	52	81	5	15
1—2	18,537	8,966	9,571	8,902	9,485	43	81	21	5
2—3	32,530	16,096	16,434	15,970	16,239	88	178	38	17
3—4	31,747	15,632	16,115	15,473	15,848	113	247	46	20
4—5	29,051	14,678	14,373	14,491	13,977	129	361	58	35
Total 0—5	*151,528*	*75,316*	*76,212*	*74,723*	*75,172*	*425*	*948*	*168*	*92*
5—10	142,186	72,098	70,088	70,851	65,314	1,094	4,513	153	261
10—15	125,354	69,129	56,225	63,160	34,483	5,616	20,836	353	906
15—20	108,125	58,976	49,149	39,595	3,708	18,608	42,735	773	2,706
20—25	122,530	62,310	60,220	25,718	994	34,446	51,882	2,146	7,344
25—30	116,480	61,068	55,412	15,295	536	42,175	43,564	3,598	11,312
30—35	107,173	54,509	52,664	9,056	439	40,542	36,176	4,911	16,049
35—40	79,181	42,772	36,409	5,069	251	32,616	22,397	5,087	13,761
40—45	86,850	42,376	44,474	4,774	279	30,409	20,928	7,193	23,267
45—50	52,377	28,800	23,577	2,775	131	19,880	9,897	6,145	13,549
50—55	65,257	31,933	33,324	3,031	159	19,751	8,882	9,151	24,283
55—60	26,217	14,519	11,698	1,048	61	8,618	2,960	4,853	8,677
60—65	37,697	16,745	20,952	1,268	84	8,769	2,677	6,708	18,191
65—70	11,308	5,969	5,339	411	38	3,019	649	2,539	4,652
70 and over	15,919	7,033	8,886	423	56	2,970	583	3,640	8,247
BUDDHIST	**10,721,228**	**5,286,142**	**5,435,086**	**3,034,592**	**2,821,318**	**2,027,490**	**2,039,165**	**224,060**	**574,603**
0—1	256,119	124,119	132,000	124,112	131,996	7	4	..	..
1—2	248,831	121,972	126,859	121,971	126,852	1	7	..	..
2—3	302,465	147,952	154,513	147,944	154,508	8	5	..	..
3—4	343,373	169,515	173,858	169,504	173,851	11	7	..	..
4—5	308,411	150,934	157,477	150,914	157,466	20	10	..	1
Total 0—5	*1,459,199*	*714,492*	*744,707*	*714,445*	*744,673*	*47*	*33*	..	*1*
5—10	1,449,789	717,752	732,037	717,480	731,814	267	205	5	18
10—15	1,271,756	652,603	619,153	651,575	614,364	1,002	4,613	26	176
15—20	1,000,827	475,438	525,389	439,467	383,490	34,590	133,574	1,381	8,325
20—25	880,679	410,315	470,364	219,047	137,185	182,369	310,010	8,899	23,169
25—30	835,169	403,385	431,784	107,329	60,524	281,955	343,389	14,101	27,871
30—35	802,142	406,495	395,647	57,817	35,502	330,092	325,004	18,586	35,141
35—40	661,733	345,486	316,247	34,849	22,612	292,253	254,309	18,384	39,326
40—45	599,864	299,489	300,375	24,906	20,753	253,012	226,983	21,571	52,639
45—50	418,343	215,518	202,825	15,634	13,222	181,575	143,593	18,309	46,010
50—55	406,745	197,724	209,021	14,864	14,993	160,440	122,321	22,420	71,707
55—60	256,930	126,557	130,373	9,653	9,589	99,780	70,823	17,124	49,961
60—65	298,453	147,045	151,408	10,738	12,778	108,009	57,373	28,298	81,257
65—70	138,455	69,354	69,101	6,815	6,194	46,406	23,469	16,133	39,438
70 and over	241,144	104,489	136,655	10,473	13,625	55,693	23,466	38,323	99,564
ZOROASTRIAN	**100,096**	**51,123**	**48,973**	**29,463**	**23,799**	**19,492**	**18,520**	**2,168**	**6,654**
0—1	2,155	1,165	990	1,165	985	..	5	..	..
1—2	1,212	594	618	590	614	4	4	..	..
2—3	1,619	800	819	794	807	6	12	..	..
3—4	1,918	950	968	945	956	5	11	..	1
4—5	1,931	950	981	948	970	1	10	1	1
Total 0—5	*8,835*	*4,459*	*4,376*	*4,442*	*4,332*	*16*	*42*	*1*	*2*
5—10	9,917	4,981	4,936	4,928	4,867	49	63	4	6
10—15	10,065	5,130	4,935	5,036	4,774	86	149	8	12
15—20	9,721	4,825	4,896	4,624	4,119	196	745	5	32
20—25	10,257	5,026	5,231	4,171	2,805	831	2,332	24	94
25—30	9,408	4,836	4,572	2,924	1,421	1,861	2,940	51	211
30—35	8,547	4,515	4,032	1,601	647	2,815	3,095	99	290
35—40	7,076	3,788	3,288	825	328	2,823	2,525	140	435
40—45	7,089	3,733	3,356	454	218	3,076	2,383	203	755
45—50	4,999	2,703	2,296	220	72	2,258	1,558	225	666
50—55	4,838	2,527	2,311	114	59	2,103	1,250	310	1,002
55—60	2,856	1,508	1,348	44	75	1,230	628	234	645
60—65	2,990	1,418	1,572	41	51	1,096	443	281	1,078
65—70	1,484	785	699	16	10	545	194	224	495
70 and over	2,014	889	1,125	23	21	507	173	359	931

TABLE VII.—Age, Sex and Civil Condition. Part I.—General Table—India—*concld.*

Age and Religion.	Population.			Unmarried.		Married.		Widowed.	
	Persons.	Males.	Females.	Males.	Females.	Males.	Females.	Males.	Females.
1	2	3	4	5	6	7	8	9	10
MUSALMAN	**65,841,928**	**34,303,609**	**31,538,319**	**18,065,851**	**11,966,196**	**14,645,695**	**14,919,006**	**1,592,063**	**4,653,117**
0—1	2,362,195	1,186,673	1,175,522	1,185,902	1,174,462	736	951	35	109
1—2	1,048,116	516,640	531,476	515,960	530,310	658	1,098	22	68
2—3	2,012,902	983,652	1,029,250	982,014	1,025,313	1,572	3,771	66	166
3—4	2,177,767	1,061,909	1,115,858	1,058,532	1,108,203	3,248	7,146	129	509
4—5	2,077,277	1,042,253	1,035,024	1,036,948	1,022,550	5,068	11,193	237	1,281
Total 0—5	*9,678,257*	*4,791,127*	*4,887,130*	*4,779,356*	*4,860,838*	*11,282*	*24,159*	*489*	*2,133*
5—10	10,115,194	5,233,618	4,881,576	5,148,684	4,549,833	81,418	317,467	3,516	14,276
10—15	7,346,814	4,143,060	3,203,754	3,821,742	1,908,648	310,042	1,258,842	11,276	36,264
15—20	5,608,230	2,858,032	2,750,198	2,079,463	370,322	750,379	2,294,742	28,190	79,134
20—25	5,591,014	2,676,219	2,914,795	1,104,490	101,877	1,501,129	2,673,566	70,600	139,352
25—30	5,855,309	3,000,342	2,854,967	571,341	51,696	2,306,091	2,572,937	122,910	230,334
30—35	5,221,343	2,730,829	2,490,514	245,169	37,074	2,333,090	2,088,791	152,570	363,749
35—40	3,632,092	2,045,336	1,586,756	95,811	18,453	1,818,897	1,199,229	130,628	369,074
40—45	3,804,880	2,000,997	1,803,883	85,185	21,715	1,735,914	1,125,088	179,898	657,080
45—50	2,136,270	1,203,060	983,210	35,393	8,196	1,041,600	492,387	126,067	432,627
50—55	2,638,123	1,388,701	1,249,422	40,117	11,800	1,141,077	466,047	207,507	772,075
55—60	944,529	530,265	414,264	11,859	3,468	428,404	138,905	90,002	271,891
60—65	1,687,108	838,198	848,910	23,882	7,600	610,512	165,403	203,804	675,907
65—70	506,784	317,552	189,232	5,630	1,896	251,451	37,640	60,471	149,696
70 and over	1,075,762	546,264	529,498	17,724	6,207	324,405	63,702	204,135	459,499
Age Unspecified	219	9	210	5	83	4	101	..	26
CHRISTIAN	**3,876,196**	**2,010,724**	**1,865,472**	**1,132,463**	**857,526**	**806,992**	**787,336**	**71,269**	**220,610**
0—1	117,956	58,407	59,549	58,343	59,478	58	64	6	7
1—2	85,050	41,994	43,056	41,951	42,980	42	71	1	5
2—3	115,999	57,291	58,708	57,207	58,531	79	165	5	12
3—4	122,615	60,046	62,569	59,906	62,252	133	301	7	16
4—5	109,210	54,881	54,329	54,683	53,941	189	369	9	19
Total 0—5	*550,830*	*272,619*	*278,211*	*272,090*	*277,182*	*501*	*970*	*28*	*59*
5—10	527,495	264,223	263,272	262,353	259,070	1,726	3,879	144	323
10—15	460,668	241,013	219,655	233,692	194,146	6,976	24,915	345	594
15—20	353,668	177,347	176,321	146,959	73,695	29,487	100,546	901	2,080
20—25	381,351	203,568	177,783	118,272	22,895	83,065	149,159	2,211	5,729
25—30	358,231	191,933	166,298	57,915	11,034	129,720	144,832	4,298	10,432
30—35	289,344	151,832	137,512	18,613	6,147	127,987	115,776	5,232	15,589
35—40	230,268	127,664	102,604	9,173	2,831	112,933	81,369	5,558	17,404
40—45	206,605	109,091	97,514	5,047	3,206	96,498	65,687	7,551	28,621
45—50	141,166	76,850	64,316	2,901	1,927	67,192	39,405	6,757	22,984
50—55	136,397	70,653	65,744	2,086	1,594	59,450	30,118	9,117	34,032
55—60	71,431	38,262	33,169	1,074	892	31,139	13,681	6,049	18,596
60—65	84,269	42,334	41,935	1,032	922	31,825	10,225	9,477	30,788
65—70	32,478	17,676	14,802	457	343	12,881	3,410	4,338	11,049
70 and over	51,995	25,659	26,336	799	642	15,507	3,364	9,263	22,330
ANIMISTIC	**10,217,544**	**5,088,241**	**5,129,303**	**2,743,194**	**2,307,464**	**2,172,149**	**2,234,399**	**172,898**	**587,440**
0—1	358,094	177,294	180,800	176,976	180,482	305	301	13	17
1—2	222,281	107,530	114,751	107,299	114,462	215	266	16	23
2—3	347,723	167,200	180,523	166,554	179,834	617	644	29	45
3—4	416,342	198,425	217,917	197,508	216,563	889	1,147	28	207
4—5	374,272	183,942	190,330	182,694	188,620	1,206	1,403	42	307
Total 0—5	*1,718,712*	*834,391*	*884,321*	*831,031*	*879,961*	*3,239*	*3,761*	*128*	*599*
5—10	1,585,779	805,461	780,318	797,397	761,553	7,730	17,526	334	1,239
10—15	1,051,868	559,448	492,420	528,052	401,636	30,562	88,218	834	2,566
15—20	794,031	382,924	411,107	284,508	154,517	95,341	247,463	3,075	9,127
20—25	834,348	366,467	467,881	149,001	51,194	208,757	397,954	8,709	18,733
25—30	933,099	449,099	484,000	78,314	22,585	355,170	432,805	15,615	28,610
30—35	870,432	439,200	431,232	34,942	14,091	385,215	370,634	19,043	46,507
35—40	590,751	315,191	275,560	14,555	5,902	284,849	228,322	15,787	41,336
40—45	604,863	320,665	284,198	10,561	5,860	288,632	193,903	21,472	84,435
45—50	302,762	162,289	140,473	4,173	2,228	144,858	89,619	13,258	48,626
50—55	373,425	190,761	182,664	4,407	3,085	164,339	80,605	22,015	99,024
55—60	132,281	66,656	65,625	1,487	1,019	55,859	31,611	9,310	32,995
60—65	236,693	109,743	126,950	2,290	1,951	86,503	28,979	20,950	96,020
65—70	54,901	27,052	27,849	706	538	20,638	8,749	5,708	18,562
70 and over	133,599	58,894	74,705	1,770	1,394	40,464	14,250	16,660	59,061
MINOR AND UNSPECIFIED	**58,081**	**28,818**	**29,263**	**10,876**	**8,282**	**16,377**	**17,438**	**1,565**	**3,543**
0—1	1,896	984	912	961	911	2	1	1	..
1—2	1,177	556	621	540	576	16	45	..	..
2—3	1,871	936	935	900	892	36	43	..	..
3—4	1,783	851	932	710	743	136	180	5	9
4—5	1,753	840	913	528	533	302	359	10	21
Total 0—5	*8,480*	*4,167*	*4,313*	*3,659*	*3,655*	*492*	*628*	*16*	*30*
5—10	7,255	3,586	3,669	2,111	2,007	1,433	1,630	42	32
10—15	6,245	3,245	3,000	1,766	1,447	1,420	1,531	59	22
15—20	5,101	2,605	2,496	1,385	570	1,168	1,884	52	42
20—25	6,041	2,722	3,319	973	260	1,668	2,960	81	99
25—30	5,206	2,509	2,697	468	151	1,956	2,400	85	146
30—35	4,784	2,334	2,450	221	94	2,000	2,101	113	255
35—40	3,227	1,687	1,540	103	32	1,487	1,264	97	244
40—45	3,642	1,854	1,788	73	27	1,613	1,267	168	494
45—50	1,855	957	898	37	14	822	571	98	313
50—55	2,447	1,220	1,227	34	11	974	600	212	616
55—60	962	535	427	10	4	435	202	90	221
60—65	1,568	741	827	12	6	526	247	203	574
65—70	414	240	174	9	..	165	59	66	115
70 and over	854	416	438	15	4	218	94	183	343

TABLE VII.—Age, Sex and Civil Condition. Part II.—By Provinces and States.

ASSAM.

Age and Religion.	Population.			Unmarried.		Married.		Widowed.	
	Persons.	Males	Females.	Males.	Females.	Males.	Females.	Males.	Females.
1	2	3	4	5	6	7	8	9	10
ALL RELIGIONS.	**6,713,635**	**3,467,621**	**3,246,014**	**1,919,469**	**1,351,758**	**1,382,704**	**1,362,071**	**165,448**	**532,185**
0—1	234,441	116,880	117,561	116,880	117,561	..	..	..	..
1—2	122,976	60,229	62,747	60,220	62,747	..	..	..	..
2—3	225,419	109,370	116,049	109,367	116,048	3	1	..	..
3—4	237,104	114,576	122,528	114,569	122,513	7	14	..	1
4—5	230,577	114,000	116,577	113,989	116,511	11	57	..	9
Total 0—5	*1,050,517*	*515,055*	*535,463*	*515,034*	*535,380*	*21*	*72*	..	*10*
5—10	1,066,870	538,132	528,738	536,324	516,625	1,752	11,449	56	664
10—15	666,772	368,755	298,017	359,949	208,896	8,450	86,006	356	3,115
15—20	535,579	258,656	276,923	221,560	61.406	35,277	203,506	1,819	12,011
20—25	560,297	257,371	302,926	139,090	16.630	110.445	263,013	6,936	23,283
25—30	645,436	324,151	321,285	82,836	5,888	224,708	276,685	16,607	38,712
30—35	564,712	298,161	266,551	32,113	2,923	245,163	210,013	20,885	53,615
35—40	424,368	248,488	175,880	13,556	1,433	214,754	120,801	20,178	53,646
40—45	379,356	212,183	167,173	7,790	1,068	183.163	90.724	21,230	75,381
45—50	213,926	125,221	88,705	3,431	422	107,371	38,053	14,419	50.230
50—55	242,469	131,512	110,957	3,060	429	106,755	32,815	19,697	77,713
55—60	93,834	52,621	41,213	1,015	142	42,154	10,530	9,452	30,541
60—65	143,947	72,540	71,407	1,387	266	55,470	10,570	15,683	60,571
65—70	33,839	17,970	15,869	429	57	13,227	2,613	4,314	13,199
70 and over	91,713	46,805	44,908	995	193	31,994	5,221	13,816	39,494
HINDU	**3,637,400**	**1,898,460**	**1,738,940**	**1,025,538**	**679,057**	**761,824**	**729,939**	**111,098**	**329,944**
0—1	122,026	60,756	61,270	60,756	61,270	..	..	..	..
1—2	61,335	30,319	31,016	30,319	31,016	..	..	..	..
2—3	110,148	53,439	56,709	53,437	56,709	2	..	..	..
3—4	118,337	56,839	61,498	56,837	61,491	2	6	..	1
4—5	115,661	57,457	58,204	57,453	58,159	4	41	..	4
Total 0—5	*527,507*	*258,810*	*268,697*	*258,802*	*268,645*	*8*	*47*	..	*5*
5—10	547,914	276,606	271,308	275,521	263,037	1,042	7,851	43	420
10—15	348,077	192,117	155,960	186,791	104,177	5.057	49,875	269	1,908
15—20	281,179	140,184	140,995	120,783	30.575	18,325	103,439	1,076	6,981
20—25	310,760	147,399	163,361	84,900	7,278	58,461	141.416	4,038	14,672
25—30	366,536	186,900	179,636	52,846	2,368	123,692	151,564	10,362	25,704
30—35	325,086	172,654	152,432	23,107	1,188	135,660	116,070	13,887	35,174
35—40	249,246	147,010	102,236	9,575	649	123,538	66,060	13,897	35,527
40—45	215,797	122,642	93,155	5,649	477	102,418	46,257	14,575	46,421
45—50	124,594	73,690	50,904	2.562	182	60,971	19,179	10,157	31,543
50—55	140,115	76,285	63,830	2,310	200	60,047	16,203	13,928	47,427
55—60	57,332	32,039	25,293	793	67	24,367	5.119	6,879	20,107
60—65	79,423	39,609	39,814	1,039	114	27,845	4,257	10,725	35,443
65—70	18,539	9,706	8,833	270	31	6,552	935	2,884	7,867
70 and over	45,295	22,809	22,486	590	74	13,841	1,667	8,378	20,745
MUSALMAN	**1,886.528**	**977,463**	**909,065**	**567,671**	**389,550**	**383,147**	**389,071**	**26,645**	**130,444**
0—1	70,702	35,527	35,175	35,527	35,175	..	..	..	..
1—2	33,025	16,033	16,992	16,033	16,992	..	..	..	..
2—3	69,378	33,509	35,869	33,508	35,868	1	1	..	..
3—4	72,507	35,044	37,463	35,039	37,460	5	3	..	..
4—5	71,774	35,440	36,334	35,437	36,327	3	6	..	1
Total 0—5	*317,386*	*155,553*	*161,833*	*155,544*	*161,822*	*9*	*10*	..	*1*
5—10	339,821	170,949	168,872	170,485	165,624	455	3,048	9	200
10—15	199,076	114,561	84,515	112,447	52,749	2,072	30,776	42	990
15—20	159,304	75,206	84,098	65,020	5,960	9,859	74.058	327	3,180
20—25	155,508	69,021	86,487	36,034	1,439	31,641	80,292	1,346	4,756
25—30	174,379	87,733	86,646	19,603	700	64,943	78,250	3,187	7,696
30—35	144,541	77,941	66,600	4.711	464	69,698	54,056	3,532	12,080
35—40	102,874	62,566	40,308	1,614	234	57,880	27,867	3,072	12,207
40—45	92,821	52,010	40,811	951	224	47,932	20.831	3,127	19,756
45—50	50,068	30,310	19,758	398	83	27,955	7,451	1,957	12.224
50—55	59,845	32,169	27,676	338	82	29,075	6,933	2,756	20,661
55—60	18,888	11,302	7,586	98	31	10,090	1,402	1,114	6,153
60—65	39,052	19,934	19,118	173	76	17,154	2,162	2,607	16,860
65—70	7,569	4,334	3,235	111	7	3.594	318	629	2,910
70 and over	25,396	13,874	11,522	144	55	10,790	697	2,940	10,770
ANIMISTIC	**1,109,187**	**549,200**	**559,987**	**302,245**	**264,798**	**220,948**	**227,795**	**26,807**	**67,394**
0—1	39,105	19,316	19,789	19,316	19,789	..	..	..	..
1—2	26,887	12,989	13,898	12,989	13,898	..	..	..	..
2—3	43,342	21,150	22,192	21,150	22,192	..	..	..	..
3—4	43,631	21,388	22,243	21,388	22,238	..	5	..	..
4—5	40,603	19,860	20,743	19,856	20,729	4	10	..	4
Total 0—5	*193,368*	*94,703*	*98,865*	*94,699*	*98,846*	*4*	*15*	..	*4*
5—10	167,916	84,871	83,045	84,641	82,475	226	529	4	41
10—15	110,922	57,391	53,531	56,095	48.141	1,254	5,185	42	205
15—20	87,615	39,536	48,079	32.452	22,944	6,696	23,402	388	1,733
20—25	86,443	37,110	49,333	17,013	7,366	18,662	38.329	1,435	3,638
25—30	96,100	45,057	51,043	9,180	2,585	33,043	43,489	2,834	4,969
30—35	88,502	43,888	44,614	3,748	1,158	36,909	37,459	3,231	5,997
35—40	66,915	35,748	31.167	2,076	496	30,686	25,196	2,986	5,475
40—45	66,460	35,112	31.348	1,030	324	30,752	22,376	3,330	8,648
45—50	36,676	19,743	16,933	395	144	17,177	10.780	2,171	6,0[illegible]
50—55	40,107	21,693	18,414	350	138	18,510	9.204	2,833	9,072
55—60	16,490	8,651	7,839	107	37	7,173	3,808	1,371	3,994
60—65	24,164	12,315	11,849	160	72	9.922	3.966	2,238	7,811
65—70	7,290	3,718	3,572	43	13	2,906	1,303	769	2,256
70 and over	20,019	9,664	10,355	256	59	7,028	2,754	2,380	7,542

TABLE VII.—Age, Sex and Civil Condition.

BENGAL.

Age and Religion.	Population.			Unmarried.		Married.		Widowed.	
	Persons.	Males.	Females.	Males.	Females.	Males.	Females.	Males.	Females.
1	2	3	4	5	6	7	8	9	10
ALL RELIGIONS	**45,483,077**	**23,365,225**	**22,117,852**	**11,943,838**	**7,425,421**	**10,608,998**	**10,255,111**	**812,389**	**4,437,320**
0—1	1,429,476	708,602	720,874	708,538	720,740	60	126	4	8
1—2	693,595	334,157	359,438	334,054	359,005	101	412	2	21
2—3	1,450,685	696,511	754,174	695,880	752,023	619	2,028	12	123
3—4	1,512,638	721,006	791,632	719,704	786,821	1,274	4,465	28	346
4—5	1,374,216	679,581	694,635	676,891	684,974	2,606	8,331	84	1,330
Total 0—5	*6,460,610*	*3,139,857*	*3,390,753*	*3,135,067*	*3,303,563*	*4,660*	*15,363*	*130*	*1,898*
5—10	7,060,569	3,586,877	3,473,692	3,544,385	3,116,188	41,100	341,749	1,392	15,755
10—15	4,943,345	2,771,240	2,172,105	2,608,517	817,184	163,322	1,302,687	4,401	52,234
15—20	4,266,348	2,028,187	2,238,161	1,458,982	94,584	556,772	2,007,066	12,433	136,511
20—25	3,931,491	1,835,229	2,096,262	659,156	35,872	1,146,206	1,856,847	29,867	203,543
25—30	4,253,343	2,180,746	2,072,597	310,545	22,457	1,809,748	1,730,018	60,453	320,122
30—35	3,434,764	1,846,305	1,588,459	96,621	12,857	1,679,671	1,173,201	70,018	402,401
35—40	2,698,722	1,557,682	1,141,040	45,457	6,917	1,438,189	708,328	74,036	425,795
40—45	2,465,514	1,331,787	1,133,727	33,516	6,022	1,206,656	536,512	91,615	591,193
45—50	1,531,098	862,590	668,508	16,879	2,411	768,208	235,473	77,503	430,624
50—55	1,632,192	827,744	804,448	15,319	2,601	711,520	189,169	100,905	612,678
55—60	735,022	391,576	343,446	6,624	1,005	324,881	59,429	60,071	283,012
60—65	1,060,967	506,611	554,356	8,919	1,731	401,368	60,272	96,324	492,353
65—70	314,518	157,661	156,857	2,706	541	119,372	15,984	35,583	140,332
70 and over	694,574	341,133	353,441	6,145	1,488	237,325	23,014	97,663	328,939
HINDU	**20,377,793**	**10,545,714**	**9,832,079**	**5,129,507**	**2,857,760**	**4,909,314**	**4,443,512**	**506,893**	**2,530,807**
0—1	620,956	306,603	314,353	306,570	314,266	32	82	1	5
1—2	269,983	129,317	140,666	129,264	140,471	52	179	1	16
2—3	563,745	271,902	291,843	271,644	290,984	252	783	6	76
3—4	584,983	278,554	306,429	277,958	304,241	579	1,980	17	208
4—5	528,428	262,606	265,822	261,346	261,213	1,210	3,968	50	641
Total 0—5	*2,568,095*	*1,248,982*	*1,319,113*	*1,246,782*	*1,311,175*	*2,125*	*6,992*	*75*	*946*
5—10	2,806,101	1,426,027	1,380,074	1,409,779	1,205,575	15,590	166,061	658	8,438
10—15	2,102,162	1,183,311	918,851	1,108,907	268,290	72,317	619,191	2,087	31,370
15—20	1,956,439	954,764	1,001,675	686,740	32,455	261,839	876,053	6,186	93,167
20—25	1,841,542	905,714	935,828	341,172	14,323	549,555	780,784	14,987	140,721
25—30	1,965,411	1,033,871	931,540	174,158	9,213	827,856	713,009	31,857	209,318
30—35	1,605,638	877,139	728,499	64,356	5,580	772,852	481,762	39,931	241,157
35—40	1,291,379	737,219	554,160	32,374	3,055	659,819	304,370	45,026	246,735
40—45	1,207,523	654,732	552,791	23,883	2,913	671,135	230,757	59,714	319,121
45—50	775,902	427,631	348,271	12,579	1,351	362,321	108,110	52,731	238,810
50—55	800,507	400,105	400,402	10,944	1,369	322,012	81,410	67,149	317,623
55—60	403,153	206,827	196,326	5,322	566	159,123	30,079	42,382	165,681
60—65	525,336	243,504	281,832	6,250	833	175,350	26,882	61,904	254,117
65—70	176,355	83,732	92,623	2,092	304	57,432	7,991	24,208	84,328
70 and over	352,250	162,156	190,094	4,169	758	99,989	10,061	57,998	179,275
MUSALMAN	**23,989,719**	**12,245,542**	**11,744,177**	**6,502,631**	**4,321,806**	**5,454,867**	**5,578,144**	**288,044**	**1,844,227**
0—1	776,057	385,701	390,356	385,676	390,317	22	36	3	3
1—2	403,394	194,970	208,424	194,922	208,205	47	214	1	5
2—3	849,730	406,487	443,243	406,263	441,983	218	1,215	6	45
3—4	885,955	422,450	463,505	421,902	460,927	537	2,442	11	136
4—5	809,275	399,000	410,275	397,642	405,322	1,324	4,274	34	679
Total 0—5	*3,724,411*	*1,808,608*	*1,915,803*	*1,806,405*	*1,906,754*	*2,148*	*8,181*	*55*	*868*
5—10	4,075,289	2,070,369	2,004,920	2,044,815	1,823,572	24,855	174,160	699	7,188
10—15	2,716,623	1,521,470	1,195,153	1,430,596	502,003	88,629	672,675	2,245	20,475
15—20	2,211,844	1,027,156	1,184,688	735,436	45,904	285,732	1,097,202	5,988	41,582
20 25	1,997,316	886,807	1,110,509	298,213	16,770	574,484	1,033,749	14,110	59,990
25—30	2,185,014	1,095,043	1,089,971	125,867	11,092	942,076	972,049	27,100	106,830
30—35	1,740,967	922,538	818,429	28,311	6,162	865,909	656,339	28,318	155,928
35—40	1,341,959	782,247	559,712	11,104	3,252	743,805	382,198	27,338	174,262
40—45	1,197,194	642,355	554,839	8,455	2,595	604,033	287,432	29,867	264,812
45—50	720,943	414,703	306,240	3,746	805	387,549	118,851	23,408	186,584
50—55	793,780	406,590	387,190	3,889	1,001	370,926	99,836	31,775	286,353
55—60	315,958	175,848	140,110	1,107	332	158,113	26,387	16,628	113,391
60—65	511,204	250,538	260,666	2,408	765	215,772	30,432	32,358	229,460
65—70	131,689	70,569	61,120	525	190	59,340	7,172	10,704	53,758
70 and over	325,528	170,701	154,827	1,754	609	131,496	11,481	37,451	142,737
ANIMISTIC	**730,182**	**371,248**	**358,934**	**195,956**	**161,452**	**164,166**	**157,482**	**11,126**	**40,000**
0—1	22,222	11,093	11,129	11,093	11,125	..	4	..	..
1—2	13,483	6,455	7,028	6,453	7,019	2	9	..	..
2—3	25,851	12,447	13,404	12,303	13,378	144	24	..	2
3—4	29,718	14,036	15,682	13,885	15,644	151	36	..	2
4—5	25,704	12,470	13,234	12,415	13,153	55	71	..	10
Total 0—5	*116,978*	*56,501*	*60,477*	*56,149*	*60,319*	*352*	*144*	..	*14*
5—10	124,773	62,759	62,019	62,193	60,587	536	1,319	30	113
10—15	[illegible]9,305	42,402	36,903	40,518	28,119	1,831	8,458	58	326
15—20	61,226	27,782	33,444	20,433	8,381	7,142	23,777	207	1,286
20—25	56,487	24,069	32,418	8,925	2,071	14,617	28,395	527	1,952
25—30	66,520	32,226	34,294	4,636	937	26,564	30,565	1,026	2,792
30—35	56,935	29,400	27,535	1,520	423	26,726	23,560	1,154	3,552
35—40	42,955	25,274	17,681	616	185	23,543	14,354	1,115	3,142
40—45	39,997	23,312	16,685	417	174	21,580	11,886	1,815	4,625
45—50	21,000	[illegible]2,743	8,257	132	53	11,759	6,011	852	3,193
50—55	23,743	13,552	10,191	179	74	12,162	4,881	1,211	5,236
55—60	9 445	5 368	4,077	53	30	4,695	1,770	620	2,277
60—65	15,974	8,395	7,579	93	43	6,980	1,842	1,322	5,694
65—70	3,838	1,970	1,868	24	6	1,594	505	352	1,357
70 and over	11,001	5,495	5,506	78	50	4,085	1,015	1,337	4,441

Part II.—By Provinces and States—*continued.*

BIHAR AND ORISSA.

Age and Religion.	Population.			Unmarried.		Married.		Widowed.	
	Persons.	Males.	Females.	Males.	Females.	Males.	Females.	Males.	Females.
1	2	3	4	5	6	7	8	9	10
ALL RELIGIONS	**34,490,084**	**16,859,929**	**17,630,155**	**7,385,507**	**5,386,311**	**8,603,957**	**9,028,628**	**930,465**	**3,215,216**
0—1	1,138,199	562,762	575,437	561,415	573,207	1,251	1,774	96	456
1—2	425,267	207,010	218,257	205,663	215,631	1,250	2,410	97	216
2—3	917,706	438,271	479,435	433,222	469,572	4,810	9,315	239	548
3—4	1,119,945	524,886	595,059	512,459	567,658	11,835	25,954	592	1,447
4—5	1,024,592	501,400	523,192	476,814	474,554	23,485	45,387	1,101	3,251
Total 0—5	*4,625,709*	*2,234,329*	*2,391,380*	*2,189,573*	*2,300,622*	*42,631*	*84,840*	*2,125*	*5,918*
5—10	5,295,755	2,678,342	2,617,413	2,339,779	2,031,561	324,415	555,145	14,148	30,707
10—15	3,851,142	2,087,732	1,763,410	1,467,614	777,348	592,302	939,047	27,816	47,015
15—20	2,670,320	1,356,690	1,313,630	646,381	146,999	676,986	1,108,348	33,323	58,283
20—25	2,715,964	1,224,404	1,491,560	303,094	40,907	873,770	1,352,732	47,540	97,921
25—30	3,097,921	1,468,410	1,629,511	167,758	28,597	1,226,577	1,432,461	74,075	168,453
30—35	2,871,988	1,382,909	1,489,079	80,543	18,999	1,217,489	1,198,687	84,877	271,393
35—40	2,186,262	1,093,806	1,092,456	41,215	10,276	972,082	801,089	80,509	281,091
40—45	1,996,900	961,796	1,035,104	29,713	9,886	838,097	611,616	93,986	413,602
45—50	1,299,588	646,050	653,538	15,711	4,595	549,108	348,696	81,231	300,247
50—55	1,365,275	645,131	720,144	16,550	5,714	523,478	265,671	105,103	448,759
55—60	645,994	305,727	340,267	7,862	2,427	238,716	136,394	59,149	201,446
60—65	991,725	411,332	580,393	9,601	4,037	297,068	105,317	104,663	471,039
65—70	296,078	126,962	169,116	2,984	1,193	87,683	37,793	36,295	130,130
70 and over	579,463	236,309	343,154	7,129	3,150	143,555	50,792	85,025	289,212
HINDU	**28,360,589**	**13,886,520**	**14,474,069**	**5,804,985**	**4,158,561**	**7,267,497**	**7,586,827**	**814,038**	**2,728,681**
0—1	923,763	457,122	466,641	455,947	464,690	1,086	1,563	89	388
1—2	333,325	161,852	171,473	160,656	169,073	1,108	2,201	88	199
2—3	739,844	353,641	386,203	349,062	377,328	4,361	8,399	218	476
3—4	896,484	420,781	475,703	409,322	450,248	10,907	24,196	552	1,259
4—5	819,369	401,475	417,894	378,945	372,690	21,506	42,340	1,024	2,864
Total 0—5	*3,712,785*	*1,794,871*	*1,917,914*	*1,753,932*	*1,834,029*	*38,968*	*78,699*	*1,971*	*5,186*
5—10	4,272,397	2,161,291	2,111,106	1,845,452	1,575,041	302,384	507,724	13,455	28,341
10—15	3,132,069	1,699,866	1,432,203	1,140,910	572,443	532,895	817,289	26,061	42,471
15—20	2,186,805	1,116,315	1,070,490	502,175	92,114	584,036	928,016	30,104	50,360
20—25	2,256,675	1,025,335	1,231,340	243,412	23,422	740,067	1,124,344	41,856	83,574
25—30	2,567,567	1,224,289	1,343,278	136,007	18,512	1,023,976	1,181,988	64,306	142,778
30—35	2,400,660	1,160,783	1,239,877	68,047	13,436	1,018,997	995,910	73,739	230,531
35—40	1,826,795	916,286	910,509	36,191	7,017	809,561	664,526	70,534	238,966
40—45	1,670,579	804,192	866,387	25,577	7,071	696,316	508,858	82,299	350,458
45—50	1,092,001	543,670	548,331	14,042	3,337	457,959	289,713	71,669	255,281
50—55	1,141,997	540,009	601,988	14,676	4,023	433,391	219,171	91,942	378,794
55—60	542,953	257,388	285,565	7,027	1,749	198,371	112,418	51,930	171,398
60—65	828,073	341,948	486,125	8,550	2,974	243,119	85,989	90,279	397,162
65—70	250,100	106,687	143,413	2,701	918	72,171	30,755	31,815	111,740
70 and over	479,133	193,590	285,543	6,226	2,475	115,286	41,427	72,078	241,641
MUSALMAN	**3,666,861**	**1,766,496**	**1,900,365**	**837,591**	**622,660**	**849,286**	**934,333**	**79,619**	**343,372**
0—1	122,624	60,402	62,222	60,293	61,991	103	165	6	66
1—2	45,975	22,711	23,264	22,607	23,090	100	160	4	14
2—3	105,230	49,943	55,287	49,554	54,423	372	813	17	51
3—4	124,941	57,677	67,264	56,869	65,638	771	1,495	37	131
4—5	118,307	57,480	60,827	55,882	57,907	1,531	2,692	67	228
Total 0—5	*517,077*	*248,213*	*268,864*	*245,205*	*263,049*	*2,877*	*5,325*	*131*	*490*
5—10	599,152	303,859	295,293	283,404	249,957	19,843	43,423	612	1,913
10—15	404,231	221,809	182,422	171,905	85,340	48,395	93,527	1,509	3,555
15—20	267,399	135,057	132,342	72,826	11,949	59,937	115,467	2,294	4,926
20—25	273,853	116,334	157,519	31,655	3,646	80,950	144,711	3,729	9,162
25—30	324,038	145,176	178,862	16,885	2,546	121,850	158,543	6,441	17,773
30—35	301,053	137,783	163,270	6,867	1,985	123,242	132,293	7,674	28,992
35—40	226,204	111,406	114,798	2,613	1,096	102,037	82,854	6,756	30,848
40—45	207,703	98,008	109,695	2,383	1,002	87,734	63,968	7,891	44,725
45—50	134,917	67,009	67,908	830	395	59,459	33,978	6,720	33,535
50—55	141,457	65,085	76,372	1,138	640	55,247	27,179	8,700	48,553
55—60	63,493	30,121	33,372	437	214	24,928	12,551	4,756	20,607
60—65	107,662	44,415	63,247	653	427	34,076	11,484	9,686	51,336
65—70	30,524	13,369	17,155	158	91	10,002	3,618	3,214	13,446
70 and over	68,098	28,852	39,246	637	323	18,709	5,412	9,506	33,511
ANIMISTIC	**2,220,526**	**1,086,231**	**1,134,295**	**613,284**	**544,690**	**439,687**	**459,353**	**33,260**	**130,252**
0—1	82,858	40,739	42,119	40,682	42,071	56	46	1	2
1—2	40,131	19,560	20,571	19,520	20,523	36	45	4	3
2—3	65,221	31,138	34,083	31,070	33,971	64	94	4	18
3—4	88,887	41,748	47,139	41,612	46,837	133	247	3	55
4—5	78,509	38,307	40,202	37,868	39,711	481	887	8	154
Total 0—5	*355,606*	*171,492*	*184,114*	*170,752*	*183,113*	*770*	*769*	*20*	*232*
5—10	384,677	193,668	191,009	191,544	186,769	2,051	3,816	73	424
10—15	282,131	148,548	133,583	137,880	106,127	10,446	26,509	222	947
15—20	196,309	95,354	100,955	63,955	38,851	30,549	59,283	850	2,821
20—25	166,659	74,040	92,619	24,944	12,644	47,287	75,177	1,809	4,798
25—30	187,155	89,347	97,808	13,266	7,087	73,038	83,513	3,043	7,258
30—35	153,050	75,741	77,309	5,042	3,276	67,558	63,214	3,141	10,819
35—40	119,582	59,031	60,551	2,085	1,992	54,059	48,256	2,887	10,303
40—45	107,038	53,678	53,360	1,540	1,677	48,734	34,945	3,404	16,738
45—50	65,106	31,639	33,467	704	787	28,395	22,336	2,540	10,344
50—55	73,728	35,894	37,834	636	977	31,224	17,420	4,034	19,437
55—60	35,384	16,342	19,042	278	368	13,836	10,236	2,228	8,438
60—65	50,611	22,540	28,071	342	585	17,992	7,127	4,206	20,359
65—70	13,942	6,253	7,689	104	168	5,015	3,061	1,134	4,440
70 and over	29,548	12,664	16,884	212	319	8,783	3,671	3,669	12,894

TABLE VII.—Age, Sex and Civil Condition.

BOMBAY.

Age and Religion.	Population.			Unmarried.		Married.		Widowed.	
	Persons.	Males.	Females.	Males.	Females.	Males.	Females.	Males.	Females.
1	2	3	4	5	6	7	8	9	10
ALL RELIGIONS	**19,672,642**	**10,245,847**	**9,426,795**	**4,833,435**	**2,955,603**	**4,847,531**	**4,802,977**	**564,881**	**1,668,215**
0—1	667,697	333,992	333,705	331,757	330,708	2,173	2,900	62	97
1—2	344,592	168,819	175,773	166,953	172,126	1,767	3,544	99	103
2—3	589,364	288,494	300,870	284,261	292,528	4,032	8,114	201	228
3—4	592,749	288,856	303,893	284,187	293,216	4,461	10,373	208	304
4—5	576,586	289,122	287,464	283,097	271,882	5,729	15,003	296	579
Total 0—5	*2,770,988*	*1,369,283*	*1,401,705*	*1,350,255*	*1,360,460*	*18,162*	*39,934*	*866*	*1,311*
5—10	2,494,579	1,288,925	1,205,654	1,241,386	1,008,257	45,417	191,979	2,122	5,418
10—15	2,026,567	1,132,045	894,522	971,587	893,172	154,403	484,678	6,055	16,672
15—20	1,610,697	856,239	754,458	546,763	83,996	299,084	642,238	10,392	28,224
20—25	1,816,520	904,559	911,961	332,328	35,414	549,933	820,118	22,298	56,429
25—30	1,887,830	998,580	889,250	182,304	20,622	778,674	779,839	37,602	88,789
30—35	1,714,260	893,020	821,249	86,891	16,732	757,197	665,886	48,932	138,631
35—40	1,240,569	685,591	554,978	40,841	9,629	595,657	404,329	49,093	141,020
40—45	1,264,897	655,252	609,645	31,546	10,037	554,953	356,877	68,753	242,731
45—50	748,807	409,203	339,604	15,397	4,407	339,253	168,514	54,553	166,683
50—55	844,615	431,661	412,954	14,627	5,285	336,602	138,014	80,432	269,655
55—60	337,609	184,044	153,565	5,527	1,996	137,754	44,367	40,763	107,202
60—65	522,493	248,036	274,457	7,654	3,157	169,305	43,557	71,077	227,743
65—70	142,762	71,937	70,825	2,012	795	46,255	9,628	23,670	60,402
70 and over	249,440	117,472	131,968	4,317	1,644	64,882	13,019	48,273	117,305
HINDU	**14,922,311**	**7,660,148**	**7,262,163**	**3,448,194**	**2,125,696**	**3,788,816**	**3,788,288**	**423,138**	**1,348,179**
0—1	498,883	248,133	250,750	246,190	248,052	1,891	2,617	52	81
1—2	283,845	138,719	145,126	137,025	141,785	1,615	3,255	79	86
2—3	454,519	221,228	233,291	217,418	225,581	3,659	7,504	151	206
3—4	443,799	213,554	230,245	209,445	220,455	3,957	9,519	152	271
4—5	429,353	213,705	215,648	208,386	201,399	5,113	13,778	206	471
Total 0—5	*2,110,399*	*1,035,339*	*1,075,060*	*1,018,464*	*1,037,272*	*16,235*	*36,673*	*640*	*1,115*
5—10	1,860,597	948,490	912,107	906,275	729,479	40,431	177,755	1,784	4,873
10—15	1,553,735	855,367	698,368	712,860	248,646	137,183	434,479	5,324	15,243
15—20	1,239,911	648,987	590,924	383,996	39,910	256,250	526,454	8,741	24,560
20—25	1,368,302	668,815	699,487	205,980	19,563	445,802	633,364	17,033	46,560
25—30	1,425,497	746,259	679,238	102,562	12,849	616,350	593,513	27,347	72,876
30—35	1,275,845	653,619	622,226	44,405	11,270	574,982	498,386	34,172	112,570
35—40	948,754	515,747	433,007	22,907	6,677	457,230	310,154	35,610	116,176
40—45	950,954	483,865	467,089	18,714	7,244	415,508	265,337	49,643	194,508
45—50	581,207	312,844	268,363	9,695	3,300	261,333	128,959	41,816	136,104
50—55	642,601	320,559	322,042	9,433	3,892	250,580	102,465	60,546	215,685
55—60	269,704	145,346	124,358	3,892	1,535	108,804	33,884	32,650	88,939
60—65	398,164	183,630	214,534	4,765	2,388	124,759	31,271	54,106	180,875
65—70	115,171	57,309	57,862	1,434	538	36,885	7,172	18,990	50,152
70 and over	181,470	83,972	97,498	2,752	1,133	46,484	8,422	34,736	87,943
MUSALMAN	**4,024,485**	**2,190,195**	**1,834,290**	**1,180,268**	**702,749**	**887,455**	**862,798**	**122,472**	**268,743**
0—1	146,014	74,423	71,591	74,211	71,399	211	189	1	3
1—2	48,200	23,985	24,215	23,891	24,001	91	205	3	9
2—3	115,770	57,866	57,904	57,596	57,487	260	402	10	15
3—4	129,333	65,912	63,421	65,543	62,865	355	530	14	26
4—5	128,486	65,999	62,487	65,509	61,575	457	821	33	91
Total 0—5	*567,803*	*288,185*	*279,618*	*286,750*	*277,327*	*1,374*	*2,147*	*61*	*144*
5—10	551,137	298,230	252,907	294,070	241,683	3,968	10,815	192	409
10—15	400,718	236,574	164,144	222,106	122,027	13,986	41,019	482	1,098
15—20	304,913	171,424	133,489	135,634	33,880	34,536	96,628	1,254	2,981
20—25	366,697	189,285	177,412	99,830	10,694	85,048	158,621	4,407	8,097
25—30	386,762	208,977	177,785	65,116	5,134	134,847	159,816	9,014	12,835
30—35	374,887	204,003	170,884	36,106	4,042	154,690	145,093	13,147	21,749
35—40	243,579	141,350	102,229	14,790	2,159	114,748	79,598	11,812	20,472
40—45	269,227	146,844	122,383	11,005	2,145	118,954	79,446	16,885	40,792
45—50	139,767	80,246	59,521	4,627	801	64,735	33,239	10,884	25,481
50—55	173,869	95,961	77,908	4,435	1,139	74,192	30,715	17,334	46,054
55—60	55,047	31,408	23,639	1,308	368	23,586	8,688	6,514	14,583
60—65	107,824	56,206	51,618	2,573	684	38,900	10,808	14,733	40,131
65—70	22,079	11,642	10,437	440	215	7,501	2,001	3,701	8,221
70 and over	60,176	29,860	30,316	1,418	451	16,390	4,169	12,052	25,696
JAIN	**212,309**	**117,519**	**94,790**	**54,815**	**26,648**	**53,087**	**44,952**	**9,617**	**23,190**
0—1	5,556	2,768	2,788	2,746	2,742	19	36	3	10
1—2	3,330	1,611	1,719	1,577	1,683	17	34	17	2
2—3	5,191	2,517	2,674	2,454	2,593	28	77	35	4
3—4	4,817	2,314	2,503	2,232	2,398	43	102	39	3
4—5	4,602	2,408	2,194	2,325	2,041	37	144	46	9
Total 0—5	*23,496*	*11,618*	*11,878*	*11,334*	*11,457*	*144*	*393*	*140*	*28*
5—10	22,410	11,376	11,034	11,075	9,492	221	1,482	80	60
10—15	23,089	13,636	9,453	12,345	4,720	1,162	4,518	129	215
15—20	20,107	11,901	8,206	8,165	412	3,535	7,346	201	448
20—25	22,725	13,107	9,618	5,308	180	7,348	8,362	456	1,076
25—30	20,947	12,342	8,605	2,748	110	8,932	6,889	662	1,606
30—35	18,278	10,149	8,129	1,357	85	7,959	5,754	833	2,290
35—40	13,982	8,344	5,638	744	43	6,749	3,457	851	2,138
40—45	14,194	7,456	6,738	625	53	5,673	3,208	1,158	3,477
45—50	8,544	5,033	3,511	352	23	3,729	1,463	952	2,025
50—35	9,596	5,011	4,585	354	31	3,377	1,322	1,280	3,352
55—60	4,430	2,550	1,880	148	10	1,565	354	837	1,516
60—65	5,877	2,778	3,099	144	13	1,610	331	1,024	2,755
65—70	1,687	1,002	885	60	6	515	90	427	789
70 and over	2,747	1,216	1,531	61	13	568	83	587	1,435

Part II.—By Provinces and States—*continued.*

BURMA.

Age and Religion.	Population.			Unmarried.		Married.		Widowed.	
	Persons.	Males.	Females.	Males.	Females.	Males.	Females.	Males.	Females.
1	2	3	4	5	6	7	8	9	10
ALL RELIGIONS	**12,039,083**	**6,145,471**	**5,893,612**	**3,495,418**	**3,056,086**	**2,393,102**	**2,218,321**	**256,951**	**619,205**
0—1	276,258	134,170	142,068	134,170	142,068	..	..	..	..
1—2	272,896	133,736	139,160	133,736	139,160	..	..	..	..
2—3	333,112	163,221	169,891	163,216	169,887	5	4	..	..
3—4	376,269	185,763	190,506	185,758	190,499	5	7	..	..
4—5	337,042	165,191	171,851	165,176	171,841	14	9	1	1
Total 0—5	*1,595,577*	*782,081*	*813,496*	*782,056*	*813,475*	*24*	*20*	*1*	*1*
5—10	1,573,950	784,144	789,806	784,071	789,621	72	183	1	2
10—15	1,377,509	714,400	663,109	713,429	658,678	951	4,285	20	146
15—20	1,118,007	548,748	569,259	504,069	413,064	43,008	147,578	1,671	8,617
20—25	1,047,189	526,720	520,469	292,186	151,289	223,588	344,270	10,946	24,910
25—30	1,006,278	528,466	476,812	160,724	67,149	350,184	379,470	17,558	30,193
30—35	959,031	519,988	439,043	91,009	40,979	405,596	358,938	23,383	39,126
35—40	756,862	416,295	340,567	49,953	24,319	344,213	273,718	22,129	42,530
40—45	692,906	365,155	327,751	36,448	22,734	302,370	245,609	26,337	59,408
45—50	460,548	246,019	214,529	20,151	14,022	203,921	151,047	20,947	49,460
50—55	453,584	227,471	226,113	19,262	16,303	182,359	131,000	25,850	78,810
55—60	272,842	136,952	135,890	10,921	10,078	107,347	73,448	18,684	52,364
60—65	321,844	161,527	160,317	12,616	13,616	118,133	59,902	30,778	86,799
65—70	147,671	75,936	71,735	6,956	6,490	50,949	24,148	18,031	41,097
70 and over	257,285	112,569	144,716	11,567	14,269	60,387	24,705	40,615	105,742
BUDDHIST	**10,384,544**	**5,113,437**	**5,271,107**	**2,941,543**	**2,747,153**	**1,954,195**	**1,968,438**	**217,699**	**555,516**
0—1	247,995	119,972	128,023	119,972	128,023	..	..	..	..
1—2	243,043	119,054	123,989	119,054	123,989	..	..	..	..
2—3	292,955	143,253	149,702	143,253	149,702	..	..	..	..
3—4	332,616	164,109	168,507	164,109	168,507	..	..	..	..
4—5	299,006	146,150	152,856	146,150	152,856	..	..	..	..
Total 0—5	*1,415,615*	*692,538*	*723,077*	*692,538*	*723,077*	..	..	..	..
5—10	1,401,609	693,184	708,425	693,184	708,415	..	10	..	..
10—15	1,232,952	632,177	600,775	631,848	597,978	317	2,676	12	121
15—20	969,399	459,826	509,573	426,365	375,832	32,135	125,778	1,326	7,963
20—25	851,894	396,442	455,452	212,342	134,723	175,448	298,256	8,662	22,473
25—30	806,072	388,774	417,298	104,343	50,487	270,754	330,825	13,677	26,986
30—35	775,207	392,117	383,090	56,390	34,974	317,719	314,329	18,008	33,787
35—40	642,997	335,152	307,845	33,947	22,343	283,269	247,391	17,936	38,111
40—45	580,508	289,304	291,204	24,267	20,525	244,102	220,188	20,935	50,491
45—50	406,044	208,786	197,258	15,290	13,092	175,634	139,783	17,862	44,383
50—55	392,906	190,614	202,292	14,555	14,856	154,403	118,699	21,656	68,737
55—60	250,457	123,095	127,362	9,489	9,524	96,871	69,291	16,735	48,547
60—65	288,976	142,413	146,563	10,501	12,668	104,475	55,580	27,437	78,306
65—70	135,376	67,737	67,639	6,223	6,143	45,237	22,896	16,277	38,600
70 and over	234,532	101,278	133,254	10,261	13,516	53,831	22,727	37,186	97,011
MUSALMAN	**420,769**	**271,421**	**149,348**	**143,348**	**76,239**	**117,760**	**59,264**	**10,313**	**13,845**
0—1	7,002	4,002	3,900	4,002	3,900	..	..	..	..
1—2	8,577	4,189	4,388	4,189	4,388	..	..	..	..
2—3	10,978	5,499	5,479	5,495	5,477	4	2	..	..
3—4	11,593	5,797	5,796	5,796	5,796	1	..	..	..
4—5	10,573	5,343	5,220	5,337	5,225	5	3	1	1
Total 0—5	*49,624*	*24,830*	*24,794*	*24,819*	*24,788*	*10*	*5*	*1*	*1*
5—10	47,711	24,617	23,094	24,600	23,078	16	15	1	1
10—15	39,015	22,877	16,138	22,750	15,672	127	463	..	3
15—20	40,503	25,228	15,275	21,638	6,311	3,487	8,698	103	266
20—25	51,268	35,824	15,444	20,261	2,328	14,822	12,382	741	734
25—30	50,584	37,290	13,294	12,560	1,455	23,524	10,986	1,206	853
30—35	42,632	31,398	11,234	7,073	741	22,877	9,397	1,448	1,096
35—40	26,951	20,365	6,586	3,294	377	15,900	5,272	1,171	937
40—45	24,296	17,246	7,050	2,563	309	13,402	5,053	1,281	1,598
45—50	13,049	9,435	3,614	1,367	227	7,255	2,369	813	1,018
50—55	13,719	8,862	4,857	1,034	308	6,884	2,386	944	2,163
55—60	5,790	3,739	2,060	337	149	2,831	909	571	1,002
60—65	7,718	4,913	2,805	557	217	3,547	754	809	1,834
65—70	2,748	1,858	890	204	50	1,280	240	374	600
70 and over	5,152	2,930	2,213	291	139	1,798	335	850	1,739
ANIMISTIC	**625,539**	**330,270**	**295,269**	**187,657**	**146,513**	**128,963**	**113,004**	**13,650**	**35,752**
0—1	10,956	5,544	5,413	5,544	5,412	..	..	..	..
1—2	12,674	6,172	6,502	6,172	6,502	..	..	..	..
2—3	17,572	8,656	8,916	8,656	8,916	..	..	..	..
3—4	19,654	9,620	10,034	9,620	10,034	..	..	..	..
4—5	16,727	8,203	8,524	8,203	8,524	..	..	..	..
Total 0—5	*77,583*	*38,195*	*39,388*	*38,195*	*39,388*	..	..	..	..
5—10	78,418	42,444	35,974	42,444	35,974	..	..	..	..
10—15	62,219	33,386	28,833	33,353	28,570	31	248	2	15
15—20	55,210	27,748	27,462	25,557	20,763	2,064	6,443	127	256
20—25	59,265	29,598	29,667	19,061	9,798	9,899	18,698	638	1,171
25—30	55,918	29,917	26,001	12,149	3,892	16,774	20,512	994	1,607
30—35	62,709	33,722	28,987	7,666	3,877	24,383	21,919	1,673	3,191
35—40	38,296	22,313	15,983	3,443	852	17,634	13,709	1,236	2,422
40—45	44,815	24,774	20,041	2,323	1,096	20,592	13,540	1,859	5,405
45—50	20,607	12,073	8,534	951	363	10,080	5,542	1,042	2,629
50—55	27,309	13,822	13,487	973	712	11,239	7,066	1,610	5,709
55—60	9,487	5,318	4,169	337	223	4,272	2,109	709	1,837
60—65	15,584	7,773	7,811	493	431	5,956	2,485	1,334	4,895
65—70	6,375	4,239	2,136	228	199	3,149	628	862	1,309
70 and over	11,744	4,948	6,796	484	385	2,890	1,105	1,574	5,306

TABLE VII.—Age, Sex and Civil Condition.

CENTRAL PROVINCES AND BERAR.

Age and Religion.	Population.			Unmarried.		Married.		Widowed.	
	Persons.	Males.	Females.	Males.	Females.	Males.	Females.	Males.	Females.
1	2	3	4	5	6	7	8	9	10
ALL RELIGIONS	**13,916,308**	**6,930,392**	**6,985,916**	**3,013,394**	**2,186,710**	**3,594,937**	**3,692,210**	**322,061**	**1,106,996**
0—1	530,007	265,289	264,718	264,765	263,094	517	605	7	29
1—2	310,022	150,858	159,164	150,291	158,050	549	1,085	18	20
2—3	444,088	214,537	229,551	213,165	226,214	1,337	3,269	35	66
3—4	490,418	233,179	257,239	231,172	250,886	1,933	6,222	74	131
4—5	431,895	214,485	217,410	211,327	207,097	3,070	9,962	88	351
Total 0—5	*2,206,430*	*1,078,348*	*1,128,082*	*1,070,720*	*1,106,941*	*7,406*	*21,933*	*222*	*608*
5—10	1,867,126	936,087	931,039	891,235	763,391	43,529	163,482	1,323	4,166
10—15	1,265,160	687,471	577,689	528,531	238,495	155,282	331,098	3,658	8,096
15—20	932,503	470,554	461,949	236,622	37,768	227,922	414,324	6,010	9,857
20—25	1,196,845	537,922	658,923	135,820	15,481	388,171	620,655	13,931	22,787
25—30	1,345,065	662,846	682,219	69,014	7,625	568,254	635,093	25,578	39,501
30—35	1,281,315	652,104	629,211	33,789	6,221	585,501	549,426	32,814	73,564
35—40	837,953	440,793	397,160	14,330	2,831	399,914	321,678	26,549	72,651
40—45	913,158	463,490	449,678	12,981	3,219	413,815	293,545	37,684	152,914
45—50	475,693	250,224	225,469	5,150	1,106	219,788	126,980	25,286	97,383
50—55	643,451	318,708	324,743	6,464	1,704	267,665	117,127	44,579	205,912
55—60	203,275	102,835	100,440	1,915	519	83,560	36,815	17,351	63,106
60—65	438,013	194,377	243,636	3,824	1,131	146,445	39,460	44,108	203,045
65—70	88,516	42,047	46,469	794	255	30,203	8,404	11,050	37,810
70 and over	221,805	92,596	129,209	2,205	723	58,473	12,890	31,918	115,596
HINDU	**11,496,486**	**5,731,936**	**5,764,550**	**2,421,027**	**1,723,743**	**3,035,156**	**3,111,683**	**275,753**	**929,124**
0—1	441,974	221,271	220,603	220,816	219,975	451	609	4	19
1—2	256,849	125,254	131,595	124,754	130,624	486	950	14	21
2—3	366,093	177,690	180,306	176,405	186,253	1,166	3,002	29	53
3—4	399,994	190,619	209,375	188,885	203,470	1,671	5,801	63	104
4—5	348,848	173,394	175,454	170,559	165,672	2,758	9,490	77	293
Total 0—5	*1,814,563*	*888,228*	*926,335*	*881,509*	*905,994*	*6,532*	*19,852*	*187*	*489*
5—10	1,530,642	767,544	763,098	725,092	602,377	41,239	156,912	1,213	3,809
10—15	1,050,889	571,449	479,440	421,096	167,572	146,966	304,357	3,397	7,511
15—20	774,322	391,716	382,606	179,831	20,274	205,522	353,848	5,368	8,494
20—25	987,708	444,308	543,400	98,201	9,809	334,192	514,402	11,915	19,189
25—30	1,107,673	548,395	559,278	51,127	4,889	475,683	520,932	21,585	33,407
30—35	1,049,006	534,729	514,277	25,875	4,372	481,166	448,285	27,686	61,620
35—40	697,889	367,290	330,590	11,359	2,025	332,968	266,544	22,937	62,021
40—45	749,983	378,795	371,188	10,214	2,347	336,386	241,344	32,195	127,407
45—50	400,789	210,329	190,460	4,211	819	184,116	106,746	23,002	82,805
50—55	534,958	265,200	269,758	5,290	1,295	221,829	96,981	38,081	171,482
55—60	172,447	87,269	85,178	1,560	406	70,628	31,053	15,081	53,719
60—65	364,740	162,713	202,027	3,175	808	123,121	32,722	37,417	168,497
65—70	75,675	36,213	39,462	664	203	25,928	7,109	9,621	32,150
70 and over	185,202	77,749	107,453	1,823	553	48,863	10,546	27,063	90,354
MUSALMAN	**564,909**	**292,047**	**272,862**	**144,173**	**99,391**	**133,757**	**126,638**	**14,117**	**46,833**
0—1	19,438	9,690	9,748	9,660	9,722	20	21	1	5
1—2	9,908	4,840	5,068	4,814	5,027	24	37	2	4
2—3	16,887	8,190	8,697	8,132	8,618	55	75	3	4
3—4	18,324	8,696	9,628	8,616	9,496	78	120	2	12
4—5	16,534	8,160	8,374	8,081	8,223	73	130	6	21
Total 0—5	*81,091*	*39,576*	*41,515*	*39,319*	*41,086*	*250*	*383*	*14*	*46*
5—10	76,213	38,000	38,213	37,314	36,382	642	1,713	44	118
10—15	54,823	30,688	24,135	28,708	16,446	1,882	7,466	98	223
15—20	39,624	21,055	18,569	16,347	2,496	4,545	15,590	163	483
20—25	52,419	25,743	26,676	11,854	937	13,201	24,410	688	1,309
25—30	53,564	28,077	25,487	5,356	605	21,461	22,872	1,260	1,020
30—35	51,609	27,047	24,562	2,392	457	23,124	20,667	1,531	3,418
35—40	31,925	18,056	13,869	938	190	15,045	10,626	1,173	3,044
40—45	38,147	19,670	18,477	845	234	17,220	11,415	1,605	6,798
45—50	17,536	9,966	7,570	259	93	8,765	3,847	942	3,630
50—55	27,251	14,050	13,201	362	136	11,806	4,334	1,883	8,731
55—60	7,589	4,331	3,258	91	30	3,529	951	711	2,277
60—65	18,796	8,839	9,957	208	93	6,752	1,513	1,879	8,361
65—70	3,719	1,955	1,764	37	21	1,407	304	511	1,439
70 and over	10,603	4,994	5,609	150	66	3,229	407	1,615	5,046
ANIMISTIC	**1,744,921**	**847,167**	**897,754**	**416,814**	**346,042**	**401,355**	**430,754**	**28,998**	**120,958**
0—1	65,056	32,520	32,536	32,478	32,472	41	59	1	5
1—2	41,377	19,844	21,533	19,800	21,437	33	93	2	4
2—3	57,286	27,255	30,031	27,141	29,838	112	183	2	10
3—4	68,973	32,370	36,603	32,191	36,300	173	290	6	18
4—5	63,857	31,581	32,276	31,346	31,916	230	324	5	36
Total 0—5	*296,549*	*143,570*	*152,979*	*142,965*	*151,963*	*589*	*948*	*16*	*68*
5—10	247,449	124,058	123,306	122,417	118,806	1,579	4,290	57	210
10—15	146,807	79,375	69,432	73,337	52,094	5,881	17,061	157	277
15—20	108,971	52,706	56,265	36,861	13,804	15,411	41,653	434	718
20—25	143,500	60,095	83,405	21,373	4,270	37,544	77,271	1,178	1,864
25—30	172,130	79,357	92,773	9,974	1,826	66,888	87,353	2,495	3,594
30—35	171,271	85,165	86,106	4,555	1,236	77,309	77,275	3,301	7,595
35—40	101,476	51,743	49,733	1,631	497	47,965	42,507	2,147	6,729
40—45	118,519	61,622	56,897	1,637	560	56,454	39,152	3,541	17,185
45—50	53,544	27,754	25,790	555	157	25,173	15,678	2,026	9,955
50—55	76,704	37,220	39,484	660	246	32,392	15,185	4,168	24,058
55—60	21,456	10,247	11,209	224	60	8,690	4,638	1,333	6,516
60—65	51,598	21,510	30,088	363	215	16,763	5,024	4,384	24,644
65—70	8,403	3,530	4,873	69	28	2,665	943	796	3,903
70 and over	24,549	9,220	15,329	208	98	6,052	1,781	2,965	13,450

PART II.—BY PROVINCES AND STATES—*continued.*

MADRAS.

Age and Religion.	Population.			Unmarried.		Married.		Widowed.	
	Persons.	Males.	Females.	Males.	Females.	Males.	Females.	Males.	Females.
1	2	3	4	5	6	7	8	9	10
ALL RELIGIONS	**41,405,404**	**20,382,955**	**21,022,449**	**10,862,162**	**7,832,583**	**8,734,806**	**9,286,460**	**785,987**	**3,903,406**
0—1	1.178,725	581,536	597,189	580,895	596,343	627	809	14	37
1—2	725,199	352,865	372,334	352,393	371,504	461	794	11	36
2—3	1,174,191	575,854	598,337	574,608	595,634	1,210	2,608	36	95
3—4	1,291,751	629,108	662,643	627,491	657,972	1,560	4,521	48	150
4—5	1,167,111	577,242	589,869	574,927	581,469	2,239	7,985	76	415
Total 0—5	*5,536,977*	*2,716,605*	*2,820,372*	*2,710,314*	*2,802,922*	*6,106*	*16,717*	*185*	*733*
5—10	5,478,675	2,719,251	2,759,424	2,693,690	2,610,708	24,721	144,403	840	4,313
10—15	4,783,768	2,488,739	2,295,029	2,392,606	1,695,352	93,763	580,380	2,370	19,297
15—20	3,565,464	1,786,461	1,779,003	1,516,127	478,870	264,907	1,242,795	5,427	57,338
20—25	3,659,493	1,666,171	1,993,322	871,853	111,631	773,960	1,744,389	20,358	137,302
25—30	3,371,623	1,615,787	1,755,836	353,390	44,166	1,224,619	1,521,813	37,728	189,907
30—35	3,235,354	1,519,466	1,715,888	136,306	29,391	1,332,332	1,367,008	50,828	319,489
35—40	2,319,162	1,200,641	1,118,521	58,175	15,389	1,092,122	817,603	50,344	285,529
40—45	2,688,861	1,309,728	1,379,133	49,226	15,739	1,178,223	817,652	82,279	545,742
45—50	1,579,038	834,930	744,108	22,805	7,873	743,421	380,855	68,704	355,380
50—55	1,908,022	924,872	983,150	24,266	8,256	787,626	357,339	112,980	617,555
55—60	839,235	443,441	395,794	10,039	3,111	366,246	119,618	67,156	273,065
60—65	1,272,879	600,920	671,959	12,396	4,848	464,573	112,545	123,951	554,566
65—70	380,924	191,301	189,623	3,344	1,345	141,391	29,291	46,566	158,987
70 and over	785,929	364,692	421,237	7,625	2,982	240,796	34,052	116,271	384,203
HINDU	**36,806,604**	**18,108,939**	**18,697,665**	**9,565,052**	**6,841,901**	**7,830,301**	**8,317,188**	**713,586**	**3,538,576**
0—1	1,043,319	514,169	529,150	513,584	528,384	572	735	13	31
1—2	631,650	306,656	324,994	306,222	324,242	424	719	10	33
2—3	1,033,695	506,045	527,650	504,920	525,123	1,091	2,442	34	85
3—4	1,144,031	556,271	587,760	554,767	583,358	1,463	4,264	41	138
4—5	1,023,324	505,073	518,251	502,932	510,199	2,069	7,669	72	383
Total 0—5	*4,876.019*	*2,388.214*	*2,487.805*	*2,382,495*	*2,471,306*	*5,619*	*15,829*	*170*	*670*
5—10	4,831,593	2,396,025	2,435,568	2,371,681	2,290,919	23,555	140,596	789	4,053
10—15	4,234,295	2,203,385	2,030,910	2,111,171	1,464,161	89,973	548,498	2,241	18,251
15—20	3,146,737	1,584,406	1,562,331	1,332,602	406,078	247,057	1,105,189	4,747	51,064
20—25	3,236,716	1,474,240	1,762,476	761,180	94,659	695,611	1,544,411	17,449	123,406
25—30	2,996,472	1,435,563	1,560,909	312,400	37,585	1,090,374	1,351,813	32,789	171,511
30—35	2,889,546	1,355,237	1,534,309	122,611	25,493	1,187,420	1,218,681	45,206	290,135
35—40	2,066,826	1,067,758	999,068	52,343	18,156	970,311	728,685	45,104	257,227
40—45	2,420,620	1,177,549	1,243,080	45,065	13,583	1,057,505	734,298	74,979	495,190
45—50	1,419,442	749,270	670,172	20,781	6,855	665,624	342,030	62,865	321,278
50—55	1,726,242	835,487	890,755	22,298	7,328	709,326	321,860	103,863	561,567
55—60	758,061	399,640	358,421	9,188	2,682	328,824	107,760	61,628	247,079
60—65	1,151,473	542,194	609,279	11,351	4,280	417,128	100,940	113,715	504,059
65—70	343,583	171,914	171,669	2,992	1,169	126,510	26,296	42,412	144,204
70 and over	708,970	328,057	380,913	6,964	2,647	215,464	30,293	105,629	347,973
MUSALMAN	**2,740,408**	**1,351,119**	**1,389,289**	**786,724**	**572,968**	**523,355**	**573,912**	**41,040**	**242,409**
0—1	81,879	40,904	40,975	40,883	40,946	21	27	..	2
1—2	59,723	29,447	30,276	29,426	30,229	20	44	1	3
2—3	84,857	42,379	42,478	42,315	42,391	63	82	1	5
3—4	85,877	42,659	43,218	42,610	43,087	43	128	6	3
4—5	83,386	41,979	41,407	41,914	41,249	62	142	3	16
Total 0—5	*395,722*	*197,368*	*198,354*	*197,148*	*197,902*	*209*	*423*	*11*	*29*
5—10	383,175	191,677	191,498	191,160	188,969	488	2,368	29	161
10—15	335,377	174,578	160,799	172,561	137,545	1,939	22,489	78	765
15—20	254,570	123,839	130,731	113,759	35,114	9,616	90,510	464	5,107
20—25	258,679	118,492	140,187	70,897	6,740	45,530	122,905	2,065	10,542
25—30	216,566	103,087	113,479	24,716	2,362	75,214	98,474	3,157	12,643
30—35	201,939	94,581	107,358	7,751	1,468	83,475	85,757	3,355	20,133
35—40	143,774	75,733	68,041	2,991	762	69,875	48,766	2,867	18,513
40—45	156,795	75,354	81,441	2,178	856	69,371	47,088	3,810	33,497
45—50	91,737	49,056	42,681	979	316	45,184	20,569	2,893	21,796
50—55	109,381	52,581	56,800	1,024	368	46,537	19,245	5,020	37,187
55—60	47,241	25,769	21,472	446	130	22,348	5,789	2,975	15,544
60—65	74,660	35,071	39,589	575	227	28,687	6,284	5,809	33,078
65—70	22,395	11,652	10,743	173	68	9,230	1,406	2.249	9,269
70 and over	48,397	22,281	26,116	371	132	15,652	1,839	8,258	24,145
CHRISTIAN	**1,191,266**	**586,836**	**604,430**	**329,210**	**269,694**	**238,689**	**248,583**	**18,937**	**86,153**
0—1	35,401	17,609	17,792	17,585	17,761	23	28	1	3
1—2	24,774	12,327	12,447	12,317	12,422	10	25	..	..
2—3	36,159	17,960	18,199	17,937	18,151	22	45	1	3
3—4	39,085	19,129	19,956	19,097	19,890	31	60	1	6
4—5	34,982	17,666	17,316	17,622	17,241	44	68	..	7
Total 0—5	*170,401*	*84,691*	*85,710*	*84,558*	*85,465*	*130*	*226*	*3*	*19*
5—10	162,065	79,894	82,171	79,660	81,421	220	704	14	46
10—15	143,100	72,997	70,103	72,211	64,100	766	5,837	20	166
15—20	107,016	51,594	55,422	47,651	24,359	3,884	30,423	59	640
20—25	105,047	47,383	57,664	27,021	6,502	20,044	48,991	318	2,171
25—30	97,891	46,530	51,361	9,919	2,684	35,821	44,777	790	3,900
30—35	87,119	41,632	45,487	3,175	1,585	37,375	37,718	1,082	6,184
35—40	66,016	34,284	31,732	1,674	982	31,463	24,208	1,147	6,542
40—45	69,680	34,179	35,501	1,182	901	31,184	23,133	1,813	11,467
45—50	45,145	23,679	21,466	686	546	21,252	12,299	1,741	8,621
50—55	49,196	24,398	24,798	560	418	21,312	10,881	2,526	13,499
55—60	24,094	12,867	11,227	290	229	10,854	3,973	1,728	7,025
60—65	32,550	16,406	16,144	294	259	13,091	3,454	3,021	12,451
65—70	11,250	5,890	5,360	127	85	4,345	1,000	1,418	4,275
70 and over	20,696	10,412	10,284	202	158	6,948	959	3,262	9,167

TABLE VII.—Age, Sex and Civil Condition.

N.-W. F. PROVINCE.

Age and Religion.	Population.			Unmarried.		Married.		Widowed.	
	Persons.	Males.	Females.	Males.	Females.	Males.	Females.	Males.	Females.
1	2	3	4	5	6	7	8	9	10
ALL RELIGIONS	**2,196,933**	**1,182,102**	**1,014,831**	**688,241**	**460,643**	**438,901**	**440,819**	**54,960**	**113,369**
0—1	84,539	42,864	41,675	42,864	41,675	..	..	..	..
1—2	31,378	15,725	15,653	15,725	15,653	..	..	..	..
2—3	66,882	32,852	34,030	32,852	34,030	..	..	..	..
3—4	75,519	37,426	38,093	37,426	38,093	..	..	..	..
4—5	76,048	38,890	37,158	38,890	37,155	..	3	..	..
Total 0—5	*334,366*	*167,757*	*166,609*	*167,757*	*166,606*	..	*3*	..	..
5—10	346,536	184,933	161,603	184,538	160,663	392	912	3	28
10—15	238,483	139,514	98,969	135,818	87,366	3,592	11,328	104	275
15—20	164,114	91,540	72,574	77,690	25,536	13,331	46,070	519	969
20—25	173,721	89,223	84,498	52,313	7,450	34,923	74,451	1,987	2,597
25—30	184,136	97,035	87,101	33,353	3,689	59,924	78,565	3,758	4,847
30—35	197,897	103,466	94,431	17,823	3,107	79,752	82,936	5,891	8,388
35—40	109,459	61,724	47,735	6,219	1,383	51,302	39,647	4,203	6,705
40—45	136,238	70,931	65,307	5,349	1,942	59,229	47,666	6,353	15,699
45—50	68,067	38,468	29,599	2,247	977	32,105	18,903	4,116	9,719
50—55	93,625	51,599	42,026	2,210	818	42,272	20,860	7,117	20,348
55—60	30,805	17,977	12,828	594	260	14,440	6,048	2,943	6,520
60—65	63,514	35,536	27,978	1,293	408	26,684	8,281	7,559	19,289
65—70	14,029	8,080	5,949	250	157	5,781	1,680	2,049	4,112
70 and over	41,943	24,319	17,624	787	282	15,174	3,469	8,358	13,873
HINDU	**119,942**	**71,397**	**48,545**	**37,957**	**19,177**	**28,457**	**21,465**	**4,983**	**7,903**
0—1	4,009	2,066	1,943	2,066	1,943	..	..	..	..
1—2	1,398	753	645	753	645	..	..	..	..
2—3	2,888	1,413	1,475	1,413	1,475	..	..	..	..
3—4	3,081	1,562	1,519	1,562	1,519	..	..	..	..
4—5	2,928	1,438	1,490	1,438	1,490	..	..	..	..
Total 0—5	*14,304*	*7,939*	*7,079*	*7,939*	*7,079*	..	..	..	..
5—10	14,650	7,704	6,976	7,673	6,896	31	75	..	5
10—15	12,136	7,154	4,982	6,904	4,030	232	936	18	16
15—20	11,001	6,952	4,049	5,427	693	1,451	3,258	74	98
20—25	14,055	9,005	5,050	4,957	164	3,745	4,531	303	356
25—30	12,826	8,344	4,482	2,653	90	5,220	3,886	462	506
30—35	10,571	6,514	4,057	1,188	100	4,738	3,321	588	626
35—40	7,122	4,653	2,469	555	32	3,612	1,861	486	576
40—45	7,157	4,243	2,914	455	30	3,127	1,661	661	1,223
45—50	4,264	2,595	1,669	244	16	1,933	785	418	868
50—55	4,848	2,868	1,980	340	31	1,913	592	615	1,357
55—60	1,733	1,106	627	83	4	741	191	282	432
60—65	2,848	1,648	1,200	134	7	1,013	220	501	973
65—70	698	417	281	28	4	234	69	155	208
70 and over	1,600	962	737	84	8	458	79	420	650
SIKH	**30,345**	**19,967**	**10,378**	**10,790**	**3,987**	**7,842**	**4,843**	**1,335**	**1,546**
0—1	874	467	407	467	407	..	..	..	..
1—2	269	130	139	130	139	..	..	..	..
2—3	639	330	309	330	309	..	..	..	..
3—4	712	366	346	366	346	..	..	..	..
4—5	630	333	297	333	297	..	..	..	..
Total 0—5	*3,124*	*1,626*	*1,498*	*1,626*	*1,498*	..	..	..	..
5—10	3,246	1,788	1,458	1,781	1,438	6	20	1	..
10—15	2,811	1,778	1,033	1,720	788	56	237	2	8
15—20	2,953	2,066	887	1,643	158	394	706	29	23
20—25	4,473	3,382	1,091	1,972	43	1,305	999	105	40
25—30	3,625	2,617	1,008	1,082	12	1,387	907	148	89
30—35	2,804	1,953	851	443	15	1,319	705	191	131
35—40	1,988	1,429	559	223	7	1,048	426	158	126
40—45	1,659	1,079	580	108	4	846	369	125	207
45—50	935	564	371	40	3	434	212	90	166
50—55	984	645	339	75	3	460	125	110	211
55—60	351	229	122	14	3	163	38	52	81
60—65	702	368	334	23	13	222	56	123	265
65—70	254	175	79	15	..	65	14	95	65
70 and over	436	268	168	25	2	137	29	106	137
MUSALMAN	**2,039,994**	**1,085,276**	**954,718**	**634,835**	**436,931**	**401,850**	**413,927**	**48,591**	**103,860**
0—1	79,550	40,274	39,276	40,274	39,276	..	..	..	..
1—2	29,626	14,791	14,835	14,791	14,835	..	..	..	..
2—3	63,288	31,069	32,219	31,069	32,219	..	..	..	..
3—4	71,646	35,459	36,187	35,459	36,187	..	..	..	..
4—5	72,399	37,068	35,331	37,068	35,328	..	3	..	..
Total 0—5	*316,509*	*158,661*	*157,848*	*158,661*	*157,845*	..	*3*	..	..
5—10	328,360	175,322	153,038	174,965	152,198	355	817	2	23
10—15	223,426	130,529	92,897	127,144	82,492	3,301	10,154	84	251
15—20	149,970	82,403	67,567	70,509	24,644	11,478	42,078	416	845
20—25	152,903	74,688	78,215	43,274	7,195	29,840	68,827	1,574	2,193
25—30	165,973	84,543	81,430	28,221	3,556	53,182	73,625	3,140	4,249
30—35	183,763	94,403	89,360	15,792	2,976	73,501	78,767	5,110	7,617
35—40	99,929	55,331	44,598	5,268	1,328	46,513	37,274	3,550	5,996
40—45	127,204	65,438	61,766	4,748	1,903	55,133	45,597	5,557	14,266
45—50	62,747	35,219	27,528	1,948	955	29,667	17,881	3,604	8,692
50—55	87,716	48,040	39,676	1,792	777	39,864	20,134	6,384	18,765
55—60	28,697	16,626	12,071	494	250	13,525	5,817	2,607	6,004
60—65	59,942	33,512	26,430	1,136	388	25,443	8,000	6,933	18,042
65—70	13,064	7,482	5,582	207	152	5,477	1,596	1,798	3,834
70 and over	39,791	23,079	16,712	676	272	14,571	3,357	7,832	13,063

PART II.—BY PROVINCES AND STATES—*continued.*

PUNJAB.

Age and Religion.	Population.			Unmarried.		Married.		Widowed.	
	Persons.	Males.	Females.	Males.	Females.	Males.	Females.	Males.	Females.
1	2	3	4	5	6	7	8	9	10
ALL RELIGIONS	**19,974,956**	**10,992,067**	**8,982,889**	**5,836,603**	**3,441,792**	**4,239,986**	**4,282,756**	**915,478**	**1,258,341**
0—1	829,085	424,654	404,431	424,625	404,386	27	40	2	5
1—2	325,061	166,049	159,012	166,026	158,984	21	26	2	2
2—3	490,656	252,884	237,772	252,793	237,601	87	159	4	12
3—4	558,711	286,965	271,746	286,783	271,293	174	413	8	40
4—5	554,959	291,617	263,342	291,245	262,444	332	818	40	80
Total 0—5	*2,758,472*	*1,422,169*	*1,336,303*	*1,421,472*	*1,334,708*	*641*	*1,456*	*56*	*139*
5—10	2,742,025	1,482,324	1,259,701	1,463,416	1,208,744	17,334	48,055	1,574	2,902
10—15	2,252,887	1,321,272	931,615	1,207,247	666,951	107,528	258,190	6,497	6,474
15—20	1,720,943	994,090	726,853	704,711	153,913	270,949	556,226	18,430	16,714
20—25	1,718,066	927,244	790,822	417,517	32,688	469,551	721,879	40,176	36,255
25—30	1,749,734	958,670	791,064	254,756	13,155	638,649	721,264	65,265	56,645
30—35	1,597,353	861,472	735,881	133,722	9,032	645,093	635,831	82,657	91,018
35—40	1,046,911	585,457	461,454	60,924	4,941	452,470	374,222	72,063	82,291
40—45	1,226,664	649,967	576,697	57,018	5,193	489,946	398,555	103,003	172,949
45—50	733,092	415,690	317,402	29,290	2,640	307,523	199,755	78,877	115,007
50—55	917,686	511,235	406,451	33,571	3,129	353,408	188,938	124,256	214,384
55—60	338,281	200,006	138,275	12,012	991	131,285	62,159	56,709	75,125
60—65	498,887	237,490	261,397	19,804	2,194	104,589	70,219	113,097	188,984
65—70	306,926	241,200	65,726	5,884	685	196,324	18,083	38,992	46,958
70 and over	367,029	183,781	183,248	15,259	2,828	54,696	27,924	113,826	152,496
HINDU	**6,682,818**	**3,686,923**	**2,995,895**	**1,859,178**	**1,016,494**	**1,479,054**	**1,475,495**	**348,691**	**503,906**
0—1	259,727	132,344	127,383	132,332	127,363	11	16	1	4
1—2	106,699	54,104	52,595	54,098	52,586	4	9	2	..
2—3	154,321	79,483	74,838	79,451	74,759	31	73	1	6
3—4	176,920	90,136	86,784	90,049	86,591	83	176	4	17
4—5	166,757	87,777	78,980	87,562	78,568	185	372	30	40
Total 0—5	*864,424*	*443,844*	*420,580*	*443,492*	*419,867*	*314*	*646*	*38*	*67*
5—10	852,819	459,369	393,450	449,869	368,013	8,761	24,181	739	1,256
10—15	748,757	436,692	312,065	381,147	187,755	52,227	120,977	3,318	3,333
15—20	633,535	369,505	264,030	235,122	27,898	124,860	227,215	9,523	8,917
20—25	624,533	339,655	284,878	132,178	5,358	189,381	260,757	18,096	19,763
25—30	596,046	329,827	266,219	77,788	1,965	226,165	237,643	25,874	26,611
30—35	534,758	290,957	243,801	44,358	1,497	214,691	201,059	31,908	41,245
35—40	355,123	200,811	154,312	23,128	786	149,234	117,455	28,449	36,071
40—45	433,978	231,233	202,745	23,283	973	165,457	125,684	42,493	76,088
45—50	244,192	140,606	103,586	12,740	405	96,709	57,772	31,157	45,409
50—55	318,478	176,345	142,133	14,917	581	112,554	55,740	48,874	85,812
55—60	113,067	67,773	45,294	5,508	186	40,310	17,114	21,955	27,994
60—65	164,274	74,836	89,438	8,002	453	25,851	18,734	40,983	70,251
65—70	93,542	73,301	20,241	2,450	123	57,265	4,321	13,586	15,797
70 and over	105,292	52,169	53,123	5,196	634	15,275	6,197	31,698	46,292
SIKH	**2,093,804**	**1,197,922**	**895,882**	**646,538**	**317,632**	**435,408**	**445,162**	**115,976**	**133,088**
0—1	84,974	45,444	39,530	45,440	39,524	3	6	1	..
1—2	35,522	19,163	16,359	19,161	16,356	2	3	..	..
2—3	49,259	27,005	22,254	26,992	22,242	12	12	1	..
3—4	53,815	29,120	24,695	29,110	24,678	10	17	..	
4—5	52,606	29,586	23,020	29,555	22,986	28	29	3	5
Total 0—5	*276,176*	*150,318*	*125,858*	*150,258*	*125,786*	*55*	*67*	*5*	*5*
5—10	271,528	154,257	117,271	152,593	113,417	1,440	3,463	224	391
10—15	231,994	145,040	86,954	132,490	61,517	11,464	24,819	1,086	618
15—20	181,181	112,679	68,502	79,843	11,549	30,459	55,509	2,377	1,444
20—25	180,218	101,856	78,362	46,428	1,788	50,630	73,331	4,798	3,243
25—30	185,303	103,334	81,969	29,796	1,009	64,999	75,098	8,539	5,862
30—35	157,985	86,122	71,863	16,092	567	60,270	62,664	9,760	8,632
35—40	110,640	62,461	48,179	8,953	459	41,579	39,556	8,929	8,164
40—45	125,178	66,617	58,561	8,416	408	46,939	41,698	11,262	16,455
45—50	86,559	49,824	36,735	5,193	225	33,998	23,927	10,633	12,583
50—55	102,199	57,908	44,291	5,818	242	36,873	21,714	15,217	22,335
55—60	43,285	25,772	17,513	2,509	103	15,383	8,334	7,880	9,076
60—65	58,259	29,048	29,211	3,838	218	11,403	8,599	13,807	20,394
65—70	35,418	26,946	8,472	1,254	78	19,899	2,473	5,793	5,921
70 and over	47,881	25,740	22,141	3,057	266	7,017	3,910	15,666	17,965
MUSALMAN	**10,955,721**	**5,967,408**	**4,988,313**	**3,246,973**	**2,059,995**	**2,278,948**	**2,317,941**	**441,487**	**610,377**
0—1	474,264	241,538	232,726	241,525	232,708	13	17	..	1
1—2	178,484	90,669	87,815	90,655	87,800	14	13	..	2
2—3	280,853	143,181	137,672	143,139	137,593	40	73	2	6
3—4	320,321	163,859	156,462	163,786	156,227	69	213	4	22
4—5	328,627	170,594	158,033	170,477	157,591	111	410	6	32
Total 0—5	*1,582,549*	*809,841*	*772,708*	*809,582*	*771,919*	*247*	*726*	*12*	*63*
5—10	1,584,465	850,907	733,558	843,322	712,159	6,998	20,178	587	1,221
10—15	1,246,584	725,002	521,582	679,894	408,619	43,069	110,503	2,039	2,460
15—20	886,746	500,906	385,840	381,638	111,318	112,913	268,358	6,355	6,164
20—25	885,377	466,715	418,662	225,449	24,309	224,400	380,531	16,866	13,822
25—30	942,606	508,928	433,678	139,303	9,418	339,539	400,793	30,086	23,467
30—35	885,317	473,371	411,946	70,984	6,550	362,307	365,224	40,080	40,172
35—40	568,862	315,104	253,758	27,802	3,476	253,368	212,995	33,934	37,287
40—45	654,351	344,717	309,634	24,706	3,655	271,873	227,060	48,138	78,919
45—50	394,222	220,916	173,306	11,040	1,875	173,640	115,397	36,236	56,034
50—55	488,333	272,063	216,270	12,549	2,206	200,571	109,532	58,943	104,532
55—60	178,786	104,646	74,140	3,873	660	74,452	36,065	26,321	37,415
60—65	271,755	131,415	140,340	7,826	1,469	66,427	42,041	57,162	95,830
65—70	174,956	138,591	36,365	2,129	475	117,242	11,023	19,220	24,867
70 and over	210,812	104,286	106,526	6,876	1,887	31,902	17,515	65,508	87,124

TABLE VII.—Age, Sex and Civil Condition.

UNITED PROVINCES.

Age and Religion.	Population.			Unmarried.		Married.		Widowed.	
	Persons.	Males.	Females.	Males.	Females.	Males.	Females.	Males.	Females.
1	2	3	4	5	6	7	8	9	10
ALL RELIGIONS	**47,182,044**	**24,641,831**	**22,540,213**	**11,065,446**	**6,887,907**	**11,650,777**	**11,777,845**	**1,925,608**	**3,874,461**
0—1 . .	1,543,660	788,584	757,076	787,101	755,219	1,420	1,719	63	138
1—2 . .	712,829	354,510	358,319	353,348	356,609	1,130	1,627	32	83
2—3 . .	1,057,332	520,736	536,596	517,665	531,815	2,977	4,007	94	174
3—4 . .	1,231,706	603,154	628,552	596,347	618,246	6,468	9,619	339	687
4—5 . .	1,164,849	591,179	573,670	582,712	561,680	8,040	10,723	427	1,267
Total 0—5 .	*5,712,376*	*2,858,163*	*2,854,213*	*2,837,173*	*2,823,569*	*20,035*	*28,295*	*955*	*2,349*
5—10 . .	6,288,077	3,299,487	2,988,590	3,134,779	2,672,150	157,444	301,580	7,264	14,860
10—15 . .	5,336,920	3,020,421	2,316,499	2,348,803	1,076,155	647,699	1,208,174	23,919	32,170
15—20 . .	3,822,362	2,118,003	1,704,359	1,061,451	137,977	1,006,680	1,510,616	49,872	55,766
20—25 . .	4,231,772	2,137,990	2,093,782	607,090	48,767	1,429,577	1,930,600	101,323	114,415
25—30 . .	4,270,682	2,213,629	2,057,053	368,647	29,820	1,696,150	1,851,127	148,632	176,097
30—35 . .	4,084,878	2,092,492	1,992,386	230,234	30,802	1,677,692	1,662,487	184,566	299,097
35—40 . .	2,796,535	1,471,021	1,325,514	124,091	13,667	1,188,833	1,035,622	158,097	270,225
40—45 . .	3,309,266	1,706,616	1,602,650	128,654	20,063	1,333,752	1,007,302	244,210	575,285
45—50 . .	1,756,630	940,593	816,037	61,802	6,304	715,121	467,992	163,670	341,741
50—55 . .	2,307,948	1,177,356	1,130,592	70,707	10,963	831,084	415,023	275,565	704,606
55—60 . .	779,486	414,572	364,914	24,563	3,619	276,335	139,611	113,674	221,684
60—65 . .	1,414,879	677,618	737,261	36,768	7,000	410,135	136,816	230,715	593,445
65—70 . .	311,573	161,944	149,629	9,340	1,233	91,238	32,538	61,366	115,858
70 and over .	758,253	351,656	406,597	21,191	5,743	168,905	50,011	161,560	350,843
Age Unspecified.	407	270	137	153	66	97	51	20	20
HINDU .	**40,122,238**	**20,949,641**	**19,172,597**	**9,344,262**	**5,735,596**	**9,956,912**	**10,053,360**	**1,648,467**	**3,383,641**
0—1 . .	1,287,430	657,921	629,509	656,663	627,938	1,215	1,458	43	113
1—2 . .	609,972	303,074	306,898	302,069	305,395	977	1,433	28	70
2—3 . .	893,136	440,118	453,018	437,377	448,843	2,657	4,024	84	151
3—4 . .	1,044,790	512,243	532,547	506,292	523,557	5,653	8,387	298	603
4—5 . .	986,179	501,359	484,820	493,781	474,156	7,203	9,533	375	1,131
Total 0—5 .	*4,821,507*	*2,414,715*	*2,406,792*	*2,396,182*	*2,379,889*	*17,705*	*24,835*	*828*	*2,068*
5—10 . .	5,329,120	2,799,054	2,530,066	2,650,165	2,250,018	142,446	266,979	6,443	13,069
10—15 . .	4,522,769	2,562,346	1,960,423	1,964,776	871,674	576,775	1,059,900	20,795	28,849
15—20 . .	3,242,433	1,802,723	1,439,710	878,904	100,516	880,775	1,289,639	43,044	49,555
20—25 . .	3,588,198	1,812,570	1,775,628	502,539	36,254	1,223,737	1,638,010	86,294	101,364
25—30 . .	3,653,545	1,894,782	1,758,763	317,172	22,553	1,450,234	1,579,207	127,376	157,003
30—35 . .	3,503,396	1,704,429	1,708,967	204,057	23,283	1,431,706	1,418,735	158,666	266,949
35—40 . .	2,404,275	1,261,808	1,142,467	112,478	10,615	1,012,442	885,880	136,888	245,972
40—45 . .	2,835,949	1,462,139	1,373,810	115,377	14,842	1,134,864	851,475	211,898	507,493
45—50 . .	1,509,285	807,007	702,278	56,300	4,688	607,861	396,009	142,846	301,581
50—55 . .	1,963,802	999,509	964,293	63,801	8,211	698,510	345,432	237,198	610,650
55—60 . .	665,689	352,535	313,154	22,511	2,765	231,824	116,913	98,200	193,476
60—65 . .	1,194,764	565,689	629,075	32,835	5,063	337,910	112,818	194,944	511,194
65—70 . .	262,754	135,065	127,689	8,479	819	74,886	26,754	51,700	100,116
70 and over .	624,359	285,009	339,350	18,538	4,343	135,144	40,724	131,327	294,288
Age Unspecified.	393	261	132	148	63	93	50	20	19
MUSALMAN .	**6,658,373**	**3,466,287**	**3,192,086**	**1,605,554**	**1,090,180**	**1,601,348**	**1,638,291**	**259,385**	**463,615**
0—1 . .	245,341	123,986	121,355	123,771	121,086	196	246	19	23
1—2 . .	97,783	48,827	48,956	48,674	48,755	150	188	3	13
2—3 . .	155,686	76,280	79,406	75,958	78,823	312	565	10	18
3—4 . .	177,732	86,352	91,380	85,520	90,110	794	1,197	38	73
4—5 . .	169,743	85,059	84,684	84,226	83,408	783	1,144	50	132
Total 0—5 .	*846,285*	*420,504*	*425,781*	*418,149*	*422,182*	*2,235*	*3,340*	*120*	*259*
5—10 . .	910,941	475,009	435,932	459,959	400,854	14,272	33,382	778	1,696
10—15 . .	769,716	432,694	337,022	362,765	192,816	66,959	141,067	2,970	3,189
15—20 . .	542,631	294,483	248,148	170,791	33,936	117,352	208,554	6,340	5,658
20—25 . .	595,448	295,221	300,227	87,906	10,984	193,285	277,375	14,030	11,868
25—30 . .	576,929	294,581	282,348	42,440	6,405	231,984	258,311	20,157	17,632
30—35 . .	548,698	279,668	269,030	22,684	6,976	232,754	232,090	24,230	29,964
35—40 . .	369,210	195,813	173,397	9,746	2,721	166,367	142,264	19,700	28,412
40—45 . .	448,285	230,905	217,380	11,809	4,922	188,917	148,439	30,179	64,019
45—50 . .	232,895	125,232	107,663	4,670	1,437	101,337	68,361	19,225	37,865
50—55 . .	326,725	168,619	158,106	6,177	2,579	126,594	66,346	35,848	89,181
55—60 . .	106,592	57,883	48,709	1,730	792	41,839	21,520	14,314	26,397
60—65 . .	209,570	106,511	103,059	3,537	1,852	69,303	22,832	33,671	78,375
65—70 . .	45,950	25,248	20,711	731	385	15,537	5,490	8,980	14,836
70 and over .	128,475	63,907	64,568	2,455	1,336	32,609	8,919	28,843	54,313
Age Unspecified.	14	9	5	5	3	4	1	..	1
CHRISTIAN .	**177,949**	**100,818**	**77,131**	**56,560**	**30,966**	**38,547**	**37,708**	**5,711**	**8,457**
0—1 . .	5,699	2,876	2,823	2,871	2,812	4	9	1	2
1—2 . .	2,447	1,264	1,183	1,264	1,180	..	3	..	..
2—3 . .	3,744	1,807	1,937	1,802	1,930	5	5	..	2
3—4 . .	4,343	2,125	2,218	2,111	2,200	12	14	2	4
4—5 . .	4,143	2,172	1,971	2,137	1,949	35	19	..	3
Total 0—5 .	*20,376*	*10,244*	*10,132*	*10,185*	*10,071*	*56*	*50*	*3*	*11*
5—10 . .	22,039	11,425	10,614	11,053	9,876	349	690	23	48
10—15 . .	18,681	10,284	8,397	8,399	5,099	1,808	3,232	77	66
15—20 . .	15,385	8,006	7,379	4,862	2,630	2,936	4,610	208	139
20—25 . .	24,794	17,037	7,757	12,188	1,224	4,497	6,259	352	274
25—30 . .	19,610	12,331	7,279	6,224	661	5,646	6,229	461	389
30—35 . .	14,778	8,293	6,485	1,775	423	5,928	5,439	590	623
35—40 . .	9,403	5,324	4,079	825	278	4,094	3,328	405	473
40—45 . .	10,678	5,753	4,925	422	231	4,650	3,472	681	1,222
45—50 . .	5,323	2,947	2,376	195	157	2,358	1,562	394	657
50—55 . .	6,955	3,742	3,213	149	137	2,800	1,453	793	1,623
55—60 . .	2,475	1,370	1,105	88	48	1,004	518	278	539
60—65 . .	4,251	2,313	1,938	85	58	1,478	528	750	1,352
65—70 . .	993	549	444	34	25	323	131	192	288
70 and over .	2,208	1,200	1,008	76	48	620	207	504	753

Part II.—By Provinces and States—*continued.*

BARODA STATE.

Age and Religion.	Population.			Unmarried.		Married.		Widowed.	
	Persons.	Males.	Females.	Males.	Females.	Males.	Females.	Males.	Females.
1	2	3	4	5	6	7	8	9	10
ALL RELIGIONS	**2,032,798**	**1,055,935**	**976,863**	**452,515**	**277,315**	**523,391**	**527,460**	**80,029**	**172,088**
0—1 . .	82,269	41,605	40,664	41,034	39,705	541	933	30	26
1—2 . .	40,114	19,811	20,303	19,126	18,638	661	1,637	24	28
2—3 . .	66,874	33,382	33,493	31,955	30,233	1,333	3,199	93	60
3—4 . .	64,131	30,881	33,250	29,205	29,898	1,598	3,303	78	49
4—5 . .	61,061	31,545	29,516	29,363	25,461	2,071	3,964	111	88
Total 0—5 .	*314,449*	*157,224*	*157,225*	*150,684*	*143,938*	*6,204*	*13,030*	*336*	*251*
5—10 . .	222,500	120,508	101,992	106,446	83,261	13,298	19,199	764	532
10—15 . .	179,303	98,702	80,601	74,306	37,354	23,329	41,524	1,067	1,723
15—20 . .	173,517	93,573	79,944	50,445	8,882	40,634	68,434	2,494	2,628
20—25 . .	202,772	102,468	100,304	32,028	2,115	65,527	92,697	4,913	5,492
25—30 . .	202,402	104,135	98,267	15,762	973	81,219	88,236	7,154	9,059
30—35 . .	176,124	88,699	87,425	7,305	551	73,993	72,668	7,402	14,206
35—40 . .	139,291	75,184	64,107	5,347	336	62,567	48,242	7,270	15,529
40—45 . .	139,215	70,320	68,895	3,625	401	56,848	39,894	9,847	28,600
45—50 . .	78,560	42,995	35,565	1,904	107	33,830	17,992	7,261	17,466
50—55 . .	91,580	46,421	45,159	2,025	124	33,149	14,081	11,247	30,954
55—60 . .	32,641	17,983	14,658	776	109	11,908	4,869	5,299	9,680
60—65 . .	48,739	23,236	26,503	972	101	13,350	4,247	7,914	22,155
65—70 . .	12,810	6,650	6,160	340	21	3,517	1,062	2,793	5,077
70 and over . .	18,895	8,837	10,058	550	43	4,019	1,279	4,268	8,736
HINDU . .	**1,697,146**	**884,474**	**812,672**	**369,755**	**217,465**	**445,451**	**448,268**	**69,268**	**146,939**
0—1 . .	68,562	34,653	33,909	34,117	32,985	506	898	30	26
1—2 . .	33,692	16,575	17,117	15,914	15,471	637	1,618	24	28
2—3 . .	55,844	27,925	27,919	26,538	24,730	1,294	3,132	93	57
3—4 . .	52,779	25,390	27,389	23,778	24,146	1,534	3,198	78	46
4—5 . .	49,981	25,973	24,008	23,877	20,200	1,988	3,731	108	77
Total 0—5 .	*260,858*	*130,516*	*130,342*	*124,224*	*117,531*	*5,959*	*12,577*	*333*	*234*
5—10 . .	183,236	99,845	83,391	86,552	64,779	12,558	18,156	735	456
10—15 . .	148,169	82,216	65,953	59,623	26,697	21,597	37,626	996	1,630
15—20 . .	145,717	79,258	66,459	40,731	5,514	36,223	58,622	2,304	2,323
20—25 . .	170,834	87,089	83,745	26,277	1,240	56,387	77,845	4,425	4,660
25—30 . .	170,421	87,891	82,530	12,857	602	68,757	74,173	6,277	7,755
30—35 . .	147,769	74,840	72,929	6,030	360	62,373	60,451	6,437	12,118
35—40 . .	116,657	62,894	53,763	4,696	227	51,905	40,178	6,293	13,358
40—45 . .	117,525	59,379	58,146	3,097	234	47,637	33,036	8,645	24,876
45—50 . .	65,304	35,439	29,865	1,617	84	27,671	14,860	6,151	14,921
50—55 . .	77,360	39,081	38,279	1,738	91	27,740	11,525	9,603	26,663
55—60 . .	26,812	14,824	11,988	700	23	9,609	3,899	4,515	8,066
60—65 . .	40,701	18,503	22,198	851	47	11,020	3,447	6,632	18,704
65—70 . .	10,390	5,381	5,009	280	10	2,724	824	2,377	4,175
70 and over . .	15,393	7,318	8,075	482	26	3,291	1,049	3,545	7,000
MUSALMAN .	**160,887**	**82,986**	**77,901**	**38,633**	**24,954**	**38,255**	**39,013**	**6,098**	**13,934**
0—1 . .	6,024	3,073	2,951	3,055	2,930	18	21	..	..
1—2 . .	2,768	1,396	1,372	1,383	1,360	13	12	..	..
2—3 . .	5,154	2,534	2,620	2,516	2,569	18	49	..	2
3—4 . .	4,900	2,392	2,508	2,349	2,430	43	77	..	1
4—5 . .	4,934	2,486	2,448	2,419	2,245	65	196	2	7
Total 0—5 .	*23,780*	*11,881*	*11,899*	*11,722*	*11,534*	*157*	*355*	*2*	*10*
5—10 . .	17,408	9,239	8,169	8,841	7,466	382	677	16	26
10—15 . .	14,575	7,903	6,672	6,847	4,239	1,011	2,375	45	58
15—20 . .	13,647	7,257	6,390	4,777	1,007	2,379	5,203	101	180
20—25 . .	16,473	8,209	8,264	3,251	274	4,663	7,579	295	411
25—30 . .	15,390	7,830	7,560	1,552	144	5,733	6,771	545	645
30—35 . .	13,596	6,647	6,949	656	68	5,436	5,708	563	1,173
35—40 . .	10,234	5,477	4,757	310	33	4,648	3,553	519	1,171
40—45 . .	11,295	5,751	5,544	263	108	4,777	3,284	711	2,152
45—50 . .	6,334	3,644	2,690	124	13	2,923	1,366	597	1,311
50—55 . .	7,909	4,096	3,813	145	19	2,993	1,176	959	2,618
55—60 . .	2,671	1,472	1,199	32	25	1,059	354	381	820
60—65 . .	4,402	2,072	2,330	52	8	1,282	385	738	1,937
65—70 . .	1,138	615	523	20	8	378	102	217	413
70 and over . .	2,035	893	1,142	41	8	433	125	419	1,009
ANIMISTIC .	**115,411**	**58,858**	**56,553**	**29,942**	**25,563**	**26,605**	**26,956**	**2,311**	**4,034**
0—1 . .	5,741	2,872	2,869	2,861	2,865	11	4	..	..
1—2 . .	2,753	1,398	1,355	1,394	1,352	4	3	..	..
2—3 . .	4,400	2,156	2,244	2,147	2,230	9	5	..	..
3—4 . .	4,953	2,376	2,577	2,365	2,573	11	4	..	..
4—5 . .	4,793	2,392	2,401	2,384	2,390	8	2	..	..
Total 0—5 .	*22,640*	*11,194*	*11,446*	*11,151*	*11,428*	*43*	*18*	..	..
5—10 . .	15,559	8,150	7,409	7,982	7,261	160	147	8	1
10—15 . .	10,526	5,385	5,141	5,091	4,368	289	764	5	9
15—20 . .	8,882	4,264	4,618	3,136	1,790	1,076	2,789	52	39
20—25 . .	9,648	4,344	5,304	1,333	387	2,907	4,825	104	92
25—30 . .	11,111	5,707	5,404	635	138	4,887	5,122	185	144
30—35 . .	9,826	4,821	5,005	233	73	4,362	4,723	226	209
35—40 . .	8,486	4,838	3,648	136	50	4,450	3,290	252	308
40—45 . .	6,143	3,224	2,919	79	39	2,930	2,417	215	463
45—50 . .	4,355	2,570	1,785	52	6	2,258	1,210	260	569
50—55 . .	3,205	1,791	1,414	49	12	1,439	826	303	576
55—60 . .	1,812	983	829	8	1	767	411	308	417
60—65 . .	1,879	942	937	28	4	646	264	268	660
65—70 . .	677	355	322	19	1	234	88	102	233
70 and over . .	662	290	372	10	5	157	62	123	305

TABLE VII.—AGE, SEX AND CIVIL CONDITION.

BIHAR AND ORISSA STATES.

AGE AND RELIGION.	POPULATION.			UNMARRIED.		MARRIED.		WIDOWED.	
	Persons.	Males.	Females.	Males.	Females.	Males.	Females.	Males.	Females.
1	2	3	4	5	6	7	8	9	10
ALL RELIGIONS	**3,945,209**	**1,955,125**	**1,990,084**	**1,025,867**	**838,548**	**870,991**	**871,829**	**58,327**	**279,707**
0—1 . .	129,520	64,108	65,412	64,106	65,408	2	3	..	1
1—2 . .	76,260	37,469	38,791	37,464	38,785	4	6	1	..
2—3 . .	117,592	57,023	60,569	57,011	60,557	12	12	..	..
3—4 . .	146,776	69,841	76,935	69,792	76,825	48	108	1	2
4—5 . .	125,229	61,160	64,069	61,058	63,837	101	217	1	15
Total 0—5 .	*595,377*	*289,601*	*305,776*	*289,431*	*305,412*	*167*	*346*	*3*	*18*
5—10 . .	641,129	318,518	322,611	313,164	305,759	5,290	16,342	64	510
10—15 . .	462,981	247,043	215,938	223,446	156,615	23,335	57,699	262	1,624
15—20 . .	320,308	159,496	160,812	109,240	43,829	49,230	112,831	1,026	4,152
20—25 . .	318,668	140,688	177,980	49,137	10,674	88,685	158,736	2,866	8,570
25—30 . .	368,263	180,225	188,038	22,928	5,770	151,894	168,558	5,403	13,710
30—35 . .	337,116	170,970	166,146	8,376	3,876	156,195	136,910	6,399	25,351
35—40 . .	219,550	117,838	101,712	3,318	1,748	109,432	78,809	5,088	21,155
40—45 . .	238,818	121,320	117,498	2,649	1,778	110,680	66,206	7,991	49,519
45—50 . .	100,796	52,049	48,747	1,069	649	46,881	27,673	4,099	20,425
50—55 . .	153,754	75,057	78,697	1,246	981	65,052	26,066	8,759	51,650
55—60 . .	42,325	20,445	21,880	386	305	17,361	9,192	2,698	12,383
60—65 . .	93,304	39,611	53,693	667	620	31,099	7,017	7,845	46,056
65—70 . .	12,787	5,766	7,021	144	107	4,408	1,806	1,214	5,108
70 and over .	40,033	16,498	23,535	606	430	11,282	3,629	4,610	19,476
HINDU . .	**3,388,429**	**1,678,229**	**1,710,200**	**867,736**	**701,543**	**759,868**	**760,863**	**50,625**	**247,794**
0—1 . .	111,811	55,322	56,489	55,320	56,487	2	2	..	..
1—2 . .	64,281	31,685	32,596	31,681	32,590	3	6	1	..
2—3 . .	99,224	48,116	51,108	48,108	51,096	5	9	..	..
3—4 . .	123,089	58,350	64,739	58,311	64,645	39	92	..	2
4—5 . .	104,853	51,150	53,703	51,062	53,495	88	196	..	12
Total 0—5 .	*503,258*	*244,623*	*258,635*	*244,482*	*258,316*	*140*	*305*	*1*	*14*
5—10 . .	546,071	271,032	275,039	266,094	258,988	4,881	15,582	57	469
10—15 . .	397,843	212,452	185,391	190,450	130,002	21,773	53,929	229	1,460
15—20 . .	274,195	137,301	136,894	92,089	33,835	44,343	99,474	869	3,585
20—25 . .	274,170	121,402	152,768	40,969	7,777	77,988	137,611	2,445	7,380
25—30 . .	316,906	155,085	161,821	18,629	4,388	131,826	145,354	4,630	12,079
30—35 . .	290,537	147,240	143,297	6,725	2,975	135,031	118,030	5,484	22,292
35—40 . .	190,036	101,650	88,386	2,675	1,382	94,561	68,054	4,414	18,950
40—45 . .	206,349	104,075	102,274	2,174	1,412	95,142	57,329	6,759	43,533
45—50 . .	88,783	45,968	42,815	883	581	41,449	23,908	3,636	18,376
50—55 . .	134,062	65,220	69,442	1,060	800	56,550	22,630	7,610	46,012
55—60 . .	37,324	18,086	19,238	309	210	15,375	7,904	2,402	11,124
60—65 . .	81,715	34,478	47,237	544	501	27,013	6,106	6,921	40,630
65—70 . .	11,361	5,125	6,236	133	93	3,913	1,563	1,079	4,580
70 and over .	35,219	14,492	20,727	520	333	9,883	3,084	4,069	17,310
MUSALMAN .	**16,577**	**9,160**	**7,417**	**4,150**	**2,706**	**4,726**	**3,414**	**284**	**1,297**
0—1 . .	447	221	226	221	225	..	..	..	1
1—2 . .	205	101	104	101	104	..	..	..	..
2—3 . .	394	184	210	184	210	..	..	..	..
3—4 . .	478	227	251	223	249	4	2	..	..
4—5 . .	410	215	195	214	190	..	4	1	1
Total 0—5 .	*1,934*	*948*	*986*	*943*	*978*	*4*	*6*	*1*	*2*
5—10 . .	2,279	1,199	1,080	1,175	1,016	24	62	..	2
10—15 . .	1,659	960	699	877	505	81	185	2	9
15—20 . .	1,228	671	557	482	95	186	450	3	12
20—25 . .	1,548	814	734	348	39	452	643	14	52
25—30 . .	1,835	1,020	815	179	31	808	711	33	73
30—35 . .	1,728	1,013	715	74	14	912	553	27	148
35—40 . .	1,145	776	369	30	5	715	273	31	91
40—45 . .	1,137	653	484	17	12	592	269	44	203
45—50 . .	474	289	185	7	3	267	91	15	91
50—55 . .	737	402	335	8	3	350	96	44	236
55—60 . .	215	123	92	4	1	105	28	14	63
60—65 . .	403	180	223	1	2	150	33	29	188
65—70 . .	57	26	31	..	..	23	7	3	24
70 and over .	198	86	112	5	2	57	7	24	103
ANIMISTIC .	**499,762**	**247,429**	**252,333**	**142,208**	**124,200**	**98,257**	**99,496**	**6,964**	**28,637**
0—1 . .	15,464	7,689	7,775	7,689	7,774	..	1	..	..
1—2 . .	10,813	5,203	5,610	5,202	5,610	1	..	..	..
2—3 . .	16,362	7,942	8,420	7,938	8,417	4	3	..	..
3—4 . .	21,485	10,389	11,096	10,388	11,082	5	14	1	..
4—5 . .	18,354	8,948	9,406	8,935	9,387	13	17	..	2
Total 0—5 .	*82,478*	*40,171*	*42,307*	*40,147*	*42,270*	*23*	*35*	*1*	*2*
5—10 . .	85,975	42,883	43,092	42,514	42,399	363	657	6	36
10—15 . .	58,369	30,861	27,508	29,479	24,126	1,354	3,244	28	138
15—20 . .	41,656	20,005	21,651	15,582	9,298	4,287	11,828	136	525
20—25 . .	39,860	17,114	22,746	7,459	2,734	9,274	18,951	381	1,061
25—30 . .	45,938	22,369	23,569	3,922	1,279	17,763	20,828	684	1,462
30—35 . .	41,990	21,238	20,752	1,514	847	18,879	17,135	845	2,770
35—40 . .	26,143	14,124	12,019	577	345	12,951	9,707	596	1,967
40—45 . .	29,492	15,586	13,906	429	330	14,086	8,076	1,121	5,500
45—50 . .	10,638	5,381	5,257	147	108	4,800	3,313	434	1,836
50—55 . .	17,064	8,760	8,304	168	168	7,568	3,083	1,029	5,053
55—60 . .	4,311	2,004	2,307	67	87	1,678	1,132	259	1,088
60—65 . .	10,365	4,624	5,741	116	110	3,684	797	874	4,884
65—70 . .	1,242	552	690	9	14	425	211	118	485
70 and over .	4,241	1,757	2,484	78	85	1,227	499	452	1,000

PART II.—BY PROVINCES AND STATES—*continued.*

BOMBAY STATES.

AGE AND RELIGION.	POPULATION.			UNMARRIED.		MARRIED.		WIDOWED.	
	Persons.	Males.	Females.	Males.	Females.	Males.	Females.	Males.	Females.
1	2	3	4	5	6	7	8	9	10
ALL RELIGIONS	**7,411,675**	**3,765,401**	**3,646,274**	**1,733,149**	**1,150,512**	**1,801,593**	**1,878,749**	**230,758**	**617,013**
0—1	260,769	130,259	130,510	129,037	128,729	1,181	1,730	41	51
1—2	157,292	76,836	80,456	75,234	77,615	1,558	2,788	44	53
2—3	255,286	124,385	130,901	120,452	124,188	3,836	6,636	97	77
3—4	248,056	119,566	128,490	115,243	120,509	4,215	7,851	108	130
4—5	227,310	113,723	113,587	108,777	103,935	4,813	9,419	133	233
Total 0—5	*1,148,713*	*564,769*	*583,944*	*548,743*	*554,976*	*15,603*	*28,424*	*423*	*544*
5—10	929,919	478,482	451,437	445,732	375,340	31,854	74,303	896	1,794
10—15	700,518	386,267	314,251	322,207	156,400	61,735	152,596	2,325	5,255
15—20	605,120	325,094	280,026	197,656	35,601	122,296	235,747	5,142	8,678
20—25	687,337	330,240	357,097	106,994	9,457	212,813	329,303	10,433	18,337
25—30	686,780	347,146	339,634	51,034	5,215	280,442	305,334	15,670	29,085
30—35	633,907	312,228	321,679	23,710	4,212	268,940	268,544	19,578	48,923
35—40	445,602	232,559	213,043	11,570	2,249	202,829	163,563	18,160	47,231
40—45	510,283	253,594	256,689	10,112	2,733	214,208	154,932	29,274	99,024
45—50	264,425	143,790	120,635	4,370	1,108	118,494	64,719	20,926	54,808
50—55	352,157	177,760	174,397	5,283	1,480	135,143	59,596	37,334	113,321
55—60	110,089	60,375	49,714	1,551	383	43,687	16,507	15,137	32,824
60—65	208,614	93,541	115,073	2,358	833	60,612	17,807	30,571	96,433
65—70	46,394	23,277	23,117	591	144	14,142	3,372	8,544	19,601
70 and over	81,817	36,279	45,538	1,229	381	18,705	4,002	16,345	41,155
HINDU	**6,054,992**	**3,081,688**	**2,973,304**	**1,385,452**	**906,913**	**1,507,402**	**1,557,623**	**188,834**	**508,768**
0—1	212,978	106,263	106,715	105,122	105,046	1,103	1,620	38	49
1—2	130,376	63,776	66,600	62,263	63,910	1,476	2,643	37	47
2—3	210,310	102,427	107,883	98,687	101,463	3,654	6,352	86	68
3—4	202,264	97,373	104,891	93,372	97,444	3,909	7,334	92	113
4—5	184,075	92,078	91,997	87,635	83,158	4,333	8,646	110	193
Total 0—5	*940,003*	*461,917*	*478,086*	*447,079*	*451,021*	*14,475*	*26,595*	*363*	*470*
5—10	750,689	385,785	364,904	355,961	294,780	29,017	68,512	807	1,612
10—15	565,877	312,491	253,386	254,820	112,848	55,587	135,833	2,084	4,705
15—20	499,220	269,736	229,484	157,769	25,379	107,408	196,618	4,559	7,487
20—25	565,963	273,957	292,006	84,426	7,302	180,638	269,766	8,893	14,938
25—30	566,380	288,699	277,681	39,338	4,220	236,331	250,080	13,030	23,381
30—35	520,808	257,853	262,955	17,787	3,523	223,989	219,143	16,077	40,289
35—40	366,077	191,461	174,616	8,719	1,883	167,838	133,578	14,904	39,155
40—45	418,002	208,270	209,732	7,796	2,293	176,423	125,139	24,051	82,300
45—50	217,072	117,727	99,345	3,345	936	97,093	52,427	17,289	45,982
50—55	286,729	144,168	142,561	4,019	1,267	109,506	47,438	30,643	93,856
55—60	89,379	48,858	40,521	1,207	332	35,383	13,124	12,268	27,065
60—65	168,444	74,699	93,745	1,784	699	48,246	13,843	24,669	79,203
65—70	37,181	18,462	18,719	459	118	11,170	2,535	6,833	16,066
70 and over	63,168	27,605	35,563	943	312	14,298	2,992	12,364	32,259
MUSALMAN	**877,431**	**445,640**	**431,791**	**230,821**	**159,101**	**188,073**	**206,765**	**26,746**	**65,925**
0—1	30,543	15,398	15,145	15,339	15,080	58	64	1	1
1—2	16,389	7,951	8,438	7,901	8,373	47	62	3	3
2—3	28,993	14,282	14,711	14,163	14,556	112	150	7	6
3—4	29,516	14,391	15,125	14,273	14,921	113	200	5	4
4—5	28,035	14,121	13,914	13,979	13,660	134	245	8	9
Total 0—5	*133,476*	*66,143*	*67,333*	*65,655*	*66,589*	*464*	*721*	*24*	*23*
5—10	116,412	60,877	55,535	59,795	52,881	1,056	2,585	26	69
10—15	86,933	48,379	38,554	44,980	28,420	3,272	9,863	127	271
15—20	68,106	35,670	32,436	26,866	7,305	8,453	24,541	351	390
20—25	78,819	36,645	42,174	15,912	1,565	19,768	38,965	965	1,644
25—30	78,126	38,114	40,012	8,209	784	28,176	36,544	1,729	2,734
30—35	74,345	36,181	38,164	4,086	518	29,752	33,008	2,343	4,638
35—40	49,404	25,463	23,941	1,787	263	21,655	19,180	2,021	4,498
40—45	61,146	30,280	30,866	1,444	322	25,397	20,074	3,439	10,470
45—50	28,569	15,864	12,705	544	114	13,211	7,436	2,109	5,155
50—55	43,812	22,836	20,976	726	165	17,830	8,081	4,280	12,730
55—60	12,051	6,722	5,329	169	38	5,000	1,996	1,553	3,295
60—65	27,864	13,378	14,486	380	112	8,966	2,658	4,032	11,716
65—70	5,297	2,887	2,410	65	15	1,854	436	968	1,959
70 and over	13,071	6,201	6,870	203	60	3,219	677	2,779	6,133
JAIN	**277,643**	**137,132**	**140,511**	**68,896**	**44,464**	**56,714**	**61,595**	**11,523**	**34,452**
0—1	8,827	4,416	4,411	4,403	4,393	11	18	2	..
1—2	5,120	2,473	2,647	2,462	2,623	8	22	3	2
2—3	7,987	3,846	4,141	3,831	4,090	13	51	2	..
3—4	7,656	3,714	3,942	3,692	3,853	20	85	2	4
4—5	7,057	3,416	3,641	3,390	3,512	22	123	4	6
Total 0—5	*36,647*	*17,865*	*18,782*	*17,778*	*18,471*	*74*	*299*	*13*	*12*
5—10	33,619	16,701	16,918	16,499	15,505	186	1,343	16	70
10—15	29,433	15,684	13,749	14,687	9,088	1,001	4,417	46	244
15—20	23,108	12,223	10,885	8,405	916	3,688	9,441	130	528
20—25	24,992	11,755	13,237	4,545	179	6,846	11,446	364	1,612
25—30	24,056	11,455	12,601	2,568	83	8,244	9,760	643	2,758
30—35	22,317	10,503	11,814	1,512	63	8,128	8,166	863	3,585
35—40	17,120	8,751	8,369	879	45	6,906	5,226	966	3,098
40—45	19,478	9,106	10,372	729	46	6,968	5,106	1,409	5,220
45—50	11,090	5,961	5,129	420	27	4,343	2,256	1,198	2,846
50—55	14,524	6,981	7,543	455	18	4,647	2,283	1,879	5,242
55—60	5,708	3,158	2,550	158	4	1,959	738	1,041	1,808
60—65	8,619	3,769	4,850	176	8	2,182	728	1,411	4,114
65—70	2,781	1,409	1,372	62	8	748	219	604	1,145
70 and over	4,151	1,811	2,340	72	3	799	167	940	2,170

TABLE VII.—Age, Sex and Civil Condition.

CENTRAL INDIA AGENCY.

Age and Religion.	Population.			Unmarried.		Married.		Widowed.	
	Persons.	Males.	Females.	Males.	Females.	Males.	Females.	Males.	Females.
1	2	3	4	5	6	7	8	9	10
ALL RELIGIONS	**9,356,980**	**4,801,459**	**4,555,521**	**2,185,834**	**1,440,294**	**2,318,145**	**2,298,678**	**297,480**	**816,549**
0—1	329,210	165,912	163,298	164,137	162,040	1,688	1,178	87	80
1—2	215,313	105,705	109,518	104,330	107,957	1,356	1,434	109	127
2—3	280,580	134,639	145,941	130,940	142,550	3,548	3,165	151	226
3—4	315,001	150,353	164,730	146,646	159,158	3,485	4,491	219	1,090
4—5	282,407	143,768	138,729	136,982	131,704	6,498	6,151	338	874
Total 0—5	*1,422,691*	*700,466*	*722,225*	*682,987*	*703,409*	*16,575*	*16,419*	*904*	*2,397*
5—10	1,165,603	603,859	561,744	561,609	482,463	40,575	75,610	1,585	3,663
10—15	864,283	483,893	380,390	365,586	163,811	114,351	210,271	3,956	6,308
15—20	737,911	403,981	333,930	217,555	32,442	178,465	288,938	7,961	12,550
20—25	890,806	433,021	457,785	138,251	18,408	277,981	409,783	16,789	29,535
25—30	927,638	467,654	459,984	84,143	12,150	357,941	403,948	25,570	43,977
30—35	909,684	474,650	435,034	50,635	8,715	389,922	351,503	34,093	74,816
35—40	563,079	297,470	266,500	23,162	4,609	248,159	188,500	26,149	63,400
40—45	646,273	331,091	315,182	23,187	5,623	267,490	170,570	40,414	138,989
45—50	305,452	161,548	143,904	10,646	2,180	126,976	68,288	23,926	73,436
50—55	421,274	204,029	217,245	12,586	2,923	149,948	62,860	41,495	151,462
55—60	127,594	67,128	60,466	4,473	960	46,456	19,807	16,190	39,699
60—65	246,017	106,253	139,764	6,354	1,546	65,750	20,772	34,149	117,446
65—70	52,776	26,910	25,866	1,701	374	16,250	5,109	8,959	20,383
70 and over	84,999	39,506	45,493	2,869	612	21,306	6,392	15,331	38,489
HINDU	**8,262,638**	**4,241,694**	**4,020,944**	**1,911,990**	**1,242,469**	**2,062,058**	**2,043,176**	**267,646**	**735,299**
0—1	288,721	145,736	142,985	144,156	141,938	1,502	972	78	75
1—2	188,385	92,610	95,775	91,382	94,414	1,132	1,256	96	105
2—3	245,201	117,637	127,564	114,157	124,484	3,347	2,877	133	203
3—4	274,839	131,004	143,835	127,771	138,885	3,033	4,079	200	871
4—5	246,913	125,962	120,951	119,519	114,547	6,135	5,615	308	789
Total 0—5	*1,244,059*	*612,949*	*631,110*	*596,985*	*614,268*	*15,149*	*14,799*	*815*	*2,043*
5—10	1,029,043	533,377	495,666	493,614	420,477	38,321	71,901	1,442	3,288
10—15	767,773	431,335	336,438	318,996	135,426	108,658	195,234	3,681	5,778
15—20	654,645	360,849	293,796	188,659	24,810	164,976	257,645	7,214	11,341
20—25	784,659	383,001	401,658	118,389	14,881	249,476	360,079	15,136	26,698
25—30	817,023	412,250	404,773	73,478	10,102	315,774	354,830	22,998	39,841
30—35	803,041	418,642	384,399	45,342	7,105	342,619	309,546	30,681	67,748
35—40	489,035	261,077	227,958	20,964	3,731	217,438	166,495	23,675	57,732
40—45	572,133	292,199	279,934	20,814	4,600	234,890	150,225	36,495	125,109
45—50	272,313	143,276	129,037	9,675	1,766	112,004	60,830	21,597	66,441
50—55	374,890	180,792	194,098	11,363	2,418	132,133	55,677	37,296	136,003
55—60	114,343	59,937	54,416	3,986	804	41,232	17,687	14,719	35,915
60—65	218,231	93,348	124,883	5,731	1,278	56,981	18,223	30,636	105,382
65—70	46,289	23,357	22,932	1,464	301	14,033	4,435	7,860	18,196
70 and over	74,261	34,405	39,856	2,630	502	18,374	5,570	13,401	33,784
MUSALMAN	**511,200**	**266,494**	**244,706**	**123,001**	**81,699**	**125,872**	**119,839**	**17,621**	**43,168**
0—1	17,308	8,656	8,652	8,591	8,501	61	148	4	3
1—2	10,536	5,288	5,248	5,135	5,092	149	143	4	13
2—3	14,360	6,987	7,373	6,890	7,155	91	205	6	13
3—4	15,903	7,617	8,286	7,337	7,904	269	288	11	94
4—5	13,681	6,755	6,926	6,580	6,533	154	356	21	38
Total 0—5	*71,788*	*35,303*	*36,485*	*34,533*	*35,184*	*724*	*1,140*	*46*	*161*
5—10	59,670	30,760	28,910	29,267	26,196	1,407	2,490	86	234
10—15	46,943	25,933	21,010	22,737	12,531	2,991	8,140	205	339
15—20	39,503	21,402	18,101	14,478	2,508	6,417	14,951	507	643
20—25	50,033	24,500	25,533	9,901	1,601	13,544	22,382	1,055	1,550
25—30	50,863	26,339	24,523	5,421	918	19,346	21,620	1,570	3,090
30—35	49,400	25,973	23,427	2,625	886	21,300	18,866	2,048	3,675
35—40	29,830	16,815	13,015	1,044	469	14,407	9,625	1,364	2,921
40—45	37,761	19,836	17,925	1,154	509	16,473	10,217	2,209	7,199
45—50	16,756	9,508	7,248	357	202	7,802	3,473	1,349	3,573
50—55	25,444	13,125	12,319	611	323	10,123	3,866	2,391	8,130
55—60	7,104	4,109	2,995	251	90	3,017	954	841	1,951
60—65	15,599	7,485	8,114	359	173	5,126	1,416	2,000	6,523
65—70	3,716	2,206	1,510	133	42	1,387	344	686	1,124
70 and over	6,791	3,200	3,591	130	72	1,806	463	1,264	3,056
ANIMISTIC	**483,394**	**239,618**	**243,776**	**123,603**	**102,283**	**108,632**	**114,708**	**7,383**	**26,775**
0—1	20,313	10,008	10,305	9,888	10,256	115	49	5	..
1—2	14,661	7,069	7,592	6,992	7,564	68	20	9	8
2—3	18,580	8,806	9,774	8,699	9,712	95	59	12	3
3—4	21,910	10,527	11,383	10,356	11,163	166	98	5	122
4—5	19,595	9,855	9,740	9,665	9,550	183	150	7	40
Total 0—5	*95,059*	*46,265*	*48,794*	*45,600*	*48,245*	*627*	*370*	*38*	*173*
5—10	66,584	34,538	32,046	33,824	31,087	669	862	45	97
10—15	40,778	21,709	19,069	19,530	13,970	2,138	4,998	41	108
15—20	35,318	17,227	18,091	11,540	4,539	5,522	13,266	165	286
20—25	44,623	18,827	25,796	6,156	1,671	12,243	23,450	428	875
25—30	49,415	23,160	26,255	3,006	944	19,477	24,089	675	1,222
30—35	47,909	24,937	22,972	1,514	604	22,537	20,144	886	2,224
35—40	27,837	15,145	12,692	686	306	13,813	10,659	646	1,727
40—45	29,485	15,505	13,980	704	425	13,702	8,563	1,099	4,072
45—50	12,340	6,481	5,859	364	177	5,651	3,220	466	2,462
50—55	15,898	7,563	8,335	302	148	6,198	2,663	1,063	5,524
55—60	4,156	1,986	2,170	127	41	1,673	903	286	1,226
60—65	9,236	4,038	5,198	128	84	2,985	928	925	4,146
65—70	1,922	891	1,031	59	21	620	274	212	736
70 and over	2,834	1,346	1,488	61	31	577	295	408	1,162

PART II.—BY PROVINCES AND STATES—*continued.*

CENTRAL PROVINCES STATES.

AGE AND RELIGION.	POPULATION.			UNMARRIED.		MARRIED.		WIDOWED.	
	Persons.	Males.	Females.	Males.	Females.	Males.	Females.	Males.	Females.
1	2	3	4	5	6	7	8	9	10
ALL RELIGIONS	**2,117,002**	**1,053,630**	**1,063,372**	**520,273**	**426,275**	**498,638**	**509,817**	**34,719**	**127,280**
0—1	76,634	38,176	38,458	38,147	38,396	25	56	4	6
1—2	60,410	29,485	30,925	29,431	30,831	50	87	4	7
2—3	67,529	32,369	35,160	32,244	34,917	119	233	6	10
3—4	90,124	42,332	47,792	42,137	47,222	185	545	10	25
4—5	72,634	35,222	37,412	34,779	36,687	427	654	16	71
Total 0—5	*367,331*	*177,584*	*189,747*	*176,738*	*188,053*	*806*	*1,575*	*40*	*119*
5—10	332,280	166,820	165,460	160,935	153,869	5,738	11,122	147	469
10—15	210,735	115,298	95,437	97,090	59,745	17,889	35,037	319	655
15—20	146,659	74,787	71,872	42,271	14,120	31,727	56,326	789	1,426
20—25	172,134	75,699	96,435	19,944	4,309	53,703	88,913	2,052	3,213
25—30	200,855	97,114	103,741	12,234	2,144	81,477	96,180	3,403	5,417
30—35	184,259	94,061	90,198	4,809	1,550	86,326	79,476	3,926	9,172
35—40	129,925	69,127	60,798	2,262	676	63,551	51,393	3,314	8,729
40—45	122,262	65,391	56,871	1,579	623	59,412	38,735	4,400	17,513
45—50	63,402	32,907	30,495	664	241	29,672	19,965	2,571	10,289
50—55	74,569	37,884	36,685	726	346	32,844	15,039	4,314	21,300
55—60	24,608	11,284	13,324	183	86	9,670	6,788	1,431	6,450
60—65	52,252	22,016	30,236	431	276	17,355	5,376	4,230	24,584
65—70	9,777	4,015	5,762	116	45	2,943	1,554	956	4,163
70 and over	25,954	9,643	16,311	291	192	6,525	2,338	2,827	13,781
HINDU	**1,311,388**	**650,807**	**660,581**	**302,654**	**243,914**	**325,708**	**331,715**	**22,445**	**84,952**
0—1	48,423	24,091	24,332	24,073	24,285	17	43	1	4
1—2	36,193	17,746	18,447	17,711	18,379	31	63	4	5
2—3	40,000	19,251	20,749	19,166	20,584	83	160	3	5
3—4	52,612	24,684	27,928	24,534	27,486	145	425	5	17
4—5	42,639	20,761	21,878	20,307	21,291	361	541	13	46
Total 0—5	*219,867*	*106,533*	*113,334*	*105,881*	*112,025*	*626*	*1,232*	*26*	*77*
5—10	199,063	99,789	99,294	94,579	89,161	5,100	9,825	110	318
10—15	128,275	70,384	57,891	55,472	31,159	14,680	26,319	232	413
15—20	91,238	47,026	44,212	23,153	6,395	23,319	36,927	554	890
20—25	108,219	47,899	60,320	10,385	1,867	36,197	56,458	1,317	1,995
25—30	126,511	61,546	64,965	6,559	1,084	52,721	60,429	2,266	3,452
30—35	115,265	58,961	56,304	2,788	864	53,594	49,586	2,579	5,844
35—40	81,585	42,747	38,838	1,341	384	39,240	32,769	2,166	5,685
40—45	77,694	40,920	36,774	970	356	37,105	24,788	2,845	11,630
45—50	41,200	20,973	20,227	439	123	18,832	13,120	1,702	6,984
50—55	48,474	24,194	24,280	462	193	20,990	9,719	2,742	14,368
55—60	16,413	7,345	9,067	116	43	6,307	4,576	922	4,448
60—65	34,081	13,868	20,213	261	145	10,952	3,600	2,655	16,568
65—70	6,563	2,579	3,984	69	22	1,909	1,028	601	2,934
70 and over	16,931	6,043	10,888	179	103	4,136	1,439	1,728	9,346
MUSALMAN	**20,120**	**10,180**	**9,940**	**4,787**	**3,304**	**4,947**	**4,922**	**446**	**1,714**
0—1	690	355	335	354	335	1	..	..	..
1—2	415	202	213	201	212	1	1	..	..
2—3	519	254	265	252	264	2	1	..	..
3—4	585	263	322	262	313	1	9	..	..
4—5	518	246	272	246	262	..	8	..	2
Total 0—5	*2,727*	*1,320*	*1,407*	*1,315*	*1,386*	*5*	*19*	..	*2*
5—10	2,618	1,355	1,263	1,321	1,180	31	72	3	3
10—15	1,906	1,034	872	918	540	112	311	4	12
15—20	1,435	790	645	528	90	255	533	7	22
20—25	1,882	904	978	323	32	535	899	46	47
25—30	2,120	1,034	1,086	164	15	807	985	63	86
30—35	1,981	940	901	70	19	833	832	38	140
35—40	1,332	761	571	56	7	657	424	46	140
40—45	1,409	732	677	42	4	643	414	47	250
45—50	665	357	308	21	2	315	149	21	157
50—55	830	405	425	11	4	343	149	51	272
55—60	255	136	119	3	..	120	42	13	77
60—65	587	236	351	6	6	178	65	52	280
65—70	100	54	46	2	..	35	12	17	34
70 and over	323	122	201	5	1	79	16	38	184
ANIMISTIC	**745,434**	**372,384**	**373,050**	**201,130**	**169,218**	**159,834**	**165,012**	**11,411**	**38,826**
0—1	25,896	12,928	12,968	12,918	12,953	7	13	3	2
1—2	22,130	10,698	11,432	10,680	11,408	18	22		3
2—3	25,614	12,207	13,407	12,170	13,330	34	72	3	5
3—4	34,973	16,461	18,512	16,417	18,393	30	111	5	8
4—5	27,900	13,458	14,442	13,370	14,316	76	103	3	23
Total 0—5	*136,513*	*65,752*	*70,761*	*65,564*	*70,400*	*174*	*321*	*14*	*40*
5—10	123,559	62,151	61,408	61,531	60,068	587	1,193	33	147
10—15	75,816	41,172	34,644	38,095	26,412	3,002	8,016	75	216
15—20	51,269	25,576	25,693	17,594	7,291	7,764	17,913	218	489
20—25	59,133	25,610	33,523	8,891	2,347	16,061	30,057	658	1,119
25—30	69,062	33,001	36,061	5,373	1,004	26,595	33,243	1,033	1,814
30—35	63,927	32,532	31,395	1,903	650	29,361	27,686	1,268	3,059
35—40	44,806	24,417	20,389	840	272	22,500	17,329	1,068	2,788
40—45	41,261	22,690	18,571	544	253	20,686	12,938	1,460	5,380
45—50	20,540	11,050	9,490	196	113	10,038	6,349	816	3,037
50—55	24,040	12,640	11,400	243	140	10,925	4,875	1,473	6,385
55—60	7,421	3,573	3,848	56	40	3,041	2,016	476	1,792
60—65	16,756	7,555	9,201	160	120	5,924	1,743	1,471	7,338
65—70	2,959	1,319	1,640	45	23	953	465	321	1,132
70 and over	8,363	3,346	5,017	105	85	2,214	848	1,027	4,084

TABLE VII.—Age, Sex and Civil Condition.

HYDERABAD STATE.

Age and Religion.	Population.			Unmarried.		Married.		Widowed.	
	Persons.	Males.	Females.	Males.	Females.	Males.	Females.	Males.	Females.
1	2	3	4	5	6	7	8	9	10
ALL RELIGIONS	**13,374,676**	**6,797,118**	**6,577,558**	**3,022,032**	**1,941,134**	**3,495,695**	**3,473,758**	**279,391**	**1,162,666**
0—1 . .	371,040	179,458	191,582	178,918	190,433	520	1,074	20	75
1—2 . .	254,336	120,746	133,590	120,085	131,764	638	1,681	23	145
2—3 . .	470,646	226,711	243,935	224,800	238,348	1,853	5,416	58	171
3—4 . .	413,504	197,604	215,900	194,879	208,150	2,661	7,443	64	307
4—5 . .	414,133	206,101	208,032	202,028	195,173	3,920	12,299	153	560
Total 0—5 .	*1,923,659*	*930,620*	*993,039*	*920,710*	*963,868*	*9,592*	*27,913*	*318*	*1,258*
5—10 . .	1,695,021	857,599	837,422	823,363	648,795	32,646	183,093	1,590	5,534
10—15 . .	1,392,802	764,794	628,008	641,523	204,488	119,116	412,333	4,155	11,187
15—20 . .	1,004,122	499,688	504,434	296,326	38,004	198,711	451,683	4,651	14,747
20—25 . .	1,164,165	536,898	627,267	163,080	21,189	365,008	574,410	8,810	31,668
25—30 . .	1,223,496	631,250	592,246	79,219	15,370	536,552	528,970	15,479	47,906
30—35 . .	1,190,977	584,516	606,461	35,722	14,398	528,124	501,640	20,670	90,423
35—40 . .	727,312	402,969	324,343	14,903	7,316	369,837	241,615	18,229	75,412
40—45 . .	972,672	504,379	468,293	17,431	10,358	453,174	278,107	33,774	179,828
45—50 . .	438,854	253,855	184,999	6,822	3,237	225,555	90,414	21,478	91,348
50—55 . .	686,953	353,934	333,019	9,859	5,809	299,528	109,122	44,547	218,088
55—60 . .	174,675	99,381	75,294	3,011	1,305	80,377	21,149	15,493	52,840
60—65 . .	461,796	222,792	239,004	5,400	3,748	171,388	35,773	46,004	199,483
65—70 . .	80,558	42,351	38,207	1,091	674	30,995	5,182	10,265	32,401
70 and over .	237,614	112,092	125,522	3,572	2,575	74,592	12,404	33,928	110,543
HINDU . .	**11,626,146**	**5,897,158**	**5,728,988**	**2,561,643**	**1,627,038**	**3,088,085**	**3,074,231**	**247,430**	**1,027,719**
0—1 . .	324,100	156,497	167,603	155,986	166,508	492	1,028	19	67
1—2 . .	225,778	107,072	118,706	106,425	116,919	624	1,646	23	141
2—3 . .	412,897	198,821	214,076	196,981	208,575	1,787	5,334	53	167
3—4 . .	362,487	173,378	189,109	170,779	181,599	2,537	7,209	62	301
4—5 . .	359,006	178,881	180,125	175,102	167,719	3,638	11,867	141	539
Total 0—5 .	*1,684,268*	*814,649*	*869,619*	*805,273*	*841,320*	*9,078*	*27,084*	*298*	*1,215*
5—10 . .	1,469,492	743,647	725,845	711,568	544,901	30,635	175,795	1,444	5,149
10—15 . .	1,204,040	662,127	541,913	545,570	146,113	112,848	385,520	3,709	10,280
15—20 . .	871,698	432,742	438,956	241,533	23,842	186,826	401,539	4,383	13,575
20—25 . .	1,006,989	461,425	545,564	121,819	16,462	331,661	500,677	7,945	28,425
25—30 . .	1,065,817	549,561	516,256	58,256	12,047	477,598	461,267	13,707	42,942
30—35 . .	1,036,323	508,357	527,966	27,144	12,172	462,946	435,009	18,267	80,785
35—40 . .	636,756	350,714	286,042	11,685	6,288	322,911	211,782	16,118	67,972
40—45 . .	844,916	437,735	407,181	14,055	8,980	393,586	239,093	30,094	159,108
45—50 . .	386,557	222,189	164,368	5,768	2,863	197,176	79,439	19,245	82,066
50—55 . .	596,775	306,266	290,509	8,180	4,992	258,358	93,673	39,728	191,844
55—60 .	152,500	86,044	66,456	2,551	1,123	69,611	18,286	13,882	47,047
60—65 . .	398,649	191,004	207,645	4,463	3,232	146,140	30,296	40,401	174,117
65—70 . .	69,961	36,389	33,572	900	578	26,463	4,447	9,026	28,552
70 and over .	201,405	94,309	107,096	2,878	2,130	62,248	10,324	29,183	94,642
MUSALMAN .	**1,380,990**	**706,821**	**674,169**	**352,479**	**240,559**	**328,278**	**317,986**	**26,064**	**115,624**
0—1 . .	36,059	17,648	18,411	17,647	18,411	1	..	..	..
1—2 . .	22,435	10,778	11,657	10,778	11,656	..	1	..	..
2—3 . .	42,674	20,629	22,045	20,625	22,045	4	..	..	..
3—4 . .	36,507	17,372	19,135	17,324	19,063	48	72	..	..
4—5 . .	40,621	20,226	20,395	20,019	20,140	207	255	..	..
Total 0—5 .	*178,296*	*86,653*	*91,643*	*86,393*	*91,315*	*260*	*328*	..	..
5—10 . .	170,504	85,612	84,892	84,101	80,230	1,393	4,364	118	298
10—15 . .	148,779	80,349	68,430	75,149	45,457	4,873	22,210	327	763
15—20 . .	107,026	53,754	53,272	44,156	11,380	9,398	40,933	200	959
20—25 . .	124,630	59,415	65,215	31,666	3,733	27,086	58,728	663	2,754
25—30 . .	125,685	65,089	60,596	15,868	2,767	47,828	53,497	1,393	4,332
30—35 . .	121,511	59,198	62,313	5,926	1,698	51,331	52,422	1,941	8,193
35—40 . .	73,303	41,878	31,425	2,472	872	37,738	24,003	1,668	6,560
40—45 . .	103,692	53,349	50,343	2,675	1,121	47,634	31,370	3,040	17,852
45—50 . .	43,253	25,887	17,366	842	307	23,223	8,973	1,822	8,086
50—55 . .	74,118	38,725	35,393	1,417	694	33,353	12,173	3,955	22,526
55—60 . .	18,730	11,090	7,640	375	147	9,421	2,417	1,294	5,076
60—65 . .	52,606	26,187	26,419	735	417	20,789	4,418	4,663	21,584
65—70 . .	9,056	5,015	4,041	131	84	3,854	545	1,030	3,412
70 and over .	29.801	14,620	15,181	573	337	10,097	1,605	3,950	13,239
ANIMISTIC .	**285,722**	**149,023**	**136,699**	**84,100**	**58,731**	**60,861**	**63,830**	**4,062**	**14,138**
0—1 . .	8,488	4,149	4,339	4,128	4,291	21	43	..	5
1—2 . .	4,850	2,309	2,541	2,298	2,507	11	30	..	4
2—3 . .	12,614	6,094	6,520	6,043	6,446	47	72	4	2
3—4 . .	12,068	5,697	6,371	5,628	6,219	67	149	2	3
4—5 . .	12,200	5,902	6,298	5,844	6,128	47	150	11	20
Total 0—5 .	*50,220*	*24,151*	*26,069*	*23,941*	*25,591*	*193*	*444*	*17*	*34*
5—10 . .	44,880	23,251	21,629	22,730	18,983	498	2,578	23	68
10—15 . .	31,273	17,636	13,637	16,440	10,326	1,092	3,290	104	121
15—20 . .	18,846	9,954	8,892	8,106	1,925	1,793	6,823	55	144
20—25 . .	23,273	10,593	12,680	5,952	691	4,468	11,672	173	317
25—30 . .	23,902	11,957	11,945	3,284	347	8,416	11,203	257	395
30—35 . .	25,990	13,167	12,823	2,067	376	10,774	11,398	326	1,049
35—40 . .	12,677	7,720	4,957	499	91	6,910	4,346	311	520
40—45 . .	18,836	10,333	8,503	466	189	9,403	6,195	462	2,119
45—50 . .	6,536	4,268	2,268	127	28	3,889	1,485	252	755
50—55 . .	12,488	6,922	5,566	184	86	6,185	2,679	553	2,801
55—60 . .	2,377	1,585	792	46	14	1,345	323	194	465
60—65 . .	8,276	4,350	3,926	136	79	3,561	880	653	2,967
65—70 . .	1,061	677	384	37	12	506	105	134	287
70 and over .	5,087	2,459	2,628	83	93	1,828	409	548	2,126

PART II.—BY PROVINCES AND STATES—*continued.*

KASHMIR STATE.

Age and Religion.	Population.			Unmarried.		Married.		Widowed.	
	Persons.	Males.	Females.	Males.	Females.	Males.	Females.	Males.	Females.
1	2	3	4	5	6	7	8	9	10
ALL RELIGIONS	**3,103,501**	**1,644,978**	**1,458,523**	**865,570**	**565,366**	**689,990**	**716,962**	**89,418**	**176,195**
0—1 . .	140,651	71,021	69,630	71,014	69,623	7	6	..	1
1—2 . .	35,648	18,235	17,413	18,233	17,409	2	4	..	..
2—3 . .	86,165	43,482	42,683	43,468	42,628	14	54	..	1
3—4 . .	103,754	52,238	51,516	52,147	51,304	88	208	3	4
4—5 . .	98,026	50,218	47,808	50,127	47,551	89	241	2	16
Total 0—5 .	*464,244*	*235,194*	*229,050*	*234,989*	*228,515*	*200*	*513*	*5*	*22*
5—10 . .	457,859	237,499	220,360	234,769	209,139	2,614	10,817	116	404
10—15 . .	347,154	192,256	154,898	176,511	98,344	15,392	55,329	353	1,225
15—20 . .	270,870	143,115	127,755	99,719	18,240	42,080	105,834	1,316	3,681
20—25 . .	265,671	131,613	134,058	53,657	4,847	74,581	123,161	3,375	6,050
25—30 . .	251,282	129,198	122,084	28,392	1,987	95,086	111,911	5,720	8,186
30—35 . .	244,218	130,041	114,177	14,067	1,351	108,162	100,218	7,812	12,608
35—40 . .	165,087	91,287	73,800	6,274	614	78,520	61,723	6,493	11,463
40—45 . .	187,231	98,037	89,194	6,154	754	81,961	64,595	9,922	23,845
45—50 . .	95,752	54,395	41,357	2,702	294	45,394	27,213	6,299	13,850
50—55 . .	130,547	72,463	58,084	3,088	385	57,581	29,152	11,794	28,547
55—60 . .	37,104	22,292	14,812	953	95	17,031	6,973	4,308	7,744
60—65 . .	100,869	56,967	43,902	2,217	379	40,829	12,562	13,921	30,961
65—70 . .	19,383	12,014	7,369	456	85	8,272	2,279	3,286	5,005
70 and over .	66,230	38,607	27,623	1,622	337	22,287	4,682	14,698	22,604
HINDU . .	**689,047**	**371,805**	**317,242**	**190,494**	**95,615**	**152,145**	**155,597**	**29,166**	**66,030**
0—1 . .	24,980	12,710	12,270	12,710	12,270	..	..	..	..
1—2 . .	7,174	3,686	3,488	3,686	3,487	..	1	..	..
2—3 . .	14,271	7,193	7,078	7,190	7,064	3	13	..	1
3—4 . .	17,592	8,872	8,720	8,851	8,669	19	51	2	..
4—5 . .	17,683	9,011	8,672	8,995	8,595	14	69	2	8
Total 0—5 .	*81,700*	*41,472*	*40,228*	*41,432*	*40,085*	*36*	*134*	*4*	*9*
5—10 . .	85,762	43,449	42,313	42,907	37,809	497	4,328	45	176
10—15 . .	71,020	40,544	30,476	37,571	14,289	2,873	15,615	100	572
15—20 . .	57,895	30,716	27,179	22,862	1,960	7,547	23,808	307	1,411
20—25 . .	58,050	30,282	27,768	15,410	422	14,023	24,804	849	2,542
25—30 . .	62,877	33,540	29,337	10,873	267	20,789	24,849	1,878	4,221
30—35 . .	60,146	32,486	27,660	6,313	241	23,707	21,428	2,466	5,991
35—40 . .	40,207	22,983	17,224	3,385	97	17,320	11,977	2,278	5,150
40—45 . .	47,812	25,307	22,505	3,263	137	18,591	12,894	3,453	9,474
45—50 . .	25,461	14,977	10,484	1,592	41	11,065	5,164	2,320	5,279
50—55 . .	34,490	19,349	15,141	1,921	83	13,392	5,286	4,036	9,772
55—60 . .	11,532	6,970	4,562	594	19	4,704	1,520	1,672	3,023
60—65 . .	27,076	15,116	11,960	1,328	80	9,446	2,189	4,342	9,691
65—70 . .	6,075	3,722	2,353	236	11	2,352	627	1,134	1,715
70 and over .	18,944	10,892	8,052	807	74	5,803	974	4,282	7,094
BUDDHIST .	**36,322**	**18,170**	**18,152**	**7,644**	**8,023**	**9,463**	**8,102**	**1,063**	**2,027**
0—1 . .	878	418	460	415	459	3	1	..	..
1—2 . .	385	172	213	171	213	1	..	..	..
2—3 . .	612	284	328	280	327	4	1	..	..
3—4 . .	836	403	433	396	431	7	2	..	..
4—5 . .	753	349	404	336	404	13	..	..	..
Total 0—5 .	*3,464*	*1,626*	*1,838*	*1,598*	*1,834*	*28*	*4*	..	..
5—10 . .	4,036	2,025	2,011	1,872	1,985	150	23	3	3
10—15 . .	3,232	1,633	1,599	1,332	1,510	295	86	6	3
15—20 . .	3,122	1,562	1,560	906	1,121	642	429	14	10
20—25 . .	2,942	1,471	1,471	465	603	969	818	37	50
25—30 . .	2,927	1,524	1,403	339	302	1,140	1,035	45	66
30—35 . .	2,872	1,453	1,419	223	168	1,182	1,165	48	86
35—40 . .	2,345	1,180	1,165	166	94	978	966	36	105
40—45 . .	2,541	1,236	1,305	176	94	1,000	1,025	60	186
45—50 . .	1,977	1,011	966	149	57	803	754	59	155
50—55 . .	1,855	896	959	102	67	684	616	110	276
55—60 . .	1,148	597	551	80	39	459	350	58	162
60—65 . .	1,677	821	856	93	56	548	444	180	356
65—70 . .	836	435	401	65	39	267	205	103	157
70 and over .	1,348	700	648	78	54	318	182	304	412
MUSALMAN .	**2,344,206**	**1,236.565**	**1,107,641**	**657,268**	**455,445**	**521,035**	**545,853**	**58,262**	**106,343**
0—1 . .	113,167	57,024	56,143	57,020	56,137	4	5	..	1
1—2 . .	27,730	14,175	13,555	14,174	13,552	1	3	..	..
2—3 . .	70,327	35,532	34,795	35,526	34,757	6	38	..	..
3—4 . .	84,197	42,406	41,791	42.344	41,633	62	154	..	4
4—5 . .	78,441	40,265	38,176	40,204	38,001	61	167	..	8
Total 0—5 .	*373,862*	*189,402*	*184,460*	*189,268*	*184,080*	*134*	*367*	..	*13*
5—10 . .	362,751	189,229	173,522	187,216	166,931	1,947	6,370	66	221
10—15 . .	269,009	147,868	121,141	135,496	81,436	12,129	39,065	243	640
15—20 . .	206,851	109,196	97,655	74,703	15,032	33,509	80,385	984	2,238
20—25 . .	201,927	98,479	103,448	37,176	3,791	58,834	96,260	2,469	3,397
25—30 . .	182,640	92,634	90,006	16,836	1,403	72,063	84,778	3,735	3,825
30—35 . .	178,470	94,655	83,815	7,398	924	82,039	76,505	5,218	6,386
35—40 . .	120,767	66,076	54,691	2,639	410	59,319	48.202	4,118	6,079
40—45 . .	134,961	70,476	64,485	2,051	511	61,519	50,067	6,306	13,907
45—50 . .	67,303	37,781	29,522	923	192	33,012	21,049	3,846	8,281
50—55 . .	92,878	51,442	41,436	1,028	227	42,893	23,009	7,521	18,200
55—60 . .	24,015	14.469	9,546	265	36	11,691	5,044	2,513	4,466
60—65 . .	71,187	40,483	30,704	780	236	30,427	9,838	9,276	20,630
65—70 . .	12,245	7,711	4,534	149	35	5,545	1,430	2,017	3,069
70 and over .	45,340	26,664	18,676	720	201	15,974	3,484	9,970	14,991

TABLE VII.—Age, Sex and Civil Condition.

MADRAS STATES.

Age and Religion.	Population.			Unmarried.		Married.		Widowed.	
	Persons.	Males.	Females.	Males.	Females.	Males.	Females.	Males.	Females.
1	2	3	4	5	6	7	8	9	10
ALL RELIGIONS	**4,811,841**	**2,411,758**	**2,400,083**	**1,317,948**	**1,049,767**	**993,415**	**993,088**	**100,395**	**357,228**
0—1	135,072	65,091	69,981	65,086	69,977	5	4	..	..
1—2	110,952	54,415	56,537	54,413	56,534	2	2	..	1
2—3	144,917	71,441	73,476	71,432	73,462	8	13	1	1
3—4	145,400	71,566	73,834	71,545	73,801	21	31	..	2
4—5	124,601	62,228	62,373	62,211	62,348	16	24	1	1
Total 0—5	*660,942*	*324,741*	*336,201*	*324,687*	*336,122*	*52*	*74*	*2*	*5*
5—10	638,121	320,282	317,839	319,496	315,968	640	1,568	146	303
10—15	578,458	299,590	278,868	296,655	253,524	2,662	24,496	273	848
15—20	454,565	223,542	231,023	195,175	94,613	27,263	131,336	1,104	5,074
20—25	425,683	202,241	223,442	106,664	24,066	91,699	187,179	3,878	12,197
25—30	428,354	208,802	219,552	45,618	10,080	156,052	189,949	7,132	19,523
30—35	345,988	172,752	173,236	14,157	5,107	150,324	142,538	8,271	25,591
35—40	319,620	172,146	147,474	6,543	3,239	156,735	113,357	8,868	30,878
40—45	257,323	132,731	124,502	3,402	2,325	119,547	80,060	9,782	42,307
45—50	202,433	109,003	93,430	2,083	1,548	97,006	52,742	9,914	39,140
50—55	170,328	84,403	85,925	1,411	1,145	71,408	34,858	11,584	49,922
55—60	111,471	58,570	52,901	716	679	48,171	17,873	9,683	34,349
60—65	105,111	49,670	55,441	617	680	37,167	10,628	11,886	44,133
65—70	47,649	23,943	23,706	289	274	17,106	3,534	6,548	19,898
70 and over	65,795	29,342	36,453	435	497	17,583	2,896	11,324	33,060
HINDU	**3,321,755**	**1,652,659**	**1,669,096**	**912,634**	**719,306**	**666,605**	**674,017**	**73,420**	**275,773**
0—1	92,709	44,733	47,976	44,728	47,972	5	4	..	..
1—2	73,164	35,877	37,287	35,875	37,284	2	2	..	1
2—3	96,450	47,698	48,752	47,689	48,742	8	10	1	..
3—4	98,603	48,485	50,118	48,466	50,089	19	27	..	2
4—5	84,141	42,116	42,025	42,101	42,003	14	22	1	..
Total 0—5	*445,067*	*218,909*	*226,158*	*218,859*	*226,090*	*48*	*65*	*2*	*3*
5—10	426,523	214,294	212,229	213,736	210,880	452	1,116	106	233
10—15	388,248	200,951	187,297	199,473	171,652	1,298	14,981	180	664
15—20	311,303	151,584	159,719	138,510	71,867	12,268	83,683	806	4,169
20—25	292,505	138,006	154,499	81,398	19,175	53,578	125,190	3,030	10,134
25—30	298,220	143,951	154,269	36,551	7,707	101,889	130,683	5,511	15,879
30—35	243,637	119,981	123,656	11,684	4,046	101,808	99,268	6,489	20,342
35—40	224,427	119,374	105,053	5,869	2,534	107,300	78,617	6,705	23,902
40—45	184,900	93,993	90,907	2,776	1,679	84,017	56,694	7,200	32,534
45—50	143,688	76,466	67,222	1,650	1,220	67,744	36,433	7,072	29,569
50—55	123,658	60,357	63,301	1,106	882	50,911	24,247	8,340	38,172
55—60	79,691	41,291	38,400	540	501	33,942	11,756	6,809	26,143
60—65	77,103	35,752	41,351	476	501	26,710	7,084	8,566	33,766
65—70	34,319	16,770	17,549	203	202	11,944	2,281	4,623	15,066
70 and over	48,466	20,980	27,486	303	370	12,696	1,919	7,961	25,197
MUSALMAN	**314,498**	**160,692**	**153,806**	**91,578**	**69,931**	**64,124**	**64,115**	**4,990**	**19,760**
0—1	8,875	4,315	4,560	4,315	4,560	..	..	..	..
1—2	7,478	3,698	3,780	3,698	3,780	..	..	..	..
2—3	10,234	5,051	5,183	5,051	5,181	..	1	..	1
3—4	10,179	5,098	5,081	5,097	5,078	1	3	..	..
4—5	9,101	4,495	4,606	4,495	4,603	..	2	..	1
Total 0—5	*45,867*	*22,657*	*23,210*	*22,656*	*23,202*	*1*	*6*	..	*2*
5—10	44,389	22,286	22,103	22,260	22,001	17	88	9	14
10—15	39,617	20,751	18,866	20,665	17,421	76	1,398	10	52
15—20	29,597	14,788	14,809	13,641	5,234	1,071	9,176	76	399
20—25	28,680	13,716	14,964	7,989	1,072	5,443	13,113	284	779
25—30	27,383	13,346	14,037	2,958	350	9,896	12,598	492	1,089
30—35	21,857	11,106	10,751	848	177	9,819	9,056	439	1,518
35—40	20,196	11,214	8,982	282	187	10,545	7,040	436	1,805
40—45	16,318	8,727	7,591	134	131	8,173	4,925	420	2,535
45—50	11,939	6,807	5,132	54	49	6,337	2,954	416	2,129
50—55	10,047	5,346	4,701	55	50	4,722	1,939	569	2,712
55—60	6,163	3,550	2,613	22	33	3,110	882	418	1,698
60—65	6,303	3,167	3,136	24	40	2,572	627	571	2,469
65—70	2,517	1,461	1,056	21	10	1,127	160	318	886
70 and over	3,625	1,770	1,855	18	24	1,215	158	537	1,673
CHRISTIAN	**1,154,209**	**587,412**	**566,797**	**308,163**	**256,063**	**257,729**	**250,061**	**21,500**	**60,673**
0—1	32,891	15,755	17,136	15,755	17,136	..	..	..	..
1—2	29,997	14,690	15,307	14,690	15,307	..	..	..	..
2—3	37,648	18,411	19,237	18,411	19,235	..	2	..	..
3—4	36,017	17,695	18,322	17,694	18,321	1	1	..	..
4—5	30,785	15,306	15,479	15,304	15,479	2	..	..	..
Total 0—5	*167,338*	*81,857*	*85,481*	*81,854*	*85,478*	*3*	*3*	..	..
5—10	164,393	82,208	82,185	82,009	81,772	169	358	30	56
10—15	148,174	76,643	71,531	75,283	63,361	1,278	8,040	82	130
15—20	111,696	56,235	55,461	42,190	17,051	13,829	37,927	216	483
20—25	102,587	49,726	52,861	16,877	3,665	32,303	47,961	546	1,235
25—30	100,630	50,504	50,126	5,932	1,977	43,480	45,669	1,092	2,480
30—35	78,819	40,839	37,980	1,582	866	37,960	33,459	1,297	3,655
35—40	73,361	40,613	32,748	912	560	38,031	27,103	1,670	5,085
40—45	54,828	29,268	25,560	480	412	26,691	18,031	2,097	7,117
45—50	45,875	25,165	20,710	372	269	22,415	13,095	2,378	7,346
50—55	35,900	18,282	17,618	245	206	15,404	8,511	2,633	8,901
55—60	25,179	13,456	11,723	153	145	10,895	5,151	2,408	6,427
60—65	21,313	10,539	10,774	117	137	7,720	2,868	2,702	7,769
65—70	10,666	5,619	5,047	64	62	3,967	1,076	1,588	3,909
70 and over	13,450	6,458	6,992	113	102	3,584	809	2,761	6,081

Part II.—By Provinces and States—*continued.*

MYSORE STATE.

Age and Religion.	Population.			Unmarried.		Married.		Widowed.	
	Persons.	Males.	Females.	Males.	Females.	Males.	Females.	Males.	Females.
1	2	3	4	5	6	7	8	9	10
ALL RELIGIONS	**5,806,193**	**2,934,621**	**2,871,572**	**1,597,180**	**1,106,337**	**1,197,404**	**1,205,726**	**140,037**	**559,509**
0—1	143,543	69,993	73,550	69,993	73,550	..	..	..	..
1—2	79,555	38,326	41,229	38,324	41,228	2	1	..	..
2—3	160,083	77,168	82,915	77,166	82,914	2	1	..	..
3—4	163,121	78,274	84,847	78,272	84,844	2	3	..	..
4—5	152,872	75,054	77,818	75,051	77,805	3	12	..	1
Total 0—5	*699,174*	*338,815*	*360,359*	*338,806*	*360,341*	*9*	*17*	..	*1*
5—10	752,260	368,259	384,001	368,167	380,959	90	2,987	2	55
10—15	719,828	368,867	350,961	367,068	272,948	1,771	76,343	28	1,670
15—20	526,809	272,949	253,860	249,258	56,630	23,336	189,290	355	7,940
20—25	521,166	253,713	267,453	150,526	13,511	101,014	232,838	2,173	21,104
25—30	466,944	238,075	228,869	64,271	5,808	168,865	193,515	4,939	29,546
30—35	419,756	208,346	211,410	23,848	4,239	176,597	164,160	7,901	43,011
35—40	339,609	183,837	155,772	11,043	2,656	163,083	109,404	9,711	43,712
40—45	363,715	186,879	176,836	8,739	3,008	162,997	101,374	15,143	72,454
45—50	248,586	136,455	112,131	4,890	1,635	117,389	54,456	14,176	56,040
50—55	268,695	134,785	133,910	4,396	1,943	109,378	44,904	21,011	87,063
55—60	128,028	70,039	57,989	1,949	701	55,047	15,628	13,043	41,660
60—65	176,177	87,401	88,776	2,356	1,130	63,920	13,259	21,125	74,357
65—70	58,307	30,113	28,194	671	281	20,944	3,389	8,498	24,524
70 and over	117,139	56,088	61,051	1,192	547	33,964	4,132	20,932	56,372
HINDU	**5,340,908**	**2,689,851**	**2,651,057**	**1,457,658**	**1,011,812**	**1,101,037**	**1,113,987**	**131,156**	**525,258**
0—1	130,636	63,678	66,958	63,678	66,958	..	..	..	..
1—2	72,776	35,018	37,758	35,016	37,757	2	1	..	..
2—3	146,236	70,305	75,931	70,303	75,930	2	1	..	..
3—4	149,388	71,639	77,749	71,637	77,747	2	2	..	..
4—5	139,024	68,243	70,781	68,240	70,769	3	11	..	1
Total 0—5	*638,060*	*308,883*	*329,177*	*308,874*	*329,161*	*9*	*15*	..	*1*
5—10	687,651	336,193	351,458	336,118	348,560	74	2,845	1	53
10—15	663,213	338,483	324,730	336,838	250,363	1,619	72,761	26	1,606
15—20	483,607	250,359	233,248	227,972	51,252	22,054	174,497	333	7,499
20—25	477,278	230,927	246,351	135,164	12,164	93,764	214,210	1,999	19,977
25—30	428,139	216,911	211,228	57,845	5,329	154,545	178,009	4,521	27,890
30—35	386,359	190,673	195,686	21,833	3,866	161,572	151,273	7,268	40,547
35—40	314,145	169,114	145,031	10,258	2,453	149,731	101,360	9,125	41,218
40—45	336,757	172,350	164,407	8,204	2,812	149,952	93,503	14,194	68,098
45—50	231,333	126,443	104,890	4,635	1,537	108,398	50,562	13,410	52,791
50—55	248,989	124,506	124,483	4,148	1,818	100,530	41,381	19,328	81,284
55—60	119,438	65,122	54,316	1,828	654	50,946	14,510	12,348	39,152
60—65	163,186	80,522	82,664	2,204	1,063	57,591	12,136	20,727	69,465
65—70	54,435	27,897	26,538	821	265	19,289	3,124	7,987	23,149
70 and over	108,318	51,468	56,850	1,116	515	30,963	3,801	19,389	52,534
MUSALMAN	**314,494**	**165,824**	**148,670**	**94,002**	**62,841**	**66,142**	**62,432**	**5,680**	**23,397**
0—1	8,890	4,392	4,498	4,392	4,498	..	..	..	..
1—2	4,567	2,244	2,323	2,244	2,323	..	..	..	..
2—3	9,538	4,693	4,845	4,693	4,845	..	..	..	..
3—4	9,357	4,483	4,874	4,483	4,873	..	1	..	..
4—5	9,650	4,733	4,917	4,733	4,917	..	..	..	..
Total 0—5	*42,002*	*20,545*	*21,457*	*20,545*	*21,456*	..	1	..	..
5—10	44,824	22,278	22,546	22,269	22,443	9	101	..	2
10—15	38,207	20,756	17,451	20,674	14,973	80	2,440	2	38
15—20	29,083	15,405	13,678	14,511	2,893	878	10,488	16	297
20—25	28,758	14,811	13,947	9,745	498	4,958	12,714	108	735
25—30	25,721	13,976	11,745	3,921	159	9,779	10,489	276	1,097
30—35	22,303	11,813	10,490	1,111	147	10,269	8,657	433	1,686
35—40	16,842	9,822	7,020	434	49	9,035	5,332	353	1,639
40—45	18,145	9,779	8,366	303	64	8,880	5,289	596	3,013
45—50	11,264	6,541	4,723	139	36	5,977	2,553	425	2,134
50—55	13,465	7,001	6,464	131	46	6,146	2,432	724	3,984
55—60	5,720	3,320	2,400	53	16	2,887	727	430	1,657
60—65	9,088	4,833	4,255	88	38	3,841	786	904	3,431
65—70	2,619	1,533	1,086	31	3	1,173	178	329	905
70 and over	6,453	3,411	3,042	47	18	2,280	245	1,084	2,779
ANIMISTIC	**72,196**	**36,999**	**35,197**	**20,694**	**15,063**	**14,756**	**15,379**	**1,549**	**4,755**
0—1	1,796	817	979	817	979	..	..	..	..
1—2	1,110	534	576	534	576	..	..	..	..
2—3	2,277	1,131	1,146	1,131	1,146	..	..	..	..
3—4	2,247	1,086	1,161	1,086	1,161	..	..	..	..
4—5	2,185	1,087	1,098	1,087	1,097	..	1	..	..
Total 0—5	*9,615*	*4,655*	*4,960*	*4,655*	*4,959*	..	*1*	..	..
5—10	10,298	5,136	5,162	5,131	5,135	4	27	1	..
10—15	9,368	4,973	4,395	4,935	3,776	38	603	..	16
15—20	6,235	3,168	3,067	2,947	881	218	2,146	3	38
20—25	6,142	2,814	3,328	1,727	165	1,053	3,049	24	114
25—30	5,524	2,787	2,737	713	40	2,014	2,508	60	189
30—35	5,325	2,666	2,659	303	34	2,269	2,310	94	315
35—40	3,728	2,087	1,641	94	7	1,903	1,337	90	297
40—45	4,394	2,321	2,073	74	27	2,090	1,457	157	589
45—50	2,783	1,625	1,158	29	3	1,441	711	155	444
50—55	3,313	1,747	1,566	35	14	1,493	702	219	85[illegible]
55—60	1,397	810	587	31	4	655	207	134	376
60—65	2,214	1,204	1,010	18	11	899	221	287	778
65—70	600	337	263	3	2	251	44	83	217
70 and over	1,360	669	591	9	5	426	54	233	532

TABLE VII.—AGE, SEX AND CIVIL CONDITION.

PUNJAB STATES.

Age and Religion.	Population.			Unmarried.		Married.		Widowed.	
	Persons.	Males.	Females.	Males.	Females.	Males.	Females.	Males.	Females.
1	2	3	4	5	6	7	8	9	10
ALL RELIGIONS	**4,212,794**	**2,322,908**	**1,889,886**	**1,191,597**	**660,783**	**926,409**	**936,373**	**204,902**	**292,730**
0—1	161,096	82,173	78,923	82,112	78,903	61	18	..	2
1—2	57,064	29,051	28,013	28,964	27,983	85	28	2	2
2—3	101,331	52,184	49,147	52,075	49,066	108	80	1	1
3—4	113,969	57,627	56,342	57,391	56,132	234	205	2	5
4—5	108,386	56,885	51,501	56,616	51,180	263	290	6	22
Total 0—5	*541,846*	*277,920*	*263,926*	*277,158*	*263,273*	*751*	*621*	*11*	*32*
5—10	541,585	292,002	249,583	285,739	235,920	5,895	13,042	368	621
10—15	448,880	261,878	187,002	235,728	122,534	24,769	62,785	1,381	1,683
15—20	386,418	224,525	161,893	155,705	26,216	64,394	131,070	4,426	4,607
20—25	379,667	204,336	175,331	88,990	5,099	105,923	161,140	9,423	9,092
25—30	375,335	204,805	170,530	54,826	2,094	135,441	154,690	14,538	13,746
30—35	355,599	190,924	164,675	32,931	1,759	139,160	140,849	18,833	22,067
35—40	225,559	128,293	97,266	15,136	695	97,175	77,419	15,982	19,152
40—45	282,823	150,642	132,181	15,432	1,072	110,509	87,648	24,701	43,461
45—50	146,865	86,424	60,441	7,505	400	61,878	36,081	17,041	23,960
50—55	213,284	120,917	92,367	9,605	644	80,958	39,406	30,354	52,317
55—60	69,765	42,609	27,156	3,108	194	27,079	11,141	12,422	15,821
60—65	139,076	77,048	62,028	5,327	406	44,295	13,866	27,426	47,756
65—70	30,025	18,461	11,564	1,373	61	9,672	2,497	7,416	9,006
70 and over	76,067	42,124	33,943	3,034	416	18,510	4,118	20,580	29,409
HINDU	**2,090,803**	**1,134,108**	**956,695**	**554,187**	**310,336**	**482,837**	**487,013**	**97,084**	**159,346**
0—1	73,757	37,310	36,447	37,249	36,427	61	18	..	2
1—2	28,981	14,552	14,329	14,465	14,303	85	25	2	1
2—3	48,129	24,288	23,841	24,185	23,777	103	63	..	1
3—4	55,038	27,214	27,824	27,000	27,675	212	144	2	5
4—5	50,865	25,935	24,930	25,692	24,682	240	228	3	20
Total 0—5	*256,670*	*129,299*	*127,371*	*128,591*	*126,864*	*701*	*478*	*7*	*29*
5—10	256,811	135,816	120,995	131,917	112,292	3,754	8,432	145	271
10—15	219,973	125,617	94,356	110,136	55,219	14,777	38,182	704	955
15—20	198,435	112,173	86,262	73,040	10,584	36,812	72,751	2,321	2,927
20—25	191,611	101,270	90,341	40,141	1,973	56,374	82,796	4,755	5,572
25—30	186,245	99,996	86,249	24,507	849	68,532	77,401	6,957	7,999
30—35	178,220	94,515	83,705	15,225	675	70,336	70,466	8,954	12,564
35—40	116,500	65,532	50,968	7,534	303	50,310	39,780	7,688	10,885
40—45	141,966	74,871	67,095	7,830	531	55,415	42,888	11,626	23,676
45—50	74,418	43,472	30,946	3,819	219	31,621	18,040	8,032	12,687
50—55	108,147	60,492	47,655	4,992	342	41,095	19,933	14,405	27,380
55—60	36,746	22,247	14,499	1,668	112	14,693	5,857	5,886	8,530
60—65	72,108	38,986	33,122	2,772	179	23,215	6,905	12,999	26,038
65—70	15,887	9,746	6,141	663	34	5,556	1,242	3,527	4,865
70 and over	37,066	20,076	16,990	1,352	160	9,646	1,862	9,078	14,968
MUSALMAN	**1,319,756**	**728,535**	**591,221**	**386,283**	**229,130**	**280,989**	**282,904**	**61,263**	**79,187**
0—1	54,637	27,861	26,776	27,861	26,776	..	..	..	..
1—2	15,679	7,938	7,741	7,938	7,737	..	3	..	1
2—3	33,249	17,133	16,116	17,130	16,102	3	14	..	..
3—4	37,760	19,184	18,576	19,171	18,522	13	54	..	..
4—5	38,042	20,124	17,918	20,107	17,863	16	53	1	2
Total 0—5	*179,367*	*92,240*	*87,127*	*92,207*	*87,000*	*32*	*124*	*1*	*3*
5—10	186,351	101,424	84,927	99,924	81,667	1,346	3,015	154	245
10—15	143,249	84,281	58,968	77,731	43,915	6,151	14,613	399	440
15—20	110,353	62,979	47,374	46,411	10,512	15,409	35,848	1,159	1,014
20—25	113,472	59,678	53,794	28,325	2,395	28,887	49,216	2,466	2,183
25—30	117,661	64,104	53,557	17,891	1,003	42,060	49,012	4,153	3,542
30—35	115,443	62,315	53,128	10,759	921	45,853	46,281	5,703	5,926
35—40	66,544	38,355	28,189	3,597	322	30,183	23,115	4,575	4,752
40—45	89,631	48,342	41,289	3,753	468	36,703	28,846	7,886	11,075
45—50	42,279	25,054	17,225	1,343	144	18,755	10,847	4,956	6,234
50—55	64,449	37,090	27,359	1,801	264	26,117	12,216	9,172	14,879
55—60	17,776	10,698	7,078	431	70	7,047	3,073	3,220	3,935
60—65	41,617	23,921	17,696	1,052	199	14,210	4,478	8,659	13,019
65—70	7,212	4,530	2,682	219	25	2,322	642	1,989	2,015
70 and over	24,352	13,524	10,828	839	225	5,014	1,578	6,771	9,025
SIKH	**789,925**	**453,673**	**336,252**	**247,814**	**119,015**	**159,895**	**164,031**	**45,964**	**53,206**
0—1	32,351	16,825	15,526	16,825	15,526	..	..	..	..
1—2	12,347	6,470	5,877	6,470	5,877	..	..	..	..
2—3	19,661	10,615	9,046	10,612	9,043	2	3	1	..
3—4	20,887	11,077	9,810	11,068	9,803	9	7	..	..
4—5	19,206	10,674	8,532	10,667	8,524	6	8	1	..
Total 0—5	*104,452*	*55,661*	*48,791*	*55,642*	*48,773*	*17*	*18*	*2*	..
5—10	96,908	53,968	42,940	53,121	41,260	780	1,582	67	98
10—15	84,400	51,284	33,116	47,248	22,924	3,764	9,915	272	277
15—20	76,538	48,767	27,771	35,870	4,938	11,959	22,190	938	648
20—25	73,443	42,800	30,643	20,278	634	20,346	28,726	2,176	1,283
25—30	70,247	40,065	30,182	12,250	174	24,439	27,864	3,376	2,144
30—35	60,891	33,508	27,383	6,830	116	22,551	23,765	4,127	3,502
35—40	41,745	23,981	17,764	3,929	52	16,387	14,278	3,665	3,434
40—45	50,435	27,022	23,413	3,773	54	18,121	15,674	5,128	7,085
45—50	29,634	17,592	12,042	2,306	15	11,288	7,074	3,998	4,953
50—55	40,139	23,043	17,096	2,774	30	13,578	7,135	6,691	9,931
55—60	14,929	9,487	5,442	994	6	5,231	2,149	3,262	3,287
60—65	24,928	13,937	10,991	1,470	19	6,763	2,412	5,695	8,560
65—70	6,769	4,107	2,662	486	1	1,749	585	1,872	2,076
70 and over	14,467	8,451	6,016	834	19	2,922	664	4,695	5,333

Part II.—By Provinces and States—*continued.*

RAJPUTANA AGENCY.

Age and Religion.	Population.			Unmarried.		Married.		Widowed.	
	Persons.	Males.	Females.	Males.	Females.	Males.	Females.	Males.	Females.
1	2	3	4	5	6	7	8	9	10
ALL RELIGIONS	**10,530,432**	**5,515,275**	**5,015,157**	**2,723,755**	**1,590,523**	**2,418,819**	**2,512,649**	**372,701**	**911,985**
0—1	408,016	205,088	202,928	205,034	202,791	52	135	2	2
1—2	157,664	77,956	79,708	77,918	79,548	33	157	5	3
2—3	309,229	152,439	156,790	152,219	156,047	206	732	14	11
3—4	351,175	172,961	178,214	172,409	176,702	534	1,482	18	30
4—5	295,831	150.418	145,413	149,634	143,294	746	2,048	38	71
Total 0—5	*1,521,915*	*758,862*	*763,053*	*757,214*	*758,383*	*1,571*	*4,554*	*77*	*117*
5—10	1,263,376	668,685	594,691	655,242	555,234	12,849	38,416	594	1,041
10—15	936,507	536,201	400,306	476,160	223,292	57,816	173,193	2,225	3,821
15—20	904,837	509,037	395,800	344,487	35,947	157,489	347,484	7,061	12,369
20—25	994,864	495,995	498,369	202,775	6,363	276,765	464,187	16,455	28,319
25—30	1,000,180	527,560	472,620	114,896	2,927	386,032	427,273	26,632	42,420
30—35	1,006,639	522,519	484,120	64,448	2,968	420,532	400,819	37,539	80,333
35—40	576,283	313,514	262,769	26,832	1,155	258,783	200,951	27,899	60,663
40—45	786,742	396,186	390,556	29,483	1,742	315,484	227,620	51,219	161,194
45—50	337,797	184,652	153,145	12,918	515	141,788	79,794	29,946	72,836
50—55	576,769	294,396	282,373	19,843	899	208,582	91,374	65,971	190,100
55—60	145,169	81,263	63,906	5,434	175	53,629	21,386	22,200	42,345
60—65	324,752	150,526	174,226	9,226	574	89,724	26,797	51,576	146,855
65—70	51,333	27,627	23,756	1,707	94	15,210	3,773	10,710	19,889
70 and over	103,219	48,252	54,967	3,090	256	22,565	5,028	22,597	49,683
HINDU	**8,752,045**	**4,600,170**	**4,151,875**	**2,259,610**	**1,280,955**	**2,023,352**	**2,099,204**	**317,208**	**771,716**
0—1	334,345	168,183	166,162	168,135	166,037	46	123	2	2
1—2	127,345	63,143	64,202	63,111	64,058	29	142	3	2
2—3	252,752	124,774	127,978	124,577	127,307	186	663	11	8
3—4	286,603	141,353	145,250	140,858	143,864	479	1,360	16	26
4—5	241,807	123,101	118,706	122,399	116,815	671	1,830	31	61
Total 0—5	*1,242,852*	*620,554*	*622.298*	*619,080*	*618,081*	*1,411*	*4,118*	*63*	*99*
5—10	1,037,134	550,244	486,890	538,434	451,775	11,321	34,195	489	920
10—15	774,378	446,299	328,079	393,832	173,750	50,565	151,009	1,902	3,320
15—20	755,732	428,219	327,513	287,722	25,004	134,411	291,872	6,086	10,637
20—25	827,586	415,318	412,268	170,606	4,256	230,817	384,143	13,895	23,869
25—30	833,066	442,302	390,764	98,628	2,060	321,019	353,246	22,655	35,458
30—35	843,033	439,238	403,795	55,834	2,189	351,298	333,684	32,106	67,922
35—40	480,550	261,992	218,558	23,383	824	214,958	166,709	23,651	51,025
40—45	662,839	334,313	328,526	25,876	1,236	264,530	190,147	43,907	137,143
45—50	283,287	154,933	128,354	11,207	363	118,359	66,560	25,367	61,431
50—55	487,258	249,082	238,176	17,681	646	174,847	76,233	56,554	161,297
55—60	121,645	68,060	53,585	4,866	121	44,446	17,768	18,748	35,696
60—65	274,308	127,087	147,221	8,256	397	74,754	22,280	44,077	124,544
65—70	42,735	22,808	19,927	1,499	64	12,375	3,138	8,934	16,725
70 and over	85,642	39,721	45,921	2,706	189	18,241	4,102	18,774	41,630
MUSALMAN	**985,825**	**517,560**	**468,265**	**254,316**	**161,975**	**229,838**	**235,011**	**33,406**	**71,279**
0—1	38,062	19,189	18,873	19,184	18,865	5	8	..	..
1—2	15,895	7,802	8,093	7,800	8,083	1	9	1	1
2—3	26,503	13,050	13,453	13,038	13,410	9	43	3	..
3—4	30,376	14,980	15,396	14,948	15,310	31	83	1	3
4—5	26,110	13,140	12,970	13,083	12,795	54	170	3	5
Total 0—5	*136.946*	*68.161*	*68,785*	*68,053*	*68,463*	*100*	*313*	*8*	*9*
5—10	121,682	63,808	57,874	62,474	54,322	1,265	3,460	69	92
10—15	102,642	57,559	45,083	51,753	29,550	5,558	15,197	248	336
15—20	89,448	49,598	39,850	33,947	6,576	14,956	32,416	695	858
20—25	92,867	46,119	46,748	17,887	1,195	26,644	43,596	1,588	1,957
25—30	86,445	45,612	40,833	8,869	469	34,448	37,719	2,295	2,645
30—35	87,390	44,619	42,771	4.990	437	36,552	36,504	3,077	5,530
35—40	49,187	27,061	22,126	1,642	167	23,139	17,915	2,280	4,044
40—45	71,150	35,975	35,175	1,879	317	29,836	23,088	4,260	11,770
45—50	29,743	16,858	12,885	747	91	13,707	7,705	2,404	5,089
50—55	53,762	28,353	25,409	965	162	21,728	10,076	5,660	15,171
55—60	13,713	8,087	5,626	220	30	5,953	2,277	1,914	3,310
60—65	32,717	16,084	16,633	527	125	10,566	3,280	4,991	13,228
65—70	5,203	3,121	2,082	104	13	1,956	430	1,061	1,639
70 and over	12,930	6,545	6,385	259	49	3,430	735	2,856	5,601
ANIMISTIC	**444,702**	**226,508**	**218,194**	**121,138**	**93,413**	**98,708**	**102,909**	**6,662**	**21,872**
0—1	22,411	11,065	11,346	11,064	11,344	1	2	..	..
1—2	10,137	4,919	5,218	4,918	5,212	1	6	..	..
2—3	20,493	9,854	10,639	9,847	10,622	7	17	..	..
3—4	24,541	11,803	12,738	11,786	12,709	16	28	1	1
4—5	19,706	10,014	9,662	10,028	9,624	15	37	1	1
Total 0—5	*97,388*	*47,685*	*49,603*	*47,643*	*49,511*	*40*	*90*	*2*	*2*
5—10	63,600	33,644	29,956	33,453	29,425	172	518	19	13
10—15	29,054	16,302	12,752	15,405	9,757	862	2,963	35	32
15—20	30,987	16,661	14,326	12,552	3,108	3,959	11,090	150	128
20—25	40,539	18,695	21,844	7,361	675	10,875	20,855	459	314
25—30	47,259	23,341	23,918	3,037	288	19,530	22,985	774	645
30—35	45,194	23,757	21,437	985	249	21,749	19,684	1,023	1,504
35—40	24,631	13,241	11,390	280	127	12,363	9,918	598	1,345
40—45	28,142	14,745	13,397	220	138	13,577	8,493	948	4,766
45—50	9,769	5,163	4,606	57	35	4,692	2,592	414	1,979
50—55	15,929	7,813	8,116	80	52	6,704	2,503	1,020	5,561
55—60	2,782	1,392	1,390	15	6	1,188	517	194	867
60—65	7,291	3,060	4,231	20	30	2,322	543	718	3,658
65—70	782	350	432	6	3	263	70	81	359
70 and over	1,455	659	796	15	9	417	88	227	699

TABLE VII.—Age, Sex and Civil Condition. Part II.—By Provinces and States—*concld.*

UNITED PROVINCES STATES.

Age and Religion.	Population.			Unmarried.		Married.		Widowed.	
	Persons.	Males.	Females.	Males.	Females.	Males.	Females.	Males.	Females.
1	2	3	4	5	6	7	8	9	10
ALL RELIGIONS	**832,036**	**431,440**	**400,596**	**201,515**	**131,098**	**202,343**	**213,810**	**27,582**	**55,688**
0—1	31,955	16,163	15,792	16,160	15,790	3	2	..	..
1—2	12,192	5,963	6,229	5,962	6,220	1	9	..	..
2—3	21,845	10,621	11,224	10,604	11,175	17	49	..	..
3—4	22,532	10,805	11,727	10,782	11,650	23	76	..	1
4—5	23,181	11,669	11,512	11,608	11,367	60	134	1	11
Total 0—5	*111,705*	*55,221*	*56,484*	*55,116*	*56,202*	*104*	*270*	*1*	*12*
5—10	110,864	57,856	53,008	56,476	48,945	1,363	3,973	17	90
10—15	88,765	49,016	39,749	40,461	20,717	8,353	18,697	202	335
15—20	64,834	35,259	29,575	20,286	2,560	14,430	26,468	543	547
20—25	74,210	37,209	37,001	12,463	823	23,151	34,939	1,595	1,239
25—30	72,988	37,483	35,505	6,526	427	28,680	33,287	2,277	1,791
30—35	75,408	39,078	36,330	4,854	497	31,057	32,365	3,167	3,448
35—40	47,732	25,714	22,018	1,580	190	21,902	18,937	2,232	2, 91
40—45	59,705	31,359	28,346	1,680	293	25,809	20,144	3,870	7,[illegible]09
45—50	27,341	14,838	12,503	555	64	12,408	8,585	1,875	3,854
50—55	42,322	21,546	20,776	750	146	16,893	8,917	3,903	11,713
55—60	13,040	6,659	6,381	186	15	5,251	3,044	1,222	3,322
60—65	26,019	12,324	13,695	325	79	8,433	2,871	3,566	10,745
65—70	5,211	2,598	2,613	65	14	1,711	526	822	2,073
70 and over	11,687	5,280	6,407	192	46	2,798	687	2,290	5,674
Age Unspecified	205	..	205	..	80	..	100	..	25
HINDU	**583,115**	**299,931**	**283,184**	**138,638**	**89,909**	**143,133**	**154,716**	**18,160**	**38,559**
0—1	21,148	10,634	10,514	10,631	10,513	3	1	..	..
1—2	8,702	4,226	4,476	4,225	4,468	1	8	..	..
2—3	14,618	7,037	7,581	7,021	7,557	16	24	..	..
3—4	15,667	7,470	8,197	7,448	8,139	22	57	..	1
4—5	16,185	8,201	7,984	8,151	7,882	49	95	1	7
Total 0—5	*76,320*	*37,568*	*38,752*	*37,476*	*38,559*	*91*	*185*	*1*	*8*
5—10	77,386	40,259	37,127	39,229	34,159	1,016	2,906	14	62
10—15	62,851	34,400	28,451	28,102	14,001	6,158	14,198	140	252
15—20	47,107	25,515	21,592	14,263	1,629	10,883	19,545	369	418
20—25	52,342	26,102	26,240	8,150	484	16,895	24,902	1,057	854
25—30	51,144	26,031	25,113	4,142	250	20,423	23,629	1,466	1,234
30—35	52,354	26,875	25,479	3,570	299	21,274	22,806	2,031	2,374
35—40	34,090	18,102	15,988	1,117	126	15,512	13,843	1,473	2,019
40—45	40,842	21,180	19,662	1,170	178	17,486	14,223	2,524	5,261
45—50	20,001	10,654	9,347	386	40	9,002	6,478	1,266	2,829
50—55	29,048	14,718	14,330	517	80	11,596	6,474	2,605	7,776
55—60	9,731	4,842	4,889	139	11	3,898	2,412	805	2,466
60—65	18,169	8,325	9,844	204	48	5,774	2,234	2,347	7,562
65—70	4,034	1,969	2,065	44	13	1,303	424	622	1,628
70 and over	7,696	3,391	4,305	129	32	1,822	457	1,440	3,816
MUSALMAN	**246,358**	**130,132**	**116,226**	**62,279**	**40,777**	**58,544**	**58,478**	**9,309**	**16,971**
0—1	10,695	5,476	5,219	5,476	5,218	..	1	..	..
1—2	3,465	1,724	1,741	1,724	1,740	..	1	..	..
2—3	7,151	3,544	3,607	3,543	3,582	1	25	..	..
3—4	6,797	3,305	3,492	3,304	3,474	1	18	..	..
4—5	6,927	3,445	3,482	3,434	3,439	11	39	..	4
Total 0—5	*35,035*	*17,494*	*17,541*	*17,481*	*17,453*	*13*	*84*	..	*4*
5—10	33,124	17,409	15,715	17,062	14,629	344	1,058	3	28
10—15	25,659	14,460	11,199	12,237	6,682	2,162	4,436	61	81
15—20	17,517	9,630	7,887	5,967	925	3,494	6,833	169	129
20—25	21,630	10,980	10,650	4,282	334	6,167	9,941	531	375
25—30	21,588	11,315	10,273	2,367	173	8,148	9,552	800	548
30—35	22,819	12,071	10,748	1,276	188	9,679	9,476	1,116	1,084
35—40	[illegible]	7,525	5,963	456	61	6,316	5,034	758	868
40—45	18,675	10,076	8,599	504	113	8,237	5,870	1,335	2,616
45—50	7,268	4,146	3,122	168	24	3,372	2,082	606	1,016
50—55	13,163	6,767	6,396	231	66	5,254	2,428	1,282	3,902
55—60	3,276	1,802	1,474	46	3	1,347	621	409	850
60—65	7,778	3,956	3,822	119	31	2,634	633	1,203	3,158
65—70	1,170	626	544	21	1	406	102	199	441
70 and over	3,963	1,875	2,088	62	14	971	228	842	1,846
Age Unspecified	205	..	205	..	80	..	100	..	25
CHRISTIAN	**1,745**	**[illegible]**	**821**	**406**	**289**	**463**	**444**	**55**	**26**
0—1	84	40	44	40	44	..	..	..	..
1—2	21	10	11	10	11	..	..	..	..
2—3	50	27	23	27	23	..	..	..	..
3—4	47	18	29	18	28	..	1	..	..
4—5	44	13	31	13	31	..	..	..	..
Total 0—5	*246*	*108*	*138*	*108*	*137*	..	*1*	..	..
5—10	249	136	113	133	108	3	5	..	..
10—15	172	106	86	83	19	23	46	..	1
15—20	138	72	66	37	3	33	63	2	..
20—25	165	88	77	20	4	64	68	4	5
25—30	173	89	84	12	4	70	76	7	4
30—35	169	93	76	6	8	77	64	10	4
35—40	106	58	48	3	3	51	43	4	2
40—45	134	76	58	2	2	66	37	8	19
45—50	39	19	20	..	..	19	15	..	5
50—55	65	32	33	..	..	28	12	6	21
55—60	22	8	14	1	1	5	10	2	3
60—65	44	26	18	1	..	19	3	6	15
65—70	5	3	2	..	..	2	..	1	2
70 and over	18	10	8	..	..	5	1	5	7

TABLE VIII.

Education.

1. This table, like Table VII, is divided into two parts. Part I is a summary statement for the whole of India. Part II contains the statistics for the total population and three main religions of the larger Provinces and States. The figures for persons literate in English (columns 11 to 13) are included in those for total literate (columns 5 to 7).

2. The population here dealt with falls short of that shown in Table I by 1,741,007 persons (males 920,465, females 820,542) as detailed in the margin and of that shown in Table VI by 132,451 persons, *viz.* :—Hindu, 399 males, 47 females ; Arya, one male ; Sikh, 24 males, 2 females ; Buddhist, 133 males, 92 females ; Musalman, 28,977 males, 25,145 females ; Christian, 5 males, 2 females, and Animistic, 38,691 males, 38,933 females. A further difference between the number of Hindus, Aryas and Brahmos as shown in this table and in Table VI is due to the fact that in the Punjab the figures for Aryas and Brahmos were amalgamated with those for Hindus. As in Table VII, Jews who were shown separately in Table VI, have been included under the head "Minor and Unspecified." This table includes 771,696 persons in Baluchistan who were omitted from Table VII. The figures for Madras States in Part II include those for Cochin and Travancore.

	Males.	Females.
Andamans and Nicobars	818	874
Burma	38,023	38,111
Kashmir	29,389	25,236
N.-W. F. Provinces	852,235	756,321

3. The figures in the body of the table refer to Christians of all races. Some statistics for Indian Christians only are noted below :—

(1)—Number of Indian Christians who are literate.

Province or State.	Total number of Indian Christians.		Literate.		Illiterate.		Literate in English.	
	Males.	Females.	Males.	Females.	Males.	Females.	Males.	Females.
TOTAL	**1,816,120**	**1,759,857**	**413,853**	**168,347**	**1,402,267**	**1,591,510**	**80,209**	**30,532**
Ajmer-Merwara	1,477	1,490	928	912	549	578	393	128
Andamans and Nicobars	150	87	63	20	87	67	48	17
Assam	31,762	32,075	6,762	3,380	25,000	28,695	1,370	416
Baluchistan	495	257	201	74	294	183	104	29
Bengal	43,641	40,821	12,487	8,021	31,154	32,800	4,923	2,384
Bihar and Orissa	127,490	131,054	13,677	5,865	113,813	125,189	3,622	653
Bombay	112,351	91,404	31,109	13,442	81,242	77,962	15,864	5,427
Burma	94,980	90,562	30,868	17,696	64,112	72,866	5,073	2,057
Central Provinces and Berar	31,878	30,702	5,148	3,473	26,730	27,229	1,926	756
Coorg	1,787	1,421	560	196	1,227	1,225	157	37
Madras	573,433	594,154	117,136	50,303	456,297	543,851	25,278	8,972
North-West Frontier Province	552	325	223	79	329	246	128	35
Punjab	90,776	73,218	3,991	2,583	86,785	70,635	1,807	1,157
United Provinces	72,951	65,238	9,039	8,385	63,912	56,853	4,270	3,667
Baroda	3,731	3,231	756	358	2,975	2,873	133	100
Central India	2,158	2,053	999	707	1,159	1,346	376	64
Cochin	116,549	114,019	36,310	12,654	80,239	101,365	2,162	516
Hyderabad	23,635	22,273	3,633	2,130	20,003	20,143	1,422	738
Kashmir	475	234	46	17	429	217	21	7
Mysore	24,278	22,276	7,973	3,550	16,305	18,726	2,980	1,317
Rajputana	1,429	1,119	691	427	738	692	243	107
Sikkim	138	129	73	26	65	103	22	3
Travancore	460,004	441,715	131,180	34,049	328,824	407,666	8,063	3,046

Note 1—For the purpose of this statement the Feringis of East Bengal (males 593, females 609) and of Assam (males 4, female 1) have been included in Indian Christians.
Note 2—The figures include the States attached to each Province, but those for Madras exclude Cochin and Travancore.

(2)—Distribution by sect of literate Indian Christians in Southern India.

Province or State.	Sect.	Total Strength of Sect.		Literate.		Illiterate.	
		Males.	Females.	Males.	Females.	Males.	Females.
Bombay	Protestants	32,105	30,080	7,704	5,459	24,401	24,621
	Roman Catholics	80,238	61,322	23,397	7,983	56,841	53,339
	Syrians	8	2	8	...	...	2
Coorg	Protestants	197	181	132	95	65	86
	Roman Catholics	1,590	1,240	428	101	1,162	1,139
Madras	Protestants	231,760	236,355	45,305	28,240	186,455	208,115
	Roman Catholics	329,709	346,382	67,748	20,675	261,961	325,707
	Syrians	11,964	11,417	4,083	1,388	7,881	10,029
Baroda	Protestants	3,465	3,097	537	245	2,928	2,852
	Roman Catholics	266	134	219	113	47	21
Cochin	Protestants	1,063	1,166	403	154	660	1,012
	Roman Catholics	49,003	46,394	14,969	5,124	34,034	41,270
	Syrians	66,483	66,459	20,938	7,376	45,545	59,083
Hyderabad	Protestants	15,288	14,297	2,427	1,465	12,861	12,832
	Roman Catholics	8,347	7,975	1,206	664	7,141	7,311
	Syrians	...	1	...	1	...	...
Mysore	Protestants	4,353	4,257	3,400	1,934	1,053	2,323
	Roman Catholics	19,917	16,017	5,565	1,615	14,352	16,402
	Syrians	8	2	8	1	...	1
Travancore	Protestants	80,710	77,003	10,041	6,635	61,069	70,268
	Roman Catholics	86,880	85,182	22,109	5,141	64,771	80,041
	Syrians	292,414	279,530	90,030	22,273	202,384	257,257

Note—For the purpose of this statement persons whose sect was not returned or whose beliefs were indefinite have been treated as Protestants. See also Note 2 above.

TABLE VIII.—Education.

Age and Religion.	POPULA					
	Total.			Literate.		
	Persons.	Males.	Females.	Persons.	Males.	Females.
1	2	3	4	5	6	7
All Religions . Total .	**313,415,389**	**160,418,470**	**152,996,910**	**18,539,578**	**16,938,815**	**1,600,763**
0—10 .	86,355,954	43,368,002	42,987,952	626,298	510,122	116,176
10—15 .	33,863,282	18,640,581	15,222,701	2,019,491	1,765,917	253,574
15—20 .	26,181,473	13,567,760	12,613,713	2,222,803	1,954,187	268,616
20 and over .	166,242,372	84,424,709	81,817,663	13,661,303	12,698,942	962,361
Age Unspecified .	772,308	417,418	354,890	9,683	9,647	36
Hindu (Brahmanic) Total .	**217,438,980**	**110,783,537**	**106,655,443**	**11,997,471**	**11,189,898**	**807,573**
0—10 .	58,129,945	29,121,822	29,008,123	419,962	357,205	62,757
10—15 .	23,245,466	12,753,469	10,491,997	1,344,491	1,209,229	135,262
15—20 .	18,017,663	9,429,880	8,587,783	1,439,667	1,301,985	137,682
20 and over .	118,028,411	59,468,512	58,559,899	8,788,250	8,316,387	471,863
Age Unspecified .	17,495	9,854	7,641	5,101	5,092	9
Arya . . . Total .	**142,661**	**79,651**	**63,010**	**37,129**	**31,357**	**5,772**
0—10 .	33,140	17,752	15,388	2,411	1,741	670
10—15 .	16,906	10,057	6,849	5,579	4,400	1,179
15—20 .	14,241	8,277	5,964	5,071	4,137	934
20 and over .	78,374	43,565	34,809	24,068	21,079	2,989
Brahmo . . Total .	**4,804**	**2,543**	**2,261**	**3,344**	**1,879**	**1,465**
0—10 .	1,236	614	622	343	170	173
10—15 .	613	313	300	518	261	257
15—20 .	532	248	284	472	228	244
20 and over .	2,423	1,368	1,055	2,011	1,220	791
Sikh . . Total .	**3,014,440**	**1,734,773**	**1,279,667**	**201,443**	**184,163**	**17,280**
0—10 .	778,177	429,524	348,653	3,249	2,153	1,096
10—15 .	327,527	203,114	124,413	16,316	13,781	2,535
15—20 .	269,334	169,208	100,126	21,868	19,276	2,592
20 and over .	1,636,057	931,128	704,929	158,947	147,893	11,054
Age Unspecified .	3,345	1,799	1,546	1,063	1,060	3
Jain . . . Total .	**1,248,182**	**643,553**	**604,629**	**342,705**	**318,585**	**24,120**
0—10 .	293,714	147,414	146,300	10,852	8,610	2,242
10—15 .	125,354	69,129	56,225	36,323	31,643	4,680
15—20 .	108,125	58,976	49,149	41,437	37,622	3,815
20 and over .	720,989	368,034	352,955	254,093	240,710	13,383

Part I.—General Table—India.

TION.						
Illiterate.			Literate in English.			Age and Religion.
Persons.	Males.	Females.	Persons.	Males.	Females.	
8	9	10	11	12	13	14
294,875,811	**143,479,655**	**151,396,156**	**1,670,387**	**1,518,361**	**152,026**	**Total All Religions.**
85,729,656	42,857,880	42,871,776	39,974	28,427	11,547	0—10
31,843,791	16,874,664	14,969,127	166,940	146,498	20,442	10—15
23,958,670	11,613,573	12,345,097	266,991	243,137	23,854	15—20
152,581,069	71,725,767	80,855,302	1,196,410	1,100,227	96,183	20 and over
762,625	407,771	354,854	72	72	...	Age Unspecified
205,441,509	**99,593,639**	**105,847,870**	**1,028,996**	**1,006,392**	**22,604**	**Total Hindu (Brahmanic).**
57,709,983	28,764,617	28,945,366	15,660	14,409	1,251	0—10
21,900,975	11,544,240	10,356,735	107,227	103,114	4,113	10—15
16,577,996	8,127,895	8,450,101	177,131	172,151	4,980	15—20
109,240,161	51,152,125	58,088,036	728,964	716,704	12,260	20 and over
12,394	4,762	7,632	14	14	...	Age Unspecified
105,532	**48,294**	**57,238**	**5,868**	**5,725**	**143**	**Total Arya.**
30,729	16,011	14,718	99	94	5	0—10
11,327	5,657	5,670	661	644	17	10—15
9,170	4,140	5,030	1,015	979	36	15—20
54,306	22,486	31,820	4,093	4,008	85	20 and over
1,460	**664**	**796**	**2,391**	**1,479**	**912**	**Total Brahmo.**
893	444	449	120	61	59	0—10
95	52	43	370	191	179	10—15
60	20	40	390	200	190	15—20
412	148	264	1,511	1,027	484	20 and over
2,812,997	**1,550,610**	**1,262,387**	**11,728**	**11,490**	**238**	**Total Sikh.**
774,928	427,371	347,557	38	29	9	0—10
311,211	189,333	121,878	1,079	1,048	31	10—15
247,466	149,932	97,534	2,558	2,498	60	15—20
1,477,110	783,235	693,875	8,052	7,914	138	20 and over
2,282	739	1,543	1	1	...	Age Unspecified
905,477	**324,968**	**580,509**	**13,239**	**13,030**	**209**	**Total Jain**
282,862	138,804	144,058	69	54	15	0—10
89,031	37,486	51,545	1,612	1,573	39	10—15
66,688	21,354	45,334	2,939	2,901	38	15—20
466,896	127,324	339,572	8,619	8,502	117	20 and over

TABLE VIII.—EDUCATION.

POPULA

Age and Religion.	Total. Persons.	Total. Males.	Total. Females.	Literate. Persons.	Literate. Males.	Literate. Females.
1	2	3	4	5	6	7
Buddhist . . Total .	**10,721.228**	**5,286,142**	**5,435,086**	**2,451,719**	**2,134,381**	**317,338**
0—10 .	2,908,988	1,432,244	1,476,744	54,935	39,585	15,350
10—15 .	1,271,756	652,603	619,153	237,115	193,665	43,450
15—20 .	1,000,827	475,438	525,389	301,957	246,788	55,169
20 and over .	5,539,657	2,725,857	2,813,800	1,857,712	1,654,343	203,369
Zoroastrian . Total .	**100,096**	**51,123**	**48,973**	**71,213**	**39,995**	**31,218**
0—10 .	18,752	9,440	9,312	3,965	2,115	1,850
10—15 .	10,065	5,130	4,935	8,028	4,237	3,791
15—20 .	9,721	4,825	4,896	8,493	4,417	4,076
20 and over .	61,558	31,728	29,830	50,727	29,226	21,501
Musalman . . Total .	**66,593,177**	**34,709,365**	**31,883,812**	**2,527,573**	**2,389,766**	**137,807**
0—10 .	19,793,451	10,024,745	9,768,706	83,806	72,385	11,421
10—15 .	7,346,814	4,143,060	3,203,754	265,603	243,940	21,663
15—20 .	5,608,230	2,858,032	2,750,198	288,639	267,850	20,789
20 and over .	33,093,214	17,277,763	15,815,451	1,886,006	1,802,096	83,910
Age Unspecified .	751,468	405,765	345,703	3,519	3,495	24
Christian . . Total .	**3,876,196**	**2,010,724**	**1,865,472**	**840,865**	**588,570**	**252,295**
0—10 .	1,078,325	536,842	541,483	44,317	24,315	20,002
10—15 .	460,668	241,013	219,655	98,971	59,138	39,833
15—20 .	353,668	177,347	176,321	107,767	65,296	42,471
20 and over .	1,983,535	1,055,522	928,013	589,810	439,821	149,989
Animistic . . Total .	**10.217,544**	**5,088,241**	**5,129,303**	**56,820**	**53,833**	**2,987**
0—10 .	3,304,491	1,639,852	1,664,639	1,825	1,491	334
10—15 .	1,051,868	559,448	492,420	5,288	4,850	438
15—20 .	794,031	382,924	411,107	6,304	5,866	438
20 and over .	5,067,154	2,506,017	2,561,137	43,403	41,626	1,777
Minor and Unspecified Total.	**58,081**	**28,818**	**29,263**	**9,296**	**6,388**	**2,908**
0—10 .	15,735	7,753	7,982	633	352	281
10—15 .	6,245	3,245	3,000	1,259	773	486
15—20 .	5,101	2,603	2,496	1,128	722	406
20 and over .	31,000	15,215	15,785	6,276	4,541	1,735

PART I.—GENERAL TABLE—INDIA—*concluded.*

...TION. Illiterate. Persons.	Illiterate. Males.	Illiterate. Females.	Literate in English. Persons.	Literate in English. Males.	Literate in English. Females.	Age and Religion.
8	9	10	11	12	13	14
8,269,509	**3,151,761**	**5,117,748**	**23,150**	**21,767**	**1,383**	**Total Buddhist.**
2,854,053	1,392,659	1,461,394	342	269	73	0—10
1,034,641	458,938	575,703	2,458	2,190	268	10—15
698,870	228,650	470.220	4,697	4,386	311	15—20
3,681,945	1,071,514	2,610,431	15,653	14,922	731	20 and over
28,883	**11,128**	**17,755**	**33,681**	**25,334**	**8,347**	**Total Zoroastrian.**
14,787	7,325	7,462	606	368	238	0—10
2,037	893	1,144	2,892	1,843	1,049	10—15
1,228	408	820	4,537	3,096	1,441	15—20
10,831	2,502	8,329	25,616	20,027	5,619	20 and over
64,065,604	**32,319,599**	**31,746,005**	**179.991**	**176,051**	**3,940**	**Total Musalman.**
19,709,645	9,952,360	9,757,285	2,860	2,615	245	0—10
7,081,211	3,899,120	3,182,091	18,946	18,359	587	10—15
5,319,591	2,590,182	2,729,409	33,714	33,032	682	15—20
31,207,208	15,475,667	15,731,541	124,414	121,988	2,426	20 and over
747,949	402,270	345,679	57	57	...	Age Unspecified
3,035,331	**1,422,154**	**1,613,177**	**365,234**	**252,591**	**112,643**	**Total Christian.**
1,034,008	512,527	521,481	19,867	10,348	9,519	0—10
361,697	181,875	179,822	30,926	17,036	13,890	10—15
245,901	112,051	133,850	39,047	23,182	15,865	15—20
1,393,725	615,701	778,024	275,394	202,025	73,369	20 and over
10,160,724	**5,034,408**	**5,126,316**	**1,595**	**1,521**	**74**	**Total Animistic.**
3,302,666	1,638,361	1,664,305	28	27	1	0—10
1,046,580	554,598	491,982	162	152	10	10—15
787,727	377,058	410,669	295	286	9	15 - 20
5,023,751	2,464,391	2,559,360	1,110	1,056	54	20 and over
48,785	**22,430**	**26,355**	**4,514**	**2,981**	**1,533**	**Total Minor and Unspecified.**
15,102	7,401	7,701	285	153	132	0—10
4,986	2,472	2,514	607	348	259	10—15
3,973	1,883	2,090	668	426	242	15—20
24,724	10,674	14,050	2,954	2,054	900	20 and over

TABLE VIII.—EDUCATION

Age and Religion.	POPULATION. Total. Persons.	Total. Males.	Total. Females.	Literate. Persons.	Literate. Males.	Literate. Females.	Illiterate. Persons.	Illiterate. Males.	Illiterate. Females.	Literate in English. Persons.	Literate in English. Males.	Literate in English. Females.
1	2	3	4	5	6	7	8	9	10	11	12	13
Assam.												
ALL RELIGIONS	**6,713,635**	**3,467,621**	**3,246,014**	**326,566**	**306,030**	**20,536**	**6,387,069**	**3,161,591**	**3,225,478**	**35,296**	**33,792**	**1,504**
0—10	2,117,387	1,053,187	1,064,200	18,686	16,326	2,360	2,098,701	1,036,861	1,061,840	495	427	68
10—15	666,772	368,755	298,017	38,991	35,637	3,354	627,781	333,118	294,663	3,507	3,351	156
15—20	535,579	258,656	276,923	36,918	33,415	3,503	498,661	225,241	273,420	5,484	5,256	228
20 and over	3,393,897	1,787,023	1,606,874	231,971	220,652	11,319	3,161,926	1,566,371	1,595,555	25,810	24,758	1,052
HINDU	**3,637,400**	**1,898,460**	**1,738,940**	**244,719**	**230,825**	**13,894**	**3,392,681**	**1,667,635**	**1,725,046**	**25,852**	**25,543**	**309**
0—10	1,075,421	535,416	540,005	14,550	12,743	1,807	1,060,871	522,673	538,198	349	333	16
10—15	348,077	192,117	155,960	28,848	26,561	2,287	319,229	165,556	153,673	2,620	2,570	50
15—20	281,179	140,184	140,995	27,210	24,905	2,305	253,969	115,279	138,690	4,127	4,057	70
20 and over	1,932,723	1,030,743	901,980	174,111	166,616	7,495	1,758,612	864,127	894,485	18,756	18,583	173
MUSALMAN	**1,886,528**	**977,463**	**909,065**	**58,119**	**56,318**	**1,801**	**1,828,409**	**921,145**	**907,264**	**4,586**	**4,526**	**60**
0—10	657,207	326,502	330,705	3,273	3,018	255	653,934	323,484	330,450	51	50	1
10—15	199,076	114,561	84,515	7,527	7,194	333	191,549	107,367	84,182	589	581	8
15—20	159,304	75,206	84,098	6,380	6,075	305	152,924	69,131	83,793	871	851	20
20 and over	870,941	461,194	409,747	40,939	40,031	908	830,002	421,163	408,839	3,075	3,044	31
ANIMISTIC	**1,109,187**	**549,200**	**559,987**	**8,600**	**7,939**	**661**	**1,100,587**	**541,261**	**559,326**	**547**	**517**	**30**
0—10	361,484	179,574	181,910	275	228	47	361,209	179,346	181,863	2	2	..
10—15	110,922	57,391	53,531	867	775	92	110,055	56,616	53,439	58	52	6
15—20	87,615	39,536	48,079	1,096	983	113	86,519	38,553	47,966	82	78	4
20 and over	549,166	272,699	276,467	6,362	5,953	409	542,804	266,746	276,058	405	385	20
Bengal.												
ALL RELIGIONS	**45,483,077**	**23,365,225**	**22,117,852**	**3,522,044**	**3,272,493**	**249,551**	**41,961,033**	**20,092,732**	**21,868,301**	**494,499**	**466,102**	**28,397**
0—10	13,521,179	6,726,734	6,794,445	167,206	144,433	22,773	13,353,973	6,582,301	6,771,672	14,786	12,198	2,588
10—15	4,943,345	2,771,240	2,172,105	417,903	379,245	38,658	4,525,442	2,391,995	2,133,447	61,299	57,399	3,900
15—20	4,266,348	2,028,187	2,238,161	427,428	385,565	41,863	3,838,920	1,642,622	2,196,298	82,843	78,811	4,032
20 and over	22,752,205	11,839,064	10,913,141	2,509,507	2,363,250	146,257	20,242,698	9,475,814	10,766,884	335,571	317,694	17,877
HINDU	**20,377,793**	**10,545,714**	**9,832,079**	**2,434,928**	**2,239,744**	**195,184**	**17,942,865**	**8,305,970**	**9,636,895**	**380,127**	**372,088**	**8,039**
0—10	5,374,196	2,675,009	2,699,187	121,959	105,587	16,372	5,252,237	2,569,422	2,682,815	9,173	8,549	624
10—15	2,102,162	1,183,311	918,851	296,384	266,477	29,907	1,805,778	916,834	888,944	47,331	45,993	1,338
15—20	1,956,439	954,764	1,001,675	304,210	270,046	34,164	1,652,229	684,718	967,511	64,462	62,910	1,552
20 and over	10,944,996	5,732,630	5,212,366	1,712,375	1,597,634	114,741	9,232,621	4,134,996	5,097,625	259,161	254,636	4,525
MUSALMAN	**23,989,719**	**12,245,542**	**11,744,177**	**991,551**	**964,405**	**27,146**	**22,998,168**	**11,281,137**	**11,717,031**	**62,301**	**61,454**	**847**
0—10	7,799,700	3,878,977	3,920,723	38,920	35,288	3,632	7,760,780	3,843,689	3,917,091	1,466	1,373	93
10—15	2,716,623	1,521,470	1,195,153	111,455	106,491	4,964	2,605,168	1,414,979	1,190,189	8,672	8,512	160
15—20	2,211,844	1,027,156	1,184,688	112,824	108,656	4,168	2,099,020	918,500	1,180,520	13,202	13,053	149
20 and over	11,261,552	5,817,939	5,443,613	728,352	713,970	14,382	10,533,200	5,103,969	5,429,231	38,961	38,516	445
ANIMISTIC	**730,182**	**371,248**	**358,934**	**3,537**	**3,392**	**145**	**726,645**	**367,856**	**358,789**	**68**	**66**	**2**
0—10	241,756	119,260	122,496	156	123	33	241,600	119,137	122,463	..	..	..
10—15	79,305	42,402	36,903	304	291	13	79,001	42,111	36,890	4	4	..
15—20	61,226	27,782	33,444	357	237	20	60,869	27,445	33,424	9	9	..
20 and over	347,895	181,804	166,091	2,720	2,641	79	345,175	179,163	166,012	55	53	2
Bihar and Orissa.												
ALL RELIGIONS	**34,490,084**	**16,859,929**	**17,630,155**	**1,419,138**	**1,348,000**	**71,138**	**33,070,946**	**15,511,929**	**17,559,017**	**79,182**	**73,978**	**5,204**
0—10	9,921,464	4,912,671	5,008,793	53,968	46,926	7,042	9,867,496	4,865,745	5,001,751	2,068	1,613	455
10—15	3,851,142	2,087,732	1,763,410	155,833	145,291	10,542	3,695,309	1,942,441	1,752,868	7,703	7,219	484
15—20	2,670,320	1,356,690	1,313,630	157,587	147,646	9,941	2,512,733	1,209,044	1,303,689	11,484	10,889	595
20 and over	18,047,158	8,502,836	9,544,322	1,051,750	1,008,137	43,613	16,995,408	7,494,699	9,500,709	57,927	54,257	3,670
HINDU	**28,360,589**	**13,886,520**	**14,474,069**	**1,226,804**	**1,175,543**	**51,261**	**27,133,785**	**12,710,977**	**14,422,808**	**54,786**	**53,794**	**992**
0—10	7,985,182	3,956,162	4,029,020	44,280	39,453	4,827	7,940,902	3,916,709	4,024,193	952	890	62
10—15	3,132,069	1,699,866	1,432,203	132,879	125,638	7,241	2,999,190	1,574,228	1,424,962	5,583	5,472	111
15—20	2,186,805	1,116,315	1,070,490	135,664	128,378	7,286	2,051,141	987,937	1,063,204	8,296	8,156	140
20 and over	15,056,533	7,114,177	7,942,356	913,981	882,074	31,907	14,142,552	6,232,108	7,910,449	39,955	39,276	679
MUSALMAN	**3,666,861**	**1,766,496**	**1,900,365**	**148,639**	**139,063**	**9,576**	**3,518,222**	**1,627,433**	**1,890,789**	**11,325**	**11,091**	**234**
0—10	1,116,229	552,072	564,157	6,825	5,715	1,110	1,109,404	546,357	563,047	312	290	22
10—15	404,231	221,809	182,422	16,473	15,004	1,469	387,758	206,805	180,953	982	955	27
15—20	267,399	135,057	132,342	16,099	14,850	1,249	251,300	120,207	131,093	1,591	1,566	25
20 and over	1,879,002	857,558	1,021,444	109,242	103,494	5,748	1,769,760	754,064	1,015,696	8,440	8,280	160
ANIMISTIC	**2,220,526**	**1,086,231**	**1,134,295**	**13,021**	**12,161**	**860**	**2,207,505**	**1,074,070**	**1,133,435**	**327**	**321**	**6**
0—10	740,288	365,160	375,123	701	534	167	739,582	364,626	374,956	4	4	..
10—15	282,131	148,548	133,583	1,628	1,488	140	280,503	147,060	133,443	46	46	..
15—20	196,309	95,354	100,955	1,817	1,717	100	194,492	93,637	100,855	88	86	2
20 and over	1,001,803	477,169	524,634	8,675	8,422	453	992,925	468,747	524,181	189	185	4

Part II.—By Provinces and States.

Age and Religion.	Population.									Literate in English.		
	Total.			Literate.			Illiterate.					
	Persons.	Males.	Females.	Persons.	Males.	Females.	Persons.	Males.	Females.	Persons.	Males.	Females.
1	2	3	4	5	6	7	8	9	10	11	12	13
Bombay.												
ALL RELIGIONS	**19,672,642**	**10,245,847**	**9,426,795**	**1,372,826**	**1,236,206**	**136,620**	**18,299,816**	**9,009,641**	**9,290,175**	**202,454**	**175,691**	**26,763**
0—10 . .	5,265,567	2,658,208	2,607,359	47,137	35,950	11,187	5,218,430	2,622,258	2,596,172	4,363	2,407	1,956
10—15 . .	2,026,567	1,132,045	894,522	153,579	132,079	21,500	1,872,988	999,966	873,022	16,418	13,001	3,417
15—20 . .	1,610,697	856,239	754,458	168,631	146,876	21,755	1,442,066	709,363	732,703	30,196	25,876	4,320
20 and over .	10,769,811	5,599,355	5,170,456	1,003,479	921,301	82,178	9,766,332	4,678,054	5,088,278	151,477	134,407	17,070
HINDU . .	**14,922,311**	**7,660,148**	**7,262,163**	**984,858**	**917,660**	**67,198**	**13,937,453**	**6,742,488**	**7,194,965**	**100,162**	**97,089**	**3,073**
0—10 . .	3,970,996	1,983,829	1,987,167	31,209	25,538	5,671	3,939,787	1,958,291	1,981,496	489	411	78
10—15 . .	1,553,735	855,367	698,368	112,485	100,725	11,760	1,441,250	754,642	686,608	8,204	7,666	538
15—20 . .	1,239,911	648,987	590,924	122,324	111,146	11,178	1,117,587	537,841	579,746	17,427	16,745	682
20 and over .	8,157,669	4,171,965	3,985,704	718,840	680,251	38,589	7,438,829	3,491,714	3,947,115	74,042	72,267	1,775
MUSALMAN .	**4,024,485**	**2,190,195**	**1,834,290**	**174,736**	**162,536**	**12,200**	**3,849,749**	**2,027,659**	**1,822,090**	**11,955**	**11,569**	**386**
0—10 . .	1,118,940	586,415	532,525	5,252	4,301	951	1,113,688	582,114	531,574	78	65	13
10—15 . .	400,718	236,574	164,144	18,243	16,427	1,816	382,475	220,147	162,328	898	855	43
15—20 . .	304,913	171,424	133,489	19,625	17,905	1,720	285,288	153,519	131,769	1,919	1,836	83
20 and over .	2,199,914	1,195,782	1,004,132	131,616	123,903	7,713	2,068,298	1,071,879	996,419	9,060	8,813	247
JAIN . .	**212,309**	**117,519**	**94,790**	**67,816**	**61,683**	**6,133**	**144,493**	**55,836**	**88,657**	**3,909**	**3,838**	**71**
0—10 . .	45,906	22,994	22,912	2,292	1,680	612	43,614	21,314	22,300	18	11	7
10—15 . .	23,089	13,636	9,453	7,464	6,332	1,132	15,625	7,304	8,321	471	455	16
15—20 . .	20,107	11,901	8,206	8,778	7,717	1,061	11,329	4,184	7,145	736	718	18
20 and over .	123,207	68,988	54,219	49,282	45,954	3,328	73,925	23,034	50,891	2,684	2,654	30
Burma.												
ALL RELIGIONS	**12,039,083**	**6,145,471**	**5,893,612**	**2,670,878**	**2,312,883**	**357,995**	**9,368,205**	**3,832,588**	**5,535,617**	**67,837**	**55,803**	**12,034**
0—10 . .	3,169,527	1,566,225	1,603,302	61,760	43,542	18,218	3,107,767	1,522,683	1,585,084	2,562	1,498	1,064
10—15 . .	1,377,509	714,400	663,109	253,133	204,084	49,049	1,124,376	510,316	614,060	6,497	4,665	1,832
15—20 . .	1,118,007	548,748	569,259	324,498	262,684	61,814	793,509	286,064	507,445	9,823	7,878	1,945
20 and over .	6,374,040	3,316,098	3,057,942	2,031,487	1,802,573	228,914	4,342,553	1,513,525	2,829,028	48,955	41,762	7,193
MUSALMAN .	**420,769**	**271,421**	**149,348**	**75,028**	**63,455**	**11,573**	**345,741**	**207,966**	**137,775**	**5,924**	**5,204**	**720**
0—10 . .	97,335	49,447	47,888	1,713	1,172	541	95,622	48,275	47,347	120	96	24
10—15 . .	39,015	22,877	16,138	5,031	3,680	1,351	33,984	19,197	14,787	441	365	76
15—20 . .	40,503	25,228	15,275	8,375	6,560	1,815	32,128	18,668	13,460	795	693	102
20 and over .	243,916	173,869	70,047	59,909	52,043	7,866	184,007	121,826	62,181	4,568	4,050	518
BUDDHIST .	**10,384,544**	**5,113,437**	**5,271,107**	**2,423,629**	**2,107,738**	**315,891**	**7,960,915**	**3,005,699**	**4,955,216**	**21,189**	**19,916**	**1,273**
0—10 . .	2,817,224	1,385,722	1,431,502	54,398	39,110	15,288	2,762,826	1,346,612	1,416,214	313	245	68
10—15 . .	1,232,952	632,177	600,775	235,116	191,823	43,293	997,836	440,354	557,482	2,247	1,992	255
15—20 . .	969,399	459,826	509,573	299,085	244,142	54,943	670,314	215,684	454,630	4,399	4,108	291
20 and over .	5,364,969	2,635,712	2,729,257	1,835,030	1,632,663	202,367	3,529,939	1,003,049	2,526,890	14,230	13,571	659
ANIMISTIC .	**625,539**	**330,270**	**295,269**	**20,459**	**19,588**	**871**	**605,080**	**310,682**	**294,398**	**470**	**443**	**27**
0—10 . .	156,001	80,639	75,362	261	222	39	155,740	80,417	75,323	19	19	..
10—15 . .	62,219	33,386	28,833	936	828	108	61,283	32,558	28,725	28	24	4
15—20 . .	56,210	27,748	27,462	1,418	1,274	144	53,792	26,474	27,318	77	75	2
20 and over .	352,109	188,497	163,612	17,844	17,264	580	334,265	171,233	163,032	346	325	21
Central Provinces and Berar.												
ALL RELIGIONS	**13,916,308**	**6,930,392**	**6,985,916**	**496,236**	**473,716**	**22,520**	**13,420,072**	**6,456,676**	**6,963,396**	**46,102**	**42,054**	**4,048**
0—10 . .	4,073,556	2,014,435	2,059,121	10,998	9,342	1,656	4,062,558	2,005,093	2,057,465	772	457	315
10—15 . .	1,265,160	687,471	577,689	55,835	52,084	3,751	1,209,325	635,387	573,938	2,994	2,554	440
15—20 . .	932,503	470,554	461,949	59,868	56,033	3,835	872,635	414,521	458,114	6,500	5,930	570
20 and over .	7,645,089	3,757,932	3,887,157	369,535	356,257	13,278	7,275,554	3,401,675	3,873,879	35,836	33,113	2,723
HINDU . .	**11,496,486**	**5,731,936**	**5,764,550**	**401,676**	**389,634**	**12,042**	**11,094,810**	**5,342,302**	**5,752,508**	**27,594**	**27,292**	**302**
0—10 . .	3,345,205	1,655,772	1,689,433	8,180	7,343	837	3,337,025	1,648,429	1,688,596	69	65	4
10—15 . .	1,050,889	571,440	479,449	46,023	43,846	2,177	1,004,866	527,603	477,263	1,762	1,720	42
15—20 . .	774,322	391,716	382,606	48,291	46,335	1,956	726,031	345,381	380,650	4,410	4,353	57
20 and over .	6,326,070	3,112,999	3,213,071	299,182	292,110	7,072	6,026,888	2,820,889	3,205,999	21,353	21,154	199
MUSALMAN .	**564,909**	**292,047**	**272,862**	**51,374**	**48,747**	**2,627**	**513,535**	**243,300**	**270,235**	**4,671**	**4,621**	**50**
0—10 . .	157,304	77,576	79,728	1,177	985	192	156,127	76,591	79,536	11	11	..
10—15 . .	54,823	30,688	24,135	5,160	4,754	406	49,663	25,934	23,729	259	256	3
15—20 . .	39,624	21,055	18,569	5,799	5,421	378	33,825	15,634	18,191	738	722	16
20 and over .	313,158	162,728	150,430	39,238	37,587	1,651	273,920	125,141	148,779	3,663	3,632	31
ANIMISTIC .	**1,744,921**	**847,167**	**897,754**	**4,446**	**4,371**	**75**	**1,740,475**	**842,796**	**897,679**	**32**	**32**	**..**
0—10 . .	543,998	267,623	276,375	99	96	3	543,899	267,527	276,372	..	..	..
10—15 . .	148,807	79,375	69,432	554	541	13	148,253	78,834	69,419	1	1	..
15—20 . .	108,971	52,706	56,265	736	726	10	108,235	51,980	56,255	9	9	..
20 and over .	943,145	447,463	495,682	3,057	3,008	49	940,088	444,455	495,633	22	22	..

TABLE VIII.—EDUCATION.

Age and Religion.	Population.									Literate in English.		
	Total.			Literate.			Illiterate.					
	Persons.	Males.	Females.	Persons.	Males.	Females.	Persons.	Males.	Females.	Persons.	Males.	Females.
1	2	3	4	5	6	7	8	9	10	11	12	13
Madras.												
ALL RELIGIONS	41,405,404	20,382,955	21,022,449	3,093,560	2,810,208	283,352	38,311,844	17,572,747	20,739,097	274,625	247,392	27,233
0—10 . .	11,015,652	5,435,856	5,579,796	93,528	75,484	18,044	10,922,124	5,360,372	5,561,752	4,664	3,275	1,389
10—15 . .	4,783,768	2,488,739	2,295,029	344,199	293,178	51,021	4,439,569	2,195,561	2,244,008	27,320	23,152	4,168
15—20 . .	3,565,464	1,786,461	1,779,003	380,969	329,508	51,461	3,184,495	1,456,953	1,727,542	45,833	40,741	5,092
20 and over .	22,040,520	10,671,899	11,368,621	2,274,864	2,112,038	162,826	19,765,656	8,559,861	11,205,795	196,808	180,224	16,584
HINDU . .	36,806,604	18,108,939	18,697,665	2,647,884	2,445,014	202,870	34,158,720	15,663,925	18,494,795	195,960	192,198	3,762
0—10 . .	9,707,612	4,784,239	4,923,373	77,826	65,060	12,766	9,629,786	4,719,179	4,910,607	1,914	1,772	142
10—15 . .	4,234,295	2,203,385	2,030,910	292,255	255,212	37,043	3,942,040	1,948,173	1,993,867	18,742	18,000	742
15—20 . .	3,146,737	1,584,406	1,562,331	322,406	285,444	36,962	2,824,331	1,298,962	1,525,369	33,717	32,854	863
20 and over .	19,717,960	9,536,909	10,181,051	1,955,397	1,839,298	116,099	17,762,563	7,697,611	10,064,952	141,587	139,572	2,015
MUSALMAN .	2,740,408	1,351,119	1,389,289	238,838	223,891	14,947	2,501,570	1,127,228	1,374,342	12,595	12,401	194
0—10 . .	778,897	389,045	389,852	5,165	4,318	847	773,732	384,727	389,005	139	132	7
10—15 . .	335,377	174,578	160,799	21,941	19,415	2,526	313,436	155,163	158,273	1,004	969	35
15—20 . .	254,570	123,839	130,731	28,200	25,669	2,531	226,370	98,170	128,200	2,031	1,999	32
20 and over .	1,371,564	663,657	707,907	183,532	174,489	9,043	1,188,032	489,168	698,864	9,421	9,301	120
CHRISTIAN .	1,191,266	586,836	604,430	197,670	132,870	64,800	993,596	453,966	539,630	65,276	42,174	23,102
0—10 . .	332,466	164,585	167,881	10,325	5,934	4,391	322,141	158,651	163,490	2,582	1,353	1,229
10—15 . .	143,100	72,997	70,103	29,135	17,796	11,339	113,965	55,201	58,764	7,488	4,125	3,363
15—20 . .	107,016	51,594	55,422	29,175	17,343	11,832	77,841	34,251	43,590	9,980	5,822	4,158
20 and over .	608,684	297,660	311,024	129,035	91,797	37,238	479,649	205,863	273,786	45,226	30,874	14,352
North-West Frontier Province.												
ALL RELIGIONS	2,196,933	1,182,102	1,014,831	72,986	66,984	6,002	2,123,947	1,115,118	1,008,829	10,543	9,788	755
0—10 . .	680,902	352,690	328,212	1,434	1,011	423	679,468	351,679	327,789	170	107	63
10—15 . .	238,483	139,514	98,969	6,015	5,162	853	232,468	134,352	98,116	472	448	24
15—20 . .	164,114	91,540	72,574	8,435	7,567	868	155,679	83,973	71,706	1,234	1,193	41
20 and over .	1,113,434	598,358	515,076	57,102	53,244	3,858	1,056,332	545,114	511,218	8,667	8,040	627
HINDU . .	119,942	71,397	48,545	29,412	26,665	2,747	90,530	44,732	45,798	2,563	2,536	27
0—10 . .	28,984	14,936	14,048	612	415	197	28,372	14,521	13,851	6	5	1
10—15 . .	12,136	7,154	4,982	2,661	2,198	463	9,475	4,956	4,519	202	199	3
15—20 . .	11,001	6,952	4,049	3,619	3,199	420	7,382	3,753	3,629	558	549	9
20 and over .	67,821	42,355	25,466	22,520	20,853	1,667	45,301	21,502	23,799	1,797	1,783	14
MUSALMAN .	2,039,994	1,085,276	954,718	27,427	26,288	1,139	2,012,567	1,058,988	953,579	1,969	1,953	16
0—10 . .	644,869	333,983	310,886	407	343	64	644,462	333,640	310,822	10	10	..
10—15 . .	223,426	130,529	92,897	2,502	2,327	175	220,924	128,202	92,722	196	195	1
15—20 . .	149,970	82,403	67,567	3,530	3,306	224	146,440	79,097	67,343	490	487	3
20 and over .	1,021,729	538,361	483,368	20,988	20,312	676	1,000,741	518,049	482,692	1,273	1,261	12
SIKH . .	30,345	19,967	10,378	10,496	9,130	1,366	19,849	10,837	9,012	508	499	9
0—10 . .	6,370	3,414	2,956	249	153	96	6,121	3,261	2,860	..	..	..
10—15 . .	2,811	1,778	1,033	795	603	192	2,016	1,175	841	30	30	..
15—20 . .	2,953	2,066	887	1,164	982	182	1,789	1,084	705	83	83	..
20 and over .	18,211	12,709	5,502	8,288	7,392	896	9,923	5,317	4,606	395	386	9
Punjab.												
ALL RELIGIONS	19,974,956	10,992,067	8,982,889	774,845	717,384	57,461	19,200,111	10,274,683	8,925,428	109,101	98,730	10,371
0—10 . .	5,500,497	2,904,493	2,596,004	12,412	8,781	3,631	5,488,085	2,895,712	2,592,373	1,848	997	851
10—15 . .	2,252,887	1,321,272	931,615	68,838	59,519	9,319	2,184,049	1,261,753	922,296	8,052	6,752	1,300
15—20 . .	1,720,943	994,090	726,853	93,434	83,365	10,069	1,627,509	910,725	716,784	17,204	15,665	1,539
20 and over .	10,500,629	5,772,212	4,728,417	600,161	565,719	34,442	9,900,468	5,206,493	4,693,975	81,997	75,316	6,681
HINDU . .	6,682,818	3,686,923	2,995,895	404,387	380,096	24,291	6,278,431	3,306,827	2,971,604	42,969	41,742	1,227
0—10 . .	1,717,243	903,213	814,030	5,567	4,115	1,452	1,711,676	899,098	812,578	156	128	28
10—15 . .	748,757	436,692	312,065	35,200	30,610	4,590	713,557	406,082	307,475	3,508	3,155	353
15—20 . .	633,535	369,505	264,030	51,015	45,720	5,295	582,520	323,785	258,735	8,577	8,041	536
20 and over .	3,583,283	1,977,513	1,605,770	312,605	299,651	12,954	3,270,678	1,677,862	1,592,816	30,728	30,418	310
MUSALMAN .	10,955,721	5,967,408	4,988,313	176,704	166,937	9,767	10,779,017	5,800,471	4,978,546	22,820	22,473	347
0—10 . .	3,167,014	1,660,748	1,506,266	2,559	2,103	456	3,164,455	1,658,645	1,505,810	89	72	17
10—15 . .	1,246,584	725,002	521,582	17,059	15,687	1,372	1,229,525	709,315	520,210	1,921	1,872	49
15—20 . .	886,746	500,906	385,840	21,917	20,410	1,507	864,829	480,496	384,333	4,590	4,520	70
20 and over .	5,655,377	3,080,752	2,574,625	135,169	128,737	6,432	5,520,208	2,952,015	2,568,193	16,220	16,009	211
SIKH . .	2,093,804	1,197,922	895,882	145,184	132,362	12,822	1,948,620	1,065,560	883,060	8,353	8,240	113
0—10 . .	547,704	304,575	243,129	2,394	1,572	822	545,310	303,003	242,307	17	15	2
10—15 . .	231,994	145,040	86,954	13,237	11,203	2,034	218,757	133,837	84,920	853	839	14
15—20 . .	181,181	112,679	68,502	16,630	14,660	1,970	164,551	98,019	66,532	1,980	1,950	30
20 and over .	1,132,925	635,628	497,297	112,923	104,927	7,996	1,020,002	530,701	489,301	5,503	5,436	67

PART II.—BY PROVINCES AND STATES—*continued.*

AGE AND RELIGION.	POPULATION.									LITERATE IN ENGLISH.		
	TOTAL.			LITERATE.			ILLITERATE.					
	Persons.	Males.	Females.	Persons.	Males.	Females.	Persons.	Males.	Females.	Persons.	Males.	Females.
1	2	3	4	5	6	7	8	9	10	11	12	13
United Provinces.												
ALL RELIGIONS	**47,182,044**	**24,641,831**	**22,540,213**	**1,618,465**	**1,505,945**	**112,520**	**45,563,579**	**23,135,886**	**22,427,693**	**136,616**	**121,529**	**15,087**
0—10 . .	12,000,453	6,157,650	5,842,803	60,981	51,285	9,696	11,939,472	6,106,365	5,833,107	4,072	2,719	1,353
10—15 . .	5,336,920	3,020,421	2,316,499	197,283	180,877	16,406	5,139,637	2,839,544	2,300,093	12,658	10,833	1,825
15—20 . .	3,822,362	2,118,003	1,704,359	192,081	176,686	15,395	3,630,281	1,941,317	1,688,964	20,048	18,101	1,947
20 and over . .	26,021,902	13,345,487	12,676,415	1,168,120	1,097,097	71,023	24,853,782	12,248,390	12,605,392	99,838	89,876	9,962
Age Unspecified.	407	270	137	..	..	..	407	270	137	..	..	..
HINDU . .	**40,122,238**	**20,949,641**	**19,172,597**	**1,281,803**	**1,213,997**	**67,806**	**38,840,435**	**19,735,644**	**19,104,791**	**64,877**	**63,782**	**1,095**
0—10 . .	10,150,627	5,213,769	4,936,858	45,273	39,852	5,421	10,105,354	5,173,917	4,931,437	1,061	989	72
10—15 . .	4,522,769	2,562,346	1,960,423	158,671	148,997	9,674	4,364,098	2,413,349	1,950,749	6,613	6,442	171
15—20 . .	3,242,433	1,802,723	1,439,710	152,781	143,582	9,199	3,089,652	1,659,141	1,430,511	11,308	11,112	196
20 and over .	22,206,016	11,370,542	10,835,474	925,078	881,566	43,512	21,280,938	10,488,976	10,791,962	45,895	45,239	656
Age Unspecified.	393	261	132	..	..	..	393	261	132	..	..	..
MUSALMAN .	**6,658,373**	**3,466,287**	**3,192,086**	**224,288**	**205,212**	**19,076**	**6,434,085**	**3,261,075**	**3,173,010**	**21,521**	**20,966**	**555**
0—10 . .	1,757,226	895,513	861,713	8,642	7,261	1,381	1,748,584	888,252	860,332	334	316	18
10—15 . .	769,716	432,694	337,022	26,062	23,241	2,821	743,654	409,453	334,201	2,233	2,141	92
15—20 . .	542,631	294,483	248,148	26,772	24,190	2,582	515,859	270,293	245,566	4,108	4,025	83
20 and over .	3,588,786	1,843,588	1,745,198	162,812	150,520	12,292	3,425,974	1,693,068	1,732,906	14,846	14,484	362
Age Unspecified.	14	9	5	..	..	..	14	9	5	..	..	..
CHRISTIAN .	**177,949**	**100,818**	**77,131**	**53,299**	**35,213**	**18,086**	**124,650**	**65,605**	**59,045**	**43,591**	**30,399**	**13,192**
0—10 . .	42,415	21,669	20,746	3,851	1,794	2,057	38,564	19,875	18,689	2,556	1,303	1,253
10—15 . .	18,681	10,284	8,397	4,794	2,278	2,516	13,887	8,006	5,881	3,070	1,540	1,530
15—20 . .	15,385	8,006	7,379	4,910	2,489	2,421	10,475	5,517	4,958	3,510	1,894	1,625
20 and over .	101,468	60,859	40,609	39,744	28,652	11,092	61,724	32,207	29,517	34,446	25,662	8,784
Baroda State.												
ALL RELIGIONS	**2,032,798**	**1,055,935**	**976,863**	**204,947**	**184,883**	**20,064**	**1,827,851**	**871,052**	**956,799**	**9,741**	**9,304**	**437**
0—10 . .	536,949	277,732	259,217	9,248	6,771	2,477	527,701	270,961	256,740	39	21	18
10—15 . .	179,303	98,702	80,601	33,016	27,175	5,841	146,287	71,527	74,760	936	862	74
15—20 . .	173,517	93,573	79,944	27,419	24,189	3,230	146,098	69,384	76,714	2,620	2,505	115
20 and over .	1,143,029	585,928	557,101	135,264	126,748	8,516	1,007,765	459,180	548,585	6,146	5,916	230
HINDU . .	**1,697,146**	**884,474**	**812,672**	**159,763**	**146,056**	**13,707**	**1,537,383**	**738,418**	**798,965**	**7,548**	**7,412**	**136**
0—10 . .	444,094	230,361	213,733	7,458	5,489	1,969	436,636	224,872	211,764	9	8	1
10—15 . .	148,169	82,216	65,953	26,800	22,402	4,398	121,369	59,814	61,555	730	708	22
15—20 . .	145,717	79,258	66,459	21,807	19,584	2,223	123,910	59,674	64,236	2,122	2,088	34
20 and over .	959,166	492,639	466,527	103,698	98,581	5,117	855,468	394,058	461,410	4,687	4,608	79
MUSALMAN .	**160,887**	**82,986**	**77,901**	**20,576**	**19,231**	**1,345**	**140,311**	**63,755**	**76,556**	**350**	**344**	**6**
0—10 . .	41,188	21,120	20,068	620	475	145	40,568	20,645	19,923	..	..	..
10—15 . .	14,575	7,903	6,672	2,663	2,306	357	11,912	5,597	6,315	22	21	1
15—20 . .	13,647	7,257	6,390	2,486	2,274	212	11,161	4,983	6,178	54	54	..
20 and over .	91,477	46,706	44,771	14,807	14,176	631	76,670	32,530	44,140	274	269	5
ANIMISTIC .	**115,411**	**58,858**	**56,553**	**867**	**784**	**83**	**114,544**	**58,074**	**56,470**	..	..	..
0—10 . .	38,199	19,344	18,855	65	52	13	38,134	19,292	18,842	..	..	..
10—15 . .	10,526	5,385	5,141	230	209	21	10,296	5,176	5,120	..	..	..
15—20 . .	8,882	4,264	4,618	112	102	10	8,770	4,162	4,608	..	..	..
20 and over .	57,804	29,865	27,939	460	421	39	57,344	29,444	27,900	..	..	..
Bihar and Orissa States.												
ALL RELIGIONS	**3,945,209**	**1,955,125**	**1,990,084**	**90,412**	**85,979**	**4,433**	**3,854,797**	**1,869,146**	**1,985,651**	**2,706**	**2,589**	**117**
0—10 . .	1,236,506	608,119	628,387	2,772	2,384	388	1,233,734	605,735	627,999	69	57	12
10—15 . .	462,981	247,043	215,938	9,292	8,555	737	453,689	238,488	215,201	287	275	12
15—20 . .	320,308	159,496	160,812	9,717	9,119	598	310,591	150,377	160,214	404	388	16
20 and over .	1,925,414	940,467	984,947	68,631	65,921	2,710	1,856,783	874,546	982,237	1,946	1,869	77
HINDU . .	**3,388,429**	**1,678,229**	**1,710,200**	**86,843**	**82,797**	**4,046**	**3,301,586**	**1,595,432**	**1,706,154**	**2,393**	**2,350**	**43**
0—10 . .	1,049,329	515,655	533,674	2,645	2,295	350	1,046,684	513,360	533,324	56	52	4
10—15 . .	397,843	212,452	185,391	8,994	8,313	681	388,849	204,139	184,710	274	268	6
15—20 . .	274,195	137,301	136,894	9,366	8,807	559	264,829	128,491	136,335	375	369	6
20 and over .	1,667,062	812,821	854,241	65,838	63,382	2,456	1,601,224	749,439	851,785	1,688	1,661	27
MUSALMAN .	**16,577**	**9,160**	**7,417**	**1,765**	**1,693**	**72**	**14,812**	**7,467**	**7,345**	**92**	**91**	**1**
0—10 . .	4,213	2,147	2,066	41	36	5	4,172	2,111	2,061	2	2	..
10—15 . .	1,659	960	699	100	89	11	1,559	871	688	2	2	..
15—20 . .	1,228	671	557	112	104	8	1,116	567	549	4	3	1
20 and over .	9,477	5,382	4,095	1,512	1,464	48	7,965	3,918	4,047	84	84	..
ANIMISTIC .	**499,762**	**247,429**	**252,333**	**822**	**782**	**40**	**498,940**	**246,647**	**252,293**	**12**	**12**	..
0—10 . .	168,453	83,054	85,399	48	38	10	168,405	83,016	85,389	..	..	..
10—15 . .	58,369	30,861	27,508	111	103	8	58,258	30,758	27,500	2	2	..
15—20 . .	41,656	20,005	21,651	139	135	4	41,517	19,870	21,647	7	7	..
20 and over .	231,284	113,509	117,775	524	506	18	230,760	113,003	117,757	3	3	..

TABLE VIII.—EDUCATION.

Age and Religion.	Population. Total. Persons.	Total. Males.	Total. Females.	Literate. Persons.	Literate. Males.	Literate. Females.	Illiterate. Persons.	Illiterate. Males.	Illiterate. Females.	Literate in English. Persons.	Literate in English. Males.	Literate in English. Females.
1	2	3	4	5	6	7	8	9	10	11	12	13
Bombay States.												
ALL RELIGIONS	**7,411,675**	**3,765,401**	**3,646,274**	**487,667**	**445,829**	**41,838**	**6,924,008**	**3,319,572**	**3,604,436**	**28,472**	**27,708**	**764**
0—10	2,078,632	1,043,251	1,035,381	21,045	17,486	3,559	2,057,587	1,025,765	1,031,822	85	56	29
10—15	700,518	386,267	314,251	62,825	54,970	7,855	637,693	331,297	306,396	3,126	3,031	95
15—20	605,120	325,094	280,026	62,080	55,149	6,931	543,040	269,945	273,095	6,760	6,632	128
20 and over	4,027,405	2,010,789	2,016,616	341,717	313,224	23,493	3,685,688	1,692,565	1,993,123	18,501	17,989	512
HINDU	**6,054,992**	**3,081,688**	**2,973,304**	**342,739**	**314,936**	**27,803**	**5,712,253**	**2,766,752**	**2,945,501**	**20,793**	**20,572**	**221**
0—10	1,690,692	847,702	842,990	14,345	12,093	2,252	1,676,347	835,609	840,738	23	18	5
10—15	565,877	312,491	253,386	42,807	37,877	4,930	523,070	274,614	248,456	2,185	2,154	31
15—20	499,220	269,736	229,484	44,297	39,643	4,654	454,923	230,093	224,830	4,982	4,940	42
20 and over	3,290,203	1,651,759	1,647,444	241,290	225,323	15,967	3,057,913	1,426,436	1,631,477	13,603	13,460	143
MUSALMAN	**877,431**	**445,640**	**431,791**	**65,814**	**62,000**	**3,814**	**811,617**	**383,640**	**427,977**	**1,867**	**1,839**	**28**
0—10	249,888	127,020	122,868	2,511	2,255	256	247,377	124,765	122,612	5	5	..
10—15	86,933	48,379	38,554	8,822	8,194	628	78,111	40,185	37,926	188	183	5
15—20	68,106	35,670	32,436	7,720	7,151	569	60,386	28,519	31,867	399	393	6
20 and over	472,504	234,571	237,933	46,761	44,400	2,361	425,743	190,171	235,572	1,275	1,258	17
JAIN	**277,643**	**137,132**	**140,511**	**73,107**	**64,743**	**8,364**	**204,536**	**72,389**	**132,147**	**3,922**	**3,895**	**27**
0—10	70,266	34,566	35,700	3,833	2,938	895	66,433	31,628	34,805	5	4	1
10—15	29,433	15,684	13,749	10,368	8,405	1,963	19,065	7,279	11,786	611	605	6
15—20	23,108	12,223	10,885	9,315	7,922	1,393	13,793	4,301	9,492	1,159	1,153	6
20 and over	154,836	74,659	80,177	49,591	45,478	4,113	105,245	29,181	76,064	2,147	2,133	14
Central India Agency.												
ALL RELIGIONS	**9,356,980**	**4,801,459**	**4,555,521**	**242,820**	**231,203**	**11,617**	**9,114,160**	**4,570,256**	**4,543,904**	**18,144**	**16,868**	**1,276**
0—10	2,588,294	1,304,325	1,283,969	7,060	6,257	803	2,581,234	1,298,068	1,283,166	292	194	98
10—15	864,283	483,893	380,390	23,031	21,600	1,431	841,252	462,293	378,959	1,109	985	124
15—20	737,911	403,981	333,930	26,117	24,448	1,669	711,794	379,533	332,261	2,362	2,167	195
20 and over	5,166,492	2,609,260	2,557,232	186,612	178,898	7,714	4,979,880	2,430,362	2,549,518	14,381	13,522	859
HINDU	**8,262,638**	**4,241,694**	**4,020,944**	**184,966**	**179,002**	**5,964**	**8,077,672**	**4,062,692**	**4,014,980**	**10,476**	**10,315**	**161**
0—10	2,273,102	1,146,326	1,126,776	5,220	4,814	406	2,267,882	1,141,512	1,126,370	84	76	8
10—15	767,773	431,335	336,438	17,965	17,244	721	749,808	414,091	335,717	733	715	18
15—20	654,645	360,849	293,796	20,118	19,302	816	634,527	341,547	292,980	1,663	1,632	31
20 and over	4,567,118	2,303,184	2,263,934	141,663	137,642	4,021	4,425,455	2,165,542	2,259,913	7,996	7,892	104
MUSALMAN	**511,200**	**266,494**	**244,706**	**31,284**	**28,437**	**2,847**	**479,916**	**238,057**	**241,859**	**1,776**	**1,745**	**31**
0—10	131,458	66,063	65,395	882	686	196	130,576	65,377	65,199	20	19	1
10—15	46,943	25,933	21,010	2,806	2,418	388	44,137	23,515	20,622	139	134	5
15—20	39,503	21,402	18,101	3,216	2,853	363	36,287	18,549	17,738	260	254	6
20 and over	293,296	153,096	140,200	24,380	22,480	1,900	268,916	130,616	138,300	1,357	1,338	19
ANIMISTIC	**483,394**	**239,618**	**243,776**	**303**	**295**	**8**	**483,091**	**239,323**	**243,768**	**3**	**3**	..
0—10	161,643	80,803	80,840	6	6	..	161,637	80,797	80,840	..	..	..
10—15	40,778	21,709	19,069	22	21	1	40,756	21,688	19,068	..	..	..
15—20	35,318	17,227	18,091	41	39	2	35,277	17,188	18,089	..	..	..
20 and over	245,655	119,879	125,776	234	229	5	245,421	119,650	125,771	3	3	..
Central Provinces States.												
ALL RELIGIONS	**2,117,002**	**1,053,630**	**1,063,372**	**24,951**	**23,825**	**1,126**	**2,092,051**	**1,029,805**	**1,062,246**	**1,148**	**1,047**	**101**
0—10	699,611	344,404	355,207	467	400	67	699,144	344,004	355,140	21	12	9
10—15	210,735	115,298	95,437	3,190	2,950	240	207,545	112,348	95,197	73	67	6
15—20	146,659	74,787	71,872	3,578	3,393	185	143,081	71,394	71,687	193	188	5
20 and over	1,059,997	519,141	540,856	17,716	17,082	634	1,042,281	502,059	540,222	861	780	81
HINDU	**1,311,388**	**650,807**	**660,581**	**21,212**	**20,385**	**827**	**1,290,176**	**630,422**	**659,754**	**785**	**776**	**9**
0—10	418,950	206,322	212,628	373	322	51	418,577	206,000	212,577	3	3	..
10—15	128,275	70,384	57,891	2,773	2,573	200	125,502	67,811	57,691	59	57	2
15—20	91,238	47,026	44,212	3,066	2,934	132	88,172	44,092	44,080	161	160	1
20 and over	672,925	327,075	345,850	15,000	14,556	444	657,925	312,519	345,406	562	556	6
MUSALMAN	**20,129**	**10,189**	**9,940**	**1,897**	**1,698**	**109**	**18,313**	**8,492**	**9,831**	**109**	**107**	**2**
0—10	5,345	2,675	2,670	28	23	5	5,317	2,652	2,665	..	..	..
10—15	1,906	1,034	872	164	146	18	1,742	888	854	4	4	..
15—20	1,435	790	645	222	203	19	1,213	587	626	15	15	..
20 and over	11,434	5,681	5,753	1,398	1,326	67	10,041	4,355	5,686	90	88	2
ANIMISTIC	**745,434**	**372,384**	**373,050**	**995**	**970**	**25**	**744,439**	**371,414**	**373,025**	**10**	**10**	..
0—10	260,072	127,903	132,169	37	36	1	260,035	127,867	132,168	..	..	..
10—15	75,816	41,172	34,644	171	163	8	75,645	41,009	34,636	2	2	..
15—20	51,269	25,576	25,603	184	177	7	51,085	25,399	25,686	1	1	..
20 and over	358,277	177,733	180,544	603	594	9	357,674	177,139	180,535	7	7	..

Part II.—By Provinces and States—*continued*.

Age and Religion.	Population. Total. Persons.	Males.	Females.	Literate. Persons.	Males.	Females.	Illiterate. Persons.	Males.	Females.	Literate in English. Persons.	Males.	Females.
1	2	3	4	5	6	7	8	9	10	11	12	13
Hyderabad State.												
ALL RELIGIONS	**13,374,676**	**6,797,118**	**6,577,558**	**368,166**	**344,089**	**24,077**	**13,006,510**	**6,453,029**	**6,553,481**	**26,526**	**22,965**	**3,561**
0—10	3,618,680	1,788,219	1,830,461	9,493	7,621	1,872	3,609,187	1,780,598	1,828,589	773	490	283
10—15	1,392,802	764,794	628,008	34,190	30,670	3,520	1,358,612	734,124	624,488	2,290	1,829	461
15—20	1,004,122	499,688	504,434	38,249	34,574	3,675	965,873	465,114	500,759	3,347	2,820	527
20 and over	7,359,072	3,744,417	3,614,655	286,234	271,224	15,010	7,072,838	3,473,193	3,599,645	20,116	17,826	2,290
HINDU	**11,626,146**	**5,897,158**	**5,728,988**	**266,968**	**256,095**	**10,873**	**11,359,178**	**5,641,063**	**5,718,115**	**8,838**	**8,483**	**355**
0—10	3,153,760	1,558,296	1,595,464	6,209	5,288	921	3,147,551	1,553,008	1,594,543	170	143	27
10—15	1,204,040	662,127	541,913	24,619	23,054	1,565	1,179,421	639,073	540,348	825	766	59
15—20	871,698	432,742	438,956	27,234	25,654	1,580	844,464	407,088	437,376	1,190	1,120	70
20 and over	6,396,648	3,243,993	3,152,655	208,906	202,099	6,807	6,187,742	3,041,894	3,145,848	6,653	6,454	199
MUSALMAN	**1,380,990**	**706,821**	**674,169**	**81,260**	**72,783**	**8,477**	**1,299,730**	**634,038**	**665,692**	**7,020**	**6,692**	**328**
0—10	348,800	172,265	176,535	2,259	1,703	556	346,541	170,562	175,979	150	110	40
10—15	148,779	80,349	68,430	7,518	6,263	1,255	141,261	74,086	67,175	727	665	62
15—20	107,026	53,754	53,272	9,042	7,657	1,385	97,984	46,097	51,887	1,230	1,172	58
20 and over	776,385	400,453	375,932	62,441	57,160	5,281	713,944	343,293	370,651	4,913	4,745	168
ANIMISTIC	**285,722**	**149,023**	**136,699**	**247**	**216**	**31**	**285,475**	**148,807**	**136,668**	..	..	..
0—10	95,100	47,402	47,698	14	10	4	95,086	47,392	47,694	..	..	..
10—15	31,273	17,636	13,637	55	45	10	31,218	17,591	13,627	..	..	..
15—20	18,846	9,954	8,892	32	28	4	18,814	9,926	8,888	..	..	..
20 and over	140,503	74,031	66,472	146	133	13	140,357	73,898	66,459	..	..	..
Kashmir State.												
ALL RELIGIONS	**3,103,501**	**1,644,978**	**1,458,523**	**64,936**	**63,251**	**1,685**	**3,038,565**	**1,581,727**	**1,456,838**	**6,132**	**5,972**	**160**
0—10	922,103	472,693	449,410	835	752	83	921,268	471,941	449,327	99	91	8
10—15	347,154	192,256	154,898	4,565	4,349	216	342,589	187,907	154,682	736	724	12
15—20	270,870	143,115	127,755	6,188	5,952	236	264,682	137,163	127,519	1,212	1,197	15
20 and over	1,563,374	836,914	726,460	53,348	52,198	1,150	1,510,026	784,716	725,310	4,085	3,960	125
HINDU	**689,047**	**371,805**	**317,242**	**41,753**	**40,771**	**982**	**647,294**	**331,034**	**316,260**	**4,818**	**4,783**	**35**
0—10	167,462	84,921	82,541	582	531	51	166,880	84,390	82,490	81	79	2
10—15	71,020	40,544	30,476	3,131	2,989	142	67,889	37,555	30,334	637	630	7
15—20	57,895	30,716	27,179	3,966	3,815	151	53,929	26,901	27,028	1,009	1,002	7
20 and over	392,670	215,624	177,046	34,074	33,436	638	358,596	182,188	176,408	3,091	3,072	19
MUSALMAN	**2,344,206**	**1,236,565**	**1,107,641**	**18,247**	**18,000**	**247**	**2,325,959**	**1,218,565**	**1,107,394**	**760**	**757**	**3**
0—10	736,613	378,631	357,982	166	156	10	736,447	378,475	357,972	7	6	1
10—15	269,009	147,868	121,141	1,115	1,091	24	267,894	146,777	121,117	59	58	1
15—20	206,851	109,196	97,655	1,755	1,710	36	205,096	107,477	97,619	153	153	..
20 and over	1,131,733	600,870	530,863	15,211	15,034	177	1,116,522	585,836	530,686	541	540	1
BUDDHIST	**36,322**	**18,170**	**18,152**	**1,322**	**1,283**	**39**	**35,000**	**16,887**	**18,113**	**1**	**1**	..
0—10	7,500	3,651	3,849	..	..	..	7,500	3,651	3,849	..	..	..
10—15	3,232	1,633	1,599	28	27	1	3,204	1,606	1,598	..	..	..
15—20	3,122	1,562	1,560	94	93	1	3,028	1,469	1,559	..	..	..
20 and over	22,468	11,324	11,144	1,200	1,163	37	21,268	10,161	11,107	1	1	..
Madras States.												
ALL RELIGIONS	**4,811,841**	**2,411,758**	**2,400,083**	**688,822**	**575,283**	**113,539**	**4,123,019**	**1,836,475**	**2,286,544**	**38,706**	**33,942**	**4,764**
0—10	1,299,063	645,023	654,040	19,828	13,405	6,423	1,279,235	631,618	647,617	747	539	208
10—15	578,458	299,590	278,868	70,039	50,784	19,255	508,419	248,806	259,613	4,238	3,307	931
15—20	454,565	223,542	231,023	89,229	67,887	21,342	365,336	155,655	209,681	7,636	6,458	1,178
20 and over	2,479,755	1,243,603	1,236,152	509,726	443,207	66,519	1,970,029	800,396	1,169,633	26,085	23,638	2,447
HINDU	**3,321,755**	**1,652,659**	**1,669 096**	**440,999**	**377,191**	**63,808**	**2,880,756**	**1,275,468**	**1,605,288**	**23,290**	**21,915**	**1,375**
0—10	871,590	433,203	438,387	11,932	8,310	3,622	859,658	424,893	434,765	343	258	85
10—15	388,248	200,951	187,297	42,931	32,371	10,560	345,317	168,580	176,737	2,356	2,013	343
15—20	311,303	151,584	159,719	55,368	43,415	11,953	255,935	108,169	147,766	4,203	3,832	371
20 and over	1,750,614	866,921	883,693	330,768	293,095	37,673	1,419,846	573,826	846,020	16,388	15,812	576
MUSALMAN	**314,498**	**160,692**	**153,806**	**28,732**	**27,015**	**1,717**	**285,766**	**133,677**	**152,089**	**552**	**540**	**12**
0—10	90,256	44,943	45,313	479	368	111	89,777	44,575	45,202	8	8	..
10—15	39,617	20,751	18,866	1,951	1,695	256	37,666	19,056	18,610	59	59	..
15—20	29,597	14,788	14,809	3,078	2,823	255	26,519	11,965	14,554	102	98	4
20 and over	155,028	80,210	74,818	23,224	22,129	1,095	131,804	58,081	73,723	383	375	8
CHRISTIAN	**1,154,209**	**587,412**	**566,797**	**218,665**	**170,722**	**47,943**	**935,544**	**416,690**	**518,854**	**14,805**	**11,439**	**3,366**
0—10	331,731	164,065	167,666	7,413	4,726	2,687	324,318	159,339	164,079	396	273	123
10—15	148,174	76,643	71,531	25,123	16,689	8,434	123,051	59,954	63,097	1,821	1,234	587
15—20	111,696	56,235	55,461	30,740	21,618	9,122	80,956	34,617	46,339	3,321	2,520	801
20 and over	562,608	290,469	272,139	155,389	127,689	27,700	407,219	162,780	244,439	9,267	7,412	1,855

TABLE VIII.—Education. Part II.—By Provinces and States—*concluded.*

Age and Religion.	Population. Total. Persons.	Total. Males.	Total. Females.	Literate. Persons.	Literate. Males.	Literate. Females.	Illiterate. Persons.	Illiterate. Males.	Illiterate. Females.	Literate in English. Persons.	Literate in English. Males.	Literate in English. Females.
1	2	3	4	5	6	7	8	9	10	11	12	13
Mysore State.												
ALL RELIGIONS	5,806,193	2,934,621	2,871,572	364,998	328,816	36,182	5,441,195	2,605,805	2,835,390	40,641	34,469	6,172
0—10 . .	1,451,434	707,074	744,360	17,268	13,326	3,942	1,434,166	693,748	740,418	1,267	761	506
10—15 . .	719,828	368,867	350,961	45,059	37,933	7,126	674,769	330,934	343,835	4,259	3,373	886
15—20 . .	526,809	272,949	253,860	43,395	37,318	6,077	483,414	235,631	247,783	5,934	4,983	951
20 and over .	3,108,122	1,585,731	1,522,391	259,276	240,239	19,037	2,848,846	1,345,492	1,503,354	29,181	25,352	3,829
HINDU . .	5,340,908	2,689,851	2,651,057	298,711	276,967	21,744	5,042,197	2,412,884	2,629,313	23,883	23,221	662
0—10 . .	1,325,711	645,076	680,635	14,168	11,490	2,678	1,311,543	633,586	677,957	342	313	29
10—15 . .	663,213	338,483	324,730	37,637	32,910	4,727	625,576	305,573	320,003	2,539	2,398	141
15—20 . .	483,607	250,359	233,248	35,636	31,838	3,798	447,971	218,521	229,450	4,051	3,894	157
20 and over .	2,868,377	1,455,933	1,412,444	211,270	200,729	10,541	2,657,107	1,255,204	1,401,903	16,951	16,616	335
MUSALMAN .	314,494	165,824	148,670	39,320	33,175	6,145	275,174	132,649	142,525	2,002	1,952	50
0—10 . .	86,826	42,823	44,003	1,539	1,024	515	85,287	41,799	43,488	12	12	..
10—15 . .	38,207	20,756	17,451	4,248	3,109	1,139	33,959	17,647	16,312	152	145	7
15—20 . .	29,083	15,405	13,678	4,531	3,530	1,001	24,552	11,875	12,677	291	275	16
20 and over .	160,378	86,840	73,538	29,002	25,512	3,490	131,376	61,328	70,048	1,547	1,520	27
ANIMISTIC .	72,196	36,999	35,197	458	416	42	71,738	36,583	35,155	4	4	..
0—10 . .	19,913	9,791	10,122	34	30	4	19,879	9,761	10,118	..	..	..
10—15 . .	9,368	4,973	4,395	60	55	5	9,308	4,918	4,390	..	..	..
15—20 . .	6,235	3,168	3,067	47	39	8	6,188	3,129	3,059	..	..	..
20 and over .	36,680	19,067	17,613	317	292	25	36,363	18,775	17,588	4	4	..
Punjab States.												
ALL RELIGIONS	4,212,794	2,322,908	1,889,886	124,350	119,079	5,271	4,088,444	2,203,829	1,884,615	8,460	7,977	483
0—10 . .	1,083,431	569,922	513,509	1,082	850	232	1,082,349	569,072	513,277	92	55	37
10—15 . .	448,880	261,878	187,002	6,884	6,375	509	441,996	255,503	186,493	572	544	28
15—20 . .	386,418	224,525	161,893	12,931	12,120	811	373,487	212,405	161,082	1,554	1,484	70
20 and over .	2,294,065	1,266,583	1,027,482	103,453	99,734	3,719	2,190,612	1,166,849	1,023,763	6,242	5,894	348
HINDU .	2,090,803	1,134,108	956,695	80,483	77,842	2,641	2,010,320	1,056,266	954,054	4,791	4,722	69
0—10 .	513,481	265,115	248,366	588	488	100	512,893	264,627	248,266	14	14	..
10—15 . .	219,973	125,617	94,356	4,357	4,052	305	215,616	121,565	94,051	367	360	7
15—20 . .	198,435	112,173	86,262	8,501	8,066	435	189,934	104,107	85,827	903	886	17
20 and over .	1,158,914	631,203	527,711	67,037	65,236	1,801	1,091,877	565,967	525,910	3,507	3,462	45
MUSALMAN .	1,319,756	728,535	591,221	16,861	16,095	766	1,302,895	712,440	590,455	1,724	1,691	33
0—10 . .	365,718	193,664	172,054	185	150	35	365,533	193,514	172,019	10	8	2
10—15 . .	143,249	84,281	58,968	1,156	1,084	72	142,093	83,197	58,896	105	100	5
15—20 .	110,353	62,979	47,374	1,917	1,795	122	108,436	61,184	47,252	310	304	6
20 and over .	700,436	387,611	312,825	13,603	13,066	537	686,833	374,545	312,288	1,299	1,279	20
SIKH . .	789,925	453,673	336,252	24,196	22,808	1,388	765,729	430,865	334,864	982	968	14
0—10 . .	201,360	109,629	91,731	228	168	60	201,132	109,461	91,671	2	1	1
10—15 . .	84,400	51,284	33,116	1,231	1,124	107	83,169	50,160	33,009	68	66	2
15—20 . .	76,538	48,767	27,771	2,225	2,024	201	74,313	46,743	27,570	262	254	8
20 and over .	427,627	243,993	183,634	20,512	19,492	1,020	407,115	224,501	182,614	650	647	3
Rajputana Agency.												
ALL RELIGIONS	10,530,432	5,515,275	5,015,157	340,470	327,960	12,510	10,189,962	5,187,315	5,002,647	12,257	11,437	820
0—10 . .	2,785,291	1,427,547	1,357,744	4,400	3,952	448	2,780,891	1,423,595	1,357,296	223	149	74
10—15 . .	936,507	536,201	400,306	22,817	21,856	961	913,690	514,345	399,345	893	808	85
15—20 . .	904,837	509,037	395,800	37,130	35,612	1,518	867,707	473,425	394,282	1,807	1,721	86
20 and over .	5,903,797	3,042,490	2,861,307	276,123	266,540	9,583	5,627,674	2,775,950	2,851,724	9,334	8,759	575
HINDU . .	8,752,045	4,600,170	4,151,875	228,672	220,829	7,843	8,523,373	4,379,341	4,144,032	7,624	7,524	100
0—10 . .	2,279,986	1,170,798	1,109,188	2,599	2,368	231	2,277,387	1,168,430	1,108,957	42	37	5
10—15 . .	774,378	446,299	328,079	14,876	14,287	589	759,502	432,012	327,490	492	480	12
15—20 . .	755,732	428,219	327,513	25,145	24,224	921	730,587	403,995	326,592	1,224	1,206	18
20 and over .	4,941,949	2,554,854	2,387,095	186,052	179,950	6,102	4,755,897	2,374,904	2,380,993	5,866	5,801	65
MUSALMAN .	985,825	517,560	468,265	24,106	22,889	1,219	961,717	494,671	467,046	1,602	1,582	20
0—10 . .	258,628	131,969	126,659	282	241	41	258,346	131,728	126,618	10	8	2
10—15 . .	102,642	57,559	45,083	1,422	1,302	120	101,220	56,257	44,963	97	96	1
15—20 . .	89,448	49,598	39,850	2,429	2,245	184	87,019	47,353	39,666	226	225	1
20 and over .	535,107	278,434	256,673	19,975	19,101	874	515,132	259,333	255,799	1,269	1,253	16
JAIN . .	332,397	161,856	170,541	83,545	81,408	2,137	248,852	80,448	168,404	849	845	4
0—10 . .	81,797	41,342	40,455	1,252	1,188	64	80,545	40,154	40,391	3	3	..
10—15 . .	28,805	14,940	13,865	6,052	5,918	134	22,753	9,022	13,731	71	70	1
15—20 . .	27,088	13,565	13,523	9,058	8,842	216	18,030	4,723	13,307	172	171	1
20 and over .	194,707	92,009	102,698	67,183	65,460	1,723	127,524	26,549	100,975	603	601	2

TABLE IX.

Education by Selected Castes, Tribes or Races.

1. This table has been prepared for all Provinces and States except the Andamans and Nicobars. Its object is to throw light on the progress made in education by the different classes of the community. In the Provincial volumes all the more important castes have been dealt with. In this Table for the whole of India statistics are given only for a sufficient number of castes to illustrate the degree of education in the various social strata. The statistics for Ajmer-Merwara, Coorg and Sikkim have here been left out of account, as the number of persons dealt with is relatively insignificant. The figures for Provinces include those for the States attached to them, except in the case of Bombay, where this Table was compiled for British Territory only, and Madras, where they exclude those for Cochin and Travancore.

2. Within each Province, State or Agency, the castes are arranged in order of merit, *i.e.* according to the proportion of literate persons in each.

3. As in Table VIII, the figures for persons literate in English (columns 8 to 10) are included in those for total literate (columns 5 to 7).

4. The total strength of a caste in this Table does not necessarily tally with that in Table XIII, as the latter includes figures added in the course of classification which the present Table does not. The strength of a few castes is also not the same as in Tables XII-A and XIV owing to the fact that figures have been compiled for different local areas. Finally the same castes have not always been selected for the purpose of each of the three Tables.

TABLE IX.—Education by selected

Province and Caste, Tribe or Race.	Population.			Literate.			Literate in English.		
	Persons.	Males.	Females.	Persons.	Males.	Females.	Persons.	Males.	Females.
1	2	3	4	5	6	7	8	9	10
ASSAM.									
Kayastha	81,177	43,600	37,577	29,232	24,795	4,437	6,811	6,719	92
Brahman	124,506	68,361	56,145	40,359	37,318	3.041	6,092	6,032	60
Sudra	115,141	59,400	55,741	10,392	9,967	425	625	623	2
Kaibartta (Chasi)	63,552	33,295	30,257	5,218	4.969	249	373	371	2
Kalita	220,640	114,886	105,754	17,460	16,904	556	1,793	1,791	2
Ahom	192,560	99,418	93,142	11,652	11,361	291	1,686	1,670	16
Kewat	88,047	44,891	43.156	5,206	5,055	151	532	528	4
Jogi (Jugi)	167,521	85,287	82,234	9,865	9,470	395	299	298	1
Rajbansi	127,946	65,747	62,199	7,192	7,037	155	218	218	...
Chutiya	82,392	42,478	39,914	4,152	4,081	71	340	339	1
Kshatriya (Manipuri)	248,279	128,656	124,623	11,912	11,655	257	487	485	2
Kachari (Hindu)	52,379	28,487	23,892	2,413	2,368	45	382	381	1
Koch	203,775	103,960	99,815	9.201	8,970	231	667	665	2
Nadiyal	63,281	32,026	31,255	2,347	2,251	96	176	174	2
Patni (Hindu)	110,858	56,721	54,137	4,023	3,792	231	91	90	1
Khasi	115,664	54,627	61,037	2,665	2,129	536	374	349	25
Kachari (Animist)	168,429	84,277	84,152	1,213	1,201	12	27	25	2
Synteng	42,124	19,629	22,495	276	242	34	22	21	1
Mikir	102,212	52,180	50,032	354	348	6	12	12	...
Garo (Animist)	137,338	69,048	68,290	183	180	3	5	5	...
BALUCHISTAN.									
Saiyid	21,296	11,008	10,288	361	357	4	5	5	...
Lasi	27,779	14,857	12,922	189	185	4	...	...	...
Jatt	78,397	42,670	35,727	445	441	4	3	3	...
Pathan	188,093	102,148	85,945	940	938	2	22	22	
Baluch (Biloch)	169,190	91,959	77,231	639	627	12	6	6	...
Brahui	167,787	93,095	74,692	542	538	4	4	4	...
BENGAL.									
Baidya	88,324	43,988	44,336	46,995	31,663	15,332	18,441	17,535	906
Subarnabanik	27,565	15,263	12,302	12,429	10,420	2,009	6,029	5,908	121
Brahman	1,185,170	638,032	547,138	472,342	410,771	61,571	129,223	126,974	2,249
Kayastha	1,107,337	567,003	540,334	384,783	322,407	62,376	108,512	105,790	2,722
Teli and Tili	391,767	201,868	189,899	68,965	60,996	2,969	7,566	7,340	226
Barui	155,031	79,052	75,979	23,703	22,303	1,400	2,788	2,742	46
Kamar	245,371	126,427	118,944	36,752	35,215	1,537	2,789	2,754	35
Tanti	275,306	144,035	131,271	39,820	37,196	2,624	5,622	5,436	186
Pod	415,880	236,788	179,092	58,582	57,668	914	1,275	1,273	2
Sadgop	527,131	264,947	262,184	73,618	69,929	3,689	9,809	9,554	255
Jogi (Jugi)	337,669	170,631	167,038	43,791	42,739	1.052	1,733	1,717	16
Bairagi	408,302	185,311	222,991	45,531	42,285	3,246	2,816	2,722	94
Napit (Nai)	435.994	223,476	212,518	48,117	46,442	1,675	3,793	3,761	32
Magh	125,394	61,482	63,912	13,757	12,946	811	630	622	8
Kaibartta (Chasi)	2,036,129	1,019,753	1,016,376	220,092	211.993	8,099	14,748	14,626	122
Sutradhar	160,764	82,369	78,395	13,774	13,239	535	1,053	1,043	10
Goala (Ahir)	608,253	334,035	274,218	46,716	45,069	1,647	3,940	3,875	65
Dhoba (Hindu)	215,322	111,604	103,718	11,863	11,528	335	596	592	4
Rajbansi	1,454,173	749,129	705,044	73,686	72,482	1,204	1,221	1,213	8
Namasudra	1,860,705	941,851	918,854	91,625	89,613	2,012	4,163	4,133	30
Jolaha	267,244	141,995	125,249	11,755	11,399	356	348	340	8
Kaibartta (Jaliya)	285,020	144,960	140,060	12,413	12,066	347	588	576	12
Chamar	105,825	67,533	38,292	3,142	3,054	88	109	108	1
Malo	215,366	109,253	106,113	6,067	5,886	181	386	385	1
Bagdi	772,890	345,964	426,926	14,769	14,305	464	583	562	21
Dom	137,584	69,973	67,611	1,062	1,009	53	40	40	...
Hari	150,960	75,695	75,265	2,059	1,997	62	39	36	3
Mochi (Muchi)	424,304	225,464	198,840	5,252	5,153	99	237	234	3
Bauri	293,750	143,496	150,254	2.906	2,838	68	81	67	14
Santal	539,400	273,286	266,114	2,208	2,137	71	30	30	...

Castes, Tribes or Races.

Province and Caste, Tribe or Race.	Population.			Literate.			Literate in English.		
	Persons.	Males.	Females.	Persons.	Males.	Females.	Persons.	Males.	Females.
1	2	3	4	5	6	7	8	9	10
BIHAR AND ORISSA.									
Kayastha	309,838	156,450	153,388	102,932	94,416	8,516	17,066	16,776	290
Karan	140,559	67,813	72,746	36,097	33,388	2,709	2,775	2,755	20
Saiyid	88,893	43,307	45,586	15,795	13,940	1,855	3,056	3,028	28
Brahman	1,530,252	765,905	764,347	256,332	242,701	13,631	12,423	11,960	463
Babhan	943,683	478,647	465,036	96,229	89,666	6,563	1,468	1,466	2
Kalwar	150,885	74,086	76,799	15,123	14,855	268	300	294	6
Rajput	1,088,793	552,298	536,495	100,017	97,022	2,995	2,456	2,436	20
Khandait	760,441	361,152	399,289	52,676	50,969	1,707	1,278	1,270	8
Teli	1,052,937	516,834	536,103	40,643	39,768	875	397	385	12
Kurmi	1,270,669	627,229	643,440	38,560	37,762	798	517	509	8
Chasa	826,293	407,170	419,123	24,753	24,127	626	136	135	1
Koiri	1,261,593	625,095	636,498	27,289	26,783	506	320	317	3
Jolaha	810,278	374,759	435,519	16,487	15,468	1,019	605	539	66
Kandu	479,663	230,823	248,840	9,447	9,280	167	123	121	2
Kewat	392,329	191,813	200,516	6,862	6,723	139	53	53	...
Kahar	501,054	233,964	267,090	8,413	7,932	481	358	348	10
Tanti	525,951	250,291	275,660	8,322	8,102	220	153	148	5
Hajjam (Nai) (Hindu)	329,624	159,762	169,862	4,592	4,367	225	231	143	88
Lohar	244,747	120,496	124,251	3,354	3,227	127	64	63	1
Gaura	709,016	343,448	365,568	9,586	9,285	301	90	90	...
Kumhar	487,031	239,767	247.264	6,411	6,201	210	151	145	6
Dhanuk	439,028	210,183	228,845	5,765	5,664	101	38	38	...
Goala (Ahir)	3,206,004	1,602,855	1,603,149	39,510	38,275	1,235	714	701	13
Dhunia	198,150	92,476	105,674	2,063	1,922	141	49	47	2
Nunia	304,609	143,308	161,301	2,884	2,808	76	37	37	...
Dhoba (Hindu)	357,030	173,828	183,202	3,011	2,872	139	33	32	1
Ho (Animist)	325,384	156,299	169.085	2,436	2,377	59	93	93	...
Panika	400,808	196,209	204,599	2,290	2,230	60	30	30	...
Munda (Animist)	245,920	122,474	123.446	1,317	1,186	131	38	38	...
Santal (Animist)	1,051,627	525,544	526,083	5,331	5,234	97	71	71	...
Oraon	321,369	156,767	164,602	1,461	1,317	144	32	28	4
Santal (Hindu)	259,591	125,209	134,382	1,027	970	57	11	11	...
Dosadh	1,108,564	530.580	577,984	4,028	3,842	186	47	47	...
Chamar	935,936	415,718	520,218	3,030	2,878	152	37	37	...
Kandh (Hindu and Animist)	237,045	115,764	121,281	552	530	22	4	4	...
Musahar	592,693	293,235	299,458	636	562	74	19	19	...
BOMBAY.									
Shrimali	33,921	17,137	16,784	15,052	12.656	2,396	1,345	1,327	18
Oswal	20,342	12,527	7,815	7,940	7,553	387	377	364	13
Brahman	173,828	90,706	83,122	59,798	53,594	6,204	10,818	10,628	190
Bhatia	4,705	2,373	2,332	1,467	1,326	141	366	362	4
Bohora, Khoja, Memon, Teli and Ghanchi	71,431	35,536	35,895	15,920	14,722	1,198	407	395	12
Lohana	453,025	246,335	206,690	93,635	88,576	5,059	8,197	8,056	141
Indian Christian	88,855	46,344	42,511	12,222	9,099	3,123	6,166	4,607	1.559
Sonar	37,831	18,973	18,858	4,380	4,259	121	104	103	1
Teli, Ganigar or Ghauchi	51,580	25,683	25,897	4,060	3,934	126	71	71	...
Lingaiat	933,123	474,207	458,916	66,051	64,377	1,674	1,413	1,408	5
Rajput	137,211	74,329	62,882	8,623	8.016	607	179	177	2
Sutar	51,884	25,846	26,038	2,934	2,808	126	62	62	...
Kunbi	1,054,694	521,299	533,395	51,391	48,872	2,519	1,408	1,385	23
Koli	852,494	443,074	409,420	21,907	21,436	471	89	85	4
Maratha	1,462,220	719,025	743,195	34,879	33,417	1,462	1,601	1,571	30
Chamar	40,738	20,603	20,135	925	883	42	27	27	...
Agri	213,259	106,839	106,420	4,363	4,303	60	43	42	1
Bhangi	37,801	19,383	18,418	420	410	10	2	2	...
Bharvad	592,570	299,839	292,731	5,194	5,044	150	67	66	1
Dubla	90,263	45,509	44,754	656	642	14	2	2	...
Ramoshi	40,511	20,643	19,868	215	213	2	...	...	...
Mahar, Holiya or Dhed	233,719	113,508	120,211	1,134	1,095	39	11	11	...
Bhil	399,741	201,919	197,822	494	483	11	13	13	...
Mang	71,104	34,393	36,711	69	67	2	...	...	...

TABLE IX.—EDUCATION BY SELECTED

Province and Caste, Tribe or Race.	Population.			Literate.			Literate in English.		
	Persons.	Males.	Females.	Persons.	Males.	Females.	Persons.	Males.	Females.
1	2	3	4	5	6	7	8	9	10
BURMA.									
Chinese	104,641	79,830	24,811	28,321	25,578	2,743	1,912	1,842	70
Talaing	320,629	159,235	161,394	70,833	58,256	12,577	619	334	285
Arakanese	344,123	177,089	167,034	58,022	54,790	3,232	1,165	1,081	84
Danu	70,947	35,264	35,683	9,400	8,112	1,288	2	...	2
Karen	903,626	450,971	452,655	114,152	86,098	28,054	4,277	3,045	1,232
Shan	941,724	465,609	476,115	94,962	84,340	10,622	140	118	22
Taungthu	183,054	91,597	91,457	10,553	8,227	2,326	18	13	5
Chin	243,066	119,373	123,693	6,923	6,473	450	39	33	6
Wa-Palaung	150,375	74,600	75,775	4,202	3,172	1,030	..	...	...
Kachin	162,368	80,764	81,604	1,449	937	512	14	13	1
CENTRAL PROVINCES AND BERAR.									
Baniya	194,820	100,683	94,137	47,641	45,883	1,758	1,560	1,543	17
Brahman	445,627	237,567	208,060	107,796	102,404	5,392	16,209	16,038	171
Sonar	126,864	63,830	63,034	15,990	15,629	361	379	371	8
Bairagi	37,984	19,649	18,335	3,470	3,392	78	31	31	...
Maratha	93,879	46,701	47,178	7,072	6,825	247	550	543	7
Rajput	440,323	223,103	217,220	27,840	27,032	808	1,464	1,445	19
Kalar	195,295	96,393	98,902	11.095	10,888	207	365	362	3
Barhai	108,815	56.297	52,518	4,847	4,763	84	141	140	1
Kurmi	284,311	141,079	143,232	9,961	9,836	125	150	149	1
Kunbi	1,342,000	675,302	666,698	41,681	41,261	420	923	916	7
Nai (Hajjam)	146,090	72,797	73,293	4,182	4,047	135	119	118	1
Lodhi	312,374	155,174	157,200	7,159	7,051	108	58	58	...
Teli	869,336	427,124	442,212	19,615	19,247	368	272	270	2
Lohar	181,311	90,929	90,382	3,541	3,445	96	109	108	1
Mali	561,232	279,589	281,643	9,504	9,207	297	234	234	...
Kumhar	118,501	60,047	58,454	1,650	1,615	35	24	24	...
Kachhi	115,930	58,181	57,749	1,417	1,374	43	27	27	...
Dhobi	164,573	80,673	83,900	1,784	1,737	47	31	30	1
Panika	132,978	63,642	69,336	1,236	1,218	18	3	3	...
Mahar	1,164,383	575.028	589,355	9,933	9,775	158	219	213	6
Ahir	727,733	361,600	366,133	5,262	5,076	186	163	163	...
Dhimar	283,413	140,734	142,679	1,967	1,893	74	99	96	3
Gond	2,227,540	1,085,536	1,142,004	7,177	7,006	171	81	80	1
Chamar	901,522	443,017	458,505	2,060	2,025	35	33	33	...
MADRAS.									
Brahman (Tamil)	480,063	238,594	241,469	200,567	171,616	28,951	53,814	53,130	684
" (Telugu)	460,819	229,290	231,529	179,305	156,354	22,951	34,303	33,809	494
" (Canarese)	93,726	45.842	47,884	28,754	26,289	2,465	5,631	5,579	52
Komati	498,295	250,043	248,252	136,604	130,383	6,221	3,802	3,786	66
Kanakkan	63,360	31,640	31,720	16,571	15,743	828	1,007	996	11
Nayar	412,102	198,196	213,906	107,564	83,091	24,473	6,113	5,895	218
Brahman (Oriya)	143,655	69,820	73,835	33,458	32,570	888	1,802	1,788	14
Chetti	350,251	171,058	179,193	69,040	66,957	2,083	1,709	1,671	38
Vaniyan	194,802	95,028	99,774	31,669	30,116	1,553	1,088	1,062	26
Lingaiat	134,592	66,375	68,217	18,995	18,523	472	322	317	5
Kammalan	559,205	274,693	284,512	74,201	71,930	2,271	1,232	1,199	33
Labbai	401,703	184,923	216,780	53,113	51,455	1,658	625	612	13
Kamsala	295,583	146,482	149,101	38,723	36,708	2,015	799	786	13
Vellala	2,535,791	1,248,052	1,287,739	329,598	306,678	22,920	26,957	26,462	495
Saiyid	170,125	85,730	84,395	21,507	19,381	2,126	2,364	2,330	34

Castes, Tribes or Races—*continued.*

Province and Caste, Tribe or Race.	Population.			Literate.			Literate in English.		
	Persons.	Males.	Females.	Persons.	Males.	Females.	Persons.	Males.	Females.
1	2	3	4	5	6	7	8	9	10
MADRAS—*contd.*									
Pathan	106,920	54,536	52,384	12,913	11,838	1,075	1,353	1,334	19
Kshatriya	158,521	80,372	78,149	19,108	17,137	1,971	2,034	2,004	30
Kaikolan	368,347	179,467	188,880	43,668	40,960	2,708	696	683	13
Balija	1,041,246	514,769	526,477	118,322	107,598	10,724	13,671	13,411	260
Bant	126,296	61,364	64,932	12,463	11,265	1,198	270	261	9
Tiyan	639,832	316,012	323,820	63,079	55,590	7,489	3,284	2,897	387
Shanan	641,976	314,733	327,243	59,167	56,993	2,174	945	940	5
Sheikh	892,873	442,866	450,007	81,870	75,400	6,470	7,097	6,988	109
Kallan	535,227	258,756	276,471	41,818	40,689	1,129	719	705	14
Nattaman	162,786	79,298	83,488	12,102	11,928	174	61	61	...
Kamma	1,126,095	564,432	561,663	72,873	68,966	3,907	1,172	1,142	30
Telaga	498,762	245,812	252,950	29,151	26,688	2,463	3,260	3,215	45
Mappilla	1,032,757	514,555	518,202	58,339	55,360	2,979	486	486	...
Idaiyan	734,767	360,154	374,613	40,600	38,793	1,807	2,131	2,095	36
Palli	2,820,156	1,383,560	1,436,596	137,362	134,016	3,346	2,691	2,618	73
Kapu	2,678,925	1,329,624	1,349,301	125,178	119,422	5,756	2,986	2,946	40
Pallan	866,132	414,945	451,187	16,778	16,397	381	152	151	1
Paraiyan	2,363,802	1,153,356	1,210,446	34,014	32,440	1,574	1,789	1,722	67
Golla	904,192	445,827	458,365	13,002	12,328	674	759	753	6
Mal	1,511,312	747,652	763,660	10,856	10,251	605	254	243	11
Madiga	807,986	406,089	401,897	3,617	3,352	265	42	38	4
Cheruman	255,395	121,567	133,828	467	419	48	3	3	...
NORTH-WEST FRONTIER PROVINCE.									
Khatri	35,720	21,662	14,058	10,108	8,819	1,289	1,213	1,195	18
Arora	69,144	37,909	31,235	17,474	15,472	2,002	1,001	991	10
Rajput	15,157	10,637	4,520	2,255	2,184	71	249	246	3
Jat	86,097	48,873	37,224	4,502	4,363	139	197	196	1
Moghal	14,865	8,269	6,596	540	526	14	71	71	...
Saiyid	75,115	39,230	35,885	2,321	2,171	150	239	237	2
Swathi	38,329	20,181	18,148	494	478	16	12	12	...
Pathan	845,183	449,500	395,683	10,672	10,420	252	941	937	4
Awan	275,711	149,550	126,161	3,474	3,306	168	291	290	1
Tarkhan	42,618	22,764	19,854	307	295	12	13	13	...
Lohar	28,589	15,331	13,258	187	181	6	6	6	...
Kumbar	22,664	11,705	10,959	140	135	5	7	7	...
Tanaoli	63,985	33,349	30,636	373	325	48	17	17	...
Gujar	113,871	61,711	52,160	636	610	26	29	29	...
Dhund	30,464	15,773	14,691	145	141	4	10	10	...
Mochi	23,040	12,383	10,657	105	96	9	4	4	...
Nai (Hajjam)	24,777	13,075	11,702	107	100	7	7	7	...
Jolaha	37,390	19,999	17,391	110	107	3	4	4	...
PUNJAB.									
Khatri	426,634	235,239	191,395	106,836	95,309	11,527	19,034	18,842	192
Agarwal	364,583	196,926	167,657	77,185	75,035	2,150	4,251	4,108	143
Arora	673,519	362,613	310,906	141,733	133,166	8,567	8,264	8,170	94
Brahman	1,014,987	560,935	454,052	114,853	109,358	5,495	11,564	11,124	440
Saiyid	246,947	131,740	115,207	20,483	19,132	1,351	2,917	2,880	37
Sheikh	334,762	185,213	149,549	24,871	22,888	1,983	5,105	5,038	67
Pathan	291,749	166,017	125,732	15,335	14,291	1,044	2,590	2,554	36
Kashmiri	178,095	95,790	82,305	6,094	5,477	617	1,378	1,355	23
Rajput	1,581,172	869,145	712,027	41,625	39,534	2,091	4,607	4,555	52
Tarkhan	643,018	354,706	288,312	14,808	13,958	850	836	831	5
Labana (Banjara)	57,762	31,296	26,466	1,325	1,292	33	34	34	
Kanet	403,762	207,180	196,582	6,840	6,619	221	211	210	1
Jat	4,944,894	2,802,974	2,141,920	82,089	78,510	3,579	5,017	4,988	29
Lohar	323,175	176,015	147,160	4,572	4,366	206	294	293	1
Awan	425,921	226,984	198,937	5,728	5,624	104	415	412	3

TABLE IX.—EDUCATION BY SELECTED

Province and Caste, Tribe or Race.	Population			Literate.			Literate in English.		
	Persons.	Males.	Females.	Persons.	Males.	Females.	Persons.	Males.	Females.
1	2	3	4	5	6	7	8	9	10
PUNJAB—*contd.*									
Nai (Hajjam)	350,263	192,207	158,056	4,500	4,343	157	224	224	...
Mirasi	225,670	121,073	104,597	2,478	2,430	48	68	67	1
Arain	977,245	540,988	436,257	10,606	10,101	505	1,510	1,482	28
Jhinwar	338,560	186,875	151,685	3,669	3,540	129	220	218	2
Jolaha (Julaha)	632,030	343.633	288,397	5,029	4,894	135	226	226	...
Ahir	207,884	115,988	91,896	1,653	1,625	28	118	118	...
Baluch (Biloch)	531,465	289,080	242,385	4,029	3,874	155	254	251	3
Kasai	118,751	62,317	56,434	886	857	29	52	52	...
Teli	295,934	162,424	133,510	1,701	1,629	72	108	108	...
Kumhar	549,433	299,168	250,265	2,334	2,241	93	137	137	...
Chamar	1,106.589	601.715	504,874	4,219	4,108	111	44	44	...
Mochi	417,230	228,004	189,226	1,564	1,520	44	63	63	...
Machhi	228,868	125,186	103.682	612	597	15	41	41	...
Chuhra	925,053	510,513	414,540	1,290	1,216	74	53	42	11
UNITED PROVINCES OF AGRA AND OUDH.									
Kayastha	483,443	255,775	227,668	156,989	139,247	17,742	20,723	20,250	473
Agarwal	284,578	158,680	125,898	69,215	65,445	3,770	5,438	5,346	92
Saiyid	245,982	127,564	118,418	39,684	35,376	4,308	4,751	4,604	147
Brahman	4,642,107	2,444,205	2,197,902	551,518	529,348	22,170	20,209	19,803	406
Sheikh	1,307,633	689,945	617,688	81,379	73,989	7,390	8,375	8,188	187
Rajput	3,629,498	1,937,556	1,691,942	221,639	209,567	12,072	6,312	6,149	163
Pathan	957,967	498,600	459,367	47,361	43,480	3,881	3,816	3,735	81
Jat	730,052	412,637	317,415	17,990	17,113	877	738	709	29
Barhai	584,314	311,910	272,904	7,522	7,098	424	269	262	7
Jolaha (Julaha)	980,513	504,123	476,390	12,166	11,281	885	316	307	9
Lohar	580,759	303,716	277,043	6,780	6,084	696	121	117	4
Kurmi	1,160,763	601,875	558,888	13,517	13,165	352	268	268	...
Teli	869,077	450,748	418,329	9,725	9,498	227	153	151	2
Nai (Hajjam)	907,413	472,280	435,133	7,771	7,320	451	230	217	13
Gujar	328,729	186,827	141,902	2,491	2,340	151	44	41	3
Dom	306,494	158,186	148,308	1,898	1,831	67	13	13	..
Lodha	1,079,870	569,406	510,464	6,009	5,863	146	88	86	2
Kahar	1,104,806	571,902	532,904	5,659	5,236	423	163	159	4
Mallah	231,016	107,825	123,191	1,095	1,051	44	19	15	4
Ahir	2,221,096	1,171,769	1,049,327	10,153	9,702	451	314	313	1
Kumhar	722,319	372,218	350,101	1,907	1,780	127	41	39	2
Gadaria	982,894	515,579	467,315	2,594	2,427	167	131	131	...
Kewat	114,564	57,708	56,856	260	232	28	3	3	...
Bhangi	360,509	189,709	170,800	693	611	82	26	26	2
Dhobi	716,100	369,650	346,450	1,154	1,013	141	19	18	1
Pasi	1,303,100	665,847	637,253	1,817	1,714	103	18	17	1
Bhar	386,812	190,905	195,907	527	489	38	6	6	...
Chamar	6,068,382	3,099,321	2,969,061	6,794	6,274	520	215	214	1
BARODA STATE.									
Brahman (Anavala)	9,893	5,313	4,580	3,616	3,291	325	273	269	4
Brahman (Andich)	40,628	20,876	19,752	12,292	11,529	763	612	606	6
Kshatriya	14,732	8,044	6,738	3,447	3,086	411	398	374	24
Kunbi Lewa	183,289	99,960	83,329	33,895	31,681	2,264	1,222	1,215	7
Rajput	64,202	34,531	29,671	5,096	4,779	317	74	72	2
Kunbi Kadwa	172,641	88,955	83,686	12,739	12,096	643	242	242	...
Koli	370,943	194,746	176,197	8,048	7,521	527	21	21	...
Dhed	99,727	50,487	49,240	2,140	1,940	200	21	20	1
Vaghri	28,129	14,702	13,427	195	170	25	1	1	...

Castes, Tribes or Races—*continued.*

Province and Caste, Tribe or Race.	Population.			Literate.			Literate in English.		
	Persons.	Males.	Females.	Persons.	Males.	Females.	Persons.	Males.	Females.
1	2	3	4	5	6	7	8	9	10
CENTRAL INDIA AGENCY.									
Oswal (Jain)	32,956	16,764	16,192	8,331	7,960	371	162	159	3
Mahesri	21,412	10,008	11,404	3,685	3.378	307	185	183	2
Porwal (Jain)	22,703	11,417	11,286	3,519	3,296	223	36	36	
Porwal (Hindu)	16,356	8,616	7,740	2,238	2,192	46	39	39	...
Agarwal	58,288	27,710	30,578	7,762	7,519	243	504	464	40
Oswal (Hindu)	14,309	6.072	8,237	1,773	1,701	72	122	122	
Saiyid	32,197	17,459	14,738	3,881	3,561	320	450	447	3
Baniya	48,338	25.303	23,035	3,830	3,682	148	18	18	
Pathan	138,522	73,476	65,046	8,890	8,203	687	452	446	6
Sheikh	147,216	76,259	70,957	9,059	8,501	558	687	680	7
Brahman	577,968	289,803	288,165	29,529	28,803	726	1,104	1,078	26
Rajput	338,456	185,738	152,718	11,775	10,959	816	632	616	16
Gujar	185,728	105,834	79,894	2,020	1,966	54	97	97	..
Bhil (Hindu)	25,831	13,693	12,138	15	15	...	...	...	..
Bhil (Animist)	269,910	134,045	135,865	144	142	2	2	2	..
Gond (Animist)	71,387	34,611	36,776	36	35	1	...	...	...
Gond (Hindu)	163,285	76,753	86,532	80	78	2	...	...	...
Bhilala (Hindu)	33,764	16,351	17,413	13	12	1	...	...	
Bhilala (Animist)	89,612	44,821	44,791	33	32	1	1	1	...
COCHIN STATE.									
Brahman	35,532	18,794	16,738	13,892	11,663	2,229	2,981	2,847	134
Nayar	121,206	58,720	62.486	32,826	24,276	8,550	2,981	2,551	430
Indian Christian	230,568	116,549	114,019	48,964	36,310	12,654	2,678	2,162	516
Kammalan	34,558	17,089	17,469	3,705	3,554	151	9	9	
Iluvan	208,453	102,817	105,636	17,171	15,910	1,261	290	280	10
Jonakan	51,469	26,274	25,195	3,367	3,223	144	52	51	1
Kudumi Chetti	12,371	6,500	5,871	555	544	11	7	7	...
Pulaiyan	72,787	35,284	37,503	346	328	18	2	2	..
HYDERABAD STATE.									
Brahman	261,241	133,192	128,049	68,325	65,069	3,256	3,026	2,947	79
Komati	223,380	114,121	109,259	39,303	37,944	1,359	292	279	13
Satani	27,883	14,589	13,294	3,210	3,079	131	54	53	1
Moghal	33,411	17,685	15,726	3,657	3,188	469	370	344	26
Saiyid	189,574	99,142	90,432	18,319	15,837	2,482	2,047	1,941	106
Pathan	135,148	71,167	63,981	10,372	9,397	975	926	900	26
Rajput	61,637	31,296	30,341	4,494	4,087	407	351	324	27
Sonar (Sunar)	88,037	45,278	42.759	5,795	5,667	128	32	31	1
Sheikh	985,019	499,495	485,524	48,451	43,961	4,490	3,640	3,472	168
Lingaiat	757,611	381,201	376,410	32,102	31,331	771	189	185	4
Panchala	117,710	59,990	57,720	4,606	4,528	78	18	17	1
Kapu	648,254	330,902	317,352	16,273	15,882	391	322	318	4
Munnur	228,354	115,120	113,234	3,621	3,516	105	120	117	3
Sale	343,130	175,968	167,162	4,562	4,479	83	33	30	3
Telaga	458,622	233,206	225,416	5,989	5,555	434	641	598	43
Maratha	1,538,874	772,878	765,996	18,119	17,448	671	410	388	22
Muthrasi	260,770	134,473	126,297	3,008	2,938	70	71	71	...
Koli	266,840	134,432	132,408	1,424	1,397	27	11	11	...
Golla	460,760	234,629	226,131	2,124	2,037	87	222	207	15
Mahar and Mala	1,137,589	574,385	563,204	3,984	3,693	291	1,204	1,160	44
Madiga and Mang	1,145,352	581,519	563,833	801	738	63	48	45	3
KASHMIR STATE.									
Kashmiri Pandit (Brahman)	55,097	30,724	24,373	17,911	17,814	97	3,136	3,122	14
Khatri	15,855	9,160	6,695	3,916	3,675	241	664	653	11
Mahajan	17,984	9,902	8,082	3,616	3,537	79	97	96	1
Rajput	50,264	29,540	20,724	3,562	3,497	65	139	138	1
Brahman	173,795	93,115	80,680	10,026	9,662	364	480	469	11
Babazada	48,843	24,233	24,610	2,520	2,434	93	49	48	1

TABLE IX.—Education by Selected Castes, Tribes or Races—*concld.*

Province and Caste, Tribe or Race.	Population.			Literate.			Literate in English.		
	Persons.	Males.	Females.	Persons.	Males.	Females.	Persons.	Males.	Females.
1	2	3	4	5	6	7	8	9	10
KASHMIR STATE—*contd.*									
Pathan	19,902	10,871	9,031	358	307	51	32	32	...
Thakkar	93,596	49,419	44,177	1,598	1,580	18	26	25	1
Moghal	33,269	17,696	15,573	471	455	16	26	26	...
Sheikh	105,338	58,197	47,141	1,152	1,116	36	121	121	...
Jat	23,888	12,464	10,924	190	184	6	8	8	...
Awan	25,831	13,922	11,909	184	181	3	6	6	...
Malik	53,451	27,072	26,379	368	355	13	8	8	...
Bat	152,210	82,012	70,198	609	604	5	26	26	...
Dar	98,525	53,150	45,375	282	278	4	6	6	...
MYSORE STATE.									
Brahman	194,570	98,597	95,973	81,125	69,674	11,451	15,802	15,346	456
Saiyid	57,671	30,298	27,373	7,278	5,931	1,347	408	390	18
Panchala	128,098	65,790	62,308	15,729	15.294	435	134	131	3
Sheikh	176,482	91,495	84,987	20,787	17,483	3,304	980	957	23
Pathan	44.689	23,469	21,220	5,005	4,193	812	277	274	3
Banajiga	132,955	67,216	65,739	12,998	11,659	1,339	1,211	1,165	46
Neygi	96,466	48,571	47,895	9,401	9,066	335	215	207	8
Lingaiat	729,431	365,091	364,340	66,826	64,580	2,246	828	809	19
Ganiga	40,469	20,311	20,158	2,264	2,188	76	30	28	2
Vakkaliga	1,331,029	665,707	665,322	42,574	41,274	1,300	828	811	17
Kumhar	41,810	21,324	20,486	1,123	1,091	32	9	8	1
Golla	150,842	76,617	74,225	2,644	2,536	108	151	150	1
Kuruba	403,366	201,967	201,399	6,221	6,028	193	109	108	1
Beda	268,454	135,597	132,857	3,835	3,607	228	61	61	...
Besta	156,863	78,228	78,635	2,168	2,053	115	26	25	1
Agasa	97,772	49,112	48,660	1,188	1,145	43	16	16	...
Holiya	613,248	309,536	303,712	5,522	5,150	372	620	615	5
Vadda	142,482	72,572	69,910	665	633	32	10	10	...
Lambani (Banjara)	41,223	21,358	19,865	123	100	23	...	...	...
Madiga	308,083	155,585	152,498	771	712	59	10	10	...
RAJPUTANA AGENCY.									
Mahajan	707,404	352,999	354,405	161,695	159,010	2,685	1,989	1,977	12
Saiyid	28,954	15,242	13,712	3,793	3,494	299	402	397	5
Brahman	920,286	474,622	445,664	76,437	74,210	2,227	3,108	3,068	40
Sonar	69,014	35,556	33,458	5,159	5,095	64	42	42	...
Pathan	108,225	57,471	50,754	5,549	5,331	218	379	374	5
Sheikh	181,704	96,638	85,066	6,890	6,561	329	589	581	8
Rajput	663,996	372,557	291,439	17,724	15,131	2,593	726	711	15
Darzi	45,200	23,068	22,132	643	625	18	17	17	...
Teli	78,427	40,628	37,799	503	493	10	10	10	...
Fakir	55,208	29,024	26,184	282	280	2	...	...	...
Nai	162,235	84,751	77,484	761	742	19	33	33	...
Jat	925,391	500,001	425,390	3,467	3,365	102	113	112	1
Mali	336,874	174,965	161,909	1,007	957	50	56	56	...
Gujar	498,607	270,412	228,195	1,367	1,313	54	37	37	...
Mina	558,687	296,205	262,482	1,489	1,467	22	7	7	...
Meo	165,689	87,346	78,343	344	343	1	2	2	...
Dhobi	45,801	23,348	22,453	73	67	6	1	1	...
Kumhar	309,228	159,672	149,556	464	457	7	7	7	...
Koli	104,047	53,499	50,548	147	138	9	7	7	...
Bhangi	82,808	42,432	40,376	53	50	3	1	1	...
TRAVANCORE STATE.									
Brahman (Malayala)	10,325	5,841	4,484	4,671	3,667	1,004	31	28	3
Brahman (others)	45,349	23,892	21,457	15,700	13,320	2,380	3,007	2,941	66
Ambalavasi	10,852	5,448	5,404	3,161	2,485	676	107	107	...
Nayar	592,489	295,703	296,786	144,946	120,263	24,683	5,446	5,088	358
Indian Christian	901,719	460,004	441,715	165,229	131,180	34.049	10,129	8,083	2,046
Chetti	20,881	10,535	10,346	3,497	3,271	226	67	62	5
Iluvan	546,265	271,677	274,588	55,192	50,517	4,675	1,441	1,359	82
Shanan	166,195	84,638	81,557	9,206	8,821	385	295	241	54
Pulaiyan	185,814	93,335	91,979	1,496	1,446	50	21	21	...
Kuravan	61,827	30,183	31,644	413	360	53	4	4	...

TABLE X.

Language.

1. The population dealt with in this Table falls short of that in Table I by 1,663,181 persons who were enumerated in tracts where language was not recorded, *viz.*, 54,625 in the Gilgit Agency in Kashmir and 1,608,556 in the Agencies and Tribal areas of the N.-W. F. Province. The figures for Madras States include those for Cochin and Travancore which are detailed at page 119.

2. The areas which have been included in this Table for the first time are as follows :—

Assam—Sema and Eastern Angami Villages in the Naga Hills.

Baluchistan—The whole except the areas (population 48,707) which were enumerated in 1901 on the standard schedule.

Burma—Karenni, Kachin districts of North Hsenwi, Chin Hills, Pakokku Hill Tracts, West Manglun and Kokang; and parts of Bhamo, Myitkyina, and Upper Chindwin.

Punjab—Biloch Trans-Frontier area.

3. The Table is divided into four parts. Part I is a general statement showing the number of persons who speak A. Vernaculars of India, B. Vernaculars of other Asiatic countries and Africa and C. European languages. In Part II the languages are arranged according to linguistic families. Part III shows the territorial distribution of each language and Part IV the linguistic distribution of the inhabitants of each Province, State or Agency. In Parts III and IV the languages have been arranged alphabetically. The more important dialects are shown in italics below the languages to which they appertain.

4. Dialects have been dealt with in the manner indicated in the Index of Indian languages printed at pages 261—292 of the India Administrative Volume, 1901, with such modifications (suggested by Sir George Grierson) as have been found necessary in view of the progress since made by the Linguistic Survey. In a few cases, as noted below, this later information was not available in time for use in the Provincial Language Tables, and the classification here made differs from that adopted in the Provincial volumes :—

Language.	Classification in the Provincial Tables.	Classification in the India Table.	Language.	Classification in the Provincial Tables.	Classification in the India Table.
Ahirwātī	Western Hindī	Rajasthanī.	Labanī, Lakankī or Lamanī	Gipsy	Rajasthanī.
Bahrūpiā	Gipsy	Ditto.	Magh	Burmese	Arakanese.
Banjarī or Labhanī	Ditto	Ditto.	Malvī	Gujarati	Rajasthanī.
Baori	Ditto	Bhil.	Panchālī	Marāthi	Bhil.
Bhilāli	Rajasthānī	Ditto.	Pardhi or Tākankārī	Gipsy	Ditto.
Chārani	Gipsy	Ditto.	Siyalgiri	Gujarātī	Ditto.
Gujarī	Western Pahārī	Ditto.	Western Pahārī	Western Group	Northern Group.

5. At the last census persons returning Hindī as their language were classified in some provinces under the three heads, Western Hindī, Eastern Hindī and Bihārī with reference to their birthplace. On the present occasion it has been thought desirable to relegate all such manipulation of the census figures to the Subsidiary Tables in the Report Volume. Consequently all persons returning their language as Hindī without further specification have been shown under this head without any attempt at classification. The figures under Western Hindī, Eastern Hindī and Bihārī in this Table include only those persons whose language is known from the entries in the language column of the Schedule, to fall under one or other of these heads. Thus the figures for Western Hindī include persons whose language was returned as Bundelkhandī, Urdū, Brij Bhāshā, etc.; and Bihārī includes those returning Bihārī, Pūrbī, Māgadhī or Maithilī as their language.

6. The following statement shows the designations under which certain languages and dialects which are known by more than one name have been entered in Parts III and IV of the Table :—

Language or Dialect.	Entered as	Language or Dialect.	Entered as	Language or Dialect.	Entered as
Andhra	Telugu.	Knweymi	Khāmi.	Mungi	Munjānī.
Arniya	Khowar.	Kuī	Kandh.	Myen	Lolo.
Bāltī	Bhotiā of Bāltistan	Kumi	Khāmi.	Orāoñ	Kurukh.
Chatrari	Khowar.	Ladakhī	Bhotiā of Ladakh.	Pahī	Padhī.
Coorgi	Kodagu.	Lahndā	Western Panjābī.	Pahrī	Padhī.
Denjongke	Bhotiā of Sikkim.	Lahu Hsi	Kwi.	Patnī	Manchātī.
Dulien	Lushei.	Lepcha	Rong.	Peguan	Mōn.
Eastern Pahārī	Naipālī.	Lhoke	Bhotiā of Bhutān.	Ponnu	Manipurī.
Gondla	Rangloī.	Lisaw	Lisu.	Selon	Selung.
Hår	Santālī.	Maler	Malto.	Singpho	Kachin.
Hmeng	Miao.	Mech	Bodo.	Talaing	Mōn.
Jangshen	Thādo.	Meithei	Manipurī.	Tibetan	Bhotiā of Tibet.
Kachārī	Bodo.	Mrung	Tipurā.	Tinūn	Rangloī.
Kachchā Nāgā	Empeo.	Muhso	Lahu.	Tsontsū	Lhotā.
Kathe	Manipurī.	Multhānī	Kanaurī.	Vāyū	Hāyū.
Kaw	Akha.				

TABLE X.—LANGUAGE. PART I.—

Province, State or Agency.	Population. Persons.	Males.	Females.
1	2	3	4
INDIA.	**313,493,215**	**160,457,311**	**153,035,904**
Provinces.	**244,267,542**	**124,873,691**	**119,393,851**
1. Ajmer-Merwara	501,395	266,198	235,197
2. Andamans and Nicobars	26,459	19,570	6,889
3. Assam	6,713,635	3,467,621	3,246,014
4. Baluchistan	414,412	239,181	175,231
5. Bengal	45,483,077	23,365,225	22,117,852
6. Bihar and Orissa	34,490,084	16,859,929	17,630,155
7. Bombay	19,672,642	10,245,847	9,426,795
8. Burma	12,115,217	6,183,494	5,931,723
9. Central Provinces and Berar	13,916,308	6,930,392	6,985,916
10. Coorg	174,976	97,279	77,697
11. Madras	41,405,404	20,382,955	21,022,449
12. North-West Frontier Province (*Districts and Administered Territories*).	2,196,933	1,182,102	1,014,831
13. Punjab	19,974,956	10,992,067	8,982,889
14. United Provinces of Agra and Oudh	47,182,044	24,641,831	22,540,213
States and Agencies.	**69,225,673**	**35,583,620**	**33,642,053**
15. Assam State (Manipur)	346,222	170,666	175,556
16. Baluchistan States	420,291	227,238	193,053
17. Baroda State	2,032,798	1,055,935	976,863
18. Bengal States	822,565	438,368	384,197
19. Bihar and Orissa States	3,945,209	1,955,125	1,990,084
20. Bombay States	7,411,675	3,765,401	3,646,274
21. Central India Agency	9,356,980	4,801,459	4,555,521
22. Central Provinces States	2,117,002	1,053,630	1,063,372
23. Hyderabad State	13,374,676	6,797,118	6,577,558
24. Kashmir State	3,103,501	1,644,978	1,458,523
25. Madras States	4,811,841	2,411,758	2,400,083
26. Mysore State	5,806,193	2,934,621	2,871,572
27. North-West Frontier Province (*Agencies and Tribal areas*)	13,538	12,641	897
28. Punjab States	4,212,794	2,322,908	1,889,886
29. Rajputana Agency	10,530,432	5,515,275	5,015,157
30. Sikkim State	87,920	45,059	42,861
31. United Provinces States	832,036	431,440	400,596

GENERAL STATEMENT.

A.—Vernaculars of India.			B.—Vernaculars of other Asiatic Countries and Africa.			C.—European Languages.			Serial No.
Persons.	Males.	Females.	Persons.	Males.	Females.	Persons.	Males.	Females.	
5	6	7	8	9	10	11	12	13	
312,948,881	**160,099,429**	**1 52,849.452**	**223,110**	**149,039**	**74,071**	**321,224**	**208,843**	**112,381**	
243,775,224	**124,548,500**	**119,226,724**	**207,261**	**139,455**	**67,806**	**285,057**	**185,736**	**99,321**	
498,630	264,213	234,417	33	19	14	2,732	1,966	766	1
25,982	19,190	6,792	140	140	...	337	240	97	2
6,710,704	3,465,509	3,245,195	308	291	17	2,623	1,821	802	3
406,341	232,958	173,383	3,740	2,779	961	4,331	3,444	887	4
45,430,769	23,332,954	22,097,815	6,527	4,613	1,914	45,781	27,658	18,123	5
34,480,681	16,854,410	17,626,271	107	90	17	9,296	5,429	3,867	6
19,542,178	10,163,032	9,379,146	72,788	44,455	28,333	57,676	38,360	19,316	7
11,979,583	6,087,874	5,891,709	110,459	79,217	31,242	25,175	16,403	8,772	8
13,904,489	6,922,403	6,982,086	450	294	156	11,369	7,695	3,674	9
174,548	97,031	77,517	6	6	...	422	242	180	10
41,362,019	20,359,371	21,002,648	1,269	927	342	42,116	22,657	19,459	11
2,187,680	1,175,195	1,012,485	3,486	1,988	1,498	5,767	4,919	848	12
19,937,290	10,964,719	8,972,571	2,526	1,485	1,041	35,140	25,863	9,277	13
47,134,330	24,609,641	22,524,689	5,422	3,151	2,271	42,292	29,039	13,253	14
69,173,657	**35,550,929**	**33.622.728**	**15,849**	**9,584**	**6,265**	**36,167**	**23,107**	**13,060**	
346,185	170,641	175,544	...	...	...	37	25	12	15
420,069	227,089	192,980	195	126	69	27	23	4	16
2,032,464	1,055,757	976,707	45	29	16	289	149	140	17
822,510	438,330	384,180	18	16	2	37	22	15	18
3,945,074	1,955,052	1,990,022	2	2	...	133	71	62	19
7,405,472	3,762,073	3,643,399	5,300	2,737	2,563	903	591	312	20
9,349,693	4,795,954	4,553,739	1,405	888	517	5,882	4,617	1,265	21
2,116,627	1,053,423	1,063,204	119	67	52	256	140	116	22
13,359,710	6,786,852	6,572,858	5,977	4,028	1,949	8,989	6,238	2,751	23
3,103,131	1,644,750	1,458,381	96	79	17	274	149	125	24
4,808,563	2,409,900	2,398,663	288	177	111	2,990	1,681	1,309	25
5,790,952	2,925,938	2,865,014	1,703	933	770	13,538	7,750	5,788	26
13,062	12,264	798	357	278	79	119	99	20	27
4,211,710	2,322,280	1,889,430	218	129	89	866	499	367	28
10,528,569	5,514,185	5,014,384	82	68	14	1,781	1,022	759	29
87,875	45,028	42,847	26	13	13	19	18	1	30
831,991	431,413	400,578	18	14	4	27	13	14	31

Family, Sub-Family, Branch and Sub-Branch.	Group and Sub-Group.	Language.	Population. Persons.	Males.	Females.
1	2	3	4	5	6
	INDIA.		**313,493,215**	**160,457,311**	**153,035,904**
	A.—Vernaculars of India.		**312,948,881**	**160,099,429**	**152,849,452**
Malayo-Polynesian Family.			**6,179**	**3,292**	**2,887**
	Malay Group.	Selung or Selon . . .	1,871	955	916
		Malay	4,308	2,337	1,971
Austro Asiatic Family.			**4,398,640**	**2,188,632**	**2,210,008**
Mon-Khmer Sub-Family.			***555,417***	***274,126***	***281,291***
	Mōn-Khmēr languages proper.	Mōn, Talaing or Peguan . .	**179,444**	**91,302**	**88,142**
	The Palaung-Wa group of the Salwin and neighbourhood.		**166,683**	**83,917**	**82,766**
		Palaung	149,252	75,000	74,252
		Wa	16,511	8,450	8,061
		Yao	274	136	138
		Miao (Hmeng)	646	331	315
	Khāsi.	Khāsi	**200,872**	**94,462**	**106,410**
	Nicobarese.	Nicobarese	**8,418**	**4,445**	**3,973**
Munda Sub-Family.			***3,843,223***	***1,914,506***	***1,928,717***
		KHERWĀRI	3,357,661	1,671,520	1,686,141
		Santāli or Har	*2,138,015*	*1,069,844*	*1,068,171*
		Mundārī	*599,580*	*298,611*	*300,969*
		Bhumij	*132,471*	*65,179*	*67,292*
		Birhār	*1,093*	*566*	*527*
		Kōdā	*24,103*	*12,623*	*11,480*
		Hō	*420,108*	*203,016*	*217,092*
		Tūrī	*10,047*	*5,009*	*5,038*
		Asurī	*4,246*	*2,191*	*2,055*
		Agariā	*1,471*	*775*	*696*
		Korwā	*26,527*	*13,706*	*12,821*
		Kūrkū	136,909	68,204	68,705
		Khariā	126,583	63,802	62,781
		Juāng	12,313	6,121	6,192
		Savara	166,280	83,478	82,802
		Gadaba	43,477	21,381	22,096
Tibeto-Chinese Family.			**12,972,512**	**6,403,805**	**6,568,707**
Tibeto-Burman Sub-Family.			***10,932,775***	***5,385,063***	***5,547,712***
TIBETO-HIMALAYAN BRANCH.			**439,552**	**223,266**	**216,286**
	Tibetan Group.		**230,269**	**116,292**	**113,977**
		BHOTIA	229,837	115,955	113,882
		Bhotiā of Tibet or Tibetan .	*6,020*	*3,734*	*2,286*
		Bhotiā of Bāltistan, or Bālti	*132,199*	*65,569*	*66,630*
		Bhotiā of Ladakh or Ladakhi	*54,761*	*27,811*	*26,950*
		Sharpā Bhotiā	*5,186*	*2,724*	*2,462*
		Bhotiā of Sikkim or Denjongke	*11,562*	*5,933*	*5,629*
		Bhotiā of Bhutān or Lhoke .	*8,680*	*4,234*	*4,446*
		Bhotiā (others) . . .	*11,429*	*5,950*	*5,479*
		Lāhulī	432	337	95
	Non-pronominalized Himālayan Group		**94,072**	**50,424**	**43,648**
		Gūrung	2,054	1,335	719
		Murmī	37,569	19,306	18,263
		Sunvār	4,516	2,420	2,096
		Mangar	19,318	11,537	7,781
		Newārī	7,712	4,247	3,465
		Padhī, Pahrī or Pahī . .	1,051	571	480
		Rong or Lepcha . . .	20,616	10,306	10,310
		Kāmī	177	106	71
		Mānjhī	800	447	353
		Toto	259	149	110

Note.—The entries in italics relate to certain dialects of the language below which they are shown.

Distribution by Linguistic Families.

Family, Sub-Family, Branch and Sub-Branch.	Group and Sub-Group.	Language.	Population. Persons.	Males.	Females.
1	2	3	4	5	6
	Pronominalized Himâlayan Group.		**115,211**	**56,550**	**58,661**
	Eastern Sub-Group.		**84,148**	**42,274**	**41,874**
		Dhîmâl	544	289	255
		Thâmi	334	212	122
		Limbû	24,263	12,707	11,556
		Kirânti Yâkhâ	1,725	977	748
		Kirânti Khambû	2,170	1,569	601
		Kirânti Jimdâr	55,111	26,519	28,592
		Hâyû (Vâyû)	1	1	...
	Western Sub-Group.		**31,063**	**14,276**	**16,787**
		Kanauri or Multhâni	22,542	10,207	12,335
		Kanâshi	376	183	193
		Manchâti or Patnî	4,797	2,325	2,472
		Rangloî, Gondla or Tinân	725	362	363
		Chamba Lâhuli	1,173	589	584
		Bunân	1,261	517	744
		Janggali	189	93	96
North Assam Branch			**58,036**	**29,640**	**28,396**
		Aka	35	34	1
		Daflâ	951	527	424
		Abor-Miri	56,795	28,932	27,863
		Mishmi	255	147	108
Assam-Burmese Branch			**10,435,187**	**5,132,157**	**5,303,030**
	Bodo Group.		**682,324**	**347,676**	**334,648**
		Bodo, Mech or Plains Kachâri	282,981	142,489	140,492
		Lalung	12,187	5,940	6,247
		Dimâ-sâ	16,586	8,285	8,301
		Chutiâ	3,107	1,431	1,676
		Gâro	192,539	99,908	92,631
		Rabhâ	28,699	14,305	14,394
		Tipurâ or Mrung	135,945	70,286	65,659
		Morân	24	6	18
		Kôch	10,256	5,026	5,230
	Nâgâ Group.		**219,711**	**108,618**	**111,093**
	Nâgâ-Bodo Sub-Group.		**26,425**	**12,833**	**13,592**
		Empeo or Kachchâ Nâgâ	8,169	4,160	4,009
		Kabui	17,230	8,178	9,052
		Khoirâo	1,026	495	531
	Nâgâ-Kuki Sub-Group.		**43,687**	**21,218**	**22,469**
		Marâm	3,259	1,593	1,666
		Maring	2,674	1,294	1,380
		Tangkhul	27,285	12,868	14,417
		Sopvomâ	10,100	5,287	4,813
		Kwoireng	369	176	193
	Western Nâgâ Sub-Group.		**81,060**	**41,050**	**40,010**
		Angâmi	38,714	20,059	18,655
		Kezhâmâ	5,035	2,600	2,435
		Rengmâ	4,389	2,025	2,364
		Semâ	32,922	16,366	16,556
	Central Nâgâ Sub-Group.		**48,827**	**23,333**	**25,494**
		Âo	29,068	13,744	15,324
		Lhotâ or Tsontsü	19,627	9,512	10,115
		Yachumi	132	77	55

TABLE X.—LANGUAGE. PART II.—

Family, Sub-Family, Branch and Sub-Branch.	Group and Sub-Group.	Language.	Population. Persons.	Males.	Females.
1	2	3	4	5	6
	Eastern Nâgâ Sub-Group.		2,940	1,424	1,516
		Tableng	299	163	136
		Tamlu	1,998	940	1,058
		Mojung	643	321	322
	Nâgâ Unclassed.	Nâgâ Unclassed	16,772	8,760	8,012
	Kuki Chin Group.		890,337	439,673	450,664
	Meithei Sub-Group.	Manipuri, Meithei, Kathe or Ponnu	313,794	156,196	157,598
	Old Kuki Sub-Group.		20,926	10,142	10,784
		Rângkhol	785	362	423
		Hallâm	3,308	1,791	1,517
		Mhâr	5,430	2,476	2,954
		Chaw	249	128	121
		Chiru	1,298	593	705
		Koireng	1,026	493	533
		Kom	2,087	960	1,127
		Purum	1,036	510	526
		Anal	2,659	1,370	1,289
		Aimol	416	224	192
		Hiroi-Lamgang	136	66	70
		Chote	193	134	59
		Vaiphei	2,303	1,035	1,268
	Northern Chin Sub-Group.		54,003	26,010	27,993
		Thâdo or Jangshen	26,571	13,030	13,541
		Siyin	151	76	75
		Paithe	15,567	7,336	8,231
		Râltê	7,493	3,405	4,088
		Soktê	4,221	2,163	2,058
	Central Chin Sub-Group.		74,856	34,973	39,883
		Zahao	3,523	1,701	1,822
		Lushei or Dulien	69,407	32,325	37,082
		Banjogi	2	2	...
		Baungshe	1,924	945	979
	Southern Chin Sub-Group.		294,561	144,981	149,580
		Yindu	4,348	2,138	2,210
		Khyang	501	229	272
		Khâmi, Khweymi or Kumi	17,532	8,785	8,747
		Anu	474	235	239
		That	80	38	42
		Chin (Unspecified)	233,661	114,552	119,109
		Chinbôk	18,179	8,916	9,263
		Taungtha	17,244	8,817	8,427
		Daingnet	919	445	474
		M'hang	23	8	15
		Chinbôn	1,600	818	782
	Mikir.	Mikir	103,063	52,766	50,297
	Unclassed Languages.	Kuki (Unspecified)	29,134	14,605	14,529
	Kachin Group.		172,024	84,951	87,073
	Kachin.	Kachin or Singpho	171,294	84,442	86,852
	Kachin-Burma Hybrids.		730	509	221
		Szi Lepai	205	122	83
		Maru	209	108	101
		Maingtha	316	279	37

Distribution by Linguistic Families—*continued.*

Family, Sub-Family, Branch and Sub-Branch.	Group and Sub-Group.	Language.	Population. Persons.	Males.	Females.
1	2	3	4	5	6
	Burma Group.		**8,405,243**	**4,118,209**	**4,287,034**
		Mrū	14,045	7,091	6,954
		Burmese	7,893,504	3,858,003	4,035,501
		Arakanese	389,831	198,819	191,012
		Taungyo	19,317	9,569	9,748
		Intha	55,880	27,707	28,173
		Danu	18,694	10,076	8,618
		Hpón	342	157	185
		Tavoyan	46	44	2
		Kadu	11,069	5,537	5,532
		Chaungtha	2,515	1,206	1,309
	Lolo Group.		**65,548**	**33,030**	**32,518**
		Lolo (Myen)	339	166	173
		Lisu (Lisaw)	9,066	4,407	4,659
		Lahu (Muhso)	18,500	9,375	9,125
		Kwi (Lahu Hsi)	3,924	2,007	1,917
		Akha (Kaw)	32,925	16,666	16,259
		Akö	794	409	385
Siamese-Chinese Sub-Family.			***2,039,737***	***1,018,742***	***1,020,995***
	Sinitic Group.	Karen	**1,067,464**	**534,820**	**532,644**
		Brè	*6,918*	*3,149*	*3,769*
		Karenbyu	*777*	*420*	*357*
		Karennet	*728*	*494*	*234*
		Karenni	*21,203*	*11,257*	*9,946*
		Manó	*2,182*	*955*	*1,227*
		Padaung	*8,516*	*4,106*	*4,410*
		Sgau Karen, Pwo-Karen and Karen (Unspecified).	*850,756*	*425,748*	*425,008*
		Sinsin	*899*	*522*	*377*
		Taungthu	*168,326*	*84,512*	*83,814*
		Yinbaw	*2,166*	*1,032*	*1,134*
		Zayein	*4,892*	*2,574*	*2,318*
	Tai Group.		**972,273**	**483,922**	**488,351**
		Siamese	8,908	5,064	3,844
		Lü	13,262	6,892	6,370
		Khün	48,408	23,925	24,483
		Shān	898,832	446,475	452,357
		Phākial	361	182	179
		Khāmtī	2,063	1,142	921
		Aiton	412	233	179
		Kob	27	9	18
Dravidian Family.			**62,718,961**	**31,223,555**	**31,495,406**
	Dravida Group.		**37,094,393**	**18,392,256**	**18,702,137**
		Tamil	18,128,365	8,895,607	9,232,758
		Malayālam	6,792,277	3,389,877	3,402,400
		Kanarese	10,525,739	5,280,001	5,245,738
		Kodagu or Coorgi	42,881	21,789	21,092
		Tulu	563,453	278,772	284,681
		Toda	730	407	323
		Kota	1,280	628	652
		Kurukh or Orāoñ	800,328	395,530	404,798
		Malhar	236	113	123
		Malto or Maler	64,875	32,360	32,515
		Brahūī	174,229	97,172	77,057

TABLE X.—Language. Part II.—

Family, Sub-Family, Branch and Sub-Branch.	Group and Sub-Group.	Language.	Population. Persons.	Males.	Females.
1	2	3	4	5	6
	Intermediate Languages.	Goṇḍ, etc.	**1,527,157**	**735,051**	**792,106**
	Andhra Group.		**24,097,411**	**12,096.248**	**12,001,163**
		Telugu or Andhra	23,542,861	11,820,129	11,722,732
		Kandh or Kuī	530,476	263,968	266,508
		Kolāmī	24,074	12,151	11,923
Indo-European Family.			**232,822,511**	**120,264,826**	**112,557,685**
Aryan Sub-Family.			***232,822,511***	***120,264,826***	***112,557,685***
ERANIAN BRANCH	**Eastern Group.**		**2,066,654**	**1,130,554**	**936,100**
		Baloch	504,586	276,324	228,262
		Pashto	1,554,465	850,105	704,360
		Munjānī or Mungi	4	4	...
		Dehwari	7,579	4,111	3,468
		Ormurī	20	10	10
INDIAN BRANCH			**230,755,857**	**119,134,272**	**111,621,585**
NON-SANSKRITIC SUB-BRANCH.			*1,207,159*	*649,514*	*557,645*
	Shina Khowar Group.		**1,207,159**	**649,514**	**557,645**
		Khowar, Arniya or Chatrari	56	52	4
		Shina	21,562	11,236	10,326
		Kashmīrī	1,180,632	635,522	545,110
		Kôhistānī	4,893	2,688	2,205
		Pashai	16	16	...
SANSKRITIC SUB-BRANCH.			*229,548,698*	*118,484.758*	*111,063,940*
	Sanskrit Group.	Sanskrit	**360**	**286**	**74**
	North-Western Group.		**8,449,073**	**4,544,479**	**3,904,594**
		Lahndā, or Western Panjābī	4,779,138	2,560,933	2,218,205
		Siraikī	*206,452*	*111,384*	*95,068*
		Sindhī	3,669,935	1,983,546	1,686,389
		Kachchhī	*389,736*	*202,476*	*187,260*
	Southern Group.	Marāthī	**19,806,636**	**9,967,689**	**9,838,947**
		Goanese	*24,284*	*17,851*	*6,433*
		Kônkanī	*495,902*	*254,192*	*241,710*
		Singhalese	*341*	*269*	*72*
		Mahl	*3,675*	*1,837*	*1,838*
	Eastern Group.		**60,462,352**	**30,524,127**	**29,938,225**
		Oriyā	10,162,321	5,001,782	5,160,539
		Bihārī	398,294	197,650	200,644
		Bengali	48,367,915	24,538,603	23,829,312
		Assamese	1,533,822	786,092	747,730
	Mediate Group.		**84,426,627**	**43,358.384**	**41,068,246**
		Hindī*	82,003,235	42,149,140	39,854,095
		Eastern Hindī	2,423,392	1,209,244	1,214,148

* *Vide* paragraph 5 of the Explanatory Note in the Title page.

DISTRIBUTION BY LINGUISTIC FAMILIES—*continued.*

Family, Sub-Family, Branch and Sub-Branch.	Group and Sub-Group.	Language.	POPULATION.		
			Persons.	Males.	Females.
1	2	3	4	5	6
	Western Group.		**54,664,478**	**29,167,657**	**25,496,821**
		Western Hindī	14,037,882	7,460,757	6,577,125
		Rājasthānī	14,067,590	7,348,611	6,718,979
		Banjārī	*504,809*	*265,861*	*238,948*
		Gujarī	*297,673*	*156,731*	*140,942*
		Gujarātī	10,682,248	5,517,977	5,164,271
		Bhīl languages . . .	*1,435,445*	*719,408*	*716,037*
		Khāndēshī	*8,516*	*4,337*	*4,179*
		Panjābī * . . .	15,876,758	8,840,312	7,036,446
	Northern Group.		**1,739,172**	**922,136**	**817,036**
		Central Pahari . . .	3,765	3,049	716
		Eastern Pahārī or Naipālī . .	208,932	126,328	82,604
		Western Pahārī* . . .	1,526,475	792,759	733,716
Unclassified Languages.			**29,618**	**15,088**	**145 30**
		Andamanese	1,324	632	692
		Gipsy languages . . .	28,294	14,456	13,838
Language not returned.			**460**	**231**	**229**
B.—Vernaculars of other Asiatic Countries and Africa			**223,110**	**149,039**	**74,071**
Indo-European Family.			**57,041**	**31,634**	**25.407**
	Eranian Group.	Persian	**56,589**	**31,305**	**25,284**
	Armenian Group.	Armenian	**452**	**329**	**123**
Semitic Family.			**43,570**	**29,317**	**14,253**
		Arabic	42,102	28,556	13,546
		Hebrew	1,457	750	707
		Syriac	11	11	...
Hamitic Family.			**7,024**	**4,765**	**2,259**
		African Dialects . . .	**5**	**3**	**2**
	Ethiopic Group.		**7,019**	**4,762**	**2,257**
		Somali	6,901	4,696	2,205
		Abyssinian (including Negro) .	118	66	52
Caucasian Family.		Caucasian	**20**	**18**	**2**
Mongolian Family.			**115,350**	**83,208**	**32,142**
	Ural-Altaic Group.		**770**	**494**	**276**
		Mongolian	1	...	1
		Turkish Dialects . . .	769	494	275
		Osmanli (Turki) .	*27*	*22*	*5*
	Japanese Group.	Japanese	**1,130**	**436**	**694**
	Monosyllabic Group.	Chinese .	**113,450**	**82,278**	**31,172**

* The dialects of Panjābī and Western Pahārī which were separately tabulated in the Punjab will be found on pages 115 and 120 under the heads Punjab and Punjab States.

TABLE X.—Language. Part II.—Distribution by Linguistic Families—*concluded.*

Family, Sub-Family, Branch and Sub-Branch.	Group and Sub-Group.	Language.	Population.		
			Persons.	Males.	Females.
1	2	3	4	5	6
Malayo-Polynesian Family.	**Malayan Group.**	Tagala	53	53	...
Bantu Family.			52	44	8
		Swahili (Zanzibari)	18	16	2
		Sidi	31	26	5
		Kaffir (Bantu)	3	2	1
C.—European Languages.			321,224	208,843	112,381
Indo-European Family.			321,201	208,825	112,376
	Indo-Aryan Group.	Romany	59	50	9
	Greek Group.	Greek (Romaic)	352	297	55
	Romance Group.		14,492	9,614	4,878
		Italian	1,102	962	140
		Latin	9	9	...
		Maltese	7	7	...
		Roumanian	7	3	4
		French	1,499	893	606
		Spanish	120	70	50
		Portuguese	11,748	7,670	4,078
	Celtic Group.		51	35	16
		Welsh	11	7	4
		Gaelic (Scotch)*	4	4	...
		Irish	36	24	12
	Balto-Slavonic Group (Slavonic).		180	80	100
		Russian	148	50	98
		Bohemian (Czech)	1	...	1
		Polish	1	...	1
		Bulgarian	1	1	...
		Slav	29	29	...
	Teutonic Group.		306,067	196,749	107,318
		English	303,515	196,927	106,588
		Dutch	160	129	31
		Flemish	24	16	8
		Norwegian	94	80	14
		Swedish	129	70	59
		Danish	65	34	31
		German	2,080	1,493	587
Basque Family.		Basque	5	5	...
Mongolian Family.	**Ural-Altaic Group.**		17	12	5
		Finnish	4	4	...
		Hungarian (Magyar)	13	8	5
Language not returned.			1	1	...

TABLE X.—LANGUAGE. PART III.—TERRITORIAL DISTRIBUTION OF EACH LANGUAGE.

LANGUAGE AND PROVINCE.	POPULATION.		
	Persons.	Males.	Females.
1	2	3	4
All Languages	**313,493,215**	**160,457,311**	**153,035,904**
A.—Vernaculars of India	**312,948,881**	**160,099,429**	**152,849,452**
ABOR-MIRI	**56,795**	**28,932**	**27,863**
Assam	56,794	28,931	27,863
Bengal	1	1	...
AGARIÂ	**1,471**	**775**	**696**
Bengal	36	33	3
Bihar and Orissa	1,435	742	693
AIMOL (Assam State)	**416**	**224**	**192**
AITON (Assam)	**412**	**233**	**179**
AKA (Assam)	**35**	**34**	**1**
AKHA (KAW) (Burma)	**32,925**	**16,666**	**16,259**
AKŎ (Burma)	**794**	**409**	**385**
ANAL (Assam State)	**2,659**	**1,370**	**1,289**
ANDAMANESE	**1,324**	**632**	**692**
Andamans and Nicobars	1,317	628	689
Bengal	7	4	3
ANGÂMI (NÂGÂ)	**38,714**	**20,059**	**18,655**
Assam	38,699	20,048	18,651
Assam State	15	11	4
ANU (Burma)	**474**	**235**	**239**
ÂO (NÂGÂ) (Assam)	**29,068**	**13,744**	**15,324**
ARAKANESE	**389,831**	**198,819**	**191,012**
Bengal	64,259	35,982	28,277
Burma	323,962	161,994	161,968
Bengal States	1,610	843	767
ASSAMESE	**1,533,822**	**786,092**	**747,730**
Assam	1,532,332	784,889	747,443
Bengal	737	628	109
Bengal States	458	412	46
Other Provinces	295	163	132
ASURI	**4,246**	**2,191**	**2,055**
Bengal	790	443	347
Bihar and Orissa	3,216	1,623	1,593
Other Provinces	240	125	115
BALOCH	**504,586**	**276,324**	**228,262**
Baluchistan	71,698	39,547	32,151
Bombay	195,022	107,785	87,237
Punjab	69,231	39,147	30,084
Baluchistan States	161,289	85,645	75,644
Bombay States	4,236	2,177	2,059
Punjab States	1,444	968	476
Rajputana Agency	945	519	426
Other Provinces	721	536	185
A.—Vernaculars of India—*contd.*			
BANJOGÎ (Assam)	**2**	**2**	..
BAUNGSHE (Burma)	**1,924**	**945**	**979**
BENGALI	**48,367,915**	**24,538,603**	**23,829,312**
Ajmer-Merwara	291	132	159
Andamans and Nicobars	1,648	1,534	114
Assam	3,224,130	1,665,230	1,558,900
Bengal	41,899,210	21,180,083	20,719,127
Bihar and Orissa	2,186,020	1,105,850	1,080,170
Bombay	1,752	1,437	315
Burma	248,310	164,405	83,905
C. P. and Berar	2,386	1,396	990
Madras	1,166	1,016	150
Punjab	2,116	1,355	761
United Provinces	22,500	10,597	11,903
Assam State	474	370	104
Bengal States	666,618	349,195	317,423
Bihar and Orissa States	108,924	54,735	54,189
Central India Agency	894	289	605
Rajputana Agency	619	355	264
Other Provinces	857	624	233
BHOTIÂ *	**229,837**	**115,955**	**113,882**
Assam	1,295	899	396
Bengal	13,973	7,338	6,635
Punjab	5,901	3,142	2,759
United Provinces	5,225	2,598	2,627
Kashmir State	186,513	92,939	93,574
Punjab States	4,404	2,537	1,867
Sikkim State	12,433	6,418	6,015
Other Provinces	93	84	9
BHOTIA OF BALTISTAN	***132,199***	***65,569***	***66,630***
Kashmir State	132,161	65,537	66,624
Other Provinces	38	32	6
BHOTIA OF BHUTAN	***8,680***	***4,234***	***4,446***
Assam	536	413	123
Bengal	3,989	2,009	1,980
United Provinces	4,150	1,809	2,341
Other Provinces	5	3	2
BHOTIA OF LADAKH	***54,761***	***27,811***	***26,950***
United Provinces	513	456	57
Kashmir State	54,237	27,346	26,891
Other Provinces	11	9	2
BHOTIA OF SIKKIM	***11,562***	***5,933***	***5,629***
Bengal	1,151	581	570
Sikkim State	10,411	5,352	5,059
BHOTIA OF TIBET	***6,020***	***3,734***	***2,286***
Assam	759	486	273
Punjab	821	655	166
United Provinces	558	330	228
Punjab States	3,763	2,204	1,559
Other Provinces	119	59	60

* This includes Bhotia of Baltistan, Bhotia of Bhutan, etc., separate figures for which are given below.

TABLE X.—LANGUAGE. PART III.—TERRITORIAL

LANGUAGE AND PROVINCE.	POPULATION.		
	Persons.	Males.	Females.
1	2	3	4
A.—Vernaculars of India—contd.			
SHARPA BHOTIA	***5,186***	***2,724***	***2,462***
Bengal	3,691	1,972	1,719
Sikkim State	1,495	752	743
BHOTIA (OTHERS)	***11,429***	***5,950***	***5,479***
Bengal	5,142	2,776	2,366
Punjab	5,045	2,457	2,588
Punjab States	631	325	306
Sikkim State	523	312	211
Other Provinces	88	80	8
BHUMIJ	**132,471**	**65,179**	**67,292**
Assam	5,342	2,668	2,674
Bengal	21,246	10,585	10,661
Bihar and Orissa	42,142	20,310	21,832
Bengal States	17	8	9
Bihar and Orissa States	63,724	31,608	32,116
BIHÂRÎ	**398,294**	**197,650**	**200,644**
Ajmer-Merwara	1,484	847	637
Bengal	22,775	12,586	10,189
Bihar and Orissa	278,836	134,374	144,462
N.-W. Frontier Province	359	333	26
United Provinces	540	363	177
Bihar and Orissa States	11,811	5,956	5,855
Central India Agency	78,398	40,681	37,717
Rajputana Agency	3,476	2,092	1,384
Other Provinces	615	418	197
BIRHÂR	**1,093**	**566**	**527**
Bihar and Orissa	941	481	460
Other Provinces	152	85	67
BODO (MECH, KACHÂRÎ)	**282,981**	**142,489**	**140,492**
Assam	261,112	130,528	130,584
Bengal	21,379	11,680	9,699
Assam State	143	77	66
Bengal States	347	204	143
BRÂHÛÎ	**174,229**	**97,172**	**77,057**
Baluchistan	21,170	11,997	9,173
Bombay	28,900	16,328	12,572
Baluchistan States	124,129	68,831	55,298
Bombay States	30	16	14
BUNÂN (Punjab)	**1,261**	**517**	**744**
BURMESE	**7,893,504**	**3,858,003**	**4,035,501**
Andamans and Nicobars	1,620	1,602	18
Bengal	8,288	722	7,566
Burma	7,883,299	3,855,510	4,027,789
Other Provinces	297	169	128

LANGUAGE AND PROVINCE.	POPULATION.		
	Persons.	Males.	Females.
1	2	3	4
A.—Vernaculars of India—contd.			
CENTRAL PAHÂRÎ	**3,765**	**3,049**	**716**
Baluchistan	298	286	12
Punjab	872	810	62
United Provinces	1,298	832	466
Punjab States	567	453	114
Rajputana Agency	530	479	51
Other Provinces	200	189	11
CHAMBA LÂHULÎ (Punjab States).	**1,173**	**589**	**584**
CHAUNGTHA (Burma)	**2,515**	**1,206**	**1,309**
CHAW (Burma)	**249**	**128**	**121**
CHIN (UNSPECIFIED) (Burma)	**233,661**	**114,552**	**119,109**
CHINBÔK (Burma)	**18,179**	**8,916**	**9,263**
CHINBÔN (Burma)	**1,600**	**818**	**782**
CHIRU (Assam State)	**1,298**	**593**	**705**
CHOTE (Assam and Assam State)	**193**	**134**	**59**
CHUTIÂ (Assam)	**3,107**	**1,431**	**1,676**
DAFLA (Assam)	**951**	**527**	**424**
DAINGNET (Burma)	**919**	**445**	**474**
DANU (Burma)	**18,694**	**10,076**	**8,618**
DEHWARI (Baluchistan and Baluchistan States).	**7,579**	**4,111**	**3,468**
DHÎMÂL	**544**	**289**	**255**
Assam	100	58	42
Bengal	444	231	213
DIMÂ-SÂ	**16,586**	**8,285**	**8,301**
Assam	16,483	8,230	8,253
Bengal States	103	55	48
EASTERN HINDÎ	**2,423,392**	**1,209,244**	**1,214,148**
Bihar and Orissa	899	437	462
Bombay	534	232	302
C. P. and Berar	1,032,832	501,732	531,100
Madras	2,668	1,368	1,300
Bihar and Orissa States	2,596	1,345	1,251
Central India Agency	1,376,523	700,224	676,299
Central Provinces States	651	343	308
Hyderabad State	6,609	3,507	3,102
Other Provinces	80	56	24
EMPEO OR KACHCHÂ NÂGÂ.	**8,169**	**4,160**	**4,009**
Assam	6,885	3,455	3,430
Assam State	1,284	705	579

Distribution of each Language—*continued.*

Language and Province.	Population. Persons.	Males.	Females.
1	2	3	4
A.—Vernaculars of India—*contd.*			
GADABA	**43,477**	**21,381**	**22,096**
Madras	43,009	21,152	21,857
Bihar and Orissa States	162	88	74
Central Provinces States	306	141	165
GĀRO	**192,539**	**99,908**	**92,631**
Assam	153,766	77,607	76,159
Bengal	37,918	21,681	16,237
Bengal States	855	620	235
GIPSY LANGUAGES	**28,294**	**14,456**	**13,838**
Ajmer-Merwara	209	98	111
Bombay	8,362	4,269	4,093
C. P. and Berar	2,274	1,156	1,118
Punjab	5,640	2,871	2,769
United Provinces	1,673	755	918
Baroda State	536	263	273
Bombay States	2,326	1,248	1,078
Central India Agency	1,097	569	528
Hyderabad State	4,566	2,359	2,207
Punjab States	474	227	247
Rajputana Agency	456	232	224
Other Provinces	681	409	272
GOṆḌ	**1,527,157**	**735,051**	**792,106**
Assam	10,306	5,380	4,926
Bihar and Orissa	247	122	125
C. P. and Berar	917,113	449,449	467,664
Madras	57,392	30,235	27,157
Bihar and Orissa States	3,965	1,964	2,001
Central India Agency	214,276	83,524	130,752
Central Provinces States	249,902	125,470	124,432
Hyderabad State	73,939	38,890	35,049
Other Provinces	17	17	...
GUJARĀTĪ *	**10,682,248**	**5,517,977**	**5,164,271**
Ajmer-Merwara	1,516	871	645
Andamans and Nicobars	309	284	25
Assam	306	238	68
Baluchistan	501	336	165
Bengal	4,195	3,012	1,183
Bihar and Orissa	2,567	1,782	785
Bombay	3,347,490	1,759,369	1,588,121
Burma	7,896	6,049	1,847
C. P. and Berar	70,241	38,217	32,024
Madras	98,774	50,453	48,321
Punjab	2,565	1,608	957
United Provinces	4,043	2,352	1,691
Baroda State	1,901,868	984,832	917,036
Bihar and Orissa States	471	353	118
Bombay States	4,279,544	2,183,953	2,095,591
Central India Agency	421,853	211,480	210,373
Central Provinces States	441	328	113
Hyderabad State	22,918	12,603	10,315
Madras States	4,196	2,274	1,922
Cochin	*1,060*	*663*	*397*
Travancore	*2,220*	*1,187*	*1,033*

Language and Province.	Population. Persons.	Males.	Females.
1	2	3	4
A.—Vernaculars of India—*contd.*			
GUJARĀTĪ—*contd.*			
Mysore State	2,776	1,617	1,159
Punjab States	3,855	2,081	1,774
Rajputana Agency	503,399	253,525	249,874
Other Provinces	524	360	164
BHIL LANGUAGES	***1,435,445***	***719,408***	***716,037***
Ajmer-Merwara	302	150	152
Bengal	282	145	137
Bombay	300,052	149,142	150,910
C. P. and Berar	24,557	12,116	12,441
Punjab	773	452	321
Baroda State	145,561	73,754	71,807
Bombay States	117,558	59,591	57,967
Central India Agency	349,932	174,852	175,080
Hyderabad State	7,858	3,884	3,974
Punjab States	3,683	1,952	1,731
Rajputana Agency	484,887	243,370	241,517
KHANDESHI	***8,516***	***4,337***	***4,179***
Central India Agency	8,272	4,197	4,075
Other Provinces	244	140	104
GŪRUNG	**2.054**	**1.335**	**719**
Assam	1,001	723	278
Bengal	1,030	599	431
Other Provinces	23	13	10
HALLĀM	**3,308**	**1,791**	**1.517**
Assam	367	218	149
Bengal States	2,941	1,573	1,368
HĀYŪ (VĀYŪ) (Sikkim)	**1**	**1**	..
HINDĪ	**82.003,235**	**42.149,140**	**39.854.095**
Ajmer-Merwara	49,251	26,311	22,940
Andamans and Nicobars	4,785	4,154	631
Assam	428,822	242,904	185,918
Bengal	1,712,602	1,149,329	563,273
Bihar and Orissa	24,146,192	11,799,895	12,346,297
Bombay	106,216	72,086	34,130
Burma	40,293	32,805	7,488
C. P. and Berar	6,044,184	3,005,689	3,038,495
Madras	749	329	420
Punjab	1,462,892	791,020	671,872
United Provinces	43,465,654	22,666,649	20,799,005
Assam State	1,956	1,548	408
Baroda State	3,203	2,360	843
Bengal States	27,575	21,315	6,260
Bihar and Orissa States	104,378	53,923	50,455
Bombay States	60,353	31,011	29,342
Central India Agency	1,060,582	556,619	503,963
Central Provinces States	1,461,980	723,493	738,487
Hyderabad State	12,261	7,837	4,424
Kashmir State	556	375	181
Punjab States	315,984	173,621	142,363
Rajputana Agency	1,190,083	636,297	553,786
Sikkim State	391	350	41
United Provinces States	302,137	149,138	152,999
Other Provinces	156	82	74

* This includes Bhil languages and Khāndēshī separate figures for which are given below.

TABLE X.—Language. Part III.—Territorial

Language and Province.	Population. Persons.	Males.	Females.
1	2	3	4
A.—Vernaculars of India—*contd.*			
HIROI-LAMGANG (Assam State).	**136**	**66**	**70**
HŌ	**420,108**	**203,016**	**217,092**
Assam	122	76	46
Bengal	3,530	1,734	1,796
Bihar and Orissa	258,224	123,413	134,811
Bihar and Orissa States	158,232	77,793	80,439
HPŌN (Burma)	**342**	**157**	**185**
INTHA (Burma)	**55,880**	**27,707**	**28,173**
JANGGALĪ (Assam)	**189**	**93**	**96**
JUĀNG (Bihar and Orissa and its States).	**12,313**	**6,121**	**6,192**
KABUI (NĀGĀ) (Assam and Assam State).	**17,230**	**8,178**	**9,052**
KACHIN OR SINGPHO	**171,294**	**84,442**	**86,852**
Assam	1,880	992	888
Burma	169,414	83,450	85,964
KADU (Burma)	**11,069**	**5,537**	**5,532**
KĀMĪ	**177**	**106**	**71**
Assam	111	63	48
Bengal	66	43	23
KANARESE	**10,525,739**	**5,280,001**	**5,245,738**
Andamans and Nicobars	305	295	10
Bombay	2,462,195	1,244,868	1,217,327
C. P. and Berar	4,397	2,020	2,377
Coorg	71,557	37,618	33,939
Madras	1,589,487	783,599	805,888
Bombay States	549,641	278,799	270,842
Central India Agency	281	126	155
Hyderabad State	1,680,005	843,815	836,190
Madras States	19,847	10,027	9,820
Cochin	*4,152*	*2,180*	*1,972*
Travancore	*1,901*	*1,053*	*848*
Mysore State	4,147,765	2,078,682	2,069,083
Other Provinces	259	152	107
KANĀSHĪ (Punjab)	**376**	**183**	**193**
KANAURI OR MULTHĀNĪ	**22,542**	**10,207**	**12,335**
Punjab States	22,359	10,083	12,276
Other Provinces	183	124	59
KANDH OR KUĪ	**530,476**	**263,968**	**266,508**
Assam	3,966	1,885	2,081
Bihar and Orissa	51,060	24,909	26,151
Madras	389,799	194,802	194,997
Bihar and Orissa States	85,651	42,372	43,279
KAREN *	**1,067,464**	**534,820**	**532,644**
Burma	1,067,363	534,769	532,594
Other Provinces	101	51	50
***BRE* (Burma)**	***6,918***	***3,149***	***3,769***
***KARENBYU* (Burma)**	***777***	***420***	***357***
***KARENNET* (Burma)**	***728***	***494***	***234***
***KARENNI* (Burma)**	***21,903***	***11,957***	***9,946***
***MANŌ* (Burma)**	***2,182***	***955***	***1,227***
***PADAUNG* (Burma)**	***8,516***	***4,106***	***4,410***
***SGAU KAREN, PWO-KAREN AND KAREN (UNSPECIFIED)* (Burma).**	***850,756***	***425,748***	***425,008***
***SINSIN* (Burma)**	***899***	***522***	***377***
***TAUNGTHU* (Burma)**	***168,326***	***84,512***	***83,814***
***YINBAW* (Burma)**	***2,166***	***1,032***	***1,134***
***ZAYEIN* (Burma)**	***4,892***	***2,574***	***2,318***
KASHMĪRĪ	**1,180,632**	**635,522**	**545,110**
N.-W. Frontier Province	533	445	88
Punjab	6,480	4,880	1,600
Kashmir State	1,172,487	629,512	542,975
Punjab States	710	387	323
Other Provinces	422	298	124
KEZHĀMĀ (NĀGĀ) (Assam)	**5,035**	**2,600**	**2,435**
KHĀMI	**17,532**	**8,785**	**8,747**
Assam	51	27	24
Bengal	1,050	528	522
Burma	16,431	8,230	8,201
KHĀMTĪ (Assam)	**2,063**	**1,142**	**921**
KHARIĀ	**126,583**	**63,802**	**62,781**
Assam	4,718	2,848	1,870
Bengal	6,437	3,671	2,766
Bihar and Orissa	64,041	31,754	32,287
C. P. and Berar	985	447	538
Bihar and Orissa States	43,149	21,469	21,680
Central Provinces States	7,253	3,613	3,640
KHĀSĪ	**200,872**	**94,462**	**106,410**
Assam	200,795	94,417	106,378
Other Provinces	77	45	32
KHOIRĀO (NĀGĀ) (Assam State).	**1,026**	**495**	**531**
KHOWAR OR CHATRARI	**56**	**52**	**4**
N.-W. Frontier Province	41	41	...
Other Provinces	15	11	4
KHUN (Burma)	**48,408**	**23,925**	**24,483**
KHYANG (Bengal and Bengal States).	**501**	**229**	**272**
KIRĀNTĪ (JĪMDĀR)	**55,111**	**26,519**	**28,592**
Bengal	39,260	18,518	20,742
Sikkim State	15,803	7,963	7,840
Other Provinces	48	38	10

* This includes Brē, Karenbyu, Karennet, etc., separate figures for which are given below.

Distribution of each Language—*continued.*

Language and Province.	Population. Persons.	Males.	Females.
1	2	3	4
A.—Vernaculars of India—*contd.*			
KIRĀNTĪ (KHAMBŪ)	**2,170**	**1,569**	**601**
Assam	1,320	1,058	262
Bengal	823	509	314
Other Provinces	27	2	25
KIRANTĪ (YĀKHĀ)	**1,725**	**977**	**748**
Assam	390	336	54
Bengal	1,311	634	677
Sikkim State	24	7	17
KOB (Assam State)	**27**	**9**	**18**
KŌCH	**10,256**	**5,026**	**5,230**
Assam	3,658	1,831	1.827
Bengal	6,598	3,195	3,403
KŌDĀ	**24,103**	**12,623**	**11,480**
Assam	68	47	21
Bengal	19,958	10,496	9,462
Bihar and Orissa	4,077	2,080	1,997
KODAGU OR COORGI	**42,881**	**21,789**	**21,092**
Coorg	42,784	21,718	21,066
Other Provinces	97	71	26
KŌHISTĀNI	**4,893**	**2,688**	**2,205**
Kashmir State	4,750	2,590	2,160
Other Provinces	143	98	45
KOIRENG	**1,026**	**493**	**533**
Assam	392	195	197
Assam State	634	298	336
KOLĀMĪ (C. P. and Berar)	**24,074**	**12,151**	**11,923**
KOM (Assam State)	**2,087**	**960**	**1,127**
KORWĀ	**26,527**	**13,706**	**12,821**
Assam	775	365	410
Bihar and Orissa	8,717	4,609	4,108
C. P. and Berar	343	168	175
Bihar and Orissa States	1,614	763	851
Central Provinces States	14,889	7,690	7,199
Other Provinces	189	111	78
KOTA	**1,280**	**628**	**652**
Assam	9	6	3
Madras	1,271	622	649
KUKI (UNSPECIFIED)	**29,134**	**14,605**	**14,529**
Assam	12,920	6,258	6,662
Bengal	3,305	1,696	1,609
Assam State	6,687	3,482	3,205
Bengal States	6,222	3,169	3,053
KŪRKŪ	**136,909**	**68,204**	**68,705**
Assam	1,990	1,206	784
C. P. and Berar	132,078	65,546	66,532
Central Provinces States	2,751	1,419	1,332
Other Provinces	90	33	57

Language and Province.	Population. Persons.	Males.	Females.
1	2	3	4
A.—Vernaculars of India—*contd.*			
KURUKH OR ORĀOÑ	**800,328**	**395,530**	**404,798**
Assam	19,813	10,706	9,107
Bengal	116,992	64,015	52,977
Bihar and Orissa	460,149	218,525	241,624
C. P. and Berar	2,940	1,432	1,508
Bengal States	264	131	133
Bihar and Orissa States	99,346	49,728	49,618
Central Provinces States	100,824	50,993	49,831
KWI (LAHU HSI) (Burma)	**3,924**	**2,007**	**1,917**
KWOIRENG (NĀGĀ) (Assam State).	**369**	**176**	**193**
LAHU (MUHSO) (Burma)	**18,500**	**9,375**	**9,125**
LĀHULĪ (Punjab and Punjab States).	**432**	**337**	**95**
LĀLUNG (Assam)	**12,187**	**5,940**	**6,247**
LHOTĀ OR TSONTSŪ (NĀGĀ) (Assam).	**19,627**	**9,512**	**10,115**
LIMBŪ	**24,263**	**12,707**	**11,556**
Assam	1,874	1,298	576
Bengal	13,944	7,255	6,689
Sikkim State	8,445	4,154	4,291
LISU (*LISAW*) (Burma)	**9,066**	**4,407**	**4,659**
LOLO (MYEN) (Burma)	**339**	**166**	**173**
LŪ (Burma)	**13,262**	**6,892**	**6,370**
LUSHEI OR DULIEN	**69,407**	**32,325**	**37,082**
Assam	68,713	31,979	36,734
Bengal States	561	274	287
Other Provinces	133	72	61
MAINGTHA (Burma)	**316**	**279**	**37**
MALAY	**4,308**	**2,337**	**1,971**
Burma	4,190	2,237	1,953
Other Provinces	118	100	18
MALAYĀLAM	**6,792,277**	**3,389,877**	**3,402,400**
Bombay	1,450	1,054	396
Burma	736	719	17
Coorg	28,825	18,616	10,209
Madras	3,098,979	1,525,343	1,573,636
Hyderabad State	243	215	28
Madras States	3,656,961	1,839,445	1,817,516
Cochin	*820,129*	*407,228*	*412,901*
Travancore	*2,836,728*	*1,432,139*	*1,404,589*
Mysore State	4,692	4,142	550
Other Provinces	391	343	48
MALHAR	**236**	**113**	**123**
Bengal	15	10	5
Bihar and Orissa and its States.	221	103	118
MALTO OR MALER	**64,875**	**32,360**	**32,515**
Bengal	1,667	825	842
Bihar and Orissa	63,207	31,534	31,673
Bengal States	1	1	..
MANCHĀTI OR PATNĪ (Punjab)	**4,797**	**2,325**	**2,472**

TABLE X.—LANGUAGE. PART III.—TERRITORIAL

Language and Province.	Population.		
	Persons.	Males.	Females.
1	2	3	4
A.—Vernaculars of India —contd.			
MANGAR	**19,318**	**11,537**	**7,781**
Assam	2,745	1,817	928
Bengal	13,521	8,162	5,359
Bihar and Orissa	26	13	13
Sikkim State	3,026	1,545	1,481
MANIPURĪ	**313,794**	**156,196**	**157,598**
Assam	83,734	42,900	40,834
Bengal	232	116	116
Burma	1,629	694	935
Assam State	211,691	103,695	107,996
Bengal States	16,381	8,717	7,664
Other Provinces	127	74	53
MĀNJHĪ	**800**	**447**	**353**
Assam	64	48	16
Bengal	363	209	154
Sikkim State	373	190	183
MARĀM (NAGA) (Assam State)	**3,259**	**1,593**	**1,666**
MARATHĪ *	**19,806,636**	**9,967,689**	**9,838,947**
Ajmer-Merwara	688	372	316
Andamans and Nicobars	671	662	9
Assam	1,396	865	531
Baluchistan	786	693	93
Bengal	2,403	1,478	925
Bihar and Orissa	1,049	560	489
Bombay	9,016,228	4,551,726	4,464,502
Burma	2,212	1,806	406
C. P. and Berar	4,865,980	2,427,510	2,438,470
Coorg	4,437	2,633	1,804
Madras	298,998	150,346	148,652
N.-W. Frontier Province	219	204	15
Punjab	756	507	249
United Provinces	6,029	3,478	2,551
Baroda State	36,145	19,483	16,662
Bihar and Orissa States	284	164	120
Bombay States	1,725,812	865,445	860,367
Central India Agency	65,913	32,076	33,837
Central Provinces States	146,119	73,444	72,675
Hyderabad State	3,498,751	1,763,997	1,734,754
Madras States	41,869	22,018	19,851
Cochin	*22,225*	*11,544*	*10,681*
Travancore	*17,820*	*9,561*	*8,259*
Mysore State	87,476	46,755	40,721
Rajputana Agency	2,028	1,105	923
Sikkim State	222	222	...
Other Provinces	165	140	25
GOANESE	***24,284***	***17,851***	***6,433***
Bengal	352	318	34
Bombay	22,396	16,286	6,110
Burma	351	342	9
C. P. and Berar	256	170	86
Bombay States	277	192	85
Other Provinces	652	543	109
A.—Vernaculars of India —contd.			
KONKANI	***495,909***	***254,199***	***241,710***
Bombay	158,558	82,417	76,141
Coorg	2,696	1,619	1,077
Madras	169,837	84,837	85,000
Bombay States	123,151	61,889	61,262
Madras States	32,207	17,112	15,095
Cochin	*21,153*	*11,226*	*9,927*
Travancore	*11,052*	*5,886*	*5,166*
Mysore State	9,358	6,243	3,115
Other Provinces	95	75	20
***MAHL* (Madras)**	***3,675***	***1,837***	***1,838***
SINGHALESE	***341***	***269***	***72***
Burma	150	102	48
Other Provinces	191	167	24
MARING (NĀGĀ) (Assam State)	**2,674**	**1,294**	**1,380**
MARU (Burma)	**209**	**108**	**101**
M'HANG (Burma)	**23**	**8**	**15**
MHĀR	**5,430**	**2,476**	**2,954**
Assam	3,196	1,416	1,780
Assam State	2,234	1,060	1,174
MIAO (HMENG) (Burma)	**646**	**331**	**315**
MIKIR (Assam)	**103,063**	**52,766**	**50,297**
MISHMI (Assam)	**255**	**147**	**108**
MOJUNG (NĀGĀ) (Assam)	**643**	**321**	**322**
MÖN, TALAING OR PEGUAN	**179,444**	**91,302**	**88,142**
Assam	1	1	...
Burma	179,443	91,301	88,142
MORĀN (Assam)	**24**	**6**	**18**
MRŪ	**14,045**	**7,091**	**6,954**
Assam	43	33	10
Bengal	11,073	5,601	5,472
Burma	2,718	1,343	1,375
Bengal States	211	114	97
MUNDĀRĪ	**599,580**	**298,611**	**300,969**
Assam	72,836	37,093	35,743
Bengal	50,183	26,718	23,465
Bihar and Orissa	404,044	198,111	205,933
Bihar and Orissa States	71,372	35,888	35,484
Central Provinces States	871	655	216
Other Provinces	274	146	128
MUNJĀNĪ OR MUNGI (Assam)	**4**	**4**	...
MURMĪ	**37,569**	**19,306**	**18,263**
Assam	1,615	1,030	585
Bengal	28,599	14,593	14,006
Sikkim State	7,355	3,683	3,672
NĀGĀ (UNCLASSED)	**16,772**	**8,760**	**8,012**
Assam	12,531	6,707	5,824
Assam State	4,238	2,052	2,186
Other Provinces	3	1	2

* This includes Goanese, Konkani, Mahl and Singhalese separate figures for which are given below.

Distribution of each Language—*continued.*

Language and Province.	Population. Persons.	Males.	Females.
1	2	3	4
A.—Vernaculars of India—*contd.*			
NAIPĀLĪ (KHAS)	**208,932**	**126,328**	**82,604**
Assam	45,214	28,513	16,701
Baluchistan	1,956	1,591	365
Bengal	90,388	50,907	39,481
Bihar and Orissa	2,623	1,372	1,251
Burma	3,970	2,323	1,647
N.-W. Frontier Province	5,179	4,359	820
Punjab	7,356	5,379	1,977
United Provinces	18,266	13,512	4,754
Assam State	1,896	1,168	728
Bengal States	456	357	99
Kashmir State	1,844	1,534	310
Punjab States	1,297	800	497
Sikkim State	28,078	14,324	13,754
Other Provinces	409	189	220
NEWĀRĪ	**7,712**	**4,247**	**3,465**
Assam	831	509	322
Bengal	5,590	3,035	2,555
Sikkim State	1,270	685	585
Other Provinces	21	18	3
NICOBARESE (Andamans and Nicobars).	**8,418**	**4,445**	**3,973**
ORIYĀ	**10,162,321**	**5,001,782**	**5,160,539**
Andamans and Nicobars	322	291	31
Assam	61,182	30,537	30,645
Bengal	293,168	193,476	99,692
Bihar and Orissa	4,905,470	2,365,092	2,540,378
Burma	19,112	18,276	836
C. P. and Berar	200,181	99,666	100,515
Madras	1,663,272	799,507	863,765
Bengal States	876	650	226
Bihar and Orissa States	2,914,788	1,442,173	1,472,615
Central Provinces States	102,454	51,315	51,139
Hyderabad State	265	137	128
Mysore State	976	500	476
Other Provinces	255	162	93
ŌRMURĪ (N.-W. F. Province)	**20**	**10**	**10**
PADHĪ, PAHRĪ OR PAHĪ (Assam)	**1,051**	**571**	**480**
PAITHE	**15,567**	**7,336**	**8,231**
Assam	7,239	3,016	4,223
Assam State	8,328	4,320	4,008
PALAUNG (Burma)	**149,252**	**75,000**	**74,252**
PANJĀBI	**15,876,758**	**8,840,312**	**7,036,446**
Ajmer-Merwara	1,598	1,299	299
Andamans and Nicobars	1,620	1,479	141
Assam	823	683	140
Baluchistan	25,191	19,320	5,871
Bengal	5,533	4,657	876
Bihar and Orissa	972	739	233
Bombay	34,790	24,482	10,308
Burma	22,938	19,493	3,445
C. P. and Berar	4,486	3,713	773
N.-W. Frontier Province	843,493	458,431	385,062
Punjab	11,900,238	6,600,539	5,299,699
United Provinces	26,946	19,461	7,485
A.—Vernaculars of India—*contd.*			
PANJĀBĪ—*contd.*			
Baluchistan States	2,351	1,345	1,006
Baroda State	234	163	71
Bombay States	1,091	905	186
Central India Agency	19,092	10,754	8,338
Hyderabad State	3,414	2,143	1,271
Kashmir State	730,074	395,632	334,442
Mysore State	407	355	52
N.-W. Frontier Province (*Agencies and Tribal areas*).	4,781	4,472	309
Punjab States	2,210,977	1,249,835	961,142
Rajputana Agency	35,081	19,901	15,180
United Provinces States	358	300	58
Other Provinces	270	211	59
PASHAI (N.-W. F. Province)	**16**	**16**	...
PASHTO	**1,554,465**	**850,105**	**704,360**
Andamans and Nicobars	493	479	14
Assam	702	664	38
Baluchistan	225,341	123,775	101,566
Bengal	2,770	2,613	157
Bihar and Orissa	732	704	28
Bombay	12,159	9,852	2,307
Burma	1,587	1,490	97
C. P. and Berar	2,372	2,108	264
N.-W. Frontier Province	1,221,839	648,400	573,439
Punjab	66,084	43,161	22,923
United Provinces	1,990	1,791	199
Baluchistan States	2,212	1,211	1,001
Bombay States	998	871	127
Central India Agency	1,659	1,200	459
Hyderabad State	786	618	168
Kashmir State	2,745	1,951	794
N.-W. Frontier Province (*Agencies and Tribal areas*).	7,740	7,349	391
Punjab States	1,090	922	168
Rajputana Agency	572	420	152
Other Provinces	594	526	68
PHĀKIAL (Assam)	**361**	**182**	**179**
PURUM (Assam State)	**1,036**	**510**	**526**
RĀBHĀ	**28,699**	**14,305**	**14,394**
Assam	27,995	13,925	14,070
Bengal	704	380	324
RĀJASTHĀNĪ *	**14,067,590**	**7,348,611**	**6,718,979**
Ajmer-Merwara	411,243	216,589	194,654
Assam	11,611	8,790	2,821
Baluchistan	302	286	16
Bengal	18,336	12,665	5,671
Bihar and Orissa	18,891	10,591	8,300
Bombay	228,058	134,901	93,157
Burma	504	382	122
C. P. and Berar	174,389	94,374	80,015
Madras	41,530	22,678	18,852
N.-W. F. Province	25,668	15,174	10,494
Punjab	514,160	279,787	234,373
United Provinces	11,533	6,350	5,183
Baroda State	3,660	2,246	1,414

* This includes Banjārī and Gujarī separate figures for which are given below.

TABLE X.—LANGUAGE. PART III.—TERRITORIAL

Language and Province.	Population. Persons.	Males.	Females.
1	2	3	4
A.—Vernaculars of India—*contd.*			
RÂJASTHÂNÎ—*contd.*			
Bengal States	809	752	57
Bihar and Orissa States	5,189	2,694	2,495
Bombay States	23,949	13,413	10,536
Central India Agency	3,452,158	1,761,092	1,691,066
Central Provinces States	9,380	4,998	4,382
Hyderabad State	288,107	152,517	135,590
Kashmir State	254,888	132,859	122,029
Madras States	563	296	267
Mysore State	44,915	23,421	21,494
Punjab States	229,782	122,599	107,183
Rajputana Agency	8,297,636	4,328,902	3,968,734
Other Provinces	329	255	74
BANJARI	*504,809*	*265,861*	*238,948*
Bihar and Orissa	1,781	833	948
Bombay	33,100	18,743	14,357
C. P. and Berar	103,158	53,160	49,998
Madras	39,744	21,267	18,477
Punjab	1,558	771	787
United Provinces	7,131	4,031	3,100
Baroda State	250	121	129
Bihar and Orissa States	3,966	1,962	2,004
Bombay States	1,816	897	919
Central India Agency	17,126	9,555	7,571
Central Provinces States	6,670	3,456	3,214
Hyderabad State	237,899	124,852	113,047
Kashmir State	2,061	1,069	992
Madras States	561	294	267
Mysore State	43,667	22,437	21,230
Rajputana Agency	4,299	2,398	1,901
Other Provinces	22	15	7
GUJARI	*297,673*	*156,731*	*140,942*
N.-W. Frontier Province	25,619	15,135	10,484
Punjab	15,126	7,995	7,131
Central India Agency	2,836	1,139	1,697
Kashmir State	252,692	131,712	120,980
Punjab States	1,400	750	650
RÂLTE	**7,493**	**3,405**	**4,088**
Assam	4,015	1,709	2,306
Assam State	3,478	1,696	1,782
RÂNGKHOL	**785**	**362**	**423**
Assam	229	99	130
Bengal States	556	263	293
RÂNGLOÎ OR TINÛN (Punjab).	**725**	**362**	**363**
RENGMA (NÂGÂ) (Assam)	**4,389**	**2,025**	**2,364**
RONG OR LEPCHA	**20,616**	**10,306**	**10,310**
Assam	10	10	..
Bengal	11,328	5,483	5,845
Sikkim State	9,278	4,813	4,465
SANSKRIT	**360**	**286**	**74**
Madras	312	246	66
Other Provinces	48	40	8
SANTÂLÎ OR HÂR	**2,138,015**	**1,069,844**	**1,068,171**
Assam	54,173	27,968	26,205
Bengal	663,720	335,551	328,169
Bihar and Orissa	1,172,460	585,242	587,218

Language and Province.	Population. Persons.	Males.	Females.
1	2	3	4
A.—Vernaculars of India—*contd.*			
SANTÂLÎ OR HÂR—*contd.*			
Bengal States	739	373	366
Bihar and Orissa States	246,897	120,698	126,199
Other Provinces	26	12	14
SAVARA	**166,280**	**83,478**	**82,802**
Assam	503	294	209
Madras	165,777	83,184	82,593
SELUNG OR SELON (Burma)	**1,271**	**655**	**616**
SEMÂ (NAGÂ)	**32,922**	**16,366**	**[16,556]**
Assam	32,921	16,365	16,556
Assam State	1	1	...
SHÂN	**898,832**	**446,475**	**452,357**
Assam	1,029	541	488
Burma	897,803	445,934	451,869
SHINA (Kashmir State)	**21,562**	**11,236**	**10,326**
SIAMESE	**8,908**	**5,064**	**3,844**
Bengal	6	6	...
Burma	8,902	5,058	3,844
SINDHI*	**3,669,935**	**1,983,546**	**1,686,389**
Baluchistan	6,346	4,011	2,335
Bengal	235	173	62
Bihar and Orissa	282	194	88
Bombay	2,897,267	1,586,656	1,310,611
C. P. and Berar	1,583	1,137	446
Madras	495	339	156
Punjab	1,997	1,431	566
United Provinces	362	218	144
Baluchistan States	63,628	34,088	29,540
Baroda State	16,089	7,874	8,215
Bombay States	599,287	302,051	297,236
Central India Agency	462	227	235
Hyderabad State	307	268	39
Madras States	730	393	337
Cochin	*352*	*191*	*161*
Travancore	*378*	*202*	*176*
Mysore State	209	138	71
Punjab States	22,169	12,260	9,909
Rajputana Agency	58,118	31,772	26,346
Other Provinces	369	316	53
KACHCHHI	*389,736*	**202,476**	**187,260**
Bihar and Orissa	258	175	83
Bombay	82,073	49,173	32,900
C. P. and Berar	1,539	1,100	439
Madras	420	270	150
Baroda State	15,268	7,309	7,959
Bombay States	288,486	143,372	145,114
Hyderabad State	307	268	39
Madras States	730	393	337
Cochin	*352*	*191*	*161*
Travancore	*378*	*202*	*176*
Other Provinces	655	416	239
SIYIN (Burma)	**151**	**76**	**75**
SOKTÊ (Assam State)	**4,221**	**2,163**	**2,058**

* This includes Kachchhi separate figures for which are given below.

Distribution of each Language—*continued.*

Language and Province.	Population. Persons.	Males.	Females.
1	2	3	4
A.—Vernaculars of India —*contd.*			
SOPVOMĀ (NAGĀ) (Assam State)	**10,100**	**5,287**	**4,813**
SUNVĀR	**4,516**	**2,420**	**2,096**
Bengal . . .	3,556	1,898	1,658
Sikkim State . .	908	484	424
Other Provinces . .	52	38	14
SZI LEPAI (Burma) . .	**205**	**122**	**83**
TABLENG (NĀGĀ) (Assam) .	**299**	**163**	**136**
TAMIL	**18,128,365**	**8,895,607**	**9,232,758**
Andamans and Nicobars	886	746	140
Assam . . .	738	455	283
Bengal . . .	2,953	1,619	1,334
Bihar and Orissa .	346	213	133
Bombay . . .	15,366	8,864	6,502
Burma . . .	125,670	87,917	37,753
C. P. and Berar . .	5,063	2,673	2,390
Coorg . . .	4,291	2,326	1,965
Madras . . .	16,692,417	8,152,474	8,539,943
Punjab . . .	288	211	77
United Provinces .	573	329	244
Bombay States . .	318	195	123
Central India Agency .	933	516	417
Hyderabad State .	32,425	17,116	15,309
Madras States . .	1,000,537	492,610	507,927
Cochin . . .	*55,231*	*27,858*	*27,373*
Travancore . .	*554,618*	*278,585*	*276,033*
Mysore State . .	244,947	126,995	117,952
Other Provinces . .	614	348	266
TAMLU (NĀGĀ) (Assam) .	**1,998**	**940**	**1,058**
TANGKHUL (NĀGĀ) . .	**27,285**	**12,868**	**14,417**
Assam . . .	13	13	...
Assam State . .	27,272	12,855	14,417
TAUNGTHA (Burma) . .	**17,244**	**8,817**	**8,427**
TAUNGYO (Burma) . . .	**19,317**	**9,569**	**9,748**
TAVOYAN (Burma) . . .	**46**	**44**	**2**
TELUGU OR ANDHRA . .	**23,542,861**	**11,820,129**	**11,722,732**
Andamans and Nicobars	447	384	63
Assam . .	20,742	11,072	9,670
Bengal . . .	10,232	5,521	4,711
Bihar and Orissa .	13,450	6,894	6,556
Bombay . .	121,029	62,751	58,278
Burma . . .	123,162	102,875	20,287
C. P. and Berar . .	125,033	62,571	62,462
Coorg . . .	2,688	1,471	1,217
Madras . . .	15,735,835	7,802,004	7,933,831
United Provinces .	651	315	336
Baroda State . .	265	139	126
Bengal States . .	451	235	216
Bihar and Orissa States	7,330	3,723	3,607
Bombay States . .	13,556	6,865	6,691
Central India Agency .	1,270	928	342
Central Provinces States	15,380	7,756	7,624
Hyderabad State .	6,367,578	3,249,365	3,118,213
Madras States . .	64,101	32,075	32,026
Cochin . . .	*11,224*	*5,511*	*5,713*
Travancore . .	*6,452*	*3,460*	*2,992*
Mysore State . .	919,410	463,035	456,375
Other Provinces . .	251	150	101

Language and Province.	Population. Persons.	Males.	Females.
1	2	3	4
A.—Vernaculars of India —*contd.*			
THĀDO OR JANGSHEN .	**26,571**	**13,030**	**13,541**
Assam . . .	116	51	65
Assam State . .	26,455	12,979	13,476
THĀMĪ	**334**	**212**	**122**
Assam . . .	42	25	17
Bengal . . .	292	187	105
THAT (Burma) . . .	**80**	**38**	**42**
TIPURĀ OR MRUNG . .	**135,945**	**70,286**	**65,659**
Assam . . .	9,676	4,917	4,759
Bengal . . .	32,289	16,652	15,637
Bengal States . .	93,980	48,717	45,263
TODA (Madras) . . .	**730**	**407**	**323**
TOTO	**259**	**149**	**110**
Assam . .	3	3	...
Bengal . . .	256	146	110
TULU	**563,453**	**278,772**	**284,681**
Bombay . . .	364	270	94
Coorg . . .	14,226	9,548	4,678
Madras . . .	514,354	246,201	268,153
Bombay States . .	205	137	68
Madras States . .	2,309	1,594	715
Cochin . .	*546*	*405*	*141*
Travancore . .	*1,762*	*1,189*	*573*
Mysore State . .	31,995	21,022	10,973
TŪRĪ	**10,047**	**5,009**	**5,038**
Assam . .	2,396	1,251	1,145
Bengal . . .	3,719	1,854	1,865
Bihar and Orissa .	2,343	1,132	1,211
Bihar and Orissa States	358	151	207
Central Provinces States	1,032	536	496
Other Provinces . .	199	83	114
VAIPHEI (Assam State) .	**2,303**	**1,035**	**1,268**
WA	**16,511**	**8,450**	**8,061**
Assam . . .	6	5	1
Burma . . .	16,505	8,445	8,060
WESTERN HINDI . . .	**14,037,882**	**7,460,757**	**6,577,125**
Ajmer-Merwara . .	31,574	17,190	14,384
Andamans and Nicobars	2,696	1,768	928
Baluchistan . .	10,873	8,379	2,494
Bengal . . .	154,402	90,539	63,863
Bihar and Orissa .	385,481	180,784	204,697
Bombay . . .	901,999	488,066	413,933
Burma . . .	144,589	118,028	26,561
C. P. and Berar .	290,896	148,891	142,005
Coorg . . .	5,527	2,975	2,552
Madras . . .	964,713	492,839	471,874
N.-W. Frontier Province	16,971	10,268	6,703
Punjab . . .	1,966,344	1,093,848	872,496

TABLE X.—LANGUAGE. PART III.—TERRITORIAL

Language and Province.	Population. Persons.	Males.	Females.
1	2	3	4
A.—Vernaculars of India—*concld.*			
WESTERN HINDÎ—*contd.*			
United Provinces	3,566,444	1,879,651	1,686,793
Baroda State	69,956	38,066	31,890
Bihar and Orissa States	2,140	1,117	1,023
Bombay States	130,552	67,679	62,873
Central India Agency	2,653,608	1,395,289	1,258,319
Central Provinces States	1,589	778	811
Hyderabad State	1,367,175	691,193	675,982
Kashmir State	1,924	1,399	525
Madras States	17,257	9,074	8,183
Cochin	*2,247*	*1,211*	*1,036*
Travancore	*4,659*	*2,625*	*2,034*
Mysore State	305,182	159,136	146,046
N.-W. Frontier Province (*Agencies and Tribal areas*).	460	390	70
Punjab States	81,247	43,303	37,944
Rajputana Agency	434,852	238,203	196,649
United Provinces States	529,285	281,790	247,495
Other Provinces	146	114	32
WESTERN PAHÂRÎ	**1,526,475**	**792,759**	**733,716**
Punjab	228,553	118,331	110,222
Central India Agency	304	169	135
Kashmir State	549,245	284,780	264,465
Punjab States	748,284	389,405	358,879
Other Provinces	89	74	15
WESTERN PANJÂBÎ*	**4,779,138**	**2,560,933**	**2,218,205**
Ajmer-Merwara	287	128	159
Baluchistan	41,359	22,388	18,971
Bombay	162,394	87,647	74,747
N.-W. Frontier Province	72,918	37,162	35,756
Punjab	3,688,009	1,972,856	1,715,153
Baluchistan States	58,615	31,642	26,973
Bombay States	13,031	7,001	6,030
Kashmir State	176,331	89,800	86,531
Punjab States	565,557	311,984	253,573
Rajputana Agency	459	217	242
Other Provinces	178	108	70
SIRAIKI	***206,452***	***111,384***	***95,068***
Baluchistan	738	402	336
Bombay	162,178	87,475	74,703
Baluchistan States	30,516	16,512	14,004
Bombay States	13,020	6,995	6,025
YACHUMI (NÂGÂ) (Assam)	**132**	**77**	**55**
YAO (Burma)	**274**	**136**	**138**
YINDU (Burma)	**4,348**	**2,138**	**2,210**
ZAHAO (Assam)	**3,523**	**1,701**	**1,822**
LANGUAGE NOT RETURNED (Bombay and Bombay States)	**460**	**231**	**229**

Language and Province.	Population. Persons.	Males.	Females.
1	2	3	4
B.—Vernaculars of other Asiatic Countries and Africa.	**223,110**	**149,039**	**74,071**
ABYSSINIAN (INCLUDING NEGRO) (Bombay and Bombay States).	**118**	**66**	**52**
AFRICAN DIALECTS	**5**	**3**	**2**
Bombay	1	...	1
Rajputana Agency	4	3	1
ARABIC	**42,102**	**28,556**	**13,546**
Bengal	840	516	324
Bombay	32,005	21,444	10,561
Burma	201	130	71
C. P. and Berar	58	48	10
Madras	423	398	25
Punjab	94	77	17
United Provinces	435	407	28
Baluchistan States	54	50	4
Baroda State	32	22	10
Bombay States	961	642	319
Central India Agency	618	466	152
Hyderabad State	5,683	3,881	1,802
Madras States	247	154	93
Cochin	*111*	*70*	*41*
Travancore	*136*	*84*	*52*
Mysore State	293	205	88
Rajputana Agency	43	35	8
Other Provinces	115	81	34
ARMENIAN	**452**	**329**	**123**
Bengal	354	254	100
Other Provinces	98	75	23
CAUCASIAN (Burma)	**20**	**18**	**2**
CHINESE	**113,450**	**82,278**	**31,172**
Andamans and Nicobars	140	140	...
Assam	244	237	7
Bengal	3,417	2,928	489
Bombay	248	240	8
Burma	108,877	78,364	30,513
Madras	125	120	5
Punjab	51	30	21
United Provinces	77	51	26
Punjab States	178	98	80
Other Provinces	93	70	23
HEBREW	**1,457**	**750**	**707**
Bengal	618	321	297
Bombay	261	127	134
Burma	476	259	217
Other Provinces	102	43	59
JAPANESE	**1,130**	**436**	**694**
Bengal	126	33	93
Bombay	363	174	189
Burma	558	199	359
United Provinces	31	6	25
Other Provinces	52	24	28

* This includes Siraiki separate figures for which are given below.

Distribution of each Language—*continued.*

Language and Province.	Population.		
	Persons.	Males.	Females.
1	2	3	4
B.—Vernaculars of other Asiatic Countries and Africa—*contd.*			
KAFFIR (Bombay)	3	2	1
MONGOLIAN (Bombay)	1	..	1
PERSIAN	56,589	31,305	25,284
Assam	46	36	10
Baluchistan	3,700	2,765	935
Bengal	1,161	552	609
Bihar and Orissa	35	34	1
Bombay	32,218	17,271	14,947
Burma	240	163	77
C. P. and Berar	380	236	144
Madras	686	386	300
N.-W. Frontier Province	3,454	1,969	1,485
Punjab	2,341	1,353	988
United Provinces	4,841	2,672	2,169
Baluchistan States	133	68	65
Bombay States	4,322	2,086	2,236
Central India Agency	787	422	365
Central Provinces States	107	56	51
Hyderabad State	256	129	127
Kashmir State	58	50	8
Mysore State	1,384	716	668
N.-W. Frontier Province (*Agencies and Tribal areas*).	357	278	79
Punjab States	30	23	7
Other Provinces	53	40	13
SIDI (Bombay)	31	26	5
SOMALI	6,901	4,696	2,205
Bombay	6,899	4,694	2,205
Hyderabad State	2	2	...
SWAHILI (ZANZIBARI)	18	16	2
Bengal	5	5	...
Other Provinces	13	11	2
SYRIAC	11	11	...
Madras States	7	7	...
Other Provinces	4	4	...
TAGALA (Burma)	53	53	...
TURKISH DIALECTS *	769	494	275
Bombay	614	385	229
Other Provinces	155	109	46
OSMANLI (TURKI)	*27*	*22*	*5*
Punjab	26	22	4
Mysore State	1	...	1

Language and Province.	Population.		
	Persons.	Males.	Females.
1	2	3	4
C.—European languages	321,224	208.843	112,381
BASQUE (Madras States)	5	5	...
BOHEMIAN (CZECH) (United Provinces)	1	...	1
BULGARIAN (Burma)	1	1	...
DANISH	65	34	31
Madras	38	15	23
Other Provinces	27	19	8
DUTCH	160	129	31
Bengal	30	24	6
Burma	41	36	5
Madras	66	52	14
Other Provinces	23	17	6
ENGLISH	303,515	196,927	106,588
Ajmer-Merwara	2,520	1,825	695
Andamans and Nicobars	336	239	97
Assam	2,569	1,789	780
Baluchistan	4,323	3,437	886
Bengal	44,602	26,763	17,839
Bihar and Orissa	9,050	5,282	3,768
Bombay	47,944	31,772	16,172
Burma	24,355	15,756	8,599
C. P. and Berar	11,058	7,482	3,576
Coorg	345	201	144
Madras	39,252	21,048	18,204
N.-W. Frontier Province	5,720	4,876	844
Punjab	34,945	25,728	9,217
United Provinces	41,620	28,461	13,159
Assam State	37	25	12
Baroda State	261	132	129
Bihar and Orissa States	124	66	58
Bombay States	743	457	286
Central India Agency	5,850	4,600	1,250
Central Provinces States	249	135	114
Hyderabad State	8,843	6,174	2,669
Kashmir State	257	141	116
Madras States	2,636	1,455	1,181
Cochin	*412*	*243*	*169*
Travancore	*2,167*	*1,181*	*986*
Mysore State	13,120	7,468	5,652
N.-W. Frontier Province (*Agencies and Tribal areas*).	119	99	20
Punjab States	855	491	364
Rajputana Agency	1,684	957	727
Other Provinces	98	68	30

* This includes Osmanli (Turki) separate figures for which are given below.

TABLE X.—LANGUAGE. PART III.—TERRITORIAL DISTRIBUTION OF EACH LANGUAGE—*concld.*

LANGUAGE AND PROVINCE.	POPULATION.		
	Persons.	Males.	Females.
1	2	3	4
C.—European languages—*contd.*			
FINNISH	4	4	...
Bombay	2	2	...
Burma	2	2	...
FLEMISH	24	16	8
Punjab	13	13	...
Other Provinces	11	3	8
FRENCH	1,499	893	606
Ajmer-Merwara	35	21	14
Bengal	150	79	71
Bihar and Orissa	77	47	30
Bombay	285	147	138
Burma	135	72	63
Madras	406	226	180
United Provinces	151	143	8
Mysore State	130	88	42
Other Provinces	130	70	60
GAELIC (Scotch)	4	4	...
Bengal	3	3	...
Mysore State	1	1	...
GERMAN	2,080	1,493	587
Bengal	322	265	57
Bihar and Orissa	146	88	58
Bombay	579	463	116
Burma	186	169	17
C. P. and Berar	30	23	7
Madras	558	371	187
Punjab	46	25	21
United Provinces	54	23	31
Mysore State	40	6	34
Other Provinces	119	60	59
GREEK (ROMAIC)	352	297	55
Bengal	94	79	15
Bombay	174	144	30
Burma	50	46	4
Other Provinces	34	28	6
HUNGARIAN (Magyar)	13	8	5
Bombay	7	5	2
Other Provinces	6	3	3
IRISH	36	24	12
Bombay	16	10	6
Other Provinces	20	14	6
C.—European languages—*concld.*			
ITALIAN	1,102	962	140
Bengal	107	78	29
Bombay	374	343	31
Burma	122	115	7
Madras	30	16	14
United Provinces	285	280	5
Hyderabad State	36	8	28
Mysore State	102	95	7
Other Provinces	46	27	19
LATIN (Madras States)	9	9	...
MALTESE (Bombay)	7	7	...
NORWEGIAN	94	80	14
Bombay	41	37	4
Other Provinces	53	43	10
POLISH (Bengal)	1	...	1
PORTUGUESE	11,748	7,670	4,078
Ajmer-Merwara	175	118	57
Bengal	392	334	58
Bombay	7,966	5,252	2,714
Burma	212	159	53
C. P. and Berar	183	137	46
Coorg	67	35	32
Madras	1,725	904	821
N.-W. Frontier Province	34	34	...
Punjab	82	73	9
United Provinces	150	109	41
Bombay States	150	125	25
Hyderabad State	70	44	26
Madras States	272	171	101
Cochin	*237*	*140*	*97*
Travancore	*35*	*31*	*4*
Mysore State	125	77	48
Rajputana Agency	59	40	19
Other Provinces	86	58	28
ROMANY (Bombay)	59	50	9
ROUMANIAN (Bengal)	7	3	4
RUSSIAN	148	50	98
Bengal	48	15	33
Bombay	53	10	43
Other Provinces	47	25	22
SLAV (Bombay)	29	29	...
SPANISH	120	70	50
Bombay	77	38	39
Other Provinces	43	32	11
SWEDISH	129	70	59
Bombay	40	32	8
C. P. and Berar	47	16	31
Other Provinces	42	22	20
WELSH	11	7	4
Mysore State	7	7	...
Other Provinces	4	...	4
LANGUAGE NOT RETURNED (Bombay).	1	1	...

TABLE X.—LANGUAGE. PART IV.—LINGUISTIC DISTRIBUTION OF EACH PROVINCE, STATE OR AGENCY.

LANGUAGE.	POPULATION.		
	Persons.	Males.	Females.
1	2	3	4
AJMER-MERWARA.			
TOTAL	**501,395**	**266,198**	**235,197**
A.—Vernaculars of India	**498,630**	**264,213**	**234,417**
Bengali	291	132	159
Bihārī	1,484	847	637
Gipsy Languages	209	98	111
Gujarātī	1,516	871	645
Bhil languages	*302*	*150*	*152*
Hindī	49,251	26,311	22,940
Marāthī	688	372	316
Panjābī	1,598	1,299	299
Pashto	191	176	15
Rājasthānī	411,243	216,589	194,654
Tamil	158	94	64
Western Hindī	31,574	17,190	14,384
Western Panjābī	287	128	159
Other languages	140	106	34
B.—Vernaculars of other Asiatic Countries and Africa.	**33**	**19**	**14**
C.—European languages	**2,732**	**1,966**	**766**
English	2,520	1,825	695
French	35	21	14
Portuguese	175	118	57
Other languages	2	2	...
ANDAMANS AND NICOBARS.			
TOTAL	**26,459**	**19,570**	**6,889**
A.—Vernaculars of India	**25,982**	**19,190**	**6,792**
Andamanese	1,317	628	689
Bengali	1,648	1,534	114
Burmese	1,620	1,602	18
Gujarātī	309	284	25
Hindī	4,785	4,154	631
Kanarese	305	295	10
Marāthī	671	662	9
Nicobarese	8,418	4,445	3,973
Oriya	322	291	31
Panjābī	1,620	1,479	141
Pashto	493	479	14
Sindhī	151	150	1
Tamil	886	746	140
Telugu	447	384	63
Western Hindī	2,696	1,768	928
Other languages	294	289	5
B.—Vernaculars of other Asiatic Countries and Africa.	**140**	**140**	...
Chinese	140	140	...
C.—European languages	**337**	**240**	**97**
English	336	239	97
Other languages	1	1	...
ASSAM.			
TOTAL	**6,713,635**	**3,467,621**	**3,246,014**
A.—Vernaculars of India	**6,710,764**	**3,465,569**	**3,245,195**
Abor-Miri	56,794	28,931	27,863
Aiton	412	233	179
Angami (Nāgā)	38,699	20,048	18,651
Ao (Nāgā)	29,068	13,744	15,324
Assamese	1,532,332	784,889	747,443
Asurī	135	67	68
Baloch	109	96	13
Bengali	3,224,130	1,665,230	1,558,900

LANGUAGE.	POPULATION.		
	Persons.	Males.	Females.
1	2	3	4
ASSAM—*contd.*			
A.—Vernaculars of India—*contd.*			
Bhotiā	1,295	899	396
Bhotiā of Bhutān	*536*	*413*	*123*
Bhotiā of Tibet	*759*	*486*	*273*
Bhumij	5,342	2,668	2,674
Bodo (Mech, Kachārī)	261,112	130,528	130,584
Burmese	146	85	61
Chutiā	3,107	1,431	1,676
Daflā	951	527	424
Dhīmāl	100	58	42
Dimā-sā	16,483	8,230	8,253
Empeo or Kachchā Nāgā	6,885	3,455	3,430
Gāro	153,766	77 607	76,159
Gond	10,306	5,380	4,926
Gujarātī	306	238	68
Gūrung	1,001	723	278
Hallām	367	218	149
Hindī	428,822	242,904	185,918
Hō	122	76	46
Janggalī	189	93	96
Kachin or Singpho	1,880	992	888
Kāmī	111	63	48
Kandh or Kuī	3,966	1,885	2,081
Kezhāmā (Nāgā)	5,035	2,60[illegible]	2,435
Khāmtī	2,063	1,142	921
Khariā	4,718	2,848	1,870
Khāsī	200,795	94,417	106,378
Kirāntī (Khambū)	1,320	1,058	262
Kirāntī (Yākhā)	390	336	54
Kōch	3,658	1,831	1,827
Koireng	392	195	197
Korwā	775	365	410
Kuki (Unspecified)	12,920	6,258	6,662
Kūrkū	1,990	1,206	784
Kurukh or Orāoṅ	19,813	10,706	9,107
Lalung	12,187	5,940	6,247
Lhotā or Tsontsü (Nāgā)	19,627	9,512	10,115
Limbū	1,874	1,298	576
Lushei or Dulien	68,713	31,979	36,734
Mangar	2,745	1,817	928
Manipurī	83,734	42,900	40,834
Marāthī	1,396	865	531
Mhār	3,196	1,416	1,780
Mikir	103,063	52,766	50,297
Mishmi	255	147	108
Mojung (Nāgā)	643	321	322
Mundārī	72,836	37,093	35,743
Murmī	1,615	1,030	585
Nāgā (Unclassed)	12,531	6,707	5,824
Naipālī (Khās)	45,214	28,513	16,701
Newārī	831	509	322
Oriya	61,182	30,537	30,645
Padhī, Pahrī or Pahī	1,051	571	480
Paithe	7,239	3,016	4,223
Panjābī	823	683	140
Pashto	702	664	38
Phākial	361	182	179
Rābhā	27,995	13,925	14,070
Rājasthānī	11,611	8,790	2,821
Raltē	4,015	1,709	2,306
Rāngkhol	229	99	130
Rengmā (Nāgā)	4,389	2,025	2,364
Santālī or Har	54,173	27,968	26,205
Savara	503	294	2[illegible]9
Semā (Nāgā)	32,921	16.365	16.556
Shān	1,029	541	488

TABLE X.—LANGUAGE. PART IV.—LINGUISTIC

Language.	Population. Persons.	Males.	Females.
1	2	3	4
ASSAM—concld.			
A.—Vernaculars of India—contd.			
Tableng (Nāgā)	299	163	136
Tamil	738	455	283
Tamlu (Nāgā)	1,998	940	1,058
Telugu	20,742	11,072	9,670
Thādo or Jangshen	116	51	65
Tipurā or Mrung	9,676	4,917	4,759
Tūrī	2,396	1,251	1,145
Yachumi (Nāgā)	132	77	55
Zahao	3,523	1,701	1,822
Other languages	596	440	156
B.—Vernaculars of other Asiatic Countries and Africa.	**308**	**291**	**17**
Chinese	244	237	7
Persian	46	36	10
Other languages	18	18	...
C.—European Languages	**2,623**	**1,821**	**802**
English	2,569	1,789	780
Other languages	54	32	22
BALUCHISTAN.			
TOTAL	**414,412**	**239,181**	**175,231**
A.—Vernaculars of India	**406,341**	**232,958**	**173,383**
Baloch	71,698	39,547	32,151
Bihārī	144	120	24
Brāhūī	21,170	11,997	9,173
Central Pahārī	298	286	12
Gipsy languages	197	111	86
Gujarātī	501	336	165
Marāthī	786	693	93
Naipālī (Khas)	1,956	1,591	365
Panjābī	25,191	19,320	5,871
Pashto	225,341	123,775	101,566
Rājasthānī	302	286	16
Sindhī	6,346	4,011	2,335
Western Hindī	10,873	8,379	2,494
Western Panjābī	41,359	22,388	18,971
Siraikī	*738*	*402*	*336*
Other languages	179	118	61
B.—Vernaculars of other Asiatic Countries and Africa.	**3,740**	**2,779**	**961**
Persian	3,700	2,765	935
Other languages	40	14	26
C.—European languages	**4,331**	**3,444**	**887**
English	4,323	3,437	886
Other languages	8	7	1
BENGAL.			
TOTAL	**45,483,077**	**23,365,225**	**22,117,852**
A.—Vernaculars of India	**45,430,769**	**23,332,954**	**22,097,815**
Arakanese	64,259	35,982	28,277
Assamese	737	628	109
Asurī	790	443	347
Bengali	41,899,210	21,180,083	20,719,127
Bhotiā	13,973	7,338	6,635
Bhotiā of Bhuiān	*3,989*	*2,009*	*1,980*
Bhotiā of Sikkim	*1,151*	*581*	*570*
Sharpā Bhotiā	*3,691*	*1,972*	*1,719*
Bhotiā (others)	*5,142*	*2,776*	*2,366*
Bhumij	21,246	10,585	10,661
Bihārī	22,775	12,586	10,189
Bodo (Mech, Kachārī)	21,379	11,680	9,699
BENGAL—contd.			
A.—Vernaculars of India—contd.			
Burmese	8,288	722	7,566
Dhīmāl	444	231	213
Gāro	37,918	21,681	16,237
Gujarātī	4,195	3,012	1,183
Bhīl languages	*282*	*145*	*137*
Gūrung	1,030	599	431
Hindī	1,712,602	1,149,329	563,273
Hō	3,530	1,734	1,796
Khāmi or Kumi	1,050	528	522
Khariā	6,437	3,671	2,766
Khyang	498	226	272
Kirāntī (Jīmdār)	39,260	18,518	20,742
Kirāntī (Khambū)	823	509	314
Kirāntī (Yākhā)	1,311	634	677
Kōch	6,598	3,195	3,403
Kōdā	19,958	10,496	9,462
Korwā	187	109	78
Kuki (Unspecified)	3,305	1,696	1,609
Kurukh or Orāoñ	116,992	64,015	52,977
Limbū	13,944	7,255	6,689
Malayālam	155	141	14
Malto or Maler	1,667	825	842
Mangar	13,521	8,162	5,359
Manipurī	232	116	116
Mānjhī	363	209	154
Marāthī	2,403	1,478	925
Goanese	*352*	*318*	*34*
Mrū	11,073	5,601	5,472
Mundārī	50,183	26,718	23,465
Murmī	28,599	14,593	14,006
Naipālī (Khas)	90,388	50,907	39,481
Newārī	5,590	3,035	2,555
Oriyā	293,168	193,476	99,692
Panjābī	5,533	4,657	876
Pashto	2,770	2,613	157
Rābhā	704	380	324
Rājasthānī	18,336	12,665	5,671
Rong or Lepcha	11,328	5,483	5,845
Santālī or Hār	663,720	335,551	328,169
Sindhī	235	173	62
Kachchhī	*146*	*86*	*60*
Sunvār	3,556	1,898	1,658
Tamil	2,953	1,619	1,334
Telugu	10,232	5,521	4,711
Thāmī	292	187	105
Tipurā or Mrung	32,289	16,652	15,637
Toto	256	146	110
Tūrī	3,719	1,854	1,865
Western Hindī	154,402	90,539	63,863
Other languages	363	270	93
B.—Vernaculars of other Asiatic Countries and Africa.	**6,527**	**4,613**	**2,914**
Arabic	840	516	324
Armenian	354	254	100
Chinese	3,417	2,928	489
Hebrew	618	321	297
Japanese	126	33	93
Persian	1,161	552	609
Other languages	11	9	2

Distribution of each Province, State or Agency—*continued.*

Language.	Population. Persons.	Males.	Females.
1	2	3	4
BENGAL.—*concld.*			
C.—European languages	**45,781**	**27,658**	**18,123**
Dutch	30	24	6
English	44,602	26,763	17,839
French	150	79	71
German	322	265	57
Greek	94	79	15
Italian	107	78	29
Portuguese	392	334	58
Russian	48	15	33
Other languages	36	21	15
BIHAR AND ORISSA.			
TOTAL	**34,490,084**	**16,859,929**	**17,630,155**
A.—Vernaculars of India	**34,480,681**	**16,854,410**	**17,626,271**
Agaria	1,435	742	693
Asurī	3,216	1,623	1,593
Bengali	2,186,020	1,105,850	1,080,170
Bhumij	42,142	20,310	21,832
Bihārī	278,836	134,374	144,462
Birhár	941	481	460
Eastern Hindī	899	437	462
Gipsy languages	186	98	88
Goṇḍ	247	122	125
Gujarātī	2,567	1,782	785
Hindī	24,146,192	11,799,895	12,346,297
Hô	258,224	123,413	134,811
Kandh or Kuī	51,060	24,909	26,151
Kharia	64,041	31,754	32,287
Kōda	4,077	2,080	1,997
Korwa	8,717	4,609	4,108
Kurukh or Orāoñ	460,149	218,525	241,624
Malhar	111	52	59
Malto or Maler	63,207	31,534	31,673
Marāthī	1,049	560	489
Mundārī	404,044	198,111	205,933
Naipālī (Khas)	2,623	1,372	1,251
Oriya	4,905,470	2,365,092	2,540,378
Panjabī	972	739	233
Pashto	732	704	28
Rājasthānī	18,891	10,591	8,300
Banjārī	*1,781*	*833*	*948*
Santālī or Hār	1,172,460	585,242	587,218
Sindhī	282	194	88
Kachchhī	*258*	*175*	*83*
Tamil	346	213	133
Telugu	13,450	6,894	6,556
Tūrī	2,343	1,132	1,211
Western Hindī	385,481	180,784	204,697
Other languages	271	192	79
B.—Vernaculars of other Asiatic Countries and Africa.	**107**	**90**	**17**
Persian	35	34	1
Other languages	72	56	16
C.—European languages	**9,296**	**5,429**	**3,867**
English	9,050	5,282	3,768
French	77	47	30
German	146	88	58
Other languages	23	12	11
BOMBAY.			
TOTAL	**19,672,642**	**10,245,847**	**9,426,795**
A.—Vernaculars of India	**19,542,178**	**10,163,032**	**9,379,146**
Baloch	195,022	107,785	87,237
Bengali	1,752	1,437	315

Language.	Population. Persons.	Males.	Females.
1	2	3	4
BOMBAY—*contd.*			
A.—Vernaculars of India—*contd.*			
Bihari	191	164	27
Brāhūī	28,900	16,328	12,572
Eastern Hindī	534	232	302
Gipsy languages	8,362	4,269	4,093
Gujarātī	3,347,490	1,759,369	1,588,121
Bhīl languages	*300,052*	*149,142*	*150,910*
Khāndēshī	*185*	*111*	*74*
Hindī	106,216	72,086	34,130
Kanarese	2,462,195	1,244,868	1,217,327
Malayālam	1,450	1,054	396
Marāthī	9,016,228	4,551,726	4,464,502
Goanese	*22,396*	*16,286*	*6,110*
Kōnkanī	*158,558*	*82,417*	*76,141*
Panjābī	34,790	24,482	10,308
Pashto	12,159	9,852	2,307
Rājasthānī	228,058	134,901	93,157
Banjārī	*33,100*	*18,743*	*14,357*
Sindhī	2,897,267	1,586,656	1,310,611
Kachchhī	*82,073*	*49,173*	*32,900*
Tamil	15,366	8,864	6,502
Telugu	121,029	62,751	58,278
Tulu	364	270	94
Western Hindī	901,999	488,066	413,933
Western Panjābī	162,394	87,647	74,747
Siraikī	*162,178*	*87,475*	*74,703*
Other languages	209	126	83
Language not returned	203	99	104
B.—Vernaculars of other Asiatic Countries and Africa.	**72,788**	**44,455**	**28,333**
Abyssinian	112	66	46
Arabic	32,005	21,444	10,561
Chinese	248	240	8
Hebrew	261	127	134
Japanese	363	174	189
Persian	32,218	17,271	14,947
Sidi	31	26	5
Somali	6,899	4,694	2,205
Turkish Dialects	614	385	229
Other languages	37	28	9
C.—European languages	**57,676**	**38,360**	**19,316**
English	47,944	31,772	16,172
French	285	147	138
German	579	463	116
Greek	174	144	30
Italian	374	343	31
Norwegian	41	37	4
Portuguese	7,966	5,252	2,714
Romany	59	50	9
Russian	53	10	43
Spanish	77	38	39
Swedish	40	32	8
Other languages	83	71	12
Language not returned	1	1	...
BURMA.			
TOTAL	**12,115,217**	**6,183,494**	**5,931,723**
A.—Vernaculars of India	**11,979,583**	**6,087,874**	**5,891,709**
Akha (Kaw)	32,925	16,666	16,259
Akö	794	409	385
Anu	474	235	239
Arakanese	323,962	161,994	161,968
Assamese	151	81	70
Baungshe	1,924	945	979

TABLE X.—Language. Part IV.—Linguistic

Language.	Population.		
	Persons.	Males.	Females.
1	2	3	4
BURMA—*contd.*			
A.—Vernaculars of India—*contd.*			
Bengali	248,310	164,405	83,905
Burmese	7,883,299	3,855,510	4,027,789
Chaungtha	2,515	1,206	1,309
Chaw	249	128	121
Chin (Unspecified)	233,661	114,552	119,109
Chinbôk	18,179	8,916	9,263
Chinbôn	1,600	818	782
Daingnet	919	445	474
Danu	18,694	10,076	8,618
Gujarātī	7,896	6,049	1,847
Hindī	40,293	32,805	7,488
Hpón	342	157	185
Intha	55,880	27,707	28,173
Kachin or Singpho	169,414	83,450	85,964
Kadu	11,069	5,537	5,532
Karen	1,067,363	534,769	532,594
Brè	*6,918*	*3,149*	*3,769*
Karenbyu	*777*	*420*	*357*
Karennet	*728*	*494*	*234*
Karenni	*21,203*	*11,257*	*9,946*
Manó	*2,182*	*955*	*1,227*
Padaung	*8,516*	*4,106*	*4,410*
Sgau Karen, Pwo-Karen and Karen (Unspecified).	*850,756*	*425,748*	*425,008*
Sinsin	*899*	*522*	*377*
Taungthu	*168,326*	*84,512*	*83,814*
Yinbaw	*2,166*	*1,032*	*1,134*
Zayein	*4,892*	*2,574*	*2,318*
Khāmi or Kumi	16,431	8,230	8,201
Khün	48,408	23,925	24,483
Kwi (Lahu Hsi)	3,924	2,007	1,917
Lahu (Muhso)	18,500	9,375	9,125
Lisu (Lisaw)	9,066	4,407	4,659
Lolo (Myen)	339	166	173
Lü	13,262	6,892	6,370
Maingtha	316	279	37
Malay	4,190	2,237	1,953
Malayālam	736	719	17
Manipurī	1,629	694	935
Marāthī	2,212	1,806	406
Goanese	*351*	*342*	*9*
Singhalese	*150*	*102*	*48*
Maru	209	108	101
Miao (Hmeng)	646	331	315
Môn, Talaing or Peguan	179,443	91,301	88,142
Mrū	2,718	1,343	1,375
Naipālī (Khas)	3,970	2,323	1,647
Oriyā	19,112	18,276	836
Palaung	149,252	75,000	74,252
Panjābī	22,938	19,493	3,445
Pashto	1,587	1,490	97
Rājasthānī	504	382	122
Selung	1,871	955	916
Shān	897,803	445,934	451,869
Siamese	8,902	5,058	3,844
Siyin	151	76	75
Szi Lepai	205	122	83
Tamil	125,670	87,917	37,753
Taungtha	17,244	8,817	8,427
Taungyo	19,317	9,569	9,748
Telugu	123,162	102,875	20,287
Wa	16,505	8,445	8,060
Western Hindī	144,589	118,028	26,561
Yao	274	136	138
Yindu	4,348	2,138	2,210
Other languages	237	160	77
BURMA—*concld.*			
B.—Vernaculars of other Asiatic Countries and Africa.	**110,459**	**79,217**	**31,242**
Arabic	201	130	71
Chinese	108,877	78,364	30,513
Hebrew	476	259	217
Japanese	558	199	359
Persian	240	163	77
Tagala	53	53	...
Other languages	54	49	5
C.—European languages	**25,175**	**16,403**	**8,772**
English	24,355	15,756	8,599
Dutch	41	36	5
French	135	72	63
German	186	169	17
Greek	50	46	4
Italian	122	115	7
Portuguese	212	159	53
Other languages	74	50	24
CENTRAL PROVINCES AND BERAR.			
TOTAL	**13,916,308**	**6,930,392**	**6,985,916**
A.—Vernaculars of India	**13,904,489**	**6,922,403**	**6,982,086**
Baloch	148	104	44
Bengali	2,386	1,396	990
Eastern Hindī	1,032,832	501,732	531,100
Gipsy languages	2,274	1,156	1,118
Goṇḍ	917,113	449,449	467,664
Gujarātī	70,241	38,217	32,024
Bhil languages	*24,557*	*12,116*	*12,441*
Hindī	6,044,184	3,005,689	3,038,495
Kanarese	4,397	2,020	2,377
Khariā	985	447	538
Kolāmī	24,074	12,151	11,923
Korwā	343	168	175
Kurkū	132,078	65,546	66,532
Kurukh or Orāoñ	2,940	1,432	1,508
Marāthī	4,865,980	2,427,510	2,438,470
Goanese	*256*	*170*	*86*
Mundārī	158	77	81
Naipālī (Khas)	100	63	37
Oriyā	200,181	99,666	100,515
Panjābī	4,486	3,713	773
Pashto	2,372	2,108	264
Rājasthānī	174,389	94,374	80,015
Banjārī	*103,158*	*53,160*	*49,998*
Sindhī	1,583	1,137	446
Kachchhī	*1,539*	*1,100*	*439*
Tamil	5,063	2,673	2,390
Telugu	125,033	62,571	62,462
Tūrī	170	69	101
Western Hindī	290,896	148,891	142,005
Other languages	83	44	39
B.—Vernaculars of other Asiatic Countries and Africa.	**450**	**294**	**156**
Arabic	58	48	10
Persian	380	236	144
Other languages	12	10	2
C.—European languages	**11,369**	**7,695**	**3,674**
English	11,058	7,482	3,576
German	30	23	7
Portuguese	183	137	46
Swedish	47	16	31
Other languages	51	37	14

Distribution of each Province, State or Agency—*continued.*

COORG.

Language.	Population. Persons.	Males.	Females.
1	2	3	4
TOTAL	**174,976**	**97,279**	**77,697**
A.—Vernaculars of India	**174,548**	**97,031**	**77,517**
Gujarātī	130	70	60
Kanarese	71,557	37,618	33,939
Kodagu or Coorgi	42,784	21,718	21,066
Malayālam	28,825	18,616	10,209
Marāthī	4,437	2,633	1,804
Kōnkanī	*2,696*	*1,619*	*1,077*
Tamil	4,291	2,326	1,965
Telugu	2,688	1,471	1,217
Tulu	14,226	9,548	4,678
Western Hindī	5,527	2,975	2,552
Other languages	83	56	27
B.—Vernaculars of other Asiatic Countries and Africa.	**6**	**6**	...
C.—European languages	**422**	**242**	**180**
English	345	201	144
Portuguese	67	35	32
Other languages	10	6	4

MADRAS.

Language.	Population. Persons.	Males.	Females.
TOTAL	**41,405,404**	**20,382,955**	**21,022,449**
A.—Vernaculars of India	**41,362,019**	**20,359,371**	**21,002,648**
Bengali	1,166	1,016	150
Eastern Hindī	2,668	1,368	1,300
Gadaba	43,009	21,152	21,857
Gonḍ	57,392	30,235	27,157
Gujarātī	98,774	50,453	48,321
Hindī	749	329	420
Kanarese	1,589,487	783,599	805,888
Kandh or Kui	389,799	194,802	194,997
Kota	1,271	622	649
Malayālam	3,098,979	1,525,343	1,573,636
Marāthī	298,998	150,346	148,652
Kōnkanī	*169,837*	*84,837*	*85,000*
Mahl	*3,675*	*1,837*	*1,838*
Singhalese	*120*	*108*	*12*
Oriyā	1,663,272	799,507	863,765
Rājasthānī	41,530	22,678	18,852
Banjārī	*39,744*	*21,267*	*18,477*
Sanskrit	312	246	66
Savara	165,777	83,184	82,593
Sindhī	495	339	156
Kachchhī	*420*	*270*	*150*
Tamil	16,692,417	8,152,474	8,539,943
Telugu	15,735,835	7,802,004	7,933,831
Toda	730	407	323
Tulu	514,354	246,201	268,153
Western Hindī	964,713	492,839	471,874
Other languages	292	227	65
B.—Vernaculars of other Asiatic Countries and Africa.	**1,269**	**927**	**342**
Arabic	423	398	25
Chinese	125	120	5
Persian	686	386	300
Other languages	35	23	12
C.—European languages.	**42,116**	**22,657**	**19,459**
English	39,252	21,048	18,204
French	406	226	180
German	558	371	187
Portuguese	1,725	904	821
Danish	38	15	23
Dutch	66	52	14
Italian	30	16	14
Other languages	41	25	16

NORTH-WEST FRONTIER PROVINCE.

Language.	Population. Persons.	Males.	Females.
1	2	3	4
TOTAL	**2,196,933**	**1,182,102**	**1,014,831**
A.—Vernaculars of India	**2,187,680**	**1,175,195**	**1,012,485**
Bihārī	359	333	26
Kashmīrī	533	445	88
Kōhistānī	117	87	30
Marāthī	219	204	15
Naipālī (Khas)	5,179	4,359	820
Panjābī	843,493	458,431	385,062
Pashto	1,221,839	648,400	573,439
Rājasthānī	25,668	15,174	10,494
Gujarī	*25,619*	*15,135*	*10,484*
Western Hindī	16,971	10,268	6,703
Western Panjābī	72,918	37,162	35,756
Other languages	384	332	52
B.—Vernaculars of other Asiatic Countries and Africa.	**3,486**	**1,988**	**1,498**
Persian	3,454	1,969	1,485
Other languages	32	19	13
C.—European languages	**5,767**	**4,919**	**848**
English	5,720	4,876	844
Portuguese	34	34	...
Other languages	13	9	4

PUNJAB.

Language.	Population. Persons.	Males.	Females.
TOTAL	**19,974,956**	**10,992,067**	**8,982,889**
A.—Vernaculars of India	**19,937,290**	**10,964,719**	**8,972,571**
Balooh	69,231	39,147	30,084
Bengali	2,116	1,355	761
Bhotiā	5,901	3,142	2,759
Bhotiā of Tibet	*821*	*655*	*166*
Bhotiā (others)	*5,045*	*2,457*	*2,588*
Bunān	1,261	517	744
Central Pahārī	872	810	62
Gipsy languages	5,640	2,871	2,769
Gujarātī	2,565	1,608	957
Bhīl languages	*773*	*452*	*321*
Hindī	1,462,892	791,020	671,872
Kanāshī	376	183	193
Kanaurī or Multhānī	179	120	59
Kashmīrī	6,480	4,880	1,600
Lāhulī	302	231	71
Manchātī or Patnī	4,797	2,325	2,472
Marāthī	756	507	249
Naipālī (Khas)	7,356	5,379	1,977
Panjābī	11,900,238	6,600,539	5,299,699
Standard	*11,162,265*	*6,208,843*	*4,953,422*
Dogrī	*737,973*	*391,696*	*346,277*
Pashto	66,084	43,161	22,923
Rājasthānī	514,160	279,787	234,373
Banjārī	*1,558*	*771*	*787*
Gujarī	*15,126*	*7,995*	*7,131*
Rangloi, Gondla or Tinān	725	362	363
Sindhī	1,997	1,431	566
Tamil	288	211	77
Telugu	147	86	61
Western Hindī	1,966,344	1,093,848	872,496
Western Pahārī	228,553	118,331	110,222
Simla Group	*22,806*	*12,880*	*9,926*
Kulu Group	*106,064*	*52,508*	*53,556*
Mandi Group	*4,543*	*2,644*	*1,899*
Chamba Group	*20,241*	*10,856*	*9,385*
Murree Kahuta Group.	*73,981*	*38,698*	*35,283*
Unspecified	*918*	*745*	*173*
Western Panjābī	3,688,009	1,972,856	1,715,153
Other languages	21	12	9
B.—Vernaculars of other Asiatic Countries and Africa.	**2,526**	**1,485**	**1,041**
Arabic	94	77	17
Chinese	51	30	21
Persian	2,341	1,353	988
Other languages	40	25	15

TABLE X.—Language. Part IV.—Linguistic

Language.	Population. Persons.	Males.	Females.
1	2	3	4
PUNJAB—contd.			
C.—European languages	**35,140**	**25,863**	**9,277**
English	34,945	25,728	9,217
German	46	25	21
Portuguese	82	73	9
Other languages	67	37	30
UNITED PROVINCES OF AGRA AND OUDH.			
TOTAL	**47,182,044**	**24,641,831**	**22,540,213**
A.—Vernaculars of India	**47,134,330**	**24,609,641**	**22,524,689**
Bengali	22,500	10,597	11,903
Bhotiā	5,225	2,598	2,627
Bhotiā of Bhutān	*4,150*	*1,809*	*2,341*
Bhotiā of Ladakh	*513*	*456*	*57*
Bhotiā of Tibet	*558*	*330*	*228*
Bihārī	540	363	177
Central Pahārī	1,298	832	466
Gipsy languages	1,673	755	918
Gujarātī	4,043	2,352	1,691
Hindī	43,465,654	22,666,649	20,799,005
Kanarese	168	91	77
Manipurī	118	65	53
Marāthī	6,029	3,478	2,551
Naipālī (Khas)	18,266	13,512	4,754
Oriyā	100	81	19
Panjābī	26,946	19,461	7,485
Pashto	1,990	1,791	199
Rājasthānī	11,533	6,350	5,183
Banjārī	*7,131*	*4,031*	*3,100*
Sindhī	362	218	144
Tamil	573	329	244
Telugu	651	315	336
Western Hindī	3,566,444	1,879,651	1,686,793
Other languages	217	153	64
B.—Vernaculars of other Asiatic Countries and Africa.	**5,422**	**3,151**	**2,271**
Arabic	435	407	28
Chinese	77	51	26
Japanese	31	6	25
Persian	4,841	2,672	2,169
Other languages	38	15	23
C.—European languages	**42,292**	**29,039**	**13,253**
English	41,620	28,461	13,159
French	151	143	8
German	54	23	31
Italian	285	280	5
Portuguese	150	109	41
Other languages	32	23	9
ASSAM STATE.			
TOTAL	**346,222**	**170,666**	**175,556**
A.—Vernaculars of India	**346,185**	**170,641**	**175,544**
Aimol	416	224	192
Anal	2,659	1,370	1,289
Bengali	474	370	104
Bodo (Mech, Kachārī)	143	77	66
Chiru	1,298	593	705
Chote	180	130	50
Empeo or Kachchā Nāgā	1,284	705	579
Hindī	1,956	1,548	408
Hiroi-Lamgang	136	66	70
Kabui (Nāgā)	17,212	8,166	9,046
Karea	100	51	49
Khoirāo (Nāgā)	1,026	495	531

Language.	Population. Persons.	Males.	Females.
1	2	3	4
ASSAM STATE—contd.			
A.—Vernaculars of India—contd.			
Koireng	634	298	336
Kom	2,087	960	1,127
Kuki (Unspecified)	6,687	3,482	3,205
Kwoireng (Nāgā)	369	176	193
Lushei or Dulien	113	63	50
Manipurī	211,691	103,695	107,996
Marām (Nāgā)	3,259	1,593	1,666
Maring (Nāgā)	2,674	1,294	1,380
Mhār	2,234	1,060	1,174
Nāgā (Unclassed)	4,238	2,052	2,186
Naipālī (Khas)	1,896	1,168	728
Paithe	8,328	4,320	4,008
Purum	1,036	510	526
Raltē	3,478	1,696	1,782
Soktē	4,221	2,163	2,058
Sopvomā (Nāgā)	10,100	5,287	4,813
Tangkhul (Nāgā)	27,272	12,855	14,417
Thādo or Jangshen	26,455	12,979	13,476
Vaiphei	2,303	1,035	1,268
Other languages	226	160	66
C.—European languages	**37**	**25**	**12**
English	37	25	12
BALUCHISTAN STATES.			
TOTAL	**420,291**	**227,238**	**193,053**
A.—Vernaculars of India	**420,069**	**227,089**	**192,980**
Baloch	161,289	85,645	75,644
Brāhūī	124,129	68,831	55,298
Dehwari	7,511	4,073	3,438
Panjābī	2,351	1,345	1,006
Pashto	2,212	1,211	1,001
Sindhī	63,628	34,088	29,540
Western Hindī	110	81	29
Western Panjābī	58,615	31,642	26,973
Siraikī	*30,516*	*16,512*	*14,004*
Other languages	224	173	51
B.—Vernaculars of other Asiatic Countries and Africa.	**195**	**126**	**69**
Arabic	54	50	4
Persian	133	68	65
Other languages	8	8	...
C.—European languages	**27**	**23**	**4**
BARODA STATE.			
TOTAL	**2,032,798**	**1,055,935**	**976,863**
A.—Vernaculars of India	**2,032,464**	**1,055,757**	**976,707**
Baloch	179	100	79
Gipsy languages	536	263	273
Gujarātī	1,901,868	984,832	917,036
Bhil languages	*145,561*	*73,754*	*71,807*
Hindī	3,203	2,360	843
Marāthī	36,145	19,483	16,662
Goanese	*144*	*112*	*32*
Panjābī	234	163	71
Pashto	145	119	26
Rājasthānī	3,660	2,246	1,414
Banjārī	*250*	*121*	*129*
Sindhī	16,089	7,874	8,215
Kachchhī	*15,268*	*7,309*	*7,959*
Telugu	265	139	126
Western Hindī	69,956	38,066	31,890
Other languages	184	112	72

Distribution of each Province, State or Agency—*continued.*

Language.	Population. Persons.	Males.	Females.
1	2	3	4
BARODA STATE—*contd.*			
B.—Vernaculars of other Asiatic Countries and Africa.	**45**	**29**	**16**
Arabic	32	22	10
Other languages	13	7	6
C.—European languages	**289**	**149**	**140**
English	261	132	129
Other languages	28	17	11
BENGAL STATES.			
TOTAL	**822,565**	**438,368**	**384,197**
A.—Vernaculars of India	**822,510**	**438,330**	**384,180**
Arakanese	1,610	843	767
Assamese	458	412	46
Bengali	666,618	349,195	317,423
Bodo (Mech, Kachārī)	347	204	143
Dimā-sā	103	55	48
Gāro	855	620	235
Gujarātī	149	91	58
Hallam	2,941	1,573	1,368
Hindī	27,575	21,315	6,260
Kuki (Unspecified)	6,222	3,169	3,053
Kurukh or Orāoñ	264	131	133
Lushei or Dulien	561	274	287
Manipurī	16,381	8,717	7,664
Mrū	211	114	97
Mundārī	115	68	47
Naipālī (Khas)	456	357	99
Oriyā	876	650	226
Rājasthānī	809	752	57
Rāngkhol	556	263	293
Santālī or Hār	739	373	366
Telugu	451	235	216
Tipurā or Mrung	93,980	48,717	45,263
Other languages	233	202	31
B.—Vernaculars of other Asiatic Countries and Africa.	**18**	**16**	**2**
C.—European languages	**37**	**22**	**15**
BIHAR AND ORISSA STATES.			
TOTAL	**3,945,209**	**1,955,125**	**1,990,084**
A.—Vernaculars of India	**3,945,074**	**1,955,052**	**1,990,022**
Bengali	108,924	54,735	54,189
Bhumij	63,724	31,608	32,116
Bihārī	11,811	5,956	5,855
Eastern Hindī	2,596	1,345	1,251
Gadaba	162	88	74
Goṇḍ	3,965	1,964	2,001
Gujarātī	471	353	118
Hindī	104,378	53,923	50,455
Hō	158,232	77,793	80,439
Juāng	12,300	6,108	6,192
Kandh or Kui	85,651	42,372	43,279
Khariā	43,149	21,469	21,680
Korwā	1,614	763	851
Kurukh or Orāoñ	99,346	49,728	49,618
Malhar	110	51	59
Marāthī	284	164	120
Mundārī	71,372	35,888	35,484
Oriyā	2,914,788	1,442,173	1,472,615
Rājasthānī	5,189	2,694	2,495
Banjārī	*3,966*	*1,962*	*2,004*
BIHAR AND ORISSA STATES—*contd.*			
A.—Vernaculars of India—*contd.*			
Santālī or Hār	246,897	120,698	126,199
Telugu	7,330	3,723	3,607
Tūrī	358	151	207
Western Hindī	2,140	1,117	1,023
Other languages	283	188	95
B.—Vernaculars of other Asiatic Countries and Africa.	**2**	**2**	...
C.—European languages	**133**	**71**	**62**
English	124	66	58
Other languages	9	5	4
BOMBAY STATES.			
TOTAL	**7,411,675**	**3,765,401**	**3,646,274**
A.—Vernaculars of India	**7,405,472**	**3,762,073**	**3,643,399**
Baloch	4,236	2,177	2,059
Gipsy languages	2,326	1,248	1,078
Gujarātī	4,279,544	2,183,953	2,095,591
Bhil languages	*117,558*	*59,591*	*57,967*
Hindī	60,353	31,011	29,342
Kanarese	549,641	278,799	270,842
Malayālam	104	98	6
Marāthī	1,725,812	865,445	860,367
Goanese	*277*	*192*	*85*
Kōnkanī	*123,151*	*61,889*	*61,262*
Panjābī	1,091	905	186
Pashto	998	871	127
Rājasthānī	23,949	13,413	10,536
Banjārī	*1,816*	*897*	*919*
Sindhī	599,287	302,051	297,236
Kachchhī	*288,486*	*143,372*	*145,114*
Tamil	318	195	123
Telugu	13,556	6,865	6,691
Tulu	205	137	68
Western Hindī	130,552	67,679	62,873
Western Panjābī	13,031	7,001	6,030
Siraikī	*13,020*	*6,995*	*6,025*
Other languages	212	93	119
Language not returned	257	132	125
B.—Vernaculars of other Asiatic Countries and Africa.	**5,300**	**2,737**	**2,563**
Arabic	961	642	319
Persian	4,322	2,086	2,236
Other languages	17	9	8
C.—European languages	**903**	**591**	**312**
English	743	457	286
Portuguese	150	125	25
Other languages	10	9	1
CENTRAL INDIA AGENCY.			
TOTAL	**9,356,980**	**4,801,459**	**4,555,521**
A.—Vernaculars of India	**9,349,693**	**4,795,954**	**4,553,739**
Bengali	894	289	605
Bihārī	78,398	40,681	37,717
Eastern Hindī	1,376,523	700,224	676,299
Gipsy languages	1,097	569	528
Goṇḍ	214,276	83,524	130,752
Gujarātī	421,853	211,480	210,373
Bhil language	*349,932*	*174,852*	*175,080*
Khāndēshī	*8,272*	*4,197*	*4,075*
Hindī	1,060,582	556,619	503,963
Kanarese	281	126	155

LANGUAGE.	POPULATION.		
	Persons.	Males.	Females.
1	2	3	4
CENTRAL INDIA AGENCY—*contd.*			
A.—Vernaculars of India—*contd.*			
Marāthī . . .	65,913	32,076	33,837
Goanese . . .	*164*	*147*	*17*
Panjābī . . .	19,092	10,754	8,338
Pashto . . .	1,659	1,200	459
Rajasthānī . . .	3,452,158	1,761,092	1,691,066
Banjārī . . .	*17,126*	*9,555*	*7,571*
Gujarī . . .	*2,836*	*1,139*	*1,697*
Sindhī . . .	462	227	235
Tamil . . .	933	516	417
Telugu . . .	1,270	928	342
Western Hindī . .	2,653,608	1,395,289	1,258,319
Western Pahārī . .	304	169	135
Other languages . .	390	191	199
B.—Vernaculars of other Asiatic Countries and Africa.	**1,405**	**888**	**517**
Arabic . . .	618	466	152
Persian . . .	787	422	365
C.—European languages .	**5.882**	**4,617**	**1,265**
English . . .	5,850	4,600	1,250
Other languages . .	32	17	15
CENTRAL PROVINCES STATES.			
TOTAL .	**2,117,002**	**1,053,630**	**1,063,372**
A.—Vernaculars of India .	**2,116,627**	**1,053,423**	**1,063,204**
Asurī . . .	105	58	47
Bengali . . .	154	100	54
Bihārī . . .	118	39	79
Eastern Hindī . .	651	343	308
Gadaba . . .	306	141	165
Goṇḍ . . .	249,902	125,470	124,432
Gujarātī . . .	441	328	113
Hindī . . .	1,461,980	723,493	738,487
Khariā . . .	7,253	3,613	3,640
Korwā . . .	14,889	7,690	7,199
Kūrkū . . .	2,751	1,419	1,332
Kurukh or Orāoñ .	100,824	50,993	49,831
Marāthī . . .	146,119	73,444	72,675
Mundārī . . .	871	655	216
Oriyā . . .	102,454	51,315	51,139
Pashto . . .	112	86	26
Rājasthānī . . .	9,380	4,998	4,382
Banjārī . .	*6,670*	*3,456*	*3,214*
Tamil . . .	146	74	72
Telugu . . .	15,380	7,756	7,624
Tūrī . . .	1,032	536	496
Western Hindī . .	1,589	778	811
Other languages . .	170	94	76
B.—Vernaculars of other Asiatic Countries and Africa.	**119**	**67**	**52**
Persian . . .	107	56	51
Other languages . .	12	11	1
C.—European languages .	**256**	**140**	**116**
English . . .	249	135	114
Portuguese . . .	7	5	2
HYDERABAD STATE.			
TOTAL .	**13,374,676**	**6,797,118**	**6,577,558**
A.—Vernaculars of India .	**13,359,710**	**6,786,852**	**6,572,858**
Bengali . . .	194	171	23
Bihārī . . .	142	83	59

LANGUAGE.	POPULATION.		
	Persons.	Males.	Females.
1	2	3	4
HYDERABAD STATE—*contd.*			
A.—Vernaculars of India—*contd.*			
Eastern Hindī . .	6,609	3,507	3,102
Gipsy languages . .	4,566	2,359	2,207
Goṇḍ . . .	73,939	38,890	35,049
Gujarātī . . .	22,918	12,603	10,315
Bhil languages .	*7,858*	*3,884*	*3,974*
Hindī . . .	12,261	7,837	4,424
Kanarese . . .	1,680,005	843,815	836,190
Malayālam . . .	243	215	28
Marāthī . . .	3,498,751	1,763,997	1,734,754
Oriyā . . .	265	137	128
Panjābī . . .	3,414	2,143	1,271
Pashto . . .	786	618	168
Rājasthānī . . .	288,107	152,517	135,590
Banjārī . . .	*237,899*	*124,852*	*113,047*
Sindhī (*Kachchhī*) .	307	268	39
Tamil . . .	32,425	17,116	15,309
Telugu . . .	6,367,578	3,249,365	3,118,213
Western Hindī . .	1,367,175	691,193	675,982
Other languages . .	25	18	7
B.—Vernaculars of other Asiatic Countries and Africa.	**5,977**	**4,028**	**1,949**
Arabic . . .	5,683	3,881	1,802
Persian . . .	256	129	127
Other languages . .	38	18	20
C.—European languages .	**8,989**	**6,238**	**2,751**
English . . .	8,843	6,174	2,669
Italian . . .	36	8	28
Portuguese . . .	70	44	26
Other languages . .	40	12	28
KASHMIR STATE.			
TOTAL .	**3,103,501**	**1,644,978**	**1,458,523**
A.—Vernaculars of India	**3,103,131**	**1,644,750**	**1,458,381**
Bhotiā . . .	186,513	92,939	93,574
Bhotiā of Bāltistan .	*132,161*	*65,537*	*66,624*
Bhotiā of Ladakh .	*54,237*	*27,346*	*26,891*
Bhotiā of Tibet .	*115*	*56*	*59*
Hindī . . .	556	375	181
Kashmīrī . . .	1,172,487	629,512	542,975
Kōhistānī . . .	4,750	2,590	2,160
Naipālī (Khas) . .	1,844	1,534	310
Panjābī . . .	730,074	395,632	334,442
Pashto . . .	2,745	1,951	794
Rājasthānī . . .	254,888	132,859	122,029
Banjārī . . .	*2,061*	*1,069*	*992*
Gujarī . . .	*252,692*	*131,712*	*120,980*
Shina . . .	21,562	11,236	10,326
Western Hindī . .	1,924	1,399	525
Western Pahārī . .	549,245	284,780	264,465
Western Panjābī . .	176,331	89,800	86,531
Other languages . .	212	143	69
B.—Vernaculars of other Asiatic Countries and Africa.	**96**	**79**	**17**
Persian . . .	58	50	8
Other languages . .	38	29	9
C.—European languages .	**274**	**149**	**125**
English . . .	257	141	116
Other languages . .	17	8	9

DISTRIBUTION OF EACH PROVINCE, STATE OR AGENCY—*continued.*

LANGUAGE.	POPULATION.		
	Persons.	Males.	Females.
1	2	3	4
MADRAS STATES.*			
TOTAL	**4,811,841**	**2,411,758**	**2,400,083**
A.—Vernaculars of India	**4,808,563**	**2,409,900**	**2,398,663**
Gujarātī	4,196	2,274	1,922
Hindī	126	60	66
Kanarese	19,847	10,027	9,820
Malayālam	3,656,961	1,839,445	1,817,516
Marāthī	41,869	22,018	19,851
Kōnkanī	*32,207*	*17,112*	*15,095*
Rājasthānī	563	296	267
Banjārī	*561*	*294*	*267*
Sindhī (*Kachchhī*)	730	393	337
Tamil	1,000,537	492,610	507,927
Telugu	64,101	32,075	32,026
Tulu	2,309	1,594	715
Western Hindī	17,257	9,074	8,183
Other languages	67	34	33
B.—Vernaculars of other Asiatic Countries and Africa.	**288**	**177**	**111**
Arabic	247	154	93
Other languages	41	23	18
C.—European languages.	**2,990**	**1,681**	**1,309**
English	2,636	1,455	1,181
Portuguese	272	171	101
Other languages	82	55	27
COCHIN STATE.			
TOTAL	**918,110**	**457,342**	**460,768**
A.—Vernaculars of India	**917,289**	**456,847**	**460,442**
Gujarātī	1,060	663	397
Hindī	121	55	66
Kanarese	4,152	2,180	1,972
Malayālam	820,129	407,228	412,901
Marāthī	22,225	11,544	10,681
Kōnkanī	*21,153*	*11,226*	*9,927*
Sindhī (*Kachchhī*)	352	191	161
Tamil	55,231	27,858	27,373
Telugu	11,224	5,511	5,713
Tulu	546	405	141
Western Hindī	2,247	1,211	1,036
Other languages	2	1	1
B.—Vernaculars of other Asiatic Countries and Africa.	**142**	**85**	**57**
Arabic	111	70	41
Other languages	31	15	16
C.—European languages	**679**	**410**	**269**
English	412	243	169
Portuguese	237	140	97
Other languages	30	27	3
TRAVANCORE STATE.			
TOTAL	**3,428,975**	**1,731,363**	**1,697,612**
A.—Vernaculars of India	**3,426,576**	**1,730,032**	**1,696,544**
Gujarātī	2,220	1,187	1,033
Kanarese	1,901	1,053	848
Malayālam	2,836,728	1,432,139	1,404,589
Marāthī	17,820	9,561	8,259
Kōnkanī	*11,052*	*5,886*	*5,166*
Sindhī (*Kachchhī*)	378	202	176
TRAVANCORE STATE—contd.			
A.—Vernaculars of India—*contd.*			
Tamil	554,618	278,585	276,033
Telugu	6,452	3,460	2,992
Tulu	1,762	1,189	573
Western Hindī	4,659	2,625	2,034
Other languages	38	31	7
B.—Vernaculars of other Asiatic Countries and Africa.	**146**	**92**	**54**
Arabic	136	84	52
Other languages	10	8	2
C.—European languages	**2,253**	**1,239**	**1,014**
English	2,167	1,181	986
Portuguese	35	31	4
Other languages	51	27	24
MYSORE STATE.			
TOTAL	**5,806,193**	**2,934,621**	**2,871,572**
A.—Vernaculars of India	**5,790,952**	**2,925,938**	**2,865,014**
Gujarātī	2,776	1,617	1,159
Kanarese	4,147,765	2,078,682	2,069,083
Malayālam	4,692	4,142	550
Marāthī	87,476	46,755	40,721
Kōnkanī	*9,358*	*6,243*	*3,115*
Oriyā	976	500	476
Panjābī	407	355	52
Rājasthānī	44,915	23,421	21,494
Banjārī	*43,667*	*22,437*	*21,230*
Sindhī	209	138	71
Kachchhī	*150*	*91*	*59*
Tamil	244,947	126,995	117,952
Telugu	919,410	463,035	456,375
Tulu	31,995	21,022	10,973
Western Hindī	305,182	159,136	146,046
Other languages	202	140	62
B.—Vernaculars of other Asiatic Countries and Africa.	**1,703**	**933**	**770**
Arabic	293	205	88
Persian	1,384	716	668
Other languages	26	12	14
C.—European languages	**13,538**	**7,750**	**5,788**
English	13,120	7,468	5,652
French	130	88	42
German	40	6	34
Italian	102	95	7
Portuguese	125	77	48
Other languages	21	16	5
N.-W. F. PROVINCE *(Agencies and Tribal areas).*			
TOTAL	**13,538**	**12,641**	**897**
A.—Vernaculars of India	**13,062**	**12,264**	**798**
Panjābī	4,781	4,472	309
Pashto	7,740	7,349	391
Western Hindī	460	390	70
Other languages	81	53	28

* Inclusive of Cochin and Travancore separate figures for which are given below.

TABLE X.—LANGUAGE. PART IV.—LINGUISTIC DISTRIBUTION OF EACH PROVINCE, STATE OR AGENCY—*concluded.*

LANGUAGE.	POPULATION.		
	Persons.	Males.	Females.
1	2	3	4
N.-W. F. PROVINCE *(Agencies and Tribal areas)*—contd.			
B.—Vernaculars of other Asiatic Countries and Africa (Persian).	357	278	79
C.—European languages (English).	119	99	20
PUNJAB STATES.			
TOTAL	**4,212,794**	**2,322,908**	**1,889,886**
A.—Vernaculars of India	**4,211,710**	**2,322,280**	**1,889,430**
Baloch	1,444	968	476
Bhotia	4,404	2,537	1,867
Bhotiā of Tibet	*3,763*	*2,204*	*1,559*
Bhotiā (others)	*631*	*325*	*306*
Central Pahārī	567	453	114
Chamba Lāhulī	1,173	589	584
Gipsy languages	474	227	217
Gujarātī	3,855	2,081	1,774
Bhil languages	*3,683*	*1,952*	*1,731*
Hindī	315,984	173,621	142,363
Kanaurī or Multhānī	22,359	10,083	12,276
Kashmīrī	710	387	323
Lāhulī	130	106	24
Naipālī (Khas)	1,297	800	497
Panjābī	2,210,977	1,249,835	961,142
Standard	*2,191,575*	*1,238,188*	*953,387*
Dogri	*19,402*	*11,647*	*7,755*
Pashto	1,090	922	168
Rājasthānī	229,782	122,599	107,183
Gujarī	*1,400*	*750*	*650*
Sindhī	22,169	12,260	9,909
Western Hindī	81,247	43,303	37,944
Western Pahārī	748,284	389,405	358,879
Simla Group	*382,202*	*200,289*	*181,913*
Kulu Group	*16,906*	*8,722*	*8,184*
Mandi Group	*232,834*	*120,634*	*112,200*
Chamba Group	*115,897*	*59,468*	*56,429*
Unspecified	*445*	*292*	*153*
Western Panjābī	565,557	311,984	253,573
Other languages	207	120	87
B.—Vernaculars of other Asiatic Countries and Africa.	**218**	**129**	**89**
Chinese	178	98	80
Persian	30	23	7
Other languages	10	8	2
C.—European languages	**866**	**499**	**367**
English	855	491	364
Other languages	11	8	3
RAJPUTANA AGENCY.			
TOTAL	**10,530,432**	**5,515,275**	**5,015,157**
A.—Vernaculars of India	**10,528,569**	**5,514,185**	**5,014,384**
Baloch	945	519	426
Bengali	619	355	264
Bihārī	3,476	2,092	1,384
Central Pahārī	530	479	51
Gipsy languages	456	232	224
Gujarātī	503,399	253,525	249,874
Bhil languages	*484,887*	*243,370*	*241,517*
Hindī	1,190,083	636,297	553,786
Marāthī	2,028	1,105	923
Panjābī	35,081	19,901	15,180
Pashto	572	420	152
Rājasthānī	8,297,636	4,328,902	3,968,734
Banjārī	*4,299*	*2,398*	*1,901*

LANGUAGE.	POPULATION.		
	Persons.	Males.	Females.
1	2	3	4
RAJPUTANA AGENCY—*contd.*			
A.—Vernaculars of India— *contd.*			
Sindhī	58,118	31,772	26,346
Kachchhī	*153*	*100*	*53*
Western Hindī	434,852	238,203	196,649
Western Panjābī	459	217	242
Other languages	315	166	149
B.—Vernaculars of other Asiatic Countries and Africa.	**82**	**68**	**14**
Arabic	43	35	8
Other languages	39	33	6
C.—European languages	**1,781**	**1,022**	**759**
English	1,684	957	727
Portuguese	59	40	19
Other languages	38	25	13
SIKKIM STATE.			
TOTAL	**87,920**	**45,059**	**42,861**
A.—Vernaculars of India	**87,875**	**45,028**	**42,847**
Bhotia	12,433	6,418	6,015
Bhotiā of Sikkim	*10,411*	*5,352*	*5,059*
Sharpā Bhotiā	*1,495*	*752*	*743*
Bhotiā (others)	*523*	*312*	*211*
Hindī	391	350	41
Kirāntī (Jimdār)	15,803	7,963	7,840
Limbū	8,445	4,154	4,291
Mangar	3,026	1,545	1,481
Mānjhī	373	190	183
Marāthī	222	222	...
Murmī	7,355	3,683	3,672
Naipālī (Khas)	28,078	14,324	13,754
Newārī	1,270	685	585
Rājasthānī	166	134	32
Rong or Lepcha	9,278	4,813	4,465
Sunvār	908	484	424
Other languages	127	63	64
B.—Vernaculars of other Asiatic Countries and Africa.	**26**	**13**	**13**
C.—European languages	**19**	**18**	**1**
UNITED PROVINCES STATES.			
TOTAL	**832,036**	**431,440**	**400,596**
A.—Vernaculars of India	**831,991**	**431,413**	**400,578**
Bengali	112	104	8
Hindī	302,137	149,138	152,999
Panjābī	358	300	58
Western Hindī	529,285	281,790	247,495
Other languages	99	81	18
B.—Vernaculars of other Asiatic Countries and Africa.	**18**	**14**	**4**
C.—European languages	**27**	**13**	**14**

TABLE XI.

Birthplace.

This Table is divided into four parts :—

Part I—Is a general summary giving for the whole of India and for each Province, State or Agency the number of persons born in India, in other Asiatic countries, in Europe, in Africa, and so on. The distinction made in 1901 between Asiatic countries adjacent to India and other Asiatic countries has not been maintained Some countries are adjacent in a geographical sense, but the bulk of the migration which takes place follows other channels than the common boundary. This is the case for instance with China and Persia.

Part II—The general groups of Part I are here distributed amongst the particular countries of which they are made up, and details are given for the whole of India and for each Province or State, showing the number of persons born in different parts of India, in Afghanistan, China, the United Kingdom, Cape Colony, Canada, etc.

Part III—Illustrates internal migration. Column 2 gives the total number of immigrants, that is to say of persons born in other parts of India, who were enumerated in the Provinces or States entered in the first column. Column 3 treats as emigrants those persons who were born in the Provinces or States shown in column 1, but were enumerated in other parts of India. The fourth column shows the balance of emigration or immigration in each case, and the subsequent columns give particulars of the net interchange of population which goes to make up the balance for or against any given Province or State. The details working up to the totals will be found in Part II. To take a simple instance—46 persons born in Ajmer-Merwara were enumerated in Assam, and 6 persons born in Assam were enumerated in Ajmer-Merwara. The difference 40 represents the net emigration from Ajmer-Merwara to Assam and appears first in column 5 as the net gain of Assam from Ajmer-Merwara. and again in column 7 as the net loss of Ajmer-Merwara to Assam. Of the gross figures 46 is shown with details of sex in Part II under Assam, while 6 is entered under Ajmer-Merwara. As Part III deals only with internal migration, immigrants born outside India (including French and Portuguese Settlements) as well as those Indians whose birthplace was not specified are excluded from the statistics. An attempt will be made in the body of the Census Report to strike a balance between immigration and emigration for India as a whole.

Part IV—Shows the distribution according to the place of Enumeration at the census of the persons born in each Province, State or Country.

2. In Parts II, III and IV Cochin and Travancore have been treated as separate units, but under each Province, State or Country their figures have been included, except where otherwise stated, in those for Madras States.

TABLE XI.—Birthplace. Part I.—General

Province, State or Agency, where enumerated.	Total Population.			COUNTRY A.—Born in India.		
	Persons.	Males.	Females.	Persons.	Males.	Females.
1	2	3	4	5	6	7
INDIA.	**315,156,396**	**161,338,935**	**153,817,461**	**312,783,652**	**159,978,045**	**152,805,607**
Provinces.	**244,267,542**	**124,873,691**	**119,393,851**	**243,615,181**	**124,433,660**	**119,181,521**
1. Ajmer-Merwara	501,395	266,198	235,197	499,929	264,902	235,027
2. Andamans and Nicobars	26,459	19,570	6,889	26,176	19,306	6,870
3. Assam	6,713,635	3,467,621	3,246,014	6,663,866	3,433,745	3,230,121
4. Baluchistan	414,412	239,181	175,231	398,572	226,980	171,592
5. Bengal	45,483,077	23,365,225	22,117,852	45,352,023	23,286,484	22,065,539
6. Bihar and Orissa	34,490,084	16,859,929	17,630,155	34,450,413	16,845,252	17,605,161
7. Bombay	19,672,642	10,245,847	9,426,795	19,608,736	10,195,018	9,413,718
8. Burma	12,115,217	6,183,494	5,931,723	11,958,945	6,076,040	5,882,905
9. Central Provinces and Berar	13,916,308	6,930,392	6,985,916	13,909,535	6,924,588	6,984,947
10. Coorg	174,976	97,279	77,697	174,868	97,208	77,660
11. Madras	41,405,404	20,382,955	21,022,449	41,391,070	20,373,334	21,017,786
12. N.-W. F. Province (*Districts and Administered Territories*)	2,196,933	1,182,102	1,014,831	2,144,871	1,147,639	997,232
13. Punjab	19,974,956	10,992,067	8,982,889	19,923,707	10,948,968	8,974,739
14. United Provinces of Agra and Oudh	47,182,044	24,641,831	22,540,213	47,112,470	24,594,196	22,518,274
States and Agencies.	**70,888,854**	**36,465,244**	**34,423,610**	**69,168,471**	**35,544,385**	**33,624,086**
15. Assam State (Manipur)	346,222	170,666	175,556	345,041	169,887	175,154
16. Baluchistan States	420,291	227,238	193,053	419,940	227,019	192,921
17. Baroda State	2,032,798	1,055,935	976,863	2,032,268	1,055,631	976,637
18. Bengal States	822,565	438,368	384,197	821,857	437,729	384,128
19. Bihar and Orissa States	3,945,209	1,955,125	1,990,084	3,945,076	1,955,019	1,990,057
20. Bombay States	7,411,675	3,765,401	3,646,274	7,408,872	3,763,134	3,645,738
21. Central India Agency	9,356,980	4,801,459	4,555,521	9,353,116	4,798,154	4,554,962
22. Central Provinces States	2,117,002	1,053,630	1,063,372	2,116,857	1,053,530	1,063,327
23. Hyderabad State	13,374,676	6,797,118	6,577,558	13,367,080	6,790,681	6,576,399
24. Kashmir State	3,158,126	1,674,367	1,483,759	3,101,113	1,642,978	1,458,135
25. Madras States	4,811,841	2,411,758	2,400,083	4,810,400	2,410,924	2,399,476
26. Mysore States	5,806,193	2,934,621	2,871,572	5,801,487	2,930,862	2,870,625
27. N.-W. F. Province (*Agencies and Tribal areas*)	1,622,094	864,876	757,218	12,394	11,512	882
28. Punjab States	4,212,794	2,322,908	1,889,886	4,209,776	2,320,525	1,889,251
29. Rajputana Agency	10,530,432	5,515.275	5,015,157	10,529,368	5,514,546	5,014,822
30. Sikkim State	87,920	45,059	42,861	61,893	30,890	31,003
31. United Provinces States	832,036	431,440	400,596	831,933	431,364	400,569

Distribution of Population by Birthplace.

WHERE BORN.

B.—Born in other Asiatic Countries.			C.—Born in Europe.			D.—Born in Africa.			E.—Born in America.			Serial Number.
Persons.	Males.	Females.	Persons.	Males.	Females.	Persons.	Males.	Females.	Persons.	Males.	Females.	
8	9	10	11	12	13	14	15	16	17	18	19	
504,113	**330,675**	**173,438**	**131,968**	**109,594**	**22,374**	**10,270**	**6,921**	**3,349**	**2,760**	**1,525**	**1,235**	
461,979	**303,650**	**158,329**	**118,340**	**98,260**	**20,080**	**9,236**	**6,306**	**2,930**	**2,468**	**1,390**	**1,078**	
170	150	20	1,266	1,131	135	9	6	3	9	4	5	1
96	96	...	182	164	18	...	...	..	3	2	1	2
48,185	32,649	15,536	1,483	1,156	327	14	13	1	58	33	25	3
12,467	9,240	3,227	3,311	2,916	395	8	6	2	34	24	10	4
116,672	67,948	48,724	13,489	10,242	3,247	232	157	75	311	175	136	5
36,678	12,610	24,068	2,836	1,982	854	29	12	17	66	30	36	6
32,474	25,609	6,865	23,443	19,700	3,743	7,546	5,275	2,271	263	147	116	7
88,268	70,368	17,900	8,337	7,060	1,277	53	42	11	403	277	126	8
1,431	1,231	200	5,100	4,413	687	42	35	7	140	71	69	9
6	4	2	95	63	32	3	2	1	2	2	...	10
5,202	3,149	2,053	7,891	5,761	2,130	886	503	383	255	151	104	11
47,166	30,040	17,126	4,820	4,373	447	22	11	11	23	18	5	12
27,144	22,706	4,438	23,620	20,124	3,496	115	75	40	266	126	140	13
46,020	27,850	18,170	22,467	19,175	3,292	277	169	108	635	330	305	14
42,134	**27,025**	**15,109**	**13,628**	**11,334**	**2,294**	**1,034**	**615**	**419**	**292**	**135**	**157**	
1,168	771	397	13	8	5	...	...	...	...	...	...	15
334	204	130	12	10	2	...	...	...	3	3	...	16
191	144	47	70	44	26	257	110	147	12	6	6	17
692	628	64	13	9	4	...	...	..	1	1	...	18
107	93	14	25	13	12	1	...	1	...	...	...	19
1,758	1,577	181	537	402	135	460	259	201	24	11	13	20
355	248	107	3,283	2,916	367	129	101	28	89	32	57	21
102	70	32	32	25	7	4	3	1	5	...	5	22
3,507	2,882	625	3,936	3,444	492	98	87	11	40	13	27	23
2,233	1,860	373	126	76	50	6	2	4	10	6	4	24
1,039	579	460	380	242	138	8	4	4	12	8	4	25
283	162	121	4,263	3,498	765	46	34	12	76	42	34	26
1,068	1,067	1	71	57	14	2	2	...	3	3	...	27
2,721	2,176	545	286	202	84	7	3	4	1	...	1	28
466	336	130	561	371	190	16	10	6	16	10	6	29
26,013	14,155	11,858	14	14	...	...	...	...	...	...	...	30
97	73	24	6	3	3	...	...	...	...	...	...	31

TABLE XI.—BIRTHPLACE. PART I.—GENERAL DISTRIBUTION OF POPULATION BY BIRTHPLACE—*concluded.*

Province, State or Agency, where enumerated.	Country where born.									Not enumerated by birthplace.		
	F.—Born in Australasia.			G.—Born at Sea.			H.—Birthplace unspecified or not returned.					
	Persons.	Males.	Females.	Persons.	Males.	Females.	Persons.	Males.	Females.	Persons.	Males.	Females.
1	20	21	22	23	24	25	26	27	28	29	30	31
INDIA.	**1,267**	**873**	**394**	**124**	**65**	**59**	**245**	**190**	**55**	**1,721,997**	**911,047**	**810,950**
Provinces.	**1,175**	**808**	**367**	**114**	**59**	**55**	**43**	**24**	**19**	**59,006**	**29,534**	**29,472**
1. Ajmer-Merwara	12	5	7	...	...	...	...	...	...	...	...	...
2. Andamans and Nicobars	2	2	...	...	...	..	...	...	...	...	...	...
3. Assam	25	21	4	4	4	...	...	...	...	...	...	...
4. Baluchistan	17	13	4	3	2	1	...	...	...	...	...	...
5. Bengal	304	193	111	46	26	20	...	...	...	...	...	...
6. Bihar and Orissa	40	32	8	22	11	11	...	...	...	...	...	...
7. Bombay	126	76	50	17	3	14	37	19	18	..	...	...
8. Burma	205	173	32	..	...	...	...	...	...	59,006	29,534	29,472
9. Central Provinces and Berar	59	53	6	1	1	...	...	...	...	...	...	...
10. Coorg	2	...	2	...	...	...	...	...	...	...	...	...
11. Madras	97	55	42	3	2	1	...	...	...	...	...	...
12. N.-W. F. Province (*Districts and Administered Territories*)	28	20	8	3	1	2	...	...	...	...	...	...
13. Punjab	104	68	36	...	...	...	...	...	...	...	...	...
14. United Provinces of Agra and Oudh	154	97	57	15	9	6	6	5	1	...	...	...
States and Agencies.	**92**	**65**	**27**	**10**	**6**	**4**	**202**	**166**	**36**	**1,662,991**	**881,513**	**781,478**
15. Assam State (Manipur)	...	...	...	...	...	...	...	...	...	...	...	...
16. Baluchistan States	2	2	...	...	...	...	...	...	...	...	...	...
17. Baroda State	...	...	...	...	...	...	...	...	...	...	...	...
18. Bengal States	2	1	1	...	...	...	...	...	...	...	...	...
19. Bihar and Orissa States	...	...	...	...	...	...	...	...	...	...	...	...
20. Bombay States	24	18	6	...	...	...	...	...	...	...	...	...
21. Central India Agency	8	8	..	...	...	...	...	...	...	...	...	...
22. Central Provinces States	1	1	...	1	1	...	...	...	...	...	...	...
23. Hyderabad State	11	9	2	4	2	2	...	...	...	..	...	...
24. Kashmir State	1	1	.	...	...	...	202	166	36	54,435	29,278	25,157
25. Madras States	2	1	1	...	...	...	...	...	...	.	...	...
26. Mysore State	34	20	14	4	3	1	...	...	...	...	...	...
27. N.-W. F. Province (*Agencies and Tribal areas*)		...	...	...	...	...	...	...	...	1,608,556	852,235	756,321
28. Punjab States	3	2	1	...	...	...	...	...	...	...	...	...
29. Rajputana Agency	4	2	2	1	...	1	...	...	...	...	...	...
30. Sikkim State	...	...	...	...	...	...	...	...	...	...	...	...
31. United Provinces States	...	...	...	...	...	...	...	...	...	...	...	...

TABLE XI.—Birthplace. Part II.—Detailed Distribution of Population by Birthplace.

Birthplace.	Population. Persons.	Males.	Females.
1	2	3	4
INDIA	**315,156.396**	**161,338,935**	**153,817.461**
A—Born in India	**312,783,652**	**159,978,045**	**152,805,607**
Provinces	*243,302,388*	*124,262,034*	*119.130,354*
Ajmere-Merwara	488,927	268,965	219,962
Andamans and Nicobars	13,024	7,093	5,931
Assam	5,908,503	3,013,465	2,895,038
Baluchistan	400,971	220,273	180,698
Bengal	44,165,012	22,409,216	21,755,796
Bihar and Orissa	36,181,814	17,974,366	18,207,448
Bombay	19,139,366	9,841,967	9,297,399
Burma	11,477,899	5,660,168	5,817,731
C. P. and Berar	13,578,202	6,723,548	6,854,654
Coorg	133,299	67,931	65,368
Madras	42,002,913	20,783,962	21,218,951
N.-W. F. Province	2,079,173	1,102,438	976,735
Punjab	19,899,998	10,991,129	8,908,86[illegible]
United Provinces	47,923,287	25,197,513	22,725,774
States and Agencies	*69,286.347*	*35,651,592*	*33,634.755*
Assam State	343,025	168,840	174,185
Baluchistan States	451,263	244.690	206,573
Baroda State	2,045,364	1,061,440	983,924
Bengal States	722,439	371,010	351,429
Bihar and Orissa States	3,704,800	1,831,055	1,873,745
Bombay States	7,526,656	3,882,122	3,644,534
Central India Agency	9,418,572	4,817,075	4,601,497
Central Provinces States	2,019,638	1,003,420	1,016,218
Hyderabad State	13,420,235	6,800,140	6,620,095
Kashmir State	3,108,647	1,652,333	1,456,314
Madras States	4,723,398	2,371,692	2,351,706
Cochin	*891,225*	*444,243*	*446,982*
Travancore	*3,394,080*	*1,714,027*	*1,680,053*
Mysore State	5,624,542	2,825,556	2,798,986
N.-W. F. Province (*Agencies and Tribal areas*)	62,670	39,867	22,803
Punjab States	4,131,706	2,275.477	1,856,229
Rajputana Agency	11,082,504	5,840,126	5,242,378
Sikkim State	61,530	30,259	31,271
United Provinces States	839,358	436,490	402,868
India, Unspecified	*17,282*	*11,565*	*5,717*
French and Portuguese Settlements	*87,635*	*52,854*	*34,781*
B.—Born in other Asiatic Countries	**504,113**	**330,675**	**173.438**
Afghanistan	91,640	67,451	24,189
Arabia	23,078	18,540	4,538
Armenia	40	14	26
Asia Minor	1	1	..
Bhotan	2,647	1,605	1.042
Bokhara	7	7	..
Ceylon	6,165	3,778	2,387
China	80,307	64,784	15,523
Chinese Tartary	30	24	6
Chinese Turkistan	14	8	6
French Indo-China	35	23	12
Hong Kong	74	52	22
Japan	1,261	567	694
Maldives	29	28	1
Mongolia	7	6	1
Nepal	280,248	160,974	119,274
Persia	6,772	4,605	2,167
Russia in Asia	150	130	20
Russian Turkistan	77	61	16
Siam	4,093	2,783	1,310
Straits Settlements and Malaya	1,873	1,294	579
Tibet	4,509	3,238	1.271
Turkey in Asia	937	616	321
Asia, *Unspecified*	119	86	33
C.—Born in Europe	**131,968**	**109.594**	**22,374**
United Kingdom	122,919	103,425	19.494
England and Wales	*95,436*	*80,605*	*14,831*
Scotland	*13,913*	*11,676*	*2,237*
Ireland	*12,244*	*9,953*	*2,291*
Channel Islands and Isle of Man	*59*	*41*	*18*
United Kingdom, Unspecified	*1,267*	*1,150*	*117*
INDIA—*contd.*			
C.—Born in Europe—*contd.*			
Austria-Hungary	599	408	191
Belgium	353	212	141
Bulgaria	1	1	..
Cyprus	4	3	1
Denmark	103	62	41
France	1,478	757	721
Germany	1,860	1,321	539
Gibraltar	93	45	48
Greece	274	245	29
Holland	235	200	35
Iceland	9	7	2
Italy	894	657	237
Malta	172	85	87
Norway	109	88	21
Portugal	948	763	185
Rumania	21	13	8
Russia	314	134	180
Spain	153	101	52
Sweden	222	145	77
Switzerland	287	190	97
Turkey in Europe	111	81	30
Europe, *Unspecified*	809	651	158
D.—Born in Africa	**10,270**	**6,921**	**3.349**
Abyssinia	2	1	1
British East Africa	6,518	4,701	1.817
Cape Colony	56	38	18
Congo	1	..	1
Egypt	301	221	80
Mauritius	514	258	256
Mozambique	1	..	1
Natal	553	296	257
Seychelles	1	..	1
Somaliland	6	6	..
St. Helena	10	6	4
Sudan	1	1	..
Transvaal	18	10	8
Zanzibar	169	87	82
Africa, *Unspecified*	2,119	1,296	823
E.—Born in America	**2,760**	**1,525**	**1,235**
Argentine Republic	3	2	1
Bermudas	12	10	2
Brazil	8	7	1
British Guiana	11	8	3
California	1	..	1
Canada	313	182	131
Chile	2	1	1
Cuba	1	1	..
Honduras	2	2	..
Jamaica	38	15	23
Mexico	2	1	1
Newfoundland	14	9	5
United States	255	125	130
West Indies	348	185	163
America, *Unspecified*	1,750	977	773
F.—Born in Australasia	**1,267**	**873**	**394**
Australia	882	572	310
Borneo	12	10	2
Fiji Islands	34	21	13
Java	94	82	12
Manilla	2	2	..
Melanesia	1	..	1
New Zealand	144	101	3
Philippines	57	53	4
Polynesia	9	9	..
Sumatra	9	5	4
Tasmania	13	9	4
Australasia, *Unspecified*	10	9	1
G.—Born at Sea	**124**	**65**	**59**
H.—Birthplace Unspecified or not returned	**245**	**190**	**55**
Not enumerated by Birthplace	**1,721,997**	**911,847**	**810,950**

TABLE XI.—Birthplace. Part II.—Detailed.

Birthplace.	Population. Persons.	Males.	Females.
1	2	3	4
AJMER-MERWARA	**501,395**	**266,198**	**235,197**
A.—Born in India	**499,929**	**264,902**	**235,027**
Provinces	*422,979*	*232,591*	*190.388*
Ajmer-Merwara	404,817	221,690	183,127
Assam	6	4	2
Baluchistan	23	13	10
Bengal	289	137	152
Bihar and Orissa	112	89	23
Bombay	1,570	926	644
Burma	21	13	8
Central Provinces and Berar	341	174	167
Madras	218	123	95
N.-W. F. Province	105	84	21
Punjab	3,496	2,380	1,116
United Provinces	11,981	6,958	5,023
States and Agencies	*76,691*	*32,122*	*44,569*
Baroda State	224	133	91
Bombay States	347	183	164
Central India Agency	2,046	983	1,063
Hyderabad State	247	134	113
Kashmir State	35	27	8
Madras States	6	3	3
Mysore State	64	33	31
N.-W. F. Province (*Agencies and Tribal areas*)	1	..	1
Punjab States	615	398	217
Rajputana Agency	72,972	30,144	42,828
United Provinces States	134	84	50
India, Unspecified	*13*	*5*	*8*
French and Portuguese Settlements	*246*	*184*	*62*
B.—Born in other Asiatic Countries.	**170**	**150**	**20**
Afghanistan	134	124	10
Arabia	8	7	1
Ceylon	5	4	1
China	1	..	1
Japan	2	1	1
Nepal	17	13	4
Persia	1	..	1
Tibet	1	1	..
Turkey in Asia	1	..	1
C.—Born in Europe	**1,266**	**1,131**	**135**
United Kingdom	1,223	1,099	124
England and Wales	*1,094*	*1,013*	*81*
Scotland	*77*	*50*	*27*
Ireland	*52*	*36*	*16*
France	29	24	5
Greece	1	1	..
Norway	1	1	..
Portugal	5	4	1
Russia	2	1	1
Spain	2	1	1
Sweden	1	..	1
Switzerland	2	..	2
D.—Born in Africa	**9**	**6**	**3**
Mauritius	1	1	..
Africa, *Unspecified*	8	5	3
E.—Born in America	**9**	**4**	**5**
Bermudas	1	1	..
Canada	1	1	..
United States	2	1	1
America, *Unspecified*	5	1	4
F.—Born in Australasia (Australia)	**12**	**5**	**7**
ANDAMANS AND NICOBARS	**26,459**	**19,570**	**6,889**
A.—Born in India	**26,176**	**19,306**	**6,870**
Provinces	*24,983*	*18,170*	*6,813*
Ajmer-Merwara	12	8	4
Andamans and Nicobars	12,057	6,371	5,686
Assam	132	128	4
Baluchistan	39	39	..
Bengal	1,221	1,089	132
Bihar and Orissa	872	777	95
Bombay	987	857	130
Burma	1,719	1,700	19
Central Provinces and Berar	887	752	135
Coorg	1	1	..
ANDAMANS AND NICOBARS—*contd.*			
Madras	1,489	1,328	161
N.-W. F. Province	459	459	..
Punjab	1,947	1,788	159
United Provinces	3,161	2,873	288
States and Agencies	*731*	*705*	*26*
Assam State	30	30	..
Baroda State	8	8	..
Bengal States	58	58	..
Bihar and Orissa States	14	14	..
Bombay States	43	43	..
Central India Agency	156	150	6
Hyderabad State	87	83	4
Kashmir State	1	1	..
Mysore State	8	7	1
Punjab States	125	125	..
Rajputana Agency	162	150	12
United Provinces States	39	36	3
India, Unspecified	*457*	*426*	*31*
French and Portuguese Settlements	*5*	*5*	..
B.—Born in other Asiatic Countries	**96**	**96**	..
Afghanistan	34	34	..
Ceylon	4	4	..
China	35	35	..
Mongolia	1	1	..
Nepal	14	14	..
Siam	7	7	..
Straits Settlements and Malaya	1	1	..
C.—Born in Europe	**182**	**164**	**18**
United Kingdom	181	163	18
England and Wales	*179*	*162*	*17*
Scotland	*1*	*1*	..
Ireland	*1*	..	*1*
Germany	1	1	..
E.—Born in America (America, *Unspecified*)	**3**	**2**	**1**
F.—Born in Australasia (New Zealand)	**2**	**2**	..
ASSAM.	**6,713,635**	**3,467,621**	**3,246,014**
A.—Born in India	**6,663,866**	**3,433,745**	**3,230,121**
Provinces	*6,696,613*	*3,410,960*	*3,215,653*
Ajmer-Merwara	46	22	24
Andamans and Nicobars	6	3	3
Assam	5,831,226	2,968,599	2,862,627
Baluchistan	190	164	26
Bengal	191,612	109,460	82,152
Bihar and Orissa	392,698	217,492	175,206
Bombay	841	648	193
Burma	2,251	1,086	1,165
Central Provinces and Berar	72,471	36,960	35,511
Coorg	2	2	..
Madras	34,497	17,049	17,448
N.-W. F. Province	86	75	11
Punjab	2,859	2,137	722
United Provinces	97,828	57,263	40,565
States and Agencies	*37,149*	*22,726*	*14,416*
Assam State	3,559	2,271	1,288
Baluchistan States	17	15	2
Bengal States	1,963	1,029	934
Bihar and Orissa States	6,166	3,067	3,099
Bombay States	1,703	924	779
Central India Agency	7,102	3,783	3,319
Central Provinces States	4,530	2,321	2,209
Hyderabad State	119	81	38
Kashmir State	18	11	7
Madras States	23	21	2
Cochin	*7*	*6*	*1*
Travancore	*4*	*3*	*1*
Mysore State	140	81	59
N.-W. F. Province (*Agencies and Tribal areas*)	18	16	2
Punjab States	114	93	21
Rajputana Agency	11,505	8,925	2,580

DISTRIBUTION OF POPULATION BY BIRTHPLACE—*continued.*

Birthplace.	Population. Persons.	Males.	Females.
1	2	3	4
ASSAM—*contd.*			
Sikkim State	49	27	22
United Provinces States	116	61	55
India, Unspecified	*75*	*38*	*37*
French and Portuguese Settlements	*36*	*21*	*15*
B.—Born in other Asiatic Countries.	**48,185**	**32,649**	**15,536**
Afghanistan	662	649	13
Arabia	15	15	..
Bhotan	714	552	162
Ceylon	9	5	4
China	270	260	10
French Indo-China	1	..	1
Hong Kong	1	1	..
Nepal	46,491	31,151	15,340
Persia	9	6	3
Russian Turkistan	4	2	2
Siam	1	1	..
Straits Settlements and Malaya	4	3	1
Tibet	8	8	..
Turkey in Asia	1	1	..
C.—Born in Europe	**1,483**	**1,156**	**327**
United Kingdom	1,415	1,111	304
England and Wales	*876*	*658*	*218*
Scotland	*442*	*380*	*62*
Ireland	*97*	*73*	*24*
Austria-Hungary	1	1	..
Cyprus	1	1	..
Denmark	4	3	1
Germany	28	17	11
Gibraltar	1	1	..
Greece	2	2	..
Italy	16	8	8
Portugal	1	1	..
Russia	6	6	..
Spain	1	1	..
Sweden	2	2	..
Switzerland	8	1	2
Turkey in Europe	2	1	1
D.—Born in Africa	**14**	**13**	**1**
Cape Colony	1	1	..
Egypt	3	3	..
Natal	4	4	..
Africa, *Unspecified*	6	5	1
E.—Born in America	**58**	**33**	**25**
Argentine Republic	2	2	..
Bermudas	1	1	..
Brazil	2	2	..
Canada	9	6	3
Newfoundland	1	1	..
United States	18	..	18
America, *Unspecified*	25	21	4
F.—Born in Australasia	**25**	**21**	**4**
Australia	14	12	2
Fiji Islands	5	4	1
New Zealand	4	3	1
Tasmania	2	2	..
G.—Born at Sea	**4**	**4**	..
BALUCHISTAN	**414,412**	**239,181**	**175,231**
A.—Born in India	**398,572**	**226,980**	**171,592**
Provinces	*387,801*	*219,304*	*168,497*
Ajmer-Merwara	206	192	14
Assam	10	6	4
Baluchistan	350,442	190,154	160,288
Bengal	123	78	45
Bihar and Orissa	62	52	10
Bombay	4,158	3,031	1,127
Burma	39	19	20
Central Provinces and Berar	124	66	58
Madras	134	78	56
N.-W. F. Province	3,555	2,852	703
Punjab	22,983	17,923	5,060
United Provinces	5,965	4,853	1,112
States and Agencies	*10,490*	*7,459*	*3,031*
Baluchistan States	6,898	4,324	2,574
Baroda State	7	5	2
Bombay States	308	244	64
Central India Agency	132	98	34
BALUCHISTAN—*contd.*			
Hyderabad State	74	59	15
Kashmir State	883	786	97
Madras States (*Travancore*)	5	3	2
Mysore State	56	29	27
N.-W. F. Province (*Agencies and Tribal areas*)	525	523	2
Punjab States	765	659	106
Rajputana Agency	811	715	96
United Provinces States	26	14	12
India, Unspecified	*121*	*77*	*44*
French and Portuguese Settlements	*160*	*140*	*20*
B.—Born in other Asiatic Countries.	**12,467**	**9,240**	**3,227**
Afghanistan	10,575	7,660	2,915
Bhotan	1	..	1
Ceylon	1	1	..
China	7	4	3
Japan	7	1	6
Nepal	1,677	1,439	238
Persia	174	121	53
Russian Turkistan	7	5	2
Tibet	1	1	..
Turkey in Asia	17	8	9
C.—Born in Europe	**3,311**	**2,916**	**395**
United Kingdom	3,276	2,899	377
England and Wales	*2,266*	*1,982*	*284*
Scotland	*125*	*102*	*23*
Ireland	*881*	*812*	*69*
Channel Islands and Isle of Man	*4*	*3*	*1*
Austria-Hungary	1	..	1
Belgium	1	1	..
France	6	3	3
Germany	9	6	3
Gibraltar	6	1	5
Italy	3	2	1
Malta	5	2	3
Portugal	1	1	..
Russia	1	..	1
Sweden	1	..	1
Switzerland	1	1	..
D.—Born in Africa	**8**	**6**	**2**
British East Africa	1	1	..
Cape Colony	5	4	1
Mauritius	2	1	1
E.—Born in America	**34**	**24**	**10**
Canada	19	15	4
United States	6	3	3
West Indies	3	2	1
America, *Unspecified*	6	4	2
F.—Born in Australasia	**17**	**13**	**4**
Australia	16	13	3
Sumatra	1		1
G.—Born at Sea	**3**	**2**	**1**
BENGAL	**45,463,077**	**23,365,225**	**22,117,852**
A.—Born in India	**45,352,023**	**23 286.484**	**22,065,539**
Provinces	*45,261,802*	*23,229,943*	*22,031,859*
Ajmer-Merwara	650	506	144
Andamans and Nicobars	80	48	32
Assam	36,290	21,344	14,946
Baluchistan	97	69	28
Bengal	43,536,925	22,007,837	21,529,088
Bihar and Orissa	1,229,981	868,437	361 544
Bombay	5,923	4,244	1,679
Burma	2,596	1.260	1,336
Central Provinces and Berar	18,016	10,310	7.796
Coorg	3	2	1
Madras	13,170	7,338	5,832
N.-W. F. Province	1,011	876	135
Punjab	17,482	13,490	3,992
United Provinces	399,578	294,182	105,396
States and Agencies	*87,777*	*55,080*	*32,697*
Assam State	135	83	52
Baluchistan States	19	7	12
Baroda State	124	88	36
Bengal States	33,683	17,728	15,955

TABLE XI.—BIRTHPLACE. PART II.—DETAILED

BIRTHPLACE.	POPULATION.		
	Persons.	Males.	Females.
1	2	3	4
BENGAL—*contd.*			
Bihar and Orissa States	3,962	2,276	1,686
Bombay States	2,475	1,859	616
Central India Agency	3,123	2,434	689
Central Provinces States	1,599	799	800
Hyderabad State	244	114	130
Kashmir State	293	242	51
Madras States	103	72	31
Cochin	*48*	*35*	*13*
Travancore	*54*	*37*	*17*
Mysore State	427	287	140
Punjab States	1,012	805	207
Rajputana Agency	35,744	25,640	10,104
Sikkim State	3,354	1,629	1,725
United Provinces States	1,480	1,017	463
India, Unspecified	*106*	*60*	*46*
French and Portuguese Settlements	*2,338*	*1,401*	*937*
B.—Born in other Asiatic Countries.	**116,672**	**67,948**	**48,724**
Afghanistan	2,624	2,541	83
Arabia	475	346	129
Armenia	15	3	12
Bhotan	1,796	950	846
Ceylon	123	80	43
China	3,085	2,698	387
Chinese Turkistan	2	2	..
Hong Kong	39	31	8
Japan	146	38	108
Maldives	22	22	..
Mongolia	1	..	1
Nepal	106,132	59,697	46,435
Persia	429	351	78
Russian Turkistan	4	3	1
Siam	9	9	..
Straits Settlements and Malaya	101	52	49
Tibet	1,532	1,056	476
Turkey in Asia	130	64	66
Asia, *Unspecified*	7	5	2
C.—Born in Europe	**13,489**	**10,242**	**3,247**
United Kingdom	12,172	9,350	2,822
England and Wales	*8,963*	*6,918*	*2,045*
Scotland	*2,392*	*1,875*	*517*
Ireland	*814*	*555*	*259*
Channel Islands and Isle of Man	*3*	*2*	*1*
Austria-Hungary	156	102	54
Belgium	65	56	9
Denmark	11	9	2
France	175	104	71
Germany	305	243	62
Gibraltar	9	6	3
Greece	81	66	15
Holland	34	32	2
Italy	130	76	54
Malta	21	13	8
Norway	6	3	3
Portugal	16	14	2
Rumania	5	2	3
Russia	120	41	79
Spain	34	23	11
Sweden	34	22	12
Switzerland	50	34	16
Turkey in Europe	63	44	19
Europe, *Unspecified*	2	2	..
D.—Born in Africa	**232**	**157**	**75**
Abyssinia	1	..	1
Cape Colony	8	3	5
Egypt	24	19	5
Mauritius	49	32	17
Natal	44	32	12
St. Helena	2	2	..
Transvaal	4	1	3
Zanzibar	12	7	5
Africa, *Unspecified*	88	61	27
E.—Born in America	**311**	**175**	**136**
British Guiana	11	8	3
Canada	47	22	25
Newfoundland	3	2	1
United States	29	12	17
West Indies	20	17	3
America, *Unspecified*	201	114	87
F.—Born in Australasia	**304**	**193**	**111**
Australia	223	124	99
Borneo	1	1	..
Java	32	32	..
Manilla	2	2	..

BIRTHPLACE.	POPULATION.		
	Persons.	Males.	Females.
1	2	3	4
BENGAL—*contd.*			
New Zealand	39	28	11
Philippines	5	4	1
Tasmania	2	2	..
G.—Born at Sea	**46**	**26**	**20**
BIHAR AND ORISSA	**34,490,084**	**16,859,929**	**17,630,155**
A.—Born in India	**34,450,413**	**16,845,252**	**17,605,161**
Provinces	*34,369,779*	*16,811,485*	*17,551,994*
Ajmer-Merwara	141	79	62
Andamans and Nicobars	13	5	8
Assam	3,135	2,597	538
Baluchistan	15	14	1
Bengal	153,351	85,259	68,092
Bihar and Orissa	34,041,032	16,643,044	17,397,988
Bombay	1,883	1,273	610
Burma	155	92	63
Central Provinces and Berar	19,743	9,843	9,900
Coorg	5	1	4
Madras	16,795	7,930	8,865
N.-W. F. Province	321	271	50
Punjab	4,086	2,914	1,172
United Provinces	122,104	58,163	63,941
States and Agencies	*87,509*	*33,706*	*53,796*
Assam State	20	15	5
Baroda State	99	67	32
Bengal States	49	34	15
Bihar and Orissa States	60,572	18,487	42,085
Bombay States	849	617	232
Central India Agency	3,056	2,013	1,043
Central Provinces States	7,883	3,266	4,617
Hyderabad State	193	129	64
Kashmir State	81	64	17
Madras States	19	12	7
Cochin	*3*	*2*	*1*
Travancore	*16*	*10*	*6*
Mysore State	190	106	84
Punjab States	370	236	134
Rajputana Agency	13,672	8,348	5,324
Sikkim State	12	10	2
United Provinces States	437	302	135
India, Unspecified	*44*	*17*	*27*
French and Portuguese Settlements	*88*	*44*	*44*
B.—Born in other Asiatic Countries.	**36,678**	**12,610**	**24,068**
Afghanistan	600	593	7
Arabia	22	17	5
Bhotan	8	3	5
Ceylon	31	9	22
China	18	13	5
French Indo-China	5	5	..
Hong Kong	3	2	1
Japan	9	7	2
Mongolia	1	1	..
Nepal	35,944	11,932	24,012
Persia	18	13	5
Siam	2	..	2
Straits Settlements and Malaya	3	2	1
Tibet	8	8	..
Turkey in Asia	2	2	..
Asia, *Unspecified*	4	3	1
C.—Born in Europe	**2,836**	**1,982**	**854**
United Kingdom	2,560	1,851	709
England and Wales	*2,052*	*1,514*	*538*
Scotland	*311*	*205*	*106*
Ireland	*197*	*132*	*65*
Austria-Hungary	11	6	5
Belgium	53	27	26
Denmark	3	1	2
France	26	10	16
Germany	140	57	83
Greece	2	2	..
Holland	2	2	..
Italy	19	12	7
Malta	3	1	2
Norway	6	5	1
Portugal	1	1	..
Rumania	1	1	..
Russia	1	1	..
Spain	1	1	..
Sweden	2	2	..
Switzerland	4	2	2
Turkey in Europe	1	..	1

Distribution of Population by Birthplace—*continued.*

Birthplace.	Population. Persons.	Males.	Females.
1	2	3	4
BIHAR AND ORISSA—*contd.*			
D.—Born in Africa	**29**	**12**	**17**
Cape Colony	2	..	2
Egypt	3	3	..
Mauritius	10	3	7
Africa, *Unspecified*	14	6	8
E.—Born in America	**66**	**30**	**36**
Canada	4	2	2
United States	6	2	4
West Indies	1	1	..
America, *Unspecified*	55	25	30
F.—Born in Australasia	**40**	**32**	**8**
Australia	37	30	7
New Zealand	3	2	1
G.—Born at Sea	**22**	**11**	**11**
BOMBAY	**19,672,642**	**10,245,847**	**9,426,795**
A.—Born in India	**19,608,736**	**10,195,018**	**9,413,718**
Provinces	***18,537,610***	***9,647,307***	***8,890,303***
Ajmer-Merwara	24,976	17,868	7,108
Andamans and Nicobars	31	16	15
Assam	108	100	8
Baluchistan	42,658	24,493	18,165
Bengal	6,347	4,720	1,627
Bihar and Orissa	757	587	170
Bombay	18,249,571	9,453,304	8,796,267
Burma	521	296	225
Central Provinces and Berar	33,075	15,507	17,568
Coorg	8	3	5
Madras	33,629	21,083	12,546
N.-W. F. Province	6,881	5,458	1,423
Punjab	49,527	36,530	12,997
United Provinces	89,521	67,342	22,179
States and Agencies	***1,012,917***	***507,931***	***504,986***
Assam State	34	29	5
Baluchistan States	26,202	14,482	11,720
Baroda State	143,661	60,795	82,866
Bengal States	30	25	5
Bihar and Orissa States	119	83	36
Bombay States	559,019	284,492	274,527
Central India Agency	15,133	8,992	6,141
Central Provinces States	40	33	7
Hyderabad State	132,228	53,582	78,646
Kashmir State	722	625	97
Madras States	467	310	157
Cochin	*381*	*241*	*140*
Travancore	*84*	*67*	*17*
Mysore State	13,791	6,492	7,299
Punjab States	3,268	2,204	1,064
Rajputana Agency	118,189	75,786	42,403
Sikkim State	14	1	13
India, Unspecified	***5,947***	***4,263***	***1,684***
French and Portuguese Settlements	***52,262***	***35,517***	***16,745***
B.—Born in other Asiatic Countries	**32,474**	**25,609**	**6,865**
Afghanistan	7,460	6,413	1,047
Arabia	17,700	14,210	3,490
Armenia	20	8	12
Bhotan	6	4	2
Ceylon	218	157	61
China	536	471	65
French Indo-China	5	..	5
Hong Kong	3	2	1
Japan	327	158	169
Mongolia	1	1	..
Nepal	304	249	55
Persia	5,179	3,399	1,780
Russia in Asia	114	104	10
Russian Turkistan	8	5	3
Siam	21	11	10
Straits Settlements and Malaya	49	47	2
Tibet	1	1	..
Turkey in Asia	458	317	141
Asia, *Unspecified*	64	52	12
C.—Born in Europe	**23,443**	**19,700**	**3,743**
United Kingdom	21,015	17,942	3,073
England and Wales	*18,140*	*15,620*	*2,520*
Scotland	*1,031*	*802*	*229*
Ireland	*1,337*	*1,518*	*319*
Channel Islands and Isle of Man	*5*	*2*	*3*
United Kingdom, Unspecified	*2*	..	*2*
BOMBAY—*contd.*			
Austria-Hungary	220	140	80
Belgium	42	29	13
Denmark	12	11	1
France	163	68	95
Germany	350	259	91
Gibraltar	30	7	23
Greece	80	71	9
Holland	14	10	4
Iceland	5	5	..
Italy	204	163	41
Malta	31	11	20
Norway	47	39	8
Portugal	361	265	96
Rumania	12	9	3
Russia	77	23	54
Spain	21	12	9
Sweden	62	39	23
Switzerland	107	95	12
Turkey in Europe	6	6	..
Europe, *Unspecified*	584	496	88
D.—Born in Africa	**7,546**	**5,275**	**2,271**
Abyssinia	1	1	..
British East Africa	6,506	4,695	1,811
Cape Colony	5	4	1
Egypt	78	58	20
Mauritius	148	59	89
Mozambique	1	..	1
Natal	3	2	1
Somaliland	5	5	..
St. Helena	2	1	1
Transvaal	3	2	1
Zanzibar	68	36	32
Africa, *Unspecified*	726	412	314
E.—Born in America	**263**	**147**	**116**
Brazil	1	..	1
Canada	4	4	..
Chile	1	1	..
Jamaica	4	4	..
Mexico	1	1	..
Newfoundland	1	1	..
United States	14	6	8
West Indies	2	2	..
America, *Unspecified*	235	128	107
F.—Born in Australasia	**126**	**76**	**50**
Australia	85	47	38
Java	13	9	4
New Zealand	24	19	5
Sumatra	3	1	2
Tasmania	1	..	1
G.—Born at Sea	**17**	**3**	**14**
H.—Birthplace Unspecified or not returned	**37**	**19**	**18**
BURMA.	**12,115,217**	**6,183,494**	**5,931,723**
A.—Born in India	**11,958,945**	**6,076,040**	**5,882,905**
Provinces	***11,947,268***	***6,066,223***	***5,881,045***
Ajmer-Merwara	199	196	3
Andamans and Nicobars	451	427	24
Assam	340	309	31
Baluchistan	30	27	3
Bengal	134,985	121,011	13,974
Bihar and Orissa	8,392	6,036	2,356
Bombay	12,782	10,646	2,136
Burma	11,465,246	5,652,871	5,812,375
Central Provinces and Berar	548	417	131
Coorg	5	4	1
Madras	247,360	205,907	41,453
N.-W. F. Province	740	704	36
Punjab	25,595	22,572	3,023
United Provinces	50,595	45,096	5,499
States and Agencies	***8,718***	***7,241***	***1,477***
Assam State	678	533	145
Baroda State	136	121	15
Bengal States	771	759	12
Bombay States	39	29	10
Central India Agency	221	166	55

TABLE XI.—BIRTHPLACE. PART II.—DETAILED

Birthplace.	Population. Persons.	Males.	Females.
1	2	3	4
BURMA—*contd.*			
Central Provinces States	75	73	2
Hyderabad State	1,575	1,302	273
Kashmir State	433	275	158
Madras States	881	649	232
Cochin	*53*	*46*	*7*
Travancore	*124*	*76*	*48*
Mysore State	933	823	110
N.-W. F. Province (*Agencies and Tribal areas*)	3	1	2
Punjab States	505	411	94
Rajputana Agency	1,780	1,407	283
United Provinces States	688	602	86
India, Unspecified	***2,114***	***1,836***	***278***
French and Portuguese Settlements	***845***	***740***	***105***
B.—Born in other Asiatic Countries	**88,268**	**70,368**	**17,900**
Afghanistan	109	109	..
Arabia	133	101	32
Armenia	3	3	..
Bhotan	4	4	..
Ceylon	846	752	94
China	75,365	60,699	14,666
French Indo-China	1	...	1
Hong Kong	6	1	5
Japan	666	310	356
Maldives	3	3	..
Mongolia	1	1	..
Nepal	5.097	4,783	1,314
Persia	147	123	24
Russian Turkistan	2	2	..
Siam	3,995	2,706	1,289
Straits Settlements and Malaya	789	655	134
Turkey in Asia	200	115	85
Asia, *Unspecified*	1	1	..
C.—Born in Europe	**8,337**	**7,060**	**1,277**
United Kingdom	7,354	6,279	1,075
England and Wales	*5,105*	*4,326*	*779*
Scotland	*1,040*	*907*	*133*
Ireland	*1,209*	*1,046*	*163*
Austria-Hungary	137	123	14
Belgium	15	12	3
Denmark	4	4	..
France	211	113	98
Germany	214	184	30
Gibraltar	13	8	5
Greece	71	70	1
Holland	59	55	4
Italy	33	24	9
Malta	3	3	..
Norway	17	17	..
Portugal	6	6	..
Russia	31	17	14
Spain	16	14	2
Sweden	44	44	..
Switzerland	7	4	3
Europe, *Unspecified*	102	83	19
D.—Born in Africa	**53**	**42**	**11**
Cape Colony	15	13	2
Egypt	1	1	..
Mauritius	1	1	..
Africa, *Unspecified*	36	27	9
E.—Born in America	**403**	**277**	**126**
Canada	2	2	..
Newfoundland	1	1	..
United States	21	20	1
America, *Unspecified*	379	254	125
F.—Born in Australasia	**205**	**173**	**32**
Australia	140	119	30
Java	2	..	2
New Zealand	7	7	..
Philippines	47	47	..
Not enumerated by Birth-place	**59,006**	**29,534**	**29,472**
C. P. AND BERAR	**13,916,308**	**6,930,392**	**6,985,916**
A.—Born in India	**13,909,535**	**6,924,588**	**6,984,947**
Provinces	***13,462,006***	***6,708,325***	***6,753,681***
Ajmer-Merwara	2,644	1,647	997
Andamans and Nicobars	19	7	12
Assam	146	67	79
Baluchistan	1,064	971	93
Bengal	3,540	1,990	1,550
C. P. AND BERAR—*contd.*			
Bihar and Orissa	93,785	49,991	43,794
Bombay	85,642	42,647	42,995
Burma	229	139	90
Central Provinces and Berar	13,141,365	6,524,757	6,616,608
Coorg	12	8	4
Madras	5,357	3,039	2,318
N.-W. F. Province	617	526	91
Punjab	9,480	7,413	2,067
United Provinces	118,106	75,123	42,983
States and Agencies	***446,730***	***215,689***	***231,041***
Assam State	40	20	20
Baroda State	375	237	138
Bengal States	2	..	2
Bihar and Orissa States	4,889	2,162	2,727
Bombay States	14,715	11,364	3,351
Central India Agency	177,717	84,422	93,295
Central Provinces States	103,357	43,167	60,190
Hyderabad State	90,778	39,565	51,213
Kashmir State	103	60	43
Madras States	28	20	8
Cochin	*12*	*9*	*3*
Travancore	*15*	*11*	*4*
Mysore State	716	381	335
N.-W. F. Province (*Agencies and Tribal areas*)	1	..	1
Punjab States	930	639	291
Rajputana Agency	52,331	33,122	19,209
Sikkim State	2	1	1
United Provinces States	746	529	217
French and Portuguese Settlements	***799***	***574***	***225***
B.—Born in other Asiatic Countries	**1,431**	**1,231**	**200**
Afghanistan	1,004	950	54
Arabia	70	57	13
Bhotan	2	2	..
Ceylon	20	9	11
China	35	12	23
Hong Kong	1	1	..
Japan	4	4	..
Nepal	218	147	71
Persia	61	39	22
Straits Settlements and Malaya	2	2	..
Turkey in Asia	8	7	1
Asia, *Unspecified*	6	1	5
C.—Born in Europe	**5,100**	**4,413**	**687**
United Kingdom	4,815	4,251	564
England and Wales	*4,417*	*3,949*	*468*
Scotland	*181*	*124*	*57*
Ireland	*207*	*168*	*39*
Channel Islands and Isle of Man	*10*	*10*	..
Belgium	5	4	1
Denmark	2	2	..
France	101	29	72
Germany	74	47	27
Greece	10	10	..
Holland	1	1	..
Iceland	1	..	1
Italy	39	36	3
Malta	1	..	1
Norway	4	4	..
Portugal	6	5	1
Russia	2	1	1
Spain	1	1	..
Sweden	35	19	16
Switzerland	2	2	..
Europe, *Unspecified*	1	1	..
D.—Born in Africa	**42**	**35**	**7**
Egypt	3	2	1
Mauritius	2	..	2
Somaliland	1	1	..
Africa, *Unspecified*	36	32	4
E.—Born in America	**140**	**71**	**69**
Canada	19	13	6
United States	9	3	6
America, *Unspecified*	112	55	57
F.—Born in Australasia	**59**	**53**	**6**
Australia	49	46	3
Java	1	..	1
New Zealand	5	5	..
Philippines	3	1	2
Tasmania	1	1	..
G.—Born at Sea	**1**	**1**	..

DISTRIBUTION OF POPULATION BY BIRTHPLACE—*continued.*

Birthplace.	Population. Persons.	Males.	Females.
1	2	3	4
COORG	**174,976**	**97,279**	**77,697**
A.—Born in India	**174,868**	**97,208**	**77,660**
Provinces	*158,593*	*87,935*	*70,658*
Ajmer-Merwara	1	1	..
Bengal	6	4	2
Bihar and Orissa	2	2	..
Bombay	518	437	81
Burma	4	2	2
Central Provinces and Berar	14	12	2
Coorg	129,441	66,077	63,364
Madras	28,581	21,378	7,203
Punjab	10	9	1
United Provinces	16	13	3
States and Agencies	*16,263*	*9,262*	*7,001*
Bihar and Orissa States	1	1	..
Bombay States	31	28	3
Hyderabad State	66	49	17
Madras States	46	34	12
Cochin	*35*	*27*	*8*
Travancore	*9*	*6*	*3*
Mysore State	16,117	9,148	6,969
Rajputana Agency	2	2	..
French and Portuguese Settlements	*12*	*11*	*1*
B.—Born in other Asiatic Countries.	**6**	**4**	**2**
Ceylon	5	4	1
China	1	..	1
C.—Born in Europe.	**95**	**63**	**32**
United Kingdom	82	58	24
England and Wales	*64*	*44*	*20*
Scotland	*16*	*12*	*4*
Ireland	*2*	*2*	..
France	6	1	5
Germany	4	3	1
Switzerland	3	1	2
D.—Born in Africa	**3**	**2**	**1**
Transvaal	1	1	..
Africa, *Unspecified*	2	1	1
E.—Born in America (Canada)	**2**	**2**	..
F.—Born in Australasia	**2**	..	**2**
New Zealand	1	..	1
Tasmania	1	..	1
MADRAS	**41,405,404**	**20,382,955**	**21,022,449**
A.—Born in India	**41,391,070**	**20,373,334**	**21,017,736**
Provinces	*41,168,789*	*20,266,874*	*20,901,915*
Ajmer-Merwara	120	78	42
Andamans and Nicobars	65	48	17
Assam	204	182	22
Baluchistan	126	116	10
Bengal	6,537	3,107	3,430
Bihar and Orissa	426	302	124
Bombay	16,952	10,741	6,211
Burma	1,991	977	1,014
Central Provinces and Berar	6,281	3,537	2,744
Coorg	737	463	274
Madras	41,132,296	20,245,089	20,887,207
N.-W. F. Province	79	54	25
Punjab	874	692	182
United Provinces	2,101	1,488	613
States and Agencies	*199,769*	*96,298*	*103,464*
Baroda State	318	258	60
Bihar and Orissa States	975	562	413
Bombay States	1,518	1,235	283
Central India Agency	503	310	193
Central Provinces States	915	526	389
Hyderabad State	60,412	29,215	31,197
Kashmir State	28	26	2
Madras States	41,106	18,375	22,731
Cochin	*9,641*	*4,805*	*4,836*
Travancore	*10,417*	*6,156*	*4,261*
Mysore State	92,503	44,661	47,842
Rajputana Agency	1,484	1,130	354
India, Unspecified	*381*	*104*	*277*
French and Portuguese Settlements	*22,138*	*10,058*	*12,080*
MADRAS—*contd.*			
B.—Born in other Asiatic Countries	**5,202**	**3,149**	**2,053**
Afghanistan	118	83	35
Arabia	274	253	21
Bhotan	17	17	..
Ceylon	3,586	2,021	1,565
China	148	123	25
Chinese Turkistan	5	2	3
French Indo-China	14	9	5
Hong Kong	7	5	2
Japan	28	19	9
Maldives	4	3	1
Nepal	17	14	3
Persia	177	144	33
Russian Turkistan	3	2	1
Siam	13	8	5
Straits Settlements and Malaya	764	427	337
Turkey in Asia	21	16	5
Asia, *Unspecified*	6	3	3
C.—Born in Europe	**7,891**	**5,761**	**2,130**
United Kingdom	6,488	4,901	1,587
England and Wales	*5,461*	*4,256*	*1,205*
Scotland	*533*	*387*	*146*
Ireland	*488*	*253*	*235*
Channel Islands and Isle of Man.	*6*	*5*	*1*
Austria-Hungary	38	22	16
Belgium	48	18	30
Denmark	39	14	25
France	503	239	264
Germany	402	314	88
Gibraltar	2	1	1
Greece	3	3	..
Holland	96	74	22
Italy	80	43	37
Norway	18	15	3
Portugal	72	61	11
Russia	13	8	5
Spain	3	..	3
Sweden	27	14	13
Switzerland	56	31	25
Turkey in Europe	2	2	..
Europe, *Unspecified*	1	1	..
D.—Born in Africa	**886**	**503**	**383**
Cape Colony	5	1	4
Mauritius	193	117	76
Natal	427	215	212
St. Helena	1	..	1
Sudan	1	1	..
Africa, *Unspecified*	259	169	90
E.—Born in America	**255**	**151**	**104**
Brazil	2	2	..
Canada	41	32	9
United States	36	28	8
West Indies	4	3	1
America, *Unspecified*	172	86	86
F.—Born in Australasia	**97**	**55**	**42**
Australia	58	32	26
Borneo	11	9	2
Java	12	8	4
New Zealand	15	6	9
Tasmania	1	..	1
G.—Born at Sea	**3**	**2**	**1**
N.-W. F. PROVINCE	**2,196,933**	**1,182,102**	**1,014,831**
A.—Born in India	**2,144,871**	**1,147,639**	**997,232**
Provinces	*2,082,239*	*1,107,943*	*974,296*
Ajmer-Merwara	16	11	5
Andamans and Nicobars	11	4	7
Assam	10	10	..
Baluchistan	200	158	42
Bengal	272	149	123
Bihar and Orissa	22	15	7
Bombay	549	424	125
Burma	29	12	17
Central Provinces and Berar	85	51	34
Madras	63	32	31
N.-W. F. Province	2,012,429	1,056,975	956,454
Punjab	63,780	47,631	16,149
United Provinces	4,773	3,471	1,302

TABLE XI.—Birthplace. Part II.—Detailed

Birthplace.	Population. Persons.	Males.	Females.
1	2	3	4
N.-W. F. PROVINCE—*contd.*			
States and Agencies	*62,330*	*39,486*	*22,844*
Assam State	10	3	7
Baroda State	11	11	..
Bombay States	108	108	..
Central India Agency	90	71	19
Central Provinces States	1	1	..
Hyderabad State	94	62	32
Kashmir State	4,489	3,639	850
Madras States (*Travancore*)	2	1	1
Mysore State	41	28	13
N.-W. F. Province (*Agencies and Tribal areas*)	54,434	33,000	21,434
Punjab States	1,440	1,203	237
Rajputana Agency	1,475	1,265	210
United Provinces States	135	94	41
India, Unspecified	*200*	*112*	*88*
French and Portuguese Settlements	*102*	*98*	*4*
B.—Born in other Asiatic Countries	**47,166**	**30,040**	**17,126**
Afghanistan	42,163	25,892	16,271
Arabia	27	16	11
Asia Minor	1	1	..
Ceylon	16	9	7
China	7	4	3
Hong Kong	2	2	..
Nepal	4,911	4,093	818
Persia	5	5	..
Russia in Asia	19	11	8
Straits Settlements and Malaya	9	5	4
Tibet	1	1	..
Turkey in Asia	5	1	4
C.—Born in Europe	**4,820**	**4,373**	**447**
United Kingdom	4,765	4,333	432
England and Wales	*3,620*	*3,295*	*325*
Scotland	*182*	*149*	*33*
Ireland	*954*	*885*	*69*
Channel Islands and Isle of Man	*9*	*4*	*5*
Austria-Hungary	1	1	..
Cyprus	2	2	..
Denmark	1	..	1
France	10	7	3
Germany	8	6	2
Gibraltar	4	2	2
Italy	1	1	..
Malta	10	8	2
Portugal	1	1	..
Russia	2	1	1
Spain	8	6	2
Switzerland	3	2	1
Turkey in Europe	3	2	1
Europe, *Unspecified*	1	1	..
D.—Born in Africa	**22**	**11**	**11**
Cape Colony	2	1	1
Egypt	2	1	1
Natal	6	3	3
St. Helena	1	1	..
Africa, *Unspecified*	11	5	6
E.—Born in America	**23**	**18**	**5**
Bermudas	2	1	1
Canada	6	5	1
Cuba	1	1	..
Jamaica	2	2	..
Newfoundland	3	2	1
West Indies	2	1	1
America, *Unspecified*	7	6	1
F.—Born in Australasia	**28**	**20**	**8**
Australia	18	12	6
New Zealand	7	6	1
Tasmania	3	2	1
G.—Born at Sea	**3**	**1**	**2**
PUNJAB	**19,974,956**	**10,992,067**	**8,982,889**
A.—Born in India	**19,923,707**	**10,948,968**	**8,974,739**
Provinces	*19,291,881*	*10,680,646*	*8,611,935*
Ajmer-Merwara	1,317	734	583
Andamans and Nicobars	109	72	37
Assam	98	64	34
Baluchistan	3,570	2,309	1,261
PUNJAB—*contd.*			
Bengal	3,752	2,194	1,558
Bihar and Orissa	1,147	566	581
Bombay	6,282	3,919	2,363
Burma	1,412	810	602
Central Provinces and Berar	1,375	838	537
Madras	1,044	649	395
N.-W. F. Province	34,521	22,635	11,886
Punjab	19,036,839	10,544,507	8,492,332
United Provinces	200,415	101,349	99,066
States and Agencies	*630,613*	*267,841*	*362,772*
Assam State	30	24	6
Baluchistan States	30	27	3
Baroda State	178	107	71
Bengal States	28	22	6
Bihar and Orissa States	44	32	12
Bombay States	566	353	213
Central India Agency	3,127	1,684	1,443
Central Provinces States	3	1	2
Hyderabad State	566	306	260
Kashmir State	69,711	36,584	33,127
Madras States	27	26	1
Cochin	*2*	*2*	..
Travancore	*19*	*18*	*1*
Mysore State	259	150	109
N.-W. F. Province (*Agencies and Tribal areas*)	192	167	25
Punjab States	372,706	138,695	234,011
Rajputana Agency	182,187	89,075	93,112
Sikkim State	3	..	3
United Provinces States	956	588	368
India, Unspecified	*1,140*	*423*	*717*
French and Portuguese Settlements	*73*	*58*	*15*
B.—Born in other Asiatic Countries	**27,144**	**22,706**	**4,438**
Afghanistan	20,575	17,441	3,134
Arabia	195	144	51
Bhotan	20	13	7
Ceylon	30	18	12
China	384	221	163
Japan	12	2	10
Nepal	4,821	4,012	809
Persia	266	186	80
Russia in Asia	11	10	1
Russian Turkistan	17	16	1
Straits Settlements and Malaya	24	16	8
Tibet	761	601	160
Turkey in Asia	25	24	1
Asia, *Unspecified*	3	2	1
C.—Born in Europe	**23,620**	**20,124**	**3,496**
United Kingdom	23,045	19,762	3,283
England and Wales	*18,378*	*15,842*	*2,536*
Scotland	*1,766*	*1,500*	*266*
Ireland	*2,892*	*2,413*	*479*
United Kingdom, Unspecified	*9*	*7*	*2*
Austria-Hungary	17	4	13
Belgium	61	35	26
Denmark	3	2	1
France	49	27	22
Germany	68	43	25
Greece	8	6	2
Holland	12	11	1
Iceland	1	..	1
Italy	29	17	12
Malta	58	21	37
Norway	2	1	1
Portugal	141	129	12
Russia	11	3	8
Spain	23	4	19
Sweden	5	1	4
Switzerland	17	11	6
Turkey in Europe	4	3	1
Europe, *Unspecified*	66	44	22
D.—Born in Africa	**115**	**75**	**40**
Cape Colony	10	9	1
Congo	1	..	1
Egypt	10	9	1
Natal	1	..	1
Transvaal	5	3	2
Africa, *Unspecified*	88	54	34

Distribution of Population by Birthplace—*continued.*

Birthplace.	Population. Persons.	Males.	Females.
1	2	3	4
PUNJAB—*contd.*			
E.—Born in America	**266**	**126**	**140**
Bermudas	7	7	..
Brazil	3	3	..
Canada	34	18	16
Honduras	1	1	..
Mexico	1	..	1
Newfoundland	2	..	2
United States	14	2	12
West Indies	7	5	2
America, *Unspecified*	197	90	107
F.—Born in Australasia	**104**	**68**	**36**
Australia	66	40	26
Fiji Islands	2	1	1
Java	3	2	1
Melanesia	1	..	1
New Zealand	19	13	6
Polynesia	9	9	..
Sumatra	4	3	1
UNITED PROVINCES	**47,182,044**	**24,641,831**	**22,540,213**
A.—Born in India	**47,112,470**	**24,594,196**	**22,518,274**
Provinces	*46,736,314*	*24,443,398*	*22,292,916*
Ajmer-Merwara	2,415	1,336	1,079
Andamans and Nicobars	154	78	76
Assam	994	543	451
Baluchistan	566	428	138
Bengal	25,578	11,854	13,724
Bihar and Orissa	104,993	34,628	70,365
Bombay	8,776	5,198	3,578
Burma	722	403	319
Central Provinces and Berar	14,558	6,423	8,135
Coorg	1	1	..
Madras	2,254	1,294	960
N.-W. F. Province	1,895	1,575	320
Punjab	115,702	57,555	58,147
United Provinces	46,457,706	24,322,082	22,135,624
States and Agencies	*375,500*	*150,403*	*225,097*
Assam State	170	113	57
Baroda State	298	171	127
Bengal States	81	30	51
Bihar and Orissa States	68	48	20
Bombay States	506	309	197
Central India Agency	195,815	71,506	124,309
Central Provinces States	240	140	100
Hyderabad State	1,342	865	477
Kashmir State	1,937	1,480	457
Madras States	98	54	44
Cochin	*25*	*22*	*3*
Travancore	*41*	*26*	*15*
Mysore State	414	231	183
N.-W. F. Province (*Agencies and Tribal areas.*)	1	..	1
Punjab States	5,803	4,061	1,742
Rajputana Agency	102,929	43,991	58,938
Sikkim State	7	4	3
United Provinces States	65,791	27,400	38,391
India, Unspecified	*320*	*116*	*204*
French and Portuguese Settlements	*336*	*279*	*57*
B.—Born in other Asiatic Countries.	**46,020**	**27,850**	**18,170**
Afghanistan	1,571	1,407	164
Arabia	158	116	42
Bhotan	12	9	3
Ceylon	97	65	32
China	151	93	58
Chinese Turkistan	6	3	3
French Indo-China	3	3	..
Hong Kong	5	2	3
Japan	44	19	25
Nepal	43,320	25,722	17,598
Persia	43	25	18
Russian Turkistan	24	18	6
Siam	4	1	3
Straits Settlements and Malaya	2	2	..
Tibet	525	323	202
Turkey in Asia	34	30	4
Asia, *Unspecified*	21	12	9
C.—Born in Europe	**22,467**	**19,175**	**3,292**
United Kingdom	22,003	18,844	3,159
England and Wales	*14,609*	*12,372*	*2,237*
Scotland	*4,344*	*3,890*	*454*
Ireland	*1,779*	*1,430*	*349*
Channel Islands and Isle of Man	*17*	*11*	*6*
United Kingdom, Unspecified	*1,254*	*1,141*	*113*
UNITED PROVINCES—*contd.*			
Austria-Hungary	1	..	1
Belgium	18	10	8
Denmark	14	13	1
France	35	26	9
Germany	130	87	43
Gibraltar	18	16	2
Greece	9	9	..
Holland	7	6	1
Italy	125	98	27
Malta	31	22	9
Norway	5	2	3
Portugal	7	4	3
Rumania	1	..	1
Russia	26	20	6
Spain	11	9	2
Sweden	1	..	1
Switzerland	14	3	11
Turkey in Europe	6	4	2
Europe, *Unspecified*	5	2	3
D.—Born in Africa	**277**	**169**	**108**
British East Africa	4	1	3
Egypt	38	15	23
Mauritius	29	15	14
Natal	57	30	27
Seychelles	1	..	1
St. Helena	1	..	1
Transvaal	2	2	..
Africa, *Unspecified*	145	106	39
E.—Born in America	**635**	**330**	**305**
Canada	41	28	13
Jamaica	29	9	20
Newfoundland	2	1	1
United States	50	19	31
West Indies	305	152	153
America, *Unspecified*	208	121	87
F.—Born in Australasia	**154**	**97**	**57**
Australia	101	58	43
Fiji Islands	26	16	10
Java	15	15	..
New Zealand	8	6	2
Philippines	2	1	1
Tasmania	1	1	..
Australasia, *Unspecified*	1	..	1
G.—Born at Sea	**15**	**9**	**6**
H.—Birthplace Unspecified or not returned	**6**	**5**	**1**
ASSAM STATE (MANIPUR)	**346,222**	**170,666**	**175,556**
A.—Born in India	**345,041**	**169,887**	**175,154**
Provinces	*6,609*	*4,037*	*2,572*
Assam	4,777	2,584	2,193
Bengal	300	198	102
Bihar and Orissa	503	402	101
Bombay	12	9	3
Burma	48	26	22
Central Provinces and Berar	20	15	5
Madras	10	7	3
N.-W. F. Province	5	2	3
Punjab	447	432	15
United Provinces	487	362	125
States and Agencies	*338,432*	*165,850*	*172,582*
Assam State	338,227	165,661	172,566
Bombay States	7	7	..
Central India Agency	2	2	..
Kashmir State	1	1	..
Mysore State	1	1	..
Punjab States	75	74	1
Rajputana Agency	115	101	14
Sikkim State	3	3	..
United Provinces States	1	..	1
B.—Born in other Asiatic Countries	**1,168**	**771**	**397**
Afghanistan	5	2	3
Nepal	1,163	769	394
C.—Born in Europe	**13**	**8**	**5**
United Kingdom	12	8	4
England and Wales	*9*	*5*	*4*
Scotland	*1*	*1*	..
Ireland	*2*	*2*	..
Germany	1	..	1

TABLE XI.—BIRTHPLACE. PART II.—DETAILED

Birthplace.	Population. Persons.	Males.	Females.
1	2	3	4
BALUCHISTAN STATES	420,291	227,238	193,053
A.—Born in India	419,940	227,019	192,921
Provinces	*1,900*	*1,235*	*665*
Ajmer-Merwara	1	1	..
Baluchistan	997	572	425
Bengal	2	2	..
Bihar and Orissa	1	1	..
Bombay	412	318	94
Madras	1	1	..
N.-W. F. Province	20	16	4
Punjab	423	292	131
United Provinces	43	32	11
States and Agencies	*418,011*	*225,757*	*192,254*
Baluchistan States	417,866	225,647	192,219
Bombay States	80	67	13
Central India Agency	1	1	..
Hyderabad State	2	2	..
Kashmir State	16	8	8
Mysore State	1	1	..
Punjab States	5	4	1
Rajputana Agency	39	26	13
United Provinces States	1	1	..
India, Unspecified	*6*	*4*	*2*
French and Portuguese Settlements	*23*	*23*	..
B.—Born in other Asiatic Countries	334	204	130
Afghanistan	50	34	16
Arabia	230	129	101
China	1	1	..
Persia	40	27	13
Russian Turkistan	7	7	..
Straits Settlements and Malaya	6	6	..
C.—Born in Europe	12	10	2
United Kingdom	11	9	2
England and Wales	*9*	*7*	*2*
Scotland	*2*	*2*	..
Austria-Hungary	1	1	..
E.—Born in America (United States)	3	3	..
F.—Born in Australasia (Australia)	2	2	..
BARODA STATE.	2,032,798	1,055,935	976,863
A.—Born in India	2,032,268	1,055,631	976,637
Provinces	*140,189*	*55,939*	*84,250*
Ajmer-Merwara	179	106	73
Assam	6	2	4
Bengal	332	226	106
Bihar and Orissa	150	141	9
Bombay	134,062	51,241	82,821
Burma	63	48	15
Central Provinces and Berar	321	211	110
Madras	228	131	97
N.-W. F. Province	39	35	4
Punjab	910	703	207
United Provinces	3,899	3,095	804
States and Agencies	*1,891,453*	*999,335*	*892,118*
Baluchistan States	41	31	10
Baroda State	1,809,841	965,918	843,923
Bombay States	73,686	28,537	45,149
Central India Agency	1,413	822	591
Hyderabad State	164	106	58
Kashmir State	18	14	4
Mysore State	32	13	19
Punjab States	11	11	..
Rajputana Agency	6,239	3,877	2,362
United Provinces States	8	6	2
India, Unspecified	*67*	*66*	*1*
French and Portuguese Settlements	*559*	*291*	*268*
B.—Born in other Asiatic Countries	191	144	47
Afghanistan	87	71	16
Arabia	37	27	10
Bhotan	3	2	1
Chinese Tartary	2	2	..
Nepal	49	29	20
Persia	13	13	..
BARODA STATE—*contd.*			
C.—Born in Europe	70	44	26
United Kingdom	55	35	20
England and Wales	*48*	*30*	*18*
Scotland	*2*	*2*	..
Ireland	*5*	*3*	*2*
Austria-Hungary	1	..	1
France	6	3	3
Germany	1	1	..
Italy	1	1	..
Malta	1	..	1
Portugal	2	2	..
Spain	1	1	..
Switzerland	2	1	1
D.—Born in Africa	257	110	147
Mauritius	54	19	35
Zanzibar	5	2	3
Africa, *Unspecified*	198	89	109
E.—Born in America (United States)	12	6	6
BENGAL STATES	822,565	438,368	384,197
A.—Born in India	821,857	437,729	384,128
Provinces	*134,905*	*85,396*	*49,509*
Ajmer-Merwara	3	3	..
Assam	30,799	16,787	14,012
Bengal	78,496	48,032	30,464
Bihar and Orissa	18,420	15,904	2,516
Bombay	26	25	1
Burma	4	4	..
Central Provinces and Berar	1,362	784	578
Madras	1,070	556	514
N.-W. F. Province	23	23	..
Punjab	82	63	19
United Provinces	4,620	3,215	1,405
States and Agencies	*686,929*	*352,310*	*334,619*
Assam State	86	55	31
Bengal States	685,760	351,314	334,446
Bihar and Orissa States	8	6	2
Bombay States	103	56	47
Central India Agency	38	27	11
Mysore State	1	..	1
Rajputana Agency	915	844	71
United Provinces States	18	8	10
French and Portuguese Settlements	*23*	*23*	..
B.—Born in other Asiatic Countries	692	628	64
Afghanistan	86	86	..
Arabia	3	3	..
Bhotan	3	3	..
Ceylon	1	1	..
China	2	..	2
Nepal	595	533	62
Persia	1	1	..
Straits Settlements and Malaya	1	1	..
C.—Born in Europe	13	9	4
United Kingdom	7	5	2
England and Wales	*6*	*4*	*2*
Scotland	*1*	*1*	..
Greece	4	2	2
Norway	1	1	..
Turkey in Europe	1	1	..
E.—Born in America (United States)	1	1	..
F.—Born in Australasia (Australia)	2	1	1
BIHAR AND ORISSA STATES.	3,945,209	1,955,125	1,990,084
A.—Born in India	3,945,076	1,955,019	1,990,057
Provinces	*308,973*	*146,414*	*162,559*
Ajmer-Merwara	2	2	..
Assam	7	5	2
Baluchistan	4	4	..
Bengal	11,982	6,255	5,727

DISTRIBUTION OF POPULATION BY BIRTHPLACE—*continued.*

BIRTHPLACE.	POPULATION.		
	Persons.	Males.	Females.
1	2	3	4
BIHAR AND ORISSA STATES—*contd.*			
Bihar and Orissa	256,708	119,409	137,299
Bombay	319	259	60
Burma	18	2	16
Central Provinces and Berar	18,712	9,306	9,406
Madras	18,694	9,385	9,309
N.-W. F. Province	30	29	1
Punjab	797	554	243
United Provinces	1,700	1,204	496
States and Agencies	*3,636,109*	*1,808,605*	*1,827,497*
Baroda State	9	9	..
Bengal States	2	2	..
Bihar and Orissa States	3,627,269	1,803,935	1,823,334
Bombay States	380	284	96
Central India Agency	532	303	229
Central Provinces States	6,298	3,114	3,184
Hyderabad State	11	8	3
Kashmir State	2	1	1
Mysore State	14	9	5
Punjab States	45	38	7
Rajputana Agency	1,538	900	638
United Provinces States	2	2	..
French and Portuguese Settlements	*1*	..	*1*
B.—Born in other Asiatic Countries	**107**	**93**	**14**
Afghanistan	57	54	3
Ceylon	2	1	1
China	2	2	..
Nepal	10	10	..
Persia	29	19	10
Tibet	1	1	..
Asia, *Unspecified*	6	6	..
C.—Born in Europe	**25**	**13**	**12**
United Kingdom	12	8	4
England and Wales	*7*	*5*	*2*
Scotland	*3*	*2*	*1*
Ireland	*2*	*1*	*1*
Belgium	4	2	2
Germany	8	3	5
Italy	1	..	1
D.—Born in Africa (Cape Colony).	**1**	..	**1**
BOMBAY STATES	**7,411,675**	**3,765,401**	**3,646,274**
A.—Born in India	**7,408,872**	**3,763,134**	**3,645,738**
Provinces	*425,492*	*167,565*	*257,927*
Ajmer-Merwara	11,392	6,611	4,781
Andamans and Nicobars	7	2	5
Baluchistan	511	408	103
Bengal	495	359	136
Bihar and Orissa	368	213	155
Bombay	401,520	152,099	249,421
Burma	111	62	49
Central Provinces and Berar	1,645	845	800
Coorg	3	2	1
Madras	1,853	974	879
N.-W. F. Province	260	205	55
Punjab	2,563	2,097	466
United Provinces	4,764	3,688	1,076
States and Agencies	*6,975,155*	*3,592,039*	*3,383,116*
Assam State	1	1	..
Baluchistan States	2	2	..
Baroda State	85,646	31,005	54,641
Bengal States	2	2	..
Bihar and Orissa States	12	9	3
Bombay States	6,852,946	3,542,899	3,310,047
Central India Agency	4,111	2,803	1,308
Central Provinces States	4	4	..
Hyderabad State	8,762	3,763	4,999
Kashmir State	29	25	4
Madras States	61	44	17
Cochin	*10*	*8*	*2*
Travancore	*51*	*36*	*15*
Mysore State	431	220	211
Punjab States	86	41	45
Rajputana Agency	23,062	11,221	11,841
India, unspecified	*2,353*	*1,283*	*1,070*
French and Portuguese Settlements	*5,872*	*2,247*	*3,625*

BIRTHPLACE.	POPULATION.		
	Persons.	Males.	Females.
1	2	3	4
BOMBAY STATES—*contd.*			
B.—Born in other Asiatic Countries.	**1,758**	**1,577**	**181**
Afghanistan	787	758	29
Arabia	676	576	100
Bhotan	1	1	..
Ceylon	12	9	3
China	2	2	..
French Indo-China	6	6	..
Japan	1	1	..
Nepal	210	164	46
Persia	16	14	2
Siam	40	40	..
Straits Settlements and Malaya	1	1	..
Turkey in Asia	6	5	1
C.—Born in Europe	**537**	**402**	**135**
United Kingdom	229	150	79
England and Wales	*182*	*120*	*62*
Scotland	*27*	*19*	*8*
Ireland	*20*	*11*	*9*
Austria-Hungary	2	2	..
Belgium	13	9	4
Denmark	1	1	..
France	1	..	1
Germany	3	2	1
Greece	1	1	..
Holland	1	1	..
Italy	9	9	..
Malta	1	1	..
Portugal	276	226	50
D.—Born in Africa	**460**	**259**	**201**
British East Africa	7	4	3
Mauritius	11	3	8
Natal	4	4	..
Zanzibar	84	42	42
Africa, *Unspecified*	354	206	148
E.—Born in America (America, *Unspecified*)	**24**	**11**	**13**
F.—Born in Australasia	**24**	**18**	**6**
Australia	10	6	4
Java	12	12	..
New Zealand	2	..	2
CENTRAL INDIA AGENCY	**9,356,980**	**4,801,459**	**4,555,521**
A.—Born in India	**9,353,116**	**4,798,154**	**4,554,962**
Provinces	*312,730*	*137,253*	*175,477*
Ajmer-Merwara	5,226	3,585	1,641
Assam	8	6	2
Baluchistan	20	18	2
Bengal	1,004	649	355
Bihar and Orissa	1,047	503	544
Bombay	47,165	26,940	20,225
Burma	13	7	6
Central Provinces and Berar	80,057	31,244	48,813
Madras	1,033	635	398
N.-W. F. Province	563	419	144
Punjab	7,859	5,118	2,741
United Provinces	168,735	68,129	100,606
States and Agencies	*9,040,194*	*4,660,768*	*4,379,426*
Baluchistan States	10	7	3
Baroda State	2,482	1,426	1,056
Bihar and Orissa States	68	15	53
Bombay States	6,946	3,644	3,302
Central India Agency	8,882,725	4,586,467	4,296,258
Central Provinces States	4	4	..
Hyderabad State	2,177	1,437	740
Kashmir State	70	65	5
Madras States (*Travancore*)	2	..	2
Mysore State	491	233	258
Punjab States	423	300	123
Rajputana Agency	144,401	66,978	77,423
United Provinces States	395	192	203
French and Portuguese Settlements	*192*	*133*	*59*
B.—Born in other Asiatic Countries	**355**	**248**	**107**
Afghanistan	178	144	34
Arabia	53	23	30
Ceylon	3	..	3

TABLE XI.—Birthplace. Part II.—Detailed

Birthplace.	Population. Persons.	Males.	Females.
1	2	3	4
CENTRAL INDIA AGENCY—*contd.*			
Japan	4	2	2
Nepal	88	58	30
Persia	11	5	6
Turkey in Asia	18	16	2
C.—Born in Europe	**3,283**	**2,916**	**367**
United Kingdom	3,192	2,841	351
England and Wales	*2,731*	*2,441*	*290*
Scotland	*99*	*80*	*19*
Ireland	*362*	*320*	*42*
France	24	20	4
Germany	16	13	3
Italy	2	1	1
Portugal	48	40	8
Russia	1	1	..
D.—Born in Africa	**129**	**101**	**28**
Egypt	127	99	28
Africa, *Unspecified*	2	2	..
E.—Born in America	**89**	**32**	**57**
Canada	74	25	49
United States	1	..	1
America, *Unspecified*	14	7	7
F.—Born in Australasia (Australasia, *Unspecified*).	**8**	**8**	..
CENTRAL PROVINCES STATES	**2,117,002**	**1,053,630**	**1,063,372**
A.—Born in India	**2,116,857**	**1,053,530**	**1,063,327**
Provinces	***194,348***	***88,469***	***105,879***
Ajmer-Merwara	29	17	12
Assam	5	5	..
Bengal	2,252	1,384	868
Bihar and Orissa	29,291	14,960	14,331
Bombay	361	216	145
Burma	7	4	3
Central Provinces and Berar	143,916	61,215	82,701
Coorg	3	3	..
Madras	4,862	2,413	2,449
N.-W. F. Province	80	62	18
Punjab	849	536	313
United Provinces	12,693	7,654	5,039
States and Agencies	***1,922,488***	***965,046***	***957,442***
Baroda State	34	21	13
Bengal States	4	2	2
Bihar and Orissa States	633	358	275
Bombay States	349	294	55
Central India Agency	20,843	11,042	9,801
Central Provinces States	1,894,687	949,970	944,717
Hyderabad State	1,953	1,136	817
Kashmir State	2	2	..
Madras States (*Travancore*)	3	..	3
Mysore State	32	17	15
Punjab States	396	248	148
Rajputana Agency	3,530	1,946	1,584
United Provinces States	22	10	12
French and Portuguese Settlements	***21***	***15***	***6***
B.—Born in other Asiatic Countries	**102**	**70**	**32**
Afghanistan	60	57	3
Arabia	4	2	2
Ceylon	2	2	..
Nepal	35	9	26
Straits Settlements and Malaya	1	..	1
C.—Born in Europe	**32**	**25**	**7**
United Kingdom	31	24	7
England and Wales	*25*	*19*	*6*
Scotland	*5*	*5*	..
Ireland	*1*	..	*1*
Holland	1	1	..
D.—Born in Africa (Africa, *Unspecified*)	**4**	**3**	**1**
E.—Born in America (America, *Unspecified*)	**5**	..	**5**
F.—Born in Australasia (Australia)	**1**	**1**	..
G.—Born at Sea	**1**	**1**	..
COCHIN STATE	**918,110**	**457,342**	**460,768**
A.—Born in India	**918,034**	**457,281**	**460,753**
Provinces	***31,064***	***15,366***	***15,698***
Bengal	22	14	8
Bihar and Orissa	25	23	2
Bombay	464	339	125
Central Provinces and Berar	12	7	5
Coorg	1	..	1
Madras	30,485	14,941	15,544
N.-W. F. Province	1	1	..
Punjab	3	3	..
United Provinces	51	38	13
States and Agencies	***886,853***	***441,810***	***445,043***
Bombay States	611	385	226
Central India Agency	38	30	8
Cochin State	870,844	434,379	436,465
Hyderabad State	27	16	11
Madras States*	3	..	3
Mysore State	108	73	35
Rajputana Agency	15	5	10
Travancore State	15,207	6,922	8,285
India, Unspecified	***30***	***24***	***6***
French and Portuguese Settlements	***87***	***81***	***6***
B.—Born in other Asiatic Countries	**22**	**17**	**5**
Ceylon	13	11	2
Persia	2	2	..
Straits Settlements and Malaya	4	1	3
Turkey in Asia	3	3	..
C.—Born in Europe	**50**	**42**	**8**
United Kingdom	20	14	6
England and Wales	*18*	*12*	*6*
Scotland	*2*	*2*	..
Belgium	1	1	..
France	2	2	..
Germany	4	2	2
Spain	23	23	..
E.—Born in America (West Indies)	**3**	**2**	**1**
F.—Born in Australasia (New Zealand)	**1**	..	**1**
HYDERABAD STATE	**13,374,676**	**6,797,118**	**6,577,558**
A.—Born in India	**13,367,080**	**6,790,681**	**6,576,399**
Provinces	***229,385***	***109,537***	***119,848***
Ajmer-Merwara	6,698	4,188	2,510
Assam	5	4	1
Baluchistan	110	100	10
Bengal	717	534	183
Bihar and Orissa	17	13	4
Bombay	118,653	50,702	67,951
Burma	185	72	113
Central Provinces and Berar	20,945	8,956	11,989
Coorg	1	...	1
Madras	67,821	34,700	33,121
N.-W. F. Province	364	317	47
Punjab	4,470	3,324	1,146
United Provinces	9,399	6,627	2,772
States and Agencies	***13,133,732***	***6,678,394***	***6,455,338***
Baluchistan States	71	71	..
Baroda State	204	106	98
Bombay States	177	170	7
Central India Agency	565	264	301
Central Provinces States	2	1	1
Hyderabad State	13,113,963	6,665,244	6,448,719
Kashmir State	83	64	19
Madras States	16	7	9
Cochin	*10*	*5*	*5*
Travancore	*6*	*2*	*4*
Mysore State	3,880	2,547	1,333
Punjab States	399	233	166
Rajputana Agency	14,271	9,612	4,659
United Provinces States	101	75	26
India, Unspecified	***3,675***	***2,566***	***1,109***
French and Portuguese Settlements	***288***	***184***	***104***

* Excluding Cochin and Travancore.

DISTRIBUTION OF POPULATION BY BIRTHPLACE—*continued.*

Birthplace.	Population. Persons.	Males.	Females.
1	2	3	4
HYDERABAD STATE—*contd.*			
B.—Born in other Asiatic Countries	**3,507**	**2,882**	**625**
Afghanistan	468	367	101
Arabia	2,864	2,394	470
Bhotan	12	12	..
Ceylon	20	9	11
Hong Kong	1	1	..
Japan	3	..	3
Nepal	19	12	7
Persia	90	59	31
Straits Settlements and Malaya	29	27	2
Turkey in Asia	1	1	..
C.—Born in Europe	**3,936**	**3,444**	**492**
United Kingdom	3,790	3,359	431
England and Wales	*3,615*	*3,238*	*377*
Scotland	*72*	*53*	*19*
Ireland	*103*	*68*	*35*
Austria-Hungary	5	1	4
Belgium	1	1	..
France	12	6	6
Germany	3	2	1
Gibraltar	1	..	1
Italy	66	42	24
Malta	1	..	1
Rumania	1	1	..
Russia	11	6	5
Spain	3	2	1
Switzerland	1	1	..
Turkey in Europe	13	13	..
Europe, *Unspecified*	28	10	18
D.—Born in Africa	**98**	**87**	**11**
Egypt	8	8	..
Mauritius	1	..	1
Africa, *Unspecified*	89	79	10
E.—Born in America	**40**	**13**	**27**
Canada	1	..	1
Jamaica	3	..	3
Newfoundland	1	1	
United States	1	..	1
America, *Unspecified*	34	12	22
F.—Born in Australasia	**11**	**9**	**2**
Australia	4	3	1
Java	4	4	..
New Zealand	2	1	1
Tasmania	1	1	..
G.—Born at Sea	**4**	**2**	**2**
KASHMIR STATE	**3,158,126**	**1,674,367**	**1,483,759**
A.—Born in India	**3,101,113**	**1,642,978**	**1,458,135**
Provinces	*71,105*	*34,516*	*36,589*
Ajmer-Merwara	27	23	4
Andamans and Nicobars	7	2	5
Baluchistan	20	17	3
Bengal	131	83	48
Bihar and Orissa	79	58	21
Bombay	166	121	45
Central Provinces and Berar	11	8	3
Madras	27	23	4
N.-W. F. Province	11,168	6,220	4,948
Punjab	58,500	27,191	31,309
United Provinces	974	770	204
States and Agencies	*3,030,000*	*1,608,454*	*1,421,546*
Baroda State	4	3	1
Bombay States	18	18	..
Central India Agency	35	28	7
Hyderabad State	11	8	3
Kashmir State	3,026,716	1,606,428	1,420,288
Mysore State	10	3	7
N.-W. F. Province (*Agencies and Tribal areas*)	1,741	973	768
Punjab States	1,207	829	378
Rajputana Agency	250	156	94
United Provinces States	8	8	..
French and Portuguese Settlements	*8*	*8*	..
KASHMIR STATE—*contd.*			
B.—Born in other Asiatic Countries.	**2,233**	**1,860**	**373**
Afghanistan	943	806	137
Arabia	1	1	..
Bhotan	2	2	..
China	2	1	1
Chinese Tartary	28	22	6
Nepal	1,077	926	151
Persia	29	26	3
Russia in Asia	1	1	..
Tibet	149	74	75
Turkey in Asia	1	1	..
C.—Born in Europe	**126**	**76**	**50**
United Kingdom	109	69	40
England and Wales	*90*	*58*	*32*
Scotland	*10*	*6*	*4*
Ireland	*9*	*5*	*4*
Denmark	1	..	1
France	3	3	..
Germany	6	1	5
Holland	2	2	..
Sweden	1	1	..
Switzerland	4	..	4
D.—Born in Africa (Africa, *Unspecified*)	**6**	**2**	**4**
E.—Born in America (America, *Unspecified*)	**10**	**6**	**4**
F.—Born in Australasia (Australia)	**1**	**1**	..
H.—Birthplace Unspecified or not returned	**202**	**166**	**36**
Not enumerated by Birthplace	**54,435**	**29,278**	**25,157**
MADRAS STATES *	**464,756**	**2**	**241,703**
A.—Born in India	**463,943**	**222,625**	**241,318**
Provinces	*47,148*	*16,944*	*30,204*
Bengal	10	6	4
Bombay	352	168	184
Burma	30	13	17
Central Provinces and Berar	10	7	3
Coorg	4	1	3
Madras	46,734	16,741	29,993
N.-W. F. Province	3	3	..
Punjab	1	1	..
United Provinces	4	4	..
States and Agencies	*416,754*	*205,669*	*211,085*
Baroda State	2	2	..
Cochin State	2	..	2
Hyderabad State	280	130	150
Madras States †	416,205	205,411	210,794
Mysore State	229	106	123
Rajputana Agency	7	7	..
Travancore State	29	13	16
India, Unspecified	*5*	*2*	*3*
French and Portuguese Settlements	*36*	*10*	*26*
B.—Born in other Asiatic Countries	**788**	**416**	**372**
Arabia	2	2	..
Ceylon	756	396	360
Japan	2	2	..
Nepal	1	1	..
Straits Settlements and Malaya	27	15	12

* Excluding Cochin and Travancore for which details are given on pages 136 and 140.
† *Vide* footnote on page 136.

Birthplace.	Population. Persons.	Males.	Females.
1	2	3	4
MADRAS STATES—*contd.*			
C.—Born in Europe	**18**	**9**	**9**
United Kingdom	9	7	2
England and Wales	*7*	*6*	*1*
Scotland	*1*	..	*1*
Ireland	*1*	*1*	..
Belgium	3	..	3
France	1	1	..
Germany	1	..	1
Holland	1	1	..
Sweden	3	..	3
D.—Born in Africa	**7**	**3**	**4**
Mauritius	5	2	3
Africa, *Unspecified*	2	1	1
MYSORE STATE	**5,806,193**	**2,934,621**	**2,871,572**
A.—Born in India	**5,801,487**	**2,930,862**	**2,870,625**
Provinces	*300,032*	*166,152*	*133,880*
Ajmer-Merwara	37	34	3
Andamans and Nicobars	14	10	4
Assam	13	10	3
Baluchistan	8	5	3
Bengal	412	243	169
Bihar and Orissa	59	40	19
Bombay	28,762	15,513	13,249
Burma	273	137	136
Central Provinces and Berar	1,183	667	516
Coorg	3,071	1,363	1,708
Madras	263,362	145,737	117,625
N.-W. F. Province	288	275	13
Punjab	1,644	1,426	218
United Provinces	906	692	214
States and Agencies	*5,500,658*	*2,764,243*	*2,736,415*
Baluchistan States	3	3	..
Baroda State	46	22	24
Bengal States	1	1	..
Bombay States	1,009	645	364
Central India Agency	85	41	44
Hyderabad State	4,342	2,456	1,886
Kashmir State	42	22	20
Madras States	443	273	170
Cochin	*206*	*129*	*77*
Travancore	*182*	*115*	*67*
Mysore State	5,493,285	2,759,662	2,733,623
Punjab States	18	11	7
Rajputana Agency	1,378	1,102	276
Sikkim State	1	1	..
United Provinces States	5	4	1
India, Unspecified	*59*	*11*	*48*
French and Portuguese Settlements	*738*	*456*	*282*
B.—Born in other Asiatic Countries	**283**	**162**	**121**
Afghanistan	24	22	2
Arabia	23	11	12
Armenia	2	..	2
Ceylon	140	72	68
China	18	16	2
Chinese Turkistan	1	1	..
Hong Kong	6	4	2
Japan	4	1	3
Nepal	9	7	2
Persia	5	4	1
Russia in Asia	1	..	1
Siam	1	..	1
Straits Settlements and Malaya	48	23	25
Asia, *Unspecified*	1	1	..
C.—Born in Europe	**4,263**	**3,498**	**765**
United Kingdom	3,939	3,289	650
England and Wales	*2,642*	*2,121*	*521*
Scotland	*1,051*	*997*	*54*
Ireland	*242*	*167*	*75*
Channel Islands and Isle of Man	*3*	*3*	..
United Kingdom, Unspecified	*1*	*1*	..
MYSORE STATE—*contd.*			
Austria-Hungary	2	2	.
Cyprus	1	..	1
Denmark	5	2	3
France	90	52	38
Germany	52	14	38
Gibraltar	8	3	5
Greece	1	1	..
Holland	4	3	1
Iceland	1	1	..
Italy	127	118	9
Malta	4	2	2
Portugal	2	1	1
Rumania	1	..	1
Russia	9	4	5
Spain	2	1	1
Switzerland	1	1	..
Turkey in Europe	8	3	5
Europe, *Unspecified*	6	1	5
D.—Born in Africa	**46**	**34**	**12**
Egypt	2	2	..
Mauritius	1	1	..
Natal	7	6	1
St. Helena	3	2	1
Transvaal	1	1	..
Africa, *Unspecified*	32	22	10
E.—Born in America	**76**	**42**	**34**
Bermudas	1	..	1
Canada	6	4	2
Chile	1	..	1
United States	25	14	11
America, *Unspecified*	43	24	19
F.—Born in Australasia	**34**	**20**	**14**
Australia	29	17	12
New Zealand	5	3	2
G.—Born at Sea	**4**	**3**	**1**
N.-W.F. PROVINCE (*Agencies and Tribal areas.*)	**1,622,094**	**864,876**	**757,218**
A.—Born in India	**12,394**	**11,512**	**882**
Provinces	*6,136*	*5,820*	*316*
Assam	1	1	..
Baluchistan	69	68	1
Bengal	12	6	6
Bihar and Orissa	2	2	..
Bombay	9	9	..
Central Provinces and Berar	1	1	..
Madras	9	9	..
N.-W. F. Province	2,531	2,448	83
Punjab	3,352	3,143	209
United Provinces	150	133	17
States and Agencies	*6,247*	*5,681*	*566*
Central India Agency	1	1	..
Kashmir State	166	165	1
Mysore State	4	4	..
N.-W. F. Province (*Agencies and Tribal areas*)	5,732	5,168	564
Punjab States	321	320	1
Rajputana Agency	17	17	..
United Provinces States	6	6	..
India, Unspecified	*11*	*11*	..
B.—Born in other Asiatic Countries	**1,068**	**1,067**	**1**
Afghanistan	317	317	..
Arabia	4	4	..
Bhotan	1	1	..
China	1	1	..
Nepal	742	741	1
Straits Settlements and Malaya	1	1	..
Tibet	2	2	..
C.—Born in Europe	**71**	**57**	**14**
United Kingdom	71	57	14
England and Wales	*52*	*44*	*8*
Scotland	*10*	*7*	*3*
Ireland	*8*	*5*	*3*
Channel Islands and Isle of Man	*1*	*1*	..

DISTRIBUTION OF POPULATION BY BIRTHPLACE—*continued.*

Birthplace.	Population.		
	Persons.	Males.	Females.
1	2	3	4
N.-W. F. PROVINCE (*Agencies and Tribal areas.*)—*contd.*			
D.—Born in Africa	2	2	..
Cape Colony	1	1	..
Africa, *Unspecified*	1	1	..
E.—Born in America	3	3	..
Canada	2	2	..
Honduras	1	1	..
Not enumerated by Birthplace.	1,608,556	852,235	756,321
PUNJAB STATES	4,212,794	2,322,906	1,889,886
A.—Born in India	4,209,776	2,320,525	1,889,251
Provinces	*422,210*	*176,977*	*245,233*
Ajmer-Merwara	226	84	142
Assam	23	12	11
Baluchistan	92	50	42
Bengal	235	140	95
Bihar and Orissa	254	218	36
Bombay	3,590	2,100	1,490
Burma	138	77	61
Central Provinces and Berar	122	80	42
Madras	39	26	13
N.-W. F. Province	539	368	171
Punjab	398,977	163,507	235,470
United Provinces	17,975	10,315	7,660
States and Agencies	*3,787,524*	*2,143,521*	*1,644,003*
Assam State	1	1	..
Baluchistan States	12	9	3
Baroda State	47	35	12
Bengal States	4	3	1
Bombay States	145	112	33
Central India Agency	503	273	230
Hyderabad State	123	70	53
Kashmir State	2,658	1,636	1,022
Mysore State	14	9	5
N.-W. F. Province (*Agencies and Tribal areas*)	19	16	3
Punjab States	3,719,009	2,116,227	1,602,782
Rajputana Agency	64,422	24.815	39,607
United Provinces States	567	315	252
India, Unspecified	*15*	*10*	*5*
French and Portuguese Settlements.	*27*	*17*	*10*
B.—Born in other Asiatic Countries.	2,721	2,176	545
Afghanistan	664	585	79
Arabia	46	44	2
Ceylon	4	3	1
China	211	118	93
Nepal	609	466	148
Persia	13	12	1
Russia in Asia	4	4	..
Russian Turkistan	1	1	..
Straits Settlements and Malaya	3	3	..
Tibet	1,166	940	226
C.—Born in Europe	286	202	84
United Kingdom	266	192	74
England and Wales	*218*	*163*	*55*
Scotland	*24*	*13*	*11*
Ireland	*23*	*15*	*8*
United Kingdom, Unspecified.	*1*	*1*	..
Austria-Hungary	2	1	1
France	2	1	1
Germany	8	4	4
Gibraltar	1	..	1
Malta	2	1	1
Spain	1	..	1
Sweden	1	..	1
Turkey in Europe	2	2	..
Europe, *Unspecified*	1	1	..
D.—Born in Africa	7	3	4
Cape Colony	1	1	..
Egypt	2	1	1
Africa, *Unspecified*	4	1	3
E.—Born in America (West Indies.)	1	..	1
F.—Born in Australasia	3	2	1
Australia	2	2	..
Fiji Islands	1	..	1

Birthplace.	Population.		
	Persons.	Males.	Females.
1	2	3	4
RAJPUTANA AGENCY	10,530,432	5,515,275	5,015,157
A.—Born in India	10,529,368	5,514,546	5,014,822
Provinces	*170,396*	*65,191*	*105,205*
Ajmer-Merwara	27,543	9,941	17,602
Assam	102	40	62
Baluchistan	119	75	44
Bengal	736	376	360
Bihar and Orissa	398	268	130
Bombay	6,624	3,279	3,345
Burma	32	14	18
Central Provinces and Berar	936	500	436
Madras	283	153	130
N.-W. F. Province	504	413	91
Punjab	63,655	24,590	39,065
United Provinces	69,464	25,542	43,922
States and Agencies	*10,358,797*	*5,449,225*	*4,909,572*
Assam State	3	1	2
Baluchistan States	91	65	26
Baroda State	1,601	888	713
Bengal States	1	1	..
Bombay States	7,934	3,193	4,741
Central India Agency	99,329	38,291	61,038
Hyderabad State	321	172	149
Kashmir State	90	67	23
Madras States	7	4	3
Mysore State	67	28	39
N.-W. F. Province (*Agencies and Tribal areas*)	3	3	..
Punjab States	21,871	7,457	14,414
Rajputana Agency	10,226,879	5,398,594	4,828,285
United Provinces States	600	461	139
India, Unspecified	*5*	..	*5*
French and Portuguese Settlements.	*170*	*130*	*40*
B.—Born in other Asiatic Countries.	466	336	130
Afghanistan	243	214	29
Arabia	36	28	8
Bokhara	7	7	..
Ceylon	15	9	6
China	8	4	4
Japan	1	1	..
Nepal	140	63	77
Persia	7	6	1
Straits Settlements and Malaya	2	2	..
Tibet	6	2	4
Turkey in Asia	1	..	1
C.—Born in Europe	561	371	190
United Kingdom	521	342	179
England and Wales	*367*	*252*	*115*
Scotland	*112*	*65*	*47*
Ireland	*41*	*25*	*16*
Channel Islands and Isle of Man	*1*	..	*1*
Belgium	2	2	..
Bulgaria	1	1	..
Denmark	1	..	1
France	20	17	3
Germany	8	4	4
Greece	1	1	..
Italy	4	2	2
Russia	1	1	..
Spain	1	1	..
Switzerland	1	..	1
D.—Born in Africa	16	10	6
Mauritius	7	4	3
Transvaal	2	..	2
Africa, *Unspecified*	7	6	1
E.—Born in America	16	10	6
Argentine Republic	1	..	1
California	1	..	1
Canada	1	1	..
United States	7	5	2
America, *Unspecified*	6	4	2
F.—Born in Australasia	4	2	2
Australia	3	1	2
Sumatra	1	1	..
G.—Born at Sea	1	..	1

TABLE XI.—BIRTHPLACE. PART II.—DETAILED DISTRIBUTION OF POPULATION BY BIRTHPLACE—*concluded.*

Birthplace.	Population.		
	Persons.	Males.	Females.
1	2	3	4
SIKKIM STATE	**87,920**	**45,059**	**42,861**
A.—Born in India	**61,893**	**30,890**	**31,003**
Provinces	*3,717*	*2,221*	*1,496*
Ajmer-Merwara	2	2	..
Bengal	3,052	1,592	1,460
Bihar and Orissa	189	176	13
Bombay	228	228	..
Burma	10	6	4
Punjab	138	126	12
United Provinces	98	91	7
States and Agencies	*58,176*	*28,669*	*29,507*
Assam State	1	..	1
Baluchistan States	1	..	1
Baroda State	1	1	..
Bombay States	4	4	..
Central India Agency	2	2	..
Punjab States	9	9	..
Rajputana Agency	73	70	3
Sikkim State	58,085	28,583	29,502
B.—Born in other Asiatic Countries	**26,013**	**14,155**	**11,858**
Afghanistan	2	2	..
Bhotan	45	30	15
China	15	5	10
Mongolia	2	2	..
Nepal	25,610	13,903	11,707
Tibet	339	213	126
C.—Born in Europe	**14**	**14**	..
United Kingdom	11	11	..
England and Wales	*10*	*10*	..
Scotland	*1*	*1*	..
Germany	3	3	..
TRAVANCORE STATE	**3,428,975**	**1,731,363**	**1,697,612**
A.—Born in India	**3,428,423**	**1,731,018**	**1,697,405**
Provinces	*49,977*	*25,503*	*24,474*
Bengal	124	100	24
Bihar and Orissa	2	2	..
Bombay	171	81	90
Burma	22	11	11
Central Provinces and Berar	41	36	5
Coorg	1	..	1
Madras	49,511	25,211	24,300
N.-W. F. Province	8	7	1
Punjab	38	18	20
United Provinces	59	37	22
States and Agencies	*3,378,161*	*1,705,298*	*1,672,863*
Baroda State	4	2	2
Bombay States	26	11	15
Central India Agency	1	1	..
Cochin State	9,946	4,527	5,419
Hyderabad State	67	44	23
Kashmir State	1	1	..
Madras States*	9	7	2
Mysore State	281	171	110
Punjab States	1	1	..
Rajputana Agency	15	8	7
Travancore State	,367,810	1,700,525	1,667,285
India, Unspecified	*135*	*111*	*24*
French and Portuguese Settlements	*150*	*106*	*44*
B.—Born in other Asiatic Countries	**229**	**146**	**83**
Afghanistan	6	3	3
Arabia	7	6	1
Ceylon	206	127	79
China	1	1	..
Japan	1	1	..
Nepal	1	1	..
Straits Settlements and Malaya	2	2	..
Turkey in Asia	5	5	..
TRAVANCORE STATE—*contd.*			
C.—Born in Europe	**312**	**191**	**121**
United Kingdom	237	160	77
England and Wales	*174*	*118*	*56*
Scotland	*48*	*35*	*13*
Ireland	*15*	*7*	*8*
Austria-Hungary]	3	2	1
Belgium	21	5	16
Denmark	2	..	2
France	2	1	1
Germany	11	4	7
Holland	1	1	..
Iceland	1	1	..
Italy	5	4	1
Norway	2	..	2
Portugal	2	2	..
Spain	1	1	..
Sweden	3	1	2
Switzerland	9	..	9
Europe, *Unspecified*	12	9	3
D.—Born in Africa (Africa, *Unspecified*)	**1**	**1**	..
E.—Born in America (America, *Unspecified*)	**9**	**6**	**3**
F.—Born in Australasia (Australasia, *Unspecified*)	**1**	**1**	..
UNITED PROVINCES STATES.	**832,036**	**431,440**	**400,596**
A.—Born in India	**831,933**	**431,364**	**400,569**
Provinces	*64,415*	*26,395*	*38,020*
Ajmer-Merwara	2	..	2
Assam	58	56	2
Baluchistan	1	1	..
Bengal	160	128	32
Bihar and Orissa	20	15	5
Bombay	36	25	11
Burma	10	5	5
Central Provinces and Berar	25	19	6
Madras	4	2	2
N.-W. F. Province	53	51	2
Punjab	630	464	166
United Provinces	63,416	25,629	37,787
States and Agencies	*767,515*	*404,969*	*362,546*
Baroda State	4	1	3
Bombay States	8	8	..
Central India Agency	127	65	62
Hyderabad State	7	2	5
Kashmir State	19	14	5
Mysore State	2	2	..
Punjab States	177	145	32
Rajputana Agency	95	57	38
United Provinces States	767,076	404,675	362,401
India, Unspecified	*3*	..	*3*
B.—Born in other Asiatic Countries.	**97**	**73**	**24**
Afghanistan	34	33	1
Arabia	15	8	7
China	1	..	1
Nepal	27	16	11
Persia	7	5	2
Tibet	13	11	2
C.—Born in Europe	**6**	**3**	**3**
United Kingdom	3	2	1
England and Wales	*2*	*1*	*1*
Scotland	*1*	*1*	..
France	1	..	1
Germany	2	1	1

* Excluding Cochin and Travancore.

TABLE XI.—BIRTHPLACE. PART III.—INTERNAL MIGRATION.

Province, State or Agency.	Immigrants born in India.	Emigrants born in Province or State.	Excess of Immigrants (+) or Emigrants (—).	Net Interchange of Population between Provinces and States.							
				Ajmer-Merwara.	Andamans and Nicobars.	Assam.	Baluchistan.	Bengal.	Bihar and Orissa.	Bombay.	Burma.
1	2	3	4	5	6	7	8	9	10	11	12
Provinces	**7,723,431**	**7,590,996**	**+132,435**	**+ 14,581**	**— 11,987**	**—753,914**	**+ 11,219**	**—1,197,284**	**+1,511,502**	**— 141,176**	**— 470,333**
1. Ajmer-Merwara	94,853	84,110	+ 10,743	...	— 12	— 40	— 183	— 361	— 29	— 23,406	— 178
2. Andamans and Nicobars	13,657	967	+ 12,690	+ 12	...	+ 126	+ 39	+ 1,141	+ 859	+ 956	+ 1,268
3. Assam	832,529	77,277	+ 755,252	+ 40	— 126	...	+ 180	+ 155,322	+ 389,563	+ 733	+ 1,911
4. Baluchistan	47,849	50,529	— 2,680	+ 183	— 39	— 180	...	+ 26	+ 47	— 38,500	+ 9
5. Bengal	1,812,654	628,087	+1,184,567	+ 361	— 1,141	— 155,322	— 26	...	+1,076,630	— 424	— 132,389
6. Bihar and Orissa	409,249	2,140,782	—1,731,533	+ 29	— 859	— 389,563	— 47	—1,076,630	...	+ 1,126	— 8,237
7. Bombay	1,300,956	889,795	+ 411,161	+ 23,406	— 956	— 733	+ 38,500	+ 424	— 1,126	...	— 12,261
8. Burma	490,740	12,653	+ 478,087	+ 178	— 1,268	— 1,911	— 9	+ 132,389	+ 8,237	+ 12,261	...
9. Central Provinces and Berar	767,371	436,837	+ 330,534	+ 2,303	— 868	— 72,325	+ 940	— 14,476	+ 74,042	+ 52,567	— 319
10. Coorg	45,415	3,858	+ 41,557	+ 1	— 1	— 2	...	+ 3	— 3	+ 510	— 1
11. Madras	236,255	870,617	— 634,362	— 98	— 1,424	— 34,293	— 8	— 6,633	— 16,369	— 16,677	— 245,369
12. N.-W. F. Province (*Districts and Administered Territories*).	132,140	66,744	+ 65,396	— 89	— 448	— 76	— 3,355	— 739	— 299	— 6,332	— 711
13. Punjab	885,655	863,159	+ 22,496	— 2,179	— 1,838	— 2,761	— 19,413	— 13,730	— 2,939	— 43,245	— 34,168
14. United Provinces	654,108	1,465,581	— 811,473	— 9,566	— 3,007	— 96,834	— 5,399	— 374,000	— 17,111	— 80,745	— 49,873
States and Agencies	**3,578,987**	**3,711,422**	**—132,435**	**—25,324**	**— 763**	**— 1,338**	**— 8,539**	**+ 12,697**	**+220,031**	**—269,985**	**— 7,754**
15. Assam State (Manipur)	6,814	4,798	+ 2,016	...	— 30	+ 1,218	...	+ 165	+ 483	— 22	— 630
16. Baluchistan States	2,045	33,397	— 31,352	+ 1	...	— 17	— 5,901	— 17	+ 1	— 25,790	...
17. Baroda State	221,801	235,523	— 13,722	— 45	— 8	+ 6	— 7	+ 208	+ 51	— 9,599	— 73
18. Bengal States	136,074	36,679	+ 99,395	+ 3	— 58	+ 28,836	...	+ 44,813	+ 18,371	— 4	— 767
19. Bihar and Orissa States	317,806	77,531	+ 240,275	+ 2	— 14	— 6,159	+ 4	+ 8,020	+ 196,136	+ 200	+ 18
20. Bombay States	547,701	673,710	— 126,009	+ 11,045	— 36	— 1,703	+ 203	— 1,980	— 481	— 157,499	+ 72
21. Central India Agency	470,199	535,847	— 65,648	+ 3,180	— 156	— 7,094	— 112	— 2,119	— 2,009	+ 32,032	— 208
22. Central Provinces States	222,149	124,951	+ 97,198	+ 29		— 4,525	...	+ 653	+ 21,408	+ 321	— 68
23. Cochin State	47,073	20,381	+ 26,602	...	...	— 7	...	— 26	+ 22	+ 83	— 53
24. Hyderabad State	249,154	306,272	— 57,118	+ 6,451	— 87	— 114	+ 36	+ 473	— 176	— 13,575	— 1,300
25. Kashmir State	74,389	81,931	— 7,542	— 8	+ 6	— 18	— 863	— 162	— 2	— 556	— 433
26 Madras States*	47,697	21,888	+ 25,809	— 6	...	— 12	..	+ 9	...	+ 350	— 674
27. Mysore State	307,405	131,257	+ 176,148	— 27	+ 6	— 127	— 48	— 15	— 131	+ 14,971	— 660
28. N.-W. F. Province (*Agencies and Tribal areas*).	6,651	56,938	— 50,287	— 1	...	— 17	— 456	+ 12	+ 2	+ 9	— 3
29. Punjab States	490,725	412,697	+ 78,028	— 380	— 125	— 91	— 673	— 777	— 116	+ 332	— 367
30. Rajputana Agency	302,314	855,625	— 553,311	— 45,429	— 162	— 11,403	— 692	— 35,006	— 13,274	— 111,565	— 1,748
31. Sikkim State	3,808	3,445	+ 363	+ 2	...	— 49	...	— 302	+ 177	+ 214	+ 10
32. Travancore State	60,328	26,270	+ 34,058	...		— 4	— 5	+ 70	— 14	+ 87	— 102
33. United Provinces States	64,854	72,282	— 7,428	— 132	— 39	— 58	— 25	— 1,320	— 417	+ 36	— 678

* Excluding Cochin and Travancore for which figures are given separately.

TABLE XI.—BIRTHPLACE

Province, State or Agency.	Net Interchange of Population											
	Central Provinces and Berar.	Coorg.	Madras.	N.-W. F. Province.	Punjab.	United Provinces.	*Total Provinces.*	Assam State. (Manipur)	Baluchistan States.	Baroda State.	Bengal States.	Bihar and Orissa States.
1	13	14	15	16	17	18	19	20	21	22	23	24
Provinces	**—153,123**	**— 28,378**	**+348,098**	**—19,540**	**+62,779**	**+327,536**	...	**— 1,903**	**+31,266**	**+ 5,250**	**—98,240**	**—232,163**
1. Ajmer-Merwara	— 2,303	— 1	+ 98	+ 89	+ 3,179	+ 9,566	*— 14,581*	...	— 1	+ 45	— 3	— 2
2. Andamans and Nicobars	+ 868	+ 1	+ 1,434	+ 448	+ 1,638	+ 3,007	*+ 11,987*	+ 30	...	+ 8	+ 58	+ 14
3. Assam	+ 72,325	+ 2	+ 34,398	+ 76	+ 2,761	+ 96,834	*+ 753,914*	— 1,218	+ 17	— 6	—29,836	+ 6,159
4. Baluchistan	— 940	...	+ 8	+ 3,355	+ 19,413	+ 5,399	*— 11,219*	...	+ 5,901	+ 7	...	— 4
5. Bengal	+ 14,476	— 3	+ 6,633	+ 739	+ 13,730	+374,000	*+1,197,264*	— 165	+ 17	— 206	—44,813	— 8,020
6. Bihar and Orissa	— 74,042	+ 3	+ 16,369	+ 299	+ 2,939	+ 17,111	*—1,511,502*	— 483	— 1	— 51	—18,371	— 196,136
7. Bombay	— 52,667	— 510	+ 16,677	+ 6,332	+ 43,245	+ 80,745	*+ 141,176*	+ 22	+ 25,790	+ 9,599	+ 4	— 200
8. Burma	+ 319	+ 1	+245,369	+ 711	+ 24,183	+ 49,878	*+ 470,333*	+ 690	...	+ 73	+ 767	— 18
9. Central Provinces and Berar		— 2	— 924	+ 532	+ 8,105	+103,548	*+ 153,123*	+ 20	...	+ 54	— 1,360	— 13,823
10. Coorg	+ 2	...	+ 27,844	...	+ 10	+ 15	*+ 28,378*	...	...	...	...	+ 1
11. Madras	+ 924	— 27,844	...	+ 16	— 170	— 153	*— 348,098*	— 10	— 1	+ 90	— 1,070	— 17,719
12. N.-W. F. Province (*Districts and Administered Territories*).	— 532	...	— 16	...	+ 29,259	+ 2,878	*+ 19,540*	+ 5	— 20	— 28	— 23	— 30
13. Punjab	— 8,105	— 10	+ 170	— 29,259	...	+ 84,713	*— 62,779*	— 417	— 393	— 732	— 54	— 758
14. United Provinces	—103,548	— 15	+ 153	— 2,878	— 84,713	...	*— 327,536*	— 317	— 43	— 3,601	— 4,539	— 1,632
States and Agencies	**—177,411**	**— 13,179**	**+286,264**	**—45,856**	**—85,275**	**—16,063**	**—132,485**	**— 113**	**+ 86**	**+8,472**	**—1,155**	**— 3,112**
15. Assam State (Manipur)	— 20	...	+ 10	— 5	+ 417	+ 317	*+ 1,903*	...	...	...	— 86	...
16. Baluchistan States	...	...	+ 1	+ 20	+ 393	+ 43	*— 31,266*	...	...	— 41	...	...
17. Baroda State	— 54	...	— 90	+ 28	+ 732	+ 3,601	*— 5,250*	...	+ 41	...	...	— 9
18. Bengal States	+ 1,360	...	+ 1,070	+ 23	+ 54	+ 4,539	*+ 98,240*	+ 86	...	...	...	+ 6
19. Bihar and Orissa States	+ 13,823	— 1	+ 17,719	+ 30	+ 753	+ 1,632	*+ 232,163*	...	...	+ 9	— 6	...
20. Bombay States	— 13,070	— 28	+ 335	+ 152	+ 1,997	+ 4,258	*— 156,735*	— 6	— 78	+ 11,960	— 101	— 368
21. Central India Agency	— 97,660	..	+ 530	+ 473	+ 4,732	— 27,080	*— 95,491*	— 2	+ 9	+ 1,069	— 38	— 464
22. Central Provinces States	+ 40,559	+ 3	+ 3,947	+ 79	+ 846	+ 12,453	*+ 75,705*	...	...	+ 34	+ 4	— 5,665
23. Cochin State	...	— 34	+ 20,844	+ 1	+ 1	+ 26	*+ 20,857*	...	...	...	...	...
24. Hyderabad State	— 69,833	— 65	+ 7,409	+ 270	+ 3,904	+ 8,057	*— 58,640*	...	+ 69	+ 40	...	— 11
25. Kashmir State	— 92	...	— 1	+ 6,674	— 11,211	— 963	*— 7,629*	— 1	— 16	— 14	...	— 2
26. Madras States*	+ 9	+ 2	+ 25,686	+ 3	— 5	— 28	*+ 25,334*	...	...	+ 2	...	...
27. Mysore State	+ 467	— 13,046	+170,859	+ 247	+ 1,385	+ 492	*+ 174,373*	— 1	+ 2	+ 14	...	— 14
28. N.-W. F. Province (*Agencies and Tribal areas*).	...	...	+ 9	— 51,903	+ 3,160	+ 149	*— 49,039*	...	...	...	..	...
29. Punjab States	— 806	...	+ 39	— 901	+ 26,271	+ 12,173	*+ 34,557*	— 74	+ 7	+ 36	+ 4	— 45
30. Rajputana Agency	— 51,395	— 2	— 1,201	— 971	—118,632	— 33,465	*— 424,847*	— 112	+ 52	— 4,638	— 914	— 1,538
31. Sikkim State	— 2	...	...	...	+ 135	+ 91	*+ 276*	— 2	+ 1	+ 1	..	...
32. Travancore State	+ 26	— 8	+ 39,094	+ 6	+ 19	+ 18	*+ 39,157*	...	...	+ 4	..	...
33. United Provinces States	— 721	...	+ 4	— 82	— 326	— 2,375	*— 6,133*	— 1	— 1	— 4	— 18	— 2

* Excluding Cochin and Travancore.

Part III.—Internal Migration—*concluded*.

BETWEEN PROVINCES AND STATES.

Bombay States.	Central India Agency.	Central Provinces States.	Cochin State.	Hyderabad State.	Kashmir State.	Madras States.*	Mysore State.	N.-W. F. Province (*Agencies and Tribal areas.*)	Punjab States.	Rajputana Agency.	Sikkim State.	Travancore State.	United Provinces States.	*Total States and Agencies.*	Serial No.
25	26	27	28	29	30	31	32	33	34	35	36	37	38	39	
+156,735	+95,491	—75,765	—26,857	+58,640	+ 7,629	—25,334	—174,373	+49,039	—34,557	+424.847	— 276	—39,187	+ 6,133	+132,435	
—11,045	— 3,180	— 29	..	— 6,451	+ 8	+ 6	+ 27	+ 1	+ 389	+ 45,429	— 2	..	+ 132	+ *25,324*	1
+ 36	+ 156	...	...	+ 87	— 6	...	— 6	...	+ 125	+ 162	...	...	+ 39	+ *703*	2
+ 1,703	+ 7,094	+ 4,525	+ 7	+ 114	+ 18	+ 12	+ 127	+ 17	+ 91	+ 11,403	+ 49	+ 4	+ 58	+ *1,338*	3
— 203	+ 112	...	...	— 36	+ 863	...	+ 48	+ 456	+ 673	+ 692		+ 5	+ 25	+ *8,539*	4
+ 1,980	+ 2,119	— 653	+ 26	— 473	+ 162	— 9	+ 15	— 12	+ 777	+ 35,008	+ 302	— 70	+ 1,320	— *12,697*	5
+ 481	+ 2,009	—21,408	— 22	+ 176	+ 2	...	+ 131	— 2	+ 116	+ 13,274	— 177	+ 14	+ 417	— *220,031*	6
+157,499	—32,032	— 321	— 83	+ 13,575	+ 556	— 350	— 14,971	— 9	— 322	+ 111,565	— 214	— 87	— 36	+ *269,985*	7
— 72	+ 208	+ 68	+ 58	+ 1,390	+ 433	+ 674	+ 660	+ 3	+ 367	+ 1,748	— 10	+ 102	+ 678	+ *7,754*	8
+13,070	+97,660	—40,559	..	+ 69,833	+ 92	— 9	— 467	...	+ 808	+ 51,395	+ 2	— 26	+ 721	+ *177,411*	9
+ 28	...	— 3	+ 34	+ 65	...	— 2	+ 13,046	...	...	+ 2	..	+ 8		+ *13,179*	10
— 335	— 580	— 3,947	— 20,844	— 7,409	+ 1	— 25,656	— 170,859	— 9	— 39	+ 1,201	..	— 39,094	— 4	— *286,264*	11
— 152	— 473	— 79	— 1	— 270	— 6,674	— 8	— 247	+ 51,903	+ 901	+ 971	...	— 6	+ 82	+ *45,856*	12
— 1,997	— 4,732	— 846	— 1	— 3,904	+ 11,211	+ 5	— 1,385	— 3,160	— 26,271	+ 118 532	— 135	— 19	+ 326	+ *85,275*	13
— 4,258	+27,080	—12,453	— 26	— 8,057	+ 963	+ 28	— 402	— 140	— 12,172	+ 33,465	— 91	— 18	+ 2,375	+ *16,063*	14
—38,726	—29,843	—21,493	— 5,835	— 1,522	— 87	— 475	— 1,775	+ 1,248	—43,471	+128,464	— 87	+ 5,129	+ 1,295		
+ 6	+ 2	..	...	...	+ 1		+ 1	.	+ 74	+ 112	+ 2	..	+ 1	+ *113*	15
+ 78	— 9	..	...	— 69	+ 16	..	— 2	..	— 7	— 52	— 1		+ 1	— *86*	16
—11,060	— 1,060	— 34	...	— 40	+ 14	— 2	— 14	..	— 36	+ 4,638	— 1	— 4	+ 4	— *8,472*	17
+ 101	+ 38	— 4	...		..	...	...		— 4	+ 914			+ 18	+ *1,155*	18
+ 368	+ 464	+ 5,665	...	+ 11	+ 2	...	+ 14		+ 45	+ 1,538		..	+ 2	+ *8,112*	19
..	— 2,835	— 345	— 601	+ 8,585	+ 11	...	— 578		— 59	+ 15,128	— 4	+ 25	— 8	+ *30,726*	20
+ 2,835	...	—20,839	— 38	+ 1,612	+ 35	...	+ 406	— 1	— 80	+ 45,072	— 2	+ 1	+ 268	+ *29,843*	21
+ 345	+ 20,889	...		+ 1,951	+ 2	...	+ 32		+ 396	+ 3,530	...	+ 3	+ 22	+ *21,493*	22
+ 601	+ 38		...	+ 17	...	+ 1	— 98			+ 15	...	+ 5,261		+ *5,835*	23
— 8,585	— 1,612	— 1,951	— 17		+ 72	— 280	— 462	.	+ 276	+ 13,950	...	— 61	+ 94	+ *1,522*	24
— 11	— 35	— 2	..	— 72		...	— 32	+ 1,575	— 1,451	+ 160	...	— 1	— 11	+ *87*	25
...	..	...	— 1	+ 280	..	...	+ 174	...	...	...	...	+ 20		+ *475*	26
+ 578	— 406	— 32	+ 98	+ 462	+ 32	— 174	..	— 4	+ 4	+ 1,311	+ 1	— 90	+ 3	+ *1,775*	27
...	+ 1	...	...		— 1,575	...	+ 4	..	+ 302	+ 14			+ 6	— *1,248*	28
+ 59	+ 80	— 396	..	— 276	+ 1,451	...	— 4	— 302		+ 42,551	9	— 1	+ 390	+ *43,471*	29
— 15,128	—45,072	— 3,530	— 15	— 13,950	— 160	...	— 1,311	— 14	— 42,551		73	— 15	505	— *128,464*	30
+ 4	+ 2	...			...	...	— 1		+ 9	+ 73	...			+ *87*	31
— 25	— 1	— 3	— 5,261	+ 61	+ 1	— 20	+ 90		+ 1	+ 15	...	...		— *5,129*	32
+ 8	— 268	— 22	...	— 94	+ 11	...	— 3	— 6	— 390	— 505	...	...		— *1,295*	33

for which figures are separately given.

TABLE XI.—BIRTHPLACE. PART IV—DISTRIBUTION

Birthplace and Place of Enumeration.	Population. Persons.	Males.	Females.
1	2	3	4
A—Born in India	**312,783,652**	**159,978,045**	**152,805,607**
Born in Ajmer-Merwara	**488,927**	**268,965**	**219,962**
Enumerated in :—			
Provinces	*437,560*	*244,368*	*193,192*
Ajmer-Merwara	404,817	221,690	183,127
Andamans and Nicobars	12	8	4
Assam	46	22	24
Baluchistan	206	192	14
Bengal	650	506	144
Bihar and Orissa	141	79	62
Bombay	24,976	17,868	7,108
Burma	199	196	3
Central Provinces and Berar	2,644	1,647	997
Coorg	1	1	..
Madras	120	78	42
N.-W. F. Province	16	11	5
Punjab	1,317	734	583
United Provinces	2,415	1,336	1,079
States and Agencies	*51,367*	*24,597*	*26,770*
Baluchistan States	1	1	..
Baroda State	179	106	73
Bengal States	3	3	..
Bihar and Orissa States	2	2	..
Bombay States	11,392	6,611	4,781
Central India Agency	5,226	3,585	1,641
Central Provinces States	29	17	12
Hyderabad State	6,698	4,188	2,510
Kashmir State	27	23	4
Mysore State	37	34	3
Punjab States	226	84	142
Rajputana Agency	27,543	9,941	17,602
Sikkim State	2	2	..
United Provinces States	2	..	2
Born in Andamans and Nicobars	**13,024**	**7,093**	**5,931**
Enumerated in :—			
Provinces	*12,996*	*7,079*	*5,917*
Andamans and Nicobars	12,057	6,371	5,686
Assam	6	3	3
Bengal	80	48	32
Bihar and Orissa	13	5	8
Bombay	31	16	15
Burma	451	427	24
Central Provinces and Berar	19	7	12
Madras	65	48	17
N.-W. F. Province	11	4	7
Punjab	109	72	37
United Provinces	154	78	76
States and Agencies	*28*	*14*	*14*
Bombay States	7	2	5
Kashmir State	7	2	5
Mysore State	14	10	4
Born in Assam	**5,908,503**	**3,013,465**	**2,895,038**
Enumerated in :—			
Provinces	*5,872,699*	*2,993,953*	*2,878,746*
Ajmer-Merwara	6	4	2
Andamans and Nicobars	132	128	4
Assam	5,831,226	2,968,599	2,862,627
Baluchistan	10	6	4
Bengal	36,290	21,344	14,946
Bihar and Orissa	3,135	2,597	538
Bombay	108	100	8
Burma	340	309	31
Central Provinces and Berar.	146	67	79
Madras	204	182	22
N.-W. F. Province	10	10	..
Punjab	98	64	34
United Provinces	994	543	451
States and Agencies	*35,804*	*19,512*	*16,292*
Assam State	4,777	2,584	2,193
Baroda State	6	2	4
Bengal States	30,799	16,787	14,012
Bihar and Orissa States	7	5	2
Central India Agency	8	6	2
Central Provinces States	5	5	..
Hyderabad State	5	4	1
Mysore State	13	10	3
N.-W. F. Province (*Agencies and Tribal areas*)	1	1	..
Punjab States	23	12	11
Rajputana Agency	102	40	62
United Provinces States	58	56	2

Birthplace and Place of Enumeration.	Population. Persons.	Males.	Females.
1	2	3	4
Born in Baluchistan	**400,971**	**220,273**	**180,698**
Enumerated in :—			
Provinces	*399,020*	*218,955*	*180,065*
Ajmer-Merwara	23	13	10
Andamans and Nicobars	39	39	..
Assam	190	164	26
Baluchistan	350,442	190,154	160,288
Bengal	97	69	28
Bihar and Orissa	15	14	1
Bombay	42,658	24,493	18,165
Burma	30	27	3
Central Provinces and Berar	1,064	971	93
Madras	126	116	10
N.-W. F. Province	200	158	42
Punjab	3,570	2,309	1,261
United Provinces	566	428	138
States and Agencies	*1,951*	*1,318*	*633*
Baluchistan States	997	572	425
Bihar and Orissa States	4	4	..
Bombay States	511	408	103
Central India Agency	20	18	2
Hyderabad State	110	100	10
Kashmir State	20	17	3
Mysore State	8	5	3
N.-W. F. Province (*Agencies and Tribal areas*).	69	68	1
Punjab States	92	50	42
Rajputana Agency	119	75	44
United Provinces States	1	1	..
Born in Bengal	**44,165,612**	**22,409,216**	**21,755,796**
Enumerated in :—			
Provinces	*44,064,538*	*22,348,889*	*21,715,649*
Ajmer-Merwara	289	137	152
Andamans and Nicobars	1,221	1,089	132
Assam	191,612	109,460	82,152
Baluchistan	123	78	45
Bengal	43,536,925	22,007,837	21,529,088
Bihar and Orissa	153,351	85,259	68,092
Bombay	6,347	4,720	1,627
Burma	134,985	121,011	13,974
Central Provinces and Berar	3,540	1,990	1,550
Coorg	6	4	2
Madras	6,537	3,107	3,430
N.-W. F. Province	272	149	123
Punjab	3,752	2,194	1,558
United Provinces	25,578	11,854	13,724
States and Agencies	*100,474*	*60,327*	*40,147*
Assam State	300	198	102
Baluchistan States	2	2	..
Baroda State	332	226	106
Bengal States	78,496	48,032	30,464
Bihar and Orissa States	11,982	6,255	5,727
Bombay States	495	359	136
Central India Agency	1,004	649	355
Central Provinces States	2,252	1,384	868
Hyderabad State	717	534	183
Kashmir State	131	83	48
Madras States	156	120	36
Cochin	*22*	*14*	*8*
Travancore	*124*	*100*	*24*
Mysore State	412	243	169
N.-W. F. Province (*Agencies and Tribal areas*)	12	6	6
Punjab States	235	140	95
Rajputana Agency	736	376	360
Sikkim State	3,052	1,592	1,460
United Provinces States	160	128	32
Born in Bihar and Orissa	**36,181,814**	**17,974,366**	**18,207,448**
Enumerated in :—			
Provinces	*35,874,281*	*17,822,018*	*18,052,263*
Ajmer-Merwara	112	89	23
Andamans and Nicobars	872	777	95
Assam	392,698	217,492	175,206
Baluchistan	62	52	10
Bengal	1,229,981	868,437	361,544
Bihar and Orissa	34,041,032	16,643,044	17,397,988
Bombay	757	587	170
Burma	8,392	6,036	2,356
Central Provinces and Berar	93,785	49,991	43,794
Coorg	2	2	..
Madras	426	302	124
N.-W. F. Province	22	15	7
Punjab	1,147	566	581
United Provinces	104,993	34,628	70,365
States and Agencies	*307,533*	*152,348*	*155,185*
Assam State	503	402	101
Baluchistan States	1	1	..
Baroda State	150	141	9
Bengal States	18,420	15,904	2,516
Bihar and Orissa States	256,708	119,409	137,299

OF BIRTHPLACE BY PLACE OF ENUMERATION.

BIRTHPLACE AND PLACE OF ENUMERATION.	POPULATION.		
	Persons.	Males.	Females.
1	2	3	4
Born in Bihar and Orissa—*contd.*			
Bombay States	368	213	155
Central India Agency	1,047	503	544
Central Provinces States	29,291	14,960	14,331
Hyderabad State	17	13	4
Kashmir State	79	58	21
Madras States	27	25	2
Cochin	*25*	*23*	*2*
Travancore	*2*	*2*	..
Mysore State	59	40	19
N.-W. F. Province (*Agencies and Tribal areas*)	2	2	..
Punjab States	254	218	36
Rajputana Agency	398	268	130
Sikkim State	189	176	13
United Provinces States	20	15	5
Born in Bombay Enumerated in :—	**19,139,366**	**9,841,967**	**9,297,399**
Provinces	*18,396,434*	*9,538,295*	*8,858,139*
Ajmer-Merwara	1,570	926	644
Andamans and Nicobars	987	857	130
Assam	841	648	193
Baluchistan	4,158	3,031	1,127
Bengal	5,923	4,244	1,679
Bihar and Orissa	1,883	1,273	610
Bombay	18,249,571	9,453,304	8,796,267
Burma	12,782	10,646	2,136
Central Provinces and Berar	85,642	42,647	42,995
Coorg	518	437	81
Madras	16,952	10,741	6,211
N.-W. F. Province	549	424	125
Punjab	6,282	3,919	2,363
United Provinces	8,776	5,198	3,578
States and Agencies	*742,932*	*303,672*	*439,260*
Assam State	12	9	3
Baluchistan States	412	318	94
Baroda State	134,062	51,241	82,821
Bengal States	26	25	1
Bihar and Orissa States	319	259	60
Bombay States	401,520	152,099	249,421
Central India Agency	47,165	26,940	20,225
Central Provinces States	361	216	145
Hyderabad State	118,653	50,702	67,951
Kashmir State	166	121	45
Madras States	987	588	399
Cochin	*464*	*339*	*125*
Travancore	*171*	*81*	*90*
Mysore State	28,762	15,513	13,249
N.-W. F. Province (*Agencies and Tribal areas*).	9	9	..
Punjab States	3,590	2,100	1,490
Rajputana Agency	6,624	3,279	3,345
Sikkim State	228	228	..
United Provinces States	36	25	11
Born in Burma Enumerated in :—	**11,477,899**	**5,660,168**	**5,817,731**
Provinces	*11,476,935*	*5,659,680*	*5,817,255*
Ajmer-Merwara	21	13	8
Andamans and Nicobars	1,719	1,700	19
Assam	2,251	1,086	1,165
Baluchistan	39	19	20
Bengal	2,596	1,260	1,336
Bihar and Orissa	155	92	63
Bombay	521	296	225
Burma	11,465,246	5,652,871	5,812,375
Central Provinces and Berar	229	139	90
Coorg	4	2	2
Madras	1,991	977	1,014
N.-W. F. Province	29	12	17
Punjab	1,412	810	602
United Provinces	722	403	319
States and Agencies	*964*	*488*	*476*
Assam State	48	26	22
Baroda State	63	48	15
Bengal States	4	4	..
Bihar and Orissa States	18	2	16
Bombay States	111	62	49
Central India Agency	13	7	6
Central Provinces States	7	4	3
Hyderabad State	185	72	113
Madras States	52	24	28
Travancore	*22*	*11*	*11*
Mysore State	273	137	136
Punjab States	138	77	61
Rajputana Agency	32	14	18
Sikkim State	10	6	4
United Provinces States	10	5	5

BIRTHPLACE AND PLACE OF ENUMERATION.	POPULATION.		
	Persons.	Males.	Females.
1	2	3	4
Born in C. P. and Berar Enumerated in :—	**13,578,202**	**6,723,548**	**6,854,654**
Provinces	*13,308,883*	*6,609,647*	*6,699,236*
Ajmer-Merwara	341	174	167
Andamans and Nicobars	887	752	135
Assam	72,471	36,960	35,511
Baluchistan	124	66	58
Bengal	18,016	10,310	7,706
Bihar and Orissa	19,743	9,843	9,900
Bombay	33,075	15,507	17,568
Burma	548	417	131
Central Provinces and Berar	13,141,365	6,524,757	6,616,608
Coorg	14	12	2
Madras	6,281	3,537	2,744
N.-W. F. Province	85	51	34
Punjab	1,375	838	537
United Provinces	14,558	6,423	8,135
States and Agencies	*269,319*	*113,901*	*155,418*
Assam State	20	15	5
Baroda State	321	211	110
Bengal States	1,362	784	578
Bihar and Orissa States	18,712	9,306	9,406
Bombay States	1,645	845	800
Central India Agency	80,057	31,244	48,813
Central Provinces States	143,916	61,215	82,701
Hyderabad State	20,945	8,956	11,989
Kashmir State	11	8	3
Madras States	63	50	13
Cochin	*12*	*7*	*5*
Travancore	*41*	*36*	*5*
Mysore State	1,183	667	516
N.-W. F. Province (*Agencies and Tribal areas*)	1	1	..
Punjab States	122	80	42
Rajputana Agency	936	500	436
United Provinces States	25	19	6
Born in Coorg Enumerated in :—	**133,299**	**67,931**	**65,368**
Provinces	*130,215*	*66,562*	*63,653*
Andamans and Nicobars	1	1	..
Assam	2	2	..
Bengal	3	2	1
Bihar and Orissa	5	1	4
Bombay	8	3	5
Burma	5	4	1
Central Provinces and Berar	12	8	4
Coorg	129,441	66,077	63,364
Madras	737	463	274
United Provinces	1	1	..
States and Agencies	*3,084*	*1,369*	*1,715*
Bombay States	3	2	1
Central Provinces States	3	3	..
Hyderabad State	1	..	1
Madras States	6	1	5
Cochin	*1*	..	*1*
Travancore	*1*	..	*1*
Mysore State	3,071	1,363	1,708
Born in Madras Enumerated in :—	**42,002,913**	**20,783,962**	**21,218,951**
Provinces	*41,516,887*	*20,532,317*	*20,984,570*
Ajmer-Merwara	218	123	95
Andamans and Nicobars	1,489	1,328	161
Assam	34,497	17,049	17,448
Baluchistan	134	78	56
Bengal	13,170	7,338	5,832
Bihar and Orissa	16,795	7,930	8,865
Bombay	33,629	21,083	12,546
Burma	247,360	205,907	41,453
Central Provinces and Berar	5,357	3,039	2,318
Coorg	28,581	21,378	7,203
Madras	41,132,296	20,245,089	20,887,207
N.-W. F. Province	63	32	31
Punjab	1,044	649	395
United Provinces	2,254	1,294	960
States and Agencies	*486,026*	*251,645*	*234,381*
Assam State	10	7	3
Baluchistan States	1	1	..
Baroda State	228	131	97
Bengal States	1,070	556	514
Bihar and Orissa States	18,694	9,385	9,309
Bombay States	1,853	974	879
Central India Agency	1,033	635	398
Central Provinces States	4,862	2,413	2,449
Hyderabad State	67,82[illegible]	34,700	33,121
Kashmir State	27	23	4

BIRTHPLACE AND PLACE OF ENUMERATION.	POPULATION.		
	Persons.	Males.	Females.
1	2	3	4
Born in Madras—*contd.*			
Madras States	126,730	56,893	69,837
Cochin	*30,485*	*14,941*	*15,544*
Travancore	*49,511*	*25,211*	*24,300*
Mysore State	263,362	145,737	117,625
N.-W. F. Province (*Agencies and Tribal areas*)	9	9	..
Punjab States	39	26	13
Rajputana Agency	283	153	130
United Provinces States	4	2	2
Born in N.-W. F. Province Enumerated in :—	**2,079,173**	**1,102,438**	**976,735**
Provinces	***2,062,699***	***1,091,544***	***971,155***
Ajmer-Merwara	105	84	21
Andamans and Nicobars	459	459	..
Assam	86	75	11
Baluchistan	3,555	2,852	703
Bengal	1,011	876	135
Bihar and Orissa	321	271	50
Bombay	6,881	5,458	1,423
Burma	740	704	36
Central Provinces and Berar	617	526	91
Madras	79	54	25
N.-W. F. Province	2,012,429	1,055,975	956,454
Punjab	34,521	22,635	11,886
United Provinces	1,895	1,575	320
States and Agencies	***16,474***	***10,894***	***5,580***
Assam State	5	2	3
Baluchistan States	20	16	4
Baroda State	39	35	4
Bengal States	23	23	..
Bihar and Orissa States	30	29	1
Bombay States	260	205	55
Central India Agency	563	419	144
Central Provinces States	80	62	18
Hyderabad State	364	317	47
Kashmir State	11,163	6,220	4,943
Madras States	12	11	1
Cochin	*1*	*1*	..
Travancore	*8*	*7*	*1*
Mysore State	288	275	13
N.-W. F. Province (*Agencies and Tribal areas*)	2,531	2,448	83
Punjab States	539	368	171
Rajputana Agency	504	413	91
United Provinces States	53	51	2
Born in Punjab Enumerated in :—	**19,899,998**	**10,991.129**	**8,908,869**
Provinces	***19,354,660***	***10,757,541***	***8,597,119***
Ajmer-Merwara	3,496	2,380	1,116
Andamans and Nicobars	1,947	1,788	159
Assam	2,859	2,137	722
Baluchistan	22,983	17,923	5,060
Bengal	17,482	13,490	3,992
Bihar and Orissa	4,086	2,914	1,172
Bombay	49,527	36,530	12,997
Burma	25,595	22,572	3,023
Central Provinces and Berar	9,480	7,413	2,067
Coorg	10	9	1
Madras	874	692	182
N.-W. F. Province	63,780	47,631	16,149
Punjab	19,036,839	10,544,507	8,492,332
United Provinces	115,702	57,555	58,147
States and Agencies	***545,338***	***233,588***	***311,730***
Assam State	447	432	15
Baluchistan States	423	292	131
Baroda State	910	703	207
Bengal States	82	63	19
Bihar and Orissa States	797	554	243
Bombay States	2,563	2,097	466
Central India Agency	7,859	5,118	2,741
Central Provinces States	849	536	313
Hyderabad State	4,470	3,324	1,146
Kashmir State	58,500	27,191	31,309
Madras States	42	22	20
Cochin	*3*	*3*	..
Travancore	*38*	*18*	*20*
Mysore State	1,644	1,426	218
N.-W. F. Province (*Agencies and Tribal areas*)	3,352	3,143	209
Punjab States	398,977	163,507	235,470
Rajputana Agency	63,655	24,590	39,065
Sikkim State	138	126	12
United Provinces States	630	464	166
Born in United Provinces Enumerated in :—	**47,923,287**	**25,197,513**	**22,725,774**
Provinces	***47,563,850***	***25,040,256***	***22,523,594***
Ajmer-Merwara	11,981	6,958	5,023
Andamans and Nicobars	3,161	2,873	288
Assam	97,828	57,263	40,565
Baluchistan	5,965	4,853	1,112
Bengal	399,578	294,182	105,396
Born in United Provinces—*contd.*			
Bihar and Orissa	122,104	58,163	63,941
Bombay	89,521	67,342	22,179
Burma	50,595	45,096	5,499
Central Provinces and Berar	118,106	75,123	42,983
Coorg	16	13	3
Madras	2,101	1,488	613
N.-W. F. Province	4,773	3,471	1,302
Punjab	200,415	101,349	99,066
United Provinces	46,457,706	24,322,082	22,135,624
States and Agencies	***359,437***	***157,257***	***202,180***
Assam State	487	362	125
Baluchistan States	43	32	11
Baroda State	3,899	3,095	804
Bengal States	4,620	3,215	1,405
Bihar and Orissa States	1,700	1,204	496
Bombay States	4,764	3,688	1,076
Central India Agency	168,735	68,129	100,606
Central Provinces States	12,693	7,654	5,039
Hyderabad State	9,399	6,627	2,772
Kashmir State	974	770	204
Madras States	114	79	35
Cochin	*51*	*38*	*13*
Travancore	*59*	*37*	*22*
Mysore State	906	692	214
N.-W. F. Province (*Agencies and Tribal areas*)	150	133	17
Punjab States	17,975	10,315	7,660
Rajputana Agency	69,464	25,542	43,922
Sikkim State	98	91	7
United Provinces States	63,416	25,629	37,787
Born in Assam State (*Manipur*) **Enumerated in :—**	**343,025**	**168,840**	**174,185**
Provinces	***4,706***	***3,121***	***1,585***
Andamans and Nicobars	30	30	..
Assam	3,559	2,271	1,288
Bengal	135	83	52
Bihar and Orissa	20	15	5
Bombay	34	29	5
Burma	678	533	145
Central Provinces and Berar	40	20	20
N.-W. F. Province	10	3	7
Punjab	30	24	6
United Provinces	170	113	57
States and Agencies	***338,319***	***165,719***	***172,600***
Assam State	338,227	165.661	172,566
Bengal States	86	55	31
Bombay States	1	1	..
Punjab States	1	1	..
Rajputana Agency	3	1	2
Sikkim State	1	..	1
Born in Baluchistan States Enumerated in :—	**451,263**	**244,690**	**206,573**
Provinces	***33,166***	***18,855***	***14,311***
Assam	17	15	2
Baluchistan	6,898	4,324	2,574
Bengal	19	7	12
Bombay	26,202	14,482	11,720
Punjab	30	27	3
States and Agencies	***418,097***	***225,835***	***192,262***
Baluchistan States	417,866	225,647	192,219
Baroda State	41	31	10
Bombay States	2	2	..
Central India Agency	10	7	3
Hyderabad State	71	71	..
Mysore State	3	3	..
Punjab States	12	9	3
Rajputana Agency	91	65	26
Sikkim State	1	..	1
Born in Baroda State Enumerated in :—	**2,045,364**	**1,061,440**	**983,924**
Provinces	***145,439***	***62,001***	***83,438***
Ajmer-Merwara	224	133	91
Andamans and Nicobars	8	8	..
Baluchistan	7	5	2
Bengal	124	88	36
Bihar and Orissa	99	67	32
Bombay	143,661	60,795	82,866
Burma	136	121	15
Central Provinces and Berar	375	237	138
Madras	318	258	60
N.-W. F. Province	11	11	..
Punjab	178	107	71
United Provinces	298	171	127

OF BIRTHPLACE BY PLACE OF ENUMERATION—*continued.*

Birthplace and Place of Enumeration.	Population.		
	Persons.	Males.	Females.
1	2	3	4
Born in Baroda State—*cont'd.*			
States and Agencies	*1,899,925*	*999,439*	*900,486*
Baroda State	1,809,841	965,918	843,923
Bihar and Orissa States	9	9	..
Bombay States	85,646	31,005	54,641
Central India Agency	2,482	1,426	1,056
Central Provinces States	34	21	13
Hyderabad State	204	106	98
Kashmir State	4	3	1
Madras States	6	4	2
Travancore	*4*	*2*	*2*
Mysore State	46	22	24
Punjab States	47	35	12
Rajputana Agency	1,601	888	713
Sikkim State	1	1	..
United Provinces States	4	1	3
Born in Bengal States Enumerated in :—	**722,439**	**371,010**	**351,429**
Provinces	*36,665*	*19,685*	*16,980*
Andamans and Nicobars	58	58	..
Assam	1,963	1,029	934
Bengal	33,683	17,728	15,955
Bihar and Orissa	49	34	15
Bombay	30	25	5
Burma	771	759	12
Central Provinces and Berar	2	..	2
Punjab	28	22	6
United Provinces	81	30	51
States and Agencies	*685,774*	*351,325*	*334,449*
Bengal States	685,760	351,314	334,446
Bihar and Orissa States	2	2	..
Bombay States	2	2	..
Central Provinces States	4	2	2
Mysore State	1	1	..
Punjab States	4	3	1
Rajputana Agency	1	1	..
Born in Bihar and Orissa States Enumerated in :—	**3,704,800**	**1,831,055**	**1,873,745**
Provinces	*76,810*	*26,732*	*50,078*
Andamans and Nicobars	14	14	..
Assam	6,166	3,067	3,099
Bengal	3,962	2,276	1,686
Bihar and Orissa	60,572	18,487	42,085
Bombay	119	83	36
Central Provinces and Berar	4,889	2,162	2,727
Coorg	1	1	..
Madras	975	562	413
Punjab	44	32	12
United Provinces	68	48	20
States and Agencies	*3,627,990*	*1,804,323*	*1,823,667*
Bengal States	8	6	2
Bihar and Orissa States	3,627,269	1,803,935	1,823,334
Bombay States	12	9	3
Central India Agency	68	15	53
Central Provinces States	633	358	275
Born in Bombay States Enumerated in :—	**7,526,656**	**3,882,122**	**3,644,534**
Provinces	*582,227*	*301,788*	*280,439*
Ajmer-Merwara	347	183	164
Andamans and Nicobars	43	43	..
Assam	1,703	924	779
Baluchistan	308	244	64
Bengal	2,475	1,859	616
Bihar and Orissa	849	617	232
Bombay	559,019	284,492	274,527
Burma	39	29	10
Central Provinces and Berar	14,715	11,364	3,351
Coorg	31	28	3
Madras	1,518	1,235	283
N.-W. F. Province	108	108	..
Punjab	566	353	213
United Provinces	506	309	197
States and Agencies	*6,944,429*	*3,580,334*	*3,364,095*
Assam State	7	7	..
Baluchistan States	80	67	13
Baroda State	73,686	28,537	45,149
Bengal States	103	56	47
Bihar and Orissa States	380	284	96
Bombay States	6,852,946	3,542,899	3,310,047
Central India Agency	6,946	3,644	3,302
Central Provinces States	349	294	55
Hyderabad State	177	170	7
Kashmir State	18	18	..
Madras States	637	396	241
Cochin	*611*	*385*	*226*
Travancore	*26*	*11*	*15*
Mysore State	1,009	645	364
Punjab States	145	112	33
Rajputana Agency	7,934	3,193	4,741
Sikkim State	4	4	..
United Provinces States	8	8	..
Born in Central India Agency Enumerated in :—	**9,418,572**	**4,817,075**	**4,601,497**
Provinces	*408,221*	*176,612*	*231,609*
Ajmer-Merwara	2,046	983	1,063
Andamans and Nicobars	156	150	6
Assam	7,102	3,783	3,319
Baluchistan	132	98	34
Bengal	3,123	2,434	689
Bihar and Orissa	3,056	2,013	1,043
Bombay	15,133	8,992	6,141
Burma	221	166	55
Central Provinces and Berar	177,717	84,422	93,295
Madras	503	310	193
N.-W. F. Province	90	71	19
Punjab	3,127	1,684	1,443
United Provinces	195,815	71,506	124,309
States and Agencies	*9,010,351*	*4,640,463*	*4,369,888*
Assam State	2	2	..
Baluchistan States	1	1	..
Baroda State	1,413	822	591
Bengal States	38	27	11
Bihar and Orissa States	532	303	229
Bombay States	4,111	2,803	1,308
Central India Agency	8,882,725	4,586,467	4,296,258
Central Provinces States	20,843	11,042	9,801
Hyderabad State	565	264	301
Kashmir State	35	28	7
Madras States	39	31	8
Cochin	*38*	*30*	*8*
Travancore	*1*	*1*	..
Mysore State	85	41	44
N.-W. F. Province (*Agencies and Tribal areas*)	1	1	..
Punjab States	503	273	230
Rajputana Agency	99,329	38,291	61,038
Sikkim State	2	2	..
United Provinces States	127	65	62
Born in Central Provinces States Enumerated in :—	**2,019,638**	**1,003,420**	**1,016,218**
Provinces	*118,643*	*50,327*	*68,316*
Assam	4,530	2,321	2,209
Bengal	1,599	799	800
Bihar and Orissa	7,883	3,266	4,617
Bombay	40	33	7
Burma	75	73	2
Central Provinces and Berar	103,357	43,167	60,190
Madras	915	526	389
N.-W. F. Province	1	1	..
Punjab	3	1	2
United Provinces	240	140	100
States and Agencies	*1,900,995*	*953,093*	*947,902*
Bihar and Orissa States	6,298	3,114	3,184
Bombay States	4	4	..
Central India Agency	4	4	..
Central Provinces States	1,894,687	949,970	944,717
Hyderabad State	2	1	1
Born in Cochin State Enumerated in :—	**891,225**	**444,243**	**446,982**
Provinces	*10,207*	*5,195*	*5,012*
Assam	7	6	1
Bengal	48	35	13
Bihar and Orissa	3	2	1
Bombay	381	241	140
Burma	53	46	7
Central Provinces and Berar	12	9	3
Coorg	35	27	8
Madras	9,641	4,805	4,836
Punjab	2	2	..
United Provinces	25	22	3
States and Agencies	*881,018*	*439,048*	*441,970*
Bombay States	10	8	2
Cochin State	870,844	434,379	436,465
Hyderabad State	10	5	5
Madras States *	2	..	2
Mysore State	206	129	77
Travancore State	9,946	4,527	5,419
Born in Hyderabad State Enumerated in :—	**13,420,235**	**6,800,140**	**6,620,095**
Provinces	*288,025*	*125,546*	*162,479*
Ajmer-Merwara	247	134	113
Andamans and Nicobars	87	83	4
Assam	119	81	38
Baluchistan	74	59	15
Bengal	244	114	130

* Excluding Cochin and Travancore.

TABLE XI.—BIRTHPLACE. PART IV—DISTRIBUTION

Birthplace and Place of Enumeration.	Population. Persons.	Males.	Females.
1	2	3	4
Born in Hyderabad State—*contd.*			
Bihar and Orissa	193	120	64
Bombay	132,228	53,582	78,646
Burma	1,575	1,302	273
Central Provinces and Berar	90,778	39,565	51,213
Coorg	66	49	17
Madras	60,412	20,215	31,197
N.-W. F. Province	94	62	32
Punjab	566	306	260
United Provinces	1,342	865	477
States and Agencies	***13,139,910***	***6,674,594***	***6,457,616***
Baluchistan States	2	2	..
Baroda State	164	106	58
Bihar and Orissa States	11	8	3
Bombay States	8,762	3,763	4,999
Central India Agency	2,177	1,437	740
Central Provinces States	1,953	1,136	817
Hyderabad State	13,113,963	6,665,244	6,448,719
Kashmir State	11	8	3
Madras States	374	190	184
Cochin	*27*	*16*	*11*
Travancore	*67*	*44*	*23*
Mysore State	4,342	2,456	1,886
Punjab States	123	70	53
Rajputana Agency	321	172	149
United Provinces States	7	2	5
Born in Kashmir State Enumerated in :—	**3,108,647**	**1,652,333**	**1,456,314**
Provinces	***78,734***	***43,820***	***34,914***
Ajmer-Merwara	35	27	8
Andamans and Nicobars	1	1	..
Assam	18	11	7
Baluchistan	883	786	97
Bengal	293	242	51
Bihar and Orissa	81	64	17
Bombay	722	625	97
Burma	433	275	158
Central Provinces and Berar	103	60	43
Madras	28	26	2
N.-W. F. Province	4,489	3,639	850
Punjab	69,711	36,584	33,127
United Provinces	1,937	1,480	457
States and Agencies	***3,029,913***	***1,608,313***	***1,421,400***
Assam State	1	1	..
Baluchistan States	16	6	8
Baroda State	18	14	4
Bihar and Orissa States	2	1	1
Bombay States	29	25	4
Central India Agency	70	65	5
Central Provinces States	2	2	..
Hyderabad State	83	64	19
Kashmir State	3,026,716	1,606,428	1,420,288
Madras States (*Travancore*)	1	1	..
Mysore State	42	22	20
N.-W. F. Province (*Agencies and Tribal areas*)	166	165	1
Punjab States	2,658	1,636	1,022
Rajputana Agency	90	67	23
United Provinces States	19	14	5
Born in Madras States * Enumerated in :—	**438,093**	**213,422**	**224,671**
Provinces	***21,814***	***7,971***	***13,843***
Ajmer-Merwara	6	3	3
Assam	12	12	..
Bengal	1	..	1
Bombay	2	2	..
Burma	704	527	177
Central Provinces and Berar	1	..	1
Coorg	2	1	1
Madras	21,048	7,414	13,634
Punjab	6	6	..
United Provinces	32	6	26
States and Agencies	***416,279***	***205,451***	***210,828***
Cochin State	3	..	3
Madras States *	416,205	205,411	210,794
Mysore State	55	29	26
Rajputana Agency	7	4	3
Travancore State	9	7	2
Born in Mysore State Enumerated in :—	**5,624,542**	**2,825,556**	**2,798,986**
Provinces	***125,659***	***62,457***	***63,202***
Ajmer-Merwara	64	33	31
Andamans and Nicobars	8	7	1
Assam	140	81	59
Baluchistan	56	29	27
Bengal	427	287	140
Born in Mysore State—*contd.*			
Bihar and Orissa	190	106	84
Bombay	13,791	6,492	7,299
Burma	933	823	110
Central Provinces and Berar	716	381	335
Coorg	16,117	9,148	6,969
Madras	92,503	44,661	47,842
N.-W. F. Province	41	28	13
Punjab	259	150	109
United Provinces	414	231	183
States and Agencies.	***5,498,883***	***2,763,099***	***2,735,784***
Assam State	1	1	..
Baluchistan States	1	1	..
Baroda State	32	13	19
Bengal States	1	..	1
Bihar and Orissa States	14	9	5
Bombay States	431	220	211
Central India agency	491	233	258
Central Provinces States	32	17	15
Hyderabad State	3,880	2,547	1,333
Kashmir State	10	3	7
Madras States	618	350	268
Cochin	*108*	*73*	*35*
Travancore	*281*	*171*	*110*
Mysore State	5,493,285	2,759,662	2,733,623
N.-W. F. Province (*Agencies and Tribal areas*)	4	4	..
Punjab States	14	9	5
Rajputana Agency	67	28	39
United Provinces States	2	2	..
Born in N.-W. F. Province (*Agencies and Tribal areas*) Enumerated in :—	**62,670**	**39,867**	**22,803**
Provinces	***55,175***	***33,707***	***21,468***
Ajmer-Merwara	1	..	1
Assam	18	16	2
Baluchistan	525	523	2
Burma	3	1	2
Central Provinces and Berar	1	..	1
N.-W. F. Province	54,434	33,000	21,434
Punjab	192	167	25
United Provinces	1	..	1
States and Agencies	***7,495***	***6,160***	***1,335***
Kashmir State	1,741	973	768
N.-W. F. Province (*Agencies and Tribal areas*)	5,732	5,168	564
Punjab States	19	16	3
Rajputana Agency	3	3	..
Born in Punjab States Enumerated in :—	**4,131,706**	**2,275,477**	**1,856,229**
Provinces	***387,653***	***149,599***	***238,194***
Ajmer-Merwara	615	398	217
Andamans and Nicobars	125	125	..
Assam	114	93	21
Baluchistan	765	659	106
Bengal	1,012	805	207
Bihar and Orissa	370	236	134
Bombay	3,268	2,204	1,064
Burma	505	411	94
Central Provinces and Berar	930	639	291
N.-W. F. Province	1,440	1,203	237
Punjab	372,706	138,695	234,011
United Provinces	5,803	4,061	1,742
States and Agencies	***3,744,053***	***2,125,948***	***1,618,105***
Assam State	75	74	1
Baluchistan States	5	4	1
Baroda State	11	11	..
Bihar and Orissa States	45	38	7
Bombay States	86	41	45
Central India Agency	423	300	123
Central Provinces States	396	248	148
Hyderabad State	399	233	166
Kashmir State	1,207	829	378
Madras States (*Travancore*)	1	1	..
Mysore State	18	11	7
N.-W. F. Province (*Agencies and Tribal areas*)	321	320	1
Punjab States	3,719,009	2,116,227	1,602,782
Rajputana Agency	21,871	7,457	14,414
Sikkim State	9	9	..
United Provinces States	177	145	32
Born in Rajputana Agency. Enumerated in :—	**11,082,504**	**5,840,126**	**5,242,378**
Provinces	***595,243***	***319,790***	***275,453***
Ajmer-Merwara	72,972	30,144	42,828
Andamans and Nicobars	162	150	12
Assam	11,505	8,925	2,580
Baluchistan	811	715	96

* Excluding Cochin and Travancore for which details are given on pages 147 and 149.

of Birthplace by Place of Enumeration—*continued.*

Birthplace and Place of Enumeration.	Population. Persons.	Males.	Females.
1	2	3	4
Born in Rajputana Agency—*contd.*			
Bengal	35,744	25,640	10,104
Bihar and Orissa	13,672	8,348	5,324
Bombay	118,189	75,786	42,403
Burma	1,780	1,497	283
Central Provinces and Berar	52,331	33,122	19,209
Coorg	2	2	..
Madras	1,484	1,130	354
N.-W. F. Province	1,475	1,265	210
Punjab	182,187	89,075	93,112
United Provinces	102,929	43.991	58,938
States and Agencies	*10,487.261*	*5,520,336*	*4,966,995*
Assam State	115	101	14
Baluchistan States	39	26	13
Baroda State	6,239	3,877	2,362
Bengal States	915	844	71
Bihar and Orissa States	1,538	900	638
Bombay States	23,062	11,221	11,841
Central India Agency	144,401	66,978	77,423
Central Provinces States	3,530	1,946	1,584
Hyderabad State	14,271	9,612	4,659
Kashmir State	250	156	94
Madras States	37	20	17
Cochin	*15*	*5*	*10*
Travancore	*15*	*8*	*7*
Mysore State	1,878	1,102	276
N.-W. F. Province (*Agencies and Tribal areas*)	17	17	..
Punjab States	64,422	24,815	39,607
Rajputana Agency	10,226,879	5,398,594	4,828,285
Sikkim State	73	70	3
United Provinces States	95	57	38
Born in Sikkim State Enumerated in :—	**61.530**	**30,259**	**31,271**
Provinces	*3,441*	*1,673*	*1,760*
Assam	49	27	22
Bengal	3,354	1,629	1,725
Bihar and Orissa	12	10	2
Bombay	14	1	13
Central Provinces and Berar	2	1	1
Punjab	3	..	3
United Provinces	7	4	3
States and Agencies	*58,089*	*28,587*	*29,502*
Assam State	3	3	..
Mysore State	1	1	..
Sikkim State	58,085	28,583	29,502
Born in Travancore State. Enumerated in :—	**3,394.080**	**1,714,027**	**1.680.053**
Provinces	*10,790*	*6,414*	*4,376*
Assam	4	3	1
Baluchistan	5	3	2
Bengal	54	37	17
Bihar and Orissa	16	10	6
Bombay	84	67	17
Burma	124	76	48
Central Provinces and Berar	15	11	4
Coorg	9	6	3
Madras	10,417	6,156	4,261
N.-W. F. Province	2	1	1
Punjab	19	18	1
United Provinces	41	26	15
States and Agencies	*3,383,290*	*1,707,613*	*1,675,677*
Bombay States	51	36	15
Central India Agency	2	..	2
Central Provinces States	3	..	3
Cochin State	15,207	6,922	8,285
Hyderabad State	6	2	4
Madras States *	29	13	16
Mysore State	182	115	67
Travancore State	3,367,810	1,700,525	1,667,285
Born in United Provinces States. Enumerated in :—	**839,358**	**436,490**	**402,868**
Provinces	*70,548*	*30,727*	*39,821*
Ajmer-Merwara	134	84	50
Andamans and Nicobars	39	36	3
Assam	116	61	55
Baluchistan	26	14	12
Bengal	1,480	1,017	463
Bihar and Orissa	437	302	135
Burma	688	602	86
Central Provinces and Berar	746	529	217
N.-W. F. Province	135	94	41
Punjab	956	588	368
United Provinces	65,791	27,400	38,391
Born in United Provinces States—*contd.*			
States and Agencies	*768,810*	*405,763*	*363,047*
Assam State	1	..	1
Baluchistan States	1	1	..
Baroda State	8	6	2
Bengal States	18	8	10
Bihar and Orissa States	2	2	..
Central India Agency	395	192	203
Central Provinces States	22	10	12
Hyderabad State	101	75	26
Kashmir State	8	8	..
Mysore State	5	4	1
N.-W. F. Province (*Agencies and Tribal areas*)	6	6	..
Punjab States	567	315	252
Rajputana Agency	600	461	139
United Provinces States	767,076	404,675	362,401
Born in India, *Unspecified* **Enumerated in :—**	**17,282**	**11,565**	**5,717**
Provinces	*10,918*	*7,477*	*3,441*
Ajmer-Merwara	13	5	8
Andamans and Nicobars	457	426	31
Assam	75	38	37
Baluchistan	121	77	44
Bengal	106	60	46
Bihar and Orissa	44	17	27
Bombay	5,947	4,263	1,684
Burma	2,114	1,836	278
Madras	381	104	277
N.-W. F. Province	200	112	88
Punjab	1,140	423	717
United Provinces	320	116	204
States and Agencies	*6,364*	*4,088*	*2,276*
Baluchistan States	6	4	2
Baroda State	67	66	1
Bombay States	2,353	1,283	1,070
Hyderabad State	3,675	2,566	1,109
Madras States	170	137	33
Cochin	*30*	*24*	*6*
Travancore	*135*	*111*	*24*
Mysore State	59	11	48
N.-W. F. Province (*Agencies and Tribal areas*)	11	11	..
Punjab States	15	10	5
Rajputana Agency	5		5
United Provinces States	3		3
Born in French and Portuguese Settlements Enumerated in :—	**87,635**	**52,854**	**34,781**
Provinces	*79,440*	*49,130*	*30,310*
Ajmer-Merwara	246	184	62
Andamans and Nicobars	5	5	..
Assam	36	21	15
Baluchistan	160	140	20
Bengal	2,338	1,401	937
Bihar and Orissa	88	44	44
Bombay	52.262	35,517	16,745
Burma	845	740	105
Central Provinces and Berar	799	574	225
Coorg	12	11	1
Madras	22,138	10,058	12,080
N.-W. F. Province	102	98	4
Punjab	73	58	15
United Provinces	336	279	57
States and Agencies	*8.195*	*3,724*	*4,471*
Baluchistan States	23	23	..
Baroda State	559	291	268
Bengal States	23	23	..
Bihar and Orissa States	1	.	1
Bombay States	5,872	2,247	3,625
Central India Agency	192	133	59
Central Provinces States	21	15	6
Hyderabad State	288	184	104
Kashmir State	8	8	..
Madras States	273	197	76
Cochin	*57*	*81*	*6*
Travancore	*150*	*106*	*44*
Mysore State	738	456	282
Punjab States	27	17	10
Rajputana Agency	170	130	40

*Excluding Cochin and Travancore.

TABLE XI.—BIRTHPLACE. PART IV.—DISTRIBUTION

Birthplace and Place of Enumeration.	Population. Persons.	Males.	Females.
1	2	3	4
B.—Born in other Asiatic Countries	**504,113**	**330,675**	**173,438**
Enumerated in :—			
Ajmer-Merwara	170	150	20
Andamans and Nicobars	96	96	..
Assam	48,185	32,649	15,536
Baluchistan	12,467	9,240	3,227
Bengal	116,672	67,948	48,724
Bihar and Orissa	36,678	12,610	24,068
Bombay	32,474	25,609	6,865
Burma	88,268	70,368	17,900
Central Provinces and Berar	1,431	1,231	200
Coorg	6	4	2
Madras	5,202	3,149	2,053
N.-W. F. Province	47,166	30,040	17,126
Punjab	27,144	22,706	4,438
United Provinces	46,020	27,850	18,170
Assam State	1,168	771	397
Baluchistan States	334	204	130
Baroda State	191	144	47
Bengal States	692	628	64
Bihar and Orissa States	107	93	14
Bombay States	1,758	1,577	181
Central India Agency	355	248	107
Central Provinces States	102	70	32
Hyderabad State	3,507	2,882	625
Kashmir State	2,233	1,860	373
Madras States	1,039	579	460
Cochin	*22*	*17*	*5*
Travancore	*229*	*146*	*83*
Mysore State	283	162	121
N.-W. F. Province (*Agencies and Tribal areas*)	1,068	1,067	1
Punjab States	2,721	2,176	545
Rajputana Agency	466	336	130
Sikkim State	26,013	14,155	11,858
United Provinces States	97	73	24
Born in Afghanistan	**91,640**	**67,451**	**24,189**
Enumerated in :—			
Ajmer-Merwara	134	124	10
Andamans and Nicobars	34	34	..
Assam	662	649	13
Baluchistan	10,575	7,660	2,915
Bengal	2,624	2,541	83
Bihar and Orissa	600	593	7
Bombay	7,460	6,413	1,047
Burma	109	109	..
Central Provinces and Berar	1,004	950	54
Madras	118	83	35
N.-W. F. Province	42,163	25,892	16,271
Punjab	20,575	17,441	3,134
United Provinces	1,571	1,407	164
Assam State	5	2	3
Baluchistan States	50	34	16
Baroda State	87	71	16
Bengal States	86	86	..
Bihar and Orissa States	57	54	3
Bombay States	787	758	29
Central India Agency	178	144	34
Central Provinces States	60	57	3
Hyderabad State	468	367	101
Kashmir State	943	806	137
Madras States (*Travancore*)	6	3	3
Mysore State	24	22	2
N.-W. F. Province (*Agencies and Tribal areas*)	317	317	..
Punjab States	664	585	79
Rajputana Agency	243	214	29
Sikkim State	2	2	..
United Provinces States	34	33	1
Born in Arabia	**23,078**	**18,540**	**4,538**
Enumerated in :—			
Ajmer-Merwara	8	7	1
Assam	15	15	..
Bengal	475	346	129
Bihar and Orissa	22	17	5
Bombay	17,700	14,210	3,490
Burma	133	101	32
Central Provinces and Berar	70	57	13
Madras	274	253	21
N.-W. F. Province	27	16	11
Punjab	195	144	51
United Provinces	158	116	42
Baluchistan States	230	129	101
Baroda State	37	27	10
Bengal States	3	3	..
Bombay States	676	576	100
Central India Agency	53	23	30
Central Provinces States	4	2	2
Hyderabad State	2,864	2,394	470
Kashmir State	1	1	..
Madras States	9	8	1
Travancore	*7*	*6*	*1*
Mysore State	23	11	12
Born in Arabia—*contd.*			
N.-W. F. Province (*Agencies and Tribal areas*)	4	4	..
Punjab States	46	44	2
Rajputana Agency	36	28	8
United Provinces States	15	8	7
Born in Armenia	**40**	**14**	**26**
Enumerated in :—			
Bengal	15	3	12
Bombay	20	8	12
Burma	3	3	..
Mysore State	2	..	2
Born in Asia Minor	**1**	**1**	..
Enumerated in :—			
N.-W. F Province	1	1	..
Born in Bhotan	**2,647**	**1,605**	**1,042**
Enumerated in :—			
Assam	714	552	162
Baluchistan	1	..	1
Bengal	1,796	950	846
Bihar and Orissa	8	3	5
Bombay	6	4	2
Burma	4	4	..
Central Provinces and Berar	2	2	..
Madras	17	17	..
Punjab	20	13	7
United Provinces	12	9	3
Baroda State	3	2	1
Bengal States	3	3	..
Bombay States	1	1	..
Hyderabad State	12	12	..
Kashmir State	2	2	..
N.-W. F. Province (*Agencies and Tribal areas*)	1	1	..
Sikkim State	45	30	15
Born in Bokhara	**7**	**7**	..
Enumerated in :—			
Rajputana Agency	7	7	..
Born in Ceylon	**6,165**	**3,778**	**2,387**
Enumerated in :—			
Ajmer-Merwara	5	4	1
Andamans and Nicobars	4	4	..
Assam	9	5	4
Baluchistan	1	1	..
Bengal	123	80	43
Bihar and Orissa	31	9	22
Bombay	218	157	61
Burma	846	752	94
Central Provinces and Berar	20	9	11
Coorg	5	4	1
Madras	3,586	2,021	1,565
N.-W. F. Province	16	9	7
Punjab	30	18	12
United Provinces	97	65	32
Bengal States	1	1	..
Bihar and Orissa States	2	1	1
Bombay States	12	9	3
Central India Agency	3	..	3
Central Provinces States	2	2	..
Hyderabad State	20	9	11
Madras States	975	534	441
Cochin	*13*	*11*	*2*
Travancore	*206*	*127*	*79*
Mysore State	140	72	68
Punjab States	4	3	1
Rajputana Agency	15	9	6
Born in China	**80,307**	**64,784**	**15,523**
Enumerated in :—			
Ajmer-Merwara	1	..	1
Andamans and Nicobars	35	35	..
Assam	270	260	10
Baluchistan	7	4	3
Bengal	3,085	2,698	387
Bihar and Orissa	18	13	5
Bombay	536	471	65
Burma	75,365	60,699	14,666
Central Provinces and Berar	35	12	23
Coorg	1	..	1
Madras	148	123	25
N.-W. F. Province	7	4	3
Punjab	384	221	163
United Provinces	151	93	58
Baluchistan States	1	1	..
Bengal States	2	..	2
Bihar and Orissa States	2	2	..
Bombay States	2	2	..
Kashmir State	2	1	1
Madras States (*Travancore*)	1	1	..
Mysore State	18	16	2

…OF BIRTHPLACE BY PLACE OF ENUMERATION—*continued.*

Birthplace and Place of Enumeration.	Population. Persons.	Males.	Females.
1	2	3	4
Born in China—*contd.*			
N.-W. F. Province (*Agencies and Tribal areas*)	1	1	..
Punjab States	211	118	93
Rajputana Agency	8	4	4
Sikkim State	15	5	10
United Provinces States	1	..	1
Born in Chinese Tartary	**30**	**24**	**6**
Enumerated in :—			
Baroda State	2	2	..
Kashmir State	28	22	6
Born in Chinese Turkistan	**14**	**8**	**6**
Enumerated in :—			
Bengal	2	2	..
Madras	5	2	3
United Provinces	6	3	3
Mysore State	1	1	..
Born in French Indo-China	**35**	**23**	**12**
Enumerated in :—			
Assam	1	..	1
Bihar and Orissa	5	5	..
Bombay	5	..	5
Burma	1	..	1
Madras	14	9	5
United Provinces	3	3	..
Bombay States	6	6	..
Born in Hong Kong	**74**	**52**	**22**
Enumerated in :—			
Assam	1	1	..
Bengal	39	31	8
Bihar and Orissa	3	2	1
Bombay	3	2	1
Burma	6	1	5
Central Provinces and Berar	1	1	..
Madras	7	5	2
N.-W. F. Province	2	2	..
United Provinces	5	2	3
Hyderabad State	1	1	..
Mysore State	6	4	2
Born in Japan	**1,261**	**567**	**694**
Enumerated in :—			
Ajmer-Merwara	2	1	1
Baluchistan	7	1	6
Bengal	146	38	108
Bihar and Orissa	9	7	2
Bombay	327	158	169
Burma	666	310	356
Central Provinces and Berar	4	4	..
Madras	28	19	9
Punjab	12	2	10
United Provinces	44	19	25
Bombay States	1	1	..
Central India Agency	4	2	2
Hyderabad State	3	..	3
Madras States	3	3	..
Travancore	*1*	*1*	..
Mysore State	4	1	3
Rajputana Agency	1	1	..
Born in Maldives	**29**	**28**	**1**
Enumerated in :—			
Bengal	22	22	..
Burma	3	3	..
Madras	4	3	1
Born in Mongolia	**7**	**6**	**1**
Enumerated in :—			
Andamans and Nicobars	1	1	..
Bengal	1	..	1
Bihar and Orissa	1	1	..
Bombay	1	1	..
Burma	1	1	..
Sikkim State	2	2	..
Born in Nepal	**280,248**	**160,974**	**119,274**
Enumerated in :—			
Ajmer-Merwara	17	13	4
Andamans and Nicobars	14	14	..
Assam	46,491	31,151	15,340
Baluchistan	1,677	1,439	238
Bengal	106,132	59,697	46,435
Bihar and Orissa	35,944	11,932	24,012
Bombay	304	249	55
Burma	5,997	4,783	1,214
Central Provinces and Berar	218	147	71
Madras	17	14	3
N.-W. F. Province	4,911	4,093	818
Punjab	4,821	4,012	809
United Provinces	43,320	25,722	17,598
Assam State	1,163	769	394

Birthplace and Place of Enumeration.	Population. Persons.	Males.	Females.
1	2	3	4
Born in Nepal—*contd.*			
Baroda State	49	29	20
Bengal States	595	533	62
Bihar and Orissa States	10	10	..
Bombay States	210	164	46
Central India Agency	88	58	30
Central Provinces States	35	9	26
Hyderabad State	19	12	7
Kashmir State	1,077	926	151
Madras States	2	2	..
Travancore	*1*	*1*	..
Mysore State	9	7	2
N.-W. F. Province (*Agencies and Tribal areas*)	742	741	1
Punjab States	609	466	143
Rajputana Agency	140	63	77
Sikkim State	25,610	13,903	11,707
United Provinces States	27	16	11
Born in Persia	**6,772**	**4,605**	**2,167**
Enumerated in :—			
Ajmer-Merwara	1	..	1
Assam	9	6	3
Baluchistan	174	121	53
Bengal	429	351	78
Bihar and Orissa	18	13	5
Bombay	5,179	3,399	1,780
Burma	147	123	24
Central Provinces and Berar	61	39	22
Madras	177	144	33
N.-W. F. Province	5	5	..
Punjab	266	186	80
United Provinces	43	25	18
Baluchistan States	40	27	13
Baroda State	13	13	..
Bengal States	1	1	..
Bihar and Orissa States	29	19	10
Bombay States	16	14	2
Central India Agency	11	5	6
Hyderabad State	90	59	31
Kashmir State	29	26	3
Madras States (*Cochin*)	2	2	..
Mysore State	5	4	1
Punjab States	13	12	1
Rajputana Agency	7	6	1
United Provinces States	7	5	2
Born in Russia in Asia	**150**	**130**	**20**
Enumerated in :—			
Bombay	114	104	10
N.-W. F. Province	19	11	8
Punjab	11	10	1
Kashmir State	1	1	..
Mysore State	1	..	1
Punjab States	4	4	..
Born in Russian Turkistan	**77**	**61**	**16**
Enumerated in :—			
Assam	4	2	2
Baluchistan	7	5	2
Bengal	4	3	1
Bombay	8	5	3
Burma	2	2	..
Madras	3	2	1
Punjab	17	16	1
United Provinces	24	18	6
Baluchistan States	7	7	..
Punjab States	1	1	..
Born in Siam	**4,093**	**2,783**	**1,310**
Enumerated in :—			
Andamans and Nicobars	7	7	..
Assam	1	1	..
Bengal	9	9	..
Bihar and Orissa	2	..	2
Bombay	21	11	10
Burma	3,995	2,706	1,289
Madras	13	8	5
United Provinces	4	1	3
Bombay States	40	40	..
Mysore State	1	..	1
Born in Straits Settlements and Malaya	**1,873**	**1,294**	**579**
Enumerated in :—			
Andamans and Nicobars	1	1	..
Assam	4	3	1
Bengal	101	52	49
Bihar and Orissa	3	2	1
Bombay	49	47	2
Burma	789	655	134
Central Provinces and Berar	2	2	..
Madras	764	427	337
N.-W. F. Province	9	5	4
Punjab	24	16	8

TABLE XI.—BIRTHPLACE. PART IV.—DISTRIBUTION

Birthplace and Place of Enumeration.	Population. Persons.	Males.	Females.
1	2	3	4
Born in Straits Settlements and Malaya—*contd.*			
United Provinces	2	2	..
Baluchistan States	6	6	..
Bengal States	1	1	..
Bombay States	1	1	..
Central Provinces States	1	..	1
Hyderabad State	29	27	2
Madras States	33	18	15
Cochin	*4*	*1*	*3*
Travancore	*2*	*2*	..
Mysore State	48	23	25
N.-W. F. Province (*Agencies and Tribal areas*)	1	1	..
Punjab States	3	3	..
Rajputana Agency	2	2	..
Born in Tibet	**4,509**	**3,238**	**1,271**
Enumerated in :—			
Ajmer-Merwara	1	1	..
Assam	3	3	..
Baluchistan	1	1	..
Bengal	1,532	1,056	476
Bihar and Orissa	8	8	..
Bombay	1	1	..
N.-W. F. Province	1	1	..
Punjab	761	601	160
United Provinces	525	323	202
Bihar and Orissa States	1	1	..
Kashmir State	149	74	75
N.-W. F. Province (*Agencies and Tribal areas*)	2	2	..
Punjab States	1,166	940	226
Rajputana Agency	6	2	4
Sikkim State	339	213	126
United Provinces States	13	11	2
Born in Turkey in Asia	**937**	**616**	**321**
Enumerated in :—			
Ajmer-Merwara	1	..	1
Assam	1	1	..
Baluchistan	17	8	9
Bengal	130	64	66
Bihar and Orissa	2	2	..
Bombay	458	317	141
Burma	200	115	85
Central Provinces and Berar	8	7	1
Madras	21	16	5
N.-W. F. Province	5	1	4
Punjab	25	24	1
United Provinces	34	30	4
Bombay States	6	5	1
Central India Agency	18	16	2
Hyderabad State	1	1	..
Kashmir State	1	1	..
Madras States	8	8	..
Cochin	*3*	*3*	..
Travancore	*5*	*5*	..
Rajputana Agency	1	..	1
Born in Asia, ***Unspecified***	**119**	**86**	**33**
Enumerated in :—			
Bengal	7	5	2
Bihar and Orissa	4	3	1
Bombay	64	52	12
Burma	1	1	..
Central Provinces and Berar	6	1	5
Madras	6	3	3
Punjab	3	2	1
United Provinces	21	12	9
Bihar and Orissa States	6	6	..
Mysore State	1	1	..
C.—Born in Europe	**131,968**	**109,594**	**22,374**
Enumerated in :			
Ajmer-Merwara	1,266	1,131	135
Andamans and Nicobars	182	164	18
Assam	1,483	1,156	327
Baluchistan	3,311	2,916	395
Bengal	13,489	10,242	3,247
Bihar and Orissa	2,836	1,982	854
Bombay	23,443	19,700	3,743
Burma	8,337	7,060	1,277
Central Provinces and Berar	5,100	4,413	687
Coorg	95	63	32
Madras	7,891	5,761	2,130
N.-W. F. Province	4,820	4,373	447
Punjab	23,620	20,124	3,496
United Provinces	22,467	19,175	3,292
Assam State	13	8	5
C.—Born in Europe—*contd.*			
Baluchistan States	12	10	2
Baroda State	70	44	26
Bengal States	13	9	4
Bihar and Orissa States	25	13	12
Bombay States	537	402	135
Central India Agency	3,283	2,916	367
Central Provinces States	32	25	7
Hyderabad State	3,936	3,444	492
Kashmir State	126	76	50
Madras States	380	242	138
Cochin	*50*	*42*	*8*
Travancore	*312*	*191*	*121*
Mysore State	4,263	3,498	765
N.-W. F. Province (*Agencies and Tribal areas*)	71	57	14
Punjab States	286	202	84
Rajputana Agency	561	371	190
Sikkim State	14	14	..
United Provinces States	6	3	3
Born in United Kingdom*	**122,919**	**103,425**	**19,494**
Enumerated in :—			
Ajmer-Merwara	1,223	1,099	124
Andamans and Nicobars	181	163	18
Assam	1,415	1,111	304
Baluchistan	3,276	2,899	377
Bengal	12,172	9,350	2,822
Bihar and Orissa	2,560	1,851	709
Bombay	21,015	17,942	3,073
Burma	7,354	6,279	1,075
Central Provinces and Berar	4,815	4,251	564
Coorg	82	58	24
Madras	6,488	4,901	1,587
N.-W. F. Province	4,765	4,333	432
Punjab	23,045	19,762	3,283
United Provinces	22,003	18,844	3,159
Assam State	12	8	4
Baluchistan States	11	9	2
Baroda State	55	35	20
Bengal States	7	5	2
Bihar and Orissa States	12	8	4
Bombay States	229	150	79
Central India Agency	3,192	2,841	351
Central Provinces States	31	24	7
Hyderabad State	3,790	3,359	431
Kashmir State	109	69	40
Madras States	266	181	85
Cochin	*20*	*14*	*6*
Travancore	*237*	*160*	*77*
Mysore State	3,939	3,289	650
N.-W. F. Province (*Agencies and Tribal areas*)	71	57	14
Punjab States	266	192	74
Rajputana Agency	521	342	179
Sikkim State	11	11	..
United Provinces States	3	2	1
Born in England and Wales	***95,436***	***80,605***	***14,831***
Enumerated in :—			
Ajmer-Merwara	1,094	1,013	81
Andamans and Nicobars	179	162	17
Assam	876	658	218
Baluchistan	2,266	1,982	284
Bengal	8,963	6,918	2,045
Bihar and Orissa	2,052	1,514	538
Bombay	18,140	15,620	2,520
Burma	5,105	4,326	779
Central Provinces and Berar	4,417	3,949	468
Coorg	64	44	20
Madras	5,461	4,256	1,205
N.-W. F. Province	3,620	3,295	325
Punjab	18,378	15,842	2,536
United Provinces	14,609	12,372	2,237
Assam State	9	5	4
Baluchistan States	9	7	2
Baroda State	48	30	18
Bengal States	6	4	2
Bihar and Orissa States	7	5	2
Bombay States	182	120	62
Central India Agency	2,731	2,441	290
Central Provinces States	25	19	6
Hyderabad State	3,615	3,238	377
Kashmir State	90	58	32
Madras States	199	136	63
Cochin	*18*	*12*	*6*
Travancore	*174*	*118*	*56*
Mysore State	2,642	2,121	521
N.-W. F. Province (*Agencies and Tribal areas*)	52	44	8
Punjab States	218	163	55
Rajputana Agency	367	252	115
Sikkim State	10	10	..
United Provinces States	2	1	1

* Separate figures for England and Wales, Scotland, Ireland, etc., are given below.

of Birthplace by Place of Enumeration—*continued.*

Birthplace and Place of Enumeration.	Population. Persons.	Males.	Females.
1	2	3	4
Born in Scotland	***13,913***	***11,676***	***2,237***
Enumerated in :—			
Ajmer-Merwara	77	50	27
Andamans and Nicobars	1	1	..
Assam	442	380	62
Baluchistan	125	102	23
Bengal	2,392	1,875	517
Bihar and Orissa	311	205	106
Bombay	1,031	802	229
Burma	1,040	907	133
Central Provinces and Berar	181	124	57
Coorg	16	12	4
Madras	533	387	146
N.-W. F. Province	182	149	33
Punjab	1,766	1,500	266
United Provinces	4,344	3,890	454
Assam State	1	1	..
Baluchistan States	2	2	..
Baroda State	2	2	..
Bengal States	1	1	..
Bihar and Orissa States	3	2	1
Bombay States	27	19	8
Central India Agency	99	80	19
Central Provinces States	5	5	..
Hyderabad State	72	53	19
Kashmir State	10	6	4
Madras States	51	37	14
Cochin	*2*	*2*	..
Travancore	*48*	*35*	*13*
Mysore State	1,051	997	54
N.-W. F. Province (*Agencies and Tribal areas*)	10	7	3
Punjab States	24	13	11
Rajputana Agency	112	65	47
Sikkim State	1	1	..
United Provinces States	1	1	..
Born in Ireland	***12,244***	***9,953***	***2,291***
Enumerated in :—			
Ajmer-Merwara	52	36	16
Andamans and Nicobars	1	..	1
Assam	97	73	24
Baluchistan	981	812	69
Bengal	814	555	259
Bihar and Orissa	197	132	65
Bombay	1,837	1,518	319
Burma	1,209	1,046	163
Central Provinces and Berar	207	168	39
Coorg	2	2	..
Madras	488	253	235
N.-W. F. Province	954	885	69
Punjab	2,892	2,413	479
United Provinces	1,779	1,430	349
Assam State	2	2	..
Baroda State	5	3	2
Bihar and Orissa States	2	1	1
Bombay States	20	11	9
Central India Agency	362	320	42
Central Provinces States	1	..	1
Hyderabad State	103	68	35
Kashmir State	9	5	4
Madras States	16	8	8
Travancore	*15*	*7*	*8*
Mysore State	242	167	75
N.-W. F. Province (*Agencies and Tribal areas*)	8	5	3
Punjab States	23	15	8
Rajputana Agency	41	25	16
Born in Channel Islands and Isle of Man	***59***	***41***	***18***
Enumerated in :—			
Baluchistan	4	3	1
Bengal	3	2	1
Bombay	5	2	3
Central Provinces and Berar	10	10	..
Madras	6	5	1
N.-W. F. Province	9	4	5
United Provinces	17	11	6
Mysore State	3	3	..
N.-W. F. Province (*Agencies and Tribal areas*)	1	1	..
Rajputana Agency	1	..	1
Born in United Kingdom, Unspecified	***1,267***	***1,150***	***117***
Enumerated in :—			
Bombay	2	..	2
Punjab	9	7	2
United Provinces	1,254	1,141	113
Mysore State	1	1	..
Punjab States	1	1	..
Born in Austria-Hungary	**599**	**408**	**191**
Enumerated in :—			
Assam	1	1	..
Baluchistan	1	..	1
Bengal	156	102	54
Bihar and Orissa	11	6	5
Bombay	220	140	80
Born in Austria-Hungary —*contd.*			
Burma	137	123	14
Madras	38	22	16
N.-W. F. Province	1	1	..
Punjab	17	4	13
United Provinces	1	..	1
Baluchistan States	1	1	..
Baroda State	1	..	1
Bombay States	2	2	..
Hyderabad State	5	1	4
Madras States (*Travancore*)	3	2	1
Mysore State	2	2	..
Punjab States	2	1	1
Born in Belgium	**353**	**212**	**141**
Enumerated in :—			
Baluchistan	1	1	..
Bengal	65	56	9
Bihar and Orissa	53	27	26
Bombay	42	29	13
Burma	15	12	3
Central Provinces and Berar	5	4	1
Madras	48	18	30
Punjab	61	35	26
United Provinces	18	10	8
Bihar and Orissa States	4	2	2
Bombay States	13	9	4
Hyderabad State	1	1	..
Madras States	25	6	19
Cochin	*1*	*1*	..
Travancore	*21*	*5*	*16*
Rajputana Agency	2	2	..
Born in Bulgaria	**1**	**1**	..
Enumerated in :—			
Rajputana Agency	1	1	..
Born in Cyprus	**4**	**3**	**1**
Enumerated in :—			
Assam	1	1	..
N.-W. F. Province	2	2	..
Mysore State	1	..	1
Born in Denmark	**103**	**62**	**41**
Enumerated in :—			
Assam	4	3	1
Bengal	11	9	2
Bihar and Orissa	3	1	2
Bombay	12	11	1
Burma	4	4	..
Central Provinces and Berar	2	2	..
Madras	39	14	25
N.-W. F. Province	1	..	1
Punjab	3	2	1
United Provinces	14	13	1
Bombay States	1	1	..
Kashmir State	1	..	1
Madras States (*Travancore*)	2	..	2
Mysore State	5	2	3
Rajputana Agency	1	..	1
Born in France	**1,478**	**757**	**721**
Enumerated in :—			
Ajmer-Merwara	29	24	5
Baluchistan	6	3	3
Bengal	175	104	71
Bihar and Orissa	26	10	16
Bombay	163	68	95
Burma	211	113	98
Central Provinces and Berar	101	29	72
Coorg	6	1	5
Madras	503	239	264
N.-W. F. Province	10	7	3
Punjab	49	27	22
United Provinces	35	26	9
Baroda State	6	3	3
Bombay States	1	..	1
Central India Agency	24	20	4
Hyderabad State	12	6	6
Kashmir State	3	3	..
Madras States	5	4	1
Cochin	*2*	*2*	..
Travancore	*2*	*1*	*1*
Mysore State	90	52	38
Punjab States	2	1	1
Rajputana Agency	20	17	3
United Provinces States	1	..	1
Born in Germany	**1,860**	**1,321**	**539**
Enumerated in :—			
Andamans and Nicobars	1	1	..
Assam	28	17	11
Baluchistan	9	6	3
Bengal	305	243	62
Bihar and Orissa	140	57	83
Bombay	350	259	91
Burma	214	184	30
Central Provinces and Berar	74	47	27

TABLE XI.—Birthplace. Part IV—Distribution

Birthplace and Place of Enumeration.	Population. Persons.	Males.	Females.
1	2	3	4
Born in Germany—*contd.*			
Coorg	4	3	1
Madras	402	314	88
N.-W. F. Province	8	6	2
Punjab	68	43	25
United Provinces	130	87	43
Assam State	1	..	1
Baroda State	1	1	..
Bihar and Orissa States	8	3	5
Bombay States	3	2	1
Central India Agency	16	13	3
Hyderabad State	3	2	1
Kashmir State	6	1	5
Madras States	16	6	10
Cochin	*4*	*2*	*2*
Travancore	*11*	*4*	*7*
Mysore State	52	14	38
Punjab States	8	4	4
Rajputana Agency	8	4	4
Sikkim State	3	3	..
United Provinces States	2	1	1
Born in Gibraltar	93	45	48
Enumerated in :—			
Assam	1	1	..
Baluchistan	6	1	5
Bengal	9	6	3
Bombay	30	7	23
Burma	13	8	5
Madras	2	1	1
N.-W. F. Province	4	2	2
United Provinces	18	16	2
Hyderabad State	1	..	1
Mysore State	8	3	5
Punjab States	1	..	1
Born in Greece	274	245	29
Enumerated in :—			
Ajmer-Merwara	1	1	.
Assam	2	2	.
Bengal	81	66	15
Bihar and Orissa	2	2	..
Bombay	80	71	9
Burma	71	70	1
Central Provinces and Berar	10	10	..
Madras	3	3	..
Punjab	8	6	2
United Provinces	9	9	..
engal States	4	2	2
Bombay States	1	1	..
Mysore State	1	1	..
Rajputana Agency	1	1	..
Born in Holland	235	200	35
Enumerated in :—			
Bengal	34	32	2
Bihar and Orissa	2	2	..
Bombay	14	10	4
Burma	59	55	4
Central Provinces and Berar	1	1	.
Madras	96	74	22
Punjab	12	11	1
United Provinces	7	6	1
Bombay States	1	1	..
Central Provinces States	1	1	..
Kashmir State	2	2	..
Madras States	2	2	..
Travancore	*1*	*1*	..
Mysore State	4	3	1
Born in Iceland	9	7	2
Enumerated in :—			
Bombay	5	5	..
Central Provinces and Berar	1	..	1
Punjab	1	..	1
Madras States (*Travancore*)	1	1	..
Mysore State	1	1	..
Born in Italy	894	657	237
Enumerated in :—			
Assam	16	8	8
Baluchistan	3	2	1
Bengal	130	76	54
Bihar and Orissa	19	12	7
Bombay	204	163	41
Burma	33	24	9
Central Provinces and Berar	39	36	3
Madras	80	43	37
N.-W. F. Province	1	1	..
Punjab	29	17	12
United Provinces	125	98	27
Baroda State	1	1	..
Bihar and Orissa States	1	..	1
Bombay States	9	9	..
Central India Agency	2	1	1
Hyderabad State	66	42	24
Madras States (*Travancore*)	5	4	1
Mysore State	127	118	9
Rajputana Agency	4	2	2
Born in Malta	172	85	87
Enumerated in :—			
Baluchistan	5	2	3
Bengal	21	13	8
Bihar and Orissa	3	1	2
Bombay	31	11	20
Burma	3	3	..
Central Provinces and Berar	1	..	1
N.-W. F. Province	10	8	2
Punjab	58	21	37
United Provinces	31	22	9
Baroda State	1	..	1
Bombay States	1	1	..
Hyderabad State	1	..	1
Mysore State	4	2	2
Punjab States	2	1	1
Born in Norway	109	88	21
Enumerated in :—			
Ajmer-Merwara	1	1	..
Bengal	6	3	3
Bihar and Orissa	6	5	1
Bombay	47	39	8
Burma	17	17	..
Central Provinces and Berar	4	4	..
Madras	18	15	3
Punjab	2	1	1
United Provinces	5	2	3
Bengal States	1	1	..
Madras States (*Travancore*)	2	..	2
Born in Portugal	948	763	185
Enumerated in :—			
Ajmer-Merwara	5	4	1
Assam	1	1	..
Baluchistan	1	1	..
Bengal	16	14	2
Bihar and Orissa	1	1	..
Bombay	361	265	96
Burma	6	6	..
Central Provinces and Berar	6	5	1
Madras	72	61	11
N.-W. F. Province	1	1	..
Punjab	141	129	12
United Provinces	7	4	3
Baroda State	2	2	..
Bombay States	276	226	50
Central India Agency	48	40	8
Madras States (*Travancore*)	2	2	..
Mysore State	2	1	1
Born in Rumania	21	13	8
Enumerated in :—			
Bengal	5	2	3
Bihar and Orissa	1	1	..
Bombay	12	9	3
United Provinces	1	..	1
Hyderabad State	1	1	..
Mysore State	1	..	1
Born in Russia	314	134	180
Enumerated in :—			
Ajmer-Merwara	2	1	1
Assam	6	6	..
Baluchistan	1	..	1
Bengal	120	41	79
Bihar and Orissa	1	1	..
Bombay	77	23	54
Burma	31	17	14
Central Provinces and Berar	2	1	1
Madras	13	8	5
N.-W. F. Province	2	1	1
Punjab	11	3	8
United Provinces	26	20	6
Central India Agency	1	1	..
Hyderabad State	11	6	5
Mysore State	9	4	5
Rajputana Agency	1	1	..
Born in Spain	153	101	52
Enumerated in :—			
Ajmer Merwara	2	1	1
Assam	1	1	..
Bengal	34	23	11
Bihar and Orissa	1	1	..
Bombay	21	12	9
Burma	16	14	2
Central Provinces and Berar	1	1	..
Madras	3	..	3
N.-W. F. Province	8	6	2
Punjab	23	4	19
United Provinces	11	9	2
Baroda State	1	1	..
Hyderabad State	3	2	1
Madras States	24	24	..
Cochin	*23*	*23*	..
Travancore	*1*	*1*	..
Mysore State	2	1	1
Punjab States	1	..	1
Rajputana Agency	1	1	..

OF BIRTHPLACE BY PLACE OF ENUMERATION—*continued.*

Birthplace and Place of Enumeration.	Population. Persons.	Males.	Females.
1	2	3	4
Born in Sweden	**222**	**145**	**77**
Enumerated in :—			
Ajmer-Merwara	1	..	*1*
Assam	2	2	..
Baluchistan	1	..	1
Bengal	34	22	12
Bihar and Orissa	2	2	..
Bombay	62	39	23
Burma	44	44	..
Central Provinces and Berar	35	19	16
Madras	27	14	13
Punjab	5	1	4
United Provinces	1	..	1
Kashmir State	1	1	..
Madras States	6	1	5
Travancore	*3*	*1*	*2*
Punjab States	1	..	1
Born in Switzerland	**287**	**190**	**97**
Enumerated in :—			
Ajmer-Merwara	2	..	2
Assam	3	1	2
Baluchistan	1	1	..
Bengal	50	34	16
Bihar and Orissa	4	2	2
Bombay	107	95	12
Burma	7	4	3
Central Provinces and Berar	2	2	..
Coorg	3	1	2
Madras	56	31	25
N.-W. F. Province	3	2	1
Punjab	17	11	6
United Provinces	14	3	11
Baroda State	2	1	1
Hyderabad State	1	1	..
Kashmir State	4	..	4
Madras States (*Travancore*)	9	..	9
Mysore State	1	1	..
Rajputana Agency	1	..	1
Born in Turkey in Europe	**111**	**81**	**30**
Enumerated in :—			
Assam	2	1	1
Bengal	63	44	19
Bihar and Orissa	1	..	1
Bombay	6	6	..
Madras	2	2	..
N.-W. F. Province	3	2	1
Punjab	4	3	1
United Provinces	6	4	2
Bengal States	1	1	..
Hyderabad State	13	13	..
Mysore State	8	3	5
Punjab States	2	2	..
Born in Europe, *Unspecified*	**809**	**651**	**158**
Enumerated in :—			
Bengal	2	2	..
Bombay	584	496	88
Burma	102	83	19
Central Provinces and Berar	1	1	..
Madras	1	1	..
N.-W. F. Province	1	1	..
Punjab	66	44	22
United Provinces	5	2	3
Hyderabad State	28	10	18
Madras States (*Travancore*)	12	9	3
Mysore State	6	1	5
Punjab States	1	1	..
B.—Born in Africa	**10,270**	**6,921**	**3,349**
Enumerated in :—			
Ajmer-Merwara	9	6	3
Assam	14	13	1
Baluchistan	8	6	2
Bengal	232	157	75
Bihar and Orissa	29	12	17
Bombay	7,546	5,275	2,271
Burma	53	42	11
Central Provinces and Berar	42	35	7
Coorg	3	2	1
Madras	886	503	383
N.-W. F. Province	22	11	11
Punjab	115	75	40
United Provinces	277	169	108
Baroda State	257	110	147
Bihar and Orissa States	1	..	1
Bombay States	460	259	201
Central India Agency	129	101	28
Central Provinces States	4	3	1
Hyderabad State	98	87	11
Kashmir State	6	2	4
Madras States	8	4	4
Travancore	*1*	*1*	..
Mysore State	46	34	12
N.-W. F. Province (*Agencies and Tribal areas*)	2	2	..
Punjab States	7	3	4
Rajputana Agency	16	10	6
Born in Abyssinia	**2**	**1**	**1**
Enumerated in :—			
Bengal	1	..	1
Bombay	1	1	..
Born in British East Africa	**6,518**	**4,701**	**1,817**
Enumerated in :—			
Baluchistan	1	1	..
Bombay	6,506	4,695	1,811
United Provinces	4	1	3
Bombay States	7	4	3
Born in Cape Colony	**56**	**38**	**18**
Enumerated in :—			
Assam	1	1	..
Baluchistan	5	4	1
Bengal	8	3	5
Bihar and Orissa	2	..	2
Bombay	5	4	1
Burma	15	13	2
Madras	5	1	4
N.-W. F. Province	2	1	1
Punjab	10	9	1
Bihar and Orissa States	1	..	1
N.-W. F. Province (*Agencies and Tribal areas*)	1	1	..
Punjab States	1	1	..
Born in Congo	**1**	..	**1**
Enumerated in :—			
Punjab	1	..	1
Born in Egypt	**301**	**221**	**80**
Enumerated in :—			
Assam	3	3	..
Bengal	24	19	5
Bihar and Orissa	3	3	..
Bombay	78	58	20
Burma	1	1	..
Central Provinces and Berar	3	2	1
N.-W. F. Province	2	1	1
Punjab	10	9	1
United Provinces	38	15	23
Central India Agency	127	99	28
Hyderabad State	8	8	..
Mysore State	2	2	..
Punjab States	2	1	1
Born in Mauritius	**514**	**258**	**256**
Enumerated in :—			
Ajmer-Merwara	1	1	..
Baluchistan	2	1	1
Bengal	49	32	17
Bihar and Orissa	10	3	7
Bombay	148	59	89
Burma	1	1	..
Central Provinces and Berar	2	..	2
Madras	193	117	76
United Provinces	29	15	14
Baroda State	54	19	35
Bombay States	11	3	8
Hyderabad State	1	..	1
Madras States	5	2	3
Mysore State	1	1	..
Rajputana Agency	7	4	3
Born in Mozambique	**1**	..	**1**
Enumerated in :—			
Bombay	1	..	1
Born in Natal	**553**	**296**	**257**
Enumerated in :—			
Assam	4	4	..
Bengal	44	32	12
Bombay	3	2	1
Madras	427	215	212
N.-W. F. Province	6	3	3
Punjab	1	..	1
United Provinces	57	30	27
Bombay States	4	4	..
Mysore State	7	6	1
Born in Seychelles	**1**	..	**1**
Enumerated in :—			
United Provinces	1	..	1
Born in Somaliland	**6**	**6**	..
Enumerated in :—			
Bombay	5	5	..
Central Provinces and Berar	1	1	..
Born in St. Helena	**10**	**6**	**4**
Enumerated in :—			
Bengal	2	2	..
Bombay	2	1	1
Madras	1	..	1
N.-W. F. Province	1	1	..
United Provinces	1	..	1
Mysore State	3	2	1
Born in Sudan	**1**	**1**	..
Enumerated in :—			
Madras	1	1	..

BIRTHPLACE AND PLACE OF ENUMERATION.	POPULATION.		
	Persons.	Males.	Females.
1	2	3	4
Born in Transvaal	18	10	8
Enumerated in :—			
Bengal	4	1	3
Bombay	3	2	1
Coorg	1	1	..
Punjab	5	3	2
United Provinces	2	2	..
Mysore State	1	1	..
Rajputana Agency	2	..	2
Born in Zanzibar	169	87	82
Enumerated in :—			
Bengal	12	7	5
Bombay	68	36	32
Baroda State	5	2	3
Bombay States	84	42	42
Born in Africa, ***Unspecified***	2,119	1,296	823
Enumerated in :—			
Ajmer-Merwara	8	5	3
Assam	6	5	1
Bengal	88	61	27
Bihar and Orissa	14	6	8
Bombay	726	412	314
Burma	36	27	9
Central Provinces and Berar	36	32	4
Coorg	2	1	1
Madras	259	169	90
N.-W. F. Province	11	5	6
Punjab	88	54	34
United Provinces	145	106	39
Baroda State	198	89	109
Bombay States	354	206	148
Central India Agency	2	2	..
Central Provinces States	4	3	1
Hyderabad State	89	79	10
Kashmir State	6	2	4
Madras States	3	2	1
Travancore	*1*	*1*	..
Mysore State	32	22	10
N.-W. F. Province (*Agencies and Tribal areas*)	1	1	..
Punjab States	4	1	3
Rajputana Agency	7	6	1
E.—Born in America	2,760	1,525	1,235
Enumerated in :—			
Ajmer-Merwara	9	4	5
Andamans and Nicobars	3	2	1
Assam	58	33	25
Baluchistan	34	24	10
Bengal	311	175	136
Bihar and Orissa	66	30	36
Bombay	263	147	116
Burma	403	277	126
Central Provinces and Berar	140	71	69
Coorg	2	2	..
Madras	255	151	104
N.-W. F. Province	23	18	5
Punjab	266	126	140
United Provinces	635	330	305
Baluchistan States	3	3	..
Baroda State	12	6	6
Bengal States	1	1	..
Bombay States	24	11	13
Central India Agency	89	32	57
Central Provinces States	5	..	5
Hyderabad State	40	13	27
Kashmir State	10	6	4
Madras States	12	8	4
Cochin	*3*	*2*	*1*
Travancore	*9*	*6*	*3*
Mysore State	76	42	34
N.-W. F. Province (*Agencies and Tribal areas*)	3	3	..
Punjab States	1	..	1
Rajputana Agency	16	10	6
Born in Argentine Republic	3	2	1
Enumerated in :—			
Assam	2	2	..
Rajputana Agency	1	..	1
Born in Bermudas	12	10	2
Enumerated in :—			
Ajmer-Merwara	1	1	..
Assam	1	1	..
N.-W. F. Province	2	1	1
Punjab	7	7	..
Mysore State	1	..	1
Born in Brazil	8	7	1
Enumerated in :—			
Assam	2	2	..
Bombay	1	..	1
Madras	2	2	..
Punjab	3	3	..
Born in British Guiana	11	8	3
Enumerated in :—			
Bengal	11	8	3
Born in California	1	..	1
Enumerated in :—			
Rajputana Agency	1	..	1
Born in Canada	313	182	131
Enumerated in :—			
Ajmer-Merwara	1	1	..
Assam	9	6	3
Baluchistan	19	15	4
Bengal	47	22	25
Bihar and Orissa	4	2	2
Bombay	4	4	..
Burma	2	2	..
Central Provinces and Berar	19	13	6
Coorg	2	2	..
Madras	41	32	9
N.-W. F. Province	6	5	1
Punjab	34	18	16
United Provinces	41	28	13
Central India Agency	74	25	49
Hyderadad State	1	..	1
Mysore State	6	4	2
N.-W. F. Province (*Agencies and Tribal areas*)	2	2	..
Rajputana Agency	1	1	..
Born in Chile	2	1	1
Enumerated in :—			
Bombay	1	1	..
Mysore State	1	..	1
Born in Cuba	1	1	..
Enumerated in :—			
N.-W. F. Province	1	1	..
Born in Honduras	2	2	..
Enumerated in :—			
Punjab	1	1	..
N.-W. F. Province (*Agencies and Tribal areas*)	1	1	..
Born in Jamaica	38	15	23
Enumerated in :—			
Bombay	4	4	..
N.-W. F. Province	2	2	..
United Provinces	29	9	20
Hyderabad State	3	..	3
Born in Mexico	2	1	1
Enumerated in :—			
Bombay	1	1	..
Punjab	1	..	1
Born in Newfoundland	14	9	5
Enumerated in :—			
Assam	1	1	..
Bengal	3	2	1
Bombay	1	1	..
Burma	1	1	..
N.-W. F. Province	3	2	1
Punjab	2	..	2
United Provinces	2	1	1
Hyderabad State	1	1	..
Born in United States	255	125	130
Enumerated in :—			
Ajmer-Merwara	2	1	1
Assam	18	..	18
Baluchistan	6	3	3
Bengal	29	12	17
Bihar and Orissa	6	2	4
Bombay	14	6	8
Burma	21	20	1
Central Provinces and Berar	9	3	6
Madras	36	28	8
Punjab	14	2	12
United Provinces	50	19	31
Baluchistan States	3	3	..
Baroda State	12	6	6
Bengal States	1	1	..
Central India Agency	1	..	1
Hyderabad State	1	..	1
Mysore State	25	14	11
Rajputana Agency	7	5	2
Born in West Indies	348	185	163
Enumerated in :—			
Baluchistan	3	2	1
Bengal	20	17	3
Bihar and Orissa	1	1	..
Bombay	2	2	..
Madras	4	3	1
N.-W. F. Province	2	1	1
Punjab	7	5	2
United Provinces	305	152	153
Madras States (*Cochin*)	3	2	1
Punjab States	1	..	1

OF BIRTHPLACE BY PLACE OF ENUMERATION—*concluded.*

Birthplace and Place of Enumeration.	Population. Persons.	Males.	Females.
1	2	3	4
Born in America, ***Unspecified***	**1,750**	**977**	**773**
Enumerated in :—			
Ajmer-Merwara	5	1	4
Andamans and Nicobars	3	2	1
Assam	25	21	4
Baluchistan	6	4	2
Bengal	201	114	87
Bihar and Orissa	55	25	30
Bombay	235	128	107
Burma	379	254	125
Central Provinces and Berar	112	55	57
Madras	172	86	86
N.-W. F. Province	7	6	1
Punjab	197	90	107
United Provinces	208	121	87
Bombay States	24	11	13
Central India Agency	14	7	7
Central Provinces States	5	..	5
Hyderabad State	34	12	22
Kashmir State	10	6	4
Madras States (*Travancore*)	9	6	3
Mysore State	43	24	19
Rajputana Agency	6	4	2
F.—Born in Australasia	**1,267**	**873**	**394**
Enumerated in :—			
Ajmer-Merwara	12	5	7
Andamans and Nicobars	2	2	..
Assam	25	21	4
Baluchistan	17	13	4
Bengal	304	193	111
Bihar and Orissa	40	32	8
Bombay	126	76	50
Burma	205	173	32
Central Provinces and Berar	59	53	6
Coorg	2	..	2
Madras	97	55	42
N.-W. F. Province	28	20	8
Punjab	104	68	36
United Provinces	154	97	57
Baluchistan States	2	2	..
Bengal States	2	1	1
Bombay States	24	18	6
Central India Agency	8	8	..
Central Provinces States	1	1	..
Hyderabad State	11	9	2
Kashmir State	1	1	..
Madras States	2	1	1
Cochin	*1*	..	*1*
Travancore	*1*	*1*	..
Mysore State	34	20	14
Punjab States	3	2	1
Rajputana Agency	4	2	2
Born in Australia	**882**	**572**	**310**
Enumerated in :—			
Ajmer-Merwara	12	5	7
Assam	14	12	2
Baluchistan	16	13	3
Bengal	223	124	99
Bihar and Orissa	37	30	7
Bombay	85	47	38
Burma	149	119	30
Central Provinces and Berar	49	46	3
Madras	58	32	26
N.-W. F. Province	18	12	6
Punjab	66	40	26
United Provinces	101	58	43
Baluchistan States	2	2	..
Bengal States	2	1	1
Bombay States	10	6	4
Central Provinces States	1	1	..
Hyderabad State	4	3	1
Kashmir State	1	1	..
Mysore State	29	17	12
Punjab States	2	2	..
Rajputana Agency	3	1	2
Born in Borneo	**12**	**10**	**2**
Enumerated in :—			
Bengal	1	1	..
Madras	11	9	2
Born in Fiji Islands	**34**	**21**	**13**
Enumerated in :—			
Assam	5	4	1
Punjab	2	1	1
United Provinces	26	16	10
Punjab States	1	..	1
Born in Java	**94**	**82**	**12**
Enumerated in :—			
Bengal	32	32	..
Bombay	13	9	4
Burma	2	..	2
Central Provinces and Berar	1	..	1
Madras	12	8	4
Punjab	3	2	1
United Provinces	15	15	..
Bombay States	12	12	..
Hyderabad State	4	4	..
Born in Manilla	**2**	**2**	..
Enumerated in :—			
Bengal	2	2	..
Born in Melanesia	**1**	..	**1**
Enumerated in :—			
Punjab	1	..	1
Born in New Zealand	**144**	**101**	**43**
Enumerated in :—			
Andamans and Nicobars	2	2	..
Assam	4	3	1
Bengal	39	28	11
Bihar and Orissa	3	2	1
Bombay	24	19	5
Burma	7	7	..
Central Provinces and Berar	5	5	..
Coorg	1	..	1
Madras	15	6	9
N.-W. F. Province	7	6	1
Punjab	19	13	6
United Provinces	8	6	2
Bombay States	2	..	2
Hyderabad State	2	1	1
Madras States (*Cochin*)	1	..	1
Mysore State	5	3	2
Born in Philippines	**57**	**53**	**4**
Enumerated in :—			
Bengal	5	4	1
Burma	47	47	..
Central Provinces and Berar	3	1	2
United Provinces	2	1	1
Born in Polynesia	**9**	**9**	..
Enumerated in :—			
Punjab	9	9	..
Born in Sumatra	**9**	**5**	**4**
Enumerated in :—			
Baluchistan	1	..	1
Bombay	3	1	2
Pun!ab	4	3	1
Rajputana Agency	1	1	..
Born in Tasmania	**13**	**9**	**4**
Enumerated in :—			
Assam	2	2	..
Bengal	2	2	..
Bombay	1	..	1
Central Provinces and Berar	1	1	..
Coorg	1	..	1
Madras	1	..	1
N.-W. F. Province	3	2	1
United Provinces	1	1	..
Hyderabad State	1	1	..
Born in Australasia, ***Unspecified***	**10**	**9**	**1**
Enumerated in :—			
United Provinces	1	..	1
Central India Agency	8	8	..
Madras States (*Travancore*)	1	1	..
G.—Born at Sea	**124**	**65**	**59**
Enumerated in :—			
Assam	4	4	..
Baluchistan	3	2	1
Bengal	46	26	20
Bihar and Orissa	22	11	11
Bombay	17	3	14
Central Provinces and Berar	1	1	..
Madras	3	2	1
N.-W. F. Province	3	1	2
United Provinces	15	9	6
Central Provinces States	1	1	..
Hyderabad State	4	2	2
Mysore State	4	3	1
Rajputana Agency	1	..	1
H.—Birthplace Unspecified or not returned	**245**	**190**	**55**
Enumerated in :—			
Bombay	37	19	18
United Provinces	6	5	1
Kashmir State	202	166	36
Not enumerated by Birthplace	**1,721,997**	**911,047**	**810,950**
Burma	59,006	29,534	29,472
Kashmir State	54,435	29,278	25,157
N.-W. F. Province (*Agencies and Tribal areas*)	1,608,556	852,235	756,321

TABLE XII.

Infirmities.

1. This Table is divided into two parts. Part I contains a general summary showing by Provinces and States the total number of persons recorded as suffering from each infirmity. Part II shows the distribution of these persons by age for India and the main Provinces and States.

2. The procedure adopted in the different Provinces and States in dealing with persons suffering from more than one infirmity has not been quite uniform. As a general rule, they were shown separately under each head, but were counted only once for the purpose of columns 2 to 4 of the Table. The population afflicted does not therefore correspond with the aggregate of the figures for the several infirmities. Further details regarding persons afflicted with more than one infirmity will be found on page 1¢2.

3. In Burma infirmities were not recorded in the Pakokku Hill Tracts or in the estimated areas of Karenni, West Manglun and Kokang. Nor were they recorded in the States under the Political Agent, Gilgit, in Kashmir ; nor in the Agency Tracts (including British Posts) in the North-West Frontier Province ; nor in the estimated population of the Andaman and Nicobar Islands. The population of these tracts is noted on the margin.*

	Persons.	Males.	Females.
*TOTAL . . .	[illegible]	[illegible]	821,[illegible]
Andamans and Nicobars	[illegible]	918	574
Burma . . .	76,134	[illegible]	[illegible],111
N.-W. F. Province . .	1,622,094	864,876	757,218
Kashmir . . .	54,625	29,389	25,236

4. The figures for Madras States include those for Cochin and Travancore which are as follows :—

STATE.	POPULATION AFFECTED.		INSANE.		DEAF-MUTES.		BLIND.		LEPERS.	
	Males.	Females.	Males.	Females.	Males.	Females.	Males.	Females.	Males.	Females.
Cochin . . .	1,370	994	156	137	178	153	609	576	333	139
Travancore . . .	2,508	1,445	349	279	588	405	724	493	847	268

5. In addition to the infirmities for which information was collected throughout India, 4,217 persons (2,393 males and 1,824 females) were recorded as afflicted with elephantiasis in Travancore.

TABLE XII.—INFIRMITIES.

Province, State or Agency.	Population afflicted.			Insane.		
	Persons.	Males.	Females.	Persons.	Males.	Females.
1	2	3	4	5	6	7
INDIA.	**831,474**	**470,887**	**360,587**	**81,006**	**50,043**	**30,963**
Provinces.	676,032	386,163	289,869	68,158	42,064	26,094
1. Ajmer-Merwara	1,558	794	764	95	66	29
2. Andamans and Nicobars	238	235	3	175	175	...
3. Assam	18,975	11,512	7,463	3,068	1,818	1,250
4. Baluchistan	1,136	738	398	130	106	24
5. Bengal	99,464	61,011	38,453	19,442	11,652	7,790
6. Bihar and Orissa	84,556	50,229	34,327	4,138	2,720	1,418
Bihar	*58,916*	*35,288*	*23,628*	*2,593*	*1,724*	*869*
Orissa	*12,472*	*8,063*	*4,409*	*799*	*556*	*243*
Chota Nagpur	*13,168*	*6,878*	*6,290*	*746*	*440*	*306*
7. Bombay (*Presidency*)	54,800	32,024	22,776	6,270	4,173	2,097
Bombay	*41,078*	*23,781*	*17,297*	*4,135*	*2,735*	*1,400*
Sind	*13,669*	*8,206*	*5,463*	*2,130*	*1,434*	*696*
Aden	*53*	*37*	*16*	*5*	*4*	*1*
8. Burma	42,119	22,859	19,260	9,582	5,220	4,362
9. Central Provinces and Berar	45,602	21,958	23,644	2,205	1,391	814
Central Provinces	*35,136*	*16,250*	*18,886*	*1,750*	*1,103*	*647*
Berar	*10,466*	*5,708*	*4,758*	*455*	*288*	*167*
10. Coorg	192	103	89	19	11	8
11. Madras	90,244	51,883	38,361	8,309	4,833	3,476
12. North-West Frontier Province (*Districts and Administered Territories*)	6,706	4,078	2,628	884	634	250
13. Punjab	76,847	43,574	33,273	5,517	3,611	1,906
14. United Provinces of Agra and Oudh	153,595	85,165	68,430	8,324	5,654	2,670
Agra	*107,280*	*60,198*	*47,087*	*6,013*	*4,098*	*1,915*
Oudh	*46,315*	*24,972*	*21,343*	*2,311*	*1,556*	*755*
States and Agencies.	155,442	84,724	70,718	12,848	7,979	4,869
15. Assam State (Manipur)	208	116	92	48	22	26
16. Baluchistan States	2,035	1,171	864	240	162	78
17. Baroda State	4,748	2,307	2,441	523	319	204
18. Bengal States	2,217	1,428	789	536	303	233
19. Bihar and Orissa States	6,596	3,810	2,786	414	279	135
20. Bombay States	19,063	9,858	9,205	1,604	1,029	575
21. Central India Agency	15,256	7,934	7,322	751	485	266
22. Central Provinces States	4,801	2,425	2,376	261	160	101
23. Hyderabad State	26,831	15,025	11,806	2,560	1,547	1,013
24. Kashmir State	10,370	6,064	4,306	1,228	786	442
25. Madras States	7,327	4,398	2,929	1,019	569	450
26. Mysore State	12,245	6,804	5,441	1,334	764	570
27. Punjab States	13,755	8,203	5,552	783	500	283
28. Rajputana Agency	27,491	13,692	13,799	1,426	973	453
29. Sikkim State	291	163	128	9	6	3
30. United Provinces States	2,208	1,326	882	112	75	37

Part I.—Distribution by Provinces.

Deaf-mutes.			Blind.			Lepers.			Serial No.
Persons.	Males.	Females.	Persons.	Males.	Females.	Persons.	Males.	Females.	
8	9	10	11	12	13	14	15	16	
199,891	**119,251**	**80,640**	**443,653**	**221,916**	**221,737**	**109,094**	**81,024**	**28,070**	
168,922	**100,838**	**68,084**	**348,347**	**175,214**	**173,133**	**92,433**	**69,190**	**23,243**	
82	60	22	1,370	661	709	11	7	4	1
13	10	3	7	7	...	43	43	...	2
5,365	3,132	2,233	6,291	3,351	2,940	4,359	3,268	1,091	3
299	223	76	686	394	292	23	17	6	4
31,469	18,751	12,718	32,170	18,132	14,038	17,027	12,871	4,156	5
26,075	15,955	10,120	38,603	19,565	19,038	15,943	12,121	3,822	6
20,122	*12,308*	*7,814*	*27,705*	*14,308*	*13,397*	*8,641*	*7,039*	*1,602*	
2,701	*1,758*	*943*	*4,286*	*2,258*	*2,028*	*4,694*	*3,495*	*1,199*	
3,252	*1,889*	*1,363*	*6,612*	*2,999*	*3,613*	*2,608*	*1,587*	*1,021*	
12,690	7,853	4,837	27,234	13,898	13,336	8,606	6,100	2,506	7
8,956	*5,323*	*3,633*	*19,584*	*9,744*	*9,840*	*8,403*	*5,979*	*2,424*	
3,707	*2,511*	*1,196*	*7,629*	*4,140*	*3,489*	*203*	*121*	*82*	
27	*19*	*8*	*21*	*14*	*7*	...	...	...	
8,564	4,731	3,833	16,935	8,066	8,869	7,038	4,842	2,196	8
6,620	3,849	2,771	30,494	12,621	17,873	6,283	4,097	2,186	9
5,281	*3,085*	*2,196*	*23,805*	*9,438*	*14,367*	*4,300*	*2,624*	*1,676*	
1,339	*764*	*575*	*6,689*	*3,183*	*3,506*	*1,983*	*1,473*	*510*	
87	41	46	81	46	35	6	6	...	10
32,053	17,778	14,275	33,595	16,972	16,623	16,663	12,526	4,137	11
2,100	1,336	764	3,440	1,904	1,536	282	204	78	12
16,943	10,693	6,250	52,875	28,146	24,729	2,006	1,454	552	13
26,562	16,426	10,136	104,566	51,451	53,115	14,143	11,634	2,509	14
20,077	*12,519*	*7,558*	*71,765*	*35,995*	*35,770*	*9,425*	*7,581*	*1,844*	
6,485	*3,907*	*2,578*	*32,801*	*15,456*	*17,345*	*4,718*	*4,053*	*665*	
30,969	**18,413**	**12,556**	**95,306**	**46,702**	**48,604**	**16,661**	**11,834**	**4,827**	
34	20	14	117	66	51	13	11	2	15
369	259	110	1,366	701	665	60	49	11	16
425	302	123	3,361	1,363	1,998	445	327	118	17
656	417	239	577	339	238	458	374	84	18
1,643	989	654	2,648	1,333	1,315	1,892	1,210	682	19
3,938	2,378	1,560	11,824	5,197	6,627	1,697	1,254	443	20
2,159	1,302	857	11,058	5,253	5,805	1,288	894	394	21
882	499	383	2,634	1,230	1,404	1,024	536	488	22
4,421	2,522	1,899	16,263	8,287	7,976	3,758	2,762	996	23
3,043	1,767	1,276	4,747	2,534	2,213	1,352	977	375	24
1,761	1,003	758	2,789	1,508	1,281	1,771	1,327	444	25
4,472	2,513	1,959	5,749	3,055	2,694	767	528	239	26
3,300	1,979	1,321	8,646	4,978	3,668	1,085	779	306	27
3,069	1,992	1,077	22,346	10,212	12,134	650	515	135	28
234	134	100	25	16	9	24	7	17	29
563	337	226	1,156	630	526	377	284	93	30

Particulars of persons suffering from more than one infirmity.

The statement below shows the number of persons suffering from more than one infirmity who have been included in the figures for each infirmity but counted only once for the purpose of columns 2 to 4 " population afflicted."

Province or State.	Sex.	Insane and deaf-mute.	Insane and blind.	Insane and leper.	Deaf-mute and blind.	Deaf-mute and leper.	Blind and leper.	Insane, deaf-mute and blind.	Insane, blind and leper.	Blind, deaf-mute and leper.
TOTAL	**Males**	**765**	**118**	**40**	**249**	**68**	**105**	**3**	**1**	**1**
	Females	**462**	**94**	**15**	**168**	**30**	**44**	**4**	...	**1**
Assam	Males	34	4	2	8	2	8	1	...	..
	Females	27	5	1	11	2	4	1	...	...
Baluchistan	Males	1	1	...	...	...	...	...	...	...
	Females	...	...	...	...	...	...	...	...	...
Bengal	Males	282	22	18	43	13	20	...	...	1
	Females	173	25	7	31	6	10	...	...	1
Bihar and Orissa	Males	57	8	3	25	10	21	...	...	...
	Females	31	7	1	16	5	11	...	...	..
Coorg	Males	1	...	...	...	...	...	...	...	...
	Females	...	...	...	...	...	...	...	...	...
Madras	Males	99	19	6	56	11	35	1	1	...
	Females	76	17	2	35	8	11	2	...	...
Punjab	Males	207	47	9	86	2	12	...	...	...
	Females	96	30	3	54	3	4	...	...	...
Baroda State	Males	1	...	...	1	2	...	...	...	...
	Females	1	...	...	1	...	...	...	...	...
Hyderabad State	Males	53	9	1	14	8	8	...	...	...
	Females	48	9	1	14	3	3	...	...	...
Mysore State	Males	30	6	1	14	3	...	1	...	...
	Females	10	1	...	5	2	1	1	...	...
Cochin State	Males	...	2	..	2	...	1	...	...	..
	Females	...	...	...	1	...	..	...	...	...
Sikkim State	Males	...	...	...	..	..	...	...	...	...
	Females	...	...	...	...	1	...	...	...	...

NOTE.—The figures in this statement include the States attached to each Province, but those for Madras exclude Cochin and Travancore.

In Ajmer-Merwara, Rajputana and Kashmir persons suffering from more than one infirmity were counted twice or three times over for the purpose of columns 2 to 4. In the remaining provinces and states such persons were treated as suffering from one infirmity only, the others being ignored. In Bombay this procedure has resulted in the omission from the Table of 11 (9 + 2) blind persons who were also lepers and of 45 (41 + 4) who were also insane: of 4 (1 + 3) deaf-mutes who were also lepers, 155 (134 + 21) who were also insane and 28 (15 + 13) who were also blind.

TABLE XII.—Infirmities. Part II.—Details by Age.

Age.	Population afflicted.			Insane.		Deaf-Mutes.		Blind.		Lepers.	
	Persons.	Males.	Females.	Males.	Females.	Males.	Females.	Males.	Females.	Males.	Females.
1	2	3	4	5	6	7	8	9	10	11	12
					India.						
0—1	1,983	1,153	830	10	8	160	120	955	685	29	17
1—2	1,540	892	648	11	22	121	116	746	496	14	15
2—3	3,807	2,153	1,654	60	57	553	535	1,502	1,032	47	38
3—4	6,377	3,611	2,766	169	155	1,560	1,238	1,827	1,340	74	48
4—5	8,127	4,681	3,446	258	185	2,398	1,770	1,960	1,437	81	70
Total 0—5	*21,834*	*13,490*	*9,344*	*508*	*427*	*4,786*	*3,779*	*6,990*	*4,990*	*245*	*188*
5—10	54,353	32,713	21,640	2,715	1,760	17,318	11,633	12,296	7,947	568	419
10—15	60,525	37,007	23,518	4,131	2,696	16,166	11,697	13,218	8,097	1,692	1,144
15—20	57,084	34,076	23,008	4,663	3,165	14,455	9,837	11,944	8,296	3,185	1,814
20—25	62,012	37,088	24,924	5,543	3,372	13,564	9,104	13,344	10,083	4,752	2,344
25—30	64,860	40,062	24,798	6,208	3,120	12,456	7,841	14,260	11,256	7,174	2,653
30—35	69,490	41,546	27,944	6,528	3,466	10,415	6,929	15,182	14,276	9,517	3,327
35—40	53,957	33,361	20,596	4,830	2,431	6,767	4,258	12,069	11,195	9,761	2,764
40—45	71,042	41,196	29,846	4,760	3,067	6,847	4,916	17,126	18,342	12,542	3,558
45—50	45,392	26,868	18,524	2,849	1,759	3,675	2,430	11,800	12,118	8,508	2,262
50—55	68,345	36,482	31,863	2,765	2,174	3,960	2,971	20,198	23,730	9,617	3,026
55—60	30,520	16,492	14,028	1,187	915	1,609	1,125	9,753	10,750	3,974	1,260
60—65	70,969	33,087	37,882	1,478	1,325	2,307	1,966	23,807	32,680	5,563	1,961
65—70	22,605	11,320	11,285	480	371	768	552	8,646	9,808	1,437	472
70 and over	75,106	35,037	40,069	853	751	1,685	1,329	30,105	37,135	2,438	892
Age Unspecified	3,380	2,062	1,318	446	174	473	183	1,079	944	66	17
Total	**831,474**	**470,887**	**360,587**	**50,043**	**30,963**	**119,251**	**80,640**	**221,916**	**221,737**	**81,094**	**28,070**
					Assam.						
0—1	23	13	10	..	...		..	11	10	2	...
1—2	28	16	12	1	...	5	3	10	8	...	1
2—3	90	59	40	2	1	25	21	30	20	2	...
3—4	208	119	89	7	2	77	64	34	22	3	2
4—5	236	128	108	5	4	83	68	39	35	3	2
Total 0—5	*594*	*335*	*259*	*15*	*7*	*190*	*156*	*124*	*95*	*9*	*5*
5—10	1,270	777	493	67	52	511	331	185	104	24	14
10—15	1,469	866	603	80	81	525	362	170	108	90	57
15—20	1,325	747	578	123	117	362	278	130	107	129	80
20—25	1,459	856	603	187	127	330	264	134	117	199	97
25—30	1,769	1,098	671	274	155	349	238	164	148	316	141
30—35	1,874	1,179	695	279	187	260	188	211	174	485	148
35—40	1,495	999	496	218	124	193	113	173	156	416	106
40—45	1,637	1,080	557	185	122	143	104	225	215	535	118
45—50	1,034	672	362	111	71	77	49	198	169	290	75
50—55	1,364	834	530	122	83	81	52	307	303	327	94
55—60	616	351	265	41	34	23	28	172	165	116	44
60—65	1,303	704	590	55	57	40	36	389	457	220	81
65—70	362	210	152	18	10	13	7	130	121	50	16
70 and over	1,404	804	600	34	23	27	27	630	506	113	45
Total	**18,975**	**11,512**	**7,463**	**1,818**	**1,250**	**3.132**	**2,233**	**3,351**	**2,940**	**3,968**	**1,091**
					Bengal						
0—1	149	87	62	...	...	17	13	69	46	1	3
1—2	114	64	50	1	1	9	22	52	25	2	2
2—3	428	254	174	5	10	101	88	147	75	4	5
3—4	834	475	359	22	31	290	208	149	124	22	4
4—5	998	574	424	37	35	364	283	161	98	20	14
Total 0—5	*2,523*	*1,454*	*1,069*	*65*	*77*	*781*	*614*	*578*	*368*	*49*	*28*
5—10	7,718	4,686	3,032	632	429	2,975	1,983	1,041	603	99	56
10—15	8,628	5,449	3,179	947	642	3,186	1,859	1,106	552	271	162
15—20	8,283	4,941	3,342	1,074	796	2,369	1,762	973	552	581	261
20—25	7,730	4,722	3,008	1,201	800	1,935	1,347	860	544	758	329
25—30	9,093	5,895	3,198	1,630	873	1,958	1,207	1,015	619	1,329	432
30—35	8,355	5,445	2,910	1,512	868	1,364	958	1,008	672	1,581	428
35—40	7,598	5,129	2,469	1,264	677	1,137	723	978	633	1,787	454
40—45	7,909	5,142	2,767	1,130	750	1,040	698	1,203	856	1,788	476
45—50	5,610	3,608	2,002	675	441	559	407	1,034	795	1,354	377
50—55	6,802	4,015	2,787	617	596	545	408	1,593	1,359	1,271	430
55—60	3,556	2,147	1,409	285	243	241	151	967	802	665	218
60—65	6,236	3,301	2,935	314	330	305	272	1,962	2,069	731	275
65—70	2,134	1,169	965	97	83	93	73	769	728	211	83
70 and over	7,289	3,908	3,381	209	185	263	166	3,043	2,886	396	148
Total	**99,464**	**61,011**	**38,453**	**11,652**	**7,790**	**18,751**	**12,718**	**18,132**	**14,038**	**12,871**	**4,156**
					Bihar and Orissa.						
0—1	369	230	150	2	...	64	45	167	103	6	2
1—2	167	96	71	...	1	22	21	74	48	...	1
2—3	515	293	222	5	3	89	99	197	117	4	4
3—4	824	451	373	9	6	219	176	220	179	6	13
4—5	1,003	592	411	5	2	318	225	264	174	8	10
Total 0—5	*2,898*	*1,671*	*1,227*	*21*	*12*	*712*	*566*	*922*	*621*	*24*	*30*
5—10	7,018	4,345	2,673	104	58	2,496	1,595	1,673	963	88	69
10—15	7,462	4,701	2,761	108	117	2,626	1,601	1,630	881	266	170
15—20	6,402	3,915	2,577	207	121	2,031	1,273	1,217	808	475	293
20—25	6,658	4,114	2,544	257	150	1,811	1,185	1,358	926	700	290
25—30	7,556	4,779	2,777	348	132	1,864	1,067	1,470	1,216	1,104	373
30—35	7,499	4,768	2,731	428	154	1,454	821	1,461	1,301	1,832	459
35—40	5,958	3,883	2,075	311	123	890	494	1,120	1,086	1,569	279
40—45	6,579	4,157	2,422	270	147	740	483	1,273	1,332	1,869	462
45—50	4,569	2,846	1,723	186	85	421	270	943	1,050	1,302	316
50—55	5,474	3,171	2,303	142	106	349	268	1,321	1,547	1,371	385
55—60	2,670	1,499	1,171	73	46	166	121	726	861	536	146
60—65	5,723	2,785	2,938	93	94	208	193	1,674	2,397	823	257
65—70	2,010	942	1,068	20	25	73	56	634	927	207	60
70 and over	5,990	2,653	3,337	49	47	115	127	2,134	3,032	355	131
Total	**84,556**	**50,229**	**34,327**	**2,720**	**1,418**	**15,955**	**10,120**	**19,565**	**19,038**	**12,121**	**3,322**

TABLE XII.—INFIRMITIES.

Age.	Population afflicted.			Insane.		Deaf-Mutes.		Blind.		Lepers.	
	Persons.	Males.	Females.	Males.	Females.	Males.	Females.	Males.	Females.	Males.	Females.
1	2	3	4	5	6	7	8	9	10	11	12
Bombay.											
0—1	174	98	76	1	1	7	10	89	65	1	...
1—2	147	90	57	1	1	13	9	72	42	4	5
2—3	275	155	120	6	4	36	30	108	84	5	2
3—4	451	266	185	13	11	97	66	153	106	3	2
4—5	535	315	220	26	19	145	106	139	88	5	7
Total 0—5	*1,582*	*924*	*658*	*47*	*36*	*298*	*221*	*561*	*385*	*18*	*16*
5—10	3,440	2,120	1,320	288	140	1,007	658	797	493	38	29
10—15	3,864	2,440	1,424	360	232	1,121	587	812	492	138	113
15—20	3,605	2,236	1,369	413	247	843	474	706	516	275	132
20—25	4,099	2,567	1,532	520	264	849	485	766	563	432	221
25—30	4,312	2,730	1,582	548	205	812	407	801	639	569	241
30—35	4,680	2,893	1,787	566	223	746	445	874	777	707	348
35—40	3,923	2,406	1,427	416	156	494	289	779	672	807	310
40—45	4,853	2,844	2,009	359	201	408	327	1,031	1,133	956	348
45—50	3,115	1,929	1,186	191	113	305	163	791	707	642	203
50—55	4,481	2,470	2,011	229	128	330	233	1,246	1,410	665	240
55—60	1,996	1,120	876	81	39	186	90	645	642	258	105
60—65	4,606	2,220	2,386	81	70	207	187	1,547	1,994	385	135
65—70	1,444	734	710	22	13	51	46	551	631	110	30
70 and over	4,800	2,301	2,409	43	30	157	185	1,991	2,295	110	41
Total	**54,800**	**32,024**	**22,776**	**4,173**	**2,097**	**7,853**	**4,837**	**13,898**	**13,336**	**6,106**	**2,506**
Burma.											
0—1	36	18	18	2	2	4	...	11	14	1	2
1—2	60	30	30	3	4	9	8	18	18	...	...
2—3	133	73	60	8	10	35	30	27	18	3	3
3—4	221	112	109	22	26	55	48	34	33	1	2
4—5	294	148	146	30	31	71	61	41	48	6	6
Total 0—5	*744*	*381*	*363*	*65*	*73*	*174*	*147*	*131*	*131*	*11*	*19*
5—10	1,809	1,022	787	168	167	513	368	296	217	46	35
10—15	2,687	1,527	1,160	322	264	676	509	370	285	159	102
15—20	3,519	2,018	1,501	532	390	701	586	444	333	341	192
20—25	4,160	2,287	1,873	667	503	669	670	497	453	454	247
25—30	3,379	2,034	1,345	602	428	441	308	420	375	571	234
30—35	3,941	2,337	1,604	671	508	449	347	511	470	706	270
35—40	3,003	1,859	1,144	534	347	220	187	473	419	632	191
40—45	3,338	1,966	1,372	557	420	266	188	591	564	552	200
45—50	2,473	1,383	1,090	300	296	114	124	563	511	406	159
50—55	2,730	1,460	1,270	294	295	134	115	663	679	369	181
55—60	2,159	985	1,174	143	196	90	84	562	764	190	130
60—65	2,778	1,327	1,451	166	199	101	68	868	1,061	202	123
65—70	1,993	897	1,096	91	111	78	58	638	874	90	53
70 and over	3,406	1,376	2,030	108	165	106	74	1,049	1,724	113	67
Total	**42,119**	**22,859**	**19,260**	**5,220**	**4,362**	**4,731**	**3,533**	**8,066**	**8,369**	**4,842**	**2,196**
Central Provinces and Berar.											
0—1	175	101	74	...	...	2	3	90	71	...	...
1—2	136	90	46	...	1	1	3	89	43	...	...
2—3	245	138	107	3	1	15	11	119	93	1	2
3—4	391	225	166	6	4	54	51	160	106	5	5
4—5	428	248	180	6	7	103	60	138	110	2	3
Total 0—5	*1,375*	*802*	*573*	*15*	*13*	*174*	*127*	*605*	*423*	*8*	*10*
5—10	2,509	1,512	907	81	64	649	402	775	509	8	23
10—15	2,375	1,399	976	135	95	595	400	613	406	66	75
15—20	2,143	1,202	941	148	117	421	395	506	448	127	81
20—25	2,883	1,582	1,301	167	94	456	360	727	671	252	167
25—30	3,326	1,829	1,497	197	72	414	308	817	918	401	204
30—35	3,967	2,094	1,873	178	79	385	310	1,000	1,312	531	272
35—40	2,883	1,540	1,343	109	64	219	128	760	917	452	234
40—45	4,050	2,075	1,975	121	73	202	165	1,114	1,486	638	262
45—50	2,567	1,298	1,269	82	35	113	81	671	970	432	183
50—55	4,333	1,926	2,407	75	47	93	84	1,233	2,006	525	268
55—60	1,659	727	932	25	8	30	28	502	804	170	92
60—65	5,238	1,857	3,381	31	34	57	49	1,452	3,090	317	208
65—70	1,286	499	787	14	8	20	15	407	731	58	33
70 and over	5,008	1,616	3,392	13	12	33	25	1,439	3,280	132	75
Total	**45,602**	**21,958**	**23,644**	**1,391**	**814**	**3,849**	**2,771**	**12,621**	**17,873**	**4,697**	**2,186**
Madras.											
0—1	121	61	60	1	1	9	9	49	49	3	1
1—2	144	68	76	...	6	15	15	53	54	..	2
2—3	368	197	171	2	6	74	77	114	83	7	5
3—4	724	403	321	15	10	228	204	154	106	7	...
4—5	1,010	570	440	21	13	403	305	142	124	6	1
Total 0—5	*2,367*	*1,299*	*1,068*	*39*	*36*	*729*	*610*	*512*	*418*	*23*	*9*
5—10	6,677	3,823	2,854	208	186	2,600	1,981	937	678	100	50
10—15	8,127	4,608	3,519	350	297	2,895	2,307	1,188	776	262	160
15—20	7,437	4,177	3,260	373	307	2,327	1,830	1,009	831	496	312
20—25	7,824	4,342	3,482	498	366	2,083	1,738	1,053	1,009	731	393
25—30	7,123	4,275	2,848	519	340	1,678	1,320	1,094	859	1,009	342
30—35	7,793	4,656	3,137	646	368	1,506	1,254	1,081	1,086	1,430	456
35—40	6,003	3,806	2,197	509	307	997	736	931	776	1,382	382
40—45	8,197	4,999	3,198	514	413	1,091	951	1,877	1,296	2,030	540
45—50	5,215	3,380	1,835	347	218	603	416	1,007	850	1,432	350
50—55	6,648	3,866	2,782	341	286	862	465	1,463	1,575	1,518	463
55—60	3,366	1,985	1,381	165	128	334	307	860	852	744	200
60—65	5,537	2,785	2,752	189	141	288	238	1,533	2,108	781	272
65—70	2,013	1,038	975	55	34	64	96	680	771	241	75
70 and over	5,917	2,844	3,073	80	74	131	124	2,312	2,758	330	124
Total	**90,244**	**51,883**	**38,361**	**4,838**	**3,476**	**17,778**	**14,275**	**18,972**	**16,693**	**12,526**	**4,137**

PART II.—DETAILS BY AGE—*continued.*

Age.	Population Afflicted.			Insane.		Deaf-Mutes.		Blind.		Lepers.	
	Persons.	Males.	Females.	Males.	Females.	Males.	Females.	Males.	Females.	Males.	Females.
1	2	3	4	5	6	7	8	9	10	11	12
					North-West Frontier Province.						
0—1	16	9	7	2	...	2	3	5	3	...	1
1—2	8	6	2	...	...	1	1	5	1	...	...
2—3	44	16	28	...	1	3	13	13	13	...	1
3—4	86	57	29	8	4	31	14	17	11	1	
4—5	100	59	41	5	3	37	27	14	10	3	1
Total 0—5	*254*	*147*	*107*	*15*	*8*	*74*	*58*	*54*	*38*	*4*	*3*
5—10	668	427	241	56	32	238	121	119	78	14	10
10—15	621	375	246	70	33	181	123	113	79	11	11
15—20	523	331	192	59	36	163	72	91	78	18	6
20—25	481	315	166	79	29	109	52	107	78	20	7
25—30	451	276	175	74	15	83	73	105	84	14	3
30—35	597	373	224	78	32	126	75	147	107	22	10
35—40	372	250	112	46	7	80	37	113	66	20	3
40—45	481	285	109	46	15	77	55	146	123	16	6
45—50	311	183	128	37	11	41	26	95	88	10	3
50—55	477	277	200	31	11	63	28	167	156	16	5
55—60	178	101	77	12	8	21	6	61	61	7	2
60—65	477	253	224	15	11	38	19	183	188	17	6
65—70	136	73	63	3	...	6	6	62	56	2	1
70 and over	676	408	273	13	2	36	13	341	256	13	2
Total	**6,706**	**4,078**	**2,628**	**634**	**250**	**1,336**	**764**	**1,904**	**1,536**	**204**	**78**
					Punjab.						
0—1	65	35	30	...	...	2	1	31	26	2	3
1—2	111	65	46	2	2	8	3	52	39	3	2
2—3	272	145	127	2	...	35	30	109	96	...	1
3—4	505	285	220	9	10	110	87	168	121	1	3
4—5	690	391	308	12	14	198	166	183	128	2	2
Total 0—5	*1,652*	*921*	*731*	*25*	*26*	*353*	*287*	*543*	*410*	*8*	*11*
5—10	4,779	2,977	1,802	220	136	1,507	909	1,183	758	20	18
10—15	4,969	3,153	1,816	281	191	1,407	887	1,304	746	25	10
15—20	4,543	2,847	1,606	409	214	1,249	715	1,173	757	60	32
20—25	4,465	2,806	1,659	464	217	1,163	631	1,156	802	70	20
25—30	4,758	2,993	1,765	471	202	1,121	581	1,331	950	104	42
30—35	4,961	2,919	2,042	454	216	979	565	1,396	1,226	120	53
35—40	3,720	2,189	1,531	276	141	561	344	1,208	983	152	68
40—45	5,639	2,999	2,640	288	180	651	393	1,876	1,996	198	82
45—50	3,762	2,170	1,592	194	104	364	205	1,460	1,249	161	41
50—55	6,652	3,542	3,110	166	119	431	264	2,758	2,672	198	65
55—60	2,997	1,665	1,332	64	40	152	99	1,375	1,167	79	20
60—65	8,106	4,083	4,023	109	72	245	166	3,606	3,748	141	45
65—70	2,971	1,675	1,296	35	12	77	61	1,523	1,217	45	9
70 and over	12,873	6,635	6,238	65	36	263	143	6,254	6,048	73	27
Total	**76,847**	**43,574**	**33,273**	**3,611**	**1,906**	**10,693**	**6,250**	**28,146**	**24,729**	**1,454**	**552**
					United Provinces.						
0—1	400	248	152	1	4	34	19	203	126	10	3
1—2	242	141	101	1	4	17	21	122	76	1	...
2—3	516	308	208	8	8	63	58	234	140	3	2
3—4	898	523	375	24	15	177	135	315	224	7	1
4—5	1,257	764	493	39	15	329	197	385	274	11	7
Total 0—5	*3,313*	*1,984*	*1,329*	*73*	*46*	*620*	*430*	*1,259*	*840*	*32*	*13*
5—10	8,539	5,276	3,263	376	173	2,232	1,455	2,626	1,617	42	18
10—15	9,267	5,868	3,399	400	219	2,265	1,247	3,016	1,872	97	61
15—20	8,614	5,384	3,230	517	265	1,757	1,034	2,917	1,817	193	114
20—25	10,690	6,688	4,002	626	301	2,004	1,056	3,644	2,407	414	148
25—30	11,650	7,303	4,347	691	247	1,846	904	4,044	2,914	722	192
30—35	13,097	7,657	5,440	719	301	1.514	978	4,232	3,884	1,192	277
35—40	9,782	5,793	3,989	470	163	929	550	3,140	3,071	1,254	205
40-45	14,523	8,165	6,358	497	262	1,004	741	4,651	4,004	2,013	361
45—50	8,902	5.001	3,901	292	138	513	302	2,811	3,243	1,385	218
50—55	15,134	7,728	7,406	253	171	657	492	4,963	6,394	1,835	349
55—60	6,139	3,030	3,109	122	85	260	159	1,977	2,723	671	142
60—65	15,451	6,851	8,600	159	117	383	362	5,200	7,866	1,109	255
65—70	4,286	2,073	2,213	58	33	176	71	1,608	2,059	231	50
70 and over	13,939	6,167	7,772	114	77	266	265	5,343	7,324	444	106
Age Unspecified	269	197	72	197	72	...		...	..	...	...
Total	**153,595**	**85,165**	**68,430**	**5,654**	**2,670**	**16,426**	**10,136**	**51,451**	**53,115**	**11,634**	**2,509**
					Baroda State.						
0—1	27	11	16	...	...	1	..	10	16		...
1—2	18	10	8	1	...	1	..	8	8		...
2—3	37	19	18	1	...	2	1	14	17	2	...
3—4	38	23	15	...	3	9	1	14	11	...	...
4—5	41	26	15	1	3	3	3	21	9	1	...
Total 0—5	*161*	*89*	*72*	*3*	*6*	*16*	*5*	*67*	*61*	*3*	..
5—10	204	199	105	35	21	57	26	93	55	4	3
10—15	209	175	124	28	19	41	21	103	81	4	3
15—20	293	175	118	31	26	40	14	82	69	22	0
20—25	330	177	153	38	29	34	17	77	93	28	15
25—30	321	182	139	43	22	33	9	76	92	30	16
30—35	349	175	174	35	30	20	12	71	116	40	16
35—40	333	159	174	30	15	15	7	68	133	47	19
40—45	357	175	182	27	10	14	4	78	154	57	14
45—50	323	141	182	17	3	12	5	84	167	28	7
50—55	453	186	267	12	10	5	1	147	246	22	10
55—60	165	87	78	5	2	5	1	67	73	10	3
60—65	506	185	321	9	6	4	1	155	313	17	2
65—70	152	51	101	2	1	3	...	43	99	3	1
70 and over	412	161	251	4	4	5	..	152	247	3	...
Total	**4,748**	**2,307**	**2,441**	**319**	**204**	**302**	**123**	**1,363**	**1,998**	**327**	**118**

TABLE XII.—Infirmities.

Age.	Population afflicted.			Insane.		Deaf-Mutes.		Blind.		Lepers.	
	Persons.	Males.	Females.	Males.	Females.	Males.	Females.	Males.	Females.	Males.	Females.
1	2	3	4	5	6	7	8	9	10	11	12
					Bengal States.						
0—1	9	4	5	...	...	1	2	3	3	...	..
1—2	1	...	1	...	..	...	...	...	1	...	..
2—3	10	4	6	1	..	3	4	...	2	...	...
3—4	13	11	2	1	..	7	2	4	...	...	...
4—5	30	19	11	6	3	7	4	5	5	1	...
Total 0—5	*63*	*38*	*25*	*8*	*3*	*18*	*12*	*12*	*11*	*1*	...
5—10	195	104	91	32	27	51	46	20	17	1	1
10—15	218	137	81	46	38	64	38	27	4	...	3
15—20	209	125	84	43	39	56	33	20	6	7	6
20—25	159	100	59	23	27	43	20	10	9	15	3
25—30	188	124	64	27	19	47	26	15	13	35	6
30—35	100	131	50	32	24	32	17	24	13	44	5
35—40	169	123	46	21	10	38	14	20	14	45	8
40—45	201	144	57	29	10	28	15	27	19	60	13
45—50	125	80	45	16	10	12	10	17	17	36	8
50—55	165	111	54	19	8	13	3	34	28	45	15
55—60	67	44	33	3	5	3	2	13	12	25	6
60—65	108	72	36	1	5	8	1	30	23	24	7
65—70	37	22	15	...	3	1	2	8	10	13	..
70 and over	123	73	50	3	5	3	...	44	42	23	3
Total	**2.217**	**1,428**	**789**	**303**	**233**	**417**	**239**	**339**	**238**	**374**	**84**
					Bihar and Orissa States.						
0—1	27	21	6	...	...	2	1	19	4	...	1
1—2	18	12	6	...	...	...	...	12	8	...	...
2—3	55	30	25	1	1	11	9	14	13	4	2
3—4	65	35	30	1	1	16	16	13	7	5	6
4—5	79	45	34	1	...	19	9	22	22	3	3
Total 0—5	*244*	*143*	*101*	*3*	*2*	*48*	*35*	*80*	*59*	*12*	*12*
5—10	549	315	234	24	17	144	99	128	97	10	21
10—15	678	375	283	33	17	156	118	128	108	58	45
15—20	579	344	235	35	16	124	78	112	85	73	56
20—25	536	325	211	24	8	88	55	96	83	117	63
25—30	594	381	213	26	20	102	40	118	85	135	50
30—35	647	412	235	47	10	86	41	116	90	163	85
35—40	457	284	173	25	11	52	31	71	68	136	68
40—45	501	320	262	24	11	50	38	84	111	171	102
45—50	265	169	96	11	5	32	15	44	51	83	98
50—55	513	286	220	15	8	38	44	107	103	126	74
55—60	160	98	62	4	3	19	6	42	30	33	14
60—65	448	201	247	4	3	27	27	111	177	59	40
65—70	70	32	38	...	1	7	2	18	33	7	2
70 and over	283	116	167	4	2	16	16	78	127	18	21
Total	**6,596**	**3,810**	**2,786**	**279**	**135**	**989**	**654**	**1,333**	**1,315**	**1,210**	**682**
					Bombay States.						
0—1	63	35	28	1	...	10	2	28	26	1	..
1—2	51	26	25	...	...	6	4	20	21	...	...
2—3	110	62	48	1	1	11	10	48	36	2	1
3—4	135	71	64	2	3	18	33	50	38	1	...
4—5	170	98	72	10	8	34	27	54	34	...	3
Total 0—5	*529*	*292*	*237*	*14*	*12*	*79*	*66*	*195*	*155*	*4*	*4*
5—10	1,019	589	430	49	45	297	200	238	182	5	8
10—15	1,189	748	441	106	63	296	180	315	183	32	16
15—20	1,244	769	475	115	82	302	147	300	215	53	31
20—25	1,357	812	545	184	62	287	165	313	284	78	34
25—30	1,367	802	565	139	63	255	162	318	309	90	42
30—35	1,525	878	697	140	54	217	146	310	427	152	70
35—40	1,181	638	543	90	20	143	100	257	378	148	36
40—45	1,857	930	927	87	54	150	131	481	682	200	60
45—50	1,062	561	501	43	34	88	58	202	379	138	30
50—55	1,950	910	1,040	53	41	108	81	571	807	178	51
55—60	693	356	337	19	5	41	22	246	291	50	19
60—65	2,042	803	1,239	26	10	67	54	632	1,133	78	33
65—70	590	267	323	6	6	18	15	225	297	18	5
70 and over	1,458	553	905	8	7	41	43	488	845	21	10
Total	**19,063**	**9,858**	**9,205**	**1,029**	**575**	**2,378**	**1,560**	**5,197**	**6,627**	**1,254**	**463**
					Central India Agency.						
0—1	51	28	23	..	..	2	6	26	16	...	1
1—2	56	37	19	...	..	4	2	32	16	1	1
2—3	129	80	40	5	1	6	6	68	41	1	1
3—4	160	100	60	6	1	20	11	74	46	...	2
4—5	176	96	80	4	1	20	19	71	59	1	1
Total 0—5	*572*	*341*	*231*	*15*	*3*	*52*	*44*	*271*	*178*	*3*	*6*
5—10	961	578	383	19	25	185	110	371	245	3	3
10—15	891	554	337	53	28	168	85	318	216	15	8
15—20	883	540	343	58	23	133	86	326	219	23	15
20—25	1,111	668	443	40	30	154	89	400	290	56	34
25—30	1,243	698	545	74	32	160	93	381	371	83	40
30—35	1,371	766	605	46	25	154	80	452	453	114	47
35—40	945	546	390	45	13	69	61	338	201	94	34
40—45	1,479	774	705	42	32	80	63	465	556	187	54
45—50	767	388	379	28	12	42	24	243	306	75	37
50—55	1,534	670	864	27	10	48	45	470	743	125	57
55—60	532	256	276	6	4	14	18	207	244	29	10
60—65	1,504	612	982	13	14	22	40	525	800	52	20
65—70	380	176	213	6	2	4	3	154	208	12	5
70 and over	984	367	617	4	4	17	16	323	591	23	6
Total	**15,256**	**7,934**	**7,322**	**485**	**206**	**1,302**	**857**	**5,258**	**5,805**	**894**	**394**

Part II.—Details by Age—*continued.*

Age.	Population Afflicted.			Insane.		Deaf-Mutes.		Blind.		Lepers.	
	Persons.	Males.	Females.	Males.	Females.	Males.	Females.	Males.	Females.	Males.	Females.
1	2	3	4	5	6	7	8	9	10	11	12
	Central Provinces States.										
0—1	13	10	3	..	..	..	..	10	3	..	..
1—2	12	7	5	..	..	..	..	6	5	1	..
2—3	24	10	14	..	..	2	2	7	10	1	2
3—4	49	28	21	..	..	7	13	15	6	6	2
4—5	68	39	29	2	..	15	12	10	14	3	3
Total 0—5	*166*	*94*	*72*	*2*	..	*24*	*27*	*57*	*38*	*11*	*7*
5—10	352	192	160	11	10	97	74	70	53	14	23
10—15	371	210	161	32	10	74	59	71	57	33	35
15—20	362	187	175	22	11	69	54	63	64	33	46
20—25	337	172	165	16	11	49	46	69	68	38	40
25—30	405	196	209	19	14	45	32	73	112	59	51
30—35	397	210	187	15	14	37	25	97	97	61	51
35—40	346	192	154	9	6	33	11	88	91	62	46
40—45	425	245	180	16	9	26	15	126	87	77	69
45—50	226	111	115	4	2	12	8	50	78	45	27
50—55	363	154	209	3	4	13	16	101	145	37	44
55—60	125	65	60	5	2	6	2	36	46	18	10
60—65	408	177	231	4	7	6	10	138	191	29	23
65—70	88	44	44	1	..	2	1	37	37	4	6
70 and over	430	176	254	1	1	6	3	154	240	15	10
Total	**4,801**	**2,425**	**2,376**	**160**	**101**	**499**	**383**	**1,239**	**1,404**	**536**	**489**
	Hyderabad State.										
0—1	124	72	52	..	..	..	1	72	51	..	..
1—2	123	71	52	1	1	3	..	66	51	1	..
2—3	231	136	95	3	5	12	10	121	79	..	1
3—4	260	139	121	3	13	41	29	96	79	..	2
4—5	356	199	157	25	8	57	59	117	91	1	1
Total 0—5	*1,094*	*617*	*477*	*32*	*27*	*113*	*99*	*472*	*351*	*3*	*4*
5—10	2,000	1,146	854	122	77	358	286	664	485	18	12
10—15	2,254	1,321	933	179	127	375	296	722	480	56	44
15—20	1,807	1,025	782	134	133	251	216	561	398	89	48
20—25	2,282	1,312	970	162	113	329	212	674	570	152	86
25—30	2,284	1,386	898	193	100	282	186	676	530	246	88
30—35	2,576	1,441	1,135	170	112	256	146	688	736	327	144
35—40	1,563	936	627	113	54	129	95	423	400	272	81
40—45	2,493	1,429	1,064	150	87	188	150	626	673	473	150
45—50	1,218	753	465	81	36	68	56	373	308	239	65
50—55	2,237	1,229	1,008	95	73	88	71	646	738	402	130
55—60	617	383	234	32	12	19	13	218	182	118	28
60—65	2,099	1,014	1,085	46	37	46	45	700	934	228	74
65—70	412	204	208	11	7	8	6	144	184	43	11
70 and over	1,895	829	1,066	18	18	17	22	700	1,007	96	23
Total	**26,831**	**15,025**	**11,806**	**1,547**	**1,013**	**2,522**	**1,899**	**8,287**	**7,976**	**2,762**	**996**
	Kashmir State.										
0—1	13	8	5	..	..	1	..	7	5	..	..
1—2	9	7	2	..	..	1	..	6	2	..	..
2—3	54	33	21	5	..	10	10	15	8	3	3
3—4	108	63	45	9	6	32	26	19	12	3	1
4—5	140	79	61	9	6	55	45	15	10	..	..
Total 0—5	*324*	*190*	*134*	*23*	*12*	*99*	*81*	*62*	*37*	*6*	*4*
5—10	860	462	398	72	35	268	242	112	102	10	19
10—15	954	550	404	87	59	275	222	157	96	31	27
15—20	970	564	406	96	43	256	203	156	135	56	25
20—25	993	554	439	95	56	228	157	171	175	60	51
25—30	746	440	306	63	38	147	116	149	121	81	31
30—35	805	515	290	93	47	165	71	168	121	89	51
35—40	582	371	211	51	30	97	55	123	101	100	25
40—45	807	497	310	71	41	109	55	176	169	141	45
45—50	450	259	191	32	20	29	17	119	131	79	23
50—55	655	413	242	42	24	37	22	210	166	124	30
55—60	169	103	66	11	6	15	7	58	49	19	4
60—65	781	444	337	25	13	21	17	288	264	110	23
65—70	169	107	62	8	2	10	1	75	56	14	3
70 and over	1,105	595	510	17	16	11	10	510	470	57	14
Total	**10,370**	**6,064**	**4,306**	**786**	**442**	**1,767**	**1,276**	**2,534**	**2,213**	**977**	**375**
	Madras States.										
0—1	12	4	8	..	..	..	1	3	7	1	..
1—2	19	10	9	..	..	2	1	7	7	1	1
2—3	33	13	20	..	1	3	7	9	11	1	2
3—4	41	24	17	1	..	9	8	12	7	2	2
4—5	55	31	24	1	..	17	13	10	9	3	2
Total 0—5	*160*	*82*	*78*	*2*	*1*	*31*	*30*	*41*	*41*	*8*	*7*
5—10	389	222	167	10	5	101	95	103	66	9	2
10—15	467	280	187	11	4	137	95	99	74	34	15
15—20	535	322	213	26	15	138	95	101	72	57	31
20—25	592	364	228	52	29	128	85	93	73	91	41
25—30	713	436	277	70	47	112	94	119	80	136	57
30—35	635	378	257	72	64	56	52	115	95	135	46
35—40	681	451	230	86	56	74	48	127	78	164	48
40—45	688	410	278	76	68	59	36	104	123	173	51
45—50	530	334	196	52	58	46	37	88	67	148	34
50—55	536	327	209	33	35	42	35	124	99	128	40
55—60	409	269	140	24	25	28	12	101	76	116	27
60—65	443	255	188	30	20	31	21	122	128	74	21
65—70	195	100	95	8	12	7	8	52	64	33	11
70 and over	354	168	186	17	11	13	15	119	147	21	13
Total	**7,327**	**4,398**	**2,929**	**569**	**450**	**1,068**	**758**	**1,566**	**1,281**	**1,327**	**446**

TABLE XII.—Infirmities. Part II.—Details by Age—*concluded*.

Age.	Population afflicted.			Insane.		Deaf-Mutes.		Blind.		Lepers.	
	Persons.	Males.	Females.	Males.	Females.	Males.	Females.	Males.	Females.	Males.	Females.
1	2	3	4	5	6	7	8	9	10	11	12
					Mysore State.						
0—1	20	6	14	..	..	..	2	6	12	..	..
1—2	15	7	8	..	..	..	..	7	8	..	..
2—3	71	35	36	1	1	6	9	26	25	2	1
3—4	83	40	43	2	3	16	17	21	23	1	..
4—5	152	63	89	2	5	40	44	20	37	1	3
Total 0—5	*341*	*151*	*190*	*5*	*9*	*62*	*72*	*80*	*105*	*4*	*4*
5—10	1,116	627	489	41	28	374	286	216	173	4	4
10—15	1,463	808	655	85	76	445	346	277	231	13	7
15—20	1,279	720	559	71	74	344	265	291	213	22	12
20—25	1,187	673	514	83	70	315	235	254	194	33	16
25—30	952	587	365	70	33	263	169	223	147	36	17
30—35	825	455	370	77	52	163	150	186	147	34	28
35—40	699	415	284	76	42	145	104	151	126	44	12
40—45	872	479	393	79	54	123	107	209	201	69	32
45—50	614	370	244	57	31	91	58	157	133	66	22
50—55	789	411	378	50	49	75	76	214	226	73	28
55—60	354	204	150	24	14	36	27	105	97	39	12
60—65	653	340	313	25	25	39	31	233	227	43	31
65—70	255	142	113	6	4	11	11	112	91	13	7
70 and over	846	422	424	15	9	27	22	847	383	35	12
Total	**12,245**	**6,804**	**5,441**	**764**	**570**	**2,513**	**1,959**	**3,055**	**2,694**	**528**	**239**
					Punjab States.						
0—1	19	13	6	..	..	1	1	11	5	1	..
1—2	25	17	8	..	..	3	1	14	7	..	..
2—3	49	29	20	1	..	4	3	24	16	1	1
3—4	98	56	42	1	3	26	20	29	19	1	1
4—5	74	45	29	3	1	23	18	18	10	1	1
Total 0—5	*265*	*160*	*105*	*5*	*4*	*57*	*43*	*96*	*57*	*4*	*3*
5—10	818	507	311	38	12	257	176	213	122	6	3
10—15	865	531	334	51	38	245	165	224	124	14	13
15—20	897	534	363	59	39	237	179	213	129	28	19
20—25	857	503	354	54	30	185	163	238	139	31	24
25—30	806	521	285	56	19	195	101	224	153	50	13
30—35	940	567	373	63	36	186	113	247	189	73	37
35—40	703	441	262	31	20	105	69	213	143	95	30
40—45	1,143	685	458	45	34	142	93	354	279	145	53
45—50	656	406	250	16	12	65	40	255	177	71	21
50—55	1,280	738	542	27	11	104	62	488	434	119	37
55—60	529	339	190	15	4	35	17	248	157	41	12
60—65	1,611	882	729	25	13	80	54	721	636	58	28
65—70	423	273	150	6	1	18	5	234	140	15	4
70 and over	1,962	1,116	846	9	10	68	41	1,015	789	29	9
Total	**13,755**	**8,203**	**5,552**	**560**	**283**	**1,979**	**1,321**	**4,978**	**3,668**	**779**	**396**
					Rajputana Agency.						
0—1	44	26	18	..	..	1	..	25	18	..	..
1—2	25	15	10	..	..	..	2	15	8	..	..
2—3	91	58	33	..	1	5	3	53	29	..	..
3—4	158	92	66	8	1	15	12	69	53	..	..
4—5	190	129	61	7	6	43	14	79	41	..	..
Total 0—5	*508*	*320*	*188*	*15*	*8*	*64*	*31*	*241*	*149*	..	..
5—10	1,092	674	418	51	19	239	119	380	277	4	3
10—15	1,144	756	388	66	38	234	124	445	219	11	7
15—20	1,231	779	452	96	46	210	91	455	308	18	7
20—25	1,499	943	556	130	45	242	104	548	394	23	18
25—30	1,510	898	612	125	33	199	100	536	468	38	11
30—35	2,033	1,060	973	129	53	204	107	663	791	64	22
35—40	1,280	664	616	68	30	115	49	440	528	41	9
40—45	2,458	1,099	1,359	90	70	128	100	774	1,166	107	23
45—50	1,330	658	672	51	17	54	43	511	604	42	8
50—55	3,263	1,473	1,790	82	40	117	85	1,186	1,648	88	17
55—60	1,188	572	616	20	10	35	19	494	586	23	1
60—65	4,324	1,684	2,640	33	32	68	65	1,546	2,534	37	9
65—70	1,074	536	538	1	2	25	7	500	525	10	4
70 and over	3,557	1,576	1,981	16	10	58	83	1,498	1,937	9	1
Total	**27,491**	**13.692**	**13,799**	**973**	**453**	**1,992**	**1,077**	**10,212**	**12,134**	**515**	**135**
					United Provinces States.						
0—1	5	2	3	..	..	..	..	2	3	..	..
1—2	9	5	4	..	1	1	1	4	2	..	..
2—3	7	3	4	..	1	1	1	2	2	..	..
3—4	9	5	4	..	..	2	2	3	2	..	..
4—5	20	12	8	1	..	5	3	6	5	..	..
Total 0—5	*50*	*27*	*23*	*1*	*2*	*9*	*7*	*17*	*14*	..	..
5—10	169	86	83	5	6	47	41	32	36	2	..
10—15	157	96	61	3	5	45	34	43	21	5	1
15—20	158	94	64	6	3	45	31	36	27	7	3
20—25	169	105	64	6	5	43	30	42	25	14	4
25—30	153	96	57	6	2	31	22	43	27	16	6
30—35	184	117	67	14	2	29	15	39	36	35	14
35—40	139	91	48	7	2	16	5	36	32	32	9
40—45	216	143	73	10	4	17	4	57	39	59	26
45—50	106	75	31	5	1	11	8	31	13	28	9
50—55	204	118	86	3	1	20	14	48	60	47	11
55—60	78	46	32	1	1	5	2	26	24	14	5
60—65	181	111	70	5	3	10	6	83	58	13	3
65—70	55	32	23	1	..	4	1	20	22	7	..
70 and over	189	89	100	2	..	5	6	77	92	5	2
Total	**2,208**	**1,326**	**882**	**75**	**37**	**337**	**226**	**630**	**526**	**284**	**98**

TABLE XII-A.

Infirmities by Selected Castes, Tribes or Races.

1. The principle followed in selecting castes for this Table is practically the same as that described in the explanatory note to Table IX. For the reason there given the total strength of a caste in this Table does not necessarily tally with that in Table XIII.

2. Within each Province, State or Agency the castes are arranged in alphabetical order.

3. The statistics for Ajmer-Merwara, Andamans and Nicobars, Coorg and Sikkim have been omitted, as the number of persons there dealt with is relatively insignificant. The figures for Provinces include those for the States attached to them, except in the case of Bombay, where this Table was compiled for British Territory only, and Madras, where they exclude the figures for Cochin and Travancore.

TABLE XII-A.—Infirmities by

Province and Caste, Tribe or Race.	Population dealt with.			Insane.			Deaf-Mutes.			Blind.			Lepers.		
	Persons.	Males.	Females.	Persons.	Males.	Females.	Persons.	Males.	Females.	Persons.	Males.	Females.	Persons.	Males.	Females.
1	2	3	4	5	6	7	8	9	10	11	12	13	14	15	16
ASSAM.															
Ahom	197,444	101,961	95,483	100	67	33	218	132	86	137	68	69	257	173	84
Brahman	126,015	69,396	56,619	87	67	20	92	54	38	68	42	26	40	32	8
Chamar	54,234	27,911	26,323	4	3	1	8	6	2	53	20	33	13	10	3
Chutiya	88,825	45,603	43,222	38	29	9	87	45	42	62	34	28	66	43	23
Garo	144,350	72,569	71,781	53	26	27	79	41	38	212	98	114	110	66	44
Jogi (Jugi)	169,097	86,171	82,926	81	42	39	116	77	39	182	80	102	101	74	27
Kachari	230,102	117,487	112,615	63	37	26	194	96	98	164	82	82	182	131	51
Kalita	221,942	115,506	106,436	111	72	39	218	115	103	243	125	118	114	80	34
Kayastha	81,967	44,377	37,590	62	44	18	45	25	20	58	36	22	28	22	6
Khasi	120,894	57,328	63,566	33	11	22	64	39	25	111	65	46	26	14	12
Koch	242,054	123,187	118,867	90	54	36	178	102	76	160	85	75	132	87	45
Kshatriya	250,541	124,764	125,777	70	31	39	43	23	20	74	51	23	49	36	13
Kshatriya Manipuri.	*20,015*	*9,871*	*10,144*	*47*	*20*	*27*	*25*	*11*	*14*	*26*	*16*	*10*	*41*	*30*	*11*
Kuki	69,819	34,625	35,194	19	9	10	7	2	5	27	17	10	3	3	...
Lushai	15,749	7,333	8,416	80	29	51	2	2	...	12	7	5	...	...	...
Mech	94,606	47,177	47,429	72	46	26	92	45	47	67	38	29	161	137	24
Mikir	105,077	53,642	51,435	30	18	12	55	21	34	131	73	58	188	130	58
Munda	91,268	47,214	44,054	21	17	4	42	22	20	52	23	29	45	28	17
Nadiyal	68,350	34,891	33,459	22	12	10	69	35	34	37	16	21	23	13	10
Naga	201,290	97,692	103,598	56	26	30	743	381	362	364	165	199	33	21	12
Patni	111,206	56,901	54,305	56	27	29	62	39	23	122	72	50	101	80	21
Rajbansi	133,078	68,584	64,494	114	69	45	112	73	39	144	77	67	152	118	34
Sudra	118,512	61,148	57,364	43	33	10	39	29	10	94	44	50	58	45	13
Synteng	42,145	19,633	22,512	36	18	18	31	16	15	39	21	18	12	10	2
BALUCHISTAN.															
Baluch (Biloch)	169,190	91,959	77,231	78	51	27	162	116	46	534	296	238	18	15	3
Brahui	167,787	93,095	74,692	84	58	26	127	79	48	303	162	141	26	19	7
Jatt	78,397	42,670	35,727	24	16	8	93	64	29	372	198	174	1	1	...
Lasi	27,779	14,857	12,922	32	22	10	55	46	9	70	35	35	2	2	...
Pathan	188,093	102,148	85,945	72	58	14	139	110	29	305	170	135	10	8	2
Saiyid	21,296	11,008	10,288	7	6	1	13	8	5	35	24	11	...	...	...
BENGAL.															
Bagdi	996,310	494,644	501,666	248	157	91	630	360	270	889	456	433	1,006	758	248
Bairagi	423,985	192,137	231,848	217	130	87	271	154	117	594	294	300	357	251	106
Barui	178,168	92,748	85,420	74	50	24	129	83	46	91	54	37	21	20	1
Bauri	310,798	153,334	157,464	64	30	34	155	82	73	429	157	272	979	606	373
Brahman	1,212,687	645,955	566,732	837	603	234	707	427	280	840	532	308	369	276	93
Chamar	136,553	86,504	50,049	64	40	24	194	116	78	210	105	105	148	115	33
Dhoba (Dhobi)	228,052	118,350	109,702	74	44	30	180	122	58	155	92	63	64	51	13
Dom	145,589	74,051	71,538	48	30	18	171	96	75	194	88	106	229	148	81
Goala (Ahir)	646,438	355,941	290,497	237	137	100	437	253	184	558	293	265	508	328	180
Hari	173,706	88,123	85,583	60	34	26	170	88	82	169	92	77	145	112	33
Jogi (Jugi)	361,141	182,903	178,238	174	106	68	240	155	85	225	128	97	62	49	13
Jolaha	282,425	152,212	130,213	68	40	28	140	90	50	153	74	79	43	29	14
Kaibartta	2,487,390	1,253,287	1,234,103	704	437	267	1,355	840	515	1,715	942	773	621	488	133
Kamar	263,329	136,158	127,171	105	66	39	168	96	72	210	126	84	118	85	33
Kayastha	1,113,684	570,819	542,865	780	530	250	687	416	271	836	504	332	193	133	60
Magh	127,949	62,914	65,035	107	51	56	70	36	34	91	54	37	19	13	6
Malo	247,533	126,890	120,643	84	44	40	96	51	45	186	108	78	61	50	11
Mochi (Muchi)	455,236	243,848	211,388	83	46	37	193	111	82	171	84	87	47	37	10
Namasudra	1,908,728	967,178	941,550	804	465	339	1,333	831	502	1,167	684	483	358	283	75
Napit (Nai)	447,306	229,988	217,318	193	119	74	334	207	127	335	190	145	138	94	44
Pod	536,527	274,148	262,379	211	116	95	248	147	101	247	146	101	51	39	12
Rajbansi	1,808,790	936,264	872,526	1,022	610	412	1,266	799	467	1,235	680	555	927	745	182
Sadgop	535,166	269,855	265,311	184	136	48	352	245	107	392	257	135	505	440	65
Santal	669,420	336,384	333,036	79	50	29	248	132	116	284	138	146	307	194	113
Sheikh	5,130,616	2,654,890	2,475,726	1,593	1,007	586	3,357	1,991	1,366	4,008	2,232	1,776	1,578	1,303	275
Sutradhar	177,453	91,556	85,897	88	56	32	89	50	39	149	85	64	70	48	22
Tanti	322,983	169,924	153,059	113	81	32	252	175	77	295	154	141	142	100	42
Teli and Tili	419,122	217,730	201,392	194	125	69	295	171	124	347	187	160	386	272	114

Selected Castes, Tribes or Races.

Province and Caste, Tribe or Race.	Population dealt with.			Insane.			Deaf-Mutes.			Blind.			Lepers.		
	Persons.	Males.	Females.	Persons.	Males.	Females.	Persons.	Males.	Females.	Persons.	Males.	Females.	Persons.	Males.	Females.
1	2	3	4	5	6	7	8	9	10	11	12	13	14	15	16
BIHAR AND ORISSA.															
Babhan	1,129,735	575,940	553,795	84	67	17	605	425	180	855	513	342	313	295	18
Bhuiya	663,757	322,708	341,049	68	38	30	297	144	153	774	354	420	364	253	111
Brahman	1,755,424	874,507	880,917	340	260	80	1,285	896	389	1,719	1,076	643	914	715	199
Chamar	1,114,467	520,099	594,368	92	52	40	834	490	344	1,216	571	645	326	257	69
Chasa	846,119	415,439	430,680	109	73	36	364	235	129	576	324	252	690	534	156
Dhanuk	572,412	272,915	299,497	43	25	18	417	262	155	694	344	350	197	161	36
Dhobi (Dhoba)	376,623	183,547	193,076	58	34	24	303	178	125	452	208	244	211	154	57
Dhunia	202,208	94,550	107,658	14	7	7	240	133	107	255	131	124	72	66	6
Dosadh	1,189,274	569,733	619,541	102	68	34	983	540	443	1,825	962	863	438	380	58
Gaura	712,772	345,819	366,953	82	42	40	390	232	158	650	326	324	436	318	118
Goala (Ahir)	3,250,415	1,621,530	1,628,885	248	162	86	2,454	1,555	899	3,613	1,811	1,802	874	713	161
Hajjam	388,429	188,843	199,586	58	42	16	372	220	152	630	316	314	140	112	28
Ho	419,221	203,045	216,176	3	2	1	27	11	16	7	5	2	6	6	...
Indian Christian	268,265	133,186	135,079	23	21	2	104	57	47	192	98	94	513	253	260
Jolaha	826,391	389,075	437,316	99	55	44	808	462	346	1,131	559	572	307	237	70
Kahar	524,431	245,801	278,630	69	39	30	434	257	177	1,076	493	583	318	261	57
Kalwar	180,825	89,148	91,677	30	21	9	161	104	57	149	85	64	47	42	5
Kandh	302,883	148,079	154,804	26	18	8	86	53	33	167	73	94	187	126	61
Kandu	502,855	243,100	259,755	51	34	17	494	303	191	712	349	363	174	154	20
Karan	147,511	71,286	76,225	33	27	6	52	41	11	70	40	30	103	84	19
Kayastha	347,613	177,704	169,909	101	74	27	264	191	73	374	247	127	80	71	9
Kewat	420,506	203,450	217,056	58	44	14	267	158	109	484	256	228	266	182	84
Khandait	769,353	365,982	403,371	111	82	29	395	281	114	659	364	295	635	477	158
Koiri	1,280,655	633,680	646,975	138	93	45	1,693	1,049	644	1,667	834	833	349	297	52
Kumbhar	513,327	256,262	257,065	50	28	22	439	254	185	639	269	870	217	158	59
Kurmi	1,312,832	651,097	661,735	137	97	40	1,010	625	385	1,925	934	991	511	397	114
Munda	410,440	201,087	209,353	136	64	72	346	191	155	573	295	278	186	117	69
Musahar	626,795	309,653	317,142	36	19	17	265	151	114	540	265	275	396	261	135
Nunia	319,102	150,956	168,146	21	16	5	216	119	97	361	184	177	105	90	15
Oraon	474,673	227,273	247,400	73	40	33	261	144	117	681	316	365	63	37	26
Panika	464,046	227,359	236,687	38	26	12	227	154	73	373	187	186	293	214	79
Rajput	1,239,692	630,625	609,067	153	126	27	888	625	263	1,125	682	443	435	391	44
Saiyid	91,105	44,460	46,645	27	24	3	105	57	48	115	61	54	38	25	13
Santal	1,399,450	692,067	707,383	103	61	42	519	288	231	596	258	338	435	282	153
Tanti	613,481	290,843	322,638	56	32	24	475	298	177	723	364	359	386	262	124
Teli and Til	1,071,906	524,741	547,165	165	126	39	760	447	313	1,263	647	616	470	363	107
BOMBAY.															
Agri	222,810	112,803	110,007	36	18	18	117	78	39	241	110	131	208	119	89
Baniya	353,982	195,406	158,576	50	38	12	66	31	35	151	86	65	58	37	21
Bharvad	627,157	318,109	309,048	121	81	40	344	193	151	691	807	384	154	113	41
Bhil	512,119	258,983	253,136	72	38	34	171	90	81	511	231	280	150	115	35
Bohora, Memon, Khoja, Teli, and Ghanchi.	177,448	94,390	83,058	70	44	26	118	86	32	197	118	79	9	6	3
Brahman	769,932	410,436	359,496	328	254	74	468	295	173	904	523	381	156	114	42
Chamar	211,853	108,991	102,862	31	16	15	107	73	34	293	160	133	71	53	18
Dubla	123,418	62,953	60,465	24	12	12	114	70	44	471	192	279	140	96	44
Indian Christian	191,438	106,011	85,427	81	48	33	87	53	34	232	108	124	331	161	170
Koli	1,160,971	601,228	559,743	242	139	103	712	412	300	1,459	616	843	515	355	160
Kunbi	1,644,824	822,020	822,804	258	178	80	827	518	309	2,488	1,177	1,311	1,275	934	341
Lingaiat	1,064,955	542,866	522,089	254	176	78	671	400	271	801	460	341	207	169	38
Lohana	464,308	252,001	212,307	266	208	58	308	229	79	911	517	394	50	33	17
Mahar, Holiya or Dhed.	1,077,159	539,447	537,712	212	123	89	507	288	219	1,669	776	893	766	516	250
Mali	272,698	137,750	134,948	43	20	23	117	63	54	415	223	192	177	114	63
Mang	227,697	111,667	116,030	50	31	19	125	72	53	278	152	126	144	99	45
Maratha	2,6[illegible]0,746	1,346,609	1,284,137	451	282	169	1,196	723	473	2,838	1,446	1,392	1,839	1,359	480
Rajput	215,358	115,941	99,417	42	24	18	103	62	41	338	164	174	68	54	14
Sonar	131,639	68,155	63,484	59	44	15	74	42	32	127	85	42	41	30	11
Sutar	119,237	62,702	56,535	27	19	8	51	30	21	143	75	68	62	48	14
Teli, Ganigar or Ghanchi.	110,890	55,873	55,017	41	28	12	80	43	37	161	84	67	71	45	26

TABLE XII-A.—Infirmities by

Province and Caste, Tribe or Race.	Population dealt with.			Insane.			Deaf-Mutes.			Blind.			Lepers.		
	Persons.	Males.	Females.	Persons.	Males.	Females.	Persons.	Males.	Females.	Persons.	Males.	Females.	Persons.	Males.	Females
1	2	3	4	5	6	7	8	9	10	11	12	13	14	15	16
BURMA.															
Arakanese	344,123	177,089	167,034	209	125	84	101	56	45	102	68	34	20	6	14
Burmese	7,479,433	3,650,902	3,828,531	4,812	2,746	2,066	3,508	2,012	1,496	11.399	5,590	5,809	4,963	3,427	1,536
Chin	243,066	119,373	123,693	1,558	792	766	613	343	270	214	107	107	301	218	83
Chinese	104,641	79,830	24,811	24	17	7	154	78	76	50	29	21	33	32	1
Danu	70,947	35,264	35,683	48	29	19	56	35	21	135	58	77	11	6	5
Intha	52,685	25,771	26,914	94	45	49	42	23	19	129	51	78	122	82	40
Kachin	162,368	80,764	81,604	379	176	203	1,630	839	791	381	226	155	59	35	24
Karen	903,626	450,971	452,655	421	245	176	360	227	133	395	192	203	367	279	88
Shan	941,724	465,609	476,115	1,207	637	570	1,412	742	670	2,881	1,436	1,445	762	409	353
Talaing	320,629	159,235	161,394	109	75	34	110	76	34	110	71	39	86	68	18
Taungthu	183,054	91,597	91.457	154	32	122	108	25	83	178	48	130	43	33	10
Wa-Palaung	150,375	74,600	75,775	177	79	98	322	146	177	295	137	158	41	20	21
CENTRAL PROVINCES AND BERAR.															
Ahir	738,192	866,815	371,377	95	63	32	294	170	124	1,510	541	969	332	174	158
Baniya	199,336	103,290	96,046	39	31	8	117	74	43	461	234	227	47	42	5
Brahman	445,744	237,605	208,139	133	103	30	212	131	81	980	472	508	90	62	28
Chamar	901,594	443,059	458,535	95	45	50	278	173	105	2,733	1,035	1,698	399	270	129
Christian	73,401	39,208	34,193	34	12	22	35	16	19	119	59	60	619	302	317
Dhanagar	96,283	48,797	47,486	19	11	8	42	25	17	252	125	127	54	38	16
Dhimar	283,684	140,853	142.831	38	26	12	199	104	95	608	238	370	105	69	36
Dhobi	165,427	81,127	84,300	13	9	4	84	51	33	320	116	204	112	73	39
Gond	2,333,893	1,138,157	1,195,736	307	182	125	1,035	582	453	4,444	1,575	2.869	801	478	323
Kachhi	119,553	60,287	59,266	18	10	8	61	38	23	359	149	210	25	14	11
Kalar	195,450	96,426	99,024	38	27	11	137	75	62	392	162	230	86	50	36
Kaur	229,412	113,563	115,849	26	16	10	100	57	43	288	125	163	75	48	27
Kumhar	118,520	60,054	58,466	6	5	1	72	39	33	217	85	132	42	27	15
Kunbi	1,356.734	682.737	673,997	204	130	74	585	344	241	2,898	1,361	1,537	710	544	166
Kurmi	302,588	150,109	152,479	41	30	11	188	122	66	910	351	559	184	121	63
Lodhi	313,900	155,922	157,978	46	29	17	165	100	65	733	293	440	64	45	19
Lohar	181,590	91,183	90,407	27	18	9	123	64	59	332	143	189	81	47	34
Mahar (Mehra)	1,165,177	575,449	589,728	170	105	65	467	248	219	2,175	909	1,266	494	323	171
Mali	563,528	279,868	283,660	79	46	33	247	153	94	1,181	530	651	385	266	119
Maratha	93,901	46,716	47,185	22	15	7	39	16	23	213	103	110	37	26	11
Nai (Hajjam)	148,750	74,078	74.672	40	30	10	102	64	38	487	212	275	76	50	26
Panika (Panka)	214,894	104,032	110,862	28	18	10	73	43	30	497	207	290	100	65	35
Rajput	441,231	223,581	217,650	68	50	18	239	149	90	780	355	425	129	92	37
Sonar (Sunar)	126,878	63,844	63,034	33	24	9	89	55	34	259	137	122	33	22	11
Teli	869,370	427,126	442,244	135	74	61	450	251	199	2,132	819	1,313	737	459	278
MADRAS.															
Brahman (Canarese)	93,726	45,842	47,884	42	29	13	41	20	21	88	43	45	76	70	6
Brahman (Oriya)	143,655	69,820	73,835	5	2	3	29	2	27	26	1	25	30	26	4
Brahman (Tamil)	480,063	238,594	241,469	133	96	37	346	187	159	461	214	247	202	150	52
Brahman (Telugu)	460,819	229,290	231,529	145	112	33	409	237	172	302	156	146	90	64	26
Cheruman	255,395	121,567	133,828	26	14	12	116	54	62	521	267	254	198	125	73
Chetti	350,251	171,058	179,193	67	39	28	163	75	88	162	93	69	70	56	14
Idaiyan	734,771	360,155	374,616	225	148	77	998	570	428	934	453	481	507	381	126
Indian Christian	1,167,595	573,438	594,157	305	159	146	954	513	441	1,144	595	549	774	569	205
Kamma	1,126,095	564,432	561,663	158	98	60	810	471	339	662	363	299	148	117	31
Kammalan	667,161	327,366	339,795	113	68	45	487	287	200	512	275	237	182	139	43
Kamsala	295,583	146,482	149,101	66	41	25	224	120	104	197	114	83	110	65	45
Kapu	2,678,925	1,329,624	1,349,301	376	213	163	1,669	948	721	1,407	696	711	564	406	158
Komati	498,295	250,043	248,252	127	92	35	362	230	132	428	260	168	169	129	40
Madiga	807,986	406,089	401,897	163	80	83	672	361	311	689	349	340	337	245	92
Mal	1,511,312	747,652	763,660	305	130	175	1,046	575	471	944	495	449	723	565	158
Nayar	412,102	198,196	213,906	134	75	59	298	156	142	595	268	327	157	108	49
Pallan	866,132	414,945	451,187	138	61	77	638	320	318	847	382	465	330	254	76
Paraiyan	2,363,803	1,153,356	1,210,447	338	167	171	1,679	919	760	1,885	928	957	1,180	889	291
Tiyan	639,832	316,012	323,820	196	108	88	369	210	159	646	319	327	230	164	66
Vellala	2,535,791	1,248,052	1,287,739	362	216	146	2,002	1,128	874	1,815	856	959	817	619	198

SELECTED CASTES, TRIBES OR RACES—*continued.*

Province and Caste, Tribe or Race.	Population dealt with			Insane.			Deaf-Mutes.			Blind.			Lepers.		
	Persons.	Males.	Females.	Persons.	Males.	Females.	Persons.	Males.	Females.	Persons.	Males.	Females.	Persons.	Males.	Females.
1	2	3	4	5	6	7	8	9	10	11	12	13	14	15	16
NORTH-WEST FRONTIER PROVINCE.															
Awan	275,711	149,550	126,161	124	91	33	372	285	87	449	245	204	35	23	12
Gujar	113,871	61,711	52,160	50	32	18	116	81	35	93	54	39	31	24	7
Jat	86,097	48,873	37,224	23	16	7	69	46	23	182	89	93	14	9	5
Jolaha	37,390	19,999	17,391	18	14	4	44	33	11	58	34	24	6	5	1
Mochi	23,040	12,383	10,657	16	10	6	31	15	16	62	40	22	1	1	...
Moghal	14,865	8,269	6,596	9	8	1	16	12	4	22	15	7	4	3	1
Pathan	845,183	449,500	395,683	318	231	87	649	439	210	1,178	755	423	88	64	24
Saiyid	75,115	39,230	35,885	38	26	12	88	47	41	119	57	62	8	6	2
Swathi	38,329	20,181	18,148	18	11	7	80	48	32	41	22	19	9	9	...
Tanaoli	63,985	33,349	30,636	26	18	8	65	38	27	66	37	29	11	8	3
Tarkhan	42,618	22,764	19,854	13	8	5	56	37	19	68	35	33	4	3	1
PUNJAB.															
Ahir	208,594	116,380	92,214	17	13	4	91	64	27	552	258	294	13	13	...
Arain	977,601	541,189	436,412	253	160	93	681	417	264	1,997	1,050	947	55	39	16
Arora	674,083	362,942	311,141	252	172	80	406	264	142	1,720	932	788	16	11	5
Awan	425,931	226,991	198,940	125	84	41	492	297	195	889	541	348	28	16	12
Baluch (Biloch)	532,499	289,611	242,888	206	130	76	426	274	152	1,490	733	757	20	14	6
Brahman	1,017,743	562,036	455,707	219	165	54	889	561	328	2,740	1,475	1,265	208	157	51
Chamar	1,128,704	613,671	515,033	198	119	79	1,119	654	465	3,828	1,817	2,011	105	78	27
Chuhra	925,535	510,776	414,759	147	94	53	307	208	99	3,999	2,076	1,923	27	22	5
Dhobi	156,046	84,642	71,404	41	29	12	219	142	77	513	277	236	5	3	2
Fakir	279,722	164,237	115,485	84	44	40	220	140	80	1,242	856	386	43	35	8
Ghirath	171,129	88,778	82,351	34	24	10	507	297	210	172	86	86	118	92	26
Gujar	610,472	338,813	271,659	69	47	22	393	254	139	1,028	601	427	52	41	11
Hali	21,067	10,779	10,288	7	5	2	75	32	43	17	7	10	48	20	28
Indian Christian	163,994	90,776	73,218	40	22	18	45	33	12	278	150	128	82	42	40
Jat	4,956,536	2,808,551	2,147,985	1,045	667	378	2,838	1,857	981	11,837	6,651	5,186	270	190	80
Jhinwar	359,864	198,667	161,197	86	45	41	257	161	96	1,023	512	511	38	32	6
Jolaha (Julaha)	635,044	345,292	289,752	187	109	78	701	436	265	1,709	940	769	53	37	16
Kanet	403,815	207,202	196,613	74	43	31	738	409	329	634	296	338	461	313	148
Kasai	119,826	62,898	56,928	40	26	14	90	54	36	349	159	190	6	5	1
Khatri	432,727	238,707	194,020	133	97	36	253	145	108	937	545	392	25	20	5
Koli	175,014	90,503	84,511	33	12	21	486	247	239	317	132	185	251	183	68
Kumhar	550,450	299,738	250,712	120	69	51	563	362	201	1,656	890	766	50	32	18
Lohar	323,477	176,191	147,286	66	42	24	375	220	155	777	447	330	66	44	22
Machhi	279,666	152,562	127,104	79	54	25	226	129	97	800	373	427	20	15	5
Mirasi	227,394	122,071	105,323	68	43	25	274	180	94	896	511	385	46	33	13
Mochi	419,378	228,688	190,690	132	81	51	388	260	128	1,189	647	542	23	16	7
Nai (Hajjam)	350,456	192,266	158,190	87	54	33	295	195	100	1,093	580	513	25	20	5
Pathan	292,417	166,519	125,898	88	69	19	172	109	63	612	329	283	26	17	9
Rajput	1,635,432	898,023	737,409	405	251	154	1,435	900	535	3,560	2,033	1,527	259	201	58
Rawat	97,798	51,129	46,669	19	9	10	179	119	60	124	58	66	109	87	22
Saiyid	247,388	131,992	115,396	61	41	20	226	139	87	661	308	353	18	14	4
Sheikh	338,873	187,378	151,495	125	79	46	266	171	95	813	427	386	26	19	7
Tarkhan	646,330	356,540	289,790	126	83	43	524	321	203	1,710	956	754	71	56	15
Teli	295,971	162,444	133,527	71	36	35	242	152	90	765	411	354	17	13	4
UNITED PROVINCES OF AGRA AND OUDH.															
Ahir	3,903,764	2,043,518	1,860,246	559	373	186	2,369	1,469	900	9,204	4,377	4,827	1,239	1,024	215
Baniya	1,210,188	646,580	563,608	311	220	91	774	498	276	2,482	1,415	1,067	243	210	33
Barhai	600,887	320,537	280,350	86	59	27	314	206	108	1,388	775	613	166	148	18
Bhangi	417,863	218,995	198,868	68	41	27	233	142	91	1,169	614	555	67	56	11
Brahman	4,678,023	2,462,543	2,215,480	992	723	269	2,921	1,943	978	9,082	4,990	4,092	1,398	1,169	229
Chamar	6,083,401	3,101,884	2,981,517	798	522	276	2,640	1,560	1,080	15,027	6,438	8,589	1,706	1,341	365
Dhobi	725,720	374,851	350,869	64	35	29	361	211	150	1,700	776	924	245	207	38
Dhunia	404,740	205,869	198,871	50	30	20	189	119	70	710	330	380	95	79	16
Dom	333,781	172,011	161,770	61	35	26	723	413	310	722	402	320	466	325	141

TABLE XII-A.—Infirmities by

Province and Caste, Tribe or Race.	Population dealt with.			Insane.			Deaf-Mutes.			Blind.			Lepers.		
	Persons.	Males.	Females.	Persons	Males.	Females.	Persons.	Males.	Females.	Persons.	Males.	Females.	Persons.	Males.	Females.
1	2	3	4	5	6	7	8	9	10	11	12	13	14	15	16
UNITED PROVINCES OF AGRA AND OUDH—*contd.*															
Fakir	527,885	280,265	247,620	82	52	30	342	237	105	1,236	674	562	175	154	21
Gadaria	983,130	515,719	467,411	140	82	58	358	199	159	2,377	1,120	1,257	217	193	24
Jat	744,600	421,857	322,743	73	56	17	276	177	99	1,496	828	668	77	68	9
Jolaha	991,264	508,544	482,720	170	117	53	693	423	270	2,316	1,131	1,185	237	204	33
Kachhi	728,800	387,943	340,857	109	68	41	279	175	104	1,916	867	1,049	208	175	33
Kahar	1,112,428	575,788	536,640	209	139	70	656	417	239	2,984	1,335	1,649	358	300	58
Kisan	353,714	191,109	162,605	37	27	10	137	90	47	867	468	399	87	80	7
Kori	860,443	440,152	420,291	184	118	66	508	315	193	2,992	1,336	1,656	321	262	59
Kumhar	726,370	374,510	351,860	118	75	43	401	255	146	1,465	739	726	210	178	32
Kurmi	1,890,381	982,504	907,877	316	206	110	900	554	346	4,474	2,181	2,293	678	586	92
Lodha	1,114,409	588,157	526,252	145	93	52	515	322	193	2,612	1,229	1,383	220	193	27
Lohar	589,075	308,182	280,893	77	55	22	327	208	119	1,211	656	555	141	126	15
Mali	186,629	98,732	87,896	37	22	15	171	107	64	649	324	325	64	49	15
Murao	674,343	355,700	318,643	139	92	47	381	222	159	1,984	817	1,167	213	190	23
Nai (Hajjam)	912,882	475,383	437,499	151	99	52	429	234	195	2,600	1,320	1,280	269	231	38
Nunia	409,256	206,276	202,980	54	32	22	199	98	101	664	303	361	93	75	18
Pasi	1,311,415	670,549	640,866	184	108	76	610	330	280	3,141	1,385	1,756	504	416	88
Pathan	960,711	500,225	460,486	214	132	82	531	321	210	1,902	999	903	229	203	26
Rajput	3,657,557	1,958,225	1,699,332	646	493	153	2,550	1,614	936	6,040	3,428	2,612	1,622	1,289	333
Sheikh	1,314,828	693,681	621,147	499	338	161	1,326	777	549	4,310	2,181	2,129	371	329	42
BARODA STATE.															
Bhil	17,081	8,681	8,400	7	4	3	5	3	2	73	27	46	13	6	7
Brahman (Audich)	40,628	20,876	19,752	17	9	8	7	5	2	66	36	30	3	3	...
Chodhra	19,657	10,016	9,641	11	5	6	9	6	3	19	4	15	34	24	10
Dhanuk	16,634	8,456	8,178	6	3	3	2	1	1	22	5	17	15	11	4
Dhed	99,727	50,487	49,240	22	13	9	15	12	3	249	79	170	40	30	10
Dubla	3,399	1,774	1,625	16	5	11	25	21	4	173	57	116	60	38	22
Gamatda	22,175	11,389	10,786	14	8	6	14	10	4	28	15	13	50	41	9
Koli	370,943	194,746	176,197	41	25	16	73	49	24	523	188	335	18	12	6
Kshatriya	14,782	8,044	6,738	6	5	1	2	1	1	11	6	5	10	...	10
Kunbi	398,975	210,687	188,288	73	54	19	45	27	18	601	246	355	31	24	7
Rajput	64,202	34,531	29,671	11	11	...	10	10	...	105	49	56	7	7	...
Sheikh	31,510	16,516	14,994	19	12	7	7	3	4	63	27	36	3	3	...
Shrimali	26,913	13,168	13,745	17	6	11	8	2	6	67	38	29	3	2	1
Vaghri	28,129	14,702	13,427	7	3	4	8	8	...	46	17	29	10	9	1
Vasava	6,694	3,512	3,182	2	1	1	3	3	...	9	5	4	67	48	19
CENTRAL INDIA AGENCY.															
Agarwal	58,288	27,710	30,578	3	2	1	34	12	22	82	41	41	4	3	1
Bhil	25,831	13,693	12,138	17	11	6	65	36	29	126	54	72	68	49	19
Bhilala (Hindu)	33,764	16,351	17,413	18	11	7	55	24	31	120	63	57	40	31	9
Brahman	577,968	289,803	288,165	65	51	14	185	122	63	717	368	349	65	37	28
Chamar	859,438	435,873	423,565	49	23	26	154	91	63	1,101	502	599	108	72	36
Gond (Hindu)	163,285	76,753	86,532	9	5	4	27	17	10	165	75	90	5	5	...
Gujar	185,728	105,834	79,894	10	7	3	38	21	17	230	125	105	17	13	4
Mahesri	21,412	10,008	11,404	1	1	...	4	3	1	25	16	9	...	...	...
Oswal	14,309	6,072	8,237	9	6	3	15	5	10	62	40	22	3	1	2
Pathan	138,522	73,476	65,046	21	15	6	33	18	15	168	100	68	14	12	2
Porwal	16,356	8,616	7,740	5	5	...	13	8	5	59	32	27	4	4	...
Rajput	335,636	184,086	151,550	33	22	11	68	53	15	340	171	169	48	34	14
Saiyid	32,197	17,459	14,738	7	3	4	11	6	5	29	15	14	4	3	1
Sheikh	147,216	76,259	70,957	40	28	12	65	39	26	265	136	129	24	17	7

Selected Castes, Tribes or Races—*continued.*

Province and Caste, Tribe or Race.	Population dealt with.			Insane.			Deaf-mutes.			Blind.			Lepers.		
	Persons.	Males.	Females.	Persons.	Males.	Females.	Persons.	Males.	Females.	Persons.	Males.	Females.	Persons.	Males.	Females
1	2	3	4	5	6	7	8	9	10	11	12	13	14	15	16
COCHIN STATE.															
Iluvan	208,453	102,817	105,636	56	29	27	78	42	36	252	138	114	103	81	22
Indian Christian	230,568	116,549	114,019	77	37	40	93	57	36	252	142	110	110	90	20
Jonakan	51,469	26,274	25,195	16	5	11	28	15	13	54	35	19	24	18	6
Kammalan	34,558	17,089	17,469	15	5	10	18	8	10	38	21	17	19	11	8
Nayar	121,206	58,720	62,486	38	21	17	32	13	19	257	112	145	49	32	17
Pulaiyan	72,787	35,284	37,503	5	3	2	16	5	11	66	30	36	55	35	20
HYDERABAD STATE.															
Brahman	261,241	133,192	128,049	89	67	22	94	49	45	361	203	158	48	34	14
Dhangar	488,609	245,387	243,222	41	23	18	100	55	45	634	313	321	99	76	23
Golla	460,760	234,629	226,131	109	62	47	168	102	66	709	341	368	107	75	32
Kapu	648,254	330,902	317,352	201	124	77	242	137	105	672	383	289	139	105	34
Koli	266,840	134,432	132,408	28	21	7	103	54	49	337	156	181	76	62	14
Komati	223,380	114,121	109,259	92	65	27	129	77	52	522	301	221	101	80	21
Lingaiat	757,611	381,201	376,410	91	58	33	221	124	97	610	318	292	107	78	29
Madiga and Mang.	1,145,352	581,519	563,833	243	136	107	366	211	155	1,231	631	600	462	331	131
Mahar and Mala	1,137,589	574,385	563,204	193	95	98	311	156	155	1,406	695	711	416	315	101
Maratha	1,538,874	772,878	765,996	86	54	32	334	184	150	2,279	1,055	1,224	357	265	92
Munnur	228,354	115,120	113,234	45	28	17	75	38	37	296	147	149	95	75	20
Muthrasi	260,770	134,473	126,297	65	41	24	105	57	48	304	135	169	125	100	25
Pathan	135,148	71,167	63,981	34	24	10	29	16	13	107	53	54	21	16	5
Saiyid	189,574	99,142	90,432	49	26	23	47	27	20	135	69	66	36	29	7
Sale	343,130	175,968	167,162	74	39	35	114	69	45	327	181	146	97	75	22
Sheikh	985,019	499,495	485,524	239	170	69	291	183	108	885	469	416	240	180	60
Sonar (Sunar)	88,037	45,278	42,759	46	33	13	64	40	24	158	97	61	40	29	11
Telaga	458,622	233,206	225,416	112	54	58	192	123	69	588	301	287	170	114	56
KASHMIR STATE.															
Balti	72,439	40,597	31,842	35	24	11	318	168	150	559	191	368	21	13	8
Brahman	236,662	130,169	106,493	103	66	37	179	115	64	342	211	131	71	55	16
Chamar	38,219	20,017	18,202	17	11	6	52	33	19	69	35	34	11	10	1
Dom	51,447	26,677	24,770	14	8	6	76	44	32	90	48	42	41	37	4
Gujar	328,003	183,798	144,205	77	49	28	127	78	49	277	150	127	173	141	32
Jat	141,409	72,895	68,514	52	27	25	186	115	71	238	131	107	46	34	12
Kashmiri (Musalman)	758,044	387,821	370,223	395	252	143	860	492	368	1,268	672	596	333	216	117
Megh	75,128	39,236	35,892	20	11	9	83	32	51	163	80	83	60	43	17
Moghal	49,887	28,037	21,850	10	7	3	27	14	13	45	32	13	14	9	5
Pathan	20,822	11,159	9,663	21	12	9	41	21	20	67	40	27	17	10	7
Rajput	157,639	85,175	72,464	46	24	22	139	92	47	231	121	110	92	79	13
Saiyid	75,445	40,083	35,362	55	45	10	61	33	28	119	65	54	30	21	9
Sheikh	101,239	57,313	43,926	56	38	18	126	69	57	155	95	60	43	28	15
Sudhan	56,754	28,160	28,594	14	8	6	25	15	10	41	22	19	76	58	18
Thakkar	104,622	54,597	50,025	39	28	11	117	68	49	188	116	72	91	64	27
MYSORE STATE.															
Banajiga	132,955	67,216	65,739	32	18	14	111	61	50	137	67	70	28	20	8
Beda	268,454	135,597	132,857	72	40	32	204	113	91	279	151	128	49	33	16
Brahman	194,370	98,597	95,973	71	47	24	182	109	73	227	124	103	23	13	10
Golla	150,842	76,617	74,225	36	18	18	107	65	42	159	86	73	25	17	8

TABLE XII-A.—Infirmities by Selected Castes, Tribes or Races—*concld.*

Province and Caste, Tribe or Race.	Population dealt with.			Insane.			Deaf-Mutes.			Blind.			Lepers.		
	Persons.	Males.	Females.	Persons.	Males.	Females.	Persons.	Males.	Females.	Persons.	Males.	Females.	Persons.	Males.	Females.
1	2	3	4	5	6	7	8	9	10	11	12	13	14	15	16
MYSORE STATE—*contd.*															
Holiya . .	613,248	309,536	303,712	87	49	38	459	258	201	505	236	269	103	78	25
Kuruba . .	403,366	201,967	201,399	55	28	27	304	171	133	463	255	208	42	28	14
Lambani (Banjara).	41,223	21,358	19,865	9	6	3	23	16	7	33	18	15	3	3	...
Lingaiat . .	729,431	365,091	364,340	155	94	61	598	323	275	853	420	433	90	56	34
Madiga . .	308,083	155,585	152,498	63	33	30	252	137	115	262	142	120	63	44	19
Neygi . .	96,466	48,571	47,895	40	25	15	68	38	30	114	64	50	15	11	4
Panchala . .	128,098	65,790	62,308	25	16	9	136	81	55	128	68	60	11	9	2
Sheikh . .	176,482	91,495	84,987	80	52	28	87	58	29	101	59	42	23	20	3
Vadda .	142,482	72,572	69,910	34	18	16	139	78	61	105	58	47	12	10	2
Vakkaliga .	1,331,029	665,707	665,322	271	147	124	1,085	591	494	1,425	774	651	151	101	50
RAJPUTANA AGENCY.															
Bhangi . .	84,980	43,655	41,325	6	1	5	33	17	16	255	134	121	1	...	1
Bhil . . .	448,910	229,266	219,644	35	26	9	102	65	37	304	128	176	32	28	4
Brahman . .	922,810	475,901	446,909	175	119	56	313	213	100	2,852	1,265	1,587	57	47	10
Chamar . .	734,110	378,017	356,093	71	45	26	167	109	58	1,481	607	874	42	28	14
Darzi . .	45,203	23,069	22,134	8	5	3	19	13	6	143	67	76	2	1	1
Dhobi .	45,801	23,348	22,453	9	5	4	22	14	8	106	33	73	4	3	1
Gujar . .	500,046	271,188	228,858	47	27	20	111	67	44	722	329	393	17	12	5
Jat . . .	928,486	501,616	426,870	80	51	29	234	153	81	1,558	677	881	63	46	17
Koli . . .	104,055	53,502	50,553	12	6	6	26	14	12	264	101	163	3	3	...
Kumbar . .	309,234	159,676	149,558	30	22	8	118	76	42	635	242	393	25	15	10
Lodha . .	47,013	24,526	22,487	13	10	3	11	8	3	84	40	44	11	11	...
Mahajan . .	707,721	353,152	354,569	209	166	43	326	210	116	2,591	1,302	1,289	54	50	4
Mali . .	336,876	174,966	161,910	38	22	16	89	50	39	555	228	327	22	16	6
Meo . .	165,690	87,347	78,343	14	7	7	41	26	15	411	146	265	7	4	3
Mina . .	558,689	296,205	262,484	49	36	13	119	83	36	649	321	328	21	17	4
Nai (Hajjam) .	162,463	84,866	77,597	29	23	6	63	42	21	507	225	282	14	11	3
Pathan . .	108,291	57,505	50,786	27	20	7	30	22	8	204	100	104	5	3	2
Rajput . .	687,292	385,124	302,168	84	65	19	188	134	54	1,186	623	563	56	48	8
Saiyid . .	28,954	15,242	13,712	13	12	1	16	13	3	53	25	28	...	...	...
Sheikh . .	182,019	96,788	85,231	56	34	22	70	49	21	356	181	175	5	4	1
Sonar . .	69,034	35,569	33,465	22	17	5	21	9	12	201	99	102	6	4	2
Teli . . .	78,560	40,698	37,862	11	7	4	24	9	15	167	75	92	7	4	3
TRAVANCORE STATE.															
Asari . .	62,882	31,804	31,078	12	10	2	23	15	8	26	14	12	24	19	5
Chetti . .	20,881	10,535	10,346	4	2	2	11	10	1	7	3	4	4	3	1
Iluvan . .	546,265	271,677	274,588	108	52	56	144	84	60	159	76	83	153	119	34
Indian Christian .	901,719	460,004	441,715	225	119	106	258	154	104	294	198	96	325	250	75
Kuravan . .	61,827	30,183	31,644	2	1	1	10	6	4	21	10	11	27	14	13
Nayar . .	592,489	295,703	296,786	97	64	33	175	100	75	244	154	90	203	168	35
Pulaiyan . .	185,314	93,335	91,979	18	6	12	42	22	20	88	46	42	81	49	32
Shanan . .	166,195	84,638	81,557	39	22	17	59	39	20	69	39	30	35	31	4

TABLE XIII.

Caste, Tribe, Race or Nationality.

1. Table XIII of the last census contained statistics for all castes and tribes. It was found, however, that the compilation of figures for a great number of minor groups, many of which contained only an insignificant fraction of the population, involved an undue expenditure of time and labour. On the present occasion, therefore, permission was given to the Provincial Superintendents to lump together as 'Others' the minor groups which contain only an insignificant fraction of the population. Advantage was taken of this permission in Ajmer-Merwara, Bengal, as it stood at the time of the census, Bombay, Burma, the United Provinces, the Rajputana Agency and the Hyderabad State. In the other Provinces and States a complete Table was prepared. In this Table for the whole of India, the minor groups, including those with a strength of less than 500, have in all cases been left out of account. Nor does the Table include Christians, who are specially dealt with in Tables XVII and XVIII, or any Hindu caste in Baluchistan.

2. This Table is divided into two parts. Part I contains a general list of the castes and tribes with their distribution by religion and locality, while Part II shows the principal castes in each Province, State or Agency. In Burma the distinction by religion was not preserved, and where a caste or tribe is divided between two religions, it has been entered under the religion acknowledged by the majority.

3. The difficulties which attended the classification of castes for the purpose of Table XIII in 1901 were explained on the title page of that Table. On the present occasion the index of caste classification at pages 538 to 592 of the India Tables volume of that census was carefully examined beforehand by the Provincial Superintendents, who also prepared for their respective Provinces and States a caste index similar to the one prepared in Bengal in 1901. In this way the difficulties inseparable from a work of this kind have been greatly reduced. They could not, however, be altogether removed, as in many cases it is almost impossible to say whether groups which seem to be connected with each other should be combined or kept separate. In such cases the procedure usually adopted has been to keep them separate and give cross references, *e.g.*, Bansphor and Dom, Chuhra and Bhangi. Where the same group is known by several names it has been shown in Part I under the one most generally current, the other names being added in brackets. For example, Hajjam (Nai and Napit), Dhuniya (Bahna, Nadaf), Hari (Bhuinmali) and so on. In Part II each caste has been shown under the name most common in the Province or State concerned.

TABLE XIII. Caste, Tribe, Race or Nationality. Part I.—

Caste, Religion and Locality.	Persons.	Males.	Females.
1	2	3	4
ABDAL (*Musalman*)	**5,479**	**2,823**	**2,656**
Bengal	4,960	2,558	2,402
Elsewhere	519	265	254
ADOR (Assam)	**856**	**646**	**210**
Hindu	4	4	...
Animist	852	642	210
AFRICAN	**8,511**	**5,499**	**3,012**
Hindu	5	2	3
Musalman	8,506	5,497	3,009
Bombay	7,887	5,159	2,728
Elsewhere	624	340	284
AGAMUDAIYAN* (*Hindu*)	**349,916**	**167,871**	**182,045**
Madras	349,753	167,793	181,960
Elsewhere	163	78	85
AGARIYA (C. P. and Berar)	**9,500**	**4,710**	**4,790**
Hindu	7,029	3,446	3,583
Animist	2,471	1,264	1,207
AGARU (*Hindu*)	**988**	**461**	**527**
Coorg	1	1	...
Madras	987	460	527
AGARWAL (AGARWALA)	**1,019,698**	**547,412**	**472,286**
Hindu	931,733	499,913	431,820
Sikh	2,003	1,144	859
Jain	85,941	46,336	39,605
Buddhist	11	9	2
Musalman	10	10	...
Ajmer-Merwara	8,400	4,444	3,956
Assam	5,360	3,460	1,900
Bengal	20,682	12,897	7,785
Bihar and Orissa	30,588	16,158	14,430
C. P. and Berar	25,147	13,387	11,760
Punjab	373,622	202,186	171,436
United Provinces	291,252	161,940	129,312
Central India Agency	61,423	29,231	32,192
Rajputana Agency	199,629	101,638	97,991
Elsewhere	3,595	2,071	1,524
AGASA (*Hindu*)	**116,047**	**57,998**	**58,049**
Coorg	1,647	869	778
Madras	16,628	8,017	8,611
Mysore State	97,772	49,112	48,660
AGER (*Hindu*) (Bombay)	**3,688**	**1,983**	**1,705**
AGHARIYA	**55,411**	**27,475**	**27,936**
Hindu	55,181	27,358	27,823
Animist	230	117	113
Bihar and Orissa	27,126	13,439	13,687
C. P. and Berar	27,057	13,413	13,644
Elsewhere	1,228	623	605
AGRAHARI	**79,279**	**40,806**	**38,473**
Hindu	79,174	40,746	38,428
Sikh	100	57	43
Jain	5	3	2
United Provinces	77,283	39,831	37,452
Elsewhere	1,996	975	1,021
AGRI (AGARI)	**236,580**	**119,861**	**116,719**
Hindu	236,567	119,853	116,714
Musalman	13	8	5
Bombay	233,553	118,287	115,266
Punjab	3,027	1,574	1,453
AGURI	**87,136**	**43,174**	**43,962**
Hindu	87,127	43,165	43,962
Animist	9	9	...
Bengal	85,850	42,601	43,249
Elsewhere	1,286	573	713
AHAR	**269,809**	**150,249**	**119,560**
Hindu	269,804	150,248	119,556
Musalman	5	1	4
Andamans and Nicobars	205	184	21
United Provinces	269,604	150,065	119,539
AHERIYA (AHERI)	**40,065**	**21,009**	**19,056**
Hindu	37,256	19,454	17,802
Sikh	985	551	434
Musalman	1,824	1,004	820
Punjab	19,505	10,568	8,937
United Provinces	20,560	10,441	10,119
AHIR † (GOALA)	**9,508,456**	**4,900,981**	**4,607,505**
Hindu	9,474,805	4,884,058	4,590,747
Sikh	314	214	130
Jain	15	12	3
Musalman	17,210	8,773	8,437
Animist	16,112	7,924	8,188
Assam	55,008	31,017	23,991
Bengal	646,473	355,966	290,507
Bihar and Orissa	3,250,415	1,621,530	1,628,885
Bombay	183,919	93,946	89,973
C. P. and Berar	738,192	366,815	371,377
Punjab	208,594	116,380	92,214
United Provinces	3,903,745	2,043,505	1,860,240
Baroda State	5,197	2,745	2,452
Central India Agency	325,719	166,339	159,380
Hyderabad State	19,331	9,862	9,469
Rajputana Agency	169,129	91,171	77,958
Elsewhere	2,764	1,705	1,059
AHOM	**197,446**	**101,963**	**95,483**
Hindu	197,440	101,959	95,481
Buddhist	2	2	...
Animist	4	2	2
Assam	197,444	101,961	95,483
Bengal	2	2	...

* Vellala has been shown separately.

† Ahar and Ghosi, and in Bombay Gavli, have been shown separately.

DISTRIBUTION OF CASTES BY RELIGION AND LOCALITY.

CASTE, RELIGION AND LOCALITY.	Persons.	Males.	Females.
1	2	3	4
AITO (*Musalman*) (Kashmir State)	**7,472**	**3,821**	**3,651**
AIYARAKAM (*Hindu*) (Madras)	**16,687**	**7,707**	**8,980**
AJAT (*Hindu*) (Bihar and Orissa)	**4,804**	**2,165**	**2,639**
AJLAF (*Musalman*)	**142,706**	**74,516**	**68,190**
Bengal	142,548	74,430	68,118
Bihar and Orissa	158	86	72
AJNA (*Hindu*) (C. I. Agency)	**26,465**	**15,172**	**11,293**
AJUDHYABASI (C. P. and Berar)	**1,729**	**800**	**929**
Hindu	1,609	742	867
Jain	120	58	62
ALAVAN (*Hindu*)	**2,276**	**1,149**	**1,127**
Madras	1,406	701	705
Travancore State	870	448	422
ALIYA (*Hindu*) (Madras)	**22,179**	**10,365**	**11,814**
AMAT (*Hindu*)	**63,005**	**31,000**	**32,005**
Bihar and Orissa	62,716	30,801	31,915
Elsewhere	289	199	90
AMBALAKARAN (*Hindu*)	**185,228**	**90,356**	**94,872**
Madras	185,177	90,326	94,851
Travancore State	51	30	21
AMBALAVASI (*Hindu*)	**33,406**	**16,292**	**17,114**
Coorg	2	2	...
Madras	20,218	9,759	10,459
Cochin State	7,817	3,918	3,904
Travancore State	5,369	2,618	2,751
AMBATTAN (*Hindu*)	**235,977**	**116,706**	**119,271**
Madras	213,050	105,199	107,851
Cochin State	1,101	511	590
Travancore State	21,826	10,996	10,830
AMBI	**11,871**	**6,007**	**5,864**
Hindu	11,866	6,003	5,863
Musalman	5	4	1
Bombay	11,866	6,003	5,863
Travancore State	5	4	1
ANAPPAN* (*Hindu*) (Madras)	**15,677**	**7,882**	**7,795**
ANDAMANESE (*Animist*) (Andamans and Nicobars)	**1,315**	**628**	**687**
ANDH	**58,279**	**28,578**	**29,701**
Hindu	55,654	27,214	28,440
Animist	2,625	1,364	1,261
C. P. and Berar	52,378	25,563	26,815
Hyderabad State	5,901	3,015	2,886
ANDI	**88,410**	**42,995**	**45,415**
Hindu	88,409	42,994	45,415
Animist	1	1	...
Madras	85,427	41,445	43,982
Elsewhere	2,983	1,550	1,433
ANDURAN (*Hindu*) (Madras)	**9,894**	**4,810**	**5,084**
ARAB (*Musalman*)	**163,654**	**91,722**	**71,932**
Bombay	156,395	88,003	68,392
Madras	5,513	2,780	2,733
Elsewhere	1,746	939	807
ARAIN	**1,001,593**	**554,501**	**447,092**
Hindu	1,214	703	511
Sikh	18	16	2
Jain	1	1	...
Musalman	1,000,360	553,781	446,579
Punjab	977,601	541,189	436,412
Kashmir State	20,621	11,497	9,124
Elsewhere	3,371	1,815	1,556
ARAKALA (*Hindu*) (Madras)	**778**	**375**	**403**
ARAKANESE	**344,127**	**177,089**	**167,038**
Buddhist	344,123	177,089	167,034
Animist	4	...	4
Assam	4	...	4
Burma	344,123	177,089	167,034
ARAKH	**89,184**	**46,112**	**43,072**
Hindu	88,404	45,724	42,680
Musalman	65	61	4
Animist	715	327	388
United Provinces	84,656	43,710	40,946
Elsewhere	4,528	2,402	2,126
ARAYAN (*Hindu*)	**10,250**	**5,262**	**4,988**
Madras	5,424	2,739	2,685
Elsewhere	4,826	2,523	2,303
ARE (*Hindu*)	**2,412**	**1,178**	**1,234**
C. P. and Berar	2,289	1,125	1,164
Travancore State	123	53	70
AREKATIKA (*Hindu*) (Hyderabad State)	**14,855**	**7,719**	**7,136**
ARGHUN (*Musalman*) (Kashmir State)	**1,517**	**1,001**	**516**
ARORA	**746,838**	**403,031**	**343,807**
Hindu	554,104	299,585	254,519
Sikh	192,365	103,260	89,105
Jain	12	8	4
Musalman	357	178	179
N.-W. F. Province	69,215	37,977	31,238
Punjab	673,665	362,728	310,937
Elsewhere	3,958	2,326	1,632

* Kappiliyan has been shown separately.

TABLE XIII.—Caste, Tribe, Race or Nationality. Part I.—

Caste, Religion and Locality.	Persons.	Males.	Females.
1	2	3	4
ARUVA (*Hindu*) (Madras)	**8,755**	**3,740**	**5,015**
ASARI (*Hindu*) (Travancore State)	**62,882**	**31,804**	**31,078**
ASATHI (C. P. and Berar)	**2,568**	**1,280**	**1,288**
Hindu	2,268	1,145	1,123
Jain	300	135	165
ASUR	**5,111**	**2,551**	**2,560**
Hindu	1,767	880	887
Animist	3,344	1,671	1,673
Bihar and Orissa	3,432	1,679	1,753
Elsewhere	1,679	872	807
ATTAR (GANDHI)	**7,090**	**3,399**	**3,691**
Hindu	6,918	3,303	3,615
Musalman	172	96	76
Central India Agency	5,948	2,820	3,128
Elsewhere	1,142	579	563
AUDHELIYA (*Hindu*) (C. P. and Berar)	**880**	**455**	**425**
AWAN (*Musalman*)	**702,452**	**377,030**	**325,422**
N.-W. F. Province	276,511	150,029	126,482
Punjab	425,931	226,991	198,940
Elsewhere	10	10	..
AYIRI (*Hindu*) (Coorg)	**896**	**496**	**400**
BABHAN (BHUINHAR BRAHMAN)	**1,265,982**	**644,832**	**621,150**
Hindu	1,265,976	644,826	621,150
Musalman	6	6	...
Bihar and Orissa	1,129,735	575,940	553,795
United Provinces	134,644	67,721	66,923
Elsewhere	1,603	1,171	432
BADAGA (Madras)	**38,180**	**18,898**	**19,282**
Hindu	38,171	18,892	19,279
Animist	9	6	3
BADDUN (BADU) (Punjab)	**1,630**	**878**	**752**
Hindu	4	4	...
Musalman	1,626	874	752
BAGATA (Madras)	**33,021**	**16,105**	**16,916**
Hindu	26,544	12,709	13,835
Animist	6,477	3,396	3,081
BAGDI	**1,041,892**	**517,388**	**524,504**
Hindu	1,041,871	517,378	524,493
Animist	21	10	11
Assam	8,391	4,212	4,179
Bengal	1,015,738	504,381	511,357
Bihar and Orissa	17,763	8,795	8,968

Caste, Religion and Locality.	Persons.	Males.	Females.
1	2	3	4
BAGHBAN (BAGBAN)	**155,910**	**82,977**	**72,933**
Hindu	135,406	72,086	63,320
Musalman	20,504	10,891	9,613
N.-W. F. Province	20,471	10,881	9,590
United Provinces	135,406	72,086	63,320
Hyderabad State	33	10	23
BAGHELWAL	**4,352**	**2,358**	**1,994**
Hindu	728	380	348
Jain	3,624	1,978	1,646
C. P. and Berar	274	240	34
Rajputana Agency	4,078	2,118	1,960
BAGRI (VAGHRI)	**175,973**	**90,847**	**85,126**
Hindu	174,787	90,257	84,530
Sikh	27	14	13
Musalman	62	17	45
Animist	1,097	559	538
Bombay	82,016	43,878	38,138
Baroda State	28,129	14,702	13,427
Central India Agency	52,907	25,471	27,436
Rajputana Agency	11,112	5,756	5,356
Elsewhere	1,809	1,040	769
BAHELIYA	**44,444**	**23,326**	**21,118**
Hindu	39,774	20,880	18,894
Musalman	4,584	2,405	2,179
Animist	86	41	45
United Provinces	38,795	20,651	18,144
Elsewhere	5,649	2,675	2,974
BAHTI (Punjab)	**4,212**	**2,335**	**1,877**
Hindu	4,090	2,270	1,820
Sikh	120	64	56
Musalman	2	1	1
BAHURUPI	**2,050**	**1,053**	**997**
Hindu	1,301	656	645
Sikh	728	382	346
Musalman	21	15	6
Punjab	841	445	396
Elsewhere	1,209	608	601
BAID (*Hindu*)	**3,326**	**1,664**	**1,662**
Ajmer-Merwara	22	9	13
Rajputana Agency	3,304	1,655	1,649
BAIDYA (*Hindu*)	**99,078**	**49,618**	**49,460**
Assam	5,610	3,049	2,561
Bengal	88,796	44,345	44,451
Elsewhere	4,672	2,224	2,448
BAIGA	**53,601**	**24,490**	**29,111**
Hindu	25,097	10,380	14,717
Animist	28,504	14,110	14,394
Assam	49	15	34
C. P. and Berar	30,391	15,045	15,346
Central India Agency	23,161	9,430	13,731

Distribution of Castes by Religion and Locality—*continued.*

Caste, Religion and Locality.	Persons.	Males.	Females.
1	2	3	4
BAIRAGI (BAISHNAB, BABAJI, BAVA)	**762,125**	**378,543**	**383,582**
Hindu	760,340	377,420	382,920
Sikh	1,041	748	293
Jain	721	362	359
Musalman	1	1	...
Animist	22	12	10
Assam	11,380	5,209	6,171
Bengal	424,308	192,283	232,025
Bihar and Orissa	78,739	41,412	37,327
Bombay	47,569	26,848	20,721
C. P. and Berar	38,059	19,693	18,366
Punjab	37,979	22,529	15,450
Baroda State	9,718	6,464	3,254
Central India Agency	49,804	29,198	20,606
Rajputana Agency	57,991	31,370	26,621
Elsewhere	6,578	3,537	3,041
BAIS BANIYA *	**7,453**	**3,896**	**3,557**
Hindu	7,438	3,889	3,549
Jain	15	7	8
Assam	79	53	26
Bengal	7,374	3,843	3,531
BAITI (CHUNARI)	**4,988**	**2,454**	**2,534**
Hindu	4,831	2,388	2,443
Musalman	157	66	91
Assam	1,135	551	584
Bengal	3,853	1,903	1,950
BAJANIYA (*Hindu*)	**11,256**	**5,926**	**5,330**
Bombay	8,724	4,554	4,170
Baroda State	2,532	1,372	1,160
BALAI (BALAHI)	**413,483**	**204,478**	**209,005**
Hindu	413,010	204,213	208,797
Musalman	34	27	7
Animist	439	238	201
Ajmer-Merwara	23,773	12,234	11,539
C. P. and Berar	52,314	25,857	26,457
Central India Agency	139,885	65,313	74,572
Rajputana Agency	197,511	101,074	96,437
BALIJA (*Hindu*)	**1,046,419**	**517,285**	**529,134**
Madras	1,041,246	514,769	526,477
Elsewhere	5,173	2,516	2,657
BALTI (*Musalman*) (Kashmir State)	**72,439**	**40,597**	**31,842**
BALUCH (BILOCH, BALOCHI) (*Musalman*)	**1,335,974**	**729,153**	**606,821**
Baluchistan	172,473	93,819	78,654
Bombay	603,271	330,546	272,725
N.-W. F. Province	26,513	14,466	12,047
Punjab	532,499	289,611	242,888
Elsewhere	1,218	711	507
BANAJIGA (*Hindu*)	**145,873**	**73,676**	**72,197**
Coorg	1,278	693	585
Madras	11,640	5,767	5,873
Mysore State	132,955	67,216	65,739
BANDA (*Hindu*) (Madras)	**2,381**	**1,282**	**1,099**
BANDAWAT (*Hindu*)	**7,023**	**3,605**	**3,418**
Bengal	1	1	...
Bihar and Orissa	7,022	3,604	3,418
BANDI (*Hindu*) (Bombay)	**7,655**	**3,383**	**4,272**
BANGALI (Punjab)	**1,130**	**631**	**499**
Hindu	1,057	589	468
Sikh	6	4	2
Musalman	67	38	29
BANIYA † (VANI, MAHAJAN)	**1,125,517**	**601,621**	**523,896**
Hindu	949,890	504,913	444,977
Sikh	2,464	1,296	1,168
Jain	113,441	63,083	50,358
Musalman	59,717	32,324	27,393
Animist	5	5	...
Bengal	14,717	8,776	5,941
Bihar and Orissa	140,575	69,367	71,208
Bombay	204,239	113,867	90,372
C. P. and Berar	48,300	24,853	23,447
Punjab	43,265	24,956	18,309
United Provinces	471,603	254,488	217,115
Central India Agency	83,247	41,080	42,167
Kashmir State	79,949	43,698	36,251
Rajputana Agency	32,588	16,794	15,794
Elsewhere	7,034	3,742	3,292
BANIYA MARATHA (*Hindu*) (Bombay)	**10,983**	**5,258**	**5,725**
BANJARA (LABANA, LAMBADI, VANJARI)	**1,084,955**	**566,779**	**518,176**
Hindu	787,274	408,408	378,866
Sikh	49,007	26,588	22,419
Jain	1	...	1
Musalman	61,069	31,471	29,598
Animist	187,604	100,312	87,292
Bihar and Orissa	6,826	3,348	3,478
Bombay	143,586	74,768	68,818
C. P. and Berar	169,505	87,291	82,214
Madras	50,107	25,605	24,502
Punjab	66,439	36,130	30,309
United Provinces	93,477	50,446	43,031
Central India Agency	35,265	20,170	15,095
Hyderabad State	435,322	224,646	210,676
Kashmir State	5,457	2,971	2,486
Mysore State	51,168	26,483	24,685
Rajputana Agency	26,694	14,311	12,383
Elsewhere	1,109	610	499

* As complete figures for Bais Baniya are not available in Bihar and Orissa they have not been shown here.

† The following Baniya castes have been shown separately :—

Agarwal. Agrahari. Ajudhyabasi. Asathi. Bagaelwal. Baniya Maratha. Baranwal.
Baraseni. Benaikaya. Bhatera. Bhatiya. Bijavargi. Charnagar. Chitora.
Deshwal. Dhusar. Gahoi. Gangrada. Golalare. Golapurab. Gujar.
Gujarathi. Humbad. Jharola. Kandu. Kapol. Kasarwani. Kasaundhan. Umre.
Kesar. Khadayata. Khandelwal. Khariya. Kudale. Lad. Lingayat. Vayada.
Lohana. Mahesri. Marwari. Mawar. Mewada. Miratwal. Modh.
Nagar. Nima. Oswal. Pancham. Porwal. Rastogi. Rauniyar.
Saitwal. Sangameshwari. Saralia. Sarsogi. Shrimali. Sorathiya. Sungah.

TABLE XIII.—Caste, Tribe, Race or Nationality. Part I.—

Caste, Religion and Locality.	Persons.	Males.	Females.
1	2	3	4
BANSPHOR *	**60,209**	**32,324**	**27,885**
Hindu	59,766	32,102	27,664
Musalman	443	222	221
United Provinces	7,735	3,867	3,868
Baroda State	9	6	3
Central India Agency	52,465	28,451	24,014
BANT (*Hindu*)	**127,467**	**62,171**	**65,296**
Coorg	1,171	807	364
Madras	126,296	61,364	64,932
BARAI (BARUI)	**547,858**	**279,221**	**268,637**
Hindu	547,766	279,178	268,588
Sikh	29	13	16
Musalman	51	22	29
Animist	12	8	4
Assam	25,154	12,986	12,168
Bengal	178,168	92,748	85,420
Bihar and Orissa	130,028	64,155	65,873
C. P. and Berar	61,177	30,643	30,534
United Provinces	139,037	71,068	67,969
Central India Agency	9,588	5,196	4,392
Elsewhere	4,706	2,425	2,281
BARANWAL (BARNAWAR)	**26,637**	**13,862**	**12,775**
Hindu	26,624	13,851	12,773
Jain	13	11	2
Bihar and Orissa	16,529	8,129	8,400
United Provinces	10,009	5,673	4,336
Elsewhere	99	60	39
BARASENI (United Provinces)	**28,703**	**15,642**	**13,061**
Hindu	28,579	15,572	13,007
Jain	124	70	54
BARGAHI (BARGAHA)	**8,523**	**4,672**	**3,851**
Hindu	8,308	4,560	3,748
Animist	215	112	103
Central India Agency	4,752	2,771	1,981
Elsewhere	3,771	1,901	1,870
BARGONDA (*Hindu*) (Central India Agency)	**7,113**	**3,703**	**3,410**
BARHAI † (BARHI, BADHOYI)	**1,067,093**	**552,155**	**514,938**
Hindu	969,341	500,232	469,109
Sikh	464	328	136
Jain	36	24	12
Buddhist	5	5	...
Musalman	97,115	51,494	45,621
Animist	132	72	60
Bihar and Orissa	324,158	157,182	166,976
C. P. and Berar	108,834	56,297	52,537
Madras	18,616	9,460	9,156
United Provinces	600,887	320,537	280,350
Rajputana Agency	9,610	5,125	4,485
Elsewhere	4,988	3,554	1,434
BARI	**87,400**	**44,127**	**43,273**
Hindu	86,976	43,838	43,138
Musalman	416	285	131
Animist	8	4	4
Bombay	6,727	3,321	3,406
United Provinces	63,055	31,948	31,107
Central India Agency	13,767	6,804	6,963
Elsewhere	3,851	2,054	1,797
BARWALA (BATWAL)	**97,012**	**52,942**	**44,070**
Hindu	37,713	20,522	17,191
Sikh	63	50	13
Musalman	59,236	32,370	26,866
Punjab	85,657	46,800	38,857
Kashmir State	11,355	6,142	5,213
BARWAR (United Provinces)	**5,007**	**2,292**	**2,715**
Hindu	4,843	2,222	2,621
Musalman	164	70	94
BASITH (Kashmir State)	**7,647**	**3,735**	**3,912**
Hindu	7,372	3,604	3,768
Sikh	220	109	111
Musalman	55	22	33
BASOR ‡	**68,307**	**33,946**	**34,361**
Hindu	65,312	32,463	32,849
Musalman	2	1	1
Animist	2,993	1,482	1,511
C. P. and Berar	52,947	26,148	26,799
United Provinces	15,360	7,798	7,562
BAT (*Musalman*) (Kashmir State)	**149,315**	**79,764**	**69,551**
BATHUDI	**55,425**	**28,056**	**27,369**
Hindu	55,421	28,054	27,367
Animist	4	2	2
Bengal	608	234	374
Bihar and Orissa	54,817	27,822	26,995
BAURI (BAVURI)	**750,010**	**367,790**	**382,220**
Hindu	744,603	364,976	379,627
Sikh	358	184	174
Musalman	1	1	...
Animist	5,048	2,629	2,419
Ajmer-Merwara	271	143	128
Assam	43,952	21,369	22,583
Bengal	313,654	154,892	158,762
Bihar and Orissa	292,503	144,817	147,686
Madras	68,699	30,337	38,362
Rajputana Agency	30,931	16,232	14,699
BAVCHA (*Hindu*) (Baroda State)	**1,371**	**672**	**699**
BAWARIYA (BORIYA)	**50,788**	**26,772**	**24,016**
Hindu	44,773	23,649	21,124
Sikh	6,002	3,115	2,887
Musalman	13	8	5
Punjab	32,868	17,495	15,373
United Provinces	17,886	9,256	8,630
Kashmir State	34	21	13

* Dom and Basor have been shown separately.
† Sutradhar has been shown separately.
‡ Bansphor and Dom have been shown separately.

Distribution of Castes by Religion and Locality—*continued.*

Caste, Religion and Locality.	Persons.	Males.	Females.
1	2	3	4
BAYAR (BIYAR)	**18,388**	**8,760**	**9,628**
Hindu	18,310	8,711	9,599
Animist	78	49	29
C. P. and Berar	1,117	563	554
United Provinces	17,271	8,197	9,074
BAZIGAR (BADIGAR)	**37,852**	**20,470**	**17,382**
Hindu	24,763	13,564	11,199
Sikh	4,724	2,468	2,256
Musalman	8,365	4,438	3,927
Punjab	36,354	196,31	16,723
Elsewhere	1,498	839	659
BEDA (BEDARU) (*Hindu*)	**318,444**	**160,430**	**158,014**
Coorg	97	50	47
Madras	49,893	24,783	25,110
Mysore State	268,454	135,597	132,857
BEDEA (Bihar and Orissa)	**27,073**	**13,064**	**14,009**
Hindu	27,072	13,063	14,009
Animist	1	1	...
BEDIYA * (BERIYA)	**63,063**	**30,133**	**32,930**
Hindu	32,978	15,188	17,790
Musalman	29,894	14,839	15,055
Animist	191	106	85
Bengal	30,713	15,252	15,461
Bihar and Orissa	5,345	2,637	2,708
United Provinces	14,054	6,473	7,581
Central India Agency	7,998	3,215	4,783
Elsewhere	4,953	2,556	2,397
BEHARA	**69,228**	**35,576**	**33,652**
Hindu	23,143	12,676	10,467
Musalman	46,081	22,896	23,185
Animist	4	4	...
Assam	365	203	162
Bengal	68,863	35,373	33,490
BELDAR	**205,420**	**102,955**	**102,465**
Hindu	197,538	99,045	98,493
Sikh	3	...	3
Musalman	7,852	3,896	3,956
Animist	27	14	13
Bengal	9,294	4,818	4,476
Bihar and Orissa	88,912	44,138	44,774
Bombay	12,398	6,307	6,091
C. P. and Berar	25,616	12,905	12,711
United Provinces	39,035	19,864	19,171
Central India Agency	26,378	13,037	13,341
Elsewhere	3,787	1,886	1,901
BELWAR (*Hindu*) (United Provinces)	**1,626**	**913**	**713**
BEMARIHA (*Hindu*) (Central India Agency)	**1,021**	**334**	**687**
BENAIKAYA (C. P. and Berar)	**1,181**	**572**	**609**
Hindu	269	130	139
Jain	912	442	470
BENIYA (*Hindu*) (Madras)	**3,522**	**1,491**	**2,031**
BERAD (BEDAR)	**396,796**	**198,194**	**198,602**
Hindu	396,795	198,193	198,602
Musalman	1	1	...
Bombay	184,871	92,498	92,373
C. P. and Berar	3,829	1,893	1,936
Hyderabad State	208,096	103,803	104,293
BERUA (*Hindu*) (Bengal)	**510**	**269**	**241**
BESTA † (BESTHA) (*Hindu*)	**205,633**	**102,698**	**102,935**
Madras	47,676	23,901	23,775
Mysore State	156,863	78,228	78,635
Elsewhere	1,094	569	525
BESYA (KASBI, TAWAIF)	**38,437**	**9,567**	**28,870**
Hindu	15,249	3,212	12,037
Musalman	23,173	6,352	16,821
Animist	15	3	12
Bengal	10,981	298	10,683
United Provinces	23,171	8,238	14,933
Elsewhere	4,285	1,031	3,254
BHABRA	**11,899**	**6,578**	**5,321**
Hindu	2,178	1,142	1,036
Sikh	1,229	626	603
Jain	8,423	4,762	3,661
Musalman	69	48	21
Assam	1	...	1
Punjab	11,898	6,578	5,320
BHAINA	**18,671**	**9,091**	**9,580**
Hindu	18,212	8,943	9,269
Animist	459	148	311
C. P. and Berar	17,387	8,489	8,898
Elsewhere	1,284	602	682
BHAMBHI (BAMBHI) (*Hindu*)	**152,713**	**78,508**	**74,205**
Ajmer-Merwara	2,550	1,305	1,245
Bombay	8,593	4,378	4,215
Central India Agency	7,744	2,885	4,859
Rajputana Agency	133,826	69,940	63,886
BHAMTA (*Hindu*) (C. P. and Berar)	**4,270**	**2,120**	**2,150**
BHAND	**3,530**	**1,640**	**1,890**
Hindu	2,273	1,053	1,220
Sikh	19	6	13
Musalman	1,238	581	657
Central India Agency	2,216	1,020	1,196
Elsewhere	1,314	620	694
BHANDARI ‡ (*Hindu*)	**184,287**	**91,432**	**92,855**
Bombay	183,131	90,749	92,382
Elsewhere	1,156	683	473

* Includes Mirshikari in Bengal.

† See also Toreya.

‡ Toddy drawers.

TABLE XIII.—Caste, Tribe, Race or Nationality. Part I.—

Caste, Religion and Locality.	Persons.	Males.	Females.
1	2	3	4
BHANDARI * (BHONDARI) (*Hindu*)	**140,441**	**68,499**	**71,942**
Bihar and Orissa	117,198	57,221	59,977
Madras	22,362	10,811	11,551
Elsewhere	881	467	414
BHANGI †	**740,481**	**384,643**	**355,838**
Hindu	667,031	345,211	321,820
Sikh	1,087	601	486
Musalman	72,111	38,695	33,416
Animist	252	136	116
Ajmer-Merwara	5,361	2,832	2,529
Bombay	140,714	74,077	66,637
C. P. and Berar	7,560	3,735	3,825
United Provinces	417,792	218,952	198,840
Baroda State	26,406	13,408	12,998
Central India Agency	56,774	27,357	29,417
Rajputana Agency	84,980	43,655	41,325
Elsewhere	894	627	267
BHANSALI (*Hindu*)	**14,606**	**7,341**	**7,265**
Bombay	14,596	7,335	7,261
Baroda State	10	6	4
BHAR ‡	**454,427**	**226,087**	**228,340**
Hindu	454,421	226,083	228,338
Animist	6	4	2
Assam	14,269	7,331	6,938
Bengal	15,363	10,148	5,215
Bihar and Orissa	30,389	14,726	15,663
United Provinces	393,518	193,432	200,086
Elsewhere	888	450	438
BHARADI (*Hindu*)	**2,404**	**1,234**	**1,170**
C. P. and Berar	2,252	1,164	1,088
Hyderabad State	152	70	82
BHARAI	**58,942**	**32,466**	**26,476**
Hindu	78	55	23
Sikh	8	3	5
Musalman	58 856	32,408	26,448
Punjab	58,400	32,166	26,234
Kashmir State	542	300	242
BHARAMPAL (*Hindu*) (Bengal)	**2,876**	**1,526**	**1,350**
BHARBHUNJA	**321,833**	**169,820**	**152,013**
Hindu	308,634	162,800	145,834
Musalman	13,199	7,020	6,179
Punjab	6,017	3,345	2,672
United Provinces	301,712	159,490	142,222
Central India Agency	5,956	2,731	3,225
Elsewhere	8,148	4,254	3,894
BHAREWA (*Hindu*) (Central India Agency)	**22,709**	**12,961**	**9,748**
BHARIYA (BHUMIYA) (C. P. and Berar)	**51,006**	**24,588**	**26,418**
Hindu	22,802	11,005	11,797
Animist	28,204	13,583	14,621
BHARVAD § (BHARUD)	**896,402**	**455,662**	**440,740**
Hindu	894,733	454,850	439,883
Animist	1,669	812	857
Bombay	836,927	426,595	410,332
C. P. and Berar	2,136	1,087	1,049
Baroda State	8,489	4,373	4,116
Central India Agency	48,850	23,607	25,243
BHAT (BAROT)	**364,862**	**186,773**	**178,089**
Hindu	329,283	168,997	160,286
Sikh	2,843	1,220	1,623
Jain	9	3	6
Buddhist	13	7	6
Musalman	32,619	16,503	16,116
Animist	95	43	52
Bengal	6,779	3,206	3,573
Bihar and Orissa	27,055	12,526	14,529
Bombay	27,020	14,679	12,341
C. P. and Berar	29,972	15,049	14,923
Punjab	37,130	19,678	17,452
United Provinces	145,720	74,431	71,289
Baroda State	14,744	7,605	7,139
Central India Agency	25,793	13,547	12,246
Rajputana Agency	47,104	24,177	22,927
Elsewhere	3,545	1,875	1,670
BHATERA (Central India Agency)	**3,465**	**1,754**	**1,711**
Hindu	3,180	1,569	1,611
Jain	285	185	100
BHATIYA	**59,006**	**30,928**	**28,078**
Hindu	45,223	23,663	21,560
Sikh	8,551	4,628	3,923
Jain	120	81	39
Musalman	5,112	2,556	2,556
Bombay	26,742	13,866	12,876
Punjab	22,047	11,882	10,165
Elsewhere	10,217	5,180	5,037
BHATIYARA	**46,638**	**24,977**	**21,661**
Hindu	79	41	38
Sikh	141	69	72
Musalman	46,418	24,867	21,551
Punjab	7,930	4,118	3,812
United Provinces	34,213	18,568	15,645
Elsewhere	4,495	2,291	2,204
BHATRA (Punjab)	**938**	**473**	**465**
Hindu	320	157	163
Sikh	616	315	301
Jain	2	1	1
BHATRAZU (*Hindu*)	**29,662**	**14,444**	**15,218**
Madras	25,137	12,066	13,071
Elsewhere	4,525	2,378	2,147
BHATTI (*Musalman*) (Kashmir State)	**4,451**	**2,399**	**2,052**
BHAVAYA (BHAWAIYA) (*Hindu*)	**16,897**	**7,314**	**9,583**
Baroda State	4,468	2,022	2,446
Central India Agency	12,429	5,292	7,137

* Chiefly barbers, in Hyderabad they are musicians.
† See also Chubra, Halalkhor and Mehtar.
‡ Rajbhar has been shown separately.
§ Includes Dhangar in Bombay.

Distribution of Castes by Religion and Locality—*continued.*

Caste, Religion and Locality.	Persons.	Males.	Females.
1	2	3	4
BHIL	**1,635,988**	**828,873**	**807,115**
Hindu	626,158	319,864	306,294
Sikh	16	9	7
Musalman	3,050	1,509	1,541
Animist	1,006,764	507,491	499,273
Ajmer-Merwara	6,509	3,289	3,220
Bombay	793,252	402,295	390,957
C. P. and Berar	27,785	13,768	14,017
Baroda State	52,787	26,848	25,939
Central India Agency	295,741	147,738	148,003
Hyderabad State	9,921	5,036	4,885
Rajputana Agency	448,910	229,266	219,644
Elsewhere	1,083	633	450
BHILALA	**138,813**	**68,972**	**69,841**
Hindu	49,201	24,151	25,050
Animist	89,612	44,821	44,791
C. P. and Berar	15,437	7,800	7,637
Central India Agency	123,376	61,172	62,204
BHISTI *	**126,375**	**66,477**	**59,898**
Hindu	317	153	164
Musalman	126,058	66,324	59,734
United Provinces	98,253	51,923	46,330
Rajputana Agency	24,789	12,690	12,099
Elsewhere	3,333	1,864	1,469
BHOGTA	**92,626**	**46,290**	**46,336**
Hindu	92,406	46,171	46,235
Animist	220	119	101
Assam	11,019	5,704	5,315
Bihar and Orissa	78,500	39,056	39,444
Elsewhere	3,107	1,530	1,577
BHOI	**305,421**	**157,803**	**147,618**
Hindu	305,333	157,762	147,571
Musalman	88	41	47
Bombay	63,722	32,370	31,352
Central India Agency	51,845	29,518	22,327
Hyderabad State	177,004	89,369	87,635
Rajputana Agency	8,627	4,284	4,343
Elsewhere	4,223	2,262	1,961
BHOJAK (BHOJKI)	**1,926**	**949**	**977**
Hindu	1,219	644	575
Jain	347	124	223
Musalman	360	181	179
Punjab	1,551	811	740
Elsewhere	375	138	237
BHOKSA (*Hindu*) (United Provinces)	**6,637**	**3,536**	**3,101**
BHOPA	**1,299**	**617**	**682**
Hindu	1,290	611	679
Animist	9	6	3
C. P. and Berar	89	51	38
Central India Agency	1,210	566	644
BHOTIA (BOT)	**44,305**	**22,281**	**22,024**
Hindu	15,365	7,046	8,319
Buddhist	28,766	15,136	13,630
Musalman	1	1	...
Animist	173	98	75
Bengal	16,936	9,016	7,920
United Provinces	13,593	5,939	7,654
Sikkim State	12,414	6,429	5,985
Elsewhere	1,362	897	465
BHOYAR (C. P. and Berar)	**58,638**	**28,990**	**29,648**
Hindu	58,628	28,986	29,642
Animist	10	4	6
BHUIYA † (BHUINYA, BHUMIYA) ‡	**854,449**	**422,950**	**431,499**
Hindu	839,237	415,201	424,036
Jain	2	...	2
Musalman	9	9	...
Animist	15,201	7,740	7,461
Assam	66,670	34,765	31,905
Bengal	69,048	37,466	31,582
Bihar and Orissa	663,757	322,708	341,049
C. P. and Berar	27,620	14,126	13,494
Madras	21,891	11,092	10,799
Central India Agency	5,463	2,793	2,670
BHULIYA	**38,877**	**19,538**	**19,339**
Hindu	38,859	19,531	19,328
Buddhist	18	7	11
Bihar and Orissa	34,022	17,081	16,941
Elsewhere	4,855	2,457	2,398
BHUMIJ	**410,701**	**198,593**	**212,108**
Hindu	401,946	194,118	207,828
Buddhist	1	1	...
Animist	8,754	4,474	4,280
Assam	38,700	19,266	19,434
Bengal	90,377	44,288	46,089
Bihar and Orissa	281,624	135,039	146,585
BHUNJIYA (C. P. and Berar)	**6,921**	**3,466**	**3,455**
Hindu	2,720	1,383	1,337
Animist	4,201	2,083	2,118
BIDUR (VIDUR)	**22,169**	**10,844**	**11,325**
Hindu	22,140	10,833	11,307
Jain	7	1	6
Animist	22	10	12
C. P. and Berar	20,987	10,377	10,610
Central India Agency	1,182	467	715
BIJAVARGI	**15,786**	**7,927**	**7,859**
Hindu	15,321	7,683	7,638
Jain	465	244	221
Ajmer-Merwara	728	357	371
Central India Agency	5,179	2,455	2,724
Rajputana Agency	9,879	5,115	4,764
BILLAVA (*Hindu*)	**159,887**	**76,825**	**83,062**
Coorg	2,816	1,793	1,023
Madras	157,071	75,032	82,039

* See also Jhinwar, Kahar and Machhi.
† Includes Bhuinhar in C. P. and Berar.
‡ In C. P. and Berar Bhariyas or Bhumiyas have been shown separately.

TABLE XIII.—Caste, Tribe, Race or Nationality. Part I.—

Caste, Religion and Locality.	Persons.	Males.	Females.
1	2	3	4
BIND	**237,365**	**116,089**	**121,276**
Hindu	237,276	116,043	121,233
Animist	89	46	43
Bengal	25,400	14,653	10,747
Bihar and Orissa	134,818	62,954	71,864
United Provinces	73,507	36,211	37,296
Elsewhere	3,640	2,271	1,369
BINJHWAR (BINJHIYA)	**123,292**	**60,686**	**62,606**
Hindu	115,625	56,938	58,687
Animist	7,667	3,748	3,919
Bihar and Orissa	62,401	30,684	31,717
C. P. and Berar	59,327	29,199	30,128
Elsewhere	1,564	803	761
BIRHOR	**3,085**	**1,489**	**1,596**
Hindu	1,941	938	1,003
Animist	1,144	551	593
Bihar and Orissa	2,340	1,104	1,236
Elsewhere	745	385	360
BISATI (Rajputana Agency)	**2,246**	**1,089**	**1,157**
Hindu	78	44	34
Musalman	2,168	1,045	1,123
BISHNOI (*Hindu*)	**73,392**	**39,566**	**33,826**
Punjab	19,416	10,509	8,907
Rajputana Agency	52,879	28,492	24,387
Elsewhere	1,097	565	532
BODA (*Hindu*) (Madras)	**5,688**	**1,899**	**3,789**
BODLA (Punjab)	**2,912**	**1,528**	**1,384**
Hindu	9	7	2
Musalman	2,903	1,521	1,382
BOGAM (*Hindu*)	**37,888**	**14,804**	**23,084**
Madras	27,507	11,707	15,800
Hyderabad State	10,381	3,097	7,284
BOHRA (BORA, BOHORA, VOHORA)	**187,742**	**96,663**	**91,079**
Hindu	3,693	1,955	1,738
Jain	2	2	...
Musalman	184,045	94,704	89,341
Animist	2	2	...
Bombay	126,011	64,862	61,149
Baroda State	25,035	12,119	12,916
Central India Agency	15,922	8,473	7.449
Rajputana Agency	11,286	5.916	5,370
Elsewhere	9,488	5,293	4,195
BOLA (*Hindu*) (Rajputana Agency)	**22,736**	**11,546**	**11,190**
BOLASI (*Hindu*) (Madras)	**10,304**	**4,765**	**5,539**
BONDHIYA (*Hindu*) (Madras)	**508**	**224**	**284**
BONDILI (*Hindu*) (Madras)	**9,771**	**4,952**	**4,819**
BONKA (BANKA) (*Hindu*)	**1,772**	**848**	**924**
C. P. and Berar	16	9	7
Madras	1,756	839	917
BORIYA (Assam)	**21,513**	**10,994**	**10,519**
Hindu	21,512	10,994	10,518
Animist	1	...	1
BOSANTIYA (*Hindu*) (Madras)	**2,467**	**1,013**	**1,454**
BOTTADA (Madras)	**62,101**	**30,959**	**31,142**
Hindu	62,080	30,943	31,137
Animist	21	16	5
BOYA	**427,908**	**217,781**	**210,127**
Hindu	427,875	217,763	210,112
Animist	33	18	15
Madras	425,862	216,732	209,130
Elsewhere	2,046	1,049	997
BRAHMA-KSHATRI (*Hindu*)	**5,936**	**3,195**	**2,741**
Bombay	5.071	2,734	2 337
Baroda State	865	461	404
BRAHMAN *	**14,598,708**	**7,626,994**	**6,971,714**
Hindu	14,572,805	7,612,318	6,960,487
Sikh	24,587	13,738	10,849
Jain	863	669	194
Buddhist	47	35	12
Musalman	404	232	172
Animist	2	2	...
Ajmer-Merwara	24,220	12,977	11,243
Assam	131,317	72,235	59,082
Bengal	1,253,841	666,583	587,258
Bihar and Orissa	1,755,424	874,507	880,917
Bombay	1,067,681	562,141	505,540
Burma	21,170	16,551	4,619
C. P. and Berar	445,744	237,605	208,139
Madras	1,310,360	650,265	660,095
N.-W. F. Province	13.208	7,856	5,352
Punjab	1,017,743	562,039	455,704
United Provinces	4,701,179	2,474,642	2,226,537
Baroda State	113.412	59,526	53,886
Central India Agency	986,206	519,480	466,726
Cochin State	35,532	18,794	16,738
Hyderabad State	261,241	133,192	128,049
Kashmir State	241,362	130,254	111,108
Mysore State	194,576	98,602	95,974
Rajputana Agency	959,752	495,031	464,721
Sikkim State	5,673	2,880	2,793
Travancore State	55,674	29,733	25,941
Elsewhere	3,393	2,101	1,292
BRAHUI (*Musalman*)	**228,176**	**126,478**	**101,698**
Baluchistan	167,787	93,095	74,692
Bombay	60,389	33,383	27,006
BRITTIYAL BANIYA † (Assam)	**9,084**	**4,563**	**4,521**
Hindu	9,083	4,563	4,520
Animist	1	...	1

* Includes Acharaj, Agradani, Barna Brahman, Daibajna and Nepali Brahman. Ganak in Assam has been shown separately.

† Hari has been shown separately.

Distribution of Castes by Religion and Locality—*continued.*

Caste, Religion and Locality.	Persons.	Males.	Females.
1	2	3	4
BRUKPA (*Musalman*) (Kashmir State)	**8,890**	**3,983**	**4,907**
BUDUBUDUKALA (BUDBUDKA, BUDABUDIKE)	**4,146**	**1,943**	**2,203**
Hindu	4,142	1,939	2,203
Musalman	4	4	..
Madras	2,000	903	1,097
Elsewhere	2,146	1,040	1,106
BUNKAR (*Hindu*) (Central India Agency)	**8,187**	**4,060**	**4,127**
BURMESE *	**7,644,310**	**3,732,848**	**3,911,462**
Hindu	55	35	20
Sikh	15	14	1
Buddhist	7,644,234	3,782,797	3,911,437
Musalman	3	1	2
Animist	3	1	2
Burma	7,642,204	3,731,026	3,911,178
Elsewhere	2,106	1,822	284
BURUD (BARAR)	**42,514**	**21,710**	**20,804**
Hindu	42,118	21,509	20,609
Sikh	291	138	153
Musalman	105	63	42
Bombay	11,745	5,778	5,967
Punjab	6,119	3,300	2,819
Hyderabad State	24,498	12,538	11,960
Elsewhere	152	94	58
CHAIN (CHAI)	**155,926**	**77,169**	**78,757**
Hindu	155,924	77,167	78,757
Animist	2	2	...
Assam	37	33	4
Bengal	93,148	45,996	47,152
Bihar and Orissa	32,335	15,702	16,633
United Provinces	30,406	15,438	14,968
CHAKALA (TSAKALA) (*Hindu*)	**562,735**	**281,847**	**280,888**
Madras	387,109	192,056	195,053
Hyderabad State	175,626	89,791	85,835
CHAKAR	**58,912**	**28,476**	**30,436**
Hindu	58,629	28,358	30,271
Jain	56	22	34
Musalman	227	96	131
Rajputana Agency	58,606	28,320	30,286
Elsewhere	306	156	150
CHAKKALA (*Hindu*) (Travancore State)	**18,074**	**8,937**	**9,137**
CHAKKAN (*Hindu*)	**38,902**	**19,164**	**19,738**
Madras	36,801	18,056	18,745
Cochin State	2,101	1,108	993
CHAKKILIYAN (*Hindu*)	**528,859**	**262,805**	**266,054**
Madras	526,451	261,421	265,030
Elsewhere	2,408	1,384	1,024
CHAKMA	**58,927**	**31,173**	**27,754**
Buddhist	58,918	31,165	27,753
Animist	9	8	1
Assam	255	159	96
Bengal	58,672	31,014	27,658
CHALIYAN (*Hindu*)	**33,143**	**16,588**	**16,555**
Madras	31,324	15,637	15,687
Elsewhere	1,819	951	868
CHAMAR † **(CHAMBHAR)**	**11,493,733**	**5,854,606**	**5,639,127**
Hindu	11,305,713	5,750,637	5,555,076
Sikh	175,379	97,392	77,987
Jain	18	4	14
Buddhist	114	53	61
Musalman	10,811	5,660	5,151
Animist	1,698	860	838
Ajmer-Merwara	13,351	6,822	6,529
Assam	54,234	27,911	26,323
Bengal	136,553	86,504	50,049
Bihar and Orissa	1,114,467	520,099	594,368
Bombay	302,536	155,075	147,461
C. P. and Berar	907,927	446,240	461,687
Punjab	1,139,941	620,421	519,520
United Provinces	6,083,401	3,101,884	2,981,517
Baroda State	32,210	15,872	16,338
Central India Agency	859,438	435,873	423,565
Hyderabad State	70,618	35,993	34,625
Kashmir State	39,099	20,462	18,637
Rajputana Agency	734,110	378,017	356,093
Elsewhere	5,848	3,433	2,415
CHANAL (Punjab)	**12,448**	**6,440**	**6,008**
Hindu	12,321	6,375	5,946
Sikh	70	37	33
Musalman	57	28	29
CHANG (Punjab)	**6,373**	**3,816**	**2,557**
Hindu	4,871	2,962	1,909
Sikh	1,499	851	648
Musalman	3	3	..
CHANGAR	**40,862**	**22,286**	**18,576**
Hindu	40	31	9
Sikh	13	13	...
Musalman	40,809	22,242	18,567
Punjab	40,407	22,048	18,359
Kashmir State	455	238	217
CHAPTEGARA (*Hindu*)	**1,733**	**853**	**880**
Coorg	81	44	37
Madras	1,652	809	843

* For sub-castes see Part II.
† Includes Dabgar in Bihar and Orissa and Mochi, Mochigar or Sochi in Bombay. Sochi of Sind, however, has been shown separately. See also Khalpa.

TABLE XIII.—Caste, Tribe, Race or Nationality. Part I.—

Caste, Religion and Locality.	Persons.	Males.	Females.
1	2	3	4
CHARAN	**76,541**	**39,946**	**36,595**
Hindu	75,958	39,618	36,340
Jain	2	2	...
Animist	581	326	255
Bombay	32,510	17,221	15,289
Rajputana Agency	37,574	19,510	18,064
Elsewhere	6,457	3,215	3,242
CHARNAGAR (C. P. and Berar)	**2,521**	**1,302**	**1,219**
Hindu	108	60	48
Jain	2,413	1,242	1,171
CHARODI (*Hindu*)	**1,079**	**455**	**624**
Coorg	4	3	1
Madras	1,075	452	623
CHASA	**851,894**	**418,658**	**433,236**
Hindu	851,826	418,619	433,207
Animist	68	39	29
Bihar and Orissa	846,119	415,439	430,680
Elsewhere	5,775	3,219	2,556
CHASA DHOBA (*Hindu*) (Bengal)	**57,626**	**29,318**	**28,308**
CHASATI (*Hindu*) (Bengal)	**28,002**	**13,601**	**14,401**
CHATURTH (*Jain*) (Bombay)	**89,208**	**46,329**	**42,879**
CHAUHAN (*Hindu*) (C. P. and Berar)	**6,750**	**3,265**	**3,485**
CHAYAKKARAN (*Hindu*) (Travancore State)	**3,294**	**1,690**	**1,604**
CHENCHU	**17,002**	**8,887**	**8,115**
Hindu	15,497	8,130	7,367
Animist	1,505	757	748
Madras	7,449	3,768	3,681
Hyderabad State	9,553	5,119	4,434
CHERO (CHERU)	**19,554**	**9,728**	**9,826**
Hindu	19,532	9,719	9,813
Animist	22	9	13
Bihar and Orissa	18,066	8,914	9,152
Elsewhere	1,488	814	674
CHERUMAN * (*Hindu*)	**256,473**	**122,095**	**134,378**
Madras	255,395	121,567	133,828
Travancore State	1,078	528	550
CHETTI (*Hindu*)	**390,450**	**196,515**	**193,935**
Burma	14,366	12,663	1,703
Madras	350,251	171,058	179,193
Travancore State	20,881	10,535	10,346
Elsewhere	4,952	2,259	2,693
CHHIMBA (CHHIPA, CHHIPI)	**251,650**	**134,813**	**116,837**
Hindu	132,713	69,941	62,772
Sikh	35,973	19,892	16,081
Jain	1,128	576	552
Musalman	81,836	44,404	37,432
Bombay	15,101	7,733	7,368
C. P. and Berar	8,799	4,399	4,400
Punjab	129,338	71,594	57,744
United Provinces	33,182	17,909	15,273
Baroda State	6,499	3,197	3,302
Central India Agency	17,749	8,716	9,033
Rajputana Agency	37,940	19,645	18,295
Elsewhere	3,042	1,620	1,422
CHIDAR (CHADAR)	**39,824**	**20,164**	**19,660**
Hindu	39,817	20,159	19,658
Animist	7	5	2
C. P. and Berar	28,129	13,968	14,161
Central India Agency	11,695	6,196	5,499
CHIK (BARAIK)	**52,111**	**26,239**	**25,872**
Hindu	48,169	24,231	23,938
Buddhist	2	1	1
Animist	3,940	2,007	1,933
Assam	5,703	2,954	2,749
Bengal	4,263	2,059	2,204
Bihar and Orissa	31,611	15,655	15,956
United Provinces	10,534	5,571	4,963
CHIK (*Musalman*) (United Provinces)	**4,629**	**2,304**	**2,325**
CHIN † (*Buddhist*) (Burma)	**306,486**	**151,165**	**155,321**
CHINDA (*Hindu*) (Madras)	**622**	**358**	**264**
CHINESE	**125,585**	**91,684**	**33,901**
Buddhist	125,571	91,673	33,898
Musalman	14	11	3
Burma	122,834	89,345	33,489
Elsewhere	2,751	2,339	412
CHISHTI (*Musalman*) (Punjab)	**4,154**	**2,254**	**1,900**
CHITARI (C. P. and Berar)	**1,227**	**677**	**550**
Hindu	1,226	676	550
Animist	1	1	...
CHITORA	**5,675**	**2,723**	**2,952**
Hindu	4,795	2,296	2,499
Jain	880	427	453
Central India Agency	3,353	1,552	1,801
Elsewhere	2,322	1,171	1,151
CHITRAKATHI (*Hindu*) (C.P. and Berar)	**1,487**	**729**	**758**

* See also Pulaiyan.
† For sub-castes see Part II.

Distribution of Castes by Religion and Locality—*continued.*

Caste, Religion and Locality.	Persons.	Males.	Females.
1	2	3	4
CHODHRA	**69,504**	**35,375**	**34,129**
Hindu	49,847	25,359	24,488
Animist	19,657	10,016	9,641
Bombay	38,138	19,276	18,862
Baroda State	31,366	16,099	15,267
CHUDITIYA (*Hindu*) (Madras)	**3,202**	**1,515**	**1,687**
CHURRA * (MUSALLI, KUTANA)	**1,269,250**	**695,853**	**573,397**
Hindu	795,010	439,052	355,958
Sikh	51,579	28,702	22,877
Jain	1	1	...
Musalman	422,660	228,098	194,562
C. P. and Berar	22	14	8
N.-W. F. Province	19,047	10,823	8,224
Punjab	1,235,103	676,915	558,188
Kashmir State	15,078	8,101	6,977
CHURIHAR (CHURIGAR)	**33,359**	**17,013**	**16,346**
Hindu	617	324	293
Musalman	32,742	16,689	16,053
United Provinces	31,097	15,827	15,270
Elsewhere	2,262	1,186	1,076
CHUTIYA (Assam)	**88,825**	**45,603**	**43,222**
Hindu	86,328	44,352	41,976
Animist	2,497	1,251	1,246
DABGAR †	**1,225**	**654**	**571**
Hindu	565	303	262
Musalman	560	351	309
Punjab	676	364	312
Baroda State	549	290	259
DADUPANTHI (*Hindu*)	**7,750**	**7,580**	**170**
Rajputana Agency	7,670	7,517	153
Elsewhere	80	63	17
DAFALI (*Musalman*)	**38,265**	**20,005**	**18,260**
United Provinces	33,195	16,804	16,391
Central India Agency	5,043	3,186	1,857
Elsewhere	27	15	12
DAFLA (Assam)	**989**	**561**	**428**
Hindu	2	2	...
Animist	987	559	428
DAHAYAT	**17,456**	**8,486**	**8,970**
Hindu	17,451	8,484	8,967
Animist	5	2	3
C. P. and Berar	14,685	7,212	7,473
Central India Agency	2,771	1,274	1,497
DAI (*Musalman*)	**27,491**	**14,121**	**13,370**
Assam	465	234	231
Bengal	27,026	13,887	13,139
DAKOT (DAKOTRA) (*Hindu*)	**21,187**	**10,617**	**10,570**
Rajputana Agency	20,326	10,166	10,160
Elsewhere	861	451	410
DALU	**5,135**	**2,660**	**2,475**
Hindu	5,134	2,659	2,475
Animist	1	1	...
Assam	329	168	161
Bengal	4,806	2,492	2,314
DAMAI	**8,483**	**4,625**	**3,858**
Hindu	8,410	4,581	3,829
Buddhist	20	14	6
Animist	53	30	23
Bengal	5,425	2,960	2,465
Elsewhere	3,058	1,665	1,393
DAMMULA (*Hindu*) (Madras)	**1,259**	**640**	**619**
DANDASI (Madras)	**45,274**	**20,745**	**24,529**
Hindu	45,265	20,741	24,524
Animist	9	4	5
DANGI (*Hindu*)	**125,203**	**65,254**	**59,949**
Ajmer-Merwara	1	1	...
C. P. and Berar	24,283	12,327	11,956
Central India Agency	62,819	33,369	29,450
Rajputana Agency	38,100	19,557	18,543
DANGRI (*Hindu*) (C. P. and Berar).	**1,762**	**835**	**927**
DAOLI (DAOLA) (Punjab)	**1,617**	**890**	**727**
Hindu	1,358	757	601
Sikh	259	133	126
DAR (*Musalman*) (Kashmir State)	**98,321**	**52,085**	**46,236**
DARAIHA (*Hindu*) (C. P. and Berar)	**2,740**	**1,294**	**1,446**
DAROGA	**127,866**	**62,208**	**65,658**
Hindu	127,844	62,192	65,652
Jain	17	12	5
Musalman	5	4	1
Ajmer-Merwara	8,952	4,550	4,402
Rajputana Agency	118,914	57,658	61,256
DARUGAR	**1,245**	**737**	**508**
Hindu	655	403	252
Musalman	590	334	256
Central India Agency	649	397	252
Elsewhere	596	340	256
DARZADA (*Musalman*) (Baluchistan)	**10,257**	**5,215**	**5,042**

* See also Bhangi, Halalkhor and Mehtar.

† In Bihar and Orissa included in Chamar.

TABLE XIII.—Caste, Tribe, Race or Nationality. Part I.—

Caste, Religion and Locality.	Persons.	Males.	Females.
1	2	3	4
DARZI* (DARJI)	**705,733**	**363,815**	**341,918**
Hindu	460,370	238,478	221,892
Sikh	1,414	813	601
Jain	1,674	827	847
Buddhist	32	20	12
Musalman	242,166	123,633	118,533
Animist	77	44	33
Bihar and Orissa	37,087	17,667	19,420
Bombay	141,423	71,819	69,604
C. P. and Berar	51,301	26,113	25,188
Punjab	35,827	18,790	17,037
United Provinces	252,885	132,001	120,884
Baroda State	13,323	6,377	6,946
Central India Agency	59,321	31,924	27,397
Hyderabad State	47,947	24,828	23,119
Mysore State	11,564	5,909	5,655
Rajputana Agency	45,203	23,069	22,134
Elsewhere	9,852	5,318	4,534
DASARI (DASRI) (*Hindu*)	**49,972**	**24,666**	**25,306**
Madras	33,438	16,020	17,418
Hyderabad State	11,942	6,320	5,622
Elsewhere	4,592	2,326	2,266
DASI (*Hindu*)	**7,965**	**3,046**	**4,919**
Madras	7,037	2,710	4,327
Elsewhere	928	336	592
DATIYA (*Musalman*) (Assam)	**937**	**502**	**435**
DAUDPUTRA (*Musalman*) (Punjab)	**21,229**	**11,737**	**9,492**
DEHAN (*Hindu*) (Assam)	**1,152**	**613**	**539**
DEHWAR (*Musalman*) (Baluchistan)	**7,326**	**4,009**	**3,317**
DESHWAL (DESHAVAL, DISAVAL)	**11,009**	**5,441**	**5,568**
Hindu	10,684	5,260	5,424
Jain	325	181	144
Baroda State	6,145	2,860	3,285
Elsewhere	4,864	2,581	2,283
DESWALI	**50,859**	**26,675**	**24,184**
Hindu	41,580	21,754	19,776
Musalman	9,318	4,910	4,408
Animist	11	11	...
Ajmer-Merwara	2,449	1,413	1,036
C. P. and Berar	7,761	3,978	3,783
Central India Agency	33,780	17,787	15,993
Rajputana Agency	6,869	3,497	3,372
DEVADIGA (*Hindu*)	**25,757**	**11,889**	**13,868**
Coorg	136	73	63
Madras	25,621	11,816	13,805
DEVANGA† (DEVANG) (*Hindu*)	**451,355**	**225,526**	**225,829**
Bombay	88,113	43,851	44,262
Madras	286,504	142,672	143,832
Hyderabad State	71,400	36,257	35,143
Elsewhere	5,338	2,746	2,592
DEVLI (*Hindu*) (Bombay)	**6,254**	**3,077**	**3,177**
DEWAR (C. P. and Berar)	**2,433**	**1,115**	**1,318**
Hindu	2,145	984	1,161
Animist	288	131	157
DHAKAD (DHAKAR)	**160,105**	**78,331**	**81,774**
Hindu	160,101	78,330	81,771
Musalman	4	1	3
Central India Agency	63,463	29,291	34,172
Rajputana Agency	93,365	47,662	45,703
Elsewhere	3,277	1,378	1,899
DHAMI (*Hindu*)	**687**	**343**	**344**
C. P. and Berar	53	24	29
Central India Agency	634	319	315
DHAMIN (DHAMI) (*Hindu*)	**1,486**	**797**	**689**
Bengal	91	63	28
Bihar and Orissa	1,395	734	661
DHANGAR ‡ (DHANAGAR)	**673,439**	**339,404**	**334,035**
Hindu	673,432	339,400	334,032
Animist	7	4	3
C. P. and Berar	110,708	55,986	54,722
Central India Agency	5,608	3,027	2,581
Hyderabad State	556,543	280,114	276,429
Elsewhere	580	277	303
DHANUK (DHANAK, DHANKA, DHANKIYA)	**859,767**	**424,756**	**435,011**
Hindu	842,409	415,896	426,513
Sikh	626	343	283
Musalman	78	46	32
Animist	16,654	8,471	8,183
Bengal	14,366	8,185	6,181
Bihar and Orissa	572,412	272,915	299,497
C. P. and Berar	6,601	3,215	3,386
Punjab	83,256	44,220	39,036
United Provinces	129,314	69,092	60,222
Baroda State	18,667	9,414	9,253
Central India Agency	7,736	3,767	3,969
Rajputana Agency	25,521	12,822	12,699
Elsewhere	1,894	1,126	768
DHANWAR	**19,242**	**9,502**	**9,740**
Hindu	14,861	7,394	7,467
Animist	4,381	2,108	2,273
C. P. and Berar	18,637	9,181	9,456
Elsewhere	605	321	284
DHARI (DHADI)	**7,367**	**3,566**	**3,801**
Hindu	6,642	3,173	3,469
Musalman	674	349	325
Animist	51	44	7
Bihar and Orissa	6,277	2,968	3,309
Elsewhere	1,090	598	492

* In Bombay, Baroda and Hyderabad Darzi includes Shimpi, Sai or Merai.
† Includes Koshti in Bombay.
‡ Includes Hatgar in C. P. and Berar and Hatkar in Hyderabad. Dhangar in Bombay included in Bharvad.

Distribution of Castes by Religion and Locality—*continued.*

Caste, Religion and Locality.	Persons.	Males.	Females.
1	2	3	4
DHARKAR	**39,058**	**19,834**	**19,224**
Hindu	38,995	19,799	19,196
Musalman	17	5	12
Animist	46	30	16
United Provinces	38,729	19,661	19,068
Elsewhere	329	173	156
DHAUGRI (DHOGRI) (*Hindu*) (Punjab)	**3,874**	**1,949**	**1,925**
DHAWA (*Musalman*) (Bengal)	**12,080**	**6,158**	**5,922**
DHED* (DHER, DHERA)	**118,518**	**60,267**	**58,251**
Hindu	118,510	60,263	58,247
Musalman	8	4	4
Baroda State	99,806	50,541	49,265
Rajputana Agency	16,830	8,826	8,004
Elsewhere	1,882	900	982
DHIMAR	**384,504**	**191,805**	**192,699**
Hindu	384,409	191,756	192,653
Musalman	54	28	26
Animist	41	21	20
C. P. and Berar	283,684	140,853	142,831
Baroda State	5,410	2,693	2,717
Central India Agency	88,776	45,111	43,665
Elsewhere	6,634	3,148	3,486
DHIRKAR (*Hindu*) (Central India Agency)	**5,413**	**2,297**	**3,116**
DHOBI (DHOBA)	**2,074,405**	**1,056,638**	**1,017,767**
Hindu	1,749,760	886,251	863,509
Sikh	2,177	1,319	858
Jain	1	1	...
Musalman	322,239	168,962	153,277
Animist	228	105	123
Assam	33,946	17,621	16,325
Bengal	231,890	120,316	111,574
Bihar and Orissa	427,079	207,675	219,404
Bombay	79,707	41,185	38,522
C. P. and Berar	165,427	81,127	84,300
Madras	33,265	16,065	17,200
N.-W. F. Province	14,877	8,100	6,777
Punjab	156,046	84,642	71,404
United Provinces	725,719	374,844	350,875
Central India Agency	82,405	41,941	40,464
Hyderabad State	66,598	33,600	32,998
Kashmir State	5,991	3,362	2,629
Rajputana Agency	45,801	23,348	22,453
Elsewhere	5,654	2,812	2,842
DHODIYA	**130,105**	**65,187**	**64,918**
Hindu	115,110	57,547	57,563
Animist	14,995	7,640	7,355
Bombay	109,615	54,680	54,935
Baroda State	20,490	10,507	9,983
DHOLI† (DAMAMI)	**67,832**	**35,000**	**32,832**
Hindu	65,271	33,757	31,514
Musalman	1,020	490	530
Animist	1,541	753	788
Ajmer-Merwara	5,378	2,766	2,612
Assam	11,292	5,590	5,702
C. P. and Berar	4,914	2,508	2,406
Central India Agency	15,340	8,009	7,331
Rajputana Agency	30,908	16,127	14,781
DHOR (*Hindu*)	**26,747**	**13,723**	**13,024**
Bombay	13,506	6,893	6,613
Hyderabad State	13,241	6,830	6,411
DHUND	**71,235**	**36,956**	**34,279**
Hindu	14	...	14
Musalman	71,221	36,956	34,265
N.-W. F. Province	30,464	15,773	14,691
Punjab	24,913	13,316	11,597
Kashmir State	15,858	7,867	7,991
DHUNIYA (BAHNA, NADAF)	**719,265**	**357,401**	**361,864**
Hindu	29,578	15,439	14,139
Musalman	689,687	341,962	347,725
Bengal	8,536	4,878	3,658
Bihar and Orissa	202,208	94,550	107,658
C. P. and Berar	48,407	24,045	24,362
United Provinces	404,738	205,867	198,871
Central India Agency	24,368	12,323	12,045
Hyderabad State	30,721	15,574	15,147
Elsewhere	287	164	123
DHURI (*Hindu*) (C. P. and Berar)	**3,204**	**1,521**	**1,683**
DHUSAR (DHUSAR-BHARGAVA)	**3,881**	**2,019**	**1,862**
Hindu	3,880	2,019	1,861
Musalman	1	...	1
United Provinces	2,283	1,237	1,046
Elsewhere	1,598	782	816
DOAI (*Hindu*)	**12,517**	**6,247**	**6,270**
Assam	22	19	3
Bengal	12,495	6,228	6,267
DOANIYA (Assam)	**1,847**	**1,060**	**787**
Hindu	156	78	78
Buddhist	1,691	982	709
DOGAR (Punjab)	**68,473**	**38,030**	**30,443**
Hindu	94	68	26
Sikh	20	10	10
Jain	1	1	...
Musalman	68,358	37,951	30,407
DOLUVA (*Hindu*) (Madras)	**17,099**	**8,386**	**8,713**
DOM ‡ (DUM, DUMNA)	**925,820**	**471,785**	**454,035**
Hindu	898,541	457,843	440,698
Sikh	1,313	735	578
Buddhist	11	7	4
Musalman	23,132	11,826	11,306
Animist	2,823	1,374	1,449
Assam	30,412	15,387	15,025
Bengal	173,991	88,101	85,890
Bihar and Orissa	241,903	119,393	122,510
C. P. and Berar	9,344	4,660	4,684
Punjab	79,916	42,697	37,219
United Provinces	333,781	172,011	161,770
Kashmir State	52,099	27,330	24,769
Elsewhere	4,374	2,206	2,168

* In Bombay Dhed has been included in Mahar.
† See also Nagarchi.
‡ In N.-W. F. Province included in Paracha. See also Bansphor and Basor.

TABLE XIII.—Caste, Tribe, Race or Nationality. Part I.—

Caste, Religion and Locality.	Persons.	Males.	Females.
1	2	3	4
DOMAL (*Musalman*) (Kashmir State)	**6,953**	**3,264**	**3,689**
DOMBO (Madras)	**62,976**	**31,370**	**31,606**
Hindu	60,669	30,191	30,478
Animist	2,307	1,179	1,128
DOMMARA (DOMBAR)	**25,605**	**12,722**	**12,883**
Hindu	25,474	12,670	12,804
Animist	131	52	79
Madras	17,714	8,872	8,842
Elsewhere	7,891	3,850	4,041
DOSADH (DUSADH)	**1,316,388**	**642,765**	**673,623**
Hindu	1,315,490	642,187	673,303
Jain	2	2	..
Musalman	26	26	...
Animist	870	550	320
Assam	10,038	5,641	4,397
Bengal	46,863	33,072	12,791
Bihar and Orissa	1,189,274	569,733	619,541
C. P. and Berar	269	154	115
United Provinces	70,944	34,165	36,779
DUBLA *	**168,846**	**85,739**	**83,107**
Hindu	165,447	83,965	81,482
Animist	3,399	1,774	1,625
Bombay	127,870	65,204	62,666
Baroda State	40,976	20,535	20,441
DUDEKULA (Madras)	**71,612**	**36,076**	**35,536**
Hindu	277	90	187
Musalman	71,335	35,986	35,349
DUMAL (*Hindu*)	**67,052**	**33,142**	**33,910**
Bengal	75	41	34
Bihar and Orissa	66,977	33,101	33,876
EKKALA (Hyderabad State)	**42,480**	**20,986**	**21,494**
Hindu	40,467	20,017	20,450
Animist	2,013	969	1,044
ĒRUMAN (*Hindu*)	**4,899**	**2,284**	**2,615**
Assam	5	3	2
Madras	4,894	2,281	2,313
FAKIR †	**979,293**	**531,678**	**447,615**
Hindu	175,902	102,335	73,567
Sikh	16,187	12,631	3,556
Jain	80	40	40
Musalman	787,124	416,672	370,452
Bengal	7,817	4,155	3,662
Bihar and Orissa	67,568	32,599	34,969
C. P. and Berar	9,095	4,526	4,569
Punjab	282,361	165,569	116,792
United Provinces	527,885	280,265	247,620
Central India Agency	11,871	6,361	5,510
Kashmir State	9,275	4,906	4,369
Rajputana Agency	55,265	29,054	26,211
Elsewhere	8,156	4,243	3,913
GABIT (GAPIT) (*Hindu*)	**24,961**	**12,168**	**12,793**
Bombay	24,818	12,025	12,793
Madras	143	143	...
GADABA	**45,773**	**23,333**	**22,440**
Hindu	42,458	21,655	20,803
Animist	3,315	1,678	1,637
C. P. and Berar	658	322	336
Madras	45,115	23,011	22,104
GADARIYA (GADRI, GAREBI)	**1,368,990**	**712,840**	**656,150**
Hindu	1,368,010	712,183	655,827
Sikh	61	38	23
Musalman	834	562	272
Animist	85	57	28
Bihar and Orissa	92,435	44,230	48,205
C. P. and Berar	40,207	20,244	19,963
Punjab	21,946	12,393	9,553
United Provinces	983,099	515,703	467,396
Central India Agency	159,762	82,682	77,080
Rajputana Agency	65,128	33,743	31,385
Elsewhere	6,413	3,845	2,568
GADDI ‡ (*Hindu*) (Punjab)	**27,618**	**13,420**	**14,198**
GADI (GABRI, GADDI)	**73,337**	**39,139**	**34,198**
Hindu	10,551	5,164	5,387
Musalman	62,786	33,975	28,811
Punjab	4,068	2,234	1,834
United Provinces	55,022	29,721	25,301
Kashmir State	10,563	5,172	5,391
Elsewhere	3,684	2,012	1,672
GAGRA (Punjab)	**3,155**	**1,680**	**1,475**
Hindu	1,149	624	525
Sikh	10	3	7
Musalman	1,996	1,053	943
GAHOI (GAHOHI)	**54,128**	**28,564**	**25,564**
Hindu	54,109	28,553	25,556
Jain	19	11	8
C. P. and Berar	6,775	3,402	3,373
United Provinces	22,271	11,505	10,766
Central India Agency	25,082	13,657	11,425

* Includes Talaviyā in Bombay.

† Includes Darvesh in Kashmir State.

‡ A geographical term applied to semi-pastoral and semi-agricultural inhabitants of the mountainous country between Kangra and Chamba.

Distribution of Castes by Religion and Locality—*continued*.

Caste, Religion and Locality.	Persons.	Males.	Females.
1	2	3	4
GAKKHAR	**34,648**	**17,446**	**17,202**
Hindu	335	184	151
Sikh	5	1	4
Musalman	34,308	17,261	17,047
N.-W. F. Province	6,807	3,676	3,131
Punjab	27,841	13,770	14,071
GAMALLA (*Hindu*) (Madras)	**153,658**	**76,517**	**77,141**
GAMTA (GAMIT)	**59,508**	**30,292**	**29,216**
Hindu	37,333	18,903	18,430
Animist	22,175	11,389	10,786
Bengal	1	...	1
Bombay	9,892	5,032	4,860
Baroda State	49,615	25,260	24,355
GAM-VAKKAL (*Hindu*) (Bombay)	**12,132**	**5,655**	**6,477**
GANAI (*Musalman*) (Kashmir State)	**46,424**	**21,795**	**24,629**
GANAK * (*Hindu*) (Assam)	**21,489**	**10,516**	**10,973**
GANDA	**364,826**	**179,960**	**184,866**
Hindu	360,843	177,961	182,882
Animist	3,983	1,999	1,984
Bengal	1,264	660	604
Bihar and Orissa	211,775	105,015	106,760
C. P. and Berar	151,787	74,285	77,502
GANDHABANIK (*Hindu*)	**145,034**	**72,536**	**72,498**
Assam	2,077	1,104	973
Bengal	119,425	59,516	59,909
Bihar and Orissa	23,532	11,916	11,616
GANDHAMALI (*Hindu*)	**6,222**	**2,940**	**3,282**
Bihar and Orissa	5,528	2,733	2,795
Elsewhore	694	207	487
GANDHILA (Punjab)	**779**	**422**	**357**
Hindu	677	370	307
Sikh	25	13	12
Musalman	77	39	38
GANDLA (*Hindu*)	**49,001**	**24,697**	**24,304**
Madras	35,986	17,809	18,177
Hyderabad State	13,015	6,888	6,127
GANGAI (GANESH)	**71,558**	**34,481**	**37,077**
Hindu	71,555	34,478	37,077
Buddhist	3	3	...
Assam	7	6	1
Bengal	20,786	10,615	10,171
Bihar and Orissa	50,765	23,860	26,905
GANGAUTA (*Hindu*)	**83,003**	**39,812**	**43,191**
Bihar and Orissa	82,633	39,538	43,095
Elsewhere	370	274	96
GANGRADA (*Hindu*) (C. P. and Berar)	**1,165**	**615**	**550**
GANIGA	**61,353**	**30,638**	**30,715**
Hindu	61,352	30,638	30,714
Animist	1	...	1
Madras	17,584	8,694	8,890
Mysore State	40,469	20,311	20,158
Elsewhere	3,300	1,633	1,667
GANRAR (GANDAPAL) (*Hindu*)	**2,913**	**1,500**	**1,413**
Assam	973	505	468
Bengal	1,940	995	945
GARA	**49,412**	**27,175**	**22,237**
Hindu	1	1	..
Musalman	49,411	27,174	22,237
Punjab	369	194	175
United Provinces	49,043	26,981	22,062
GARO	**187,351**	**94,263**	**93,088**
Hindu	2,897	1,502	1,395
Animist	184,454	92,761	91,693
Assam	144,350	72,569	71,781
Bengal	43,001	21,694	21.307
GARODA (GARODIYA) (*Hindu*)	**17,235**	**8,927**	**8,308**
Ajmer-Merwara	91	47	44
Baroda State	6,281	3,125	3,156
Rajputana Agency	10,863	5,755	5,108
GARPAGARI (*Hindu*) (C. P. and Berar)	**9,048**	**4,500**	**4,548**
GARRI † (*Hindu*) (Punjab)	**555**	**285**	**270**
GATTI (*Hindu*) (Madras)	**2,232**	**1,082**	**1,150**
GAURA (GAUDA)	**900,192**	**437,610**	**462,582**
Hindu	898,869	436,806	462,063
Jain	1	1	..
Animist	1,322	803	519
Bihar and Orissa	712,772	345,819	366,953
Coorg	12,994	6,923	6,071
Madras	169,261	81,838	87,423
Elsewhore	5,165	3,030	2,135
GAVADA (*Hindu*) (Bombay)	**6,750**	**3,005**	**3,745**
GAVANDI ‡ (*Hindu*) (Bombay)	**39,409**	**19,489**	**19,920**
GAVARA (*Hindu*) (Madras)	**60,515**	**29,076**	**31,439**
GAVLI § (*Hindu*) (Bombay)	**38,542**	**19,262**	**19,280**

* Acharaj, Agradani, etc., have been included in Brahman.
† A caste of travelling actors, minstrels and mountebanks; different from Gadi (Garri).
‡ Includes Uppar or Chunara in Bombay.
§ Ahir has been shown separately.

TABLE XIII.—Caste, Tribe, Race or Nationality. Part I.—

Caste, Religion and Locality.	Persons.	Males.	Females.
1	2	3	4
GAWARIYA (Rajputana Agency)	**2,599**	**1,332**	**1,267**
Hindu	2,586	1,324	1,262
Musalman	1	...	1
Animist	12	8	4
GAYINTA (*Hindu*) (Madras)	**1,665**	**801**	**864**
GHAI (Punjab)	**2,498**	**1,391**	**1,107**
Hindu	2,426	1,351	1,075
Musalman	72	40	32
GHANCHA	**19,355**	**10,213**	**9,142**
Hindu	18,464	9,730	8,734
Jain	1	1	...
Musalman	890	482	408
Ajmer-Merwara	3	1	2
Rajputana Agency	19,352	10,212	9,140
GHANCHI (Baroda State)	**16,481**	**8,437**	**8,044**
Hindu	11,862	6,038	5,824
Jain	5	2	3
Musalman	4,614	2,397	2,217
GHANTRA (GHONTORA)	**2,884**	**1,523**	**1,361**
Hindu	2,832	1,501	1,331
Animist	52	22	30
Bihar and Orissa	1,572	759	813
Elsewhere	1,312	764	548
GHARTI	**5,078**	**2,665**	**2,413**
Hindu	5,068	2,657	2,411
Animist	10	8	2
Bengal	3,991	2,070	1,921
Elsewhere	1,087	595	492
GHARUK (*Hindu*)	**1,019**	**525**	**494**
Bengal	1	1	...
United Provinces	1,018	524	494
GHASI (GHASIYA)	**134,076**	**65,864**	**68,212**
Hindu	123,804	60,942	62,862
Animist	10,272	4,922	5,350
Assam	15,114	7,580	7,534
Bengal	5,900	3,278	2,622
Bihar and Orissa	69,920	34,125	35,795
C. P. and Berar	43,142	20,881	22,261
GHATWAL	**79,557**	**37,726**	**41,831**
Hindu	79,459	37,684	41,775
Animist	98	42	56
Assam	4,068	2,000	2,068
Bengal	5,575	3,261	2,314
Bihar and Orissa	69,914	32,465	37,449
GHIRATH (Punjab)	**171,129**	**88,778**	**82,351**
Hindu	168,144	87,181	80,963
Sikh	2,968	1,593	1,375
Musalman	17	4	13
GHOSI *	**51,927**	**26,929**	**24,998**
Hindu	9,960	5,110	4,850
Musalman	41,809	21,702	20,107
Animist	158	117	41
C. P. and Berar	9,739	4,999	4,740
United Provinces	35,825	18,564	17,261
Elsewhere	6,363	3,366	2,997
GHULAM (GOLAM) (*Musalman*)	**24,946**	**12,202**	**12,744**
Baluchistan	21,078	10,007	11,071
Elsewhere	3,868	2,195	1,673
GHULAMAZAD (*Musalman*) (Baluchistan)	**7,738**	**4,233**	**3,505**
GINGRA (*Hindu*) (Bihar and Orissa)	**3,424**	**1,641**	**1,783**
GODARI (*Hindu*) (Madras)	**2,246**	**1,549**	**697**
GOKHA (*Hindu*)	**47,262**	**23,004**	**24,258**
Bihar and Orissa	47,139	22,960	24,179
Elsewhere	123	44	79
GOLA	**74,747**	**37,501**	**37,246**
Hindu	74,737	37,497	37,240
Musalman	10	4	6
Bihar and Orissa	55,571	27,806	27,765
Bombay	13,791	7,020	6,771
Baroda State	5,220	2,592	2,628
Elsewhere	165	83	82
GOLANALAL (*Jain*) (Central India Agency)	**1,487**	**787**	**700**
GOLAPURAB (C. P. and Berar)	**5,801**	**2,952**	**2,849**
Hindu	640	304	336
Jain	5,161	2,648	2,513
GOLLA (GOLAR)	**1,538,021**	**767,889**	**770,132**
Hindu	1,535,322	766,532	768,790
Animist	2,699	1,357	1,342
C. P. and Berar	16,710	8,080	8,630
Madras	904,192	445,827	458,365
Hyderabad State	460,760	234,629	226,131
Mysore State	150,842	76,617	74,225
Elsewhere	5,517	2,736	2,781
GOND †	**2,917,950**	**1,423,804**	**1,494,146**
Hindu	840,980	409,773	431,207
Musalman	6	2	4
Animist	2,076,964	1,014,029	1,062,935
Assam	51,572	26,917	24,655
Bihar and Orissa	235,671	116,669	119,002
C. P. and Berar	2,339,361	1,140,862	1,198,499
Madras	32,257	16,848	15,409
Central India Agency	234,672	111,364	123,308
Hyderabad State	24,090	10,883	13,207
Elsewhere	327	261	66

* Ahir has been shown separately.
† The U. P. Gonds have been classed under Gour except those of the Jhansi district who are shown under Gond.

DISTRIBUTION OF CASTES BY RELIGION AND LOCALITY—*continued.*

Caste, Religion and Locality.	Persons.	Males.	Females.
1	2	3	4
GONDHALI (*Hindu*)	**9,538**	**4,836**	**4,702**
Hyderabad State	5,193	2,622	2,571
Elsewhere	4,345	2,214	2,131
GONR *	**183,404**	**90,281**	**93,123**
Hindu	183,394	90,277	93,117
Musalman	3	1	2
Animist	7	3	4
Bengal	9,390	7,436	1,954
Bihar and Orissa	63,883	29,663	34,220
United Provinces	110,131	53,182	56,949
GONRHI (GORIYA)	**228,669**	**113,361**	**115,308**
Hindu	224,246	111,127	113,119
Musalman	4,423	2,234	2,189
Bengal	11,325	6,996	4,329
Bihar and Orissa	130,106	63,137	66,969
United Provinces	87,238	43,228	44,010
GORAIT	**7,746**	**4,128**	**3,618**
Hindu	6,788	3,642	3,146
Buddhist	9	3	6
Animist	949	483	466
Assam	3,547	1,792	1,755
Bengal	4,199	2,336	1,863
GOSAIN (GOSAVI)	**262,054**	**140,546**	**121,508**
Hindu	261,932	140,475	121,457
Sikh	73	45	28
Jain	4	3	1
Musalman	8	4	4
Animist	37	19	18
Bihar and Orissa	24,486	12,405	12,081
C. P. and Berar	42,272	22,107	20,165
Punjab	11,701	6,941	4,760
United Provinces	93,997	50,196	43,801
Baroda State	6,628	3,663	2,965
Central India Agency	21,443	11,801	9,642
Hyderabad State	29,988	16,036	13,952
Rajputana Agency	27,806	15,418	12,388
Elsewhere	3,733	1,979	1,754
GOUNDLA (*Hindu*) (Hyderabad State)	**306,071**	**156,381**	**149,690**
GOWARI (C. P. and Berar)	**157,580**	**77,300**	**80,280**
Hindu	152,502	74,746	77,756
Jain	1	1	...
Animist	5,077	2,553	2,524
BASSIYA (Rajputana Agency)	**17,419**	**8,918**	**8,501**
Hindu	16,268	8,331	7,937
Animist	1,151	587	564
GUDALA (*Hindu*) (Madras)	**4,442**	**2,182**	**2,260**
GUJAR (GUJJAR)	**2,199,196**	**1,216,863**	**982,335**
Hindu	1,239,826	687,777	552,049
Sikh	4,212	2,522	1,690
Jain	8	6	2
Musalman	955,150	526,557	428,593
Animist	2	1	1
Ajmer-Merwara	35,059	18,609	16,450
C. P. and Berar	55,798	28,607	27,191
N.-W. F. Province	113,871	61,711	52,160
Punjab	610,472	338,813	271,659
United Provinces	366,191	206,156	160,035
Central India Agency	185,728	105,834	79,894
Kashmir State	328,003	183,798	144,205
Rajputana Agency	500,046	271,188	228,858
Elsewhere	4,030	2,147	1,883
GUJARATHI (GUJRATI)	**2,645**	**1,373**	**1,272**
Hindu	1,808	980	828
Jain	837	393	444
Hyderabad State	969	529	440
Elsewhere	1,676	844	832
GULGULIYA	**853**	**491**	**362**
Hindu	799	464	335
Animist	54	27	27
Bihar and Orissa	824	474	350
Elsewhere	29	17	12
GUNI (*Hindu*) (Madras)	**1,523**	**735**	**788**
GURAV † **(GURAO)**	**97,489**	**49,249**	**48,240**
Hindu	97,481	49,246	48,235
Jain	8	3	5
Bombay	65,538	32,890	32,648
C. P. and Berar	14,172	6,994	7,178
Central India Agency	257	98	159
Hyderabad State	17,522	9,267	8,255
GURIYA (GODIYA) (*Hindu*)	**158,294**	**76,897**	**81,397**
Bihar and Orissa	146,777	71,090	75,687
Madras	10,604	5,017	5,587
Elsewhere	913	790	123
GURKHA (GORKHA)	**22,068**	**16,084**	**5,984**
Hindu	22,018	16,062	5,956
Sikh	3	3	...
Buddhist	1	1	...
Musalman	46	18	28
N.-W. F. Province	6,343	5,163	1,180
Punjab	8,297	5,587	2,710
United Provinces	6,076	4,151	1,925
Elsewhere	1,352	1,183	169
GURUNG	**19,593**	**10,470**	**9,123**
Hindu	19,432	10,372	9,060
Buddhist	112	69	43
Animist	49	29	20
Bengal	10,961	5,673	5,288
Sikkim State	6,058	3,063	2,995
Elsewhere	2,574	1,734	840

* *Vide* footnote to Gond.

† Includes Hugar in Bombay.

TABLE XIII.—CASTE, TRIBE, RACE OR NATIONALITY. PART I.—

CASTE, RELIGION AND LOCALITY.	Persons.	Males.	Females.
1	2	3	4
HABURA (*Hindu*) (United Provinces)	**1,818**	**1,027**	**791**
HADI (*Hindu*) (Bengal) . .	**26,212**	**13,415**	**12,797**
HAJANG	**33,304**	**17,302**	**16,002**
Hindu . . .	33,296	17,296	16,000
Animist . . .	8	6	2
Assam . . .	8,288	4,324	3,964
Bengal . . .	25,016	12,978	12,038
HAJJAM (NAI, NAPIT) . .	**3,013,399**	**1,552,613**	**1,460,786**
Hindu . . .	2,417,456	1,238,454	1,179,002
Sikh	34,428	19,554	14,874
Jain . . .	35	27	8
Musalman . . .	561,230	294,438	266,792
Animist . . .	250	140	110
Ajmer-Merwara . .	6,503	3,297	3,206
Assam . . .	39,781	20,825	18,956
Bengal . . .	458,035	236,006	222,029
Bihar and Orissa .	455,758	221,623	234,135
Bombay . . .	196,460	101,203	95,257
C. P. and Berar . .	148,750	74,078	74,672
N.-W. F. Province .	24,777	13,075	11,702
Punjab . . .	350,456	192,266	158,190
United Provinces .	912,828	475,341	437,487
Baroda State . .	26,266	13,261	13,005
Central India Agency .	156,395	77,464	78,931
Kashmir State . .	34,456	18,697	15,759
Mysore State . .	39,414	19,977	19,437
Rajputana Agency .	162,463	84,866	77,597
Elsewhere . . .	1,057	634	423
HALALKHOR * . .	**20,607**	**10,369**	**10,238**
Hindu . . .	20,568	10,358	10,210
Musalman . . .	17	11	6
Animist . . .	22	...	22
Bihar and Orissa .	18,586	9,187	9,399
Elsewhere . . .	2,021	1,182	839
HALBA (C. P. and Berar) .	**100,211**	**48,836**	**51,375**
Hindu . . .	100,033	48,723	51,310
Animist . . .	178	113	65
HALEPAIK (*Hindu*) . .	**54,634**	**27,605**	**27,029**
Bombay . . .	48,493	24,817	23,676
Coorg . . .	39	18	21
Madras . . .	6,102	2,770	3,332
HALI (Punjab)	**21,067**	**10,779**	**10,288**
Hindu . . .	21,065	10,777	10,288
Sikh . . .	1	1	...
Buddhist . . .	1	1	...
HALWAI	**254,844**	**131,646**	**123,198**
Hindu . . .	220,439	113,683	106,756
Sikh . . .	21	19	2
Jain . . .	4	2	2
Musalman . . .	34,378	17,941	16,437
Animist . . .	2	1	1
Bengal . . .	13,690	8,796	4,894
Bihar and Orissa .	142,003	70,679	71,324
United Provinces .	91,291	48,085	43,206
Elsewhere . . .	7,860	4,086	3,774
HANBAR (*Hindu*) (Bombay) .	**17,451**	**8,837**	**8,614**
HANJI (*Musalman*) (Kashmir State)	**18,275**	**10,244**	**8,031**
HARI† (HADDI, BHUINMALI)	**454,174**	**228,002**	**226,172**
Hindu . . .	454,045	227,924	226,121
Animist . . .	129	78	51
Assam . . .	40,826	21,045	19,781
Bengal . . .	265,679	134,513	131,166
Bihar and Orissa .	119,468	58,560	60,908
Madras . . .	28,201	13,884	14,317
HARKANTA (*Hindu*) (Bombay)	**7,902**	**3,934**	**3,968**
HARNI (*Musalman*) . . .	**4,034**	**2,145**	**1,889**
Punjab . . .	3,380	1,798	1,582
Kashmir State . .	654	347	307
HEGGADE (*Hindu*) . . .	**5,282**	**2,591**	**2,691**
Coorg . . .	1,830	988	842
Madras . . .	3,452	1,603	1,849
HESI (Punjab)	**1,475**	**751**	**724**
Hindu . . .	1,433	730	703
Buddhist . . .	42	21	21
HIRA (*Hindu*) (Assam) . .	**16,351**	**8,063**	**8,288**
HO	**420,571**	**203,823**	**216,748**
Hindu . . .	61,035	30,446	30,589
Animist . . .	359,536	173,377	186,159
Bihar and Orissa .	419,221	203,045	216,176
Elsewhere . . .	1,350	778	572
HOLEYA‡ (HOLIYA) (*Hindu*) .	**771,513**	**383,147**	**388,366**
Coorg . . .	22,107	12,419	9,688
Madras . . .	136,109	61,164	74,945
Mysore State . .	613,248	309,536	308,712
Travancore State .	49	28	21
HUMBAD (HAMAR, UMAD, UMAR)	**42,112**	**21,805**	**20,307**
Hindu . . .	30,155	15,911	14,244
Jain	11,957	5,894	6,063
United Provinces .	29,992	15,815	14,177
Rajputana Agency .	8,583	4,257	4,326
Elsewhere . . .	3,537	1,733	1,804

* See also Bhangi, Chuhra and Mehtar.

† In Assam Brittiyal Baniya has been shown separately.

‡ In Bombay Holiya has been included in Mahar.

Distribution of Castes by Religion and Locality—*continued.*

Caste, Religion and Locality.	Persons.	Males.	Females.
1	2	3	4
IDAIYAN (ITAYAN) (*Hindu*)	**744,372**	**364,899**	**379,473**
Madras	734,767	360,154	374,613
Cochin State	380	189	191
Travancore State	9,225	4,556	4,669
IDIGA (*Hindu*)	**324,957**	**159,207**	**165,750**
Madras	261,235	126,756	134,479
Hyderabad State	24,911	12,582	12,329
Mysore State	38,758	19,836	18,922
Elsewhere	53	33	20
ILAMAGAN (*Hindu*) (Madras)	**7,160**	**3,114**	**4,046**
ILAVANIYAN (*Hindu*) (Travancore State)	**6,116**	**3,055**	**3,061**
ILAVATTI (*Hindu*) (Travancore State)	**6,671**	**3,211**	**3,460**
ILAYATU (ELAYAD) (*Hindu*)	**4,796**	**2,498**	**2,298**
Madras	447	214	233
Travancore State	4,349	2,284	2,065
ILUVAN (IZHAVAN) (*Hindu*)	**875,856**	**431,989**	**443,867**
Madras	121,138	57,495	63,643
Cochin State	208,453	102,817	105,636
Travancore State	546,265	271,677	274,588
INDRA (*Hindu*) (Madras)	**56,774**	**26,535**	**30,239**
IRALIGA (Mysore State)	**2,043**	**1,073**	**970**
Hindu	154	78	76
Animist	1,889	995	894
IRAQI (*Musalman*) (United Provinces)	**8,751**	**4,070**	**4,681**
IRULA (Madras)	**100,659**	**50,095**	**50,564**
Hindu	95,278	47,349	47,929
Animist	5,381	2,746	2,635
JAGA (*Hindu*)	**3,681**	**1,798**	**1,883**
Rajputana Agency	2,842	1,424	1,418
Elsewhere	839	374	465
JAGGALI (Madras)	**4,280**	**1,514**	**2,766**
Hindu	4,246	1,497	2,749
Animist	34	17	17
JAISWAL (JESWAL)	**3,945**	**2,271**	**1,674**
Hindu	127	75	52
Jain	3,818	2,196	1,622
Central India Agency	1,981	1,148	833
Rajputana Agency	1,964	1,123	841
JALADHA (Assam)	**6,709**	**3,360**	**3,349**
Hindu	5,372	2,697	2,675
Animist	1,337	663	674
JALABI (*Hindu*) (Madras)	**23,560**	**11,170**	**12,390**
JANAPPAN (GONIGA) (*Hindu*)	**43,705**	**20,295**	**23,410**
Madras	42,707	19.842	22,865
Mysore State	998	453	545
JANGAM	**113,692**	**55,895**	**57,797**
Hindu	113,676	55,887	57,789
Jain	16	8	8
C. P. and Berar	3,601	1,836	1,765
Madras	110,091	54,059	56,032
JANJUA	**3,587**	**2,054**	**1,533**
Hindu	4	2	2
Sikh	5	..	5
Musalman	3,578	2,052	1,526
Punjab	3,570	2,038	1,532
Mysore State	17	16	1
JAPANESE (*Buddhist*)	**666**	**212**	**454**
Burma	542	180	362
Elsewhere	124	32	92
JAT	**6,964,286**	**3,912,211**	**3,052,075**
Hindu	2,817,501	1,564,844	1,252,657
Sikh	1,642,016	968,641	673,375
Jain	118	99	19
Musalman	2,504,651	1,378,627	1,126,024
Ajmer-Merwara	30,497	16,526	13,971
Baluchistan	5,680	3,151	2,529
Bombay	11,378	6,350	5,028
C. P. and Berar	9,959	5,753	4,206
N.-W. F. Province	86,097	48,873	37,224
Punjab	4,956,536	2,808,551	2,147,985
United Provinces	744,600	421,857	322,743
Central India Agency	47,160	24,661	22,499
Kashmir State	141,439	72,895	68,544
Rajputana Agency	928,486	501,616	426,870
Elsewhere	2,454	1,978	476
JATAPU	**93,273**	**45,371**	**47,902**
Hindu	63,054	30,709	32,345
Animist	30,219	14,662	15,557
Assam	753	419	334
Madras	92,520	44,952	47,568
JATT (*Musalman*) (Baluchistan)	**78,400**	**42,673**	**35,727**
JETTI (*Hindu*) (Madras)	**622**	**405**	**217**

TABLE XIII.—Caste, Tribe, Race or Nationality. Part I.—

Caste, Religion and Locality.	Persons.	Males.	Females.
1	2	3	4
JHABEL (Punjab)	**14,046**	**7,856**	**6,190**
Hindu	1	1	...
Musalman	14,045	7,855	6,190
JHAROLA (Baroda State)	**2,054**	**964**	**1,090**
Hindu	2,029	952	1,077
Jain	25	12	13
JHINWAR * (JHIWAR)	**375,694**	**207,478**	**168,216**
Hindu	238,418	132,983	105,435
Sikh	45,773	25,242	20,531
Jain	4	2	2
Musalman	91,499	49,251	42,248
Punjab	359,864	198,667	161,197
Kashmir State	13,500	7,285	6,215
Elsewhere	2,330	1,526	804
JHOJHA (JHOJA)	**30,987**	**17,012**	**13,975**
Hindu	1	...	1
Jain	14	...	14
Musalman	30,972	17,012	13,960
Punjab	262	135	127
United Provinces	30,725	16,877	13,848
JHORA	**839**	**407**	**432**
Hindu	767	362	405
Animist	72	45	27
Assam	703	325	378
Bengal	136	82	54
JINGAR (ZEENGAR) (*Hindu*)	**12,529**	**6,115**	**6,414**
Hyderabad State	9,824	4,719	5,105
Elsewhere	2,705	1,396	1,309
JOGI † (JUGI)	**814,365**	**417,748**	**396,617**
Hindu	769,159	394,648	374,511
Sikh	307	203	104
Musalman	44,740	22,802	21,938
Animist	159	95	64
Assam	169,113	86,180	82,933
Bengal	361,141	182,903	178,238
Bihar and Orissa	35,321	17,716	17,605
Bombay	5,296	2,696	2,600
C. P. and Berar	15,402	7,753	7,649
Madras	23,190	11,644	11,546
Punjab	83,412	44,887	38,525
Central India Agency	15,100	7,806	7,294
Hyderabad State	5,907	3,288	2,619
Kashmir State	5,553	3,125	2,428
Mysore State	15,061	7,587	7,474
Rajputana Agency	77,052	40,644	36,408
Elsewhere	2,817	1,519	1,298
JOLAHA ‡ (JULAHA, MOMIN)	**2,858,399**	**1,460,654**	**1,397,745**
Hindu	98,651	53,371	45,280
Sikh	6,233	3,444	2,789
Buddhist	42	18	24
Musalman	2,753,473	1,403,821	1,349,652
Assam	7,207	3,763	3,444
Bengal	282,705	152,352	130,353
Bihar and Orissa	826,391	389,075	437,316
Bombay	10,478	5,140	5,338
N.-W. F. Province	37,390	19,999	17,391
Punjab	635,044	345,292	289,752
United Provinces	991,263	508,543	482,720
Central India Agency	12,270	6,554	5,716
Hyderabad State	5,194	2,755	2,439
Kashmir State	26,830	14,795	12,035
Rajputana Agency	18,333	9,478	8,855
Elsewhere	5,294	2,908	2,386
JONAKAN (JONAGAN) (*Musalman*)	**117,280**	**59,257**	**58,023**
Madras	8,780	3,568	5,212
Cochin State	51,469	26,274	25,195
Travancore State	57,031	29,415	27,616
JOSHI (*Hindu*)	**20,227**	**10,167**	**10,060**
C. P. and Berar	5,906	2,831	3,075
Central India Agency	9,581	5,015	4,566
Elsewhere	4,740	2,321	2,419
JUANG	**12,845**	**6,499**	**6,346**
Hindu	1,315	625	690
Animist	11,530	5,874	5,656
Assam	5	5	...
Bihar and Orissa	12,840	6,494	6,346
KABBALIGAR (KABBER, KABBERA) (*Hindu*)	**79,916**	**41,683**	**38,233**
Bombay	59,815	31,993	27,822
Madras	20,101	9,690	10,411
KACHARI	**231,912**	**118,424**	**113,488**
Hindu	62,041	33,411	28,630
Buddhist	3	3	...
Animist	169,868	85,010	84,858
Assam	230,102	117,487	112,615
Bengal	1,810	937	873
KACHERA	**9,568**	**4,751**	**4,817**
Hindu	8,086	3,998	4,088
Jain	5	5	...
Musalman	1,477	748	729
Central India Agency	6,394	3,197	3,197
Elsewhere	3,174	1,554	1,620

* Bhisti, Kahar and Machhi have been shown separately.
† Includes Nath in Rajputana and Ajmer-Merwara. In Central India Agency Nath has been shown separately.
‡ Includes Bafinda in Kashmir State. Hindu Jolaha in Bengal and Bihar and Orissa included in Tanti and Tatwa.

Distribution of Castes by Religion and Locality—*continued.*

Caste, Religion and Locality.	Persons.	Males.	Females.
1	2	3	4
KACHHI (KACHHIYA)	**1,304,296**	**674,402**	**629,894**
Hindu	1,302,309	673,001	629,308
Sikh	123	71	52
Jain	4	2	2
Buddhist	1	1	...
Musalman	1,852	1,322	530
Animist	7	5	2
Bombay	12,757	6,654	6,103
C. P. and Berar	119,553	60,287	59,266
United Provinces	728,800	387,943	340,857
Baroda State	8,029	4,257	3,772
Central India Agency	372,496	182,357	190,139
Rajputana Agency	60,666	31,766	28,900
Elsewhere	1,995	1,138	857
KACHIN (SINGPHO)	**162,822**	**81,010**	**81,812**
Hindu	2	1	1
Buddhist	162,526	80,854	81,672
Animist	294	155	139
Assam	454	246	208
Burma	162,368	80,764	81,604
KACHIN-BURMA HYBRIDS AND LOLO GROUP* (*Buddhist*) (Burma)	**77,585**	**40,225**	**37,360**
KADAN	**1,238**	**609**	**629**
Hindu	791	399	392
Animist	447	210	237
Madras	791	399	392
Cochin State	447	210	237
KADHERA (KADERA, KADAR)	**26,790**	**14,294**	**12,496**
Hindu	26,656	14,226	12,430
Musalman	36	18	18
Animist	98	50	48
United Provinces	23,491	12,645	10,846
Elsewhere	3,299	1,649	1,650
KADIYA (*Hindu*) (Bombay)	**10,439**	**4,849**	**5,590**
KADUPPATTAN (*Hindu*)	**34,294**	**16,777**	**17,517**
Madras	19,971	9,703	10,268
Cochin State	14,323	7,074	7,249
KAHAR †	**1,838,698**	**941,631**	**897,067**
Hindu	1,831,305	937,804	893,501
Sikh	369	2[illegible]8	81
Jain	13	9	4
Musalman	6,965	3,502	3,463
Animist	46	28	18
Assam	13,366	7,331	6,035
Bengal	89,[illegible]94	61,[illegible]36	27,758
Bihar and Orissa	524,431	245,[illegible]01	278,630
C. P. and Berar	28,357	11,[illegible]3	11,474
United Provinces	1,112,421	575,784	536,637
Central India Agency	56,835	29,086	27,749
Rajputana Agency	15,164	7,9[illegible]7	7,197
Elsewhere	3,430	1,843	1,587
KAHUT (Punjab)	**10,648**	**5,566**	**5,082**
Hindu	86	59	27
Sikh	3	...	3
Musalman	10,559	5,507	5,052
KAIBARTTA, CHASI (MAHISYA) (*Hindu*)	**2,231,218**	**1,123,625**	**1,107,593**
Assam	65,312	34,304	31,008
Bengal	2,137,948	1,075,562	1,062,386
Bihar and Orissa	27,958	13,759	14,199
KAIBARTTA, JALIYA	**375,936**	**191,428**	**184,508**
Hindu	375,934	191,427	184,507
Animist	2	1	1
Assam	45,098	23,331	21,767
Bengal	326,655	165,836	160,819
Bihar and Orissa	4,183	2,261	1,922
KAIBARTTA (UNSPECIFIED)	**104,806**	**52,747**	**52,059**
Hindu	104,795	52,744	52,051
Animist	11	3	8
Assam	20,843	10,624	10,219
Bengal	22,800	11,891	10,909
Bihar and Orissa	61,163	30,232	30,931
KAIKADI	**11,925**	**5,785**	**6,140**
Hindu	11,920	5,782	6,138
Animist	5	3	2
Bombay	9,614	4,681	4,933
C. P. and Berar	2,311	1,104	1,207
KAIKOLAN (KAIKKALAVAN) (*Hindu*)	**373,297**	**181,890**	**191,407**
Madras	368,347	179,467	188,880
Elsewhere	4,950	2,423	2,527
KAIMKHANI (*Musalman*)	**28,882**	**15,130**	**13,752**
Ajmer-Merwara	542	306	236
Rajputana Agency	28,340	14,824	13,516
KALANGA (*Hindu*)	**5,825**	**2,811**	**3,014**
Bihar and Orissa	4,066	1,937	2,129
Elsewhere	1,759	874	885
KALBELIYA (*Hindu*) (Central India Agency)	**5,163**	**3,063**	**2,100**
KALINGI (*Hindu*) (Madras)	**83,442**	**39,978**	**43,464**
KALINJI (*Hindu*) (Madras)	**51,558**	**22,809**	**28,749**
KALITA (*Hindu*)	**222,021**	**115,557**	**106,464**
Assam	221,942	115,506	106,436
Bengal	79	51	28
KALLAN (*Hindu*)	**536,629**	**259,619**	**277,010**
Madras	535,572	258,972	276,600
Elsewhere	1,057	647	410

* For sub-castes see Part II.

† See also Bhisti, Jhinwar and Machhi.

TABLE XIII.—Caste, Tribe, Race or Nationality. Part I.—

Caste, Religion and Locality.	Persons.	Males.	Females.
1	2	3	4
KALLASARI (*Hindu*) (Travancore State)	**7,992**	**4,051**	**3,941**
KALOTA (*Hindu*) (Central India Agency)	**22,033**	**12,378**	**9,655**
KALU	**158,092**	**80,090**	**78,002**
Hindu	158,083	80,084	77,999
Jain	3	3	...
Musalman	5	2	3
Animist	1	1	...
Assam	2,031	1,356	675
Bengal	111,562	56,332	55,230
Bihar and Orissa	44,499	22,402	22,097
KALWAR * (KALAL, KALAR, KALAN)	**954,241**	**483,811**	**470,430**
Hindu	876,095	444,912	431,183
Sikh	12,695	6,895	5,800
Jain	963	531	432
Buddhist	4	2	2
Musalman	64,283	31,361	32,922
Animist	201	110	91
Bengal	12,929	8,700	4,229
Bihar and Orissa	217,504	105,889	111,615
Bombay	7,860	3,949	3,911
C. P. and Berar	195,450	96,426	99,024
Punjab	48,706	26,313	22,393
United Provinces	287,576	148,140	139,436
Central India Agency	63,663	32,766	30,897
Hyderabad State	75,339	38,366	36,973
Rajputana Agency	39,860	20,334	19,526
Elsewhere	5,354	2,928	2,426
KAMANGAR	**2,476**	**1,321**	**1,155**
Hindu	302	217	85
Musalman	2,174	1,104	1,070
Punjab	1,779	946	833
Elsewhere	697	375	322
KAMAR †	**314,105**	**161,654**	**152,451**
Hindu	306,299	157,762	148,537
Sikh	2	2	...
Jain	3	3	...
Animist	7,801	3,887	3,914
Assam	43,285	21,923	21,362
Bengal	263,329	136,158	127,171
C. P. and Berar	7,438	3,542	3,896
Elsewhere	53	31	22
KAMATHI (*Hindu*)	**3,512**	**1,905**	**1,607**
Bombay	3,370	1,835	1,535
C. P. and Berar	142	70	72
KAMBOH	**179,067**	**98,634**	**80,433**
Hindu	36,372	19,968	16,401
Sikh	71,871	39,379	32,492
Musalman	70,824	39,287	31,537
Punjab	172,434	95,004	77,430
United Provinces	6,633	3,630	3,003
KAMI	**20,570**	**11,043**	**9,527**
Hindu	20,401	10,941	9,460
Buddhist	49	32	17
Animist	120	70	50
Bengal	13,667	7,345	6,322
Elsewhere	6,903	3,698	3,205
KAMKAR (United Provinces)	**36,845**	**17,116**	**19,729**
Hindu	36,717	17,045	19,672
Musalman	128	71	57
KAMMA (*Hindu*)	**1,126,531**	**564,628**	**561,903**
Madras	1,126,095	564,432	561,663
Elsewhere	436	196	240
KAMMALAN ‡ (KAMSALA) (*Hindu*)	**1,047,752**	**516,280**	**531,472**
Coorg	167	80	87
Madras	962,744	473,848	488,896
Cochin State	37,301	18,323	18,978
Travancore State	47,540	24,029	23,511
KANADI (*Hindu*) (C. P. and Berar)	**1,127**	**584**	**543**
KANAKKAN (*Hindu*)	**71,073**	**35,532**	**35,541**
Madras	63,360	31,640	31,720
Cochin State	7,527	3,790	3,737
Mysore State	186	102	84
KANCHAN (KANJAR)	**6,291**	**2,571**	**3,720**
Hindu	189	92	97
Musalman	6,102	2,479	3,623
Punjab	5,979	2,437	3,542
Kashmir State	312	134	178
KANDERA (*Hindu*)	**28,438**	**14,591**	**13,847**
Ajmer-Merwara	17	9	8
Central India Agency	19,792	10,148	9,644
Rajputana Agency	8,629	4,434	4,195
KANDH (KHOND)	**673,346**	**332,438**	**340,908**
Hindu	237,569	116,091	121,478
Animist	435,777	216,347	219,430
Assam	5,138	2,657	2,481
Bengal	601	446	155
Bihar and Orissa	302,883	148,079	154,804
C. P. and Berar	9,587	4,643	4,944
Madras	355,137	176,613	178,524
KANDRA (KADMA) (*Hindu*)	**192,753**	**93,637**	**99,116**
Bengal	36,947	18,562	18,385
Bihar and Orissa	155,806	75,075	80,731
KANDU	**664,423**	**328,935**	**335,488**
Hindu	664,363	328,906	335,457
Sikh	48	20	28
Jain	3	3	...
Buddhist	1	1	...
Musalman	1	...	1
Animist	7	5	2
Bengal	12,603	9,658	2,945
Bihar and Orissa	502,855	243,100	259,755
United Provinces	146,892	74,866	72,026
Elsewhere	2,073	1,311	762

* Includes Musalman Pasi in Bihar and Orissa (males 171, females 174).
† Lohar has been shown separately.
‡ Panchala has been treated as a main caste and shown separately.

DISTRIBUTION OF CASTES BY RELIGION AND LOCALITY—*continued.*

Caste, Religion and Locality.	Persons.	Males.	Females.
1	2	3	4
KANERA (Punjab)	**2,825**	**1,580**	**1,245**
Hindu	50	36	14
Sikh	1	1	...
Musalman	2,774	1,543	1,231
KANET (Punjab)	**403,815**	**207,202**	**196,613**
Hindu	394,718	202,762	191,956
Sikh	2,982	1,526	1,456
Buddhist	6,104	2,903	3,201
Musalman	11	11	...
KANIKKARAN (*Animist*) (Travancore State)	**4,034**	**2,166**	**1,868**
KANIYAN * (*Hindu*)	**1,272**	**645**	**627**
Coorg	198	133	65
Madras	1,074	512	562
KANIYAN † (KANISAN) (*Hindu*)	**30,920**	**15,265**	**15,655**
Madras	15,689	7,486	8,203
Cochin State	3,244	1,624	1,620
Travancore State	11,987	6,155	5,832
KANJAR	**23,983**	**11,947**	**12,036**
Hindu	22,511	11,192	11,319
Musalman	1,445	742	703
Animist	27	13	14
United Provinces	18,345	9,256	9,089
Elsewhere	5,638	2,691	2,947
KANNADIYAN (KANADA) (*Hindu*)	**32,281**	**16,552**	**15,729**
Madras	28,375	14,556	13,819
Elsewhere	3,906	1,996	1,910
KANSARI (KANSARA, KASERA, KASAR)	**89,050**	**45,214**	**43,836**
Hindu	88,501	44,974	43,527
Sikh	162	71	91
Jain	87	31	56
Musalman	73	37	36
Animist	227	101	126
Bengal	16,147	8,126	8,021
Bihar and Orissa	29,771	14,872	14,899
C. P. and Berar	20,175	10,210	9,965
Hyderabad State	14,522	7,689	6,833
Elsewhere	8,435	4,317	4,118
KAORA (KAONRA)	**129,529**	**64,815**	**64,714**
Hindu	129,520	64,811	64,709
Animist	9	4	5
Bengal	112,281	56,072	56,209
C. P. and Berar	15,339	7,791	7,548
Elsewhere	1,909	952	957
KAPALI (*Hindu*)	**156,024**	**79,851**	**76,173**
Bengal	154,418	79,037	75,381
Elsewhere	1,606	814	792

Caste, Religion and Locality.	Persons.	Males.	Females.
1	2	3	4
KAPOL (KAPOLA) (*Hindu*)	**16,772**	**8,739**	**8,033**
Bombay	14,270	7,392	6,878
Baroda State	2,502	1,347	1,155
KAPPILIYAN ‡ (*Hindu*) (Madras)	**38,493**	**19,123**	**19,370**
KAPU (KAPEWAR)	**3,361,621**	**1,682,716**	**1,678,905**
Hindu	3,355,186	1,679,103	1,676,083
Animist	6,435	3,613	2,822
Burma	14,964	12,588	2,376
C. P. and Berar	18,489	9,131	9,358
Madras	2,678,925	1,329,624	1,349,301
Hyderabad State	648,254	330,902	317,352
Elsewhere	989	471	518
KARAIYAN (*Hindu*) (Madras)	**4,565**	**2,312**	**2,253**
KARAN (KARNAM)	**255,689**	**126,107**	**129,582**
Hindu	255,597	126,063	129,534
Animist	92	44	48
Bengal	53,106	27,001	26,105
Bihar and Orissa	147,511	71,286	76,225
C. P. and Berar	963	547	416
Madras	54,109	27,273	26,836
KAREN § (*Buddhist*) (Burma)	**1,102,695**	**549,758**	**552,937**
KARIMPALAN (*Hindu*) (Madras)	**2,898**	**1,362**	**1,536**
KARMALI (Bihar and Orissa)	**21,842**	**11,072**	**10,770**
Hindu	16,341	8,356	7,985
Animist	5,501	2,716	2,785
KARNABATTU (*Hindu*) (Madras)	**9,477**	**4,926**	**4,551**
KARUMPURATTAN (*Hindu*) (Madras)	**11,620**	**5,256**	**6,364**
KASAI (KASSAB, QASSAB)	**363,123**	**189,088**	**174,035**
Hindu	2,221	1,149	1,072
Sikh	2	1	1
Musalman	360,900	187,938	172,962
Bihar and Orissa	14,232	6,870	7,362
Bombay	8,958	4,462	4,496
N.-W. F. Province	8,721	4,559	4,162
Punjab	119,826	62,898	56,928
United Provinces	171,725	90,088	81,637
Rajputana Agency	29,400	15,006	14,394
Elsewhere	10,261	5,205	5,056
KASARWANI	**81,217**	**40,324**	**40,893**
Hindu	81,069	40,252	40,817
Sikh	107	49	58
Jain	41	23	18
Bihar and Orissa	27,951	13,937	14,014
C. P. and Berar	6,579	3,339	3,240
United Provinces	46,383	22,864	23,519
Elsewhere	304	184	120

* A forest-tribe.
† Astrologers and Herbalists.
‡ Anappan has been shown separately.
§ For sub-castes see Part II.

TABLE XIII.—Caste, Tribe, Race or Nationality. Part I.—

Caste, Religion and Locality.	Persons.	Males.	Females.
1	2	3	4
KASAUNDHAN (KASAUNDHA) (*Hindu*)	**96,919**	**49,861**	**47,058**
Bengal	23	9	14
C. P. and Berar	5,567	2,598	2,969
United Provinces	82,542	43,041	39,501
Central India Agency	8,787	4,213	4,574
KASBATI (*Musalman*) (Baroda State)	**6,323**	**3,454**	**2,869**
KASHMIRI	**206,893**	**111,104**	**95,789**
Hindu	554	307	247
Sikh	10	8	2
Musalman	206,329	110,789	95,540
Assam	21	15	6
N.-W. F. Province	28,631	15,198	13,433
Punjab	178,241	95,891	82,350
KASTHA (*Hindu*) (Bengal)	**20,750**	**10,580**	**10,170**
KATASAN (*Hindu*)	**1,366**	**642**	**724**
Madras	1,315	619	696
Travancore State	51	23	28
KATHI (*Hindu*)	**32,053**	**16,660**	**15,393**
Bombay	28,580	14,816	13,764
Baroda State	3,473	1,844	1,629
KATIYA	**41,997**	**20,653**	**21,344**
Hindu	41,852	20,572	21,280
Animist	145	81	64
C. P. and Berar	41,311	20,202	21,109
Central India Agency	686	451	235
KATKARI (KATHODIYA)	**91,841**	**45,803**	**46,038**
Hindu	91,447	45,610	45,837
Animist	394	193	201
Bombay	91,319	45,541	45,778
Baroda State	522	262	260
KATTU-MAHRATI (*Hindu*) (Madras)	**858**	**526**	**332**
KATTU-NAYAKKAN (*Hindu*) (Madras)	**2,475**	**1,311**	**1,164**
KAVANDAN (*Hindu*)	**12,096**	**5,943**	**6,153**
Madras	10,311	5,059	5,252
Elsewhere	1,785	884	901
KAVATI (*Hindu*) (Travancore State)	**5,946**	**3,055**	**2,891**
KAVUTIYAN (*Hindu*) (Madras)	**6,365**	**3,240**	**3,125**
KAWAR (KAUR)	**233,423**	**115,768**	**117,655**
Hindu	204,876	101,337	103,539
Animist	28,547	14,431	14,116
C. P. and Berar	229,412	113,563	115,849
Elsewhere	4,011	2,205	1,806
KAYASTHA (KAYASTH)	**2,178,390**	**1,130,439**	**1,047,951**
Hindu	2,176,711	1,129,652	1,047,059
Sikh	196	101	95
Jain	180	101	79
Buddhist	1	1	...
Musalman	1,302	584	718
Assam	81,967	44,377	37,590
Bengal	1,113,684	570,819	542,865
Bihar and Orissa	347,613	177,704	169,909
C. P. and Berar	33,584	17,580	16,004
Punjab	13,374	7,477	5,897
United Provinces	485,073	256,730	228,343
Central India Agency	71,392	38,434	32,958
Rajputana Agency	23,610	12,853	10,757
Elsewhere	8,093	4,465	3,628
KEHAL (Punjab)	**1,909**	**1,022**	**887**
Hindu	23	9	14
Musalman	1,886	1,013	873
KELASI (*Hindu*) (Madras)	**7,313**	**3,631**	**3,682**
KESAR (*Hindu*) (Central India Agency)	**14,469**	**7,433**	**7,036**
KEWAT (KEVUTO)	**1,215,616**	**596,256**	**619,360**
Hindu	1,215,504	596,197	619,307
Musalman	17	6	11
Animist	95	53	42
Assam	94,777	48,245	46,532
Bengal	22,066	11,998	10,068
Bihar and Orissa	420,506	203,450	217,056
C. P. and Berar	169,395	81,704	87,691
Madras	34,447	15,034	19,413
United Provinces	445,121	223,414	221,707
Central India Agency	29,304	12,411	16,893
KHADAL	**4,267**	**2,086**	**2,181**
Hindu	4,168	2,041	2,127
Animist	99	45	54
Assam	4,266	2,085	2,181
Bengal	1	1	...
KHADAYATA	**23,763**	**12,340**	**11,423**
Hindu	23,761	12,338	11,423
Jain	2	2	...
Bombay	20,986	10,801	10,185
Baroda State	2,777	1,539	1,238
KHAGI (*Hindu*) (United Provinces)	**49,249**	**26,107**	**23,142**
KHAIRA (KHOIRA)	**64,078**	**31,339**	**32,739**
Hindu	64,067	31,330	32,737
Animist	11	9	2
Bengal	41,435	20,302	21,133
Bihar and Orissa	20,738	10,169	10,569
Elsewhere	1,905	868	1,037

Distribution of Castes by Religion and Locality—*continued.*

Caste, Religion and Locality.	Persons.	Males.	Females.
1	2	3	4
KHAKAR (*Musalman*) (Mysore State)	**520**	**255**	**265**
KHALPA * (*Hindu*) (Bombay)	**9,358**	**4,918**	**4,440**
KHALSA (Punjab)	**16,610**	**10,481**	**6,129**
Hindu	30	21	9
Sikh	16,580	10,460	6,120
KHAMBU (JIMDAR)	**65,210**	**33,727**	**31,483**
Hindu	64,874	33,518	31,356
Buddhist	145	96	49
Animist	191	113	78
Bengal	45,101	22,831	22,270
Sikkim State	15,872	7,939	7,933
Elsewhere	4,237	2,957	1,280
KHAMI (*Animist*) (Bengal)	**1,461**	**747**	**714**
KHAMTI (Assam)	**1,868**	**1,014**	**854**
Hindu	2	2	...
Buddhist	1,850	996	854
Animist	16	16	...
KHANDAYAT	**807,106**	**395,381**	**411,725**
Hindu	807,105	395,380	411,725
Animist	1	1	...
Bengal	36,408	28,605	7,803
Bihar and Orissa	769,358	365,982	403,371
Elsewhere	1,345	794	551
KHANDELWAL	**82,414**	**43,663**	**38,751**
Hindu	71,870	38,081	33,789
Jain	10,544	5,582	4,962
United Provinces	5,739	3,017	2,722
Central India Agency	9,981	4,861	5,120
Rajputana Agency	63,064	33,918	29,146
Elsewhere	3,630	1,867	1,763
KHANGAR (KANGAR)	**83,098**	**42,606**	**40,492**
Hindu	82,167	42,120	40,047
Musalman	930	485	445
Animist	1	1	...
C. P. and Berar	12,815	6,422	6,393
United Provinces	28,704	14,419	14,285
Central India Agency	38,443	20,173	18,270
Elsewhere	3,136	1,592	1,544
KHANZADA (*Musalman*)	**30,665**	**15,897**	**14,768**
United Provinces	17,804	9,183	8,621
Rajputana Agency	9,198	4,712	4,486
Elsewhere	3,663	2,002	1,661
KHARIYA	**148,358**	**73,268**	**75,090**
Hindu	67,601	33,705	33,896
Animist	80,757	39,563	41,194
Assam	12,857	6,417	5,940
Bengal	16,105	8,353	7,752
Bihar and Orissa	105,472	51,909	53,563
C. P. and Berar	9,927	4,789	5,138
Central India Agency	4,497	1,800	2,697
KHAROL (*Hindu*)	**12,541**	**6,205**	**6,336**
Rajputana Agency	7,861	4,003	3,858
Elsewhere	4,680	2,202	2,478
KHARRAL (KARRAL)	**57,994**	**30,574**	**27,420**
Hindu	594	310	284
Sikh	344	150	194
Musalman	57,056	30,114	26,942
N.-W. F. Province	22,106	11,316	10,790
Punjab	35,886	19,256	16,630
Mysore State	2	2	...
KHARURA (KHODURA)	**14,956**	**7,301**	**7,655**
Hindu	14,952	7,298	7,654
Buddhist	4	3	1
Bihar and Orissa	10,871	5,243	5,628
Elsewhere	4,085	2,058	2,027
KHARVA (KHARVI)	**45,286**	**23,288**	**21,998**
Hindu	45,046	23,176	21,870
Musalman	240	112	128
Bombay	37,844	19,367	18,477
Elsewhere	7,442	3,921	3,521
KHARWAR (KHERWAR)	**147,231**	**72,742**	**74,489**
Hindu	145,146	71,689	73,457
Animist	2,085	1,053	1,032
Assam	7,234	3,855	3,379
Bengal	11,938	6,193	5,745
Bihar and Orissa	85,876	42,278	43,598
C. P. and Berar	19,651	9,529	10,122
United Provinces	15,458	7,370	8,088
Central India Agency	454	178	276
Rajputana Agency	6,620	3,339	3,281
KHAS	**21,485**	**11,910**	**9,575**
Hindu	21,384	11,853	9,531
Buddhist	10	7	3
Animist	91	50	41
Assam	2,014	1,281	733
Bengal	13,261	7,351	5,910
Sikkim State	6,210	3,278	2,932
KHASI (KHASIA)	**120,933**	**57,354**	**63,579**
Hindu	1,197	622	575
Buddhist	2	...	2
Animist	119,734	56,732	63,002
Assam	120,894	57,328	63,566
Bengal	39	26	13
KHATI	**250,596**	**128,329**	**122,267**
Hindu	250,530	128,276	122,254
Sikh	35	22	13
Musalman	31	31	...
Ajmer-Merwara	6,839	3,620	3,219
Central India Agency	107,428	54,785	52,643
Rajputana Agency	134,992	69,245	65,747
Elsewhere	1,337	679	658

* Chamar has been shown separately.

TABLE XIII.—Caste, Tribe, Race or Nationality. Part I.—

Caste, Religion and Locality.	Persons.	Males.	Females.
1	2	3	4
KHATIK (KATIKE)	**299,357**	**156,923**	**142,434**
Hindu	287,236	150,233	137,003
Sikh	44	24	20
Musalman	12,059	6,654	5,405
Animist	18	12	6
C. P. and Berar	12,596	6,315	6,281
Punjab	23,081	12,855	10,226
United Provinces	182,495	94,885	87,610
Central India Agency	20,566	11,547	9,019
Rajputana Agency	51,276	26,380	24,896
Elsewhere	9,343	4,941	4,402
KHATRI * (KHATTRI)	**599,159**	**331,914**	**267,245**
Hindu	498,627	276,993	221,634
Sikh	99,806	54,551	45,255
Jain	464	265	199
Musalman	262	105	157
Bengal	10,956	7,506	3,450
Bihar and Orissa	35,073	17,732	17,341
N.-W. F. Province	35,720	21,662	14,058
Punjab	432,727	238,707	194,020
United Provinces	44,489	23,520	20,969
Kashmir State	18,517	10,705	7,812
Rajputana Agency	10,410	5,441	4,969
Elsewhere	11,267	6,641	4,626
KHATRI † (KSHATRI, CHHATRI)	**119,584**	**63,477**	**56,107**
Hindu	112,116	59,628	52,488
Musalman	7,468	3,849	3,619
Bombay	106,930	56,882	50,048
Hyderabad State	9,133	4,683	4,450
Elsewhere	3,521	1,912	1,609
KHATTAR (*Musalman*) (Punjab)	**14,817**	**7,733**	**7,084**
KHATWE	**116,928**	**55,448**	**61,480**
Hindu	116,927	55,447	61,480
Animist	1	1	...
Bihar and Orissa	116,842	55,367	61,475
Elsewhere	86	81	5
KHAVAS (*Hindu*)	**31,424**	**15,417**	**16,007**
Bombay	31,173	15,286	15,887
Baroda State	251	131	120
KHAWASWAL (Rajputana Agency)	**1,203**	**727**	**476**
Hindu	1,201	725	476
Musalman	2	2	...
KHEN (KHYAN) (*Hindu*)	**23,162**	**11,601**	**11,561**
Assam	983	482	501
Bengal	22,179	11,119	11,060
KHETAURI (KHETARI) (*Hindu*)	**27,442**	**13,194**	**14,248**
Bengal	1	1	...
Bihar and Orissa	27,441	13,193	14,248
KHOJA	**127,215**	**66,240**	**60,975**
Hindu	7	5	2
Sikh	1	1	...
Musalman	127,207	66,234	60,973
Bombay	52,476	26,464	26,012
Punjab	62,869	33,335	29,534
Kashmir State	5,816	3,162	2,654
Elsewhere	6,054	3,279	2,775
KHOKHAR	**61,375**	**33,450**	**27,925**
Hindu	14	7	7
Sikh	3	3	...
Musalman	61,358	33,440	27,918
Punjab	59,956	32,666	27,290
Elsewhere	1,419	784	635
KHUMRA (Punjab)	**564**	**282**	**282**
Hindu	5	...	5
Sikh	4	4	...
Musalman	555	278	277
KHWAJA (*Musalman*) (Kashmir State)	**1,462**	**672**	**790**
KHYANG (Bengal)	**791**	**353**	**438**
Hindu	4	4	...
Buddhist	459	203	256
Animist	328	146	182
KIR (*Hindu*)	**35,729**	**18,474**	**17,255**
Ajmer-Merwara	974	497	477
C. P. and Berar	6,711	3,526	3,185
Central India Agency	6,370	3,214	3,156
Rajputana Agency	21,674	11,237	10,437
KIRAR	**151,452**	**78,473**	**72,979**
Hindu	148,413	76,930	71,483
Animist	3,039	1,543	1,496
C. P. and Berar	47,793	24,036	23,757
United Provinces	1,933	1,240	693
Central India Agency	89,922	47,088	42,834
Rajputana Agency	11,804	6,109	5,695
KISAN ‡	**393,436**	**210,571**	**182,865**
Hindu	367,497	197,967	169,530
Musalman	13	10	3
Animist	25,926	12,594	13,332
Bengal	1,455	792	663
Bihar and Orissa	38,276	18,675	19,601
United Provinces	353,705	191,104	162,601
KOCH §	**370,490**	**188,226**	**182,264**
Hindu	367,722	186,783	180,939
Jain	3	3	...
Animist	2,765	1,440	1,325
Assam	242,054	123,187	118,867
Bengal	125,046	63,315	61,731
Bihar and Orissa	3,390	1,724	1,666

* Kshatriya has been shown separately. See also next entry.
† They are mostly weavers.
‡ Nagesiya has been shown separately.
§ Rajbansi has been shown separately.

Distribution of Castes by Religion and Locality—*continued.*

Caste, Religion and Locality.	Persons.	Males.	Females.
1	2	3	4
KODAGA (*Hindu*)	**39,232**	**19,729**	**19,503**
Coorg	39,228	19,726	19,502
Madras	4	3	1
KOIRI (KOERI)	**1,766,796**	**888,698**	**878,098**
Hindu	1,766,035	888,669	877,366
Jain	3	3	...
Musalman	726	16	710
Animist	32	10	22
Assam	14,000	8,064	5,936
Bengal	25,814	19,902	5,912
Bihar and Orissa	1,280,655	633,680	646,975
United Provinces	446,322	227,049	219,273
Sikkim State	5	3	2
KOKNA (KOKANA)	**79,129**	**40,338**	**38,791**
Hindu	74,584	38,100	36,484
Animist	4,545	2,238	2,307
Bombay	72,678	37,123	35,555
Baroda State	6,451	3,215	3,236
KOL	**344,790**	**167,650**	**177,140**
Hindu	314,687	153,019	161,668
Animist	30,103	14,631	15,472
Assam	3,898	1,895	2,003
C. P. and Berar.	82,598	40,857	41,741
United Provinces	65,647	32,291	33,356
Central India Agency	192,647	92,607	100,040
KOLAM (C. P. and Berar)	**24,976**	**12,331**	**12,645**
Hindu	8,359	4,174	4,185
Animist	16,617	8,157	8,460
KOLAYAN (*Hindu*)	**22,241**	**10,755**	**11,486**
Coorg	290	248	42
Madras	21,951	10,507	11,444
KOLGHA	**6,541**	**3,223**	**3,318**
Hindu	5,874	2,891	2,983
Animist	667	332	335
Bombay	5,849	2,875	2,974
Baroda State	692	348	344
KOLHATI (*Hindu*) (Hyderabad State)	**1,143**	**520**	**623**
KOLI (KOHLI, KULI, DAGI)	**3,171,978**	**1,636,616**	**1,535,362**
Hindu	3,169,404	1,635,271	1,534,133
Sikh	2,193	1,153	1,040
Jain	7	6	1
Buddhist	141	67	74
Musalman	204	107	97
Animist	29	12	17
Ajmer-Merwara	6,565	3,480	3,085
Bombay	2,006,121	1,040,310	965,811
C. P. and Berar	61,775	31,039	30,736
Punjab	175,014	90,503	84,511
Baroda State	370,953	194,754	176,199
Central India Agency	173,645	84,956	88,689
Hyderabad State	266,840	134,432	132,408
Rajputana Agency	104,055	53,502	50,553
Elsewhere	7,010	3,640	3,370
KOLIYAN (*Hindu*) (Madras)	**1,081**	**551**	**530**
KOLTA	**159,821**	**79,482**	**80,339**
Hindu	159,756	79,455	80,301
Animist	65	27	38
Bihar and Orissa	123,526	61,407	62,119
C. P. and Berar	36,295	18,075	18,220
KOMARPAIK (*Hindu*) (Bombay)	**10,059**	**4,876**	**5,183**
KOMATI (KOMTI)	**765,535**	**387,206**	**378,329**
Hindu	765,531	387,202	378,329
Musalman	1	1	...
Animist	3	3	...
Bombay	21,865	12,003	9,862
C. P. and Berar	10,766	5,396	5,370
Madras	498,295	250,043	248,252
Hyderabad State	223,380	114,121	109,259
Mysore State	9,813	5,042	4,771
Elsewhere	1,416	601	815
KONAI (*Hindu*)	**9,428**	**4,746**	**4,682**
Assam	12	8	4
Bengal	9,416	4,738	4,678
KONDA DORA (Madras)	**89,775**	**44,932**	**44,843**
Hindu	75,647	37,139	38,508
Animist	14,128	7,793	6,335
KONDRA (*Hindu*) (Madras)	**8,543**	**3,758**	**4,785**
KONKANI	**12,557**	**6,562**	**5,995**
Hindu	12,402	6,441	5,961
Musalman	155	121	34
Travancore State	10,219	5,356	4,863
Elsewhere	2,338	1,206	1,132
KORA	**99,319**	**49,390**	**49,929**
Hindu	86,053	42,768	43,285
Animist	13,266	6,622	6,644
Assam	3,839	1,991	1,848
Bengal	46,497	23,087	23,410
Bihar and Orissa	48,983	24,312	24,671
KORAGA (*Hindu*) (Madras)	**4,391**	**2,006**	**2,385**
KORI	**918,820**	**472,535**	**446,285**
Hindu	917,633	471,901	445,732
Sikh	25	19	6
Musalman	1,162	615	547
C. P. and Berar	39,628	20,397	19,231
Punjab	18,050	11,578	6,472
United Provinces	860,434	440,144	420,290
Elsewhere	708	416	292

TABLE XIII.—Caste, Tribe, Race or Nationality. Part I.—

Caste, Religion and Locality.	Persons.	Males.	Females.
1	2	3	4
KORKU	**177,734**	**86,919**	**90,815**
Hindu	104,555	50,925	53,630
Animist	73,179	35,994	37,185
C. P. and Berar	152,363	75,559	76,804
Central India Agency	25,371	11,360	14,011
KORWA	**52,799**	**26,631**	**26,168**
Hindu	15,380	7,680	7,700
Buddhist	1	1	...
Animist	37,418	18,950	18,468
Bihar and Orissa	14,231	7,123	7,108
C. P. and Berar	34,000	17,164	16,836
Elsewhere	4,568	2,344	2,224
KOSHTA * (KOSHTI)	**163,822**	**81,902**	**81,920**
Hindu	163,752	81,870	81,882
Musalman	5	5	...
Animist	65	27	38
Bihar and Orissa	6,974	3,521	3,453
C. P. and Berar	154,599	77,288	77,311
Elsewhere	2,249	1,093	1,156
KOTA (*Hindu*) (Madras)	**1,163**	**547**	**616**
KOTAL (KOTWAL)	**27,664**	**14,817**	**12,847**
Hindu	27,138	14,562	12,576
Jain	523	254	269
Animist	3	1	2
Assam	55	26	29
Central India Agency	27,609	14,791	12,818
KOTARI (*Hindu*) (Madras)	**1,497**	**723**	**774**
KOTEGARA (*Hindu*)	**11,690**	**5,750**	**5,940**
Coorg	68	37	31
Madras	11,622	5,713	5,909
KOTTIYA (Madras)	**19,801**	**10,038**	**9,763**
Hindu	11,692	6,025	5,667
Animist	8,109	4,013	4,096
KOTWALIYA (Baroda State)	**1,658**	**798**	**860**
Hindu	583	277	306
Animist	1,075	521	554
KOYI	**203,763**	**101,899**	**101,864**
Hindu	52,755	26,157	26,598
Animist	151,008	75,742	75,266
Madras	79,422	39,316	40,106
Hyderabad State	124,341	62,583	61,758
KRISHNANVAKA (*Hindu*) (Travancore State)	**10,429**	**5,309**	**5,120**

Caste, Religion and Locality	Persons.	Males.	Females.
1	2	3	4
KSHATRIYA † (KSHATTRIYA)	**468,456**	**235,479**	**232,977**
Hindu	468,170	235,312	232,858
Sikh	130	89	41
Buddhist	4	2	2
Animist	152	76	76
Assam	250,541	124,764	125,777
Bengal	16,419	8,472	7,947
Madras	158,521	80,372	78,149
Mysore State	37,927	19,294	18,633
Elsewhere	5,048	2,577	2,471
KUCHRIYA (*Hindu*) (Bombay)	**4,037**	**1,771**	**2,266**
KUDALE (*Hindu*) (Bombay)	**10,927**	**5,338**	**5,589**
KUDIYA	**4,661**	**2,311**	**2,350**
Hindu	4,660	2,310	2,350
Animist	1	1	...
Coorg	541	258	283
Madras	4,120	2,053	2,067
KUDUB (*Hindu*) (Madras)	**10,366**	**5,183**	**5,183**
KUDUMI CHETTI (*Hindu*)	**20,578**	**10,863**	**9,715**
Cochin State	12,371	6,500	5,871
Travancore State	8,207	4,363	3,844
KUDUMO (*Hindu*)	**22,792**	**11,309**	**11,483**
Madras	22,772	11,300	11,472
Travancore State	20	9	11
KUKI ‡	**88,370**	**43,855**	**44,515**
Hindu	8,922	4,459	4,463
Buddhist	178	94	84
Animist	79,270	39,302	39,968
Assam	77,196	38,252	38,944
Bengal	11,174	5,603	5,571
KULU (*Musalman*)	**78,352**	**40,184**	**38,168**
Bengal	74,296	38,217	36,079
Bihar and Orissa	4,056	1,967	2,089
KUMAWAT (*Hindu*)	**5,219**	**2,578**	**2,641**
C. P. and Berar	2	2	...
Central India Agency	5,217	2,576	2,641

* In Bombay Koshti has been included in Devanga.
† In Assam and Bengal they are almost all Manipuris who on conversion to Hinduism claim to be classed as Kshatriyas. See also Khatri.
‡ For the details of individual tribes see Assam Table.

Distribution of Castes by Religion and Locality—*continued*.

Caste, Religion and Locality.	Persons.	Males.	Females.
1	2	3	4
KUMHAR (KUMBHAR, KUMMARA, KUMBARA)	**3,424,815**	**1,765,686**	**1,659,129**
Hindu	2,973,159	1,521,692	1,451,467
Sikh	25,022	13,948	11,074
Jain	15	10	5
Musalman	426,185	229,816	196,369
Animist	434	220	214
Ajmer-Merwara	14,120	7,218	6,902
Assam	27,913	14,428	13,485
Bengal	294,545	151,617	142,928
Bihar and Orissa	513,327	256,262	257,065
Bombay	254,542	128,471	126,071
C. P. and Berar	118,520	60,054	58,466
Madras	190,505	95,409	95,096
N.-W. F. Province	22,664	11,705	10,959
Punjab	550,450	299,738	250,712
United Provinces	726,361	374,504	351,857
Baroda State	43,733	22,233	21,500
Central India Agency	145,274	74,442	70,832
Hyderabad State	151,986	77,980	74,006
Kashmir State	18,958	10,154	8,804
Mysore State	41,810	21,324	20,486
Rajputana Agency	309,234	159,676	149,558
Elsewhere	873	471	402
KUNBI (KANBI,* KULMI)	**4,512,737**	**2,273,980**	**2,238,757**
Hindu	4,511,261	2,273,191	2,238,070
Jain	1,470	784	686
Animist	6	5	1
Bombay	2,489,230	1,249,016	1,240,214
C. P. and Berar	1,356,734	682,737	673,997
Baroda State	402,657	212,799	189,858
Central India Agency	215,359	104,235	111,124
Rajputana Agency	48,202	24,910	23,292
Elsewhere	555	283	272
KUNDRA (*Hindu*) (Bihar and Orissa)	**824**	**408**	**416**
KUNJRA	**279,257**	**136,328**	**142,929**
Hindu	893	512	381
Musalman	278,364	135,816	142,548
Bihar and Orissa	188,610	89,186	99,424
United Provinces	73,606	37,984	35,622
Elsewhere	17,041	9,158	7,883
KUNNAVAN (*Hindu*) (Madras)	**4,351**	**2,127**	**2,224**
KURAMWAR (*Hindu*) (C. P. and Berar)	**3,792**	**1,890**	**1,902**
KURAVAN (KORAVA, KORACHA, KORAMA)	**224,211**	**110,807**	**113,404**
Hindu	203,347	100,328	103,019
Animist	20,864	10,479	10,385
Bombay	23,254	12,187	11,067
Madras	110,157	53,877	56,280
Mysore State	26,988	13,568	13,420
Travancore State	62,974	30,766	32,208
Elsewhere	838	409	429
KURIC'CHAN (*Hindu*) (Madras)	**9,722**	**4,917**	**4,805**
KURMI	**3,735,651**	**1,919,716**	**1,815,935**
Hindu	3,734,837	1,919,259	1,815,578
Sikh	6	5	1
Musalman	335	205	130
Animist	473	247	226
Assam	24,520	14,296	10,224
Bengal	176,779	106,108	70,671
Bihar and Orissa	1,312,832	651,097	661,735
C. P. and Berar	302,588	150,109	152,479
United Provinces	1,890,371	982,497	907,874
Hyderabad State	23,078	11,819	11,259
Elsewhere	5,483	3,790	1,693
KURNI (KARNI) (*Hindu*)	**11,418**	**9,243**	**2,175**
Madras	9,644	8,351	1,293
Elsewhere	1,774	892	882
KURUKKAL (*Hindu*)	**1,632**	**830**	**802**
Cochin State	258	119	139
Travancore State	1,374	711	663
KURUMBAN (KURUBA, KURMA)	**947,619**	**480,792**	**466,827**
Hindu	935,238	474,375	460,863
Animist	12,381	6,417	5,964
Coorg	7,394	3,905	3,489
Madras	385,686	196,474	189,212
Cochin State	9	7	2
Hyderabad State	144,688	75,144	69,544
Mysore State	409,842	205,262	204,580
KUSAVAN (*Hindu*)	**159,991**	**78,754**	**81,237**
Madras	153,127	75,222	77,905
Elsewhere	6,864	3,532	3,332
KUSIARI (*Hindu*) (Assam)	**1,999**	**991**	**1,008**
KUTTADI (*Hindu*)	**4,182**	**2,037**	**2,145**
Madras	4,175	2,035	2,140
Travancore State	7	2	5
LABBAI (*Musalman*)	**424,724**	**197,629**	**227,095**
Coorg	332	225	107
Madras	401,703	184,923	216,780
Mysore State	7,995	5,200	2,795
Travancore State	14,694	7,281	7,413
LAD (LOD)	**35,572**	**17,995**	**17,577**
Hindu	32,970	16,776	16,194
Jain	2,602	1,219	1,383
Bombay	11,781	6,402	5,379
C. P. and Berar	5,383	2,691	2,692
Baroda State	8,500	4,173	4,327
Hyderabad State	8,776	4,175	4,601
Elsewhere	1,132	554	578
LAHERI (LAKHERA)	**24,345**	**12,787**	**11,558**
Hindu	23,438	12,295	11,143
Jain	1	1	..
Musalman	906	491	415
Central India Agency	9,500	5,164	4,336
Rajputana Agency	10,752	5,539	5,213
Elsewhere	4,093	2,084	2,009

* For sub-castes in Baroda see Part II.

TABLE XIII.—Caste, Tribe, Race or Nationality. Part I.—

Caste, Religion and Locality.	Persons.	Males.	Females.
1	2	3	4
LAKHER (*Animist*) (Assam)	**3,647**	**1,756**	**1,891**
LALBEGI	**4,065**	**2,270**	**1,795**
Hindu	3,160	1,770	1,390
Sikh	2	2	…
Musalman	898	496	402
Animist	5	2	3
C. P. and Berar	2,573	1,418	1,155
Elsewhere	1,492	852	640
LALUNG (Assam)	**39,219**	**19,222**	**19,997**
Hindu	492	259	233
Buddhist	4	4	…
Animist	38,723	18,959	19,764
LASI * (PANJ RAJ) (*Musalman*) (Baluchistan)	**34,980**	**18,573**	**16,407**
LEPCHA	**18,881**	**9,446**	**9,435**
Hindu	89	47	42
Buddhist	18,789	9,397	9,392
Animist	3	2	1
Assam	7	7	…
Bengal	9,843	4,763	5,080
Sikkim State	9,031	4,676	4,355
LILARI (NILARI, NIRALI)	**31,656**	**17,091**	**14,565**
Hindu	564	374	190
Sikh	11	7	4
Musalman	31,081	16,710	14,371
Punjab	31,540	17,007	14,533
Elsewhere	116	84	32
LIMBU	**24,363**	**15,426**	**8,937**
Hindu	23,750	15,015	8,735
Buddhist	395	269	126
Animist	218	142	76
Bengal	16,878	9,183	7,695
Elsewhere	7,485	6,243	1,242
LINGAYAT	**2,976,293**	**1,504,073**	**1,472,220**
Hindu	2,976,270	1,504,061	1,472,209
Jain	23	12	11
Bombay	1,339,248	683,472	655,776
C. P. and Berar	7,793	4,204	3,589
Coorg	7,558	3,697	3,861
Madras	134,592	66,375	68,217
Hyderabad State	757,611	381,201	376,410
Mysore State	729,431	365,091	364,340
Elsewhere	60	33	27
LODA (*Hindu*)	**21,656**	**10,927**	**10,729**
Central India Agency	13,943	6,822	7,121
Rajputana Agency	7,713	4,105	3,608
LODHA (LODHI)	**1,732,230**	**904,321**	**827,909**
Hindu	1,731,326	903,829	827,497
Sikh	6	3	3
Buddhist	6	6	…
Musalman	412	227	185
Animist	480	256	224
Bengal	7,403	3,793	3,610
C. P. and Berar	313,900	155,922	157,978
Punjab	9,413	5,159	4,254
United Provinces	1,114,408	588,156	526,252
Central India Agency	228,235	120,311	107,924
Rajputana Agency	47,013	24,526	22,487
Elsewhere	11,858	6,454	5,404
LOHAIT KURI	**1,701**	**910**	**791**
Hindu	1,696	905	791
Jain	5	5	…
Assam	598	377	221
Bengal	1,103	533	570
LOHANA (LUHANA) (*Hindu*)	**605,482**	**322,474**	**283,008**
Bombay	593,584	316,426	277,158
Baroda State	11,588	5,959	5,629
Elsewhere	310	89	221
LOHAR † (LUHAR, LOHARA)	**2,070,372**	**1,066,887**	**1,003,485**
Hindu	1,646,697	840,402	806,295
Sikh	35,414	19,578	15,836
Jain	19	14	5
Buddhist	405	205	200
Musalman	361,052	193,435	167,617
Animist	26,785	13,253	13,532
Assam	12,191	6,390	5,801
Bengal	48,522	25,101	23,421
Bihar and Orissa	479,817	235,129	244,688
Bombay	121,126	62,875	58,251
C. P. and Berar	181,590	91,183	90,407
Madras	8,038	3,788	4,250
N.-W. F. Province	28,589	15,331	13,258
Punjab	323,477	176,191	147,286
United Provinces	589,008	308,138	280,870
Baroda State	19,258	9,494	9,764
Central India Agency	96,989	49,835	47,154
Hyderabad State	47,844	24,828	23,016
Kashmir State	28,884	15,101	13,783
Rajputana Agency	80,822	41,247	39,575
Elsewhere	4,217	2,256	1,961
LOI (*Hindu*) (Assam)	**18,170**	**8,880**	**9,290**
LOK (*Hindu*) (Rajputana Agency)	**2,027**	**1,085**	**942**
LON (*Musalman*) (Kashmir State)	**56,931**	**29,718**	**27,213**
LONARI ‡ (*Hindu*)	**10,218**	**5,105**	**5,113**
Bombay	7,728	3,877	3,851
Elsewhere	2,490	1,228	1,262
LORI (*Musalman*) (Baluchistan)	**10,936**	**5,912**	**5,024**
LUSHAI §	**80,484**	**36,782**	**43,702**
Hindu	93	58	35
Animist	80,391	36,724	3,667
Assam	80,425	36,758	43,667-
Bengal	59	24	35
LYNG-NGAM (*Animist*) (Assam)	**1,993**	**1,003**	**990**

* Includes Sheikh in Baluchistan.
† Kamar has been shown separately, except in Bihar and Orissa.
‡ Nuniya has been shown separately.
§ For the details of individual tribes see Assam Table.

Distribution of Castes by Religion and Locality—*continued.*

Caste, Religion and Locality.	Persons.	Males.	Females.
1	2	3	4
MACHHI *	**325,814**	**175,037**	**150,777**
Hindu	41,856	20,174	21,682
Musalman	283,958	154,863	129,095
Bombay	39,300	18,696	20,604
Punjab	279,666	152,562	127,104
Elsewhere	6,848	3,779	3,069
MADIGA † **(MADGI)**	**1,931,017**	**977,514**	**953,503**
Hindu	1,931,007	977,508	953,499
Animist	10	6	4
C. P. and Berar	8,574	4,243	4,331
Madras	807,986	406,089	401,897
Hyderabad State	804,393	410,474	393,919
Mysore State	308,083	155,585	152,498
Elsewhere	1,981	1,123	858
MAGH	**128,545**	**63,273**	**65,272**
Hindu	645	476	169
Sikh	52	19	33
Buddhist	127,599	62,647	64,952
Musalman	26	16	10
Animist	223	115	108
Bengal	127,949	62,914	65,035
Elsewhere	596	359	237
MAHAR ‡ **(MEHRA)**	**3,342,680**	**1,666,578**	**1,676,102**
Hindu	3,342,105	1,666,276	1,675,829
Jain	32	20	12
Musalman	2	...	2
Animist	541	282	259
Bihar and Orissa	7,982	3,935	4,047
Bombay	1,470,992	735,841	735,151
C. P. and Berar	1,165,177	575,449	589,728
Central India Agency	6,280	3,056	3,224
Hyderabad State	689,543	346,974	342,569
Elsewhere	2,706	1,323	1,383
MAHARANA (*Hindu*) (Bihar and Orissa)	**1,376**	**695**	**681**
MAHESRI	**149,411**	**74,862**	**74,549**
Hindu	146,870	73,315	73,555
Sikh	1	1	...
Jain	2,532	1,538	994
Musalman	8	8	...
Ajmer-Merwara	5,414	2,924	2,490
C. P. and Berar	14,107	7,443	6,664
United Provinces	9,712	5,177	4,535
Central India Agency	23,150	11,056	12,094
Rajputana Agency	91,106	44,597	46,509
Elsewhere	5,922	3,665	2,257
MAHIFAROSH (*Musalman*)	**5,675**	**2,905**	**2,770**
Assam	2	2	...
Bengal	5,673	2,903	2,770
MAHIMAL (*Musalman*)	**78,090**	**39,484**	**38,606**
Assam	77,379	39,102	38,277
Bengal	711	382	329
MAHLI	**88,704**	**44,504**	**44,200**
Hindu	73,250	36,993	36,257
Animist	15,454	7,511	7,943
Assam	8,274	4,321	3,953
Bengal	15,965	8,013	7,952
Bihar and Orissa	64,189	32,026	32,163
C. P. and Berar	276	144	132
MAHTAM (Punjab)	**81,811**	**43,602**	**38,209**
Hindu	17,518	9,372	8,146
Sikh	50,056	26,384	23,672
Musalman	14,237	7,846	6,391
MAHTON (Punjab)	**6,841**	**3,861**	**2,980**
Hindu	6,292	3,570	2,722
Sikh	549	291	258
MAHURI	**25,239**	**11,193**	**14,046**
Hindu	25,238	11,192	14,046
Jain	1	1	...
Bihar and Orissa	25,066	11,082	13,984
Elsewhere	173	111	62
MAJHWAR (C. P. and Berar)	**14,216**	**7,196**	**7,014**
Hindu	9,849	4,969	4,880
Animist	4,361	2,227	2,134
MAJI (*Hindu*) (Central India Agency)	**20,611**	**13,372**	**7,239**
MAJJULU (*Hindu*) (Madras)	**10,643**	**4,761**	**5,882**
MAKRANI (*Musalman*)	**20,353**	**11,067**	**9,286**
Baluchistan	9,030	4,703	4,327
Bombay	10,420	5,904	4,516
Elsewhere	903	460	443
MAL (MALA)	**2,135,329**	**1,071,050**	**1,064,279**
Hindu	2,134,934	1,070,859	1,064,075
Musalman	1	...	1
Animist	394	191	203
Assam	6,695	3,766	2,929
Bengal	108,163	54,117	54,046
Bihar and Orissa	24,406	12,018	12,388
Burma	21,248	18,106	3,142
C. P. and Berar	15,459	7,980	7,479
Madras	1,511,312	747,652	763,660
Hyderabad State	448,046	227,411	220,635
MALAIMAN (*Hindu*) (Madras)	**57,034**	**27,478**	**29,556**
MALAK (*Musalman*) (Kashmir State)	**8,897**	**4,622**	**4,275**
MALANKURAVAN (*Animist*) (Travancore State)	**997**	**514**	**483**
MALASAR (MALA-URALI, MALA-ULLATAN)	**4,817**	**2,553**	**2,264**
Hindu	3,303	1,809	1,494
Animist	1,514	744	770
Madras	4,199	2,250	1,949
Elsewhere	618	303	315

* See also Bhisti, Jhinwar and Kahar. † See also Megh. ‡ Includes Dhed and Holiya in Bombay.

TABLE XIII.—Caste, Tribe, Race or Nationality. Part I.—

Caste, Religion and Locality.	Persons.	Males.	Females.
1	2	3	4
MALAVA (*Hindu*) (Madras)	2,766	1,322	1,444
MALAVETAN (*Animist*) (Travancore State)	5,051	2,584	2,467
MALAY (*Musalman*) (Burma)	4,239	2,265	1,974
MALAYALI (*Hindu*)	64,973	32,610	32,363
Madras	63,487	31,395	32,092
Elsewhere	1,486	1,215	271
MALAYAN (MALAYARAYAN)	14,675	7,364	7,311
Hindu	9,602	4,790	4,812
Animist	5,073	2,574	2,499
Madras	9,602	4,790	4,812
Elsewhere	5,073	2,574	2,499
MALERU (Mysore State)	1,757	771	986
Hindu	1,756	770	986
Animist	1	1	...
MALI (MALIAR, MALAKAR)	2,035,843	1,041,531	994,312
Hindu	1,916,491	978,562	937,929
Sikh	1,124	640	484
Jain	113	49	64
Musalman	117,141	61,884	55,257
Animist	974	396	578
Ajmer-Merwara	14,340	7,499	6,841
Assam	14,231	7,450	6,781
Bengal	38,858	20,414	18,444
Bihar and Orissa	139,619	69,643	69,976
Bombay	302,205	153,066	149,139
C. P. and Berar	572,864	284,397	288,467
Madras	34,337	16,776	17,561
N.-W. F. Province	19,950	10,412	9,538
Punjab	193,579	105,104	88,475
United Provinces	186,593	98,714	87,879
Central India Agency	72,462	37,403	35,059
Hyderabad State	107,097	54,230	52,867
Rajputana Agency	336,876	174,966	161,910
Elsewhere	2,829	1,457	1,372
MALIK (MALEK) (*Musalman*)	53,681	27,736	25,945
Baroda State	7,519	3,972	3,547
Kashmir State	46,162	23,764	22,398
MALLAH	738,780	360,355	378,425
Hindu	658,918	317,090	341,828
Sikh	12	4	8
Musalman	79,756	43,211	36,545
Animist	94	50	44
Bengal	27,472	19,882	7,590
Bihar and Orissa	362,727	169,924	192,803
Punjab	77,837	41,693	36,144
United Provinces	248,656	117,196	131,460
Central India Agency	7,928	3,152	4,776
Elsewhere	14,160	8,508	5,652
MALLIK (*Musalman*)	38,286	18,711	19,575
Assam	40	21	19
Bengal	17,510	9,212	8,298
Bihar and Orissa	20,736	9,478	11,258
MALO	268,014	138,444	129,570
Hindu	268,008	138,439	129,569
Jain	2	2	...
Animist	4	3	1
Assam	20,357	11,295	9,062
Bengal	247,200	126,890	120,310
Bihar and Orissa	457	259	198
MAL PAHARIA *	54,069	27,198	26,871
Hindu	48,272	24,238	24,034
Animist	5,797	2,960	2,837
Assam	3,533	1,823	1,710
Bengal	11,739	6,185	5,554
Bihar and Orissa	38,797	19,190	19,607
MANA (C. P. and Berar)	49,037	23,835	25,202
Hindu	49,014	23,820	25,194
Animist	23	15	8
MANBHAO	6,694	3,579	3,115
Hindu	6,679	3,570	3,109
Jain	15	9	6
C. P. and Berar	3,951	2,095	1,856
Hyderabad State	2,743	1,484	1,259
MANG (MADIG)	700,069	347,759	352,310
Hindu	700,028	347,738	352,290
Jain	1	...	1
Animist	40	21	19
Bombay	274,037	134,852	139,185
C. P. and Berar	83,660	41,106	42,554
Hyderabad State	340,959	171,045	169,914
Elsewhere	1,413	756	657
MANGALA (*Hindu*)	260,514	129,985	130,529
Madras	184,000	90,231	93,769
Hyderabad State	76,514	39,754	36,760
MANGAR	32,790	18,712	14,078
Hindu	31,999	18,254	13,745
Buddhist	37	26	11
Animist	754	432	322
Assam	7,201	4,716	2,485
Bengal	21,533	11,745	9,788
Elsewhere	4,056	2,251	1,805
MANGELA (*Hindu*) (Bombay)	13,867	6,896	6,971
MANGRIK (Kashmir State)	98,508	48,558	49,950
Buddhist	35,616	17,691	17,925
Musalman	62,892	30,867	32,025
MANIHAR (MANIAR)	94,534	49,940	44,594
Hindu	4,939	2,394	2,545
Musalman	89,595	47,546	42,049
Punjab	7,276	3,949	3,327
United Provinces	75,488	40,043	35,445
Rajputana Agency	8,978	4,672	4,306
Elsewhere	2,792	1,276	1,516

* See also Sauria Paharia.

Distribution of Castes by Religion and Locality—*continued.*

Caste, Religion and Locality.	Persons.	Males.	Females.
1	2	3	4
MANIPURI	**4,183**	**2,037**	**2,146**
Hindu	3,353	1,626	1,727
Musalman	830	411	419
Assam	830	411	419
Burma	3,353	1,626	1,727
MANJHI	**4,933**	**2,713**	**2,220**
Hindu	4,558	2,513	2,045
Sikh	7	6	1
Buddhist	7	5	2
Animist	361	189	172
Assam	2,662	1,425	1,237
Bengal	2,271	1,288	983
MANKAR (*Hindu*) (Central India Agency)	**9,065**	**4,339**	**4,726**
MANNEWAR (C. P. and Berar)	**1,601**	**825**	**776**
Hindu	1,559	798	761
Animist	42	27	15
MAPPILLA (*Musalman*)	**1,046,834**	**524,121**	**522,713**
Coorg	7,196	5,032	2,164
Madras	1,032,757	514,555	518,202
Elsewhere	6,881	4,534	2,347
MARAKKAN (*Hindu*) (Travancore State)	**14,604**	**7,274**	**7,330**
MARAKKAYAR (*Musalman*) (Madras)	**2,461**	**1,245**	**1,216**
MARATHA (MAHRATTA, MAHRATI)	**5,087,436**	**2,582,346**	**2,505,090**
Hindu	5,087,430	2,582,342	2,505,088
Jain	6	4	2
Bombay	3,279,496	1,672,212	1,607,284
C. P. and Berar	93,901	46,716	47,185
Madras	79,247	39,078	40,169
Baroda State	14,785	8,047	6,738
Central India Agency	28,008	14,821	13,187
Hyderabad State	1,538,874	772,878	765,996
Mysore State	45,898	23,909	21,989
Elsewhere	7,227	4,685	2,542
MARAVAN (*Hindu*)	**375,042**	**182,976**	**192,066**
Madras	364,762	177,785	186,977
Mysore State	15	15	...
Travancore State	10,265	5,176	5,089
MARAYAN (MARAN) (*Hindu*)	**43,873**	**21,550**	**22,323**
Madras	14,555	6,889	7,666
Travancore State	29,318	14,661	14,657
MARIJA (Punjab)	**1,992**	**1,047**	**945**
Hindu	1,962	1,034	928
Musalman	30	13	17
MARTA (Coorg)	**1,476**	**1,438**	**38**
Hindu	1,412	1,375	37
Animist	64	63	1
MARU (*Hindu*) (Central India Agency)	**2,903**	**1,426**	**1,477**
MARWARI (MARWADI)	**45,412**	**24,983**	**20,429**
Hindu	44,968	24,606	20,362
Jain	444	377	67
Hyderabad State	38,264	20,372	17,892
Elsewhere	7,148	4,611	2,537
MASALCHI (*Musalman*) (Bengal)	**1,239**	**678**	**561**
MATAK (Assam)	**9,246**	**5,208**	**4,038**
Hindu	9,242	5,206	4,036
Buddhist	4	2	2
MAULIK (NAIYA)	**4,307**	**2,235**	**2,072**
Hindu	4,291	2,223	2,068
Animist	16	12	4
Assam	4,227	2,193	2,034
Bengal	80	42	38
MAVILAN (*Hindu*)	**2,536**	**1,373**	**1,163**
Coorg	19	10	9
Madras	2,517	1,363	1,154
MAWAR (MAHAWAR) (*Hindu*) (Rajputana Agency)	**9,753**	**5,052**	**4,701**
MAWASI (MAVCHI)	**6,230**	**3,106**	**3,124**
Hindu	6,221	3,099	3,122
Animist	9	7	2
Baroda State	989	537	452
Central India Agency	5,241	2,569	2,672
MAYRA	**151,889**	**79,592**	**72,297**
Hindu	151,861	79,576	72,285
Animist	28	16	12
Assam	2,186	1,033	1,153
Bengal	126,386	66,836	59,550
Bihar and Orissa	23,317	11,723	11,594
MAZHABI	**21,779**	**12,229**	**9,550**
Hindu	58	27	31
Sikh	21,699	12,180	9,519
Musalman	22	22	...
Punjab	21,691	12,192	9,499
Kashmir State	88	37	51
MECH	**115,056**	**57,896**	**57,160**
Hindu	77,472	38,775	38,697
Animist	37,584	19,121	18,463
Assam	94,606	47,177	47,429
Bengal	20,450	10,719	9,731
MEDARA (MEDA) (*Hindu*)	**27,818**	**14,041**	**13,777**
Coorg	529	273	256
Madras	20,511	10,291	10,220
Mysore State	6,778	3,477	3,301

TABLE XIII.—Caste, Tribe, Race or Nationality. Part I.—

Caste, Religion and Locality.	Persons.	Males.	Females.
1	2	3	4
MEGH * (MEGHWAL).	**174,218**	**92 033**	**82,185**
Hindu	173,318	91,564	81,754
Sikh	673	348	325
Musalman	227	121	106
Punjab	40,020	21,988	18,032
Kashmir State	75,409	39,331	36,078
Rajputana Agency	57,621	30,152	27,469
Elsewhere	1,168	562	606
MEHTAR †	**26,526**	**13,850**	**12,676**
Hindu	25,933	13,525	12,408
Musalman	569	309	260
Animist	24	16	8
Bengal	5,825	3,246	2,579
C. P. and Berar	13,012	6,642	6,370
Rajputana Agency	6,151	3,124	3,027
Elsewhere	1,538	838	700
MELAKKARAN (*Hindu*) (Madras)	**10,925**	**5,045**	**5,880**
MEMON	**114,529**	**54,014**	**60,515**
Hindu	130	97	33
Musalman	114,399	53,917	60,482
Bombay	97,283	44,874	52,409
Baroda State	13,540	6,431	7,109
Elsewhere	3,706	2,709	997
MEN (Punjab)	**24,173**	**12,881**	**11,292**
Hindu	31	25	6
Musalman	24,142	12,856	11,286
MENGHWAR (*Animist*) (Bombay)	**3,526**	**1,923**	**1,603**
MEO (MEWATI).	**403,868**	**213,154**	**190,714**
Hindu	37,820	19,735	18,085
Musalman	366,048	193,419	172,629
Bombay	26,228	13,520	12,708
Punjab	124,993	66,379	58,614
United Provinces	73,966	39,553	34,413
Central India Agency	12,786	6,243	6,543
Rajputana Agency	165,690	87,347	78,343
Elsewhere	205	112	93
MER	**44,135**	**23,002**	**21,133**
Hindu	44,052	22,962	21,090
Musalman	83	40	43
Ajmer-Merwara	21,803	11,634	10,169
Central India Agency	8,620	4,212	4,408
Rajputana Agency	13,712	7,156	6,556
MERAT GORAT (*Hindu*).	**2,051**	**1,316**	**735**
Ajmer-Merwara	2,025	1,300	725
Rajputana Agency	26	16	10
MERAT KATHAT (*Musalman*)	**19,876**	**10,914**	**8,962**
Ajmer-Merwara	17,626	9,651	7,975
Rajputana Agency	2,250	1,263	987

Caste, Religion and Locality.	Persons.	Males.	Females.
1	2	3	4
METTAN (*Musalman*) (Travancore State)	**66,864**	**33,768**	**33,096**
MEWADA (Baroda State).	**1,692**	**872**	**820**
Hindu	956	515	441
Jain	736	357	379
MHALI (C.P. and Berar).	**37,489**	**19,115**	**18,374**
Hindu	37,469	19,101	18,368
Jain	15	10	5
Musalman	3	2	1
Animist	2	2	...
MIKIR (Assam)	**105,077**	**53,642**	**51,435**
Hindu	736	385	351
Animist	104,341	53,257	51,084
MINA	**639,908**	**338,039**	**301,869**
Hindu	589,840	312,548	277,292
Sikh	1	1	...
Musalman	454	264	190
Animist	49,613	25,226	24,387
Central India Agency	74,636	38,127	36,509
Rajputana Agency	558,689	296,205	262,484
Elsewhere	6,583	3,707	2,876
MIR (*Musalman*)	**78,597**	**42,765**	**35,832**
Kashmir State	77,532	42,204	35,328
Elsewhere	1,065	561	504
MIRASI (MIRIASIN)	**270,664**	**144,592**	**126,072**
Hindu	2,783	1,519	1,214
Sikh	69	44	25
Buddhist	4	4	...
Musalman	267,858	143,025	124,833
N.-W. F. Province	11,790	6,134	5,656
Punjab	227,891	122,362	105,529
Kashmir State	7,699	4,097	3,602
Rajputana Agency	21,729	11,200	10,529
Elsewhere	1,555	799	756
MIRATWAL (MARETWAL) (*Hindu*)	**3,392**	**1,805**	**1,587**
Central India Agency	2,907	1,569	1,338
Rajputana Agency	485	236	249
MIRDHA.	**17,009**	**11,613**	**5,396**
Hindu	16,936	11,545	5 391
Musalman	73	68	5
Central India Agency	16,936	11,545	5,391
Elsewhere	73	68	5
MIRI (Assam)	**57,792**	**29,335**	**28,457**
Hindu	13,460	6,872	6,588
Animist	44,332	22,463	21,869
MIRSHIKARI ‡ (*Musalman*) (Assam)	**924**	**437**	**487**
MISHWANI (*Musalman*) (N.-W. F. Province)	**4,888**	**2,404**	**2,484**

* See also Madiga.

† See also Bhangi, Chuhra and Halalkhor.

‡ In Bengal included in Bediya.

DISTRIBUTION OF CASTES BY RELIGION AND LOCALITY—*continued*.

CASTE, RELIGION AND LOCALITY.	Persons.	Males.	Females.
1	2	3	4
MOCHI (MUCHI)	**1,018,366**	**548,181**	**470,185**
Hindu	561,777	299,997	261,780
Sikh	195	139	56
Musalman	456,120	247,891	208.229
Animist	274	154	120
Assam	13,697	7,839	5,868
Bengal	455,448	244,012	211,436
Bihar and Orissa	31,339	15,757	15,582
Madras	6,285	2,964	3,321
N.-W. F. Province	23,209	12,526	10,683
Punjab	419,378	228,688	190,690
United Provinces	8,869	4,920	3,949
Baroda State	8,954	4,737	4,217
Central India Agency	7,126	3,511	3,615
Hyderabad State	7,023	3,999	3,024
Kashmir State	14,694	7,644	7,050
Rajputana Agency	15,428	8,101	7,327
Elsewhere	6,916	3,493	3,423
MODH (MOD)	**30,414**	**15,254**	**15,160**
Hindu	30,183	15,140	15,043
Jain	231	114	117
Bombay	21,819	11,087	10,732
Elsewhere	8,595	4,167	4,428
MOGER	**43,097**	**20,151**	**22,946**
Hindu	3,949	1,975	1,974
Animist	39,148	18,176	20,972
Bombay	3,949	1,975	1,974
Madras	39,148	18,176	20,972
MOGHAL * (MUGHAL) (*Musalman*)	**358,022**	**192,579**	**165,443**
Bengal	14,627	8,158	6,469
Bihar and Orissa	7,073	3,422	3,651
Bombay	6,268	3,384	2,884
C. P. and Berar	9,045	4,640	4,405
Madras	18,628	9,702	8,926
N.-W. F. Province	14,865	8,269	6,596
Punjab	98,574	53,529	45,045
United Provinces	60,362	31,562	28,800
Central India Agency	18,468	9,973	8,495
Hyderabad State	33,411	17,685	15,726
Kashmir State	49,875	28,037	21,838
Mysore State	8,151	4,299	3,852
Rajputana Agency	14,121	7,469	6,652
Elsewhere	4,554	2,450	2,104
MOGHIYA	**15,511**	**8,138**	**7,373**
Hindu	15,440	8,092	7,348
Animist	71	46	25
Central India Agency	11,197	5,927	5,270
Rajputana Agency	4,314	2,211	2,103
MOILI (*Hindu*) (Madras)	**3,534**	**1,776**	**1,758**
MOKERI (*Musalman*) (Central India Agency)	**2,507**	**1,242**	**1,265**
MOLESALAM (*Musalman*)	**21,335**	**11,150**	**10,185**
Bombay	12,369	6,334	6,035
Baroda State	8,966	4,816	4,150
MOMNA † (*Musalman*)	**13,822**	**7,323**	**6,499**
Bombay	6,639	3,285	3,354
Baroda State	7,183	4,038	3,145
MONDI (*Hindu*) (Madras)	**1,930**	**820**	**1,110**
MORAN (*Hindu*) (Assam)	**1,405**	**805**	**600**
MORIYA (*Musalman*) (Assam)	**1,582**	**900**	**682**
MUDALI (*Hindu*) (Mysore State)	**17,896**	**9,369**	**8,527**
MUDUGAR (*Animist*) (Madras)	**1,210**	**603**	**607**
MUKHI (Assam)	**2,718**	**1,377**	**1,341**
Hindu	2,717	1,377	1,340
Animist	1	...	1
MUKKUVAN	**21,300**	**10,909**	**10,391**
Hindu	2,085	1,138	947
Animist	19,215	9,771	9,444
Madras	19,215	9,771	9,444
Elsewhere	2,085	1,138	947
MUKRI (*Hindu*) (Bombay)	**4,946**	**2,390**	**2,556**
MULI (Madras)	**5,243**	**2,719**	**2,524**
Hindu	4,666	2,372	2,294
Animist	577	347	230
MUNDA (MURHA)	**574,434**	**286,401**	**288,033**
Hindu	194,261	97,831	96,430
Buddhist	3	3	...
Animist	380,170	188,567	191,603
Assam	91,298	47,227	44,071
Bengal	67,252	35,217	32,035
Bihar and Orissa	410,140	201,087	209,353
C. P. and Berar	5,444	2,870	2,574
MUNI (*Hindu*) (Madras)	**1,623**	**743**	**880**
MUNNUR (*Hindu*) (Hyderabad State)	**228,354**	**115,120**	**113,234**
MUPPAN (*Hindu*) (Madras)	**7,958**	**3,878**	**4,080**
MURAO	**674,346**	**355,703**	**318,643**
Hindu	673,878	355,346	318,532
Sikh	173	100	73
Musalman	295	257	38
Bengal	3	3	...
United Provinces	674,313	355,700	318,643
MURIYARI	**6,221**	**3,254**	**2,967**
Hindu	6,129	3,211	2,918
Animist	92	43	49
Assam	1,027	555	472
Bengal	5,194	2,699	2,495
MURMI	**41,358**	**21,404**	**19,954**
Hindu	3,161	2,036	1,125
Buddhist	37,937	19,234	18,703
Animist	260	134	126
Bengal	30,900	15,851	15,049
Sikkim State	7,436	3,705	3,731
Elsewhere	3,022	1,848	1,174

* See also Turk.

† Momin has been included in Jolaha.

TABLE XIII.—Caste, Tribe, Race or Nationality. Part I.—

Caste, Religion and Locality.	Persons.	Males.	Females.
1	2	3	4
MURUNG (MRU)	**12,393**	**6,340**	**6,053**
Hindu	1,109	582	527
Buddhist	44	24	20
Animist	11,240	5,734	5,506
Assam	2	1	1
Bengal	12,391	6,339	6,052
MUSAHAR	**699,207**	**347,755**	**351,452**
Hindu	698,615	347,274	351,341
Musalman	411	365	46
Animist	181	116	65
Assam	14,284	7,555	6,729
Bengal	11,874	7,001	4,873
Bihar and Orissa	626,795	309,653	317,142
United Provinces	46,254	23,546	22,708
MUSSAD (*Hindu*) (Madras)	**1,121**	**521**	**600**
MUTALI (Travancore State)	**585**	**308**	**277**
Hindu	555	289	266
Musalman	30	19	11
MUTRASI (MUTRACHA) (*Hindu*)	**414,674**	**212,066**	**202,608**
C. P. and Berar	482	225	257
Madras	153,422	77,368	76,054
Hyderabad State	260,770	134,473	126,297
MUTTAN (*Hindu*) (Madras)	**9,696**	**4,882**	**4,814**
MUTTIRIYAN (*Hindu*)	**86,926**	**43,357**	**43,569**
Madras	86,856	43,321	43,535
Cochin State	70	36	34
MUVVARI (*Hindu*) (Madras)	**3,005**	**1,268**	**1,737**
NADIYAL (*Hindu*) (Assam)	**68,350**	**34,891**	**33,459**
NADOR (*Hindu*) (Bombay)	**6,586**	**3,507**	**3,079**
NAGA *	**220,034**	**108,575**	**111,459**
Hindu	70	58	12
Animist	219,964	108,517	111,447
Assam	220,033	108,575	111,458
Bengal	1	...	1
NAGAR (*Hindu*)	**27,720**	**13,434**	**14,286**
Bengal	18,537	8,818	9,719
Bombay	5,146	2,602	2,544
Elsewhere	4,037	2,014	2,023
NAGARALU (*Hindu*) (Madras)	**14,569**	**6,752**	**7,817**
NAGARCHI †	**34,729**	**17,386**	**17,343**
Hindu	5,495	2,654	2,841
Musalman	28,397	14,341	14,056
Animist	837	391	446
Assam	3,588	1,925	1,663
Bengal	24,902	12,470	12,432
C. P. and Berar	6,239	2,991	3,248
NAGARTA (*Hindu*) (Mysore State)	**7,782**	**3,865**	**3,917**
NAGAVASULU (*Hindu*) (Madras)	**24,983**	**12,278**	**12,705**
NAGESIYA ‡ (NAGASIYA)	**52,712**	**26,484**	**26,228**
Hindu	48,191	24,244	23,947
Animist	4,521	2,240	2,281
Bihar and Orissa	6,021	2,907	3,114
C. P. and Berar	44,165	22,207	21,958
Elsewhere	2,526	1,370	1,156
NAHURA (*Hindu*) (Central India Agency)	**1,055**	**473**	**582**
NAIK (NAYAK, NAIKDA)	**125,524**	**64,152**	**61,372**
Hindu	118,954	60,841	58,113
Sikh	5	3	2
Musalman	166	93	73
Animist	6,399	3,215	3,184
Bombay	48,258	23,852	24,406
Punjab	6,674	3,708	2,966
United Provinces	5,314	2,506	2,808
Baroda State	10,030	5,053	4,977
Central India Agency	9,776	5,301	4,475
Rajputana Agency	42,391	22,111	20,280
Elsewhere	3,081	1,621	1,460
NAIKARU (*Hindu*) (C. P. and Berar)	**2,192**	**1,088**	**1,104**
NALAKEYAVA (*Hindu*) (Madras)	**1,365**	**668**	**697**
NALIYA (NALUA) (*Musalman*) (Bengal)	**6,264**	**2,962**	**3,302**
NAMASUDRA	**2,087,162**	**1,059,420**	**1,027,742**
Hindu	2,087,129	1,059,397	1,027,732
Musalman	32	22	10
Animist	1	1	...
Assam	172,753	89,347	83,406
Bengal	1,909,794	967,760	942,034
Bihar and Orissa	4,615	2,313	2,302
NARODA (*Hindu*) (Bombay)	**4,841**	**2,394**	**2,447**
NAT (NATUVA)	**126,428**	**63,292**	**63,136**
Hindu	95,163	47,456	47,707
Sikh	40	16	24
Jain	1	1	...
Musalman	30,850	15,633	15,217
Animist	374	186	188
Assam	5,143	2,557	2,586
Bengal	9,979	4,855	5,124
Bihar and Orissa	5,651	2,611	3,040
C. P. and Berar	11,385	5,419	5,966
United Provinces	68,376	34,370	34,006
Central India Agency	10,090	5,455	4,635
Rajputana Agency	8,447	4,392	4,055
Elsewhere	7,357	3,633	3,724
NATH § (*Hindu*) (Central India Agency)	**12,309**	**6,829**	**5,480**
NATTAMAN (*Hindu*) (Madras)	**162,786**	**79,298**	**83,488**
NAU MUSLIM (NASYA) (*Musalman*)	**133,318**	**72,402**	**60,916**
Bombay	92,535	52,088	40,447
United Provinces	35,440	17,780	17,660
Elsewhere	5,343	2,634	2,809

* For the details of individual tribes see Assam Table. † See also Dholi. ‡ Kisan has been shown separately. § Jogi has been shown separately.

Distribution of Castes by Religion and Locality—*continued*.

Caste, Religion and Locality.	Persons.	Males.	Females.
1	2	3	4
NAVAYAT (*Musalman*)	**2,938**	**1,602**	**1,336**
Madras	1,761	1,042	719
Elsewhere	1,177	560	617
NAYADI (NAYATI)	**843**	**446**	**397**
Hindu	566	291	275
Animist	277	155	122
Madras	535	273	262
Elsewhere	308	173	135
NAYAR (NAIR)	**1,129,466**	**555,185**	**574,281**
Hindu	1,129,465	555,184	574,281
Animist	1	1	...
Madras	412,618	198,422	214,196
Cochin State	121,991	59,128	62,863
Travancore State	592,655	295,781	296,874
Elsewhere	2,202	1,854	348
NAYATA (*Musalman*) (Central India Agency)	**5,553**	**2,983**	**2,570**
NEPALI	**4,271**	**2,720**	**1,551**
Hindu	3,192	2,114	1,078
Buddhist	891	485	406
Animist	188	121	67
Assam	2,917	1,907	1,010
Bengal	1,354	813	541
NEWAR	**14,473**	**8,119**	**6,354**
Hindu	14,208	7,973	6,235
Buddhist	56	41	15
Animist	209	105	104
Bengal	9,602	5,341	4,261
Elsewhere	4,871	2,778	2,093
NEYGI (*Hindu*) (Mysore State)	**96,466**	**48,571**	**47,895**
NEYYALA* (*Hindu*) (Madras)	**11,717**	**5,020**	**6,697**
NHAVI (*Hindu*) (Hyderabad State)	**58,974**	**30,019**	**28,955**
NICOBARESE † (Andamans and Nicobars).	**8,370**	**4,446**	**3,924**
Buddhist	12	10	2
Musalman	3	2	1
Animist	8,355	4,434	3,921
NIHAL (NAHAL) (C. P. and Berar).	**12,403**	**6,064**	**6,339**
Hindu	8,777	4,259	4,518
Animist	3,626	1,805	1,821
NIKARI (*Musalman*)	**46,913**	**23,514**	**23,399**
Assam	1,631	810	821
Bengal	45,282	22,704	22,578
NIMA (NEMA)	**19,894**	**10,407**	**9,487**
Hindu	10,260	4,787	5,473
Jain	9,634	5,620	4,014
Bombay	5,174	2,478	2,696
Central India Agency	10,322	5,739	4,583
Elsewhere	4,398	2,190	2,208
NIYARIA (Punjab)	**2,271**	**1,130**	**1,141**
Hindu	199	106	93
Sikh	10	6	4
Musalman	2.062	1,018	1,044
NOKKAN (*Hindu*) (Madras)	**4,528**	**2,150**	**2,378**
NOLIYA (*Hindu*) (Madras)	**2,361**	**848**	**1,513**
NULAYAN (*Hindu*) (Travancore State)	**3,393**	**1,764**	**1,629**
NUNIYA ‡ (LUNIYA, NUNGAR)	**799,880**	**414,590**	**385,290**
Hindu	798,433	413,747	384,686
Sikh	296	156	140
Jain	8	1	7
Buddhist	3	1	2
Musalman	1,063	620	443
Animist	77	65	12
Assam	14,358	9,222	5,136
Bengal	42,121	40,106	2.015
Bihar and Orissa	319,102	150,956	168,146
Punjab	9,987	5,390	4,597
United Provinces	409,256	206,276	202,980
Elsewhere	5,056	2,640	2,416
OC'CHAN (*Hindu*)	**5,692**	**2,724**	**2,968**
Madras	5,177	2,481	2,696
Travancore State	515	243	272
OD § (ODDE, ORH, ODH).	**610,162**	**308,976**	**301,186**
Hindu	597,556	302,391	295,165
Sikh	145	68	77
Musalman	12,339	6,457	5,882
Animist	122	60	62
Madras	550,109	277,375	272.734
Punjab	32,246	17,188	15,058
United Provinces	9.071	4 502	4,569
Rajputana Agency	7,839	4,159	3,680
Elsewhere	10,897	5,752	5,145
OJALI	**11,695**	**5,689**	**6,006**
Hindu	6,836	3,409	3,427
Animist	4,859	2,280	2,579
Assam	42	17	25
Madras	11,653	5,672	5,981
OMAITO (*Hindu*) (Madras)	**11,501**	**5,769**	**5,732**
ORAON	**751,983**	**373,095**	**378,888**
Hindu	157,414	82,086	75.328
Animist	594,569	291,009	303,560
Assam	28,583	14,670	13,913
Bengal	165,628	89,236	76,392
Bihar and Orissa	474,673	227,273	247,400
C. P. and Berar	83,099	41,916	41,183
ORIYA (ODIYA, URIYA).	**118,835**	**60,504**	**58,331**
Hindu	117,982	60,066	57,916
Animist	853	438	415
Assam	5.964	3,237	2,727
Burma	10,411	9,810	601
Madras	101.312	46,783	54,529
Elsewhere	1,148	674	474
OSTA (*Musalman*) (Travancore State)	**1,029**	**528**	**501**

* See also Noliya. † For details see Part II. ‡ Lonari has been shown separately. § In Bombay included in Vadda.

TABLE XIII.—Caste, Tribe, Race or Nationality. Part I.—

Caste, Religion and Locality.	Persons.	Males.	Females.
1	2	3	4
OSWAL	**427,778**	**212,945**	**214,833**
Hindu	31,054	16,512	14,542
Sikh	12	7	5
Jain	396,702	196,416	200,286
Animist	10	10	...
Ajmer-Merwara	14,228	7,566	6,662
Bombay	132,588	67,521	65,067
C. P. and Berar	9,612	5,498	4,114
Punjab	5,662	3,012	2,650
Central India Agency	47,795	23,139	24,656
Rajputana Agency	209,965	100,685	109,280
Elsewhere	7,928	5,524	2,404
OTARI	**3,121**	**1,531**	**1,590**
Hindu	3,070	1,493	1,577
Animist	51	38	13
C. P. and Berar	2,634	1,271	1,363
Elsewhere	487	260	227
PACHAHDA (*Musalman*) (Punjab)	**32,425**	**16,833**	**15,592**
PADIYACHI (*Hindu*) (Burma)	**11,808**	**8,085**	**3,723**
PADTI (*Hindu*) (Bombay)	**3,908**	**2,029**	**1,879**
PAIDI (Madras)	**48,610**	**23,913**	**24,697**
Hindu	40,242	19,839	20,403
Animist	8,368	4,074	4,294
PAIK	**3,194**	**1,548**	**1,646**
Hindu	3,130	1,519	1,611
Animist	64	29	35
Assam	3	...	3
C. P. and Berar	3,191	1,548	1,643
PAKHIWARA (PAKHIWAS) (Punjab)	**4,167**	**2,351**	**1,816**
Hindu	1	1	...
Musalman	4,166	2,350	1,816
PALA (*Hindu*) (Central India Agency)	**710**	**395**	**315**
PALE (Coorg)	**4,120**	**2,897**	**1,223**
Hindu	4,101	2,887	1,214
Animist	19	10	9
PALIYAN (*Hindu*) (Madras)	**1,538**	**846**	**692**
PALLAN (*Hindu*)	**877,354**	**420,150**	**457,204**
Madras	866,132	414,945	451,187
Travancore State	11,222	5,205	6,017
PALLI (PALI)	**2,828,792**	**1,389,568**	**1,439,224**
Hindu	2,828,751	1,389,549	1,439,202
Animist	41	19	22
Burma	5,861	4,527	1,334
Madras	2,820,156	1,383,560	1,436,596
Elsewhere	2,775	1,481	1,294
PANAN (*Hindu*)	**20,935**	**10,408**	**10,527**
Madras	14,717	7,238	7,479
Elsewhere	6,218	3,170	3,048
PANCHALA * (PANCHAL)	**392,327**	**199,504**	**192,823**
Hindu	392,318	199,495	192,823
Musalman	5	5	...
Animist	4	4	...
Bombay	81,083	41,462	39,621
C. P. and Berar	8,712	4,241	4,471
Coorg	2,003	1,068	935
Madras	54,721	26,953	27,768
Hyderabad State	117,710	59,990	57,720
Mysore State	128,098	65,790	62,308
PANCHAM	**12,349**	**6,294**	**6,055**
Hindu	155	93	62
Jain	12,194	6,201	5,993
Bombay	12,194	6,201	5,993
C. P. and Berar	155	93	62
PANCHKALSHI (SOMAVANSHI-KSHATRI) (*Hindu*) (Bombay)	**14,357**	**7,179**	**7,178**
PANDARAM (PANTARAM) (*Hindu*)	**86,535**	**42,987**	**43,548**
Madras	66,868	32,983	33,885
Travancore State	15,239	7,719	7,520
Elsewhere	4,428	2,285	2,143
PANDIT (*Musalman*) (Kashmir State)	**3,326**	**1,696**	**1,630**
PANDITATTAN (*Hindu*) (Cochin State)	**2,456**	**1,342**	**1,114**
PANDITO (*Hindu*) (Madras)	**1,158**	**559**	**599**
PANDRA (*Hindu*) (Bihar and Orissa)	**4,639**	**2,297**	**2,342**
PANGUL (*Hindu*)	**1,918**	**974**	**944**
C. P. and Berar	1,854	941	913
Hyderabad State	64	33	31
PANIKA (PAN, PANO, PANKA)	**796,973**	**390,728**	**406,245**
Hindu	776,843	380,706	396,137
Animist	20,130	10,022	10,108
Assam	17,939	8,739	9,200
Bihar and Orissa	464,046	227,359	236,687
C. P. and Berar	214,894	104,032	110,862
Madras	71,323	35,651	35,672
Central India Agency	26,656	13,732	12,924
Elsewhere	2,115	1,215	900

* See also Kammalan.

Distribution of Castes by Religion and Locality—*continued.*

Caste, Religion and Locality.	Persons.	Males.	Females.
1	2	3	4
PANIKKAN (*Hindu*)	**30,801**	**14,860**	**15,941**
Madras	30,083	14,537	15,546
Travancore State	718	323	395
PANISAVAN (*Hindu*) (Madras)	**19,553**	**9,640**	**9,913**
PANIYAN (*Hindu*) (Madras)	**34,574**	**17,501**	**17,073**
PARACHA *	**16,160**	**8,698**	**7,462**
Hindu	5	3	2
Musalman	16,155	8,695	7,460
N.-W. F. Province	12,330	6,670	5,660
Punjab	3,830	2,028	1,802
PARAI (*Musalman*) (Kashmir State)	**15,629**	**8,448**	**7,181**
PARAIYAN (PARAYAN, PARAYA) (*Hindu*)	**2,448,295**	**1,195,155**	**1,253,140**
Madras	2,365,433	1,154,107	1,211,326
Cochin State	8,356	4,135	4,221
Travancore State	73,581	36,731	36,850
Elsewhere	925	182	743
PARAVAN (*Hindu*)	**14,736**	**7,286**	**7,450**
Madras	5,396	2,623	2,773
Travancore State	9,313	4,648	4,665
Elsewhere	27	15	12
PARDHAN	**118,677**	**57,740**	**60,937**
Hindu	25,217	12,232	12,985
Animist	93,460	45,508	47,952
Assam	47	29	18
C. P. and Berar	118,630	57,711	60,919
PARDHI (SHIKARI)	**65,902**	**31,721**	**34,181**
Hindu	65,538	31,541	33,997
Musalman	1	...	1
Animist	363	180	183
Bombay	17,896	9,994	7,902
C. P. and Berar	12,890	6,506	6,384
Central India Agency	24,594	9,749	14,845
Hyderabad State	10,522	5,472	5,050
PARHAIYA	**9,674**	**4,988**	**4,686**
Hindu	9,531	4,885	4,646
Animist	143	103	40
Bihar and Orissa	9,452	4,867	4,585
Elsewhere	222	121	101
PARIVARAM	**20,805**	**10,103**	**10,702**
Hindu	20,804	10,102	10,702
Animist	1	1	...
Coorg	20	13	7
Madras	20,785	10,090	10,695

Caste, Religion and Locality.	Persons.	Males.	Females.
1	2	3	4
PASI †	**1,499,825**	**767,382**	**732,443**
Hindu	1,499,232	767,054	732,178
Jain	1	...	1
Musalman	432	247	185
Animist	160	81	79
Assam	6,943	3,492	3,451
Bengal	15,043	9,827	5,216
Bihar and Orissa	150,142	75,345	74,797
United Provinces	1,311,415	670,549	640,866
Central India Agency	8,085	3,472	4,613
Elsewhere	8,197	4,697	3,500
PATANE PRABHU (*Hindu*) (Bombay)	**3,293**	**1,730**	**1,563**
PATEL	**55,804**	**27,755**	**28,049**
Hindu	55,803	27,754	28,049
Jain	1	1	...
Ajmer-Merwara	6	4	2
Rajputana Agency	55,798	27,751	28,047
PATELIYA (*Hindu*) (Bombay)	**13,859**	**7,038**	**6,821**
PATHAN (*Musalman*)	**3,796,816**	**2,021,298**	**1,775,518**
Ajmer-Merwara	11,429	6,181	5,248
Assam	13,673	7,932	5,741
Baluchistan	214,517	118,582	95,935
Bengal	314,652	173,599	141,053
Bihar and Orissa	220,707	106,287	114,420
Bombay	161,095	89,515	71,580
Burma	8,041	6,967	1,074
C. P. and Berar	143,972	74,082	69,890
Madras	106,920	54,536	52,384
N.-W. F. Province	845,183	449,500	395,683
Punjab	292,689	166,664	126,025
United Provinces	960,711	500,225	460,486
Baroda State	16,420	8,732	7,688
Central India Agency	138,522	73,476	65,046
Hyderabad State	135,148	71,167	63,981
Kashmir State	52,263	27,931	24,332
Mysore State	44,689	23,469	21,220
Rajputana Agency	108,653	57,815	50,838
Elsewhere	7,532	4,638	2,894
PATIAL (PATIKAR) (*Hindu*)	**12,810**	**6,429**	**6,381**
Assam	4,190	2,147	2,043
Bengal	8,620	4,282	4,338
PATLIYA (Central India Agency)	**21,625**	**13,573**	**8,052**
Hindu	21,616	13,568	8,048
Animist	9	5	4
PATNI	**174,738**	**89,249**	**85,489**
Hindu	174,727	89,243	85,484
Jain	11	6	5
Assam	111,206	56,901	54,305
Bengal	63,447	32,294	31,153
Bihar and Orissa	85	54	31

NOTE.—Patharwat has been included in Silawat
* Includes Dom in N.-W. F. Province
† In Bihar and Orissa Musalman Pasi has been included in Kalwar

TABLE XIII.—Caste, Tribe, Race or Nationality. Part I.—

Caste, Religion and Locality.	Persons.	Males.	Females.
1	2	3	4
PATNULKARAN (PATNUL) (*Hindu*)	**96,132**	**47,013**	**49,119**
Madras	92,840	45,444	47,396
Travancore State	3,292	1,569	1,723
PATRA (ORIYA) (*Hindu*)	**39,310**	**18,660**	**20,650**
Bihar and Orissa	37,216	17,583	19,633
Elsewhere	2,094	1,077	1,017
PATRA (TELUGU) (*Hindu*) (Madras)	**16,103**	**7,967**	**8,136**
PATRAMELA (*Hindu*) (Madras)	**1,078**	**466**	**612**
PATTANAVAN (PATTAPU) (*Hindu*) (Madras)	**48,847**	**24,523**	**24,324**
PATVEKARI (PATVEGARA) (*Hindu*)	**2,790**	**1,393**	**1,397**
Bombay	2,291	1,134	1,157
Elsewhere	499	259	240
PATWA	**60,023**	**30,523**	**29,500**
Hindu	58,659	29,922	28,737
Jain	74	26	48
Musalman	493	199	294
Animist	797	376	421
Bihar and Orissa	16,824	8,307	8,517
C. P. and Berar	7,073	3,470	3,603
United Provinces	27,153	13,662	13,491
Elsewhere	8,973	5,084	3,889
PENJA (PINJARI, PINJARA, PINARA)	**74,270**	**37,570**	**36,700**
Hindu	3,536	1,646	1,890
Jain	8	8	...
Musalman	70,731	35,921	34,810
Ajmer-Merwara	1,006	555	451
Bombay	15,658	7,642	8,016
Punjab	13,023	7,176	5,847
Baroda State	5,408	2,792	2,616
Central India Agency	18,991	9,149	9,842
Mysore State	5,886	2,968	2,918
Rajputana Agency	14,298	7,288	7,010
PENTIYA (*Hindu*) (Madras)	**4,213**	**2,009**	**2,204**
PERIKA (PERIKE, PERKI)	**61,771**	**30,854**	**30,917**
Hindu	61,770	30,853	30,917
Animist	1	1	...
C. P. and Berar	3,968	1,877	2,091
Madras	24,965	12,560	12,405
Hyderabad State	32,838	16,417	16,421
PERNA (Punjab)	**2,246**	**1,199**	**1,047**
Hindu	91	54	37
Musalman	2,155	1,145	1,010
PHAKIYAL (Assam)	**506**	**253**	**253**
Hindu	1	1	...
Buddhist	505	252	253

Caste, Religion and Locality.	Persons.	Males.	Females.
1	2	3	4
PIC'CHIGUNTA (Madras)	**8,977**	**4,583**	**4,394**
Hindu	8,938	4,565	4,373
Animist	39	18	21
PICHHAKUNTALA (*Hindu*) (Hyderabad State)	**3,269**	**1,598**	**1,671**
PILLE (*Hindu*) (Mysore State)	**1,251**	**677**	**574**
PINDARI (PINDARA)	**6,413**	**3,283**	**3,130**
Hindu	100	49	51
Musalman	6,313	3,234	3,079
Central India Agency	4,014	2,074	1,940
Elsewhere	2,399	1,209	1,190
POD	**536,591**	**274,197**	**262,394**
Hindu	536,590	274,197	262,393
Animist	1	..	1
Assam	23	16	7
Bengal	536,568	274,181	262,387
POROJA	**98,598**	**50,824**	**47,774**
Hindu	74,137	37,915	36,222
Animist	24,461	12,909	11,552
Assam	5,861	3,032	2,829
Madras	92,737	47,792	44,945
PORWAL (PARWAR, PORVAD)	**135,030**	**67,405**	**67,625**
Hindu	30,325	15,991	14,334
Jain	104,705	51,414	53,291
Bombay	24,402	12,300	12,102
C. P. and Berar	29,445	15,119	14,326
Baroda State	8,613	4,737	3,876
Central India Agency	39,369	20,233	19,136
Rajputana Agency	33,140	14,955	18,185
Elsewhere	61	61	...
PRABHU * (PARBHU) (*Hindu*)	**33,280**	**17,043**	**16,237**
Bombay	27,120	13,884	13,236
Elsewhere	6,160	3,159	3,001
PUJARI	**1,245**	**621**	**624**
Hindu	1,239	616	623
Jain	6	5	1
Madras	231	128	103
Punjab	1,014	493	521
PULAIYAN† (PULAYAN) (*Hindu*)	**262,416**	**130,571**	**131,845**
Madras	4,315	1,952	2,363
Cochin State	72,787	35,284	37,503
Travancore State	185,314	93,335	91,979
PULLUVAN (*Hindu*)	**6,813**	**3,005**	**3,808**
Madras	6,625	2,946	3,679
Cochin State	188	59	129

* Includes Kayasth Prabhu in Bombay

† See also Cheruman

Distribution of Castes by Religion and Locality—*continued.*

Caste, Religion and Locality.	Persons.	Males.	Females.
1	2	3	4
PULUVAN (*Hindu*)	**3,757**	**1,919**	**1,838**
Madras	1,908	901	1,007
Elsewhere	1,849	1,018	831
PUNDARI (PURO)	**15,788**	**8,068**	**7,720**
Hindu	15,780	8,060	7,720
Animist	8	8	...
Assam	81	73	8
Bengal	15,707	7,995	7,712
PURBIYA	**4,671**	**2,931**	**1,740**
Hindu	4,561	2,874	1,687
Sikh	98	54	44
Musalman	12	3	9
Punjab	4,647	2,922	1,725
Travancore State	24	9	15
PUSHPAKAN (*Hindu*) (Travancore State)	**1,925**	**1,012**	**913**
QURESHI (KURESHI) (*Musalman*)	**92,232**	**48,704**	**43,528**
N.-W. F. Province	20,939	11,058	9,881
Punjab	70,922	37,418	33,509
Elsewhere	371	233	138
RABARI (REBARI, RAHBARI)	**310,566**	**163,133**	**147,433**
Hindu	310,543	163,113	147,430
Sikh	8	6	2
Musalman	14	13	1
Animist	1	1	...
Bombay	130,009	68,708	61,301
Baroda State	44,916	23,649	21,267
Rajputana Agency	129,918	67,760	62,158
Elsewhere	5,723	3,016	2,707
RABHA *	**79,756**	**39,889**	**39,867**
Hindu	34,934	17,569	17,365
Animist	44,822	22,320	22,502
Assam	79,022	39,504	39,518
Bengal	734	385	349
RACHEWAR (*Hindu*)	**3,223**	**1,582**	**1,641**
Coorg	44	15	29
Mysore State	3,179	1,567	1,612
RADDI (*Hindu*) (Bombay)	**50,115**	**25,370**	**24,745**
RADHA (*Hindu*) (United Provinces)	**2,956**	**1,439**	**1,517**
RAIGAR	**101,426**	**51,774**	**49,652**
Hindu	101,391	51,757	49,634
Musalman	11	4	7
Animist	24	13	11
Ajmer-Merwara	19,858	10,148	9,710
Rajputana Agency	81,568	41,626	39,942
RAINA (*Musalman*) (Kashmir State)	**3,264**	**1,434**	**1,830**
RAJ (Punjab)	**14,604**	**7,382**	**7,222**
Hindu	5,403	2,787	2,616
Sikh	795	431	364
Musalman	8,406	4,164	4,242
RAJAPURI (*Hindu*) (Madras)	**11,420**	**5,671**	**5,749**
RAJBANSI †	**2,049,454**	**1,061,322**	**988,132**
Hindu	2,049,422	1,061,297	988,125
Jain	10	10	...
Animist	22	15	7
Assam	133,078	68,584	64,494
Bengal	1,808,790	936,264	872,526
Bihar and Orissa	107,586	56,474	51,112
RAJBHAR ‡	**18,276**	**11,259**	**7,017**
Hindu	18,080	11,154	6,926
Animist	196	105	91
Bengal	10,278	7,211	3,067
Elsewhere	7,998	4,048	3,950
RAJJHAR (LAJJHAR) (C. P. and Berar)	**7,554**	**3,649**	**3,905**
Hindu	6,998	3,375	3,623
Animist	556	274	282
RAJPUT (CHHATRI)	**9,430,095**	**5,068,043**	**4,362,052**
Hindu	7,758,193	4,168,103	3,590,090
Sikh	27,716	16,191	11,525
Jain	846	752	94
Buddhist	37	22	15
Musalman	1,643,155	882,877	760,278
Animist	148	98	50
Ajmer-Merwara	14,302	8,225	6,077
Assam	27,670	17,536	10,134
Bengal	130,221	84,358	45,863
Bihar and Orissa	1,239,826	630,717	609,109
Bombay	457,723	242,964	214,759
Burma	10,942	9,296	1,646
C. P. and Berar	441,231	223,581	217,650
Madras	17,603	8,899	8,704
N.-W. F. Province	15,263	10,715	4,548
Punjab	1,635,432	898,023	737,409
United Provinces	3,657,557	1,958,225	1,699,332
Baroda State	64,287	34,582	29,705
Central India Agency	755,819	411,527	344,292
Hyderabad State	61,637	31,296	30,341
Kashmir State	211,328	111,396	99,932
Rajputana Agency	687,292	385,124	302,168
Elsewhere	1,962	1,579	383
RAJU (*Hindu*)	**113,160**	**57,411**	**55,749**
Bengal	61,064	31,164	29,900
Bihar and Orissa	52,096	26,247	25,849

* Includes Totla in Assam (males 3,684, females 3,777)
† Kcch has been shown separately
‡ Bhar has been shown separately

TABLE XIII.—Caste, Tribe, Race or Nationality. Part I.—

Caste, Religion and Locality.	Persons.	Males.	Females.
1	2	3	4
RAJWAR (MOWAR)	**192,613**	**96,857**	**95,756**
Hindu	187,667	94,396	93,271
Animist	4,946	2,461	2,485
Assam	8,338	4.291	4,047
Bengal	22,301	11,582	10,719
Bihar and Orissa	131,971	65,880	66,091
C. P. and Berar	30,003	15,104	14,899
RAMOSHI (RAMOSI) (*Hindu*)	**60,064**	**30,555**	**29,509**
Bombay	59,914	30,478	29,436
C. P. and Berar	150	77	73
RANA	**11,823**	**5,976**	**5,847**
Hindu	9,764	4,988	4,776
Musalman	2,059	988	1,071
Rajputana Agency	11,808	5,967	5,841
Elsewhere	15	9	6
RANGHAR (*Musalman*) (United Provinces)	**1,170**	**835**	**335**
RANGREZ (RANGARI)	**122,923**	**63,612**	**59,311**
Hindu	65,088	32,952	32,136
Sikh	54	37	17
Jain	69	35	34
Musalman	57,197	30,331	26,866
Animist	515	257	258
Bombay	6,584	3,258	3,326
C. P. and Berar	16,846	8,414	8,432
Madras	15,309	7,727	7,582
United Provinces	34,012	18,231	15,781
Central India Agency	6,234	3,208	3,026
Hyderabad State	22,508	11,521	10,987
Rajputana Agency	15,485	8,049	7,436
Elsewhere	5,945	3,204	2,741
RAO	**12,895**	**6,513**	**6,382**
Hindu	12,880	6,506	6,374
Musalman	15	7	8
Ajmer-Merwara	324	178	146
Rajputana Agency	12,571	6,335	6,236
RASTOGI (RUSTOGI)	**12,013**	**6,223**	**5,790**
Hindu	11,987	6,217	5,770
Jain	26	6	20
United Provinces	11,698	6,047	5,651
Elsewhere	315	176	139
RATHAR (*Musalman*) (Kashmir State)	**33,951**	**18,151**	**15,800**
RATHI (Punjab)	**97,798**	**51,129**	**46,669**
Hindu	97,776	51,112	46,664
Sikh	8	3	5
Musalman	14	14	...
RAUNIYAR (RAUNIHAR, NONIYAR)	**94,086**	**47,788**	**46,298**
Hindu	94,084	47,786	46,298
Jain	1	1	...
Musalman	1	1	...
Bihar and Orissa	83,482	42,061	41,421
United Provinces	7,768	4,024	3,744
Elsewhere	2,836	1,703	1,133
RAUTIYA	**17,597**	**9,372**	**8,225**
Hindu	17,395	9,268	8,127
Sikh	1	...	1
Jain	2	2	...
Animist	199	102	97
C. P. and Berar	12,037	6,267	5,770
Elsewhere	5,560	3,105	2,455
RAVALIYA (*Hindu*)	**69,189**	**36,120**	**33,069**
Bombay	46,707	24,398	22,309
Baroda State	22,482	11,722	10,760
RAVULO (*Hindu*) (Madras)	**5,702**	**2,862**	**2,840**
RAVUTTAN (*Musalman*)	**9,632**	**4,995**	**4,637**
Cochin State	8,430	4,311	4,119
Travancore State	1,202	684	518
RAWAL	**4,815**	**2,431**	**2,384**
Hindu	4,813	2,430	2,383
Jain	2	1	1
Baroda State	2	1	1
Rajputana Agency	4,813	2,430	2,383
RAWAT (RAOT, RAWA)	**155,070**	**82,239**	**72,831**
Hindu	140,397	73,922	66,475
Sikh	42	28	14
Jain	16	10	6
Musalman	14,600	8,268	6,332
Animist	15	11	4
Ajmer-Merwara	47,905	24,963	22,942
Punjab	15,419	8,652	6,767
United Provinces	14,226	7,933	6,293
Central India Agency	63,601	32,982	30,619
Rajputana Agency	13,754	7,580	6,174
Elsewhere	165	129	36
RAZU (RAJU) (*Hindu*)	**103,123**	**51,486**	**51,637**
Madras	102,845	51,349	51,496
Elsewhere	278	137	141
REHAR (REHARA) (*Hindu*) (Punjab)	**1,438**	**735**	**703**
REHEWARI (REWARI) (*Hindu*)	**3,779**	**2,005**	**1,774**
C. P. and Berar	38	28	10
Central India Agency	3,741	1,977	1,764
RELLI	**21,478**	**9,843**	**11,635**
Hindu	20,960	9,587	11,373
Animist	518	256	262
Assam	6	6	...
Madras	21,472	9,837	11,635
RIGZANG (TARAKCHOS) (Kashmir State)	**4,888**	**2,555**	**2,333**
Buddhist	862	561	301
Musalman	4,026	1,994	2,032

DISTRIBUTION OF CASTES BY RELIGION AND LOCALITY—*continued.*

CASTE, RELIGION AND LOCALITY.	Persons.	Males.	Females.
1	2	3	4
RISHI (*Musalman*) (Kashmir State)	**7,685**	**3,964**	**3,721**
RONA (Madras)	**39,166**	**19,773**	**19,393**
Hindu	32,443	16,553	15,890
Animist	6,723	3,220	3,503
ROR (Punjab)	**41,431**	**23,121**	**18,310**
Hindu	41,115	22,949	18,166
Sikh	302	164	138
Musalman	14	8	6
RUWALA (*Hindu*) (Central India Agency)	**3,377**	**1,727**	**1,650**
SAD (Rajputana Agency)	**28,544**	**15,573**	**12,971**
Hindu	28,538	15,569	12,969
Animist	6	4	2
SADAR (*Hindu*) (Madras)	**3,715**	**1,840**	**1,875**
SADGOP (*Hindu*)	**575,931**	**291,779**	**284,152**
Bengal	550,093	277,638	272,455
Bihar and Orissa	23,940	12,941	10,999
Elsewhere	1,898	1,200	698
SADHU (SADH)	**18,280**	**10,909**	**7,371**
Hindu	17,633	10,690	6,943
Sikh	17	10	7
Jain	630	209	421
Rajputana Agency	10,519	6,451	4,068
Elsewhere	7,761	4,458	3,303
SADU (*Hindu*) (Bombay)	**3,465**	**2,208**	**1,257**
SAGAR (*Hindu*)	**13,120**	**6,803**	**6,317**
Bombay	11,538	6,000	5,538
Baroda State	1,582	803	779
SAINI	**181,989**	**101,648**	**80,341**
Hindu	131,633	73,413	58,220
Sikh	47,035	26,237	20,798
Musalman	3,321	1,998	1,323
Punjab	112,719	63,085	49,634
United Provinces	69,270	38,563	30,707
SAINTHWAR (*Hindu*) (United Provinces)	**119,086**	**60,412**	**58,674**
SAITWAL (SAILWAL)	**7,091**	**3,466**	**3,625**
Hindu	459	247	212
Jain	6,632	3,219	3,413
C. P. and Berar	7,017	3,426	3,591
Rajputana Agency	74	40	34

CASTE, RELIGION AND LOCALITY.	Persons.	Males.	Females.
1	2	3	4
SAIYID (*Musalman*)	**1,655,525**	**863,366**	**792,159**
Ajmer-Merwara	5,199	2,823	2,376
Assam	14,134	7,498	6,636
Baluchistan	22,183	11,662	10,521
Bengal	143,757	75,567	68,190
Bihar and Orissa	91,105	44,460	46,645
Bombay	150,492	77,679	72,813
Burma	6,871	5,398	1,473
C. P. and Berar	47,936	24,656	23,280
Madras	170,125	85,730	84,395
N.-W. F. Province	75,115	39,230	35,885
Punjab	247,388	131,992	115,396
United Provinces	250,204	129,843	120,361
Baroda State	8,772	4,576	4,196
Central India Agency	32,197	17,459	14,738
Kashmir State	102,195	54,066	48,129
Hyderabad State	189,574	99,142	90,432
Mysore State	57,671	30,298	27,373
Rajputana Agency	28,954	15,242	13,712
Travancore State	10,425	5,319	5,106
Elsewhere	1,228	726	502
SALE (SALI, SALVI)	**786,408**	**398,121**	**388,287**
Hindu	786,406	398,120	388,286
Jain	1	...	1
Musalman	1	1	...
Bombay	57,763	30,102	27,661
C. P. and Berar	14,289	6,911	7,378
Madras	358,482	178,389	180,093
Hyderabad State	343,130	175,968	167,162
Travancore State	9,919	4,953	4,966
Elsewhere	2,825	1,798	1,027
SALOI (*Hindu*) (Assam)	**9,334**	**4,651**	**4,683**
SAMAGARA (SEMMAN) (*Hindu*)	**3,294**	**1,599**	**1,695**
Coorg	14	8	6
Madras	3,280	1,591	1,689
SAMANTA (SAMANTAN) (*Hindu*)	**5,519**	**2,727**	**2,792**
Madras	4,663	2,293	2,370
Elsewhere	856	434	422
SAMANTIYA (*Hindu*) (Madras)	**14,750**	**6,959**	**7,791**
SANGAMESHVARI (*Hindu*) (Bombay)	**12,700**	**5,766**	**6,934**
SANGAR (*Hindu*) (Bombay)	**6,823**	**3,354**	**3,469**
SANKHARI (SONKARI) (*Hindu*)	**6,339**	**3,160**	**3,179**
Bengal	5,612	2,733	2,879
Elsewhere	727	427	300

TABLE XIII.—Caste, Tribe, Race or Nationality. Part I.—

Caste, Religion and Locality.	Persons.	Males.	Females.
1	2	3	4
SANNYASI (SWAMI, ATITH)	**147,016**	**76,071**	**70,945**
Hindu	146,922	76,048	70,874
Jain	90	19	71
Animist	4	4	...
Bihar and Orissa	73,593	35,132	38,461
United Provinces	29,703	15,182	14,521
Rajputana Agency	33,297	19,890	13,407
Elsewhere	10,423	5,867	4,556
SANSI	**32,481**	**17,444**	**15,037**
Hindu	28,668	15,350	13,318
Sikh	595	303	292
Musalman	2,849	1,597	1,252
Animist	369	194	175
Punjab	26,990	14,863	12,127
Elsewhere	5,491	2,581	2,910
SANSIYA	**1,978**	**945**	**1,033**
Hindu	1,924	916	1,008
Animist	54	29	25
C. P. and Berar	1,106	528	578
Elsewhere	872	417	455
SANTAL (SAONTA)	**2,138,310**	**1,064,085**	**1,074,225**
Hindu	467,489	230,884	236,605
Buddhist	1	1	...
Animist	1,670,820	833,200	837,620
Assam	59,008	30,322	28,686
Bengal	669,420	336,384	333,036
Bihar and Orissa	1,399,450	692,067	707,383
C. P. and Berar	10,432	5,312	5,120
SAPPALIGA (*Hindu*) (Madras)	**2,513**	**1,195**	**1,318**
SARAK	**18,707**	**9,521**	**9,186**
Hindu	16,659	8,442	8,217
Jain	215	99	116
Buddhist	1,833	980	853
Bihar and Orissa	14,729	7,551	7,178
Elsewhere	3,978	1,970	2,008
SARALIA (Punjab)	**7,456**	**4,236**	**3,220**
Hindu	7,341	4,165	3,176
Sikh	101	63	38
Jain	14	8	6
SARAOGI	**61,625**	**32,240**	**29,385**
Hindu	8,521	4,126	4,395
Jain	53,104	28,114	24,990
Central India Agency	17,967	8,990	8,977
Rajputana Agency	38,041	19,835	18,206
Elsewhere	5,617	3,415	2,202
SARERA (SARABA)	**21,876**	**11,725**	**10,151**
Hindu	12,017	6,362	5,655
Sikh	1,322	724	598
Musalman	8,537	4,639	3,898
N.-W. F. Province	8,507	4,616	3,891
Punjab	10,743	5,779	4,964
Kashmir State	2,626	1,330	1,296
SARGARA	**27,359**	**14,296**	**13,063**
Hindu	27,274	14,254	13,020
Animist	85	42	43
Rajputana Agency	26,520	13,865	12,655
Elsewhere	839	431	408
SARKI	**3,832**	**2,152**	**1,680**
Hindu	3,766	2,112	1,654
Buddhist	30	21	9
Animist	36	19	17
Bengal	2,974	1,659	1,315
Elsewhere	858	493	365
SATANI (*Hindu*)	**99,760**	**50,043**	**49,717**
Madras	47,921	23,533	24,388
Hyderabad State	27,883	14,589	13,294
Mysore State	23,038	11,472	11,566
Elsewhere	918	449	469
SATHAVARA (*Hindu*)	**45,468**	**22,957**	**22,511**
Assam	1	1	...
Bombay	39,637	20,049	19,588
Baroda State	5,830	2,907	2,923
SATTI (Punjab)	**19,366**	**9,769**	**9,597**
Hindu	60	36	24
Musalman	19,306	9,733	9,573
SAUNTI (*Hindu*) (Bihar and Orissa)	**22,659**	**11,147**	**11,512**
SAURIA PAHARIA* (MALE)	**64,617**	**32,213**	**32,404**
Hindu	6,194	3,222	2,972
Animist	58,423	28,991	29,432
Bihar and Orissa	62,796	31,201	31,595
Elsewhere	1,821	1,012	809
SAVAR (SAHAR, SAVARA, SAHARIYA)	**582,342**	**287,597**	**294,745**
Hindu	400,841	196,610	204,231
Musalman	2	2	...
Animist	181,499	90,985	90,514
Bihar and Orissa	218,167	106,055	112,112
C. P. and Berar	74,181	36,041	38,140
Madras	186,128	92,348	93,780
Central India Agency	81,042	41,560	39,482
Rajputana Agency	13,801	6,998	6,803
Elsewhere	9,023	4,595	4,428
SAYAKKARAN (*Hindu*) (Madras)	**2,763**	**1,260**	**1,503**
SEGIDI (*Hindu*) (Madras)	**56,404**	**25,470**	**30,934**
SEMBADAVAN (*Hindu*)	**66,113**	**32,731**	**33,382**
Madras	64,403	31,905	32,498
Travancore State	1,710	826	884
SENAIKKUDAIYAN (*Hindu*) (Madras)	**38,133**	**18,827**	**19,306**

* See also Mal Paharia.

Distribution of Castes by Religion and Locality—*continued.*

Caste, Religion and Locality.	Persons.	Males.	Females.
1	2	3	4
SEPI (*Hindu*) (Punjab)	**1,851**	**956**	**895**
SEVAG	**10,329**	**5,000**	**5,329**
Hindu	10,209	4,931	5,278
Jain	120	69	51
Ajmer-Merwara	254	137	117
Rajputana Agency	10,075	4,863	5,212
SHAGIRDPESHA (*Hindu*)	**47,361**	**20,754**	**26,607**
Bengal	902	419	483
Bihar and Orissa	46,459	20,335	26,124
SHAHA (SUNRI)	**800,849**	**398,453**	**402,396**
Hindu	800,342	398,185	402,157
Musalman	303	157	146
Animist	204	111	93
Assam	56,929	28,867	28,062
Bengal	444,252	221,331	222,921
Bihar and Orissa	257,114	126,901	130,213
C. P. and Berar	5,470	2,731	2,739
Madras	36,756	18,455	18,301
Elsewhere	328	168	160
SHAN *	**996,946**	**495,995**	**500,951**
Hindu	3	3	...
Buddhist	996,943	495,992	500,951
Assam	526	292	234
Burma	996,420	495,703	500,717
SHANAN (CHANNAN) (*Hindu*)	**808,264**	**399,419**	**408,845**
Madras	641,976	314,733	327,243
Travancore State	166,195	84,638	81,557
Elsewhere	93	48	45
SHARIF (ASHRAF) (*Musalman*)	**2,813**	**1,773**	**1,040**
Madras	1,712	1,188	524
Elsewhere	1,101	585	516
SHEIKH † (*Musalman*)	**32,131,342**	**16,442,047**	**15,689,295**
Ajmer-Merwara	25,130	13,380	11,750
Assam	1,769,666	916,488	853,178
Bengal	22,952,944	11,698,628	11,254 316
Bihar and Orissa	1,708,932	841,111	867,821
Bombay	954,504	495,015	459,489
Burma	237,568	152,412	85,156
C. P. and Berar	280,314	144,434	135,880
Madras	892,910	442,885	450,025
N.-W. F. Province	17,892	10.013	7,879
Punjab	338,873	187,378	151,495
United Provinces	1,314,828	693,681	621,147
Baroda State	31,510	16,516	14,994
SHEIKH (*Musalman*)—*contd.*			
Central India Agency	147,216	76,259	70,957
Hyderabad State	985,019	499,495	485,524
Kashmir State	105,285	59,662	45,623
Mysore State	176,482	91,495	84,987
Rajputana Agency	182,019	96,788	85,231
Elsewhere	10,250	6,407	3,843
SHENVA (SHINDHAVA) (*Hindu*)	**14,289**	**7,405**	**6,884**
Bombay	6,702	3,487	3,215
Baroda State	7,587	3,918	3,669
SHIN (*Musalman*) (Kashmir State)	**11,080**	**5,930**	**5,150**
SHINDE (*Hindu*) (Bombay)	**10,250**	**4,570**	**5,680**
SHORAGAR (Punjab)	**787**	**531**	**256**
Hindu	658	462	196
Musalman	129	69	60
SHRIMALI	**217,226**	**110,025**	**107,201**
Hindu	36,665	18,974	17,691
Jain	180,561	91,051	89,510
Bombay	184,632	93,826	90,806
Baroda State	31,965	15,872	16,093
Elsewhere	629	327	302
SIKLIGAR (SAIQALGAR)	**5,922**	**3,048**	**2,874**
Hindu	4,548	2,319	2,229
Sikh	818	444	374
Musalman	556	285	271
Rajputana Agency	2,096	1,033	1,063
Elsewhere	3,826	2,015	1,811
SILAWAT (SALAT, PATHRAT)	**17,264**	**8,709**	**8,555**
Hindu	10,499	5,186	5,313
Musalman	6,765	3,523	3,242
Central India Agency	6,335	3,171	3,164
Rajputana Agency	7,858	3,922	3,936
Elsewhere	3,071	1 616	1.455
SINDHI ‡ (*Musalman*)	**1,701,158**	**935,075**	**766,083**
Bombay	1,664.209	915,321	748.888
Rajputana Agency	33,277	17,775	15,502
Elsewhere	3,672	1,979	1,693
SIOLO (*Hindu*) (Madras)	**1,658**	**1,301**	**357**
***SIRKIBAND (Punjab)**	**3,354**	**1,816**	**1,538**
Hindu	2,608	1,435	1,173
Sikh	244	116	128
Musalman	502	265	237

* For sub-castes see Part II

† In Baluchistan included in Lasi

‡ This includes 1,625,387 persons belonging to the indigenous tribes of Sind, *viz.*:—

	Males.	Females.
Dahar Sindhi	5,210	3,868
Dahoreja Chachar	3,620	2,817
Indhar	1,297	1,090
Jat Sindhi	48,441	38,706
Mahar Sindhi	13,788	11,663
Mirbahar or Muhanı	73,001	60,198
Saman	718,381	586,709
Sumras	31,472	25,042
Others	56	28
Total	895,266	730,121

TABLE XIII.—Caste, Tribe, Race or Nationality. Part I.—

Caste, Religion and Locality.	Persons.	Males.	Females.
1	2	3	4
SIRVI (*Hindu*)	**64,650**	**33,648**	**31,002**
Ajmer-Merwara	10	7	3
Central India Agency	13,645	6,990	6,655
Rajputana Agency	50,995	26,651	24,344
SIYALGIR (*Hindu*)	**722**	**374**	**348**
Bengal	492	253	239
Bihar and Orissa	230	121	109
SOCHI * (*Hindu*) (Bombay)	**3,942**	**2,150**	**1,792**
SOKIAR (*Hindu*)	**14,161**	**6,655**	**7,506**
Bengal	18	18	..
Bihar and Orissa	14,143	6,637	7,506
SOLAGA (SOLIGA)	**3,740**	**1,875**	**1,865**
Hindu	1,944	981	963
Animist	1,796	894	902
Madras	1,944	981	963
Mysore State	1,796	894	902
SONAR (SUNAR, SONI, SARNAKAR)	**1,262,978**	**655,479**	**607,499**
Hindu	1,191,180	617,527	573,653
Sikh	28,331	15,359	12,972
Jain	57	33	24
Buddhist	5	5	..
Musalman	42,987	22,336	20,651
Animist	418	219	199
Bengal	56,305	30,464	25,841
Bihar and Orissa	212,454	104,963	107,491
Bombay	179,357	91,995	87,362
C. P. and Berar	126,878	63,844	63,034
N.-W. F. Province	9,714	5,033	4,681
Punjab	158,318	85,587	72,731
United Provinces	267,020	143,295	123,725
Baroda State	10,659	5,325	5,334
Central India Agency	66,612	34,387	32,225
Hyderabad State	88,037	45,278	42,759
Kashmir State	6,379	3,366	3,013
Rajputana Agency	69,034	35,569	33,465
Elsewhere	12,211	6,373	5,838
SONDHIYA (*Hindu*)	**102,239**	**49,680**	**52,559**
Central India Agency	70,546	32,662	37,884
Rajputana Agency	31,693	17,018	14,675
SONJHARA (C. P. and Berar)	**1,447**	**742**	**705**
Hindu	1,289	666	623
Animist	158	76	82
SOR (SUAR) (*Hindu*)	**15,877**	**6,994**	**8,883**
Central India Agency	13,783	5,924	7,859
Rajputana Agency	2,094	1,070	1,024
SORATHIYA	**12,054**	**5,959**	**6,095**
Hindu	12,026	5,945	6,081
Jain	28	14	14
Bombay	11,601	5,737	5,864
Baroda State	453	222	231
SUBARNABANIK (*Hindu*)	**129,567**	**66,003**	**63,564**
Assam	598	370	228
Bengal	109,429	55,740	53,689
Bihar and Orissa	19,540	9,893	9,647
SUD	**20,682**	**11,388**	**9,294**
Hindu	19,791	10,894	8,897
Sikh	888	492	396
Musalman	3	2	1
C. P. and Berar	37	23	14
Punjab	20,645	11,365	9,280
SUDARMAN (*Hindu*) (Madras)	**46,707**	**22,970**	**23,737**
SUDH (SUDHA, SUDDHO)	**97,650**	**47,801**	**49,849**
Hindu	97,645	47,798	49,847
Animist	5	3	2
Bengal	19	13	6
Bihar and Orissa	79,334	38,981	40,353
Madras	18,297	8,807	9,490
SUDHAN (*Musalman*) (Kashmir State)	**56,800**	**28,206**	**28,594**
SUDRA	**295,437**	**153,931**	**141,506**
Hindu	295,431	153,926	141,505
Jain	6	5	1
Assam	118,512	61,148	57,364
Bengal	148,778	70,892	77,886
Burma	26,806	21,350	5,456
Elsewhere	1,341	541	800
SUNGAH (Rajputana Agency)	**1,320**	**673**	**647**
Hindu	1,318	672	646
Jain	2	1	1
SUNKAR (SONKAR) (*Hindu*)	**10,002**	**5,529**	**4,473**
United Provinces	9,406	5,257	4,149
Central India Agency	596	272	324
SUNNI (*Musalman*)	**667**	**406**	**261**
Cochin State	560	312	248
Elsewhere	107	94	13
SUNUWAR	**5,583**	**2,931**	**2,652**
Hindu	5,564	2,917	2,647
Buddhist	4	2	2
Animist	15	12	3
Bengal	4,323	2,259	2,064
Elsewhere	1,260	672	588
SURAHIYA (*Hindu*)	**5,062**	**4,056**	**1,006**
Assam	716	588	128
Bengal	4,346	3,468	878

* The figures refer only to Sind. In other parts of Bombay Sochi has been classed under Chamar—*vide* footnote to Chamar

Distribution of Castes by Religion and Locality—*continued.*

Caste, Religion and Locality.	Persons.	Males.	Females.
1	2	3	4
SUTRADHAR * (SUTAR, CHHUTAR, BADIG)	**649,445**	**334,890**	**314,555**
Hindu	649,356	334,848	314,508
Sikh	12	8	4
Jain	5	4	1
Musalman	71	29	42
Animist	1	1	...
Assam	15,982	8,368	7,614
Bengal	177,453	91,556	85,897
Bombay	199,968	103,312	96,656
Baroda State	20,790	10,855	9,935
Central India Agency	115,167	59,400	55,767
Hyderabad State	69,205	35,118	34,087
Rajputana Agency	45,941	23,692	22,249
Elsewhere	4,939	2,589	2,350
SWATHI (*Musalman*) (N.-W. F. Province)	**38,329**	**20,181**	**18,148**
SYNTENG (Assam)	**42,145**	**19,633**	**22,512**
Hindu	1	1	...
Animist	42,144	19,632	22,512
TAGA (TAGAH)	**150,088**	**83,906**	**66,182**
Hindu	115,707	65,481	50,226
Sikh	10	10	...
Musalman	34,371	18,415	15,956
Punjab	13,223	7,323	5,900
United Provinces	136,865	76,583	60,282
TAI (*Musalman*)	**5,229**	**2,429**	**2,800**
Bombay	2,299	1,052	1,247
Baroda State	2,930	1,377	1,553
TAKARI	**7,288**	**3,719**	**3,569**
Hindu	7,266	3,709	3,557
Musalman	22	10	12
C. P. and Berar	7,002	3,585	3,417
Hyderabad State	286	134	152
TALAING (*Buddhist*) (Burma)	**320,629**	**159,235**	**161,394**
TALAVIYA † (Baroda State)	**9,647**	**5,253**	**4,394**
Hindu	8,919	4,874	4,045
Animist	728	379	349
TAMBALLA (*Hindu*) (Madras)	**3,433**	**1,810**	**1,623**
TAMBAT (TAMERA)	**36,228**	**19,359**	**16,869**
Hindu	36,226	19,357	16,869
Animist	2	2	...
Bombay	25,913	13,769	12,144
C. P. and Berar	4,572	2,402	2,170
Central India Agency	5,743	3,188	2,555
TAMBOLI (TAMBULI)	**180,312**	**92,936**	**87,376**
Hindu	179,762	92,594	87,168
Sikh	8	5	3
Musalman	539	334	205
Animist	3	3	...
Bengal	48,685	24,406	24,279
Bihar and Orissa	39,789	19,767	20,022
United Provinces	68,200	35,414	32,786
Central India Agency	15,149	8,736	6,413
Elsewhere	8,489	4,613	3,876
TANAOLI (*Musalman*)	**64,096**	**33,414**	**30,682**
N.-W. F. Province	63,985	33,349	30,636
Punjab	111	65	46
TANTAN (*Hindu*) (Travancore State)	**21,641**	**10,836**	**10,805**
TANTI AND TATWA ‡	**980,071**	**482,378**	**497,693**
Hindu	979,879	482,275	497,604
Sikh	1	1	...
Jain	1	1	...
Animist	190	101	89
Assam	41,528	20,689	20,839
Bengal	322,983	169,924	153,059
Bihar and Orissa	613,277	290,732	322,545
Elsewhere	2,283	1,033	1,250
TANTRE (*Musalman*) (Kashmir State)	**8,056**	**4,431**	**3,625**
TARAKAN	**7,497**	**3,666**	**3,831**
Hindu	7,494	3,664	3,830
Musalman	3	2	1
Madras	6,781	3,335	3,446
Elsewhere	716	331	385
TARKHAN	**716,959**	**394,486**	**322,473**
Hindu	176,866	97,944	78,922
Sikh	183,170	102,811	80,359
Jain	5	3	2
Buddhist	23	10	13
Musalman	356,895	193,718	163,177
N.-W. F. Province	42,618	22,764	19,854
Punjab	646,330	356,540	289,790
Kashmir State	27,871	15,080	12,791
Elsewhere	140	102	38
TATTAN (*Hindu*) (Travancore State)	**21,350**	**10,718**	**10,632**
TELAGA (TELINGA)	**967,218**	**484,229**	**482,989**
Hindu	964,660	482,834	481,826
Animist	2,558	1,395	1,163
Assam	9,131	4,832	4,299
Bengal	703	379	324
Madras	498,762	245,812	252,950
Hyderabad State	458,622	233,206	225,416

* Barhai has been shown separately. † In Bombay included in Dubla.
‡ Includes Hindu Jolaha in Bengal and Bihar and Orissa.

Caste, Religion and Locality.	Persons.	Males.	Females.
1	2	3	4
TELI AND TILI *	**4,233,250**	**2,147,937**	**2,085,313**
Hindu	3,600,427	1,807,373	1,793,054
Sikh	35	19	16
Jain	2	...	2
Buddhist	1	1	...
Musalman	632,637	340,468	292,169
Animist	148	76	72
Assam	38,757	20,399	18,358
Bengal	419,122	217,730	201,392
Bihar and Orissa	1,071,906	524,741	547,165
Bombay	168,848	85,247	83,601
C. P. and Berar	869,370	427,126	442,244
Madras	47,912	23,063	24,849
N.-W. F. Province	6,932	3,678	3,254
Punjab	295,971	162,444	133,527
United Provinces	968,132	504,507	463,625
Central India Agency	186,820	96,985	89,835
Hyderabad State	56,944	28,620	28,324
Kashmir State	19,309	10,206	9,103
Rajputana Agency	78,560	40,698	37,862
Elsewhere	4,667	2,493	2,174
TELIKULA (*Hindu*) (Madras)	**9,397**	**4,502**	**4,895**
THAKUR (THAKKAR)	**245,784**	**128,206**	**117,578**
Hindu	235,256	123,253	112,003
Sikh	1	1	...
Buddhist	1	1	...
Musalman	10,526	4,951	5,575
Bombay	132,180	68,487	63,693
Punjab	6,982	4,051	2,931
Kashmir State	104,613	54,588	50,025
Elsewhere	2,009	1,080	929
THARU (THIYAR)	**67,191**	**35,650**	**31,541**
Hindu	67,170	35,636	31,534
Musalman	1	1	...
Animist	20	13	7
Bihar and Orissa	35,060	17,816	17,244
United Provinces	27,720	14,933	12,787
Elsewhere	4,411	2,901	1,510
THATHERA (THATHIYAR)	**51,393**	**26,065**	**25,328**
Hindu	49,697	25,111	24,586
Sikh	451	257	194
Buddhist	24	15	9
Musalman	1,216	677	539
Animist	5	5	...
Bihar and Orissa	26,617	12,862	13,755
United Provinces	20,379	10,800	9,579
Elsewhere	4,397	2,403	1,994
THORI	**44,952**	**24,119**	**20,833**
Hindu	44,056	23,656	20,400
Sikh	510	275	235
Buddhist	8	3	5
Musalman	378	185	193
Punjab	16,451	8,903	7,548
Rajputana Agency	28,413	15,167	13,246
Elsewhere	88	49	39
TIGALA (*Hindu*)	**69,234**	**35,426**	**33,808**
Coorg	1	...	1
Mysore State	69,233	35,426	33,807

Caste, Religion and Locality.	Persons.	Males.	Females.
1	2	3	4
TIPARA	**139,765**	**71,213**	**68,552**
Hindu	120,541	61,329	59,212
Buddhist	992	515	477
Animist	18,232	9,369	8,863
Assam	9,740	5,002	4,738
Bengal	130,025	66,211	63,814
TIRMALI (*Hindu*)	**704**	**314**	**390**
C. P. and Berar	365	148	217
Hyderabad State	339	166	173
TIYAN (*Hindu*)	**641,606**	**317,483**	**324,123**
Coorg	1,774	1,471	303
Madras	639,832	316,012	323,820
TIYAR (TIYORO) (*Hindu*)	**280,510**	**139,400**	**141,110**
Bengal	215,270	108,209	107,061
Bihar and Orissa	60,897	28,968	31,929
Elsewhere	4,343	2,223	2,120
TOBA (Punjab)	**569**	**325**	**244**
Hindu	1	1	...
Musalman	568	324	244
TODA (Madras)	**748**	**426**	**322**
Hindu	45	28	17
Animist	703	398	305
TOGATA (*Hindu*) (Madras)	**67,028**	**34,278**	**32,750**
TOHALA (*Hindu*) (Madras)	**1,966**	**1,074**	**892**
TOKAR (*Hindu*) (Assam)	**942**	**479**	**463**
TOLKOLLAN (*Hindu*) (Madras)	**3,304**	**1,664**	**1,640**
TONDAMAN (*Hindu*) (Madras)	**2,837**	**1,393**	**1,444**
TOREYA †	**10,501**	**5,222**	**5,279**
Hindu	10,500	5,222	5,278
Animist	1	...	1
Coorg	527	280	247
Madras	9,974	4,942	5,032
TOTTIYAN (*Hindu*)	**156,535**	**77,113**	**79,422**
Madras	155,748	76,656	79,092
Elsewhere	787	457	330
TULUKKAN (*Musalman*) (Travancore State)	**61,095**	**31,417**	**29,678**
TURAHA (TURHA) (*Hindu*)	**76,288**	**36,118**	**40,170**
Bihar and Orissa	64,164	29,056	35,108
United Provinces	7,917	3,328	4,589
Elsewhere	4,207	3,734	473

Note.—Totla has been included in Rabha

* Includes Ganiger or Ghanchi in Bombay

† See also Besta

Distribution of Castes by Religion and Locality—*continued.*

Caste, Religion and Locality.	Persons.	Males.	Females.
1		3	4
TURI	**90,378**	**45,064**	**45,314**
Hindu	83,823	41,904	41,919
Buddhist	1	...	1
Animist	6,554	3,160	3,394
Assam	16,501	8,523	7,978
Bengal	17,666	9,154	8,512
Bihar and Orissa	47,399	23,077	24,322
Elsewhere	8,812	4,310	4,502
TURK* (*Musalman*)	**84,607**	**44,631**	**39,976**
United Provinces	77,166	40,758	36,408
Elsewhere	7,441	3,873	3,568
TURUNG (Assam)	**541**	**291**	**250**
Buddhist	515	277	238
Animist	26	14	12
UDAIYAN (*Hindu*) (Madras)	**12,489**	**5,723**	**6,766**
UDIYA (*Hindu*) (Bihar and Orissa)	**12,514**	**6,120**	**6,394**
ULEMA (*Musalman*)	**22,923**	**12,186**	**10,737**
Punjab	22,921	12,185	10,736
Travancore State	2	1	1
ULLATAN	**4,511**	**2,390**	**2,121**
Hindu	3,974	2,129	1,845
Animist	537	261	276
Cochin State	537	261	276
Travancore State	3,974	2,129	1,845
UMRE (*Hindu*) (C. P. and Berar)	**1,867**	**924**	**943**
UPPARA (UPPILIYAN) (*Hindu*)	**326,199**	**163,931**	**162,268**
Madras	160,657	80,053	80,604
Hyderabad State	57,000	29,098	27,902
Mysore State	108,131	54,541	53,590
Elsewhere	411	239	172
URALI (*Hindu*)	**67,692**	**33,081**	**34,611**
Madras	61,747	30,125	31,622
Travancore State	5,945	2,956	2,989
VADDA † (VODDA VADDAR, WADDAR)	**390,119**	**199,439**	**190,680**
Hindu	389,809	199,291	190,518
Musalman	276	126	150
Animist	34	22	12
Bombay	102,842	52,542	50,300
C. P. and Berar	12,869	6,551	6,318
Coorg	127	78	49
Hyderabad State	131,799	67,696	64,103
Mysore State	142,482	72,572	69,910
VADI (*Hindu*) (Baroda State)	**511**	**286**	**225**
VADUGAN (VADUKAN) (*Hindu*)	**59,118**	**28,810**	**30,308**
Madras	58,124	28,327	29,797
Cochin State	991	483	511
VAGHER (*Hindu*) (Baroda State)	**4,277**	**2,226**	**2,051**
VAISYA	**40,067**	**20,962**	**19,105**
Hindu	40,062	20,959	19,103
Jain	5	3	2
Madras	6,042	3,050	2,992
Mysore State	26,497	13,780	12,717
Elsewhere	7,528	4,132	3,396
VAITI (*Hindu*) (Bombay)	**2,699**	**1,498**	**1,201**
VAKKALIGA (VAKKAL, WAKLIGAR)	**1,507,093**	**753,207**	**753,886**
Hindu	1,501,940	750,595	751,345
Jain	5,153	2,612	2,541
Bombay	41,040	20,747	20,293
Coorg	10,576	5,829	4,747
Madras	80,798	38,931	41,867
Hyderabad State	38,497	19,381	19,116
Mysore State	1,336,182	668,319	667,863
VALAIYAN (VALAN) (*Hindu*)	**383,948**	**185,463**	**198,485**
Madras	358,848	172,554	186,294
Cochin State	7,827	4,046	3,781
Travancore State	17,273	8,863	8,410
VALLAMBAN (*Hindu*) (Madras)	**25,322**	**11,993**	**13,329**
VALLUVAN (*Hindu*)	**64,977**	**32,438**	**32,539**
Madras	63,493	31,694	31,799
Elsewhere	1,484	744	740
VALUVADI (*Hindu*) (Madras)	**6,407**	**3,218**	**3,189**
VALVI (Baroda State)	**1,046**	**522**	**524**
Hindu	565	268	297
Animist	481	254	227
VANIYAN (*Hindu*)	**212,130**	**103,599**	**108,531**
Madras	194,802	95,028	99,774
Travancore State	16,235	8,115	8,120
Elsewhere	1,093	456	637
VANNAN (MANNAN)	**288,544**	**143,719**	**144,825**
Hindu	287,305	143,072	144,233
Animist	1,239	647	592
Madras	274,572	136,732	137,840
Cochin State	97	54	43
Travancore State	13,875	6,933	6,942
VANZA (*Hindu*) (Baroda State)	**1,391**	**715**	**676**
VARLI	**192,609**	**97,134**	**95,475**
Hindu	190,354	95,967	94,387
Animist	2,255	1,167	1,088
Bombay	190,237	95,915	94,322
Elsewhere	2,372	1,219	1,153
VASUDEVA (WASUDEO) (*Hindu*)	**7,940**	**4,043**	**3,897**
C. P. and Berar	2,458	1,242	1,216
Hyderabad State	5,482	2,801	2,681

NOTE.—Umar has been included in Humbad and Vaghri in Bagri

* See also Moghal

† Includes Od in Bombay

TABLE XIII.—Caste, Tribe, Race or Nationality.

Part I.—Distribution of Castes by Religion and Locality—*concluded.*

Caste, Religion and Locality.	Persons.	Males.	Females.
1	2	3	4
VAYADA (*Hindu*) (Baroda State)	**740**	**399**	**341**
VEDAN (*Hindu*) (Madras)	**46,799**	**23,039**	**23,760**
VELAKKATTALAVAN (*Hindu*)	**13,297**	**6,560**	**6,737**
Madras	10,026	4,936	5,090
Cochin State	3,271	1,624	1,647
VELAMA (*Hindu*)	**571,822**	**284,317**	**287,505**
C. P. and Berar	738	367	371
Madras	487,297	241,245	246,052
Hyderabad State	83,787	42,705	41,082
VELAN (*Hindu*)	**25,673**	**12,597**	**13,076**
Madras	3,394	1,652	1,742
Cochin State	9,322	4,595	4,727
Travancore State	12,957	6,350	6,607
VELAN * (*Hindu*) (Travancore State)	**5,782**	**2,931**	**2,851**
VELLALA † (*Hindu*)	**2,603,089**	**1,283,129**	**1,319,960**
Burma	6,012	4,119	1,893
Madras	2,535,791	1,248,052	1,287,739
Cochin State	7,012	3,541	3,471
Travancore State	49,479	24,774	24,705
Elsewhere	4,795	2,643	2,152
VELUTTEDAN (*Hindu*)	**26,391**	**12,828**	**13,563**
Madras	11,654	5,521	6,133
Cochin State	3,381	1,589	1,792
Travancore State	11,356	5,718	5,638
VETTUVAN	**86,119**	**41,424**	**44,695**
Hindu	86,115	41,422	44,693
Animist	4	2	2
Madras	79,372	38,241	41,131
Cochin State	5,261	2,437	2,824
Travancore State	1,486	746	740
WA-PALAUNG, MIAO-YAO AND SALON ‡ (*Buddhist*) (Burma).	**175,636**	**89,055**	**86,581**
WAR (*Animist*) (Assam)	**6,445**	**2,903**	**3,542**
YAKHA	**1,462**	**727**	**735**
Hindu	1,450	722	728
Buddhist	2	2	...
Animist	10	3	7
Bengal	1,283	615	668
Elsewhere	179	112	67
YANADI	**121,839**	**62,221**	**59,618**
Hindu	43,157	22,080	21,077
Animist	78,682	40,141	38,541
Madras	121,549	62,091	59,458
Hyderabad State	290	130	160
YASHKUN (*Musalman*) (Kashmir State)	**35,011**	**17,965**	**17,046**
YATA (*Hindu*) (Madras)	**50,411**	**21,517**	**28,894**
YERAVA (YERRAVALA)	**18,264**	**9,355**	**8,909**
Hindu	2,751	1,374	1,377
Animist	15,513	7,981	7,532
Coorg	15,338	7,918	7,420
Elsewhere	2,926	1,437	1,489
YERUKALA	**88,319**	**44,775**	**43,544**
Hindu	83,835	42,580	41,255
Animist	4,484	2,195	2,289
C. P. and Berar	78	47	31
Madras	88,241	44,728	43,513
ZERBADI (*Musalman*) (Burma)	**59,729**	**28,047**	**31,682**

* A potter caste. † Agamudaiyan has been shown separately. ‡ For sub-castes see Part II

TABLE XIII.

Caste, Tribe, Race or Nationality.

Part II.—PRINCIPAL CASTES IN EACH PROVINCE, STATE OR AGENCY.

Caste.	Persons.	Males.	Females.
1	2	3	4
AJMER-MERWARA.			
Agarwal	8,400	4,444	3,956
Balai	23,773	12,234	11,539
Bambhi	2,550	1,305	1,245
Bhangi	5,361	2,832	2,529
Bhil	6,509	3,289	3,220
Brahman	24,220	12,977	11,243
Chamar	13,351	6,822	6,529
Chhipa	2,652	1,418	1,234
Daroga	8,952	4,550	4,402
Darzi	2,250	1,226	1,024
Deswali	2,449	1,413	1,036
Dhobi	2,882	1,479	1,403
Dholi	5,378	2,766	2,612
Gujar	35,059	18,609	16,450
Jat	30,497	16,526	13,971
Jogi	2,534	1,381	1,153
Kahar	3,043	1,580	1,463
Kayastha	2,439	1,320	1,119
Khati	6,839	3,620	3,219
Khatik	3,552	1,793	1,759
Koli	6,565	3,480	3,085
Kumhar	14,120	7,218	6,902
Lohar	4,214	2,256	1,958
Maheshri	5,414	2,924	2,490
Mali	14,340	7,499	6,841
Mer	21,803	11,634	10,169
Merat Gorat	2,025	1,300	725
Merat Kathat	17,626	9,651	7,975
Mina	4,223	2,442	1,781
Nai	6,503	3,297	3,206
Naik (Nayak)	2,497	1,298	1,199
Oswal	14,228	7,566	6,662
Pathan	11,429	6,181	5,248
Raigar	19,858	10,148	9,710
Rajput	14,302	8,225	6,077
Rawat	47,905	24,963	22,942
Rebari	2,033	1,085	948
Sadhu	4,638	2,552	2,086
Saiyid	5,199	2,823	2,376
Saraogi	3,223	1,858	1,365
Sheikh	25,130	13,380	11,750
Sunar	3,200	1,674	1,526
Teli	4,406	2,284	2,122
ANDAMANS AND NICOBARS.			
Andamanese	1,315	628	687
Nicobarese (excluding Shom Pen)	7,995	4,256	3,739
,, (Shom Pen)	375	190	185
Sheikh	2,496	2,147	349
ASSAM.			
Agarwala	5,360	3,460	1,900
Ahir	55,008	31,017	23,991
Ahom	197,444	101,961	95,483
Bagdi	8,391	4,212	4,179
Baidya	5,610	3,049	2,561
Baishnab (Bairagi)	11,380	5,209	6,171
Barui	25,154	12,986	12,168
Bauri	43,952	21,369	22,583
Bhar	14,269	7,331	6,938
Bhogta	11,019	5,704	5,315
Bhuiya	66,670	34,765	31,905
Bhumij	38,700	19,266	19,434
Boriya	21,513	10,994	10,519
Brahman	131,317	72,235	59,082
Brittiyal Baniya	9,084	4,563	4,521
Chamar	54,234	27,911	26,323
Chik (Baraik)	5,703	2,954	2,749
Chutiya	88,825	45,603	43,222
Dhoba	33,946	17,621	16,325
Dholi	11,292	5,590	5,702
Dom	30,412	15,387	15,025
Dosadh	10,038	5,641	4,397
Ganak (Grahabipra)	21,489	10,516	10,973
Garo	144,350	72,569	71,781
Ghasi	15,114	7,580	7,534
Gond	51,572	26,917	24,655
Hajang	8,288	4,324	3,964
Hajjam	39,781	20,825	18,956
Hari	40,826	21,045	19,781
Hira	16,351	8,063	8,288
Jalandha	6,709	3,360	3,349
Jogi (Jugi)	169,113	86,180	82,933
Jolaha	7,207	3,763	3,444
Kachari	230,102	117,487	112,615
Kahar	13,366	7,331	6,035
Kaibartta, Chasi (Mahisya)	65,312	34,304	31,008
Kaibartta, Jaliya	45,098	23,331	21,767
Kaibartta (Unspecified)	20,843	10,624	10,219
Kalita	221,942	115,506	106,436
Kamar	43,285	21,923	21,362
ASSAM—contd.			
Kandh	5,138	2,657	2,481
Kayastha	81,967	44,377	37,590
Kewat	94,777	48,245	46,532
Khariya	12,357	6,417	5,940
Kharwar	7,234	3,855	3,379
Khasi	120,894	57,328	63,566
Kooh	242,054	123,187	118,867
Koiri	14,000	8,064	5,936
Kshattriya (Manipuri)	250,541	124,764	125,777
Kuki	77,196	38,252	38,944
Kumhar	27,913	14,428	13,485
Kurmi	24,520	14,296	10,224
Lalung	39,219	19,222	19,997
Lohar	12,191	6,390	5,801
Loi	18,170	8,880	9,290
Lushai	80,425	36,758	43,667
Mahimal	77,379	39,102	38,277
Mahli	8,274	4,321	3,953
Mal	6,695	3,766	2,929
Mali	14,234	7,450	6,784
Malo	20,357	11,295	9,062
Mangar	7,201	4,716	2,485
Matak	9,246	5,208	4,038
Mech	94,606	47,177	47,429
Mikir	105,077	53,642	51,435
Miri	57,792	29,335	28,457
Muchi	13,697	7,829	5,868
Munda	91,298	47,227	44,071
Musahar	14,284	7,555	6,729
Nadiyal	68,350	34,891	33,459
Naga	220,033	108,575	111,458
Namasudra	172,753	89,347	83,406
Nat	5,143	2,557	2,586
Nuniya	14,358	9,222	5,136
Oraon	28,583	14,670	13,913
Oriya	5,964	3,237	2,727
Pan (Panika)	17,939	8,739	9,200
Pasi	6,943	3,492	3,451
Pathan	13,673	7,932	5,741
Patni	111,206	56,901	54,305
Poroja	5,861	3,032	2,829
Rabha	79,022	39,504	39,518
Rajbansi	133,078	68,584	64,494
Rajput (Chhatri)	27,670	17,536	10,134
Rajwar	8,338	4,291	4,047
Saiyid	14,134	7,498	6,636
Saloi	9,334	4,651	4,683
Santal	59,008	30,322	28,686
Shaha (Sunri)	56,929	28,867	28,062
Sheikh	1,769,666	916,488	853,178
Sudra	118,512	61,148	57,364
Sutradhar	15,982	8,368	7,614
Synteng	42,145	19,633	22,512
Tanti	41,528	20,689	20,839
Teli (Tili)	38,757	20,399	18,358
Telinga	9,131	4,832	4,299
Tipara	9,740	5,002	4,738
Turi	16,501	8,523	7,978
War	6,445	2,903	3,542
BALUCHISTAN.			
Baloch	172,473	93,819	78,654
Brahui	167,787	93,095	74,692
Darzada	10,257	5,215	5,042
Dehwar	7,326	4,009	3,317
Ghulam	21,078	10,007	11,071
Ghulamazad	7,738	4,233	3,505
Jat	5,680	3,151	2,529
Jatt	78,400	42,673	35,727
Lasi (Panj Raj)	34,980	18,573	16,407
Lori	10,936	5,912	5,024
Nakib*	6,536	3,444	3,092
Pathan	214,517	118,582	95,935
Saiyid	22,183	11,662	10,521
BENGAL.			
Agarwala	20,682	12,897	7,785
Aguri	85,850	42,601	43,249
Ajlaf	142,548	74,430	68,118
Bagdi	1,015,738	504,381	511,357
Baidya	88,796	44,345	44,451
Bais Baniya	7,374	3,843	3,531
Baishnab (Bairagi)	424,308	192,283	232,025
Baniya	14,717	8,776	5,941
Barui	178,168	92,748	85,420

*Included in Makrani in Part I

Principal Castes in each Province, State or Agency.

Caste.	Persons.	Males.	Females.
1	2	3	4
BENGAL—*contd.*			
Bauri	313,654	154,892	158,762
Bediya	30,713	15,252	15,461
Behara	68,863	35,373	33,490
Beldar	9,294	4,818	4,476
Besya	10,981	298	10,683
Bhar	15,363	10,148	5,215
Bhat	6,779	3,206	3,573
Bhotia	16,936	9,016	7,920
Bhuiya	69,048	37,466	31,582
Bhumij	90,377	44,288	46,089
Bind	25,400	14,653	10,747
Brahman	1,253,841	666,583	587,258
Chain	93,148	45,996	47,152
Chakma	58,672	31,014	27,658
Chamar	136,553	86,504	50,049
Chasa Dhoba	57,626	29,318	28,308
Chasati	28,002	13,601	14,401
Dai	27,026	13,887	13,139
Damai	5,425	2,960	2,465
Dhanuk	14,366	8,185	6,181
Dhawa	12,080	6,158	5,922
Dhoba	231,890	120,316	111,574
Dhuniya	8,536	4,878	3,658
Doai	12,495	6,228	6,267
Dom	173,991	88,101	85,890
Dosadh	45,863	33,072	12,791
Fakir	7,817	4,155	3,662
Gandhabanik	119,425	59,516	59,909
Gangai (Ganesh)	20,786	10,615	10,171
Garo	43,001	21,694	21,307
Ghasi	5,900	3,278	2,622
Ghatwal	5,575	3,261	2,314
Goala	646,473	355,966	290,507
Gonr	9,390	7,436	1,954
Gonrhi	11,325	6,996	4,329
Gurung	10,961	5,673	5,288
Hadi	26,212	13,415	12,797
Hajang	25,016	12,978	12,038
Halwai	13,690	8,796	4,894
Hari	265,679	134,513	131,166
Jogi and Jugi	361,141	182,903	178,238
Jolaha	282,705	152,352	130,353
Kahar	89,694	61,936	27,758
Kaibartta, Chasi (Mahisya)	2,137,948	1,075,562	1,062,386
Kaibartta, Jaliya	326,655	165,826	160,819
Kaibartta (Unspecified)	22,800	11,891	10,909
Kalu	111,562	56,332	55,230
Kalwar	12,929	8,700	4,229
Kamar (Karmakar)	263,329	136,158	127,171
Kami	13,667	7,345	6,322
Kandra (Kadma)	36,947	18,562	18,385
Kandu	12,603	9,658	2,945
Kansari (Kasera)	16,147	8,126	8,021
Kaora	112,281	56,072	56,209
Kapali	154,418	79,037	75,381
Karan	53,106	27,001	26,105
Kastha	20,750	10,580	10,170
Kayastha	1,113,684	570,819	542,865
Kewat	22,066	11,998	10,068
Khaira	41,435	20,302	21,133
Khambu	45,101	22,831	22,270
Khandayat	36,408	28,605	7,803
Kharia	16,105	8,353	7,752
Kharwar	11,938	6,193	5,745
Khas	13,261	7,351	5,910
Khatri	10,956	7,506	3,450
Khen (Khyan)	22,179	11,119	11,060
Koch	125,046	63,315	61,731
Koiri	25,814	19,902	5,912
Konai	9,416	4,738	4,678
Kora	46,497	23,087	23,410
Kshatriya	16,419	8,472	7,947
Kuki	11,174	5,603	5,571
Kulu	74,296	38,217	36,079
Kumhar	294,545	151,617	142,928
Kurmi	176,779	106,108	70,671
Lepcha	9,843	4,763	5,080
Limbu	16,878	9,183	7,695
Lodha	7,403	3,793	3,610
Lohar	48,522	25,101	23,421
Magh	127,949	62,914	65,035
Mahifarosh	5,673	2,903	2,770
Mahli	15,965	8,013	7,952
Mal	108,163	54,117	54,046
Mali (Malakar)	38,858	20,414	18,444
Mallah	27,472	19,882	7,590
Mallik	17,510	9,212	8,298
Malo	247,200	126,890	120,310
Mal Paharia	11,739	6,185	5,554
Mangar	21,533	11,745	9,788
Mayra	126,386	66,836	59,550
Mech	20,450	10,719	9,731
Mehtar	5,825	3,246	2,579
Muchi	455,448	244,012	211,436
Mughal	14,627	8,158	6,469
BENGAL—*concld.*			
Munda	67,252	35,217	32,035
Muriyari	5,194	2,699	2,495
Murmi	30,900	15,851	15,049
Murung (Mru)	12,391	6,339	6,052
Musahar	11,874	7,001	4,873
Nagar	18,537	8,818	9,719
Nagarchi	24,902	12,470	12,432
Naliya (Nalua)	6,204	2,902	3,302
Namasudra	1,909,794	967,760	942,034
Napit	458,035	236,006	222,029
Nat	9,979	4,855	5,124
Newar	9,602	5,341	4,261
Nikari	45,282	22,704	22,578
Nuniya	42,121	40,106	2,015
Oraon	165,628	89,236	76,392
Pasi	15,043	9,827	5,216
Pathan	314,652	173,599	141,053
Patial (Patikar)	8,620	4,282	4,338
Patni	63,447	32,294	31,153
Pod	536,568	274,181	262,387
Pundari (Puro)	15,707	7,995	7,712
Rajbansi	1,808,790	936,264	872,526
Rajbhar	10,278	7,211	3,067
Rajput (Chhatri)	130,221	84,358	45,863
Ra u	61,064	31,164	29,900
Rajwar	22,301	11,582	10,719
Sadgop	550,093	277,638	272,455
Saiyid	143,757	75,567	68,190
Sankhari	5,612	2,733	2,879
Santal	669,420	336,384	333,036
Shaha (Sunri)	444,252	221,331	222,921
Sheikh	22,952,944	11,698,628	11,254,316
Sonar (Sarnakar)	56,305	30,464	25,841
Subarnabanik	109,429	55,740	53,689
Sudra	148,778	70,892	77,886
Sutradhar (Chhutar)	177,453	91,556	85,897
Tambuli	48,685	24,406	24,279
Tanti and Tatwa	322,983	169,924	153,059
Teli and Tili	419,122	217,730	201,392
Tipara	130,025	66,211	63,814
Tiyar	215,270	108,209	107,061
Turi	17,666	9,154	8,512
BIHAR AND ORISSA.			
Agariya	27,126	13,439	13,687
Agarwala	30,588	16,158	14,430
Ahir (Goala)	3,250,415	1,621,530	1,628,885
Amat	62,716	30,801	31,915
Babhan	1,129,735	575,940	553,795
Bagdi	17,763	8,795	8,968
Baishnab (Bairagi)	78,739	41,412	37,327
Bandawat	7,022	3,604	3,418
Baniya	140,575	69,367	71,208
Banjara	6,826	3,348	3,478
Barai	130,028	64,155	65,873
Barhi	324,158	157,182	166,976
Barnawar	16,529	8,129	8,400
Bathudi	54,817	27,822	26,995
Bauri	292,503	144,817	147,686
Bedea	27,073	13,064	14,009
Bediya	5,345	2,637	2,708
Beldar	88,912	44,138	44,774
Bhandari	117,198	57,221	59,977
Bhar	30,389	14,726	15,663
Bhat	27,055	12,526	14,529
Bhogta	78,500	39,056	39,444
Bhuiya	663,757	322,708	341,049
Bhuiliya	34,022	17,081	16,941
Bhumij	281,624	135,039	146,585
Bind	134,818	62,954	71,864
Binjhiya	62,401	30,684	31,717
Brahman	1,755,424	874,507	880,917
Chain	32,335	15,702	16,633
Chamar	1,114,467	520,099	594,368
Chasa	846,119	415,439	430,680
Chero	18,066	8,914	9,152
Chik (Baraik)	31,611	15,655	15,956
Darzi	37,087	17,667	19,420
Dhanuk	572,412	272,915	299,497
Dhari	6,277	2,968	3,309
Dhobi	427,079	207,675	219,404
Dhuniya	202,208	94,550	107,658
Dom	241,903	119,393	122,510
Dosadh	1,189,274	569,733	619,541
Dumal	66,977	33,101	33,876
Fakir	67,568	32,599	34,969
Ganda	211,775	105,015	106,760
Gandhabanik	23,532	11,916	11,616
Gandhamali	5,528	2,733	2,795
Gangai (Ganesh)	50,765	23,860	26,905

TABLE XIII—CASTE, TRIBE, RACE OR NATIONALITY. PART II.—

Caste.	Persons.	Males.	Females.
1	2	3	4
BIHAR AND ORISSA—*contd.*			
Gangauta	82,633	39,533	43,095
Gareri	92,435	44,230	48,205
Gaura	712,772	345,819	366,953
Ghasi	69,920	34,125	35,795
Ghatwal	69,914	32,465	37,449
Gokha	47,139	22,960	24,179
Gola	55,571	27,806	27,765
Gond	235,671	116,669	119,002
Gonr	63,883	29,663	34,220
Gonrhi	130,106	63,137	66,969
Gosain	24,486	12,405	12,081
Guriya	146,777	71,090	75,687
Hajjam (Napit)	455,758	221,623	234,135
Halalkhor	18,586	9,187	9,399
Halwai	142,003	70,679	71,324
Hari	119,468	58,560	60,908
Ho	419,221	203,045	216,176
Jogi and Jugi	35,321	17,716	17,605
Jolaha	826,391	389,075	437,316
Juang	12,840	6,494	6,346
Kahar	524,431	245,801	278,630
Kaibartta, Chasi (Mahisya)	27,958	13,759	14,199
Kaibartta, Jaliya	4,183	2,261	1,922
Kaibartta (Unspecified)	61,163	30,232	30,931
Kalu	44,499	22,402	22,097
Kalwar (Kalal)	217,504	105,889	111,615
Kandh	302,883	148,079	154,804
Kandra (Kadma)	155,806	75,075	80,731
Kandu	502,855	243,100	259,755
Kansari (Kasera)	29,771	14,872	14,899
Karan	147,511	71,286	76,225
Karmali	21,842	11,072	10,770
Kasai (Kassab)	14,232	6,870	7,362
Kasarwani	27,951	13,937	14,014
Kayastha	347,613	177,714	169,909
Kewat	420,506	203,450	217,056
Khaira	20,738	10,169	10,569
Khandayat	769,353	365,982	403,371
Khariya	105,472	51,909	53,563
Kharura	10,871	5,243	5,628
Kharwar	85,876	42,278	43,598
Khatri	35,073	17,732	17,341
Khatwe	116,842	55,367	61,475
Khetauri	27,441	13,193	14,248
Kisan	38,276	18,675	19,601
Koiri	1,280,655	633,680	646,975
Koita	123,526	61,407	62,119
Kora	48,983	24,312	24,671
Korwa	14,231	7,123	7,108
Koshta	6,974	3,521	3,453
Kumhar	513,327	256,262	257,065
Kunjra	188,610	89,186	99,424
Kurmi	1,312,832	651,097	661,735
Lohar (Kamar)	479,817	235,129	244,688
Mahar	7,982	3,935	4,047
Mahli	64,189	32,026	32,163
Mahuri	25,066	11,082	13,984
Mal	24,406	12,018	12,388
Mali (Malakar)	139,619	69,643	69,976
Mallah	362,727	169,924	192,803
Mallik	20,736	9,478	11,258
Mal Paharia	38,797	19,190	19,607
Mayra	23,317	11,723	11,594
Muchi	31,339	15,757	15,582
Mughal	7,073	3,422	3,651
Munda	410,440	201,087	209,353
Musahar	626,795	309,653	317,142
Nagesiya	6,021	2,907	3,114
Nat	5,651	2,611	3,040
Nuniya	319,102	150,956	168,146
Oraon	474,673	227,273	247,400
Pan (Panika)	464,046	227,359	236,687
Parhaiya	9,452	4,867	4,585
Pasi	150,142	75,345	74,797
Pathan	220,707	106,287	114,420
Patra	37,216	17,583	19,633
Patwa	16,824	8,307	8,517
Rajbansi	107,586	56,474	51,112
Rajput (Chhatri)	1,239,826	630,717	609,109
Raju	52,096	26,247	25,849
Rajwar	131,971	65,880	66,091
Rauniyar (Noniyar)	83,482	42,061	41,421
Sadgop	23,940	12,941	10,999
Saiyid	91,105	44,460	46,645
Sannyasi (Atith)	73,593	35,132	38,461
Santal	1,399,450	692,067	707,383
Sarak	14,729	7,551	7,178
Saunti	22,659	11,147	11,512
Sauria Paharia	62,796	31,201	31,595
Savar (Sahar)	218,167	106,055	112,112
Shagirupesha	46,459	20,335	26,124
Sheikh	1,708,932	841,111	867,821
Sokiar	14,143	6,637	7,506
Sonar	212,454	104,963	107,491
Subarnabanik	19,540	9,893	9,647
Sudh (Sudha)	79,334	38,981	40,353
BIHAR AND ORISSA—*concld.*			
Sunri	257,114	126,901	130,213
Tambuli	39,789	19,767	20,022
Tanti and Tatwa	613,277	290,732	322,545
Teli and Tili	1,071,906	524,741	547,165
Tharu	35,060	17,816	17,244
Thathera	26,617	12,862	13,755
Tiyar	60,897	28,968	31,929
Turaha	64,164	29,056	35,108
Turi	47,399	23,077	24,322
Udiya	12,514	6,120	6,394
BOMBAY.			
Agri	233,553	118,287	115,266
Ahir	183,919	93,946	89,973
Ambi	11,866	6,003	5,863
Arab	156,395	88,003	68,392
Bairagi (Bava)	47,569	26,848	20,721
Bajaniya	8,724	4,554	4,170
Balochi	603,271	330,546	272,725
Bandi	7,655	3,383	4,272
Baniya	204,239	113,867	90,372
Baniya Maratha	10,983	5,258	5,725
Bari	6,727	3,321	3,406
Beldar	12,398	6,307	6,091
Berad (Bedar)	184,871	92,498	92,373
Bhambhi	8,593	4,378	4,215
Bhandari	183,131	90,749	92,382
Bhangi	140,714	74,077	66,637
Bhansali	14,596	7,335	7,261
Bharvad	836,927	426,595	410,332
Bhat	27,020	14,679	12,341
Bhatiya	26,742	13,866	12,876
Bhil	793,252	402,295	390,957
Bhoi	63,722	32,370	31,352
Bohora	126,011	64,862	61,149
Brahma Kshatri	5,071	2,734	2,337
Brahman	1,067,681	562,141	505,540
Brahui	60,389	33,383	27,006
Burud (Medar)	11,745	5,778	5,967
Chamar	302,536	155,075	147,461
Charan	32,510	17,221	15,289
Chaturth	89,208	46,329	42,879
Chhipa	15,101	7,733	7,368
Chodhra	38,138	19,276	18,862
Darji	141,423	71,819	69,604
Devli	6,254	3,077	3,177
Dhobi	79,707	41,185	38,522
Dhodiya	109,615	54,680	54,935
Dhor	13,506	6,893	6,613
Dubla (Talaviya)	127,870	65,204	62,666
Gabit (Gapit)	24,818	12,025	12,793
Gamta (Gamit)	9,892	5,032	4,860
Gam-Vakkal	12,132	5,655	6,477
Gavada	6,750	3,005	3,745
Gavandi (Uppar)	39,409	19,489	19,920
Gavli	38,542	19,262	19,280
Gola	13,791	7,020	6,771
Gurav (Hugar)	65,538	32,890	32,648
Hajjam	196,460	101,203	95,257
Halepaik	48,493	24,817	23,676
Hanbar	17,451	8,837	8,614
Harkanta	7,922	3,934	3,988
Jat	11,378	6,350	5,028
Jogi	5,296	2,696	2,600
Kabbaligar (Kabber)	59,815	31,993	27,822
Kachhiya	12,757	6,654	6,103
Kadiya	10,439	4,849	5,590
Kaikadi	9,614	4,681	4,933
Kalal	7,860	3,949	3,911
Kapol	14,270	7,392	6,878
Kasai	8,958	4,462	4,496
Kathi	28,580	14,816	13,764
Katkari	91,319	45,541	45,778
Kayasth Prabhu	27,120	13,884	13,236
Khadayata	20,986	10,801	10,185
Khalpa	9,358	4,918	4,440
Kharva (Kharvi)	37,844	19,367	18,477
Khatri*	106,930	56,882	50,048
Khavas	31,173	15,286	15,887
Khoja	52,476	26,464	26,012
Kokna	72,678	37,123	35,555
Koigha	5,849	2,875	2,974
Koli	2,006,121	1,040,310	965,811
Komarpaik	10,059	4,876	5,183
Komti	21,865	12,003	9,862
Korava	23,254	12,187	11,067
Koshti†	88,113	43,851	44,262
Kudale	10,927	5,338	5,589
Kumbhar	254,542	128,471	126,071
Kunbi	2,489,230	1,249,016	1,240,214
Lad	11,781	6,402	5,379

* Mostly weavers

† Included in Devanga in Part I

Principal Castes in each Province, State or Agency—*continued.*

Caste.	Persons.	Males.	Females.
1	2	3	4
BOMBAY—*contd.*			
Lingayat	1,339,248	683,472	655,776
Lohana	593,584	316,426	277,158
Lohar	121,126	62,875	58,251
Lonari	7,728	3,877	3,851
Machhi	39,300	18,696	20,604
Mahar (Holiya or Dhed)	1,470,992	735,841	735,151
Makrani	10,420	5,904	4,516
Mali	302,205	153,066	149,139
Mang (Madig)	274,037	134,852	139,185
Mangela	13,807	6,836	6,971
Maratha	3,279,496	1,672,212	1,607,284
Memon	97,283	44,874	52,409
Mo *	26,228	13,520	12,708
Modh	21,819	11,087	10,732
Molesalam	12,369	6,334	6,035
Momin	10,478	5,140	5,338
Momna	6,639	3,285	3,354
Mughal	6,268	3,384	2,884
Nador	6,586	3,507	3,079
Nagar	5,146	2,602	2,544
Naikda	48,258	23,852	24,406
Nau Muslim	92,535	52,088	40,447
Nema (Nima)	5,174	2,478	2,696
Oswal	132,588	67,521	65,067
Panchal	81,083	41,462	39,621
Pancham	12,194	6,201	5,993
Panchkalshi (Somavanshikshatri)	14,357	7,179	7,178
Pardhi (Shikari)	17,896	9,994	7,902
Pateliya	13,859	7,038	6,821
Pathan	161,095	89,515	71,580
Pinjari	15,658	7,642	8,016
Porwal (Porvad)	24,402	12,300	12,102
Rabari	130,009	68,708	61,301
Raddi	50,115	25,370	24,745
Rajput	457,723	242,964	214,759
Ramoshi	59,914	30,478	29,436
Rangari	6,584	3,258	3,326
Ravaliya	46,707	24,398	22,309
Sagar	11,538	6,000	5,538
Saiyid	150,492	77,679	72,813
Sali (Salvi)	57,763	30,102	27,661
Sangameshvari	12,700	5,766	6,934
Sangar	6,823	3,354	3,469
Sathavara	39,637	20,049	19,588
Sheikh	954,504	495,015	459,489
Shinde	10,250	4,570	5,680
Shindhava	6,702	3,487	3,215
Shrimali	184,632	93,826	90,806
Siddi † (Somali)	7,887	5,159	2,728
Sindhi	1,664,209	915,321	748,888
Sonar	179,357	91,995	87,362
Sorathiya	11,601	5,737	5,864
Sutar (Badig)	199,968	103,312	96,656
Tambat	25,913	13,769	12,144
Teli	168,848	85,247	83,601
Thakur	132,180	68,487	63,693
Vaddar (Od)	102,842	52,542	50,300
Vaghri	82,016	43,878	38,138
Vakkal	41,040	20,747	20,293
Vanjari (Lamani)	143,586	74,768	68,818
Varli	190,237	95,915	94,322
BURMA.			
Arakanese	344,123	177,089	167,034
Brahman	21,170	16,551	4,619
Burmese	7,642,204	3,731,026	3,911,178
Burmese	*7,479,433*	*3,650,902*	*3,828,531*
Chaungtha	*2,506*	*1,194*	*1,312*
Danu	*70,947*	*35,264*	*35,683*
Hpon	*378*	*176*	*202*
Intha	*52,685*	*25,771*	*26,914*
Kadu	*11,196*	*5,600*	*5,596*
Mrō	*2,708*	*1,342*	*1,366*
Taman	*527*	*281*	*246*
Taungyo	*19,656*	*9,271*	*10,385*
Tavoyan	*523*	*397*	*126*
Yabein	*1,549*	*775*	*774*
Yaw	*96*	*53*	*43*
Chetti	14,366	12,663	1,703
Chin	306,486	151,165	155,321
Anu	*479*	*235*	*244*
Baungshe	*14,216*	*7,056*	*7,160*
Chaw	*249*	*128*	*121*
Chin (Unspecified)	*131,323*	*65,113*	*66,210*
Chinbok	*18,179*	*8,916*	*9,263*
Chinbon	*1,600*	*818*	*782*
Daingnet	*954*	*496*	*458*
Kadoe	*1,009*	*497*	*512*
Kamhon	*10,882*	*5,389*	*5,493*
Khami	*16,372*	*8,243*	*8,129*
BURMA—*contd.*			
Klang	*6,926*	*3,385*	*3,541*
Kwangli	*3,701*	*1,661*	*2,040*
Kyunakya	*364*	*162*	*202*
Laiyo	*6,403*	*3,028*	*3,375*
Lamban	*4,463*	*2,057*	*2,406*
Naga	*1,263*	*672*	*591*
Nagawn	*3,831*	*1,839*	*1,992*
Seintaung	*7,918*	*3,900*	*4,018*
Siyin	*3,108*	*1,526*	*1,582*
Sokte	*11,368*	*5,616*	*5,752*
Tashon	*6,143*	*2,840*	*3,303*
Taungtha	*17,462*	*8,888*	*8,574*
Whamah	*3,383*	*1,570*	*1,813*
Wi	*832*	*422*	*410*
Yakaw	*8,949*	*4,227*	*4,722*
Yaun	*13,568*	*7,007*	*6,561*
Yindu	*4,348*	*2,138*	*2,210*
Yoe	*3,918*	*1,890*	*2,028*
Yokwa	*2,849*	*1,239*	*1,610*
Minor Chin Tribes	*426*	*207*	*219*
Chinese	122,834	89,345	33,489
Kachin	162,368	80,764	81,604
Kachin-Burma Hybrids and Lolo Group.	77,585	40,285	37,300
Akha (Kaw)	*33,181*	*17,685*	*15,496*
Ako	*4,119*	*2,878*	*1,241*
Kwi (Lahu Hsi)	*3,189*	*832*	*2,357*
Lahu (Muhso)	*18,103*	*9,200*	*8,903*
Lashi	*2,908*	*1,423*	*1,485*
Lisu	*8,487*	*4,395*	*4,092*
Lolo (Myen)	*339*	*166*	*173*
Maingtha	*401*	*362*	*39*
Maru	*3,855*	*1,966*	*1,889*
Tsi	*3,003*	*1,378*	*1,625*
Kapu	14,964	12,588	2,376
Karen	1,102,695	549,758	552,937
Bre	*6,911*	*3,149*	*3,762*
Karenbyu	*790*	*446*	*344*
Karennet	*3,721*	*1,791*	*1,930*
Karenni	*19,008*	*9,252*	*9,756*
Mano	*1,445*	*221*	*1,224*
Padaung	*8,516*	*4,106*	*4,410*
Sgau-Karen, Pwo-Karen and Karen unspecified.	*872,825*	*436,014*	*436,811*
Sinsin	*533*	*156*	*377*
Taungthu	*183,054*	*91,597*	*91,457*
Yinbaw	*911*	*467*	*444*
Zayein	*4,981*	*2,559*	*2,422*
Mala	21,248	18,106	3,142
Oriya	10,411	9,810	601
Padiyachi	11,808	8,085	3,723
Pali	5,861	4,527	1,334
Pathan	8,041	6,967	1,074
Rajput	10,942	9,296	1,646
Saiyid	6,871	5,398	1,473
Shan	996,420	495,703	500,717
Daye	*201*	*87*	*114*
Khün	*42,366*	*21,663*	*20,703*
Lü	*17,331*	*8,426*	*8,905*
Shan (Unspecified)	*926,879*	*460,444*	*466,435*
Siamese	*9,643*	*5,083*	*4,560*
Sheikh	237,568	152,412	85,156
Sudra	26,806	21,350	5,456
Talaing	320,629	159,235	161,394
Vellala	6,012	4,119	1,893
Wa-Palaung, Miao-Yao and Salon	175,636	89,055	86,581
Danaw	*1,724*	*1,201*	*523*
En (In)	*3,455*	*1,660*	*1,795*
Lamet	*231*	*231*	..
Miao	*646*	*331*	*315*
Palaung	*144,139*	*72,563*	*71,576*
Pale	*68*	*35*	*33*
Pyin	*275*	*155*	*120*
Salon Mawken	*1,984*	*1,020*	*964*
Wa	*14,674*	*7,503*	*7,171*
Yao	*512*	*362*	*150*
Yin Riang	*7,928*	*3,994*	*3,934*
Zerbadi	59,729	28,047	31,682
CENTRAL PROVINCES AND BERAR.			
Agariya	9,500	4,710	4,790
Agarwal	25,147	13,387	11,760
Aghariya	27,057	13,413	13,644
Ahir	738,192	366,815	371,377
Andh	52,378	25,563	26,815
Bahna	48,407	24,045	24,362
Baiga	30,391	15,045	15,346
Bairagi	38,059	19,693	18,366
Balahi	52,314	25,857	26,457
Baniya	48,300	24,853	23,447
Banjara	169,505	87,291	82,214

* Included in Meo in Part I
† Included in African in Part I

CASTE.	Persons.	Males.	Females.
1	2	3	4
C. P. AND BERAR—contd.			
Barai	61,177	30,643	30,534
Barhai	108,834	56,297	52,537
Basor	52,947	26,148	26,799
Beldar	25,616	12,905	12,711
Bhaina	17,387	8,489	8,898
Bhangi	7,560	3,735	3,825
Bhariya (Bhumiya)	51,006	24,588	26,418
Bhat	29,972	15,049	14,923
Bhil	27,785	13,768	14,017
Bhilala	15,437	7,800	7,637
Bhoyar	58,638	28,990	29,648
Bhulnbar	27,620	14,126	13,494
Bhunjiya	6,921	3,466	3,455
Bidur	20,987	10,377	10,610
Binjhwar	59,327	29,199	30,128
Brahman	445,744	237,605	208,139
Chadar	28,129	13,968	14,161
Chamar (Dohor)	907,927	446,240	461,687
Chauhan	6,750	3,265	3,485
Chhipa	8,799	4,399	4,400
Dahayat	14,685	7,212	7,473
Dangi	24,283	12,327	11,956
Darji	51,301	26,113	25,188
Deswali	7,761	3,978	3,783
Dhanagar (Hatgar)	110,708	55,986	54,722
Dhanuk	6,601	3,215	3,386
Dhanwar	18,637	9,181	9,456
Dhimar	283,684	140,853	142,831
Dhobi	165,427	81,127	84,300
Dom	9,344	4,660	4,684
Fakir	9,095	4,526	4,569
Gadariya	40,207	20,244	19,963
Gahoi	6,775	3,402	3,373
Ganda	151,787	74,285	77,502
Garpagari	9,048	4,500	4,548
Ghasiya	43,142	20,881	22,261
Ghosi	9,739	4,999	4 740
Golapurab	5,801	2,952	2,849
Golar	16,710	8,080	8,630
Gond	2,339,361	1,140,862	1,198,499
Gosain	42,272	22,107	20,165
Gowari	157,580	77,300	80,280
Gujar	55,798	28,607	27,191
Guiao	14,172	6,994	7,178
Halba	100,211	48,836	51,375
Jat	9,959	5,753	4,206
Jogi	15,402	7,753	7,649
Joshi	5,906	2,831	3,075
Kachhi	119,553	60,287	59,266
Kahar	23,357	11,883	11,474
Kalar	195,450	96,426	99,024
Kamar	7,438	3,542	3,896
Kandh (Khond)	9,587	4,643	4,944
Kaonra	15,339	7,791	7,548
Kapu (Kapewar)	18,489	9,131	9,358
Kasari	20,175	10,210	9,965
Kasarwani	6,579	3,339	3,240
Kasaundha	5,567	2,598	2,969
Katiya	41,311	20,202	21,109
Kawar	229,412	113,563	115,849
Kayasth	33,584	17,580	16,004
Kewat	169,395	81,704	87,691
Khangar	12,815	6,422	6,393
Khariya	9,927	4,789	5,138
Kharwar	19,651	9,529	10,122
Khatik	12,596	6,315	6,281
Kir	6.711	3,526	3,185
Kirar	47,793	24,036	23,757
Kol	82,598	40,857	41,741
Kolam	24,976	12,331	12,645
Koli (Kohli)	61,775	31,039	30,736
Kolta	36,295	18,075	18,220
Komti	10,766	5,396	5,370
Kori	39,628	20,397	19.231
Korku	152,363	75,559	76,804
Korwa	34,000	17,164	16,836
Koshti (Koskati)	154,599	77.288	77,311
Kumhar	118,520	60,054	58,466
Kunbi	1,356,734	682,737	673,997
Kurmi	302,588	150,109	152,479
Lingayat	7,793	4.204	3,589
Lod	5,383	2,691	2,692
Lodhi	313,900	155,922	157,978
Lohar	181,590	91,183	90,407
Madgi	8,574	4,243	4,331
Maheshri	14,107	7,443	6,664
Majhwar	14,210	7,196	7,014
Mala (Mal)	15,459	7,980	7,479
Mali	572,864	284,397	288,467
Mana	49,037	23,835	25,202
Mang	83,660	41.106	42,554
Maratha	93,901	46,716	47,185
Mehra	1,165,177	575,449	589,728
Mehtar	13,012	6,642	6,370
Mhali	37,489	19,115	18,374
C. P. AND BERAR—concld.			
Moghal	9,045	4,640	4,405
Munda (Murha)	5,444	2,870	2,574
Nagarchi	6,239	2,991	3,248
Nagasiya	44,165	22,207	21,958
Nai	148,750	74,078	74.672
Nat	11,385	5,419	5,966
Nihal (Nahal)	12,403	6.064	6,339
Oraon	83,099	41,916	41,183
Oswal	9,612	5,498	4,114
Panchal	8,712	4,241	4,471
Panka	214,894	104,032	110,862
Pardhan	118,630	57,711	60,919
Pardhi	12,890	6,506	6,384
Parwar	29,445	15,119	14,326
Pathan	143,972	74,082	69,890
Patwa	7,073	3,470	3,603
Rajjhar (Lajjhar)	7,554	3,649	3,905
Rajput	441,231	223,581	217,650
Rajwar (Mowar)	30,003	15,104	14,899
Rangari	16,846	8,414	8,432
Rautiya	12,037	6,267	5,770
Saitwal	7,017	3,426	3,591
Seiyid	47,936	24,656	23,280
Sali	14,289	6,911	7,378
Santal (Saonta)	10,432	5,312	5,120
Savara	74,181	36,041	38,140
Sheikh	280,314	144,434	135,880
Sunar	126,878	63,844	63,034
Sundi *	5,470	2,731	2,739
Takari	7,002	3,585	3,417
Teli	869,370	427,126	442,244
Waddar	12,869	6,551	6,318
COORG.			
Billava	2,816	1,793	1,023
Brahman	2,521	1,349	1,172
Devanga	2,933	1,539	1,394
Gauda	12,994	6,923	6,071
Holeya	22,107	12,419	9,688
Kodaga	39,228	19,726	19,502
Kuruba	7,394	3,905	3,489
Lingayat	7,558	3,697	3,861
Mahratta	2,145	1,338	807
Mappilla	7,196	5,032	2,164
Pale	4,120	2,897	1,223
Panchala	2,003	1,068	935
Sheikh	3,752	2,063	1,669
Vakkaliga	10,576	5,829	4,747
Yerava	15,338	7,918	7,420
MADRAS.			
Agamudaiyan	349,753	167,793	181,960
Agasa	16,628	8,017	8,611
Aiyarakam	16,687	7,707	8,980
Aiya	22,179	10,365	11,814
Ambalakaran	185,177	90,326	94,851
Ambalavasi	20,218	9,759	10,459
Ambattan	213,050	105,199	107,851
Anappan	15,677	7,882	7,795
Andi	85,427	41,445	43,982
Anduran	9,894	4,810	5,084
Arab	5,518	2,780	2,738
Arayan	5.424	2,739	2,685
Aruva	8,755	3,740	5,015
Badaga	38,180	18,898	19,282
Badhoyi	18,616	9,460	9,156
Bagata	33,021	16,105	16,916
Ball'a	1,041,246	514,769	526,477
Bana iga	11,640	5,767	5.873
Bant	126,296	61,364	64,932
Bavuri	68,699	30,337	38,362
Bedaru	49,893	24,783	25.110
Bestha	47,676	23,901	23,775
Bhatrazu	25,137	12,066	13,071
Bhondari	22,362	10,811	11,551
Bhumiya	21,891	11,092	10,799
Billava	157,071	75,032	82,039
Boda	5,688	1,899	3,789
Bogam	27,507	11,707	15,800
Bolasi	10.304	4,765	5,539
Bondili	9,771	4,952	4,819
Bottada	62,101	30,959	31,142
Boya	425,862	216,732	209,130
Brahman	1,310,360	650,265	660,095
Chakkan	36,801	18,056	18,745
Chakkiliyan	526,451	261,421	265,030
Chaliyan	31,324	15,637	15,687
Chenchu	7,449	3,768	3,681

* Included in Shaha in Part I

Principal Castes in each Province, State or Agency—*continued*.

Caste.	Persons.	Males.	Females.
1	2	3	4
MADRAS—*contd.*			
Cheruman	255,395	121,567	133,828
Chetti	350,251	171,058	179,103
Dandasi	45,274	20,745	24,529
Dasari	33,438	16,020	17,418
Dasi	7,037	2,710	4,327
Devadiga	25,621	11,816	13,805
Devanga	286,504	142,672	143,832
Dhobi	33,265	16,065	17,200
Doluva	17,099	8,386	8,713
Dombo	62,976	31,370	31,606
Dommara	17,714	8,872	8,842
Dudekula	71,612	36,076	35,536
Gadaba	45,115	23,011	22,104
Gamalla	153,658	76,517	77,141
Gandla	35,986	17,809	18,177
Ganiga	17,584	8,694	8,890
Gauda (Gaudo)	169,261	81,838	87,423
Gavara	60,515	29,076	31,439
Godiya	10,604	5,017	5,587
Golla	904,192	445,827	458,365
Gond	32,257	16,848	15,409
Haddi	28,201	13,884	14,317
Halepaik	6,102	2,770	3,332
Holeya	136,109	61,164	74,945
Idaiyan	734,767	360,154	374,613
Idiga	261,235	126,756	134,479
Ilamagan	7,160	3,114	4,046
Iluvan	121,138	57,495	63,643
Indra	56,774	26,535	30,239
Irula	100,659	50,095	50,564
Jalari	23,560	11,170	12,390
Janappan	42,707	19,842	22,865
Jangam	110,091	54,059	56,032
Jatapu	92,520	44,952	47,568
Jogi	23,190	11,644	11,546
Jonagan	8,780	3,568	5,212
Kabbera	20,101	9,690	10,411
Kaduppattan	19,971	9,703	10,268
Kaikolan	368,347	179,467	188,880
Kalingi	83,442	39,978	43,464
Kalinji	51,558	22,809	28,749
Kallan	535,572	258,972	276,600
Kamma	1,126,095	564,432	561,663
Kammalan (Kamsala)	962,744	473,848	488,896
Kanakkan	63,360	31,640	31,720
Kanisan	15,689	7,486	8,203
Kannadiyan	28,375	14,556	13,819
Kappiliyan	38,493	19,123	19,370
Kapu	2,678,925	1,329,624	1,349,301
Karnabattu	9,477	4,926	4,551
Karnam	54,109	27,273	26,836
Karumpurattan	11,620	5,256	6,364
Kavandan	10,311	5,059	5,252
Kavutiyan	6,365	3,240	3,125
Kelasi	7,313	3,631	3,682
Kevuto	34,447	15,034	19,413
Khond	355,137	176,613	178,524
Kolayan	21,951	10,507	11,444
Komati	498,295	250,043	248,252
Konda Dora	89,775	44,932	44,843
Kondra	8,543	3,758	4,785
Kotegara	11,622	5,713	5,909
Kottiya	19,801	10,038	9,763
Koyi	79,422	39,316	40,106
Kshatriya	158,521	80,372	78,149
Kudub	10,366	5,183	5,183
Kudumo	22,772	11,300	11,472
Kumbara (Kumbhar, Kummara)	190,505	95,409	95,096
Kuravan	110,157	53,877	56,280
Kuric'chan	9,722	4,917	4,805
Kurni	9,644	8,351	1,293
Kurumban (Kuruba)	385,686	196,474	189,212
Kusavan	153,127	75,222	77,905
Labbai	401,703	184,923	216,780
Lambadi	50,107	25,605	24,502
Lingayat	134,592	66,375	68,217
Lohara	8,038	3,788	4,250
Madiga	807,986	406,089	401,897
Mahrati	79,247	39,078	40,169
Majjulu	10,643	4,761	5,882
Mala	1,511,312	747,652	763,660
Malaiman	57,034	27,478	29,556
Malayali	63,487	31,395	32,092
Malayan	9,602	4,790	4,812
Mali	34,337	16,776	17,561
Mangala	184,000	90,231	93,769
Mappilla	1,032,757	514,555	518,202
Maravan	364,762	177,785	186,977
Marayan	14,555	6,889	7,666
Medara	20,511	10,291	10,220
Melakkaran	10,925	5,045	5,880
Moger	39,148	18,176	20,072
Moghal	18,628	9,702	8,926
Muc'chi*	6,285	2,964	3,321
Mukkuvan	19,215	9,771	9,444
MADRAS—*concld.*			
Muli	5,243	2,719	2,524
Muppan	7,958	3,878	4,080
Mutracha	153,422	77,368	76,054
Muttan	9,696	4,882	4,814
Muttiriyan	86,856	43,321	43,535
Nagaralu	14,569	6,752	7,817
Nagavasulu	24,983	12,278	12,705
Nattaman	162,786	79,298	83,488
Nayar	412,618	198,422	214,196
Neyyala	11,717	5,020	6,697
Oc'chan	5,177	2,481	2,696
Odde	550,109	277,375	272,734
Odiya	101,312	46,783	54,529
Ojali	11,653	5,672	5,981
Omaito	11,501	5,769	5,732
Paidi	48,610	23,913	24,697
Pallan	866,132	414,945	451,187
Palli	2,820,156	1,383,560	1,436,596
Panan	14,717	7,238	7,479
Panchala	54,721	26,953	27,768
Pandaram	66,868	32,983	33,885
Panikkan	30,083	14,537	15,546
Panisavan	19,553	9,640	9,913
Paniyan	34,574	17,501	17,073
Pano	71,323	35,651	35,672
Paraiyan	2,365,433	1,154,107	1,211,326
Paravan	5,396	2,623	2,773
Parivaram	20,785	10,090	10,695
Pathan	106,920	54,536	52,384
Patnulkaran	92,840	45,444	47,396
Patra (Telugu)	16,103	7,967	8,136
Pattanavan	48,847	24,523	24,324
Periko	24,965	12,560	12,405
Pic'chigunta	8,977	4,583	4,394
Poroja	92,737	47,792	44,945
Puluvan	6,625	2,946	3,679
Rajapuri	11,420	5,671	5,749
Rajput	17,603	8,899	8,704
Rangari	15,309	7,727	7,582
Ravulo	5,702	2,862	2,840
Razu	102,845	51,349	51,496
Relli	21,472	9,837	11,635
Rona	39,166	19,773	19,393
Saiyid	170,125	85,730	84,395
Sale	358,482	178,389	180,093
Samantiya	14,750	6,959	7,791
Satani	47,921	23,533	24,388
Savara	186,128	92,348	93,780
Segidi	56,404	25,470	30,934
Sembadavan	64,403	31,905	32,498
Senaikkudaiyan	38,133	18,827	19,306
Shanan	641,976	314,733	327,243
Sheikh	892,910	442,885	450,025
Sondi †	36,756	18,455	18,301
Sudarman	46,707	22,970	23,737
Suddho	18,297	8,807	9,490
Tarakan	6,781	3,335	3,446
Telaga	498,762	245,812	252,950
Teli	47,912	23,063	24,849
Telikula	9,397	4,502	4,895
Tiyan	639,832	316,012	323,820
Togata	67,028	34,278	32,750
Toreya	9,974	4,942	5,032
Tottiyan	155,748	76,656	79,092
Tsakala	387,109	192,056	195,053
Udaiyan	12,489	5,723	6,766
Uppara (Uppiliyan)	160,657	80,053	80,604
Urali	61,747	30,125	31,622
Vadugan	58,124	28,327	29,797
Vaisya	6,042	3,050	2,992
Vakkaliga	80,798	38,931	41,867
Valaiyan	358,848	172,554	186,294
Vallamban	25,322	11,993	13,329
Valluvan	63,493	31,694	31,799
Valuvadi	6,407	3,218	3,189
Vaniyan	194,802	95,028	99,774
Vannan (Mannan)	274,572	136,732	137,840
Vedan	46,709	23,039	23,760
Velakkattalavan	10,026	4,936	5,090
Velama	487,297	241,245	246,052
Vellala	2,535,791	1,248,052	1,287,739
Veluttedan	11,654	5,521	6,133
Vettuvan	79,372	38,241	41,131
Yanadi	121,549	62,091	59,458
Yata	50,411	21,517	28,894
Yerukala	88,241	44,728	43,513
NORTH-WEST FRONTIER PROVINCE.			
Arain	3,343	1,797	1,546
Arora	69,215	37,977	31,238
Awan	276,511	150,029	126,482
Baghban	20,471	10,881	9,590
Baluch	26,513	14,466	12,047

* Included in Mochi in Part I

† Included in Shaha in Part I

TABLE XIII.—Caste, Tribe, Race or Nationality. Part II.—

Caste.	Persons.	Males.	Females.
1	2	3	4
N.-W. F. PROVINCE—*contd.*			
Bhatiya	4,086	2,095	1,991
Bhatiyara	4,331	2,209	2,122
Brahman	13,208	7,856	5,352
Chamar	4,686	2,674	2,012
Chuhra (Musalli, Kutana)	19,047	10,823	8,224
Darzi	2,278	1,278	1,000
Dhobi	14,877	8,100	6,777
Dhund	30,464	15,773	14,691
Gakkhar	6,807	3,676	3,131
Gujar	113,871	61,711	52,160
Gurkha	6,343	5,163	1,180
Jat	86,097	48,873	37,224
Jhinwar	2,327	1,524	803
Jolaha	37,390	19,999	17,391
Karal	22,106	11,316	10,790
Kashmiri	28,631	15,198	13,433
Khatri	35,720	21,662	14,058
Khoja	2,974	1,676	1,298
Kumhar	22,664	11,705	10,959
Lohar	28,589	15,331	13,258
Machhi	4,031	2,175	1,856
Maliar	19,950	10,412	9,538
Mallah	4,805	2,696	2,109
Mirasi	11,790	6,134	5,656
Mishwani	4,888	2,404	2,484
Mochi	23,209	12,526	10,683
Moghal	14,865	8,269	6,596
Nai	24,777	13,075	11,702
Paracha	12,330	6,670	5,660
Pathan	845,183	449,500	395,683
Qassab	8,721	4,559	4,162
Qureshi	20,939	11,058	9,881
Rajput	15,263	10,715	4,548
Rangrez	3,933	2,198	1,735
Saiyid	75,115	39,230	35,885
Sarara	8,507	4,616	3,891
Sheikh	17,892	10,013	7,879
Sonar	9,714	5,033	4,681
Swathi	38,329	20,181	18,148
Tanaoli	63,985	33,349	30,636
Tarkhan	42,618	22,764	19,854
Teli	6,932	3,678	3,254
Turk	4,499	2,309	2,190
PUNJAB.			
Agarwal	373,622	202,186	171,436
Aheri	19,505	10,568	8,937
Ahir	208,594	116,380	92,214
Arain	977,601	541,189	436,412
Arora	673,665	362,728	310,937
Awan	425,931	226,991	198,940
Bairagi	37,979	22,529	15,450
Baniya	43,265	24,956	18,309
Banjara	66,439	36,130	30,309
Barar	6,119	3,300	2,819
Barwala (Batwal)	85,657	46,800	38,857
Bawariya	32,868	17,495	15,373
Bazigar	36,354	19,631	16,723
Bhabra	11,898	6,578	5,320
Bharai	58,400	32,166	26,234
Bharbhunja	6,017	3,345	2,672
Bhat	37,130	19,678	17,452
Bhatiya	22,047	11,882	10,165
Bhatiyara	7,930	4,118	3,812
Biloch	532,499	289,611	242,888
Bishnoi	19,416	10,509	8,907
Brahman	1,017,743	562,039	455,704
Chamar	1,139,941	620,421	519,520
Chanal	12,448	6,440	6,008
Chang	6,373	3,816	2,557
Changar	40,407	22,048	18,359
Chhimba	129,338	71,594	57,744
Chuhra	1,235,103	676,915	558,183
Darzi	35,827	18,790	17,037
Daudputra	21,229	11,737	9,492
Dhanak	83,256	44,220	39,036
Dhobi	156,046	84,642	71,404
Dhund	24,913	13,316	11,597
Dogar	68,473	38,030	30,443
Dumna	79,916	42,697	37,219
Fakir	282,361	165,569	116,792
Gadariya	21,946	12,393	9,553
Gaddi	27,618	13,420	14,198
Gakkhar	27,841	13,770	14,071
Ghirath	171,129	88,778	82,351
Gosain	11,701	6,941	4,760
Gujjar	610,472	339,813	271,659
Gurkha	8,297	5,587	2,710
Hali	21,067	10,779	10,288
Jat	4,956,536	2,808,551	2,147,985
Jhabel	14,046	7,856	6,190
Jhinwar	359,864	198,667	161,197
Jogi	83,412	44,887	38,525
Julaha	635,044	345,292	289,752
PUNJAB—*contd.*			
Kahut	10,648	5,566	5,082
Kalwar (Kalal)	48,706	26,313	22,393
Kamboh	172,434	95,004	77,430
Kanet	403,815	207,202	196,613
Kanjar	5,979	2,437	3,542
Kashmiri	178,241	95,891	82,350
Kayasth	13,374	7,477	5,897
Khalsa	16,610	10,481	6,129
Kharral	35,886	19,256	16,630
Khatik	23,081	12,855	10,226
Khatri	432,727	238,707	194,020
Khattar	14,817	7,733	7,084
Khoja	62,869	33,335	29,534
Khokhar	59,956	32,666	27,290
Koli and Dagi	175,014	90,503	84,511
Kori	18,050	11,578	6,472
Kumhar	550,450	299,738	250,712
Lilari	31,540	17,007	14,533
Lodha	9,413	5,159	4,254
Lohar	323,477	176,191	147,286
Machhi	279,666	152,562	127,104
Mahtam	81,811	43,602	38,209
Mahton	6,841	3,861	2,980
Mali (Maliar)	193,579	105,104	88,475
Mallah	77,837	41,693	36,144
Maniar	7,276	3,949	3,327
Mazhabi	21,691	12,192	9,499
Megh	40,020	21,988	18,032
Men	24,173	12,881	11,292
Meo (Mewati)	124,993	66,379	58,614
Mirasi	227,891	122,362	105,529
Mochi	419,378	228,688	190,690
Moghal	98,574	53,529	45,045
Nai	350,456	192,266	158,190
Naik	6,674	3,708	2,966
Nungar	9,987	5,390	4,597
Od (Odh)	32,246	17,188	15,058
Oswal	5,662	3,012	2,650
Pachahda	32,425	16,833	15,592
Pathan	292,689	166,664	126,025
Penja	13,023	7,176	5,847
Qassab	119,826	62,898	56,928
Qureshi	70,922	37,413	33,509
Raj	14,604	7,382	7,222
Rajput	1,635,432	898,023	737,409
Rathi	97,798	51,129	46,669
Rawat	15,419	8,652	6,767
Ror	41,431	23,121	18,310
Saini	112,719	63,085	49,634
Saiyid	247,388	131,992	115,396
Sansi	26,990	14,863	12,127
Saralia	7,456	4,236	3,220
Sarera	10,743	5,779	4,964
Satti	19,366	9,769	9,597
Sheikh	338,873	187,378	151,495
Sud	20,645	11,365	9,280
Sunar	158,318	85,587	72,731
Tagah	13,223	7,323	5,900
Tarkhan	646,330	356,540	289,790
Teli	295,971	162,444	133,527
Thakkar	6,982	4,051	2,931
Thori	16,451	8,903	7,548
Ulema	22,921	12,185	10,736
UNITED PROVINCES.			
Agarwal	291,252	161,940	129,312
Agrahari	77,283	39,831	37,452
Ahar	269,604	150,065	119,539
Aheriya	20,560	10,441	10,119
Ahir	3,903,745	2,043,505	1,860,240
Arakh	84,656	43,710	40,946
Atith	29,703	15,182	14,521
Baghban	135,406	72,086	63,320
Baheliya	38,795	20,651	18,144
Baniya	471,603	254,488	217,115
Banjara	93,477	50,446	43,031
Bansphor	7,735	3,867	3,868
Barai	139,037	71,068	67,969
Baranwal	10,009	5,673	4,336
Baraseni	28,703	15,642	13,061
Barhai	600,887	320,537	280,350
Bari	63,055	31,948	31,107
Barwar	5,007	2,292	2,715
Basor	15,360	7,798	7,562
Bayar	17,271	8,197	9,074
Beldar	39,035	19,864	19,171
Beriya	14,054	6,473	7,581
Bhangi	417,792	218,952	198,840
Bhar	398,518	193,432	200,086
Bharbhunja	301,712	159,490	142,222
Bhat	145,720	74,431	71,289
Bhathiyara	34,213	18,568	15,645
Bhisti	98,253	51,923	46,330
Bhoksa	6,637	3,536	3,101

PRINCIPAL CASTES IN EACH PROVINCE, STATE OR AGENCY—*continued*.

CASTE.	Persons.	Males.	Females.
1	2	3	4
UNITED PROVINCES—*contd.*			
Bhotia	13,593	5,939	7,654
Bhuinhar	134,644	67,721	66,923
Bind	73,507	36,211	37,296
Boriya	17,886	9,256	8,630
Brahman	4,701,179	2,474,642	2,226,537
Chain (Chai)	30,406	15,438	14,968
Chamar	6,083,401	3,101,884	2,981,517
Chhipi	33,182	17,909	15,273
Chik *	10,534	5,571	4,963
Churihar	31,097	15,827	15,270
Dafali	33,195	16,804	16,391
Darzi	252,885	132,001	120,884
Dhanuk	129,314	69,092	60,222
Dharkar	38,729	19,661	19,068
Dhobi	725,719	374,844	350,875
Dhuniya	404,738	205,867	198,871
Dom	333,781	172,011	161,770
Dusadh	70,944	34,165	36,779
Fakir	527,885	280,265	247,620
Gadariya	983,099	515,703	467,396
Gaddi	55,022	29,721	25,301
Gahoi	22,271	11,505	10,766
Gara	49,043	26,981	22,062
Ghosi	35,825	18,564	17,261
Gond (Gonr) †	110,232	53,232	57,000
Goriya	87,238	43,228	44,010
Gosain	93,997	50,196	43,801
Gujar	366,191	206,156	160,035
Gurkha	6,076	4,151	1,925
Halwai	91,291	48,085	43,206
Iraqi	8,751	4,070	4,681
Jat	744,600	421,857	322,743
Jhojha	30,725	16,877	13,848
Julaha	991,263	508,543	482,720
Kachhi	728,800	387,943	340,857
Kadhera	23,491	12,645	10,846
Kahar	1,112,421	575,784	536,637
Kalwar	287,576	148,140	139,436
Kamboh	6,633	3,630	3,003
Kamkar	36,845	17,116	19,729
Kandu	146,892	74,866	72,026
Kanjar	18,345	9,256	9,089
Kasarwani	46,383	22,864	23,519
Kasaundhan	82,542	43,041	39,501
Kayastha	485,073	256,730	228,343
Kewat	445,121	223,414	221,707
Khagi	49,249	26,107	23,142
Khandelwal	5,739	3,017	2,722
Khangar	28,704	14,419	14,285
Khanzada	17,804	9,183	8,621
Kharwar	15,458	7,370	8,088
Khatik	182,495	94,885	87,610
Khattri	44,489	23,520	20,969
Kisan	353,705	191,104	162,601
Koeri	446,322	227,049	219,273
Kol	65,647	32,291	33,356
Kori	860,434	440,144	420,290
Kumhar	726,361	374,504	351,857
Kunjra	73,606	37,984	35,622
Kurmi	1,890,371	982,497	907,874
Lodha	1,114,408	588,156	526,252
Lohar	589,008	308,138	280,870
Luniya	409,256	206,276	202,980
Mahesri	9,712	5,177	4,535
Mali	186,593	98,714	87,879
Mallah	248,656	117,196	131,460
Manihar	75,488	40,043	35,445
Meo	73,966	39,553	34,413
Mochi	8,869	4,920	3,949
Mughal	60,362	31,562	28,800
Murao	674,343	355,700	318,643
Musahar	46,254	23,546	22,708
Nai	912,828	475,341	437,487
Naik	5,314	2,506	2,808
Nat	68,376	34,370	34,006
Nau Muslim	35,440	17,780	17,660
Orh	9,071	4,502	4,569
Pasi	1,311,415	670,549	640,866
Pathan	960,711	500,225	460,486
Patwa	27,153	13,662	13,491
Qassab	171,725	90,088	81,637
Rajput	3,657,557	1,958,225	1,699,332
Rangrez	34,012	18,231	15,781
Rauniyar	7,768	4,024	3,744
Rawa	14,226	7,933	6,293
Rustogi	11,698	6,047	5,651
Saini	69,270	38,563	30,707
Sainthwar	119,086	60,412	58,674
Saiyid	250,204	129,843	120,361
Sheikh	1,314,828	693,681	621,147
Sonar	267,020	143,295	123,725
Sunkar	9,406	5,257	4,149
Taga	136,865	76,583	60,282
Tamboli	68,200	35,414	32,786
Tawaif	23,171	8,238	14,933
UNITED PROVINCES—*concld.*			
Teli	968,132	504,507	463,625
Tharu	27,720	14,938	12,787
Thathera	20,379	10,800	9,579
Turha	7,917	3,328	4,589
Turk	77,166	40,758	36,408
Umar	29,992	15,815	14,177
BARODA STATE.			
Ahir	5,197	2,745	2,452
Bajaniya	2,532	1,372	1,160
Bava	9,718	6,464	3,254
Bhangi	26,406	13,408	12,998
Bharvad	8,489	4,373	4,116
Bhat	14,744	7,605	7,139
Bhil	52,787	26,848	25,939
Bhoi	4,165	2,223	1,942
Brahman	113,412	59,526	53,886
Chamar	32,210	15,872	16,338
Chhipa	6,499	3,197	3,302
Chodhra	31,366	16,099	15,267
Darji	13,323	6,377	6,946
Dhanka	18,667	9,414	9,253
Dhed	99,806	50,541	49,265
Dhimar	5,410	2,693	2,717
Dhobi	2,676	1,271	1,405
Dhodiya	20,490	10,507	9,983
Disaval	6,145	2,860	3,285
Dubla	40,976	20,535	20,441
Fakir	4,639	2,471	2,168
Gamit	49,615	25,260	24,355
Garoda	6,281	3,125	3,156
Ghanchi	16,481	8,437	8,044
Gola	5,220	2,592	2,628
Gosain	6,628	3,663	2,965
Hajjam	26,266	13,261	13,005
Jharola	2,054	964	1,090
Kachhiya	8,029	4,257	3,772
Kanbi	402,657	212,799	189,858
Anjana	*30,920*	*15,732*	*15,188*
Kadwa	*172,856*	*89,059*	*83,797*
Lewa	*184,810*	*100,800*	*84,010*
Others	*14,071*	*7,208*	*6,863*
Kansara	2,142	1,081	1,061
Kapol	2,502	1,347	1,155
Kasbati	6,323	3,454	2,869
Kathi	3,473	1,844	1,629
Khadayata	2,777	1,539	1,238
Kharva	2,313	1,142	1,171
Khatri	3,516	1,907	1,609
Kokana	6,451	3,215	3,236
Koli	370,953	194,754	176,199
Kumbhar	43,733	22,233	21,500
Lad	8,500	4,173	4,327
Luhana	11,588	5,959	5,629
Luhar	19,258	9,494	9,764
Machhi	2,621	1,502	1,119
Malek	7,519	3,972	3,547
Mali	2,786	1,437	1,349
Maratha Kshatriya ‡	14,785	8,047	6,738
Memon	13,540	6,431	7,109
Mochi	8,954	4,737	4,217
Modh	3,560	1,875	1,685
Molesalam	8,966	4,816	4,150
Momna	7,183	4,038	3,145
Nagar	3,657	1,792	1,865
Nayakda	10,030	5,053	4,977
Oswal	2,944	1,568	1,376
Pathan	16,420	8,732	7,688
Pinjara	5,408	2,792	2,616
Porvad	8,613	4,737	3,876
Prabhu	3,153	1,622	1,531
Rabari	44,916	23,649	21,267
Rajput	64,287	34,582	29,705
Ravaliya	22,482	11,722	10,760
Saiyid	8,772	4,576	4,196
Sathavara	5,830	2,907	2,923
Shaikh	31,510	16,516	14,994
Shenva	7,587	3,918	3,669
Shrimali	31,965	15,872	16,093
Sindhi	3,548	1,920	1,628
Sonar (Soni)	10,659	5,325	5,334
Sutar	20,790	10,855	9,935
Tai	2,930	1,377	1,553
Talaviya	9,647	5,253	4,394
Targala §	4,468	2,022	2,446
Vagher	4,277	2,226	2,051
Vaghri	28,129	14,702	13,427
Vohora	25,035	12,119	12,916

* These are all Hindu Chiks
† *Vide* footnote to Gond in Part I

‡ Included in Maratha in Part I
§ Included in Bhavaya in Part I

Caste.	Persons.	Males.	Females.
1	2	3	4
CENTRAL INDIA AGENCY.			
Agarwal	61,423	29,231	32,192
Ahir	325,719	166,339	159,380
Ajna	26,465	15,172	11,293
Bagri	52,907	25,471	27,436
Baiga	23,161	9,430	13,731
Bairagi	49,804	29,198	20,606
Balai	139,885	65,313	74,572
Baniya	83,247	41,080	42,167
Banjara	35,265	20,170	15,095
Bansphor	52,465	28,451	24,014
Baraí	9,588	5,196	4,392
Bargunda	7,113	3,703	3,410
Bari	13,767	6,804	6,963
Bediya	7,998	3,215	4,783
Behena *	24,368	12,323	12,045
Beldar	26,378	13,037	13,341
Bhambhi	7,744	2,885	4,859
Bhangi	56,774	27,357	29,417
Bharbhunja	5,956	2,731	3,225
Bharewa	22,709	12,961	9,748
Bharud	48,850	23,607	25,243
Bhat	25,793	13,547	12,246
Bhawaiya	12,429	5,292	7,137
Bhil	295,741	147,738	148,003
Bhilala	123,376	61,172	62,204
Bhoi	51,845	29,518	22,327
Bhumiya	5,463	2,793	2,670
Bijavargi	5,179	2,455	2,724
Bohra	15,922	8,473	7,449
Brahman	986,206	519,480	466,726
Bunkar	8,187	4,060	4,127
Chamar	859,438	435,873	423,565
Chhipa	17,749	8,716	9,033
Chidar	11,695	6,196	5,499
Dafali	5,043	3,186	1,857
Dangi	62,819	33,369	29,450
Darzi	59,321	31,924	27,397
Deswali	33,780	17,787	15,993
Dhakad	63,463	29,291	34,172
Dhangar	5,608	3,027	2,581
Dhanuk	7,733	3,767	3,966
Dhimar	88,776	45,111	43,665
Dhirkar	5,413	2,297	3,116
Dhobi	82,405	41,941	40,464
Dholi	15,340	8,000	7,331
Fakir	11,871	6,361	5,510
Gadariya	159,762	82,682	77,080
Gahohi	25,082	13,657	11,425
Gandhi	5,948	2,820	3,128
Gond	234,672	111,364	123,308
Gosain	21,443	11,801	9,642
Gujar	185,728	105,834	79,894
Jat	47,160	24,661	22,499
Jogi	15,100	7,806	7,294
Jolaha	12,270	6,554	5,716
Joshi	9,581	5,015	4,566
Kachera	6,394	3,197	3,197
Kachhi	372,496	182,357	190,139
Kahar	56,835	29,086	27,749
Kalal	63,663	32,766	30,897
Kalbeliya	5,163	3,063	2,100
Kalota	22,033	12,378	9,655
Kandera	19,792	10,148	9,644
Kasaundhan	8,787	4,213	4,574
Kayastha	71,392	38,434	32,958
Kesar	14,469	7,433	7,036
Kewat	29,304	12,411	16,893
Khandelwal	9,981	4,861	5,120
Khangar	38,443	20,173	18,270
Khati	107,428	54,785	52,643
Khatik	20,566	11,547	9,019
Kir	6,370	3,214	3,156
Kirar	89,922	47,088	42,834
Kol	192,647	92,607	100,040
Koli	173,645	84,956	88,689
Korku	25,371	11,360	14,011
Kotwal	27,609	14,791	12,818
Kulmi	215,359	104,235	111,124
Kumawat	5,217	2,576	2,641
Kumhar	145,274	74,442	70,832
Lakhera	9,500	5,164	4,336
Loda	13,943	6,822	7,121
Lodhi	228,235	120,311	107,924
Lohar	96,989	49,835	47,154
Mahar	6,280	3,056	3,224
Mahesri	23,150	11,056	12,094
Maji	20,611	13,372	7,239
Mali	72,462	37,403	35,059
Mallah	7,928	3,152	4,776
Mankar	9,065	4,339	4,726
Maratha	28,008	14,821	13,187
Mawasi	5,241	2,569	2,672
Mewati	12,786	6,243	6,543
Mina	74,636	38,127	36,509
Mir	8,620	4,212	4,408
Mirdha	16,936	11,545	5,391
CENTRAL INDIA AGENCY—contd.			
Mochi	7,126	3,511	3,615
Moghiya	11,197	5,927	5,270
Mughal	18,468	9,973	8,495
Nai	156,395	77,464	78,931
Naik	9,776	5,301	4,475
Nat	10,090	5,455	4,635
Nath	12,309	6,829	5,480
Nayata	5,553	2,983	2,570
Nima	10,322	5,739	4,583
Oswal	47,795	23,139	24,656
Panika	26,656	13,732	12,924
Pardhi	24,594	9,749	14,845
Pasi	8,085	3,472	4,613
Pathan	138,522	73,476	65,046
Patliya	21,625	13,573	8,052
Pinjara	18,991	9,149	9,842
Porwal	39,369	20,233	19,136
Rajput	755,819	411,527	344,292
Rangrez (Rangara)	6,234	3,208	3,026
Rawat	63,601	32,982	30,619
Sahariya	81,042	41,560	39,482
Saiyid	32,197	17,459	14,738
Saraogi	17,967	8,990	8,977
Sheikh	147,216	76,259	70,957
Silawat	6,335	3,171	3,164
Sirvi	13,645	6,990	6,655
Sonar	66,612	34,387	32,225
Sondhiya	70,546	32,662	37,884
Sor	13,783	5,924	7,859
Sutar	115,167	59,400	55,767
Tambat	5,743	3,188	2,555
Tamboli	15,149	8,736	6,413
Teli	186,820	96,985	89,835
COCHIN STATE.			
Ambalavasi	7,817	3,913	3,904
Arayan	4,766	2,505	2,261
Brahman	35,532	18,794	16,738
Chakkan	2,101	1,108	993
Chetti	4,606	2,092	2,514
Devanga	2,349	1,176	1,173
Iluvan	208,453	102,817	105,636
Jonakan	51,469	26,274	25,195
Kaduppattan	14,323	7,074	7,249
Kaikalan	4,121	2,011	2,110
Kammalan	37,301	18,323	18,978
Kanakkan	7,527	3,790	3,737
Kaniyan	3,244	1,624	1,620
Kudumi Chetti	12,371	6,500	5,871
Kusavan	3,557	1,829	1,728
Malayan	2,461	1,280	1,181
Nayar	121,991	59,128	62,863
Odde	2,815	1,368	1,447
Panan	2,902	1,491	1,411
Pandaram	3,715	1,886	1,829
Panditattan	2,456	1,342	1,114
Parayan	8,356	4,135	4,221
Pulayan	72,787	35,284	37,503
Ravuttan	8,430	4,311	4,119
Valan	7,827	4,046	3,781
Velakkattalavan	3,271	1,624	1,647
Velan	9,322	4,595	4,727
Vellala	7,012	3,541	3,471
Veluttedan	3,381	1,589	1,792
Vettuvan	5,261	2,437	2,824
HYDERABAD STATE.			
Andh	5,901	3,015	2,886
Arekatika	14,855	7,719	7,136
Bedar	208,096	103,803	104,293
Bhil	9,921	5,036	4,885
Bhoi	177,004	89,369	87,635
Bogam	10,381	3,097	7,284
Brahman	261,241	133,192	128,049
Burud	24,498	12,538	11,960
Chakala	175,626	89,791	85,835
Chambhar	70,618	35,093	34,625
Chenchu	9,553	5,119	4,434

* Included in Dhuniya in Part I

Principal Castes in each Province, State or Agency—*continued.*

Caste.	Persons.	Males.	Females.
1	2	3	4
Hyderabad State—*contd.*			
Darzi	47,947	24,828	23,119
Dasri	11,942	6,320	5,622
Devang	71,400	36,257	35,143
Dhangar (Hatkar)	556,543	280,114	276,429
Dhobi	66,598	33,600	32,998
Dhor	13,241	6,830	6,411
Erkala	42,480	20,986	21,494
Gandla	13,015	6,888	6,127
Golla	460,760	234,629	226,131
Gond	24,090	10,883	13,207
Gondhali	5,193	2,622	2,571
Gosain	29,988	16,036	13,952
Gouli *	19,331	9,862	9,469
Goundla	306,071	156,381	149,690
Gurav	17,522	9,267	8,255
Idiga	24,911	12,582	12,329
Jogi	5,907	3,288	2,619
Kalal	75,339	38,366	36,973
Kapu	648,254	330,902	317,352
Kasar	14,522	7,689	6,833
Khatri	9,133	4,683	4,450
Koli	266,840	134,432	132,408
Komati	223,380	114,121	109,259
Koyi	124,341	62,583	61,758
Kumbhar (Kummara)	151,986	77,080	74,906
Kurma	144,688	75,144	69,544
Kurmi	23,078	11,819	11,259
Lad	8,776	4,175	4,601
Lada †	30,721	15,574	15,147
Lingayat	757,611	381,201	376,410
Lohar	47,844	24,828	23,016
Madiga	804,393	410,474	393,919
Mahar	689,543	346,974	342,569
Mala	448,046	227,411	220,635
Mali	107,097	54,230	52,867
Mang	340,959	171,045	169,914
Mangala	76,514	39,754	36,760
Maratha	1,538,874	772,878	765,996
Marwadi	38,264	20,372	17,892
Mochi	7,023	3,999	3,024
Momin	5,194	2,755	2,439
Mughal	33,411	17,685	15,726
Munnur	228,354	115,120	113,234
Mutrasi	260,770	134,473	126,297
Nhavi	58,974	30,019	28,955
Panchal	117,710	59,990	57,720
Pardhi	10,522	5,472	5,050
Pathan	135,148	71,167	63,981
Perika	32,838	16,417	16,421
Rajput	61,637	31,296	30,341
Rangari	22,508	11,521	10,987
Saiyid	189,574	99,142	90,432
Sale	343,130	175,968	167,162
Satani	27,983	14,589	13,294
Sheikh	985,019	499,495	485,524
Sunar	88,037	45,278	42,759
Sutar	69,205	35,118	34,087
Telaga	458,622	233,206	225,416
Teli	56,944	28,620	28,324
Uppara	57,000	29,098	27,902
Vaddar	131,799	67,696	64,103
Vanjari (Lambadi)	435,322	224,646	210,676
Velama	83,787	42,705	41,082
Wakligar	38,497	19,381	19,116
Wasudeo	5,482	2,801	2,681
Zeengar	9,824	4,719	5,105
Kashmir State.			
Aito	7,472	3,821	3,651
Arain	20,621	11,497	9,124
Arora	3,527	2,082	1,445
Balti	72,439	40,597	31,842
Banjara	5,457	2,971	2,486
Barwala	11,355	6,142	[illegible],213
Basith	7,647	3,735	3,912
Bat	149,315	79,764	69,551
Beldar	2,418	1,226	1,192
Bhatti	4,451	2,399	2,052
Brahman	241,362	130,254	111,108
Brukpa	8,890	3,983	4,907
Chamar	39,099	20,462	18,637
Chuhra	15,078	8,101	6,977
Dar	98,321	52,085	46,236
Darzi	3,958	1,996	1,962
Dhobi	5,991	3,362	2,629
Dhund	15,858	7,867	7,991
Domal	6,953	3,264	3,689
Dum	52,099	27,330	24,769
Fakir (Darvesh)	9,275	4,906	4,369
Gaddi	10,563	5,172	5,391
Ganai	46,424	21,795	24,629
Gujjar	328,003	183,798	144,205
Hajjam	34,456	18,697	15,759
Hanji	18,275	10,244	8,031
Jat	141,439	72,895	68,544
Jhiwar	13,500	7,285	6,215
Kashmir State—*contd.*			
Jogi	5,553	3,125	2,428
Julaha (Bafinda)	26,830	14,795	12,035
Khatri	18,517	10,705	7,812
Khoja	5,816	3,162	2,654
Kumhar	18,958	10,154	8,804
Lohar	28,884	15,101	13,783
Lon	56,931	29,718	27,213
Mahajan	79,949	43,698	36,251
Malak	8,897	4,622	4,275
Malik	46,162	23,764	22,398
Mangrik	98,508	48,558	49,950
Megh	75,409	39,331	36,078
Mir	77,532	42,204	35,328
Mirasi	7,699	4,097	3,602
Mochi	14,694	7,644	7,050
Mughal	49,875	28,037	21,838
Pandit	3,326	1,696	1,630
Parai	15,629	8,448	7,181
Pathan	52,263	27,931	24,332
Raina	3,264	1,434	1,830
Rajput	211,328	111,396	99,932
Rathar	33,951	18,151	15,800
Rigzang	4,888	2,555	2,333
Rishi	7,685	3,964	3,721
Sadhu	3,068	1,882	1,186
Saiyid	102,195	54,066	48,129
Saryara ‡	2,626	1,330	1,296
Sheikh	105,285	59,662	45,623
Shin	11,080	5,930	5,150
Sudhan	56,090	28,206	28,594
Tantre	8,056	4,431	3,625
Tarkhan	27,871	15,080	12,791
Teli	19,309	10,206	9,103
Thakkar	104,613	54,588	50,025
Thiyar	2,755	1,345	1,410
Turk	2,407	1,200	1,207
Yashkun	35,011	17,965	17,046
Zargar §	6,379	3,366	3,013
Mysore State.			
Agasa	97,772	49,112	48,660
Banajiga	132,955	67,216	65,739
Beda	268,454	135,597	132,857
Besta	156,863	78,228	78,635
Brahman	194,576	98,602	95,974
Darzi	11,564	5,909	5,655
Ganiga	40,469	20,311	20,158
Golla	150,842	76,617	74,225
Holeya	613,248	309,536	303,712
Idiga	38,758	19,836	18,922
Jogi	15,061	7,587	7,474
Komati	9,813	5,042	4,771
Koracha (Korama)	26,988	13,568	13,420
Kshatriya	37,927	19,294	18,633
Kumbara	41,810	21,324	20,486
Kuruba	409,842	205,262	204,580
Labbai	7,995	5,200	2,795
Lambani	51,168	26,483	24,685
Lingayat	729,431	365,091	864,340
Madiga	308,083	155,585	152,498
Mahratta	45,898	23,909	21,989
Meda	6,778	3,477	3,301
Mudali	17,896	9,369	8,527
Mughal	8,151	4,299	3,852
Nagarta	7,782	3,865	3,917
Nayinda ‖	39,414	19,977	19,437
Neygi	96,466	48,571	47,895
Panchala	128,098	65,790	62,308
Pathan	44,689	23,469	21,220
Pinjari	5,886	2,968	2,918
Saiyid	57,671	30,298	27,373
Satani	23,038	11,472	11,566
Sheikh	176,482	91,495	84,987
Tigala	69,233	35,426	33,807
Uppara	108,131	54,541	53,590
Vaisya	26,497	13,780	12,717
Vodda	142,482	72,572	69,910
Vakkaliga	1,336,182	668,319	667,863
Rajputana Agency.			
Agarwal	199,629	101,638	97,991
Ahir	169,129	91,171	77,958
Bagri	11,112	5,756	5,356
Bairagi	57,991	31,370	26,621
Balai	197,511	101,074	96,437

* Included in Ahir in Part I
† Included in Dhuniya in Part I
‡ Included in Sarera in Part I
§ Included in Sonar in Part I
‖ Included in Hajjam in Part I

TABLE XIII.—Caste, Tribe, Race or Nationality. Part II.—Principal Castes in each Province, State or Agency—*concluded.*

Caste.	Persons.	Males.	Females.
1	2	3	4
RAJPUTANA AGENCY—*contd.*			
Bambhi	133,826	69,940	63,886
Baniya	32,588	16,794	15,794
Banjara	26,694	14,311	12,383
Barhai	9,610	5,125	4,485
Bauri	30,931	16,232	14,699
Bhangi	84,980	43,655	41,325
Bhat	47,104	24,177	22,927
Bhil	448,910	229,266	219,644
Bhisti	24,789	12,690	12,099
Bhoi	8,627	4,284	4,343
Bijavargi	9,879	5,115	4,764
Bishnoi	52,879	28,492	24,387
Bohra	11,286	5,916	5,370
Bola	22,736	11,546	11,190
Brahman	959,752	495,031	464,721
Chakar	58,606	28,320	30,286
Chamar	734,110	378,017	356,093
Charan	37,574	19,510	18,064
Chhipa	37,940	19,645	18,295
Dadupanthi	7,670	7,517	153
Dakot	20,326	10,166	10,160
Dangi	38,100	19,557	18,543
Daroga	118,914	57,658	61,256
Darzi	45,203	23,069	22,134
Deswali	6,869	3,497	3,372
Dhakar	93,365	47,662	45,703
Dhanak	25,521	12,822	12,699
Dhed	16,830	8,826	8,004
Dhobi	45,801	23,348	22,453
Dholi	30,908	16,127	14,781
Fakir	55,265	29,054	26,211
Gadariya	65,128	33,743	31,385
Garoda	10,863	5,755	5,108
Ghancha	19,352	10,212	9,140
Gosain	27,806	15,418	12,388
Grassiya	17,419	8,918	8,501
Gujar	500,046	271,188	228,858
Hamar (Humbad)	8,583	4,257	4,326
Jat	928,486	501,616	426,870
Jogi	77,052	40,644	36,408
Julaha	18,333	9,478	8,855
Kachhi	60,666	31,766	28,900
Kahar	15,164	7,967	7,197
Kaimkhani	28,340	14,824	13,516
Kalal	39,860	20,334	19,526
Kandera	8,629	4,434	4,195
Kasai	29,400	15,006	14,394
Kayastha	23,610	12,853	10,757
Khandelwal	63,064	33,918	29,146
Khanzada	9,198	4,712	4,486
Kharol	7,861	4,003	3,858
Kharwar	6,620	3,339	3,281
Khati	134,992	69,245	65,747
Khatik	51,276	26,380	24,896
Khatri	10,410	5,441	4,969
Kir	21,674	11,237	10,437
Kirar	11,804	6,109	5,695
Koli	104,055	53,502	50,553
Kumhar	309,234	159,676	149,558
Kunbi	48,202	24,910	23,292
Lakhera	10,752	5,539	5,213
Loda	7,713	4,105	3,608
Lodha	47,013	24,526	22,487
Lohar	80,822	41,247	39,575
Maheari	91,106	44,597	46,509
Mali	336,876	174,966	161,910
Manihar	8,978	4,672	4,306
Mawar (Mahawar)	9,753	5,052	4,701
Megh	57,621	30,152	27,469
Mehtar	6,151	3,124	3,027
Meo	165,690	87,347	78,343
Mer	13,712	7,156	6,556
Mina	558,689	296,205	262,484
Mirasi	21,729	11,200	10,529
Mochi	15,428	8,101	7,327
Moghal	14,121	7,469	6,652
Nai	162,463	84,866	77,597
Naik	42,391	22,111	20,280
Nat	8,447	4,392	4,055
Od (Odh)	7,839	4,159	3,680
Oswal	209,965	100,686	109,280
Patel	55,798	27,751	28,047
Pathan	108,653	57,815	50,838
Pinara	14,298	7,288	7,010
Porwal	33,140	14,955	18,185
Raigar	81,568	41,626	39,942
Rajput	687,292	385,124	302,168
Rana	11,808	5,967	5,841
Rangrez	15,485	8,049	7,436
Rao	12,571	6,335	6,236
Rawat	13,754	7,580	6,174
Rebari	129,918	67,760	62,158
Sad	28,544	15,573	12,971
RAJPUTANA AGENCY—*concld.*			
Sadhu	10,519	6,451	4,068
Sahar	13,801	6,998	6,803
Saiyid	28,954	15,242	13,712
Saraogi	38,041	19,835	18,206
Sargara	26,520	13,865	12,655
Sevag	10,075	4,863	5,212
Sheikh	182,019	96,788	85,231
Silawat	7,858	3,922	3,936
Sindhi	33,277	17,775	15,502
Sirvi	50,995	26,651	24,344
Sondhiya	31,693	17,018	14,675
Sunar	69,034	35,569	33,465
Sutar	45,941	23,692	22,249
Swami	34,297	19,890	13,407
Teli	78,560	40,698	37,862
Thori	28,413	15,167	13,246
SIKKIM STATE.			
Bhotia	12,414	6,429	5,985
Brahman	5,673	2,880	2,793
Gurung	6,058	3,063	2,995
Kami	4,778	2,436	2,342
Khambu	15,872	7,939	7,933
Khas	6,210	3,278	2,932
Lepcha	9,031	4,676	4,355
Limbu	4,566	4,178	388
Mangar	3,182	1,616	1,566
Murmi	7,436	3,705	3,731
Newar	2,937	1,583	1,354
TRAVANCORE STATE.			
Ambalavasi	5,369	2,618	2,751
Ampattan	21,826	10,996	10,830
Asari	62,882	31,804	31,078
Balija	2,060	1,025	1,035
Brahman	55,674	29,733	25,941
Chakkala	18,074	8,937	9,137
Channan (Shanan)	166,195	84,638	81,557
Chayakkaran	3,294	1,690	1,604
Chetti	20,881	10,535	10,346
Ilavaniyan	6,116	3,055	3,061
Ilayatu	4,349	2,284	2,065
Itayan	9,225	4,556	4,669
Ishavan	546,265	271,677	274,588
Ishavatti	6,671	3,211	3,460
Jonakan	57,031	29,415	27,616
Kallasari	7,992	4,051	3,941
Kammalan	47,540	24,029	23,511
Kanikkaran	4,034	2,166	1,868
Kaniyan	11,987	6,155	5,832
Kavati	5,946	3,055	2,891
Konkani	10,219	5,356	4,863
Krishnanvaka	10,429	5,309	5,120
Kshatriya	3,190	1,599	1,591
Kudumi	8,207	4,363	3,844
Kuravan	62,974	30,766	32,208
Kusavan	3,307	1,703	1,604
Labbai	14,694	7,281	7,413
Malavetan	5,051	2,584	2,467
Malayarayan	2,612	1,294	1,318
Mappilla	4,624	2,545	2,079
Marakkan	14,604	7,274	7,330
Maran	29,318	14,661	14,657
Maratti *	4,471	2,770	1,701
Maravan	10,265	5,176	5,089
Mettan	66,864	33,768	33,096
Naikkan †	2,770	1,478	1,292
Nayar	592,655	295,781	296,874
Nulayan	3,393	1,764	1,629
Pallan	11,222	5,205	6,017
Panan	3,316	1,679	1,637
Pantaram	15,239	7,719	7,520
Paravan	9,313	4,648	4,665
Parayan	73,581	36,731	36,850
Pathan	4,037	2,437	1,600
Patnul	3,292	1,569	1,723
Pulayan	185,314	93,335	91,979
Saiyid	10,425	5,319	5,106
Saliyan ‡ (Chaliya)	9,919	4,953	4,966
Sheikh	3,565	1,926	1,639
Tantan	21,641	10,836	10,805
Tattan	21,350	10,718	10,632
Tulukkan	61,095	31,417	29,678
Ullatan	3,974	2,129	1,845
Urali	5,945	2,956	2,9[illegible]
Valan	17,273	8,863	8,410
Vaniyan	16,235	8,115	8,120
Vannan	13,875	6,933	6,942
Velan	12,957	6,350	6,607
Velan §	5,782	2,931	2,851
Vellala	49,479	24,774	24,705
Velutteden	11,356	5,718	5,638

* Included in Maratha in Part I
† Included in Palli in Part I
‡ Included in Sale in Part I
§ A potter caste

TABLE XIV.

Civil Condition by Age for Selected Castes.

1. This Table contains statistics of civil condition by age for selected castes and tribes, whereas Table VII deals with the total population. The object of the table is to illustrate the relative prevalence of infant marriage and the prohibition of the remarriage of widows among the various social strata in different parts of India. For the reason given on the title page of Table IX the total strength of a caste in this Table does not necessarily tally with that in Table XIII.

2. Within each Province, State or Agency the castes are arranged according to the frequency of infant marriage, *i.e.*, according to the proportion which the number of married females under 12 years of age bears to the total female population. As in Part II of Table XIII, each caste has been shown under the name most common in the Province or State concerned.

3. The figures for Provinces include those for the States attached to them, except in the case of Bombay, where this Table was compiled for British territory only, and Madras, where they exclude the figures for Cochin and Travancore.

TABLE XIV.—Civil Condition by

Caste, Tribe or Race.	Locality.	Sex.	Population dealt with.	Unmarried.							
				Total.	0—5.	5—12.	12—15.	15—20.	20—40.	40 & over.	Total.
1	2	3	4	5	6	7	8	9	10	11	12
AJMER-MERWARA.											
JAT (Hindu)	Ajmer-Merwara	Male	15,850	6,365	2,150	2,003	475	617	982	138	7,795
		Female	13,881	3,491	1,878	1,448	120	35	9	1	7,610
GUJAR (Ditto)	Ditto	Male	18,415	7,918	2,685	2,547	705	806	1,082	148	8,783
		Female	16,279	4,961	2,690	1,983	177	75	18	8	8,782
RAWAT (Ditto)	Ditto	Male	24,953	13,896	4,471	3,790	978	1,638	2,885	134	9,912
		Female	22,966	8,371	4,475	3,143	421	261	50	21	11,374
MER (Ditto)	Ditto	Male	11,623	6,095	1,685	1,728	618	847	1,121	96	4,850
		Female	10,151	3,782	1,690	1,540	352	144	44	3	4,893
ASSAM.											
PATNI (Hindu)	Surma valley	Male	56,721	30,215	7,096	10,489	3,171	4,029	5,101	329	23,767
		Female	54,137	16,322	7,577	8,150	244	118	139	94	24,162
RAJBANSI (Ditto)	Goalpara	Male	65,747	37,235	9,798	13,217	3,565	4,592	5,719	344	25,449
		Female	62,199	21,830	10,477	10,071	749	376	143	14	27,378
BRAHMAN (Ditto)	Assam	Male	68,361	36,227	8,457	12,015	3,794	4,711	6,424	826	28,127
		Female	56,145	19,143	8,541	9,574	604	246	139	39	23,952
JOGI (JUGI) (Ditto)	Ditto	Male	85,287	48,090	12,239	16,931	5,108	5,982	7,297	533	32,617
		Female	82,234	29,375	12,632	14,259	1,311	840	277	56	33,479
SUDRA (Ditto)	Sylhet	Male	59,400	35,852	7,168	11,359	3,688	4,773	8,177	687	20,916
		Female	55,741	18,707	7,586	10,400	488	124	87	22	21,225
GARO (Animist)	Garo Hills and contiguous districts of Assam.	Male	69,048	36,839	12,505	14,245	3,884	3,779	2,135	201	31,263
		Female	68,290	29,958	11,957	12,371	2,748	2,005	856	21	34,961
KALITA (Hindu)	Brahmaputra valley	Male	114,886	68,356	17,911	23,117	7,303	8,700	10,671	654	41,023
		Female	105,754	46,673	18,332	21,548	3,947	2,153	644	49	40,301
MECH (Ditto)	Goalpara	Male	34,170	19,734	6,860	8,103	1,977	1,465	1,219	110	13,232
		Female	34,421	16,838	7,284	7,320	1,434	599	229	22	14,458
MECH (Animist)	Ditto	Male	12,606	6,692	2,493	2,619	566	491	487	36	4,914
		Female	12,431	5,968	2,657	2,518	476	221	92	4	5,374
KEWAT (Hindu)	Brahmaputra Valley	Male	44,891	26,863	7,205	9,417	2,793	3,308	3,878	262	15,860
		Female	43,156	19,536	7,311	9,056	1,726	1,100	320	23	16,136
KOCH (Ditto)	Ditto	Male	103,960	62,097	16,610	21,886	6,478	7,523	9,056	544	36,694
		Female	99,815	45,838	17,062	20,672	4,114	3,024	902	64	37,272
KSHATTRIYA (MANIPURI) (Ditto).	Manipur, Cachar and Sylhet	Male	123,656	72,500	19,613	27,627	7,276	10,142	7,389	453	46,035
		Female	124,623	57,054	19,541	26,611	6,488	3,547	712	155	47,696
MIKIR (Animist)	Assam	Male	52,180	29,769	9,775	10,770	2,555	3,321	3,128	220	20,856
		Female	50,632	25,621	10,178	9,921	2,207	2,348	879	88	20,289
KACHARI (Ditto)	Brahmaputra Valley	Male	84,277	46,645	16,737	17,323	4,435	3,676	4,220	254	33,857
		Female	84,152	41,042	17,788	16,580	3,471	2,167	971	65	33,870
KACHARI (Hindu)	Cachar and Brahmaputra Valley	Male	26,487	16,245	4,606	5,336	1,678	1,905	2,523	197	10,385
		Female	23,892	12,414	4,465	4,691	1,558	1,389	297	14	8,934
CHUTIYA (Hindu and Animist)	Upper Brahmaputra Valley	Male	42,478	25,092	6,465	8,961	2,536	3,100	3,811	219	14,673
		Female	39,914	19,626	6,600	8,808	1,975	1,767	439	37	14,969
LUSHAI (Animist)	Lushai Hills	Male	36,672	20,794	5,213	7,179	3,275	3,197	2,787	143	14,378
		Female	43,633	21,397	5,931	7,538	2,423	3,328	2,009	178	14,477
AHOM (Hindu)	Brahmaputra Valley	Male	99,418	60,262	16,124	21,622	6,074	7,334	8,717	391	33,295
		Female	93,142	46,976	16,993	20,717	5,079	5,179	960	48	33,024
NADIYAL (Ditto)	Ditto	Male	32,026	19,041	5,420	6,969	1,999	2,186	2,334	133	11,664
		Female	31,255	15,183	5,822	6,911	1,248	874	305	23	11,476
SYNTENG (Animist)	Khasi and Jaintia Hills	Male	19,629	10,758	3,707	3,883	1,264	1,818	570	66	7,669
		Female	22,495	9,637	4,048	3,775	1,050	631	104	29	8,292
KHASI (Ditto)	Ditto	Male	54,627	30,497	9,653	10,387	3,116	3,968	3,195	178	21,190
		Female	61,637	28,753	10,278	10,269	3,306	3,197	1,629	74	22,168
NAGA (Ditto)	Naga Hills and Manipur	Male	87,639	46,188	13,134	16,614	4,786	5,394	5,714	546	35,517
		Female	90,445	42,213	13,872	16,729	4,555	4,536	2,350	171	36,280
BENGAL.											
POD (Hindu)	24-Parganas and Khulna.	Male	239,737	116,458	35,438	48,789	14,607	11,617	5,487	520	115,136
		Female	230,272	68,519	36,493	29,555	1,315	404	542	210	114,729
MUCHI (Ditto)	Bengal	Male	207,983	89,535	25,189	36,959	11,921	9,167	5,659	640	110,040
		Female	182,022	53,160	25,698	23,814	2,134	929	464	121	94,118
JOLAHA (Musalman).	Ditto	Male	144,679	64,444	17,696	26,361	8,584	6,907	4,267	629	74,740
		Female	124,889	37,204	17,570	16,874	1,505	722	449	84	65,345
GOALA (Hindu)	Ditto	Male	335,942	145,693	33,461	48,765	19,850	20,570	20,292	2,755	168,908
		Female	275,639	68,062	34,091	29,936	2,118	804	867	246	125,564
TELI AND TILI (Ditto)	Ditto	Male	206,577	94,432	28,320	32,484	13,791	12,380	10,670	1,787	96,292
		Female	193,259	47,619	23,256	20,653	1,862	1,078	629	141	89,595
DOM (Ditto)	West Bengal and Calcutta.	Male	64,228	27,254	7,053	10,925	3,895	3,101	1,887	393	33,210
		Female	62,119	16,368	7,265	7,577	1,061	247	159	59	32,779
SADGOP (Ditto)	West and Central Bengal.	Male	247,210	117,629	27,311	39,345	16,621	16,835	14,988	2,579	109,959
		Female	244,732	58,471	28,018	27,091	1,977	740	392	258	111,049
KAIBARTTA, CHASI (Ditto)	Bengal	Male	962,469	475,486	122,812	168,486	68,852	64,687	45,846	5,303	433,668
		Female	963,361	268,874	127,599	128,018	8,768	4,645	3,397	1,447	446,902
TANTI AND TATWA (Ditto)	Ditto	Male	124,062	55,605	14,411	18,859	8,091	7,428	5,799	1,017	61,213
		Female	113,123	36,862	14,186	18,689	1,420	982	379	206	53,332
BAGDI (Ditto)	West and Central Bengal.	Male	419,512	197,448	51,592	73,646	28,458	26,184	15,932	1,636	200,473
		Female	423,325	111,775	53,918	51,709	3,310	1,188	1,183	467	200,576
NAMASUDRA (Ditto)	Bengal	Male	909,512	462,593	122,901	171,414	57,398	58,869	46,576	5,440	397,461
		Female	885,348	268,937	127,946	128,191	8,253	2,261	1,679	607	387,769
NAPIT (HAJJAM) (Ditto)	Ditto	Male	225,940	109,678	26,955	39,483	14,519	15,483	11,920	1,318	102,094
		Female	213,300	60,795	28,105	29,368	2,029	623	488	182	95,796

Age for Selected Castes.

Married.						Widowed.							Caste, Tribe or Race.
0—5.	5—12.	12—15.	15—20.	20—40.	40 & over.	Total.	0—5.	5—12.	12—15.	15—20.	20—40	40 & over.	
13	14	15	16	17	18	19	20	21	22	23	24	25	26
													AJMER-MERWARA.
20 79	298 492	272 412	676 933	4,531 4,622	1,998 1,072	1,690 2,780	1 3	26 11	18 14	55 47	703 732	887 1,973	JAT (Hindu).
26 95	298 561	244 420	653 1,133	5,048 5,217	2,514 1,356	1,714 2,596	.. ..	15 14	16 13	56 23	727 524	900 2,022	GUJAR (Ditto).
7 19	27 90	20 227	217 1,161	5,458 7,810	4,183 2,058	1,145 3,163	.. ..	.. 3	2 2	17 11	299 398	827 2,749	RAWAT (Ditto).
1 7	20 42	34 121	125 615	2,811 3,189	1,859 919	678 1,476	1 1	1 3	.. ..	13 5	217 235	446 1,232	MER (Ditto).
													ASSAM.
.. 5	20 1,512	65 2,249	670 4,996	13,696 13,254	9,316 2,146	2,739 13,653	.. ..	2 53	.. 79	6 351	798 5,009	1,938 8,161	PATNI (Hindu).
.. 3	49 1,652	119 2,273	755 5,052	13,742 14,179	10,777 4,219	3,070 12,991	.. ..	2 70	3 117	13 497	871 5,091	2,181 7,216	RAJBANSI (Ditto).
.. 1	78 1,333	168 2,249	872 4,448	16,174 13,164	10,835 2,757	4,007 13,050	.. 1	2 40	6 83	38 410	1,154 4,292	2,807 8,224	BRAHMAN (Ditto).
.. 1	46 1,617	107 2,449	779 5,817	18,591 19,756	18,094 3,839	4,580 19,380	.. ..	3 35	4 103	17 497	1,325 6,772	3,281 11,973	JOGI (JUGI) (Ditto).
.. ..	16 881	30 1,696	242 4,265	10,994 12,419	9,634 1,964	2,632 15,809	.. ..	.. 38	.. 67	5 386	618 5,752	2,009 9,566	SUDRA (Ditto).
.. ..	102 583	290 1,587	1,784 5,837	16,099 18,861	12,988 8,113	946 3,351	.. ..	2 5	2 26	21 131	278 957	643 2,282	GARO (Animist).
.. ..	84 643	106 1,396	678 5,257	21,960 27,216	18,195 5,789	5,507 18,780	.. ..	2 17	9 27	20 150	1,510 4,923	3,966 13,663	KALITA (Hindu).
.. ..	24 194	149 681	623 1,924	6,812 8,567	5,624 3,092	1,204 3,125	.. ..	.. 2	6 7	17 45	329 643	852 2,428	MECH (Ditto).
.. ..	7 50	45 234	209 687	2,437 3,180	2,216 1,228	400 1,089	.. ..	.. ..	.. 3	.. 16	124 166	276 904	MECH (Animist).
.. ..	19 172	37 350	218 1,841	8,432 11,206	7,154 2,567	2,168 7,484	.. ..	1 3	2 12	14 63	591 1,897	1,560 5,509	KEWAT (Hindu).
1 ..	37 273	77 709	446 4,535	20,227 25,998	15,906 5,757	5,169 16,705	.. ..	.. 3	3 19	36 159	1,588 4,371	3,542 12,153	KOCH (Ditto).
.. 6	72 225	106 863	963 7,171	24,618 28,393	20,276 11,028	5,121 19,853	.. ..	.. 28	5 48	87 683	1,557 5,364	3,472 13,760	KSHATTRIYA (MANIPURI) (Ditto).
.. ..	67 92	92 281	589 1,847	10,942 12,687	9,216 5,382	1,555 4,122	.. ..	.. 3	3 9	22 76	531 972	999 3,062	MIKIR (Animist).
.. ..	72 121	221 800	1,078 4,029	19,951 22,377	12,585 6,543	3,775 9,240	.. ..	5 5	6 12	32 88	1,842 2,174	2,390 6,961	KACHARI (Ditto).
.. ..	11 31	20 129	209 955	6,436 6,088	3,710 1,781	1,857 2,544	.. 1	.. 3	2 7	21 51	750 768	1,084 1,714	KACHARI (Hindu).
.. ..	28 55	33 112	199 1,668	8,522 10,397	5,891 2,787	2,713 5,319	.. ..	.. 6	4 5	25 41	980 1,299	1,704 3,968	CHUTIYA (Hindu and Animist).
3 8	34 38	27 55	255 875	7,025 9,350	7,034 4,151	1,509 7,759	.. 3	1 21	1 6	45 192	772 2,348	681 5,189	LUSHAI (Animist).
.. ..	49 80	64 365	431 3,240	19,988 23,210	12,758 6,129	5,871 11,142	.. ..	3 9	10 11	33 106	2,152 2,988	3,673 8,028	AHOM (Hindu).
.. ..	11 25	20 131	152 1,538	6,505 8,052	4,396 1,730	1,901 4,596	.. ..	.. 3	2 7	20 96	766 1,458	1,113 3,032	NADIYAL (Ditto).
.. ..	4 8	20 70	417 1,245	4,587 5,251	2,581 1,718	1,262 4,566	.. ..	1 1	1 21	54 280	604 1,621	602 2,643	SYNTENG (Animist).
.. ..	4 21	31 112	483 2,151	12,154 14,639	8,527 5,237	2,931 10,124	.. ..	.. 5	5 16	58 312	1,136 3,372	1,782 6,419	KHASI (Ditto).
.. ..	19 20	37 160	675 1,581	17,341 21,483	17,445 13,036	5,334 11,952	.. ..	.. ..	.. 7	33 275	1,980 3,225	3,371 8,445	NAGA (Ditto).
													BENGAL.
92 1,650	1,593 15,958	2,850 13,089	10,154 23,343	61,596 48,873	38,851 11,812	8,143 47,033	9 35	33 452	27 768	196 2,652	1,881 16,443	6,047 26,683	POD (Hindu).
57 229	1,191 9,517	2,712 9,737	8,955 17,549	61,491 46,177	35,643 10,909	8,399 34,744	.. 23	30 286	103 585	472 1,406	2,599 10,314	5,195 22,130	MUCHI (Ditto).
42 197	1,014 6,292	2,081 6,426	6,030 12,014	42,020 32,587	23,553 7,829	5,495 22,340	1 8	18 165	48 213	176 511	1,915 5,788	3,337 15,655	JOLAHA (Musalman).
138 288	1,039 13,953	2,818 14,784	10,857 24,152	95,772 56,571	58,284 15,866	21,241 81,413	6 19	34 622	110 1,198	519 4,192	5,954 27,370	14,618 48,012	GOALA (Hindu).
34 187	727 9,393	2,369 10,087	8,670 17,387	58,191 40,046	33,301 12,495	13,853 56,045	.. 23	12 396	59 791	485 2,793	3,689 18,541	9,608 33,501	TELI AND TILI (Ditto).
26 98	411 2,798	1,083 3,356	3,457 6,808	17,475 15,108	10,758 4,626	3,764 12,972	.. 4	3 87	17 197	178 576	1,257 3,743	2,314 8,365	DOM (Ditto).
27 228	799 10,780	2,747 13,489	9,167 22,208	57,027 49,418	40,192 14,926	19,622 75,212	1 18	36 437	99 1,036	740 3,584	4,766 24,042	13,980 46,095	SADGOP (Ditto).
631 1,440	2,788 41,093	7,617 49,249	38,982 95,061	235,981 199,421	152,769 54,688	53,314 253,585	8 66	228 1,929	525 4,800	1,710 14,539	14,483 87,647	36,360 144,604	KAIBARTTA, CHASI (Ditto).
14 100	328 4,637	1,118 5,698	4,479 10,038	34,127 24,849	21,147 8,010	7,244 28,929	'9 6	24 152	40 386	304 1,360	2,292 9,700	4,575 17,325	TANTI AND TATWA (Ditto).
91 468	1,660 16,936	3,588 22,880	15,861 40,204	109,301 96,075	69,977 25,463	21,596 111,974	.. 29	22 658	150 1,609	455 5,500	5,168 37,147	15,796 66,131	BAGDI (Ditto).
273 783	3,945 34,839	6,668 40,143	23,612 81,022	219,115 187,013	143,853 43,969	49,458 228,642	7 182	187 1,774	664 3,001	1,782 20,810	18,100 82,256	33,718 120,669	NAMASUDRA (Ditto).
29 206	581 8,127	1,582 10,255	6,798 20,722	56,984 45,385	36,125 11,151	13,268 56,709	.. 17	26 384	35 757	304 2,561	3,519 19,418	9,390 33,577	NAPIT (HAJJAM) (Ditto).

TABLE XIV.—Civil Condition by Age

Caste, Tribe or Race.	Locality.	Sex.	Population dealt with.	Unmarried. Total.	0—5.	5—12.	12—15.	15—20.	20—40.	40 & over.	Total.
1	2	3	4	5	6	7	8	9	10	11	12
BENGAL—*continued.*											
KAMAR (Hindu)	Bengal	Male	116,924	55,135	18,564	19,276	7,781	7,604	5,998	812	54,554
		Female	110,788	31,105	14,509	14,341	1,264	528	361	102	51,465
JOGI (JUGI) (Ditto)	Ditto	Male	160,595	82,166	19,914	30,290	10,736	11,199	8,763	1,264	70,966
		Female	156,864	46,493	20,904	23,505	1,002	348	643	96	72,069
HARI (Ditto)	Ditto	Male	73,769	33,593	9,048	13,671	4,432	3,659	2,439	344	35,813
		Female	72,449	21,686	9,937	9,970	966	410	237	166	36,277
DHOBA (Ditto)	Ditto	Male	100,167	48,849	11,882	17,724	6,584	6,789	5,332	529	45,847
		Female	93,310	28,061	12,484	13,914	1,017	280	322	64	42,693
CHAMAR (Ditto)	Ditto	Male	65,354	20,169	5,341	7,076	2,543	2,369	2,532	308	42,308
		Female	35,563	9,851	4,733	4,398	408	147	138	27	19,721
KAIBARTTA, JALIYA (Ditto).	Ditto	Male	151,010	75,090	18,412	27,083	10,215	9,446	8,951	893	67,946
		Female	144,839	44,886	20,024	21,054	1,619	1,425	638	126	65,951
BAISHNAB (Ditto)	Ditto	Male	182,214	82,117	19,623	29,057	11,084	10,380	8,853	3,170	85,670
		Female	219,653	45,929	20,967	20,936	1,839	815	986	386	89,753
MALO (Ditto)	Ditto	Male	96,020	48,011	11,553	16,360	6,008	6,405	7,050	640	42,019
		Female	93,189	27,205	12,608	12,734	1,248	228	359	38	40,213
RAJBANSI (Ditto)	North Bengal and Faridpur.	Male	734,639	392,527	97,460	144,041	43,921	47,345	55,051	4,709	299,188
		Female	691,417	239,216	109,755	116,407	8,581	2,063	1,940	470	292,123
BAURI (Ditto)	West Bengal	Male	128,838	61,545	16,645	26,095	10,315	5,841	2,172	477	61,137
		Female	133,347	43,439	18,521	21,161	2,662	591	362	133	66,623
BRAHMAN (Ditto)	Bengal	Male	637,290	308,928	71,998	101,400	40,559	44,423	42,509	8,039	295,487
		Female	559,519	165,958	73,276	81,366	7,368	2,230	1,288	430	252,787
KAYASTH (Ditto)	Ditto	Male	565,968	298,475	68,453	97,209	40,221	45,262	42,343	4,987	241,957
		Female	540,147	169,073	69,348	87,423	8,603	1,879	1,449	371	225,485
BAIDYA (Ditto)	Ditto	Male	37,166	20,858	5,070	7,093	2,762	3,498	2,198	237	15,105
		Female	36,531	13,190	5,259	6,768	938	109	99	17	15,810
SANTAL (Ditto)	Ditto	Male	75,193	38,623	11,072	15,791	4,767	3,715	3,062	216	33,855
		Female	72,944	31,164	11,729	14,274	3,027	1,497	543	94	33,719
SANTAL (Animist)	Ditto	Male	235,506	128,204	35,811	51,943	16,706	13,489	9,544	711	98,871
		Female	231,664	104,288	33,231	47,505	10,370	5,560	2,185	437	98,760
MAGH (Buddhist)	East Bengal	Male	61,482	35,906	8,961	13,270	4,600	5,432	3,348	295	23,512
		Female	63,912	27,342	8,705	12,278	3,253	2,372	649	85	26,328
BIHAR AND ORISSA.											
DHANUK (Hindu)	Bihar	Male	247,765	70,081	30,531	30,544	3,977	2,585	1,838	661	160,931
		Female	271,166	50,170	30,680	17,144	983	477	679	257	169,415
TANTI AND TATWA (Ditto)	Bihar, Orissa and Manbhum.	Male	226,796	81,887	29,561	32,299	8,339	6,560	4,437	691	131,994
		Female	252,402	59,796	28,865	24,488	3,869	1,379	866	329	146,314
GOALA (AHIR) (Ditto)	Bihar and Chota Nagpur Plateau.	Male	1,551,272	534,566	186,415	226,174	46,770	35,837	33,311	6,059	897,309
		Female	1,556,632	393,275	190,938	163,929	20,359	8,636	6,287	3,126	901,117
DHUNIYA (Musalman)	North and South Bihar.	Male	90,516	35,946	13,034	16,953	2,816	1,739	1,162	242	50,126
		Female	103,275	28,040	14,107	11,994	981	387	439	132	58,683
KUMHAR (Hindu)	North Bihar, Orissa and Chota Nagpur Plateau	Male	139,215	53,649	18,342	21,704	5,844	4,517	2,749	493	78,050
		Female	140,904	41,883	18,631	16,906	3,446	1,397	968	535	77,334
TELI AND TILI (Ditto)	Bihar and Chota Nagpur Plateau.	Male	360,159	131,163	47,328	55,158	12,073	8,499	6,736	1,369	205,426
		Female	374,516	98,376	48,138	41,276	4,517	2,214	1,439	792	212,033
MUSAHAR (Ditto)	North and South Bihar	Male	264,901	97,949	34,953	47,046	8,558	4,427	2,298	667	153,148
		Female	270,190	82,011	38,371	37,623	3,090	1,462	1,090	375	156,533
CHAMAR (Ditto)	Bihar, Cuttack and Chota Nagpur Plateau.	Male	492,039	186,678	68,704	82,651	16,251	10,696	6,868	1,508	280,946
		Female	567,383	158,515	74,816	69,533	7,443	3,246	2,497	980	321,807
HAJJAM (NAPIT) (Ditto)	Bihar and Chota Nagpur Plateau.	Male	182,487	69,095	24,508	29,814	6,145	4,836	3,314	978	101,594
		Female	195,380	52,385	25,212	21,963	2,478	1,011	1,107	614	109,502
KOIRI (Ditto)	Ditto	Male	533,865	195,876	67,197	81,298	17,522	13,408	14,077	2,374	297,159
		Female	544,916	145,602	70,829	63,094	6,103	2,594	2,143	839	304,965
JOLAHA (Musalman)	Ditto	Male	380,091	162,372	58,127	73,810	14,513	8,693	5,994	1,235	196,564
		Female	426,779	129,985	60,259	58,898	5,479	2,245	2,046	1,058	233,129
NUNIYA (Hindu)	Bihar.	Male	130,363	51,818	18,429	21,750	5,181	3,602	2,400	456	71,135
		Female	149,142	42,860	20,229	18,484	2,201	909	763	274	81,500
KURMI (Ditto)	Bihar and Chota Nagpur Plateau.	Male	605,279	232,326	70,646	87,690	29,629	24,548	16,060	3,753	310,725
		Female	621,898	179,825	74,352	77,494	12,469	9,750	3,919	1,841	322,551
DHOBI (Ditto)	Bihar and Orissa (Whole Province).	Male	147,023	61,051	19,351	24,971	6,824	5,670	3,747	488	77,987
		Female	156,265	47,676	19,830	21,143	3,800	1,480	815	608	82,272
KANDU (Ditto)	Bihar	Male	149,755	60,421	19,926	26,768	5,668	4,080	3,472	517	79,055
		Female	162,080	44,123	21,426	21,096	1,891	780	666	264	85,875
KAHAR (Ditto)	Bihar and Chota Nagpur Plateau.	Male	161,877	66,415	22,179	30,152	6,722	3,951	2,909	502	84,915
		Female	185,961	50,427	23,363	23,231	2,019	719	778	317	98,310
LOHAR (Ditto)	Ditto	Male	114,048	50,785	16,466	21,372	5,641	3,886	2,841	579	57,310
		Female	122,093	40,283	17,331	18,023	2,466	1,185	947	331	62,580
BRAHMAN (Ditto)	Bihar and Orissa (Whole Province).	Male	772,460	364,005	87,099	136,326	44,747	39,565	45,749	10,519	351,994
		Female	772,577	216,770	90,816	107,346	11,556	3,341	2,363	1,348	354,894
BHUIYA (Ditto)	Bihar and Chota Nagpur Plateau.	Male	258,497	125,153	38,470	53,901	14,139	10,257	7,222	1,164	120,599
		Female	276,935	107,241	42,664	46,082	9,078	5,004	2,836	1,577	131,402
BABHAN (Ditto)	Bihar and Hazaribagh	Male	460,917	226,834	48,390	83,456	23,687	22,165	39,461	9,675	198,507
		Female	445,537	129,973	48,449	68,660	8,069	2,508	1,490	797	198,925
RAJPUT (Ditto)	Bihar and Chota Nagpur Plateau.	Male	526,259	277,754	57,705	98,807	30,059	29,200	50,486	11,497	209,940
		Female	523,756	159,816	58,630	82,165	11,754	3,946	2,343	972	222,320
KEWAT (Ditto)	Orissa	Male	101,827	48,781	13,561	19,426	6,533	5,329	3,761	171	49,393
		Female	108,247	37,795	14,105	18,525	3,536	1,087	420	122	51,322
GAURA (Ditto)	Ditto	Male	166,051	83,174	21,529	32,417	12,006	10,006	6,878	338	76,392
		Female	182,516	59,690	22,237	29,206	5,891	1,583	607	166	85,633

FOR SELECTED CASTES—*continued*.

MARRIED.							WIDOWED.						
0—5.	5—12.	12—15.	15—20.	20—40.	40 & over.	Total.	0—5.	5—12.	12—15.	15—20.	20—40.	40 & over.	CASTE, TRIBE OR RACE.
13	14	15	16	17	18	19	20	21	22	23	24	25	26
													BENGAL—*continued*.
20 87	345 4,174	1,800 5,723	3,718 10,567	29,958 24,177	19,513 6,737	**7,235 28,218**	1 16	11 178	59 355	228 1,480	2,077 9,219	4,859 16,970	KAMAR (Hindu).
13 71	403 5,895	783 7,528	3,912 15,341	39,414 35,708	26,441 7,466	**7,463 38,362**	1 8	8 217	34 315	106 1,397	1,676 12,760	5,638 23,665	JOGI (JUGI) (Ditto).
19 80	267 2,622	835 3,190	2,860 7,140	19,715 18,478	12,117 4,767	**4,363 14,477**	.. 3	8 87	44 172	206 539	1,474 4,362	2,631 9,314	HARI (Ditto).
25 72	310 3,173	856 4,256	2,991 9,209	25,549 21,038	16,116 4,945	**5,480 22,536**	.. 12	11 105	49 259	109 940	1,554 7,881	3,757 13,339	DHOBA (Ditto).
37 33	494 1,172	1,362 1,508	3,378 3,378	24,321 10,919	12,716 2,711	**2,877 5,901**	.. 1	13 31	36 52	130 198	1,283 1,804	1,406 3,905	CHAMAR (Ditto).
21 126	311 4,557	972 6,831	4,169 13,896	38,085 32,470	24,388 7,171	**8,064 34,893**	1 17	17 154	20 631	168 1,423	2,175 12,012	5,683 20,656	KAIBARTTA, JALIYA (Ditto).
51 194	612 6,762	1,893 8,360	6,005 16,103	44,445 43,900	33,164 14,434	**14,427 83,971**	1 17	30 380	54 753	255 2,637	3,629 27,482	10,458 52,722	BAISHNAB (Ditto).
15 30	150 2,710	528 4,160	2,082 8,152	22,305 20,808	16,939 4,853	**5,990 25,771**	2 3	6 115	16 255	170 1,183	1,540 8,800	4,256 15,415	MALO (Ditto).
122 410	1,197 19,908	3,871 25,369	18,552 61,811	157,633 156,858	117,813 27,767	**42,324 160,078**	4 65	50 1,027	58 1,374	526 5,176	12,503 59,655	29,174 92,781	RAJBANSI (Ditto).
24 76	1,154 3,766	2,812 6,356	7,713 13,001	31,796 31,719	17,638 11,705	**6,156 23,294**	.. 2	7 124	29 225	396 988	2,206 7,567	3,518 14,388	BAURI (Ditto).
146 249	1,428 14,853	4,262 26,681	17,619 53,044	162,471 120,419	109,561 37,541	**32,875 140,774**	1 42	51 603	127 1,350	846 5,451	8,323 42,357	23,527 90,971	BRAHMAN (Ditto).
82 172	1,162 7,986	2,400 20,955	10,355 48,830	131,379 116,212	96,579 31,330	**25,536 145,589**	1 39	32 420	133 1,071	1,024 4,861	6,008 44,792	18,338 94,406	KAYASTH (Ditto).
8 9	37 343	81 1,095	548 3,517	8,188 8,271	6,243 2,575	**1,203 7,531**	.. ..	.. 20	2 32	28 184	289 1,973	884 5,322	BAIDYA (Ditto).
16 29	170 665	585 1,702	2,237 5,586	18,198 19,368	12,649 6,369	**2,715 8,061**	2 ..	3 38	18 86	86 347	894 2,597	1,712 4,993	SANTAL (Ditto).
57 73	757 1,744	1,471 4,958	6,097 16,378	52,609 57,561	37,886 18,046	**8,430 28,616**	2 5	24 72	154 210	334 1,198	2,584 8,266	5,332 18,865	SANTAL (Animist).
1 ..	47 281	63 969	448 3,957	12,581 15,808	10,372 5,313	**2,064 10,242**	.. ..	.. 7	1 30	20 309	630 2,634	1,413 7,262	MAGH (Buddhist).
													BIHAR AND ORISSA.
1,613 3,514	22,853 32,326	9,917 11,446	15,681 18,736	67,831 76,511	43,036 26,882	**16,893 51,581**	64 185	1,135 1,874	698 722	1,172 965	5,204 11,788	8,420 36,047	DHANUK (Hindu).
1,527 2,670	16,038 21,547	7,250 10,226	10,797 16,695	57,511 70,335	38,871 24,841	**12,915 46,293**	83 100	923 1,321	384 561	903 1,069	3,421 10,735	7,001 32,507	TANTI AND TATWA (Ditto).
8,560 14,805	99,335 132,779	52,506 64,481	82,630 101,059	411,266 434,010	248,012 153,983	**119,397 262,240**	400 1,000	5,270 8,041	3,415 4,137	6,315 6,608	40,584 62,735	68,418 179,719	GOALA (AHIR) (Ditto).
311 562	4,854 9,070	2,839 3,931	4,520 6,106	22,800 28,755	14,793 10,259	**4,444 16,552**	11 27	131 322	93 111	218 543	1,499 3,705	2,492 11,844	DHUNIYA (Musalman).
646 1,556	7,133 10,785	4,343 6,449	7,622 10,095	35,435 36,028	22,871 12,421	**7,516 21,687**	28 53	306 485	281 414	513 923	2,220 5,111	4,168 14,701	KUMHAR (Hindu).
1,771 2,963	20,442 29,648	12,104 16,485	19,818 25,092	95,784 102,998	55,507 34,847	**23,570 64,107**	175 178	1,030 1,504	768 1,028	1,441 1,811	7,536 14,881	12,620 44,705	TELI AND TILI (Ditto).
1,076 2,070	14,217 21,001	8,523 10,602	14,604 18,448	70,030 77,059	44,698 27,353	**13,704 31,556**	75 102	630 947	417 500	897 908	4,347 8,294	7,338 21,805	MUSAHAR (Ditto).
2,432 5,028	31,386 41,759	16,668 21,653	25,123 35,376	128,784 164,311	76,553 53,680	**24,415 86,961**	132 264	1,178 2,224	973 1,126	1,513 1,683	7,416 20,479	13,203 61,205	CHAMAR (Ditto).
713 1,298	8,956 14,028	6,649 8,413	10,926 13,178	46,361 54,001	27,989 18,584	**11,798 33,493**	153 74	466 768	484 629	774 1,047	8,719 7,810	6,202 23,165	HAJJAM (NAPIT) (Ditto).
1,701 3,070	25,083 38,211	16,876 21,662	26,245 34,690	140,726 153,118	86,528 54,214	**40,839 94,349**	173 853	1,037 1,995	762 1,081	1,607 1,908	13,217 23,406	24,034 65,606	KOIRI (Ditto).
935 1,902	15,026 26,304	12,691 18,503	20,125 27,235	88,937 117,528	58,850 41,657	**21,155 63,665**	57 131	509 782	603 723	1,435 1,221	6,085 14,049	12,466 46,759	J LAHA (Musalman).
565 1,020	6,682 8,754	4,003 4,788	6,295 8,236	32,964 43,479	20,626 15,223	**7,410 24,782**	36 53	361 466	447 183	538 598	1,988 5,755	4,040 17,727	NUNIYA (Hindu).
1,794 3,702	19,380 33,913	19,993 26,485	39,584 46,016	135,081 151,634	94,943 60,801	**62,219 119,522**	164 502	874 2,621	694 3,916	4,042 5,316	24,054 32,566	32,391 74,601	KURMI (Ditto).
410 824	5,781 8,233	3,462 5,574	6,365 10,678	38,588 43,231	23,381 13,732	**7,965 26,317**	80 94	230 397	171 280	372 626	2,367 6,287	4,815 18,633	DHOBI (Ditto).
355 646	5,435 8,340	4,347 5,827	7,046 9,385	38,508 46,117	23,364 15,560	**10,279 30,082**	9 41	225 372	191 235	513 484	3,643 7,078	5,698 21,872	KANDU (Ditto).
270 489	4,148 8,211	4,609 7,111	7,733 11,473	42,419 53,379	25,736 17,647	**10,547 37,244**	7 47	165 426	170 344	514 519	3,896 8,633	5,795 27,270	KAHAR (Ditto).
196 486	3,115 4,903	3,277 4,079	5,550 7,670	27,985 33,844	17,187 11,598	**5,953 19,230**	7 68	119 293	160 254	288 494	1,969 4,478	3,410 13,643	LOHAR (Ditto).
515 1,063	5,510 23,491	11,343 31,245	27,634 51,828	184,201 182,748	122,791 64,519	**56,461 200,913**	56 134	354 1,360	653 1,874	1,577 5,420	14,537 60,572	39,284 131,553	BRAHMAN (Ditto).
640 1,088	3,118 6,695	4,478 9,372	10,611 20,749	64,717 70,376	37,035 23,122	**12,745 38,292**	13 124	125 555	349 825	1,092 1,607	4,160 10,467	7,006 24,714	BH IYA (Ditto).
467 624	3,970 8,802	6,470 11,275	15,511 25,433	100,442 111,407	71,638 41,384	**35,576 116,639**	67 108	231 661	189 640	631 2,143	9,915 33,395	24,543 79,692	BABHAN (Ditto).
325 1,158	3,208 9,764	5,920 11,271	15,066 26,181	106,961 127,863	78,460 40,083	**38,556 141,626**	77 123	321 829	326 854	802 2,657	11,080 42,148	25,950 95,015	RAJPUT (Ditto).
9 11	505 2,041	1,087 3,181	3,074 7,204	27,934 30,270	16,784 8,906	**3,653 19,130**	.. 1	3 46	4 68	39 221	1,007 4,409	2,600 14,385	KEWAT (Ditto).
6 10	745 3,122	1,770 5,997	4,382 12,523	42,531 49,700	26,958 14,281	**6,465 37,193**	.. ..	10 74	19 180	62 492	1,776 8,730	4,618 27,717	GAURA (Ditto).

TABLE XIV.—Civil Condition by Age.

Caste, Tribe or Race.	Locality.	Sex.	Population dealt with.	Unmarried.							
				Total.	0—5.	5—12.	12—15.	15—20.	20—40.	40 & over.	Total.
1	2	3	4	5	6	7	8	9	10	11	12
BIHAR AND ORISSA —continued.											
SAIYID (Musalman).	Bihar and Orissa (Whole Province).	Male	43,728	22,371	5,743	9,080	2,779	2,481	1,973	315	19,074
		Female	46,664	16,588	5,991	7,926	1,548	658	325	140	20,037
KAYASTH (Hindu)	Bihar	Male	125,858	61,481	14,098	21,576	7,119	7,222	9,288	2,188	53,633
		Female	126,424	40,791	14,496	20,657	3,771	1,154	488	225	53,717
CHASA (Ditto)	Orissa	Male	287,102	152,864	36,470	56,720	21,730	20,565	16,804	575	124,595
		Female	299,297	112,571	39,055	55,247	13,137	3,671	1,125	336	132,645
KHANDAYAT (Ditto)	Ditto	Male	362,259	199,550	45,201	71,059	28,982	29,526	23,905	877	149,183
		Female	400,042	143,436	47,576	67,879	19,119	7,192	1,287	377	166,505
MUNDA (Animist)	Ranchi	Male	107,339	59,049	17,747	22,582	7,672	6,352	4,067	679	44,011
		Female	116,468	52,778	17,691	22,465	6,214	3,816	1,843	749	43,662
SANTAL (Ditto)	Chota Nagpur Plateau	Male	525,309	298,419	97,065	116,169	38,174	28,662	17,156	1,193	211,753
		Female	529,762	257,180	97,419	104,296	30,369	17,445	6,773	878	225,024
PAN (Hindu)	Orissa, Angul and Orissa States.	Male	181,660	101,740	25,888	41,067	13,741	12,221	8,415	413	74,840
		Female	191,801	83,427	28,344	39,830	9,667	3,861	1,446	279	79,990
ORAON (Animist)	Ranchi	Male	141,159	71,827	27,223	28,268	9,888	4,693	1,488	267	64,330
		Female	161,628	63,607	26,860	28,029	5,656	1,997	770	295	72,183
KANDH (Hindu)	Angul and Orissa States.	Male	56,738	30,890	8,239	11,261	3,617	3,803	3,700	270	24,090
		Female	59,964	26,300	9,207	10,982	2,843	2,223	882	163	24,384
KARAN (Ditto)	Orissa	Male	67,751	37,343	7,382	12,124	5,130	5,568	6,653	486	27,533
		Female	72,809	26,533	7,604	12,324	3,999	2,187	317	102	28,327
KANDH (Animist)	Angul and Orissa States.	Male	81,348	46,186	12,182	16,570	5,291	5,825	5,969	349	32,688
		Female	84,582	39,858	13,020	16,222	4,530	3,992	1,843	251	33,161
BOMBAY.											
BERAD (BEDAR) (Hindu)	Belgaum	Male	25,954	11,119	3,770	4,140	1,536	1,018	593	62	12,754
		Female	25,591	6,741	3,466	2,553	306	138	150	128	14,048
BHARVAD (Ditto)	Ahmadabad, Deccan and Karnatak.	Male	299,839	121,272	40,720	44,722	15,531	10,962	8,115	1,222	160,686
		Female	292,731	71,056	39,616	26,751	2,427	771	1,076	415	166,589
BHANGI (Ditto)	Gujarat	Male	19,383	7,833	3,069	2,754	631	746	564	69	10,556
		Female	15,418	4,967	2,962	1,678	144	106	79	18	10,972
LINGAYAT (Ditto)	Karnatak	Male	474,207	199,588	60,795	67,624	30,161	22,173	16,894	1,941	235,190
		Female	458,916	112,668	56,268	45,566	5,741	1,804	2,504	785	240,673
TELI, GANIGAR OR GHANCHI (Ditto).	Surat, Khandesh East and Ratnagiri.	Male	25,683	10,494	3,756	4,313	1,148	787	410	80	13,912
		Female	25,397	6,633	3,754	2,625	121	43	72	18	14,763
MANG (Ditto)	Bijapur and Sholapur	Male	34,393	15,413	5,131	5,806	1,806	1,510	1,889	271	17,297
		Female	36,711	12,995	5,037	3,310	454	616	2,235	1,343	18,890
KUNBI (Ditto)	Ahmadabad, Kaira, Thana, Khandesh East, Ahmadnagar and Ratnagiri.	Male	521,290	221,956	73,192	83,395	24,005	20,105	17,794	3,465	269,681
		Female	533,395	137,378	74,207	55,716	4,504	1,017	1,421	513	298,956
MAHAR, HOLIYA OR DHED (Ditto).	Ahmadabad, Satara and Ratnagiri.	Male	113,508	52,175	17,434	19,554	5,867	5,414	3,405	501	56,767
		Female	120,211	33,436	18,066	12,777	915	454	903	321	63,520
CHAMAR, (Ditto)	Ahmadabad and Poona	Male	20,603	8,716	3,229	3,023	871	848	678	67	10,978
		Female	20,135	5,652	3,209	2,055	195	83	66	44	11,302
MARATHA (Ditto)	Poona, Satara, Ratnagiri and Sholapur.	Male	719,025	341,428	94,714	125,676	45,501	39,330	31,409	4,798	337,064
		Female	743,195	202,949	98,670	88,687	6,709	1,958	5,039	1,891	364,425
RAJPUT (Ditto)	Ahmadabad, Kaira and Khandesh West.	Male	59,303	26,875	8,350	8,616	2,694	3,079	3,736	400	29,254
		Female	53,772	14,536	7,918	5,628	560	198	174	58	27,761
KOLI (Ditto)	Gujarat and Nasik	Male	417,755	185,476	68,435	68,502	17,061	20,300	19,505	1,673	204,971
		Female	387,744	116,992	63,851	44,978	4,450	1,305	1,586	372	211,380
AGRI (Ditto)	Thana and Kolaba	Male	106,839	51,590	15,750	20,696	5,870	5,214	3,720	340	50,836
		Female	106,426	36,558	16,463	17,567	1,725	350	853	100	54,655
BRAHMAN (Ditto)	Most parts of the Presidency.	Male	90,796	45,132	10,911	13,003	5,830	6,847	7,049	1,492	38,694
		Female	83,122	24,001	10,683	11,522	1,814	227	202	53	38,178
BHIL (Hindu and Animist)	Panch Mahals, Khandesh West and Nasik.	Male	169,390	86,843	31,183	32,613	8,818	7,747	5,952	530	78,703
		Female	171,601	72,954	34,039	28,228	5,394	3,554	1,470	269	83,870
OSWAL (Hindu and Jain)	Ahmadnagar and Bombay City.	Male	12,597	5,430	803	1,360	767	1,002	1,301	197	6,357
		Female	7,815	2,521	1,086	1,208	169	51	41	16	3,689
INDIAN CHRISTIAN	Broach, Thana, Ahmadnagar, Kanara and Sind.	Male	46,344	23,997	5,888	7,662	3,339	3,441	3,395	322	20,410
		Female	42,511	17,359	6,018	7,325	2,062	1,192	644	118	18,966
LOHANA (Hindu)	Sind	Male	236,228	129,484	30,235	42,900	15,849	14,473	23,125	2,902	92,406
		Female	202,433	76,414	30,739	34,084	8,292	2,304	862	133	92,940
SHRIMALI (Hindu and Jain)	Ahmadabad and Kaira.	Male	17,137	8,190	1,983	2,350	1,030	1,073	1,528	276	7,545
		Female	16,784	4,646	1,894	2,114	487	77	58	18	7,505
BALUCH (Musalman)	Sind	Male	315,861	173,873	45,502	59,889	18,400	17,360	28,800	4,422	126,033
		Female	260,931	109,958	42,173	46,293	11,497	5,843	3,450	702	121,327
BURMA.											
KAREN (Buddhist)	Tenasserim Div., S. Shan States and the rural portions of the Deltaic Plain.	Male	450,971	266,240	68,494	85,476	30,439	38,654	41,692	6,485	165,951
		Female	452,655	253,384	66,458	86,186	30,400	35,191	28,411	6,743	163,894
CHINESE (Ditto)	Distributed all over Burma.	Male	79,830	46,529	5,296	7,970	3,193	5,687	19,875	4,508	29,716
		Female	24,811	12,418	2,990	3,662	1,627	1,985	1,444	710	9,927
TALAING (Ditto)	Amherst and Thatôn mainly.	Male	159,235	96,572	25,053	31,388	11,650	13,946	12,881	2,154	57,310
		Female	161,394	93,093	25,680	32,607	11,826	14,001	7,643	1,886	58,376
TAUNGTHU (Ditto)	Southern Shan States and Thatôn.	Male	91,597	52,661	16,506	16,500	5,959	6,796	5,555	1,345	33,311
		Female	91,457	49,221	12,889	15,160	8,575	6,793	4,636	1,168	32,826
DANU (Ditto)	Shan States and Mandalay.	Male	35,964	19,643	4,505	5,787	2,697	2,946	2,820	888	12,694
		Female	35,653	18,869	4,856	6,474	2,745	2,526	1,668	545	13,706

FOR SELECTED CASTES—*continued.*

Married.						Widowed.							Caste, Tribe or Race.
0—5.	5—12.	12—15.	15—20.	20—40.	40 & over	Total.	0—5.	5—12.	12—15.	15—20.	20—40.	40 & over.	
13	14	15	16	17	18	19	20	21	22	23	24	25	26
													BIHAR AND ORISSA —*continued.*
50 45	225 589	293 915	801 2,847	9,780 11,586	7,925 4,055	2,283 9,459	10 18	16 78	47 121	89 158	595 2,351	1,526 6,733	SAIYID (Musalman).
83 122	755 1,330	1,295 2,492	3,253 6,864	27,567 31,723	20,680 11,186	10,744 31,916	10 15	74 138	105 112	268 540	2,901 8,938	7,886 22,173	KAYASTH (Hindu).
10 15	493 2,488	998 6,277	3,970 18,992	69,712 80,931	49,412 23,942	9,643 54,061	.. ..	4 50	15 146	41 555	2,304 12,057	7,279 41,273	CHASA (Ditto).
11 9	537 2,999	1,374 7,554	4,569 25,924	83,877 100,620	58,815 29,399	13,526 90,107	.. ..	10 129	16 326	85 1,257	2,859 24,541	10,556 63,854	KHANDAYAT (Ditto).
77 57	377 714	1,234 1,736	4,186 5,309	23,600 25,211	14,537 10,635	4,279 13,968	10 16	39 103	29 182	112 363	1,735 3,371	2,354 9,938	MUNDA (Animist).
340 466	1,144 2,763	9,129 23,698	19,025 30,816	121,722 127,175	60,393 40,106	15,137 47,558	2 92	13 156	149 351	614 1,751	5,563 12,649	8,796 32,559	SANTAL (Ditto).
5 12	492 1,094	554 2,060	2,483 11,298	45,722 52,735	25,584 12,791	5,680 28,384	.. 2	5 47	17 71	54 344	1,551 7,725	3,453 20,195	PAN (Hindu).
107 249	562 599	736 3,196	9,554 10,165	35,552 36,116	17,819 21,858	4,993 25,838	6 13	29 214	50 466	193 515	1,656 5,924	3,059 18,706	ORAON (Animist).
2 2	112 258	167 350	709 2,545	14,498 17,059	8,602 4,170	1,758 9,250	.. ..	2 16	5 12	23 86	631 2,382	1,097 6,784	KANDH (Hindu).
3 5	56 210	78 533	443 3,543	14,665 18,071	12,288 5,965	2,875 17,949	.. ..	.. 10	3 34	8 140	536 4,363	2,328 13,402	KARAN (Ditto).
1 5	113 185	189 552	1,026 3,716	20,102 23,406	11,257 5,297	2,474 11,563	.. ..	1 8	6 29	41 437	915 3,006	1,511 8,083	KANDH (Animist).
													BOMBAY.
78 409	551 2,040	629 1,200	1,137 1,731	6,208 6,789	4,151 1,879	2,081 4,802	1 11	41 66	34 77	69 171	432 1,163	1,504 3,314	BERAD (BEDAR) (Hindu).
915 3,595	5,501 21,743	6,793 14,328	13,056 21,687	80,994 79,806	53,427 25,430	17,881 55,086	70 67	278 672	312 574	593 1,089	4,078 12,442	12,550 40,242	BHARVAD (Ditto).
96 219	758 1,314	384 637	946 1,294	5,688 6,080	2,684 1,428	994 2,459	12 7	33 24	17 15	44 29	50 553	538 1,831	BHANGI (Ditto).
924 4,830	6,200 31,296	10,289 23,218	19,152 33,315	120,471 114,979	78,144 33,035	39,439 105,575	116 121	563 1,302	911 1,450	1,295 2,506	10,395 28,495	26,159 71,701	LINGAYAT (Ditto).
54 73	713 1,894	776 1,280	1,236 2,119	6,645 7,117	4,488 2,283	1,277 4,501	.. 2	9 30	10 54	31 74	317 936	910 3,405	TELI, GANIGAR OR GHANCHI (Ditto).
55 389	338 2,307	457 1,291	1,124 2,317	8,897 9,275	6,426 3,311	1,683 4,826	.. 5	16 43	10 32	30 211	380 877	1,247 3,658	MANG (Ditto).
2,255 3,987	9,009 29,620	10,309 23,245	21,440 39,554	137,677 155,683	88,991 46,867	29,662 97,061	127 138	286 595	344 663	813 1,205	8,245 22,866	19,848 71,594	KUNBI (Ditto).
567 866	1,504 6,431	1,187 4,636	3,850 8,430	29,024 32,894	20,635 10,263	4,566 23,255	5 14	43 198	90 180	107 329	920 5,151	3,461 17,433	MAHAR, HOLIYA OR DHED (Ditto).
69 141	420 1,068	359 774	891 1,438	5,748 6,092	3,491 1,789	909 3,181	1 7	8 24	8 29	27 44	265 709	600 2,368	CHAMAR (Ditto).
2,055 3,452	6,054 35,984	5,784 29,420	16,322 47,756	172,923 186,049	133,916 61,764	40,593 175,821	11 53	150 1,327	186 1,729	376 4,393	7,885 49,439	32,085 118,880	MARATHA (Ditto).
162 247	679 2,103	734 1,580	2,155 3,755	16,803 16,018	8,721 4,058	3,674 11,475	7 14	31 55	31 33	101 140	1,166 3,424	2,338 7,809	RAJPUT (Ditto).
1,017 1,647	5,946 13,478	6,164 11,624	15,903 26,844	117,692 125,670	58,249 32,117	27,308 59,372	43 57	182 477	208 427	827 821	10,000 14,058	16,048 43,532	KOLI (Ditto).
130 158	477 2,829	911 3,657	3,216 7,833	29,865 32,192	16,237 7,986	4,413 15,207	19 3	25 43	12 57	44 141	1,189 3,254	3,124 11,709	AGRI (Ditto).
51 79	192 1,296	572 3,362	2,095 7,163	21,234 19,768	14,550 6,510	6,880 20,943	2 5	20 52	30 110	114 594	1,634 6,566	5,080 13,616	BRAHMAN (Ditto).
358 416	665 2,060	892 3,278	4,061 10,534	49,409 54,335	23,318 13,247	3,844 14,777	9 11	28 40	15 20	75 99	1,153 2,586	2,569 12,071	BHIL (Hindu and Animist).
7 10	32 98	50 235	331 716	4,363 2,178	1,574 452	740 1,605	.. 1	2 3	1 4	4 45	197 543	536 1,009	OSWAL (Hindu and Jain).
49 55	163 500	191 763	784 2,474	11,438 11,799	7,785 3,375	1,937 6,156	2 4	12 13	11 13	25 42	473 1,579	1,414 4,535	INDIAN CHRISTIAN.
10 13	548 1,638	1,688 4,847	5,323 13,129	58,718 58,456	31,124 14,857	14,338 33,079	.. 1	8 28	20 54	130 318	4,943 9,074	9,237 23,604	LOHANA (Hindu).
21 22	44 76	89 316	576 1,241	4,289 4,522	2,576 1,328	1,402 4,631	3 5	6 4	8 8	15 46	364 1,391	1,011 3,177	SHRIMALI (Hindu and Jain).
25 24	568 1,311	1,261 3,820	5,451 12,634	67,456 73,341	61,272 80,197	15,955 29,646	.. ..	4 10	17 27	139 254	5,427 7,349	10,368 22,006	BALUCH (Musalman).
													BURMA.
.. ..	.. 353	186 299	2,497 8,976	91,854 105,682	71,414 48,584	18,780 35,377	.. ..	.. 4	1 2	150 509	5,033 8,129	13,596 26,733	KAREN (Buddhist).
.. ..	1 9	9 43	1,159 816	17,061 6,123	11,486 2,936	3,585 2,466	.. ..	.. ..	.. ..	115 30	1,228 567	2,242 1,869	CHINESE (Ditto).
.. ..	.. 51	12 54	701 3,177	32,326 37,109	24,271 17,985	5,353 9,925	.. ..	.. ..	.. ..	17 129	1,466 2,241	3,870 7,555	TALAING (Ditto).
.. ..	.. 18	25 25	1,653 4,708	16,091 17,863	15,542 10,212	5,625 9,416	.. ..	.. ..	.. ..	354 421	1,928 2,583	3,343 6,406	TAUNGTHU (Ditto).
.. ..	1 3	.. 66	670 912	5,917 7,520	6,106 5,205	2,927 3,168	.. ..	.. ..	.. 27	82 28	1,106 806	1,739 2,307	DANU (Ditto).

TABLE XIV.—Civil Condition by Age

Caste, Tribe or Race.	Locality.	Sex.	Population dealt with.	Unmarried. Total.	0—5.	5—12.	12—15.	15—20.	20—40.	40 & over.	Total.
1	2	3	4	5	6	7	8	9	10	11	12
BURMA—*continued*.											
SHAN (Buddhist)	Shan States, Northern Hill Districts and a part of the Deltaic Plain.	Male	465,609	248,014	58,576	75,063	29,227	37,009	36,079	12,060	182,552
		Female	476,115	216,439	55,979	72,677	26,766	30,151	17,669	13,197	194,429
CHIN (Ditto)	Most part of Burma	Male	119,373	66,955	16,463	21,475	7,660	10,542	9,348	1,467	47,165
		Female	123,693	61,200	18,165	21,579	5,933	8,037	6,122	1,364	50,035
ARAKANESE (Ditto)	Arakan Division and Bassein.	Male	177,069	88,312	19,167	28,210	12,378	15,434	9,795	3,333	70,248
		Female	167,934	78,130	18,962	28,300	10,813	10,647	6,227	3,161	66,851
KACHIN (Ditto)	Northern Hill Districts and Shan States.	Male	80,764	46,061	6,071	12,793	6,606	8,037	10,087	2,467	31,421
		Female	81,604	40,657	7,011	11,168	4,908	6,339	9,090	2,141	30,393
WA-PALAUNG (Ditto)	Shan States and a part of Ruby Mines.	Male	74,600	41,369	9,564	9,211	4,962	6,383	6,733	4,516	28,153
		Female	75,775	37,123	9,279	10,949	4,165	6,249	3,839	2,642	30,602
CENTRAL PROVINCES AND BERAR.											
KUNBI (Hindu)	Marhatta Div., Chindwara, Nimar and Betul.	Male	675,302	237,066	92,918	94,053	21,211	12,947	13,250	2,687	394,170
		Female	666,698	147,376	90,567	49,040	1,876	1,761	3,189	937	402,961
MALI (Ditto)	C. P. and Berar	Male	279,589	104,740	42,969	41,516	8,393	5,984	4,965	913	159,267
		Female	281,643	74,955	43,396	26,622	2,279	1,133	997	528	161,338
TELI (Ditto)	Ditto	Male	427,124	164,263	70,609	65,417	12,660	8,259	6,321	997	245,382
		Female	442,212	123,097	70,985	46,266	2,957	943	1,348	598	255,211
BARHAI (Ditto)	Ditto	Male	56,297	22,255	7,601	8,751	2,354	1,704	1,601	244	30,950
		Female	52,518	14,634	7,552	6,153	408	140	284	97	29,054
KURMI (Ditto)	Nerbudda Valley, Plateau and Chhattisgarh Divs.	Male	141,079	58,132	21,525	22,390	5,198	4,170	4,351	498	76,479
		Female	143,232	41,294	21,986	17,246	1,420	263	271	108	78,642
MARATHA (Ditto)	C. P. and Berar	Male	46,701	19,002	5,740	6,740	2,039	1,909	2,154	420	24,481
		Female	47,178	12,625	6,169	5,132	456	233	481	154	23,659
SUNAR (Ditto)	Ditto	Male	63,830	27,549	8,661	10,684	3,045	2,376	2,350	433	32,649
		Female	63,034	18,240	9,010	8,145	560	206	230	89	32,744
KUMHAR (Ditto)	Ditto	Male	60,047	25,004	8,855	9,702	2,348	1,949	1,894	256	32,217
		Female	58,454	18,392	9,493	7,588	681	269	275	86	31,173
NAI (Ditto)	Ditto	Male	72,797	30,708	10,591	12,220	3,175	2,342	2,113	267	38,450
		Female	73,293	22,216	10,973	9,772	855	293	244	79	38,986
MEHRA (Ditto)	Ditto	Male	575,028	249,238	97,499	95,055	22,325	17,967	14,683	1,709	303,895
		Female	589,355	189,433	98,824	74,428	7,729	3,308	4,035	1,109	315,835
DHOBI (Ditto)	Ditto	Male	80,673	34,212	12,906	13,785	3,219	2,284	1,774	244	43,126
		Female	83,900	26,359	13,485	10,687	939	740	333	175	44,517
RAJPUT (Ditto)	Ditto	Male	223,103	96,904	29,747	34,086	9,891	8,962	12,394	1,824	114,124
		Female	217,220	64,194	30,668	28,126	3,361	928	854	257	111 179
CHAMAR (Ditto)	Ditto	Male	443,017	182,940	76,766	69,573	13,555	11,865	9,599	882	244,798
		Female	458,505	141,931	79,865	56,086	3,385	1,085	1,045	465	258,792
KALAR (Ditto)	Ditto	Male	96,393	41,833	14,681	16,153	3,972	3,231	3,388	413	50,000
		Female	98,902	31,269	15,317	13,462	1,317	529	434	150	51,901
BANIYA (Hindu and Jain)	Ditto	Male	100,683	45,157	11,820	15,087	5,165	4,662	6,906	1,567	47,964
		Female	94,137	26,114	12,109	12,129	1,040	250	404	182	45,502
LOHAR (Hindu)	Ditto	Male	90,929	41,501	14,096	16,143	4,223	3,487	3,057	493	45,388
		Female	90,382	31,750	14,776	13,313	1,810	864	814	182	45,889
LODHI (Ditto)	Ditto	Male	155,174	73,372	24,425	27,292	7,243	6,350	7,364	698	75,104
		Female	157,200	50,712	24,128	22,894	2,571	643	376	100	79,417
AHIR (Ditto)	Ditto	Male	354,669	162,505	57,466	64,311	15,557	12,372	11,488	1,311	177,367
		Female	358,407	125,767	59,558	54,801	6,392	2,648	1,876	492	181,333
DHIMAR (Ditto)	Ditto	Male	140,734	63,657	22,592	24,121	6,261	5,438	4,714	531	71,036
		Female	142,679	49,392	23,854	20,460	2,302	1,402	905	469	72,380
BRAHMAN (Ditto)	Ditto	Male	237,567	112,964	27,962	35,607	12,675	12,512	19,565	4,643	107,402
		Female	206,060	61,294	27,381	29,878	2,469	591	669	236	95,666
PANKA (Ditto)	Mandla, Seoni, Balaghat and Chhattisgarh Div.	Male	63,642	27,020	10,366	10,476	2,220	1,960	1,778	220	34,065
		Female	60,336	21,723	11,151	9,037	832	277	334	92	36,721
KACHHI (Ditto)	Nerbudda Valley and Plateau Division.	Male	58,181	26,721	9,154	9,999	2,566	2,433	2,390	179	28,679
		Female	57,749	18,578	9,329	8,349	615	125	129	31	29,455
GOND (Ditto)	C. P. and Berar	Male	174,683	80,898	28,449	30,073	7,644	6,860	7,191	681	86,087
		Female	185,243	64,536	29,705	27,786	3,946	1,640	1,147	312	91,696
GOND (Animist)	Ditto	Male	910,853	456,582	154,346	171,472	45,339	41,333	40,382	3,760	422,649
		Female	956,761	379,417	161,633	161,052	30,032	16,205	8,893	1,602	451,029
MADRAS.											
KAMSALA (Hindu)	Vizagapatam and Gódavari.	Male	47,290	22,323	5,283	8,622	3,198	2,984	1,993	243	22,897
		Female	48,411	12,418	5,773	5,815	383	219	165	63	22,968
KAPU (Ditto)	Vizagapatam and Cuddapah.	Male	365,421	175,487	41,016	67,502	22,931	21,016	20,120	2,393	176,094
		Female	377,961	107,882	42,475	51,214	8,306	2,928	1,751	408	189,610
BRAHMAN (ORIYA) (Ditto).	Ganjam and Madras	Male	60,812	28,717	7,558	11,515	4,273	3,149	1,977	245	29,970
		Female	65,142	17,822	7,976	8,730	257	344	342	173	30,664
BRAHMAN (TELUGU) (Ditto).	Ganjam, Kistna and Madras.	Male	55,376	28,369	6,561	10,259	4,082	3,887	2,762	818	24,432
		Female	55,665	12,938	5,976	6,258	244	229	195	36	26,005
KOMATI (Ditto)	Kistna, Nellore and Guntur.	Male	84,709	41,571	10,229	14,397	6,038	5,392	4,592	923	39,488
		Female	87,480	22,816	10,570	11,063	759	143	220	61	42,344
MALA (Ditto)	Godávari and Kistna	Male	289,454	151,845	42,501	62,875	19,603	15,779	10,044	1,043	128,698
		Female	297,258	109,774	41,488	51,278	9,157	3,622	3,183	1,046	138,710
BRAHMAN (TAMIL) (Ditto).	Madras and Tanjore	Male	75,248	33,112	8,240	11,451	5,023	4,924	2,805	669	38,612
		Female	74,453	19,232	8,181	9,313	883	352	347	156	36,822
BALIJA (Ditto)	Cuddapah, Salem and North and South Arcot.	Male	112,274	61,268	13,329	18,749	8,117	8,957	10,513	1,603	45,588
		Female	112,772	38,898	13,156	18,236	4,411	1,781	960	355	47,788

FOR SELECTED CASTES—*continued.*

Married.						Widowed.							Caste, Tribe or Race.
0—5.	5—12.	12—15.	15—20.	20—40.	40 & over.	Total.	0—5.	5—12.	12—15.	15—20.	20—40.	40 & over.	
13	14	15	16	17	18	19	20	21	22	23	24	25	26
													BURMA—*continued.*
..	1	385	9,257	88,942	83,967	35,043	..	..	2	3,888	11,983	19,170	SHAN (Buddhist).
..	6	585	18,674	103,885	71,279	65,247	..	..	46	3,582	19,650	41,969	
..	..	13	761	25,487	20,904	5,253	..	..	..	53	1,851	3,349	CHIN (Ditto).
..	1	50	3,454	32,191	14,330	12,458	..	..	1	133	2,645	9,679	
..	..	85	10,328	32,612	27,228	18,529	..	..	..	1,324	8,192	9,013	ARAKANESE (Ditto).
..	..	32	6,905	40,499	19,435	22,053	..	..	..	843	7,439	13,771	
..	..	..	2,316	14,805	14,300	3,282	..	..	4	56	1,323	1,899	KACHIN (Ditto).
..	..	52	5,134	15,669	9,538	10,554	..	..	..	176	2,858	7,520	
..	1	1	3,033	12,873	12,245	5,078	..	..	..	225	2,127	2,726	WA-PALAUNG (Ditto).
..	..	169	2,349	17,140	10,944	8,050	..	..	..	399	1,865	5,786	
													CENTRAL PROVINCES AND BERAR.
2,252	16,349	18,902	30,023	186,250	140,394	44,066	39	520	597	1,851	12,982	28,577	KUNBI (Hindu).
6,725	61,565	27,540	43,541	192,519	71,091	116,347	224	1,949	1,245	1,653	20,857	90,419	
550	6,214	7,775	12,646	78,880	58,202	15,582	110	230	208	445	4,557	10,032	MALI (Ditto).
1,735	20,107	10,399	17,870	81,150	30,077	45,359	54	646	429	644	7,494	36,083	
812	11,911	12,407	21,593	128,908	74,751	17,479	21	217	209	455	5,455	11,122	TELI (Ditto).
2,258	28,857	17,667	28,051	133,743	44,025	63,904	65	589	470	640	9,605	52,535	
53	555	990	2,410	16,335	10,607	3,092	3	21	28	79	945	2,016	BARHAI (Ditto).
190	2,954	2,011	3,317	15,472	5,110	8,830	8	86	82	121	1,579	6,954	
157	3,886	3,664	6,859	40,389	21,524	6,468	3	79	57	140	2,120	4,069	KURMI (Ditto).
469	7,542	5,500	9,580	48,249	12,302	23,296	5	108	80	187	4,353	18,568	
92	463	601	1,278	12,692	9,855	3,218	3	31	26	68	881	2,209	MARATHA (Ditto).
314	2,194	1,716	2,956	11,841	4,638	10,894	24	75	129	221	2,615	7,830	
189	555	1,099	2,564	17,280	11,012	3,632	6	22	39	120	1,096	2,355	SUNAR (Ditto).
210	3,070	2,388	4,186	17,439	5,451	12,050	10	91	131	238	2,626	8,954	
95	1,101	1,089	2,339	17,408	10,190	2,826	3	29	30	87	895	1,782	KUMHAR (Ditto).
227	2,759	1,996	3,497	17,486	5,208	8,889	4	69	44	91	1,790	6,891	
97	1,041	1,466	3,025	20,791	12,080	3,639	11	28	75	93	1,139	2,293	NAI (Ditto).
271	3,285	2,580	4,477	21,838	6,540	12,691	28	72	62	137	2,238	9,559	
925	6,328	9,378	18,677	161,063	107,524	21,295	48	146	280	565	5,901	15,046	MEHRA (Ditto).
2,517	25,825	18,315	36,393	175,408	57,377	84,067	104	869	1,040	2,529	15,145	64,400	
106	1,200	1,517	3,283	23,790	18,230	3,335	4	39	23	74	1,057	2,138	DHOBI (Ditto).
215	3,660	2,808	5,367	25,808	7,164	13,024	32	108	99	136	2,490	10,159	
317	4,001	4,131	7,787	59,900	37,988	12,075	11	67	85	261	3,520	8,131	RAJPUT (Ditto).
575	8,706	7,829	13,223	60,906	19,940	41,947	60	202	244	550	9,213	31,578	
663	8,904	7,375	16,759	135,368	75,729	15,979	11	173	140	548	5,594	9,516	CHAMAR (Ditto).
1,423	17,919	13,267	27,522	151,924	46,737	57,782	75	310	153	438	9,671	47,135	
84	1,497	1,701	3,535	26,871	16,312	4,555	7	28	32	118	1,360	3,010	KALAR (Ditto).
214	3,885	3,331	5,902	29,484	9,135	15,792	12	82	78	153	2,908	12,564	
101	674	1,436	3,714	26,023	16,016	7,562	3	37	72	169	2,228	5,058	BANIYA (Hindu and Jain).
235	3,330	3,596	6,709	24,641	6,991	22,521	23	131	192	496	6,290	15,889	
127	889	1,351	3,226	24,643	15,152	4,040	10	43	106	278	1,186	2,417	LOHAR (Hindu).
275	2,716	2,555	5,191	26,805	8,347	12,734	24	81	138	259	2,835	9,897	
121	2,005	2,685	5,776	41,157	23,860	6,698	2	35	54	103	2,059	4,445	LODHI (Ditto).
239	4,644	4,912	9,669	46,888	13,065	27,071	19	103	110	269	6,228	20,347	
293	4,221	5,147	12,054	100,507	55,145	14,797	8	116	99	334	5,412	8,828	AHIR (Ditto).
619	10,155	9,422	19,671	110,446	31,020	51,307	30	214	218	398	9,305	41,142	
370	1,310	1,612	4,218	40,096	23,430	6,041	7	42	46	242	1,747	3,957	DHIMAR (Ditto).
407	3,772	3,996	8,687	43,410	12,158	20,907	4	96	88	298	4,079	16,342	
181	1,337	2,207	6,922	58,568	38,187	17,201	4	57	69	283	4,643	12,195	BRAHMAN (Ditto).
320	5,709	7,422	13,414	52,529	16,272	51,170	17	229	306	992	14,382	35,244	
68	788	799	2,126	19,381	10,953	2,557	5	20	16	85	1,097	1,334	PANKA (Ditto).
93	1,818	1,553	3,686	22,588	6,988	10,892	12	38	20	58	1,820	8,944	
22	456	780	1,968	17,006	8,447	2,781	2	10	9	33	940	1,787	KACHHI (Ditto).
79	1,508	1,747	3,607	18,397	4,122	9,716	3	19	33	98	2,297	7,271	
141	918	1,479	4,615	48,744	30,190	7,696	10	34	39	201	2,687	4,777	GOND (Ditto).
278	2,557	3,372	9,588	58,317	17,584	29,611	16	92	86	240	5,251	23,326	
540	3,378	5,322	18,049	248,628	151,737	31,622	24	124	207	686	11,380	19,251	GOND (Animist).
1,356	9,750	14,819	44,318	294,923	85,863	126,315	107	530	268	906	22,578	101,926	
													MADRAS.
16	253	522	1,728	11,881	8,502	2,070	..	4	22	62	409	1,573	KAMSALA (Hindu).
75	3,283	2,186	3,553	10,474	3,397	13,225	3	125	147	652	4,092	8,206	
118	3,241	4,749	11,206	84,154	72,626	13,840	..	95	132	167	2,308	11,138	KAPU (Ditto).
951	20,982	14,295	24,265	95,129	33,988	81,269	20	592	666	1,551	21,332	57,108	
70	268	602	2,436	15,518	11,081	2,125	2	10	81	48	392	1,642	BRAHMAN (ORIYA) (Ditto).
373	2,581	3,649	4,673	14,375	5,013	16,656	12	86	175	446	4,472	11,465	
10	203	557	2,248	11,961	9,453	2,575	..	..	3	36	390	2,146	BRAHMAN (TELUGU) (Ditto).
38	2,382	2,675	4,675	11,309	4,926	16,122	5	61	126	422	3,978	11,530	
8	105	477	2,295	18,915	17,688	3,650	..	4	11	49	644	2,942	KOMATI (Ditto).
51	3,656	5,212	7,247	18,880	7,348	22,320	1	111	170	661	5,631	15,746	
45	1,249	1,383	6,881	66,534	52,606	8,911	1	32	32	126	1,921	6,799	MALA (Ditto).
215	7,368	9,337	21,508	74,424	25,858	48,774	9	171	289	1,746	12,631	33,928	
14	73	478	2,977	19,862	15,208	4,124	..	1	5	33	595	3,490	BRAHMAN (TAMIL) (Ditto.)
33	1,399	3,490	6,542	17,794	7,564	18,399	3	17	45	312	3,998	14,024	
25	74	97	337	21,613	22,942	5,418	..	9	8	8	784	4,609	BALIJA (Ditto).
86	1,231	2,315	7,170	27,740	9,246	26,085	2	36	55	280	6,124	19,588	

TABLE XIV.—Civil Condition by Age

Caste, Tribe or Race.	Locality.	Sex.	Population dealt with.	Unmarried.							
				Total.	0—5.	5—12.	12—15.	15—20.	20—40.	40 & over.	Total.
1	2	3	4	5	6	7	8	9	10	11	12
MADRAS—*continued.*											
PARAIYAN (Hindu)	South Arcot and Tanjore.	Male	447,856	245,090	73,125	86,020	30,533	34,559	18,663	1,290	191,475
		Female	473,521	195,870	76,249	82,465	19,440	12,372	4,491	853	212,495
KAIKOLAN (Ditto)	Coimbatore and Salem	Male	49,623	25,530	6,882	8,801	3,637	3,490	2,344	376	21,088
		Female	51,451	22,235	7,043	9,170	2,923	1,765	988	346	22,225
CHETTI (Ditto)	Coimbatore and Rámnád.	Male	46,774	24,376	6,159	8,077	3,287	3,406	3,060	387	20,368
		Female	52,942	19,238	6,304	8,109	2,704	1,484	428	209	22,833
KAMMALAN (Ditto)	Madura, Rámnád and Tinnevelly.	Male	98,113	54,411	13,166	17,549	6,986	8,216	7,738	806	40,339
		Female	105,035	42,729	14,191	18,086	5,507	3,362	1,237	346	44,225
VELLALA (Ditto)	Salem and Coimbatore	Male	432,134	234,412	52,578	73,115	32,396	37,058	34,947	4,318	179,351
		Female	439,394	179,376	54,011	74,593	27,155	18,553	4,280	784	183,168
TIYAN (Ditto)	Malabar	Male	297,410	170,168	41,129	53,970	23,778	27,922	22,922	447	115,552
		Female	305,888	133,673	41,134	51,349	18,797	14,333	7,403	657	115,463
SHANAN (Ditto)	Tinnevelly	Male	132,277	77,681	18,672	24,666	9,959	12,329	11,686	369	49,974
		Female	137,248	62,776	19,246	25,539	8,887	7,321	1,450	333	52,838
CHERUMAN (Ditto)	Malabar	Male	116,100	63,587	17,144	20,649	9,764	10,064	5,799	167	47,462
		Female	128,331	52,235	17,269	20,182	7,424	5,193	2,012	205	51,290
NORTH-WEST FRONTIER PROVINCE.											
JAT (Hindu, Musalman and Sikh).	N.-W. F. Province	Male	48,873	27,212	5,951	8,953	2,780	3,145	6,010	373	19,315
		Female	37,224	16,184	5,769	7,589	1,732	728	309	57	16,922
ARORA (Hindu and Sikh)	Ditto	Male	37,909	20,906	4,608	6,580	2,834	2,717	3,546	621	14,405
		Female	31,235	12,725	4,559	5,551	1,804	506	255	50	13,221
TANAOLI (Musalman)	Ditto	Male	33,349	19,120	4,808	6,914	2,594	2,348	2,260	196	12,778
		Female	30,636	13,421	5,076	5,564	1,701	735	267	78	14,405
TARKHAN (Hindu, Musalman and Sikh).	Ditto	Male	22,764	12,711	3,369	4,336	1,746	1,468	1,562	230	8,798
		Female	19,854	9,054	3,393	3,737	1,119	508	197	100	8,904
SWATHI (Musalman)	Ditto	Male	20,181	11,933	2,977	4,398	1,595	1,404	1,394	165	7,510
		Female	16,148	8,867	2,918	3,832	991	438	659	29	7,455
PATHAN (Ditto)	Ditto	Male	449,500	271,356	67,797	83,860	42,389	29,453	42,851	5,006	161,692
		Female	395,683	181,373	64,079	71,282	27,144	9,772	7,048	2,048	168,804
GUJAR (Hindu, Musalman and Sikh).	Ditto	Male	61,711	35,997	8,961	11,947	5,067	4,326	5,138	558	22,986
		Female	52,160	23,128	8,717	10,098	2,655	1,128	410	110	24,477
AWAN (Musalman)	Ditto	Male	149,550	87,591	21,283	28,463	13,349	10,140	13,064	1,292	55,041
		Female	126,161	56,795	22,522	23,241	7,517	3,316	1,715	484	53,446
PUNJAB.											
CHAMAR (Hindu)	Punjab	Male	509,230	230,194	65,798	81,415	29,010	27,141	22,585	4,245	233,767
		Female	430,895	135,882	63,339	59,285	9,871	2,341	758	288	234,983
JAT (Ditto)	Ditto	Male	592,554	288,465	68,817	88,317	34,088	35,480	46,935	14,828	238,259
		Female	458,441	140,968	62,134	63,350	11,525	3,098	556	305	244,585
ARAIN (Musalman)	Central Punjab, Plains	Male	431,899	218,589	58,270	76,176	28,570	24,710	26,868	3,965	171,426
		Female	345,733	137,637	56,414	58,551	14,516	5,253	2,298	605	168,840
CHAMAR (Sikh)	Punjab	Male	92,091	44,210	12,045	14,364	5,706	5,952	5,268	875	38,587
		Female	73,714	25,777	11,328	10,966	2,429	826	175	53	38,328
JHINWAR (Hindu)	Ditto	Male	124,003	60,430	14,922	19,746	7,967	8,366	7,875	1,554	49,544
		Female	96,516	33,930	14,369	15,107	3,188	947	249	70	48,968
KUMHAR (Ditto)	Central Punjab, Plains and Eastern Punjab.	Male	82,394	39,004	10,619	12,528	5,601	6,180	4,256	820	35,498
		Female	67,689	21,870	9,802	9,403	2,034	470	113	48	35,417
RAJPUT (Ditto)	Punjab	Male	209,738	115,110	22,012	31,999	14,313	16,808	23,778	6,200	77,183
		Female	158,555	47,204	18,394	21,895	4,860	1,426	461	168	73,704
KANET (Ditto)	Central Punjab, Hills	Male	172,176	80,587	17,983	26,313	11,036	10,545	12,288	2,427	81,245
		Female	165,496	55,383	18,822	24,634	6,019	3,334	1,820	704	84,152
BRAHMAN (Ditto)	Punjab	Male	555,516	278,808	58,168	84,199	36,270	39,281	53,729	17,156	205,831
		Female	456,270	142,699	55,889	66,827	14,690	3,725	1,076	492	202,566
AHIR (Ditto)	Delhi Division	Male	63,968	30,889	7,458	10,423	4,112	3,757	4,004	1,135	26,500
		Female	50,962	16,729	7,230	7,580	1,595	254	45	25	25,987
CHUHRA (Ditto)	Central Punjab, Plains and Eastern Punjab.	Male	416,811	223,769	63,058	77,185	29,825	27,959	22,971	2,771	161,651
		Female	339,562	138,798	58,879	58,875	13,948	4,754	2,041	301	163,437
TELI (Musalman)	Central Punjab, Plains	Male	111,251	58,552	15,672	20,458	7,860	6,930	6,495	1,137	42,975
		Female	89,665	34,728	14,406	14,804	3,498	1,494	354	172	43,268
SHEIKH (Ditto)	Punjab	Male	185,213	92,431	21,067	28,709	12,620	12,394	15,323	2,318	78,001
		Female	149,549	55,770	20,352	24,116	6,319	3,177	1,279	527	72,493
JAT (Sikh)	Ditto	Male	951,572	525,166	114,967	153,947	66,893	69,877	92,437	27,045	329,756
		Female	667,760	226,239	90,074	97,182	27,106	8,755	2,288	834	335,637
NAI (Musalman)	Central Punjab, Plains	Male	64,543	32,900	8,973	11,281	4,386	3,638	3,906	716	25,438
		Female	53,140	21,372	8,319	9,123	2,429	1,033	372	96	25,210
LOHAR (Ditto)	Ditto	Male	66,763	35,181	9,738	11,884	4,706	4,075	4,079	649	25,735
		Female	55,203	22,782	8,816	9,764	2,878	991	238	95	26,180
KUMHAR (Ditto)	Ditto	Male	124,194	65,692	17,933	22,583	8,647	7,487	7,930	1,112	48,140
		Female	102,039	41,511	16,607	17,692	4,609	1,862	592	149	47,601
TARKHAN (Sikh)	Ditto	Male	95,258	49,573	11,900	15,875	6,383	6,248	7,208	1,959	35,175
		Female	75,826	27,011	11,050	11,893	2,941	754	237	136	37,419
MUCHI (Musalman)	Ditto	Male	134,983	70,766	19,313	24,151	9,608	8,060	8,340	1,294	52,121
		Female	109,911	44,440	18,015	18,676	4,998	1,952	649	150	52,252
AGARWAL (Hindu)	Eastern Punjab and Phulkian States.	Male	156,591	78,658	18,140	25,193	9,832	8,731	12,585	4,227	59,400
		Female	134,779	44,695	17,396	21,584	4,515	924	183	93	60,671
JULAHA (Musalman)	Punjab	Male	308,231	161,865	42,171	54,157	21,150	19,368	21,722	3,297	119,478
		Female	258,735	104,928	40,510	44,633	11,789	5,539	2,056	401	122,152
KHATRI (Hindu)	Central Punjab, Plains and Western Punjab.	Male	172,200	96,123	18,809	27,784	13,041	12,574	18,961	4,954	62,047
		Female	139,215	49,944	19,173	21,882	6,815	1,533	380	175	61,758

FOR SELECTED CASTES—*continued.*

Married. 0—5.	Married. 5—12.	Married. 12—15.	Married. 15—20.	Married. 20—40.	Married. 40 & over.	Widowed. Total.	Widowed. 0—5.	Widowed. 5—12.	Widowed. 12—15.	Widowed. 15—20.	Widowed. 20—40.	Widowed. 40 & over.	Caste, Tribe or Race.
13	14	15	16	17	18	19	20	21	22	23	24	25	26
													MADRAS—*continued.*
129 235	446 8,327	555 5,806	4,772 29,968	99,634 129,978	85,939 43,281	11,291 65,156	2 10	10 92	14 93	63 607	2,036 13,560	9,166 50,794	PARAIYAN (Hindu).
15 7	84 297	210 751	1,186 2,836	11,150 12,353	8,443 5,981	3,005 6,991	1 1	4 8	3 11	29 65	620 1,586	2,348 5,370	KAIKOLAN (Ditto).
11 25	75 179	175 665	976 2,908	10,013 13,546	9,118 5,510	2,030 10,871	1 2	1 11	3 18	12 98	456 2,393	1,557 8,349	CHETTI (Ditto).
18 20	133 318	155 872	716 5,947	20,440 27,049	18,877 10,019	3,363 18,051	1 1	.. 10	1 29	11 147	744 4,282	2,606 13,612	KAMMALAN (Ditto).
79 117	322 1,192	909 3,600	4,676 16,712	89,431 114,850	83,984 46,697	18,371 76,850	2 12	13 55	11 80	46 568	3,074 16,574	15,225 59,561	VELLALA (Ditto).
.. 1	34 326	172 3,118	2,063 16,663	66,485 75,673	46,798 19,682	11,690 56,752	.. ..	2 12	4 199	145 1,784	5,173 18,225	6,366 36,532	TIYAN (Ditto).
9 24	31 99	46 267	387 4,306	25,522 35,672	23,979 12,470	4,622 22,234	2 1	5 9	3 4	12 40	686 4,502	3,914 17,678	SHANAN (Ditto).
.. ..	4 100	49 1,415	1,400 7,968	28,317 33,156	17,692 8,656	5,051 24,506	.. ..	.. 5	6 59	123 653	1,998 7,593	2,924 16,496	CHERUMAN (Ditto).
													NORTH-WEST FRONTIER PROVINCE.
.. 1	30 144	105 303	839 1,352	11,898 11,197	6,443 3,925	2,346 4,118	.. ..	.. ..	1 2	37 32	960 887	1,348 3,247	JAT (Hindu, Musalman and Sikh).
.. ..	19 110	109 449	645 1,917	8,192 8,530	5,440 2,215	2,598 5,289	.. ..	1 ..	9 12	36 62	813 1,441	1,739 3,774	ARORA (Hindu and Sikh).
.. ..	7 65	154 335	323 1,412	6,073 9,155	6,221 3,438	1,451 2,810	.. ..	.. ..	.. 1	12 34	359 508	1,080 2,267	TANAOLI (Musalman).
.. ..	2 37	126 200	361 1,052	4,623 5,495	3,686 2,120	1,255 1,896	.. ..	.. ..	2 4	10 22	416 421	827 1,449	TARKHAN (Hindu, Musalman and Sikh).
.. ..	10 29	20 153	160 1,034	3,578 4,468	3,747 1,751	738 1,826	.. ..	.. ..	.. 3	8 10	179 364	551 1,449	SWATHI (Musalman).
.. ..	282 620	654 3,148	3,588 14,726	83,432 106,539	73,741 43,771	16,452 45,506	.. ..	1 14	38 76	170 262	4,032 8,643	12,211 36,511	PATHAN (Ditto).
.. ..	86 79	140 654	751 2,671	10,592 15,023	11,437 6,050	2,728 4,555	.. ..	.. 1	3 12	20 38	701 755	2,004 3,749	GUJAR (Hindu, Musalman and Sikh).
.. ..	146 178	384 1,093	1,825 6,408	27,342 34,116	25,844 11,651	6,918 13,929	.. ..	1 2	7 36	51 177	2,086 2,638	4,773 11,067	AWAN (Musalman).
													PUNJAB.
50 120	6,018 15,003	9,707 18,347	23,281 37,428	122,612 124,195	72,104 39,890	45,269 60,930	5 6	232 323	461 354	1,469 985	13,652 12,895	29,450 45,467	CHAMAR (Hindu).
63 130	5,120 9,525	10,959 18,176	26,169 36,246	119,066 132,574	76,882 47,934	65,830 72,888	8 11	343 340	839 252	2,658 944	20,084 15,318	41,898 56,023	JAT (Ditto).
15 47	2,843 6,429	4,813 8,894	12,666 21,405	86,736 92,238	64,358 39,827	41,884 39,256	.. 2	122 159	144 147	730 440	11,723 7,179	29,165 31,329	ARAIN (Musalman).
2 9	648 1,294	1,153 2,148	3,348 5,363	20,767 21,753	12,669 7,761	9,294 9,609	.. ..	39 48	68 45	207 131	2,683 1,782	6,297 7,603	CHAMAR (Sikh).
5 14	525 1,652	1,158 3,097	4,216 7,151	26,429 27,395	17,211 9,659	14,029 15,618	.. 10	31 342	69 64	321 216	4,419 3,512	9,189 11,474	JHINWAR (Hindu).
9 21	377 1,080	984 2,384	3,547 5,483	18,929 19,690	11,652 6,862	7,892 10,349	3 1	32 33	77 67	227 128	2,396 2,258	5,157 7,862	KUMHAR (Ditto).
13 27	379 2,463	969 4,682	3,959 12,669	39,390 41,201	32,473 12,762	17,445 37,647	3 4	36 90	49 144	249 764	5,054 10,378	12,054 26,267	RAJPUT (Ditto).
31 39	717 2,451	1,542 4,013	4,364 10,584	40,099 47,656	34,492 19,409	10,344 25,963	.. 1	21 52	41 130	218 361	2,773 4,960	7,291 20,459	KANET (Ditto).
34 75	1,291 6,474	4,015 11,773	15,921 33,837	106,748 110,602	77,822 40,300	60,882 105,605	7 10	141 338	331 523	1,355 2,628	17,943 30,609	41,105 70,897	BRAHMAN (Ditto).
1 3	233 715	837 1,764	2,884 4,018	13,317 13,339	9,278 6,128	6,579 5,186	.. ..	11 11	18 31	186 119	1,821 1,677	4,543 6,348	AHIR (Ditto).
28 69	1,574 4,223	3,105 7,499	11,772 28,189	90,244 95,650	54,933 32,827	31,391 37,287	2 ..	102 113	157 121	820 407	9,670 7,621	20,640 29,005	CHUHRA (Ditto).
1 11	350 1,000	812 2,110	2,865 5,870	23,605 24,759	15,342 9,518	9,824 11,609	1 ..	14 53	46 63	214 114	2,942 2,323	6,607 9,056	TELI (Musalman).
12 40	604 1,539	1,314 3,387	4,399 9,711	42,222 42,550	29,450 15,266	14,781 21,286	.. ..	38 54	56 68	278 265	4,587 4,351	9,827 16,548	SHEIKH (Ditto).
20 42	2,510 7,019	6,961 14,085	23,985 40,826	185,786 190,460	130,494 83,255	96,650 105,824	2 ..	200 300	633 296	1,914 919	27,015 19,507	66,886 84,802	JAT (Sikh).
1 1	230 555	535 1,090	1,838 2,955	13,235 14,206	9,599 6,313	6,205 6,558	.. ..	11 20	33 22	134 63	1,818 1,382	4,209 5,071	NAI (Musalman).
.. 2	178 558	461 1,191	1,716 3,338	13,480 14,768	9,950 6,328	5,897 6,241	.. ..	10 16	12 25	104 58	1,826 1,204	3,945 4,943	LOHAR (Ditto).
5 3	371 999	922 1,946	2,966 5,777	25,048 26,967	18,828 11,889	10,292 12,927	.. ..	15 20	46 31	149 76	2,965 2,571	7,117 10,220	KUMHAR (Ditto).
2 ..	230 699	714 1,724	2,625 4,818	17,587 20,867	14,017 9,311	10,510 11,396	.. ..	28 29	37 43	272 110	3,044 2,280	7,129 8,984	TARKHAN (Sikh).
1 5	351 976	859 2,190	2,981 6,498	27,371 29,145	20,558 18,438	12,096 13,219	.. 1	12 34	38 26	152 128	3,515 2,485	8,379 10,550	MOCHI (Musalman).
9 41	452 1,104	2,097 4,134	7,150 10,803	32,515 32,934	17,177 11,655	18,533 29,413	1 4	38 87	106 183	445 979	5,849 10,079	12,094 18,081	AGARWAL (Hindu).
7 26	634 2,141	1,603 4,563	5,523 14,488	62,689 72,242	49,022 28,742	26,888 31,655	.. 2	31 68	74 75	323 282	7,018 5,927	19,442 25,301	JULAHA (Musalman).
.. 1	220 1,133	647 2,460	3,669 9,452	34,266 36,008	23,236 12,704	14,039 27,513	.. ..	20 176	41 80	173 347	3,975 7,106	9,812 19,805	KHATRI (Hindu).

Caste, Tribe or Race.	Locality.	Sex.	Population dealt with.	Unmarried.							
				Total.	0—5.	5—12.	12—15.	15—20.	20—40.	40 & over.	Total.
1	2	3	4	5	6	7	8	9	10	11	12
PUNJAB—*continued.*											
MIRASI (Musalman)	Punjab	Male	120,238	64,437	16,585	21,102	8,217	7,855	9,226	1,452	46,160
		Female	103,888	41,743	15,651	17,627	4,760	2,548	914	248	48,256
RAJPUT (Ditto)	Ditto	Male	645,650	364,159	85,090	115,234	48,691	48,087	58,791	8,266	236,076
		Female	543,250	222,371	82,985	91,270	26,660	14,891	5,347	1,209	240,531
ARORA (Hindu)	Western Punjab	Male	174,596	93,511	20,434	31,727	12,021	10,521	15,450	3,358	68,139
		Female	151,424	57,698	20,788	27,591	6,518	2,148	495	158	66,833
JAT (Musalman)	Punjab	Male	1,258,825	718,485	167,254	240,566	98,382	80,292	116,483	15,508	457,346
		Female	1,015,771	437,720	156,567	189,805	56,666	23,373	9,163	2,146	462,425
TARKHAN (Ditto)	Central Punjab, Plains and Western Punjab.	Male	154,288	83,439	21,717	29,020	10,992	9,445	10,594	1,671	59,800
		Female	129,272	54,483	20,578	23,561	6,529	2,610	957	248	60,036
ARORA (Sikh)	Ditto	Male	93,246	52,028	12,178	17,742	6,694	5,932	7,488	1,994	34,438
		Female	81,280	32,362	11,869	13,781	4,892	1,323	409	88	37,282
PATHAN (Musalman)	Ditto	Male	166,017	90,999	18,821	26,176	11,278	12,600	19,580	2,544	64,828
		Female	125,732	51,902	18,142	22,079	6,465	3,230	1,520	466	56,937
MACHHI (Ditto)	Ditto	Male	125,186	70,134	18,993	23,598	9,003	7,318	9,925	1,297	46,182
		Female	103,682	44,682	17,114	19,062	5,055	2,451	788	222	47,793
SAIYID (Ditto)	Ditto	Male	131,740	71,312	16,367	23,392	9,291	9,098	11,501	1,663	50,948
		Female	115,207	47,274	15,585	19,922	5,978	3,303	1,915	571	50,668
AWAN (Ditto)	Ditto	Male	226,984	127,089	32,213	43,334	16,656	14,684	18,229	1,973	85,119
		Female	196,937	84,329	29,850	36,743	9,825	5,267	2,179	465	89,468
BILOCH (Ditto)	Ditto	Male	289,680	162,879	41,719	57,480	21,947	16,267	22,517	2,949	112,214
		Female	242,385	102,482	39,967	46,433	9,997	4,068	1,537	480	116,478
UNITED PROVINCES OF AGRA AND OUDH.											
KURMI (Hindu)	17 districts and Rampur State.	Male	601,875	234,528	65,487	79,602	20,922	18,190	31,504	8,823	324,284
		Female	558,886	135,006	64,243	58,987	6,558	2,574	1,869	775	323,162
KUMHAR (Hindu and Musalman).	Almost the whole Province	Male	372,218	147,400	46,032	60,868	15,594	11,287	10,856	2,813	195,434
		Female	350,181	99,986	45,763	46,189	4,358	1,515	1,561	600	196,827
CHAMAR (Ditto)	Ditto	Male	3,099,321	1,263,444	388,891	536,389	134,101	98,635	87,928	17,500	1,617,842
		Female	2,969,061	896,475	400,948	422,969	41,201	12,511	13,520	5,326	1,625,126
PASI (Hindu)	28 districts	Male	665,247	275,429	79,507	118,196	28,133	25,017	21,477	3,099	350,040
		Female	637,253	200,240	82,534	96,989	11,782	4,077	3,654	1,204	352,873
GADARIYA (Ditto)	Almost the whole Province.	Male	515,579	214,650	60,002	88,072	25,190	18,421	18,404	3,961	258,452
		Female	467,315	140,146	58,793	69,057	7,080	2,091	2,212	913	256,143
AHIR (Hindu and Musalman)	27 districts and Rampur State.	Male	1,171,769	497,490	125,817	192,800	58,074	47,733	60,178	12,888	580,045
		Female	1,049,327	295,558	120,738	146,873	17,159	4,959	4,555	1,774	576,212
JULAHA (Ditto)	41 districts and Rampur State.	Male	504,123	217,739	68,340	89,936	24,118	17,975	14,573	2,802	246,045
		Female	476,390	158,297	69,763	72,190	9,725	3,080	2,466	1,073	255,892
TELI (Ditto)	40 districts and Rampur State.	Male	450,748	187,667	53,289	77,367	20,598	15,562	16,988	3,863	226,760
		Female	418,329	125,475	53,645	60,048	6,217	1,953	2,414	1,198	227,154
BHAR (Hindu)	13 districts	Male	190,905	80,520	26,891	34,852	7,511	5,639	4,641	986	96,981
		Female	195,907	63,337	28,479	28,864	3,115	1,400	1,465	514	102,716
BHANGI (Hindu and Musalman).	29 districts and Rampur State.	Male	189,709	83,226	23,507	33,751	9,912	7,737	6,791	1,528	89,990
		Female	179,900	56,760	23,370	26,932	3,699	1,358	996	410	92,287
DHOBI (Ditto)	Almost the whole Province.	Male	369,650	158,625	45,073	65,837	18,601	14,056	12,720	2,338	182,999
		Female	346,450	109,323	46,132	52,607	6,369	2,007	1,590	618	186,938
LOHAR (Ditto)	United Provinces except Kumaun Division.	Male	303,716	130,690	36,278	51,293	15,097	11,793	13,407	2,822	147,893
		Female	277,943	85,971	36,032	41,516	4,590	1,696	1,427	708	147,262
LODHA (Hindu)	37 districts and Rampur State.	Male	569,406	236,818	64,277	96,548	27,235	21,451	23,099	4,208	285,736
		Female	510,464	151,703	62,726	73,877	9,321	3,559	2,207	1,013	277,760
MALLAH (Hindu and Musalman).	19 districts	Male	107,825	49,204	15,886	21,151	5,208	3,507	2,902	550	51,457
		Female	123,191	38,698	17,081	18,212	1,903	581	699	222	63,760
DOM (Ditto)	7 districts and Tehri-Garhwal State.	Male	158,186	73,790	21,750	28,290	9,095	7,721	6,325	609	78,212
		Female	148,306	50,299	24,550	22,652	3,296	1,083	580	138	80,588
KAHAR (Ditto)	Almost the whole Province.	Male	571,962	254,686	69,957	100,991	32,460	25,251	21,468	4,559	270,803
		Female	532,964	171,170	69,929	81,878	11,965	3,672	2,766	1,140	277,492
NAI (Ditto)	Ditto	Male	472,280	211,006	55,283	82,169	26,628	21,402	21,042	4,482	222,878
		Female	435,133	137,981	55,611	66,164	9,976	2,894	2,297	959	226,548
BARHAI (Ditto)	41 districts and Rampur State.	Male	311,910	138,564	35,141	52,595	17,888	14,210	15,044	3,686	145,856
		Female	272,904	85,816	34,675	41,829	6,016	1,719	1,836	741	143,476
JAT (Hindu, Musalman and Sikh).	14 districts and Rampur State.	Male	412,637	190,924	43,302	66,202	25,608	19,836	25,608	10,373	177,743
		Female	317,415	95,021	36,723	45,596	8,874	2,072	1,172	584	171,956
GUJAR (Hindu and Musalman).	15 districts.	Male	186,827	95,187	19,878	32,181	12,525	11,430	14,221	4,952	74,945
		Female	141,902	45,503	16,765	21,964	4,480	1,358	672	244	74,621
BRAHMAN (Hindu)	United Provinces	Male	2,444,295	1,216,014	251,408	390,847	141,662	130,697	221,627	80,278	1,004,309
		Female	2,197,902	636,863	239,827	309,525	55,869	16,955	10,453	4,174	1,020,398
RAJPUT (Hindu and Musalman).	Ditto	Male	1,937,556	962,072	205,856	317,859	122,444	108,101	163,587	64,225	807,578
		Female	1,691,942	518,505	194,017	248,888	48,174	14,578	9,214	4,134	824,999
AGARWAL (Hindu and Jain)	29 districts and Rampur State.	Male	156,680	73,310	15,236	23,021	9,767	8,398	11,511	5,377	62,723
		Female	125,898	41,601	14,287	19,264	4,902	1,315	996	837	57,755
SHEIKH (Musalman)	U. P. except Tehri-Garhwal State.	Male	689,945	325,000	79,913	118,866	42,048	38,708	38,680	6,785	310,164
		Female	617,688	217,376	80,842	98,622	20,078	9,020	6,239	2,575	301,733
PATHAN (Ditto)	U. P. (except Almora, Garhwal and Tehri-Garhwal State).	Male	498,690	244,879	58,365	88,737	30,760	29,896	32,110	5,011	218,304
		Female	459,367	160,204	59,039	75,000	15,709	5,545	3,511	1,400	222,457
KAYASTHA (Hindu and Musalman).	Almost the whole Province.	Male	255,775	129,586	26,402	39,514	16,635	16,897	22,564	7,574	101,739
		Female	227,668	77,146	26,578	36,227	9,705	3,102	1,090	446	101,056
SAIYID (Musalman)	Most part of the Province.	Male	127,564	65,094	15,133	21,507	8,944	8,979	9,097	1,434	53,093
		Female	112,418	44,359	14,766	19,766	5,466	2,808	1,149	404	53,430

FOR SELECTED CASTES—*continued.*

Married.						Widowed.							Caste, Tribe or Race.
0—5.	5—12.	12—15.	15—20.	20—40.	40 & over	Total.	0—5.	5—12.	12—15.	15—20	20—40.	40 & over.	
13	14	15	16	17	18	19	20	21	22	23	24	25	26
													PUNJAB—*continued.*
9 8	226 711	522 1,613	2,633 5,703	23,570 28,146	19,200 12,075	9,641 13,890	.. 1	23 32	26 43	145 120	2,782 2,515	6,665 11,179	MIRASI (Musalman).
34 123	1,103 3,617	2,519 7,711	10,246 28,802	120,691 144,362	101,483 55,916	45,415 80,357	1 6	80 172	126 227	504 992	11,541 18,427	33,163 60,533	RAJPUT (Ditto).
5 17	147 1,023	754 3,044	3,771 8,720	37,244 41,278	26,218 12,756	12,936 26,893	1 5	16 32	15 61	117 339	3,646 6,772	9,141 19,684	ARORA (Hindu).
39 85	2,055 6,165	5,514 13,210	16,531 44,715	237,538 283,166	195,669 115,084	82,994 115,626	1 8	144 248	220 278	686 769	21,315 18,783	60,628 95,540	JAT (Musalman).
4 8	322 775	776 2,208	2,896 7,099	31,059 35,450	24,743 14,501	11,649 14,753	.. ..	12 22	30 23	145 134	3,049 2,745	7,813 11,829	TARKHAN (Ditto).
4 10	165 471	299 1,290	1,734 4,667	17,682 22,045	14,554 8,799	6,774 11,636	.. ..	13 26	14 43	59 154	1,777 2,838	4,911 8,575	ARORA (Sikh).
5 7	209 647	464 1,607	2,019 6,329	34,018 34,157	28,113 14,190	10,190 16,893	1 2	35 23	15 40	155 180	3,020 3,048	6,964 13,600	PATHAN (Musalman).
4 6	184 503	496 1,465	1,877 5,403	23,945 28,105	19,676 12,311	8,876 11,197	.. 1	10 12	23 28	100 94	2,457 1,987	6,280 9,075	MACHHI (Ditto).
1 12	177 516	426 1,422	1,939 5,743	26,170 30,298	22,235 12,677	9,480 17,265	.. ..	9 30	26 60	93 201	2,632 3,840	6,720 13,134	SAIYID (Ditto).
1 2	271 868	650 2,255	2,613 9,250	44,201 54,438	37,383 22,655	14,776 25,146	.. ..	8 37	23 50	113 180	3,802 4,890	10,830 19,983	AWAN (Ditto).
18 32	368 858	892 3,405	3,417 11,732	54,247 68,383	53,272 32,068	13,937 23,495	1 9	22 57	32 33	114 181	3,113 3,092	10,705 20,053	BILOCH (Ditto).
													UNITED PROVINCES OF AGRA AND OUDH.
1,766 2,123	25,615 34,814	19,293 23,271	30,036 36,570	151,871 166,695	95,703 59,689	53,063 100,720	44 94	716 1,177	1,065 775	1,679 1,380	16,816 21,023	32,743 76,271	KURMI (Hindu).
352 594	7,910 15,241	10,370 16,092	19,725 27,393	97,879 101,801	59,198 35,706	29,384 53,288	25 40	264 387	461 491	1,217 1,004	9,326 11,196	18,091 40,170	KUMHAR (Hindu and Musalman).
2,736 4,469	60,169 114,014	81,087 130,076	158,892 214,232	828,108 858,784	486,900 303,551	218,035 447,460	124 399	2,177 3,406	3,746 4,126	10,924 8,281	73,759 97,633	127,305 333,615	CHAMAR (Ditto).
567 826	16,186 24,182	15,318 23,099	30,359 43,679	178,358 193,841	109,252 67,246	40,378 84,140	35 40	422 559	557 569	1,461 1,266	12,900 18,144	25,003 63,562	PASI (Hindu).
345 596	8,364 17,706	13,340 21,274	26,485 35,779	130,656 133,695	79,262 47,093	43,077 71,026	13 41	306 384	521 534	1,576 1,142	13,970 14,877	26,691 54,048	GADARIYA (Ditto).
839 1,033	22,215 38,919	27,616 44,886	52,645 73,328	291,924 308,517	184,806 109,529	94,234 177,557	48 55	755 969	1,051 1,202	3,051 2,824	29,472 37,536	59,857 134,971	AHIR (Hindu and Musalman).
374 644	7,326 16,570	10,146 17,540	20,637 31,617	123,857 137,936	83,705 51,585	40,339 62,261	10 46	285 423	536 452	1,384 1,064	12,194 11,604	25,930 48,612	JULAHA (Ditto).
338 483	6,890 14,632	11,051 17,879	21,405 28,835	116,711 123,196	70,365 42,129	36,321 65,700	25 23	217 350	487 468	1,273 1,266	12,240 14,159	22,079 49,434	TELI (Ditto).
332 448	3,878 6,255	4,494 6,919	8,423 11,160	50,705 58,346	29,129 19,588	13,424 29,854	25 56	168 292	245 398	662 567	4,805 7,312	7,519 21,229	BHAR (Hindu).
68 142	2,181 5,397	4,437 7,213	10,031 13,806	44,610 47,671	28,663 18,058	16,493 21,753	8 8	95 113	224 168	774 627	5,432 4,637	9,960 16,200	BHANGI (Hindu and Musalman).
271 353	5,080 10,485	7,872 13,672	17,354 25,053	95,283 102,297	57,139 35,078	28,026 50,189	17 20	178 260	319 321	960 918	9,035 10,638	17,517 38,032	DHOBI (Ditto).
277 383	4,062 8,216	6,510 11,055	13,219 19,508	76,320 80,114	47,505 28,986	25,133 43,816	11 41	167 299	302 366	763 846	7,971 9,328	15,919 32,930	LOHAR (Ditto).
152 220	7,588 15,256	13,282 22,977	27,670 33,104	147,612 148,698	89,452 52,505	46,852 81,001	18 12	236 276	478 476	1,417 1,846	15,414 17,844	29,289 60,547	LODHA (Hindu).
169 193	1,333 3,276	2,125 4,746	4,641 7,878	26,810 35,898	16,379 11,769	7,164 20,733	17 25	74 88	109 161	345 317	2,097 4,867	4,522 15,275	MALLAH (Hindu and Musalman).
41 85	727 3,719	1,760 5,873	5,215 10,759	41,680 44,225	28,789 15,927	6,184 17,421	.. 4	12 49	35 89	142 355	1,809 3,190	4,096 13,734	DOM (Ditto).
329 649	4,800 12,263	9,551 18,721	24,698 35,426	142,069 153,274	89,356 57,159	46,413 84,242	12 25	191 327	419 506	1,671 1,370	14,782 17,917	29,338 64,097	KAHAR (Ditto).
375 443	4,152 9,814	8,342 15,473	20,442 31,495	116,973 125,106	72,594 44,277	38,396 70,684	23 30	154 346	435 446	1,323 1,159	12,196 15,277	24,265 53,426	NAI (Ditto).
125 251	2,261 6,007	5,066 10,252	13,395 19,960	75,267 77,386	49,742 29,620	27,490 45,612	8 31	122 193	260 311	768 873	8,524 9,152	17,808 33,052	BARHAI (Ditto).
102 166	2,808 6,778	8,547 14,563	22,417 27,029	84,947 83,559	58,832 39,861	43,970 50,438	7 99	236 723	540 1,697	1,834 1,431	11,886 9,749	29,467 36,73[illegible]	JAT (Hindu, Musalman and Sikh).
67 69	1,702 2,951	3,194 5,771	8,116 12,734	36,086 37,685	24,880 15,411	16,695 21,778	6 14	77 96	157 125	678 420	5,000 4,977	10,777 16,146	GUJAR (Hindu and Musalman).
1,075 2,335	17,244 42,104	34,361 69,689	84,590 135,638	503,559 557,749	363,480 212,883	223,882 540,701	57 270	957 2,317	1,696 3,589	5,039 10,867	59,031 142,326	157,102 381,332	BRAHMAN (Hindu).
1,073 1,943	10,302 31,375	22,302 54,696	64,163 116,489	413,686 452,265	296,052 168,231	147,906 348,438	55 161	607 1,497	1,195 2,092	3,812 6,877	39,624 88,597	102,613 249,214	RAJPUT (Hindu and Musalman).
128 245	796 2,030	2,903 4,378	7,444 10,450	31,354 28,476	20,098 12,176	22,647 26,542	37 12	144 297	696 169	1,781 866	5,889 7,503	14,100 17,695	AGARWAL (Hindu and Jain).
511 447	4,240 10,280	7,249 16,314	18,929 39,338	163,442 171,250	115,793 64,104	54,781 96,579	21 33	205 302	463 435	1,490 2,014	17,267 20,167	35,335 75,628	SHAKH (Musalman).
207 308	2,901 6,493	4,204 10,632	11,170 26,789	111,871 128,306	87,951 49,929	35,417 76,766	6 37	94 216	221 227	597 867	10,420 14,003	24,079 61,356	PATHAN (Ditto).
77 202	908 1,689	2,081 4,376	6,860 15,250	54,028 57,517	37,785 22,022	24,450 49,464	17 52	70 179	153 274	554 971	6,610 12,443	17,046 35,545	KAYASTHA (Hindu and Musalman).
37 70	353 835	596 1,938	2,195 6,543	27,345 31,290	22,567 12,754	9,377 20,629	1 4	35 53	68 58	144 275	2,387 4,246	6,742 15,993	SAIYID (Musalman).

TABLE XIV.—Civil Condition by Age

Caste, Tribe or Race.	Locality.	Sex.	Population dealt with.	Unmarried.							
				Total.	0—5.	5—12.	12—15.	15—20.	20—40.	40 & over.	Total.
1	2	3	4	5	6	7	8	9	10	11	12
BARODA STATE.											
KANBI KADWA (Hindu)	Baroda	Male	88,955	16,915	8,076	4,053	1,132	1,327	2,036	291	62,221
		Female	83,686	6,522	5,060	1,016	276	120	46	4	60,272
DHED (Ditto)	Ditto	Male	50,487	21,267	8,102	6,548	2,139	2,277	1,840	361	26,327
		Female	49,240	13,854	8,097	4,213	835	463	241	5	27,594
VAGHRI (Ditto)	Ditto	Male	14,702	6,509	2,640	2,089	541	696	521	72	7,456
		Female	13,427	4,606	2,607	1,486	311	153	48	3	7,272
KANBI LEWA (Ditto)	Ditto	Male	99,960	42,165	12,578	12,098	4,825	4,904	6,195	1,570	47,587
		Female	83,329	21,913	11,412	8,672	1,292	341	163	33	45,065
KOLI (Ditto)	Ditto	Male	194,746	87,663	31,028	24,709	9,117	12,748	8,908	1,153	92,666
		Female	176,197	50,619	29,046	14,563	4,247	1,968	782	13	96,403
RAJPUT (Ditto)	Ditto	Male	34,531	16,396	4,427	4,357	1,834	2,254	3,085	439	15,289
		Female	29,671	7,844	3,949	2,869	670	241	94	21	14,559
KHATRI (Ditto)	Ditto	Male	1,842	734	239	282	63	77	64	9	997
		Female	1,546	424	213	167	36	8	..	..	863
BRAHMAN (ANAVALA) (Ditto).	Ditto	Male	5,313	2,567	637	694	314	264	449	209	2,187
		Female	4,580	1,333	574	630	64	3	3	9	2,171
BRAHMAN (AUDICH) (Ditto).	Ditto	Male	20,876	9,705	2,411	2,803	1,185	1,206	1,782	318	9,407
		Female	19,752	4,877	2,442	2,090	247	55	26	17	8,574
CENTRAL INDIA AGENCY.											
AGARWAL (Hindu)	Central India	Male	27,710	11,794	3,015	3,285	1,547	1,283	1,844	820	12,679
		Female	30,578	9,752	3,736	3,307	1,393	501	455	310	13,352
BANIYA* (Ditto)	Bundelkhand and Baghelkhand.	Male	25,303	10,791	3,007	3,447	1,229	1,025	1,509	574	12,234
		Female	23,035	6,893	2,926	2,538	701	295	344	89	11,452
BRAHMAN (Ditto)	Central India	Male	289,803	127,408	31,826	37,127	14,861	14,501	20,718	8,375	129,744
		Female	288,165	88,139	36,233	35,794	6,839	3,943	3,253	2,077	129,503
GOND (Ditto)	Baghelkhand	Male	76,753	35,975	11,589	11,083	4,755	3,399	3,359	1,790	35,656
		Female	86,532	36,457	14,672	12,757	3,693	2,624	1,569	1,142	38,081
PORWAL (Ditto)	Malwa	Male	8,616	3,687	883	1,013	467	454	684	186	3,553
		Female	7,740	2,635	835	817	347	390	142	104	3,397
GUJAR (Ditto)	Northern Gwalior	Male	105,834	46,281	11,970	11,184	5,375	5,248	9,846	2,658	47,828
		Female	79,894	28,159	10,398	9,957	3,299	1,486	2,244	775	39,965
RAJPUT (Ditto)	Central India	Male	185,738	84,729	20,453	21,458	11,538	11,886	14,075	5,319	80,847
		Female	152,718	56,017	20,355	18,733	6,075	4,885	3,024	2,945	68,336
PORWAL (Jain)	Northern Gwalior and Bundelkhand.	Male	11,417	4,922	1,453	1,528	661	466	631	183	5,694
		Female	11,286	3,711	1,649	1,359	341	24	254	84	5,383
OSWAL (Hindu)	Malwa	Male	6,072	2,615	627	701	327	309	452	199	2,835
		Female	8,237	3,268	960	763	415	921	115	94	3,127
MAHESRI (Ditto)	Ditto	Male	10,008	4,085	971	997	485	452	839	341	4,322
		Female	11,404	3,523	1,319	1,164	705	195	119	21	5,635
SHEIKH (Musalman)	Northern Gwalior, Indore, Bhopal and Ratlam.	Male	76,259	33,211	10,242	10,349	3,758	3,668	4,308	886	36,989
		Female	70,957	23,446	9,889	8,657	2,479	940	895	586	34,662
PATHAN (Ditto)	Northern Gwalior and Bhopal.	Male	73,476	31,886	8,658	10,200	3,851	3,653	4,494	1,030	35,487
		Female	65,046	22,675	9,273	8,840	2,172	1,039	899	452	31,962
BHILALA (Hindu)	Hilly Tracts	Male	16,351	7,784	2,281	2,756	989	823	858	77	8,069
		Female	17,413	8,141	2,890	2,623	1,186	941	466	35	7,819
OSWAL (Jain)	Malwa	Male	16,764	7,546	2,003	2,094	954	866	1,180	449	6,849
		Female	16,192	5,782	2,638	2,229	601	120	105	29	6,764
GOND (Animist)	Hilly Tracts	Male	34,611	15,718	5,485	4,065	2,022	1,816	1,615	815	16,178
		Female	36,776	13,480	6,244	4,578	918	678	691	371	17,747
BHIL (Ditto)	Ditto	Male	134,045	69,602	25,850	21,088	9,845	6,311	6,185	328	62,311
		Female	135,865	55,796	27,220	21,067	4,790	1,265	1,298	158	65,361
BHILALA (Ditto)	Ditto	Male	44,821	25,859	9,687	8,208	2,904	2,522	2,247	291	17,619
		Female	44,791	23,001	10,018	7,632	2,564	1,561	1,023	203	18,563
COCHIN STATE.											
INDIAN CHRISTIAN	Cochin	Male	116,549	64,363	18,030	21,327	9,542	9,708	5,354	407	48,048
		Female	114,019	52,268	18,069	21,058	7,496	3,923	1,450	272	47,819
JONAKAN (Musalman)	Ditto	Male	26,274	15,358	4,113	4,713	2,185	2,371	1,927	49	10,195
		Female	25,195	11,810	4,024	4,597	1,756	1,032	358	43	10,240
PULAYAN (Hindu)	Ditto	Male	35,284	19,073	5,640	6,330	2,716	2,712	1,083	92	14,759
		Female	37,503	16,444	5,646	6,359	2,355	1,458	560	66	15,705
NAYAR (Ditto)	Ditto	Male	58,720	36,966	8,339	9,872	4,631	6,042	7,626	456	18,912
		Female	62,486	25,232	8,153	9,483	3,673	2,667	1,118	138	23,010
ILUVAN (Ditto)	Ditto	Male	102,817	57,525	15,389	18,369	8,349	9,335	5,869	214	41,746
		Female	105,636	48,615	15,460	18,097	7,683	5,352	1,895	178	41,306
HYDERABAD STATE.											
MUNNUR (Hindu)	Hyderabad	Male	115,190	47,862	19,840	13,322	6,419	5,581	2,163	546	60,357
		Female	113,234	26,327	18,783	5,652	1,082	277	323	210	66,731
KAPU (Ditto)	Ditto	Male	330,902	145,184	54,433	40,264	24,759	17,338	7,801	589	178,204
		Female	317,352	85,657	44,202	34,085	5,735	1,332	202	151	179,211
KOLI (Ditto)	Ditto	Male	134,432	51,389	21,558	16,799	7,486	4,119	1,146	281	79,526
		Female	132,408	33,711	22,317	9,835	1,235	121	117	86	77,462
BRAHMAN (Ditto)	Ditto	Male	133,192	54,574	20,438	15,541	7,075	6,410	4,441	769	72,947
		Female	128,049	31,541	19,383	10,740	727	319	263	109	71,182
LINGAYAT (Ditto)	Ditto	Male	381,201	144,700	63,784	43,485	22,184	11,250	2,141	1,856	215,873
		Female	376,410	107,106	62,787	28,424	9,409	3,882	1,562	1,042	207,827

* This includes Gahoi, Kasaundhan and Kesar.

FOR SELECTED CASTES—*continued*.

MARRIED.						WIDOWED.							CASTE, TRIBE OR RACE.
0—5.	5—12.	12—15.	15—20.	20—40.	40 & over.	Total.	0—5.	5—12.	12—15.	15—20.	20—40.	40 & over.	
13	14	15	16	17	18	19	20	21	22	23	24	25	26
													BARODA STATE.
4,186 8,630	7,409 10,741	2,799 5,024	6,483 6,825	29,848 24,676	11,494 4,876	9,819 16,892	216 122	370 260	283 374	299 225	3,689 5,264	5,007 10,647	KANBI KADWA (Hindu).
125 324	760 2,128	992 2,122	2,499 3,803	14,208 14,886	7,748 4,261	2,893 7,862	17 7	35 97	43 52	140 93	911 1,786	1,747 5,827	DHED (Ditto).
41 40	184 373	341 350	719 926	4,007 4,328	2,158 1,255	743 1,547	1 ..	5 14	9 20	32 87	247 365	449 1,061	VAGHRI (Ditto).
267 270	2,164 2,206	1,838 3,117	5,169 6,139	23,547 24,920	14,602 8,433	10,208 16,331	6 7	47 96	110 92	335 234	3,332 4,379	6,378 11,523	KANBI LEWA (Ditto).
421 1,189	2,418 3,531	3,198 5,215	6,085 12,635	54,165 53,976	26,384 21,858	14,417 27,175	30 43	101 108	107 151	181 276	5,487 6,807	8,511 20,290	KOLI (Ditto).
49 96	191 569	284 815	1,227 2,093	8,253 8,628	5,285 2,358	2,846 7,268	.. 3	7 28	21 59	102 100	954 2,268	1,762 4,810	RAJPUT (Ditto).
.. 3	20 27	57 80	87 113	406 439	357 201	181 259	.. ..	2 3	.. 2	6 4	57 56	116 194	KHATRI (Ditto).
.. 2	28 80	78 242	237 307	1,184 1,118	660 422	559 1,076	.. ..	1 3	2 7	8 29	147 364	401 673	BRAHMAN (ANAVALA) (Ditto).
18 25	70 246	148 605	564 1,340	5,174 5,055	3,433 1,603	1,764 6,001	1 1	4 12	5 47	24 66	510 1,697	1,220 4,178	BRAHMAN (AUDICH) (Ditto).
													CENTRAL INDIA AGENCY.
113 199	413 1,364	886 1,693	1,802 2,367	5,629 5,480	8,836 2,299	3,237 7,474	57 100	17 146	43 220	140 367	1,106 2,350	1,874 4,291	AGARWAL (Hindu).
471 155	984 1,004	1,125 1,377	1,633 1,801	5,033 4,942	2,988 2,083	2,278 4,690	11 10	64 63	68 136	168 254	704 1,307	1,263 2,920	BANIYA (Ditto).
2,416 2,370	6,234 10,083	9,144 13,679	17,812 20,760	55,933 59,306	38,155 23,305	32,651 70,523	133 923	260 1,202	970 1,475	2,100 2,556	8,270 21,188	20,918 43,184	BRAHMAN (Ditto).
1,866 600	3,968 2,805	2,731 3,311	4,103 5,996	14,384 15,259	8,604 10,110	5,122 11,994	17 29	175 185	235 270	512 571	1,375 3,678	2,808 7,261	GOND (Ditto).
36 48	104 220	261 451	500 743	1,560 1,384	1,097 551	1,371 1,708	7 3	26 13	38 41	62 156	643 540	595 955	PORWAL (Ditto).
1,346 478	2,240 2,245	2,857 2,953	6,492 5,579	20,944 19,045	18,949 9,665	11,725 11,770	91 31	145 99	277 267	358 433	3,787 3,218	7,067 7,722	GUJAR (Ditto).
1,920 1,097	3,596 3,473	6,306 6,063	11,538 11,534	32,661 30,965	24,826 15,204	20,162 28,365	167 150	315 367	678 670	1,498 2,204	6,656 8,343	10,848 16,631	RAJPUT (Ditto).
22 41	127 273	195 442	698 832	2,600 2,664	1,452 1,131	1,401 2,192	2 10	10 17	9 31	19 33	431 759	930 1,342	PORWAL (Jain).
24 30	78 185	141 382	320 960	1,047 901	725 669	1,122 1,842	5 2	5 7	10 34	62 67	646 595	394 1,137	OSWAL (Hindu).
60 30	121 264	343 882	700 1,205	1,838 1,790	1,260 1,464	1,661 2,946	1 ..	11 16	13 37	65 166	854 828	657 1,199	MAHESRI (Ditto).
141 186	802 1,361	454 2,501	2,501 5,117	18,242 17,888	14,849 7,609	6,659 12,849	14 42	51 129	42 136	110 116	2,099 3,443	3,743 8,983	SHEIKH (Musalman).
194 191	602 1,149	1,019 2,171	3,157 4,518	18,383 17,639	12,132 6,294	6,103 10,409	11 15	65 93	54 98	127 131	2,044 2,609	3,802 7,463	PATHAN (Ditto).
13 46	125 208	531 525	1,018 1,252	4,037 3,665	2,350 2,123	496 1,453	1 2	.. 3	3 6	20 92	110 443	364 907	BHILALA (Hindu).
31 37	131 184	266 627	709 1,189	3,648 3,457	2,064 1,270	2,369 3,646	3 9	14 20	9 34	43 157	816 1,388	1,484 2,038	OSWAL (Jain).
127 56	113 348	381 660	1,519 1,964	8,687 10,943	5,351 3,781	2,715 5,549	14 3	8 17	16 11	35 63	986 1,303	1,656 4,152	GOND (Animist).
236 187	385 1,198	673 1,648	1,720 6,622	42,372 42,114	16,925 13,592	2,132 14,706	6 23	12 39	20 59	61 92	750 3,079	1,283 11,414	BHIL (Ditto).
36 12	23 213	427 480	836 2,121	10,750 12,517	5,547 3,220	1,343 3,227	.. ..	1 4	.. 18	11 21	473 618	858 2,566	BHILALA (Ditto).
													COCHIN STATE.
.. ..	44 162	95 987	1,760 6,878	29,530 30,902	16,619 8,890	4,138 13,932	.. ..	.. 7	2 9	27 106	832 2,985	3,277 10,825	INDIAN CHRISTIAN.
.. ..	.. 18	5 193	186 1,468	6,068 6,876	3,936 1,685	721 3,145	.. ..	.. 1	.. 7	12 73	237 856	472 2,208	JONAKAN (Musalman).
.. ..	9 25	10 259	378 2,014	8,451 10,321	5,911 3,088	1,452 5,354	.. ..	.. 3	1 7	23 85	441 1,411	987 3,848	PULAYAN (Hindu).
.. ..	.. 41	.. 507	189 3,385	10,469 14,596	8,254 4,481	2,842 14,944	.. ..	.. ..	.. 23	19 291	872 4,388	1,951 9,542	NAYAR (Ditto).
.. ..	6 58	48 511	450 5,307	25,609 27,861	15,633 7,571	3,546 15,713	.. ..	.. 5	1 22	38 271	1,042 4,457	2,465 10,958	ILUVAN (Ditto).
													HYDERABAD STATE.
458 385	2,267 8,850	2,580 11,169	9,136 7,959	27,189 28,711	18,727 11,657	6,961 18,176	30 31	87 166	284 208	426 662	1,406 4,118	4,668 12,991	MUNNUR (Hindu).
398 620	4,085 18,287	12,206 23,200	14,559 26,552	85,873 72,660	61,088 37,892	7,514 52,484	29 34	86 363	113 471	43 1,331	2,271 12,678	4,972 37,607	KAPU (Ditto).
135 641	2,533 6,401	7,927 11,368	8,260 13,562	35,277 33,232	25,388 12,198	3,523 21,295	33 26	60 265	91 624	79 900	857 5,134	2,403 14,346	KOLI (Ditto).
220 616	1,455 6,028	3,131 9,159	13,552 13,219	29,153 24,352	24,736 17,808	6,371 25,326	22 32	54 195	80 581	130 1,248	674 6,619	5,411 16,651	BRAHMAN (Ditto).
896 1,465	7,079 18,012	22,294 30,592	22,486 26,775	81,001 83,949	81,916 56,234	20,629 62,277	101 123	555 698	609 2,962	558 3,581	6,426 18,256	12,385 41,657	LINGAYAT (Ditto).

TABLE XIV.—Civil Condition by Age

Caste, Tribe or Race.	Locality.	Sex.	Population dealt with.	Unmarried. Total.	0—5.	5—12.	12—15.	15—20.	20—40.	40 & over.	Total.
1	2	3	4	5	6	7	8	9	10	11	12
HYDERABAD STATE —*continued.*											
KOMATI (Hindu)	Hyderabad	Male	114,121	49,348	18,255	13,260	8,612	6,673	1,901	647	60,126
		Female	109,259	32,096	15,169	11,532	4,032	789	378	246	57,170
SALE (Ditto)	Ditto	Male	175,968	79,876	32,979	25,157	12,511	7,035	1,691	503	89,143
		Female	167,162	55,206	29,382	20,870	3,238	811	580	325	91,173
MARATHA (Ditto)	Ditto	Male	772,878	314,044	112,328	92,440	48,825	29,111	24,780	6,560	420,874
		Female	765,966	222,127	109,169	78,017	25,346	4,651	4,538	406	415,428
MAHAR AND MALA (Ditto)	Ditto	Male	574,385	250,358	98,381	76,726	38,984	24,886	8,550	2,881	301,115
		Female	563,264	182,634	95,455	59,605	18,811	4,912	3,298	558	305,520
SUNAR (Ditto)	Ditto	Male	45,278	18,741	7,255	5,068	2,696	1,920	1,428	379	23,136
		Female	42,759	13,352	6,961	4,292	1,169	435	312	183	22,265
PANCHAL (Ditto)	Ditto	Male	59,990	25,600	10,058	6,931	3,788	2,991	1,449	383	30,863
		Female	57,720	18,926	9,920	6,154	1,521	815	400	116	29,576
MADIGA AND MANG (Ditto).	Ditto	Male	581,519	265,632	109,553	79,957	33,389	25,787	14,999	1,347	297,094
		Female	563,833	187,125	110,715	64,321	7,724	2,205	1,797	363	303,269
GOLLA (Ditto)	Ditto	Male	234,629	104,756	34,064	36,244	16,350	11,527	5,427	1,144	124,425
		Female	226,131	63,262	39,646	22,573	684	214	100	45	129,259
TELAGA (Ditto)	Ditto	Male	233,206	107,435	37,806	34,034	16,028	11,548	7,424	595	114,162
		Female	225,416	75,798	38,016	25,587	7,762	2,202	1,355	876	113,390
MUTRASI (Ditto)	Ditto	Male	134,473	61,086	22,502	16,652	9,217	6,221	4,011	483	66,954
		Female	126,297	37,222	22,461	11,415	2,515	644	115	72	72,084
PATHAN (Musalman)	Ditto	Male	71,167	33,573	9,391	9,868	4,645	4,595	4,278	796	34,404
		Female	63,981	23,532	9,529	8,460	3,087	1,418	974	364	31,499
SAIYID (Ditto)	Ditto	Male	99,142	47,149	12,754	13,672	6,706	5,996	6,924	1,097	47,117
		Female	90,432	32,113	12,098	12,628	4,368	1,586	1,062	371	43,569
SHEIKH (Ditto)	Ditto	Male	499,495	250,462	73,115	62,124	46,647	34,732	30,788	3,056	229,470
		Female	485,524	171,834	69,938	59,126	25,504	9,172	6,935	1,159	235,719
KASHMIR STATE.											
BRAHMAN (Hindu)	Kashmir	Male	93,115	48,568	10,102	13,905	6,015	6,297	9,554	2,695	35,973
		Female	80,680	24,523	9,775	12,101	1,501	447	477	222	36,934
THAKKAR (Ditto)	Ditto	Male	49,419	25,307	5,134	7,189	2,708	3,089	5,400	1,787	19,941
		Female	44,177	13,943	5,480	6,196	1,068	459	455	285	20,704
RAJPUT (Ditto)	Ditto	Male	29,540	16,490	3,102	4,658	2,073	2,264	3,562	831	10,822
		Female	20,724	4,802	1,806	2,466	361	106	43	20	10,597
JAT (Musalman)	Ditto	Male	58,002	31,686	8,362	11,259	3,852	3,337	4,200	676	22,617
		Female	55,561	20,694	7,881	9,101	2,416	1,256	473	117	28,722
AWAN (Ditto)	Ditto	Male	13,922	7,723	2,139	2,869	966	816	825	108	5,525
		Female	11,909	5,122	2,074	2,328	432	198	84	6	5,644
MUGHAL (Ditto)	Ditto	Male	17,696	9,575	2,639	3,501	1,214	1,129	998	94	7,304
		Female	15,573	6,525	2,520	2,964	623	226	182	10	7,442
DAR (Ditto)	Ditto	Male	53,150	27,467	8,517	10,332	3,216	2,953	2,284	165	23,146
		Female	45,375	18,600	7,945	8,592	1,532	373	122	36	22,952
MALIK (Ditto)	Ditto	Male	27,072	14,436	4,111	5,462	1,717	1,686	1,291	170	11,444
		Female	26,379	11,405	4,339	5,195	1,014	507	129	221	12,454
BAT (Ditto)	Ditto	Male	82,012	42,601	12,405	16,000	5,096	4,936	3,790	374	35,226
		Female	70,198	26,726	11,966	13,266	2,445	627	300	122	35,237
KASHMIRI PANDIT (BRAHMAN) (Hindu).	Ditto	Male	30,724	17,283	3,345	4,847	1,827	2,276	3,722	1,266	11,312
		Female	24,373	8,568	3,222	4,590	731	98	25	2	10,954
MYSORE STATE.											
BRAHMAN (Hindu)	Mysore	Male	98,597	48,163	11,277	16,079	6,714	7,511	5,326	1,256	43,624
		Female	95,973	27,822	12,172	14,762	764	70	43	11	42,932
KURUBA (Ditto)	Ditto	Male	201,967	108,049	23,504	35,593	16,156	16,881	14,705	1,210	84,482
		Female	201,399	74,799	24,838	35,598	9,353	3,344	1,229	437	86,445
PANCHALA (Ditto)	Ditto	Male	65,790	35,255	7,308	10,707	5,184	5,694	5,770	592	27,148
		Female	62,306	23,144	7,734	11,380	2,687	940	316	87	26,625
VAKKALIGA (Ditto)	Ditto	Male	665,707	359,621	74,570	115,428	53,307	58,395	53,535	4,386	277,109
		Female	665,322	249,212	79,602	119,654	33,407	12,426	3,301	822	281,956
AGASA (Ditto)	Ditto	Male	49,112	26,248	5,804	8,629	3,859	3,994	3,668	294	20,487
		Female	48,660	18,267	6,278	8,710	2,137	858	227	57	21,060
BANAJIGA (Ditto)	Ditto	Male	67,216	35,430	7,272	11,059	4,802	5,535	6,009	753	27,859
		Female	65,739	23,767	7,716	11,107	2,751	1,002	776	415	27,641
BESTA (Ditto)	Ditto	Male	78,228	42,045	9,224	14,051	6,142	6,434	5,652	542	32,739
		Female	73,635	30,453	9,782	13,823	3,722	1,582	1,049	495	33,364
MADIGA (Ditto)	Ditto	Male	155,585	86,898	19,765	28,636	11,516	12,424	13,159	1,398	62,594
		Female	152,498	66,130	21,462	28,820	6,918	3,832	3,604	1,494	63,733
NEYGI (Ditto)	Ditto	Male	48,571	25,491	5,753	8,325	3,821	4,057	3,166	369	20,133
		Female	47,895	17,852	6,058	8,707	2,178	660	185	64	20,548
BEDA (Ditto)	Ditto	Male	135,597	75,706	15,983	23,509	9,994	11,330	13,154	1,786	52,531
		Female	132,857	54,608	17,088	24,146	6,111	2,803	2,746	1,719	54,321
LINGAYAT (Ditto)	Ditto	Male	365,691	201,838	40,693	61,326	31,200	32,364	32,406	3,849	142,619
		Female	364,340	135,963	42,825	65,297	18,888	6,436	1,889	628	144,762
GOLLA (Ditto)	Ditto	Male	76,617	42,176	8,576	13,177	5,574	6,248	7,766	835	30,368
		Female	74,235	28,526	9,856	13,485	3,515	1,588	436	146	30,552
VADDA (Ditto)	Ditto	Male	72,572	39,369	9,162	13,095	5,297	5,784	5,665	416	30,092
		Female	69,916	28,167	9,642	13,828	3,255	1,429	418	100	31,254

FOR SELECTED CASTES—*continued.*

Married.						Widowed.							Caste, Tribe or Race.
0—5.	5—12.	12—15.	15—20.	20—40.	40 & over.	Total.	0—5.	5—12.	12—15.	15—20.	20—40.	40 & over.	
13	14	15	16	17	18	19	20	21	22	23	24	25	26
													HYDERABAD STATE —*continued.*
119 261	1,403 5,193	3,349 6,268	6,057 9,426	25,717 22,445	23,481 13,577	4,647 19,998	13 18	68 136	176 368	349 781	1,120 5,541	2,921 13,159	KOMATI (Hindu).
224 341	1,717 7,509	2,307 7,700	8,772 14,844	41,490 38,212	34,633 22,567	6,949 20,783	7 20	35 142	234 290	461 650	1,527 4,608	4,685 15,073	SALE (Ditto).
1,897 2,503	13,036 32,676	22,105 44,290	42,675 54,222	190,210 180,204	150,951 101,534	37,960 128,441	73 163	495 2,733	899 4,239	3,255 8,074	12,286 29,271	20,952 83,961	MARATHA (Hindu).
1,356 2,670	7,746 22,967	12,168 27,306	27,206 49,999	139,640 140,030	112,999 62,548	22,912 75,650	74 106	314 981	523 2,095	1,178 3,876	6,629 17,243	14,194 51,249	MAHAR AND MALA (Ditto).
93 169	449 1,735	899 2,180	2,201 3,233	9,871 8,870	9,623 6,078	3,401 7,142	7 15	15 87	98 140	283 243	906 1,725	2,092 4,982	SUNAR (Ditto).
112 214	477 2,269	914 2,478	2,248 4,148	14,820 13,170	12,292 7,297	3,527 9,218	14 15	45 79	82 151	134 303	851 2,075	2,401 6,595	PANCHAL (Ditto).
735 1,534	3,597 22,134	13,085 32,604	22,948 48,893	142,372 119,115	114,857 83,989	19,393 73,439	193 94	342 448	512 1,412	1,405 2,492	5,087 18,009	11,854 50,984	MADIGA AND MANG (Ditto).
352 478	2,284 8,464	8,649 22,144	9,501 24,100	57,890 49,888	45,749 24,185	5,448 33,616	24 15	148 203	251 568	445 979	1,110 8,337	3,470 23,508	GOLLA (Ditto).
356 406	1,162 8,341	2,988 9,823	8,101 18,185	55,904 50,788	45,651 25,847	11,699 36,228	7 30	49 181	78 318	745 1,004	2,896 8,121	7,834 26,574	TELAGA (Ditto).
107 388	482 3,775	878 9,643	5,305 14,848	32,556 28,616	27,626 14,814	6,433 16,991	6 62	18 162	64 135	227 547	1,460 3,773	4,658 12,312	MUTRASI (Ditto).
.. ..	236 604	517 1,781	1,910 4,540	18,007 17,047	13,734 7,527	3,190 8,656	.. ..	4 29	22 75	70 184	787 1,992	2,307 6,370	PATHAN (Musalman).
.. ..	357 843	676 3,314	2,266 5,728	22,478 23,446	21,345 10,238	4,876 14,756	.. ..	15 31	44 198	140 295	1,205 3,222	3,472 11,004	SAIYID (Ditto).
.. ..	901 4,049	2,345 11,847	8,297 30,985	114,941 132,920	102,986 55,918	19,563 77,971	.. ..	74 231	238 857	505 1,768	4,388 15,292	14,358 59,823	SHEIKH (Ditto).
													KASHMIR STATE.
8 67	232 2,562	772 2,843	2,398 5,975	16,988 18,899	15,575 6,588	3,574 19,223	1 3	9 82	118 188	361 477	2,175 5,620	5,910 12,853	BRAHMAN (Hindu).
11 87	320 1,330	902 1,585	1,674 3,390	8,842 10,785	8,192 3,577	4,171 9,536	1 1	7 54	138 120	275 183	1,118 2,181	2,632 6,991	THAKKAR (Ditto).
3 8	44 435	159 618	625 1,744	5,274 6,080	4,717 1,762	2,228 5,325	.. ..	1 19	26 24	12 73	606 1,450	1,588 3,759	RAJPUT (Ditto).
17 24	156 696	384 1,273	1,057 3,067	11,102 17,527	9,901 6,135	3,699 6,145	3 ..	4 18	10 16	22 91	956 1,227	2,704 4,794	JAT (Musalman).
3 1	38 150	87 292	269 786	2,853 3,234	2,275 1,181	674 1,143	.. ..	2 6	2 5	4 30	184 182	482 920	AWAN (Ditto).
2 ..	28 157	86 405	421 1,169	3,725 4,109	3,042 1,602	817 1,606	2 ..	6 1	18 21	28 36	213 335	550 1,213	MUGHAL (Ditto).
1 1	135 434	409 1,361	1,739 3,588	12,494 12,728	8,368 4,890	2,537 3,523	.. ..	6 4	16 37	88 95	621 627	1,806 3,060	DAR (Ditto).
5 10	86 238	187 739	770 1,921	6,058 7,062	4,338 2,484	1,192 2,520	.. ..	1 5	6 13	24 63	290 484	871 2,005	MALIK (Ditto).
10 6	156 550	657 2,235	2,691 5,636	18,676 19,312	13,036 7,498	4,185 6,235	.. 4	2 5	16 28	55 245	1,147 1,097	2,965 4,856	BAT (Ditto).
.. 2	35 152	178 522	523 1,712	6,084 6,547	4,492 2,019	2,129 4,751	.. ..	2 9	6 13	11 64	484 1,214	1,626 3,451	KASHMIRI PANDIT (BRAHMAN) (Hindu.)
													MYSORE STATE.
.. ..	14 1,559	80 4,940	1,810 8,672	24,152 20,616	17,568 7,145	6,810 25,219	.. ..	.. 26	.. 159	28 824	1,196 7,003	5,586 17,207	BRAHMAN (Hindu).
.. 2	20 1,500	144 4,432	1,869 13,201	42,435 50,379	40,014 16,931	9,436 40,155	.. ..	.. 29	.. 99	25 453	1,592 9,115	7,819 30,459	KURUBA (Ditto).
.. 1	8 452	38 1,563	507 4,600	14,178 15,171	12,422 4,838	3,387 12,539	.. ..	.. 7	.. 44	10 241	667 3,387	2,710 8,860	PANCHALA (Ditto).
2 2	64 4,778	336 14,698	5,297 42,190	139,245 163,443	132,165 56,845	28,977 134,154	.. ..	1 65	5 285	60 1,475	5,190 30,827	23,721 101,502	VAKKALIGA (Ditto).
.. ..	7 345	25 1,015	460 3,356	10,500 12,376	9,495 3,968	2,377 9,333	.. ..	.. 2	.. 28	6 121	437 2,325	1,934 6,857	AGASA (Ditto).
1 1	4 458	28 1,417	451 4,487	13,940 15,884	13,435 5,394	3,927 14,331	.. ..	.. 7	.. 31	15 241	639 3,546	3,273 10,506	BANAJIGA (Ditto).
.. 3	11 546	39 1,705	701 5,227	16,570 19,308	15,418 6,575	3,444 14,818	.. ..	.. 14	.. 36	9 222	616 3,627	2,819 10,919	BESTA (Ditto).
2 1	20 1,048	71 2,744	1,226 9,577	31,055 36,862	30,220 13,701	6,893 22,635	.. ..	.. 20	1 58	16 350	949 5,192	5,127 17,015	MADIGA (Ditto).
.. ..	6 306	30 1,113	487 3,538	10,615 11,507	8,995 4,084	2,947 9,495	.. ..	.. 3	1 27	8 180	481 2,585	2,457 6,700	NEYGI (Ditto).
.. ..	13 815	55 2,456	907 8,511	25,572 31,182	25,984 11,357	7,360 23,928	.. ..	1 18	3 51	13 272	1,059 5,558	6,284 18,029	BEDA (Ditto).
.. 1	27 2,168	164 7,881	2,517 23,835	74,259 84,852	65,652 26,025	20,634 83,615	.. ..	.. 52	2 207	39 1,147	3,401 23,237	17,192 58,972	LINGAYAT (Ditto).
.. ..	3 435	51 1,268	473 4,436	13,608 17,808	16,238 6,610	4,073 15,147	.. ..	.. 5	3 24	6 184	576 3,249	3,488 11,685	GOLLA (Ditto).
.. 2	13 348	38 1,131	541 4,622	14,776 18,197	14,724 6,954	3,111 10,489	.. ..	.. 8	3 20	10 126	597 2,254	2,501 8,081	VADDA (Ditto).

TABLE XIV.—CIVIL CONDITION BY AGE

CASTE, TRIBE OR RACE.	Locality.	Sex.	Population dealt with.	UNMARRIED.							
				Total.	0—5.	5—12.	12—15.	15—20.	20—40.	40 & over.	Total.
1	2	3	4	5	6	7	8	9	10	11	12
MYSORE STATE.—*continued.*											
HOLEYA (Hindu)	Mysore	Male	369,536	170,582	35,625	52,728	23,083	26,640	29,918	2,588	125,378
		Female	363,712	123,681	37,924	54,098	15,859	9,072	5,262	1,466	126,350
SHEIKH (Musalman)	Ditto	Male	91,495	51,861	11,595	17,111	6,804	7,980	7,913	418	36,451
		Female	84,987	35,580	12,107	17,219	3,887	1,744	489	134	35,905
RAJPUTANA AGENCY.											
TELI (Musalman)	Rajputana	Male	16,624	7,599	3,307	2,801	860	856	*684	91	7,915
		Female	15,319	4,824	2,316	2,087	299	80	31	11	8,397
JAT (Hindu)	Ditto	Male	495,744	239,133	64,512	75,437	24,450	31,589	37,046	5,999	217,639
		Female	422,799	126,647	61,352	54,638	7,713	2,345	484	120	224,766
GUJAR (Ditto)	Ditto	Male	270,412	132,191	34,899	42,801	13,590	17,364	20,421	3,116	119,234
		Female	228,195	70,258	34,218	31,080	3,489	1,054	402	115	121,901
TELI (Ditto)	Ditto	Male	24,001	10,650	3,677	3,497	868	1,126	1,325	157	11,389
		Female	22,477	6,944	3,677	2,825	303	89	35	15	11,592
KUMHAR (Ditto)	Ditto	Male	155,665	71,469	23,176	23,552	7,023	9,199	7,743	776	74,398
		Female	146,054	45,924	23,711	18,760	2,389	754	237	73	76,500
FAKIR (Musalman)	Ditto	Male	28,853	13,651	3,897	4,736	1,724	1,725	1,194	375	13,144
		Female	26,063	9,139	4,086	3,989	786	292	59	27	13,583
MALI (Hindu)	Ditto	Male	174,426	81,619	24,405	27,485	8,701	10,685	9,335	1,008	82,393
		Female	161,346	50,804	24,591	22,070	2,863	855	359	66	83,853
KOLI (Ditto)	Ditto	Male	53,499	23,251	6,841	8,369	2,639	2,943	2,217	242	26,214
		Female	50,548	15,966	7,512	7,063	945	337	104	25	26,788
SHEIKH (Musalman)	Ditto	Male	96,638	46,388	11,922	14,665	5,570	6,170	7,054	1,007	43,613
		Female	85,066	28,601	11,663	12,567	2,466	1,059	627	219	42,434
SUNAR (Hindu)	Ditto	Male	35,510	16,928	4,726	5,799	1,605	1,972	2,322	504	15,919
		Female	33,415	10,055	4,764	4,591	494	135	52	19	16,685
BHANGI (Ditto)	Ditto	Male	41,951	20,045	6,282	7,163	2,019	2,326	1,977	278	19,562
		Female	39,923	13,962	6,445	6,006	957	416	110	28	21,230
NAI (Ditto)	Ditto	Male	79,944	37,537	10,242	11,931	3,784	4,940	5,823	817	35,972
		Female	72,880	21,616	10,759	9,301	1,088	304	134	24	37,325
BRAHMAN (Ditto)	Ditto	Male	474,549	234,090	55,181	70,380	22,624	29,534	43,286	13,125	195,398
		Female	445,654	121,578	56,175	56,873	6,197	1,495	626	212	206,762
MINA (Ditto)	Ditto	Male	272,411	135,528	35,548	44,790	14,832	17,442	19,975	2,941	121,463
		Female	246,093	78,127	35,708	35,190	5,375	1,369	380	105	124,399
SAIYID (Musalman)	Ditto	Male	15,242	7,909	1,758	2,231	893	1,070	1,098	159	7,033
		Female	13,712	4,670	1,891	2,093	417	186	70	13	6,768
MAHAJAN (Hindu and Jain)	Ditto	Male	352,570	178,439	43,988	57,375	17,605	18,945	29,935	10,591	140,021
		Female	353,960	104,998	43,758	51,866	7,764	1,485	433	192	157,243
MEO (Musalman)	Ditto	Male	87,273	43,861	10,965	15,068	6,882	6,534	3,793	619	37,648
		Female	78,270	29,146	10,960	12,787	3,849	1,356	157	39	38,491
RAJPUT (Hindu)	Ditto	Male	355,348	206,017	40,904	52,197	19,272	29,551	50,677	13,326	126,886
		Female	276,878	78,751	33,989	34,810	6,463	2,433	803	253	124,695
TRAVANCORE STATE.											
BRAHMAN (OTHERS) (Hindu).	Travancore	Male	23,892	12,743	3,517	4,263	1,063	1,909	1,913	78	9,756
		Female	21,457	7,490	3,446	3,359	222	279	113	71	9,402
BRAHMAN (MALAYALA) (Ditto).	Ditto	Male	5,841	2,865	433	795	531	505	512	89	2,625
		Female	4,484	1,525	458	636	219	131	51	30	1,955
CHETTI (Ditto)	Ditto	Male	10,535	5,716	1,251	2,098	783	820	679	85	4,135
		Female	10,346	4,482	1,242	1,877	723	398	169	73	4,169
INDIAN CHRISTIAN	Ditto	Male	460,004	237,722	62,355	84,979	38,659	31,555	19,128	1,046	205,277
		Female	441,715	196,902	66,023	72,112	41,761	12,655	5,348	1,003	197,794
AMBALAVASI (Hindu)	Ditto	Male	5,446	2,999	782	858	519	348	432	60	2,097
		Female	5,404	2,350	795	782	505	158	59	51	2,030
PULAYAN (Ditto)	Ditto	Male	93,335	46,383	12,860	15,423	4,630	6,264	6,969	237	44,098
		Female	91,979	38,452	12,663	15,327	4,334	3,600	2,187	341	43,771
SHANAN (Ditto)	Ditto	Male	84,638	50,179	12,683	17,782	4,953	7,553	6,093	260	30,933
		Female	81,557	39,688	12,574	15,749	3,981	4,996	2,104	284	29,934
KURAVAN (Ditto)	Ditto	Male	30,183	15,037	4,974	5,272	1,482	2,089	1,164	56	13,614
		Female	31,644	12,905	4,529	5,134	2,193	592	402	55	13,552
IZHAVAN (Ditto)	Ditto	Male	271,677	155,051	33,270	54,901	21,280	24,307	20,728	665	104,475
		Female	274,588	127,768	34,222	52,564	18,913	14,093	7,352	624	104,095
NAYAR (Ditto)	Ditto	Male	295,793	168,545	37,915	50,851	22,777	24,592	31,071	1,339	112,795
		Female	296,786	131,389	42,363	47,206	19,513	14,201	6,791	1,315	110,855

FOR SELECTED CASTES—*concluded.*

Married.						Widowed.							Caste, Tribe or Race.
0—5.	5—12.	12—15.	15—20.	20—40.	40 & over.	Total.	0—5.	5—12.	12—15.	15—20.	20—40.	40 & over.	
13	14	15	16	17	18	19	20	21	22	23	24	25	26
													MYSORE STATE —*continued.*
3	40	139	2,010	64,468	58,718	**13,576**	..	1	2	40	2,744	10,789	HOLEYA (Hindu).
2	1,401	4,483	18,184	77,099	25,181	**53,681**	1	18	102	689	13,660	39,211	
..	8	41	468	18,618	17,316	**3,183**	..	..	2	10	644	2,527	SHEIKH (Musalman).
1	262	1,191	6,119	21,354	6,978	**13,502**	..	7	19	177	8,048	10,251	
													RAJPUTANA AGENCY.
6	178	226	699	4,150	2,656	**1,116**	1	12	8	33	311	745	TELI (Musalman).
20	427	542	1,266	4,542	1,600	**2,068**	..	3	6	20	379	1,690	
201	3,893	5,291	16,968	118,391	72,895	**38,972**	9	117	171	774	11,675	26,226	JAT (Hindu).
667	10,291	13,610	31,635	126,272	42,291	**71,386**	6	208	318	886	14,600	55,368	
68	1,684	2,567	8,196	65,038	41,681	**18,987**	2	101	88	377	6,145	12,274	GUJAR (Ditto).
180	5,671	7,009	16,546	70,207	22,288	**36,036**	3	67	115	324	7,009	28,518	
10	180	297	823	6,589	3,490	**1,962**	3	8	11	63	747	1,130	TELI (Ditto).
28	481	599	1,579	7,047	1,858	**3,941**	..	5	9	77	901	2,949	
56	1,006	1,409	5,177	41,196	25,554	**9,798**	4	34	68	272	3,064	6,356	KUMHAR (Ditto).
204	2,836	4,155	10,946	44,341	14,018	**23,630**	2	41	56	311	4,715	18,505	
3	156	272	1,100	6,982	4,631	**2,658**	..	13	9	50	519	1,467	FAKIR (Musalman).
13	471	751	1,961	7,634	2,753	**3,341**	..	13	6	39	634	2,649	
61	790	1,285	5,150	45,792	29,365	**10,414**	2	33	49	229	2,985	7,116	MALI (Hindu).
146	2,782	4,150	11,738	49,516	15,526	**26,689**	2	41	87	312	5,812	20,435	
12	272	506	1,974	14,275	9,175	**4,634**	..	11	29	128	1,147	2,719	KOLI (Ditto).
14	851	1,416	3,914	15,857	4,706	**7,774**	..	10	38	142	1,745	5,839	
12	453	705	2,577	23,124	16,742	**6,637**	4	29	35	141	1,878	4,550	SHEIKH (Musalman).
34	1,417	1,862	5,844	24,951	8,326	**14,031**	1	35	39	173	2,826	10,957	
8	127	286	1,271	8,635	5,592	**2,663**	..	15	12	52	761	1,823	SUNAR (Hindu).
15	553	955	2,419	9,488	3,255	**6,675**	3	16	18	111	1,622	4,905	
9	354	493	1,525	10,742	6,439	**2,344**	1	14	18	107	755	1,449	BHANGI (Ditto).
33	632	967	2,974	12,494	4,130	**4,731**	1	3	19	116	965	3,627	
11	285	554	2,288	19,651	13,233	**6,435**	..	24	25	130	1,922	4,334	NAI (Ditto).
44	1,079	1,774	5,150	22,061	7,217	**13,945**	2	32	27	168	2,794	10,922	
73	1,423	3,315	13,126	104,157	73,304	**45,071**	3	71	133	597	11,637	32,630	BRAHMAN (Ditto).
143	6,035	11,585	29,805	118,342	40,852	**117,314**	4	219	429	2,248	33,098	81,316	
30	1,050	2,235	7,524	66,335	44,289	**15,420**	..	24	50	247	4,224	10,875	MINA (Ditto).
67	2,734	6,294	16,081	74,467	24,756	**37,567**	5	41	128	342	7,112	29,939	
2	54	80	308	3,656	2,933	**1,060**	..	3	6	10	256	725	SAIYID (Musalman).
3	115	216	934	4,077	1,423	**2,274**	..	5	5	22	486	1,756	
45	775	2,613	11,328	77,309	47,951	**34,110**	4	53	89	459	8,822	24,688	MAHAJAN (Hindu and Jain).
77	2,827	8,944	25,325	90,708	29,362	**91,719**	7	119	267	1,679	28,671	60,976	
4	210	767	3,298	19,781	13,638	**5,764**	..	21	39	144	1,687	3,873	MEO (Musalman).
..	568	1,970	6,014	21,693	8,245	**10,631**	..	12	32	110	2,071	8,402	
45	550	835	4,320	67,770	53,366	**22,445**	5	43	64	217	5,428	16,688	RAJPUT (Hindu).
99	1,873	4,673	16,[illegible]36	78,149	23,065	**73,432**	5	131	202	1,039	18,797	53,258	
													TRAVANCORE STATE.
..	24	106	195	5,849	3,582	**1,393**	..	9	25	32	279	1,048	BRAHMAN (OTHERS) (Hindu).
..	318	719	1,640	4,811	1,914	**4,565**	..	12	18	93	954	3,488	
..	..	1	114	1,287	1,223	**351**	..	1	5	4	102	239	BRAHMAN (MALAYALA) (Ditto).
..	16	63	235	1,146	495	**1,004**	..	..	1	13	217	773	
..	15	25	169	2,121	1,805	**684**	..	2	5	10	146	521	CHETTI (Ditto).
..	29	66	558	2,406	1,110	**1,695**	..	7	16	29	391	1,252	
..	232	1,053	11,971	120,044	71,977	**17,065**	..	11	99	181	3,713	13,001	INDIAN CHRISTIAN.
..	986	6,184	30,575	120,533	39,516	**45,019**	..	42	122	361	9,138	35,356	
..	..	2	85	1,094	916	**352**	..	1	2	3	109	237	AMBALAVASI (Hindu).
..	11	37	329	1,167	486	**1,024**	..	..	3	24	196	801	
..	5	32	881	26,531	16,649	**2,854**	..	3	16	46	911	1,878	PULAYAN (Ditto).
..	137	697	5,380	30,290	7,267	**9,756**	..	4	21	156	2,397	7,178	
..	23	35	625	15,889	14,361	**3,526**	..	3	16	56	854	2,597	SHANAN (Ditto).
..	114	252	2,350	22,195	5,023	**11,935**	..	3	29	112	3,125	8,666	
..	7	22	219	6,987	6,379	**1,532**	..	1	3	9	493	1,026	KURAVAN (Ditto).
..	33	160	2,534	8,342	2,483	**5,137**	..	3	13	71	972	4,128	
..	31	121	1,580	60,622	42,121	**12,151**	..	6	31	168	4,213	7,733	IZHAVAN (Ditto).
..	201	1,165	11,515	70,416	20,798	**42,725**	..	28	112	697	12,987	28,901	
..	51	115	1,113	60,207	51,309	**14,363**	..	5	29	161	5,218	8,950	NAYAR (Ditto).
..	174	1,459	13,712	71,468	24,042	**54,542**	..	31	136	820	13,728	39,832	

TABLE XV.

Occupation or Means of Livelihood.

PART A.—GENERAL TABLE OF OCCUPATIONS.

1. For the purpose of this Table a new scheme of classification, based on that drawn up by M. Bertillon, has been adopted at the present census. All occupations are divided according to this scheme into four main Classes and sub-divided into twelve sub-classes, 55 Orders and 169 Groups. For further explanation Chapter XII of the Report Volume should be referred to.

2. This Table is divided into five parts, *viz.*—

Part A.—General Table of Occupations.

Part B.—Number of Agriculturists with subsidiary Occupations (Actual Workers only).

[Part C.—Number of persons following selected subsidiary Occupations combined with certain principal Occupations. This Part, the compilation of which was optional, was not prepared in all provinces, and even where prepared the occupations selected were not always the same. A consolidated table for India as a whole could not therefore be compiled.]

Part D.—Distribution of Occupations by religion.

Part E.—Statistics of Industries. The scope of this Part is explained in the explanatory note prefixed to it.

3. Part A is further sub-divided into two sections. The first section contains a general summary giving the total strength of each Class, Sub-class, Order and Group for (*a*) India as a whole, (*b*) British territory and (*c*) States and Agencies. The second section gives for each Province, State or Agency the total strength of each Class, Sub-class and Order, and also of those groups the total strength of which is at least 50,000. In this section, to economize space the sex details have been dispensed with except in respect of the total number of Actual workers, while for the selected groups figures for 'Total Workers and Dependants' only have been given.

4. The population dealt with falls short of that in Table I by 1,686,382 persons who were enumerated in tracts where occupation was not recorded, *viz.*:—Andamans and Nicobars (1,692), Burma (76,134), and the Agencies and Tribal areas in the North-West Frontier Province (1,608,556). The figures for Madras States in section (ii) of this Part include those for Cochin and Travancore, separate figures for which by Orders will be found on page 316.

TABLE XV—Occupation or Means of Livelihood.

Group Number.	Occupations.	INDIA. Total Workers and Dependants.	Actual Workers. Total. Males.	Actual Workers. Total. Females.	Actual Workers. Partially agriculturist. Males.	Actual Workers. Partially agriculturist. Females.	Dependants.
	1	2	3	4	5	6	7
	TOTAL POPULATION	**313,470,014**	**101,525,421**	**47,359,582**	**3,336,983**	**669,653**	**164,585,011**
	A.—PRODUCTION OF RAW MATERIALS	227,080,092	72,332,823	34,176,058	470,344	127,953	120,571,211
	I.—EXPLOITATION OF THE SURFACE OF THE EARTH	*226,550,483*	*72,122,268*	*34,078,164*	*455,208*	*121,066*	*120,350,051*
	1.—Pasture and agriculture	**224,695,900**	**71,462,868**	**33,872,511**	**376,858**	**105,187**	**119,360,521**
	(a) Ordinary Cultivation	*216,787,137*	*67,543,794*	*32,595,794*	*151,788*	*28,103*	*116,647,549*
1	Income from rent of agricultural land	7,743,507	2,113,710	731,486	..	..	4,898,311
2	Ordinary cultivators	167,015,427	51,956,508	19,139,433	..	..	95,919,486
3	Agents, managers of landed estates (not planters), clerks, rent collectors, etc.	781,868	314,892	4,320	44,441	249	462,656
4	Farm servants and field labourers	41,246,335	13,158,684	12,720,555	107,347	27,854	15,367,096
	(b) Growers of special products and market gardening	*2,012,503*	*706,173*	*495,718*	*62,747*	*25,458*	*810,612*
5	Tea, coffee, cinchona and indigo plantations	1,040,425	391,627	350,064	36,464	13,165	298,734
6	Fruit, flower, vegetable, betel, vine, areca-nut, etc., growers	972,078	314,546	145,654	26,283	12,293	511,878
	(c) Forestry	*672,093*	*217,474*	*159,831*	*21,992*	*15,040*	*294,788*
7	Forest officers, rangers, guards, etc.	89,187	34,413	1,362	3,076	100	53,412
8	Wood-cutters, fire-wood, lac, catechu, rubber, etc., collectors, and charcoal burners	582,906	183,061	158,469	18,916	14,940	241,376
	(d) Raising of farm stock	*5,176,104*	*2,984,467*	*606,224*	*131,887*	*36,501*	*1,585,413*
9	Cattle and buffalo breeders and keepers	704,556	289,835	143,933	22,490	7,528	270,788
10	Sheep, goat and pig breeders	465,596	185,497	46,845	19,797	2,793	233,254
11	Breeders of other animals (horses, mules, camels, asses, etc.)	39,955	18,640	2,191	839	87	19,124
12	Herdsmen, shepherds, goatherds, etc.	3,965,997	2,490,495	413,255	88,762	26,093	1,062,247
13	*(e) Raising of small animals* (birds, bees, silkworms, etc.)	*48,063*	*10,960*	*14,944*	*2,444*	*85*	*22,159*
	2.—Fishing and hunting	**1,854,583**	**659,400**	**205,653**	**84,350**	**15,879**	**989,530**
14	Fishing	1,783,672	630,064	201,682	82,315	15,687	951,926
15	Hunting	70,911	29,336	3,971	2,035	192	37,604
	II.—EXTRACTION OF MINERALS	*529,609*	*210,555*	*97,894*	*15,136*	*6,887*	*221,160*
	3.—Mines	**375,927**	**153,785**	**74,139**	**9,840**	**5,268**	**148,003**
16	Coal mines and petroleum wells	277,426	115,210	62,433	8,143	5,076	99,783
17	Mines and metallic minerals (gold, iron, manganese, etc.)	98,501	38,575	11,706	1,697	192	48,220
18	**4.—Quarries of hard rocks**—[Other minerals (jade, diamonds, limestone, etc.)]	**75,424**	**29,972**	**8,209**	**1,595**	**128**	**37,243**
	5.—Salt, etc.	**78,258**	**26,798**	**15,546**	**3,701**	**1,491**	**35,914**
19	Rock, sea and marsh salt	29,276	10,595	4,079	872	243	14,602
20	Extraction of saltpetre, alum and other substances soluble in water	48,982	16,203	11,467	2,829	1,248	21,312
	B.—PREPARATION AND SUPPLY OF MATERIAL SUBSTANCES	58,191,121	19,124,551	8,886,967	2,048,149	431,160	30,179,603
	III.—INDUSTRY	*35,323,041*	*11,503,467*	*6,011,763*	*1,401,566*	*299,777*	*17,807,811*
	6.—Textiles	**8,306,501**	**2,685,256**	**1,764,193**	**244,646**	**81,976**	**3,857,052**
21	Cotton ginning, cleaning and pressing	523,637	163,572	104,542	17,915	5,742	255,523
22	Cotton spinning, sizing and weaving	5,966,468	1,921,977	1,215,714	190,441	63,422	2,828,777
23	Jute spinning, pressing and weaving	362,369	189,130	42,217	6,758	332	131,022
24	Rope, twine and string	377,203	82,658	167,197	6,159	3,686	127,348
25	Other fibres (cocoanut, aloes, flax, hemp, straw, etc.)	121,458	28,898	43,269	2,072	699	49,291
26	Wool carders and spinners, weavers of woollen blankets, carpets, etc.	319,636	103,294	67,297	10,842	5,242	149,045
27	Silk spinners and weavers	257,249	77,805	64,010	2,869	1,354	115,434
28	Hair, camel and horse hair, bristles work, brush makers, etc.	7,890	2,750	1,319	310	56	3,821
29	Persons occupied with feathers	1,940	675	226	42	10	1,039
30	Dyeing, bleaching, printing, preparation and sponging of textiles	232,731	77,533	37,880	4,943	1,195	117,318
31	Other (lace, crape, embroideries, fringes, etc.), and insufficiently described textile industries	135,920	36,964	20,522	2,295	239	78,434
	7.—Hides, skins and hard materials from the animal kingdom	**698,741**	**252,445**	**42,349**	**34,638**	**4,008**	**403,947**
32	Tanners, curriers, leather dressers and dyers, etc.	474,732	171,303	31,155	24,274	3,024	272,274
33	Makers of leather articles, such as trunks, water-bags, etc.	204,786	75,112	9,635	9,810	868	120,030
34	Furriers	2,061	939	305	219	18	817
35	Bone, ivory, horn, shell, etc., workers	17,162	5,091	1,254	335	98	10,817
	8.—Wood	**3,799,892**	**1,297,527**	**433,393**	**175,087**	**23,824**	**2,068,972**
36	Sawyers, carpenters, turners and joiners, etc.	2,525,139	929,065	49,142	140,401	4,441	1,546,932
37	Basket makers and other industries of woody materials, including leaves.	1,274,753	368,462	384,251	34,686	19,383	522,040

Part A—General Table, (*i*)—Summary for All India.

British Territory. Total Workers and Dependants.	British Territory. Actual Workers. Total. Males.	British Territory. Actual Workers. Total. Females.	British Territory. Actual Workers. Partially agriculturist. Males.	British Territory. Actual Workers. Partially agriculturist. Females.	British Territory. Dependants.	States and Agencies. Total Workers and Dependants.	States and Agencies. Actual Workers. Total. Males.	States and Agencies. Actual Workers. Total. Females.	States and Agencies. Actual Workers. Partially agriculturist. Males.	States and Agencies. Actual Workers. Partially agriculturist. Females.	States and Agencies. Dependants.	Group Number.
8	9	10	11	12	13	14	15	16	17	18	19	
244,189,716	79,028,337	35,788,824	2,506,682	492,784	129,372,555	69,288,298	22,497,084	11,570,758	830,381	176,869	35,212,456	
179,948,129	57,263,835	26,150,411	353,231	87,345	96,533,883	47,131,963	15,068,988	8,025,647	117,113	40,608	24,037,328	
179,529,352	57,097,846	26,063,448	340,158	80,593	96,368,058	47,021,131	15,024,499	8,014,716	115,050	40,473	23,981,993	
177,935,894	56,547,794	25,875,926	266,821	66,132	95,512,174	46,760,906	14,915,074	7,996,585	104,037	39,055	23,848,347	
172,321,648	53,610,680	24,908,248	104,031	1,884	93,802,720	44,465,489	13,933,114	7,687,546	47,757	26,219	22,844,829	
5,467,006	1,406,106	523,492	..	..	3,537,408	2,276,501	707,604	207,994	..	..	1,360,903	1
133,724,099	41,452,817	14,653,550	..	..	77,617,732	33,291,328	10,503,691	4,485,883	..	..	18,301,754	2
696,387	277,895	2,931	48,021	191	415,561	85,481	36,997	1,389	1,420	58	47,095	3
32,434,156	10,473,862	9,728,275	61,010	1,693	12,232,019	8,812,179	2,684,822	2,992,280	46,337	26,161	3,135,077	4
1,666,145	583,655	455,053	60,233	24,703	617,437	356,358	122,518	40,665	2,514	755	193,175	
997,730	371,555	338,560	36,267	13,140	287,615	42,695	20,072	11,504	197	25	11,119	5
668,415	212,100	116,493	23,966	11,563	329,822	313,663	102,446	29,161	2,317	730	182,056	6
478,362	155,852	111,129	17,063	12,433	211,381	193,731	61,622	48,702	4,929	2,607	83,407	
67,277	25,534	1,191	2,459	87	40,552	21,910	8,879	171	617	13	12,860	7
411,085	130,318	109,938	14,604	12,346	170,829	171,821	52,743	48,531	4,312	2,594	70,547	8
3,433,495	2,187,339	386,625	83,121	27,033	859,531	1,742,609	797,128	219,599	48,766	9,468	725,882	
428,257	177,696	109,123	14,351	6,574	141,438	276,299	112,139	34,810	8,139	954	129,350	9
205,037	92,575	19,072	8,537	1,703	93,396	260,559	92,922	27,773	11,260	1,090	139,864	10
14,575	5,240	473	267	39	8,862	25,380	13,400	1,718	571	48	10,262	11
2,785,626	1,911,828	257,957	59,966	18,717	615,841	1,180,371	578,667	155,298	28,796	7,376	446,406	12
46,244	10,268	14,871	2,373	79	21,105	1,819	692	73	71	6	1,054	13
1,593,458	550,052	187,522	73,337	14,461	855,884	261,125	109,348	18,131	11,013	1,418	133,646	
1,558,881	536,633	184,928	72,100	14,312	837,320	224,791	93,431	16,754	10,215	1,375	114,606	14
34,577	13,419	2,594	1,237	149	18,564	36,334	15,917	1,377	798	43	19,040	15
418,777	165,989	86,963	13,073	6,759	165,825	110,832	44,566	10,931	2,063	135	55,335	
298,764	122,107	68,000	8,651	5,232	108,657	77,163	31,678	6,139	1,189	36	39,346	
262,746	107,679	60,207	8,114	5,065	94,860	14,680	7,531	2,226	29	11	4,922	16
36,018	14,428	7,793	537	167	13,797	62,483	24,147	3,913	1,160	25	34,423	17
58,897	23,339	6,110	1,175	102	29,448	16,527	6,633	2,099	420	26	7,795	18
61,116	20,543	12,853	3,247	1,418	27,720	17,142	6,255	2,693	454	73	8,194	
15,094	5,428	1,539	474	176	8,127	14,182	5,167	2,540	398	67	6,475	19
46,022	15,115	11,314	2,773	1,242	19,593	2,960	1,088	153	56	6	1,719	20
44,537,228	14,632,006	6,757,573	1,558,150	328,922	23,147,649	13,653,893	4,492,545	2,129,394	489,999	102,238	7,031,954	
26,791,864	8,661,737	4,566,846	1,047,889	299,484	13,563,281	8,531,177	2,841,730	1,444,917	353,684	70,293	4,244,530	
6,196,671	2,048,614	1,213,381	178,280	59,010	2,934,676	2,109,830	636,642	550,812	66,366	22,966	922,376	
362,033	115,657	65,944	12,506	4,096	180,432	161,604	47,915	38,598	5,409	1,646	75,091	21
4,583,878	1,498,365	853,897	141,595	45,657	2,231,646	1,382,590	423,642	361,817	48,846	17,765	597,131	22
359,896	187,930	41,989	6,726	332	129,977	2,473	1,200	228	32		1,045	23
216,086	42,605	98,849	4,757	3,228	74,632	161,117	40,053	68,348	1,402	458	52,716	24
64,133	18,844	17,581	1,802	468	27,708	57,325	10,054	25,688	270	231	21,583	25
160,261	48,155	42,607	5,220	3,265	69,499	159,375	55,139	24,690	5,622	1,977	79,546	26
236,635	71,609	59,020	2,718	1,332	106,006	20,614	6,196	4,990	151	22	9,428	27
5,047	1,736	858	69	4	2,453	2,843	1,014	461	241	51	1,368	28
1,474	438	213	30	10	823	466	237	13	12		216	29
128,439	41,921	17,126	2,003	463	69,392	104,292	35,612	20,754	2,940	732	47,926	30
78,789	21,384	15,297	854	155	42,108	57,131	15,580	5,225	1,441	84	36,326	31
473,041	166,301	23,353	18,132	2,289	283,387	225,700	86,144	18,996	16,506	1,719	120,560	
314,916	112,902	16,376	13,459	1,638	185,638	159,816	58,401	14,779	10,815	1,386	86,636	32
141,680	48,541	5,558	4,322	535	87,581	63,106	26,571	4,077	5,488	333	32,458	33
1,391	571	305	165	18	515	670	368	..	54	..	802	34
15,054	4,287	1,114	186	98	9,653	2,108	804	140	149	..	1,164	35
2,893,498	982,681	323,976	129,919	18,411	1,586,841	906,394	314,846	109,417	45,168	5,413	482,131	
1,936,189	707,355	37,467	102,885	3,425	1,191,367	588,950	221,710	11,675	37,516	1,016	355,565	36
957,309	275,326	286,509	27,034	14,986	395,474	317,444	93,136	97,742	7,652	4,397	126,566	37

Group Number.	OCCUPATION.	Total Workers and Dependants.	INDIA. Actual Workers. Total. Males.	Total. Females.	Partially agriculturist. Males.	Partially agriculturist. Females.	Dependants.
	1	2	3	4	5	6	7
	9.—Metals	**1,861,445**	**657,938**	**79,369**	**94,642**	**7,154**	**1,124,138**
38	Forging and rolling of iron and other metals	17,115	6,122	1,478	496	27	9,515
39	Plough and agricultural implement makers	66,881	22,733	2,792	3,953	360	41,356
40	Makers of arms, guns, etc.	20,017	9,368	316	332	2	10,333
41	Other workers in iron and makers of implements and tools, principally or exclusively of iron	1,390,042	489,512	59,419	81,554	5,955	841,111
42	Workers in brass, copper and bell-metal	288,899	100,930	12,721	6,783	695	175,248
43	Workers in other metals (tin, zinc, lead, quicksilver, etc.)	73,414	26,996	2,523	1,180	111	43,695
44	Workers in mints, die-sinkers, etc.	5,077	2,277	120	344	4	2,680
	10.—Ceramics	**2,240,210**	**767,886**	**391,282**	**120,472**	**29,887**	**1,081,042**
45	Makers of glass and crystal ware	39,469	12,290	8,565	1,277	361	18,614
46	Makers of porcelain and crockery	4,320	1,614	507	53	32	2,199
47	Potters and earthen pipe and bowl makers	1,959,956	651,882	350,900	112,507	28,819	957,174
48	Brick and tile makers	209,914	91,501	24,330	6,045	663	94,083
49	Others (mosaic, talc, mica, alabaster, etc., workers).	26,551	10,599	6,980	590	12	8,972
	11.—Chemical products properly so called, and analogous	**1,241,587**	**390,467**	**239,612**	**74,620**	**17,729**	**611,508**
50	Manufacture of matches and explosive materials	19,038	6,157	1,521	457	121	11,360
51	Manufacture of ærated and mineral waters	6,487	1,990	629	117	29	3,868
52	Manufacture of dyes, paint and ink	8,841	3,243	1,229	186	120	4,369
53	Manufacture and refining of vegetable and mineral oils	1,149,720	359,457	225,161	72,129	16,808	565,102
54	Manufacture of paper, cardboard and papier maché	7,460	3,163	643	134	46	3,654
55	Others (soap, candles, lac, cutch, perfumes and miscellaneous drugs)	50,041	16,457	10,429	1,597	605	23,155
	12.—Food industries	**3,711,675**	**806,194**	**1,327,851**	**72,080**	**35,010**	**1,577,630**
56	Rice pounders and huskers and flour grinders	1,575,122	127,920	963,342	6,924	17,693	483,860
57	Bakers and biscuit makers	96,799	30,934	15,073	1,301	182	50,792
58	Grain parchers, etc.	551,838	127,608	240,245	18,042	11,981	183,985
59	Butchers	351,603	110,296	21,522	6,653	1,290	219,785
60	Fish curers	7,248	2,716	1,477	156	32	3,055
61	Butter, cheese and ghee makers	26,155	7,254	3,573	1,241	131	15,328
62	Makers of sugar, molasses and gur	83,966	24,991	24,224	2,296	1,431	34,751
63	Sweetmeat makers, preparers of jam and condiments, etc.	281,259	104,673	24,613	5,257	851	151,973
64	Brewers and distillers	34,128	10,835	7,154	1,429	671	16,139
65	Toddy drawers	627,638	235,100	9,994	28,192	635	382,544
66	Manufacturers of tobacco, opium and ganja	75,919	23,867	16,634	589	113	35,418
	13.—Industries of dress and the toilet	**7,750,609**	**2,676,445**	**1,071,310**	**432,934**	**77,265**	**4,002,854**
67	Hat, cap and turban makers	26,270	7,004	5,968	95	68	13,298
68	Tailors, milliners, dress makers and darners, embroiderers on linen	1,273,236	425,667	211,440	35,467	6,976	636,129
69	Shoe, boot and sandal makers	2,127,864	767,921	161,180	106,128	14,825	1,198,763
70	Other industries pertaining to dress—gloves, socks, gaiters, belts, buttons, umbrellas, canes, etc.	35,549	11,578	5,130	568	123	18,841
71	Washing, cleaning and dyeing	2,125,425	676,329	524,425	122,131	46,160	924,671
72	Barbers, hairdressers and wig makers	2,140,079	783,508	153,906	167,876	8,744	1,202,665
73	Other industries connected with the toilet (tattooers, shampooers, bath houses, etc.)	22,186	4,438	9,261	669	369	8,487
	14.—Furniture industries	**39,268**	**13,723**	**4,440**	**542**	**88**	**21,105**
74	Cabinet makers, carriage painters, etc.	34,697	13,018	1,892	489	83	19,787
75	Upholsterers, tent makers, etc.	4,571	705	2,548	53	5	1,318
	15.—Building industries	**2,062,493**	**752,342**	**209,773**	**54,060**	**13,143**	**1,100,378**
76	Lime burners, cement workers	50,864	15,894	9,434	1,881	327	25,536
77	Excavators, plinth builders and well sinkers	367,826	127,365	85,666	13,983	6,536	154,795
78	Stone and marble workers, masons and bricklayers	1,294,379	478,885	90,698	30,201	4,885	724,796
79	Others (thatchers, building contractors, house painters, tilers, plumbers, locksmiths, etc.)	349,424	130,198	23,975	8,495	1,395	195,251
	16.—Construction of means of transport	**66,056**	**24,467**	**471**	**2,301**	**44**	**41,118**
80	Cart, carriage, palki, etc., makers and wheelwrights.	24,199	9,952	106	569	2	14,141
81	Saddlers, harness makers, whip and lash makers	9,420	3,462	294	310	10	5,664
82	Ship and boat builders	32,437	11,053	71	1,422	32	21,313
83	**17.—Production and transmission of physical forces (heat, light, electricity, motive power, etc.,** (Gas works, electric light and ice factories.))	**14,384**	**7,026**	**231**	**111**	..	**7,127**
	18.—Industries of luxury and those pertaining to literature and the arts and sciences	**2,141,665**	**741,425**	**81,675**	**71,540**	**4,717**	**1,318,565**
84	Printers, lithographers, engravers, etc.	89,389	36,129	409	614	2	52,851
85	Newspaper and magazine managers and editors, journalists, etc.	2,337	763	35	26	19	1,539
86	Bookbinders and stitchers, envelope makers, etc.	25,689	10,579	347	207	3	14,763
87	Makers of musical instruments	12,102	4,236	1,390	310	51	6,476
88	Makers of watches and clocks and optical, photographic and surgical instruments	15,960	5,762	111	119	31	10,087
89	Workers in precious stones and metals, enamellers, imitation jewellery makers, gilders, etc.	1,779,113	611,258	38,003	64,318	3,226	1,129,852
90	Makers of bangles, rosaries, bead and other necklaces, spangles, lingams and sacred threads	174,149	56,503	37,460	5,331	1,208	80,186
91	Toy, kite, cage, fishing tackle, etc. makers, taxidermists, etc.	23,693	8,558	2,606	381	155	12,529
92	Others, including managers, persons other than performers employed in theatres and other places of public entertainment, employés of public societies, race course service, huntsmen, etc.	19,233	7,637	1,314	234	22	10,282
93	**19.—Industries concerned with refuse matter.** (Sweepers, scavengers, dust and sweeping contractors)	**1,388,515**	**430,396**	**365,814**	**23,893**	**4,932**	**592,375**
	IV.—TRANSPORT	***5,028,978***	***2,156,943***	***237,939***	***139,229***	***11,120***	***2,634,096***
	20.—Transport by water	**962,766**	**451,404**	**30,201**	**34,318**	**1,094**	**501,161**
94	Harbour works, dockyards and pilots	48,960	26,790	3,173	402	11	18,997
95	Ship owners and their employés, ship brokers, ships' officers, engineers, mariners and firemen	180,008	88,323	349	7,374	4	91,336
96	Persons employed on the maintenance of streams, rivers and canals (including construction)	159,359	70,098	11,343	3,918	483	77,918
97	Boat owners, boat men and tow men	594,439	266,193	15,336	22,624	596	312,910

PART A—GENERAL TABLE, (*i*) SUMMARY FOR ALL INDIA—*continued.*

BRITISH TERRITORY.						STATES AND AGENCIES.						
Total Workers and Dependants.	ACTUAL WORKERS. Total.		ACTUAL WORKERS. Partially agriculturist.		Dependants.	Total Workers and Dependants.	ACTUAL WORKERS. Total.		ACTUAL WORKERS. Partially agriculturist.		Dependants.	Group Number.
	Males.	Females.	Males.	Females.			Males.	Females.	Males.	Females.		
8	9	10	11	12	13	14	15	16	17	18	19	
1,378,833	**491,896**	**43,429**	**73,964**	**4,436**	**843,508**	**482,612**	**166,042**	**35,940**	**20,678**	**2,718**	**280,630**	
13,098	4,661	863	367	17	7,574	4,017	1,461	615	129	10	1,941	38
50,617	16,779	2,166	3,055	328	31,672	16,264	5,954	626	898	32	9,684	39
16,519	7,991	108	211	2	8,420	3,498	1,377	208	121	..	1,913	40
1,010,163	360,055	30,559	63,443	3,654	619,549	379,879	129,457	28,860	18,111	2,301	221,562	41
224,762	78,485	7,633	5,654	354	138,644	64,137	22,445	5,088	1,129	341	36,604	42
60,097	22,242	2,023	911	80	35,832	13,317	4,754	500	269	31	8,063	43
3,577	1,683	77	323	1	1,817	1,500	594	43	21	3	863	44
1,646,043	**559,729**	**288,543**	**85,873**	**23,113**	**797,771**	**594,167**	**208,157**	**102,739**	**34,599**	**6,774**	**283,271**	
28,546	8,966	5,715	1,071	297	13,865	10,923	3,324	2,850	206	64	4,749	45
4,106	1,532	504	51	32	2,070	214	82	3	2	..	129	46
1,406,286	458,176	254,728	78,558	22,145	693,382	553,670	193,706	96,172	33,949	6,674	268,792	47
180,579	80,462	20,616	5,603	627	79,501	29,335	11,039	3,714	442	36	14,582	48
26,526	10,593	6,980	590	12	8,953	25	6	..	..	..	19	49
988,326	**308,216**	**200,167**	**58,171**	**14,192**	**479,943**	**253,261**	**82,251**	**39,445**	**16,449**	**3,537**	**131,565**	
14,213	4,566	1,082	352	88	8,565	4,825	1,591	439	105	33	2,795	50
5,688	1,607	621	109	29	3,460	709	383	8	8	...	408	51
6,625	2,501	745	172	116	3,379	2,216	742	484	14	4	990	52
912,509	282,790	188,154	56,081	13,425	441,565	237,211	76,667	37,007	16,048	3,383	123,537	53
5,948	2,571	554	82	46	2,823	1,512	592	89	52	...	831	54
43,343	14,181	9,011	1,375	488	20,151	6,698	2,276	1,418	222	117	3,004	55
3,033,728	**620,232**	**1,169,445**	**58,201**	**30,986**	**1,244,051**	**677,947**	**185,962**	**158,406**	**13,879**	**4,024**	**333,579**	
1,388,136	115,044	852,152	6,386	15,977	420,940	186,986	12,876	111,190	538	1,716	62,920	56
82,168	25,643	13,495	1,128	177	43,080	14,631	5,291	1,578	173	5	7,762	57
498,985	114,642	219,760	15,977	10,733	164,583	52,853	12,966	20,485	2,065	1,248	19,402	58
270,430	83,119	14,598	4,523	681	172,713	81,173	27,177	6,924	2,130	609	47,072	59
6,007	2,354	1,380	128	31	2,273	1,241	362	97	28	1	782	60
22,938	7,056	2,003	1,237	125	13,879	3,217	198	1,570	4	6	1,449	61
76,585	23,995	20,849	2,256	1,389	31,741	7,381	996	3,375	40	42	3,010	62
232,113	86,090	21,347	4,873	811	124,676	49,146	18,583	3,266	384	40	27,297	63
13,353	3,577	3,875	363	472	5,901	20,775	7,258	3,279	1,066	199	10,238	64
381,079	140,090	4,697	20,781	486	236,292	246,559	95,010	5,297	7,411	149	146,252	65
61,934	18,622	15,289	549	104	28,023	13,985	5,245	1,345	40	9	7,395	66
5,652,131	**1,925,326**	**782,725**	**320,585**	**58,480**	**2,944,080**	**2,098,478**	**751,119**	**288,585**	**112,349**	**18,785**	**1,058,774**	
24,042	6,372	5,397	72	68	12,273	2,228	632	571	23	...	1,025	67
944,377	317,413	151,775	25,521	4,653	475,189	328,859	108,254	59,665	9,946	2,323	160,940	68
1,345,132	480,942	71,348	65,571	7,631	792,842	782,732	286,979	89,832	40,557	7,194	405,921	69
29,115	9,584	3,653	474	95	15,878	6,434	1,994	1,477	94	28	2,963	70
1,639,801	517,297	409,989	98,652	39,035	712,515	485,624	159,032	114,436	23,479	7,125	212,156	71
1,649,094	589,723	131,837	129,645	6,634	927,534	490,985	193,785	22,069	38,231	2,110	275,131	72
20,570	3,995	8,726	650	364	7,849	1,616	443	535	19	5	638	73
35,677	**12,418**	**4,231**	**511**	**87**	**19,028**	**3,591**	**1,305**	**209**	**31**	**1**	**2,077**	
31,592	11,878	1,725	465	82	17,989	3,105	1,140	167	24	1	1,798	74
4,085	540	2,506	46	5	1,039	486	165	42	7	...	279	75
1,621,852	**594,116**	**164,030**	**43,880**	**11,412**	**863,706**	**440,641**	**158,226**	**45,743**	**10,180**	**1,731**	**236,672**	
37,021	11,337	6,895	1,111	289	18,789	13,843	4,557	2,539	270	38	6,747	76
323,358	112,872	77,512	13,007	6,252	132,974	44,468	14,493	8,154	976	284	21,821	77
963,994	358,529	58,789	22,423	3,586	546,676	330,385	120,356	31,909	7,778	1,299	178,120	78
297,479	111,378	20,834	7,339	1,285	165,267	51,945	18,820	3,141	1,156	110	29,984	79
56,775	**19,997**	**287**	**1,911**	**38**	**36,491**	**9,281**	**4,470**	**184**	**390**	**6**	**4,627**	
19,032	7,257	66	455	1	11,709	5,167	2,695	40	114	1	2,432	80
6,537	2,219	154	74	5	4,164	2,888	1,243	140	236	5	1,500	81
31,206	10,521	67	1,382	32	20,618	1,231	532	4	40	...	695	82
11,537	**5,872**	**229**	**103**	..	**5,436**	**2,847**	**1,154**	**2**	**8**	..	**1,691**	83
1,674,609	**580,464**	**57,295**	**57,941**	**3,073**	**1,036,850**	**467,056**	**160,961**	**24,380**	**13,599**	**1,644**	**281,715**	
80,800	32,718	384	545	2	47,698	8,589	3,411	25	69	..	5,153	84
1,994	660	33	24	19	1,301	343	103	2	2	..	238	85
23,483	9,761	313	188	3	13,409	2,206	818	34	19	..	1,354	86
10,222	3,589	1,268	280	45	5,365	1,880	647	122	30	6	1,111	87
13,465	4,887	105	111	31	8,473	2,495	875	6	8	..	1,614	88
1,369,895	470,952	22,394	51,752	1,841	876,549	409,218	140,306	15,609	12,566	1,385	253,303	89
137,602	43,689	29,525	4,481	957	64,388	36,5[illegible]7	12,814	7,935	850	251	15,798	90
21,279	7,889	2,112	364	153	11,278	2,414	669	494	17	2	1,251	91
15,869	6,319	1,161	196	22	8,389	3,364	1,318	153	38	..	1,893	92
1,129,143	**345,875**	**295,755**	**20,411**	**3,957**	**487,513**	**259,372**	**84,451**	**70,059**	**3,482**	**975**	**104,862**	93
4,336,054	*1,874,513*	*187,494*	*193,561*	*9,098*	*2,274,047*	*692,924*	*282,430*	*50,445*	*15,668*	*2,022*	*360,049*	
885,128	**412,774**	**24,501**	**32,681**	**960**	**447,853**	**97,638**	**38,630**	**5,700**	**1,637**	**114**	**53,308**	
48,708	26,707	3,166	402	11	18,835	252	83	7	..	..	162	94
160,653	82,427	280	7,117	3	77,946	19,355	5,896	69	257	1	13,390	95
139,776	60,346	9,068	3,398	376	70,362	19,583	9,752	2,275	520	107	7,556	96
535,991	243,294	11,987	21,764	590	280,710	58,448	22,899	3,349	860	6	32,200	97

*

TABLE XV.—Occupation or Means of Livelihood.

Group Number.	Occupation.	INDIA. Total Workers and Dependants.	Actual Workers. Total. Males.	Actual Workers. Total. Females.	Actual Workers. Partially agriculturist. Males.	Actual Workers. Partially agriculturist. Females.	Dependants.
	1	2	3	4	5	6	7
	21.—Transport by road	**2,781,938**	**1,181,167**	**181,337**	**80,333**	**9,475**	**1,419,434**
98	Persons employed on the construction and maintenance of roads and bridges	562,574	248,857	98,297	15,951	5,165	215,420
99	Cart owners and drivers, coachmen, stable boys, tramway, mail carriage, etc., managers and employés (excluding private servants)	1,025,229	450,521	29,699	26,969	2,571	545,009
100	Palki, etc., bearers and owners	202,482	95,909	565	14,949	42	106,008
101	Pack elephant, camel, mule, ass and bullock owners and drivers	445,850	167,374	8,742	10,943	473	269,734
102	Porters and messengers	545,803	218,506	44,034	11,521	1,224	283,263
	22.—Transport by rail	**1,062,493**	**448,992**	**25,192**	**18,827**	**514**	**588,309**
103	Railway employés of all kinds other than construction coolies	908,646	373,194	8,381	15,048	175	527,071
104	Labourers employed on railway construction	153,847	75,798	16,811	3,779	339	61,238
105	**23.—Post Office, Telegraph and Telephone services**	**201,781**	**75,380**	**1,209**	**5,751**	**37**	**125,192**
	V.—TRADE	***17,839,109***	***5,464,141***	***9,637,965***	***507,354***	***120,263***	***[9,737,696***
106	**24.—Banks, establishments of credit, exchange and insurance.** (Bank managers, money lenders, exchange and insurance agents, money changers and brokers and their employés.)	**1,220,187**	**356,625**	**64,839**	**50,902**	**3,410**	**798,723**
107	**25.—Brokerage, commission and export.** (Brokers, commission agents, commercial travellers, warehouse owners and their employés)	**240,858**	**82,388**	**6,761**	**4,070**	**235**	**151,709**
108	**26.—Trade in textiles.** (Trade in piece goods, wool, cotton, silk, hair and other textiles)	**1,277,469**	**426,139**	**86,891**	**32,425**	**3,779**	**764,439**
109	**27.—Trade in skins, leather and furs.** (Trade in skins, leather, furs, feathers, horns, etc.)	**296,712**	**103,517**	**11,040**	**12,620**	**1,269**	**182,155**
110	**28.—Trade in wood.** [Trade in wood (not firewood), cork, bark, etc.]	**224,838**	**70,529**	**38,869**	**6,192**	**1,792**	**115,440**
111	**29.—Trade in metals.** (Trade in metals, machinery, knife, tool, etc., sellers)	**59,766**	**[19,972**	**2,551**	**1,467**	**77**	**37,243**
112	**30.—Trade in pottery**	**101,981**	**29,198**	**24,961**	**4,222**	**1,315**	**47,822**
113	**31.—Trade in chemical products.** [Trade in chemical products, drugs, dyes, paints, petroleum, explosives, etc.]	**171,927**	**58,028**	**18,472**	**5,185**	**1,047**	**95,427**
	32.—Hotels, cafes, restaurants, etc.	**719,052**	**226,427**	**125,462**	**24,147**	**6,317**	**367,163**
114	Vendors of wine, liquors, ærated waters, etc.	622,192	191,915	114,487	22,930	6,091	315,790
115	Owners and managers of hotels, cookshops, sarais, etc., and their employés	96,860	34,512	10,975	1,217	226	51,373
	33.—Other trade in food stuffs	**9,478,868**	**2,808,320**	**1,668,793**	**273,556**	**72,774**	**5,001,755**
116	Fish dealers	945,026	215,653	260,273	23,566	11,228	469,100
117	Grocers and sellers of vegetable oil, salt and other condiments	2,916,236	925,467	322,442	94,167	18,498	1,668,327
118	Sellers of milk, butter, ghee, poultry, eggs, etc.	639,492	173,375	158,888	23,167	6,655	307,229
119	Sellers of sweetmeats, sugar, gur and molasses	535,545	149,158	110,798	8,500	1,982	275,589
120	Cardamom, betel-leaf, vegetables, fruit and areca nut sellers	1,584,776	426,284	414,089	42,858	16,986	744,403
121	Grain and pulse dealers	2,190,885	709,517	271,530	64,560	10,700	1,209,838
122	Tobacco, opium, ganja, etc., sellers	317,110	102,793	38,776	7,541	1,572	175,541
123	Dealers in sheep, goats and pigs	113,139	40,917	9,661	3,328	520	62,561
124	Dealers in hay, grass and fodder	236,659	65,156	82,336	5,869	4,633	89,167
125	**34.—Trade in clothing and toilet articles.** [Trade in ready-made clothing and other articles of dress and the toilet (hats, umbrellas, socks, ready-made shoes, perfumes, etc.).]	**306,701**	**101,088**	**21,775**	**6,349**	**1,308**	**183,838**
	35.—Trade in furniture	**173,413**	**56,878**	**15,570**	**3,739**	**784**	**100,965**
126	Trade in furniture, carpets, curtains and bedding	57,282	17,639	10,601	1,390	479	29,042
127	Hardware, cooking utensils, porcelain, crockery, glassware, bottles, articles for gardening, the cellar, etc.	116,131	39,239	4,969	2,349	305	71,923
128	**36.—Trade in building materials.** (Stones, bricks, plaster, cement, sand, tiles, thatch, etc.)	**84,613**	**25,875**	**13,866**	**2,217**	**729**	**44,872**
129	**37.—Trade in means of transport.** [Dealers and hirers of elephants, camels, horses, cattle, asses, mules, etc.; sellers (not makers) of carriages, saddlery, etc.]	**239,396**	**87,229**	**10,581**	**7,600**	**704**	**141,586**
130	**38.—Trade in fuel.** (Dealers in firewood, charcoal, coal, cowdung, etc.)	**524,962**	**119,366**	**215,634**	**16,634**	**12,174**	**189,962**
	39.—Trade in articles of luxury and those pertaining to letters and the arts and sciences	**522,130**	**162,854**	**71,862**	**12,750**	**3,280**	**287,414**
131	Dealers in precious stones, jewellery (real and imitation), clocks, optical instruments, etc.	102,234	33,089	5,221	1,933	210	63,924
132	Dealers in common bangles, bead necklaces, fans, small articles, toys, hunting and fishing tackle, flowers, etc.	376,401	114,732	65,072	10,227	2,939	196,597
133	Publishers, booksellers, stationers, dealers in music, pictures, musical instruments and curiosities	43,495	15,033	1,569	590	131	26,893
134	**40.—Trade in refuse matter.** (Dealers in rags, stable refuse, etc.)	**3,695**	**1,279**	**349**	**86**	**6**	**2,067**
	41.—Trade of other sorts	**2,192,584**	**728,429**	**238,989**	**49,213**	**9,178**	**1,225,116**
135	Shopkeepers otherwise unspecified.	1,984,040	651,282	227,465	44,739	8,670	1,105,293
136	Itinerant traders, pedlars, hawkers, etc.	82,998	30,486	3,951	1,245	186	48,561
137	Conjurors, acrobats, fortune tellers, reciters, exhibitors, of curiosities and wild animals	82,119	30,451	5,801	1,967	259	45,867
138	Other trades (including farmers of pounds, tolls and markets)	43,377	16,210	1,772	1,262	63	25,395

PART A.—GENERAL TABLE, (*i*) SUMMARY FOR ALL INDIA—*continued.*

British Territory.						States and Agencies.						
Total Workers and Dependants.	Actual Workers.				Dependants.	Total Workers and Dependants.	Actual Workers.				Dependants.	Group Number.
	Total.		Partially agriculturist.				Total.		Partially agriculturist.			
	Males.	Females.	Males.	Females.			Males.	Females.	Males.	Females.		
8	9	10	11	12	13	14	15	16	17	18	19	
2,343,722	**1,061,819**	**188,859**	**68,178**	**7,578**	**1,203,044**	**438,216**	**179,348**	**42,478**	**12,155**	**1,897**	**216,390**	
459,203	210,961	73,228	14,270	4,231	175,014	103,371	37,896	25,069	1,681	934	40,406	98
866,480	378,799	24,310	22,734	2,111	463,371	158,749	71,722	5,389	4,235	460	81,638	99
195,250	92,392	499	14,752	87	102,359	7,232	3,517	66	197	5	3,649	100
352,007	129,378	4,510	7,034	115	218,119	93,843	37,996	4,232	3,909	858	51,615	101
470,782	190,289	36,312	9,388	1,084	244,181	75,021	28,217	7,722	2,133	140	39,082	102
936,651	**397,012**	**22,961**	**17,545**	**505**	**516,678**	**125,842**	**51,980**	**2,231**	**1,282**	**9**	**71,631**	
802,838	329,911	7,630	14,012	167	465,297	105,808	43,283	751	1,036	8	61,774	103
133,813	67,101	15,331	3,533	338	51,381	20,034	8,697	1,480	246	1	9,857	104
170,553	**62,908**	**1,173**	**5,157**	**35**	**106,472**	**31,228**	**12,472**	**36**	**594**	**2**	**18,720**	105
13,409,310	***4,095,756***	***2,003,233***	***386,707***	***90,340***	***7,310,321***	***4,429,792***	***1,368,385***	***634,032***	***190,647***	***39,923***	***2,427,375***	
803,561	**236,390**	**42,888**	**37,927**	**2,533**	**524,283**	**416,626**	**120,235**	**21,951**	**12,975**	**877**	**274,449**	106
203,762	**70,992**	**6,060**	**3,694**	**203**	**126,650**	**37,156**	**11,396**	**701**	**376**	**32**	**25,059**	107
901,365	**308,021**	**58,003**	**25,067**	**3,004**	**535,341**	**376,104**	**118,118**	**28,888**	**7,358**	**775**	**229,098**	108
238,014	**80,755**	**6,840**	**7,816**	**572**	**150,419**	**58,698**	**22,762**	**4,200**	**4,804**	**697**	**31,736**	109
179,555	**56,369**	**27,741**	**5,325**	**1,381**	**95,445**	**45,283**	**14,160**	**11,128**	**867**	**411**	**19,995**	110
44,273	**15,415**	**1,983**	**1,041**	**47**	**26,875**	**15,493**	**4,557**	**568**	**426**	**30**	**10,368**	111
82,304	**24,510**	**19,105**	**3,463**	**724**	**38,689**	**19,677**	**4,688**	**5,856**	**759**	**591**	**9,133**	112
149,552	**50,109**	**16,284**	**4,781**	**1,020**	**83,159**	**22,375**	**7,919**	**2,188**	**384**	**27**	**12,268**	113
368,569	**123,173**	**44,826**	**11,269**	**2,393**	**200,570**	**350,483**	**103,254**	**80,636**	**12,878**	**3,924**	**166,593**	
286,939	93,141	36,120	10,250	2,184	157,678	335,253	98,774	78,367	12,680	3,907	158,112	114
81,630	30,032	8,706	1,019	209	42,892	15,230	4,480	2,269	198	17	8,481	115
7,420,566	**2,184,013**	**1,330,050**	**219,633**	**57,413**	**3,906,503**	**2,058,302**	**624,307**	**338,743**	**53,923**	**15,361**	**1,095,252**	
837,889	192,424	224,872	22,551	10,316	420,593	107,137	23,229	35,401	1,015	912	48,507	116
2,195,405	690,397	254,978	72,777	15,201	1,250,035	720,831	235,070	67,469	21,390	3,297	418,292	117
505,244	138,989	123,064	18,914	5,252	243,191	134,248	34,386	35,824	4,453	1,408	64,038	118
463,287	126,792	98,919	7,701	1,808	237,576	72,258	22,366	11,879	799	174	38,018	119
1,265,229	340,489	329,325	34,582	12,527	595,415	319,547	85,795	84,764	8,276	4,459	148,988	120
1,667,057	540,917	211,611	51,253	7,669	914,529	523,828	168,600	59,919	13,307	3,031	295,309	121
269,751	88,031	34,497	7,013	1,477	147,223	47,359	14,762	4,279	528	95	28,318	122
65,047	22,656	4,500	1,826	356	37,891	48,092	18,261	5,161	1,502	164	24,670	123
151,657	43,318	48,289	3,016	2,807	60,050	85,002	21,838	34,047	2,853	1,826	29,117	124
251,656	**80,859**	**16,484**	**4,949**	**1,095**	**154,313**	**55,045**	**20,229**	**5,291**	**1,400**	**296**	**29,525**	125
145,022	**47,138**	**12,726**	**3,217**	**587**	**85,158**	**28,391**	**9,740**	**2,844**	**522**	**197**	**15,807**	
42,713	12,966	8,253	1,127	330	21,494	14,569	4,673	2,348	253	149	7,548	126
102,309	34,172	4,473	2,090	257	63,664	13,822	5,067	496	259	48	8,259	127
65,115	**20,269**	**11,047**	**1,889**	**650**	**33,799**	**19,498**	**5,606**	**2,819**	**328**	**79**	**11,073**	128
192,143	**69,515**	**7,149**	**6,073**	**458**	**115,479**	**47,253**	**17,714**	**3,432**	**1,527**	**246**	**26,107**	129
391,165	**87,034**	**166,105**	**7,382**	**9,108**	**138,026**	**133,797**	**32,333**	**49,529**	**3,252**	**3,066**	**51,936**	130
401,988	**128,351**	**49,918**	**10,113**	**2,236**	**223,719**	**120,142**	**34,563**	**21,944**	**2,637**	**1,044**	**63,695**	
77,127	25,925	2,857	1,493	146	48,345	25,107	7,164	2,364	440	64	15,579	131
285,932	88,956	45,600	8,118	1,964	151,366	90,469	25,766	19,472	2,109	975	45,231	132
38,929	13,460	1,461	502	126	24,008	4,566	1,573	108	88	5	2,885	133
3,141	**1,133**	**232**	**83**	**5**	**1,776**	**554**	**146**	**117**	**3**	**1**	**291**	134
1,567,619	**511,710**	**185,792**	**32,985**	**6,911**	**870,117**	**624,915**	**216,719**	**53,197**	**16,223**	**2,267**	**354,999**	
1,431,919	460,118	177,679	29,643	6,496	794,122	552,121	191,164	49,786	15,096	2,174	311,171	135
45,743	17,588	3,007	746	141	25,148	37,255	12,898	944	499	45	23,413	136
59,111	22,399	3,953	1,673	220	32,759	23,008	8,052	1,848	294	39	13,108	137
30,846	11,605	1,153	923	54	18,088	12,531	4,605	619	339	9	7,307	138

*

TABLE XV.—Occupation or Means of Livelihood.

Group Number.	Occupation.	INDIA. Total Workers and Dependants.	Actual Workers. Total. Males.	Actual Workers. Total. Females.	Actual Workers. Partially agriculturist. Males.	Actual Workers. Partially agriculturist. Females.	Dependants.
	1	2	3	4	5	6	7
	C.—PUBLIC ADMINISTRATION AND LIBERAL ARTS	10,912,123	3,981,507	518,147	564,557	29,978	6,412,469
	VI.—PUBLIC FORCE	*? 398,586*	*1,059,399*	*10,025*	*178,420*	*1,039*	*1,399,169*
	42.—Army	**665,278**	**383,106**	**968**	**54,095**	**14**	**281,204**
139	Army (Imperial)	366,306	241,042	507	42,966	9	124,757
140	Army (Native States)	298,972	142,064	461	11,129	5	156,447
141	**43.—Navy**	**4,640**	**2,225**	**4**	**38**	..	**2,411**
	44.—Police	**1,728,668**	**674,068**	**9,053**	**124,287**	**1,025**	**1,045,547**
142	Police	721,202	295,477	2,235	26,115	191	423,490
143	Village watchmen	1,007,466	378,591	6,818	98,172	834	622,057
	VII.—(ORDER 45) PUBLIC ADMINISTRATION	*2,648,005*	*927,599*	*42,922*	*133,759*	*7,649*	*1,677,484*
144	Service of the State	809,427	267,455	2,823	29,132	226	539,149
145	Service of Native and Foreign States	643,078	242,056	6,441	16,611	106	394,581
146	Municipal and other local (not village) service	190,038	72,609	6,180	4,009	105	111,249
147	Village officials and servants other than watchmen	1,005,462	345,479	27,478	84,007	7,212	632,505
	VIII.—PROFESSIONS AND LIBERAL ARTS.	*5,325,357*	*1,851,053*	*402,586*	*235,313*	*20,019*	*3,071,718*
	46.—Religion	**2,769,489**	**1,008,678**	**186,451**	**147,949**	**10,314**	**1,574,360**
148	Priests, ministers, etc.	1.596,328	572,293	76,021	90,728	5,230	948,014
149	Religious mendicants, inmates of monasteries, etc.	698,036	270,117	87,362	29,108	3,378	340,557
150	Catechists, readers, church and mission service.	60,042	16,332	3,016	1,104	31	40,694
151	Temple, burial or burning ground service, pilgrim conductors, circumcisers	415,083	149,936	20,052	27,009	1,675	245,095
	47.—Law	**303,408**	**81,840**	**621**	**14,029**	**7**	**220,947**
152	Lawyers of all kinds, including Kazis, law agents and mukhtiars	175,618	41,158	522	8,164	7	133,938
153	Lawyers' clerks, petition writers, etc.	127,790	40,682	99	5,865	..	87,009
	48.—Medicine	**?26,900**	**169,004**	**101,298**	**17,692**	**4,693**	**356,598**
154	Medical practitioners of all kinds, including dentists, oculists and veterinary surgeons	436,761	137,564	13,317	15,468	798	285,880
155	Midwives, vaccinators, compounders, nurses, masseurs, etc.	190,139	21,440	87,981	2,224	3,895	70,718
156	**49.—Instruction**. [Professors and teachers of all kinds (except law, medicine, music, dancing and drawing) and clerks and servants connected with education].	**674,393**	**245,923**	**25,745**	**24,524**	**1,021**	**402,725**
	50.—Letters and arts and sciences	**951,167**	**345,608**	**88,471**	**31,119**	**3,977**	**517,088**
157	Public scribes, stenographers, etc.	12,595	4,101	375	256	5	8,119
158	Architects, surveyors, engineers, and their employés.	128,946	45,028	1,328	3,478	21	82,590
159	Others (authors, photographers, artists, sculptors, astronomers, meteorologists, botanists, astrologers, etc.)	120,192	42,617	4,052	3,464	249	73,523
160	Music composers and masters, players on all kinds of musical instruments (not military), singers, actors, and dancers	689,434	253,862	82,716	23,921	3,702	352,856
	IX.—(ORDER 51) PERSONS LIVING PRINCIPALLY ON THEIR INCOME.	*540,175*	*143,456*	*62,614*	*17,065*	*1,278*	*334,105*
161	Proprietors (other than of agricultural land), fund and scholarship holders and pensioners	540,175	143,456	62,614	17,065	1,278	334,105
	D.—MISCELLANEOUS	17,286,678	6,086,540	3,778,410	253,933	80,562	7,421,728
	X.—(ORDER 52) DOMESTIC SERVICE	*4,599,080*	*1,733,119*	*? 92,744*	*78,347*	*25,046*	*1,873,224*
162	Cooks, water carriers, doorkeepers, watchmen and other indoor servants	4,290,642	1,587,615	987,856	73,119	24,954	1,715,171
163	Private grooms, coachmen, dog boys, etc.	308,438	145,497	4,888	5,228	92	158,053
	XI.—INSUFFICIENTLY DESCRIBED OCCUPATIONS. (Order 53.—General terms which do not indicate a definite occupation)	*?.336,917*	*3,057,818*	*2,009,882*	*113,657*	*36,505*	*4,168,517*
164	Manufacturers, business men and contractors otherwise unspecified	122,596	40,698	2,727	3,162	136	79,271
165	Cashiers, accountants, book-keepers, clerks and other employés in unspecified offices, warehouses and shops	776,663	301,658	14,993	12,686	560	460,012
166	Mechanics otherwise unspecified	63,208	26,774	1,504	456	14	34,930
167	Labourers and workmen otherwise unspecified	8,273,650	2,688,688	1,990,658	97,353	35,795	3,594,304
	XII.—UNPRODUCTIVE	*3,451,381*	*1,295,610*	*775,784*	*61,929*	*19,011*	*1,379,987*
168	**54.—Inmates of jails, asylums and hospitals**	**132,610**	**117,273**	**7,290**	**699**	**70**	**8,047**
169	**55.—Beggars, vagrants, prostitutes.** (Beggars, vagrants, procurers, prostitutes, receivers of stolen goods, cattle poisoners)	**3,318,771**	**1,178,337**	**768,494**	**61,230**	**18,941**	**1,371,940**

PART A.—GENERAL TABLE (i) SUMMARY FOR ALL INDIA—*concluded*.

BRITISH TERRITORY.						STATES AND AGENCIES.						
Total Workers and Dependants.	ACTUAL WORKERS.				Dependants.	Total Workers and Dependants.	ACTUAL WORKERS.				Dependants.	Group Number.
	Total.		Partially agriculturist.				Total.		Partially agriculturist.			
	Males.	Females.	Males.	Females.			Males.	Females.	Males.	Females.		
8	9	10	11	12	13	14	15	16	17	18	19	
7,306,043	2,626,490	340,938	398,346	17,920	4,338,615	3,606,080	1,355,017	177,209	166,211	12,058	2,073,854	
1,553,589	*688,843*	*4,928*	*131,999*	*596*	*859,818*	*844,997*	*370,556*	*5,097*	*47,121*	*443*	*469,344*	
329,456	216,370	467	40,182	9	112,619	335,822	166,736	501	13,913	5	168,585	
326,682	214,571	465	40,098	9	111,646	39,624	26,471	42	2,868	..	13,111	139
2,774	1,799	2	84	..	973	296,198	140,265	459	11,045	5	155,474	140
4,511	2,211	..	38	..	2,300	129	14	4	..	..	111	141
1,219,622	470,262	4,461	91,079	587	744,899	509,046	203,806	4,592	33,208	438	300,648	
492,854	204,989	2,088	20,668	190	285,777	228,348	90,488	147	5,447	1	137,713	142
726,768	265,273	2,373	70,411	397	459,122	280,698	113,318	4,445	27,761	437	162,935	143
1,503,819	*505,171*	*21,939*	*80,099*	*3,140*	*976,709*	*1,144,193*	*429,498*	*20,983*	*53,660*	*4,509*	*700,782*	
744,018	244,227	2,310	27,601	218	497,481	65,409	23,228	513	1,531	8	41,668	144
19,212	6,566	493	600	7	12,153	623,866	235,490	5,948	16,011	99	382,428	145
158,933	60,384	4,958	3,403	80	93,591	31,105	12,225	1,222	606	25	17,658	146
581,649	193,994	14,178	48,495	2,835	373,477	423,813	151,485	13,300	35,512	4,377	59,028	147
3,881,670	*1,335,018*	*278,474*	*173,577*	*13,287*	*2,268,178*	*1,443,687*	*516,035*	*124,119*	*61,736*	*6,725*	*803,540*	
1,897,173	688,618	116,494	100,952	6,426	1,092,061	872,316	320,060	69,957	46,997	3,888	482,299	
1,247,107	448,058	53,611	69,070	3,603	745,438	349,221	124,235	22,410	21,658	1,627	202,576	148
317,952	125,721	47,091	11,352	1,491	145,140	380,084	144,396	40,271	17,756	1,887	195,417	149
39,975	9,864	2,293	784	29	27,818	20,067	6,468	723	320	2	12,876	150
292,139	104,975	13,499	19,746	1,303	173,665	122,944	44,961	6,553	7,263	372	71,430	151
255,663	68,446	572	12,860	7	186,645	47,745	13,394	49	1,169	..	34,302	
140,014	31,747	482	7,229	7	107,785	35,604	9,411	40	935	..	26,153	152
115,649	36,699	90	5,631	..	78,860	12,141	3,983	9	234	..	8,149	153
525,131	137,456	86,612	15,814	3,946	301,063	101,769	31,548	14,686	1,878	747	55,535	
368,731	111,495	11,495	13,881	710	245,741	68,030	26,069	1,822	1,587	88	40,139	154
156,400	25,961	75,117	1,933	3,236	55,322	33,739	5,479	12,864	291	659	15,396	155
530,579	194,963	20,025	21,002	773	315,651	143,814	51,020	5,720	3,522	248	87,074	156
673,124	245,595	54,771	22,949	2,135	372,758	278,043	100,013	33,700	8,170	1,842	144,330	
11,609	3,750	373	229	5	7,486	986	351	2	27	..	633	157
93,053	34,082	1,009	2,974	21	62,962	30,893	10,946	319	504	..	19,628	158
77,923	26,851	1,939	2,186	83	49,133	42,269	15,766	2,113	1,278	166	24,390	159
485,539	180,912	51,450	17,560	2,026	253,177	203,895	72,950	31,266	6,361	1,676	99,679	160
366,979	*97,458*	*35,597*	*13,371*	*897*	*233,917*	*173,203*	*45,998*	*27,017*	*3,694*	*381*	*100,188*	
366,972	97,458	35,597	13,371	897	233,917	173,203	45,998	27,017	3,694	381	100,188	161
12,398,316	4,506,006	2,539,902	196,875	58,597	5,352,408	4,888,362	1,580,534	1,238,508	57,058	21,365	2,069,320	
3,416,999	*1,309,714*	*755,900*	*57,114*	*17,976*	*1,359,078*	*1,189,088*	*423,398*	*237,544*	*21,233*	*7,070*	*521,146*	
3,176,322	1,195,801	751,691	52,835	17,898	1,228,830	1,114,320	391,814	236,165	20,284	7,056	486,341	162
240,670	113,913	3,509	4,279	78	123,248	67,768	31,584	1,379	949	14	34,805	163
6,575,606	*2,295,999*	*1,229,490*	*95,388*	*26,893*	*3,050,124*	*2,660,611*	*761,826*	*780,392*	*18,269*	*9,612*	*1,118,393*	
91,316	30,701	1,197	2,497	90	59,418	31,380	9,997	1,530	665	46	19,853	164
637,324	253,865	12,278	10,999	490	371,181	139,339	47,793	2,715	1,687	70	88,831	165
56,314	24,173	855	378	8	31,286	6,894	2,601	649	78	6	3,644	166
5,790,652	1,987,253	1,215,160	81,514	26,305	2,588,239	2,482,998	701,435	775,498	15,839	9,490	1,006,065	167
2,405,718	*900,300*	*555,212*	*44,373*	*13,728*	*950,206*	*1,045,663*	*395,310*	*220,572*	*17,556*	*5,283*	*429,781*	
106,745	97,018	5,584	628	62	6,143	23,865	20,255	1,706	71	8	1,904	168
2,298,973	803,282	549,628	43,745	13,666	944,063	1,021,798	375,055	218,866	17,485	5,275	427,877	169

TABLE XV.—Occupation or Means of Livelihood.

Serial Number.	Province, State or Agency.	CLASS A :—PRODUCTION OF RAW MATERIALS. TOTAL OF ALL CLASSES. Total Workers and Dependants.	Actual Workers. Total. Males.	Females.	Partially Agriculturist.	Dependants.	TOTAL OF CLASS A. Total Workers and Dependants.	Actual Workers. Total. Males.	Females.	Partially Agriculturist.	Dependants.	TOTAL Total Workers and Dependants.
	1	2	3	4	5	6	7	8	9	10	11	12
	INDIA.	313,479,614	101,525,421	47,359,582	4,906,636	164,585,611	227,680,092	72,332,823	34,176,058	598,297	120,571,211	226,550,483
	Provinces.	244,189,716	79,028,337	35,788,824	2,999,386	129,372,555	179,948,129	57,263,835	26,150,411	440,576	96,533,888	179,529,352
1	Ajmer-Merwara	501,395	184,143	109,669	13,044	207,583	276,227	96,485	82,030	359	97,812	275,639
2	Andamans and Nicobars	24,767	17,913	797	19	6,057	9,549	4,587	67	..	4,895	9,549
3	Assam	6,713,635	2,148,211	928,527	111,339	3,636,897	5,913,575	1,847,684	812,453	63,350	3,253,438	5,907,789
4	Baluchistan	414,412	154,742	1,976	17,066	257,694	316,685	101,193	91	3,127	215,401	315,277
5	Bengal	45,483,077	14,102,875	2,117,330	412,797	29,262,872	35,340,836	10,497,246	966,909	54,716	23,876,681	35,224,959
6	Bihar and Orissa	34,490,084	10,754,459	5,970,465	364,470	17,765,160	27,912,008	8,711,052	4,416,623	61,784	14,784,333	27,759,267
7	Bombay	19,672,642	6,419,167	2,897,784	184,183	10,355,691	13,459,714	4,120,270	2,230,718	28,084	7,108,726	13,427,708
8	Burma	12,039,083	3,813,666	2,913,743	107,823	5,311,674	8,639,688	2,622,348	2,153,325	19,149	3,864,015	8,624,395
9	C. P. and Berar	13,916,308	4,607,093	3,760,178	229,604	5,549,037	10,949,684	3,549,104	3,252,874	40,282	4,147,706	10,919,927
10	Coorg	174,976	72,035	44,238	1,765	58,703	144,570	56,942	39,974	519	47,654	144,547
11	Madras	41,405,404	12,783,881	8,249,231	585,645	20,372,292	29,266,763	9,074,054	6,254,518	41,440	13,938,191	29,249,994
12	N.-W. F. Province (*Districts and Administered Territories*).	2,196,933	677,127	45,270	12,111	1,474,536	1,487,958	421,423	23,613	149	1,042,922	1,487,673
13	Punjab	19,974,956	6,756,172	945,843	240,898	12,272,941	11,590,196	3,910,064	358,886	9,672	7,320,256	11,557,776
14	United Provinces	47,182,044	16,536,853	7,803,773	718,622	22,841,418	34,640,666	12,250,483	5,558,330	117,945	16,831,853	34,631,859
	States and Agencies	69,280,298	22,497,084	11,570,758	1,907,250	35,212,456	47,131,963	15,068,988	8,025,647	157,721	24,037,328	47,021,131
15	Assam State (Manipur)	346,222	79,273	56,659	2,009	210,290	271,339	69,888	12,226	2	189,225	270,602
16	Baluchistan States	420,291	141,211	5,355	6,466	273,725	349,976	118,066	1	3,482	231,909	349,710
17	Baroda State	2,032,798	661,522	285,247	17,946	1,086,029	1,332,881	428,515	201,132	766	703,234	1,339,756
18	Bengal States	822,565	285,599	49,675	3,929	487,291	737,111	244,599	37,167	392	455,345	737,111
19	Bihar and Orissa States	3,945,209	1,192,419	678,648	49,069	2,074,142	3,202,971	979,593	478,840	4,179	1,744,538	3,198,816
20	Bombay States	7,411,675	2,314,559	1,075,654	51,215	4,021,462	4,990,966	1,560,416	843,271	3,774	2,587,279	4,981,615
21	Central India Agency	9,356,960	3,288,363	2,032,029	168,555	4,036,588	5,953,423	2,067,030	1,356,994	38,753	2,529,399	5,949,356
22	Central Provinces States	2,117,002	659,398	506,231	13,163	951,373	1,832,531	569,813	437,489	2,569	825,229	1,832,313
23	Hyderabad State	13,374,676	4,449,847	2,722,146	288,779	6,202,683	8,406,192	2,731,179	1,865,231	83,460	3,811,782	8,389,718
24	Kashmir State	3,158,126	1,024,661	461,628	21,970	1,671,837	2,519,742	796,769	397,631	1,363	1,325,342	2,519,709
25	Madras States	4,811,841	1,362,822	713,957	24,163	2,735,562	2,729,419	778,049	308,973	2,177	1,642,397	2,726,113
26	Mysore State	5,806,193	1,448,416	349,440	55,780	4,008,337	4,296,631	1,021,469	152,180	2,318	3,124,982	4,265,644
27	N.-W. F. Province (*Agencies and Tribal areas*).	13,538	12,150	23	1,325	1,365	4,455	4,347	1	1	107	4,455
28	Punjab States	4,212,794	1,494,550	232,880	41,570	2,485,364	2,948,170	1,034,725	152,199	1,134	1,761,246	2,944,368
29	Rajputana Agency	10,530,432	3,787,701	2,336,358	249,634	4,406,373	6,832,939	2,434,749	1,742,435	15,725	2,655,755	6,819,699
30	Sikkim State	87,920	30,697	28,404	13	28,819	83,703	28,084	27,694	..	27,925	83,703
31	United Provinces States	832,036	264,396	36,424	11,662	531,216	635,514	201,697	12,183	626	421,634	635,513

Part A.—General Table, (ii) Provincial Distribution.

CLASS A :—*SUB-CLASS I.—EXPLOITATION OF THE SURFACE OF THE EARTH.*

of Sub-Class I.				Order 1.—Pasture and Agriculture. *Total of Order 1.*					Sub-Order 1 (a)—Ordinary Cultivation. *Total of Sub-Order 1 (a).*					
Actual Workers. Total. Males.	Actual Workers. Total. Females.	Partially Agri-culturist.	Dependants.	Total Workers and Dependants.	Actual Workers. Total. Males.	Actual Workers. Total. Females.	Partially Agriculturist.	Dependants.	Total Workers and Dependants.	Actual Workers. Total. Males.	Actual Workers. Total. Females.	Partially Agriculturist.	Dependants.	Serial Number.
13	14	15	16	17	18	19	20	21	22	23	24	25	26	
72,122,268	34,078,164	576,274	120,350,051	224,685,900	71,462,868	33,872,511	476,645	119,360,521	216,787,137	67,543,794	32,595,794	179,891	116,647,549	
57,097,846	26,663,448	420,751	96,368,058	177,935,894	56,547,794	25,875,926	332,953	95,512,174	172,321,648	53,610,680	24,906,248	105,915	93,862,720	
96,187	81,967	346	97,478	275,594	96,174	81,967	343	97,453	268,596	92,602	81,243	21	94,751	1
4,587	67	..	4,895	9,518	4,574	67	..	4,877	1,565	375	67	..	1,123	2
1,844,250	811,517	63,260	3,252,022	5,807,234	1,801,594	809,779	50,828	3,195,861	5,054,324	1,518,750	568,663	879	2,966,911	3
100,041	84	2,775	215,152	315,273	100,038	84	2,775	215,151	272,553	85,422	6	28	187,125	4
10,456,912	941,745	52,826	23,826,302	34,582,312	10,245,788	875,032	29,317	23,461,492	33,862,878	9,835,307	751,551	14,311	23,276,020	5
8,644,243	4,372,733	47,655	14,735,291	27,625,362	8,599,385	4,348,382	34,914	14,677,595	26,990,314	8,245,562	4,212,384	10,226	14,532,368	6
4,107,883	2,228,250	27,232	7,091,575	13,273,644	4,058,941	2,205,428	22,292	7,009,275	12,712,709	3,749,610	2,144,640	602	6,818,459	7
2,615,932	2,150,953	19,010	3,857,510	8,472,391	2,567,202	2,123,276	15,736	3,781,913	8,083,712	2,434,999	2,024,772	13	3,623,941	8
3,537,214	3,245,282	39,790	4,137,431	10,793,698	3,487,904	3,224,441	19,373	4,081,353	10,330,646	3,258,403	3,145,066	579	3,927,177	9
56,922	39,973	519	47,652	144,468	56,897	39,966	519	47,605	120,401	43,561	34,040	..	42,800	10
9,068,325	6,252,476	40,738	13,929,193	29,011,171	8,982,956	6,236,049	33,346	13,792,166	28,288,808	8,606,588	6,158,352	14,009	13,523,838	11
421,300	23,612	147	1,042,761	1,487,184	421,124	23,612	147	1,042,448	1,468,071	412,775	23,400	12	1,031,896	12
3,897,014	357,623	9,219	7,303,139	11,549,320	3,893,576	357,474	8,974	7,298,270	11,166,334	3,656,446	349,246	238	7,160,642	13
12,247,036	5,557,166	117,234	16,827,657	34,588,725	12,231,641	5,550,369	114,889	16,806,715	33,700,737	11,670,280	5,414,758	74,997	16,615,669	14
15,024,422	8,014,716	155,523	23,961,993	46,760,066	14,915,074	7,996,585	143,692	23,848,347	44,465,489	13,933,114	7,687,546	73,976	22,844,829	
69,684	11,988	1	188,930	270,451	69,638	11,983	1	188,830	269,056	69,170	11,819	..	188,067	15
117,989	1	3,482	231,720	344,160	116,370	1	3,397	227,789	288,500	97,159	1	9	191,340	16
428,474	201,129	766	703,153	1,329,961	427,679	200,684	760	701,598	1,284,365	412,281	196,193	6	675,891	17
244,599	37,167	392	455,345	733,263	242,974	36,736	157	453,553	731,499	241,667	36,703	75	453,129	18
977,999	477,107	4,136	1,743,710	3,192,480	972,228	474,522	3,351	1,735,730	3,064,668	908,398	460,016	262	1,696,254	19
1,556,814	842,693	3,718	2,582,108	4,969,083	1,552,704	841,105	3,465	2,575,274	4,665,962	1,423,946	811,237	124	2,430,779	20
2,065,646	1,356,540	38,700	2,527,170	5,936,785	2,059,905	1,355,300	37,956	2,521,580	5,660,991	1,925,526	1,307,190	27,109	2,428,275	21
569,754	437,409	2,544	825,160	1,825,173	567,310	436,038	2,199	821,825	1,721,287	524,352	416,696	19	780,239	22
2,721,445	1,862,451	80,323	3,805,822	8,281,829	2,670,018	1,856,165	71,022	3,755,646	7,619,505	2,403,868	1,737,615	45,377	3,478,022	23
796,760	397,630	1,363	1,325,319	2,515,519	795,289	397,307	1,250	1,322,923	2,474,991	777,010	392,917	16	1,305,064	24
776,730	308,483	2,176	1,640,900	2,646,631	745,770	304,918	2,044	1,595,943	2,388,421	660,688	284,047	19	1,443,686	25
1,001,581	150,921	1,077	3,093,142	4,243,435	1,000,830	150,809	992	3,091,796	4,160,550	963,004	137,261	4	3,060,285	26
4,347	1	1	107	4,455	4,347	1	1	107	4,448	4,342	1	1	105	27
1,033,215	152,052	1,093	1,759,100	2,940,525	1,031,709	152,006	1,013	1,756,810	2,849,810	930,720	146,600	18	1,722,490	28
2,429,605	1,739,266	15,125	2,650,758	6,818,961	2,429,268	1,739,246	15,059	2,650,447	5,571,957	2,313,101	1,709,930	671	2,548,926	29
28,084	27,694	..	27,925	83,703	28,084	27,694	..	27,925	83,017	27,593	27,553	..	27,871	30
201,696	12,183	626	421,634	633,592	200,951	12,070	416	420,571	626,462	195,289	11,767	266	419,406	31

TABLE XV.—Occupation or Means of Livelihood.

Serial Number.	Province, State or Agency.	CLASS A: SUB-CLASS I.—EXPLOITATION OF THE SURFACE OF THE EARTH. SUB-ORDER 1 (a)—ORDINARY CULTIVATION—contd. Group 1.—Income from rent of Agricultural land.	Group 2.—Ordinary cultivators.	Group 3.—Agents, managers of landed estates (not planters), clerks, rent collectors, etc.	Group 4.—Farm servants and field labourers.	SUB-ORDER 1 (b)—GROWERS OF SPECIAL … TOTAL OF SUB-ORDER I (b). Total Workers and Dependants.	Actual Workers. Total. Males.	Actual Workers. Total. Females.	Actual Workers. Partially Agriculturist.	Dependants.	Group 5.—Tea, coffee, cinchona and indigo plantation.
	1	27	28	29	30	31	32	33	34	35	36
	INDIA.	**7,743,507**	**167,015,427**	**781,868**	**41,246,335**	**2,012,503**	**706,173**	**495,718**	**88,295**	**810,612**	**1,040,425**
	Provinces.	**5,467,906**	**133,724,099**	**696,387**	**32,434,156**	**1,656,145**	**583,655**	**455,053**	**84,936**	**617,437**	**997,730**
1	Ajmer-Merwara	10,647	227,196	456	30,297	*892*	*438*	*34*	*12*	*420*	1
2	Andamans and Nicobars	..	1,550	..	15	*7,906*	*4,178*	..	..	*3,728*	1
3	Assam	137,104	4,824,061	8,543	84,616	*702,695*	*246,243*	*238,140*	*47,859*	*218,312*	675,359
4	Baluchistan	36,753	234,911	161	728	*747*	*547*	..	*130*	*200*	..
5	Bengal	1,192,880	29,042,174	207,287	3,420,537	*342,292*	*128,989*	*93,413*	*8,192*	*119,890*	248,426
6	Bihar and Orissa	595,641	19,770,872	173,971	6,449,830	*26,636*	*10,114*	*1,523*	*2,583*	*14,999*	4,480
7	Bombay	542,615	8,839,804	8,035	3,322,255	*40,128*	*15,473*	*5,095*	*3,315*	*19,560*	18
8	Burma	220,485	6,215,154	123	1,647,950	*238,511*	*68,447*	*68,274*	*10,966*	*101,790*	6,217
9	C. P. and Berar	122,417	6,146,166	18,086	4,043,977	*45,349*	*14,859*	*12,997*	*3,282*	*17,993*	482
10	Coorg	3,841	81,462	7	35,091	*22,292*	*12,486*	*5,558*	*449*	*4,248*	22,062
11	Madras	1,114,840	19,291,767	74,419	7,807,782	*155,567*	*53,563*	*18,582*	*4,572*	*83,422*	87,286
12	N.-W. F. Province (*Districts and Administered Territories*).	87,073	1,330,498	519	49,981	*2,728*	*953*	*11*	*29*	*1,764*	..
13	Punjab	540,556	9,615,586	8,950	1,001,242	*14,104*	*5,577*	*345*	*278*	*8,182*	624
14	United Provinces	862,154	28,102,898	195,830	4,539,855	*55,798*	*21,788*	*11,081*	*3,269*	*22,929*	2,774
	States and Agencies.	**2,276,501**	**33,291,328**	**85,481**	**8,812,179**	**356,358**	**122,518**	**40,665**	**3,360**	**193,175**	**42,695**
15	Assam State (Manipur)	2	268,710	38	306	*98*	*38*	*2*	..	*58*	1
16	Baluchistan States	40,896	241,957	164	5,483	*1,563*	*474*	..	*32*	*1,089*	..
17	Baroda State	25,681	944,994	211	318,479	*2,536*	*942*	*332*	*67*	*1,262*	..
18	Bengal States	12,386	706,492	1,059	11,562	*348*	*247*	*19*	*13*	*82*	65
19	Bihar and Orissa States	35,085	2,226,017	3,727	790,839	*1,954*	*695*	*470*	*166*	*789*	12
20	Bombay States	303,062	2,848,522	2,883	1,511,495	*9,527*	*3,156*	*876*	*114*	*5,496*	59
21	Central India Agency	123,516	4,038,048	11,024	1,488,408	*14,290*	*5,466*	*2,935*	*328*	*5,889*	150
22	Central Provinces States	7,494	1,326,239	776	386,778	*6,978*	*1,925*	*2,492*	*275*	*2,561*	5
23	Hyderabad State	731,803	4,064,950	34,540	2,788,212	*22,804*	*8,137*	*5,349*	*808*	*9,318*	..
24	Kashmir State	32,470	2,400,806	1,434	40,281	*4,407*	*1,600*	*606*	*48*	*2,201*	..
25	Madras States	121,491	1,842,177	3,887	420,866	*230,746*	*74,081*	*17,480*	*129*	*139,185*	17,602
26	Mysore State	171,549	3,811,562	67	177,372	*45,545*	*18,084*	*8,364*	*491*	*19,097*	24,805
27	N.-W. F. Province (*Agencies and Tribal areas*).	357	4,087	4	..	*5*	*5*	..	..	..	..
28	Punjab States	85,313	2,572,556	996	190,945	*6,728*	*3,392*	*1,051*	*25*	*2,285*	87
29	Rajputana Agency	580,907	5,302,327	23,753	664,970	*8,127*	*3,929*	*575*	*248*	*3,623*	4
30	Sikkim State	224	82,767	26	..	*22*	*16*	*1*	..	*5*	..
31	United Provinces States	4,265	609,117	892	12,188	*680*	*332*	*113*	*25*	*235*	15

Part A—General Table, (*ii*) Provincial Distribution—*continued*.

PRODUCTS.	CLASS A : SUB-CLASS I.—EXPLOITATION OF THE SURFACE OF THE EARTH.												
	SUB-ORDER 1 (c).—FORESTRY.							SUB-ORDER 1 (d).—RAISING OF FARM STOCK.					
	TOTAL OF SUB-ORDER 1 (c).							TOTAL OF SUB-ORDER 1 (d).					
		Actual Workers.							Actual Workers.				
		Total.							Total.				
Group 6.—Fruit, flower, vegetable, betel, vine, areca-nut, etc., growers.	Total Workers and Dependants.	Males.	Females.	Partially Agriculturist.	Dependants.	Group 7.—Forest officers, rangers, guards, etc.	Group 8.—Wood-cutters, fire-wood, lac, catechu, rubber, etc., collectors and charcoal burners.	Total Workers and Dependants.	Males.	Females.	Partially Agriculturist.	Dependants.	Serial Number.
37	38	39	40	41	42	43	44	45	46	47	48	49	
972,078	**672,093**	**217,474**	**159,831**	**37,632**	**294,788**	**89,127**	**582,966**	**5,176,104**	**2,984,467**	**606,224**	**168,388**	**1,585,413**	
656,415	**478,362**	**155,852**	**111,129**	**29,496**	**211,381**	**67,277**	**411,085**	**3,433,495**	**2,187,339**	**386,625**	**110,154**	**859,531**	
891	*1,131*	*422*	*231*	*99*	*478*	152	979	*4,975*	*2,712*	*459*	*211*	*1,804*	1
7,905	*31*	*11*	..	..	*20*	31	..	*16*	*10*	..	..	*6*	2
27,336	*3,857*	*2,107*	*190*	*250*	*1,560*	1,323	2,534	*46,231*	*34,460*	*2,748*	*1,840*	*9,023*	3
747	*779*	*303*	..	*178*	*476*	87	692	*41,194*	*13,766*	*78*	*2,439*	*27,350*	4
93,866	*29,969*	*12,262*	*4,722*	*1,154*	*12,985*	1,897	28,072	*304,518*	*260,235*	*11,288*	*3,318*	*32,995*	5
22,156	*48,283*	*14,260*	*14,582*	*2,744*	*19,141*	4.130	44,153	*559,637*	*329,267*	*119,560*	*19,323*	*110,810*	6
40,110	*104,406*	*30,356*	*27,559*	*10,362*	*46,191*	9,814	94,592	*416,217*	*263,434*	*27,827*	*5,012*	*124,956*	7
232,294	*42,765*	*12,507*	*10,599*	*1,097*	*19,659*	5,116	37,649	*105,944*	*50,884*	*19,109*	*3,630*	*35,951*	8
45,367	*72,304*	*18,628*	*27,544*	*6,610*	*26,132*	12,492	59,812	*344,790*	*195,989*	*38,806*	*8,902*	*109,995*	9
230	*1,108*	*420*	*247*	*55*	*441*	228	880	*667*	*430*	*121*	*15*	*116*	10
118,281	*69,997*	*22,268*	*9,651*	*2,631*	*38,078*	19,237	50,760	*496,472*	*300,426*	*49,388*	*22,108*	*146,658*	11
2,728	*2,297*	*840*	*22*	*11*	*1,435*	605	1,692	*14,070*	*6,553*	*179*	*95*	*7,338*	12
13,480	*42,998*	*18,380*	*2,139*	*1,630*	*22,479*	4,506	38,492	*325,865*	*213,167*	*5,744*	*6,828*	*106,954*	13
53,024	*58,437*	*23,088*	*13,043*	*2,675*	*22,306*	7,659	50,778	*772,899*	*516,006*	*111,318*	*33,433*	*145,575*	14
313,663	**193,731**	**61,622**	**48,702**	**7,536**	**83,407**	**21,910**	**171,821**	**1,742,609**	**797,128**	**219,599**	**58,234**	**725,882**	
97	*242*	*23*	*137*	..	*82*	13	229	*1,047*	*407*	*19*	*1*	*621*	15
1,563	*2,258*	*731*	..	*22*	*1,527*	15	2,243	*51,839*	*18,006*	..	*3,334*	*33,833*	16
2,536	*810*	*384*	*24*	*17*	*402*	529	281	*42,239*	*14,067*	*4,135*	*669*	*24,037*	17
283	*296*	*135*	*2*	*53*	*159*	63	233	*1,116*	*922*	*12*	*16*	*182*	18
1,942	*6,639*	*2,108*	*1,435*	*256*	*3,096*	1,393	5,246	*109,148*	*61,004*	*12,597*	*2,665*	*35,547*	19
9,468	*37,192*	*10,156*	*11,890*	*929*	*15,146*	1,976	35,216	*256,339*	*115,432*	*17,101*	*2,298*	*123,806*	20
14,140	*40,139*	*15,646*	*10,904*	*523*	*13,589*	2,851	37,288	*221,276*	*113,231*	*34,263*	*9,494*	*73,782*	21
6,973	*9,158*	*2,451*	*2,930*	*226*	*3,777*	1,456	7,702	*87,744*	*38,580*	*13,919*	*1,679*	*35,245*	22
22,804	*41,774*	*12,248*	*7,285*	*2,536*	*22,241*	869	40,906	*597,728*	*240,754*	*105,916*	*22,295*	*251,058*	23
4,407	*3,085*	*1,328*	*172*	*69*	*1,585*	2,140	945	*32,284*	*14,944*	*3,607*	*1,074*	*13,733*	24
213,144	*12,529*	*3,629*	*2,066*	*271*	*6,834*	2,605	9,924	*14,761*	*7,358*	*1,325*	*1,625*	*6,078*	25
20,850	*9,078*	*2,516*	*1,543*	*208*	*5,019*	4,211	4,867	*27,754*	*17,056*	*3,615*	*280*	*7,083*	26
5	..	..	..	..	..	..	..	*2*	..	..	..	*2*	27
6,641	*3,083*	*1,624*	*162*	*86*	*1,297*	982	2,101	*80,90[illegible]*	*45,970*	*4,193*	*884*	*30,738*	28
8,123	*27,111*	*8,480*	*10,109*	*2,317*	*8,522*	2,686	24,425	*211,740*	*103,756*	*18,619*	*11,818*	*89,365*	29
22	*65*	*34*	*18*	..	*13*	12	58	*598*	*440*	*122*	..	*36*	30
665	*272*	*129*	*25*	*23*	*118*	109	163	*6,093*	*5,201*	*156*	*102*	*736*	31

TABLE XV.—Occupation or Means of Livelihood.

Serial Number.	Province, State or Agency.	CLASS A: SUB-CLASS I.—EXPLOITATION OF THE SURFACE OF THE EARTH. SUB-ORDER 1 (d)—RAISING OF FARM STOCK—contd. Group 9.—Cattle and buffalo breeders and keepers.	Group 10.—Sheep, goat and pig breeders.	Group 12.—Herdsmen, shepherds, goat-herds, etc.	SUB-ORDER 1 (e)—RAISING OF SMALL ANIMALS. TOTAL OF SUB-ORDER 1 (e). [Group 13—Birds, Bees, Silk worms, etc.] Total Workers and Dependants.	Actual Workers. Total. Males.	Females.	Partially Agriculturist.	Dependants.
	1	50	51	52	53	54	55	56	57
	INDIA.	**704,556**	**465,596**	**3,965,997**	**48,063**	**10,960**	**14,944**	**2,539**	**22,159**
	Provinces.	**428,257**	**205,037**	**2,785,626**	**46,244**	**10,268**	**14,871**	**2,462**	**21,105**
1	Ajmer-Merwara	628	632	3,714	..	..	..	..	..
2	Andamans and Nicobars	..	..	16	..	..	..	..	..
3	Assam	18,018	96	28,114	*127*	*34*	*35*	..	*58*
4	Baluchistan	416	33,464	2,616	..	..	..	..	..
5	Bengal	40,662	1,936	261,794	*42,655*	*8,995*	*14,058*	*2,362*	*19,602*
6	Bihar and Orissa	165,685	2,198	391,427	*492*	*182*	*33*	*22*	*277*
7	Bombay	60,245	28,077	324,585	*184*	*68*	*7*	*1*	*109*
8	Burma	2,645	12,232	91,032	*1,459*	*365*	*522*	*36*	*572*
9	C. P. and Berar	30,790	3,174	310,471	*109*	*26*	*28*	..	*55*
10	Coorg	245	2	420	..	..	..	..	..
11	Madras	74,501	101,649	317,649	*327*	*111*	*46*	*26*	*170*
12	N.-W. F. Province (*Districts and Administered Territories*).	179	364	13,511	*18*	*3*	..	..	*15*
13	Punjab	18,188	4,251	301,526	*19*	*6*	..	..	*13*
14	United Provinces	16,055	16,962	738,751	*854*	*479*	*139*	*15*	*236*
	States and Agencies.	**276,299**	**260,559**	**1,180,371**	**1,819**	**692**	**73**	**77**	**1,054**
15	Assam State (Manipur)	801	..	240	*8*	..	*6*	..	*2*
16	Baluchistan States	1,670	45,623	2,796	..	..	..	..	..
17	Baroda State	25,330	9,740	5,633	*11*	*5*	..	*1*	*6*
18	Bengal States	262	187	654	*4*	*3*	..	..	*1*
19	Bihar and Orissa States	48,998	312	59,795	*71*	*23*	*4*	*2*	*44*
20	Bombay States	23,418	37,800	194,404	*63*	*15*	*1*	..	*47*
21	Central India Agency	17,745	3,366	182,763	*89*	*36*	*8*	*2*	*45*
22	Central Provinces States	2,999	137	84,582	*6*	*2*	*1*	..	*3*
23	Hyderabad State	42,418	109,739	445,158	*18*	*11*	..	*6*	*7*
24	Kashmir State	23,785	736	7,763	*752*	*407*	*5*	*52*	*340*
25	Madras States	1,220	1,547	11,841	*174*	*14*	..	..	*160*
26	Mysore State	875	1,061	25,575	*508*	*170*	*26*	*9*	*312*
27	N.-W. F. Province (*Agencies and Tribal areas*).	..	..	2	..	..	..	..	..
28	Punjab States	21,256	2,077	57,372	*3*	*3*	..	..	..
29	Rajputana Agency	65,133	48,198	95,524	*26*	*2*	*13*	*5*	*11*
30	Sikkim State	369	..	229	*1*	*1*	..	..	..
31	United Provinces States	20	16	6,040	*85*	..	*9*	..	*76*

PART A.—GENERAL TABLE, (ii) PROVINCIAL DISTRIBUTION—*continued.*

CLASS A: SUB-CLASS I.—EXPLOITATION OF THE SURFACE OF THE EARTH. ORDER 2.—FISHING AND HUNTING.							CLASS A: SUB-CLASS II.—EXTRACTION OF MINERALS.					
TOTAL OF ORDER 2.					Group 14.—Fishing.	Group 15.—Hunting.	TOTAL OF SUB-CLASS II.					
Total Workers and Dependants.	Actual Workers. Total. Males.	Actual Workers. Total. Females.	Actual Workers. Partially Agriculturist.	Dependants.			Total Workers and Dependants.	Actual Workers. Total. Males.	Actual Workers. Total. Females.	Actual Workers. Partially Agriculturist.	Dependants.	Serial Number.
58	59	60	61	62	63	64	65	66	67	68	69	
1,854,583	659,400	205,653	100,229	989,530	1,783,672	70,911	529,609	210,555	97,894	22,023	221,160	
1,593,458	550,052	187,522	87,796	855,884	1,558,881	34,577	418,777	165,989	86,963	19,825	165,825	
38	13	..	3	25	3	35	*695*	298	63	13	334	1
31	13	..	..	18	31	..	..	..	..	..	..	2
100,555	42,656	1,738	12,432	56,161	99,951	604	*5,786*	3,434	936	90	1,416	3
4	3	..	..	1	2	2	*1,408*	1,152	7	352	249	4
642,647	211,124	66,713	23,509	364,810	640,022	2,625	*115,877*	40,334	25,164	1,890	50,379	5
126,905	44,858	24,351	12,741	57,696	118,030	8,875	*159,741*	66,809	43,890	14,129	49,042	6
154,064	48,942	22,822	4,940	82,300	150,826	3,238	*32,006*	12,387	2,468	852	17,151	7
152,004	48,730	27,677	3,274	75,597	151,601	403	*15,293*	6,416	2,372	139	6,505	8
126,229	49,310	20,841	20,417	56,078	120,781	5,448	*29,757*	11,890	7,592	492	10,275	9
79	25	7	..	47	4	75	*23*	20	1	..	2	10
238,823	85,369	16,427	7,392	137,027	234,001	4,822	*16,769*	5,729	2,042	702	8,998	11
489	176	..	..	313	423	66	*985*	123	1	2	161	12
8,456	3,438	149	245	4,869	6,763	1,693	*32,330*	13,950	1,263	453	17,117	13
43,134	15,395	6,797	2,845	20,942	36,443	6,691	*8,807*	3,447	1,164	711	4,196	14
261,125	109,348	18,131	12,431	133,646	224,791	36,334	110,832	44,566	10,931	2,198	55,335	
151	46	5	..	100	151	..	*737*	204	238	1	295	15
5,550	1,619	..	85	3,931	5,502	48	*266*	77	..	..	189	16
2,795	795	445	6	1,555	2,783	12	*125*	41	3	..	81	17
3,848	1,625	431	235	1,792	3,832	16	..	..	..	..	..	18
16,336	5,771	2,585	785	7,980	15,580	756	*4,155*	1,594	1,733	43	828	19
12,532	4,110	1,588	253	6,834	11,522	1,010	*9,351*	3,602	578	56	5,171	20
12,571	5,741	1,240	744	5,590	10,687	1,884	*4,067*	1,384	454	53	2,229	21
7,140	2,444	1,371	345	3,325	6,463	677	*218*	59	30	25	79	22
107,889	51,427	6,286	9,301	50,176	78,269	29,620	*18,474*	9,734	2,780	137	5,960	23
4,190	1,471	323	104	2,396	3,326	864	*33*	9	1	..	23	24
79,482	30,960	3,565	132	44,957	79,318	164	*3,306*	1,319	490	1	1,497	25
2,209	751	112	85	1,346	1,993	216	*52,987*	19,888	1,259	1,241	31,840	26
..	..	..	..	..	..	..	..	..	..	..	..	27
3,843	1,506	47	80	2,290	3,399	441	*3,802*	1,510	146	41	2,146	28
668	337	20	66	311	78	590	*13,310*	5,144	3,169	600	4,997	29
..	..	..	..	..	..	..	..	..	..	..	..	30
1,921	745	113	210	1,063	1,888	33	*1*	1	..	..	..	31

TABLE XV.—Occupation or Means of Livelihood.

Serial Number.	Province, State or Agency.	Class A: *Sub-Class II.—Extraction of Minerals.* Order 3.—Mines. *Total of Order 3.* Total Workers and Dependants.	Actual Workers. Total. Males.	Actual Workers. Total. Females.	Actual Workers. Partially Agriculturist.	Dependants.	Group 16.—Coal mines and petroleum wells.	Group 17.—Mines and metallic minerals (gold, iron, manganese, etc).
	1	70	71	72	73	74	75	76
	INDIA.	**375,927**	**153,785**	**74,139**	**15,108**	**148,003**	**277,426**	**98,501**
	Provinces.	**298,764**	**122,107**	**68,000**	**13,883**	**108,657**	**262,746**	**36,018**
1	Ajmer-Merwara	..	..	..	..	..	..	..
2	Andamans and Nicobars	..	..	..	..	..	..	..
3	Assam	5,097	3,039	902	84	1,156	5,096	1
4	Baluchistan	1,400	1,149	7	350	244	1,395	5
5	Bengal	114,714	39,499	25,013	1,885	50,202	114,693	21
6	Bihar and Orissa	127,098	57,181	33,059	10,684	36,858	127,011	87
7	Bombay	2,740	1,748	280	40	712	1,281	1,459
8	Burma	8,173	4,682	639	31	2,852	3,319	4,854
9	C. P. and Berar	27,237	10,863	7,139	411	9,235	6,105	21,132
10	Coorg	..	..	..	..	..	..	..
11	Madras	8,515	2,655	817	311	5,043	276	8,239
12	N.-W. F. Province (*Districts and Administe ed Territories*).	45	7	..	..	38	5	40
13	Punjab	3,591	1,241	129	79	2,221	3,484	107
14	United Provinces	154	48	15	8	96	81	73
	States and Agencies.	**77,163**	**31,678**	**6,139**	**1,225**	**39,346**	**14,680**	**62,483**
15	Assam State (Manipur)	25	21	1	..	3	..	25
16	Baluchistan States	..	..	..	..	..	..	..
17	Baroda State	125	41	3	..	81	..	125
18	Bengal States	..	..	..	..	..	..	..
19	Bihar and Orissa States	3,997	1,540	1,685	35	772	21	3,976
20	Bombay States	292	57	33	1	202	120	172
21	Central India Agency	3,039	1,104	375	10	1,560	2,411	628
22	Central Provinces States	186	47	66	25	73	12	174
23	Hyderabad State	15,325	8,224	2,328	..	4,773	11,872	3,453
24	Kashmir State	33	9	1	..	23	..	33
25	Madras States	2,837	1,148	457	1	1,232	..	2,837
26	Mysore State	50,823	19,312	1,163	1,120	30,348	3	50,820
27	N.-W. F. Province (*Agencies and Tribal areas*).	..	..	..	..	..	..	..
28	Punjab States	124	34	18	3	72	5	119
29	Rajputana Agency	357	141	9	30	207	236	121
30	Sikkim State	..	..	..	..	..	..	..
31	United Provinces States	..	..	..	..	..	..	..

PART A.—GENERAL TABLE, (ii) PROVINCIAL DISTRIBUTION—*continued*.

CLASS A: *SUB-CLASS II.—EXTRACTION OF MINERALS.*										CLASS B: *PREPARATION AND SUPPLY OF MATERIAL SUBSTANCES.*					
ORDER 4.—QUARRIES OF HARD ROCKS.					ORDER 5.—SALT, ETC.										
TOTAL OF ORDER 4. [Group 18.—Other minerals (jade, diamonds, limestone, etc.)]					*TOTAL OF ORDER 5.*					*TOTAL OF CLASS B.*					
Total Workers and Dependants.	Actual Workers.			Dependants.	Total Workers and Dependants.	Actual Workers.			Dependants.	Total Workers and Dependants.	Actual Workers.			Dependants.	Serial Number.
	Total.		Partially Agriculturist.			Total.		Partially Agriculturist.			Total.		Partially Agriculturist.		
	Males.	Females.				Males.	Females.				Males.	Females.			
77	78	79	80	81	82	83	84	85	86	87	88	89	90	91	
75,424	**29,972**	**8,209**	**1,722**	**37,243**	**78,258**	**26,796**	**15,546**	**5,192**	**35,914**	**58,191,121**	**19,124,551**	**8,886,967**	**2,479,309**	**30,179,603**	
58,897	**23,339**	**6,110**	**1,277**	**29,448**	**61,116**	**20,543**	**12,853**	**4,665**	**27,720**	**44,537,228**	**14,632,006**	**6,757,573**	**1,887,072**	**23,147,649**	
691	298	59	13	334	4	..	4	..	..	161,795	61,033	19,606	8,189	81,156	1
..	..	..	..	..	..	..	..	..	..	939	509	17	11	413	2
680	395	27	6	258	9	..	7	..	2	474,581	176,912	66,341	31,725	231,328	3
..	..	..	..	..	8	3	..	2	5	49,609	23,471	522	2,862	25,616	4
885	592	147	2	146	278	243	4	3	31	6,672,775	2,336,914	789,615	250,092	3,546,246	5
3,658	1,335	1,127	38	1,196	28,985	8,293	9,704	3,407	10,988	4,310,571	1,282,464	1,044,629	229,668	1,983,478	6
24,197	8,525	1,809	469	13,863	5,069	2,114	379	343	2,576	4,306,098	1,550,897	457,372	103,069	2,297,829	7
3,896	781	1,267	50	1,848	3,224	953	466	58	1,805	2,403,804	746,832	632,683	65,800	1,024,289	8
1,883	839	216	67	828	637	188	237	14	212	2,210,067	772,863	409,849	147,892	1,027,355	9
23	20	1	..	2	..	..	..	..	..	21,792	10,972	2,833	585	7,987	10
5,505	2,306	943	264	2,256	2,749	768	282	127	1,609	8,849,524	2,743,805	1,355,637	423,351	4,750,082	11
..	..	..	..	..	240	116	1	2	123	442,625	141,516	9,778	4,017	291,331	12
14,576	7,050	383	214	7,143	14,163	5,659	751	160	7,753	6,328,536	2,063,535	440,703	172,485	3,824,298	13
2,903	1,198	131	154	1,574	5,750	2,206	1,018	549	2,526	8,304,512	2,720,283	1,527,988	447,326	4,056,241	14
16,527	**6,683**	**2,049**	**446**	**7,795**	**17,142**	**6,255**	**2,693**	**527**	**8,194**	**13,653,893**	**4,492,545**	**2,129,394**	**592,237**	**7,031,954**	
..	..	..	..	..	712	183	237	1	292	63,201	4,255	44,002	1,206	14,944	15
..	..	..	..	..	266	77	..	..	189	45,643	15,481	365	1,800	29,797	16
..	..	..	..	..	..	..	..	..	..	396,588	131,350	40,927	11,489	224,311	17
..	..	..	..	..	..	..	..	..	..	51,761	25,093	8,474	2,012	18,184	18
158	54	48	8	56	..	..	..	..	..	497,089	135,768	148,328	34,527	212,993	19
5,922	2,380	353	27	3,189	3,137	1,165	192	28	1,780	1,582,437	474,773	145,848	30,056	961,816	20
110	25	1	..	84	918	255	78	48	585	1,711,417	616,879	271,787	97,861	822,751	21
9	5	..	..	4	23	7	14	..	2	217,099	67,128	55,293	8,068	94,678	22
3,149	1,510	452	137	1,187	..	..	..	..	..	3,141,052	1,084,932	567,598	140,152	1,488,522	23
..	..	..	..	..	..	..	..	..	..	433,421	147,018	51,173	14,486	235,230	24
31	21	..	..	10	438	150	33	..	255	1,322,684	372,815	255,608	15,363	694,261	25
28	7	13	..	8	2,136	569	83	121	1,484	710,332	199,228	54,416	27,012	456,688	26
..	..	..	..	..	..	..	..	..	..	1,947	1,250	19	27	678	27
1,543	678	86	16	779	2,135	798	42	22	1,295	871,433	303,322	51,891	25,900	516,220	28
5,576	1,952	1,146	256	2,478	7,377	3,051	2,014	312	2,312	2,486,020	875,663	416,223	173,724	1,194,134	29
..	..	..	..	..	..	..	..	..	..	1,952	1,180	297	3	475	30
1	1	..	..	..	..	..	..	..	..	119,877	36,410	17,145	8,551	66,322	31

TABLE XV.—Occupation or Means of Livelihood.

CLASS B: *SUB-CLASS III.—INDUSTRY.*

Serial Number.	Province, State or Agency.	*TOTAL OF SUB-CLASS III.* Total Workers and Dependants.	Actual Workers. Total. Males.	Actual Workers. Total. Females.	Actual Workers. Partially Agriculturist.	Dependants.	ORDER 6.—TEXTILES. *TOTAL OF ORDER 6.* Total Workers and Dependants.	Actual Workers. Total. Males.	Actual Workers. Total. Females.	Actual Workers. Partially Agriculturist.	Dependants.
	1	92	93	94	95	96	97	98	99	100	101
	INDIA.	35,323,041	11,503,467	6,011,763	1,701,343	17,807,811	8,306,501	2,685,256	1,764,193	326,622	3,857,052
	Provinces.	26,791,864	8,661,737	4,566,846	1,277,366	13,563,281	6,196,671	2,048,614	1,213,381	237,290	2,934,676
1	Ajmer-Merwara	*84,701*	31,673	16,024	5,766	37,004	19,216	6,983	5,760	988	6,523
2	Andamans and Nicobars	*406*	229	2	4	175	128	107	..	..	21
3	Assam	*168,193*	54,208	35,983	13,026	78,002	15,673	2,371	8,668	977	4,634
4	Baluchistan	*18,185*	8,845	469	895	8,871	880	341	2	87	537
5	Bengal	*3,491,642*	1,124,451	539,786	119,689	1,757,405	868,411	346,653	106,537	26,872	415,221
6	Bihar and Orissa	*2,458,873*	721,415	626,892	149,653	1,110,566	361,333	109,604	80,999	24,934	170,730
7	Bombay	*2,466,375*	867,865	334,904	70,068	1,263,606	808,802	304,411	154,986	15,565	349,405
8	Burma	*806,431*	249,433	220,310	22,521	336,688	155,050	9,123	103,316	5,997	42,611
9	C. P. and Berar	*1,455,206*	503,476	295,524	116,099	656,206	390,379	133,797	102,586	30,247	153,996
10	Coorg	*11,592*	5,349	1,824	323	4,419	279	99	64	6	116
11	Madras	*5,553,170*	1,788,685	894,181	300,073	2,870,304	1,401,842	455,368	291,063	64,460	655,411
12	N.-W. F. Province (*Districts and Administered Territories*).	*252,733*	78,649	8,134	2,196	165,949	47,923	13,920	2,568	362	31,435
13	Punjab	*4,335,153*	1,373,652	395,936	124,428	2,565,565	978,442	295,026	122,340	24,828	561,076
14	United Provinces	*5,759,205*	1,853,807	1,196,877	352,625	2,708,521	1,148,313	370,861	234,492	41,966	542,960
	States and Agencies.	8,531,177	2,841,730	1,444,917	423,977	4,244,530	2,109,830	636,642	550,812	89,332	922,376
15	Assam State (Manipur)	*48,431*	1,810	36,961	1,054	9,660	43,746	543	36,068	956	7,135
16	Baluchistan States	*19,048*	6,229	364	703	12,455	1,652	564	26	39	1,062
17	Baroda State	*250,050*	85,547	31,013	8,106	133,490	52,433	16,351	9,477	2,385	26,605
18	Bengal States	*19,008*	6,751	4,594	749	7,663	1,605	604	530	89	471
19	Bihar and Orissa States	*337,569*	91,219	97,183	25,064	149,167	119,079	34,004	29,359	9,716	55,716
20	Bombay States	*935,150*	289,148	109,130	23,500	536,872	224,667	68,832	40,432	4,118	115,403
21	Central India Agency	*1,145,073*	416,117	187,117	70,677	541,839	168,024	56,378	40,065	7,733	71,586
22	Central Provinces States	*158,607*	47,699	42,252	6,487	68,656	53,351	16,491	14,503	2,082	22,357
23	Hyderabad State	*1,872,733*	676,082	318,086	85,065	878,565	517,750	174,159	106,746	18,058	236,845
24	Kashmir State	*280,397*	92,262	40,771	10,140	147,364	95,619	26,306	29,444	2,354	39,869
25	Madras States	*818,349*	228,021	169,940	9,280	420,388	211,813	50,052	86,732	909	75,029
26	Mysore State	*443,132*	126,543	28,469	19,326	288,120	101,407	29,461	6,094	3,419	66,852
27	N.-W. F. Province (*Agencies and Tribal areas*).	*823*	579	19	17	227	6	2	..	..	4
28	Punjab States	*580,144*	196,000	45,175	17,574	338,969	110,039	35,637	11,103	2,963	63,299
29	Rajputana Agency	*1,547,057*	554,508	322,460	140,070	669,789	390,522	121,730	138,064	32,898	130,728
30	Sikkim State	*425*	227	88	..	110	71	26	22	..	23
31	United Provinces States	*75,179*	22,688	11,295	6,165	41,196	18,046	5,507	3,147	1,618	9,392

PART A.—GENERAL TABLE, (ii) PROVINCIAL DISTRIBUTION—*continued.*

CLASS B : *SUB-CLASS III.—INDUSTRY.* ORDER 6.—TEXTILES—*contd.*									
Group 21.—Cotton ginning, cleaning and pressing.	Group 22.—Cotton spinning, sizing and weaving.	Group 23.—Jute spinning, pressing and weaving.	Group 24.—Rope, twine and string.	Group 25.—Other fibres (cocoanut, aloes, flax, hemp, straw, etc.).	Group 26.—Wool carders and spinners, weavers of woollen blankets, carpets, etc.	Group 27.—Silk spinners and weavers.	Group 30.—Dyeing, bleaching, printing, preparation and sponging of textiles.	Group 31.—Other (lace, crape, embroideries, fringes, etc.), and insufficiently described textile industries.	Serial Number.
102	103	104	105	106	107	108	109	110	
583,637	**5,866,468**	**362,369**	**377,203**	**121,456**	**319,636**	**257,249**	**232,731**	**135,920**	
362,033	**4,583,878**	**359,896**	**216,086**	**64,133**	**160,261**	**236,635**	**128,439**	**78,789**	
7,979	9,138	11	343	..	385	..	1,296	64	1
..	..	..	..	128	..	..	..	..	2
45	13,185	196	1,082	..	10	1,131	18	6	3
22	6	..	19	..	794	..	22	17	4
904	458,762	327,130	26,182	1,341	2,297	48,783	922	1,764	5
16,052	277,236	17,233	12,381	207	15,639	6,863	12,523	2,968	6
29,832	614,518	356	50,311	8,442	34,536	38,594	17,676	13,010	7
2,282	132,737	..	1,241	15	46	18,621	62	46	8
47,110	299,635	1,953	3,440	1,296	13,162	18,159	3,899	1,547	9
.	261	..	..	.1	16	1	..	..	10
59,119	1,114,890	5,564	74,124	13,025	37,152	74,764	17,024	3,873	11
3,431	34,598	..	253	569	485	373	7,586	628	12
81,769	789,616	1,320	4,902	30,907	15,632	13,302	17,591	22,843	13
113,488	839,296	6,133	41,808	8,202	40,107	16,044	49,820	32,023	14
161,604	**1,282,590**	**2,473**	**161,117**	**57,325**	**159,375**	**20,614**	**104,292**	**57,131**	
1	43,110	..	3	..	..	586	26	20	15
..	1,197	..	27	..	319	6	..	103	16
10,635	33,802	46	491	323	92	1,191	3,966	1,887	17
..	1,141	445	10	..	..	..	8	1	18
363	116,061	19	416	..	12	1,575	9	368	19
11,873	172,184	168	9,755	808	8,029	5,543	14,500	1,531	20
26,587	106,726	265	1,541	387	11,198	551	17,746	2,758	21
151	50,905	176	236	49	1,016	744	24	3	22
69,948	302,745	1,098	28,954	10	89,095	1,901	22,310	1,413	23
180	61,184	..	194	22	23,677	5,724	2,375	2,263	24
619	45,476	..	111,604	53,149	263	9	158	293	25
163	33,673	118	1,370	258	18,399	2,478	126	44,751	26
1	1	..	..	..	..	..	4	..	27
7,974	98,540	129	3,447	1,316	1,391	282	1,195	732	28
30,732	306,939	6	2,710	960	5,653	24	41,076	579	29
..	69	..	..	..	..	..	..	2	30
2,377	13,837	3	359	43	231	..	769	427	31

TABLE XV.—Occupation or Means of Livelihood.

Serial Number.	Province, State or Agency.	CLASS B: SUB-CLASS XII.—INDUSTRY. ORDER 7.—HIDES, SKINS AND HARD MATERIALS FROM THE ANIMAL KINGDOM. TOTAL OF ORDER 7. Total Workers and Dependants.	Actual Workers. Total. Males.	Actual Workers. Total. Females.	Actual Workers. Partially Agriculturist.	Dependants.	Group 32.—Tanners, curriers, leather dressers and dyers, etc.	Group 33.—Makers of leather articles, such as trunks, water-bags, etc.
	1	111	112	113	114	115	116	117
	INDIA.	**666,741**	**252,445**	**42,349**	**38,646**	**403,947**	**474,732**	**204,786**
	Provinces.	**473,041**	**166,301**	**23,353**	**20,421**	**283,387**	**324,916**	**141,680**
1	Ajmer-Merwara	5,150	2,139	339	777	2,672	1,307	3,835
2	Andamans and Nicobars	..	..	..	..	..	..	..
3	Assam	1,410	743	40	115	627	1,223	61
4	Baluchistan	31	17	..	..	14	14	1
5	Bengal	53,561	20,274	1,012	1,816	32,275	37,649	6,536
6	Bihar and Orissa	7,973	3,015	693	544	4,265	5,600	1,646
7	Bombay	45,782	14,650	3,857	2,591	27,275	38,206	7,022
8	Burma	624	232	59	2	333	161	207
9	C. P. and Berar	12,990	4,732	1,706	1,251	6,552	8,643	4,155
10	Coorg	1	..	1	..	..	1	..
11	Madras	132,075	46,532	4,414	3,895	81,129	32,267	99,216
12	N.-W. F. Province (*Districts and Administered Territories*)	4,304	1,135	44	21	3,125	1,774	[illegible],472
13	Punjab	78,373	24,375	2,113	1,300	51,885	66,483	11,725
14	United Provinces	130,767	48,437	9,075	8,109	73,235	121,588	4,804
	States and Agencies.	**225,700**	**86,144**	**18,996**	**18,225**	**120,560**	**150,816**	**63,106**
15	Assam State (Manipur)	22	[illegible]	1	..	12	..	22
16	Baluchistan States	176	54	..	..	122	21	155
17	Baroda State	6,032	5,760	1,105	737	9,167	14,967	1,035
18	Bengal States	556	348	3	32	205	554	..
19	Bihar and Orissa States	228	103	11	8	114	218	..
20	Bombay States	55,118	17,836	4,175	1,966	33,058	51,424	3,187
21	Central India Agency	23,670	11,171	1,369	1,412	11,130	11,036	12,630
22	Central Provinces States	797	255	108	45	434	329	468
23	Hyderabad State	15,930	6,634	1,921	374	7,375	7,061	7,946
24	Kashmir State	620	238	22	24	360	620	..
25	Madras States	1,485	550	52	29	883	128	1,270
26	Mysore State	4,055	992	196	103	2,868	1,066	2,945
27	N.-W. F. Province (*Agencies and Tribal areas*).	..	..	..	..	..	..	..
28	Punjab States	11,204	4,141	209	261	6,854	10,801	369
29	Rajputana Agency	94,932	37,735	9,802	13,159	47,395	60,818	32,977
30	Sikkim State	..	..	..	..	..	..	..
31	United Provinces States	875	269	23	75	583	773	102

PART A.—GENERAL TABLE, (ii) PROVINCIAL DISTRIBUTION—*continued.*

CLASS B : SUB-CLASS III.—INDUSTRY.													
ORDER 8.—WOOD.							ORDER 9.—METALS.						Serial Number.
TOTAL OF ORDER 8.					Group 36.—Sawyers, carpenters, turners and joiners, etc.	Group 37.—Basket makers and other industries of woody materials, including leaves.	TOTAL OF ORDER 9.						
Total Workers and Dependants.	Actual Workers. Total. Males.	Actual Workers. Total. Females.	Partially Agriculturist.	Dependants.			Total Workers and Dependants.	Actual Workers. Total. Males.	Actual Workers. Total. Females.	Partially Agriculturist.	Dependants.		
118	119	120	121	122	123	124	125	126	127	128	129		
3,799,892	**1,297,527**	**433,393**	**198,911**	**2,068,972**	**2,525,139**	**1,274,753**	**1,861,445**	**657,938**	**79,369**	**101,796**	**1,124,138**		
2,893,498	**982,681**	**323,976**	**146,330**	**1,586,841**	**1,936,189**	**957,309**	**1,378,833**	**491,896**	**43,429**	**78,400**	**843,508**		
4,998	2,210	322	742	2,466	4,140	858	4,171	1,555	329	249	2,287	1	
43	17	..	1	26	43	..	14	4	..	..	10	2	
32,893	11,687	7,532	2,807	13,674	19,287	13,606	12,755	4,783	97	1,337	7,875	3	
1,621	689	.	117	932	1,365	256	3,304	1,400	..	179	1,904	4	
366,954	123,407	44,189	13,424	199,358	227,803	139,151	184,210	68,978	1,614	7,298	113,618	5	
261,905	81,729	53,809	14,112	126,367	118,310	143,595	169,390	58,283	9,269	9,284	101,838	6	
284,648	98,129	25,784	10,953	160,735	208,672	75,976	121,833	43,518	3,289	3,292	75,026	7	
191,686	68,469	26,958	5,283	96,259	143,719	47,967	34,912	14,036	2,151	597	18,725	8	
178,729	64,046	31,340	13,654	83,343	94,773	83,956	113,264	41,030	10,277	8,471	61,957	9	
2,274	1,208	437	106	629	1,042	1,232	625	304	16	17	305	10	
633,116	198,036	82,480	29,486	352,600	411,603	221,513	216,373	73,987	7,102	9,482	135,284	11	
29,945	9,303	610	365	20,032	27,788	2,157	25,007	7,799	24	356	17,184	12	
425,701	146,990	9,434	17,568	269,277	332,258	93,443	208,948	70,013	893	8,838	138,042	13	
478,985	176,761	41,081	39,712	261,143	345,386	133,599	284,027	106,206	8,368	29,000	169,458	14	
906,394	**314,846**	**109,417**	**50,581**	**482,131**	**588,950**	**317,444**	**482,612**	**166,042**	**35,940**	**23,396**	**280,630**		
1,136	384	20	19	732	1,031	105	493	181	73	25	239	15	
3,606	1,097	80	166	2,429	2,564	1,042	4,019	1,314	..	32	2,706	16	
26,275	9,045	1,944	790	15,286	20,969	5,306	16,150	6,405	335	467	9,410	17	
2,091	1,199	138	57	754	1,492	599	536	294	11	48	231	19	
35,209	8,795	13,156	2,200	13,258	7,073	28,136	39,076	12,107	5,627	1,754	21,342	19	
116,641	36,561	10,426	5,056	69,654	83,264	33,377	50,713	16,635	852	1,549	33,226	20	
133,102	49,369	22,303	6,827	61,430	64,075	69,027	70,801	25,595	6,794	4,100	38,412	21	
18,033	5,883	4,248	429	7,902	3,556	14,477	27,187	8,587	4,876	735	13,724	22	
146,747	55,611	19,837	6,785	71,299	87,903	58,844	88,772	30,665	10,956	4,561	47,151	23	
31,045	10,154	2,400	1,423	18,491	19,999	11,046	13,104	4,675	163	825	8,266	24	
141,418	42,867	19,388	1,622	79,163	95,602	45,816	46,889	15,340	998	452	30,551	25	
40,659	13,455	2,627	1,524	24,577	27,282	13,377	23,315	6,622	221	1,025	16,472	26	
67	58	..	..	9	67	..	39	24	1	..	14	27	
59,048	21,314	1,156	2,527	36,578	46,8[illegible]1	10,657	31,148	11,122	741	1,430	19,285	28	
144,390	56,460	11,554	20,339	76,376	119,565	24,825	67,420	25,597	4,258	6,092	37,565	29	
32	27	..	..	5	32	..	55	33	6	..	16	30	
6,895	2,567	140	757	4,188	6,085	810	2,895	846	28	301	2,021	31	

TABLE XV.—Occupation or Means of Livelihood.

Serial Number.	Province, State or Agency.	CLASS B : SUB-CLASS III.—INDUSTRY. ORDER 9.—METALS—contd. Group 39.—Plough and agricultural implement makers.	Group 41.—Other workers in iron and makers of implements and tools, principally or exclusively of iron.	Group 42.—Workers in brass, copper and bell-metal.	Group 43.—Workers in other metals (tin, zinc, lead, quicksilver, etc.)	ORDER 10.—CERAMICS. TOTAL OF ORDER 10. Total Workers and Dependants.	Actual Workers. Total. Males.	Actual Workers. Total. Females.	Actual Workers. Partially Agriculturist.	Dependants.
	1	130	131	132	133	134	135	136	137	138
	INDIA.	**66,881**	**1,390,042**	**288,899**	**73,414**	**2,240,210**	**767,886**	**391,282**	**150,250**	**1,081,042**
	Provinces.	**50,617**	**1,010,163**	**224,762**	**60,097**	**1,646,043**	**559,729**	**288,543**	**108,896**	**797,771**
1	Ajmer-Merwara	95	3,230	655	170	5,605	2,081	1,478	1,022	2,046
2	Andamans and Nicobars . .	..	14	..	..	2	..	..	..	2
3	Assam	220	7,561	4,763	164	16,202	4,367	5,133	1,239	6,702
4	Baluchistan	..	2,559	118	97	216	93	..	21	123
5	Bengal	3,786	108,443	48,223	9,209	226,018	80,545	34,579	12,075	110,894
6	Bihar and Orissa . .	11,295	114,924	29,585	13,120	226,516	76,551	56,432	15,528	93,533
7	Bombay	254	82,618	24,031	10,000	134,375	44,555	23,900	6,110	65,920
8	Burma	3	29,040	554	4,759	18,821	4,656	6,687	306	7,478
9	C. P. and Berar . . .	12,819	74,785	18,714	2,454	88,375	30,920	24,421	6,380	33,034
10	Coorg	..	461	93	70	584	188	212	36	184
11	Madras	2,666	156,365	41,435	12,560	247,383	85,147	47,799	19,538	114,437
12	N.-W. F. Province (*Districts and Administered Territories*).	5,087	18,392	467	926	15,026	4,400	169	61	10,457
13	Punjab	10,938	177,277	17,702	1,306	304,151	103,300	10,125	7,864	190,726
14	United Provinces . . .	2,452	234,485	38,442	5,253	362,769	122,926	77,518	38,506	162,325
	States and Agencies.	**16,264**	**379,879**	**64,137**	**13,317**	**594,167**	**208,157**	**102,739**	**41,373**	**283,271**
15	Assam State (Manipur) . .	..	299	194	..	593	48	380	19	165
16	Baluchistan States . . .	..	3,863	90	57	506	178	..	23	328
17	Baroda State	..	13,647	2,195	277	26,743	8,599	5,157	961	12,987
18	Bengal States	2	432	38	51	1,132	540	170	37	422
19	Bihar and Orissa States . .	12	29,396	7,153	2,488	24,909	8,119	5,510	2,550	11,280
20	Bombay States . . .	1,405	40,156	6,959	1,996	76,370	24,848	10,701	2,318	40,821
21	Central India Agency . .	1,767	51,851	12,036	3,097	100,011	36,587	21,925	7,961	41,499
22	Central Provinces States . .	3,183	16,737	4,293	116	10,220	3,252	2,861	850	4,107
23	Hyderabad State . . .	9	73,586	12,925	1,096	103,514	37,591	18,566	6,434	47,357
24	Kashmir State	..	12,041	312	188	14,201	4,825	1,620	749	7,756
25	Madras States	53	37,319	8,317	1,072	20,460	6,398	4,253	557	9,809
26	Mysore State	7	19,730	1,591	1,912	26,515	6,686	1,639	1,680	18,190
27	N.-W. F. Province (*Agencies and Tribal areas*)	..	29	3	4	17	11	..	..	6
28	Punjab States	9,452	20,260	1,241	12	48,553	16,957	1,986	997	29,610
29	Rajputana Agency . . .	302	58,275	6,447	916	136,964	52,196	27,666	15,913	57,102
30	Sikkim State . . .	..	55	..	..	16	16	..	..	..
31	United Provinces States . .	72	2,203	343	35	3,443	1,306	305	329	1,832

Part A.—General Table, (*ii*) Provincial Distribution—*continued.*

CLASS B: SUB-CLASS III.—INDUSTRY.									
ORDER 10.—CERAMICS—*contd.*		ORDER 11.—CHEMICAL PRODUCTS PROPERLY SO CALLED, AND ANALOGOUS.							
		TOTAL OF ORDER 11.							
			ACTUAL WORKERS.						
Group 47.—Potters and earthen pipe and bowl makers.	Group 48.—Brick and tile makers.	Total Workers and Dependants.	Total. Males.	Total. Females.	Partially Agriculturist.	Dependants.	Group 53.—Manufacture and refining of vegetable and mineral oils.	Group 55.—Others (soap, candles, lac, cutch, perfumes and miscellaneous drugs).	Serial Number.
139	140	141	142	143	144	145	146	147	
1,959,956	**299,914**	**1,241,587**	**390,467**	**239,612**	**92,349**	**611,508**	**1,149,720**	**50,941**	
1,406,286	**180,579**	**988,326**	**308,216**	**200,167**	**72,363**	**479,943**	**912,509**	**43,343**	
5,516	89	2,558	1,040	509	495	1,009	2,188	1	1
2	..	..	..	..	..	..	..	..	2
15,165	921	5,312	1,786	736	446	2,790	4,172	1,067	3
157	59	62	39	..	6	23	21	7	4
188,721	34,665	133,064	43,266	9,448	7,547	80,350	122,622	4,136	5
184,951	10,795	143,420	42,402	43,585	10,185	57,433	124,294	17,006	6
117,924	15,460	58,036	17,700	6,606	2,968	33,730	53,832	1,288	7
15,323	3,242	10,560	4,502	1,990	102	4,068	9,110	1,145	8
67,717	19,087	33,037	9,531	10,442	2,932	13,064	30,122	1,400	9
555	29	31	19	..	4	12	26	1	10
222,342	21,230	60,823	20,614	8,189	3,978	32,020	53,112	1,857	11
12,981	1,914	5,645	1,655	80	77	3,910	5,094	119	12
244,733	56,078	110,958	34,871	3,733	4,716	72,354	104,160	1,850	13
330,199	17,010	424,820	130,791	114,849	38,907	179,180	403,756	13,466	14
553,670	**29,335**	**253,261**	**82,251**	**39,445**	**19,986**	**131,565**	**237,211**	**6,696**	
512	81	114	27	3	..	84	114	..	15
441	65	265	83	..	41	182	237	..	16
25,663	809	10,953	3,551	799	377	6,603	10,631	7	17
1,015	116	396	63	162	19	171	265	23	18
23,680	950	12,280	3,364	3,427	1,351	5,489	11,516	474	19
74,466	1,795	22,295	6,558	1,635	616	14,102	21,512	529	20
86,035	4,418	71,493	21,581	16,334	6,213	33,578	66,063	3,506	21
9,063	1,041	4,004	970	1,783	321	1,251	3,750	228	22
102,373	1,141	19,211	7,568	2,704	1,720	8,939	18,091	496	23
18,377	824	13,044	4,303	572	676	8,169	11,309	982	24
13,139	7,242	24,534	8,031	3,125	164	13,378	23,349	86	25
26,229	280	7,238	1,862	386	635	4,990	6,791	98	26
13	4	..	..	..	..	..	..	..	27
39,763	8,710	17,267	5,621	671	758	10,975	16,490	27	28
135,086	1,518	46,446	17,492	7,168	6,594	21,786	43,410	213	29
16	..	..	..	..	..	..	..	..	30
2,844	341	3,721	1,177	676	501	1,869	3,683	29	31

TABLE XV.—Occupation or Means of Livelihood.

Serial Number.	Province, State or Agency.	Class B: Sub-Class III.—Industry. Order 12.—Food Industries. Total of Order 12. Total Workers and Dependants.	Actual Workers. Total. Males.	Actual Workers. Total. Females.	Actual Workers. Partially Agriculturist.	Dependants.	Group 56.—Rice pounders and huskers and flour grinders.	Group 57.—Bakers and biscuit makers.	Group 58.—Grain parchers, etc.	Group 59.—Butchers.
	1	148	149	150	151	152	153	154	155	156
	INDIA.	**3,711,675**	**806,194**	**1,327,851**	**107,090**	**1,577,630**	**1,575,122**	**96,799**	**551,838**	**351,603**
	Provinces.	**3,033,728**	**620,232**	**1,169,445**	**89,187**	**1,244,051**	**1,388,136**	**82,168**	**498,985**	**270,430**
1	Ajmer-Merwara	3,530	880	1,176	18	1,474	1,457	159	301	981
2	Andamans and Nicobars	14	1	1	..	12	..	8	6	..
3	Assam	19,135	1,534	10,662	472	6,939	13,635	651	878	376
4	Baluchistan	1,942	1,039	24	170	879	374	503	121	566
5	Bengal	478,409	42,300	286,780	6,152	149,329	376,524	12,119	21,546	9,939
6	Bihar and Orissa	385,513	61,003	197,854	16,105	126,656	159,970	2,882	143,691	15,197
7	Bombay	190,159	48,336	52,817	3,618	89,006	77,726	8,031	13,147	29,800
8	Burma	178,255	59,889	44,845	6,475	73,521	110,623	1,234	94	6,897
9	C. P. and Berar	88,036	18,553	38,534	4,730	30,949	20,408	465	26,422	18,794
10	Coorg	3,549	1,411	553	46	1,585	585	149	22	287
11	Madras	617,563	157,036	139,953	24,571	320,574	203,949	12,970	5,906	25,582
12	N.-W. F. Province (*Districts and Administered Territories*).	25,854	7,533	2,268	170	16,053	9,061	162	4,980	8,588
13	Punjab	261,768	61,872	66,486	3,249	133,410	98,681	36,930	32,665	41,972
14	United Provinces	780,001	158,845	327,492	23,411	293,664	315,143	5,905	249,208	111,451
	States and Agencies.	**677,947**	**185,962**	**158,406**	**17,903**	**333,579**	**186,986**	**14,631**	**52,853**	**81,173**
15	Assam State (Manipur)	236	5	73	..	158	2	11	147	..
16	Baluchistan States	1,902	546	174	86	1,182	341	79	628	467
17	Baroda State	11,314	3,939	2,565	286	4,810	5,350	12	310	1,641
18	Bengal States	5,089	174	3,354	9	1,561	4,764	41	56	32
19	Bihar and Orissa States	49,186	7,091	26,904	2,828	15,191	20,201	572	23,741	73
20	Bombay States	51,364	9,008	17,768	316	24,588	25,350	327	2,172	5,277
21	Central India Agency	65,028	19,506	16,307	1,472	29,215	18,470	945	7,894	14,179
22	Central Provinces States	17,502	3,525	8,731	462	5,246	4,867	126	5,639	159
23	Hyderabad State	119,245	49,288	13,892	6,264	56,065	7,308	2,869	2,082	21,192
24	Kashmir State	20,858	7,412	2,352	356	11,094	8,736	5,638	123	4,081
25	Madras States	210,353	55,005	28,125	2,449	127,223	41,376	494	472	1,620
26	Mysore State	23,213	4,988	6,102	420	12,123	9,972	970	191	4,610
27	N.-W. F. Province (*Agencies and Tribal areas*).	74	37	..	..	37	..	..	..	39
28	Punjab States	27,916	7,061	7,436	221	13,419	14,687	1,798	3,017	4,484
29	Rajputana Agency	64,449	16,407	20,713	2,374	27,329	20,372	401	4,462	21,616
30	Sikkim State	47	15	21	..	11	..	..	..	5
31	United Provinces States	10,171	1,955	3,889	360	4,327	5,240	346	1,921	2,298

Part A.—General Table, (*ii*) Provincial Distribution—*continued*.

CLASS B : *SUB-CLASS III.—INDUSTRY.*													
ORDER 12.—FOOD INDUSTRIES—*contd.*				ORDER 13.—INDUSTRIES OF DRESS AND THE TOILET.									
				TOTAL OF ORDER 13.									
					Actual Workers.								
					Total.								
Group 62.—Makers of sugar, molasses and gur.	Group 63.—Sweetmeat makers, preparers of jam and condiments, etc.	Group 65.—Toddy drawers.	Group 66.—Manufacturers of tobacco, opium and ganja.	Total workers and Dependants.	Males.	Females.	Partially Agriculturist.	Dependants.	Group 68.—Tailors, milliners, dress makers and darners, embroiderers on linen.	Group 69.—Shoe, boot and sandal makers.	Group 71.—Washing, cleaning and dyeing.	Group 72.—Barbers, hair-dressers and wig makers.	Serial Number.
157	158	159	160	161	162	163	164	165	166	167	168	169	
88,966	**281,259**	**627,638**	**75,919**	**7,750,609**	**2,676,445**	**1,071,310**	**510,199**	**4,002,854**	**1,273,236**	**2,127,864**	**2,125,425**	**2,140,079**	
76,585	**232,113**	**381,079**	**61,934**	**5,652,131**	**1,925,326**	**782,725**	**379,065**	**2,944,080**	**944,377**	**1,345,132**	**1,639,891**	**1,649,094**	
1	616	..	..	18,230	6,954	2,791	1,231	8,485	3,273	5,095	5,027	4,810	1
..	..	..	..	129	58	..	3	71	46	18	37	28	2
45	1,029	16	42	35,090	14,005	2,097	3,828	18,988	9,166	1,797	8,908	14,934	3
..	286	..	1	3,895	2,031	102	125	1,762	1,231	1,085	1,031	521	4
7,605	31,249	2,009	2,295	514,437	177,677	32,461	28,655	304,299	114,465	61,195	122,578	208,862	5
1,738	25,440	25,299	4,143	548,198	170,460	129,826	42,587	247,912	80,032	65,196	186,378	211,516	6
772	26,131	10,657	21,400	444,035	156,171	39,007	16,852	248,857	92,782	150,575	77,549	117,815	7
8,298	2,113	35,152	13,171	116,056	45,886	23,830	2,148	46,340	60,870	11,972	23,742	4,877	8
242	12,605	1,488	3,725	352,127	129,923	52,208	38,858	169,996	58,138	114,898	77,507	92,262	9
..	118	2,170	218	2,242	887	431	55	924	535	151	1,144	410	10
26,090	19,879	302,995	12,333	1,226,286	412,434	209,502	100,606	604,350	83,423	277,179	598,104	258,116	11
91	2,430	..	318	70,697	23,161	1,473	648	46,063	10,949	29,742	6,382	21,898	12
1,864	48,161	..	1,379	994,211	327,223	50,714	33,405	616,274	133,688	461,865	156,504	235,734	13
30,839	62,056	1,293	2,914	1,326,498	458,456	238,283	110,064	629,759	295,829	164,364	874,910	477,311	14
7,881	**49,146**	**246,559**	**13,985**	**2,098,478**	**751,119**	**288,585**	**131,134**	**1,058,774**	**328,859**	**782,732**	**485,624**	**490,965**	
..	..	..	..	1,000	264	257	15	479	852	55	48	15	15
..	382	..	..	3,726	1,249	66	246	2,411	236	1,694	1,040	556	16
3	1,536	884	1,328	45,632	15,536	5,043	1,475	25,053	13,801	8,266	3,090	19,787	17
9	147	1	19	3,321	1,479	38	227	1,804	456	182	430	2,236	18
..	665	1,222	235	41,695	12,775	8,767	3,727	20,153	1,264	1,591	24,470	14,316	19
336	11,005	880	4,313	185,762	60,907	12,634	6,045	112,221	53,795	51,429	18,936	60,591	20
287	17,509	7	2,566	391,413	149,756	45,756	32,399	195,901	59,027	189,695	55,605	84,441	21
..	709	6	686	19,608	6,235	3,278	1,338	10,095	1,603	6,708	5,014	5,644	22
249	1,652	79,852	3,585	642,448	234,466	115,228	32,369	292,754	70,859	269,048	214,921	85,880	23
19	2,246	..	..	66,985	25,138	3,116	3,139	38,731	21,580	27,318	5,198	12,727	24
5,479	185	157,493	390	88,174	26,408	21,990	2,109	39,781	10,458	1,084	40,783	35,106	25
482	289	6,200	424	102,557	27,662	6,126	5,448	68,769	16,841	19,537	44,150	21,238	26
..	35	..	..	360	261	6	17	93	148	63	103	46	27
100	8,635	..	80	153,651	52,861	8,548	5,633	92,242	18,278	78,625	21,167	36,327	28
220	8,998	14	201	334,507	130,417	56,285	35,159	147,855	52,999	125,501	46,354	108,191	29
..	41	..	..	130	62	31	..	37	101	5	12	12	30
197	..	..	158	17,509	5,648	1,466	1,788	10,395	6,561	1,731	4,303	4,872	31

TABLE XV.—Occupation or Means of Livelihood.

Serial Number.	Province, State or Agency.	SUB-CLASS III.—INDUSTRY. ORDER 14.—FURNITURE INDUSTRIES. TOTAL OF ORDER 14. Total Workers and Dependants.	Actual Workers. Total. Males.	Actual Workers. Total. Females.	Actual Workers. Partially Agriculturist.	Dependants.	ORDER 15.—BUILDING INDUSTRIES. TOTAL OF ORDER 15. Total Workers and Dependants.	Actual Workers. Total. Males.	Actual Workers. Total. Females.	Actual Workers. Partially Agriculturist.	Dependants.
	1	170	171	172	173	174	175	176	177	178	179
	INDIA.	**39,268**	**13,723**	**4,440**	**630**	**21,105**	**2,062,493**	**752,342**	**209,773**	**[illegible]**	**[illegible]**
	Provinces.	**35,677**	**12,418**	**4,231**	**598**	**19,028**	**1,621,852**	**594,116**	**164,030**	**[illegible]**	**[illegible]**
1	Ajmer-Merwara	..	..	..	..	..	7,188	2,729	808	86	3,651
2	Andamans and Nicobars	..	..	..	..	..	4	1	..	..	3
3	Assam	69	45	..	2	24	8,912	4,561	412	712	3,939
4	Baluchistan	86	36	1	1	49	1,690	1,027	1	138	662
5	Bengal	9,840	2,403	3,088	101	4,349	226,781	89,844	7,975	5,541	128,962
6	Bihar and Orissa	716	283	22	19	411	134,070	50,575	23,985	7,396	59,510
7	Bombay	2,476	1,013	160	38	1,303	161,721	62,228	13,317	2,949	86,176
8	Burma	1,862	1,513	69	96	280	24,257	9,780	3,941	242	10,536
9	C. P. and Berar	255	83	13	1	159	79,450	29,780	12,887	3,394	36,783
10	Coorg	1	1	..	..	..	1,039	776	60	20	203
11	Madras	4,848	1,654	241	227	2,953	598,312	199,883	83,988	36,417	314,441
12	N.-W. F. Province (*Districts and Administered Territories*).	1,381	435	24	29	922	7,981	2,852	68	15	5,061
13	Punjab	7,858	2,647	289	29	4,922	233,711	87,684	7,983	4,350	138,044
14	United Provinces	6,285	2,305	324	56	3,656	136,736	52,396	8,605	4,064	75,735
	States and Agencies.	**3,591**	**1,305**	**209**	**32**	**2,077**	**440,641**	**158,226**	**45,743**	**11,911**	**[illegible]**
15	Assam State (Manipur)	4	..	4	..	..	46	21	2	..	23
16	Baluchistan States	14	5	..	..	9	1,501	554	18	32	929
17	Baroda State	142	46	1	3	95	12,931	4,908	635	299	7,388
18	Bengal States	18	8	..	2	10	2,303	1,154	126	130	1,023
19	Bihar and Orissa States	5	4	..	..	1	4,494	1,604	921	172	1,969
20	Bombay States	984	357	102	2	525	59,888	19,314	3,849	521	36,725
21	Central India Agency	363	158	54	..	151	28,566	11,412	2,780	686	14,374
22	Central Provinces States	4	3	..	..	1	2,114	650	599	8	865
23	Hyderabad State	255	126	..	..	129	111,194	41,344	16,678	3,617	58,172
24	Kashmir State	..	..	..	..	..	7,953	2,878	227	163	4,846
25	Madras States	277	93	[illegible]	2	174	29,567	9,705	2,456	519	17,406
26	Mysore State	357	123	12	5	222	48,714	15,229	3,569	1,798	29,916
27	N.-W. F. Province (*Agencies and Tribal areas*).	..	..	..	..	..	35	15	..	..	20
28	Punjab States	901	277	10	13	614	38,457	14,672	1,129	600	22,656
29	Rajputana Agency	228	94	16	4	118	89,039	33,577	12,729	3,280	42,783
30	Sikkim State	..	..	..	..	..	9	6	..	..	3
31	United Provinces States	39	11	..	1	28	3,830	1 183	25	89	2,622

PART A.—GENERAL TABLE, (*ii*) PROVINCIAL DISTRIBUTION—*continued*.

CLASS B: SUB-CLASS III.—INDUSTRIES.															
ORDER 15.—BUILDING INDUSTRIES.				ORDER 16.—CONSTRUCTION OF MEANS OF TRANSPORT.					ORDER 17.—PRODUCTION AND TRANSMISSION OF PHYSICAL FORCES.						
				TOTAL OF ORDER 16.					TOTAL OF ORDER 17. (Group 83.—Gas works, electric light and ice factories.)						
Group 76.—Lime burners, cement workers.	Group 77.—Excavators, plinth builders and well sinkers.	Group 78.—Stone and marble workers, masons and brick-layers.	Group 79.—Others (thatchers, building contractors, house painters, tilers, plumbers, locksmiths, etc.)	Total Workers and Dependants.	Actual Workers. Total. Males.	Actual Workers. Total. Females.	Actual Workers. Partially Agriculturist.	Dependants.	Total Workers and Dependants.	Actual Workers. Total. Males.	Actual Workers. Total. Females.	Actual Workers. Partially Agriculturist.	Dependants.	Serial Number.
180	181	182	183	184	185	186	187	188	189	190	191	192	193	
50,864	**367,826**	**1,294,379**	**349,424**	**66,056**	**24,467**	**471**	**2,345**	**41,118**	**14,384**	**7,026**	**231**	**111**	**7,127**	
37,021	**323,358**	**963,994**	**297,479**	**56,775**	**19,997**	**287**	**1,949**	**36,491**	**11,537**	**5,872**	**229**	**103**	**5,436**	
285	4	6,345	554	12	7	1	..	4	35	20	..	..	15	1
..	..	4	..	..	..	..	..	..		..	..	..	..	2
738	3,004	3,026	2,144	608	344	5	28	259	4	3	..	..	1	3
40	303	519	828	41	25	..	2	16	..	..	..	..	..	4
7,369	8,410	117,669	93,333	38,916	12,832	33	1,456	26,051	4,783	2,936	16	24	1,831	5
877	66,327	53,571	13,295	1,658	605	38	40	1,015	297	70	11	4	216	6
5,729	6,754	141,315	7,923	1,508	595	21	26	892	2,828	1,376	184	..	1,268	7
1,167	269	13,003	9,818	2,187	1,154	58	81	975	180	72	..	1	108	8
4,465	3,849	68,406	2,730	883	301	67	27	515	42	25	1	1	16	9
1	2	228	808	2	2	..	..	..	..	..	..	..	..	10
12,936	227,145	317,354	40,877	3,614	1,561	13	149	2,040	1,161	419	13	4	729	11
100	91	3,970	3,820	837	318	5	3	519	14	8	..	..	6	12
1,532	6,212	145,090	80,877	3,089	1,069	19	59	2,001	1,477	661	..	63	816	13
1,782	988	93,494	40,472	3,420	1,189	27	78	2,204	716	282	4	6	430	14
13,843	**44,468**	**330,385**	**51,945**	**9,281**	**4,470**	**184**	**396**	**4,627**	**2,847**	**1,154**	**2**	**8**	**1,691**	
11	..	18	17	32	12	..	..	20	..	..	..	..	..	15
9	319	695	478	..	..	..	..	..	..	..	..	..	..	16
334	1,222	9,253	2,122	247	122	..	5	125	101	61	..	..	40	17
130	721	430	1,022	24	24	..	..	..	1	1	..	1	..	18
260	149	3,493	592	16	4	..	..	12		..	..	..	..	19
2,122	6,164	49,238	2,364	1,352	389	41	12	922	329	136	..	..	193	20
3,182	469	17,683	7,232	1,443	713	61	124	669	95	58	1	..	36	21
65	53	1,752	244	173	79	10	5	84	3	3	..	..	..	22
643	2,149	101,530	6,872	2,910	1,832	28	139	1,050	78	42	..	..	36	23
114	5,079	..	2,760	256	119	9	..	128	208	58	..	..	150	24
2,730	3,286	21,760	1,791	455	260	..	4	195	67	18	..	..	49	25
937	16,203	27,703	3,871	1,083	395	4	59	684	1,281	497	1	6	783	26
..	..	35	..	..	..	..	..	..	..	..	..	..	..	27
273	392	18,941	18,851	442	184	1	3	257	133	33	..	1	100	28
2,952	8,245	74,625	3,217	427	177	27	9	223	542	243	..	..	290	29
..	..	9	..	..	..	..	..	..	..	..	.	..	.	30
81	17	3,220	512	421	160	3	36	258	9	4	..	..	5	31

TABLE XV.—Occupation or Means of Livelihood.

Serial Number.	Province, State or Agency.	Class B :—Sub-Class III.—Industry. Order 18.—Industries of luxury and those pertaining to literature, etc. Total of Order 18. Total Workers and Dependants.	Actual Workers. Total. Males.	Actual Workers. Total. Females.	Actual Workers. Partially Agriculturist.	Dependants.	Group 84.—Printers, Lithographers, engravers, etc.	Group 89.—Workers in precious stones and metals, enamellers, imitation jewellery makers, gilders, etc.	Group 90.—Makers of bangles, rosaries, bead and other necklaces, spangles, lingams and sacred threads.
	1	194	195	196	197	198	199	200	201
	INDIA.	**2,141,665**	**741,425**	**81,675**	**76,257**	**1,318,565**	**89,389**	**1,779,113**	**174,149**
	Provinces.	**1,674,609**	**580,464**	**57,295**	**61,014**	**1,036,850**	**80,800**	**1,369,895**	**137,602**
1	Ajmer-Merwara	7,800	2,908	867	179	4,025	546	5,848	1,235
2	Andamans and Nicobars	34	14		..	20	15	16	..
3	Assam	17,067	6,680	206	1,033	10,181	1,041	15,184	161
4	Baluchistan	871	417	2	28	452	88	670	..
5	Bengal	267,343	93,386	4,508	8,273	169,449	20,963	213,193	13,042
6	Bihar and Orissa	175,958	57,251	13,858	7,588	104,849	2,075	125,926	42,065
7	Bombay	170,267	61,006	2,768	4,600	106,493	16,075	139,689	5,068
8	Burma	58,878	23,454	4,802	970	30,622	2,981	50,232	1,297
9	C. P. and Berar	93,209	33,011	3,828	5,613	56,370	1,788	80,017	8,098
10	Coorg	875	427	24	33	424	11	826	..
11	Madras	365,672	122,782	8,660	15,623	234,230	19,354	327,038	9,821
12	N.-W. F. Province (*Districts and Administered Territories*).	11,144	3,457	80	78	7,607	114	10,118	31
13	Punjab	191,722	63,387	2,496	2,547	125,839	4,730	168,385	7,609
14	United Provinces	313,769	112,284	15,196	14,449	186,289	11,019	232,753	49,180
	States and Agencies.	**467,056**	**160,961**	**24,380**	**15,243**	**281,715**	**8,589**	**409,218**	**36,547**
15	Assam State (Manipur)	669	220	74	20	375	1	463	189
16	Baluchistan States	1,168	396	..	28	772	..	1,154	..
17	Baroda State	11,507	3,887	281	142	7,339	624	10,158	13
18	Bengal States	1,364	661	16	89	687	67	1,145	49
19	Bihar and Orissa States	7,916	2,792	1,358	543	3,766	176	5,402	1,729
20	Bombay States	66,147	20,865	957	705	44,325	1,840	59,303	1,652
21	Central India Agency	52,450	19,702	3,318	1,656	29,430	349	46,592	4,207
22	Central Provinces States	4,260	1,521	426	184	2,313	93	2,756	947
23	Hyderabad State	97,951	34,780	9,831	4,430	53,340	697	93,489	2,871
24	Kashmir State	12,254	4,804	72	296	7,378	..	10,947	765
25	Madras States	37,191	12,426	411	407	24,354	2,116	32,684	1,229
26	Mysore State	53,558	15,831	476	3,144	37,251	1,673	50,587	108
27	N.-W. F. Province (*Agencies and Tribal areas.*)	20	19	..	..	1	..	19	..
28	Punjab States	24,859	8,951	281	618	15,627	139	22,507	1,810
29	Rajputana Agency	91,692	32,880	6,729	2,736	52,083	518	68,841	21,186
30	Sikkim State	32	15	6	..	11	1	30	..
31	United Provinces States	4,018	1,211	144	245	2,663	295	3,141	292

PART A.—General Table, (*ii*) Provincial Distribution—*continued.*

CLASS B : SUB-CLASS III.—INDUSTRY. ORDER 19.—INDUSTRIES CONCERNED WITH REFUSE MATTER. TOTAL OF ORDER 19. [Group 83.—Sweepers, scavengers, dust and sweeping contractors.]					CLASS B : SUB-CLASS IV.—TRANSPORT. TOTAL OF SUB-CLASS IV.					
Total Workers and Dependants.	Actual Workers. Total. Males.	Actual Workers. Total. Females.	Partially Agriculturist.	Dependants.	Total Workers and Dependants.	Actual Workers. Total. Males.	Actual Workers. Total. Females.	Partially Agriculturist.	Dependants.	Serial Number.
202	203	204	205	206	207	208	209	210	211	
1,288,515	**420,226**	**365,814**	**28,985**	**502,475**	***5,028,973***	**2,156,942**	**237,939**	**150,349**	**2,634,092**	
1,129,142	**345,875**	**295,755**	**24,268**	**487,512**	***4,336,654***	**1,874,513**	**187,494**	**132,659**	**2,274,647**	
6,208	2,217	1,644	10	2,347	*34,630*	13,961	389	224	20,280	1
38	27	1	..	10	*292*	128	..	..	64	2
3,063	1,299	395	30	1,369	*75,128*	43,923	4,022	4,748	27,183	3
3,546	1,691	337	21	1,518	*17,979*	8,566	6	1,507	9,400	4
48,915	19,950	7,546	455	21,419	*951,543*	469,310	31,910	44,724	450,313	5
41,926	9,584	16,511	1,328	15,831	*339,823*	140,744	12,938	14,076	186,141	6
39,905	14,177	8,118	505	17,610	*618,028*	268,869	27,208	9,066	321,951	7
13,103	6,667	1,604	221	4,832	*393,652*	181,734	43,944	12,134	167,974	8
24,430	7,744	7,214	540	9,472	*203,897*	85,177	25,405	3,870	93,315	9
90	27	26	..	37	*3,089*	2,393	69	59	627	10
44,102	13,232	10,764	1,337	20,106	*566,297*	206,787	18,759	13,207	340,751	11
6,974	2,678	721	11	3,575	*47,464*	16,695	228	358	30,541	12
534,744	154,534	119,311	15,612	260,899	*638,573*	248,370	13,106	13,830	377,097	13
362,099	112,048	121,563	4,298	128,488	*445,767*	187,847	9,510	14,856	248,410	14
259,372	**84,451**	**70,059**	**4,457**	**104,862**	***692,924***	**282,430**	**40,445**	**17,690**	**370,049**	
340	96	6	..	238	*1,472*	762	7	111	703	15
513	189	..	10	324	*10,784*	3,600	..	864	7,184	16
19,590	7,337	3,671	179	8,582	*16,638*	6,773	345	292	9,520	17
572	202	46	9	324	*10,718*	8,993	168	389	1,557	18
3,476	457	2,143	155	876	*21,226*	9,051	2,165	809	10,010	19
23,520	6,853	5,558	281	11,109	*105,405*	27,591	3,543	1,049	64,271	20
38,614	14,136	10,050	94	14,428	*59,412*	28,611	3,130	1,928	25,671	21
1,351	245	829	28	277	*14,064*	5,536	1,625	211	6,903	22
6,728	1 976	1,690	314	3,058	*133,951*	51,561	18,866	4,273	63,524	23
4,250	1,352	774	135	2,124	*33,667*	14,022	3,037	806	16,608	24
5,666	873	2,400	57	2,393	*76,202*	30,998	6,308	491	38,896	25
9,180	2,740	2,017	63	4,423	*31,096*	11,833	432	703	18,831	26
207	152	12	..	43	*310*	245	..	10	65	27
56,526	17,169	11,904	1,549	27,453	*70,557*	29,057	1,225	1,795	40,275	28
85,499	29,803	27,490	1,518	28,197	*110,202*	47,196	9,353	3,662	53,653	29
33	27	2	..	4	*377*	250	7	..	120	30
3,307	844	1,449	65	1,014	*3,843*	1,351	234	297	2,258	31

TABLE XV.—Occupation or Means of Livelihood.

Serial Number.	Province, State or Agency.	Class B : *Sub-Class IV.—Transport.* Order 20.—Transport by Water. *Total of Order 20.* Total Workers and Dependants.	Actual Workers. Total. Males.	Actual Workers. Total. Females.	Actual Workers. Partially Agriculturist.	Dependants.	Group 95.—Ship owners and their employés, ship brokers, ships' officers, engineers, mariners and firemen.	Group 96.—Persons employed on the maintenance of streams, rivers and canals (including construction).	Group 97.—Boat owners, boat men and tow men.
	1	212	213	214	215	216	217	218	219
	INDIA.	**982,766**	**451,404**	**30,201**	**35,412**	**501,161**	**180,008**	**159,359**	**594,439**
	Provinces.	**885,128**	**412,774**	**24,501**	**33,661**	**447,853**	**160,653**	**139,776**	**535,991**
1	Ajmer-Merwara	95	54	..	8	41	2	93	..
2	Andamans and Nicobars	158	111	..	..	47	154	..	4
3	Assam	23,831	13,402	28	1,585	10,401	3,043	2	20,471
4	Baluchistan	399	249	1	122	149	..	399	..
5	Bengal	310,684	150,036	1,297	16,783	159,351	65,172	3,687	224,978
6	Bihar and Orissa	46,767	17,111	165	2,377	29,491	6,399	4,858	35,503
7	Bombay	148,906	74,275	5,990	4,641	68,641	57,239	28,211	38,538
8	Burma	131,071	65,770	9,546	2,674	55,755	11,539	66	118,771
9	C. P. and Berar	5,999	2,676	1,104	189	2,219	5	4,970	1,021
10	Coorg	10	8	..	4	2	4	..	6
11	Madras	74,966	30,658	826	1,005	43,482	15,912	1,778	51,983
12	N.-W. F. Province (*Districts and Administered Territories*).	2,604	932	5	15	1,667	33	944	1,627
13	Punjab	100,433	42,945	3,889	2,360	53,599	442	81,301	18,299
14	United Provinces	39,205	14,547	1,650	1,898	23,008	709	13,467	24,790
	States and Agencies.	**97,638**	**38,630**	**5,760**	**1,751**	**53,308**	**19,355**	**19,583**	**58,448**
15	Assam State (Manipur)	10	7	1	1	2	..	1	9
16	Baluchistan States	489	221	..	3	268	57	1	431
17	Baroda State	1,861	670	3	110	1,188	..	41	1,816
18	Bengal States	496	398	..	21	98	7	5	484
19	Bihar and Orissa States	5,269	2,415	19	203	2,835	11	109	5,149
20	Bombay States	28,747	9,744	254	292	18,749	18,117	1,953	8,486
21	Central India Agency	1,393	562	238	131	593	..	56	1,337
22	Central Provinces States	155	56	22	1	77	..	15	140
23	Hyderabad State	2,667	1,344	164	260	1,159	..	2,336	331
24	Kashmir State	15,968	6,402	2,985	224	6,581	67	2,524	13,377
25	Madras States	30,668	13,117	1,783	147	15,768	945	6,481	23,109
26	Mysore State	596	165	11	30	420	1	369	225
27	N.-W. F. Province (*Agencies and Tribal areas*).	17	14	..	..	3	..	17	..
28	Punjab States	7,707	2,785	31	196	4,891	49	4,800	2,849
29	Rajputana Agency	1,343	640	185	117	518	100	745	498
30	Sikkim State	4	2	..	..	2	..	..	4
31	United Provinces States	248	88	4	15	156	1	130	113

PART A.—GENERAL TABLE, (*ii*) PROVINCIAL DISTRIBUTION—*continued.*

CLASS B : *SUB-CLASS IV.—TRANSPORT.*

ORDER 21—TRANSPORT BY ROAD.

TOTAL OF ORDER 21. Total Workers and Dependants.	* Actual Workers. Total. Males.	Females.	Partially Agriculturist.	Dependants.	Group 98.—Persons employed on the construction and maintenance of roads and bridges.	Group 99.—Cart owners and drivers, coachmen, stable boys, tramway, mail carriage, etc., managers and employés (excluding private servants).	Group 100.—Palki, etc., bearers and owners.	Group 101.—Pack elephant, camel, mule, ass and bullock owners and drivers.	Group 102.—Porters and messengers.	Serial Number.
220	221	222	223	224	225	226	227	228	229	
2,781,938	**1,181,167**	**181,337**	**89,868**	**1,419,434**	**562,574**	**1,025,229**	**202,482**	**445,850**	**545,803**	
2,343,722	**1,001,819**	**138,859**	**75,756**	**1,203,044**	**459,203**	**866,480**	**195,250**	**352,007**	**470,782**	
5,784	2,741	274	154	2,769	760	2,690	69	600	1,665	1
..	..	..	..	..	..	..	..	..	..	2
32,882	20,302	2,822	2,446	9,758	13,880	9,053	3,499	23	6,427	3
11,957	4,681	5	314	7,271	863	872	6	9,988	228	4
448,817	233,632	28,485	21,166	186,700	180,226	107,032	126,022	918	34,619	5
201,604	86,489	10,836	9,145	104,279	18,074	72,562	36,857	29,920	44,191	6
282,071	116,798	17,485	3,294	147,788	21,351	89,457	143	37,002	134,118	7
230,168	96,076	33,439	9,124	100,653	91,541	132,099	149	6,304	75	8
108,256	43,989	14,313	2,732	49,954	37,270	43,450	1,595	5,884	20,057	9
2,837	2,265	69	32	503	782	1,910	..	62	83	10
340,627	128,186	16,345	9,126	196,096	31,586	213,496	2,853	1,060	91,632	11
40,002	13,506	217	256	26,279	2,471	8,349	258	24,181	4,743	12
387,216	142,679	8,035	8,581	236,502	39,628	53,177	2,205	197,209	94,997	13
251,501	110,475	6,534	9,386	134,492	20,771	132,333	21,594	38,856	37,947	14
438,216	**179,348**	**42,478**	**14,052**	**216,390**	**103,371**	**158,749**	**7,232**	**93,843**	**75,021**	
1,386	715	6	110	665	87	1,141	4	..	154	15
9,828	3,220	..	820	6,608	21	10	..	9,566	231	16
5,960	2,256	183	122	3,521	328	4,534	12	850	236	17
9,612	8,229	168	317	1,215	7,750	794	863	..	205	18
13,781	5,696	2,091	568	5,994	7,091	3,665	903	488	1,634	19
49,083	18,565	2,622	654	27,896	4,151	20,914	1,031	13,277	9,710	20
37,800	17,371	2,780	1,686	17,649	6,120	22,858	993	5,518	2,311	21
10,748	4,266	1,523	182	4,959	3,322	3,270	173	2,280	1,708	22
111,476	41,919	18,004	3,988	51,553	51,879	47,907	1,674	1,335	8,681	23
15,504	6,610	52	491	8,842	1,549	698	29	10,902	2,326	24
37,937	14,790	4,522	296	18,625	5,529	17,130	142	608	14,528	25
17,547	7,363	383	326	9,801	3,343	13,070	385	58	691	26
164	141	..	7	23	24	31	102	3	4	27
40,534	15,924	1,071	1,169	23,539	1,719	5,742	26	16,409	16,638	28
73,772	31,176	8,838	3,066	33,758	10,293	15,216	781	32,130	15,352	29
278	179	7	..	92	12	65	28	74	99	30
2,806	928	228	260	1,650	153	1,704	86	345	518	31

TABLE XV.—Occupation or Means of Livelihood.

CLASS B: *SUB-CLASS IV.—TRANSPORT.*

ORDER 22.—TRANSPORT BY RAIL.

Serial Number.	Province, State or Agency.	*TOTAL OF ORDER 22.* Total Workers and Dependants.	Actual Workers. Total. Males.	Actual Workers. Total. Females.	Actual Workers. Partially Agriculturist.	Dependants.	Group 103.—Railway employés of all kinds other than construction coolies.	Group 104.—Labourers employed on railway construction.
	1	230	231	232	233	234	235	236
	INDIA.	**1,062,493**	**448,992**	**25,192**	**19,341**	**588,309**	**906,646**	**153,847**
	Provinces.	**936,651**	**397,012**	**22,961**	**18,050**	**516,678**	**802,838**	**133,813**
1	Ajmer-Merwara . . .	27,809	10,835	115	58	16,859	27,580	229
2	Andamans and Nicobars . .	..	..	..	..	..	..	..
3	Assam	13,877	7,927	1,172	430	4,778	11,213	2,664
4	Baluchistan	4,916	3,287	..	960	1,629	4,755	161
5	Bengal	160,547	74,001	2,040	5,373	84,506	149,408	11,139
6	Bihar and Orissa . . .	80,514	33,130	1,875	2,142	45,509	76,421	4,093
7	Bombay	162,122	68,171	3,115	804	90,836	151,972	10,150
8	Burma	27,686	17,665	717	288	9,304	22,633	5,053
9	C. P. and Berar . . .	81,669	35,349	9,967	844	36,353	36,276	45,393
10	Coorg	19	9	..	1	10	17	2
11	Madras	116,457	36,836	1,519	1,872	78,102	101,450	15,007
12	N.-W. F. Province (*Districts and Administered Territories*).	3,166	1,538	2	65	1,626	2,827	339
13	Punjab	129,432	55,160	1,172	2,457	73,100	105,764	23,668
14	United Provinces . . .	128,437	53,104	1,267	2,756	74,066	112,522	15,915
	States and Agencies.	**125,842**	**51,980**	**2,231**	**1,291**	**71,631**	**105,806**	**20,034**
15	Assam State (Manipur) . .	..	..	..	..	..	..	..
16	Baluchistan States . . .	44	20	..	3	24	29	15
17	Baroda State	6,458	2,570	159	39	3,729	6,226	232
18	Bengal States	376	242	..	28	134	376	..
19	Bihar and Orissa States . .	1,399	608	46	31	745	1,270	129
20	Bombay States . . .	21,447	7,116	662	52	13,669	17,587	3,860
21	Central India Agency . .	10,923	4,689	112	71	6,122	10,194	729
22	Central Provinces States . .	2,498	966	71	23	1,461	1,707	791
23	Hyderabad State . . .	18,609	7,861	698	8	10,050	13,794	4,815
24	Kashmir State . . .	426	217	..	25	209	399	27
25	Madras States	2,284	1,144	1	6	1,139	2,092	192
26	Mysore State	9,395	3,114	84	201	6,247	8,652	743
27	N.-W. F. Province (*Agencies and Tribal areas*).	93	64	..	..	29	88	5
28	Punjab States	20,021	9,322	123	366	10,576	13,549	6,472
29	Rajputana Agency . . .	31,319	13,767	323	419	17,229	29,351	1,968
30	Sikkim State	11	9	..	..	2	11	..
31	United Provinces States . .	539	271	2	19	266	483	56

PART A.—GENERAL TABLE, (ii) PROVINCIAL DISTRIBUTION—*continued.*

CLASS B: *SUB-CLASS IV.—TRANSPORT.* ORDER 23.—POST OFFICE, TELEGRAPH & TELEPHONE SERVICES. *TOTAL OF ORDER 23.* [Group 165.—Post Office, Telegraph and Telephone services.]					CLASS B: *SUB-CLASS V.—TRADE.* *TOTAL OF SUB-CLASS V.*					
Total Workers and Dependants.	Actual Workers. Total. Males.	Actual Workers. Total. Females.	Actual Workers. Partially Agriculturist.	Dependants.	Total Workers and Dependants.	Actual Workers. Total. Males.	Actual Workers. Total. Females.	Actual Workers. Partially Agriculturist.	Dependants.	Serial Number.
237	238	239	240	241	242	243	244	245	246	
201,781	**75,380**	**1,209**	**5,788**	**125,192**	**17,839,102**	**5,464,141**	**2,637,265**	**627,617**	**9,737,696**	
170,553	**62,908**	**1,173**	**5,192**	**106,472**	**13,409,310**	**4,095,756**	**2,003,233**	**477,047**	**7,310,321**	
942	331	..	4	611	*42,464*	15,399	3,193	2,199	23,872	1
34	17	..	..	17	*341*	152	15	7	174	2
4,538	2,292	..	287	2,246	*231,960*	78,781	26,336	13,951	126,143	3
700	349	..	111	351	*13,452*	6,060	47	460	7,345	4
31,494	11,650	88	1,402	19,756	*2,299,591*	743,144	217,919	85,679	1,338,528	5
10.938	4,014	62	412	6,862	*1,511,875*	420,305	404,799	65,939	686,771	6
24,929	9,625	618	327	14,686	*1,221,695*	414,163	95,260	23,935	712,272	7
4,727	2,223	242	48	2,262	*1,203,721*	315,665	368,429	31,145	519,627	8
7.973	3,163	21	105	4,789	*550,964*	184,210	88,920	27,923	277,834	9
223	111	..	22	112	*7,111*	3,230	940	203	2,941	10
34,247	11,107	69	1,204	23,071	*2,730,057*	748,333	442,697	110,071	1,539,027	11
1,692	719	4	22	969	*142,429*	46,172	1,416	1,463	94,841	12
21,492	7,586	10	432	13,896	*1,354,810*	441,513	31,661	34,227	881,636	13
26,624	9,721	59	816	16,844	*2,099,540*	678,629	321,601	79,845	1,099,310	14
31,228	**12,472**	**36**	**596**	**18,720**	**4,429,792**	**1,368,385**	**634,032**	**150,570**	**2,427,375**	
76	40	..	..	36	*13,298*	1,683	7,034	41	4,581	15
423	139	..	38	284	*15,811*	5,652	1	233	10,158	16
2,359	1,277	..	21	1,082	*129,900*	39,030	9,569	3,091	81,301	17
234	124	..	23	110	*21,975*	9,349	3,712	874	8,914	18
777	332	9	17	436	*138,294*	35,498	48,980	8,654	53,816	19
6,128	2,166	5	51	3,957	*541,882*	148,034	33,175	5,507	360,673	20
2,296	989	..	40	1,307	*513,932*	177,151	81,540	25,256	255,241	21
663	248	9	5	406	*44,428*	13,893	11,416	1,370	19,119	22
1,199	437	..	17	762	*1,134,368*	357,289	230,646	50,814	546,433	23
1,769	793	..	66	976	*119,357*	40,734	7,365	3,540	71,258	24
5,313	1,947	2	42	3,364	*428,133*	113,796	79,360	5,592	234,977	25
3,558	1,191	4	146	2,363	*236,104*	60,852	25,515	6,983	149,737	26
36	26	..	3	10	*812*	426	..	..	386	27
2,295	1,026	..	64	1,269	*220,732*	78,265	5,491	6,531	136,976	28
3,768	1,613	7	60	2,148	*828,761*	273,659	84,410	20,992	470,692	29
84	60	..	..	24	*1,150*	703	202	3	245	30
250	64	..	3	186	*40,855*	12,371	5,616	2,089	22,868	31

TABLE XV.—Occupation or Means of Livelihood.

CLASS B: *SUB-CLASS V.—TRADE.*

Serial Number.	Province, State or Agency.	ORDER 24.—BANKS, ESTABLISHMENTS OF CREDIT, EXCHANGE AND INSURANCE. TOTAL OF ORDER 24. [Group 106.—Bank Managers, money-lenders, exchange and insurance agents, money changers and brokers and their employés.] Total Workers and Dependants.	Actual Workers. Total. Males.	Actual Workers. Total. Females.	Actual Workers. Partially Agriculturist.	Dependants.	ORDER 25.—BROKERAGE, COMMISSION AND EXPORT. TOTAL OF ORDER 25. [Group 107.—Brokers, commission agents, commercial travellers, warehouse owners and their employés.] Total Workers and Dependants.	Actual Workers. Total. Males.	Actual Workers. Total. Females.	Actual Workers. Partially Agriculturist.	Dependants.
	1	247	248	249	250	251	252	253	254	255	256
	INDIA.	**1,220,187**	**356,625**	**64,839**	**54,312**	**798,723**	**240,858**	**82,388**	**6,761**	**4,305**	**151,709**
	Provinces.	**803,561**	**236,390**	**42,888**	**40,460**	**524,283**	**203,702**	**70,992**	**6,060**	**3,897**	**126,650**
1	Ajmer-Merwara	7,191	2,455	143	456	4,593	1,545	597	9	11	939
2	Andamans and Nicobars	2	1	..	..	1	6	1	..	1	5
3	Assam	6,402	1,675	452	553	4,275	412	187	2	4	223
4	Baluchistan	288	109	..	30	179	115	58	..	8	57
5	Bengal	129,901	35,479	6,442	7,528	87,980	43,297	14,722	790	1,413	27,785
6	Bihar and Orissa	58,793	18,891	5,413	3,730	34,489	21,890	7,661	2,617	672	11,612
7	Bombay	94,234	29,026	3,725	3,184	61,483	34,793	12,989	252	173	21,552
8	Burma	17,345	6,758	2,346	698	8,241	21,415	7,608	1,423	118	12,384
9	C. P. and Berar	81,611	30,922	2,056	3,811	48,633	6,692	2,117	166	129	4,409
10	Coorg	91	19	28	2	44	3	..	..	..	3
11	Madras	102,087	23,417	12,821	4,359	65,849	19,815	5,967	225	323	13,623
12	N.-W. F. Province (*Districts and Administered Territories.*)	3,037	856	122	79	2,059	2,057	639	1	8	1,417
13	Punjab	159,948	43,214	2,625	8,159	114,109	22,389	8,383	135	220	13,921
14	United Provinces	142,631	43,568	6,715	7,871	92,348	29,273	10,113	440	817	18,720
	States and Agencies.	**416,626**	**120,235**	**21,951**	**13,852**	**274,440**	**37,156**	**11,396**	**701**	**408**	**25,059**
15	Assam State (Manipur)	6	4	..	1	2	1	..	1	..	..
16	Baluchistan States	431	145	..	..	286	97	20	..	..	68
17	Baroda State	17,600	4,967	785	654	11,848	1,200	528	1	8	671
18	Bengal States	834	318	23	61	493	1,213	774	..	59	439
19	Bihar and Orissa States	9,593	3,277	1,861	582	4,455	115	24	37	3	54
20	Bombay States	60,593	15,248	4,194	666	41,151	3,717	987	9	8	2,721
21	Central India Agency	36,093	12,065	2,642	2,067	21,386	5,195	1,874	39	38	3,282
22	Central Provinces States	3,868	1,505	237	157	2,126	267	94	11	4	162
23	Hyderabad State	22,223	7,313	2,382	832	12,528	3,588	794	532	40	2,262
24	Kashmir State	10,239	2,986	266	540	6,987	..	..	..	..	..
25	Madras States	26,345	5,958	2,012	1,311	18,375	1,139	361	32	7	746
26	Mysore State	7,217	1,759	441	336	5,017	1,698	411	14	36	1,273
27	N.-W. F. Province (*Agencies and Tribal areas*).	..	..	..	..	..	1	1	..	..	..
28	Punjab States	33,942	9,496	1,088	2,064	23,358	3,893	1,556	6	105	2,331
29	Rajputana Agency	185,988	54,837	5,955	4,560	125,196	14,894	3,917	19	80	10,958
30	Sikkim State	2	1	..	..	1	..	..	..	..	..
31	United Provinces States	1,652	356	65	21	1,231	138	46	..	20	92

PART A.—GENERAL TABLE, (ii) PROVINCIAL DISTRIBUTION—*continued.*

CLASS B: *SUB-CLASS V.—TRADE.*

ORDER 26.—TRADE IN TEXTILES. *TOTAL OF ORDER 26.* [Group 108.— Trade in piece goods, wool, cotton, silk, hair and other textiles.]					ORDER 27.—TRADE IN SKINS, LEATHER AND FURS. *TOTAL OF ORDER 27.* [Group 109.—Trade in skins, leather, furs, feathers, horns, etc.]					ORDER 28.—TRADE IN WOOD *TOTAL OF ORDER 28.* [Group 110.—Trade in wood (not firewood), cork, bark, etc.]					
Total Workers and Dependants.	Actual Workers. Total. Males.	Actual Workers. Total. Females.	Actual Workers. Partially Agriculturist.	Dependants.	Total Workers and Dependants.	Actual Workers. Total. Males.	Actual Workers. Total. Females.	Actual Workers. Partially Agriculturist.	Dependants.	Total Workers and Dependants.	Actual Workers. Total. Males.	Actual Workers. Total. Females.	Actual Workers. Partially Agriculturist.	Dependants.	Serial Number.
257	258	259	260	261	262	263	264	265	266	267	268	269	270	271	
1,277,469	**426,139**	**86,891**	**36,204**	**764,439**	**296,712**	**103,517**	**11,040**	**13,889**	**182,155**	**224,838**	**70,529**	**38,869**	**7,984**	**115,440**	
901,365	**306,021**	**58,003**	**28,071**	**535,341**	**238,014**	**80,755**	**6,840**	**8,388**	**150,419**	**179,555**	**56,369**	**27,741**	**6,706**	**95,445**	
3,262	1,178	84	37	2,000	1,150	407	25	85	718	93	32	39	5	22	1
60	23	2	2	35	..	..	..	..	..	15	11	..	..	4	2
11,779	5,543	750	666	5,486	8,046	3,402	127	533	4,517	3,184	1,303	163	230	1,718	3
2,540	1,026	1	120	1,513	88	48	..	1	40	7	5	..	..	2	4
193,266	71,187	5,290	7,022	116,789	83,681	31,065	1,124	2,681	51,492	44,806	13,029	8,257	1,413	23,520	5
94,536	28,328	11,167	3,854	55,041	33,783	11,338	2,023	2,072	20,422	30,019	10,394	8,523	1,978	11,102	6
128,966	46,496	2,848	1,817	79,622	12,332	4,321	419	348	7,592	10,748	3,233	491	116	7,024	7
74,875	21,006	22,811	2,604	31,058	1,481	525	130	26	826	21,988	7,979	2,480	408	11,529	8
49,365	18,410	3,081	1,791	27,874	7,313	2,783	586	455	3,944	6,543	2,251	1,154	1,009	3,138	9
455	263	15	25	177	81	41	1	..	39	68	26	19	2	23	10
97,873	36,232	6,475	3,968	55,166	49,235	14,238	1,753	1,429	33,244	32,706	8,335	5,251	1,043	19,120	11
13,016	3,625	128	280	9,263	2,071	544	16	13	1,511	6,093	1,803	128	6	4,162	12
99,922	30,418	692	1,758	68,812	28,217	8,544	160	411	19,513	16,346	5,581	..	286	10,765	13
131,450	44,286	4,659	4,177	82,505	10,536	3,499	476	340	6,561	6,939	2,387	1,236	210	3,316	14
376,104	**118,118**	**28,888**	**8,133**	**229,098**	**58,698**	**22,762**	**4,200**	**5,501**	**31,736**	**45,283**	**14,160**	**11,128**	**1,278**	**19,995**	
3,544	187	2,508	4	849	3	1	1	..	1	335	118	43	1	174	15
2,530	944	..	50	1,586	58	24	..	1	34	745	218	..	4	527	16
11,131	3,617	183	142	7,331	1,688	557	189	142	942	930	384	129	18	417	17
949	545	101	41	303	2,393	1,606	14	114	773	449	201	119	7	129	18
8,195	3,052	1,174	573	3,969	2,381	1,037	89	59	1,255	7,188	3,032	1,604	420	2,552	19
69,040	16,134	804	283	52,102	6,094	2,107	275	434	3,712	5,005	1,598	562	49	2,845	20
27,121	11,161	1,810	544	14,150	2,095	807	109	111	1,179	1,750	343	879	12	528	21
2,581	869	243	55	1,469	1,025	396	104	40	525	347	120	46	14	181	22
81,139	32,680	9,108	3,828	39,351	15,218	6,165	2,163	1,666	6,890	8,511	2,593	2,005	461	3,913	23
6,032	2,105	23	103	3,904	1,140	398	17	32	725	895	370	64	10	461	24
51,569	14,400	10,295	317	26,874	1,872	509	32	44	1,331	11,053	2,675	4,011	110	4,367	25
23,060	6,540	311	750	16,209	4,686	1,470	59	86	3,157	2,615	552	537	58	1,526	26
40	18	..	..	22	..	..	..	..	..	2	2	..	..	..	27
13,338	4,574	130	261	8,634	1,545	550	6	17	989	1,081	513	..	9	568	28
73,855	20,700	1,896	971	51,259	18,284	7,074	1,142	2,752	10,068	3,118	1,048	872	60	1,198	29
1	1	..	..	..	..	..	..	..	..	..	..	..	..	..	30
1,979	591	302	211	1,086	216	61	..	3	155	1,259	363	257	45	609	31

TABLE XV.—OCCUPATION OR MEANS OF LIVELIHOOD.

Serial Number.	Province, State or Agency.	CLASS B: SUB-CLASS V.—TRADE. ORDER 29.—TRADE IN METALS. TOTAL OF ORDER 29. [Group 111.—Trade in metals, machinery, knife, tool, etc., sellers.] Total Workers and Dependants.	Actual Workers. Total. Males.	Actual Workers. Total. Females.	Actual Workers. Partially Agri-culturist.	Depen-dants.	ORDER 30.—TRADE IN POTTERY. TOTAL OF ORDER 30. [Group 112—Trade in pottery.] Total Workers and Dependants.	Actual Workers. Total. Males.	Actual Workers. Total. Females.	Actual Workers. Partially Agriculturist.	Dependants.
	1	272	273	274	275	276	277	278	279	280	281
	INDIA.	**59,766**	**19,972**	**2,551**	**1,544**	**37,243**	**101,981**	**29,198**	**24,961**	**5,587**	**47,822**
	Provinces.	**44,273**	**15,415**	**1,983**	**1,088**	**26,875**	**82,304**	**24,510**	**19,105**	**4,187**	**38,689**
1	Ajmer-Merwara	41	11	..	..	30	..	..	..	..	..
2	Andamans and Nicobars	..	..	..	..	..	..	..	..	..	..
3	Assam	624	317	15	10	292	*3,170*	1,409	243	226	1,518
4	Baluchistan	19	10	..	2	9	*9*	6	..	3	3
5	Bengal	11,498	4,532	108	354	6,858	*27,236*	9,712	3,667	1,478	13,857
6	Bihar and Orissa	5,079	1,469	468	132	3,142	*13,788*	2,860	5,595	484	5,333
7	Bombay	8,881	3,529	306	86	5,046	*135*	40	7	3	88
8	Burma	1,644	444	528	72	672	*10,386*	2,425	3,784	454	4,177
9	C. P. and Berar	1,220	433	118	31	669	*1,411*	385	538	99	488
10	Coorg	33	27	..	..	6	*44*	18	10	3	16
11	Madras	3,816	1,019	155	49	2,642	*21,618*	6,038	4,655	1,391	10,925
12	N.-W. F. Province (*Districts and Administered Territories*).	229	93	..	..	136	*284*	99	3	1	182
13	Punjab	4,479	1,322	73	225	3,084	*841*	276	149	7	416
14	United Provinces	6,710	2,209	212	127	4,289	*3,382*	1,242	454	10	1,686
	States and Agencies.	**15,493**	**4,557**	**568**	**456**	**10,368**	**19,677**	**4,688**	**5,856**	**1,350**	**9,133**
15	Assam State (Manipur)	35	2	29	..	4	*38*	4	24	..	10
16	Baluchistan States	..	..	..	..	..	..	..	..	..	..
17	Baroda States	954	203	3	15	748	*94*	27	6	..	61
18	Bengal States	74	57	..	1	17	*286*	80	51	4	155
19	Bihar and Orissa States	41	18	13	1	10	*2,378*	431	928	147	1,019
20	Bombay States	2,855	748	103	42	2,004	*127*	47	3	22	77
21	Central India Agency	3,159	1,194	15	148	1,950	*18*	9	1	..	8
22	Central Provinces States	631	151	211	10	269	*135*	30	57	16	48
23	Hyderabad State	959	326	93	8	540	*11,228*	2,503	3,211	681	5,514
24	Kashmir State	..	..	..	..	..	..	..	..	..	..
25	Madras States	435	102	7	..	326	*4,509*	1,321	1,411	447	1,777
26	Mysore State	1,027	277	8	31	742	*551*	169	64	82	318
27	N.-W. F. Province (*Agencies and Tribal areas*).	..	..	..	..	..	..	..	..	..	..
28	Punjab States	1,439	225	2	16	1,212	*92*	20	27	..	45
29	Rajputana Agency	961	347	19	4	595	*221*	47	73	1	101
30	Sikkim State	..	..	..	..	..	..	..	..	..	..
31	United Provinces States	2,923	907	65	180	1,951	..	..	..	..	..

PART A.—GENERAL TABLE, (*ii*) PROVINCIAL DISTRIBUTION—*continued.*

CLASS B. *SUB-CLASS V.—TRADE.*

ORDER 31.—TRADE IN CHEMICAL PRODUCTS. TOTAL OF ORDER 31 [Group 113.—Trade in chemical products (drugs, dyes, paints, petroleum, explosives, etc.)]					ORDER 32.—HOTELS, CAFÉS, RESTAURANTS, ETC. TOTAL OF ORDER 32							
Total Workers and Dependants.	Actual Workers. Total. Males.	Actual Workers. Total. Females.	Actual Workers. Partially Agriculturist.	Dependants.	Total Workers and Dependants.	Actual Workers. Total. Males.	Actual Workers. Total. Females.	Actual Workers. Partially Agriculturist.	Dependants.	Group 114.—Vendors of wine, liquors, ærated waters, etc.	Group 115.—Owners and managers of hotels, cookshops, serais, etc., and their employés.	Serial Number.
282	283	284	285	286	287	288	289	290	291	292	293	
171,927	**58,028**	**18,472**	**6,212**	**95,427**	**719,052**	**226,427**	**125,462**	**30,464**	**367,163**	**622,192**	**96,860**	
149,552	**50,109**	**16,284**	**5,801**	**83,159**	**368,569**	**123,173**	**44,826**	**13,662**	**200,570**	**286,939**	**81,630**	
39	13	..	..	26	612	220	38	15	354	467	145	1
..	..	..	..	..	18	4	..	..	14	18	..	2
1,790	685	214	62	891	1,377	614	104	46	659	783	644	3
519	217	1	17	301	271	179	..	13	92	142	129	4
15,979	6,747	504	378	8,728	29,856	13,565	816	942	15,475	20,975	8,881	5
37,520	12,926	8,588	2,977	16,006	83,088	24,814	16,139	3,687	42,135	80,436	2,652	6
7,447	2,505	871	146	4,071	40,559	16,475	2,547	382	21,537	21,331	19,228	7
2,903	1,025	404	42	1,474	21,651	9,335	3,445	1,076	8,871	14,474	7,177	8
6,885	2,189	1,412	183	3,284	12,084	4,426	907	442	6,751	10,823	1,261	9
16	5	1	1	10	274	135	5	7	134	236	38	10
18,002	4,812	2,376	650	10,814	136,509	37,640	18,305	5,775	80,564	108,173	28,336	11
337	93	20	..	224	6,063	2,357	101	25	3,605	596	5,467	12
38,398	12,298	256	533	25,844	8,232	3,053	169	145	5,010	6,228	2,004	13
19,717	6,594	1,637	812	11,486	27,975	10,356	2,250	1,107	15,369	22,307	5,668	14
22,375	**7,919**	**2,188**	**411**	**12,268**	**350,483**	**103,254**	**80,636**	**16,802**	**166,593**	**335,253**	**15,230**	
21	2	14	..	5	544	22	424	1	98	513	31	15
371	124	..	49	247	83	30	..	..	53	73	10	16
256	64	3	..	189	3,390	1,054	92	81	2,244	2,779	611	17
45	6	18	1	21	105	75	7	2	23	66	39	18
1,134	416	71	7	647	5,978	1,868	832	520	3,278	5,859	119	19
1,062	308	53	1	701	8,462	2,676	468	222	5,318	6,226	2,236	20
6,945	2,718	988	148	3,239	24,152	8,504	2,725	1,321	12,923	22,330	1,822	21
1,727	614	419	24	694	1,710	448	543	52	719	1,697	13	22
2,454	713	394	52	1,347	241,975	69,324	65,721	12,852	106,930	241,714	261	23
..	..	..	..	..	196	84	4	9	108	109	87	24
1,107	396	9	5	702	34,221	9,507	6,975	295	17,739	27,320	6,901	25
1,913	486	119	43	1,308	11,624	3,125	492	307	8,007	10,101	1,523	26
..	..	..	..	..	57	33	..	..	24	45	12	27
4,022	1,476	57	65	2,489	1,242	545	16	37	681	1,060	182	28
676	267	34	7	375	15,752	5,638	2,214	1,078	7,905	14,658	1,094	29
..	..	..	..	..	244	84	89	3	71	72	172	30
642	329	9	9	304	748	242	34	22	472	631	117	31

TABLE XV.—Occupation or Means of Livelihood.

Serial Number.	Province, State or Agency.	CLASS B : SUB-CLASS V.—TRADE. ORDER 33.—OTHER TRADE IN FOOD STUFFS. TOTAL OF ORDER 33. Total Workers and Dependants.	Actual Workers. Total. Males.	Actual Workers. Total. Females.	Actual Workers. Partially Agriculturist.	Dependants.	Group 116.—Fish dealer.	Group 117.—Grocers and sellers of vegetable oil, salt and other condiments.	Group 118.—Sellers of milk, butter, ghee, poultry, eggs, etc.
	1	294	295	296	297	298	299	300	301
	INDIA.	**9,478,868**	**2,808,320**	**1,668,793**	**346,330**	**5,001,755**	**945,026**	**2,916,236**	**[illegible]**
	Provinces.	**7,420,566**	**2,184,013**	**1,330,050**	**277,046**	**3,906,503**	**837,889**	**2,195,405**	**566,264**
1	Ajmer-Merwara	20,194	7,634	1,345	1,062	11,215	25	11,359	1,999
2	Andamans and Nicobars	162	86	13	3	63	..	2	63
3	Assam	155,503	46,592	20,615	9,605	88,296	58,908	36,105	10,857
4	Baluchistan	6,384	3,073	43	183	3,268	8	4,525	403
5	Bengal	1,379,157	428,239	155,219	53,056	795,699	319,878	352,945	144,409
6	Bihar and Orissa	872,561	237,804	253,295	35,877	381,462	91,098	295,948	52,813
7	Bombay	644,000	210,986	61,409	13,017	371,605	25,214	348,882	31,577
8	Burma	513,911	113,579	169,795	13,412	230,537	107,111	35,978	10,378
9	C. P. and Berar	309,410	97,349	67,840	17,306	144,221	3,276	128,182	11,894
10	Coorg	5,335	2,388	702	155	2,245	83	2,542	31
11	Madras	1,816,521	482,452	330,249	72,700	1,003,820	220,531	847,687	80,961
12	N.-W. F. Province (*Districts and Administered Territories*).	48,984	16,563	548	468	31,873	14	25,059	6,017
13	Punjab	248,095	82,513	19,028	4,830	146,554	644	4,309	40,856
14	United Provinces	1,400,349	454,756	249,949	55,312	695,645	11,099	101,882	112,997
	States and Agencies.	**2,058,302**	**624,307**	**338,743**	**69,284**	**1,095,252**	**107,137**	**720,831**	**[illegible]**
15	Assam State (Manipur)	7,586	848	3,844	20	2,894	1,326	692	186
16	Baluchistan States	6,653	2,507	..	82	4,146	275	5,005	107
17	Baroda State	54,718	17,322	5,804	1,392	31,592	1,696	4,556	3,249
18	Bengal States	12,289	3,776	3,146	408	5,367	4,407	1,813	553
19	Bihar and Orissa States	73,992	18,045	29,144	4,685	26,803	5,044	23,496	6,198
20	Bombay States	283,724	79,655	19,227	2,804	184,842	5,044	153,327	15,839
21	Central India Agency	294,305	96,745	56,789	15,419	140,771	655	62,100	29,194
22	Central Provinces States	26,173	7,928	7,740	740	10,505	89	10,098	2,965
23	Hyderabad State	391,941	115,556	85,551	17,426	190,834	24,960	112,156	17,040
24	Kashmir State	82,174	28,743	5,986	2,372	47,445	..	..	23,343
25	Madras States	242,166	62,750	48,888	2,164	130,528	62,072	48,259	3,430?
26	Mysore State	130,518	32,284	17,317	3,755	80,917	1,084	61,518	8,255
27	N.-W. F. Province (*Agencies and Tribal areas*).	88	41	..	..	47	..	14	39
28	Punjab States	29,901	10,833	2,225	484	16,843	123	939	4,674
29	Rajputana Agency	395,869	139,395	48,668	16,141	207,806	60	236,206	17,118
30	Sikkim State	15	11	1	..	3	..	..	..
31	United Provinces States	26,190	7,868	4,413	1,392	13,909	463	653	1,658

Part A.—General Table, (ii) Provincial Distribution—*continued*.

CLASS B: *SUB-CLASS V.—TRADE.*

ORDER 33.—OTHER TRADE IN FOOD STUFFS—*contd.*						ORDER 34.—TRADE IN CLOTHING AND TOILET ARTICLES. *TOTAL OF ORDER 34.* [Group 125.—Trade in ready-made clothing and other articles of dress and the toilet.]					
Group 119.—Sellers of sweet-meats, sugar, gur and molasses.	Group 120.—Cardamom, betel-leaf, vegetables, fruit and areca-nut sellers.	Group 121.—Grain and pulse dealers.	Group 122.—Tobacco, opium, ganja, etc., sellers.	Group 123.—Dealers in sheep, goats and pigs.	Group 124.—Dealers in hay, grass and fodder.	Total Workers and Dependants.	Actual Workers. Total. Males.	Actual Workers. Total. Females.	Actual Workers. Partially Agriculturist.	Dependants.	Serial Number.
302	303	304	305	306	307	308	309	310	311	312	
535,545	**1,584,776**	**2,196,885**	**317,110**	**113,139**	**236,659**	**306,701**	**101,068**	**21,775**	**7,742**	**183,836**	
463,287	**1,265,229**	**1,667,057**	**269,751**	**65,047**	**151,657**	**251,656**	**80,859**	**16,484**	**6,044**	**154,313**	
1,668	1,564	1,075	579	1,455	470	436	169	4	1	263	1
27	52	18	..	..	..	..	..	..	..	..	2
3,759	19,785	23,669	2,178	144	98	1,642	576	545	51	521	3
7	544	375	105	235	182	213	96	1	7	116	4
71,181	239,787	204,377	32,845	5,777	7,898	23,755	10,655	419	440	12,681	5
52,258	136,657	199,481	31,535	2,947	9,824	12,748	4,178	2,110	571	6,460	6
7,714	90,468	98,347	17,095	8,358	16,345	17,806	5,057	983	127	11,766	7
108,839	117,309	105,332	22,362	1,058	5,544	6,531	2,813	1,103	174	2,615	8
7,187	49,108	71,535	17,142	1,433	19,743	6,379	2,033	992	237	3,354	9
115	696	1,777	61	15	15	9	3	1	1	5	10
127,690	223,495	199,733	65,733	27,558	23,113	88,998	25,643	5,707	3,337	57,648	11
1,460	6,333	3,632	672	232	5,565	3,230	944	27	28	2,259	12
8,545	82,768	82,379	6,812	7,343	14,440	31,505	10,471	634	214	20,400	13
72,837	296,663	675,327	72,632	8,492	48,420	58,404	18,221	3,958	856	36,225	14
72,258	**318,547**	**523,828**	**47,359**	**48,092**	**85,002**	**55,045**	**20,229**	**5,291**	**1,698**	**29,525**	
28	2,275	2,882	182	13	2	19	9	2	..	8	15
..	561	543	33	120	..	6	2	..	..	4	16
687	17,814	23,864	1,811	541	550	1,425	460	33	7	932	17
746	1,158	3,037	301	271	3	112	53	1	6	58	18
3,432	10,665	23,575	1,022	102	458	993	314	179	45	500	19
4,567	29,124	59,437	7,762	1,760	6,864	6,339	1,706	554	18	4,079	20
10,488	38,752	130,110	6,973	2,881	13,152	9,614	6,373	164	332	3,077	21
86	2,824	8,095	1,534	11	471	71	31	17	1	23	22
4,656	97,564	106,171	4,615	19,400	5,379	16,622	4,688	3,395	830	8,539	23
..	5,384	41,657	876	8,248	2,666	1,315	188	115	82	1,012	24
10,903	47,148	41,467	11,615	1,660	6,212	1,481	516	34	80	931	25
5,046	25,354	19,437	4,894	1,601	3,379	3,303	1,053	126	113	2,024	26
..	5	23	2	..	5	7	5	..	..	2	27
3,150	8,472	8,428	835	1,663	1,728	3,464	1,271	74	20	2,119	28
18,015	24,079	43,523	4,277	9,258	43,334	9,087	3,255	571	152	5,261	29
1	14	..	..	..	..	..	..	..	..	..	30
1,508	8,354	11,579	627	554	799	687	305	26	12	356	31

TABLE XV.—OCCUPATION OR MEANS OF LIVELIHOOD.

Serial Number.	Province, State or Agency.	Class B: Sub-Class V.—Trade. Order 35.—Trade in Furniture. Total of Order 35. Total Workers and Dependants.	Actual Workers. Total. Males.	Actual Workers. Total. Females.	Actual Workers. Partially Agriculturist.	Dependants.	Group 126.—Trade in furniture, carpets, curtains and bedding.	Group 127.—Hardware, cooking utensils, porcelain, crockery, glassware, bottles, articles for gardening, the cellar, etc.
	1	313	314	315	316	317	318	319
	INDIA.	**173,413**	**56,878**	**15,570**	**4,523**	**100,965**	**57,282**	**116,131**
	Provinces.	**145,022**	**47,138**	**12,726**	**3,804**	**85,158**	**42,713**	**102,309**
1	Ajmer-Merwara	283	76	42	..	165	219	64
2	Andamans and Nicobars	..	..	..	..	..	..	..
3	Assam	3,785	1,771	400	372	1,614	2,424	1,361
4	Baluchistan	317	146	..	10	171	287	30
5	Bengal	41,748	13,663	2,502	1,126	25,583	9,547	32,201
6	Bihar and Orissa	14,948	4,625	1,988	460	8,335	5,133	9,815
7	Bombay	13,454	4,311	737	176	8,406	3,349	10,105
8	Burma	13,496	4,487	3,445	311	5,564	7,137	6,359
9	C. P. and Berar	5,448	1,732	821	237	2,895	1,592	3,856
10	Coorg	47	40	1	..	6	..	47
11	Madras	28,313	8,475	1,655	676	18,183	7,348	20,965
12	N.-W. F. Province (*Districts and Administered Territories*)	725	353	..	19	372	686	39
13	Punjab	6,675	1,986	72	46	4,617	2,640	4,035
14	United Provinces	15,783	5,473	1,063	371	9,247	2,351	13,432
	States and Agencies.	**28,391**	**9,740**	**2,844**	**719**	**15,807**	**14,569**	**13,822**
15	Assam State (Manipur)	15	2	8	..	5	8	7
16	Baluchistan States	766	244	..	14	522	759	7
17	Baroda State	523	132	70	4	321	404	119
18	Bengal States	455	368	33	2	54	30	425
19	Bihar and Orissa States	861	249	113	39	499	75	786
20	Bombay States	4,378	1,231	225	61	2,922	2,022	2,356
21	Central India Agency	626	293	25	2	308	187	439
22	Central Provinces States	166	77	16	15	73	..	166
23	Hyderabad State	7,670	2,960	1,099	242	3,611	6,117	1,553
24	Kashmir State	147	55	7	9	85	13	134
25	Madras States	5,488	1,545	833	107	3,110	2,773	2,715
26	Mysore State	2,417	807	43	97	1,567	477	1,940
27	N.-W. F. Province (*Agencies and Tribal areas*)	..	..	..	..	..	..	..
28	Punjab States	1,952	661	93	47	1,198	590	1,362
29	Rajputana Agency	2,564	980	237	53	1,347	778	1,786
30	Sikkim State	..	..	..	..	..	..	..
31	United Provinces States	363	136	42	27	185	336	27

PART A.—GENERAL TABLE, (ii) PROVINCIAL DISTRIBUTION—*continued.*

CLASS B: *SUB-CLASS V.—TRADE.*

ORDER 36.—TRADE IN BUILDING MATERIALS. TOTAL OF ORDER 36. [Group 128.—Trade in building materials (stones, bricks, plaster, cement, sand, tiles, thatch, etc.)]					ORDER 37.—TRADE IN MEANS OF TRANSPORT. TOTAL OF ORDER 37. [Group 129.—Dealers and hirers of elephants, camels, horses, cattle, asses, mules, etc. sellers (not makers) of carriages, saddlery, etc.]					
Total Workers and Dependants.	Actual Workers. Total. Males.	Actual Workers. Total. Females.	Actual Workers. Partially Agriculturist.	Dependants.	Total Workers and Dependants.	Actual Workers. Total. Males.	Actual Workers. Total. Females.	Actual Workers. Partially Agriculturist.	Dependants.	Serial Number.
320	321	322	323	324	325	326	327	328	329	
84,613	**25,875**	**13,866**	**2,946**	**44,872**	**239,396**	**87,229**	**10,581**	**8,394**	**141,586**	
65,115	**20,269**	**11,047**	**2,539**	**33,799**	**192,143**	**69,515**	**7,149**	**6,531**	**115,479**	
7	..	5	..	2	1,250	323	69	33	858	1
..	..	..	..	..	..	..	..	..	..	2
2,290	832	313	105	1,145	2,528	1,388	193	117	947	3
22	4	..	..	18	258	97	..	6	161	4
12,862	4,144	928	483	7,790	16,341	6,260	257	757	9,824	5
5,063	1,333	1,393	302	2,337	7,515	3,304	472	343	3,739	6
8,389	3,709	882	204	3,798	19,671	7,209	682	549	11,780	7
3,057	891	1,180	82	986	15,661	6,226	2,371	518	7,064	8
1,939	652	286	152	1,001	9,859	3,869	399	404	5,591	9
64	21	24	1	19	3	2	..	..	1	10
24,734	6,562	5,640	1,067	12,532	27,671	10,248	1,006	1,007	16,417	11
88	34	..	..	54	1,553	556	5	7	992	12
2,871	975	16	86	1,880	44,220	14,734	314	1,437	29,172	13
3,729	1,112	380	57	2,237	45,613	15,299	1,381	1,353	28,933	14
19,496	**5,606**	**2,819**	**407**	**11,073**	**47,253**	**17,714**	**3,432**	**1,773**	**26,107**	
46	7	17	..	22	270	110	11	..	149	15
29	8	..	..	21	84	32	..	2	52	16
489	174	10	..	305	1,754	321	556	16	877	17
294	127	32	25	135	77	42	2	3	33	18
208	42	89	4	77	308	155	33	13	120	19
1,873	570	163	34	1,140	7,118	2,404	245	117	4,469	20
485	197	37	6	251	4,296	1,654	324	189	2,318	21
16	8	2	..	6	763	301	89	16	373	22
1,260	495	85	..	680	15,597	5,838	1,814	650	7,945	23
45	24	1	2	20	703	286	25	4	392	24
7,663	2,095	1,247	114	4,321	2,062	776	47	41	1,239	25
4,234	894	478	162	2,862	1,421	576	15	23	830	26
..	..	..	..	..	..	..	..	..	..	27
261	173	1	2	87	3,177	1,392	33	79	1,752	28
2,398	774	656	57	968	8,788	3,577	231	589	4,980	29
..	..	..	..	..	6	3	2	..	1	30
197	18	1	1	178	829	247	5	31	577	31

TABLE XV.—Occupation or Means of Livelihood.

Serial Number.	Province, State or Agency.	Class B: Sub-Class V.—Trade. Order 38.—Trade in fuel. Total of Order 38. [Group 130.—Dealers in firewood, charcoal, coal, cowdung, etc.] Total Workers and Dependants.	Actual Workers. Total. Males.	Actual Workers. Total. Females.	Actual Workers. Partially Agriculturist.	Dependants.	Order 39.—Trade in articles of luxury and those pertaining to letters, etc. Total of Order 39. Total Workers and Dependants.	Actual Workers. Total. Males.	Actual Workers. Total. Females.	Actual Workers. Partially Agriculturist.	Dependants.
	1	330	331	332	333	334	335	336	337	338	339
	INDIA.	**524,962**	**119,366**	**215,634**	**22,806**	**189,962**	**522,130**	**162,854**	**71,862**	**16,030**	**297,414**
	Provinces.	**391,165**	**87,034**	**166,105**	**16,490**	**138,026**	**401,988**	**128,351**	**49,918**	**12,349**	**228,719**
1	Ajmer-Merwara	2,720	769	1,064	262	887	389	112	97	4	180
2	Andamans and Nicobars	..	..	..	..	..	..	..	..	..	..
3	Assam	2,461	781	220	130	1,460	9,445	4,168	969	430	4,318
4	Baluchistan	357	127	..	7	230	512	249	1	7	262
5	Bengal	46,654	9,199	22,938	962	14,517	88,959	29,737	5,331	2,248	53,891
6	Bihar and Orissa	90,765	9,036	63,170	3,889	18,559	45,141	13,143	10,159	1,826	21,839
7	Bombay	35,747	10,156	11,260	1,692	14,331	50,411	16,781	4,237	644	29,393
8	Burma	10,753	3,738	2,224	334	4,791	10,961	3,883	1,488	297	5,590
9	C. P. and Berar	4,475	1,227	1,570	294	1,678	29,765	9,125	6,102	840	14,538
10	Coorg	73	1	61	1	11	290	93	50	3	147
11	Madras	85,551	21,677	29,106	5,672	34,768	87,106	25,761	9,248	3,564	52,097
12	N.-W. F. Province (*Districts and Administered Territories*)	1,069	231	47	1	791	1,080	349	18	5	712
13	Punjab	17,874	6,188	2,252	584	9,434	26,404	8,481	1,005	263	16,918
14	United Provinces	92,666	23,904	32,193	2,662	36,569	51,525	16,469	11,223	2,218	23,833
	States and Agencies.	**133,797**	**32,332**	**49,529**	**6,316**	**51,936**	**120,142**	**34,503**	**21,944**	**3,681**	**68,695**
15	Assam State (Manipur)	133	25	65	..	43	110	27	13	1	70
16	Baluchistan States	133	40	1	12	92	150	62	..	..	88
17	Baroda State	1,581	535	168	70	878	2,670	735	159	31	1,776
18	Bengal States	456	184	79	37	193	206	103	19	9	84
19	Bihar and Orissa States	18,473	1,702	11,335	1,287	5,436	2,562	819	268	159	1,475
20	Bombay States	12,207	2,750	4,091	246	5,366	12,445	3,307	629	92	8,509
21	Central India Agency	12,797	3,807	3,336	803	5,654	17,938	5,669	3,734	676	8,535
22	Central Provinces States	782	95	408	42	279	2,510	633	990	14	887
23	Hyderabad State	25,880	7,063	6,379	1,518	12,438	46,316	12,453	12,069	1,721	21,794
24	Kashmir State	3,883	1,458	613	168	1,812	3,115	841	126	36	2,148
25	Madras States	6,808	1,942	1,845	49	3,021	3,606	1,069	227	79	2,310
26	Mysore State	6,880	1,254	3,058	96	2,568	9,531	2,577	917	328	6,037
27	N.-W. F. Province (*Agencies and Tribal areas*)	..	..	..	..	..	13	2	..	..	11
28	Punjab States	5,729	1,867	636	111	3,226	2,298	613	157	24	1,528
29	Rajputana Agency	37,677	9,532	17,257	1,854	10,888	15,814	5,352	2,512	469	7,950
30	Sikkim State	..	..	..	..	..	..	..	..	..	..
31	United Provinces States	378	78	258	25	42	858	241	124	42	493

Part A.—General Table, (ii) Provincial Distribution—*continued*

Class B: Sub-Class V.—Trade.												
Order 39—*contd.*		Order 40.—Trade in Refuse Matter.					Order 41.—Trade of Other Sorts.					
Group 131.—Dealers in precious stones, jewellery (real and imitation), clock, optical instruments, etc.	Group 132.—Dealers in common bangles, bead necklaces, fans, small articles, toys, hunting and fishing tackle, flowers, etc.	*Total of Order 40.* [Group 134.—Dealers in rags, stable refuse, etc.]					*Total of Order 41.*					
		Total Workers and Dependants.	Actual Workers. Total. Males.	Actual Workers. Total. Females.	Actual Workers. Partially Agriculturist.	Dependants.	Total Workers and Dependants.	Actual Workers. Total. Males.	Actual Workers. Total. Females.	Actual Workers. Partially Agriculturist.	Dependants.	Serial Number.
340	341	342	343	344	345	346	347	348	349	350	351	
102,234	**376,401**	**3,695**	**1,279**	**349**	**92**	**2,967**	**2,192,534**	**728,429**	**238,989**	**58,391**	**1,225,116**	
77,127	**285,932**	**3,141**	**1,183**	**232**	**88**	**1,776**	**1,567,619**	**511,716**	**185,792**	**39,896**	**870,117**	
31	306	..	..	..	..	..	3,252	1,403	229	228	1,620	1
..	..	..	..	..	..	..	78	26	..	1	52	2
456	8,755	3	..	3	..	..	16,819	7,538	1,018	811	8,263	3
38	451	..	..	..	..	..	1,533	610	..	46	923	4
13,861	61,925	443	123	19	..	301	110,152	41,086	3,308	3,400	65,758	5
5,244	38,231	27	10	6	1	11	84,611	28,191	11,673	3,084	44,747	6
12,145	31,075	273	134	42	18	97	93,849	37,206	3,562	1,253	53,081	7
8,591	1,150	94	27	6	..	61	455,569	122,916	149,466	10,495	183,187	8
1,585	26,945	593	296	4	18	293	9,972	4,011	888	485	5,073	9
13	274	..	..	..	..	..	225	148	22	2	55	10
22,331	59,058	440	147	46	4	247	89,062	29,670	8,024	2,997	51,368	11
408	427	86	20	..	..	66	52,427	17,013	252	573	35,162	12
9,462	14,298	157	70	13	..	74	598,237	203,056	4,068	15,023	391,113	13
2,967	43,037	1,025	306	93	47	626	51,833	18,836	3,282	1,498	29,715	14
25,107	**90,469**	**554**	**146**	**117**	**4**	**291**	**624,915**	**216,719**	**53,197**	**18,495**	**354,999**	
7	103	..	..	..	..	..	592	315	30	13	247	15
2	148	..	..	..	..	..	3,675	1,243	..	19	2,432	16
1,759	709	97	16	49	..	32	29,400	7,934	1,329	511	20,137	17
43	159	..	..	..	..	..	1,738	1,034	67	94	637	18
931	1,502	23	14	4	..	5	3,871	1,003	1,206	110	1,662	19
4,603	6,774	13	5	8	..	..	56,830	16,553	1,562	408	38,715	20
3,614	14,021	4	3	..	..	1	67,339	23,735	7,923	3,440	35,681	21
64	2,446	4	3	1	..	..	1,652	590	282	170	780	22
7,265	38,144	..	..	..	..	..	241,787	85,825	34,645	8,007	121,317	23
1,524	1,432	180	55	..	1	125	9,293	3,141	118	172	6,034	24
1,632	1,336	92	20	16	1	56	26,517	7,854	1,439	421	17,224	25
1,572	7,560	132	27	39	2	66	22,777	6,591	1,477	728	14,709	26
..	..	..	..	..	..	..	604	324	..	..	280	27
428	1,687	..	..	..	..	..	113,356	42,500	940	3,190	69,016	28
1,659	13,708	4	3	..	..	1	42,811	16,921	2,054	1,164	23,836	29
..	..	..	..	..	..	..	882	603	110	..	169	30
4	740	5	..	..	..	5	1,791	553	15	48	1,223	31

TABLE XV.—Occupation or Means of Livelihood.

Serial Number.	Province, State or Agency.	CLASS B : SUB-CLASS V.—TRADE. ORDER 41.—TRADE OF OTHER SORTS. Group 135.—Shop keepers otherwise unspecified.	Group 136.—Itinerant traders, pedlars, hawkers, etc.	Group 137.—Conjurors, acrobats, fortune-tellers, reciters, exhibitors of curiosities and wild animals.	CLASS C : PUBLIC ADMINISTRATION AND LIBERAL ARTS. TOTAL OF CLASS C. Total Workers and Dependants.	Actual Workers. Total. Males.	Actual Workers. Total. Females.	Actual Workers. Partially Agriculturist.	Dependants.
	1	352	353	354	355	356	357	358	359
	INDIA.	**1,984,040**	**82,998**	**82,119**	**10,912,123**	**3,981,507**	**518,147**	**594,535**	**6,412,469**
	Provinces.	**1,431,919**	**45,743**	**59,111**	**7,306,043**	**2,626,490**	**340,938**	**416,266**	**4,338,815**
1	Ajmer-Merwara	2,244	658	252	**35,022**	15,430	2,827	3,807	16,765
2	Andamans and Nicobars	78	..	..	**1,875**	1,235	6	8	634
3	Assam	14,846	139	916	**120,998**	44,287	1,321	10,689	75,390
4	Baluchistan	1,364	151	9	**31,766**	22,062	200	10,067	9,504
5	Bengal	93,681	5,460	5,138	**1,167,142**	375,906	42,148	67,595	749,088
6	Bihar and Orissa	76,840	1,502	2,765	**567,036**	205,937	40,925	46,501	320,174
7	Bombay	70,949	9,008	9,547	**935,568**	344,959	40,347	41,084	550,262
8	Burma	450,939	456	3,816	**445,846**	200,019	29,839	12,477	215,988
9	C. P. and Berar	4,730	49	4,290	**483,353**	183,838	27,782	31,528	271,733
10	Coorg	154	..	41	**3,824**	1,678	112	545	2,034
11	Madras	71,492	1,804	10,371	**1,309,840**	413,089	47,211	71,645	849,540
12	N.-W. F. Province (*Districts and Administered Territories.*)	50,556	1,534	195	**132,121**	61,610	1,338	7,327	69,173
13	Punjab	569,087	10,761	16,145	**898,813**	324,629	39,152	37,124	536,032
14	United Provinces	24,959	14,221	5,606	**1,171,839**	431,811	67,730	75,919	672,298
	States and Agencies.	**552,121**	**37,255**	**23,008**	**3,606,080**	**1,355,017**	**177,209**	**178,269**	**2,072,254**
15	Assam State (Manipur)	510	..	29	**9,040**	3,842	262	760	4,936
16	Baluchistan States	3,613	39	2	**10,428**	4,282	13	790	6,133
17	Baroda State	27,755	279	1,090	**146,275**	56,806	7,084	3,321	84,385
18	Bengal States	1,350	19	242	**14,438**	6,032	218	1,210	8,188
19	Bihar and Orissa States	3,113	182	491	**85,408**	31,192	1,919	7,825	52,297
20	Bombay States	31,226	20,945	3,151	**478,538**	165,503	18,936	15,018	294,099
21	Central India Agency	62,447	2,245	2,192	**490,986**	201,939	17,860	20,761	271,187
22	Central Provinces States	459	..	1,171	**39,162**	13,947	3,380	2,037	21,835
23	Hyderabad State	239,765	30	1,992	**747,998**	297,375	36,275	35,785	414,348
24	Kashmir State	7,400	1,112	779	**104,541**	40,915	1,957	4,049	61,669
25	Madras States	21,946	83	3,528	**209,239**	65,452	6,071	4,167	137,716
26	Mysore State	12,314	913	2,635	**306,608**	86,144	6,460	21,583	214,004
27	N.-W. F. Province (*Agencies and Tribal areas*).	604	..	..	**5,887**	5,632	1	1,240	254
28	Punjab States	107,858	1,576	3,796	**178,350**	66,419	7,402	11,054	104,529
29	Rajputana Agency	29,725	9,814	1,779	**738,112**	296,108	68,115	45,179	373,889
30	Sikkim State	871	..	11	**823**	643	20	5	160
31	United Provinces States	1,165	18	120	**38,247**	12,786	1,236	1,276	24,225

PART A.—GENERAL TABLE, (*ii*) PROVINCIAL DISTRIBUTION—*continued.*

CLASS C: *SUB-CLASS VI.—PUBLIC FORCE.*

TOTAL OF SUB-CLASS VI.					ORDER 49.—ARMY. TOTAL OF ORDER 49.					Group 139—Army (Imperial).	Group 140.—Army (Native States).	Serial Number.
Total Workers and Dependants.	Actual Workers. Total. Males.	Actual Workers. Total. Females.	Actual Workers. Partially Agriculturist.	Dependants.	Total Workers and Dependants.	Actual Workers. Total. Males.	Actual Workers. Total. Females.	Actual Workers. Partially Agriculturist.	Dependants.			
360	361	362	363	364	365	366	367	368	369	370	371	
2,388,586	**1,050,899**	**10,025**	**179,450**	**1,328,162**	**665,278**	**383,106**	**968**	**54,160**	**281,204**	**368,306**	**296,972**	
1,553,589	**688,842**	**4,928**	**131,895**	**859,818**	**329,456**	**216,370**	**467**	**40,191**	**112,619**	**326,682**	**2,774**	
8,865	5,557	14	2,288	3,294	6,447	4,331	12	2,209	2,104	6,307	140	1
1,257	1,038	..	4	219	231	162	..	3	69	231	..	2
17,594	8,480	..	1,320	9,114	2,495	1,620	..	139	875	2,496	..	3
18,638	15,667	1	7,660	2,970	16,761	14,386	1	6,929	2,374	16,761	..	4
181,734	68,477	..	15,854	113,257	8,713	7,123	..	1,012	1,590	8,646	67	5
139,870	54,739	..	14,612	85,131	1,246	975	..	63	271	1,240	6	6
133,993	65,122	375	3,406	67,726	31,392	23,402	24	224	7,966	31,369	23	7
79,495	40,188	1,717	2,757	37,590	24,984	18,717	68	1,954	6,199	24,984	..	8
157,311	65,046	1,973	13,927	90,292	11,286	9,066	31	468	2,189	10,099	1,187	9
432	261	..	148	171	17	6	..	..	11	17	..	10
207,395	71,060	3	10,580	136,262	15,626	7,619	..	370	8,007	15,154	472	11
51,599	32,266	4	6,148	19,322	36,479	25,753	..	5,716	10,726	36,479	..	12
225,896	104,880	16	16,250	121,000	117,754	64,824	16	11,331	52,914	117,592	162	13
330,357	156,062	825	36,939	173,470	56,025	38,386	815	9,778	17,324	55,308	717	14
844,997	**379,556**	**5,097**	**47,564**	**460,344**	**335,822**	**166,736**	**501**	**13,918**	**168,585**	**39,626**	**296,196**	
1,291	903	..	462	388	627	550	..	445	77	610	17	15
1,759	917	..	118	842	1,758	916	..	118	842	138	1,620	16
26,904	12,276	..	980	14,628	11,560	5,718	..	323	5,842	1,009	10,551	17
2,005	846	..	230	1,159	219	102	..	10	117	8	211	18
40,566	13,187	..	4,173	27,379	109	57	..	3	52	54	55	19
105,246	38,977	1,077	5,901	65,192	8,194	3,592	8	300	4,594	1,991	6,203	20
181,938	90,182	2,321	6,933	89,435	89,551	48,815	..	2,160	40,736	11,474	78,077	21
16,429	5,372	604	1,218	10,453	35	18	..	..	17	4	31	22
164,398	68,271	278	5,005	95,849	68,750	26,328	278	700	42,144	5,554	63,196	23
20,513	10,573	18	1,207	9,922	10,706	6,970	18	781	3,718	9	10,697	24
12,509	4,672	..	518	7,837	6,919	2,211	..	203	4,708	115	6,804	25
71,729	27,262	586	4,030	43,881	21,986	9,899	..	967	12,087	10,277	11,709	26
4,237	4,176	..	878	61	4,076	4,025	..	877	51	4,076	..	27
39,835	17,352	..	3,908	22,483	19,475	9,834	..	3,206	9,641	625	18,850	28
149,019	72,370	211	11,620	76,438	86,458	44,053	197	3,694	41,308	3,307	83,151	29
349	294	..	..	55	244	236	..	..	8	244	..	30
6,270	2,926	2	275	3,342	5,155	2,512	..	66	2,643	129	5,026	31

TABLE XV.—Occupation or Means of Livelihood.

Serial Number.	Province, State or Agency.	CLASS C: SUB-CLASS VI.—PUBLIC FORCE. ORDER 43.—NAVY. TOTAL OF ORDER 43. (Group 141.—Navy.) Total Workers and Dependants.	Actual Workers. Total. Males.	Actual Workers. Total. Females.	Actual Workers. Partially Agriculturist.	Dependants.	ORDER 44.—POLICE. TOTAL OF ORDER 44. Total Workers and Dependants.	Actual Workers. Total. Males.	Actual Workers. Total. Females.	Actual Workers. Partially Agriculturist.	Dependants.
	1	372	373	374	375	376	377	378	379	380	381
	INDIA.	4,649	2,225	4	38	2,411	1,728,668	674,668	9,653	125,312	1,045,547
	Provinces.	4,511	2,211	..	38	2,300	1,219,622	470,262	4,461	91,666	744,899
1	Ajmer-Merwara	..	..	..	..	..	2,418	1,226	2	79	1,190
2	Andamans and Nicobars	..	..	..	..	..	1,026	876	..	1	150
3	Assam	..	..	..	..	..	15,099	6,860	..	1,181	8,239
4	Baluchistan	..	..	..	..	..	1,877	1,281	..	731	596
5	Bengal	15	14	..	..	1	173,006	61,340	..	14,842	111,666
6	Bihar and Orissa	..	..	..	..	..	138,624	53,764	..	14,549	84,860
7	Bombay	4,439	2,182	..	38	2,257	97,392	39,538	351	3,146	57,503
8	Burma	28	11	..	..	17	54,483	21,460	1,649	803	31,374
9	C. P. and Berar	12	..	..	..	12	146,013	55,980	1,942	13,459	88,091
10	Coorg	..	..	..	..	..	415	255	..	148	160
11	Madras	..	..	..	..	..	191,699	63,441	3	10,210	128,255
12	N.-W. F. Province (*Districts and Administered Territories*).	..	..	..	..	..	15,113	6,513	4	432	8,596
13	Punjab	..	..	..	..	..	108,142	40,056	..	4,919	68,086
14	United Provinces	17	4	..	..	13	274,315	117,672	510	27,166	156,133
	States and Agencies.	129	14	4	..	111	509,046	203,806	4,592	33,646	300,648
15	Assam State (Manipur)	..	..	..	..	..	664	353	..	17	311
16	Baluchistan States	..	..	..	..	..	1	1	..	..	..
17	Baroda State	..	..	..	..	..	15,344	[6,558	..	652	8,786
18	Bengal States	..	..	..	..	..	1,786	744	..	229	1,042
19	Bihar and Orissa States	..	..	..	..	..	40,457	13,130	..	4,170	27,327
20	Bombay States	117	10	..	..	107	96,935	35,375	1,069	5,601	60,491
21	Central India Agency	..	..	..	..	..	92,387	41,367	2,321	4,773	48,699
22	Central Provinces States	4	..	4	..	..	16,390	5,354	600	1,218	10,436
23	Hyderabad State	..	..	..	..	..	95,648	41,943	..	4,395	53,705
24	Kashmir State	..	..	..	..	..	9,807	3,603	..	426	6,204
25	Madras States	..	..	..	..	..	5,590	2,461	..	255	3,129
26	Mysore State	8	4	..	..	4	49,735	17,359	586	3,063	31,790
27	N.-W. F. Province (*Agencies and Tribal areas*).	..	..	..	..	..	161	151	..	1	10
28	Punjab States	..	..	..	..	..	20,360	7,518	..	702	12,842
29	Rajputana Agency	..	..	..	..	..	62,561	27,417	14	7,985	35,130
30	Sikkim State	..	..	..	..	..	105	58	..	..	47
31	United Provinces States	..	..	..	..	..	1,115	414	2	209	693

PART A.—GENERAL TABLE, (ii) PROVINCIAL DISTRIBUTION—continued.

ORDER 44.—POLICE—contd.		CLASS C: SUB-CLASS VII.—PUBLIC ADMINISTRATION. ORDER 45.—PUBLIC ADMINISTRATION. TOTAL OF SUB-CLASS VII AND ORDER 45.										
			Actual Workers.									
			Total.									
Group 142.—Police.	Group 143.—Village watchmen.	Total Workers and Dependants.	Males.	Females.	Partially Agriculturist.	Dependants.	Group 144.—Service of the State.	Group 145.—Service of Native and Foreign States.	Group 146.—Municipal and other local (not village) service.	Group 147.—Village officials and servants other than watchmen.	Serial Number.
382	383	384	385	386	387	388	389	390	391	392	
721,202	**1,007,466**	**2,648,005**	**927,599**	**42,922**	**141,406**	**1,677,484**	**809,427**	**643,078**	**190,038**	**1,005,462**	
492,854	**726,768**	**1,503,812**	**505,171**	**21,939**	**83,239**	**976,702**	**744,018**	**19,212**	**158,933**	**581,649**	
1,917	501	*4,778*	1,802	22	177	2,904	2,521	774	987	496	1
952	74	*397*	121	..	3	276	397	..	..	..	2
10,252	4,847	*14,313*	4,405	37	1,122	9,871	8,907	175	1,157	4,074	3
1,873	4	*6,345*	3,653	2	2,005	2,690	5,645	19	443	238	4
38,167	134,839	*130,810*	41,882	617	5,956	88,311	111,725	273	17,684	1,128	5
33,725	104,899	*57,561*	19,358	429	3,453	37,774	49,488	369	4,793	2,911	6
72,431	24,961	*359,366*	126,004	13,969	24,582	219,393	126,917	3,829	40,986	187,634	7
54,266	217	*103,108*	36,238	4,394	5,493	62,476	34,294	2,976	4,174	61,664	8
28,635	117,378	*96,482*	32,664	1,206	3,671	62,612	49,245	292	11,737	35,208	9
349	66	*1,171*	476	..	179	695	777	6	180	208	10
100,202	91,497	*343,338*	111,207	539	24,380	231,592	160,086	3,555	33,768	145,929	11
8,509	6,604	*23,199*	8,876	67	284	14,256	16,190	1,589	2,184	3,236	12
56,022	52,120	*109,984*	36,698	317	3,106	72,969	54,897	1,357	20,011	33,719	13
85,554	188,761	*253,010*	81,787	340	8,828	170,883	122,929	3,998	20,879	105,204	14
228,348	**280,698**	**1,144,193**	**422,428**	**20,983**	**58,169**	**700,782**	**65,409**	**623,866**	**31,105**	**423,813**	
518	146	*719*	283	19	71	417	219	370	3	127	15
1	..	*3,651*	1,573	..	420	2,078	859	2,784	..	8	16
9,919	5,425	*38,217*	13,853	284	747	24,080	33,318	376	1,959	2,564	17
586	1,200	*2,987*	1,331	2	320	1,654	117	2,762	90	18	18
9,717	30,740	*9,408*	3,772	106	611	5,530	150	7,767	43	1,448	19
62,644	34,291	*171,035*	58,578	2,810	5,591	109,647	16,960	110,963	4,387	38,725	20
40,707	51,680	*139,485*	54,282	2,056	3,816	83,147	4,836	108,143	2,411	24,095	21
3,898	12,492	*5,725*	2,106	161	175	3,458	101	4,309	191	1,124	22
35,135	60,513	*346,184*	149,366	7,343	20,814	189,475	4,567	130,831	8,926	201,860	23
4,672	5,135	*28,707*	11,157	241	726	17,309	34	23,617	1,765	3,291	24
5,360	230	*52,566*	16,735	236	1,396	35,595	259	44,431	654	7,222	25
18,188	31,547	*132,867*	30,524	1,251	13,802	101,092	928	38,695	5,874	87,370	26
122	39	*1,435*	1,317	..	344	118	1,398	..	7	30	27
11,302	9,058	*40,901*	14,641	467	2,619	25,793	395	23,324	2,239	14,943	28
25,450	37,111	*153,636*	58,020	5,844	6,349	89,772	1,165	110,599	2,530	39,342	29
60	45	*87*	35	..	1	52	10	42	8	27	30
69	1,046	*16,583*	4,855	163	277	11,565	93	14,853	18	1,619	31

TABLE XV.—Occupation or Means of Livelihood.

CLASS C: *SUB-CLASS VIII.—PROFESSIONS AND LIBERAL ARTS.*

Serial Number.	Province, State or Agency.	*TOTAL OF SUB-CLASS VIII.* Total Workers and Dependants.	Actual Workers. Total. Males.	Actual Workers. Total. Females.	Actual Workers. Partially Agriculturist.	Dependants.	ORDER 46.—RELIGION. *TOTAL OF ORDER 46.* Total Workers and Dependants.	Actual Workers. Total. Males.	Actual Workers. Total. Females.	Actual Workers. Partially Agriculturist.	Dependants.
	1	393	394	395	396	397	398	399	400	401	402
	INDIA.	**5,325,357**	**1,851,053**	**402,586**	**255,325**	**3,071,718**	**2,769,489**	**1,008,678**	**186,451**	**158,263**	**1,574,360**
	Provinces.	**3,881,670**	**1,335,018**	**278,474**	**186,864**	**2,268,178**	**1,897,173**	**688,618**	**116,494**	**107,378**	**1,092,061**
1	Ajmer-Merwara	*19,005*	7,542	2,523	1,262	8,940	**10,109**	4,419	1,107	696	4,583
2	Andamans and Nicobars	*214*	73	4	1	137	**4**	2	..	..	2
3	Assam	*86,150*	30,588	1,224	8,050	54,338	**50,708**	16,757	708	5,004	33,243
4	Baluchistan	*6,220*	2,629	171	379	3,420	**3,566**	1,312	53	118	2,201
5	Bengal	*803,173*	254,682	36,002	44,321	512,489	**367,637**	118,175	17,258	20,626	232,204
6	Bihar and Orissa	*360,354*	129,452	39,555	28,067	191,347	**182,691**	68,170	12,948	18,405	101,573
7	Bombay	*371,448*	135,169	19,609	10,928	216,670	**179,541**	65,802	10,820	6,925	102,919
8	Burma	*256,276*	121,417	23,235	4,148	111,624	**140,834**	79,102	11,087	1,414	50,645
9	C. P. and Berar	*217,844*	82,988	23,454	13,565	111,402	**118,698**	46,144	14,117	7,061	58,437
10	Coorg	*2,081*	901	88	207	1,092	**899**	393	30	116	476
11	Madras	*672,574*	210,042	37,310	33,654	425,222	**253,354**	82,922	11,428	17,240	159,004
12	N.-W. F. Province (*Districts and Administered Territories*).	*51,605*	18,687	1,056	822	31,862	**38,891**	14,504	631	628	23,756
13	Punjab	*514,894*	166,375	34,953	15,159	313,566	**285,782**	92,485	14,002	11,243	179,295
14	United Provinces	*519,832*	174,473	59,290	26,301	286,069	**264,459**	98,431	22,305	17,902	143,723
	States and Agencies.	**1,443,687**	**516,035**	**124,112**	**68,461**	**803,540**	**872,316**	**320,060**	**69,957**	**50,885**	**482,299**
15	Assam State (Manipur)	*6,765*	2,593	236	225	3,936	**4,581**	1,645	183	168	2,753
16	Baluchistan States	*4,949*	1,778	11	255	3,160	**3,433**	1,211	2	193	2,220
17	Baroda State	*74,692*	28,734	5,523	1,764	40,435	**51,985**	20,004	4,886	1,519	27,095
18	Bengal States	*8,766*	3,756	122	631	4,888	**3,482**	1,752	51	275	1,679
19	Bihar and Orissa States	*34,753*	14,115	1,719	3,018	18,919	**23,017**	8,652	1,365	2,178	13,000
20	Bombay States	*187,562*	64,610	12,054	3,181	110,898	**116,740**	41,861	9,172	2,217	65,707
21	Central India Agency	*138,390*	49,162	9,121	9,680	80,107	**94,629**	33,161	3,087	8,548	58,381
22	Central Provinces States	*16,860*	6,425	2,591	642	7,844	**10,792**	4,090	1,996	396	4,707
23	Hyderabad State	*209,039*	71,088	26,365	9,658	111,586	**101,187**	30,137	12,953	4,973	58,097
24	Kashmir State	*52,889*	18,434	1,528	1,959	32,927	**38,592**	13,026	1,173	1,629	24,393
25	Madras States	*136,615*	41,855	5,474	2,134	89,286	**47,647**	15,734	3,058	1,039	28,855
26	Mysore State	*81,077*	23,430	2,771	4,888	54,876	**34,564**	10,254	1,968	2,825	23,342
27	N.-W. F. Province (*Agencies and Tribal areas*).	*190*	132	1	18	57	**32**	21	..	1	11
28	Punjab States	*87,682*	31,200	6,020	3,753	50,462	**56,771**	20,197	3,574	3,106	33,000
29	Rajputana Agency	*388,899*	153,778	49,653	25,946	185,468	**277,851**	115,867	26,980	21,294	135,004
30	Sikkim State	*364*	292	20	4	52	**285**	248	16	4	21
31	United Provinces States	*14,195*	4,653	903	705	8,639	**6,728**	2,200	494	523	4,034

Part A.—General Table, (ii) Provincial Distribution—*continued.*

CLASS C: *SUB-CLASS VIII.—PROFESSIONS AND LIBERAL ARTS.*

ORDER 46.—RELIGION.—*contd.*				ORDER 47.—LAW.							
				TOTAL OF ORDER 47.							
					Actual Workers.						
					Total.						
Group 148.—Priests, ministers, etc.	Group 149.—Religious mendicants, inmates of monasteries, etc.	Group 150.—Catechists, readers, church and mission service.	Group 151.—Temple, burial or burning ground service, pilgrim conductors, circumcisers.	Total Workers and Dependants.	Males.	Females.	Partially Agriculturist.	Dependants.	Group 152.—Lawyers of all kinds, including Kazis, law agents and mukhtiars.	Group 153.—Lawyers' clerks, petition writers, etc.	Serial Number.
403	404	405	406	407	408	409	410	411	412	413	
1,596,328	**696,036**	**60,942**	**415,063**	**303,408**	**81,840**	**621**	**14,036**	**220,947**	**175,618**	**127,790**	
1,247,107	**317,952**	**39,975**	**292,139**	**255,663**	**68,446**	**572**	**12,867**	**186,645**	**140,014**	**115,649**	
1,906	6,421	157	1,625	**443**	113	..	6	330	231	212	1
1	..	3	..	**29**	10	..	1	19	..	29	2
47,456	795	042	1,515	**5,107**	1,318	..	415	3,789	2,586	2,521	3
2,219	1,176	48	123	**146**	43	..	13	103	16	130	4
308,359	47,666	4,361	7,251	**74,738**	18,624	..	5,716	56,114	48,122	26,616	5
124,092	16,388	971	41,240	**23,974**	6,654	..	1,626	17,320	14,153	9,821	6
53,560	94,764	4,303	26,905	**22,295**	5,782	34	468	16,479	13,350	8,945	7
128,642	11,638	434	120	**8,306**	2,874	393	53	5,039	6,079	2,227	8
10,786	94,933	6,440	6,539	**14,021**	3,927	65	524	10,029	9,495	4,526	9
54	3	204	638	**149**	38	..	9	111	129	20	10
82,808	6,411	13,300	150,835	**47,995**	13,196	3	2,248	34,796	20,344	27,651	11
22,949	12,848	71	3,023	**1,141**	313	3	29	825	240	901	12
261,078	3,504	3,691	17,509	**20,219**	5,506	..	554	14,713	8,639	11,580	13
203,188	21,405	5,050	34,816	**37,100**	10,048	74	1,205	26,978	16,630	20,470	14
349,221	**360,084**	**20,967**	**122,944**	**47,745**	**13,394**	**49**	**1,169**	**34,302**	**35,604**	**12,141**	
853	2	658	3,088	**11**	5	..	..	6	..	11	15
1,825	1,423	..	185	**87**	29	..	14	58	80	7	16
30,101	7,137	922	4,825	**1,670**	440	..	16	1,230	1,212	458	17
3,167	96	..	219	**1,060**	233	..	96	827	825	235	18
3,670	6,246	23	13,078	**633**	186	..	50	447	336	297	19
13,495	82,568	4,628	16,049	**8,094**	1,885	7	118	6,202	6,695	1,399	20
54,227	32,327	496	7,579	**3,663**	1,335	..	21	2,328	2,342	1,321	21
620	8,829	340	1,008	**408**	101	1	18	306	262	146	22
57,800	33,743	2,217	7,418	**6,863**	2,543	36	289	4,284	6,835	28	23
6,737	31,614	..	241	**1,523**	402	..	29	1,121	481	1,042	24
10,995	663	5,394	30,595	**11,293**	2,731	..	175	8,562	7,289	4,004	25
12,212	1,448	629	20,275	**2,687**	513	..	143	2,174	2,250	437	26
23	6	..	3	..	..	..	..	..	..	..	27
52,912	693	319	2,847	**2,827**	974	..	110	1,853	1,609	1,128	28
90,209	170,135	4,414	13,093	**6,501**	1,883	..	79	4,618	5,060	1,441	29
270	..	15	..	**9**	4	..	..	5	1	8	30
1,096	3,154	12	2,466	**416**	130	5	11	281	237	179	31

TABLE XV.—Occupation or Means of Livelihood.

Serial Number.	Province, State or Agency.	Class C: Sub Class VIII.—Professions and Liberal Arts. Order 48.—Medicine. Total of Order 48. Total Workers and Dependants.	Actual Workers. Total. Males.	Actual Workers. Total. Females.	Actual Workers. Partially Agriculturist.	Dependants.	Group 154.—Medical practitioners of all kinds, including dentists, oculists and veterinary surgeons.	Group 155.—Midwives, vaccinators, compounders, nurses, masseurs, etc.
	1	414	415	416	417	418	419	420
	INDIA.	**626,900**	**169,004**	**101,296**	**22,385**	**356,598**	**436,761**	**190,139**
	Provinces.	**525,131**	**137,456**	**86,612**	**19,760**	**301,063**	**368,731**	**156,400**
1	Ajmer-Merwara	1,102	298	199	15	605	540	562
2	Andamans and Nicobars	80	27	4	..	49	72	8
3	Assam	10,335	3,737	225	574	6,373	8,017	2,318
4	Baluchistan	792	386	70	94	336	349	443
5	Bengal	161,918	41,480	15,197	7,515	105,241	133,099	28,819
6	Bihar and Orissa	52,711	11,369	22,148	2,968	19,194	17,595	35,116
7	Bombay	31,729	9,938	3,233	324	18,558	19,857	11,872
8	Burma	52,172	18,769	6,341	1,917	27,062	49,582	2,590
9	C. P. and Berar	16,459	3,229	6,512	1,312	6,718	6,442	10,017
10	Coorg	258	103	20	24	135	177	81
11	Madras	88,865	24,226	7,056	2,884	57,583	74,552	14,313
12	N.-W. F. Province (*Districts and Administered Territories*).	2,503	791	161	52	1,551	1,861	642
13	Punjab	44,916	11,204	6,862	815	26,850	27,021	17,895
14	United Provinces	61,291	11,899	18,584	1,266	30,808	29,567	31,724
	States and Agencies.	**101,769**	**31,548**	**14,686**	**2,625**	**55,535**	**68,030**	**33,739**
15	Assam State (Manipur)	551	255	39	24	257	485	66
16	Baluchistan States	75	27	9	5	39	43	32
17	Baroda State	3,079	978	204	26	1,897	1,950	1,129
18	Bengal States	1,087	364	52	60	671	924	163
19	Bihar and Orissa States	1,295	435	73	57	787	926	369
20	Bombay States	11,200	2,881	905	101	7,414	7,654	3,546
21	Central India Agency	5,954	1,643	1,281	101	3,130	2,656	3,298
22	Central Provinces States	967	211	343	38	413	271	696
23	Hyderabad State	30,973	13,383	3,880	1,140	13,710	23,760	7,213
24	Kashmir State	2,769	928	168	63	1,673	2,093	676
25	Madras States	15,963	4,360	580	261	11,023	13,886	2,077
26	Mysore State	7,477	1,753	570	139	5,154	4,601	2,876
27	N.-W. F. Province (*Agencies and Tribal areas*).	52	30	1	5	21	40	12
28	Punjab States	4,580	1,270	751	90	2,559	2,557	2,023
29	Rajputana Agency	14,908	2,957	5,708	499	6,248	5,691	9,217
30	Sikkim State	25	17	2	..	6	10	15
31	United Provinces States	814	156	125	16	533	483	331

PART A.—GENERAL TABLE, (ii) PROVINCIAL DISTRIBUTION—*continued*.

CLASS C: *SUB-CLASS VIII.—PROFESSIONS AND LIBERAL ARTS.*

ORDER 49.—INSTRUCTION. TOTAL OF ORDER 49. [Group 156.—Professors and teachers of all kinds and clerks and servants connected with education.] Total Workers and Dependants.	Actual Workers. Total. Males.	Actual Workers. Total. Females.	Actual Workers. Partially Agri-culturist.	Dependants.	ORDER 50.—LETTERS AND ARTS AND SCIENCES. TOTAL OF ORDER 50. Total Workers and Dependants.	Actual Workers. Total. Males.	Actual Workers. Total. Females.	Actual Workers. Partially Agri-culturist.	Dependants.	Group 158. Architects, surveyors, engineers and their employés.	Group 159.—Others (authors, photographers, artists, sculptors, astronomers, meteorologists, botanists, astrologers, etc.)	Group 160.—Music composers and masters, players on all kinds of musical instruments (not military), singers, actors and dancers.	Serial Number.
421	422	423	424	425	426	427	428	429	430	431	432	433	
674,393	245,923	25,745	25,545	402,725	951,167	345,606	88,471	35,896	517,088	128,946	120,192	689,434	
530,579	194,903	20,025	21,775	315,651	673,124	245,595	54,771	25,064	372,758	96,053	77,922	485,589	
1,696	560	87	22	1,049	5,655	2,152	1,130	523	2,373	348	159	5,147	1
44	21	..	..	23	57	13	..	..	44	57	..	..	2
11,798	5,123	226	1,202	6,449	8,202	3,653	65	855	4,484	2,560	1,116	4,526	3
534	303	48	44	183	1,182	585	..	110	597	868	89	197	4
95,867	37,439	1,836	5,715	56,592	103,013	38,964	1,711	4,749	62,338	14,186	14,119	73,126	5
49,962	21,349	1,011	2,110	27,602	51,016	21,910	3,448	2,958	25,658	5,645	6,076	38,290	6
65,676	24,521	2,637	1,649	38,518	72,207	29,126	2,885	1,562	40,196	19,848	9,361	42,617	7
26,939	9,818	2,776	492	14,345	28,025	10,854	2,638	272	14,533	3,998	5,666	16,495	8
27,890	10,543	955	463	16,392	40,776	19,145	1,805	4,206	19,826	17,204	1,372	32,175	9
351	136	18	48	197	424	231	20	10	173	220	117	82	10
145,333	47,101	6,713	6,260	91,519	137,027	42,597	12,110	5,013	82,320	26,962	28,203	80,093	11
2,417	903	86	49	1,428	6,653	2,176	175	64	4,302	1,095	165	5,123	12
36,101	11,435	1,791	951	22,875	127,876	45,745	12,298	1,596	69,833	6,534	8,102	110,305	13
65,971	25,651	1,841	2,761	38,479	91,011	28,444	16,436	3,167	46,081	8,528	3,378	77,363	14
143,814	51,020	5,720	3,770	87,074	278,043	100,013	33,700	10,012	144,330	30,893	42,269	203,865	
559	233	3	14	323	1,063	455	11	24	597	156	129	778	15
72	45	..	2	27	1,282	466	..	41	816	24	28	1,230	16
9,399	4,147	179	101	5,073	8,559	3,165	254	102	5,140	2,532	420	5,607	17
975	402	11	83	562	2,162	1,005	8	117	1,149	174	70	1,918	18
4,792	2,775	63	352	1,954	5,016	2,067	218	381	2,731	969	559	3,409	19
22,316	7,399	772	290	14,145	29,212	10,584	1,198	455	17,430	4,115	3,021	21,987	20
6,951	2,761	515	171	3,675	27,193	10,362	4,238	839	12,593	1,996	2,476	22,706	21
1,758	848	64	46	846	2,935	1,175	188	144	1,572	291	79	2,565	22
23,574	8,360	1,995	893	13,219	46,442	16,665	7,501	2,363	22,276	1,166	11,502	33,774	23
3,053	1,174	18	79	1,861	6,952	2,904	169	159	3,879	3,797	1,352	1,803	24
35,195	10,865	1,036	333	23,294	26,517	8,165	800	326	17,552	5,142	9,364	11,940	25
22,110	7,146	740	1,204	14,224	14,239	3,764	498	577	9,982	4,729	2,438	6,800	26
15	9	..	..	6	91	72	..	12	19	74	..	17	27
4,030	1,444	154	105	2,432	19,474	7,315	1,541	340	10,618	937	402	17,766	28
8,041	3,061	160	81	4,820	81,598	30,010	16,810	3,993	34,778	4,776	10,260	66,440	29
39	17	2	..	20	6	6	..	..	..	5	1	..	30
935	334	8	16	593	5,302	1,833	271	139	3,196	10	78	5,285	31

TABLE XV—Occupation or Means of Livelihood.

Serial Number.	Province, State or Agency.	Class C: Sub-Class IX.—Persons living on their income. Order 51.—Persons living principally on their income. Total of Sub-Class IX and Order 51. [Group 161.—Proprietors (other than of agricultural land), fund and scholarship holders and pensioners.] Total Workers and Dependants.	Actual Workers. Total. Males.	Actual Workers. Total. Females.	Actual Workers. Partially Agri-culturist.	Dependants.	Class D: Miscellaneous. Total of Class D. Total Workers and Dependants.	Actual Workers. Total. Males.	Actual Workers. Total. Females.	Actual Workers. Partially Agri-culturist.	Dependants.
	1	434	435	436	437	438	439	440	441	442	443
	INDIA.	**540,175**	**143,456**	**62,614**	**18,343**	**334,105**	**17,286,678**	**6,086,540**	**3,778,410**	**394,695**	**7,461,728**
	Provinces.	**366,972**	**97,458**	**35,597**	**14,268**	**233,917**	**12,398,316**	**4,506,006**	**2,539,902**	**255,472**	[illegible]
1	Ajmer-Merwara	*2,424*	529	268	80	1,627	**28,851**	11,195	5,206	689	11,850
2	Andamans and Nicobars	*7*	3	2	..	2	**12,404**	11,582	707	..	115
3	Assam	*2,941*	814	60	147	2,067	**204,481**	79,328	48,412	5,685	76,741
4	Baluchistan	*563*	118	26	23	424	**16,352**	8,016	1,163	1,010	7,173
5	Bengal	*51,425*	10,865	5,529	1,464	35,031	**2,302,324**	892,800	318,658	40,294	1,090,857
6	Bihar and Orissa	*9,251*	2,388	941	369	5,922	**1,700,469**	555,006	468,288	26,517	677,175
7	Bombay	*71,531*	18,664	6,394	2,166	46,473	**971,262**	403,041	169,347	11,946	398,874
8	Burma	*6,967*	2,176	493	79	4,298	**549,745**	244,467	97,896	10,397	207,382
9	C. P. and Berar	*11,716*	3,140	1,149	365	7,427	**273,204**	101,288	69,673	9,902	102,243
10	Coorg	*140*	40	24	11	76	**4,790**	2,443	1,319	116	1,028
11	Madras	*86,603*	20,780	9,359	3,031	56,464	**1,979,277**	552,933	591,865	49,209	834,479
12	N.-W. F. Province (*Districts and Administered Territories.*)	*5,725*	1,781	211	73	3,733	**134,229**	52,578	10,541	618	71,110
13	Punjab	*49,039*	16,676	3,866	2,609	28,497	**1,156,501**	457,044	107,102	21,617	592,355
14	United Provinces	*68,640*	19,489	7,275	3,851	41,876	**3,065,627**	1,134,276	649,725	77,432	1,281,026
	States and Agencies.	**173,203**	**45,998**	**27,017**	**4,075**	**100,188**	**4,888,362**	**1,580,534**	**1,228,506**	[illegible]	[illegible]
15	Assam State (Manipur)	*265*	63	7	2	195	**2,642**	**1,288**	169	41	1,185
16	Baluchistan States	*69*	14	2	6	53	**14,244**	3,382	4,976	385	5,886
17	Baroda State	*8,462*	1,943	1,277	30	5,242	**155,054**	44,851	36,104	2,170	74,099
18	Bengal States	*680*	99	94	20	487	**19 315**	9,875	3,816	315	5,624
19	Bihar and Orissa States	*681*	118	94	23	469	**159,741**	45,866	49,561	2,538	64,314
20	Bombay States	*14,695*	3,338	2,995	345	8,362	**359,734**	113,867	67,599	2,367	178,268
21	Central India Agency	*31,173*	8,313	4,362	332	18,498	**1,201,154**	402,515	385,388	11,180	413,251
22	Central Provinces States	*148*	44	24	2	80	**28,210**	8,510	10,069	489	9,631
23	Hyderabad State	*28,377*	8,650	2,289	218	17,438	**1,077,434**	336,361	253,042	32,382	488,031
24	Kashmir State	*2,432*	751	170	157	1,511	**100,422**	39,959	10,867	2,072	49,596
25	Madras States	*7,549*	2,190	361	119	4,998	**550,499**	146,006	143,305	2,458	261,188
26	Mysore State	*20,935*	4,928	1,852	773	14,155	**490,622**	141,575	136,384	2,867	212,663
27	N.-W. F. Province (*Agencies and Tribal areas.*)	*25*	7	..	..	18	**1,249**	921	2	57	326
28	Punjab States	*9,932*	3,226	915	774	5,791	**214,341**	90,084	21,383	3,482	103,369
29	Rajputana Agency	*46.558*	11,940	12,407	1,255	22,211	**473,361**	181,181	109,585	15,006	182,595
30	Sikkim State	*23*	22	..	..	1	**1,442**	790	393	5	259
31	United Provinces States	*1,199*	352	168	19	679	**38,398**	13,503	5,860	1,209	19,085

PART A.—GENERAL TABLE, (*ii*) PROVINCIAL DISTRIBUTION—*continued.*

CLASS D : *SUB-CLASS X.—DOMESTIC SERVICE.*							CLASS D : *SUB-CLASS XI.—INSUFFICIENTLY DESCRIBED OCCUPATIONS.*					
ORDER 52.—DOMESTIC SERVICE.							ORDER 53.—GENERAL TERMS WHICH DO NOT INDICATE A DEFINITE OCCUPATION.					
TOTAL OF SUB-CLASS X AND ORDER 52.					Group 162.—Cooks, water-carriers, door-keepers, watchmen and other indoor servants.	Group 163.—Private grooms, coachmen, dog boys, etc.	*TOTAL OF SUB-CLASS XI AND ORDER 53.*					Serial Number.
Total Workers and Dependants.	ACTUAL WORKERS. Total. Males.	ACTUAL WORKERS. Total. Females.	ACTUAL WORKERS. Partially Agriculturist.	Dependants.			Total Workers and Dependants.	ACTUAL WORKERS. Total. Males.	ACTUAL WORKERS. Total. Females.	ACTUAL WORKERS. Partially Agriculturist.	Dependants.	
444	415	446	447	448	449	450	451	452	453	454	455	
4,599,080	**1,733,112**	**992,744**	**103,393**	**1,873,224**	**4,290,642**	**308,438**	**9,236,217**	**3,057,818**	**2,009,882**	**150,162**	**4,168,517**	
3,416,992	**1,309,714**	**755,200**	**75,090**	**1,352,078**	**3,176,322**	**240,670**	**6,575,606**	**2,295,992**	**1,229,490**	**122,281**	**3,050,124**	
14,738	6,172	2,195	266	6,371	13,173	1,565	*5,152*	1,609	1,491	27	2,052	1
199	145	7	..	47	199	..	*184*	130	..	..	54	2
37,490	21,526	5,510	1,177	10,454	34,448	3,042	*96,613*	38,008	16,893	3,631	41,712	3
7,158	4,191	908	759	2,059	5,702	1,456	*6,112*	2,552	38	210	3,522	4
519,851	249,691	110,915	8,878	159,245	498,789	21,062	*1,346,184*	523,207	43,349	27,594	779,628	5
692,663	215,489	206,145	12,591	271,028	644,836	47,826	*829,144*	272,436	210,273	9,880	346,435	6
331,719	147,364	53,211	3,490	131,144	307,510	24,209	*390,067*	161,395	59,630	2,942	169,042	7
85,771	47,816	10,987	1,133	26,968	82,197	3,574	*429,399*	180,246	76,922	8,789	172,231	8
142,792	51,043	40,013	5,773	51,736	131,095	11,697	*35,449*	11,164	9,441	260	14,844	9
2,318	1,149	680	44	489	2,055	263	*1,882*	1,022	450	71	410	10
203,826	62,281	47,026	4,028	94,519	184,907	18,919	*1,503,693*	887,121	471,705	31,728	644,867	11
38,845	18,195	3,380	339	17,270	35,361	3,484	*72,947*	24,094	4,852	207	44,001	12
438,844	168,184	50,237	9,490	220,423	410,245	28,599	*211,053*	81,254	12,720	3,492	117,079	13
900,779	316,468	223,986	27,122	360,325	825,805	74,974	*1,647,727*	611,754	321,726	33,400	714,247	14
1,182,088	**423,396**	**237,544**	**28,303**	**521,146**	**1,114,320**	**67,768**	**2,660,611**	**761,826**	**780,392**	**27,881**	**1,118,393**	
1,049	507	40	17	502	941	108	*1,088*	493	9	24	586	15
7,136	879	4,911	89	1,346	6,958	178	*4,644*	1,544	38	104	3,062	16
3,510	1,237	595	47	1,678	3,349	161	*142,985*	40,235	33,977	2,096	68,073	17
7,039	4,695	675	107	1,669	6,590	449	*2,746*	1,744	27	122	975	18
33,484	12,114	9,409	950	11,961	27,262	6,222	*113,195*	28,805	36,55ɼ	1,356	47,769	19
62,072	19,461	14,065	526	28,546	58,172	3,900	*160,540*	45,034	32,092	657	83,414	20
214,177	81,543	43,565	5,918	89,069	204,889	9,288	*754,480*	223,103	275,887	3,303	255,490	21
18,203	5,085	7,152	294	5,966	14,615	3,588	*2,280*	558	753	71	969	22
421,147	140,971	75,814	10,881	204,362	406,181	14,966	*380,148*	110,010	111,369	13,206	158,769	23
37,766	16,788	3,415	496	17,563	36,911	855	*23,004*	8,364	2,111	511	12,529	24
23,097	6,624	6,156	164	10,317	20,796	2,301	*515,166*	134,350	133,226	2,248	247,590	25
38,308	14,078	6,382	255	17,848	32,584	5,724	*400,349*	111,445	116,381	1,930	172,523	26
363	278	2	27	88	315	48	*696*	517	..	28	179	27
68,883	28,646	7,026	1,593	33,211	66,260	2,623	*53,577*	21,005	6,576	415	25,996	28
224,700	83,160	54,705	6,247	86,835	208,595	16,105	*92,517*	29,358	29,621	1,261	33,538	29
719	486	167	..	66	690	29	*599*	231	185	1	183	30
20,435	6,851	3,465	692	10,119	19,212	1,223	*13,367*	5,080	1.589	455	6,748	31

TABLE XV.—Occupation or Means of Livelihood.

Serial Number.	Province, State or Agency.	Class D: Sub-Class XI.—Insufficiently described occupations. Order 53.—General terms which do not indicate a definite occupation—contd. Group 164.—Manufacturers, business men and contractors otherwise unspecified.	Group 165.—Cashiers, accountants, book-keepers, clerks and other employés in unspecified offices, warehouses and shops.	Group 166.—Mechanics otherwise unspecified.	Group 167.—Labourers and workmen otherwise unspecified.	Class D: Sub-Class XII.—Unproductive. Total of Sub-Class XII. Total Workers and Dependants.	Actual Workers. Total. Males.	Actual Workers. Total. Females.	Actual Workers. Partially Agriculturist.	Dependants.
	1	456	457	458	459	460	461	462	463	464
	INDIA.	**122,696**	**776,663**	**63,208**	**8,273,650**	**3,451,381**	**1,295,610**	**775,784**	**80,940**	**1,379,987**
	Provinces.	**91,316**	**637,324**	**56,314**	**5,790,652**	**2,405,718**	**900,300**	**555,212**	**58,101**	**950,206**
1	Ajmer-Merwara	303	552	..	4,297	*8,361*	3,414	1,520	396	3,427
2	Andamans and Nicobars	..	..	..	184	*12,021*	11,307	700	..	14
3	Assam	1,801	9,713	1,472	83,627	*70,378*	19,794	26,009	767	24,575
4	Baluchistan	185	81	1	5,845	*3,082*	1,273	217	41	1,592
5	Bengal	14,080	181,450	22,258	1,128,396	*436,289*	119,911	164,394	3,922	151,984
6	Bihar and Orissa	6,395	45,186	142	777,421	*178,663*	67,081	51,870	4,046	59,712
7	Bombay	10,353	110,947	13,881	254,936	*249,476*	94,282	56,506	5,514	98,688
8	Burma	10,852	58,873	8,240	351,434	*34,575*	16,405	9,987	475	8,183
9	C. P. and Berar	2,389	4,410	1,009	27,641	*94,963*	39,081	20,219	3,869	35,663
10	Coorg	46	260	7	1,569	*590*	272	189	1	129
11	Madras	14,687	160,459	6,818	1,321,729	*271,758*	103,531	73,184	13,453	95,093
12	N.-W. F. Province (*Districts and Administered Territories*).	2,786	416	357	69,388	*22,437*	10,289	2,309	72	9,839
13	Punjab	11,680	25,873	400	173,100	*506,604*	207,606	44,145	8,635	254,853
14	United Provinces	15,759	39,104	,779	1,59 ,085	*516,521*	206,054	104,013	16,910	206,454
	States and Agencies.	**31,380**	**139,339**	**6,894**	**2,482,996**	**1,045,663**	**395,310**	**220,572**	**22,839**	**429,781**
15	Assam State (Manipur)	98	185	652	153	*505*	288	120	..	97
16	Baluchistan States	99	31	..	4,514	*2,464*	959	27	102	1,478
17	Baroda State	..	26,354	118	115,813	*9,259*	3,379	1,532	27	4,348
18	Bengal States	97	927	15	1,707	*9,530*	3,436	3,114	86	2,980
19	Bihar and Orissa States	337	970	56	111,762	*13,132*	4,947	3,601	232	4,584
20	Bombay States	3,132	53,080	3,052	101,276	*137,122*	49,372	21,442	1,184	66,308
21	Central India Agency	6,025	5,160	1,567	741,728	*232,497*	97,869	65,936	1,959	68,692
22	Central Provinces States	12	455	3	1,810	*7,727*	2,867	2,164	124	2,696
23	Hyderabad State	6,828	8,073	1,090	364,157	*276,139*	85,380	65,859	8,295	124,900
24	Kashmir State	6,543	66	167	16,228	*39,652*	14,807	5,341	1,065	19,504
25	Madras States	1,816	13,623	22	499,705	*12,236*	5,032	3,923	46	3,281
26	Mysore State	4,031	8,900	77	387,341	*51,965*	16,052	13,621	682	22,292
27	N.-W. F. Province (*Agencies and Tribal Areas*).	53	8	..	685	*190*	131	..	2	59
28	Punjab States	1,527	973	33	51,044	*92,381*	40,433	7,786	1,474	44,162
29	Rajputana Agency	448	20,058	40	71,971	*156,144*	68,663	25,259	7,498	62,222
30	Sikkim State	3	84	..	512	*124*	73	41	1	10
31	United Provinces States	331	392	2	12,642	*4,596*	1,622	806	62	2,168

PART A.—GENERAL TABLE, (ii) PROVINCIAL DISTRIBUTION—*concluded.*

CLASS D: *SUB-CLASS XII.—UNPRODUCTIVE.*

ORDER 54.—INMATES OF JAILS, ASYLUMS AND HOSPITALS. TOTAL OF ORDER 54. [Group 168.—Inmates of jails, asylums and hospitals.]					ORDER 55.—BEGGARS, VAGRANTS, PROSTITUTES. TOTAL OF ORDER 55. [Group 169.—Beggars, vagrants, procurers, prostitutes, receivers of stolen goods, cattle poisoners.]					
Total Workers and Dependants.	Actual Workers. Total. Males.	Actual Workers. Total. Females.	Actual Workers. Partially Agriculturist.	Dependants.	Total Workers and Dependants.	Actual Workers. Total. Males.	Actual Workers. Total. Females.	Actual Workers. Partially Agriculturist.	Dependants.	Serial Number.
465	466	467	468	469	470	471	472	473	474	
132,610	**117,273**	**7,290**	**769**	**8,047**	**3,318,771**	**1,178,337**	**768,494**	**80,171**	**1,371,940**	
106,745	**97,018**	**5,584**	**690**	**4,143**	**2,296,973**	**803,282**	**549,628**	**57,411**	**944,063**	
445	19	16	..	410	7,916	3,395	1,504	396	3,017	1
11,998	11,301	689	..	8	23	6	11	..	6	2
2,139	2,043	88	128	8	68,239	17,751	25,921	639	24,567	3
302	282	18	8	2	2,780	991	199	38	1,590	4
14,099	13,082	992	164	25	422,190	106,829	163,402	3,768	151,959	5
7,817	6,705	1,112	62	..	170,846	60,376	50,758	3,984	59,712	6
8,422	6,572	374	34	1,476	241,054	87,710	56,132	5,480	97,212	7
8,500	8,052	44	2	404	26,075	8,353	9,943	473	7,779	8
3,341	2,487	192	11	662	91,622	36,594	20,027	3,858	35,001	9
110	77	1	..	32	480	195	188	1	97	10
13,363	11,816	547	160	1,000	258,395	91,715	72,587	13,293	94,093	11
1,490	1,465	18	..	7	20,947	8,824	2,291	72	9,882	12
12,605	11,413	304	..	888	493,999	196,193	43,841	8,635	253,965	13
24,114	21,704	1,189	131	1,221	492,407	184,350	102,824	16,779	205,233	14
23,865	**20,255**	**1,706**	**79**	**1,904**	**1,021,796**	**375,055**	**218,866**	**22,760**	**427,877**	
117	117	..	..	..	388	171	120	..	97	15
48	46	1	..	1	2,416	913	26	102	1,477	16
802	576	97	1	129	8,457	2,803	1,435	26	4,219	17
51	42	9	..	..	9,479	3,394	3,105	86	2,980	18
1,243	1,165	78	2	..	11,889	3,782	3,523	230	4,584	19
1,888	1,655	95	17	138	135,234	47,717	21,347	1,167	66,170	20
4,148	3,004	501	44	643	228,349	94,865	65,435	1,915	68,049	21
515	406	16	..	93	7,212	2,461	2,148	124	2,603	22
3,428	3,198	131	..	99	272,711	82,182	65,728	8,295	124,801	23
658	621	18	..	19	38,994	14,186	5,323	1,065	19,485	24
1,958	1,329	106	1	523	10,278	3,703	3,817	46	2,758	25
1,434	1,237	197	..	..	50,531	14,815	13,424	682	22,292	26
61	61	..	2	..	129	70	..	..	59	27
1,800	1,687	96	..	17	90,581	38,746	7,690	1,474	44,145	28
5,219	4,630	360	12	229	150,925	64,033	24,899	7,486	61,993	29
10	10	..	..	..	114	63	41	1	10	30
485	471	1	..	13	4,111	1,151	805	62	2,155	31

Distribution by Occupation of the population of Cochin and Travancore.

Order No.	Occupation.	Cochin State. Total Workers and Dependants.	Cochin State. Actual Workers. Total. Males.	Cochin State. Actual Workers. Total. Females.	Cochin State. Actual Workers. Partially Agriculturist.	Cochin State. Dependants.	Travancore State. Total Workers and Dependants.	Travancore State. Actual Workers. Total. Males.	Travancore State. Actual Workers. Total. Females.	Travancore State. Actual Workers. Partially Agriculturist.	Travancore State. Dependants.
	1	2	3	4	5	6	7	8	9	10	11
	TOTAL OF ALL CLASSES	**918,110**	**248,247**	**127,266**	**7,982**	**542,597**	**3,428,975**	**965,102**	**456,544**	**7,005**	**2,007,329**
	A.—Production of raw materials	**483,910**	**124,717**	**63,602**	**1,730**	**295,591**	**1,907,199**	**541,764**	**141,130**	**257**	**1,224,305**
	I.—EXPLOITATION OF THE SURFACE OF THE EARTH.	***483,904***	***124,717***	***63,602***	***1,730***	***295,585***	***1,905,466***	***541,112***	***140,964***	***257***	***1,223,390***
1	Pasture and agriculture	470,607	119,343	62,641	1,623	288,623	1,839,423	515,570	138,391	241	1,185,462
	(a) Ordinary cultivation	*439,878*	*110,387*	*61,065*	..	*268,426*	*1,615,902*	*441,314*	*119,633*	*14*	*1,054,955*
	(b) Growers of special products and market gardening.	*23,196*	*5,710*	*1,209*	..	*16,277*	*206,856*	*68,164*	*16,256*	*95*	*122,436*
	(c) Forestry	*5,422*	*1,736*	*299*	*148*	*3,387*	*6,466*	*1,646*	*1,664*	*80*	*3,156*
	(d) Raising of farm stock	*1,940*	*1,499*	*68*	*1,475*	*373*	*10,196*	*4,443*	*838*	*52*	*4,915*
	(e) Raising of small animals	*171*	*11*	..	..	*160*	*3*	*3*	..	..	..
2	Fishing and hunting	13,297	5,374	961	107	6,962	66,043	25,542	2,573	16	37,928
	II.—EXTRACTION OF MINERALS	***6***	..	..	..	***6***	***1,733***	***652***	***166***	..	***915***
3	Mines	6	..	..	..	6	1,295	502	133	..	660
4	Quarries of hard rocks	..	..	..	..	..	..	..	..	..	..
5	Salt, etc.	..	..	..	..	..	438	150	33	..	255
	B.—Preparation and supply of material substances.	**316,466**	**83,875**	**52,375**	**4,368**	**180,158**	**928,685**	**265,123**	**190,533**	**4,351**	**473,029**
	III.—INDUSTRY	***192,051***	***47,088***	***42,556***	***2,586***	***102,407***	***588,410***	***168,332***	***120,615***	***2,918***	***299,463***
6	Textiles	46,825	9,381	18,632	322	18,812	160,544	38,987	67,087	217	54,470
7	Hides, skins, hard and materials from the animal kingdom.	1,179	405	48	18	726	149	58	3	..	88
8	Wood	43,232	12,459	5,761	697	25,012	93,018	28,619	13,271	349	51,128
9	Metals	9,277	2,755	360	62	6,162	35,391	11,801	603	135	22,987
10	Ceramics	4,196	1,271	914	26	2,011	14,234	4,600	2,617	54	7,017
11	Chemical products properly so called, and analogous.	4,192	1,042	365	17	2,785	20,003	6,907	2,708	146	10,388
12	Food industries	40,211	8,058	9,508	948	22,645	168,407	46,613	17,934	1,436	103,860
13	Industries of dress and the toilet	18,438	4,910	5,049	272	8,479	60,888	18,333	15,029	384	27,526
14	Furniture industries	132	37	..	2	95	127	53	..	..	74
15	Building industries	13,532	4,180	352	124	9,000	7,506	2,678	513	61	4,315
16	Construction of means of transport	66	25	..	..	41	387	233	..	4	154
17	Production and transmission of physical forces (heat, light, electricity, motive power, etc.)	1	1	..	..	..	61	16	..	..	45
18	Industries of luxury and those pertaining to literature and the arts and sciences.	7,785	2,449	48	67	5,288	25,714	8,876	305	128	16,533
19	Industries concerned with refuse matter.	2,985	115	1,519	31	1,351	1,981	558	545	4	878
	IV.—TRANSPORT	***18,856***	***7,282***	***357***	***253***	***11,217***	***54,942***	***22,724***	***5,921***	***102***	***26,297***
20	Transport by water	6,773	2,911	10	128	3,852	23,895	10,206	1,773	19	11,916
21	Transport by road	10,050	3,527	346	117	6,177	25,838	10,400	4,146	69	11,202
22	Transport by rail	1,301	569	1	2	731	929	567	..	2	362
23	Post Office, Telegraph and Telephone services.	732	275	..	6	457	4,280	1,551	2	12	2,727
	V.—TRADE	***105,501***	***29,505***	***9,462***	***1,529***	***66,534***	***285,333***	***74,067***	***63,997***	***1,331***	***147,969***
24	Banks, establishments of credit, exchange and insurance.	4,424	844	595	83	2,985	9,446	1,887	861	48	6,698
25	Brokerage, commission and export	255	85	4	..	166	827	259	26	5	542
26	Trade in textiles	5,646	1,812	86	134	3,748	45,221	12,436	9,957	154	22,828
27	Trade in skins, leather and furs	544	132	11	5	401	508	184	3	1	321
28	Trade in wood	1,305	394	8	25	903	9,031	2,094	3,732	50	3,205
29	Trade in metals	321	71	7	..	243	78	30	..	..	48
30	Trade in pottery	217	37	23	1	157	2,289	620	635	12	1,034
31	Trade in chemical products	842	301	5	3	536	131	47	..	..	84
32	Hotels, cafés, restaurants, etc.	9,690	2,346	1,411	66	5,983	23,443	6,811	5,427	138	11,205
33	Other trade in food stuffs	59,573	16,761	6,362	934	36,450	168,703	42,185	39,647	636	86,871
34	Trade in clothing and toilet articles	336	154	..	1	182	64	25	4	1	35
35	Trade in furniture	1,537	558	108	21	871	3,281	834	412	26	2,035
36	Trade in building materials	1,585	379	223	19	983	5,004	1,363	862	25	2,779
37	Trade in means of transport	797	336	11	11	450	937	331	8	1	598
38	Trade in fuel	2,043	817	92	26	1,134	4,082	1,025	1,448	3	1,609
39	Trade in articles of luxury and those pertaining to letters and the arts and sciences.	1,118	237	64	11	817	1,415	457	..	13	958
40	Trade in refuse matter	54	7	16	1	31	38	13	..	..	25
41	Trade of other sorts	15,214	4,234	436	188	10,544	10,835	3,466	975	218	6,394
	C.—Public administration and liberal arts.	**43,478**	**13,990**	**1,856**	**722**	**27,632**	**145,428**	**44,918**	**3,540**	**1,735**	**96,970**
	VI.—PUBLIC FORCE	***1,740***	***700***	..	***6***	***1,040***	***9,289***	***3,480***	..	***430***	***5,809***
42	Army	576	247	..	1	329	5,886	1,818	..	232	4,068
43	Navy	..	..	..	..	..	..	..	..	..	..
44	Police	1,164	453	..	5	711	3,403	1,662	..	198	1,741
45	***VII.—(ORDER 45) PUBLIC ADMINISTRATION.***	***10,045***	***3,507***	***224***	***160***	***6,314***	***32,695***	***10,122***	..	***413***	***22,573***
	VIII.—PROFESSIONS AND LIBERAL ARTS.	***30,564***	***9,457***	***1,616***	***594***	***19,491***	***97,729***	***29,645***	***3,256***	***844***	***64,828***
46	Religion	10,648	3,484	938	201	6,226	33,714	10,992	2,064	384	20,658
47	Law	2,163	585	..	59	1,578	8,545	2,003	..	70	6,542
48	Medicine	4,881	1,280	195	84	3,406	10,209	2,874	269	131	7,066
49	Instruction	7,417	2,289	308	121	4,820	26,365	8,111	677	138	17,577
50	Letters and arts and sciences	5,455	1,819	175	59	3,461	18,896	5,665	246	121	12,985
51	***IX.—(ORDER 51) PERSONS LIVING PRINCIPALLY ON THEIR INCOME.***	***1,129***	***326***	***16***	***39***	***787***	***5,715***	***1,671***	***284***	***48***	***3,760***
	D—Miscellaneous	**74,314**	**25,665**	**9,433**	**1,162**	**39,216**	**447,663**	**113,297**	**121,341**	**662**	**213,025**
52	***X.—(ORDER 52) DOMESTIC SERVICE.***	***5,573***	***2,351***	***1,516***	***39***	***1,706***	***15,255***	***3,481***	***4,337***	***39***	***7,437***
53	***XI.—(ORDER 53) INSUFFICIENTLY DESCRIBED OCCUPATIONS***	***66,194***	***22,306***	***7,045***	***1,109***	***36,843***	***424,789***	***106,596***	***114,635***	***623***	***203,558***
	XII.—UNPRODUCTIVE.	***2,547***	***1,008***	***872***	***14***	***667***	***7,619***	***3,220***	***2,369***	..	***2,030***
54	Inmates of jails, asylums and hospitals	157	108	7	1	42	1,740	1,164	95	..	481
55	Beggars, vagrants and prostitutes	2,390	900	865	13	625	5,879	2,056	2,274	..	1,549

TABLE XV.

Occupation or Means of Livelihood.

PART B.—NUMBER OF AGRICULTURISTS WITH SUBSIDIARY OCCUPATIONS.

1. This Part shows the number of actual workers in Groups 1 (rent receivers), 2 (rent payers) and 4 (field labourers) who have subsidiary occupations. These details are not available for the Andamans and Nicobars and the Frontier Ilaqas in the Kashmir State. Hence the total number of actual workers here shown does not quite agree with that given in Part A, section (i).

2. The figures for Provinces include those for the States attached to them, except in the case of Madras, where they exclude those for Cochin and Travancore which are shown separately.

TABLE XV—Occupation or Means of Livelihood. Part B—Number of

(1) Rent Receivers (Landlords).

Province, State or Agency.	Total number of Rent Receivers (Actual Workers).		Number of actual workers who returned subsidiary occupations. Total.		Other Agricultural Occupations.		Non-Agricultural Occupations.	
	Males.	Females.	Males.	Females.	Males.	Females.	Males.	Females.
1	2	3	4	5	6	7	8	9
INDIA.	**2,113,710**	**731,486**	**591,824**	**86,978**	**264,453**	**46,129**	**327,371**	**40,849**
Ajmer-Merwara	3,439	869	1,343	110	504	73	839	37
Assam	18,286	4,195	10,549	607	4,179	272	6,370	335
Baluchistan	22,524	7	9,439	..	1,022	..	8,417	..
Bengal	263,479	63,328	84,611	5,190	30,966	2,887	53,645	2,303
Bihar and Orissa	197,538	45,559	55,707	5,789	43,551	3,666	12,156	2,123
Bombay	224,702	56,912	60,998	7,366	25,876	4,642	35,122	2,724
Burma	59,921	68,997	7,470	6,418	2,667	2,231	4,803	4,187
Central Provinces and Berar	32,142	25,782	16,257	4,519	9,264	2,845	6,993	1,674
Coorg	1,116	878	497	132	66	66	431	66
Madras	265,504	180,590	85,411	20,332	17,920	9,347	67,491	10,985
N.-W. F. Province	25,819	3,511	4,439	147	283	99	4,156	48
Punjab	171,379	68,393	48,030	5,047	6,564	472	41,466	4,575
United Provinces	259,685	86,973	100,052	15,403	67,546	10,532	32,506	4,871
Baroda State	7,984	1,935	760	145	319	119	441	26
Central India Agency	43,762	10,279	22,320	3,220	14,318	1,960	8,002	1,260
Cochin State	2,697	700	652	68	15	1	637	67
Hyderabad State	234,108	113,407	22,539	7,864	12,521	5,295	10,018	2,569
Kashmir State	8,385	3,983	2,216	286	843	118	1,373	168
Mysore State	34,295	20,718	10,665	1,777	242	111	10,423	1,666
Rajputana Agency	215,481	19,497	45,276	2,173	24,939	1,079	20,337	1,094
Sikkim State	56	10	9	..	1	..	8	..
Travancore State	21,408	4,963	2,584	385	847	314	1,737	71

Agriculturists with Subsidiary Occupations (Actual Workers only).

(2) Rent Payers (Ordinary Cultivators).

Province, State or Agency.	Total number of Rent payers (Actual Workers).		Number of actual workers who returned subsidiary occupations.					
			Total.		Other Agricultural Occupations.		Non-Agricultural Occupations.	
	Males.	Females.	Males.	Females.	Males.	Females.	Males.	Females.
1	2	3	4	5	6	7	8	9
INDIA.	**51,929,573**	**19,139,367**	**7,606,404**	**1,765,353**	**2,032,702**	**824,478**	**5,573,702**	**940,875**
Ajmer-Merwara	79,887	66,020	8,351	1,685	1,053	631	7,298	1,054
Assam	1,525,888	566,322	257,352	46,316	19,781	3,034	237,571	43,282
Baluchistan	155,068	..	47,272	..	1,380	..	45,892	..
Bengal	8,422,860	482,998	1,186,999	35,079	282,542	9,932	904,457	25,147
Bihar and Orissa	6,621,769	2,518,805	1,320,274	324,342	374,660	130,256	945,614	194,086
Bombay	3,491,581	1,013,759	453,061	99,171	143,271	64,751	309,790	34,420
Burma	1,858,632	1,559,824	170,219	104,491	67,902	35,881	102,317	68,610
Central Provinces and Berar	2,350,713	1,756,106	323,965	181,106	81,046	86,566	242,919	94,540
Coorg	27,308	22,511	3,274	804	574	397	2,700	407
Madras	6,101,912	3,369,132	880,931	277,551	270,364	152,131	610,567	125,420
N.-W. F. Province	374,621	18,783	30,610	219	1,497	10	29,113	209
Punjab	4,017,131	302,616	326,746	7,854	58,199	1,268	268,547	6,586
United Provinces	9,913,214	3,980,964	2,021,883	586,772	628,466	307,127	1,393,417	279,645
Baroda State	310,548	86,886	13,486	1,080	2,695	662	10,791	418
Central India Agency	1,425,548	711,868	104,078	34,270	27,460	9,421	76,618	24,849
Cochin State	59,633	12,514	8,556	593	401	93	8,155	500
Hyderabad State	1,367,676	727,383	51,214	18,637	23,307	10,330	27,907	8,307
Kashmir State	725,937	381,837	117,427	8,217	12,406	826	105,021	7,391
Mysore State	845,056	82,855	103,424	5,048	2,579	271	100,845	4,777
Rajputana Agency	1,881,964	1,395,581	150,776	29,802	27,934	9,850	122,842	19,952
Sikkim State	27,527	27,543	977	281	7	..	970	281
Travancore State	345,150	55,260	25,529	2,035	5,178	1,041	20,351	994

TABLE XV—Occupation or Means of Livelihood. Part B—Number of Agriculturists with Subsidiary Occupations (Actual Workers only)—*concluded.*

(3) FARM SERVANTS AND FIELD LABOURERS.

Province, State or Agency.	Total number of Agricultural Labourers (Actual Workers).		Number of actual workers who returned subsidiary occupations. Total.		Other Agricultural Occupations.		Non-Agricultural Occupations.	
	Males.	Females.	Males.	Females.	Males.	Females.	Males.	Females.
1	2	3	4	5	6	7	8	9
INDIA.	13,158,644	12,720,554	782,921	389,547	249,226	97,925	533,695	291,622
Ajmer-Merwara	9,156	14,348	507	264	124	69	383	195
Assam	40,647	9,965	2,882	983	700	56	2,182	927
Baluchistan	4,844	..	44	..	12	..	32	..
Bengal	1,313,806	241,928	93,857	11,428	31,420	1,448	62,437	9,980
Bihar and Orissa	2,259,652	2,108,036	159,269	65,169	49,382	13,648	109,887	51,521
Bombay	1,451,444	1,885,058	82,483	47,247	14,574	5,114	67,909	42,133
Burma	516,415	395,944	45,922	26,915	7,041	4,519	38,881	22,396
Central Provinces and Berar	1,392,427	1,779,510	58,602	54,254	13,692	5,227	44,910	49,027
Coorg	15,133	10,651	290	130	78	21	212	109
Madras	2,324,605	2,760,380	101,295	60,444	28,508	14,306	72,787	46,138
N.-W. F. Province	16,521	1,107	668	15	150	..	518	15
Punjab	444,635	124,837	34,320	3,900	5,114	211	29,206	3,689
United Provinces	1,606,792	1,357,760	114,806	69,832	75,954	44,044	38,852	25,788
Baroda State	93,656	107,568	2,422	196	640	11	1,782	185
Central India Agency	452,295	584,219	38,771	22,136	6,889	2,490	31,882	19,646
Cochin State	47,527	47,846	2,825	2,012	151	11	2,674	2,001
Hyderabad State	790,731	896,825	23,135	14,596	7,028	4,321	16,107	10,275
Kashmir State	15,440	7,097	1,561	81	352	7	1,209	74
Mysore State	83,632	33,687	2,054	769	365	44	1,689	725
Rajputana Agency	205,115	294,383	12,629	8,780	5,767	2,355	6,862	6,425
Travancore State	74,171	59,405	4,579	396	1,285	23	3,294	372

TABLE XV.

Occupation or Means of Livelihood.

PART D.—DISTRIBUTION BY RELIGION.

1. This Part, the compilation of which was optional, was prepared for the Provinces, etc., noted on the margin. Statistics have been given for all these units, but to economize space details for groups have been dispensed with.

Assam.	United Provinces.
Baluchistan.	Baroda State.
Bengal.	Central India Agency.
Bihar and Orissa.	Cochin State.
Burma.	Hyderabad State.
C. P. and Berar.	Kashmir State.
Punjab.	Travancore State.

2. In Burma occupations were not recorded in the Pakokku Hill Tracts or in the estimated areas of Karenni, West Manglun and Kokang. The population of these areas has therefore been omitted. As in Tables VII and VIII, the figures for Hindus in the Punjab include Aryas and Brahmos.

TABLE XV.—Occupation or Means of Livelihood.

Order Number.	Occupation.	ASSAM. Total number of Workers and Dependants. All Religions.	Hindu.	Musalman.	Christian.	Animistic.	Others.
	1	2	3	4	5	6	7
	TOTAL POPULATION	**7,059,857**	**3,838,769**	**1,901,032**	**66,562**	**1,239,280**	**14,214**
	A.—Production of raw materials	**6,184,914**	**3,217,114**	**1,725,955**	**55,555**	**1,176,810**	**9,480**
	I.—EXPLOITATION OF THE SURFACE OF THE EARTH.	***6,178,391***	***3,212,443***	***1,725,255***	***55,450***	***1,175,980***	***9,263***
1	Pasture and agriculture	6,077,685	3,150,477	1,686,726	55,428	1,175,812	9,242
	(a) Ordinary cultivation	*5,323,380*	*2,518,817*	*1,669,069*	*45,128*	*1,081,734*	*8,632*
	(b) Growers of special products and market gardening	*702,793*	*596,644*	*12,273*	*9,295*	*84,268*	*313*
	(c) Forestry	*4,099*	*2,685*	*410*	*102*	*874*	*28*
	(d) Raising of farm stock	*47,273*	*32,316*	*4,949*	*899*	*8,845*	*269*
	(e) Raising of small animals	*135*	*15*	*25*	*4*	*91*	..
2	Fishing and hunting	100,706	61,966	38,529	22	168	21
	II.—EXTRACTION OF MINERALS	***6,523***	***4,671***	***700***	***105***	***830***	***217***
3	Mines	5,122	4,206	607	56	57	196
4	Quarries of hard rocks	680	162	92	49	356	21
5	Salt, etc.	721	303	1	..	417	..
	B.—Preparation and supply of material substances.	**537,782**	**408,706**	**96,327**	**3,270**	**26,309**	**3,170**
	III.—INDUSTRY	***216,624***	***176,197***	***27,770***	***1,114***	***11,061***	***482***
6	Textiles	59,419	53,854	1,820	98	3,641	6
7	Hides, skins and hard materials from the animal kingdom.	1,432	1,372	42	..	13	5
8	Wood	34,029	29,829	2,094	351	1,413	342
9	Metals	13,248	10,560	2,161	27	483	17
10	Ceramics	16,795	16,450	249	9	87	..
11	Chemical products properly so called, and analogous.	5,426	4,047	1,371	..	8	..
12	Food industries	19,371	9,050	7,368	38	2,908	7
13	Industries of dress and the toilet	36,090	27,139	7,963	211	739	38
14	Furniture industries	73	61	11	..	1	..
15	Building industries	8,958	5,718	2,678	54	500	8
16	Construction of means of transport	640	550	19	3	68	..
17	Production and transmission of physical forces (heat, light, electricity, motive power, etc.).	4	3	..	..	..	1
18	Industries of luxury and those pertaining to literature and the arts and sciences.	17,736	14,971	1,843	296	580	46
19	Industries concerned with refuse matter	3,403	2,593	151	27	620	12
	IV.—TRANSPORT	***76,600***	***56,247***	***12,505***	***1,091***	***6,602***	***155***
20	Transport by water	23,841	16,468	7,235	51	75	12
21	Transport by road	34,268	24,861	3,065	499	5,783	60
22	Transport by rail	13,877	11,235	1,689	436	444	73
23	Post Office, Telegraph and Telephone services	4,614	3,683	516	105	300	10
	V.—TRADE	***244,558***	***176,262***	***56,052***	***1,065***	***8,646***	***2,533***
24	Banks, establishments of credit, exchange and insurance.	6,408	5,364	678	15	68	83
25	Brokerage, commission and export	413	325	83	1	2	2
26	Trade in textiles	15,323	11,317	2,093	308	902	703
27	Trade in skins, leather, and furs	8,049	6,880	1,151	3	15	..
28	Trade in wood	3,519	1,966	1,199	5	338	11
29	Trade in metals	659	542	89	7	20	1
30	Trade in pottery	3,208	3,091	97	..	20	..
31	Trade in chemical products	1,811	988	581	21	168	53
32	Hotels, cafés, restaurants, etc.	1,921	961	364	20	576	..
33	Other trade in food stuffs	163,089	119,863	36,758	543	5,078	847
34	Trade in clothing and toilet articles	1,661	129	1,505	24	1	2
35	Trade in furniture	3,800	3,325	391	2	26	56
36	Trade in building materials	2,336	1,339	733	11	243	10
37	Trade in means of transport	2,798	1,808	714	28	231	17
38	Trade in fuel	2,594	1,090	1,150	14	334	6
39	Trade in articles of luxury and those pertaining to letters and the arts and sciences.	9,555	3,677	5,630	18	212	18
40	Trade in refuse matter	3	3	..	..	..	..
41	Trade of other sorts	17,411	13,394	2,836	45	412	724
	C.—Public administration and liberal arts.	**130,038**	**104,405**	**16,936**	**4,266**	**3,925**	**506**
	VI.—PUBLIC FORCE	***18,885***	***13,397***	***4,116***	***238***	***964***	***170***
42	Army	3,122	2,157	747	130	66	22
43	Navy	..	..	..	..	..	..
44	Police	15,763	11,240	3,369	108	898	148
45	***VII.—(ORDER 45) PUBLIC ADMINISTRATION.***	***15,032***	***10,616***	***1,711***	***487***	***2,141***	***77***
	VIII.—PROFESSIONS AND LIBERAL ARTS.	***92,915***	***77,973***	***10,754***	***3,294***	***647***	***247***
46	Religion	55,289	50,090	4,184	806	102	107
47	Law	5,118	4,411	638	34	31	4
48	Medicine	10,886	7,888	2,360	348	261	29
49	Instruction	12,357	8,097	2,300	1,784	104	72
50	Letters and arts and sciences	9,265	7,487	1,272	322	149	35
51	***IX.—(ORDER 51) PERSONS LIVING PRINCIPALLY ON THEIR INCOME.***	***3,206***	***2,419***	***355***	***247***	***173***	***12***
	D.—Miscellaneous	**207,123**	108,644	**61,814**	**3,471**	**32,236**	**1,058**
52	***X.—(ORDER 52) DOMESTIC SERVICE***	***38,539***	***22,826***	***11,885***	***763***	***2,775***	***290***
53	***XI.—(ORDER 53) INSUFFICIENTLY DESCRIBED OCCUPATIONS.***	***97,701***	***47,098***	***24,085***	***2,540***	***23,316***	***662***
	XII.—UNPRODUCTIVE	***70,883***	***38,620***	***25,844***	***168***	***6,145***	***106***
54	Inmates of jails, asylums and hospitals	2,256	1,176	820	6	253	1
55	Beggars, vagrants, prostitutes	68,627	37,444	25,024	162	5,892	105

Part D.—Distribution by Religion.

BALUCHISTAN.						BENGAL.							
Total number of Workers and Dependants.						Total number of Workers and Dependants.							
All Religions.	Hindu.	Sikh.	Musalman.	Christian.	Others.	All Religions.	Hindu.	Buddhist.	Musalman.	Christian.	Animistic.	Others.	Order Number.
8	9	10	11	12	13	14	15	16	17	18	19	20	
834,703	**37,602**	**8,390**	**782,648**	**5,085**	**978**	**46,305,642**	**20,945,379**	**246,866**	**24,237,228**	**129,746**	**730,780**	**15,643**	
666,661	**1,561**	**205**	**664,815**	**7**	**73**	**36,077,947**	**14,262,212**	**195,623**	**20,897,934**	**53,657**	**667,496**	**1,025**	
664,987	*1,440*	*160*	*663,333*	*7*	*47*	*35,962,070*	*14,164,508*	*195,623*	*20,893,492*	*53,246*	*654,176*	*1,025*	
659,433	1,440	160	657,779	7	47	35,315,575	13,557,038	194,003	20,856,622	52,763	654,124	1,025	1
561,053	*709*	*153*	*560,161*	*3*	*27*	*34,594,377*	*13,111,694*	*170,446*	*20,673,074*	*48,984*	*589,193*	*986*	
2,310	*497*	..	*1,802*	..	*11*	*342,640*	*255,555*	*20,912*	*15,026*	*3,218*	*47,896*	*33*	
3,037	*8*	*6*	*3,014*	*4*	*5*	*30,265*	*16,971*	*1,184*	*10,525*	*101*	*1,489*	*4*	
93,033	*226*	*1*	*92,802*	..	*4*	*305,634*	*156,788*	*1,461*	*131,389*	*440*	*15,554*	*2*	
..	..	..	..	..	..	*42,659*	*16,030*	..	*26,608*	*20*	*1*	..	
5,554	..	..	5,554	..	..	646,495	607,470	1,620	36,870	483	52	..	2
1,674	*121*	*45*	*1,482*	..	*26*	*115,877*	*97,704*	..	*4,442*	*411*	*13,320*	..	
1,400	121	45	1,208	..	26	114,714	96,769	..	4,216	409	13,320	..	3
..	..	..	..	..	..	885	860	..	23	2	..	..	4
274	..	..	274	..	..	278	75	..	208	..	..	..	5
95,252	**25,796**	**4,574**	**63,941**	**506**	**435**	**6,724,476**	**4,708,991**	**26,597**	**1,908,037**	**28,987**	**42,043**	**9,821**	
37,233	*6,303*	*1,207*	*29,492*	*162*	*69*	*3,440,650*	*2,371,008*	*10,693*	*1,040,685*	*7,534*	*9,136*	*1,594*	
2,532	20	10	2,501	1	..	870,016	506,702	5,424	356,136	1,385	291	78	6
207	1	..	206	..	..	54,117	51,444	21	2,556	51	42	3	7
5,227	54	334	4,838	1	..	369,045	302,920	1,899	59,435	1,364	2,702	725	8
7,323	200	136	6,967	5	15	184,746	167,721	39	16,230	356	376	24	9
722	24	..	698	..	..	227,150	214,346	23	12,198	51	528	4	10
327	39	..	287	..	1	133,460	50,423	94	82,677	240	1	25	11
3,844	764	232	2,825	12	11	483,498	283,367	1,799	193,878	491	3,923	40	12
7,621	1,011	118	6,450	26	16	517,758	395,406	642	120,675	629	58	348	13
100	8	..	92	..	..	9,858	3,276	1	6,535	35	..	11	14
3,191	341	172	2,667	..	11	229,084	88,365	447	138,580	629	1,055	8	15
41	18	..	20	2	1	38,940	32,169	16	6,537	188	14	16	16
..	..	..	..	..	..	4,784	2,956	2	1,199	558	..	69	17
2,039	444	156	1,416	9	14	268,707	225,144	272	41,495	1,503	68	225	18
4,059	3,379	49	525	106	..	49,487	46,769	14	2,554	54	78	18	19
28,756	*2,130*	*482*	*25,602*	*313*	*229*	*962,260*	*550,350*	*2,520*	*367,194*	*14,972*	*26,139*	*1,085*	
888	87	16	751	14	20	311,180	126,718	597	178,596	3,482	1,707	80	20
21,785	287	112	21,381	..	5	458,429	290,749	1,440	141,835	888	23,485	32	21
4,960	1,554	323	2,668	266	149	160,923	109,255	275	40,250	9,310	911	922	22
1,123	202	31	802	33	55	31,728	23,628	208	6,513	1,292	36	51	23
29,263	*17,363*	*2,885*	*8,847*	*31*	*137*	*2,321,566*	*1,787,633*	*13,384*	*500,158*	*6,481*	*6,768*	*7,149*	
719	601	79	33	1	5	130,735	117,089	162	12,399	465	7	613	24
212	159	18	35	..	..	44,510	32,915	20	9,323	1,054	91	1,107	25
5,070	2,849	394	1,799	1	27	194,215	142,571	924	46,820	483	320	3,097	26
146	..	..	146	..	..	86,074	65,693	8	20,152	163	25	33	27
752	2	6	744	..	..	45,255	29,339	220	13,306	78	2,288	24	28
19	6	..	13	..	..	11,572	10,234	3	1,233	63	27	12	29
9	..	..	9	..	..	27,522	24,453	1	3,045	1	18	4	30
890	686	55	136	6	7	16,024	11,743	8	3,947	207	33	86	31
354	173	31	128	7	15	29,961	21,424	148	7,619	504	154	112	32
13,037	9,153	1,524	2,303	3	54	1,391,446	1,116,655	9,490	262,866	971	772	692	33
219	16	4	195	3	1	23,867	9,153	11	14,264	158	..	178	34
1,083	35	11	1,033	..	4	42,203	33,476	435	8,149	90	17	36	35
51	..	..	51	..	..	13,156	10,229	4	2,905	15	3	..	36
342	29	1	306	..	6	16,418	5,194	186	10,965	90	18	15	37
490	42	6	437	..	5	47,110	33,323	137	10,655	62	2,922	11	38
662	292	24	331	10	5	89,165	48,133	163	40,400	222	11	236	39
..	..	..	..	..	..	443	159	..	284	..	..	..	40
5,208	3,820	732	1,148	..	8	111,990	75,850	1,411	31,826	1,855	62	886	41
42,194	**7,356**	**3,149**	**27,088**	**4,173**	**428**	**1,181,580**	**912,549**	**4,946**	**231,312**	**28,737**	**1,295**	**2,741**	
20,397	*4,851*	*2,540*	*9,128*	*3,757*	*121*	*183,739*	*115,166*	*1,211*	*60,960*	*5,304*	*713*	*385*	
18,519	4,676	2,193	7,797	3,748	105	8,932	2,334	8	2,064	4,179	1	346	42
..	..	..	..	..	..	15	13	..	..	2	..	..	43
1,878	175	347	1,331	9	16	174,792	112,819	1,203	58,896	1,123	712	39	44
9,996	*1,025*	*256*	*8,469*	*81*	*165*	*133,797*	*101,570*	*453*	*27,509*	*3,525*	*334*	*406*	45
11,169	*1,421*	*341*	*8,972*	*293*	*142*	*811,939*	*656,446*	*3,133*	*135,038*	*15,589*	*130*	*1,603*	
6,999	684	98	6,178	30	9	371,119	309,077	543	56,164	5,116	6	213	46
233	53	15	135	..	30	75,798	67,261	41	7,744	562	3	187	47
867	255	69	350	163	30	163,005	132,548	1,916	25,762	2,297	80	402	48
606	35	26	456	70	19	96,842	71,703	425	20,314	3,795	34	571	49
2,461	394	133	1,853	30	54	105,175	75,857	208	25,054	3,819	7	230	50
632	*59*	*12*	*519*	*42*	..	*52,105*	*39,367*	*149*	*7,805*	*4,319*	*118*	*347*	51
30,596	**2,889**	**462**	**26,804**	**399**	**42**	**2,321,639**	**1,061,627**	**19,700**	**1,199,945**	**18,365**	**19,946**	**2,056**	
14,294	*1,712*	*188*	*11,987*	*387*	*20*	*526,890*	*356,382*	*5,496*	*151,942*	*9,631*	*2,735*	*714*	52
10,756	*841*	*249*	*9,642*	*9*	*15*	*1,348,930*	*487,529*	*13,068*	*823,602*	*7,178*	*16,351*	*1,202*	53
5,546	*336*	*25*	*5,175*	*3*	*7*	*445,819*	*217,716*	*1,146*	*224,401*	*1,556*	*860*	*140*	
350	9	2	340	..	..	14,150	5,738	81	7,041	1,195	90	5	54
5,196	328	23	4,835	3	7	431,669	211,978	1,065	217,360	361	770	135	55

TABLE XV.—Occupation or Means of Livelihood.

Order Number.	Occupation.	BIHAR AND ORISSA.					
		Total number of Workers and Dependants.					
		All Religions.	Hindu.	Musalman.	Christian.	Animistic.	Others.
	1	21	22	23	24	25	26
	TOTAL POPULATION	**38,435,293**	**31,749,018**	**3,683,438**	**268,265**	**2,720,288**	**14,284**
	A.—Production of raw materials	**31,114,979**	**25,819,939**	**2,781,600**	**201,957**	**2,305,847**	**5,636**
	I.—EXPLOITATION OF THE SURFACE OF THE EARTH.	***30,951,083***	***25,705,596***	***2,771,226***	***201,647***	***2,267,016***	***5,598***
1	Pasture and agriculture	30,807,842	25,567,174	2,768,508	201,633	2,264,930	5,597
	(a) Ordinary cultivation	*30,054,982*	*24,943,336*	*2,729,379*	*196,460*	*2,180,266*	*5,541*
	(b) Growers of special products and market gardening	*28,590*	*25,565*	*2,113*	*507*	*405*	..
	(c) Forestry	*54,922*	*45,385*	*2,438*	*625*	*6,463*	*11*
	(d) Raising of farm stock	*668,785*	*552,396*	*34,514*	*4,040*	*77,790*	*45*
	(e) Raising of small animals	*563*	*492*	*64*	*1*	*6*	..
2	Fishing and hunting	143,241	138,422	2,718	14	2,086	1
	II.—EXTRACTION OF MINERALS	***163,896***	***114,343***	***10,374***	***310***	***38,831***	***38***
3	Mines	131,095	81,845	10,101	307	38,804	38
4	Quarries of hard rocks	3,816	3,572	214	3	27	
5	Salt, etc.	28,985	28,926	59	..	..	..
	B.—Preparation and supply of material substances.	**4,807,660**	**4,055,412**	**598,134**	**19,429**	**127,734**	**6,951**
	III.—INDUSTRY	***2,796,442***	***2,361,807***	***350,760***	***9,735***	***71,563***	***2,577***
6	Textiles	480,412	324,410	145,233	2,918	6,219	1,632
7	Hides, skins and hard materials from the animal kingdom.	8,201	7,287	752	116	43	3
8	Wood	297,114	273,845	4,710	1,065	17,372	122
9	Metals	208,466	190,124	6,926	1,495	9,630	291
10	Ceramics	251,425	230,375	9,191	987	10,869	3
11	Chemical products properly so called, and analogous.	155,700	145,723	2,700	122	7,136	19
12	Food industries	434,699	382,577	45,816	374	5,760	172
13	Industries of dress and the toilet	589,893	484,626	97,156	1,333	6,716	62
14	Furniture industries	721	525	186	9	1	..
15	Building industries	138,564	113,363	18,401	682	6,078	40
16	Construction of means of transport	1,674	1,162	364	138	10	..
17	Production and transmission of physical forces (heat, light, electricity, motive power, etc).	297	121	164	10	..	2
18	Industries of luxury and those pertaining to literature and the arts and sciences.	183,874	165,209	17,388	396	655	226
19	Industries concerned with refuse matter	45,402	42,460	1,773	90	1,074	5
	IV.—TRANSPORT	***361,049***	***289,272***	***59,017***	***6,174***	***13,287***	***299***
20	Transport by water	52,036	40,335	11,503	90	92	16
21	Transport by road	215,385	172,350	29,424	1,563	11,998	50
22	Transport by rail	81,913	61,245	15,708	3,973	759	228
23	Post Office, Telegraph and Telephone services	11,715	8,342	2,382	548	438	5
	V.—TRADE	***1,650,169***	***1,411,333***	***188,357***	***3,520***	***42,884***	***4,075***
24	Banks, establishments of credit, exchange and insurance.	68,386	62,357	4,327	241	670	791
25	Brokerage, commission and export	22,005	17,592	1,455	47	2,875	36
26	Trade in textiles	102,731	75,939	23,432	544	1,395	1,421
27	Trade in skin, leather, and furs	36,164	24,049	10,977	359	764	15
28	Trade in wood	37,207	34,047	1,668	47	1,427	18
29	Trade in metals	5,120	4,796	312	2	7	3
30	Trade in pottery	16,166	15,924	231	1	10	...
31	Trade in chemical products	38,654	34,729	1,888	259	1,737	41
32	Hotels, cafés, restaurants, etc.	89,066	77,763	9,791	282	1,188	42
33	Other trade in food stuffs	946,553	842,289	88,978	560	13,521	1,205
34	Trade in clothing and toilet articles	13,741	9,904	3,813	18	2	4
35	Trade in furniture	15,809	14,260	1,481	..	41	27
36	Trade in building materials	5,271	4,339	842	46	44	..
37	Trade in means of transport	7,823	3,369	4,414	4	13	23
38	Trade in fuel	109,238	91,720	4,331	814	12,373	..
39	Trade in articles of luxury and those pertaining to letters and the arts and sciences.	47,703	32,956	13,991	68	514	174
40	Trade in refuse matter	50	46	2	2	..	..
41	Trade of other sorts	88,482	65,254	16,424	226	6,303	275
	C.—Public Administration and liberal arts.	**652,444**	**547,351**	**78,294**	**15,010**	**11,036**	**753**
	VI.—PUBLIC FORCE	***180,436***	***151,104***	***20,417***	***1,780***	***7,108***	***27***
42	Army	1,355	409	111	835	..	..
43	Navy	..	..	..	..	..	..
44	Police	179,081	150,695	20,306	945	7,108	27
45	***VII.—(ORDER 45) PUBLIC ADMINISTRATION.***	***66,969***	***49,734***	***13,621***	***1,952***	***1,525***	***137***
	VIII.—PROFESSIONS AND LIBERAL ARTS.	***395,107***	***340,694***	***41,609***	***9,905***	***2,388***	***511***
46	Religion	205,703	192,056	6,520	5,780	1,201	151
47	Law	24,607	19,258	5,165	115	2	67
48	Medicine	54,006	46,539	6,380	696	260	131
49	Instruction	54,754	41,724	10,071	2,168	658	133
50	Letters and arts and sciences	56,032	41,117	13,473	1,146	267	29
51	***IX.—(ORDER 51) PERSONS LIVING PRINCIPALLY ON THEIR INCOME.***	***9,932***	***5,819***	***2,647***	***1,373***	***15***	***78***
	D.—Miscellaneous.	**1,860,210**	**1,326,316**	**225,410**	**31,869**	**275,671**	**944**
52	***X.—(ORDER 52) DOMESTIC SERVICE***	***726,146***	***542,334***	***102,391***	***14,277***	***66,957***	***187***
53	***XI.—(ORDER 53) INSUFFICIENTLY DESCRIBED OCCUPATIONS.***	***942,269***	***656,745***	***71,041***	***16,499***	***197,406***	***578***
	XII.—UNPRODUCTIVE	***191,795***	***127,237***	***51,978***	***1,093***	***11,308***	***179***
54	Inmates of jails, asylums and hospitals	9,060	6,735	1,943	213	162	7
55	Beggars, vagrants and prostitutes	182,735	120,502	50,035	880	11,146	172

Part D.—Distribution by Religion—*continued.*

Burma.						Central Provinces and Berar.						Order Number.
Total number of Workers and Dependants.						Total number of Workers and Dependants.						
All Religions.	Hindu.	Buddhist.	Musalman.	Animistic.	Others.	All Religions.	Hindu.	Musalman.	Christian.	Animistic.	Others.	
27	28	29	30	31	32	33	34	35	36	37	38	
12,039,083	**389,528**	**10,384,544**	**420,769**	**625,539**	**218,703**	**16,033,310**	**12,807,874**	**585,029**	**73,401**	**2490,355**	**76,651**	
8,639,688	**98,294**	**7,658,157**	**200,022**	**535,186**	**148,090**	**12,782,215**	**10,061,372**	**250,069**	**44,821**	**2,388,514**	**17,439**	
8,624,395	*94,475*	*7,647,588*	*199,065*	*535,186*	*148,081*	*12,752,240*	*10,058.372*	*248,499*	*44,677*	*2,383,363*	*17,329*	
8,472,391	91,486	7,506,898	198,507	532,867	147,633	12,618,871	9,926,800	248,194	44,671	2,381,877	17,329	1
8,083,712	*79,720*	*7,158,313*	*185,697*	*517,926*	*142,056*	*12,051,933*	*9,439,059*	*236,044*	*43,601*	*2,315,986*	*17,243*	
238,511	*5,787*	*216,857*	*2,888*	*9,282*	*3,757*	*52,827*	*51,262*	*522*	*204*	*837*	*2*	
42,765	*158*	*40,699*	*192*	*1,241*	*475*	*81,462*	*52,981*	*7,019*	*145*	*21,282*	*35*	
105,944	*5,819*	*89,715*	*4,667*	*4,399*	*1,344*	*432,534*	*383,438*	*4,569*	*721*	*43,757*	*49*	
1,459	*2*	1,314	*123*	*19*	*1*	*115*	*60*	*40*	..	*15*	..	
152,004	2,989	140,690	5,558	2,319	448	133,369	131,572	305	6	1,486	..	2
15,293	*3,749*	*10,569*	*957*	..	*18*	*29,975*	*23,000*	*1,570*	*144*	*5,151*	*110*	
8,173	3,567	3,750	846	..	10	27,423	21,153	1,405	135	4,622	108	3
3,896	182	3,605	102	..	7	1,892	1,268	107	9	506	2	4
3,224	..	3,214	9	..	1	660	579	58	..	23	..	5
2,403,894	**156,031**	**1,998,392**	**155,541**	**70,343**	**22,997**	**2,427,166**	**2,068,991**	**223,201**	**7,504**	**73,441**	**54,029**	
806,431	*58,934*	*682,304*	*39,284*	*21,089*	*4,820*	*1,613,813*	*1,461,846*	*99,253*	*2,873*	*46,148*	*3,693*	
155,050	2,377	150,811	1,221	581	60	443,730	405,647	33,627	1,068	2,753	635	6
624	20	566	5	29	4	13,787	13,498	238	11	40	..	7
101,686	2,732	178,553	2,957	6,856	588	196,762	169,480	1,446	592	25,088	156	8
34,912	2,402	30,420	1,207	772	111	140,451	127,508	4,421	246	8,157	119	9
18,821	2,107	16,193	490	..	31	98,595	96,221	1,454	17	902	1	10
10,560	5,595	2,480	2,406	2	77	37,041	35,791	870	2	358	20	11
178,255	14,923	147,973	12,597	1,980	782	105,538	84,696	15,434	97	4,187	1,124	12
116,056	16,042	77,660	11,377	9,907	1,070	371,735	342,521	26,807	313	703	1,391	13
1,862	57	462	1,245	81	17	259	166	93	..	..	..	14
24,257	1,766	19,267	2,866	148	210	81,564	69,668	8,452	127	3,276	41	15
2,187	312	1,601	148	51	75	1,056	844	87	4	121	..	16
180	2	57	9	..	112	45	35	..	9	1	..	17
58,878	3,993	51,117	1,791	608	1,369	97,469	91,927	4,604	256	503	179	18
13,103	6,606	5,144	965	74	314	25,781	23,844	1,720	131	59	27	19
393,659	*53,929*	*285,310*	*38,088*	*7,507*	*8,825*	*217,961*	*172,979*	*26,045*	*3,921*	*13,393*	*1,623*	
131,071	7,233	99,767	19,918	1,690	2,463	6,154	5,455	244	39	374	42	20
230,168	29,131	180,014	13,720	5,586	1,717	119,004	95,029	14,918	348	8,152	557	21
27,686	16,009	3,777	3,944	209	3,747	84,167	66,007	9,720	3,191	4,288	961	22
4,727	1,549	1,752	506	22	898	8,686	6,488	1,163	343	579	63	23
1,203,791	*43,175*	*1,031,978*	*78,169*	*41,747*	*9,352*	*595,392*	*434,166*	*97,903*	*710*	*13,900*	*48,713*	
17,345	3,152	11,054	1,678	204	1,257	85,479	62,760	13,444	49	791	8,435	24
21,415	2,542	15,941	1,202	1,137	593	6,959	5,673	650	12	99	525	25
74,875	2,455	59,508	9,939	2,728	245	51,946	32,554	10,952	8	201	8,231	26
1,491	92	1,043	250	80	16	8,338	6,595	1,650	33	57	3	27
21,988	1,757	18,450	994	556	231	6,890	2,884	1,225	4	2,750	27	28
1,644	39	1,365	232	2	6	1,851	1,130	592	..	99	30	29
10,386	62	10,122	63	115	24	1,546	1,436	93	..	8	9	30
2,903	285	2,212	290	51	65	8,612	6,443	1,289	7	784	89	31
21,651	1,694	14,186	2,337	3,121	313	13,794	11,454	1,634	107	406	193	32
513,911	17,421	460,704	22,729	10,992	2,065	335,583	261,642	37,220	174	6,112	30,435	33
6,531	84	5,674	235	486	52	6,450	2,529	3,724	1	41	155	34
13,496	110	12,320	843	190	33	5,614	5,258	244	4	74	34	35
3,057	37	2,914	83	20	3	1,955	1,227	706	2	18	2	36
15,661	425	11,971	2,220	997	48	10,622	6,127	4,172	25	278	20	37
10,753	754	9,118	416	401	64	5,257	3,675	942	65	571	4	38
10,961	560	8,166	1,539	574	122	32,275	14,507	17,199	131	227	211	39
94	30	46	7	..	11	597	471	124	..	..	2	40
455,569	11,676	386,484	33,112	20,093	4,204	11,624	7,801	2,043	88	1,384	308	41
445,846	**25,412**	**360,502**	**21,400**	**6,818**	**31,714**	**522,515**	**426,840**	**62,429**	**16,468**	**12,923**	**3,855**	
79,495	*12,249*	*45,730*	*9,976*	*1,261*	*10,279*	*173,740*	*141,651*	*19,486*	*5,157*	*6,140*	*1,306*	
24,984	7,736	2,844	6,157	264	7,983	11,321	2,672	3,039	4,428	5	1,177	42
28	11	10	..	..	7	16	16	..	..	..	..	43
54,483	4,502	42,876	3,819	997	2,289	162,403	138,963	16,447	729	6,135	129	44
103,108	*7,661*	*81,989*	*3,690*	*3,263*	*6,505*	*102,207*	*79,120*	*19,809*	*932*	*1,710*	*636*	45
256,276	*4,753*	*228,559*	*6,845*	*2,207*	*13,912*	*234,704*	*198,872*	*19,699*	*9,384*	*4,984*	*1,765*	
140,834	705	132,378	2,240	1,407	4,104	129,490	113,713	7,381	6,296	1,634	466	46
8,306	423	6,392	763	1	727	14,429	11,959	1,901	75	09	305	47
52,172	1,760	46,338	1,815	366	1,893	17,426	14,039	2,539	402	325	121	48
26,939	561	18,848	1,537	70	5,923	29,648	22,884	4,099	1,836	291	538	49
28,025	1,304	24,608	490	363	1,265	48,711	36,277	3,689	775	2,635	335	50
6,967	*749*	*4,294*	*889*	*87*	*1,018*	*11,864*	*7,197*	*3,435*	*995*	*89*	*148*	51
549,745	**109,861**	**366,993**	**43,806**	**13,192**	**15,893**	**301,414**	**230,671**	**49,330**	**4,608**	**15,47 7**	**1,328**	
85,771	*27,438*	*36,613*	*12,869*	*2,208*	*6,650*	*160,995*	*127,621*	*21,945*	*3,754*	*6,745*	*930*	52
429,399	*81,061*	*301,323*	*28,520*	*9,776*	*8,719*	*37,729*	*30,046*	*4,309*	*619*	*2,522*	*233*	53
34,575	*1,362*	*29,057*	*2,424*	*1,208*	*524*	*102,690*	*73,004*	*23,076*	*235*	*6,210*	*165*	
8,500	617	7,275	427	46	135	3,856	3,010	277	157	303	29	54
26,075	745	21,782	1,997	1,162	389	98,834	69,914	22,799	78	5,907	136	55

TABLE XV.—Occupation or Means of Livelihood.

Order Number.	Occupation.	PUNJAB.					
		Total number of Workers and Dependants.					
		All Religions.	Hindu.	Sikh.	Musalman.	Christian.	Others.
	1	39	40	41	42	43	44
	TOTAL POPULATION	**24,187,750**	**8,773,621**	**2,883,729**	**12,275,477**	**199,751**	**55,172**
	A.—Production of raw materials	**14,538,276**	**4,909,447**	**2,123,495**	**7,419,674**	**76,280**	**9,380**
	I.—EXPLOITATION OF THE SURFACE OF THE EARTH.	***14,509,144***	***4,894,745***	***2,122,754***	***7,398,990***	***76,279***	***9,377***
1	Pasture and agriculture	14,489,845	4,892,899	2,122,660	7,388,668	76,242	9,376
	(a) Ordinary cultivation	*14,016,144*	*4,746,626*	*2,101,987*	*7,083,146*	*75,104*	*9,281*
	(b) Growers of special products and market gardening	*20,832*	*10,815*	*215*	*9,666*	*132*	*4*
	(c) Forestry	*46,081*	*14,637*	*1,619*	*29,674*	*146*	*5*
	(d) Raising of farm stock	*406,766*	*120,815*	*18,837*	*266,168*	*860*	*86*
	(e) Raising of small animals	*22*	*6*	*2*	*14*	..	..
2	Fishing and hunting	12,299	1,846	94	10,328	30	1
	II.—EXTRACTION OF MINERALS	***36,139***	***14,709***	***741***	***20,678***	8	***3***
3	Mines	3,715	976	34	2,705	..	..
4	Quarries of hard rocks	16,119	6,861	654	8,602	..	2
5	Salt, etc.	16,298	6,865	53	9,371	8	1
	B.—Preparation and supply of material substances.	**7,199,969**	**2,968,952**	**563,884**	**3,509,549**	**76,165**	**41,419**
	III.—INDUSTRY	***4,915,297***	***1,748,971***	***346,877***	***2,752,029***	***65,067***	***2,353***
6	Textiles	1,088,481	251,342	69,733	766,429	376	601
7	Hides, skins and hard materials from the animal kingdom.	89,577	69,073	6,926	13,570	8	..
8	Wood	484,749	137,842	85,481	260,754	535	137
9	Metals	240,096	59,173	22,006	158,685	98	132
10	Ceramics	352,704	101,370	8,793	240,519	2,011	11
11	Chemical products properly so called, and analogous.	128,225	2,387	243	125,548	21	31
12	Food industries	289,684	114,403	15,494	158,539	334	914
13	Industries of dress and the toilet	1,147,862	357,987	81,777	706,584	1,206	308
14	Furniture industries	8,759	1,242	1,460	5,990	61	6
15	Building industries	272,168	74,696	17,176	179,256	998	42
16	Construction of means of transport	3,531	954	354	2,210	13	...
17	Production and transmission of physical forces (heat, light, electricity, motive power, etc.)	1,610	227	45	306	1,014	18
18	Industries of luxury and those pertaining to literature and the arts and sciences.	216,581	116,883	27,879	71,478	200	141
19	Industries concerned with refuse matter	591,270	461,392	9,508	62,166	58,192	12
	IV.—TRANSPORT	***709,130***	***231,057***	***57,904***	***412,072***	***7,207***	***890***
20	Transport by water	108,140	37,625	5,006	65,093	332	84
21	Transport by road	427,750	125,284	40,553	259,981	1,691	241
22	Transport by rail	149,453	56,836	10,903	76,563	4,723	428
23	Post Office, Telegraph and Telephone services	23,787	11,312	1,442	10,435	461	137
	V.—TRADE	***1,575,549***	***1,008,924***	***179,103***	***345,448***	***3,891***	***38,176***
24	Banks, establishments of credit, exchange and insurance.	193,890	154,376	26,120	5,296	167	7,931
25	Brokerage, commission and export	26,232	20,220	2,868	1,890	31	1,273
26	Trade in textiles	113,260	66,350	15,344	25,434	58	6,074
27	Trade in skins, leather, and furs	29,762	4,138	396	23,099	2,126	3
28	Trade in wood	17,427	6,291	1,390	9,649	31	66
29	Trade in metals	5,918	4,166	483	979	..	290
30	Trade in pottery	933	283	70	580	..	..
31	Trade in chemical products	42,420	27,413	4,537	8,402	26	2,042
32	Hotels, cafés, restaurants, etc.	9,474	4,809	1,374	3,019	177	95
33	Other trade in food stuffs	277,996	128,191	11,867	134,896	220	2,822
34	Trade in clothing and toilet articles	34,969	10,804	829	21,883	28	1,425
35	Trade in furniture	8,627	5,156	912	1,995	1	563
36	Trade in building materials	3,132	1,139	422	1,541	..	30
37	Trade in means of transport	47,397	9,841	3,037	34,305	163	51
38	Trade in fuel	23,603	9,092	1,215	13,205	50	41
39	Trade in articles of luxury and those pertaining to letters and the arts and sciences.	28,702	12,600	1,050	12,771	110	2,171
40	Trade in refuse matter	157	28	..	129	..	..
41	Trade of other sorts	711,593	544,027	107,189	46,375	703	13,299
	C.—Public administration and liberal arts	**1,078,163**	**424,369**	**101,371**	**511,678**	**37,973**	**2,780**
	VI.—PUBLIC FORCE	***265,731***	***60,574***	***41,922***	***139,094***	***23,892***	***249***
42	Army	137,229	29,120	32,713	52,143	23,173	80
43	Navy	..	..	..	..	..	..
44	Police	128,502	31,454	9,209	86,951	719	169
45	***VII.—(ORDER 45) PUBLIC ADMINISTRATION.***	***150,885***	***71,596***	***14,947***	***59,811***	***3,315***	***1,286***
	VIII.—PROFESSIONS AND LIBERAL ARTS.	***602,576***	***268,296***	***31,476***	***292,720***	***19,191***	***893***
46	Religion	342,553	196,702	13,487	128,313	3,980	71
47	Law	23,046	11,949	1,907	8,723	95	372
48	Medicine	49,496	15,203	2,223	29,995	1,945	130
49	Instruction	40,131	17,324	3,267	17,243	2,090	207
50	Letters and arts and sciences	147,350	27,118	10,592	108,446	1,081	113
51	***IX.—(ORDER 51) PERSONS LIVING PRINCIPALLY ON THEIR INCOME.***	***58,971***	***23,973***	***13,026***	***20,045***	***1,575***	***352***
	D.—Miscellaneous	**1,371,342**	**450,853**	**74,979**	**834,524**	**9,333**	**1,593**
52	***X.—(ORDER 52) DOMESTIC SERVICE***	***507,727***	***203,022***	***36,096***	***263,525***	***4,730***	***354***
53	***XI.—(ORDER 53) INSUFFICIENTLY DESCRIBED OCCUPATIONS.***	***264,630***	***107,761***	***13,010***	***139,678***	***3,659***	***522***
	XII.—UNPRODUCTIVE	***598,985***	***140,070***	***25,873***	***431,381***	***944***	***717***
54	Inmates of jails, asylums and hospitals	14,405	3,382	1,591	9,382	50	..
55	Beggars, vagrants, prostitutes	584,580	136,688	24,282	421,999	894	717

Part D.—Distribution by Religion—*continued.*

United Provinces.						Baroda State.						
Total number of Workers and Dependants.						Total number of Workers and Dependants.						Order Number.
All Religions.	Hindu.	Arya.	Musalman.	Christian.	Others.	All Religions.	Hindu.	Jain.	Musalman.	Animistic.	Others.	
45	46	47	48	49	50	51	52	53	54	55	56	
48,014,080	40,705,353	131,638	6,904,731	179,694	92,664	2,032,798	1,697,146	43,462	160,887	115,411	15,892	
35,276,180	31,641,366	86,492	3,482,712	41,407	24,203	1,332,881	1,146,220	1,991	74,279	106,169	4,222	
35,267,372	31,633,493	86,491	3,481,886	41,396	24,176	1,332,756	1,146,095	1,991	74,379	106,169	4,222	
35,222,317	31,602,064	86,482	3,468,259	41,372	24,140	1,329,961	1,143,520	1,991	74,069	106,159	4,222	1
34,327,199	30,789,455	85,567	3,390,379	37,797	24,001	1,284,365	1,099,305	1,973	73,655	105,223	4,209	
56,478	52,118	50	4,037	252	21	2,536	2,507	9	16	..	4	
58,709	45,664	62	12,855	99	29	810	585	..	45	171	9	
778,992	714,374	803	60,503	3,223	89	42,239	41,113	9	352	765	..	
939	453	..	485	1	..	11	10	..	1	..	..	
45,055	31,359	9	13,627	24	36	2,795	2,575	..	210	10	..	
8,808	7,943	1	826	11	27	125	125	..	..	..	..	2
154	109	..	42	3	..	125	125	..	..	..	..	3
2,904	2,605	..	266	7	26	..	..	..	..	..	..	4
5,750	5,229	1	518	1	1	..	..	..	..	..	..	5
8,424,389	5,921,037	28,492	2,344,391	71,898	58,571	396,588	305,488	35,481	44,460	2,894	8,265	
5,834,384	4,021,696	7,909	1,741,716	57,880	5,190	250,050	218,551	2,035	21,257	2,265	5,942	
1,166,359	463,572	1,874	698,508	1,331	1,074	52,433	37,860	1,142	7,026	16	5,489	6
131,642	118,353	465	11,972	808	44	16,032	15,843	14	118	21	36	7
485,880	404,489	1,122	77,440	2,392	437	26,275	24,571	18	683	985	18	8
286,922	215,259	280	70,885	132	366	16,150	15,595	113	434	..	8	9
366,212	336,394	64	29,619	119	16	26,743	25,942	78	698	23	2	10
428,541	310,297	100	117,906	200	38	10,953	6,870	71	4,004	..	8	11
790,172	599,914	1,350	185,873	391	2,644	11,314	8,104	340	1,961	885	24	12
1,344,007	936,693	906	402,708	3,426	274	45,632	42,667	100	2,612	166	87	13
6,324	1,953	..	4,324	39	8	142	43	7	82	..	10	14
140,566	88,935	358	50,986	236	51	12,931	10,647	104	1,978	59	143	15
3,841	2,251	2	1,518	56	14	247	221	..	2	..	24	16
725	395	7	252	61	10	101	100	..	1	..	..	17
317,787	243,656	1,351	71,875	778	127	11,507	10,628	48	742	3	86	18
365,406	299,535	23	17,850	47,911	87	19,590	19,460	..	16	107	7	19
449,610	296,919	2,837	138,197	9,879	1,778	16,638	11,959	266	3,697	303	413	
39,453	31,587	285	7,302	144	135	1,861	1,286	..	575	..	..	20
254,307	162,527	862	89,570	879	469	5,960	3,838	19	1,918	159	26	21
128,976	84,774	1,332	34,059	7,732	1,079	6,458	4,908	69	1,013	139	329	22
26,874	18,031	358	7,266	1,124	95	2,359	1,027	178	191	5	58	23
2,140,395	1,609,429	17,753	464,478	4,139	51,603	129,900	74,978	33,180	19,506	326	1,910	
144,283	120,191	3,062	9,993	371	10,666	17,600	7,195	10,111	210	2	82	24
29,411	24,925	416	3,328	93	649	1,200	336	778	82	..	4	25
133,429	95,216	2,359	30,137	333	5,384	11,131	5,323	3,045	2,695	..	68	26
10,752	3,475	5	7,140	125	7	1,688	1,538	11	99	..	40	27
8,198	5,446	20	2,613	98	21	930	564	10	86	195	75	28
9,633	7,320	211	1,720	28	354	954	84	2	862	..	6	29
3,382	1,946	..	1,434	1	1	94	71	..	23	..	..	30
20,359	12,649	442	6,636	71	561	256	166	5	65	..	20	31
28,723	21,753	405	5,383	913	269	3,390	2,071	23	240	54	1,002	32
1,426,539	1,146,298	7,220	245,613	1,016	26,392	54,718	38,775	9,074	6,694	43	132	33
59,091	14,448	291	43,751	90	511	1,425	365	48	1,011	..	1	34
16,146	13,537	154	2,088	10	357	523	324	64	135	..	..	35
3,926	2,463	14	1,417	19	13	489	399	20	70	..	..	36
46,442	9,426	34	36,902	35	45	1,754	1,569	..	185	..	..	37
93,044	78,589	25	19,343	69	18	1,581	1,160	17	372	14	18	38
52,383	25,377	266	26,273	147	320	2,670	1,596	563	504	1	6	39
1,030	898	..	121	11	..	97	97	..	..	..	..	40
53,624	23,465	2,829	20,586	709	6,035	29,400	13,345	9,469	6,173	17	456	41
1,210,086	819,279	12,933	322,452	47,806	7,614	148,275	118,539	3,831	23,363	1,153	1,389	
336,697	214,780	817	92,593	23,870	4,637	26,904	16,714	42	9,228	816	104	
61,180	24,751	66	14,472	18,412	3,479	11,560	8,428	1	3,055	3	73	42
17	5	3	4	..	5	..	..	..	..	..	..	43
275,430	190,024	748	78,047	5,458	1,153	15,344	8,286	41	6,173	813	31	44
269,593	181,363	4,778	78,090	4,106	1,256	38,917	29,391	834	7,283	192	517	45
534,097	387,393	6,669	193,619	15,089	1,364	74,692	66,506	1,093	6,076	141	876	
271,187	244,457	1,447	18,093	6,983	207	51,085	47,819	273	3,562	51	280	46
37,516	22,772	1,563	12,626	273	282	1,670	1,473	152	37	..	8	47
62,105	40,120	892	18,324	2,428	341	3,079	2,407	128	339	..	205	48
66,906	37,306	2,309	22,675	4,181	435	9,394	7,628	339	1,112	70	255	49
96,313	42,688	458	51,894	1,224	99	8,559	7,184	201	1,026	20	128	50
69,839	35,843	669	28,227	4,743	357	8,463	5,928	1,369	776	4	392	51
3,103,425	2,323,671	3,721	755,176	18,581	2,276	155,054	126,899	2,659	18,785	5,195	1,516	
921,214	646,815	1,116	267,127	5,586	570	3,510	2,518	138	564	29	261	52
1,661,094	1,383,386	2,000	263,484	10,872	1,352	142,285	117,481	2,502	16,180	5,072	1,050	53
521,117	293,470	605	224,565	2,123	354	9,259	6,900	19	2,041	94	205	
24,599	19,402	181	4,669	321	26	802	638	..	77	31	56	54
496,518	274,068	424	219,896	1,802	328	8,457	6,262	19	1,964	63	140	55

TABLE XV.—Occupation or Means of Livelihood.

Order Number.	Occupation.	CENTRAL INDIA AGENCY. Total number of Workers and Dependants. All Religions.	Hindu.	Jain.	Musalman.	Animistic.	Others.
	1	57	58	59	60	61	62
	TOTAL POPULATION	**9,356,980**	**8,262,638**	**87,471**	**511,200**	**483,394**	**12,277**
	A. Production of raw materials	**5,953,423**	**5,391,165**	**12,895**	**139,995**	**408,541**	**827**
	I.—EXPLOITATION OF THE SURFACE OF THE EARTH.	*5,949,350*	*5,388,039*	*12,876*	*139,087*	*408,532*	*822*
1	Pasture and agriculture	5,936,785	5,376,846	12,876	137,950	408,291	822
	(a) Ordinary cultivation	*5,660,991*	*5,125,204*	*12,798*	*130,397*	*391,833*	*759*
	(b) Growers of special products and market gardening	*14,290*	*13,410*	*16*	*770*	*57*	*37*
	(c) Forestry	*40,139*	*31,901*	*12*	*1,694*	6,516	*16*
	(d) Raising of farm stock	*221,276*	*206,245*	*50*	*5,087*	9,884	*10*
	(e) Raising of small animals	*89*	*86*	..	*2*	*1*	..
2	Fishing and hunting	12,571	11,193	..	1,137	241	..
	II.—EXTRACTION OF MINERALS	*4,067*	*3,126*	*19*	*908*	*9*	*5*
3	Mines	3,039	2,445	12	568	9	5
4	Quarries of hard rocks	110	107	..	3	..	..
5	Salt, etc.	913	574	7	337	..	..
	B.—Preparation and supply of material substances.	**1,711,417**	**1,477,847**	**67,963**	**156,004**	**7,972**	**1,631**
	III.—INDUSTRY	*1,145,073*	*1,047,099*	*4,391*	*91,046*	*2,290*	*317*
6	Textiles	168,024	134,758	419	31,929	895	23
7	Hides, skins and hard materials from the animal kingdom.	23,670	23,236	..	425	9	..
8	Wood	133,102	131,372	38	1,201	482	9
9	Metals	70,801	61,716	126	8,865	91	3
10	Ceramics	100,011	96,922	12	3,013	64	..
11	Chemical products properly so called, and analogous.	71,493	69,410	8	1,994	81	..
12	Food industries	65,028	49,475	3,388	11,758	372	35
13	Industries of dress and the toilet	391,413	378,352	180	12,643	100	138
14	Furniture industries	363	137	..	226	..	..
15	Building industries	28,566	22,573	40	5,873	79	1
16	Construction of means of transport	1,443	1,403	3	29	7	1
17	Production and transmission of physical forces (heat, light, electricity, motive power, etc.)	95	55	..	33	..	7
18	Industries of luxury and those pertaining to literature and the arts and sciences.	52,450	44,136	174	8,090	..	50
19	Industries concerned with refuse matter	38,614	33,554	3	4,967	40	50
	IV.—TRANSPORT	*52,412*	*38,615*	*183*	*11,685*	*837*	*1,092*
20	Transport by water	1,393	1,307	4	77	5	..
21	Transport by road	37,800	28,386	134	8,709	524	47
22	Transport by rail	10,923	7,223	43	2,460	192	1,005
23	Post Office, Telegraph and Telephone services	2,296	1,699	2	439	116	40
	V.—TRADE	*513,939*	*392,133*	*63,389*	*53,973*	*4,915*	*222*
24	Banks, establishments of credit, exchange and insurance.	36,093	23,994	10,793	1,276	14	16
25	Brokerage, commission and export	5,195	3,694	1,085	403	7	6
26	Trade in textiles	27,121	17,732	5,787	3,562	5	35
27	Trade in skins, leather and furs	2,095	1,510	297	284	3	1
28	Trade in wood	1,750	1,312	59	244	135	..
29	Trade in metals	3,159	2,178	15	940	26	..
30	Trade in pottery	18	9	5	4	..	..
31	Trade in chemical products	6,945	4,552	21	2,343	20	9
32	Hotels, cafés, restaurants, etc.	24,152	22,383	165	1,424	104	76
33	Other trade in food stuffs	294,305	234,661	32,435	24,195	2,992	22
34	Trade in clothing and toilet articles	9,614	4,655	383	4,576	..	..
35	Trade in furniture	626	527	14	85	..	..
36	Trade in building materials	485	387	..	98	..	..
37	Trade in means of transport	4,296	3,469	42	678	87	..
38	Trade in fuel	12,797	9,893	39	1,367	1,496	2
39	Trade in articles of luxury and those pertaining to letters and the arts and sciences.	17,938	13,040	921	3,973	..	4
40	Trade in refuse matter	4	4	..	..	..	..
41	Trade of other sorts	67,339	48,113	11,328	7,821	27	50
	C.—Public administration and liberal arts	**490,986**	**369,197**	**1,383**	**106,059**	**6,290**	**7,647**
	VI.—PUBLIC FORCE	*181,938*	*128,543*	*96*	*43,673*	*4,361*	*5,265*
42	Army	89,551	60,375	26	23,444	610	5,096
43	Navy	..	..	..	..	..	..
44	Police	92,387	68,168	70	20,229	3,751	169
45	*VII.—(ORDER 45) PUBLIC ADMINISTRATION.*	*139,485*	*97,349*	*897*	*38,846*	*1,451*	*942*
	VIII.—PROFESSIONS AND LIBERAL ARTS.	*138,390*	*123,585*	*571*	*13,059*	*315*	*860*
46	Religion	94,629	91,188	436	2,366	169	470
47	Law	3,663	2,617	42	988	..	16
48	Medicine	5,954	4,350	32	1,435	17	120
49	Instruction	6,951	5,520	44	1,244	8	135
50	Letters and arts and sciences	27,193	19,910	17	7,026	121	119
51	*IX.—(ORDER 51) PERSONS LIVING PRINCIPALLY ON THEIR INCOME.*	*31,173*	*19,720*	*319*	*10,481*	*73*	*580*
	D.—Miscellaneous	**1,201,154**	**1,024,429**	**4,730**	**109,142**	**60,681**	**2,172**
52	*X.—(ORDER 52) DOMESTIC SERVICE*	*214,177*	*170,491*	*1,858*	*36,886*	*3,053*	*1,889*
53	*XI.—(ORDER 53) INSUFFICIENTLY DESCRIBED OCCUPATIONS.*	*754,480*	*650,314*	*2,591*	*45,121*	*56,212*	*242*
	XII.—UNPRODUCTIVE	*232,497*	*203,624*	*281*	*27,135*	*1,416*	*41*
54	Inmates of jails, asylums and hospitals	4,148	3,399	4	417	291	37
55	Beggars, vagrants and prostitutes	228,349	200,225	277	26,718	1,125	4

PART D.—DISTRIBUTION BY RELIGION—*continued.*

HYDERABAD STATE.						KASHMIR STATE.						Order Number.
TOTAL NUMBER OF WORKERS AND DEPENDANTS.						TOTAL NUMBER OF WORKERS AND DEPENDANTS.						
All Religions.	Hindu.	Musalman.	Christian.	Animistic.	Others.	All Religions.	Hindu.	Sikh.	Buddhist.	Musalman.	Others.	
63	64	65	66	67	68	69	70	71	72	73	74	
13,374,676	**11,626,146**	**1,380,990**	**54,296**	**285,722**	**27,522**	**3,158,126**	**689,342**	**31,553**	**36,512**	**2,398,320**	**2,399**	
8,408,192	**7,455,929**	**667,212**	**29,345**	**247,150**	**8,556**	**2,519,742**	**480,750**	**25,064**	**32,732**	**1,980,762**	**434**	
8,389,718	*7,438,953*	*666,110*	*28,960*	*247,139*	*8,556*	*2,519,709*	*480,727*	*25,064*	*32,730*	*1,980,754*	*434*	
8,281,829	7,335,910	662,976	28,844	245,543	8,556	2,515,519	480,700	25,052	32,730	1,976,603	434	1
7,619,505	*6,699,604*	*652,361*	*28,146*	*231,014*	*8,380*	*2,474,991*	*470,080*	*25,022*	*31,940*	*1,947,538*	*411*	
22,804	*19,106*	*3,637*	*10*	..	*51*	*4,407*	*158*	*7*	*30*	*4,205*	*7*	
41,774	*26,301*	*2,471*	*378*	*12,604*	*20*	*3,085*	*1,594*	*2*	*52*	*1,421*	*16*	
597,728	*590,888*	*4,507*	*310*	*1,918*	*105*	*32,284*	*8,857*	*20*	*708*	*22,699*	..	
18	*11*	..	..	*7*	..	*752*	*11*	*1*	..	*740*	..	
107,889	103,043	3,134	116	1,596	..	4,190	27	12	..	4,151	..	2
18,474	*16,976*	*1,102*	*385*	*11*	..	*33*	*23*	..	*2*	*8*	..	
15,325	14,081	909	385	..	..	33	23	..	2	8	..	3
3,149	2,945	193	..	11	..	..	..	..	..	..	..	4
..	..	..	..	..	..	..	..	..	..	..	..	5
3,141,052	**2,875,372**	**226,130**	**9,836**	**17,820**	**11,894**	**433,421**	**114,783**	**3,857**	**900**	**312,632**	**1,249**	
1,872,733	*1,761,669*	*102,271*	*4,097*	*2,664*	*2,032*	*280,397*	*62,749*	*1,076*	*251*	*215,655*	*666*	
517,750	460,166	55,172	1,211	253	948	95,619	17,104	218	106	77,946	245	6
15,930	14,842	1,050	38	..	..	620	109	..	..	511	..	7
146,747	141,168	3,365	637	1,554	23	31,045	8,209	100	30	22,696	10	8
88,772	83,688	4,879	74	..	131	13,104	3,249	125	59	9,667	4	9
103,514	103,427	87	..	..	..	14,201	1,368	4	..	12,758	71	10
19,211	17,739	1,472	..	..	..	13,044	729	5	..	12,309	1	11
119,245	103,493	15,870	111	132	139	20,858	7,454	122	8	13,276	3	12
642,448	628,419	12,060	1,141	133	695	66,985	17,339	35	28	49,582	1	13
255	121	57	77	..	..	..	..	..	..	..	..	14
111,194	105,521	5,125	63	451	34	7,953	1,208	29	..	6,715	1	15
2,910	2,432	428	50	..	..	256	27	..	..	229	..	16
78	..	..	75	..	3	208	162	4	..	28	14	17
97,951	95,772	1,692	289	141	57	12,254	4,688	424	13	7,116	13	18
6,728	4,881	1,514	331	..	2	4,250	1,103	10	12	2,822	303	19
133,951	*102,818*	*21,883*	*3,946*	*4,997*	*307*	*33,667*	*4,355*	*307*	*170*	*28,728*	*107*	
2,667	2,278	389	..	..	..	15,968	644	122	2	15,188	12	20
111,476	88,958	16,655	917	4,790	156	15,504	2,787	144	135	12,430	8	21
18,609	11,265	4,067	2,924	207	146	426	117	14	..	295	..	22
1,199	317	772	105	..	5	1,769	807	27	33	815	87	23
1,134,368	*1,010,885*	*101,976*	*1,793*	*10,159*	*9,555*	*119,357*	*47,679*	*2,474*	*479*	*68,249*	*476*	
22,223	18,035	3,122	17	7	1,042	10,239	8,848	724	..	603	64	24
3,588	1,769	1,827	90	..	102	..	..	..	..	..	..	25
81,139	67,214	11,878	308	185	1,554	6,032	2,794	210	71	2,926	31	26
15,218	10,382	4,472	27	337	..	1,140	72	1	..	1,034	33	27
8,511	8,243	115	3	9	141	895	88	8	2	797	..	28
959	345	613	..	..	1	..	..	..	..	..	..	29
11,228	11,020	208	..	..	..	..	..	..	..	..	..	30
2,454	1,262	1,084	105	..	3	..	..	..	..	..	..	31
241,975	238,646	2,774	155	197	203	196	80	31	..	79	6	32
391,941	354,760	31,811	271	2,771	2,328	82,174	25,648	1,165	374	54,938	49	33
16,622	11,786	4,625	127	34	50	1,315	924	5	..	386	..	34
7,670	6,198	1,260	78	8	126	147	94	..	..	53	..	35
1,260	969	291	..	..	..	45	6	..	..	39	..	36
15,597	13,282	892	19	1,351	53	703	146	3	6	548	..	37
25,880	20,688	4,231	44	902	15	3,883	2,238	1	12	1,632	..	38
46,816	39,036	6,419	158	24	679	3,115	1,600	21	..	1,461	33	39
..	..	..	..	..	..	180	1	..	..	179	..	40
241,787	207,250	26,554	391	4,334	3,258	9,293	5,140	305	14	3,574	260	41
747,998	**527,538**	**206,322**	**9,937**	**1,003**	**3,198**	**104,541**	**60,153**	**1,535**	**1,580**	**40,681**	**592**	
164,398	*93,385*	*66,989*	*3,282*	*102*	*640*	*20,513*	*12,952*	*238*	*137*	*7,124*	*62*	
68,750	27,356	37,961	3,041	..	392	10,706	7,998	102	..	2,560	46	42
..	..	..	..	..	..	..	..	..	..	..	..	43
95,648	66,029	29,028	241	102	248	9,807	4,954	136	137	4,564	16	44
346,184	*249,272*	*92,461*	*2,230*	*826*	*1,395*	*28,707*	*18,139*	*881*	*26*	*9,412*	*249*	45
209,039	*168,531*	*35,321*	*4,061*	*75*	*1,051*	*52,889*	*27,402*	*385*	*1,416*	*23,455*	*231*	
101,187	87,303	11,053	2,303	7	515	38,592	21,216	149	1,344	15,823	60	46
6,863	3,942	2,829	76	..	16	1,523	1,051	30	..	412	30	47
30,973	25,059	5,635	244	13	22	2,769	1,052	36	14	1,631	36	48
23,574	14,018	8,314	1,019	29	195	3,053	1,478	25	1	1,495	59	49
46,442	38,203	7,490	419	27	303	6,952	2,610	145	57	4,094	46	50
28,377	*16,350*	*11,551*	*364*	..	*119*	*2,432*	*1,660*	*31*	*1*	*690*	*50*	51
1,077,434	**767,307**	**281,326**	**5,178**	**19,749**	**3,874**	**100,422**	**33,656**	**1,097**	**1,300**	**64,245**	**124**	
421,147	*222,557*	*190,387*	*1,943*	*4,168*	*2,092*	*37,766*	*17,817*	*560*	*382*	*18,966*	*41*	52
380,148	*319,587*	*45,077*	*2,757*	*11,902*	*825*	*23,004*	*10,117*	*248*	*269*	*12,338*	*32*	53
276,139	*225,163*	*45,862*	*478*	*3,679*	*957*	*39,652*	*5,722*	*289*	*649*	*32,941*	*51*	
3,428	2,401	956	15	..	58	658	9	4	1	644	..	54
272,711	222,762	44,906	463	3,679	901	38,994	5,713	285	648	32,297	51	55

TABLE XV.—Occupation or Means of Livelihood. Part D.—Distribution by Religion—*concld.*

Order Number.	Occupation.	Cochin State. Total number of Workers and Dependants. All Religions.	Hindu.	Musalman.	Christian.	Others.	Travancore State. Total number of Workers and Dependants. All Religions.	Hindu.	Musalman.	Christian.	Others.
	1	75	76	77	78	79	80	81	82	83	84
	TOTAL POPULATION	**918,110**	**615,708**	**63,822**	**233,092**	**5,488**	**3,428,975**	**2,282,617**	**226,617**	**903,868**	**15,873**
	A.—Production of raw materials	**483,910**	**342,945**	**26,528**	**110,846**	**3,591**	**1,907,199**	**1,209,457**	**149,487**	**535,405**	**12,850**
	I.—EXPLOITATION OF THE SURFACE OF THE EARTH.	*483,904*	*342,939*	*26,528*	*110,846*	*3,591*	*1,905,466*	*1,208,375*	*149,354*	*534,933*	*12,804*
1	Pasture and agriculture	470,607	334,955	26,121	105,940	3,591	1,839,423	1,184,811	138,134	503,685	12,793
2	Fishing and hunting	13,297	7,984	407	4,906	..	66,043	23,564	11,220	31,248	11
	II.—EXTRACTION OF MINERALS	*6*	*6*	..	..	..	*1,733*	*1,082*	*133*	*472*	*46*
3	Mines	6	6	..	..	..	1,295	692	106	451	46
4	Quarries of hard rocks	..	..	..	..	..	..	..	..	..	..
5	Salt, etc.	..	..	..	..	..	438	390	27	21	..
	B.—Preparation and supply of material substances.	**316,408**	**194,237**	**28,873**	**92,082**	**1,216**	**928,685**	**655,672**	**47,857**	**224,976**	**180**
	III.—INDUSTRY	*192,031*	*137,186*	*6,224*	*48,340*	*301*	*588,410*	*443,689*	*27,641*	*117,013*	*67*
6	Textiles	46,825	25,251	1,909	19,533	132	160,544	99,595	17,674	43,275	..
7	Hides, skins and hard materials from the animal kingdom.	1,179	1,033	..	146	..	149	115	11	23	..
8	Wood	43,232	30,626	1,784	10,812	10	93,018	61,810	3,829	27,312	67
9	Metals	9,277	7,093	155	1,420	..	35,391	29,871	801	4,719	..
10	Ceramics	4,196	3,417	21	758	..	14,234	9,342	641	4,251	..
11	Chemical products properly so called, and analogous.	4,192	1,679	44	2,460	..	20,003	15,375	1,008	3,620	..
12	Food industries	40,211	33,891	1,018	5,302	..	168,407	151,393	1,739	15,275	..
13	Industries of dress and the toilet	18,438	15,014	924	2,428	72	60,888	51,375	781	8,732	..
14	Furniture industries	132	13	2	117	..	127	99	2	26	..
15	Building industries	13,532	9,246	323	3,963	..	7,506	4,972	543	1,991	..
16	Construction of means of transport	66	8	2	1	55	387	263	29	95	..
17	Production and transmission of physical forces (heat, light, electricity, motive power, etc.).	1	1	..	..	..	61	17	3	41	..
18	Industries of luxury and those pertaining to literature and the arts and sciences.	7,785	6,851	10	892	32	25,714	18,436	437	6,841	..
19	Industries concerned with refuse matter	2,985	2,463	32	490	..	1,981	1,026	143	812	..
	IV.—TRANSPORT	*18,856*	*8,419*	*2,985*	*7,442*	*10*	*54,942*	*29,443*	*1,779*	*23,670*	*50*
20	Transport by water	6,773	2,313	1,443	3,012	5	23,895	7,933	946	15,016	..
21	Transport by road	10,050	4,997	1,408	3,642	3	25,838	17,627	765	7,414	32
22	Transport by rail	1,301	564	116	619	2	929	718	25	168	18
23	Post Office, Telegraph and Telephone services	732	545	18	169	..	4,280	3,165	43	1,072	..
	V.—TRADE	*103,501*	*48,632*	*19,664*	*36,300*	*905*	*285,333*	*182,540*	*18,437*	*84,293*	*63*
24	Banks, establishments of credit, exchange and insurance.	4,424	4,009	73	336	6	9,446	7,951	252	1,236	7
25	Brokerage, commission and export	255	201	17	16	21	827	579	116	132	..
26	Trade in textiles	5,646	2,258	750	2,562	76	45,221	28,795	3,231	13,172	23
27	Trade in skins, leather, and furs	544	4	50	410	80	508	397	22	89	..
28	Trade in wood	1,305	424	328	546	7	9,031	6,574	306	2,146	5
29	Trade in metals	321	114	13	194	..	78	51	15	12	..
30	Trade in pottery	217	113	55	44	5	2,289	1,375	98	816	..
31	Trade in chemical products	842	285	232	322	3	131	86	6	39	..
32	Hotels, cafés, restaurants, etc.	9,690	8,022	638	995	35	23,443	16,779	296	6,368	..
33	Other trade in food stuffs	59,573	24,481	15,468	19,075	549	168,703	102,927	11,462	54,314	..
34	Trade in clothing and toilet articles	336	76	19	241	..	64	32	14	18	..
35	Trade in furniture	1,537	432	374	731	..	3,281	2,137	327	817	..
36	Trade in building materials	1,585	765	144	676	..	5,004	3,671	175	1,158	..
37	Trade in means of transport	797	435	246	116	..	937	628	66	243	..
38	Trade in fuel	2,043	754	150	1,137	2	4,082	2,585	510	974	13
39	Trade in articles of luxury and those pertaining to letters and the arts and sciences	1,118	777	29	287	25	1,415	970	131	314	..
40	Trade in refuse matter	54	54	..	..	..	38	21	4	13	..
41	Trade of other sorts	15,214	5,428	1,078	8,612	96	10,835	6,982	1,406	2,432	15
	C.—Public administration and liberal arts	**43,478**	**34,650**	**1,994**	**6,781**	**53**	**145,428**	**107,600**	**3,689**	**34,110**	**29**
	VI.—PUBLIC FORCE	*1,740*	*1,421*	*146*	*173*	..	*9,989*	*8,958*	*239*	*92*	..
42	Army	576	576	..	..	..	5,886	5,730	91	56	..
43	Navy	..	..	..	..	..	..	..	..	..	..
44	Police	1,164	845	146	173	..	3,403	3,219	148	36	..
45	*VII.—(ORDER 45) PUBLIC ADMINISTRATION.*	*10,045*	*8,789*	*290*	*964*	*2*	*32,695*	*23,746*	*331*	*8,618*	..
	VIII.—PROFESSIONS AND LIBERAL ARTS.	*30,564*	*23,536*	*1,461*	*5,528*	*39*	*97,720*	*70,718*	*3,058*	*23,924*	*29*
46	Religion	10,648	8,463	615	1,563	7	33,714	23,327	1,421	8,945	21
47	Law	2,163	1,863	2	298	..	8,545	6,312	28	2,205	..
48	Medicine	4,881	3,517	250	1,113	1	10,200	7,858	89	2,244	..
49	Instruction	7,417	5,042	581	1,763	31	28,365	20,702	445	5,128	..
50	Letters and arts and sciences	5,455	4,651	13	791	..	18,896	12,431	1,075	5,382	8
51	*IX.—(ORDER 51) PERSONS LIVING PRINCIPALLY ON THEIR INCOME.*	*1,129*	*904*	*97*	*116*	*12*	*5,715*	*4,178*	*61*	*1,476*	..
	D.—Miscellaneous	**74,314**	**43,876**	**6,427**	**23,383**	**628**	**447,663**	**309,888**	**25,584**	**109,377**	**2,814**
52	*X.—(ORDER 52) DOMESTIC SERVICE*	*5,573*	*3,512*	*365*	*1,674*	*22*	*15,255*	*11,068*	*745*	*3,432*	*10*
53	*XI.—(ORDER 53) INSUFFICIENTLY DESCRIBED OCCUPATIONS.*	*66,194*	*38,851*	*5,878*	*20,897*	*568*	*424,789*	*294,526*	*23,953*	*103,521*	*2,789*
	XII.—UNPRODUCTIVE	*2,547*	*1,513*	*184*	*812*	*38*	*7,619*	*4,294*	*886*	*2,424*	*15*
54	Inmates of jails, asylums and hospitals	157	76	..	81	..	1,740	1,048	148	530	15
55	Beggars, vagrants, prostitutes	2,390	1,437	184	731	38	5,879	3,246	738	1,895	..

TABLE XV.

Occupation or Means of Livelihood.

PART E.—STATISTICS OF INDUSTRIES.

1. Parts A to D of Table XV which were compiled from the general schedules give the main functional distribution of the people. The statistics in this Part regarding various industrial concerns, such as mines, mills, etc., were collected in a special schedule, which was filled in by the owners or managers of all factories, etc., in which at least 20 persons were employed on the date of the Census. This Part is divided into two sections. Section I contains information for the whole Empire regarding each kind of factory, etc., distinguishing between those factories in which mechanical power is used and those in which it is not, and classifying them according to the number of persons employed. Section II gives for each Province, State, or Agency the number of persons employed in each kind of factory, etc., without these details. In the corresponding Table in the Provincial Volumes two more sections have been added showing the caste and nationality of the owners and managers of important concerns.

2. For the purpose of this Part the various industrial undertakings have been divided into 16 main heads and 111 sub-heads, minor concerns not falling under these sub-heads being grouped together as 'Others.' When two or more industries are combined in one factory, the classification has usually been made with reference to the first named in the return: thus, a cotton ginning and rice husking and flour mill has been classed under "Textile Industries (cotton)." Certain factories in the United Provinces in which hand-power or bullock-power is used have been classed in the Provincial Table as factories having mechanical power. They have here been classed with those in which mechanical power is not used. The Upper Jhelum Canal construction, which was wrongly included in Kashmir Table XV-E, has been omitted from this Table.

3. The Statement below shows the factories, etc., which have been included in 'Others' under each main head:—

I.—Growing of Special Products.

Casuarina Plantation.
Cinnamon Plantation.
Copra Out-agency.
General Produce curing yard.
General Produce Work.
Harra Factory.
Pepper Estate.
Sugarcane Plantation.

II.—Mines.

Copper Mine.
Diamond Mine.
Galena Mine.
Graphite Mine.
Jade Mine.
Magnesite Mine.
Plumbago Mine.
Ruby Mine.
Salt Mine.
Silver and Lead Mine.

III.—Quarries of Hard Rocks.

Kankar Quarry.
Slate Quarry.
Soil Quarry.

IV.—Textile Industries.

Agave fibre spinning Mill.
Fibre Factory.
Industrial Home for weaving, carpentry, shoe-making, etc.
Senna Press.
Sisal.
Textile Institute.

VI.—Wood, etc., Industries.

Cane Factory.
Cask-making Factory.

VII.—Metal Industries.

Institute for teaching mechanical works.
Lead-smelting Workshop.
Metal stamping Works.
Metal vessel Factory.
Metal Works.
Repairing and Workshop.
Surgical and veterinary instruments Factory.
Type casting Works.
Weight and Measures making Factory.

IX.—Industries connected with Chemical Products.

Briquette Factory.
Extraction of Rasaunt (Sap of berbers lycium).
Fish oil and fish manure Works.
Government Medical Store.
Ink Factory.
Manure Works.
Pencil Factory.

X.—Food Industries.

Condiment Factory.
Confectionery Factory.
Ginger-bleaching Factory.
Potato-meal Factory.

XI.—Industries of Dress.

Button and Comb Factory.
Laundry.

XIV.—Industries connected with Transport.

Aerial Ropeway.
Bridge Work including that of Railway.
Landing and Shipping Warehouse.

XVI.—Industries of Luxury.

Clock and Watch Works.
Map reproduction Factory.
Process engraving and Art printing Works.
Scientific and optical and musical instruments Workshop.
School of Arts.

4. The figures for Provinces include those for the States attached to them, except in the case of Madras, where they exclude Cochin and Travancore.

TABLE XV.—Occupation or Means of Livelihood.

Description and classification of factory, etc., according to number of persons employed.	Number of factories.	Total number of persons employed. Males.	Females.	Classification of persons employed. Direction, Supervision and Clerical Work. Europeans and Anglo-Indians. M.	F.	Indians. M.	F.	Skilled Workmen. Europeans and Anglo-Indians. M.	F.	Indians. Males.	Females.	Unskilled Labourers. Age 14 and over. Males.	Females.	Under 14. Males.	Females.
1	2	3	4	5	6	7	8	9	10	11	12	13	14	15	16
INDIA.	**7,113**	**1,521,631**	**584,793**	**9,267**	**170**	**60,681**	**713**	**6,262**	**210**	**504,560**	**43,746**	**796,330**	**446,868**	**144,031**	**93,066**
I.—Growing of Special Products.	*1,687*	*440,800*	*369,607*	*1,617*	*10*	*10,171*	*175*	*254*	*2*	*16,514*	*1,678*	*329,628*	*295,481*	*82,618*	*73,261*
Cardamom Plantations.	**10**	**724**	**450**	**4**	..	**78**	**20**	..	..	**2**	..	**560**	**348**	**80**	**82**
With mechanical power. (a) (100—200).	*2*	*200*	*95*	*2*	..	*18*	..	..	..	*2*	..	*167*	*88*	*11*	*7*
Without mechanical power.	*8*	*524*	*355*	*2*	..	*60*	*20*	..	..	..	..	*393*	*260*	*69*	*75*
20 to 50	3	68	23	..	..	6	..	..	..	..	..	50	20	12	3
50 to 100	2	93	44	1	..	45	20	..	..	..	..	45	20	2	4
100 to 200	1	75	69	..	..	..	..	..	..	..	..	56	47	19	22
200 to 400	2	288	219	1	..	9	..	..	..	..	..	242	173	36	46
Cinchona Plantations.	**5**	**684**	**460**	**5**	..	**25**	..	..	..	**11**	..	**533**	**380**	**110**	**80**
With mechanical power. (b) (400 and over)	*1*	*382*	*312*	*2*	..	*19*	..	..	..	..	..	*285*	*242*	*76*	*70*
Without mechanical power.	*4*	*302*	*148*	*3*	..	*6*	..	..	..	*11*	..	*248*	*138*	*34*	*10*
50 to 100	2	91	74	1	..	3	..	..	..	..	..	79	69	8	5
100 to 200	2	211	74	2	..	3	..	..	..	11	..	169	69	26	5
Coffee Plantations.	**482**	**32,227**	**25,396**	**247**	**2**	**1,236**	**64**	**19**	**2**	**1,366**	**610**	**25,931**	**20,593**	**3,428**	**4,125**
With mechanical power. (c)	*93*	*10,370*	*9,865*	*101*	..	*355*	*23*	*10*	*2*	*628*	*245*	*8,303*	*7,738*	*973*	*1,807*
20 to 50	12	293	128	11	..	29	11	..	2	49	11	184	89	20	15
50 to 100	14	641	347	5	..	19	1	..	..	142	100	432	196	43	50
100 to 200	28	2,564	1,660	23	..	91	..	5	..	118	29	2,055	1,434	272	197
200 to 400	25	3,847	2,860	28	..	93	6	2	..	208	96	3,143	2,207	373	561
400 and over	14	3,025	4,870	34	..	123	5	3	..	111	9	2,469	3,862	265	994
Without mechanical power.	*389*	*21,857*	*15,531*	*146*	*2*	*881*	*41*	*9*	..	*738*	*365*	*17,628*	*12,805*	*2,455*	*2,318*
20 to 50	113	2,443	1,597	24	..	130	5	2	..	117	40	1,857	1,265	313	287
50 to 100	147	6,224	4,407	48	..	280	8	1	..	284	152	4,896	3,602	715	645
100 to 200	97	7,834	5,621	47	2	287	28	6	..	195	102	6,520	4,775	779	714
200 to 400	30	4,596	3,249	25	..	114	..	..	..	139	71	3,748	2,652	570	526
400 and over	2	760	657	2	..	70	..	..	..	3	..	607	511	78	146
Indigo Plantations.	**121**	**26,544**	**4,251**	**97**	**1**	**2,073**	**3**	**12**	..	**2,168**	**306**	**16,174**	**2,199**	**6,020**	**1,742**
With mechanical power. (d)	*112*	*25,817*	*4,013*	*93*	*1*	*2,021*	*3*	*12*	..	*2,101*	*306*	*15,732*	*2,025*	*5,858*	*1,678*
20 to 50	10	334	20	7	..	68	..	..	..	43	..	206	20	10	..
50 to 100	23	1,582	91	7	..	297	..	..	..	52	..	1,083	53	143	38
100 to 200	29	3,678	364	20	1	422	1	10	..	445	5	2,172	169	609	188
200 to 400	28	6,676	1,269	17	..	491	..	1	..	327	1	4,364	736	1,476	532
400 and over	22	13,547	2,269	42	..	743	2	1	..	1,234	300	7,907	1,047	3,620	920
Without mechanical power.	*9*	*727*	*238*	*4*	..	*52*	..	..	..	*67*	..	*442*	*174*	*162*	*64*
20 to 50	4	139	12	2	..	7	..	..	..	36	..	91	8	3	4
50 to 100	2	177	16	..	..	8	..	..	..	9	..	50	6	110	10
100 to 200	2	247	83	2	..	31	..	..	..	14	..	151	48	49	35
200 to 400	1	164	127	..	..	6	..	..	..	8	..	150	112	..	15
Rubber Plantations.	**48**	**11,198**	**2,469**	**92**	**2**	**168**	**4**	**1**	..	**1,595**	**117**	**8,508**	**1,811**	**834**	**535**
With mechanical power. (e)	*2*	*292*	*113*	*4*	..	*11*	..	..	..	..	..	*240*	*55*	*37*	*58*
100 to 200	1	80	101	3	..	5	..	..	..	..	..	43	47	29	54
200 to 409	1	212	12	1	..	6	..	..	..	..	..	197	8	8	4
Without mechanical power.	*46*	*10,906*	*2,356*	*88*	*2*	*157*	*4*	*1*	..	*1,595*	*117*	*8,268*	*1,756*	*797*	*477*
20 to 50	7	190	46	7	..	10	..	..	..	45	..	116	41	12	5
50 to 100	3	201	54	5	..	5	..	..	..	41	40	131	4	19	10
100 to 200	12	1,204	428	13	..	43	..	..	..	111	..	918	362	119	66
200 to 400	15	3,211	939	29	2	52	4	1	..	220	77	2,650	705	259	151
400 and over	9	6,100	889	34	..	47	..	..	..	1,178	..	4,453	644	388	245
Tea Plantations.	**1,002**	**367,944**	**335,741**	**1,145**	**5**	**6,466**	**77**	**219**	..	**11,331**	**524**	**276,696**	**289,581**	**71,987**	**65,554**
With mechanical power. (f)	*777*	*330,415*	*304,146*	*1,032*	*5*	*5,745*	*66*	*205*	..	*10,443*	*483*	*248,439*	*243,945*	*64,551*	*59,647*
20 to 50	47	1,230	289	33	1	126	3	18	..	155	18	725	234	143	33
50 to 100	35	1,747	798	9	..	142	13	3	..	251	31	1,178	603	164	151
100 to 200	53	4,668	3,418	14	..	180	1	2	..	428	20	3,276	2,722	768	875
200 to 400	126	20,195	17,592	72	1	578	7	17	..	1,282	109	14,907	14,646	3,339	2,829
400 and over	516	302,575	282,049	904	3	4,719	42	165	..	8,297	305	228,353	225,740	60,137	55,959
Without mechanical power.	*225*	*37,429*	*31,595*	*113*	..	*721*	*11*	*14*	..	*888*	*41*	*28,257*	*25,636*	*7,436*	*5,907*
20 to 50	39	970	354	9	..	72	..	4	..	215	40	532	272	118	42
50 to 100	30	1,657	549	6	..	93	5	..	..	272	..	1,046	450	240	94
100 to 200	39	3,137	2,801	17	..	89	..	2	..	69	1	2,523	2,391	437	409
200 to 400	54	9,205	6,804	37	..	196	4	2	..	178	..	6,929	5,629	1,863	1,171
400 and over	63	22,460	21,087	44	..	271	2	6	..	154	..	17,207	16,894	4,778	4,191
Others.	**19**	**1,579**	**840**	**27**	..	**125**	**7**	**1**	..	**41**	**121**	**1,226**	**569**	**159**	**143**
With mechanical power. (g)	*4*	*266*	*153*	..	..	*15*	..	..	..	*1*	..	*219*	*122*	*31*	*31*
50 to 100	1	46	23	..	..	6	..	..	..	1	..	29	14	10	9
100 to 200	3	220	130	..	..	9	..	..	..	..	..	190	108	21	22
Without mechanical power.	*15*	*1,313*	*687*	*27*	..	*110*	*7*	*1*	..	*40*	*121*	*1,007*	*447*	*128*	*112*
20 to 50	6	89	81	..	..	29	..	..	..	8	..	39	75	13	6
50 to 100	2	105	39	..	..	..	..	..	..	..	..	105	39	..	..
100 to 200	5	406	320	3	..	13	6	1	..	32	60	306	179	51	75
200 to 400	1	292	86	..	..	6	..	..	..	..	61	265	20	21	5
400 and over	1	421	161	24	..	62	1	..	..	..	..	292	134	43	26

Power.—(*a*) Water 2. (*b*) Steam 1. (*c*) Steam 20, Oil 25, Water 42, Water and oil 3, Steam and oil 2, Gas 1. (*d*) Steam 112. (*e*) Oil 2. (*f*) Steam 683, Oil 27, Electricity and oil 3, Steam and water 20, Water 19, Steam and oil 6, Steam, water and oil 1, Electricity 7, Oil and water 5, Oil and gas 1, Gas 3, Water and wheel 1, Water, oil and electricity 1. (*g*) Steam 4.

PART E.—STATISTICS OF INDUSTRIES, (i) GENERAL STATEMENT.

Description and classification of factory, etc., according to number of persons employed.	Number of factories.	Total number of persons employed.		CLASSIFICATION OF PERSONS EMPLOYED.											
				DIRECTION, SUPERVISION AND CLERICAL WORK.				SKILLED WORKMEN.				UNSKILLED LABOURERS.			
				Europeans and Anglo-Indians.		Indians.		Europeans and Anglo-Indians.		Indians.		Age 14 and over.		Under 14.	
		Males.	Females.	M.	F.	M.	F.	M.	F.	Males.	Females.	Males.	Females.	Males.	Females.
1	2	3	4	5	6	7	8	9	10	11	12	13	14	15	16
II.—Mines	***562***	***162,219***	***61,868***	***1,160***	***4***	***4,896***	***15***	***740***	..	***68,924***	***2,731***	***79,671***	***52,503***	***7,598***	***6,615***
COLLIERIES	**353**	**99,601**	**43,276**	**326**	..	**3,842**	**4**	**27**	..	**56,276**	**765**	**34,458**	**38,038**	**4,672**	**4,469**
With mechanical power. (a)	*306*	*97,280*	*42,150*	*321*	..	*3,721*	*4*	*26*	..	*55,410*	*746*	*33,273*	*37,088*	*4,529*	*4,312*
20 to 50	34	877	341	..	..	124	..	..	..	384	24	344	295	25	22
50 to 100	48	2,311	990	7	..	190	1	..	..	1,123	33	907	886	84	70
100 to 200	62	6,611	2,814	11	..	443	3	2	..	3,721	48	2,191	2,555	243	206
200 to 400	59	11,561	5,158	35	..	538	..	1	..	7,084	205	3,376	4,463	527	490
400 and over	103	75,920	32,847	268	..	2,426	..	23	..	43,098	436	26,455	28,889	3,650	3,522
Without mechanical power.	*47*	*2,321*	*1,126*	*5*	..	*121*	..	*1*	..	*866*	*19*	*1,185*	*950*	*143*	*157*
20 to 50	26	656	253	2	..	43	..	1	..	251	19	348	228	11	8
50 to 100	12	513	286	2	..	26	..	..	..	208	..	250	264	27	22
100 to 200	5	532	256	..	..	29	..	..	..	221	..	216	178	66	78
200 to 400	4	620	331	1	..	23	..	..	..	186	..	371	282	39	49
GOLD MINES	**12**	**26,596**	**1,996**	**575**	**2**	**157**	..	**372**	..	**6,009**	..	**18,940**	**1,732**	**643**	**262**
With mechanical power. (b)	*11*	*26,535*	*1,990*	*573*	*2*	*154*	..	*372*	..	*5,990*	..	*18,810*	*1,727*	*636*	*261*
100 to 200	1	155	19	6	..	1	..	3	..	45	..	95	19	5	..
200 to 400	2	394	64	19	1	5	..	..	..	131	..	223	60	16	3
400 and over	8	25,986	1,907	548	1	148	..	360	..	5,814	..	18,492	1,648	615	258
Without mechanical power (50 to 100).	*1*	*61*	*6*	*2*	..	*3*	..	..	..	*19*	..	*30*	*5*	*7*	*1*
IRON MINES	**3**	**3,981**	**2,325**	**7**	..	**14**	..	..	..	**34**	..	**3,804**	**2,180**	**122**	**145**
With mechanical power (c) (400 and over).	*1*	*2,636*	*1,698*	*2*	..	*4*	..	..	..	*17*	..	*2,613*	*1,698*	..	..
Without mechanical power (400 and over).	*2*	*1,345*	*627*	*5*	..	*10*	..	..	..	*17*	..	*1,191*	*482*	*122*	*145*
MANGANESE MINES	**54**	**9,882**	**6,796**	**50**	**1**	**202**	**8**	**11**	..	**271**	**9**	**8,662**	**6,203**	**686**	**575**
With mechanical power. (d)	*10*	*3,990*	*2,364*	*17*	..	*53*	..	*5*	..	*142*	*1*	*3,546*	*2,130*	*227*	*233*
100 to 200	1	119	2	3	..	2	..	2	..	25	..	85	2	2	..
200 to 400	1	224	104	..	..	6	..	..	..	2	..	185	88	31	16
400 and over	8	3,647	2,258	14	..	45	..	3	..	115	1	3,276	2,(40	194	217
Without mechanical power.	*44*	*5,892*	*4,432*	*33*	*1*	*149*	*8*	*6*	..	*129*	*8*	*5,116*	*4,073*	*459*	*342*
20 to 50	7	118	119	1	1	12	..	..	..	17	6	85	111	3	1
50 to 100	8	348	209	2	..	34	4	1	..	10	..	230	167	71	38
100 to 200	13	1,032	850	11	..	28	4	4	..	8	..	883	774	98	72
200 to 400	10	1,413	1,199	10	..	29	..	1	..	26	..	1,236	1,123	111	76
400 and over	6	2,981	2,055	9	..	46	..	..	..	68	2	2,682	1,898	176	155
MICA MINES	**93**	**8,805**	**5,914**	**17**	**1**	**334**	**3**	**3**	..	**2,974**	**1,949**	**4,294**	**2,932**	**1,183**	**1,029**
With mechanical power. (e)	*18*	*3,333*	*1,892*	*10*	*1*	*90*	..	*1*	..	*1,346*	*531*	*1,602*	*1,025*	*284*	*335*
20 to 50	4	97	38	1	..	8	..	..	..	30	9	47	23	11	6
50 to 100	4	174	87	..	..	11	..	1	..	80	19	70	60	12	8
100 to 200	6	415	352	..	..	27	..	..	..	192	152	179	169	17	31
200 to 400	1	155	129	..	..	5	..	..	..	60	90	81	37	9	2
400 and over	3	2,492	1,286	9	1	39	..	..	..	984	261	1,225	736	235	288
Without mechanical power.	*75*	*5,472*	*4,022*	*7*	..	*244*	*3*	*2*	..	*1,628*	*1,418*	*2,692*	*1,907*	*899*	*694*
20 to 50	15	279	173	..	..	25	3	..	..	149	53	74	79	31	38
50 to 100	25	1,031	743	3	..	56	..	..	..	359	290	450	330	163	123
100 to 200	21	1,592	1,436	2	..	44	..	2	..	517	804	790	451	237	181
200 to 400	12	1,944	1,371	..	..	109	..	..	..	557	271	929	825	349	275
400 and over	2	626	299	2	..	10	..	..	..	46	..	449	222	119	77
PETROLEUM WELLS	**20**	**5,923**	**411**	**96**	..	**193**	..	**300**	..	**1,334**	**6**	**3,971**	**400**	**29**	**5**
With mechanical power. (f)	*20*	*5,923*	*411*	*96*	..	*193*	..	*300*	..	*1,334*	*6*	*3,971*	*400*	*29*	*5*
20 to 50	4	131	4	3	..	9	..	8	..	26	..	85	4	..	..
50 to 100	7	514	8	3	..	21	..	50	..	82	6	355	2	3	..
100 to 200	1	164	6	2	..	5	..	11	..	16	..	130	6	..	..
200 to 400	4	1,072	64	16	..	11	..	16	..	434	..	502	64	3	..
400 and over	4	4,042	329	72	..	147	..	215	..	776	..	2,809	324	23	5
OTHERS	**27**	**7,431**	**1,150**	**89**	..	**154**	..	**27**	..	**1,326**	**2**	**5,642**	**1,018**	**183**	**130**
With mechanical power. (g)	*7*	*5,076*	*450*	*84*	..	*59*	..	*22*	..	*627*	*2*	*4,183*	*381*	*101*	*67*
100 to 200	3	247	124	4	..	15	..	..	..	31	2	193	117	4	5
400 and over	4	4,829	326	80	..	44	..	22	..	596	..	3,990	264	97	62
Without mechanical power.	*20*	*2,355*	*700*	*5*	..	*95*	..	*5*	..	*699*	..	*1,459*	*637*	*92*	*63*
20 to 50	7	255	20	..	..	7	..	..	..	95	..	152	18	1	2
50 to 100	8	528	37	..	..	6	..	..	..	132	..	367	37	23	..
200 to 400	3	785	15	..	..	31	..	..	..	135	..	600	13	19	2
400 and over	2	787	628	5	..	51	..	6	..	337	..	343	569	49	59
III.—Quarries of Hard Rocks.	***53***	***9,539***	***2,734***	***22***	..	***288***	***1***	***2***	***1***	***1,116***	***99***	***7,345***	***2,229***	***766***	***411***
STONE AND MARBLE QUARRIES.	**50**	**9,166**	**2,700**	**21**	..	**256**	**1**	**2**	**1**	**1,045**	**99**	**7,124**	**2,194**	**718**	**405**
With mechanical power. (h)	*4*	*2,548*	*451*	*11*	..	*25*	..	..	.	*71*	..	*1,944*	*328*	*497*	*123*
100 to 200	1	123	6	1	..	3	..	..	..	4	..	115	6	..	..
400 and over	3	2,425	445	10	..	22	..	..	..	67	..	1,829	322	497	123
Without mechanical power.	*46*	*6,618*	*2,249*	*10*	..	*231*	*1*	*2*	*1*	*974*	*99*	*5,189*	*1,866*	*221*	*282*
20 to 50	17	492	84	..	..	29	..	..	1	254	24	197	56	12	3
50 to 100	12	630	251	..	..	20	..	..	..	271	75	207	148	33	28
100 to 200	7	631	277	2	..	26	..	..	..	103	..	440	225	60	52
200 to 400	2	387	50	..	..	8	..	..	..	154	..	225	50	..	..
400 and over	8	4,478	1,587	8	..	139	1	2	..	102	..	4,021	1,387	116	199

Power.—(a) Steam 298, Steam and electricity 8. (b) Steam 6, Steam and electricity 5. (c) Steam 1. (d) Steam 8, Oil 1, Steam and oil 1. (e) Steam 6, Oil 6, Water 6, (f) Steam 13, Steam and oil 3, Steam, oil and electricity 1, Steam and gas 3. (g) Steam 3. Steam and oil 1, Steam and water 2, Electricity 1. (h) Steam 4.

TABLE XV.—OCCUPATION OR MEANS OF LIVELIHOOD.

Description and classification of factory, etc., according to number of persons employed.	Number of factories.	Total number of persons employed.		CLASSIFICATION OF PERSONS EMPLOYED.											
				DIRECTION, SUPERVISION AND CLERICAL WORK.				SKILLED WORKMEN.				UNSKILLED LABOURERS.			
				Europeans and Anglo-Indians.		Indians.		Europeans and Anglo-Indians.		Indians.		Age 14 and over.		Under 14.	
		Males.	Females.	M.	F.	M.	F.	M.	F.	Males.	Females.	Males.	Females.	Males.	Females.
1	2	3	4	5	6	7	8	9	10	11	12	13	14	15	16
III.—Quarries of Hard Rocks—contd.															
OTHERS	**3**	**373**	**34**	**1**	..	**32**	..	..	..	**71**	..	**221**	**28**	**48**	**6**
With mechanical power (a) (20 to 50).	*1*	*36*	*10*	..	..	*8*	..	..	..	*8*	..	*20*	*10*	..	..
Without mechanical power.	*2*	*337*	*24*	*1*	..	*24*	..	..	..	*63*	..	*201*	*18*	*48*	*6*
100 to 200	1	151	..	..	..	..	..	..	..	..	..	123	..	28	..
200 to 400	1	186	24	1	..	24	..	..	..	63	..	78	18	20	6
IV.—Textile Industries.	*1,487*	*445,057*	*119,532*	*1,404*	*22*	*18,330*	*277*	*369*	*27*	*213,953*	*36,231*	*174,404*	*66,541*	*36,607*	*9,434*
(a) Cotton	*1,127*	*238,909*	*69,981*	*568*	*5*	*12,367*	*218*	*259*	*25*	*138,700*	*28,207*	*72,663*	*36,172*	*14,352*	*4,654*
COTTON GINNING, CLEANING AND PRESSING MILLS.	**823**	**44,780**	**26,295**	**73**	**2**	**4,555**	**94**	**80**	..	**8,904**	**629**	**28,901**	**23,728**	**2,267**	**1,842**
With mechanical power. (b)	*823*	*44,780*	*26,295*	*73*	*2*	*4,555*	*94*	*80*	..	*8,904*	*629*	*28,901*	*23,728*	*2,267*	*1,842*
20 to 50	209	5,596	1,721	38	..	833	33	5	..	1,299	81	3,153	1,446	268	161
50 to 100	386	17,439	10,679	12	..	1,788	28	20	..	3,307	308	11,468	9,704	844	639
100 to 200	197	16,260	10,116	11	..	1,527	19	12	..	2,805	100	10,985	9,283	920	714
200 to 400	29	4,895	3,458	10	2	379	14	43	..	1,056	140	3,177	2,979	230	323
400 and over	2	590	321	2	..	28	..	..	..	437	..	118	316	5	5
THREAD GLAZING AND POLISHING MILLS.	**1**	**35**	..	..	..	**1**	..	..	..	**2**	..	**20**	..	**12**	..
Without mechanical power (20 to 50).	*1*	*35*	..	..	..	*1*	..	..	..	*2*	..	*20*	..	*12*	..
COTTON SPINNING, WEAVING, AND OTHER MILLS.	**286**	**193,098**	**42,858**	**486**	**3**	**7,709**	**99**	**179**	**25**	**129,248**	**27,551**	**43,456**	**12,375**	**12,020**	**2,805**
With mechanical power. (c)	*221*	*189,785*	*41,697*	*474*	*1*	*7,452*	*81*	*163*	..	*126,889*	*26,698*	*42,910*	*12,133*	*11,897*	*2,784*
20 to 50	16	500	43	6	..	63	..	6	..	178	24	219	19	28	..
50 to 100	11	670	41	9	..	90	..	..	..	287	11	273	27	11	3
100 to 200	12	1,428	388	3	..	120	..	2	..	928	167	802	218	73	3
200 to 400	18	5,025	1,074	12	..	326	2	110	..	3,348	738	827	260	402	74
400 and over	164	182,162	40,151	444	1	6,853	79	45	..	122,148	25,758	41,289	11,609	11,383	2,704
Without mechanical power.	*65*	*3,313*	*1,161*	*12*	*2*	*257*	*18*	*16*	*25*	*2,359*	*853*	*546*	*242*	*123*	*21*
20 to 50	44	916	457	4	..	110	17	16	25	399	286	338	129	40	..
50 to 100	15	752	237	5	2	39	1	..	..	548	146	112	74	48	14
100 to 200	5	419	179	1	..	63	..	..	..	289	155	40	17	26	7
400 and over	1	1,226	288	2	..	45	..	..	..	1,123	266	56	22	..	..
COTTON CARPET AND RUG MANUFACTORIES.	**17**	**996**	**128**	**9**	..	**102**	**25**		..	**546**	**27**	**286**	**69**	**53**	**7**
With mechanical power. (d)	*2*	*378*	*49*	*6*	..	*12*		..	..	*154*	..	*206*	*49*	..	..
100 to 200	1	141	8	3	..	4	..	..	..	123	..	11	8	..	..
200 to 400	1	237	41	3	..	8	..	..	..	31	..	195	41	..	..
Without mechanical power.	*15*	*618*	*79*	*3*	..	*90*	*25*	..		*392*	*27*	*80*	*20*	*53*	*7*
20 to 50	12	350	47	1	..	59	17	..	..	173	4	67	19	50	7
50 to 100	2	105	17	..	..	22	8	..	..	79	8	1	1	3	..
100 to 200	1	163	15	2		9	..	..	..	140	15	12	.	..	..
(b) Jute, Hemp, etc.	*293*	*184,119*	*38,207*	*734*	..	*4,711*	*33*	*108*	..	*60,905*	*5,059*	*98,358*	*28,875*	*19,296*	*4,247*
JUTE PRESSES	**123**	**12,827**	**1,426**	**108**	.	**963**	..	**33**	..	**2,492**	**69**	**9,048**	**1,314**	**188**	**43**
With mechanical power. (e)	*98*	*11,643*	*1,331*	*105*	..	*848*	..	*33*	..	*2,187*	*16*	*8,323*	*1,272*	*147*	*43*
20 to 50	42	1,129	22	20	..	184	..	23	..	284	..	589	21	29	1
50 to 100	25	1,681	93	28	..	218	..	2	..	340	15	1,051	68	42	10
100 to 200	12	1,618	63	19	..	107	..	7	..	234	1	1,183	53	68	9
200 to 400	12	2,999	259	3	..	82	..	1	..	246	..	2,665	259	2	..
400 and over	7	4,216	894	35	..	257	..	..	..	1,083	..	2,835	871	6	23
Without mechanical power.	*25*	*1,184*	*95*	*3*	..	*115*	..	..	..	*305*	*53*	*720*	*42*	*41*	..
20 to 50	17	425	49	..	..	40	..	..	..	45	26	324	23	16	..
50 to 100	6	314	34	..	..	43	..	..	..	60	20	196	14	15	..
100 to 200	1	110	5	..	..	10	..	..	..	..	..	100	5	..	..
200 to 400	1	335	7	3	..	22	..	..	..	200	7	100	..	10	..
JUTE MILLS	**52**	**166,643**	**35,621**	**579**	..	**3,436**	..	**71**	..	**57,105**	**4,734**	**87,113**	**26,978**	**18,339**	**3,909**
With mechanical power. (f)	*52*	*166,643*	*35,621*	*579*	..	*3,436*	..	*71*	..	*57,105*	*4,734*	*87,113*	*26,978*	*18,339*	*3,909*
100 to 200	2	238	68	8	..	8	..	2	..	22	..	184	68	14	..
200 to 400	1	253	52	2	..	8	..	..	..	68	..	134	38	41	14
400 and over	49	166,152	35,501	569	..	3,420	..	69	..	57,015	4,734	86,795	26,872	18,284	3,895
ROPE WORKS	**25**	**1,897**	**157**	**4**	..	**79**	**23**	**2**	..	**989**	**76**	**550**	**49**	**273**	**9**
With mechanical power. (g)	*10*	*1,039*	*109*	*4*	..	*33*	..	*2*	..	*511*	*58*	*436*	*42*	*53*	*9*
20 to 50	5	159	23	..	..	7	..	..	..	61	..	81	19	10	6
50 to 100	1	63	..	..	..	5	..	..	..	48	..	10	..	..	..
100 to 200	2	246	26	2	..	7	..	2	..	60	10	153	13	22	3
200 to 400	2	571	58	2	..	14	..	..	..	342	48	192	10	21	..
Without mechanical power.	*15*	*858*	*48*	..	..	*46*	*23*	..	..	*478*	*18*	*114*	*7*	*220*	..
20 to 50	7	194	20	..	..	9	..	..	..	162	18	12	2	11	..
50 to 100	6	363	28	..	..	36	23	..	..	130	.	42	5	149	..
100 to 200	2	301	..	..	..	1	.	..	..	180	..	60	..	60	..

Power.—(*a*) Steam 1. (*b*) Steam 804, Steam and oil 5, Water 2, Oil 10, Gas 1, Steam and electricity 1. (*c*) Steam 218, Steam and oil 1, Water 1, Oil 1. (*d*) Oil 1, Suction-gas 1. (*e*) Steam 58, Water 22, Oil 8, Electricity 5, Steam and oil 2, Water and oil 1, Steam, oil and electricity 1, Gas 1. (*f*) Steam 51, Electricity 1. (*g*) Steam 8, Oil 1, Not stated 1.

PART E.—STATISTICS OF INDUSTRIES, (i) GENERAL STATEMENT—*continued.*

Description and Classification of factory, etc., according to number of persons employed.	Number of factories.	Total number of persons employed.		CLASSIFICATION OF PERSONS EMPLOYED.											
				DIRECTION, SUPERVISION AND CLERICAL WORK.				SKILLED WORKMEN.				UNSKILLED LABOURERS.			
				Europeans and Anglo-Indians.		Indians.		Europeans and Anglo-Indians.		Indians.		Age 14 and over.		Under 14.	
		Males.	Females.	M.	F.	M.	F.	M.	F.	Males.	Females.	Males.	Females.	Males.	Females.
1	2	3	4	5	6	7	8	9	10	11	12	13	14	15	16
XV.—Textile Industries—contd.															
COIR FACTORIES	**13**	**2,424**	**716**	**43**	..	**213**	**10**	**2**	..	**258**	**39**	**1,451**	**418**	**457**	**249**
With mechanical power (a)	*7*	*1,745*	*462*	*38*	..	*96*	..	*1*	..	*139*	..	*1,080*	*267*	*391*	*195*
20 to 50	3	107	..	6	..	10	..	1	..	26	..	64	..	..	..
50 to 100	1	52	11	2	..	2	..	..	..	4	..	44	11	..	..
200 to 400	1	267	62	1	..	15	..	..	..	103	..	13	5	135	57
400 and over	2	1,319	383	29	..	69	..	..	..	6	..	959	251	256	138
Without mechanical power.	*6*	*679*	*251*	*5*	..	*117*	*10*	*1*	..	*119*	*39*	*371*	*151*	*66*	*54*
20 to 50	2	49	23	..	..	18	5	..	..	3	..	21	5	7	13
50 to 100	1	78	9	..	..	39	3	..	..	35	3	4	3	..	..
100 to 200	1	112	4	1	..	48	2	1	..	48	2	..	..	14	..
200 to 400	1	186	50	..	..	3	..	..	..	3	2	172	45	8	3
400 and over	1	254	168	4	..	9	..	..	..	30	32	174	98	37	38
HEMP MILLS	**3**	**115**	**101**	..	..	**2**	..	..	..	..	..	**96**	**85**	**17**	**16**
With mechanical power (b) (50 to 100).	*1*	*48*	*31*	..	..	..	..	..	..	..	..	*41*	*25*	*7*	*6*
Without mechanical power (50 to 100)	*2*	*67*	*70*	..	..	*2*	..	..	..	..	..	*55*	*60*	*10*	*10*
FIBRE CLEANING WORKS.	**6**	**145**	**165**	..	..	**18**	..	..	..	**60**	**134**	**45**	**10**	**22**	**21**
Without mechanical power.	*6*	*145*	*165*	..	..	*18*	..	..	..	*60*	*134*	*45*	*10*	*22*	*21*
20 to 50	3	20	74	..	..	5	..	..	..	10	60	..	..	5	14
50 to 100	3	125	91	..	..	13	..	..	..	50	74	45	10	17	7
FIBRE MATTING AND BAG WORKS.	**1**	**61**	**21**	..	..	..	..	..	..	**1**	..	**60**	**21**	..	..
With mechanical power (c) (50 to 100).	*1*	*61*	*21*	..	..	..	..	..	..	*1*	..	*60*	*21*	..	..
(c) Wool	*47*	*6,489*	*861*	*41*	..	*340*	*11*	..	..	*4,739*	*129*	*899*	*619*	*463*	*109*
WOOL PRESSES	**1**	**46**	..	..	..	**3**	..	..	..	**8**	..	**35**	..	..	..
With mechanical power (d) (20 to 50).	*1*	*46*	..	..	..	*3*	..	..	..	*8*	..	*35*	..	..	..
WOOLLEN MILLS	**21**	**2,580**	**818**	**35**	..	**142**	**11**	..	..	**1,677**	**123**	**533**	**585**	**193**	**99**
With mechanical power. (e)	*5*	*2,450*	*284*	*35*	..	*117*	*1*	..	..	*1,646*	*113*	*474*	*92*	*178*	*78*
20 to 50	2	40	..	..	..	4	..	..	..	11	..	25	..	..	..
400 and over	3	2,410	284	35	..	113	1	..	..	1,635	113	449	92	178	78
Without mechanical power.	*16*	*130*	*534*	..	..	*25*	*10*	..	..	*31*	*10*	*59*	*493*	*15*	*21*
20 to 50	10	89	214	..	..	25	10	..	..	31	10	18	191	15	3
50 to 100	6	41	320	..	..	..	..	..	..	..	..	41	302	..	18
CARPET, BLANKET AND SHAWL FACTORIES.	**25**	**3,856**	**43**	**6**	..	**195**	..	..	..	**3,054**	**6**	**331**	**34**	**270**	**3**
With mechanical power. (f)	*2*	*646*	*5*	*4*	..	*55*	..	..	..	*564*	..	*23*	*5*	..	..
50 to 100	1	45	5	3	..	2	..	..	..	32	..	8	5	..	..
400 and over	1	601	..	1	..	53	..	..	..	532	..	15	..	..	..
Without mechanical power.	*23*	*3,210*	*38*	*2*	..	*140*	..	..	..	*2,490*	*6*	*308*	*29*	*270*	*3*
20 to 50	10	317	10	..	..	9	..	..	..	193	5	65	2	50	3
50 to 100	7	469	1	1	..	42	..	..	..	174	1	107	..	145	..
100 to 200	2	202	..	..	..	6	..	..	..	113	..	28	..	55	..
200 to 400	3	703	27	..	..	65	..	..	..	560	..	78	27	..	..
400 and over	1	1,519	..	1	..	18	..	..	..	1,450	..	30	..	20	..
(d) Silk	*49*	*11,827*	*883*	*24*	..	*709*	*4*	*1*	..	*7,665*	*680*	*1,276*	*166*	*2,152*	*33*
SILK (INCLUDING TASSAR, ETC.), FILATURES AND MILLS.	**49**	**11,827**	**883**	**24**	..	**709**	**4**	**1**	..	**7,665**	**680**	**1,276**	**166**	**2,152**	**33**
With mechanical power. (g)	*33*	*7,981*	*752*	*22*	..	*551*	*4*	*1*	..	*5,640*	*602*	*1,158*	*135*	*609*	*11*
20 to 50	3	100	18	..	..	10	..	..	..	39	5	28	13	23	..
50 to 100	8	525	55	4	..	41	..	..	..	241	12	166	41	73	2
100 to 200	12	1,703	98	7	..	131	..	1	..	787	45	426	44	351	9
200 to 400	7	1,548	181	5	..	62	1	..	..	1,200	163	194	17	87	..
400 and over	3	4,105	400	6	..	307	3	..	..	3,373	377	344	20	75	..
Without mechanical power.	*16*	*3,846*	*131*	*2*	..	*158*	..	..	..	*2,025*	*78*	*118*	*31*	*1,543*	*22*
20 to 50	8	209	30	..	..	18	..	..	..	120	18	55	5	16	7
50 to 100	2	114	36	..	..	82	..	..	..	55	2	13	19	14	15
100 to 200	2	321	6	..	..	19	..	..	..	245	5	7	1	50	..
200 to 400	2	546	47	1	..	13	..	..	..	390	47	24	..	118	..
400 and over	2	2,656	12	1	..	76	..	..	..	1,215	6	19	6	1,345	..
(e) Hair, etc.	*5*	*1,993*	*296*	*31*	*4*	*110*	..	*1*	..	*1,419*	*227*	*287*	*49*	*75*	*16*
BRUSH FACTORIES	**4**	**296**	**75**	**5**	..	**29**	..	..	..	**176**	**59**	**11**	..	**75**	**16**
With mechanical power. (h)	*3*	*270*	*75*	*5*	..	*27*	..	..	..	*154*	*59*	*9*	..	*75*	*16*
20 to 50	1	22	2	..	..	12	..	..	..	10	2	..	..	..	..
100 to 200	2	248	73	5	..	15	..	..	..	144	57	9	..	75	16
Without mechanical power (20 to 50).	*1*	*26*	..	..	..	*2*	..	..	..	*22*	..	*2*	..	..	..

Power.—(a) Steam 7. (b) Steam 1. (c) Steam 1. (d) Steam 1. (e) Steam 3, Electricity 1, Steam and water 1. (f) Steam 2. (g) Steam 31, Oil 1, Steam and oil 1. (h) Oil 1, Gas 1, Electricity 2.

TABLE XV.—Occupation or Means of Livelihood.

Description and Classification of factory, etc., according to number of persons employed.	Number of factories.	Total number of persons employed. Males.	Total number of persons employed. Females.	Direction, Supervision and Clerical Work. Europeans and Anglo-Indians. M.	Direction, Supervision and Clerical Work. Europeans and Anglo-Indians. F.	Direction, Supervision and Clerical Work. Indians. M.	Direction, Supervision and Clerical Work. Indians. F.	Skilled Workmen. Europeans and Anglo-Indians. M.	Skilled Workmen. Europeans and Anglo-Indians. F.	Skilled Workmen. Indians. Males.	Skilled Workmen. Indians. Females.	Unskilled Labourers. Age 14 and over. Males.	Unskilled Labourers. Age 14 and over. Females.	Unskilled Labourers. Under 14. Males.	Unskilled Labourers. Under 14. Females.
1	2	3	4	5	6	7	8	9	10	11	12	13	14	15	16
***IV.—Textile Industries*—concld.**															
Felt Factories	**1**	**1,627**	**221**	**26**	**4**	**81**	..	**1**	..	**1,243**	**168**	**276**	**49**	..	..
With mechanical power (a) (400 and over).	*1*	*1,627*	*221*	*26*	*4*	*81*	..	*1*	..	*1,243*	*168*	*276*	*49*	..	..
(f) Others.	***36***	***1,804***	***3,004***	***6***	***13***	***83***	***11***	..	***9***	***525***	***1,936***	***921***	***660***	***269***	***382***
Calico Printing Works.	**11**	**324**	**69**	..	..	**12**	..	..	..	**241**	**36**	**18**	**26**	**53**	**7**
Without mechanical power.	*11*	*324*	*69*	..	..	*12*	..	..	..	*241*	*36*	*18*	*26*	*53*	*7*
20 to 50	10	286	55	..	..	12	..	..	..	205	26	18	26	51	3
50 to 100	1	38	14	..	..	..	..	..	..	36	10	..	..	2	4
Lace and Embroidery Works	**15**	**293**	**1,990**	**1**	**13**	**4**	**10**	..	**2**	**220**	**1,900**	**39**	**65**	**29**	..
Without mechanical power.	*15*	*293*	*1,990*	*1*	*13*	*4*	*10*	..	*2*	*220*	*1,900*	*39*	*65*	*29*	..
20 to 50	11	228	57	..	..	2	4	..	..	170	53	39	..	17	..
50 to 100	2	65	61	1	2	2	1	..	2	50	1	..	55	12	..
100 to 200	1	..	123	..	3	..	..	..	..	..	110	..	10	..	..
400 and over	1	..	1,740	..	8	..	5	..	..	..	1,736	..	..	..	..
Others	**10**	**1,187**	**945**	**5**	..	**67**	**1**	..	..	**64**	..	**864**	**569**	**187**	**375**
With mechanical power. (b)	*5*	*597*	*504*	*4*	..	*12*	..	..	..	*23*	..	*491*	*444*	*67*	*60*
50 to 100	1	30	27	2	..	1	..	..	..	2	..	17	27	8	..
100 to 200	2	172	160	1	..	4	..	..	..	14	..	123	127	39	33
200 to 400	1	164	103	..	..	1	..	..	..	3	..	150	96	10	7
400 and over	1	231	214	1	..	6	..	..	..	4	..	201	194	10	20
Without mechanical power.	*5*	*590*	*441*	*1*	..	*55*	*1*	..	..	*41*	..	*373*	*125*	*120*	*315*
20 to 50	2	55	..	..	..	8	..	..	..	20	..	27	..	..	..
50 to 100	1	61	..	..	..	1	..	..	..	4	..	46	..	10	..
400 and over	2	474	441	1	..	46	1	..	..	17	..	300	125	110	315
V.—Leather and other Industries.	***158***	***19,508***	***1,104***	***105***	..	***891***	***8***	***108***	***4***	***5,516***	***114***	***5,135***	***919***	***893***	***66***
Bone Mills	**8**	**764**	**319**	**10**	..	**39**	..	..	..	**97**	..	**610**	**317**	**8**	**2**
With mechanical power. (c)	*8*	*764*	*319*	*10*	..	*39*	..	..	..	*97*	..	*610*	*317*	*8*	*2*
20 to 50	2	67	25	1	..	4	..	..	..	7	..	55	25	..	..
100 to 200	4	375	133	4	..	20	..	..	..	43	..	307	133	1	..
200 to 400	2	322	161	5	..	15	..	..	..	47	..	248	159	7	2
Gut Factories	**3**	**117**	**28**	..	..	**3**	**2**	..	..	**18**	..	**77**	**25**	**19**	**1**
Without mechanical power.	*3*	*117*	*28*	..	..	*3*	*2*	..	..	*18*	..	*77*	*25*	*19*	*1*
20 to 50	2	68	4	..	..	1	2	..	..	18	..	42	1	7	1
50 to 100	1	49	24	..	..	2	..	..	..	..	..	35	24	12	..
Leather Factories.	**25**	**2,837**	**148**	**54**	..	**196**	..	**94**	**4**	**1,664**	**51**	**763**	**83**	**66**	**10**
With mechanical power. (d)	*5*	*1,817*	*1*	*36*	..	*96*	..	*33*	..	*1,237*	..	*385*	*1*	*30*	..
20 to 50	1	28	..	2	..	7	..	2	..	7	..	10	..	..	..
50 to 100	2	170	1	2	..	14	..	..	..	131	..	18	1	5	..
100 to 200	1	117	..	..	..	5	..	4	..	100	..	8	..	..	..
400 and over	1	1,502	..	32	..	70	..	27	..	999	..	349	..	25	..
Without mechanical power.	*20*	*1,020*	*147*	*18*	..	*100*	..	*61*	*4*	*427*	*51*	*378*	*82*	*36*	*10*
20 to 50	8	256	21	6	..	26	..	58	4	92	..	66	15	8	2
50 to 100	10	621	40	11	..	59	..	3	..	318	12	216	27	14	1
100 to 200	2	143	86	1	..	15	..	..	..	17	39	96	40	14	7
Tanneries	**122**	**8,790**	**609**	**41**	..	**583**	**6**	**14**	..	**3,737**	**63**	**3,685**	**487**	**730**	**53**
With mechanical power. (e)	*12*	*2,067*	*132*	*20*	..	*135*	..	*4*	..	*1,224*	*2*	*535*	*110*	*149*	*20*
20 to 50	2	57	..	2	..	36	..	..	..	9	..	10	..	..	..
50 to 100	3	200	16	1	..	43	..	..	..	110	2	31	13	15	1
100 to 200	4	557	19	3	..	19	..	..	..	290	..	229	19	16	..
200 to 400	2	523	83	4	..	21	..	..	..	307	..	131	64	60	19
400 and over	1	730	14	10	..	16	..	4	..	508	..	134	14	58	..
Without mechanical power.	*110*	*6,723*	*477*	*21*	..	*448*	*6*	*10*	..	*2,513*	*61*	*3,150*	*377*	*581*	*33*
20 to 50	53	1,6 1	114	3	..	145	2	8	..	773	12	626	96	136	4
50 to 100	40	2,555	184	2	..	161	4	2	..	1,091	24	1,048	127	251	29
100 to 200	15	1,921	178	5	..	96	..	..	..	575	25	1,052	153	193	..
200 to 400	2	556	1	11	..	46	..	..	..	74	..	424	1	1	..

Power.—(a) Steam 1. (b) Steam 5. (c) Steam 8. (d) Steam 3, Electricity 1, Oil 1. (e) Steam 9, Oil 2, Steam and oil 1.

PART E.—STATISTICS OF INDUSTRIES, (i) GENERAL STATEMENT—*continued*

Description and Classification of factory, etc., according to number of persons employed.	Number of factories.	Total number of persons employed.		CLASSIFICATION OF PERSONS EMPLOYED.											
				DIRECTION, SUPERVISION AND CLERICAL WORK.				SKILLED WORKMEN.				UNSKILLED LABOURERS.			
				Europeans and Anglo-Indians.		Indians.		Europeans and Anglo-Indians.		Indians.		Age 14 and over.		Under 14.	
		Males.	Females.	M.	F.	M.	F.	M.	F.	Males.	Females.	Males.	Females.	Males.	Females.
1	2	3	4	5	6	7	8	9	10	11	12	13	14	15	16
VI.—Wood, etc., Industries.	***168***	***28,172***	***895***	***177***	***8***	***1,904***	***51***	***39***	..	***11,376***	***91***	***14,048***	***632***	***628***	***113***
CARPENTRY WORKS.	**33**	**4,945**	**118**	**46**	**2**	**187**	**2**	**14**	..	**2,915**	**32**	**1,484**	**51**	**299**	**31**
With mechanical power. (a)	*12*	*3,275*	*7*	*30*	..	*96*	..	*12*	..	*2,334*	..	*725*	*7*	*78*	..
20 to 50	1	45	..	..	..	1	..	..	..	37	..	7	..	..	..
50 to 100	6	416	7	5	..	32	..	1	..	314	..	64	7	..	..
100 to 200	3	491	..	4	..	28	..	..	..	231	..	162	..	66	..
200 to 400	1	222	..	3	..	4	..	1	..	158	..	44	..	12	..
400 and over	1	2,101	..	18	..	31	..	10	..	1,594	..	448	..	..	..
Without mechanical power.	*21*	*1,670*	*111*	*16*	*2*	*91*	*2*	*2*	..	*581*	*32*	*759*	*44*	*221*	*31*
20 to 50	11	354	8	3	..	26	..	2	..	204	1	94	7	25	..
50 to 100	6	378	31	10	1	10	1	..	..	153	1	104	17	101	11
100 to 200	2	316	31	1	..	15	1	..	..	121	30	179	..	..	..
200 to 400	1	160	40	..	..	10	..	..	..	65	..	60	20	25	20
400 and over	1	462	1	2	1	30	..	..	..	38	..	322	..	70	..
SAW MILLS	**106**	**11,790**	**700**	**114**	**6**	**1,486**	**49**	**15**	..	**2,795**	**59**	**7,164**	**506**	**216**	**80**
With mechanical power. (b)	*106*	*11,790*	*700*	*114*	*6*	*1,486*	*49*	*15*	..	*2,795*	*59*	*7,164*	*506*	*216*	*80*
20 to 50	33	1,168	73	14	..	216	6	2	..	435	20	448	42	53	5
50 to 100	38	2,422	235	43	6	368	7	2	..	383	20	1,520	175	106	27
100 to 200	18	2,161	224	14	..	254	36	3	..	575	19	1,286	138	29	31
200 to 400	12	2,916	168	26	..	387	..	8	..	566	..	1,901	151	28	17
400 and over	5	3,123	..	17	..	261	..	..	..	836	..	2,009	..	..	..
TIMBER YARDS	**27**	**11,368**	**77**	**17**	..	**227**	..	..	..	**5,650**	..	**5,398**	**75**	**76**	**2**
With mechanical power. (c)	*4*	*626*	*5*	*3*	..	*39*	..	..	..	*411*	..	*172*	*5*	*1*	..
20 to 50	1	20	..	..	..	2	..	..	..	17	..	1	..	..	..
50 to 100	2	153	5	..	..	5	..	..	..	54	..	93	5	1	..
400 and over	1	453	..	3	..	32	..	..	..	340	..	78	..	..	..
Without mechanical power.	*23*	*10,742*	*72*	*14*	..	*188*	..	..	..	*5,239*	..	*5,226*	*70*	*75*	*2*
20 to 50	12	326	..	..	..	41	..	..	..	73	..	199	..	13	..
50 to 100	3	200	14	..	..	9	..	..	..	113	..	74	13	4	1
100 to 200	4	515	33	6	..	57	..	..	..	27	..	367	32	58	1
400 and over	4	9,701	25	8	..	81	..	..	..	5,026	..	4,586	25	..	..
OTHERS	**2**	**69**	..	..	..	**4**	..	**10**	..	**16**	..	**2**	..	**37**	..
Without mechanical power (20 to 50).	*2*	*69*	..	..	..	*4*	..	*10*	..	*16*	..	*2*	..	*37*	..
VII.—Metal Industries.	***372***	***68,048***	***2,997***	***1,237***	***6***	***3,882***	***4***	***555***	..	***33,454***	***106***	***27,324***	***2,840***	***1,596***	***41***
ALUMINIUM FACTORIES.	**4**	**428**	**1**	**5**	**1**	**15**	..	**31**	..	**296**	..	**68**	..	**13**	..
With mechanical power. (d)	*4*	*428*	*1*	*5*	*1*	*15*	..	*31*	..	*296*	..	*68*	..	*13*	..
20 to 50	1	33	..	1	..	..	..	27	..	..	..	..	..	5	..
50 to 100	2	135	..	..	..	3	..	..	..	110	..	22	..	..	..
200 to 400	1	260	1	4	1	12	..	4	..	186	..	46	..	8	..
ARMS FACTORIES	**6**	**5,871**	**1**	**143**	**1**	**228**	..	**20**	..	**4,494**	..	**974**	..	**12**	..
With mechanical power. (e)	*4*	*5,790*	..	*135*	..	*217*	..	*20*	..	*4,449*	..	*957*	..	*12*	..
20 to 50	1	32	..	1	..	1	..	..	..	28	..	2	..	..	..
400 and over	3	5,758	..	134	..	216	..	20	..	4,421	..	955	..	12	..
Without mechanical power (20 to 50).	*2*	*81*	*1*	*8*	*1*	*11*	..	..	..	*45*	..	*17*	..	..	..
ARSENALS	**16**	**4,691**	**2**	**260**	..	**277**	..	**28**	..	**1,937**	..	**1,951**	**2**	**238**	..
With mechanical power. (f)	*13*	*3,878*	*2*	*233*	..	*261*	..	*15*	..	*1,367*	..	*1,819*	*2*	*183*	..
20 to 50	3	71	..	..	..	1	..	..	..	70	..	..	..	..	..
50 to 100	3	192	..	..	..	3	..	..	..	144	..	45	..	..	..
100 to 200	2	368	..	6	..	11	..	..	..	241	..	104	..	6	..
200 to 400	1	292	..	32	..	19	..	2	..	83	..	139	..	17	..
400 and over	4	2,955	2	195	..	227	..	13	..	829	..	1,531	2	160	..
Without mechanical power.	*3*	*813*	..	*27*	..	*16*	..	*13*	..	*570*	..	*132*	..	*55*	..
20 to 50	1	31	..	4	..	1	..	13	..	..	..	13	..	..	..
200 to 400	1	212	..	17	..	8	..	..	..	74	..	102	..	11	..
400 and over	1	570	..	6	..	7	..	..	..	496	..	17	..	44	..
BRASS, COPPER, AND BELL-METAL FOUNDRIES.	**36**	**1,376**	**16**	**1**	..	**113**	..	**19**	..	**737**	..	**421**	**14**	**85**	**2**
With mechanical power. (g)	*6*	*316*	..	*1*	..	*67*	..	*19*	..	*163*	..	*48*	..	*18*	..
20 to 50	4	117	..	..	..	24	..	19	..	57	..	13	..	4	..
50 to 100	1	80	..	..	..	40	..	..	..	25	..	15	..	..	..
100 to 200	1	119	..	1	..	3	..	..	..	81	..	20		14	..
Without mechanical power.	*30*	*1,060*	*16*	..	..	*46*	..	..	..	*574*	..	*373*	*14*	*67*	*2*
20 to 50	22	594	7	..	..	25	..	..	..	322	..	209	5	38	2
50 to 100	8	466	9	..	..	21	..	..	..	252	..	164	9	29	..
GUN-CARRIAGE FACTORIES.	**1**	**1,525**	..	**38**	..	**88**	..	**36**	..	**954**	..	**380**	..	**29**	..
With mechanical power(h) (400 and over).	*1*	*1,525*	..	*38*	..	*88*	..	*36*	..	*954*	..	*380*	..	*29*	..

Power.—(a) Steam 5, Oil 4, Steam, oil and gas 2, Electricity 1. (b) Steam 105, Electricity 1. (c) Electricity 1, Hydraulic 3. (d) Oil 3, Gas and electricity 1. (e) Steam 3, Electricity 1. (f) Steam 5, Oil 1, Steam and electricity 7. (g) Steam 5, Oil 1. (h) Electricity 1.

TABLE XV.—OCCUPATION OR MEANS OF LIVELIHOOD.

Description and Classification of factory, etc., according to number of persons employed.	Number of factories.	Total number of persons employed.		CLASSIFICATION OF PERSONS EMPLOYED.											
				Direction, Supervision and Clerical Work.				Skilled Workmen.				Unskilled Labourers.			
				Europeans and Anglo-Indians.		Indians.		Europeans and Anglo-Indians.		Indians.		Age 14 and over.		Under 14.	
		Males.	Females.	M.	F.	M.	F.	M.	F.	Males.	Females.	Males.	Females.	Males.	Females.
1	2	3	4	5	6	7	8	9	10	11	12	13	14	15	16
VII.—Metal Industries—contd.															
IRON FOUNDRIES	**64**	**9,416**	**646**	**107**	**1**	**420**	..	**37**	..	**4,391**	**3**	**4,250**	**616**	**211**	**26**
With mechanical power.(a)	*63*	*9,386*	*646*	*107*	*1*	*414*	..	*37*	..	*4,377*	*3*	*4,242*	*616*	*209*	*26*
20 to 50	34	1,047	18	7	..	84	..	2	..	560	2	335	16	59	..
50 to 100	15	1,070	19	6	..	48	..	4	..	564	1	422	18	26	..
100 to 200	8	1,109	..	15	..	42	..	7	..	691	..	354	..	..	..
200 to 400	2	484	..	7	..	30	..	4	..	319	..	116	..	8	..
400 and over	4	5,676	609	72	1	210	..	20	..	2,243	..	3,015	582	116	26
Without mechanical power (20 to 50).	*1*	*30*	..	..	..	*6*	..	..	..	*14*	..	*8*	..	*2*	..
IRON AND STEEL WORKS.*	**75**	**9,841**	**1,815**	**149**	..	**695**	**2**	**62**	..	**4,022**	**5**	**4,625**	**1,807**	**288**	**1**
With mechanical power.(b)	*46*	*8,835*	*1,810*	*147*	..	*595*	*2*	*62*	..	*3,568*	*3*	*4,275*	*1,804*	*188*	*1*
20 to 50	18	537	9	5	..	40	..	21	..	204	2	225	6	42	1
50 to 100	9	647	2	1	..	67	..	..	..	353	1	188	1	38	..
100 to 200	7	1,003	15	12	..	145	..	5	..	424	..	387	15	30	..
200 to 400	9	2,407	1	33	..	185	..	20	..	1,387	..	754	1	78	..
400 and over	3	4,241	1,783	96	..	208	2	16	..	1,200	..	2,721	1,781	..	..
Without mechanical power.	*29*	*1,006*	*5*	*2*	..	*100*	..	..	..	*454*	*2*	*350*	*3*	*100*	..
20 to 50	24	661	5	2	..	76	..	..	..	282	2	241	3	60	..
50 to 100	5	345	..	..	..	24	..	..	..	172	..	109	..	40	..
LOCK AND CUTLERY WORKS.	**12**	**1,046**	..	**5**	..	**42**	..	..	..	**813**	..	**121**	..	**65**	..
With mechanical power(c) (50 to 100).	*1*	*50*	..	..	..	..	..	..	..	*25*	..	*21*	..	*4*	..
Without mechanical power.	*11*	*996*	..	*5*	..	*42*	..	..	..	*788*	..	*100*	..	*61*	..
20 to 50	6	156	..	1	..	7	..	..	..	104	..	40	..	4	..
50 to 100	2	178	..	1	..	15	..	..	..	125	..	20	..	17	..
100 to 200	1	137	..	1	..	6	..	..	..	100	..	20	..	10	..
200 to 400	2	525	..	2	..	14	..	..	..	459	..	20	..	30	..
MACHINERY AND ENGINEERING WORKSHOPS.	**93**	**22,749**	**398**	**410**	**3**	**1,374**	**1**	**263**	..	**12,313**	**85**	**7,917**	**306**	**472**	**3**
With mechanical power.(d)	*84*	*21,982*	*281*	*407*	*3*	*1,334*	*1*	*259*	..	*11,891*	..	*7,644*	*274*	*447*	*3*
20 to 50	17	572	8	9	..	33	..	2	..	303	..	183	8	42	..
50 to 100	22	1,588	5	32	2	169	1	3	..	875	..	495	2	14	..
100 to 200	16	2,157	27	23	..	113	..	12	..	1,266	..	680	24	63	3
200 to 400	15	4,062	17	56	1	187	..	38	..	2,366	..	1,273	16	137	..
400 and over	14	13,603	224	287	..	832	..	204	..	7,081	..	5,008	224	191	..
Without mechanical power.	*9*	*767*	*117*	*3*	..	*40*	..	*4*	..	*422*	*85*	*273*	*32*	*25*	..
20 to 50	5	149	..	1	..	16	..	..	..	80	..	51	..	1	..
100 to 200	3	324	87	2	..	10	..	4	..	132	85	162	2	14	..
200 to 400	1	294	30	..	..	14	..	..	..	210	..	60	30	10	..
MINTS	**4**	**2,380**	..	**45**	..	**164**	..	**26**	..	**628**	..	**1,459**	..	**58**	..
With mechanical power(e) (400 and over).	*3*	*2,354*	..	*45*	..	*160*	..	*26*	..	*621*	..	*1,444*	..	*58*	..
Without mechanical power (20 to 50).	*1*	*26*	..	..	..	*4*	..	..	..	*7*	..	*15*	..	..	..
PUBLIC WORKS AND LOCAL FUND WORKSHOPS.	**10**	**1,241**	**2**	**7**	..	**81**	..	**14**	..	**559**	..	**568**	**2**	**12**	..
With mechanical power.(f)	*9*	*1,201*	*2*	*7*	..	*80*	..	*14*	..	*523*	..	*566*	*2*	*11*	..
20 to 50	3	126	..	..	..	8	..	1	..	56	..	61	..	..	..
50 to 100	3	218	..	2	..	9	..	3	..	102	..	91	..	11	..
200 to 400	3	857	2	5	..	63	..	10	..	365	..	414	2	..	..
Without mechanical power (20 to 50).	*1*	*40*	..	..	..	*1*	..	..	..	*36*	..	*2*	..	*1*	..
TIN WORKS	**31**	**5,632**	**52**	**53**	..	**282**	**1**	**6**	..	**1,396**	**13**	**3,835**	**29**	**60**	**9**
With mechanical power.(g)	*10*	*3,830*	*5*	*30*	..	*216*	..	*4*	..	*923*	..	*2,638*	*5*	*19*	..
50 to 100	1	58	..	1	..	2	..	..	..	14	..	41	..	..	..
100 to 200	6	932	1	9	..	80	..	..	..	448	..	376	1	19	..
400 and over	3	2,840	4	20	..	134	..	4	..	461	..	2,221	4	..	..
Without mechanical power.	*21*	*1,802*	*47*	*23*	.	*66*	*1*	*2*	..	*473*	*13*	*1,197*	*24*	*41*	*9*
20 to 50	12	365	2	13	..	15	..	2	..	139	..	164	2	32	..
50 to 100	3	175	34	2	..	9	..	..	..	110	9	49	19	5	6
100 to 200	4	495	10	5	..	12	..	..	..	185	4	289	3	4	3
200 to 400	1	330	..	..	..	12	..	..	..	9	..	309	..	..	..
400 and over	1	437	1	3	..	18	1	..	..	30	..	386	..	..	..
OTHERS	**20**	**1,852**	**64**	**14**	..	**103**	..	**13**	..	**914**	..	**755**	**64**	**53**	..
With mechanical power.(h)	*13*	*1,645*	*64*	*14*	..	*85*	..	*13*	..	*861*	..	*670*	*64*	*2*	..
20 to 50	6	190	..	1	..	14	..	..	..	99	..	74	..	2	..
50 to 100	4	288	..	2	..	12	..	..	..	146	..	128	..	..	..
200 to 400	2	690	5	2	..	38	..	2	..	518	..	130	5	..	..
400 and over	1	477	59	9	..	21	..	11	..	98	..	338	59	..	..
Without mechanical power (20 to 50).	*7*	*207*	..	..	..	*18*	..	..	..	*53*	..	*85*	..	*51*	..

* Including working with iron sheets (making steel trunks, despatch boxes, etc).

Power.—(*a*) Steam 50, Oil 9, Electricity 2, Steam and oil 2. (*b*) Steam 36, Oil 8, Electricity 1, Steam and oil 1. (*c*) Electricity 1. (*d*) Steam 60, Oil 12, Electricity 5, Steam and electricity 1, Oil and gas 1, Gas 1, Steam and oil 2, Steam oil and gas 1, Steam, oil, gas and electricity 1. (*e*) Steam 3. (*f*) Steam 9. (*g*) Steam 7, Water 1, Oil 2. (*h*) Steam 4, Oil 6, Steam and oil 1, Electricity 2.

PART E.—STATISTICS OF INDUSTRIES, (i) GENERAL STATEMENT—*continued.*

Description and Classification of factory, etc., according to number of persons employed.	Number of factories.	Total number of persons employed. Males.	Total number of persons employed. Females.	Direction, Supervision and Clerical Work. Europeans and Anglo-Indians. M.	Direction, Supervision and Clerical Work. Europeans and Anglo-Indians. F.	Direction, Supervision and Clerical Work. Indians. M.	Direction, Supervision and Clerical Work. Indians. F.	Skilled Workmen. Europeans and Anglo-Indians. M.	Skilled Workmen. Europeans and Anglo-Indians. F.	Skilled Workmen. Indians. Males.	Skilled Workmen. Indians. Females.	Unskilled Labourers. Age 14 and over. Males.	Unskilled Labourers. Age 14 and over. Females.	Unskilled Labourers. Under 14. Males.	Unskilled Labourers. Under 14. Females.
1	2	3	4	5	6	7	8	9	10	11	12	13	14	15	16
VIII.—Glass and Earthenware Industries.	*453*	*39,859*	*9,614*	*67*	..	*1,403*	*20*	*32*	..	*9,297*	*1,203*	*25,639*	*6,673*	*3,414*	*1,718*
BRICK AND TILE FACTORIES.	**411**	**36,893**	**9,263**	**56**	..	**1,177**	**20**	**26**	..	**7,932**	**1,162**	**24,386**	**6,376**	**3,316**	**1,705**
With mechanical power. (a)	*53*	*9,458*	*2,251*	*50*	..	*395*	*3*	*18*	..	*1,287*	*120*	*6,973*	*1,818*	*735*	*310*
20 to 50 .	7	236	19	..	..	13	..	1	..	30	..	185	17	7	2
50 to 100 .	10	657	87	3	..	47	..	..	..	134	7	417	58	56	22
100 to 200 .	15	1,873	438	6	..	76	..	..	..	236	..	1,381	341	174	97
200 to 400 .	12	2,749	606	21	..	101	..	..	..	265	5	2,117	522	245	79
400 and over .	9	3,943	1,101	20	..	158	3	17	..	622	108	2,873	880	253	110
Without mechanical power.	*358*	*27,435*	*7,012*	*6*	..	*782*	*17*	*8*	..	*6,645*	*1,042*	*17,413*	*4,558*	*2,581*	*1,395*
20 to 50 .	123	3,650	660	..	..	164	..	..	..	801	67	2,305	482	380	111
50 to 100 .	126	7,057	1,671	1	..	265	9	1	..	1,645	205	4,516	1,125	629	332
100 to 200 .	76	8,364	2,257	2	..	221	1	..	..	2,095	313	5,377	1,503	669	440
200 to 400 .	28	5,875	1,423	1	..	98	7	7	..	1,717	272	3,419	857	633	287
400 and over .	5	2,489	1,001	2	..	34	..	..	..	387	185	1,796	591	270	225
GLASS FACTORIES .	**36**	**1,265**	**76**	**5**	..	**127**	..	**6**	..	**855**	**35**	**203**	**36**	**69**	**5**
With mechanical power. (b)	*4*	*223*	*59*	*4*	..	*16*	..	*4*	..	*126*	*35*	*41*	*21*	*32*	*3*
20 to 50 .	3	89	5	4	..	5	..	3	..	55	..	18	5	4	..
100 to 200 .	1	134	54	..	..	11	..	1	..	71	35	23	15	28	3
Without mechanical power.	*32*	*1,042*	*17*	*1*	..	*111*	..	*2*	..	*729*	..	*162*	*15*	*37*	*2*
20 to 50 .	30	898	1	1	..	105	..	2	..	688	..	78	1	24	..
50 to 100 .	2	144	16	..	..	6	..	..	..	41	..	84	14	13	2
GLASS BANGLE FACTORIES.	**1**	**15**	**7**	..	..	**1**	..	..	..	**11**	..	**3**	**7**	..	..
Without mechanical power (20 to 50).	*1*	*15*	*7*	..	..	*1*	..	..	..	*11*	..	*3*	*7*	..	..
POTTERY WORKS .	**5**	**1,679**	**268**	**6**	..	**98**	..	..	..	**499**	**6**	**1,047**	**254**	**29**	**8**
With mechanical power. (c)	*4*	*1,639*	*253*	*6*	..	*93*	..	..	..	*474*	*1*	*1,037*	*244*	*29*	*8*
50 to 100 .	1	83	6	..	..	3	..	..	..	52	..	26	6	2	..
200 to 400 .	1	214	63	1	..	13	..	..	..	37	1	155	57	8	5
400 and over .	2	1,342	184	5	..	77	..	..	..	385	..	856	181	19	3
Without mechanical power (50 to 100).	*1*	*40*	*15*	..	..	*5*	..	..	..	*25*	*5*	*10*	*10*	..	..
IX.—Industries connected with Chemical Products.	*455*	*43,736*	*5,620*	*585*	*1*	*2,722*	*25*	*97*	..	*11,050*	*876*	*26,767*	*4,314*	*2,517*	*404*
ÆRATED WATER FACTORIES.	**32**	**1,351**	**11**	**36**	**1**	**145**	..	**8**	..	**282**	**4**	**768**	**6**	**112**	..
With mechanical power. (d)	*31*	*1,331*	*11*	*36*	*1*	*143*	..	*8*	..	*264*	*4*	*768*	*6*	*112*	..
20 to 50 .	22	658	11	15	1	56	..	4	..	127	4	414	6	42	..
50 to 100 .	8	540	..	11	..	67	..	4	..	105	..	284	..	69	..
100 to 200 .	1	133	..	10	..	20	..	..	..	32	..	70	..	1	..
Without mechanical power (20 to 50).	*1*	*20*	..	..	..	*2*	..	..	..	*18*	..	..	..	..	..
AMMUNITION FACTORIES.	**4**	**6,083**	**1**	**173**	..	**282**	..	**20**	..	**1,072**	..	**3,627**	**1**	**909**	..
With mechanical power (e) (400 and over).	*3*	*6,048*	..	*173*	..	*279*	..	*20*	..	*1,072*	..	*3,595*	..	*909*	..
Without mechanical power (20 to 50).	*1*	*35*	*1*	..	..	*3*	..	..	..	..	..	*32*	*1*	..	..
BULK OIL INSTALLATIONS.	**10**	**1,355**	**49**	**6**	..	**85**	..	**1**	..	**703**	..	**540**	**49**	**20**	..
With mechanical power. (f)	*10*	*1,355*	*49*	*6*	..	*85*	..	*1*	..	*703*	..	*540*	*49*	*20*	..
20 to 50 .	1	22	..	..	..	3	..	..	..	6	..	13	..	..	..
50 to 100 .	4	339	..	3	..	19	..	..	..	108	..	189	..	20	..
100 to 200 .	3	388	48	1	..	30	..	1	..	211	..	145	48	..	..
200 to 400 .	2	606	1	2	..	33	..	..	..	378	..	193	1	..	..
CARD-BOARD FACTORIES.	**1**	**26**	..	..	..	**1**	..	..	..	**25**	..	..	..	..	..
With mechanical power (g) (20 to 50).	*1*	*26*	..	..	..	*1*	..	..	..	*25*	..	..	..	..	..
CHEMICAL WORKS .	**18**	**1,499**	**97**	**17**	..	**265**	**1**	..	..	**284**	..	**857**	**81**	**76**	**15**
With mechanical power. (h)	*11*	*1,214*	*94*	*17*	..	*185*	..	..	..	*210*	..	*748*	*79*	*54*	*15*
20 to 50 .	5	161	7	3	..	20	..	..	..	26	..	111	7	1	..
100 to 200 .	4	594	42	11	..	76	..	..	..	144	..	339	35	24	7
200 to 400 .	2	459	45	3	..	89	..	..	..	40	..	298	37	29	8
Without mechanical power.	*7*	*285*	*3*	..	..	*80*	*1*	..	..	*74*	..	*109*	*2*	*22*	..
20 to 50 .	5	180	3	..	..	41	1	..	..	55	..	63	2	21	..
50 to 100 .	2	105	..	..	..	39	..	..	..	19	..	46	..	1	..
DYE WORKS . .	**30**	**2,174**	**425**	**7**	..	**119**	..	..	..	**692**	**237**	**1,262**	**178**	**94**	**10**
With mechanical power. (i)	*10*	*1,393*	*109*	*7*	..	*82*	..	..	..	*209*	*31*	*1,012*	*71*	*83*	*7*
20 to 50 .	3	78	2	..	..	13	..	..	..	27	2	22	..	16	..
50 to 100 .	3	216	9	2	..	15	..	..	..	49	9	145	..	5	..
100 to 200 .	2	267	20	..	..	14	..	..	..	103	20	146	..	4	..
200 to 400 .	1	279	1	..	..	30	..	..	..	..	..	199	1	50	..
400 and over .	1	553	77	5	..	10	..	..	..	30	..	500	70	8	7
Without mechanical power.	*20*	*781*	*316*	..	..	*37*	..	..	..	*483*	*206*	*250*	*107*	*11*	*3*
20 to 50 .	13	280	60	..	..	13	..	..	..	192	43	74	25	1	1
50 to 100 .	4	210	82	..	..	10	..	..	..	25	..	173	82	2	..
100 to 200 .	3	291	165	..	..	14	..	..	..	266	163	3	..	8	2

Power.—(a) Steam 47, Oil 4, Steam and oil 1, Steam and gas 1. (b) Steam 2, Oil 2. (c) Steam 4. (d) Steam 12, Electricity 8, Oil 9, Gas and electricity 1, Steam, oil and gas 1. (e) Steam 2, Electricity 1. (f) Steam 4, Oil 4, Steam and oil 1, Gas 1. (g) Electricity 1. (h) Steam 7, Oil 1, Electricity 1, Steam, oil and gas 1, Gas 1. (i) Steam 10.

TABLE XV.—Occupation or Means of Livelihood.

Description and Classification of factory, etc., according to number of persons employed.	Number of factories	Total number of persons employed.		CLASSIFICATION OF PERSONS EMPLOYED.											
				Direction, Supervision and Clerical Work.				Skilled Workmen.				Unskilled Labourers.			
				Europeans and Anglo-Indians.		Indians.		Europeans and Anglo-Indians.		Indians.		Age 14 and over.		Under 14.	
		Males.	Females.	M.	F.	M.	F.	M.	F.	Males.	Females.	Males.	Females.	Males.	Females.
1	2	3	4	5	6	7	8	9	10	11	12	13	14	15	16
IX.—Industries connected with Chemical Products—contd.															
Gunpowder Factories.	**1**	**138**	..	..	..	**5**	..	..	..	**109**	..	**17**	..	**7**	..
With mechanical power (a) (100 to 200).	*1*	*138*	..	..	..	*5*	..	..	..	*109*	..	*17*	..	*7*	..
Lac and cutch Factories.	**74**	**3,416**	**1,709**	**10**	..	**161**	**8**	**5**	..	**1,536**	**408**	**1,539**	**1,119**	**165**	**174**
With mechanical power. (b)	*6*	*910*	*367*	*4*	..	*37*	*1*	*3*	..	*305*	*128*	*535*	*215*	*26*	*23*
20 to 50	1	39	8	..	..	5	1	..	..	20	4	13	2	1	1
100 to 200	3	338	134	3	..	15	..	3	..	175	88	137	43	5	3
200 to 400	1	131	72	..	..	4	..	..	..	50	33	57	20	20	19
400 and over	1	402	153	1	..	13	..	..	..	60	3	328	150	..	..
Without mechanical power.	*68*	*2,506*	*1,342*	*6*	..	*124*	*7*	*2*	..	*1,231*	*280*	*1,004*	*904*	*139*	*151*
20 to 50	39	940	413	2	..	63	4	..	..	431	94	394	293	50	22
50 to 100	21	882	441	3	..	43	3	2	..	414	101	375	317	45	20
100 to 200	7	523	407	1	..	13	..	..	..	290	61	175	237	44	109
200 to 400	1	161	81	..	..	5	..	..	..	96	24	60	57	..	..
Match Factories	**6**	**491**	**146**	..	..	**39**	..	..	..	**143**	**6**	**225**	**106**	**84**	**34**
With mechanical power. (c)	*5*	*466*	*140*	..	..	*35*	..	..	..	*123*	..	*224*	*106*	*84*	*34*
20 to 50	1	23	..	..	..	2	..	..	..	..	..	12	..	9	..
50 to 100	2	81	38	..	..	10	..	..	..	36	..	15	20	20	18
200 to 400	2	362	102	..	..	23	..	..	..	87	..	197	86	55	16
Without mechanical power (20 to 50).	*1*	*25*	*6*	..	..	*4*	..	..	..	*20*	*6*	*1*	..	..	..
Oil Mills	**208**	**8,154**	**1,591**	**45**	..	**967**	**11**	**15**	..	**1,830**	**114**	**5,011**	**1,374**	**286**	**92**
With mechanical power. (d)	*138*	*5,784*	*395*	*15*	..	*809*	*11*	*15*	..	*1,371*	*14*	*3,424*	*346*	*150*	*24*
20 to 50	98	2,971	134	4	..	327	..	3	..	654	6	1,926	127	57	1
50 to 100	34	1,981	167	9	..	389	7	10	..	602	3	901	134	70	23
100 to 200	6	832	94	2	..	93	4	2	..	115	5	597	85	23	..
Without mechanical power.	*70*	*2,370*	*1,196*	*30*	..	*158*	..	..	..	*459*	*100*	*1,587*	*1,028*	*136*	*68*
20 to 50	53	1,111	464	1	..	85	..	..	..	284	62	666	396	75	6
50 to 100	13	504	263	1	..	20	..	..	..	44	..	417	255	22	8
100 to 200	1	81	31	..	..	5	..	..	..	..	..	70	25	6	6
200 to 400	1	173	60	7	..	4	..	..	..	74	..	88	60	..	..
400 and over	2	501	378	21	..	44	..	..	..	57	38	346	292	33	48
Paint Works.	**2**	**50**	**20**	**1**	..	**7**	..	..	..	**8**	..	**33**	**20**	**1**	..
With mechanical power (e) (20 to 50).	*2*	*50*	*20*	*1*	..	*7*	..	..	..	*8*	..	*33*	*20*	*1*	..
Paper Mills	**10**	**4,425**	**700**	**49**	..	**166**	..	**21**	..	**857**	**87**	**3,167**	**606**	**165**	**7**
With mechanical power. (f)	*9*	*4,404*	*700*	*49*	..	*165*	..	*21*	..	*838*	*87*	*3,166*	*606*	*165*	*7*
20 to 50	2	59	18	..	..	6	..	..	..	20	..	33	18	..	..
50 to 100	1	52	1	..	..	32	..	..	..	10	..	8	1	2	..
100 to 200	1	92	8	..	..	8	..	2	..	6	..	64	8	12	..
200 to 400	1	191	99	1	..	22	..	..	..	78	87	88	11	2	1
400 and over	4	4,010	574	48	..	97	..	19	..	724	..	2,973	568	140	6
Without mechanical power (20 to 50).	*1*	*21*	..	..	..	*1*	..	..	..	*19*	..	*1*	..	..	..
Perfumery Factories.	**7**	**194**	**6**	..	..	**58**	..	..	..	**56**	..	**68**	**6**	**12**	..
Without mechanical power (20 to 50).	*7*	*194*	*6*	..	..	*58*	..	..	..	*56*	..	*68*	*6*	*12*	..
Petroleum Refineries.	**9**	**10,811**	**47**	**212**	..	**240**	..	**9**	..	**2,933**	..	**7,250**	**47**	**167**	..
With mechanical power. (g)	*9*	*10,811*	*47*	*212*	..	*240*	..	*9*	..	*2,933*	..	*7,250*	*47*	*167*	..
20 to 50	3	110	1	2	..	6	..	..	..	34	..	61	1	7	..
50 to 100	2	141	6	1	..	7	..	1	..	65	..	61	6	6	..
400 and over	4	10,560	40	209	..	227	..	8	..	2,834	..	7,128	40	154	..
Salt crushing Mills	**4**	**1,205**	**581**	**2**	..	**12**	..	..	..	**43**	..	**1,007**	**538**	**141**	**43**
With mechanical power (h) (50 to 100).	*2*	*115*	*24*	..	..	*3*	..	..	..	*43*	..	*69*	*24*	..	..
Without mechanical power (400 and over)	*2*	*1,090*	*557*	*2*	..	*9*	..	..	..	..	..	*938*	*514*	*141*	*43*
Salt Refineries	**6**	**950**	**50**	**1**	..	**25**	..	..	..	**263**	..	**577**	**48**	**84**	**2**
With mechanical power (i) (20 to 50).	*2*	*70*	..	..	..	*8*	..	..	..	*22*	..	..	..	*40*	..
Without mechanical power.	*4*	*880*	*50*	*1*	..	*17*	..	..	..	*241*	..	*577*	*48*	*44*	*2*
100 to 200	2	353	22	1	..	10	..	..	..	83	..	226	20	33	2
200 to 400	2	527	28	..	..	7	..	..	..	158	..	351	28	11	..
Saltpetre Refineries.	**18**	**589**	**131**	..	..	**62**	**5**	..	..	**118**	**17**	**369**	**89**	**40**	**20**
With mechanical power. (j)	*2*	*77*	*49*	..	..	*18*	*5*	..	..	*3*	..	*56*	*42*	..	*2*
20 to 50	1	30	10	..	..	15	5	..	..	..	..	15	3	..	2
50 to 100	1	47	39	..	..	3	..	..	..	3	..	41	39	..	..
Without mechanical power.	*16*	*512*	*82*	..	..	*44*	..	..	..	*115*	*17*	*313*	*47*	*40*	*18*
20 to 50	13	321	67	..	..	24	..	..	..	55	7	202	42	40	18
50 to 100	3	191	15	..	..	20	..	..	..	60	10	111	5	..	..
Soap and candle Factories.	**7**	**473**	..	**6**	..	**50**	..	**4**	..	**50**	..	**254**	..	**109**	..
With mechanical power. (k)	*6*	*439*	..	*6*	..	*48*	..	*4*	..	*45*	..	*249*	..	*87*	..
20 to 50	4	132	..	1	..	28	..	..	..	18	..	68	..	17	..
50 to 100	1	71	..	3	..	6	..	2	..	..	..	52	..	8	..
200 to 400	1	236	..	2	..	14	..	2	..	27	..	129	..	62	..
Without mechanical power (20 to 50).	*1*	*34*	..	..	..	*2*	..	..	..	*5*	..	*5*	..	*22*	..

Power.—(a) Steam 1. (b) Steam 5, Water 1. (c) Steam 5. (d) Steam 130, Steam and water 4. Oil 3, Electricity 1. (e) Oil 1, Water 1. (f) Steam 8, Steam and water 1. (g) Steam 5, Steam and oil 2 Steam, oil and electricity 1, Steam, pump and oil 1. (h) Steam 1, Oil 1. (i) Steam 2. (j) Steam 1, Water 1. (k) Steam 5, Electricity 1.

PART E.—STATISTICS OF INDUSTRIES, (*i*) General STATEMENT—*continued*.

Description and Classification of factory, etc., according to number of persons employed.	Number of factories.	Total number of persons employed.		CLASSIFICATION OF PERSONS EMPLOYED.											
				DIRECTION, SUPERVISION AND CLERICAL WORK.				SKILLED WORKMEN.				UNSKILLED LABOURERS.			
				Europeans and Anglo-Indians.		Indians.		Europeans and Anglo-Indians.		Indians.		Age 14 and over.		Under 14.	
		Males.	Females.	M.	F.	M.	F.	M.	F.	Males.	Females.	Males.	Females.	Males.	Females.
1	2	3	4	5	6	7	8	9	10	11	12	13	14	15	16
IX.—Industries connected with Chemical Products—concld.															
OTHERS	**8**	**354**	**56**	**20**	..	**33**	..	**14**	..	**46**	**3**	**196**	**46**	**45**	**7**
With mechanical power. (a)	*4*	*128*	*29*	*3*	..	*8*	..	*1*	..	*23*	..	*76*	*26*	*17*	*3*
20 to 50	3	86	..	3	..	3	..	..	..	9	..	57	..	14	..
50 to 100	1	42	29	..	..	5	..	1	..	14	..	19	26	3	3
Without mechanical power.	*4*	*226*	*27*	*17*	..	*25*	..	*13*	..	*23*	*3*	*120*	*20*	*28*	*4*
20 to 50	3	74	18	..	..	7	..	..	..	12	3	32	11	23	4
100 to 200	1	152	9	17	..	18	..	13	..	11	..	88	9	5	..
X.—Food Industries	***720***	***64,204***	***10,197***	***480***	***6***	***4,780***	***89***	***373***	***13***	***10,464***	***393***	***44,588***	***8,427***	***3,519***	***1,969***
BAKERIES	**7**	**376**	..	**7**	..	**46**	..	**2**	..	**163**	..	**156**	..	..	..
With mechanical power(b) (20 to 50).	*3*	*106*	..	*1*	..	*15*	..	..	..	*57*	..	*33*	..	..	..
Without mechanical power.	*4*	*270*	..	*6*	..	*33*	..	*2*	..	*106*	..	*123*	..	..	..
20 to 50	1	27	..	1	..	3	..	..	..	17	..	6	..	..	..
50 to 100	3	243	..	5	..	30	..	2	..	89	..	117	..	..	..
BISCUIT FACTORIES	**4**	**144**	**3**	**4**	**1**	**17**	..	..	..	**38**	..	**79**	**2**	**6**	..
With mechanical power(c) (20 to 50).	*3*	*123*	*3*	*4*	*1*	*14*	..	..	..	*28*	..	*73*	*2*	*4*	..
Without mechanical power (20 to 50).	*1*	*21*	..	..	..	*3*	..	..	..	*10*	..	*6*	..	*2*	..
BREWERIES AND DISTILLERIES.	**70**	**5,006**	**156**	**56**	..	**532**	..	**8**	..	**939**	**6**	**3,336**	**142**	**135**	**2**
With mechanical power. (d)	*48*	*4,176*	*107*	*55*	..	*427*	..	*8*	..	*805*	*1*	*2,760*	*98*	*121*	*2*
20 to 50	17	599	16	7	..	59	..	2	..	88	1	414	15	29	..
50 to 100	20	1,198	51	16	..	144	..	3	..	298	..	701	43	36	2
100 to 200	8	1,070	40	12	..	110	..	3	..	142	..	796	40	7	..
200 to 400	2	717	..	11	..	40	..	..	..	134	..	493	..	39	..
400 and over	1	592	..	9	..	74	..	..	..	143	..	356	..	10	..
Without mechanical power.	*22*	*830*	*49*	*1*	..	*105*	..	..	..	*134*	*5*	*576*	*44*	*14*	..
20 to 50	16	466	26	1	..	67	..	..	..	65	..	331	26	2	..
50 to 100	6	364	23	..	..	38	..	..	..	69	5	245	18	12	..
DAIRY FARM	**14**	**876**	**89**	**42**	**1**	**65**	**1**	**19**	..	**91**	..	**654**	**83**	**5**	**4**
With mechanical power. (e)	*9*	*665*	*78*	*40*	..	*47*	..	*19*	..	*48*	..	*506*	*74*	*5*	*4*
20 to 50	2	73	8	5	..	14	..	..	..	2	..	52	8	..	..
50 to 100	6	395	27	28	..	30	..	11	..	32	..	291	27	3	..
200 to 400	1	197	43	7	..	3	..	8	..	14	..	163	39	2	4
Without mechanical power.	*5*	*211*	*11*	*2*	*1*	*18*	*1*	..	..	*43*	..	*148*	*9*	..	..
20 to 50	4	127	9	..	..	14	..	..	..	24	..	89	9	..	..
50 to 100	1	84	2	2	1	4	1	..	..	19	..	59	..	..	..
FISH CURING WORKS	**27**	**1,198**	**990**	**4**	..	**78**	..	**3**	..	**189**	**91**	**678**	**760**	**246**	**139**
With mechanical power(f) (20 to 50).	*1*	*24*	*3*	*4*	..	..	..	*3*	..	..	..	*17*	*2*	..	*1*
Without mechanical power.	*26*	*1,174*	*987*	..	..	*78*	..	..	..	*189*	*91*	*661*	*758*	*246*	*138*
20 to 50	15	301	196	..	..	30	..	..	..	96	58	138	112	37	26
50 to 100	4	115	131	..	..	11	..	..	..	20	33	70	93	14	5
100 to 200	5	410	394	..	..	14	..	..	..	50	..	252	337	94	57
200 to 400	2	348	266	..	..	23	..	..	..	23	..	201	216	101	50
FLOUR AND RICE MILLS.	**463**	**37,790**	**4,584**	**201**	..	**2,674**	**83**	**247**	**13**	**5,325**	**105**	**28,323**	**3,951**	**1,020**	**432**
With mechanical power. (g)	*393*	*37,599*	*4,469*	*201*	..	*2,643*	*83*	*242*	*13*	*5,303*	*99*	*28,196*	*3,846*	*1,014*	*428*
20 to 50	217	5,472	1,304	27	..	976	12	39	11	935	16	3,215	1,171	280	94
50 to 100	93	5,637	944	32	..	800	52	24	..	1,086	20	3,482	805	218	67
100 to 200	38	5,070	362	29	..	475	19	71	..	908	..	3,484	290	103	44
200 to 400	27	6,818	736	42	..	235	..	92	2	925	63	5,325	552	199	119
400 and over	18	14,602	1,123	71	..	157	..	16	..	1,449	..	12,690	1,019	219	104
Without mechanical power.	*10*	*191*	*115*	..	..	*31*	..	*5*	..	*22*	*6*	*127*	*105*	*6*	*4*
20 to 50	9	158	85	..	..	25	..	5	..	22	6	100	75	6	4
50 to 100	1	33	30	..	..	6	..	..	..	..	..	27	30	..	..
FORAGE PRESSES	**14**	**705**	**479**	**3**	..	**60**	..	..	..	**153**	**15**	**425**	**411**	**64**	**58**
With mechanical power. (h)	*10*	*629*	*436*	*3*	..	*58*	..	..	..	*144*	..	*363*	*383*	*61*	*53*
20 to 50	4	146	4	2	..	8	..	..	..	8	..	118	2	10	2
50 to 100	4	210	87	1	..	30	..	..	..	6	..	145	76	28	11
100 to 200	1	84	45	..	..	1	..	..	..	5	..	70	30	8	15
400 and over	1	189	300	..	..	19	..	..	..	125	..	30	275	15	25
Without mechanical power (20 to 50).	*4*	*76*	*43*	..	..	*2*	..	..	..	*9*	*15*	*62*	*28*	*3*	..
OPIUM, GANJA, TOBACCO, SNUFF AND VINEGAR FACTORIES.	**57**	**6,057**	**1,193**	**65**	**3**	**678**	**5**	**12**	..	**1,434**	**122**	**2,683**	**907**	**1,185**	**156**
With mechanical power. (i)	*17*	*3,677*	*630*	*56*	*3*	*323*	*5*	*12*	..	*877*	*119*	*1,883*	*447*	*526*	*56*
20 to 50	4	108	12	2	..	7	..	..	..	38	9	52	3	9	
50 to 100	5	324	25	4	..	22	..	3	..	135	..	100	25	60	..
100 to 200	1	94	20	1	..	5	..	..	..	9	..	51	15	28	..
200 to 400	3	851	1	4	..	49	1	..	..	490	..	207	..	101	5
400 and over	4	2,300	572	45	3	240	4	9	..	205	110	1,473	404	328	51

Power.—(*a*) Steam 4. (*b*) Steam 1, Oil 1, Electricity 1. (*c*) Steam 3. (*d*) Steam 43, Water 1, Oil 2, Steam and electricity 1, Steam and oil 1. (*e*) Steam 8, Steam and oil 1. (*f*) Steam 1. (*g*) Steam 369, Water 5, Oil 13, Steam and oil 2, Electricity 1, Steam and water 3. (*h*) Steam 6, Oil 2, Electricity 1, Steam and oil 1. (*i*) Steam 12, Oil 4, Electricity 1.

TABLE XV.—Occupation or Means of Livelihood.

Description and Classification of factory, etc., according to number of persons employed.	Number of factories.	Total number of persons employed.		CLASSIFICATION OF PERSONS EMPLOYED.											
				Direction, Supervision and Clerical Work.				Skilled Workmen.				Unskilled Labourers.			
				Europeans and Anglo-Indians.		Indians.		Europeans and Anglo-Indians.		Indians.		Age 14 and over.		Under 14.	
		Males.	Females.	M.	F.	M.	F.	M.	F.	Males.	Females.	Males.	Females.	Males.	Females.
1	2	3	4	5	6	7	8	9	10	11	12	13	14	15	16
X.—Food Industries—contd.															
Opium, etc., Factories—*contd.*															
Without mechanical power.	*40*	*2,330*	*563*	*9*	..	*355*	..	..	..	*557*	*3*	*800*	*460*	*659*	*100*
20 to 50	20	565	59	2	..	34	..	..	..	193	3	155	50	181	6
50 to 100	11	689	94	2	..	22	..	..	..	233	..	258	75	174	19
100 to 200	7	629	241	5	..	17	..	..	..	81	..	268	206	258	35
200 to 400	2	497	169	..	..	282	..	..	..	50	..	119	129	46	40
Slaughter Houses and Jerked Meat Works.	**10**	**1,529**	**1,106**	**4**	..	**52**	..	**2**	..	**146**	**1**	**874**	**749**	**451**	**356**
With mechanical power (a) (50 to 100).	*1*	*68*	*1*	*2*	..	*6*	..	*2*	..	..	..	*58*	*1*	..	..
Without mechanical power.	*9*	*1,461*	*1,105*	*2*	..	*46*	..	..	..	*146*	*1*	*816*	*748*	*451*	*356*
20 to 50	5	112	57	..	..	7	..	..	..	33	..	42	43	30	14
50 to 100	1	44	42	..	..	2	..	..	..	..	..	20	21	22	21
100 to 200	1	79	53	..	..	10	..	..	..	..	..	56	53	13	..
200 to 400	1	233	117	..	..	25	..	..	..	25	1	171	114	12	2
400 and over	1	993	836	2	..	2	..	..	..	88	..	527	517	374	319
Sugar Factories	**76**	**7,502**	**617**	**52**	..	**409**	..	**26**	..	**1,313**	**45**	**5,560**	**523**	**142**	**49**
With mechanical power. (b)	*42*	*6,569*	*433*	*51*	..	*333*	..	*22*	..	*1,220*	..	*4,831*	*404*	*112*	*29*
20 to 50	12	379	6	..	..	31	..	..	..	51	..	297	6	..	..
50 to 100	13	770	80	5	..	87	..	..	..	226	..	487	75	15	5
100 to 200	5	726	25	11	..	59	..	6	..	168	..	462	23	20	2
200 to 400	8	2,304	99	17	..	95	..	14	..	342	..	1,790	83	46	16
400 and over	4	2,390	223	18	..	111	..	2	..	433	..	1,795	217	31	6
Without mechanical power.	*34*	*933*	*184*	*1*	..	*76*	..	*4*	..	*93*	*45*	*729*	*119*	*30*	*20*
20 to 50	29	641	150	..	..	65	..	4	..	81	45	469	99	22	6
50 to 100	5	292	34	1	..	11	..	..	..	12	..	260	20	8	14
Water Works	**30**	**2,690**	**877**	**32**	..	**145**	..	**10**	..	**616**	..	**1,639**	**811**	**248**	**66**
With mechanical power. (c)	*26*	*2,308*	*675*	*29*	..	*118*	..	*10*	..	*534*	..	*1,379*	*619*	*238*	*56*
20 to 50	12	425	3	17	..	39	..	4	..	84	..	251	3	30	..
50 to 100	10	631	51	9	..	46	..	6	..	176	..	361	45	33	6
100 to 200	2	264	..	2	..	5	..	..	..	64	..	168	..	25	..
200 to 400	1	207	..	..	..	23	..	..	..	173	..	11	..	..	..
400 and over	1	781	621	1	..	5	..	..	..	37	..	588	571	150	50
Without mechanical power.	*4*	*382*	*202*	*3*	..	*27*	..	..	..	*82*	..	*260*	*192*	*10*	*10*
20 to 50	1	47	..	2	..	1	..	..	..	18	..	23	..	3	..
50 to 100	1	57	..	..	..	10	..	..	..	5	..	42	..	..	..
100 to 200	1	115	48	..	..	..	..	..	..	2	..	113	48	..	..
200 to 400	1	163	154	1	..	16	..	..	..	57	..	82	144	7	10
Others	**8**	**331**	**103**	**10**	**1**	**22**	..	**44**	..	**57**	**8**	**181**	**88**	**17**	**6**
With mechanical power. (d)	*4*	*210*	*68*	*7*	*1*	*14*	..	*43*	..	*23*	*8*	*123*	*59*	..	..
20 to 50	1	22	7	..	..	7	..	..	..	11	7	4	..	..	..
50 to 100	3	188	61	7	1	7	..	43	..	12	1	119	59	..	..
Without mechanical power.	*4*	*121*	*35*	*3*	..	*8*	..	*1*	..	*34*	..	*58*	*29*	*17*	*6*
20 to 50	3	56	15	3	..	5	..	1	..	29	..	16	12	2	3
50 to 100	1	65	20	..	..	3	..	..	..	5	..	42	17	15	3
XI.—Industries of Dress.	*90*	*9,817*	*372*	*169*	*40*	*643*	*20*	*121*	*127*	*6,986*	*29*	*1,260*	*155*	*638*	*1*
Boot and Shoe Factories.	**23**	**5,036**	**127**	**69**	**1**	**238**	**2**	**13**	..	**4,041**	..	**243**	**124**	**432**	..
With mechanical power. (e)	*5*	*3,962*	*121*	*59*	..	*121*	*2*	*4*	..	*3,244*	..	*159*	*119*	*375*	..
20 to 50	2	64	1	..	..	5	..	..	..	49	..	8	1	2	..
200 to 400	1	214	2	4	..	16	2	4	..	190	..	..	..	..	..
400 and over	2	3,684	118	55	..	100	..	..	..	3,005	..	151	118	373	..
Without mechanical power.	*18*	*1,074*	*6*	*10*	*1*	*117*	..	*9*	..	*797*	..	*84*	*5*	*57*	..
20 to 50	10	422	4	6	1	27	..	3	..	299	..	49	3	38	..
50 to 100	7	482	2	4	..	6	..	6	..	426	..	21	2	19	..
100 to 200	1	170	..	..	..	84	..	..	..	72	..	14	..	..	..
Dress Factories	**32**	**2,570**	**173**	**86**	**39**	**197**	..	**23**	**127**	**1,483**	..	**671**	**7**	**110**	..
With mechanical power(f) (20 to 50).	*2*	*65*	..	*2*	..	*10*	..	..	..	*36*	..	*11*	..	*6*	..
Without mechanical power.	*30*	*2,505*	*173*	*84*	*39*	*187*	..	*23*	*127*	*1,447*	..	*660*	*7*	*104*	..
20 to 50	18	521	7	8	3	17	..	3	..	369	..	85	4	30	..
50 to 100	3	207	3	3	1	4	..	2	2	142	..	19	..	46	..
100 to 200	6	681	130	16	3	41	..	..	125	375	..	230	2	19	..
200 to 400	2	539	32	54	32	87	..	12	..	134	..	252	..	..	..
400 and over	1	557	1	3	..	38	..	6	..	427	..	83	1	..	..
Hosiery Factories	**12**	**1,184**	**72**	**13**	..	**160**	**18**	..	..	**755**	**29**	**216**	**24**	**40**	*1*
With mechanical power. (g)	*7*	*1,037*	*64*	*13*	..	*156*	*18*	..	..	*650*	*21*	*204*	*24*	*14*	*1*
20 to 50	2	80	1	..	..	5	..	..	..	50	..	11	..	14	1
50 to 100	3	149	27	..	..	9	..	..	..	33	3	107	24	..	..
200 to 400	1	198	36	..	..	99	18	..	..	99	18	..	..	..	..
400 and over	1	610	..	13	..	43	..	..	..	468	..	86	..	..	..
Without mechanical power (20 to 50).	*5*	*147*	*8*	..	..	*4*	..	..	..	*105*	*8*	*12*	..	*26*	..

Power.—(*a*) Steam 1. (*b*) Steam 33, Oil 6, Steam and oil 1, Steam and electricity 1, Steam and water 1. (*c*) Steam 23, Electricity 2, Oil 1. (*d*) Steam 3, Oil 1, (*e*) Steam 3, Oil 1, Gas and electricity 1. (*f*) Steam 1, Steam and oil 1. (*g*) Steam 6, Oil 1.

PART E.—STATISTICS OF INDUSTRIES, (*i*) GENERAL STATEMENT—*continued.*

Description and Classification of factory, etc., according to number of persons employed.	Number of factories.	Total number of persons employed.		CLASSIFICATION OF PERSONS EMPLOYED.											
				DIRECTION, SUPERVISION AND CLERICAL WORK.				SKILLED WORKMEN.				UNSKILLED LABOURERS.			
				Europeans and Anglo-Indians.		Indians.		Europeans and Anglo-Indians.		Indians.		Age 14 and over.		Under 14.	
		Males.	Females.	M.	F.	M.	F.	M.	F.	Males.	Females.	Males.	Females.	Males.	Females.
1	2	3	4	5	6	7	8	9	10	11	12	13	14	15	16
***XI.—Industries of Dress*—contd.**															
UMBRELLA FACTORIES.	17	814	..	..	..	40	..	85	..	553	..	97	..	39	..
With mechanical power (a) (20 to 50)	*2*	*69*	..	..	..	*7*	..	..	..	*32*	..	*30*	..	..	..
Without mechanical power.	*15*	*745*	..	..	..	*33*	..	*85*	..	*521*	..	*67*	..	*39*	..
20 to 50	12	365	..	..	..	24	..	..	..	271	..	56	..	14	..
50 to 100	2	152	..	..	..	2	..	85	..	50	..	5	..	10	..
200 to 400	1	228	..	..	..	7	..	..	..	200	..	6	..	15	..
OTHERS	6	213	..	1	..	8	..	..	..	154	..	33	..	17	..
With mechanical power (b) (20 to 50).	*2*	*44*	..	*1*	..	*4*	..	..	..	*34*	..	*5*	..	..	..
Without mechanical power.	*4*	*169*	..	..	..	*4*	..	..	..	*120*	..	*28*	..	*17*	..
20 to 50	3	104	..	..	..	2	..	..	..	65	..	20	..	17	..
50 to 100	1	65	..	..	..	2	..	..	..	55	..	8	..	..	..
XII.—Furniture Industries.	*50*	*3,329*	*50*	*29*	*1*	*235*	..	*30*	..	*2,072*	..	*726*	*38*	*230*	*11*
FURNITURE FACTORIES.	46	3,060	50	26	1	219	..	29	..	1,868	..	695	38	223	11
With mechanical power (c).	*14*	*1,571*	*36*	*23*	*1*	*80*	..	*29*	..	*880*	..	*451*	*32*	*108*	*3*
20 to 50	4	156	..	2	..	13	..	26	..	89	..	21	..	5	..
50 to 100	4	322	1	6	1	26	..	2	..	175	..	113	..	..	..
100 to 200	4	475	25	9	..	24	..	1	..	352	..	84	22	5	3
200 to 400	2	618	10	6	..	17	..	..	..	264	..	233	10	98	..
Without mechanical power.	*32*	*1,489*	*14*	*3*	..	*139*	..	..	..	*988*	..	*244*	*6*	*115*	*8*
20 to 50	21	660	13	2	..	101	..	..	..	404	..	115	5	38	8
50 to 100	10	695	1	..	..	33	..	..	..	474	..	124	1	64	..
100 to 200	1	134	..	1	..	5	..	..	..	110	..	5	..	13	..
TENT FACTORIES	4	262	..	3	..	16	..	1	..	204	..	31	..	7	..
Without mechanical power.	*4*	*262*	..	*3*	..	*16*	..	*1*	..	*204*	..	*31*	..	*7*	..
20 to 50	1	27	..	1	..	3	..	1	..	10	..	10	..	2	..
50 to 100	2	131	..	2	..	3	..	..	..	112	..	14	..	..	..
100 to 200	1	104	..	..	..	10	..	..	..	82	..	7	..	5	..
XIII.—Industries connected with Buildings.	*163*	*17,015*	*5,153*	*81*	*1*	*620*	*18*	*66*	*14*	*3,054*	*158*	*12,095*	*4,312*	*1,169*	*650*
BUILDING WORKSHOPS	1	212	..	5	..	9	..	..	..	61	..	134	..	3	..
With mechanical power (d) (200 to 400).	*1*	*212*	..	*5*	..	*9*	..	..	..	*61*	..	*134*	..	*3*	..
LIME WORKS AND KILNS.	53	5,508	2,122	17	..	228	2	10	..	345	4	4,486	1,883	422	233
With mechanical power. (e)	*27*	*1,814*	*860*	*10*	..	*65*	*2*	*10*	..	*233*	*4*	*1,397*	*780*	*99*	*74*
20 to 50	12	281	79	2	..	21	2	4	..	46	4	197	63	11	10
50 to 100	4	232	72	..	..	8	..	4	..	38	..	171	63	11	9
100 to 200	7	722	312	3	..	16	..	2	..	51	..	506	278	54	34
200 to 400	4	579	397	5	..	20	..	..	..	98	..	433	376	23	21
Without mechanical power.	*26*	*3,694*	*1,262*	*7*	..	*163*	..	..	..	*112*	..	*3,089*	*1,103*	*323*	*159*
20 to 50	8	177	113	3	..	12	..	..	..	17	..	127	88	18	25
50 to 100	8	380	187	2	..	59	..	..	..	80	..	402	159	37	28
100 to 200	2	179	129	2	..	7	..	..	..	15	..	139	129	16	..
200 to 400	6	1,313	405	..	..	42	..	..	..	..	..	1,129	329	142	76
400 and over	2	1,445	428	..	..	43	..	..	..	..	..	1,292	398	110	30
STONE, MARBLE AND CEMENT WORKS	57	5,696	1,909	54	1	198	16	55	14	1,324	52	3,656	1,494	409	332
With mechanical power. (f)	*14*	*3,144*	*681*	*40*	..	*90*	*1*	*24*	..	*940*	*10*	*1,978*	*613*	*72*	*57*
20 to 50	3	60	30	..	..	2	..	1	..	24	6	31	13	2	11
50 to 100	4	261	13	27	..	17	..	..	..	39	..	176	10	2	3
100 to 200	2	195	66	..	..	8	..	..	..	67	4	97	25	23	37
200 to 400	2	461	120	6	..	26	..	12	..	128	..	289	120	..	..
400 and over	3	2,167	452	7	..	37	1	11	..	682	..	1,385	445	45	6
Without mechanical power.	*43*	*2,552*	*1,228*	*14*	*1*	*108*	*15*	*31*	*14*	*384*	*42*	*1,678*	*881*	*337*	*275*
20 to 50	17	426	110	4	1	20	..	2	..	100	11	270	71	30	27
50 to 100	16	798	297	8	..	34	1	1	..	232	16	431	209	92	71
100 to 200	7	569	363	..	..	41	14	28	14	42	14	349	222	109	99
200 to 400	2	335	222	2	..	12	..	..	..	..	..	316	220	5	2
400 and over	1	424	236	..	..	1	..	..	..	10	1	312	159	101	76
SURKI FACTORIES	52	5,599	1,122	5	..	185	..	1	..	1,324	102	3,749	935	335	85
With mechanical power. (g)	*48*	*5,278*	*989*	*5*	..	*175*	..	*1*	..	*1,288*	*102*	*3,535*	*826*	*274*	*61*
20 to 50	30	718	74	1	..	92	..	1	..	162	2	425	71	37	1
50 to 100	6	389	9	3	..	18	..	..	..	45	..	304	8	19	1
100 to 200	3	400	62	..	..	9	..	..	..	14	..	374	62	3	..
200 to 400	4	748	203	..	..	18	..	..	..	92	2	593	160	45	41
400 and over	5	3,023	641	1	..	38	..	..	..	975	98	1,839	525	170	18
Without mechanical power.	*4*	*321*	*133*	..	..	*10*	..	..	..	*36*	..	*214*	*109*	*61*	*24*
20 to 50	1	25	13	..	..	1	..	..	..	1	..	23	13	..	..
50 to 100	1	52	22	..	..	2	..	..	..	30	..	20	22	..	..
100 to 200	1	80	36	..	..	1	..	..	..	1	..	54	25	24	11
200 to 400	1	164	62	..	..	6	..	..	..	4	..	117	49	37	13
XIV.—Industries connected with Transport.	*949*	*193,590*	*1,597*	*1,974*	*98*	*4,155*	..	*2,995*	..	*77,876*	*4*	*36,515*	*1,499*	*775*	*73*
BICYCLE WORKS	3	74	..	1	..	7	..	..	..	43	..	21	..	2	..
With mechanical power (h) (20 to 50).	*1*	*24*	..	*1*	..	*1*	..	..	..	*12*	..	*8*	..	*2*	..
Without mechanical power (20 to 50).	*2*	*50*	..	..	..	*6*	..	..	..	*31*	..	*13*	..	..	..

Power.—(*a*) Steam 1, Oil 1. (*b*) Steam 1, Oil 1. (*c*) Steam 1, Electricity 7, Steam and Oil 1, Oil 5. (*d*) Steam 1. (*e*) Steam 27. (*f*) Steam 10, Oil 2, Steam and oil 1, Electricity 1. (*g*) Steam 47, Electricity 1, (*h*) Steam 1.

TABLE XV.—Occupation or Means of Livelihood.

Description and classification of factory, etc., according to number of persons employed.	Number of factories.	Total number of persons employed. Males.	Total number of persons employed. Females.	Direction, Supervision and Clerical Work. Europeans and Anglo-Indians. M.	F.	Indians. M.	F.	Skilled workmen. Europeans and Anglo-Indians. M.	F.	Indians. Males.	Females.	Unskilled labourers. Age 14 and over. Males.	Females.	Under 14. Males.	Females.
1	2	3	4	5	6	7	8	9	10	11	12	13	14	15	16
XIV.—Industries connected with Transport—contd.															
Coach-building Factories.	**40**	**2,904**	**6**	**42**	..	**183**	..	..	..	**2,011**	..	**532**	**6**	**136**	..
With mechanical power. (a)	*7*	*909*	*5*	*9*	..	*62*	..	..	..	*608*	..	*165*	*5*	*65*	..
20 to 50	1	22	..	1	..	7	..	..	..	..	..	14	..	..	..
50 to 100	2	142	3	2	..	31	..	..	..	49	..	53	3	7	..
100 to 200	3	462	..	3	..	9	..	..	..	350	..	63	..	37	..
200 to 400	1	283	2	3	..	15	..	..	..	209	..	35	2	21	..
Without mechanical power.	*33*	*1,995*	*1*	*33*	..	*121*	..	..	..	*1,403*	..	*367*	*1*	*71*	..
20 to 50	22	679	1	3	..	29	..	..	..	401	..	216	1	30	..
50 to 100	8	455	..	2	..	14	..	..	..	376	..	62	..	1	..
100 to 200	2	235	..	16	..	64	..	..	..	126	..	29	..	..	..
400 and over	1	626	..	12	..	14	..	..	..	500	..	60	..	40	..
Dredging Works	**3**	**605**	**1**	**5**	..	**21**	..	..	..	**104**	..	**475**	**1**	..	..
With mechanical power (b).	*3*	*605*	*1*	*5*	..	*21*	..	..	..	*104*	..	*475*	*1*	..	..
50 to 100	1	65	..	1	..	1	..	..	..	13	..	50	..	..	..
100 to 200	1	115	1	2	..	10	..	..	..	3	..	100	1	..	..
400 and over	1	425	..	2	..	10	..	..	..	88	..	325	..	..	..
Motor-car Works.	**18**	**1,487**	**1**	**70**	..	**106**	..	**36**	..	**1,087**	..	**184**	**1**	**4**	..
With mechanical power. (c)	*17*	*1,446*	*1*	*69*	..	*103*	..	*34*	..	*1,058*	..	*178*	*1*	*4*	..
20 to 50	8	232	1	24	..	47	..	15	..	103	..	39	1	4	..
50 to 100	2	109	..	3	..	11	..	..	..	72	..	23	..	..	..
100 to 200	5	556	..	23	..	83	..	9	..	396	..	95	..	..	..
200 to 400	2	549	..	19	..	12	..	10	..	467	..	21	..	..	..
Without mechanical power (20 to 50).	*1*	*41*	..	*1*	..	*3*	..	*2*	..	*29*	..	*6*	..	..	..
Railway Workshops.	**118**	**97,702**	**1,021**	**822**	**12**	**3,064**	..	**2,591**	..	**62,865**	**4**	**28,059**	**986**	**301**	**19**
With mechanical power. (d)	*88*	*95,444*	*1,016*	*790*	*12*	*2,973*	..	*2,507*	..	*61,930*	*4*	*27,005*	*981*	*239*	*19*
20 to 50	14	529	2	10	..	22	..	4	..	230	..	263	2	..	..
50 to 100	10	736	28	9	..	32	..	15	..	281	..	389	28	10	..
100 to 200	12	1,862	13	19	..	138	..	120	..	777	..	778	12	30	1
200 to 400	19	5,140	66	82	..	322	..	197	..	2,774	..	1,727	58	38	8
400 and over	33	87,177	907	670	12	2,459	..	2,171	..	57,868	4	23,848	881	161	10
Without mechanical power.	*30*	*2,258*	*5*	*32*	..	*91*	..	*84*	..	*935*	..	*1,054*	*5*	*62*	..
20 to 50	11	344	1	6	..	18	..	1	..	155	..	117	1	47	..
50 to 100	13	862	1	14	..	32	..	15	..	370	..	419	1	12	..
100 to 200	4	585	2	9	..	31	..	19	..	245	..	278	2	3	..
200 to 400	2	467	1	3	..	10	..	49	..	165	..	240	1	..	..
Shipwrights	**6**	**5,161**	**3**	**50**	..	**143**	..	**50**	..	**3,471**	..	**1,439**	**3**	**8**	..
With mechanical power. (e)	*6*	*5,161*	*3*	*50*	..	*143*	..	*50*	..	*3,471*	..	*1,439*	*3*	*8*	..
200 to 400	2	543	..	8	..	33	..	3	..	216	..	283	..	..	..
400 and over	4	4,618	3	42	..	110	..	47	..	3,255	..	1,156	3	8	..
Shipyards and Dockyards.*	**21**	**9,556**	**110**	**152**	**14**	**303**	..	**138**	..	**6,064**	..	**2,780**	**95**	**119**	**1**
With mechanical power. (f)	*19*	*9,272*	*110*	*152*	*14*	*302*	..	*138*	..	*5,788*	..	*2,773*	*95*	*119*	*1*
20 to 50	1	44	..	..	..	4	..	..	..	10	..	10	..	20	..
50 to 100	3	212	1	1	..	12	..	..	..	108	..	76	..	15	1
100 to 200	5	810	11	11	..	32	..	48	..	468	..	246	11	5	..
200 to 400	5	1,468	..	31	..	55	..	32	..	883	..	459	..	8	..
400 and over	5	6,788	98	109	14	199	..	58	..	4,319	..	1,982	84	71	..
Without mechanical power.	*2*	*284*	..	..	..	*1*	..	..	..	*276*	..	*7*	..	..	..
20 to 50	1	32	..	..	..	..	..	..	..	28	..	4	..	..	..
200 to 400	1	252	..	..	..	1	..	..	..	248	..	3	..	..	..
Telegraph and Postal Workshops.	**10**	**1,566**	**4**	**57**	**1**	**149**	..	**35**	..	**927**	..	**371**	**3**	**27**	..
With mechanical power. (g)	*5*	*1,036*	*3*	*54*	*1*	*82*	..	*32*	..	*624*	..	*241*	*2*	*3*	..
20 to 50	2	74	2	3	..	26	..	..	..	15	..	27	2	3	..
50 to 100	2	115	1	43	1	15	..	30	..	9	..	18	..	..	..
400 and over	1	847	..	8	..	41	..	2	..	600	..	196	..	..	..
Without mechanical power.	*5*	*530*	*1*	*3*	..	*67*	..	*3*	..	*303*	..	*130*	*1*	*24*	..
20 to 50	2	70	..	..	..	10	..	1	..	45	..	14	..	..	..
50 to 100	2	131	1	2	..	32	..	2	..	25	..	70	1	..	..
200 to 400	1	329	..	1	..	25	..	..	..	233	..	46	..	24	..
Tramway Workshops.	**14**	**2,539**	**23**	**50**	**1**	**127**	..	**45**	..	**971**	..	**1,300**	**22**	**46**	..
With mechanical power. (h)	*12*	*1,894*	*15*	*36*	*1*	*112*	..	*43*	..	*759*	..	*910*	*14*	*34*	..
20 to 50	1	34	..	..	..	3	..	2	..	15	..	14	..	..	..
50 to 100	4	287	..	9	..	9	..	12	..	121	..	136	..	..	..
100 to 200	2	222	13	2	..	13	..	20	..	66	..	107	13	14	..
200 to 400	5	1,351	2	25	1	87	..	9	..	557	..	653	1	20	..
Without mechanical power.	*2*	*645*	*8*	*14*	..	*15*	..	*2*	..	*212*	..	*390*	*8*	*12*	..
100 to 200	1	191	8	2	..	8	..	2	..	65	..	102	8	12	..
400 and over	1	454	..	12	..	7	..	..	..	147	..	288	..	..	..
Others	**9**	**1,926**	**428**	**25**	..	**52**	..	**30**	..	**333**	..	**1,354**	**375**	**132**	**53**
With mechanical power. (i)	*5*	*1,560*	*374*	*23*	..	*20*	..	*30*	..	*297*	..	*1,080*	*325*	*110*	*49*
20 to 50	2	64	..	2	..	4	..	..	..	8	..	50	..	..	..
50 to 100	1	54	..	4	..	1	..	1	..	7	..	36	..	5	..
400 and over	2	1,442	374	17	..	15	..	29	..	282	..	994	325	105	49
Without mechanical power.	*4*	*366*	*54*	*2*	..	*32*	..	..	..	*36*	..	*274*	*50*	*22*	*4*
50 to 100	2	78	31	..	..	6	..	..	..	10	..	55	30	7	1
100 to 200	1	97	12	..	..	3	..	..	..	10	..	80	9	4	3
200 to 400	1	191	11	2	..	23	..	..	..	16	..	139	11	11	..

* Inclusive of Port Commissioner's and Port Trust Workshops.

Power.—(a) Steam 1, Oil 3, Electricity 3. (b) Steam 2, Electricity 1. (c) Steam 2, Electricity 8, Oil 7. (d) Steam 71, Electricity 6, Steam and electricity 5, Steam and oil 1, Oil and Electricity 1, Steam, oil and gas 1, Steam and air 2, Oil 1. (e) Steam 6. (f) Steam 16, Steam and electricity 2, Steam and oil 1. (g) Steam 2, Electricity 2, Oil 1. (h) Steam 6, Electricity 6. (i) Steam 4, Water and electricity 1.

PART E—STATISTICS OF INDUSTRIES, (*i*) GENERAL STATEMENT—*concluded.*

Description and classification of factory, etc., according to number of persons employed.	Number of factories.	Total number of persons employed.		CLASSIFICATION OF PERSONS EMPLOYED.											
				DIRECTION, SUPERVISION AND CLERICAL WORK.				SKILLED WORKMEN.				UNSKILLED LABOURERS.			
				Europeans and Anglo-Indians.		Indians.		Europeans and Anglo-Indians.		Indians.		Age 14 and over		Under 14.	
		Males.	Females.	M.	F.	M.	F.	M.	F.	Males.	Females.	Males.	Females.	Males.	Females.
1	2	3	4	5	6	7	8	9	10	11	12	13	14	15	16
XV.—Production and transmission of Physical forces.	*64*	*8,041*	*198*	*959*	*3*	*414*	..	*90*	..	*4,940*	*21*	*3,007*	*103*	*31*	*1*
ELECTRIC POWER AND LIGHTING WORKS.	**31**	**2,003**	**47**	**117**	..	**134**	..	**80**	..	**701**	..	**953**	**46**	**18**	**1**
With mechanical power. (a)	*29*	*1,937*	*46*	*115*	..	*133*	..	*80*	..	*662*	..	*931*	*45*	*16*	*1*
20 to 50 .	17	633	6	15	..	53	..	22	..	244	..	297	6	2	..
50 to 100 .	6	363	13	13	..	48	..	3	..	111	..	187	13	3	..
100 to 200 .	4	553	5	80	..	17	..	37	..	196	..	214	4	9	1
200 to 400 .	2	386	22	7	..	15	..	18	..	111	..	233	22	2	..
Without mechanical power (20 to 50).	*2*	*66*	*1*	*2*	..	*1*	..	..	..	*39*	..	*22*	*1*	*2*	..
GAS WORKS .	**14**	**4,643**	**37**	**119**	**3**	**176**	..	**7**	..	**3,137**	**21**	**1,203**	**13**	**1**	..
With mechanical power. (b)	*13*	*4,615*	*37*	*119*	*3*	*174*	..	*7*	..	*3,126*	*21*	*1,188*	*13*	*1*	..
20 to 50 .	4	125	..	5	..	10	..	..	..	40	..	69	..	1	..
50 to 100	2	145	1	3	..	7	..	1	..	14	..	120	1	..	..
100 to 200 .	4	592	6	25	..	42	..	6	..	273	6	246	..	..	..
400 and over .	3	3,753	30	86	3	115	..	..	..	2,799	15	753	12	..	..
Without mechanical power (20 to 50).	*1*	*28*	..	..	..	*2*	..	..	..	*11*	..	*15*	..	..	..
HYDRAULIC WORKS .	**1**	**552**	..	**2**	..	**14**	..	..	..	**186**	..	**350**	..	..	..
With mechanical power (c) (400 and over).	*1*	*552*	..	*2*	..	*14*	..	..	..	*186*	..	*350*	..	..	..
ICE FACTORIES .	**18**	**843**	**44**	**21**	..	**90**	..	**3**	..	**216**	..	**501**	**44**	**12**	..
With mechanical power. (d)	*18*	*843*	*44*	*21*	..	*90*	..	*3*	..	*216*	..	*501*	*44*	*12*	..
20 to 50	13	419	4	4	..	57	..	..	..	116	..	230	4	12	..
50 to 100 .	3	184	40	9	..	13	..	1	..	45	..	116	40	..	..
100 to 200 .	2	240	..	8	..	20	..	2	..	55	..	155	..	..	..
XVI.—Industries of Luxury.	*389*	*45,179*	*395*	*601*	*40*	*4,827*	*10*	*463*	*22*	*29,368*	*12*	*8,748*	*223*	*1,172*	*18*
GAMES AND SPORT WORKS.	**4**	**365**	..	**5**	..	**34**	..	..	..	**276**	..	**30**	..	**20**	..
With mechanical power(e) (100 to 200).	*2*	*270*	..	*3*	..	*27*	..	..	..	*200*	..	*20*	..	*20*	..
Without mechanical power.	*2*	*95*	..	*2*	..	*7*	..	..	..	*76*	..	*10*	..	..	..
20 to 50 .	1	42	..	..	..	4	..	..	..	35	..	3	..	..	..
50 to 100 .	1	53	..	2	..	3	..	..	..	41	..	7	..	..	..
JEWELLERY WORKSHOPS.	**21**	**1,564**	**1**	**34**	..	**155**	..	**16**	..	**1,004**	..	**243**	**1**	**112**	..
With mechanical power. (f)	*9*	*1,035*	*1*	*30*	..	*64*	..	*13*	..	*751*	..	*136*	*1*	*41*	..
20 to 50 .	3	98	1	..	..	7	..	..	..	32	..	45	1	14	..
50 to 100 .	1	78	..	4	..	4	..	..	..	59	..	11	..	..	..
100 to 200 .	3	343	..	16	..	11	..	8	..	256	..	42	..	10	..
200 to 400 .	2	516	..	10	..	42	..	5	..	404	..	38	..	17	..
Without mechanical power.	*12*	*529*	..	*4*	..	*91*	..	*3*	..	*253*	..	*107*	..	*71*	..
20 to 50 .	8	238	..	4	..	29	..	3	..	131	..	51	..	20	..
50 to 100 .	3	184	..	..	..	57	..	..	..	62	..	56	..	9	..
100 to 200 .	1	107	..	..	..	5	..	..	..	60	..	..	..	42	..
PHOTO WORKS .	**9**	**714**	**1**	**22**	**1**	**76**	..	**4**	..	**264**	..	**336**	..	**12**	..
With mechanical power. (g)	*4*	*524*	..	*16*	..	*31*	..	*4*	..	*236*	..	*235*	..	*2*	..
20 to 50 .	1	22	..	..	..	3	..	..	..	15	..	4	..	..	..
50 to 100 .	1	68	..	2	..	2	..	2	..	41	..	19	..	2	..
100 to 200 .	1	142	..	1	..	10	..	..	..	72	..	59	..	..	..
200 to 400 .	1	292	..	13	..	16	..	2	..	108	..	153	..	..	..
Without mechanical power.	*5*	*190*	*1*	*6*	*1*	*45*	..	..	..	*28*	..	*101*	..	*10*	..
20 to 50 .	4	117	1	6	1	41	..	..	..	26	..	40	..	4	..
50 to 100 .	1	73	..	..	..	4	..	..	..	2	..	61	..	6	..
PRINTING PRESSES .	**341**	**41,294**	**304**	**477**	**23**	**4,406**	**8**	**418**	**22**	**27,136**	**12**	**7,836**	**221**	**1,019**	**15**
With mechanical power. (h)	*194*	*32,435*	*269*	*426*	*18*	*3,128*	*3*	*270*	*21*	*22,031*	*4*	*5,898*	*206*	*682*	*17*
20 to 50 .	68	2,153	9	12	..	264	2	18	..	1,247	4	504	3	113	..
50 to 100 .	40	2,970	1	14	1	453	..	12	..	1,862	..	501	..	128	..
100 to 200 .	34	4,683	16	67	9	488	..	34	3	2,921	..	1,076	4	97	..
200 to 400 .	38	8,634	211	154	5	722	..	34	..	5,730	..	1,846	189	148	17
400 and over .	19	13,995	32	179	3	1,201	1	177	18	10,271	..	1,971	10	196	..
Without mechanical power.	*147*	*8,859*	*35*	*51*	*5*	*1,280*	*5*	*148*	*1*	*5,105*	*8*	*1,938*	*15*	*337*	*1*
20 to 50 .	96	2,886	12	19	4	275	..	91	1	1,851	..	513	6	137	1
50 to 100 .	31	1,955	12	14	1	264	1	39	..	1,100	6	462	4	76	..
100 to 200 .	12	1,416	10	3	..	243	4	3	..	618	2	450	4	99	..
200 to 400 .	6	1,731	1	11	..	428	..	4	..	883	..	380	1	25	..
400 and over .	2	871	..	4	..	70	..	11	..	653	..	133	..	..	..
OTHERS .	**14**	**1,242**	**19**	**63**	**16**	**154**	**2**	**25**	..	**688**	..	**303**	**1**	**9**	..
With mechanical power. (i)	*6*	*867*	*16*	*45*	*15*	*86*	..	*7*	..	*514*	..	*211*	*1*	*4*	..
20 to 50 .	1	37	..	..	..	4	..	..	..	29	..	4	..	..	..
50 to 100 .	2	110	2	10	1	5	..	6	..	38	..	47	1	4	..
100 to 200 .	1	162	..	1	..	13	..	1	..	80	..	67	..	..	..
200 to 400 .	2	558	14	34	14	64	..	..	..	367	..	93	..	..	..
Without mechanical power.	*8*	*375*	*3*	*18*	*1*	*68*	*2*	*18*	..	*174*	..	*92*	..	*5*	..
20 to 50 .	4	116	..	8	..	8	..	..	..	51	..	44	..	5	..
50 to 100 .	4	259	3	10	1	60	2	18	..	123	..	48	..	..	..

Power.—(a) Steam 8, Electricity 8, Steam and electricity 4, Oil 1, Water 1, Hydraulic 4, Steam and oil 3. (b) Steam 9, Gas 4. (c) Steam 1. (d) Steam 18. (e) Steam 1, Oil 1. (f) Electricity 9. (g) Electricity 2, Oil 1, Electric oil engine 1. (h) Steam 56, Oil 71, Electricity 61, Steam and electricity 2, Gas 1, Oil and electricity 1, Oil and gas 1, Petroleum 1. (i) Steam 2, Electricity 3, Oil 1.

TABLE XV.—Occupation or Means of Livelihood.

Description of Factory, Mine, etc., and Province, State or Agency.	Number of factories.	Total number of persons employed.		Classification of persons employed. Direction, Supervision and Clerical Work. Europeans and Anglo-Indians		Direction, Supervision and Clerical Work. Indians.		Skilled workmen. Europeans and Anglo-Indians.		Skilled workmen. Indians.		Unskilled labourers. Age 14 and over.		Unskilled labourers. Under 14.	
		Males.	Females.	M.	F.	M.	F.	M.	F.	Males.	Females.	Males.	Females.	Males.	Females.
1	2	3	4	5	6	7	8	9	10	11	12	13	14	15	16
INDIA	**7,113**	**1,521,031**	**584,793**	**9,267**	**170**	**60,061**	**713**	**6,262**	**210**	**504,560**	**43,746**	**796,830**	**446,868**	**144,031**	**93,086**
I.—Growing of Special Products	*1,687*	*440,800*	*369,607*	*1,617*	*10*	*10,171*	*175*	*252*	*2*	*16,514*	*1,678*	*329,628*	*295,481*	*83,618*	*72,261*
Cardamom Plantations.	**10**	**724**	**450**	**4**	..	**78**	**20**	..	..	**2**	..	**560**	**348**	**80**	**82**
Madras	1	123	123	1	..	..	..	..	..	..	..	105	101	17	22
Mysore State	9	601	327	3	..	78	20	..	..	2	..	455	247	63	60
Cinchona Plantations.	**5**	**684**	**460**	**5**	..	**25**	..	..	..	**11**	..	**533**	**380**	**110**	**80**
Bengal	2	414	347	2	..	20	..	..	..	..	..	311	272	81	75
Madras	3	270	113	3	..	5	..	..	..	11	..	222	108	29	5
Coffee Plantations	**482**	**32,227**	**25,396**	**247**	**2**	**1,236**	**64**	**19**	**2**	**1,366**	**610**	**25,931**	**20,593**	**3,428**	**4,125**
Coorg	94	7,187	3,625	47	..	138	3	2	2	252	107	6,211	3,045	537	468
Madras	131	10,234	11,355	122	..	458	27	7	..	267	137	8,322	9,109	1,058	2,082
Cochin State	15	425	218	9	..	1	..	3	..	..	..	371	189	41	20
Mysore State	242	14,381	10,198	69	2	639	34	7	..	847	366	11,027	8,250	1,792	1,546
Indigo Plantations	**121**	**26,544**	**4,251**	**97**	**1**	**2,073**	**3**	**12**	..	**2,168**	**306**	**16,174**	**2,199**	**6,020**	**1,742**
Bengal	2	103	12	1	..	14	..	..	..	..	..	88	12	..	..
Bihar and Orissa	119	26,441	4,239	96	1	2,059	3	12	..	2,168	306	16,086	2,187	6,020	1,742
Rubber Plantations.	**48**	**11,198**	**2,469**	**92**	**2**	**168**	**4**	**1**	..	**1,595**	**117**	**8,508**	**1,811**	**834**	**535**
Assam	1	124	..	1	..	10	..	..	..	84	..	25	..	4	..
Burma	10	3,896	151	33	..	36	..	..	..	540	..	3,239	133	48	18
Madras	16	2,454	736	22	..	26	..	..	..	100	77	2,115	551	191	108
Cochin State	6	2,616	578	10	..	21	..	..	..	715	..	1,543	393	327	185
Mysore State	3	311	305	1	..	15	..	..	..	14	..	266	281	15	24
Travancore State	12	1,797	699	25	2	60	4	1	..	142	40	1,320	453	240	209
Tea Plantations	**1,002**	**367,844**	**335,741**	**1,145**	**5**	**6,466**	**77**	**219**	..	**11,331**	**524**	**276,696**	**269,581**	**71,987**	**65,554**
Assam	609	256,048	237,435	748	3	4,240	54	139	..	4,837	260	198,448	194,051	47,636	43,067
Bengal	240	97,784	93,502	297	1	1,594	6	46	..	4,998	210	68,389	71,558	22,460	21,727
Bihar and Orissa	6	330	205	3	..	42	..	2	..	10	..	250	163	23	42
Madras	41	5,348	2,934	60	..	103	12	21	..	203	28	4,534	2,505	427	389
Punjab	41	3,611	303	4	..	273	2	1	..	733	3	2,030	252	570	46
United Provinces	28	3,029	594	6	..	88	..	2	..	350	..	1,976	468	607	126
Travancore State	37	1,694	768	27	1	126	3	8	..	200	23	1,069	584	264	157
Others	**19**	**1,579**	[illegible]	**7**	..	**125**	**7**	**1**	..	**41**	**121**	**1,226**	**569**	**159**	**143**
Assam	2	91	63	..	..	6	..	..	..	2	..	81	57	2	6
Bengal	3	196	98	..	..	11	..	..	..	1	..	155	73	29	25
C. P. and Berar	2	30	145	..	..	3	6	..	..	..	..	10	96	26	43
Madras	11	1,216	534	27	..	81	1	1	..	38	121	980	343	89	69
Travancore State	1	37	..	..	..	24	..	..	..	..	..	..	..	13	..
II.—Mines	*569*	*163,919*	*61,868*	*1,160*	*4*	*4,896*	*15*	*740*	..	*68,994*	*3,731*	*79,671*	*59,503*	*7,598*	*6,613*
Collieries	**353**	**99,601**	**43,276**	**326**	..	**3,842**	**4**	**27**	..	**56,276**	**765**	**34,458**	**38,038**	**4,672**	**4,469**
Assam	6	2,023	787	15	..	17	..	1	..	312	..	1,638	778	40	9
Baluchistan	4	1,109	12	4	..	42	..	..	..	140	..	870	12	53	..
Bengal	129	27,114	10,593	106	..	1,282	1	5	..	15,511	111	8,441	8,962	1,769	1,519
Bihar and Orissa	199	57,912	28,966	154	..	1,993	3	11	..	35,183	461	17,861	26,158	2,710	2,344
C. P. and Berar	5	2,309	715	15	..	102	..	3	..	1,211	..	930	694	48	21
Punjab	6	1,449	2	2	..	44	..	..	..	261	..	1,094	2	48	..
C. I. Agency	2	1,272	193	5	..	20	..	..	..	1,135	193	112	..	..	..
Hyderabad State	1	6,302	1,996	25	..	334	..	7	..	2,511	..	3,425	1,423	..	573
Rajputana Agency	1	111	12	..	..	8	..	..	..	12	..	87	9	4	3
Gold Mines	**12**	**26,596**	**1,996**	**575**	**2**	**157**	..	**372**	..	**6,009**	..	**18,849**	**1,732**	**643**	**262**
Bombay	1	191	40	14	..	3	..	..	..	51	..	113	40	10	..
Madras	3	955	78	10	..	5	..	11	..	237	..	634	76	58	2
Hyderabad State	2	1,674	351	32	..	9	..	11	..	89	..	1,494	319	39	32
Mysore State	6	23,776	1,527	519	2	140	..	350	..	5,632	..	16,509	1,297	536	228
Iron Mines (Bihar and Orissa).	**3**	**3,961**	**2,325**	**7**	..	**14**	..	..	..	**34**	..	**3,804**	**2,180**	**122**	**145**
Manganese Mines.	**54**	**9,882**	**6,796**	**50**	**1**	**202**	**8**	**11**	..	**271**	**9**	**8,662**	**6,203**	**686**	**575**
Bihar and Orissa	1	119	2	3	..	2	..	2	..	25	..	85	2	2	..
Bombay	4	612	202	3	..	28	2	..	..	18	..	542	184	21	16
C. P. and Berar	40	6,609	5,169	26	1	135	6	6	..	159	8	5,844	4,794	439	360
Madras	5	1,993	1,106	15	..	23	..	1	..	58	1	1,747	941	149	164
C. I. Agency	1	224	104	..	..	6	..	..	..	2	..	185	88	31	16
Mysore State	3	325	213	3	..	8	..	2	..	9	..	259	194	44	19
Mica Mines	**93**	**8,805**	**5,914**	**17**	**1**	**334**	**3**	**3**	..	**2,974**	**1,949**	**4,294**	**2,932**	**1,183**	**1,029**
Ajmer-Merwara	2	103	11	..	..	5	..	..	..	46	8	44	3	8	..
Bengal	1	41	32	1	..	2	..	..	..	31	32	7	..	..	..
Bihar and Orissa	52	7,003	3,837	13	1	237	..	2	..	2,031	795	3,657	2,146	1,063	895
Madras	38	1,658	2,034	3	..	90	3	1	..	866	1,114	586	783	112	134
Petroleum Wells	**20**	**5,923**	**411**	**96**	..	**193**	..	**300**	..	**1,334**	**6**	**3,971**	**400**	**29**	**5**
Assam	1	803	207	15	..	32	..	..	..	260	..	473	202	23	5
Burma	19	5,120	204	81	..	161	..	300	..	1,074	6	3,498	198	6	..
Others	**27**	**7,431**	**1,150**	**89**	..	**154**	..	**27**	..	**1,326**	**2**	**5,642**	**1,018**	**193**	**130**
Assam	1	58	1	..	..	4	..	..	..	27	..	27	1	..	..
Bihar and Orissa	1	935	164	20	..	7	..	11	..	96	..	736	136	65	28
Burma	15	4,468	8	54	..	26	..	6	..	564	..	3,818	8	..	..
Madras	2	280	228	4	..	20	..	5	..	9	..	234	210	8	18
Punjab	4	843	463	1	..	60	..	..	..	350	..	348	418	64	45
C. I. Agency	1	44	61	..	..	5	..	..	..	1	2	35	56	3	3
Travancore State	3	803	225	10	..	32	..	5	..	279	..	444	189	33	36

Part E.—Statistics of Industries, (ii) Provincial Distribution—*continued.*

Description of Factory, Mine, etc., and Province, State or Agency.	Number of factories.	Total number of persons employed.		Classification of persons employed.											
				Direction, Supervision and Clerical Work.				Skilled Workmen.				Unskilled Labourers.			
				Europeans and Anglo-Indians.		Indians.		Europeans and Anglo-Indians.		Indians.		Age 14 and over.		Under 14.	
		Males.	Females.	M.	F.	M.	F.	M.	F.	Males.	Females.	Males.	Females.	Males.	Females.
1	2	3	4	5	6	7	8	9	10	11	12	13	14	15	16
III.—Quarries of Hard Rocks.	*53*	*9,539*	*2,734*	*22*	..	*288*	*1*	*2*	*1*	*1,116*	*99*	*7,345*	*2,222*	*766*	*411*
Stone and marble quarries.	**50**	**9,166**	**2,700**	**21**	..	**256**	**1**	**2**	**1**	**1,045**	**99**	**7,124**	**2,194**	**718**	**405**
Bengal	1	498	43	1	..	27	..	1	..	11	..	448	43	10	..
Bihar and Orissa	3	775	467	2	..	9	..	..	..	19	..	715	432	30	35
Bombay	31	2,722	1,026	..	..	143	1	..	1	784	99	1,685	758	110	167
Burma	1	1,442	154	8	..	6	..	..	..	40	..	901	41	487	118
C. P. and Berar	7	511	277	2	..	16	..	..	..	77	..	369	220	47	57
Punjab	3	1,878	16	4	..	10	..	..	..	26	..	1,824	16	..	..
C. I. Agency	1	850	542	1	..	32	..	1	..	18	..	779	522	19	20
Hyderabad State	2	95	24	..	..	1	..	..	..	59	..	35	24	..	..
Rajputana Agency	1	400	151	3	..	3	..	..	..	11	..	368	138	15	13
Others	**3**	**373**	**34**	**1**	..	**32**	..	..	..	**71**	..	**221**	**28**	**48**	**6**
Bombay	1	36	10	..	..	8	..	..	..	8	..	20	10	..	..
Punjab	2	337	24	1	..	24	..	..	..	63	..	201	18	48	6
IV.—Textile Industries.	*1,487*	*445,057*	*112,532*	*1,404*	*22*	*18,320*	*277*	*369*	*27*	*213,953*	*36,931*	*174,404*	*66,541*	*36,607*	*9,434*
(a) Cotton	*1,127*	*238,909*	*69,981*	*568*	*5*	*12,367*	*218*	*259*	*25*	*138,700*	*28,207*	*72,663*	*36,172*	*14,352*	*4,654*
Cotton ginning, cleaning and pressing mills.	**823**	**44,780**	**26,295**	**73**	**2**	**4,555**	**94**	**80**	..	**8,904**	**629**	**28,901**	**23,728**	**2,267**	**1,842**
Ajmer-Merwara	8	1,301	843	3	..	39	..	1	..	493	35	665	738	100	70
Bengal	4	314	600	2	..	54	2	..	..	30	4	223	589	5	5
Bombay	310	17,305	10,331	35	..	1,528	30	12	..	3,324	270	11,677	9,424	729	607
Burma	5	577	159	..	..	85	..	..	..	96	13	375	116	21	30
C. P. and Berar	153	7,895	5,696	1	..	668	19	..	..	1,385	..	5,610	5,324	231	353
Madras	41	1,824	1,090	16	..	264	1	4	..	458	36	1,036	1,027	46	26
N.-W. F. Province	2	63	..	..	..	25	..	..	..	14	..	24	..	..	..
Punjab	66	3,713	929	3	..	486	14	1	..	1,071	11	1,999	808	153	96
United Provinces	14	883	404	4	..	102	..	..	..	290	41	421	261	66	102
Baroda State	55	3,719	1,773	..	..	340	2	12	..	540	42	2,296	1,407	522	322
C. I. Agency	92	3,905	2,899	5	2	381	24	26	..	769	137	2,568	2,135	156	101
Hyderabad State	48	1,999	1,444	1	..	449	2	..	..	272	40	1,088	1,300	189	102
Mysore State	7	183	156	1	..	31	..	1	..	40	..	106	150	4	6
Rajputana Agency	18	1,099	471	2	..	94	..	23	..	122	..	813	449	45	22
Thread glazing and polishing mills (Bengal).	**1**	**35**	..	..	..	**1**	..	..	..	**2**	..	**20**	..	**12**	..
Cotton spinning, weaving and other mills.	**286**	**193,098**	**42,858**	**486**	**3**	**77 09**	**99**	**179**	**25**	**129,248**	**27,551**	**43,456**	**12,375**	**12,020**	**2,805**
Ajmer-Merwara	1	999	190	2	..	36	..	2	..	623	37	317	153	19	..
Bengal	14	9,552	1,286	45	..	179	..	12	..	4,695	259	3,815	942	806	85
Bombay	162	131,954	32,249	266	..	5,215	61	136	..	93,874	22,376	26,269	7,804	6,194	2,008
C. P. and Berar	10	10,524	2,850	9	..	771	13	1	..	6,076	1,749	3,118	942	549	146
Madras	37	17,539	3,467	77	1	609	8	15	..	9,150	1,782	4,946	1,240	2,742	436
Punjab	21	2,528	481	7	2	132	11	8	25	1,474	329	705	107	202	7
United Provinces	11	12,015	840	72	..	363	3	3	..	8,864	402	2,044	435	649	..
Baroda State	4	1,235	122	..	..	84	..	..	..	509	63	443	49	199	10
C. I. Agency	5	2,955	401	3	..	94	..	..	..	1,961	274	626	118	271	9
Cochin State	1	128	3	1	..	8	..	..	..	69	..	40	3	10	..
Hyderabad State	12	2,385	703	2	..	101	3	1	..	1,452	188	538	424	291	88
Kashmir State	2	57	..	..	..	..	..	..	..	24	..	33	..	..	..
Mysore State	1	685	149	..	..	65	..	..	..	411	92	149	41	60	16
Rajputana Agency	1	416	114	..	..	18	..	..	..	19	..	373	114	6	..
Travancore State	4	126	3	2	..	14	..	1	..	47	..	40	3	22	..
Cotton carpet and rug manufactories.	**17**	**996**	**128**	**9**	..	**102**	**25**	..	..	**546**	**27**	**286**	**69**	**53**	**7**
Bombay	9	264	60	1	..	61	25	..	..	133	8	27	20	42	7
Punjab	1	37	..	..	..	8	..	..	..	28	..	..	..	1	..
United Provinces	1	237	41	3	..	8	..	..	..	31	..	195	41	..	..
C. I. Agency	6	458	27	5	..	25	..	..	..	354	19	64	8	10	..
(b) Jute, Hemp, etc.	*223*	*184,119*	*38,907*	*734*	..	*4,711*	*33*	*108*	..	*60,905*	*5,059*	*98,358*	*28,875*	*19,296*	*4,947*
Jute presses	**123**	**12,827**	**1,426**	**108**	..	**963**	..	**33**	..	**2,492**	**69**	**9,643**	**1,314**	**188**	**43**
Bengal	109	12,422	1,420	108	..	927	..	33	..	2,356	69	8,819	1,308	179	43
Bihar and Orissa	8	230	..	..	..	24	..	..	..	129	..	77	..	..	..
Madras	6	175	6	..	..	12	..	..	..	7	..	147	6	9	..
Jute mills	**52**	**166,643**	**35,621**	**579**	..	**3,436**	..	**71**	..	**57,105**	**4,734**	**87,113**	**26,978**	**18,339**	**3,909**
Bengal	50	165,183	35,263	574	..	3,370	..	68	..	56,908	4,679	86,132	26,730	18,131	3,854
Madras	2	1,460	358	5	..	66	..	3	..	197	55	981	248	208	55
Rope works	**25**	**1,897**	**157**	**4**	..	**79**	**23**	**2**	..	**989**	**76**	**550**	**49**	**273**	**9**
Bengal	15	1,335	92	4	..	32	..	2	..	687	66	403	26	207	..
Bihar and Orissa	1	24	16	..	..	1	..	..	..	..	..	17	11	6	5
Bombay	5	277	23	..	..	36	23	..	..	180	..	7	..	54	..
Burma	1	136	17	..	..	4	..	..	..	60	10	70	4	2	8
Madras	1	37	9	..	..	1	..	..	..	1	..	35	8	..	1
Punjab	1	25	..	..	..	..	..	..	..	13	..	8	..	4	..
United Provinces	1	63	..	..	..	5	..	..	..	48	..	10	..	..	..
Coir factories	**13**	**2,424**	**716**	**43**	..	**213**	**10**	**2**	..	**258**	**39**	**1,451**	**418**	**457**	**249**
Madras	6	814	280	11	..	37	..	1	..	162	34	423	148	180	98
Cochin State	1	52	11	2	..	2	..	..	..	4	..	44	11	..	..
Travancore State	6	1,558	425	30	..	174	10	1	..	92	5	984	259	277	151
Hemp mills (Bihar and Orissa).	**3**	**115**	**101**	..	..	**2**	..	..	..	..	..	**96**	**85**	**17**	**16**

TABLE XV.—Occupation or Means of Livelihood.

Description of Factory, Mine, etc., and Province, State or Agency.	Number of factories.	Total number of persons employed.		CLASSIFICATION OF PERSONS EMPLOYED. Direction, Supervision and Clerical Work. Europeans and Anglo-Indians.		Indians.		Skilled workmen. Europeans and Anglo-Indians.		Indians.		Unskilled labourers. Age 14 and over.		Under 14.	
		Males.	Females.	M.	F.	M.	F.	M.	F.	Males.	Females.	Males.	Females.	Males.	Females.
1	2	3	4	5	6	7	8	9	10	11	12	13	14	15	16
IV.—Textile Industries—contd.															
Fibre cleaning works (Madras).	6	145	165	..	..	18	..	..	..	60	134	45	10	22	21
Fibre matting and bag works (United Provinces).	1	61	21	..	..	..	..	..	..	1	..	60	21	..	..
(c) Wool	*47*	*6,462*	*861*	*41*	..	*340*	*11*	..	..	*4,739*	*129*	*899*	*619*	*463*	*102*
Wool Presses (Punjab).	1	46	..	..	..	3	..	..	..	8	..	35	..	..	..
Woollen Mills	21	2,580	818	35	..	142	11	..	..	1,677	123	533	585	193	99
Bombay	15	437	579	5	..	31	10	..	..	201	10	200	541	..	18
Punjab	3	1,119	68	13	..	60	..	..	..	839	59	190	5	17	4
United Provinces	2	48	5	..	..	8	..	..	..	10	..	15	2	15	3
Mysore State	1	976	166	17	..	43	1	..	..	627	54	128	37	161	74
Carpet, blanket and shawl factories.	25	3,856	43	6	..	195	..	..	..	3,054	6	331	34	270	3
Bombay	1	45	5	3	..	2	..	..	..	32	..	8	5	..	..
Punjab	8	913	1	..	..	95	..	..	..	673	1	57	..	88	..
United Provinces	1	180	27	..	..	4	..	..	..	108	..	68	27	..	..
Hyderabad State	2	114	4	..	..	1	..	..	..	3	..	96	2	14	2
Kashmir State	10	2,368	6	3	..	85	..	..	..	2,180	5	57	..	43	1
Rajputana Agency	3	236	..	..	..	8	..	..	..	58	..	45	..	125	..
(d) Silk	*49*	*11,827*	*883*	*24*	..	*709*	*4*	*1*	..	*7,665*	*680*	*1,276*	*166*	*2,152*	*33*
Silk (including tassar, etc.) filatures and mills.	49	11,827	883	24	..	709	4	1	..	7,665	680	1,276	166	2,152	33
Bengal	33	6,705	243	18	..	315	1	1	..	3,546	165	809	73	2,016	4
Bihar and Orissa	2	79	36	..	..	5	..	..	..	42	2	14	19	18	15
Bombay	8	2,170	495	..	..	162	3	..	..	1,720	460	213	25	75	7
Punjab	2	332	47	..	..	12	..	..	..	302	47	10	..	8	..
Baroda State	1	33	11	..	..	5	..	..	..	..	..	25	11	3	..
Hyderabad State	1	32	28	..	..	6	..	..	..	12	6	14	22	..	..
Kashmir State	2	2,476	23	6	..	204	..	..	..	2,043	..	191	16	32	7
(e) Hair, etc.	*5*	*1,923*	*296*	*31*	*4*	*110*	..	*1*	..	*1,419*	*227*	*287*	*49*	*75*	*16*
Brush Factories	4	296	75	5	..	29	..	..	..	176	59	11	..	75	16
Bombay	1	22	2	..	..	12	..	..	..	10	2	..	..	..	..
United Provinces	2	248	73	5	..	15	..	..	..	144	57	9	..	75	16
Baroda State	1	26	..	..	..	2	..	..	..	22	..	2	..	..	..
Felt Factories (United Provinces).	1	1,627	221	26	4	81	..	1	..	1,243	168	276	49	..	..
(f) Others	*36*	*1,804*	*3,004*	*6*	*13*	*83*	*11*	..	*2*	*525*	*1,936*	*921*	*660*	*269*	*382*
Calico printing works	11	324	69	..	..	12	..	..	..	241	36	18	26	53	7
Bombay	4	111	43	..	..	..	..	..	..	106	36	..	..	5	7
United Provinces	7	213	26	..	..	12	..	..	..	135	..	18	26	48	..
Lace and embroidery works.	15	293	1,990	1	13	4	10	..	2	220	1,900	39	65	29	..
Bihar and Orissa	4	1	232	1	5	..	5	..	2	..	155	..	65	..	..
Bombay	4	136	6	..	..	2	..	..	..	122	6	..	..	12	..
Madras	1	25	..	..	..	..	..	..	..	25	..	..	..	..	..
Kashmir State	5	131	3	..	..	2	..	..	..	73	3	39	..	17	..
Travancore State	1	..	1,749	..	8	..	5	..	..	..	1,736	..	..	..	..
Others	10	1,187	945	5	..	67	1	..	..	64	..	864	569	187	375
Assam	4	513	409	4	..	9	..	..	..	17	..	438	371	45	38
Bombay	1	84	95	..	..	3	..	..	..	6	..	53	73	22	22
Madras	1	27	..	..	..	5	..	..	..	2	..	20	..	..	..
Punjab	1	61	..	..	..	1	..	..	..	4	..	46	..	10	..
C. I. Agency	1	28	..	..	..	3	..	..	..	18	..	7	..	..	..
Travancore State	2	474	441	1	..	46	1	..	..	17	..	300	125	110	315
V.—Leather and other Industries.	*158*	*12,508*	*1,104*	*105*	..	*821*	*8*	*108*	*4*	*5,516*	*114*	*5,135*	*919*	*823*	*66*
Bone Mills	8	764	319	10	..	39	..	..	..	97	..	610	317	8	2
Bengal	4	461	107	7	..	24	..	..	..	72	..	350	105	8	2
Bombay	4	308	212	3	..	15	..	..	..	25	..	260	212	..	..
Gut Factories	3	117	28	..	..	3	2	..	..	18	..	77	25	19	1
Bengal	1	45	..	..	..	..	..	..	..	18	..	21	..	6	..
Bombay	1	49	24	..	..	2	..	..	..	..	..	35	24	12	..
C. P. and Berar	1	23	4	..	..	1	2	..	..	..	..	21	1	1	1

Part E.—Statistics of Industries, (*ii*) Provincial Distribution—*continued*.

Description of Factory, Mine, etc., and Province, State or Agency.	Number of factories.	Total number of persons employed.		CLASSIFICATION OF PERSONS EMPLOYED. Direction, Supervision and Clerical Work. Europeans and Anglo-Indians.		Indians.		Skilled workmen. Europeans and Anglo-Indians.		Indians.		Unskilled labourers. Age 14 and over.		Under 14.	
		Males.	Females.	M.	F.	M.	F.	M.	F.	Males.	Females.	Males.	Females.	Males.	Females.
1	2	3	4	5	6	7	8	9	10	11	12	13	14	15	16
V.—Leather and other Industries—contd.															
Leather Factories	**25**	**2,837**	**148**	**54**	..	**196**	..	**94**	**4**	**1,664**	**51**	**763**	**83**	**66**	**10**
Bengal	4	348	..	8	..	23	..	7	..	267	..	43	..	..	..
Bombay	3	137	5	4	..	9	..	3	..	58	..	51	5	12	..
C. P. and Berar	1	45	23	..	..	6	..	..	..	..	..	39	22	..	1
Madras	2	68	4	2	..	9	..	2	..	38	..	17	4	..	..
Punjab	3	98	4	..	..	6	..	55	4	..	..	37	..	..	..
United Provinces	10	1,971	111	38	..	129	..	27	..	1,170	51	558	51	49	9
Baroda State	1	71	1	1	..	6	..	..	..	57	..	6	1	1	..
C. I. Agency	1	99	..	1	..	8	..	..	..	74	..	12	..	4	..
Tanneries	**122**	**8,790**	**609**	**41**	..	**583**	**6**	**14**	..	**3,737**	**63**	**3,685**	**487**	**730**	**53**
Bengal	10	1,161	1	18	..	101	..	..	..	149	..	882	1	11	..
Bihar and Orissa	3	227	3	3	..	13	..	..	..	163	..	48	3	..	..
Bombay	22	1,884	189	5	..	38	..	..	..	758	34	528	145	55	10
Madras	66	4,118	296	3	..	319	6	9	..	1,734	23	1,495	238	558	29
United Provinces	3	987	24	10	..	22	..	4	..	598	..	298	24	60	..
C. I. Agency	2	116	1	2	..	13	..	1	..	74	..	22	1	4	..
Hyderabad State	13	607	75	..	..	54	..	..	..	157	6	363	56	33	13
Mysore State	3	190	20	..	..	23	..	..	..	109	..	49	19	9	1
VI.—Wood, etc., Industries.	***168***	***28,172***	***895***	***177***	***8***	***1,904***	***51***	***39***	..	***11,376***	***91***	***14,048***	***639***	***628***	***113***
Carpentry Works	**33**	**4,945**	**118**	**46**	**2**	**187**	**2**	**14**	..	**2,915**	**32**	**1,484**	**51**	**299**	**31**
Assam	1	21	1	2	..	..	..	1	..	3	1	11	..	4	..
Bengal	5	463	..	13	..	11	..	1	..	365	..	69	..	4	..
Bombay	1	160	40	..	..	10	..	..	..	65	..	60	20	25	20
C. P. and Berar	3	161	31	3	1	11	1	..	..	63	1	58	17	26	11
Madras	15	1,429	46	6	1	106	1	1	..	587	30	567	14	162	..
United Provinces	4	2,567	..	22	..	39	..	11	..	1,756	..	671	..	68	..
Hyderabad State	1	45	..	..	..	3	..	..	..	28	..	13	..	6	..
Travancore State	3	99	..	..	..	7	..	..	..	53	..	35	..	4	..
Saw Mills	**106**	**11,790**	**706**	**114**	**6**	**1,486**	**49**	**15**	..	**2,795**	**59**	**7,164**	**506**	**216**	**80**
Assam	10	828	322	8	..	41	..	1	..	152	..	579	290	47	32
Bihar and Orissa	1	134	22	3	..	6	..	..	..	59	..	66	22	..	..
Bombay	6	564	36	5	..	49	3	..	..	254	6	285	11	21	16
Burma	82	9,523	310	85	6	1,305	46	7	..	2,165	53	5,813	173	148	32
Madras	3	231	..	5	..	42	..	..	..	43	..	141	..	..	..
Baroda State	1	41	10	..	..	13	..	..	..	3	..	25	10	..	..
Cochin State	2	424	..	5	..	9	..	5	..	117	..	288	..	..	..
Mysore State	1	45	..	3	..	21	..	2	..	2	..	17	..	..	..
Timber Yards	**27**	**11,368**	**77**	**17**	..	**227**	..	..	..	**5,650**	..	**5,398**	**75**	**76**	**2**
Bengal	7	320	..	..	..	20	..	..	..	174	..	70	..	56	..
Bihar and Orissa	6	9,505	25	13	..	117	..	..	..	5,027	..	4,348	25	..	..
Bombay	1	37	..	..	..	4	..	..	..	8	..	25	..	..	..
Madras	3	62	..	..	..	16	..	..	..	14	..	27	..	5	..
Hyderabad State	1	46	5	..	..	5	..	..	..	30	..	11	5	..	..
Kashmir State	9	1,398	47	4	..	65	..	..	..	397	..	917	45	15	2
Others	**2**	**69**	..	..	..	**4**	..	**10**	..	**16**	..	**2**	..	**37**	..
Punjab	1	46	..	..	..	1	..	10	..	..	..	..	..	35	..
Cochin State	1	23	..	..	..	3	..	..	..	16	..	2	..	2	..
VII.—Metal Industries.	***379***	***68,048***	***9,997***	***1,937***	***6***	***3,889***	***4***	***555***	..	***33,454***	***106***	***27,394***	***9,840***	***1,596***	***41***
Aluminium Factories.	**4**	**428**	**1**	**5**	**1**	**15**	..	**31**	..	**296**	..	**68**	..	**13**	..
Bombay	3	168	..	1	..	3	..	27	..	110	..	22	..	5	..
Madras	1	260	1	4	1	12	..	4	..	186	..	46	..	8	..
Arms Factories (Bengal).	**6**	**5,871**	**1**	**143**	**1**	**228**	..	**20**	..	**4,494**	..	**974**	..	**12**	..
Arsenals	**16**	**4,691**	**2**	**260**	..	**277**	..	**28**	..	**1,937**	..	**1,951**	**2**	**238**	..
Baluchistan	1	537	..	37	..	17	..	..	..	129	..	338	..	16	..
Bengal	1	53	..	..	..	1	..	..	..	7	..	45	..	..	..
Bombay	2	1,211	2	74	..	50	..	3	..	490	..	488	2	106	..
Burma	1	292	..	32	..	19	..	2	..	83	..	139	..	17	..
Madras	1	767	..	41	..	44	..	10	..	281	..	387	..	4	..
Punjab	8	1,230	..	66	..	138	..	..	..	451	..	524	..	51	..
United Provinces	1	570	..	6	..	7	..	..	..	496	..	17	..	44	..
Mysore State	1	31	..	4	..	1	..	13	..	..	..	13	..	..	..
Brass, copper and bell-metal foundries.	**36**	**1,376**	**16**	**1**	..	**112**	..	**19**	..	**737**	..	**421**	**14**	**85**	**2**
Bengal	22	749	4	..	..	35	..	..	..	368	..	328	4	18	..
Bombay	6	283	..	..	..	64	..	19	..	158	..	28	..	14	..
Madras	3	111	12	..	..	8	..	..	..	43	..	34	10	26	2
United Provinces	5	233	..	1	..	6	..	..	..	168	..	31	..	27	..
Gun-carriage Factories (C. P. and Berar).	**1**	**1,525**	..	**38**	..	**88**	..	**36**	..	**954**	..	**380**	..	**29**	..

TABLE XV.—Occupation or Means of Livelihood.

Description of Factory, Mine, etc., and Province, State or Agency.	Number of factories.	Total number of persons employed.		Classification of persons employed. Direction, Supervision and Clerical Work. Europeans and Anglo-Indians.		Indians.		Skilled workmen. Europeans and Anglo-Indians.		Indians.		Unskilled labourers. Age 14 and over.		Under 14.	
		Males.	Females.	M.	F.	M.	F.	M.	F.	Males.	Females.	Males.	Females.	Males.	Females.
1	2	3	4	5	6	7	8	9	10	11	12	13	14	15	16
VII.—Metal Industries—contd.															
Iron Foundries .	**64**	**9,416**	**646**	**107**	**1**	**420**	..	**37**	..	**4,391**	**3**	**4,250**	**616**	**211**	**26**
Bengal . .	34	6,945	635	74	1	304	..	13	..	3,118	3	3,261	605	175	26
Bombay . .	12	1,189	..	10	..	46	..	..	..	667	..	459	..	7	..
Burma . .	5	736	..	19	..	19	..	22	..	345	..	331	..	..	..
Punjab . .	5	250	..	1	..	34	..	..	..	154	..	51	..	10	..
United Provinces .	6	193	3	1	..	12	..	2	..	72	..	94	3	12	..
Hyderabad State .	1	61	5	..	..	3	..	..	..	12	..	46	5	..	..
Mysore State .	1	42	3	2	..	2	..	..	..	23	..	8	3	7	..
Iron and Steel Works.*	**75**	**9,841**	**1,815**	**149**	..	**695**	**2**	**62**	..	**4,022**	**5**	**4,625**	**1,807**	**288**	**1**
Bengal . .	17	2,026	3	21	..	88	..	3	..	1,215	..	617	3	82	..
Bihar and Orissa .	4	3,231	1,796	95	..	201	2	13	..	387	2	2,584	1,792	1	..
Bombay . .	8	701	4	4	..	111	..	24	..	423	3	128	1	11	..
Madras . .	16	1,220	8	16	..	98	..	15	..	572	..	432	8	87	..
Punjab . .	20	2,014	..	7	..	139	..	5	..	1,121	..	670	..	72	..
United Provinces .	7	461	4	3	..	45	..	2	..	246	..	130	3	35	1
Cochin State .	2	65	..	3	..	4	..	..	..	19	..	39	..	..	..
Kashmir State .	1	73	..	..	..	9	..	..	..	39	..	25	..	..	..
Lock and Cutlery Works.	**12**	**1,046**	..	**5**	..	**42**	..	..	..	**813**	..	**121**	..	**65**	..
Bengal . .	1	87	..	..	..	9	..	..	..	62	..	9	..	7	..
Bombay . .	2	49	..	..	..	1	..	..	..	26	..	18	..	4	..
Punjab . .	1	50	..	..	..	..	..	..	..	25	..	21	..	4	..
United Provinces .	8	860	..	5	..	32	..	..	..	700	..	73	..	50	..
Machinery and Engineering Workshops.	**93**	**22,749**	**398**	**410**	**3**	**1,374**	**1**	**263**	..	**12,313**	**85**	**7,917**	**306**	**472**	**3**
Assam . .	2	72	..	..	..	5	..	..	..	40	..	27	..	..	..
Bengal . .	37	11,706	8	253	2	796	..	121	..	6,224	..	4,068	6	239	..
Bihar and Orissa .	7	553	9	8	..	27	..	1	..	284	..	207	9	26	..
Bombay . .	18	5,100	232	55	1	253	1	37	..	2,584	..	2,071	230	100	..
Burma . .	3	852	..	28	..	27	..	4	..	550	..	243	..	..	..
C. P. and Berar .	1	207	8	..	..	10	..	3	..	100	..	86	8	8	..
Madras . .	10	1,899	5	36	..	124	..	80	..	1,100	..	543	5	16	..
United Provinces .	9	1,479	105	21	..	75	..	6	..	878	85	486	17	13	3
Rajputana Agency	5	616	31	2	..	32	..	..	..	448	..	123	31	11	..
Travancore State .	1	265	..	2	..	25	..	11	..	105	..	63	..	59	..
Mints . . .	**4**	**2,380**	..	**45**	..	**164**	..	**26**	..	**628**	..	**1,450**	..	**58**	..
Bengal . .	1	922	..	21	..	46	..	12	..	137	..	706	..	..	..
Bombay . .	1	755	..	20	..	40	..	1	..	320	..	346	..	28	..
Hyderabad State .	1	677	..	4	..	74	..	13	..	164	..	392	..	30	..
Travancore State .	1	26	..	..	..	4	..	..	..	7	..	15	..	..	..
Public Works and Local Fund Workshops.	**10**	**1,241**	**2**	**7**	..	**81**	..	**14**	..	**559**	..	**568**	**2**	**12**	..
Bengal . .	2	392	..	1	..	17	..	3	..	4	..	367	..	..	..
Bombay . .	2	334	2	1	..	26	..	..	..	251	..	56	2	..	..
Burma . .	1	70	..	2	..	3	..	..	..	31	..	33	..	1	..
Madras . .	2	303	..	3	..	29	..	11	..	169	..	81	..	10	..
Punjab . .	2	89	..	..	..	4	..	..	..	67	..	17	..	1	..
Kashmir State .	1	53	..	..	..	2	..	..	..	37	..	14	..	..	..
Tin Works . .	**31**	**5,632**	**52**	**53**	..	**282**	**1**	**6**	..	**1,396**	**13**	**3,835**	**29**	**60**	**9**
Bengal . .	5	2,723	..	22	..	162	..	4	..	608	..	1,013	..	14	..
Bombay . .	7	1,052	5	5	..	51	..	..	..	332	..	651	5	13	..
Burma . .	17	1,688	47	24	..	59	1	2	..	401	13	1,187	24	15	9
Madras . .	1	104	..	2	..	5	..	..	..	35	..	44	..	18	..
Punjab . .	1	65	..	..	..	5	..	..	..	20	..	40	..	..	..
Others . .	**20**	**1,852**	**64**	**14**	..	**103**	..	**13**	..	**914**	..	**755**	**64**	**53**	..
Bengal . .	4	109	..	..	..	10	..	..	..	47	..	32	..	20	..
Bombay . .	10	732	5	2	..	20	..	..	..	453	..	226	5	31	..
Burma . .	1	477	59	9	..	21	..	11	..	98	..	338	59	..	..
Punjab . .	2	117	..	..	..	11	..	..	..	86	..	18	..	2	..
C. I. Agency .	2	383	..	3	..	32	..	2	..	230	..	116	..	..	..
Hyderabad State .	1	34	..	..	..	9	..	..	..	..	..	25	..	..	..
VIII.—Glass and Earthenware Industries.	***453***	***39,852***	***9,614***	***67***	..	***1,408***	***30***	***32***	..	***9,297***	***1,303***	***25,639***	***6,673***	***3,414***	***1,718***
Brick and Tile Factories.	**411**	**36,893**	**9,263**	**56**	..	**1,177**	**20**	**26**	..	**7,932**	**1,162**	**24,386**	**6,376**	**3,316**	**1,705**
Assam . .	1	101	35	1	..	2	..	..	..	7	..	90	32	1	3
Bengal . .	161	17,956	4,083	4	..	360	3	1	..	4,087	299	12,318	3,081	1,186	680
Bihar and Orissa .	8	914	309	1	..	18	..	..	..	372	45	373	171	150	93
Bombay . .	26	2,146	941	2	..	77	6	..	..	110	49	1,719	738	238	148
Burma . .	2	153	..	1	..	33	..	..	..	11	..	108	..	..	..
C. P. and Berar .	5	364	346	2	..	17	..	..	..	51	23	238	262	56	61
Madras . .	49	4,344	887	6	..	152	..	7	..	332	103	3,537	681	310	103
Punjab . .	89	4,802	1,353		..	164	9	..	..	1,630	399	2,481	609	527	336
United Provinces .	32	2,578	862	6	..	137	..	..	..	733	184	1,327	505	375	173
Baroda State .	3	313	201	..	..	13	2	..	..	87	42	158	132	60	25
C. I. Agency .	2	205	23	..	..	1	..	..	..	72	..	120	23	12	..
Cochin State .	15	707	100	..	..	38	..	1	..	47	..	510	88	111	12
Hyderabad State .	1	14	11	..	..	..	..	..	..	3	1	1	4	10	6
Kashmir State .	[illegible]	532	32	..	..	14	..	..	..	163	10	325	22	30	..
Mysore State .	1	295	59	4	..	6	..	..	..	11	..	140	6	134	53
Travancore State .	8	1,469	41	29	..	145	..	17	..	216	7	946	22	116	12

* Including working with iron sheets (making steel trunks, despatch boxes, etc.).

Part E.—Statistics of Industries, (*ii*) Provincial Distribution—*continued.*

Description of Factory, Mine, etc., and Province, State or Agency.	Number of factories.	Total number of persons employed.		Classification of persons employed.											
				Direction, Supervision and Clerical Work.				Skilled workmen.				Unskilled labourers.			
				Europeans and Anglo-Indians.		Indians.		Europeans and Anglo-Indians.		Indians.		Age 14 and over.		Under 14.	
		Males.	Females.	M.	F.	M.	F.	M.	F.	Males.	Females.	Males.	Females.	Males.	Females.
1	2	3	4	5	6	7	8	9	10	11	12	13	14	15	16
***VIII.—Glass and Earthenware Industries*—contd.**															
Glass Factories	**36**	**1,265**	**76**	**5**	..	**127**	..	**6**	..	**855**	**35**	**203**	**36**	**69**	**5**
Bengal	2	93	16	..	..	2	..	..	..	50	..	22	14	19	3
Bombay	1	43	1	..	..	2	..	2	..	12	..	17	1	10	..
C. P. and Berar	1	134	54	..	..	11	..	1	..	71	35	23	16	28	2
Madras	1	10	3	2	..	3	..	2	..	11	..	1	3	..	..
Punjab	2	72	..	1	..	8	..	..	..	40	..	15	..	8	..
United Provinces	28	815	2	2	..	97	..	1	..	656	..	55	2	4	..
C. I. Agency	1	89	..	..	..	4	..	..	..	15	..	70	..	..	..
Glass bangle Factories (Bombay).	**1**	**15**	**7**	..	..	**1**	..	..	..	**11**	..	**3**	**7**	..	..
Pottery Works	**5**	**1,679**	**268**	**6**	..	**98**	..	..	..	**499**	**6**	**1,047**	**254**	**29**	**8**
Bengal	2	1,048	124	3	..	60	..	..	..	337	..	639	123	9	1
Bihar and Orissa	1	40	15	..	..	5	..	..	..	25	5	10	10	..	..
C. P. and Berar	2	591	129	3	..	33	..	..	..	137	1	398	121	20	7
IX.—Industries connected with Chemical Products.	*455*	*43,738*	*5,620*	*585*	*2*	*2,722*	*35*	*97*	..	*11,050*	*876*	*26,767*	*4,314*	*2,517*	*404*
Ærated Water Factories.	**32**	**1,351**	**11**	**36**	**1**	**145**	..	**8**	..	**282**	**4**	**768**	**6**	**112**	..
Bengal	7	362	..	12	..	33	..	..	..	54	..	219	..	44	..
Bihar and Orissa	1	22	..	1	..	1	..	1	..	1	..	18	..	..	..
Bombay	9	310	4	1	..	29	..	..	..	92	4	170	..	18	..
Burma	4	277	..	5	..	33	..	3	..	63	..	173	..	..	..
Madras	6	205	6	11	..	13	..	2	..	39	..	134	6	6	..
United Provinces	1	23	1	1	1	..	..	..	..	3	..	..	..	19	..
Mysore State	1	47	..	3	..	2	..	2	..	5	..	35	..	..	..
Hyderabad State	3	105	..	2	..	34	..	..	..	25	..	19	..	25	..
Ammunition Factories.	**4**	**6,083**	**1**	**173**	..	**282**	..	**20**	..	**1,072**	..	**3,627**	**1**	**909**	..
Bengal	2	2,954	1	50	..	114	..	2	..	460	..	1,981	1	347	..
Bombay	1	2,336	..	60	..	71	..	8	..	470	..	1,165	..	562	..
Madras	1	793	..	63	..	97	..	10	..	142	..	481	..	..	..
Bulk oil Installations.	**10**	**1,355**	**49**	**6**	..	**85**	..	**1**	..	**703**	..	**540**	**49**	**20**	..
Bengal	1	277	1	1	..	11	..	..	..	168	..	97	1	..	..
Bombay	3	512	41	1	..	42	..	..	..	271	..	198	41	..	..
Madras	6	566	7	4	..	32	..	1	..	264	..	245	7	20	..
Card-board Factories (Bengal).	**1**	**26**	..	..	..	**1**	..	..	..	**25**	..	..	..	..	..
Chemical Works	**18**	**1,499**	**97**	**17**	..	**265**	**1**	..	..	**284**	..	**857**	**81**	**76**	**15**
Bengal	11	727	45	7	..	128	1	..	..	165	..	381	37	46	7
Madras	2	351	23	8	..	41	..	..	..	73	..	219	18	10	5
Bombay	2	74	7	..	..	12	..	..	..	11	..	50	7	1	..
Punjab	1	37	..	1	..	6	..	..	..	6	..	24	..	..	..
United Provinces	1	47	..	..	..	5	..	..	..	3	..	39	..	..	..
Baroda State	1	263	22	1	..	73	..	..	..	26	..	144	19	19	3
Dye Works	**30**	**2,174**	**425**	**7**	..	**119**	..	..	..	**692**	**237**	**1,262**	**178**	**94**	**10**
Bengal	1	74	..	2	..	1	..	..	..	1	..	70	..	..	..
Bombay	16	1,286	130	5	..	19	..	..	..	531	49	720	73	11	8
Madras	8	221	294	..	..	31	..	..	..	145	188	36	104	9	2
United Provinces	1	33	..	..	..	6	..	..	..	7	..	8	..	12	..
Baroda State	4	560	1	..	..	62	..	..	..	8	..	428	1	62	..
Gunpowder Factories (C. I. Agency).	**1**	**138**	..	..	..	**5**	..	..	..	**109**	..	**17**	..	**7**	..
Lac and cutch Factories.	**74**	**3,416**	**1,709**	**10**	..	**161**	**8**	**5**	..	**1,536**	**408**	**1,539**	**1,119**	**165**	**174**
Bengal	3	542	209	2	..	19	..	..	..	144	7	377	202	..	..
Bihar and Orissa	48	1,896	910	4	..	94	5	2	..	913	184	783	615	100	106
Bombay	1	76	78	..	..	..	..	..	..	41	42	6	3	29	33
Burma	1	117	9	2	..	7	..	3	..	5	..	95	6	5	3
C. P. and Berar	5	166	148	..	..	5	..	..	..	60	7	97	137	4	4
United Provinces	15	517	271	2	..	33	3	..	..	277	84	178	156	27	28
C. I. Agency	1	102	84	..	..	3	..	..	..	96	84	3	..	..	..
Match Factories	**6**	**491**	**146**	..	..	**39**	..	..	..	**143**	**6**	**225**	**106**	**84**	**34**
Bengal	1	23	..	..	..	2	..	..	..	..	..	12	..	9	..
Bombay	4	335	73	..	..	27	..	..	..	138	6	118	45	52	22
C. P. and Berar	1	133	73	..	..	10	..	..	..	5	..	95	61	23	12
Oil Mills	**208**	**8,154**	**1,591**	**45**	..	**967**	**11**	**15**	..	**1,830**	**114**	**5,011**	**1,374**	**286**	**92**
Assam	4	131	4	..	..	12	..	..	..	38	..	81	4	..	..
Bengal	118	3,660	609	6	..	354	..	2	..	941	69	2,267	532	90	8
Bihar and Orissa	7	372	42	..	..	29	..	..	..	108	..	218	42	17	..
Bombay	8	408	70	..	..	48	2	..	..	65	..	265	51	30	17
C. P. and Berar	3	86	2	..	..	16	..	..	..	11	..	59	2	..	..
Madras	34	1,585	503	29	..	160	4	..	..	325	45	976	410	95	44
United Provinces	10	596	302	3	..	33	..	1	..	98	..	435	279	26	23
Baroda State	3	90	12	..	..	16	..	..	..	7	..	67	12	..	..
Cochin State	9	578	36	..	..	46	..	4	..	90	..	411	36	18	..
Travancore State	12	648	11	7	..	258	5	8	..	138	..	232	6	10	..

TABLE XV.—Occupation or Means of Livelihood.

Description of Factory, Mine, etc., and Province, State or Agency.	Number of factories.	Total number of persons employed.		CLASSIFICATION OF PERSONS EMPLOYED.											
				Direction, Supervision and Clerical Work.				Skilled Workmen.				Unskilled Labourers.			
				Europeans and Anglo-Indians.		Indians.		Europeans and Anglo-Indians.		Indians.		Age 14 and over.		Under 14.	
		Males.	Females.	M.	F.	M.	F.	M.	F.	Males.	Females.	Males.	Females.	Males.	Females.
1	2	3	4	5	6	7	8	9	10	11	12	13	14	15	16
IX.—Industries connected with Chemical Products—contd.															
Paint Works	**2**	**50**	**20**	**1**	..	**7**	..	..	..	**8**	..	**33**	**20**	**1**	..
Bengal	1	28	..	..	..	4	..	..	..	4	..	19	..	1	..
C. P. and Berar	1	22	20	1	..	3	..	..	..	4	..	14	20	..	..
Paper Mills	**10**	**4,425**	**700**	**49**	..	**166**	..	**21**	..	**857**	**87**	**3,167**	**606**	**165**	**7**
Bengal	6	3,350	562	42	..	88	..	13	..	651	..	2,468	556	88	6
Bombay	2	220	117	1	..	24	..	..	..	78	87	115	29	2	1
United Provinces	1	763	13	6	..	46	..	6	..	122	..	520	13	63	..
Travancore State	1	92	8	..	..	8	..	2	..	6	..	64	8	12	..
Perfumery Factories	**7**	**194**	**6**	..	..	**58**	..	..	..	**56**	..	**68**	**6**	**12**	..
Bengal	1	27	..	..	..	9	..	..	..	7	..	11	..	..	..
United Provinces	6	167	6	..	..	49	..	..	..	49	..	57	6	12	..
Petroleum Refineries	**9**	**10,811**	**47**	**212**	..	**240**	..	**9**	..	**2,933**	..	**7,250**	**47**	**167**	..
Burma	7	10,707	40	211	..	233	..	8	..	2,878	..	7,223	40	154	..
Madras	2	104	7	1	..	7	..	1	..	55	..	27	7	13	..
Salt Crushing Mills	**4**	**1,205**	**581**	**2**	..	**12**	..	..	..	**43**	..	**1,007**	**538**	**141**	**43**
Bengal	1	42	24	..	..	..	..	..	..	6	..	36	24	..	..
Madras	3	1,163	557	2	..	12	..	..	..	37	..	971	514	141	43
Salt Refineries	**6**	**950**	**50**	**1**	..	**25**	..	..	..	**263**	..	**577**	**48**	**84**	**2**
Bombay	1	181	1	1	..	6	..	..	..	71	..	98	1	5	..
United Provinces	2	70	..	..	..	8	..	..	..	22	..	..	..	40	..
Travancore State	3	699	49	..	..	11	..	..	..	170	..	479	47	39	2
Saltpetre Refineries	**18**	**589**	**131**	..	..	**62**	**5**	..	..	**118**	**17**	**369**	**89**	**40**	**20**
Bihar and Orissa	11	274	54	..	..	21	..	..	..	50	7	171	35	32	12
Punjab	4	137	23	..	..	20	5	..	..	25	..	84	10	8	8
United Provinces	2	131	15	..	..	18	..	..	..	40	10	73	5	..	..
Madras	1	47	39	..	..	3	..	..	..	3	..	41	39	..	..
Soap and Candle Factories	**7**	**473**	..	**6**	..	**50**	..	**4**	..	**50**	..	**254**	..	**109**	..
Bengal	6	402	..	3	..	44	..	2	..	50	..	202	..	101	..
United Provinces	1	71	..	3	..	6	..	2	..	..	..	52	..	8	..
Others	**8**	**354**	**56**	**20**	..	**33**	..	**14**	..	**46**	**3**	**196**	**46**	**45**	**7**
Baluchistan	1	35	..	1	..	2	..	..	..	5	..	27	..	..	..
Bengal	2	51	..	2	..	1	..	..	..	4	..	30	..	14	..
Bombay	2	182	9	17	..	23	..	13	..	15	..	98	9	16	..
Madras	1	26	10	..	..	2	..	..	..	8	3	4	3	12	4
Kashmir State	1	18	8	..	..	..	..	..	..	..	..	18	8	..	..
Mysore State	1	42	29	..	..	5	..	1	..	14	..	19	26	3	3
X.—Food Industries.	***790***	***64,304***	***10,197***	***480***	***6***	***4,780***	***89***	***373***	***13***	***10,464***	***393***	***44,588***	***8,497***	***3,519***	***1,969***
Bakeries	**7**	**376**	..	**7**	..	**48**	..	**2**	..	**163**	..	**156**	..	..	..
Bengal	1	33	..	..	..	4	..	..	..	13	..	16	..	..	..
Bombay	2	145	..	2	..	15	..	2	..	19	..	107	..	..	..
Madras	1	98	..	3	..	15	..	..	..	70	..	10	..	..	..
Punjab	2	73	..	1	..	11	..	..	..	44	..	17	..	..	..
Mysore State	1	27	..	1	..	3	..	..	..	17	..	6	..	..	..
Biscuit Factories	**4**	**144**	**3**	**4**	**1**	**17**	..	..	..	**38**	..	**79**	**2**	**6**	..
Bengal	2	58	..	..	..	4	..	..	..	25	..	23	..	6	..
Bombay	1	39	3	3	1	5	..	..	..	11	..	20	2	..	..
Punjab	1	47	..	1	..	8	..	..	..	2	..	36	..	..	..
Breweries and Distilleries	**70**	**5,006**	**156**	**56**	..	**532**	..	**8**	..	**939**	**6**	**3,336**	**142**	**135**	**8**
Ajmer-Merwara	1	21	..	..	..	1	..	..	..	1	..	19	..	..	..
Assam	1	62	4	..	..	9	..	..	..	19	..	34	4	..	..
Baluchistan	1	83	..	1	..	1	..	..	..	35	..	46	..	..	..
Bengal	3	233	10	3	..	38	..	1	..	65	..	123	10	3	..
Bihar and Orissa	6	728	23	6	..	107	..	1	..	115	..	452	23	47	..
Bombay	15	783	35	4	..	73	..	1	..	108	5	594	26	3	4
Burma	1	137	..	3	..	6	..	..	..	..	..	128	..	..	..
C. P. and Berar	6	329	25	5	..	33	..	1	..	53	..	237	25	..	..
Madras	8	332	21	2	..	31	..	..	..	83	..	193	17	23	4
Punjab	6	702	..	11	..	49	..	..	..	126	..	509	..	7	..
United Provinces	9	986	4	12	..	101	..	..	..	232	..	631	4	10	..
C. I. Agency	3	87	11	1	..	22	..	..	..	22	..	42	11	..	..
Cochin State	1	41	1	..	..	7	..	..	..	22	1	12	..	..	..
Hyderabad State	4	133	17	1	..	23	..	..	..	2	..	110	17	2	..
Mysore State	3	262	5	7	..	15	..	4	..	41	..	158	5	37	..
Rajputana Agency	2	82	..	..	..	16	..	..	..	15	..	48	..	3	..
Dairy Farms	**14**	**876**	**89**	**42**	**1**	**65**	**1**	**19**	..	**91**	..	**654**	**83**	**5**	**4**
Bengal	1	84	2	2	1	4	1	..	..	19	..	59	..	..	..
Bombay	3	281	51	11	..	10	..	9	..	15	..	282	47	4	4
C. P. and Berar	2	82	5	5	..	6	..	..	..	7	..	64	5	..	..
United Provinces	4	206	11	8	..	23	..	6	..	34	..	135	11	..	..
Punjab	2	84	4	8	..	13	..	..	..	2	..	61	4	..	..
C. I. Agency	1	55	6	3	..	4	..	4	..	..	..	43	6	1	..
Mysore State	1	84	10	5	..	5	..	..	..	14	..	60	10	..	..

PART E.—STATISTICS OF INDUSTRIES, (*ii*) PROVINCIAL DISTRIBUTION—*continued.*

Description of Factory, Mine, etc., and Province, State or Agency.	Number of factories.	Total number of persons employed.		CLASSIFICATION OF PERSONS EMPLOYED. Direction, Supervision and Clerical Work. Europeans and Anglo-Indians.		Indians.		Skilled Workmen. Europeans and Anglo-Indians.		Indians.		Unskilled Labourers. Age 14 and over.		Under 14.	
		Males.	Females.	M.	F.	M.	F.	M.	F.	Males.	Females.	Males.	Females.	Males.	Females.
1	2	3	4	5	6	7	8	9	10	11	12	13	14	15	16
X.—Food Industries —contd.															
FISH CURING WORKS.	27	1,198	990	4	..	78	..	3	..	189	91	678	760	246	139
Bombay	3	37	52	..	..	3	..	..	..	..	..	28	42	6	10
Madras	23	1,137	935	..	..	75	..	..	..	189	91	633	716	240	128
Cochin State	1	24	3	4	..	..	..	3	..	..	..	17	2	..	1
FLOUR AND RICE MILLS.	403	37,790	4,584	201	..	2,674	83	247	13	5,325	105	28,323	3,951	1,020	432
Bengal	44	1,478	456	4	..	155	1	13	..	168	3	1,025	444	93	8
Bihar and Orissa	5	244	59	..	..	20	..	..	..	98	..	121	50	10	..
Bombay	56	2,183	236	18	..	334	9	6	..	404	3	1,371	210	50	14
Burma	152	27,807	2,065	147	..	1,268	35	208	13	3,452	71	22,245	1,701	487	245
C. P. and Berar	1	11	20	..	..	1	..	..	..	5	..	5	20	..	..
Madras	81	3,246	1,475	11	..	526	38	7	..	560	8	1,848	1,276	294	153
Punjab	37	1,878	68	10	..	239	..	11	..	384	1	1,172	66	62	1
United Provinces	10	523	71	8	..	65	..	2	..	137	6	309	61	2	4
Baroda State	1	30	36	..	..	4	..	..	..	9	..	16	30	1	6
C. I. Agency	2	60	21	..	..	8	..	..	..	22	6	30	15	..	..
Cochin State	3	62	16	2	..	13	..	..	..	9	..	38	16	..	..
Hyderabad State	8	206	35	1	..	34	..	..	..	32	7	118	27	21	1
Travancore State	3	62	26	..	..	7	..	..	..	30	..	25	26	..	..
FORAGE PRESSES	14	705	479	3	..	60	..	..	..	153	15	425	411	64	53
Bengal	4	137	9	1	..	28	..	..	..	2	..	103	9	3	..
Bihar and Orissa	4	351	395	1	..	20	..	..	..	130	..	168	355	32	40
Madras	2	67	45	..	..	8	..	..	..	6	15	38	20	15	10
Punjab	1	37	..	1	..	..	..	..	..	6	..	30	..	..	..
C. I. Agency	1	40	4	..	..	2	..	..	..	..	..	28	2	10	2
Hyderabad State	1	14	22	..	..	1	..	..	..	5	..	8	22	..	..
Rajputana Agency	1	59	4	..	..	1	..	..	..	4	..	50	3	4	1
OPIUM, GANJA, TOBACCO, SNUFF AND VINEGAR FACTORIES.	57	6,057	1,193	65	3	678	5	12	..	1,434	122	2,683	907	1,185	156
Bengal	7	630	217	3	..	25	..	8	..	134	118	312	86	148	13
Bihar and Orissa	4	1,447	443	41	3	95	..	4	..	53	..	1,042	397	212	48
Bombay	6	311	358	3	..	1	..	..	..	89	1	159	307	59	50
C. P. and Berar	8	614	137	..	..	290	..	..	..	50	..	208	107	66	30
Madras	24	1,970	2	8	..	96	1	..	..	892	..	448	1	526	..
Punjab	1	29	..	1	..	3	..	..	..	8	..	1	..	16	..
United Provinces	3	733	10	9	..	152	4	..	..	107	3	407	3	58	..
Baroda State	1	60	1	..	..	3	..	..	..	19	..	38	1	..	..
Hyderabad State	1	127	25	..	..	2	..	..	..	..	..	50	5	75	20
Mysore State	2	136	..	..	..	11	..	..	..	82	..	18	..	25	..
SLAUGHTER HOUSES AND JERKED MEAT WORKS.	10	1,529	1,106	4	..	52	..	2	..	146	1	874	749	451	356
Bombay	1	68	1	2	..	6	..	2	..	..	..	58	1	..	..
C. P. and Berar	8	1,424	1,105	2	..	45	..	..	..	113	1	816	748	448	356
Punjab	1	37	..	..	..	1	..	..	..	33	..	..	..	3	..
SUGAR FACTORIES	76	7,502	617	52	..	469	..	26	..	1,312	45	5,560	523	142	49
Bengal	10	834	43	8	..	42	..	..	..	150	..	622	43	12	..
Bihar and Orissa	26	2,524	35	18	..	87	..	11	..	282	4	2,058	23	68	8
Bombay	11	212	153	..	..	19	..	4	..	34	41	153	109	2	3
Madras	5	1,462	216	16	..	137	..	10	..	267	..	999	200	33	16
N.-W. F. Province	1	62	..	..	..	4	..	..	..	18	..	40	..	..	..
Punjab	4	357	50	1	..	14	..	..	..	18	..	321	50	3	..
United Provinces	9	1,410	3	6	..	67	..	1	..	461	..	873	3	2	..
Baroda State	1	117	7	..	..	9	..	..	..	10	..	95	5	3	2
C. I. Agency	5	225	59	..	..	15	..	..	..	16	..	181	40	13	19
Mysore State	3	248	44	3	..	9	..	..	..	50	..	186	44	..	..
Rajputana Agency	1	51	7	..	..	6	..	..	..	7	..	32	6	6	1
WATER WORKS	30	2,690	877	32	..	145	..	10	..	616	..	1,639	811	248	66
Bengal	6	250	2	8	..	28	..	..	..	35	..	179	2	..	..
Bihar and Orissa	1	37	..	1	..	1	..	..	..	17	..	..	..	18	..
Bombay	1	20	..	2	..	10	..	1	..	..	..	..	..	7	..
Burma	2	50	..	4	..	..	..	..	..	12	..	34	..	..	..
C. P. and Berar	2	835	658	1	..	7	..	..	..	54	..	618	602	155	56
Madras	4	398	202	7	..	18	..	..	..	89	..	272	192	12	10
Punjab	3	185	..	2	..	20	..	..	..	49	..	95	..	19	..
United Provinces	5	438	10	4	..	19	..	1	..	109	..	277	10	28	..
Baroda State	1	57	..	..	..	10	..	..	..	5	..	42	..	..	..
Hyderabad State	1	207	..	..	..	23	..	..	..	173	..	11	..	..	..
Mysore State	3	160	3	1	..	7	..	8	..	53	..	82	3	9	..
Rajputana Agency	1	53	2	2	..	2	..	..	..	20	..	29	2	..	..
OTHERS	8	331	103	10	1	22	..	44	..	57	8	181	88	17	6
Bengal	4	139	68	10	1	14	..	44	..	19	8	50	59	2	..
Bombay	1	10	15	..	..	2	..	..	..	3	..	5	12	..	3
Madras	1	65	20	..	..	3	..	..	..	5	..	42	17	15	3
Punjab	1	91	..	..	..	1	..	..	..	10	..	80	..	..	..
Cochin State	1	26	..	..	..	2	..	..	..	20	..	4	..	..	..
XI.—Industries of Dress.	*90*	*9,817*	*379*	*169*	*40*	*643*	*90*	*191*	*197*	*6,986*	*99*	*1,960*	*155*	*632*	*7*
BOOT AND SHOE FACTORIES.	23	5,636	127	69	1	238	2	13	..	4,041	..	243	124	432	..
Bengal	7	471	..	..	..	9	..	..	..	418	..	37	..	7	..
Bombay	2	784	57	6	..	30	..	..	..	625	..	40	57	33	..
Madras	9	571	7	9	..	30	2	10	..	450	..	30	5	42	..
United Provinces	4	3,217	63	52	1	167	..	2	..	2,522	..	132	62	342	..
Mysore State	1	43	..	2	..	2	..	1	..	26	..	4	..	8	..

TABLE XV.—OCCUPATION OR MEANS OF LIVELIHOOD.

Description of Factory, Mine, etc., and Province, State or Agency.	Number of factories.	Total number of persons employed.		CLASSIFICATION OF PERSONS EMPLOYED											
				DIRECTION, SUPERVISION AND CLERICAL WORK.				SKILLED WORKMEN.				UNSKILLED LABOURERS.			
				Europeans and Anglo-Indians.		Indians.		Europeans and Anglo-Indians.		Indians.		Age 14 and over.		Under 14.	
		Males.	Females.	M.	F.	M.	F.	M.	F.	Males.	Females.	Males.	Females.	Males.	Females.
1	2	3	4	5	6	7	8	9	10	11	12	13	14	15	16
XI.—Industries of Dress—contd.															
DRESS FACTORIES	32	2,570	173	86	39	197	..	23	127	1,483	..	671	7	110	..
Bengal	9	1,056	34	69	32	115	..	17	2	538	..	290	..	27	..
Bombay	2	168	..	..	..	12	..	..	..	25	..	125	..	6	..
Madras	8	1,001	133	14	5	63	..	6	125	694	..	182	3	42	..
Punjab	8	193	..	2	..	5	..	..	..	165	..	11	..	15	..
United Provinces	1	28	3	1	2	..	..	..	..	..	..	26	1	1	..
Hyderabad State	3	87	3	..	..	1	..	..	..	44	..	30	3	12	..
Mysore State	1	32	..	..	..	1	..	..	..	17	..	7	..	7	..
HOSIERY FACTORIES.	12	1,184	72	13	..	160	18	..	..	755	29	216	24	40	1
Bengal	2	659	..	13	..	45	..	..	..	508	..	90	..	3	..
Bihar and Orissa	1	25	..	..	..	1	..	..	..	23	..	1	..	..	..
Bombay	4	347	63	..	..	108	18	..	..	132	21	107	24	..	..
Punjab	1	40	..	..	..	3	..	..	..	20	..	6	..	11	..
Kashmir State	3	82	8	..	..	..	..	..	..	62	8	5	..	15	..
Mysore State	1	31	1	..	..	3	..	..	..	10	..	7	..	11	1
UMBRELLA FACTORIES	17	814	..	..	..	40	..	85	..	553	..	97	..	39	..
Bengal	14	656	..	..	..	33	..	..	..	521	..	63	..	39	..
Bombay	3	158	..	..	..	7	..	85	..	32	..	34	..	..	..
OTHERS	6	213	..	1	..	8	..	..	..	154	..	33	..	17	..
Bengal	1	24	..	..	..	1	..	..	..	22	..	1	..	..	..
Madras	4	158	..	1	..	6	..	..	..	102	..	32	..	17	..
Punjab	1	31	..	..	..	1	..	..	..	30	..	..	..	..	..
XII.—Furniture Industries.	*50*	*3,399*	*50*	*29*	*1*	*233*	..	*30*	..	*2,079*	..	*726*	*38*	*230*	*11*
FURNITURE FACTORIES.	46	3,060	50	26	1	219	..	29	..	1,868	..	693	38	223	11
Bengal	14	905	11	18	1	39	..	29	..	678	..	134	10	7	..
Bombay	9	491	..	4	..	77	..	..	..	284	..	120	..	6	..
C. P. and Berar	4	253	4	1	..	12	..	..	..	178	..	62	4	..	..
Madras	4	310	9	1	..	14	..	..	..	217	..	35	1	43	8
Punjab	3	228	..	2	..	6	..	..	..	192	..	18	..	10	..
United Provinces	3	157	1	..	..	13	..	..	..	119	..	21	1	4	..
Baroda State	1	62	..	..	..	11	..	..	..	39	..	12	..	..	..
C. I. Agency	4	217	25	..	..	26	..	..	..	99	..	61	22	31	3
Hyderabad State	1	36	..	..	..	10	..	..	..	19	..	7	..	..	..
Kashmir State	1	26	..	..	..	2	..	..	..	20	..	4	..	..	..
Mysore State	2	375	..	..	..	9	..	..	..	23	..	221	..	122	..
TENT FACTORIES	4	262	..	3	..	16	..	1	..	204	..	31	..	7	..
Bombay	1	104	..	..	..	10	..	..	..	82	..	7	..	5	..
Punjab	1	68	..	..	..	2	..	..	..	62	..	4	..	..	..
United Provinces	2	90	..	3	..	4	..	1	..	60	..	20	..	2	..
XIII.—Industries connected with Buildings.	*163*	*17,015*	*5,153*	*81*	*1*	*620*	*18*	*66*	*14*	*3,034*	*158*	*12,025*	*4,312*	*1,169*	*650*
BUILDING WORKSHOPS (Baluchistan).	1	212	..	5	..	9	..	..	..	61	..	134	..	3	..
LIME WORKS AND KILNS.	53	5,508	2,122	17	..	228	2	10	..	345	4	4,486	1,883	422	233
Bengal	3	257	37	1	..	7	..	4	..	29	..	212	33	4	4
Bihar and Orissa	8	581	356	2	..	34	2	4	..	115	4	372	289	54	61
Bombay	12	3,038	833	..	..	114	..	..	..	..	..	2,672	727	252	106
C. P. and Berar	17	970	817	8	..	40	..	2	..	83	..	752	760	85	57
Punjab	5	244	41	1	..	12	..	..	..	24	..	191	38	16	3
United Provinces	7	367	38	3	..	16	..	..	..	94	..	251	36	3	2
C. I. Agency	1	51	..	2	..	5	..	..	..	..	..	36	..	8	..
STONE, MARBLE AND CEMENT WORKS.	57	5,698	1,909	54	1	193	16	55	14	1,394	52	3,656	1,491	409	332
Bengal	7	441	21	34	..	23	..	..	..	173	4	208	17	3	..
Bihar and Orissa	12	1,992	785	5	..	49	..	12	..	233	..	1,657	743	36	42
Bombay	3	176	145	..	..	5	1	..	..	23	16	141	124	7	4
Madras	5	481	141	6	1	53	14	40	14	58	20	313	78	11	14
United Provinces	25	1,557	766	2	..	44	1	1	..	152	1	1,053	498	305	266
C. I. Agency	2	102	..	..	..	7	..	..	..	95	..	..	..	..	..
Hyderabad State	1	902	40	6	..	16	..	..	..	563	..	270	34	45	6
Mysore State	1	28	..	..	..	..	..	2	..	10	..	14	..	2	..
Travancore State	1	17	11	1	..	1	..	..	..	15	11	..	..	..	..
SURKI FACTORIES	52	5,599	1,122	5	..	185	..	1	..	1,324	102	3,749	935	335	85
Bengal	37	4,846	979	4	..	130	..	1	..	1,172	102	3,268	816	271	61
Bihar and Orissa	1	52	22	..	..	2	..	..	..	30	..	20	22	..	..
Punjab	3	99	5	1	..	8	..	..	..	15	..	75	5	..	..
United Provinces	10	578	116	..	..	44	..	..	..	105	..	365	92	64	24
Kashmir State	1	24	..	..	..	1	..	..	..	2	..	21	..	..	..

PART E.—STATISTICS OF INDUSTRIES, (*ii*) PROVINCIAL DISTRIBUTION—*continued.*

Description of Factory, Mine, etc., and Province, State or Agency.	Number of factories.	Total number of persons employed.		CLASSIFICATION OF PERSONS EMPLOYED.											
				Direction, Supervision and Clerical Work.				Skilled workmen.				Unskilled labourers.			
				Europeans and Anglo-Indians.		Indians.		Europeans and Anglo-Indians.		Indians.		Age 14 and over.		Under 14.	
		Males.	Females.	M.	F.	M.	F.	M.	F.	Males.	Females.	Males.	Females.	Males.	Females.
1	2	3	4	5	6	7	8	9	10	11	12	13	14	15	16
XIV.—Industries connected with Transport.	***242***	***193,520***	***1,597***	***1,974***	***28***	***4,155***	..	***9,925***	..	***77,876***	***4***	***36,515***	***1,492***	***775***	***73***
BICYCLE WORKS	**3**	**74**	..	**1**	..	**7**	..	..	..	**43**	..	**21**	..	**2**	..
Bengal	2	44	..	1	..	4	..	..	..	18	..	19	..	2	..
Hyderabad State	1	30	..	..	..	3	..	..	..	25	..	2	..	..	..
COACH-BUILDING FACTORIES.	**40**	**2,904**	**6**	**42**	..	**183**	..	..	..	**2,011**	..	**532**	**6**	**136**	—
Bengal	9	1,322	3	19	..	25	..	..	..	1,066	..	144	3	68	..
Bombay	6	179	1	..	..	8	..	..	..	91	..	78	1	2	..
Madras	5	597	2	4	..	60	..	..	..	411	..	79	2	43	..
N.-W. F. Province	3	63	..	..	..	3	..	..	..	27	..	32	..	1	..
Punjab	4	182	..	3	..	10	..	..	..	131	..	36	..	2	..
United Provinces	6	171	..	2	..	12	..	..	..	50	..	107	..	..	..
Hyderabad State	3	130	..	..	..	1	..	..	..	117	..	8	..	4	..
Mysore State	3	199	..	14	..	62	..	..	..	60	..	47	..	16	..
Rajputana Agency	1	61	..	..	..	2	..	..	..	58	..	1	..	..	..
DREDGING WORKS	**3**	**605**	**1**	**5**	..	**21**	..	..	..	**104**	..	**475**	**1**	..	..
Bengal	2	180	1	3	..	11	..	..	..	16	..	150	1	..	..
Kashmir State	1	425	..	2	..	10	..	..	..	88	..	325	..	..	..
MOTOR-CAR WORKS	**18**	**1,487**	**1**	**70**	..	**106**	..	**36**	..	**1,087**	..	**184**	**1**	**4**	..
Bengal	7	963	..	46	..	41	..	22	..	729	..	125	..	..	..
Bombay	5	270	..	11	..	24	..	2	..	217	..	12	..	4	..
Madras	2	61	1	9	..	10	..	6	..	22	..	14	1	..	..
Punjab	1	104	..	..	..	4	..	1	..	80	..	19	..	..	..
United Provinces	1	25	..	1	..	20	..	..	..	..	..	4	..	..	..
Hyderabad State	1	41	..	1	..	3	..	2	..	29	..	6	..	..	..
Mysore State	1	23	..	2	..	4	..	3	..	10	..	4	..	..	..
RAILWAY WORKSHOPS	**118**	**97,702**	**1,021**	**822**	**12**	**3,064**	..	**2,591**	..	**62,865**	**4**	**28,059**	**986**	**301**	**19**
Ajmer-Merwara	3	8,373	4	65	..	237	..	299	..	5,659	4	2,027	..	86	..
Assam	5	999	4	6	..	27	..	39	..	693	..	225	4	9	..
Baluchistan	3	340	..	4	..	6	..	2	..	179	..	145	..	4	..
Bengal	15	22,272	463	219	..	775	..	319	..	15,129	..	5,780	453	50	16
Bihar and Orissa	7	10,031	238	51	..	113	..	231	..	6,726	..	2,898	238	12	..
Bombay	13	15,337	151	151	..	473	..	294	..	9,782	..	4,629	143	8	8
Burma	4	3,224	..	46	..	197	..	82	..	2,069	..	830	..	..	..
C. P. and Berar	11	1,504	78	11	..	73	..	51	..	520	..	793	77	56	..
Madras	23	12,474	6	116	2	606	..	778	..	7,207	..	3,727	4	40	—
Punjab	19	10,873	..	44	..	144	..	148	..	7,673	..	2,836	..	28	..
United Provinces	5	7,182	14	74	..	237	..	118	..	4,834	..	1,919	14	..	..
Cochin State	1	22	1	..	..	..	..	..	..	2	..	20	1	..	..
Hyderabad State	3	3,259	61	24	10	138	..	196	..	1,516	..	1,377	51	8	..
Mysore State	4	407	1	4	..	13	..	33	..	194	..	168	1	..	..
Rajputana Agency	2	1,405	..	7	..	25	..	1	..	682	..	690	..	..	..
SHIPWRIGHTS (Bombay).	**6**	**5,161**	**3**	**50**	..	**143**	..	**50**	..	**3,471**	..	**1,439**	**3**	**8**	..
SHIPYARDS AND DOCK YARDS.*	**21**	**9,556**	**110**	**152**	**14**	**368**	..	**138**	..	**6,064**	..	**2,780**	**95**	**119**	**1**
Bengal	11	7,306	1	107	..	266	..	59	..	5,012	..	1,781	1	81	..
Bombay	3	125	1	..	..	10	..	..	..	46	..	34	..	35	1
Burma	4	1,453	108	37	14	17	..	10	..	567	..	822	94	..	..
Madras	3	672	..	8	..	10	..	69	..	439	..	143	..	3	..
TELEGRAPH AND POSTAL WORKSHOPS	**10**	**1,566**	**4**	**57**	**1**	**149**	..	**35**	..	**927**	..	**371**	**3**	**27**	..
Bengal	1	847	..	8	..	41	..	2	..	600	..	196	..	..	..
Bombay	1	38	..	2	..	4	..	..	..	15	..	16	..	1	..
Burma	2	122	..	36	..	34	..	..	..	7	..	45	..	..	..
C. P. and Berar	1	60	1	7	1	3	..	30	..	2	..	18	..	..	..
Madras	3	135	3	3	..	32	..	3	..	48	..	47	3	2	..
United Provinces	1	329	..	1	..	25	..	..	..	233	..	46	..	24	..
Travancore State	1	35	..	..	..	10	..	..	..	22	..	3	..	..	..
TRAMWAY WORKSHOPS.	**14**	**2,539**	**23**	**50**	**1**	**127**	..	**45**	..	**971**	..	**1,300**	**22**	**46**	..
Bengal	4	818	..	21	..	20	..	..	..	319	..	458	..	..	..
Bombay	3	664	1	15	..	42	..	12	..	242	..	333	1	20	..
C. P. and Berar	1	133	1	..	..	6	..	..	..	55	..	62	1	10	..
Madras	1	203	..	3	..	11	..	1	..	158	..	120	..	..	..
United Provinces	1	245	1	6	1	28	..	8	..	94	..	109	..	..	..
Baroda State	1	191	8	2	..	8	..	2	..	65	..	102	8	12	..
Cochin State	1	34	..	..	..	3	..	2	..	15	..	14	..	..	..
Mysore State	2	161	12	3	..	9	..	20	..	23	..	102	12	4	..
OTHERS	**9**	**1,926**	**428**	**25**	..	**52**	..	**30**	..	**333**	..	**1,354**	**375**	**132**	**53**
Bengal	5	725	257	3	..	15	..	..	..	32	..	591	204	84	53
Madras	3	1,181	171	21	..	35	..	30	..	299	..	748	171	48	..
Baroda State	1	20	..	1	..	2	..	..	..	2	..	15	..	..	..

* Inclusive of Port Commissioner's and Port Trust Workshops.

TABLE XV.—Occupation or Means of Livelihood. Part E.—Statistics of Industries, (ii) Provincial Distribution—*concluded.*

Description of Factory, Mine, etc., and Province, State or Agency.	Number of factories.	Total number of persons employed.		Classification of persons employed.											
				Direction, Supervision and Clerical Work.				Skilled workmen.				Unskilled labourers.			
				Europeans and Anglo-Indians.		Indians.		Europeans and Anglo-Indians.		Indians.		Age 14 and over.		Under 14.	
		Males.	Females.	M.	F.	M.	F.	M.	F.	Males.	Females.	Males.	Females.	Males.	
1	2	3	4	5	6	7	8	9	10	11	12	13	14	15	16
XV.—Production and transmission of physical forces.	*64*	*8,041*	*198*	*259*	*3*	*414*	..	*90*	..	*4,940*	*21*	*3,007*	*103*	*31*	*1*
Electric power and lighting works.	**31**	**2,003**	**47**	**117**	..	**134**	..	**30**	..	**701**	..	**953**	**46**	**18**	**1**
Bombay	1	117	4	11	..	3	..	7	..	40	..	56	4	..	..
Burma	2	267	..	53	..	3	..	2	..	110	..	99	..	..	..
Madras	3	287	2	5	..	10	..	22	..	92	..	156	2	2	..
Punjab	4	350	20	7	..	35	..	..	..	142	..	162	20	4	..
United Provinces	4	177	..	3	..	11	..	2	..	98	..	61	..	2	..
Baroda State	1	58	..	..	..	17	..	..	..	9	..	32	..	..	..
C. I. Agency	3	110	13	3	..	5	..	..	..	15	..	86	13	1	..
Hyderabad State	1	34	6	..	..	3	..	..	..	15	..	16	6	..	..
Mysore State	6	389	2	33	..	26	..	46	..	112	..	163	1	9	1
Kashmir State	6	214	..	2	..	21	..	1	..	68	..	122	..	..	..
Gas Works	**14**	**4,643**	**37**	**119**	**3**	**176**	..	**7**	..	**3,137**	**21**	**1,203**	**13**	**1**	..
Bengal	8	3,402	19	107	3	132	..	7	..	2,556	15	600	1	..	..
Bombay	2	1,065	18	9	..	31	..	..	..	538	6	487	12	..	..
C. P. and Berar	1	23	..	..	..	2	..	..	..	11	..	10	..	..	..
Punjab	1	28	..	..	..	2	..	..	..	11	..	15	..	..	..
Rajputana Agency	2	125	..	3	..	9	..	..	..	21	..	91	..	1	..
Hydraulic Works (Bombay).	**1**	**552**	..	**2**	..	**14**	..	..	..	**186**	..	**350**	..	..	..
Ice Factories	**18**	**843**	**44**	**21**	..	**90**	..	**3**	..	**216**	..	**501**	**44**	**12**	..
Ajmer-Merwara	1	44	..	..	..	2	..	..	..	19	..	17	..	6	..
Bengal	4	340	..	15	..	29	..	2	..	78	..	216	..	..	..
Bihar and Orissa	1	21	1	..	..	..	..	..	..	3	..	15	1	3	..
Bombay	5	194	..	1	..	35	..	..	..	66	..	92	..	..	..
Madras	1	54	40	2	..	3	..	1	..	3	..	45	40	..	..
Punjab	1	29	..	1	..	1	..	..	..	11	..	16	..	..	..
United Provinces	3	118	3	..	..	14	..	..	..	20	..	82	3	2	..
Rajputana Agency	2	43	..	2	..	6	..	..	..	16	..	18	..	1	..
XVI.—Industries of Luxury.	*389*	*45,179*	*395*	*601*	*40*	*4,897*	*10*	*463*	*29*	*29,368*	*19*	*8,748*	*223*	*1,179*	*18*
Games and sport works.	**4**	**365**	..	**5**	..	**34**	..	..	..	**276**	..	**30**	..	**20**	..
Madras	1	53	..	2	..	3	..	..	..	41	..	7	..	..	..
Punjab	3	312	..	3	..	31	..	..	..	235	..	23	..	20	..
Jewellery workshops.	**21**	**1,564**	**1**	**34**	..	**155**	..	**16**	..	**1,004**	..	**243**	**1**	**112**	..
Bengal	10	743	..	13	..	39	..	..	..	561	..	96	..	44	..
Bihar and Orissa	1	22	..	1	..	2	..	..	..	19	..	..	..	..	..
Bombay	4	209	..	..	..	57	..	..	..	62	..	81	..	9	..
Madras	2	398	..	10	..	42	..	5	..	268	..	31	..	42	..
Punjab	1	88	1	..	..	2	..	..	..	14	..	15	1	7	..
United Provinces	1	21	..	..	..	1	..	..	..	10	..	5	..	5	..
Mysore State	2	133	..	10	..	12	..	11	..	80	..	15	..	5	..
Photo Works	**9**	**14**	**1**	**22**	**1**	**76**	..	**4**	..	**264**	..	**336**	..	**12**	..
Bengal	4	411	1	21	1	20	..	4	..	161	..	203	..	2	..
Punjab	1	22	..	..	..	3	..	..	..	15	..	4	..	..	..
United Provinces	3	253	..	1	..	44	..	..	..	74	..	124	..	10	..
Kashmir State	1	28	..	..	..	9	..	..	..	14	..	5	..	..	..
Printing Presses	**341**	**41,294**	**304**	**477**	**23**	**4,408**	**8**	**418**	**22**	**27,136**	**12**	**7,836**	**221**	**1,019**	**18**
Ajmer-Merwara	4	274	..	2	..	21	..	..	..	196	..	30	..	16	..
Assam	1	298	..	1	..	32	..	5	..	239	..	21	..	..	..
Bengal	105	12,456	35	158	6	1,317	5	137	18	8,745	2	1,904	4	195	..
Bihar and Orissa	7	360	4	1	..	59	1	..	..	256	..	36	3	8	..
Bombay	67	8,529	226	64	6	1,120	2	76	..	4,876	10	2,137	191	256	17
Burma	8	1,746	9	73	8	154	..	5	1	1,187	..	269	..	58	..
C. P. and Berar	3	495	..	11	..	54	..	3	..	351	..	76	..	..	..
Madras	52	6,783	22	53	2	518	..	85	..	4,902	..	971	19	254	1
N.-W. F. Province	2	77	..	1	..	6	..	1	..	50	..	19	..	..	..
Punjab	28	3,158	3	31	..	418	..	24	3	2,070	..	550	..	65	..
United Provinces	27	4,603	..	61	..	382	..	71	..	2,671	..	1,320	..	98	..
Baroda State	4	270	..	..	..	41	..	..	..	213	..	16	..	..	..
C. I. Agency	3	298	..	1	..	33	..	..	..	189	..	70	..	..	..
Cochin State	5	207	1	..	..	21	..	..	..	138	..	36	1	12	..
Hyderabad State	2	60	1	4	..	4	..	..	..	24	..	22	1	6	..
Kashmir State	3	259	..	..	..	43	..	..	..	95	..	121	..	..	..
Mysore State	9	714	1	12	1	110	..	11	..	429	..	102	..	41	..
Rajputana Agency	3	191	..	..	..	15	..	..	..	87	..	80	..	..	..
Travancore State	7	321	2	4	..	51	..	..	..	418	..	88	2	10	..
Others	**14**	**1,262**	**19**	**63**	**16**	**154**	**2**	**25**	..	**888**	..	**306**	**1**	**9**	..
Assam	1	162	..	1	..	13	..	1	..	80	..	67	..	..	..
Bengal	10	936	17	52	15	134	2	18	..	564	..	167	..	1	..
Bombay	2	84	1	10	1	2	..	6	..	18	..	40	..	8	..
Travancore State	1	60	1	..	..	5	..	..	..	26	..	29	1	..	..

TABLE XVI.

Occupation by selected Castes, Tribes or Races.

1. This Table was not compiled in the Andamans and Nicobars; while in Ajmer-Merwara, Burma, the North-West Frontier Province and Rajputana it was compiled only for Europeans, Anglo-Indians and Armenians. The present Table for all India contains a selection from the various Provincial tables. It is divided into two parts. Part I deals with the indigenous castes and tribes and Part II with Europeans, Anglo-Indians and Armenians. To economize space, figures for the smaller units, such as Baluchistan, Coorg, Cochin, etc., have been omitted from Part I.

2. For the purpose of this Table the occupations have been arranged under 13 main heads corresponding to the sub-classes of the scheme of classification adopted in Part A of Table XV: these heads have been subdivided where necessary, in order to distinguish between different occupations. Columns 7 to 10 of Part I are intended to throw light on the extent to which the traditional caste occupations are followed. The object of columns 11 and 12 is to make it possible to discount the tendency of functional castes to return their traditional occupations as their means of livelihood. Except in Bombay, where the contrary course has been followed, the figures in the subsequent columns are exclusive of the number of actual workers shown in columns 7 and 8 as following the traditional occupation. Statistics for columns 9 to 12 were not compiled for Bihar and Orissa, nor for the Presidency and Burdwan Divisions, Darjeeling and Cooch Behar in Bengal, nor for the State of Cochin.

3. Within each Province, State or Agency the castes are arranged in alphabetical order. The figures for Provinces include those for the States attached to them, except in the case of Bombay, where this Table was compiled for British territory only, and of Madras, where they exclude those for Cochin and Travancore. For the reasons given on the title page to Table IX the total strength of a caste in this Table does not necessarily tally with that in Table XIII.

4. As already noted, the statistics for Europeans, Anglo-Indians and Armenians are given separately in Part II of the Table. Such statistics were not compiled in Travancore, and in Cochin they were tabulated in a different form and so could not be incorporated here. In Baroda figures for Europeans and Anglo-Indians were amalgamated, while in Bombay they were compiled only for the Anglo-Indians in Sind. Columns 7 to 12 of Part I have been omitted from this Part.

5. Some supplementary statistics similar to those at pages 502-506 of the Bengal Census Tables for 1901 showing the distribution by caste of certain occupations have been compiled in Assam, Bengal, Bihar and Orissa and the Punjab. They have not been reproduced here.

TABLE XVI.—Occupation by Selected Castes, Tribes

Serial Number.	Caste, Tribe or Race.	Traditional Occupation.	Population dealt with. — Actual Workers. Males.	Population dealt with. — Actual Workers. Females.	Population dealt with. — Dependants. Males.	Population dealt with. — Dependants. Females.	Number of actual workers whose traditional caste occupation was returned as their Principal means of livelihood. Males.	Principal means of livelihood. Females.	Subsidiary means of livelihood. Males.	Subsidiary means of livelihood. Females.	Number of actual workers returning their traditional occupation as their principal means of livelihood who had some subsidiary occupation. Males.	Females.
	1	2	3	4	5	6	7	8	9	10	11	12
	ASSAM.											
1	Ahom	Cultivators	58,693	49,479	40,725	43,663	54,976	47,916	400	4	3,713	287
2	Brahman	Priests	41,[illegible]65	8,169	26,996	47,976	11,030	467	5,040	62	4,511	90
3	Jogi (Jugi)	Weavers	53,041	18,189	32,246	64,945	1,630	1,226	2,518	767	902	36
4	Kaibartta, Chasi	Cultivators	21 541	1,329	11,754	28,928	18,082	524	464	4	2,549	41
5	Kalita	Cultivators	68,309	32,024	46,577	73,730	56,624	28,150	1,239	79	4,805	655
6	Kayastha	Writers	26,280	2,372	17,320	35,205	1,851	5	411	3	602	1
7	Kewat	Fishermen	26,565	16,471	18,326	26,685	21,842	14,253	278	14	1,572	321
8	Khasi	Cultivators	33,554	36,121	21,073	24,916	24,576	26,761	1,248	1,519	6,998	8,632
9	Kshattriya (Manipuri)	Cultivators	62,152	45,436	61,504	79,187	47,640	2,412	987	183	2,474	382
10	Nadiyal	Fishermen	18,592	15,243	13,434	16,012	4,243	3,251	4,[illegible]14	2,017	1,021	382
11	Patni	Boatmen	37,111	5,343	19,610	48,794	4,848	149	2,715	12	2,134	15
12	Rajbansi	Cultivators	41,034	4,783	24,713	57,416	36,664	2,327	910	16	3,137	874
13	Sudra	Indoor servants	37,487	2,634	21,913	53,107	1,237	231	174	2	180	3
14	Synteng	Cultivators	11,825	12,469	7,804	10,028	8,822	8,457	85	118	912	1,335
	BENGAL.											
1	Bagdi	Cultivators and fishermen	272,719	119,753	149,283	305,473	205,967	73,778	..	..	..	..
2	Baidya	Physicians	19,184	1,949	24,878	42,287	4,132	117	..	..	..	..
3	Baishnab	Religious mendicants.	125,964	76,725	59,406	147,351	41,926	47,508	..	..	..	..
4	Barui	Betel leaf growers	29,492	1,492	22 304	47,924	18,345	611	1,431	20	7,447	61
5	Bauri	Labourers	97,268	64,646	15,179	80,576	49,045	35,177	..	..	..	..
6	Brahman	Priests	364,125	35,939	271,244	520,559	81,438	5,736	6,114	195	8,930	209
7	Chain	Cultivators	13,394	6,059	7,704	16,380	8,568	890	..	..	..	..
8	Chamar and Muchi	Leather workers	203,166	34,892	91,057	204,016	64,722	15,661	2,342	18	3,364	23
9	Dhoba	Washermen	63,257	17,172	40,975	82,734	29,709	13,668	..	..	..	..
10	Dom	Basket makers and scavengers	43,144	23,692	20,265	38,307	12,299	17,251	..	..	..	..
11	Goala	Herdsmen and milkmen	213,055	38,774	102,554	229,407	61,807	17,237	..	..	..	..
12	Hari	Scavengers	52,173	21,931	27,316	56,528	2,651	4,664	..	..	..	..
13	Jogi	Weavers	101,179	18,055	72,038	151,561	32,676	10,352	..	..	..	..
14	Jolaha	Weavers	91,430	14,129	51,303	111,641	32,914	7,099	..	..	..	..
15	Kaibartta, Chas	Cultivators	616,010	88,075	395,072	920,623	511,232	85,801	..	..	..	..
16	Kaibartta, Jaliya	Fishermen	92,244	17,741	54,628	123,928	51,664	9,160	..	..	..	..
17	Kalu	Oil pressers	33,042	6,491	19,658	38,029	11,041	2,582	..	..	..	..
18	Kamar	Blacksmiths	76,085	6,817	45,811	105,882	46,142	3,807	..	..	..	..
19	Kayastha	Writers	273,662	31,528	241,132	477,412	31,956	199	..	..	..	..
20	Magh	Cultivators	34,617	21,000	26,865	42,912	22,695	12,564	249	6	3,373	99
21	Malo	Boatmen and fishermen	75,102	12,896	36,963	99,253	57,258	4,505	..	..	..	..
22	Namasudra	Boatmen and cultivators	559,667	49,588	395,982	820,902	439,110	18,964	..	..	..	..
23	Napit	Barbers	132,674	18,186	84,901	191,727	65,103	7,932	..	..	..	..
24	Pod	Fishermen	160,107	12,768	111,6[illegible]4	246,638	145,047	5,502	..	..	..	..
25	Rajbansi	Cultivators	467,739	30,056	266,128	660,820	405,362	8,903	..	..	..	..
26	Sadgop	Cultivators	162,484	25,408	100,504	229,058	140,477	11,987	..	..	..	..
27	Santal (*Hindu*)	Cultivators	51,201	31,555	26,476	41,980	33,411	16,926	..	..	..	..
28	Santal (*Animist*)	Cultivators	158,124	111,895	91,960	134,031	114,468	72,026	..	..	..	..
29	Sutradhar	Carpenters	49,890	7,490	29,868	68,973	33,594	461	..	..	..	..
30	Tanti	Weavers	99,034	26,074	49,130	104,255	42,178	9,109	..	..	..	..
31	Teli and Tili	Oil pressers	116,294	20,392	69,573	157,109	10,179	2,638	..	..	..	..
	BIHAR AND ORISSA.											
1	Babhan	Agriculturists	317,492	55,284	163,959	421,831	295,566	21,326	..	..	..	..
2	Brahman	Priests	487,916	57,516	282,635	706,436	58,383	9,834	..	..	..	..
3	Chamar and Muchi	Leather workers	327,571	284,193	188,990	305,902	41,304	24,217	..	..	..	..
4	Chasa	Cultivators	250,775	33,279	155,778	388,125	229,165	17,559	..	..	..	..
5	Dhanuk	Domestic servants	161,061	97,489	86,454	174,189	72,844	43,978	..	..	..	..
6	Dhobi	Washermen	114,641	87,278	64,519	92,979	52,977	63,857	..	..	..	..
7	Dhuniya	Cotton cleaners	55,946	34,036	36,367	71,715	3,084	2,373	..	..	..	..
8	Dosadh	Labourers	370,529	276,593	193,037	349,139	199,548	190,746	..	..	..	..
9	Gaura	Herdsmen and Milkmen	220,593	122,181	123,488	243 076	46,019	28,761	..	..	..	..
10	Goala (Ahir)	Herdsmen and Milkmen	1,045,796	903,441	533,856	1,002,544	124,003	123,853	..	..	..	..
11	Hajjam (*Hindu*)	Barbers	129,289	78,586	73,201	134,866	54,183	32,156	..	..	..	..
12	Ho (*Hindu*)	Cultivators	15,235	11,187	9,197	11,345	13,254	10,334	..	..	..	..
13	Ho (*Animist*)	Cultivators	109,534	107,762	63,332	78,090	90,509	91,696	..	..	..	..
14	Jolaha	Weavers	228,877	165,842	156,715	269,419	41,287	23,666	..	..	..	..
15	Kahar	Palki-bearers	157,841	145,242	85,644	132,217	33,366	54,812	..	..	..	..
16	Kalwar	Distillers	48,754	16,120	30,176	64,193	2,541	841	..	..	..	..
17	Kandh (*Animist*)	Cultivators	52,085	43,195	29,230	41,932	48,644	38,171	..	..	..	..
18	Kandu	Grain parchers	147,246	97,870	86,172	52,330	15,667	36,558	..	..	..	..
19	Karan	Writers	39,901	4,052	27,722	68,880	7,516	38	..	..	..	..
20	Kayastha	Writers	91,223	8,805	59,767	139,685	27,032	354	..	..	..	..
21	Kewat	Fishermen	122,538	74,251	68,234	130,496	21,526	33,569	..	..	..	..
22	Khandayat	Land holders	217,063	22,970	144,832	376,237	189,430	9,959	..	..	..	..
23	Koiri	Cultivators and vegetable growers	415,176	231,987	216,869	413,368	350,760	166,932	..	..	..	..
24	Kumhar	Potters	162,633	111,866	81,001	140,654	91,619	71,630	..	..	..	..
25	Kurmi	Cultivators	233,845	131,646	134,361	259,464	205,055	112,723	..	..	..	..
26	Lohar	Blacksmiths	84,942	42,626	55,603	101,767	31,365	7,783	..	..	..	..
27	Munda (*Hindu*)	Cultivators	19,542	17,175	12,431	16,732	16,005	13,613	..	..	..	..
28	Munda (*Animist*)	Cultivators	76,766	71,024	49,466	59,876	64,920	63,822	..	..	..	..
29	Musahar	Labourers	192,764	158,881	101,421	144,249	154,750	136,680	..	..	..	..
30	Nuniya	Saltpetre refiners	91,799	71,394	54,853	93,664	18,812	19,916	..	..	..	..
31	Oraon (*Animist*)	Cultivators	91,662	94,647	65,662	79,996	75,898	77,286	..	..	..	..

Recorded principal occupation of actual workers.																				
I.—Exploitation of the surface of the soil.												II.—Extraction of minerals.				III.—Industries.				
Income from rent of land.		Cultivators of all kinds.		Agents and managers of landed estates, planters, forest officers and their clerks, rent collectors, etc.		Field labourers, wood-cutters, etc.		Raisers of livestock, milkmen and herdsmen.		Fishing and hunting.		Owners, managers, clerks, etc.		Labourers.		Owners, managers, clerks, etc.		Artisans and other workmen.		
Males.	Females.	Males.	Females.	Males.	Females.	Males.	Females.	Males.	Females.	Males.	Females.	Males.	Females.	Males.	Females.	Males.	Females.	Males.	Females.	Serial Number.
13	14	15	16	17	18	19	20	21	22	23	24	25	26	27	28	29	30	31	32	
19	17	9	770	757	..	231	101	206	18	4	..	1	..	47	1	7	..	281	62	1
2,865	365	12,742	4,011	1,277	..	612	362	1,970	354	..	..	11	..	42	1	11	..	177	1,382	2
2,518	177	43,330	14,140	54	..	1,216	369	688	27	..	..	4	..	1	..	1	..	399	538	3
1,043	83	8	90	60	..	404	50	55	..	64	1	..	..	2	7	2	..	188	218	4
425	335	19	16	380	1	1,176	142	1,352	15	..	..	1	..	48	1	4	..	1,687	1,317	5
3,274	313	10,946	1,148	635	..	287	276	40	6	..	..	5	..	20	3	22	..	997	108	6
35	55	7	371	97	..	833	539	799	17	36	31	..	..	..	..	..	..	523	320	7
9	17	..	..	4	..	945	1,431	1,794	591	8	..	7	3	165	1	..	..	664	894	8
6,580	462	482	25	27	1	524	244	69	5	49	88	..	..	17	..	6	..	1,971	33,494	9
6	13	12,365	9,867	8	..	234	56	356	31	11	86	..	..	2	..	5	..	315	293	10
5,139	311	15,346	729	1	20	1,285	1,396	309	17	3,967	217	..	..	53	..	2	..	179	637	11
388	27	14	7	281	..	1,107	101	419	1	177	..	..	..	..	..	..	..	228	666	12
970	61	30,477	1,315	273	..	621	21	40	..	2	..	..	..	6	..	3	..	1,307	554	13
23	30	..	..	1	..	302	473	1,081	148	..	..	..	1	3	..	..	..	327	912	14
382	266	..	..	1,069	35	7,130	1,234	15,468	315	..	..	10	..	113	87	52	..	15,011	24,484	1
4,232	965	1,183	288	1,601	5	34	9	30	..	..	..	32	1	4	..	119	..	281	170	2
1,660	500	41,759	4,596	1,057	24	4,397	238	594	64	69	9	20	..	68	2	821	11	11,331	6,345	3
288	55	3,909	293	71	..	166	11	3	..	..	..	..	..	1	..	5	..	431	172	4
83	87	9,938	2,200	162	4	..	..	11,997	1,181	133	66	11	4	12,463	11,106	1	..	5,074	8,226	5
54,512	10,986	68,393	7,928	18,669	230	1,039	192	191	21	..	..	393	2	235	2	2,723	4	9,990	1,703	6
3	3	..	..	12	..	1,745	430	702	525	2	..	..	..	..	..	..	..	116	1,622	7
197	77	34,735	1,514	160	94	37,327	3,389	6,393	196	58	126	4	..	1,247	222	253	48	6,646	1,166	8
640	52	22,536	1,206	279	5	2,942	256	303	21	3	2	10	..	69	4	22	..	2,036	1,084	9
57	11	5,121	354	161	3	13,588	2,297	2,743	157	73	50	..	..	669	355	49	8	308	204	10
4,782	704	79,721	5,369	1,459	14	15,072	3,084	414	26	92	4	22	..	1,168	62	187	16	11,155	5,133	11
93	22	12,974	837	1,016	22	15,028	2,758	2,689	56	619	249	14	..	302	150	36	..	3,473	6,602	12
1,522	158	34,955	1,424	295	..	2,653	61	222	9	6	2	2	..	3	..	190	27	5,130	2,473	13
620	248	23,348	631	153	13	6,102	372	1,181	37	115	15	30	2	150	40	89	..	16,095	3,674	14
6,537	1,647	1,730	89	3,162	23	11,747	335	7,941	158	746	105	69	..	75	41	714	30	18,775	29,817	15
336	62	26,173	1,394	74	..	1,600	165	140	13	662	12	..	..	13	..	9	14	1,603	3,736	16
163	74	13,444	1,136	58	4	2,048	180	601	15	109	4	10	..	74	2	62	2	1,975	1,370	17
648	313	10,034	1,373	199	12	3,737	1,805	588	41	..	..	84	..	175	7	193	8	7,891	840	18
40,460	8,872	90,871	9,253	12,978	69	2,983	120	441	24	10	..	60	1	64	..	325	8	11,135	4,413	19
188	90	2,737	1,405	52	..	291	68	157	15	665	19	..	..	1	..	..	..	374	4,955	20
115	49	6,300	352	94	76	975	234	307	8	77	10	1	..	7	..	31	2	1,264	4,758	21
3,604	1,833	5,528	1,483	1,158	67	16,581	315	4,060	128	13,851	949	311	14	122	103	122	..	30,672	13,203	22
1,200	622	46,048	2,779	820	25	2,247	132	523	62	11	2	14	9	68	3	153	..	4,549	2,714	23
210	86	1,435	47	2,062	10	1,864	8	1,227	97	..	..	..	..	3	..	140	259	2,852	3,561	24
3,787	537	9,450	207	482	1	23,230	385	1,307	152	1,025	147	..	..	107	21	26	39	4,026	9,725	25
386	162	..	..	1,103	31	658	15	3,212	24	16	38	42	..	30	3	603	2	4,013	8,038	26
16	1	27	228	11	..	4,635	4,381	2,128	220	129	21	1	..	6,136	3,857	9	..	2,784	3,203	27
9	6	587	75	21	..	15,520	13,399	11,048	1,945	7	39	..	..	4,521	3,021	30	..	4,981	10,003	28
273	122	9,790	874	60	7	674	103	153	6	9	2	1	..	45	6	10	..	2,921	4,208	29
574	328	26,129	2,528	277	2	5,420	2,255	871	26	22	..	3	..	63	5	165	17	8,203	6,853	30
2,552	1,097	55,605	4,004	535	20	5,570	444	1,302	25	96	1	23	..	196	5	257	1	9,081	6,986	31
..	..	..	..	6,252	20	5,410	2,172	1,872	61	122	7	38	4	29	5	27	2	193	555	1
22,676	3,113	351,544	32,862	4,426	150	7,612	1,980	1,773	85	..	..	366	12	496	119	86	30	731	2,839	2
903	544	116,412	62,645	1,081	1,008	140,685	163,967	7,740	1,269	286	1,495	..	..	2,827	2,446	..	..	1,014	1,985	3
1,383	333	..	..	317	2	4,092	666	5,682	164	154	3	..	..	31	28	2	..	961	9,639	4
46	10	7,037	1,448	417	95	64,804	45,752	7,434	644	14	1	..	..	196	28	2	6	945	2,760	5
849	335	44,283	14,709	278	46	10,745	6,281	2,110	187	76	48	2	..	373	199	12	..	233	207	6
212	259	24,744	9,254	177	62	18,886	17,187	1,737	105	25	108	6	..	36	10	20	1	1,345	1,245	7
1,679	1,524	116,455	50,263	3,743	679	11,903	12,266	12,604	1,459	207	131	..	..	1,933	952	..	..	2,283	3,492	8
681	205	113,624	41,571	217	2	41,628	32,100	..	..	17	5	1	..	201	144	1	..	757	7,445	9
7,729	1,893	714,105	288,522	3,876	2,664	155,578	156,175	..	..	363	54	19	14	2,670	977	29	19	2,210	4,821	10
503	581	59,743	26,858	178	395	8,165	14,180	1,947	247	61	13 1	2	..	425	232	5	1	162	391	11
..	..	..	..	..	..	35	4	1,686	173	..	..	..	..	32	229	..	..	25	28	12
155	7	..	..	223	1	4,593	6,654	6,443	791	15	4 134	1	..	197	150	..	..	381	38	13
1,595	1,068	116,589	71,704	948	30	32,427	48,735	4,418	436	320	149	88	4	2,598	1,450	98	41	5,587	3,929	14
475	443	52,325	29,230	1,730	729	46,701	47,758	3,779	477	439	..	44	..	1,359	648	55	23	2,027	1,445	15
382	63	22,651	5,477	260	24	3,054	1,937	371	32	2		1	..	35	7	61	1	432	366	16
7	2	..	..	1	..	829	292	851	81	59	20 535	11	..	..	1	..	..	303	2,803	17
770	144	70,518	25,096	752	249	35,522	25,376	2,728	270	147		..	..	286	56	..	..	4,127	1,899	18
2,473	309	21,783	1,709	891	2	1,348	123	93	10	2	1	2	..	7	1	3	..	214	1,138	19
5,547	1,232	42,447	5,174	2,927	23	822	618	59	21	3	..	46	..	9	3	46	3	410	556	20
185	92	56,184	10,761	642	120	24,513	12,667	3,854	135	..	..	..	..	73	26	..	..	2,761	7,136	21
..	..	8,265	532	877	6	2,778	100	3,295	86	5	1	1	..	69	1	239	..	1,399	9,050	22
1,610	1,209	..	..	908	739	43,690	53,739	6,721	1,041	81	1,035	21	5	685	249	12	18	886	1,164	23
1,506	1,680	51,176	21,239	201	14	7,947	9,479	2,700	470	58	2	13	..	410	478	5	1	3,443	2,995	24
1,587	409	..	..	2,017	141	12,267	11,923	2,966	746	277	64	138	241	262	101	20	6	1,324	1,514	25
281	63	39,292	19,471	319	59	7,271	10,725	1,424	435	15	105	2	..	304	112	18	2	1,361	846	26
150	60	..	..	1	4	372	301	1,163	139	3	1	..	..	6	63	..	..	197	156	27
3,592	71	..	..	64	40	1,471	1,918	2,471	520	161	9	..	..	504	89	..	..	286	103	28
142	1,278	18,627	7,056	137	1	8,554	9,727	6,694	246	232	125	..	..	191	29	..	..	508	1,338	29
162	30	44,806	24,490	409	56	18,443	19,829	1,006	292	123	23	9	..	209	365	8	7	2,894	2,839	30
4,528	2,741	..	..	101	7	2,363	4,354	2,153	614	342	51	..	..	618	474	2	..	333	376	31

TABLE XVI.—Occupation by Selected Castes, Tribes

Serial Number.	Caste, Tribe or Race.	Traditional Occupation.	RECORDED PRINCIPAL OCCUPATION — IV.—Transport. — Owners, managers, ships' officers, etc. — Males.	IV.—Transport. — Owners, managers, ships' officers, etc. — Females.	IV.—Transport. — Labourers, boatmen, carters, palki-bearers, etc. — Males.	IV.—Transport. — Labourers, boatmen, carters, palki-bearers, etc. — Females.	V.—Trade. — Males.	V.—Trade. — Females.	VI.—Public Force. — Commissioned and Gazetted Officers. — Males.	VI.—Public Force. — Commissioned and Gazetted Officers. — Females.	VI.—Public Force. — Others. — Males.	VI.—Public Force. — Others. — Females.
	1	2	33	34	35	36	37	38	39	40	41	42
	ASSAM.											
1	Ahom	Cultivators	37	..	342	..	246	12	..	..	105	..
2	Brahman	Priests	488	..	412	4	3,090	580	10	..	314	..
3	Jogi (Jugi)	Weavers	16	..	100	2	798	124	..	..	124	..
4	Kaibartta, Chasi	Cultivators	16	..	41	..	574	23	..	..	68	..
5	Kalita	Cultivators	104	..	542	1	2,559	180	..	..	70	..
6	Kayastha	Writers	590	..	216	2	3,183	141	17	..	228	..
7	Kewat	Fishermen	22	..	304	16	1,007	166	..	..	38	..
8	Khasi	Cultivators	1	..	1,241	1,868	896	1,406	..	..	23	..
9	Kshattriya, Manipuri	Cultivators	15	1	549	2	1,714	8,431	21	..	355	..
10	Nadiyal.	Fishermen	30	..	165	3	372	1,315	..	..	9	..
11	Patni	Boatmen	17	..	84	6	3,921	1,036	..	..	105	..
12	Rajbansi	Cultivators	5	..	87	1	409	543	2	..	84	..
13	Sudra	Indoor servants	11	..	117	..	1,459	93	..	..	177	..
14	Synteng	Cultivators	..	..	80	90	316	437	..	..	1	..
	BENGAL.											
1	Bagdi	Cultivators and Fishermen	96	7	1,977	81	2,161	6,210	..	..	3,984	9
2	Baidya	Physicians	736	1	73	..	1,118	123	65	..	323	2
3	Baishnab	Religious mendicants	131	4	827	39	9,875	4,260	5	..	280	9
4	Barui	Betel leaf growers	20	..	49	1	5,484	228	..	..	10	..
5	Bauri	Labourers	41	65	816	302	486	729	..	..	872	..
6	Brahman	Priests	6,558	13	4,227	2	24,343	1,465	289	..	5,673	7
7	Chain	Cultivators	..	..	494	..	336	2,082	..	..	..	..
8	Chamar and Muchi	Leather workers	182	29	7,073	356	16,674	4,729	10	..	1,233	11
9	Dhoba	Washermen	46	..	341	3	1,215	244	..	..	366	1
10	Dom	Basket makers and scavengers	8	..	447	13	576	700	..	..	1,485	14
11	Goala	Herdsmen and milkmen	451	9	10,241	32	9,533	2,530	51	..	780	3
12	Hari	Scavengers	33	227	2,620	66	2,576	2,067	1	..	1,653	2
13	Jogi	Weavers	64	..	487	7	14,343	1,422	..	..	367	..
14	Jolaha	Weavers	47	1	1,151	18	3,403	569	3	..	261	..
15	Kaibartta, Chasi	Cultivators	415	34	4,692	25	16,024	8,282	29	..	735	11
16	Kaibartta, Jaliya	Fishermen	68	..	1,662	4	6,658	1,699	9	..	112	..
17	Kalu	Oil pressers	35	..	391	5	1,675	656	..	..	43	5
18	Kamar	Blacksmiths	109	..	526	11	2,958	931	13	..	116	6
19	Kayastha	Writers	1,974	3	3,001	3	32,425	2,271	158	..	2,784	1
20	Magh	Cultivators	15	..	113	..	3,354	1,145	2	..	246	1
21	Malo	Boatmen and fishermen	43	..	2,453	2	5,026	1,878	..	..	56	..
22	Namasudra	Boatmen and cultivators	189	3	2,592	..	17,523	5,850	30	..	2,067	10
23	Napit	Barbers	186	8	515	5	3,493	1,537	12	..	410	8
24	Pod	Fishermen	65	1	345	22	1,553	1,804	4	..	109	5
25	Rajbansi	Cultivators	53	..	965	..	3,009	6,063	6	..	586	1
26	Sadgop	Cultivatoss	301	28	594	1	4,949	1,707	16	..	225	1
27	Santal (*Hindu*)	Cultivators	1	..	314	53	166	645	..	..	30	..
28	Santal (*Animist*).	Cultivators	12	..	455	244	828	4,105	..	..	84	6
29	Sutradhar	Carpenters	75	..	113	1	1,340	959	8	..	23	2
30	Tanti	Weavers	162	..	2,814	8	6,334	1,344	15	..	347	3
31	Teli and Tili	Oil pressers	157	1	1,213	37	23,642	2,527	5	..	118	2
	BIHAR AND ORISSA.											
1	Babhan	Agriculturists	100	9	854	17	810	240	58	..	769	..
2	Brahman	Priests	1,010	5	1,320	11	6,310	1,557	214	..	2,366	18
3	Chamar and Muchi	Leather workers	37	16	1,395	471	1,935	1,522	..	..	157	3
4	Chasa	Cultivators	48	..	1,280	22	1,665	2,731	..	..	148	..
5	Dhanuk	Domestic servants	30	..	3,034	188	1,063	1,225	52	..	209	3
6	Dhobi	Washermen.	18	5	300	57	244	189	22	..	67	..
7	Dhuniya	Cotton cleaners	28	13	735	135	1,753	1,251	2	..	190	7
8	Dosadh	Labourers	127	13	4,346	522	2,476	4,982	..	..	2,201	9
9	Gaura	Herdsmen and milkmen.	86	3	2,304	176	927	3,638	3	..	441	44
10	Goala (Ahir)	Herdsmen and milkmen.	243	98	9,011	674	3,779	11,426	23	..	1,689	36
11	Hajjam (*Hindu*)	Barbers	51	6	334	28	390	567	4	..	61	1
12	Ho (*Hindu*)	Cultivators	..	..	8	3	19	196	..	..	4	..
13	Ho (*Animist*)	Cultivators	12	..	489	45	115	383	..	..	154	..
14	Jolaha	Weavers	225	..	2,225	717	6,791	3,215	12	..	417	61
15	Kahar	Palki-bearers	218	9	1,971	100	2,291	1,906	8	..	381	1
16	Kalwar	Distillers	..	..	704	169	16,673	6,797	10	..	156	..
17	Kandh (*Animist*)	Cultivators	..	..	37	20	238	242	..	..	243	158
18	Kandu	Grain parchers	45	4	1,565	122	9,666	4,728	6	..	176	..
19	Karan	Writers	26	..	116	2	660	163	9	..	583	4
20	Kayastha	Writers	382	7	643	2	1,124	256	149	..	621	3
21	Kewat	Fishermen	..	..	5,382	114	3,230	5,653	..	..	104	11
22	Khandayat	Landholders	14	..	1,288	11	1,635	1,644	30	..	537	5
23	Koiri	Cultivators and vegetable growers	..	..	2,058	121	1,176	1,332	34	..	121	12
24	Kumhar	Potters	21	..	267	94	1,050	1,826	2	..	45	..
25	Kurmi	Cultivators	138	10	1,771	329	1,827	787	70	..	252	..
26	Lohar	Blacksmiths	167	..	525	41	699	737	1	..	66	1
27	Munda (*Hindu*)	Cultivators	..	..	2	1	85	431	..	..	11	..
28	Munda (*Animist*)	Cultivators	3	..	82	24	185	365	11	..	33	1
29	Musahar	Labourers	..	..	884	212	483	1,391	..	..	200	7
30	Nuniya	Saltpetre refiners	116	66	874	436	1,688	1,389	2	..	193	10
31	Oraon (*Animist*).	Cultivators	17	..	170	57	187	612	3	..	116	78

OR RACES. PART I.—INDIGENOUS CASTES, ETC.—*continued.*

OF ACTUAL WORKERS.—*contd.*

VII.—PUBLIC ADMINISTRATION.				VIII.—ARTS AND PROFESSIONS.						IX.—PERSONS LIVING ON THEIR INCOME.		X.—DOMESTIC SERVICE.		XI.—CONTRACTORS, CLERKS, CASHIERS, ETC., OTHERWISE UNSPECIFIED.		XII.—LABOURERS UNSPECIFIED.		XIII.—BEGGARS, PROSTITUTES, CRIMINALS AND INMATES OF JAILS AND ASYLUMS.		
Gazetted Officers.		Others.		Religious.		Lawyers, doctors and teachers.		Others.												
Males.	Females.	Males.	Females.	Males.	Females.	Males.	Females.	Males.	Females.	Males.	Females.	Males.	Females.	Males.	Females.	Males.	Females.	Males.	Females.	Serial Number.
43	44	45	46	47	48	49	50	51	52	53	54	55	56	57	58	59	60	61	62	
1	..	178	..	10	..	147	2	42	..	7	1	288	91	52	..	318	132	282	356	1
12	..	511	..	1,372	117	1,409	11	512	11	78	6	1,000	21	134	..	348	44	938	433	2
..	..	90	..	601	34	176	7	71	4	14	..	234	45	6	..	475	98	600	1,408	3
..	..	55	..	6	..	147	1	11	3	6	..	505	150	1	..	104	19	104	160	4
1	..	391	..	185	7	464	5	157	5	17	..	859	110	64	..	594	34	586	1,705	5
27	..	440	..	484	33	1,491	18	305	5	63	1	513	70	170	2	146	20	230	226	6
1	..	134	..	83	..	121	..	52	1	12	1	178	56	15	1	261	45	167	599	7
11	1	45	..	2	..	12	..	52	5	7	..	124	186	33	..	2,890	3,490	45	17	8
1	..	193	19	240	33	480	12	472	39	29	7	364	32	38	1	175	75	191	88	9
..	..	29	..	3	..	15	1	21	..	14	2	79	19	3	..	123	65	194	239	10
..	..	24	..	25	2	44	6	3	1	2	..	579	40	2	1	851	365	325	408	11
..	..	21	..	92	1	111	2	22	3	10	9	361	242	4	..	241	39	307	612	12
..	..	175	..	19	1	179	4	22	7	13	..	34	57	18	..	209	94	118	196	13
..	..	52	..	..	..	3	..	3	..	..	..	17	40	..	..	786	1,868	8	13	14
..	..	225	1	38	8	250	20	238	88	161	126	11,589	8,835	170	31	5,597	1,758	731	2,480	1
182	..	1,392	..	44	10	1,976	19	223	4	308	67	181	77	794	5	65	4	66	82	2
5	..	374	23	569	114	1,523	26	926	98	276	456	2,648	4,752	450	28	1,662	318	3,291	7,301	3
1	..	17	..	3	..	284	5	26	1	2	..	63	12	14	..	264	34	36	69	4
..	..	34	..	14	6	..	..	72	416	35	19	3,949	2,544	483	2	1,198	2,150	360	432	5
607	..	10,012	15	1,906	175	19,389	102	3,634	102	4,715	1,623	24,156	3,163	13,371	26	3,781	115	3,881	2,337	6
..	..	2	..	1	..	15	..	3	..	1	..	29	31	4	..	1,352	447	9	29	7
..	..	562	9	21	6	14	18	4,183	2,540	282	57	8,664	1,696	620	15	10,745	1,451	1,150	1,462	8
4	..	40	1	11	1	203	2	104	8	44	5	544	194	34	5	1,628	111	128	349	9
..	..	31	1	56	4	..	..	1,764	218	29	7	1,942	1,060	341	5	970	566	427	414	10
7	..	452	3	36	10	472	3	265	47	336	137	7,793	3,081	615	16	7,530	412	614	892	11
..	..	116	..	5	1	39	54	1,856	1,465	27	27	2,347	1,527	100	5	1,543	442	364	687	12
5	..	101	..	1,722	40	1,317	16	177	15	87	28	728	327	143	2	2,901	137	1,083	1,555	13
..	..	95	..	33	2	181	..	65	23	107	85	1,593	369	138	2	3,086	316	470	613	14
81	..	849	4	87	11	3,488	22	479	36	654	332	9,651	7,523	1,118	79	8,032	1,038	948	2,632	15
1	..	23	..	17	1	147	2	42	61	36	8	384	590	71	8	465	66	275	746	16
..	..	18	1	3	..	65	..	62	2	78	39	504	258	49	..	474	27	60	120	17
13	..	74	..	14	..	345	6	141	45	111	77	745	979	143	..	983	227	183	329	18
432	..	4,416	4	349	39	16,341	130	1,850	89	1,668	530	10,839	3,788	1,973	37	4,307	190	831	1,484	19
3	..	72	..	182	..	482	28	47	34	32	2	555	61	40	..	2,009	284	306	829	20
..	..	25	..	2	1	96	5	49	8	30	13	268	544	32	1	484	165	109	285	21
2	..	187	..	107	14	1,077	35	458	156	88	35	4,379	2,370	319	24	14,123	809	1,428	3,223	22
..	..	456	1	12	10	3,043	31	237	14	141	72	1,956	1,250	372	13	1,091	397	194	660	23
5	..	50	2	6	2	337	5	50	35	134	40	1,069	349	108	14	1,332	669	102	300	24
18	..	116	2	610	39	497	12	269	14	85	37	3,237	777	450	21	5,316	342	2,840	2,631	25
25	..	492	..	32	2	1,248	4	158	10	384	210	2,162	2,613	556	1	679	81	123	450	26
..	..	3	..	3	..	20	5	14	2	..	51	375	80	17	..	920	1,818	51	64	27
..	..	7	..	1	..	34	..	5	11	..	1	1,268	490	28	155	4,052	6,154	158	275	28
1	..	39	..	6	1	124	4	44	10	31	18	189	412	72	..	194	40	101	254	29
8	..	234	..	12	1	377	4	208	19	161	115	2,037	2,333	457	22	2,586	275	377	827	30
9	..	218	1	14	6	589	10	147	8	243	175	2,004	1,784	496	10	1,840	164	203	446	31
58	..	465	6	285	10	514	5	68	3	75	17	2,341	433	576	5	403	161	612	228	1
401	..	2,471	6	1,760	204	5,336	74	1,001	19	567	96	10,066	1,844	1,549	141	1,183	312	4,269	2,205	2
..	..	78	6	42	11	20	12	1,096	11,247	54	329	2,726	1,987	279	317	6,479	7,218	1,016	1,478	3
2	..	149	1	269	14	811	3	95	8	14	106	1,830	1,015	150	4	2,589	593	438	386	4
7	..	92	..	13	..	199	..	117	7	20	6	..	..	223	78	1,900	1,076	353	184	5
1	..	34	1	14	7	23	10	19	3	3	22	410	183	119	51	665	681	164	200	6
..	..	64	..	2	..	32	3	70	7	9	18	1,899	897	126	40	569	620	195	441	7
..	..	687	4	18	13	44	3	227	220	46	41	7,513	1,201	624	149	..	..	1,865	1,924	8
..	..	802	130	60	7	154	25	86	18	36	33	4,088	4,794	186	89	2,648	2,466	626	525	9
47	..	948	10	66	22	208	24	306	134	145	20	7,269	3,141	1,004	481	8,377	8,004	2,101	1,379	10
6	..	89	..	55	52	118	15	64	20	39	24	1,665	1,466	107	55	709	1,013	221	295	11
..	..	..	..	..	..	1	..	..	..	..	..	69	154	..	..	89	43	13	22	12
..	..	16	..	8	7	45	..	190	194	7	4	1,185	1,739	403	1	4,297	5,953	96	97	13
11	..	378	11	56	9	394	25	300	67	164	111	7,060	4,241	667	424	3,136	4,232	1,086	1,532	14
..	..	851	13	416	7	160	6	287	60	69	138	3,508	2,852	1,066	222	3,902	3,740	413	393	15
6	..	26	..	4	..	56	2	21	..	39	15	722	147	187	32	169	94	201	116	16
..	..	9	..	13	..	47	..	3	..	1	..	124	464	1	..	617	920	47	26	17
4	..	73	..	3	..	79	2	51	1	33	36	3,001	1,517	295	100	1,593	965	239	220	18
4	..	499	1	198	6	697	11	74	..	76	3	681	323	196	3	1,609	60	191	145	19
442	..	1,641	1	107	2	3,720	21	356	6	292	39	1,123	358	857	15	212	36	206	80	20
..	..	69	1	13	7	67	1	38	3	20	71	1,999	3,315	127	..	1,494	401	259	178	21
35	..	523	5	105	4	723	11	259	9	31	26	2,090	790	243	1	2,715	197	477	582	22
7	..	184	..	23	12	257	8	86	8	72	7	2,397	1,633	221	54	2,505	2,152	651	466	23
1	..	59	1	109	12	61	..	38	12	18	2	670	468	60	94	891	1,124	255	256	24
12	..	424	1	26	3	202	1	136	2	22	79	895	396	388	372	1,380	1,469	389	329	25
1	..	43	1	10	53	25	2	63	59	17	37	563	562	90	53	865	1,314	155	165	26
3	..	5	..	..	..	11	..	..	..	1	2	183	171	235	237	1,099	1,975	10	21	27
4	..	13	1	28	..	14	2	41	89	3	2	837	491	60	182	1,891	3,234	35	71	28
..	..	24	..	2	..	..	..	20	4	29	..	682	209	68	8	..	..	587	575	29
1	..	15	..	..	..	16	1	6	3	15	7	470	305	120	91	1,171	1,023	232	223	30
4	..	41	29	323	3	7	32	78	229	479	6	682	749	266	128	2,807	6,690	144	131	31

TABLE XVI.—Occupation by Selected Castes, Tribes

Serial Number.	Caste, Tribe or Race.	Traditional Occupation.	Population dealt with. Actual Workers. Males.	Actual Workers. Females.	Dependants. Males.	Dependants. Females.	Number of actual workers whose traditional caste occupation was returned as their Principal means of livelihood. .	Principal means of livelihood. Females.	Subsidiary means of livelihood. Males.	Subsidiary means of livelihood. Females.	Number of actual workers returning their traditional occupation as their principal means of livelihood who had some subsidiary occupation. Males.	Females.
	1	2	3	4	5	6	7	8	9	10	11	12
	BIHAR AND ORISSA —contd.											
32	Pan (*Hindu*)	Weavers	120,410	65,037	77,362	141,517	15,482	11,868	..	..	..	..
33	Pan (*Animist*)	Weavers	5,553	4,101	3,415	4,883	1,236	524	..	..	..	..
34	Rajput	Military servants and cultivators	399,295	47,236	212,110	536,178	358,768	37,678	..	..	..	..
35	Saiyid	....	21,547	6,541	17,082	33,788	..	..	..	..	..	..
36	Santal (*Hindu*)	Cultivators	85,699	71,724	42,795	64,405	70,485	63,750	..	..	..	..
37	Santal (*Animist*)	Cultivators	342,682	301,753	182,851	228,898	279,444	268,791	..	..	..	..
38	Tanti and Tatwa	Weavers	165,336	105,896	92,859	179,385	34,126	26,453	..	..	..	..
39	Teli	Oil pressers	322,251	168,595	200,077	361,364	60,644	72,392	..	..	..	..
	BOMBAY.											
1	Agri	Saltmakers and husbandmen	62,545	47,000	44,294	59,420	40,406	32,824	1,141	174	7,468	2,411
2	Bhangi or Halalkhor	Scavengers	11,908	8,827	7,575	9,591	3,007	2,277	261	93	611	225
3	Bharvad, Dhangar or Kurub	Shepherds	189,081	104,085	110,758	188,646	29,919	11,154	4,146	1,017	2,490	766
4	Bhil	Hunters and woodmen	117,721	92,213	84,198	105,609	2,255	2,906	103	8	164	203
5	Bohora, Khoja, Memon and Teli or Ghanchi.	Traders	30,157	6,555	24,227	44,113	6,363	612	308	15	764	25
6	Brahman	Priests and writers	50,446	7,343	40,260	75,779	9,608	809	1,220	43	1,710	41
7	Chambhar, Mochi, Machigar or Sochi.	Shoemakers	12,602	6,130	8,001	14,095	5,232	1,482	511	56	641	107
8	Dubla or Talavia	Field labourers	28,739	24,788	16,770	19,966	20,507	22,564	473	55	899	255
9	Koli	Labourers and cultivators	276,507	189,790	166,567	219,630	211,256	160,549	2,072	278	11,506	2,470
10	Kunbi	Husbandmen	319,813	229,091	201,486	304,304	184,548	100,273	1,811	944	38,931	23,367
11	Lingayat	Traders and cultivators	295,940	116,192	178,267	342,724	175,414	33,688	2,937	527	20,369	2,341
12	Lohana	Traders	150,427	5,552	95,908	201,138	70,459	1,387	1,713	7	4,513	62
13	Mahar, Holiya or Dhed	Village watchmen and menials	96,866	66,168	61,858	98,774	2,109	511	8,141	1,251	2,181	348
14	Mang or Madig	Village servants and cultivators	22,672	17,940	11,721	18,771	5,755	1,390	915	59	1,417	257
15	Maratha	Soldiers and cultivators.	426,649	251,402	292,376	491,793	263,958	132,253	3,608	732	29,103	7,070
16	Rajput		46,828	17,945	27,501	44,937	21,533	4,470	515	50	1,079	75
17	Ramoshi	Watchmen and thieves	12,222	5,251	8,421	14,017	1,187	51	1,022	18	817	6
18	Sonar	Goldsmiths	10,570	1,959	8,403	16,899	6,529	781	1,044	22	1,424	16
19	Sutar or Badig	Carpenters	15,344	5,625	10,502	20,413	9,317	193	1,605	26	1,768	21
20	Teli, Ganiger or Ghanchi	Oil pressers	14,933	9,596	10,750	16,301	1,974	962	1,794	363	892	223
21	Vani, Oswal	Traders	8,375	557	4,152	7,258	4,397	255	230	20	434	7
22	Vani, Shrimali	Traders	10,217	1,896	6,920	14,888	5,859	511	148	12	608	25
	CENTRAL PROVINCES AND BERAR.											
1	Ahir	Graziers	237,780	197,413	123,820	168,729	86,311	40,925	9,543	4,251	6,476	2,907
2	Bairagi	Devotees	13,648	7,368	6,861	10,967	6,498	2,672	1,360	239	539	116
3	Baniya	Traders	63,967	15,442	36,716	75,895	38,585	8,964	4,405	401	6,718	408
4	Barhai	Carpenters	37,378	19,870	18,919	32,648	28,153	1,017	2,911	72	4,406	107
5	Brahman	Priests	152,691	40,238	84,876	167,822	16,767	2,679	3,368	192	3,000	149
6	Chamar	Leather workers	288,544	269,290	154 473	189,305	47,401	15,489	19,836	2,194	12,965	3,026
7	Dhimar	Water carriers	92,870	86,900	47,884	56,679	45,425	27,451	6,710	3,695	13,024	8,379
8	Dhobi	Washermen	3,139	50,400	27,534	33,500	20,795	22,063	6,801	5,222	6,764	5,234
9	Gond	Agriculturists	714,958	691,139	370,578	450,865	441,625	415,567	3,058	2,734	28,672	28,291
10	Kachhi	Vegetable growers	38,333	32,403	19,948	25,346	3,977	4,572	2,599	1,738	843	856
11	Kalar	Distillers	62,491	49,628	33 902	49,274	4,143	2,447	1,299	450	562	136
12	Kumhar	Potters	46,624	33,339	20,023	25,115	29,056	24,650	5,023	2,715	4,279	2,510
13	Kunbi	Agriculturists	465,522	350,264	269,780	318,434	261,981	141,923	1,930	403	20,417	21,466
14	Kurmi	Agriculturists	91,108	70,469	49,971	72,763	71,277	53,932	596	223	6,283	1,842
15	Lodhi	Agriculturists	101,650	83,802	53,524	73,398	74,140	59,189	537	149	5,715	1,806
16	Lohar	Ironsmiths	58,769	41,850	32,169	48,532	35,770	10,232	4,859	589	7,514	1,337
17	Mali	Vegetable and fruit growers.	188,117	166,380	91,472	115,263	13,153	14,871	9,093	6,790	11,965	1,348
18	Maratha	Soldiers	32,050	17,280	14,651	20,896	1,194	..	150	..	157	..
19	Mehra (Mahar)	Cotton weavers	385,050	367,407	189,978	221,948	47,436	36,337	5,820	2,755	10,104	8,248
20	Nai	Barbers	47,685	33,339	25,112	39,954	31,947	..	7,861	..	8,939	..
21	Panka	Cotton weavers	41,762	40,865	21,880	28,471	5,483	5 003	3,312	96	896	417
22	Rajput	Soldiers	151,843	100,822	71,280	116,398	3,955	..	78	..	465	..
23	Sunar	Goldsmiths.	40,567	15,081	23,263	47,953	27,892	1,405	3,555	67	4,694	113
24	Teli	Oil pressers.	276,889	250,944	150,235	191,268	19,066	20,847	11,140	8,598	5,410	3,252
	MADRAS.											
1	Balija	Traders	69,164	38,079	43,110	74,693	8,074	4,549	840	212	713	217
2	Brahman, Canarese	Priests	10,647	2,992	6,754	15,238	762	54	909	..	189	..
3	Brahman, Oriya	Priests	36,109	7,556	26,116	58,618	3,296	445	2,107	28	850	53
4	Brahman, Tamil	Priests	35,470	4,791	27,292	62,882	4,852	70	1,140	2	972	3
5	Brahman, Telugu	Priests	27,929	6,945	23,938	44,735	3,522	135	2,849	244	560	21
6	Cheruman	Field labourers	74,171	81,766	41,929	46,625	69,409	79,649	253	134	998	3,401
7	Kaikolan	Weavers	30,544	29,157	19,079	31,294	18,715	8,585	396	67	1,133	124
8	Kalian	Cultivators	131,911	83,962	78,244	129,523	119,559	74,734	1,087	324	9,197	2,467

OR RACES. PART I.—INDIGENOUS CASTES, ETC.—*continued.*

RECORDED PRINCIPAL OCCUPATION OF ACTUAL WORKERS.																				
I.—EXPLOITATION OF THE SURFACE OF THE SOIL.												II.—EXTRACTION OF MINERALS.				III.—INDUSTRIES.				
Income from rent of land.		Cultivators of all kinds.		Agents and managers of landed estates, planters, forest officers and their clerks, rent collectors, etc.		Field labourers, wood-cutters, etc.		Raisers of livestock, milkmen and herdsmen.		Fishing and hunting.		Owners, managers, clerks, etc.		Labourers.		Owners, managers, clerks, etc.		Artisans and other workmen.		Serial Number.
Males.	Females.	Males.	Females.	Males.	Females.	Males.	Females.	Males.	Females.	Males.	Females.	Males.	Females.	Males.	Females.	Males.	Females.	Males.	Females.	
13	14	15	16	17	18	19	20	21	22	23	24	25	26	27	28	29	30	31	32	
208	29	35,973	5,969	100	11	44,394	23,809	8,151	1,484	34	21	5	..	288	296	2	..	692	4,260	32
18	1	988	363	..	..	1,634	2,030	141	41	..	..	..	..	..	..	..	..	294	24	33
..	..	..	..	9,766	272	8,054	4,439	2,763	108	69	27	151	1	989	191	67	13	486	1,085	34
3,257	1,710	8,402	1,700	1,212	117	1,155	556	164	21	13	6	12	..	133	39	34	9	565	714	35
582	147	..	..	13	..	1,976	2,724	8,775	1,197	9	5	..	..	1,396	985	..	..	70	326	36
1,890	327	..	..	567	9	8,256	8,439	33,238	5,551	580	1,710	1	..	8,171	6,924	..	..	277	1,014	37
296	62	56,092	13,604	253	92	55,268	51,330	5,511	600	27	28	2	1	254	193	55	..	3,212	5,302	38
2,144	1,233	180,860	55,847	517	118	27,753	16,769	3,774	354	78	338	13	3	835	306	50	17	1,974	6,228	39
1,485	1,049	47,894	35,481	29	..	6,379	8,848	2,466	102	4	3	..	..	39	101	8	..	596	434	1
35	6	710	113	1	1	2,585	3,561	281	70	..	..	..	..	..	..	..	..	5,327	3,677	2
2,455	1,213	90,852	25,999	735	43	42,921	56,126	31,512	7,127	539	2	4	1	66	6	37	126	11,405	8,559	3
1,001	75	43,375	10,907	101	4	54,738	75,025	5,187	404	108	47	..	..	174	142	..	..	3,613	2,184	4
673	211	11,792	1,597	12	..	1,840	2,828	159	15	2	..	..	..	1	..	15	..	3,491	629	5
6,768	1,661	9,038	1,254	182	1	398	446	53	17	1	..	6	..	1	..	384	3	1,466	692	6
333	22	940	285	359	..	1,695	2,832	134	14	..	..	..	..	21	4	5	3	8,030	2,454	7
1	1	1,292	147	10	..	21,585	22,876	2,080	197	19	22	..	..	..	..	..	..	1,006	562	8
4,125	743	150,373	27,055	56	2	84,893	141,856	4,536	984	128	49	2	..	702	62	34	..	13,196	5,969	9
5,090	2,458	213,904	124,222	94	..	66,097	94,686	11,476	1,127	8	..	..	..	11	..	690	8	7,487	3,006	10
6,666	4,056	172,048	29,526	46	..	46,113	53,727	9,503	711	422	..	4	..	36	7	117	2	22,639	16,260	11
8,240	189	17,559	129	67	..	2,693	227	204	16	..	..	..	..	121	..	107	..	15,503	2,207	12
1,390	222	37,956	23,374	1	..	19,787	25,101	3,341	322	26	..	..	..	63	3	1	4	22,350	6,678	13
117	98	3,764	1,138	1	..	9,457	11,983	1,590	124	..	..	..	..	1	..	..	..	3,974	1,427	14
6,730	4,602	293,203	139,385	126	..	63,705	90,185	19,988	1,547	517	92	1	..	152	11	25	..	11,788	4,053	15
3,565	1,006	21,118	4,224	26	..	10,136	10,447	645	61	..	..	1	..	16	2	64	2	3,785	1,027	16
201	97	4,744	1,564	10	79	3,286	3,343	1,032	128	..	..	..	..	11	17	4	..	116	67	17
225	79	1,775	1,008	2	3	130	267	32	9	..	..	..	..	..	..	1	..	7,966	269	18
56	52	2,665	2,696	9	1	695	1,930	148	99	..	..	..	..	9	..	7	..	11,318	856	19
39	18	5,480	3,339	4	..	2,674	3,536	289	11	..	..	..	..	..	..	2	5	3,541	1,317	20
96	20	476	66	..	..	28	13	8	1	..	..	..	..	..	..	10	..	280	45	21
196	80	122	29	21	..	9	19	..	1	..	..	..	..	..	..	277	..	515	710	22
413	531	92,176	77,449	496	..	43,450	58,728	..	..	38	5	7	1	328	132	35	1	2,169	1,803	1
182	283	5,751	3,359	53	..	349	701	52	2	..	..	..	..	1	1	5	..	62	50	2
827	507	12,671	3,106	210	2	2,935	3,767	179	22	1	..	14	2	56	13	104	26	1,827	1,077	3
206	96	5,326	4,653	10	..	2,162	13,372	427	19	9	..	1	..	24	16	6	..	396	279	4
4,164	1,323	61,191	20,427	2,228	..	7,489	5,368	814	199	..	..	94	..	177	24	416	8	2,760	952	5
478	8	145,609	140,842	125	7	77,556	103,260	3,869	165	9	3	..	..	608	500	11	12	3,318	2,089	6
148	146	20,614	15,696	190	..	14,220	24,590	1,895	192	2,115	612	20	1	244	139	6	..	1,897	6,578	7
230	71	18,739	15,424	..	..	10,194	11,847	1,070	74	2	1	1	..	64	18	13	..	405	176	8
..	..	..	..	931	15	224,387	253,927	24,168	2,328	193	43	4	..	1,582	1,324	29	..	5,549	5,650	9
111	61	19,574	14,689	20	..	10,895	11,438	814	51	1	..	..	..	63	82	1	..	730	511	10
506	614	35,816	29,017	181	11	12,182	14,231	1,164	56	3	..	4	..	164	61	45	..	927	479	11
119	34	7,330	4,961	41	2	1,729	2,848	837	62	15	..	..	..	14	8	3	4	482	294	12
..	..	..	..	483	35	160,194	200,105	17,051	648	78	6	16	1	449	208	71	2	6,099	2,735	13
..	..	..	..	172	4	14,532	14,986	1,678	83	4	3	1	..	54	14	2	..	556	395	14
..	..	..	..	97	2	20,599	22,557	2,704	146	2	..	18	..	258	149	39	..	944	561	15
118	195	11,837	12,462	41	5	5,550	17,835	843	74	7	6	1	..	147	76	32	4	3,207	627	16
1,503	1,042	98,294	67,608	200	..	62,233	77,475	3,585	109	3	9	..	..	242	203	20	4	2,058	1,241	17
622	406	14,832	4,063	132	2	8,041	10,281	530	47	..	..	3	..	22	5	62	..	1,677	876	18
1,368	470	89,104	68,558	402	..	162,589	234,199	16,169	2,169	257	4	..	2	2,890	2,028	80	13	12,767	8,985	19
162	90	12,835	11,688	41	3	1,416	10,269	400	36	1	..	..	..	12	8	5	1	254	3,207	20
28	19	19,530	20,456	9	..	10,500	13,580	506	178	..	3	..	..	3	12	..	..	88	74	21
1,991	939	96,872	70,496	904	3	26,640	24,274	3,570	177	45	8	14	..	218	60	67	2	3,170	1,366	22
267	139	7,191	5,703	65	..	1,669	6,025	171	43	..	..	1	..	21	8	26	..	1,223	672	23
2,673	948	157,396	136,361	141	15	70,745	82,566	6,129	241	2	7	8	..	344	97	35	5	3,367	1,940	24
2,225	1,071	37,115	16,927	455	16	7,986	10,183	672	182	62	7	..	..	59	2	5	..	5,114	2,789	1
1,486	441	7,654	2,072	5	..	9	12	..	9	..	..	..	..	..	..	..	..	20	5	2
6,426	1,594	16,938	1,389	359	26	1,504	382	79	..	..	..	..	..	..	..	..	..	395	2,400	3
11,155	2,218	7,202	672	992	15	84	7	..	..	..	..	..	..	..	..	18	..	54	11	4
9,332	3,792	8,751	2,413	364	40	79	5	8	..	..	..	..	..	..	..	..	..	47	14	5
..	..	385	117	1,928	27	62	105	970	67	5	2	..	..	9	..	..	..	869	1,663	6
170	309	4,027	2,117	33	4	1,020	728	72	15	4	..	..	..	..	5	46	45	400	578	7
..	..	..	..	268	34	47	23	1,189	148	39	..	1	1	..	14	4	17	1,773	2,927	8

TABLE XVI.—Occupation by Selected Castes, Tribes:

RECORDED PRINCIPAL OCCUPATION

Serial Number.	Caste, Tribe or Race.	Traditional Occupation.	IV.—Transport. Owners, managers, ships' officers, etc. Males.	IV.—Transport. Owners, managers, ships' officers, etc. Females.	IV.—Transport. Labourers, boatmen, carters, palki-bearers, etc. Males.	IV.—Transport. Labourers, boatmen, carters, palki-bearers, etc. Females.	V.—Trade. Males.	V.—Trade. Females.	VI.—Public Force. Commissioned and Gazetted Officers. Males.	VI.—Public Force. Commissioned and Gazetted Officers. Females.	VI.—Public Force. Others. Males.	VI.—Public Force. Others. Females.
	1	2	33	34	35	36	37	38	39	40	41	42
	BIHAR AND ORISSA—contd.											
32	Pan (*Hindu*)	Weavers	59	..	439	113	1,432	9,981	20	..	3,037	35
33	Pan (*Animist*)	Weavers	12	..	14	3	244	188	..	..	159	4
34	Rajput	Military servants and cultivators.	352	7	2,332	35	2,909	961	131	..	1,291	8
35	Saiyid	....	97	8	446	49	894	257	82	..	401	9
36	Santal (*Hindu*)	Cultivators	..	1	95	13	99	749	..	..	50	..
37	Santal (*Animist*)	Cultivators	32	..	430	81	749	1,436	..	..	170	..
38	Tanti and Tatwa	Weavers	111	58	2,723	298	1,739	3,023	12	..	383	7
39	Teli	Oil pressers	191	29	5,819	374	30,233	11,408	65	..	346	95
	BOMBAY.											
1	Agri	Saltmakers and husbandmen	3	..	1,379	49	489	124	..	..	36	..
2	Bhangi or Halalkhor	Scavengers	..	..	105	27	123	27	..	..	3	..
3	Bharvad, Dhangar or Kurub	Shepherds	35	3	1,002	109	1,934	1,983	..	..	234	6
4	Bhil	Hunters and woodmen	8	1	2,831	738	1,335	794	41	..	1,632	3
5	Bohora, Khoja, Memon and Teli or Ghanchi	Traders	44	1	1,872	43	7,738	660	..	..	108	3
6	Brahman	Priests and writers	552	3	1,040	15	5,675	326	22	..	742	..
7	Chambhar, Mochi, Machigar or Sochi.	Shoemakers	3	..	284	65	289	74	..	..	53	..
8	Dubla or Talavia	Field labourers	..	..	438	40	179	58	..	..	9	..
9	Koli	Labourers and cultivators	29	..	7,068	1,653	1,652	583	..	..	699	2
10	Kunbi	Husbandmen	51	..	2,251	153	3,913	492	1	..	349	..
11	Lingayat	Traders and cultivators	65	..	927	20	24,184	7,126	10	..	436	2
12	Lohana	Traders	502	..	9,007	326	77,074	1,492	..	..	589	..
13	Mahar, Holiya or Dhed	Village watchmen and menials	85	..	3,720	1,070	1,978	327	..	..	24	..
14	Mang or Madig	Village servants and cultivators	..	..	96	14	541	590	..	..	1,261	96
15	Maratha	Soldiers and cultivators	199	2	6,695	511	4,425	2,269	..	..	2,554	..
16	Rajput	Soldiers and cultivators	79	8	2,025	408	1,158	187	7	..	1,166	..
17	Ramoshi	Watchmen and thieves	..	..	140	38	42	79	..	..	2,066	59
18	Sonar	Goldsmiths	19	..	14	2	175	51	5	..	6	..
19	Sutar or Badig	Carpenters	108	..	46	17	95	27	..	..	3	..
20	Teli, Ganiger or Ghanchi	Oil pressers	7	1	321	112	1,944	721	..	..	29	..
21	Vani, Oswal	Traders	20	..	125	..	5,988	292	..	..	1	..
22	Vani, Shrimali	Traders	17	..	44	82	7,775	583	..	..	13	..
	CENTRAL PROVINCES AND BERAR.											
:	Ahir	Graziers	73	5	3,886	787	2,098	1,902	9	..	512	..
2	Bairagi	Devotees	4	..	63	19	218	198	..	..	27	..
3	Baniya	Traders	114	2	695	100	1,361	171	6	..	91	..
4	Barhai	Carpenters	21	8	135	39	134	106	..	..	12	..
5	Brahman	Priests	1,213	3	3,445	208	11.570	1,486	12	..	3,615	..
6	Chamar	Leather workers	8	..	3,870	1,913	2,120	1,524	..	..	289	27
7	Dhimar	Water carriers	56	5	2,105	673	2,487	9,115	..	..	115	..
8	Dhobi	Washermen	8	..	597	116	340	186	..	..	26	..
9	Gond	Agriculturists	52	7	5,572	2,148	3,107	4,423	..	..	521	78
10	Kachhi	Vegetable growers	5	..	911	163	407	416	..	..	36	..
11	Kalar	Distillers	11	..	1,109	188	4,670	2,120	9	..	60	..
12	Kumhar	Potters	16	..	266	143	277	142	1	..	10	..
13	Kunbi	Agriculturists	86	4	3,669	585	4,226	985	..	..	596	..
14	Kurmi	Agriculturists	21	2	1,116	143	574	512	..	..	76	..
15	Lodhi	Agriculturists	14	5	1,118	128	668	552	..	..	60	..
16	Lohar	Ironsmiths	26	7	365	116	278	270	2	..	39	..
17	Mali	Vegetable and fruit growers.	35	1	1,142	270	2,378	2,343	..	..	164	..
18	Maratha	Soldiers	52	..	1,437	116	968	384	..	..	89	..
19	Mehra (Mahar)	Cotton weavers	270	5	9,798	4,223	9,170	6,059	..	..	24,961	10
20	Nai	Barbers	9	..	128	58	241	294	1	..	67	..
21	Panka	Cotton weavers	5	1	514	234	436	736	..	..	3,655	42
22	Rajput	Soldiers	317	16	3,872	514	4,386	1,723	6	..	355	..
23	Sunar	Goldsmiths.	17	..	120	36	974	632	1	..	64	..
24	Teli	Oil pressers.	101	1	3,981	964	9,472	5,066	..	..	172	..
	MADRAS.											
1	Balija	Traders	18	..	1,273	47	..	..	..	..	888	..
2	Brahman, Canarese	Priests	3	..	5	..	215	92	..	..	1	..
3	Brahman, Oriya	Priests	..	..	157	217	3,354	536	1	..	42	..
4	Brahman, Tamil	Priests	556	1	73	..	2,669	1,323	..	..	141	..
5	Brahman, Telugu	Priests			56	..	416	93	..	..	80	..
6	Cheruman	Field labourers		..	380	8	46	38	..	..	..	..
7	Kaikolan	Weavers	11	..	253	34	2,447	2,633	..	..	100	..
8	Kallan	Cultivators	36	10	2,078	22	1,539	2,396	..	..	600	..

OR RACES. PART I.—INDIGENOUS CASTES, ETC.—*continued.*

OF ACTUAL WORKERS—contd.

VII.—Public Administration.				VIII.—Arts and Professions.						IX.—Persons living on their income.		X.—Domestic service.		XI.—Contractors, clerks, cashiers, etc., otherwise unspecified.		XII.—Labourers, unspecified.		XIII.—Beggars, prostitutes, criminals and inmates of jails and asylums.		
Gazetted Officers.		Others.		Religious.		Lawyers, doctors and teachers.		Others.												
Males.	Females.	Males.	Females.	Males.	Females.	Males.	Females.	Males.	Females.	Males.	Females.	Males.	Females.	Males.	Females.	Males.	Females.	Males.	Females.	Serial Number.
43	44	45	46	47	48	49	50	51	52	53	54	55	56	57	58	59	60	61	62	
..	..	401	7	48	2	59	2	229	1	5	2	2,254	320	30	10	6,197	5,962	871	855	32
..	..	1	..	..	..	..	..	5	1	1	..	151	46	7	6	606	852	42	18	33
182	..	1,376	10	111	7	799	7	284	40	257	70	4,688	1,202	1,478	79	1,051	696	941	300	34
174	..	527	7	189	21	1,176	50	138	11	94	7	1,065	627	255	20	160	79	902	524	35
..	..	11	2	2	..	11	..	5	5	16	..	1,057	751	22	3	867	841	158	225	36
..	..	140	..	7	4	41	1	287	282	7	5	3,373	1,894	22	6	4,855	4,889	145	390	37
5	..	97	..	19	2	145	7	392	44	31	18	1,578	769	203	132	2,164	2,822	638	1,045	38
10	..	78	2	128	28	218	2	115	22	139	62	2,461	804	375	112	2,888	1,516	548	536	39
..	..	177	..	17	1	38	5	11	2	4	8	923	179	7	..	461	572	100	42	1
..	..	1,096	454	53	5	4	3	122	12	1	1	43	17	33	9	168	185	1,098	659	2
..	..	1,276	22	183	115	156	39	100	14	39	17	872	591	69	4	1,112	857	1,543	1,123	3
..	..	790	24	11	1	17	3	94	18	73	4	720	196	88	4	1,094	1,331	690	308	4
2	..	272	4	176	27	353	13	75	8	190	157	702	216	363	9	50	58	227	76	5
37	..	5,296	16	9,213	987	3,301	155	637	23	983	314	2,141	862	798	13	24	60	1,688	495	6
..	..	25	3	5	..	..	2	9	..	17	2	86	96	7	..	239	228	68	46	7
..	..	624	21	3	..	7	5	10	..	57	1	719	250	212	10	434	571	54	27	8
..	..	2,449	117	72	21	201	15	143	21	63	9	2,502	1,005	657	33	2,277	9,377	650	234	9
2	..	1,177	7	150	17	672	43	94	19	242	60	2,976	1,010	694	9	1,529	1,198	655	576	10
37	..	1,355	94	5,165	1,158	1,016	89	214	59	191	154	2,464	1,342	34	6	1,018	1,050	1,230	803	11
18	..	3,128	..	1,295	147	2,399	72	352	18	697	112	6,347	432	2,670	14	378	45	1,477	126	12
..	..	4,139	835	162	47	18	..	149	4	163	42	1,066	229	13	3	1,004	963	1,430	944	13
..	..	1,038	168	9	66	2	..	31	1	2	..	301	33	1	..	163	249	323	1,953	14
1	..	2,980	12	366	147	398	34	400	41	1,516	356	4,478	3,054	366	4	3,472	2,964	2,564	2,133	15
..	..	1,023	16	74	6	143	17	42	10	57	66	983	213	185	9	171	153	359	81	16
..	..	20	9	3	3	..	..	2	..	11	1	188	57	7	..	258	269	81	41	17
..	..	40	..	23	1	33	1	9	..	12	9	35	180	9	3	11	50	26	32	18
..	..	21	..	5	2	16	1	2	2	12	16	52	98	16	1	23	66	38	61	19
..	..	48	..	..	..	41	1	7	1	24	4	121	111	101	7	208	356	53	56	20
..	..	9	..	57	30	197	..	7	..	6	23	559	45	596	2	65	8	25	12	21
1	..	209	1	37	23	287	14	17	1	66	113	64	130	500	7	6	43	39	60	22
2	..	915	19	62	25	176	20	173	110	71	10	3,312	13,871	78	14	502	669	468	406	1
1	..	67	3	..	..	109	5	57	8	11	7	78	34	14	1	11	10	35	20	2
2	..	493	..	130	15	547	24	130	19	332	111	1,950	260	211	11	190	137	306	107	3
..	..	60	..	7	1	38	3	12	4	3	7	73	73	36	..	41	134	86	48	4
104	..	9,982	105	11,586	5,530	5,030	156	874	31	950	169	5,967	1,044	651	22	481	204	1,091	300	5
..	..	..	..	62	35	..	..	93	1,304	16	7	1,474	359	14	13	801	886	993	757	6
1	..	371	11	32	2	152	26	55	32	24	15	..	..	50	10	363	506	285	200	7
..	..	111	..	37	39	64	..	65	9	5	..	..	..	11	1	98	94	264	281	8
5	..	804	15	533	164	206	19	264	140	55	22	2,971	2,787	105	35	926	1,335	1,369	1,092	9
..	..	62	..	7	..	23	3	17	5	5	4	200	87	12	6	338	311	124	59	10
2	..	281	1	10	..	213	6	29	2	31	14	558	123	119	12	170	155	132	91	11
..	..	34	2	..	1	29	1	11	1	8	9	117	46	12	1	58	62	59	48	12
2	..	3,325	14	110	16	708	12	229	60	187	59	3,298	1,029	246	16	1,129	1,309	1,328	492	13
3	..	216	5	23	2	127	8	18	3	42	..	303	154	17	4	152	123	144	97	14
1	..	130	1	12	4	62	6	18	5	15	5	328	176	18	..	206	226	199	93	15
..	..	75	2	6	1	53	7	13	6	6	12	134	120	29	2	82	197	108	94	16
1	..	632	..	63	41	285	9	84	33	35	17	1,151	363	85	11	395	481	382	249	17
..	..	973	..	45	12	248	22	154	71	86	29	725	527	92	13	211	190	355	236	18
..	..	33	..	64	53	317	90	473	710	48	11	2,701	931	193	25	500	581	3,460	1,944	19
..	..	140	3	24	14	126	11	33	70	14	3	206	7,410	12	..	35	85	76	66	20
..	..	98	..	42	19	96	4	39	19	2	..	273	113	14	5	65	60	328	307	21
25	..	1,583	..	104	13	746	37	247	52	172	61	1,768	480	268	9	412	261	641	331	22
5	..	181	..	22	1	205	12	16	12	34	20	182	178	37	5	57	106	126	84	23
3	..	466	..	59	11	124	12	59	13	58	11	1,049	334	124	1	770	1,080	545	445	24
..	..	967	..	175	54	492	48	372	102	309	67	234	128	663	87	1,212	1,439	704	431	1
1	..	116	..	..	..	183	1	17	..	8	160	103	135	53	..	5	11	1	..	2
7	..	386	..	..	..	998	17	39	1	28	32	689	212	100	..	367	64	935	241	3
4	..	2,516	..	..	..	2,498	2	370	7	200	165	704	186	1,203	1	8	5	171	108	4
10	..	1,562	..	..	..	1,612	60	273	4	98	160	204	103	194	4	..	1	421	112	5
..	..	1	..	2	..	24	1	1	..	..	..	25	14	11	1	8	4	36	10	6
1	..	103	..	206	71	216	18	443	778	12	15	266	218	97	1	1,450	3,933	452	70	7
..	..	506	..	91	16	200	14	168	47	27	23	322	337	299	30	1,998	3,080	265	109	8

TABLE XVI.—Occupation by Selected Castes, Tribes

Serial Number.	Caste, Tribe or Race.	Traditional Occupation.	Population dealt with.				Number of actual workers whose traditional caste occupation was returned as their				Number of actual workers returning their traditional occupation as their principal means of livelihood who had some subsidiary occupation.	
			Actual Workers.		Dependants.		Principal means of livelihood.		Subsidiary means of livelihood.			
			Males.	Females.	Males.	Females.	Males.	Females.	Males.	Females.	Males.	Females.
	1	2	3	4	5	6	7	8	9	10	11	12
	MADRAS—contd.											
9	Kammalan	Metal and wood-workers.	64,145	20,395	33,968	84,640	49,843	1,130	5,072	175	8,252	273
10	Kamsala		30,045	5,545	17,245	43,066	22,968	1,932	565	15	7,501	460
11	Madiga	Leather workers	79,924	56,495	33,232	55,718	19,045	4,620	813	351	13,122	2,303
12	Mala	Field labourers	196,259	167,856	93,195	129,402	140,968	146,895	6,207	3,945	10,675	12,817
13	Shanan	Toddy drawers	74,666	34,993	57,611	102,855	15,293	..	2,853	..	4,014	..
14	Tiyan	Toddy drawers	164,270	116,438	133,140	189,450	20,218	..	8,528	..	4,645	..
	PUNJAB.											
1	Agarwal	Traders	118,435	7,452	78,491	160,205	92,266	2,259	8,566	44	11,145	159
2	Ahir	Herdsmen and milkmen.	73,552	13,508	42,436	78,388	41,579	2,347	297	8	1,291	27
3	Arain	Agriculturists	321,972	24,007	219,016	412,250	276,459	10,932	5,140	268	21,032	429
4	Arora	Traders	214,846	14,428	147,767	296,478	142,702	1,585	7,143	141	18,055	100
5	Awan	Agriculturists	136,001	9,972	90,983	188,965	111,102	5,560	1,657	67	12,054	256
6	Biloch	Agriculturists	171,441	8,230	117,639	234,155	126,208	2,793	1,692	44	8,794	196
7	Brahman	Priests	364,326	54,795	196,609	399,257	87,272	12,671	40,235	2,075	17,263	975
8	Chamar	Leather workers	383,339	88,479	218,376	416,395	136,752	23,179	30,126	2,176	36,642	2,086
9	Chuhra	Sweepers and scavengers.	305,372	113,095	205,141	301,445	141,947	98,279	32,552	441	28,984	5,058
10	Jat	Agriculturists	1,732,668	117,359	1,070,314	2,024,561	1,521,979	96,416	16,411	746	115,378	2,754
11	Jhinwar	Village menials	119,613	48,749	67,262	102,936	66.190	39,341	5,480	471	14,055	3,868
12	Julaha	Weavers	212,850	55,714	130,783	232,683	146,158	35,925	7,811	452	24,040	1,438
13	Kanet	Agriculturists	142,714	47,041	64,466	149,541	133,359	44,595	469	68	6,627	333
14	Kashmiri	Traders	58,105	8,037	37,685	74,268	14,997	871	754	181	2,934	130
15	Khatri	Traders	137,544	9,935	97,695	181,460	75,419	2,577	4,497	170	11,087	218
16	Kumhar	Potters	180,317	22,125	118,851	228,140	96,644	10,519	6,847	305	22,751	589
17	Labana	Rope makers	18,579	2,863	12,717	23,603	3,854	1,149	647	26	728	34
18	Lohar	Ironsmiths	104,876	8,562	71,139	138,595	64,283	1,060	8,076	157	18,606	100
19	Machhi	Water carriers and fishermen	74,414	24,741	50,772	78,941	23,819	5,471	1,489	499	4,855	767
20	Mira	Minstrels and genealogists	75,406	15,909	45,667	88,688	33,907	7,262	2,172	162	5,780	384
21	Mochi	Shoemakers	134,387	14,737	93,617	174,489	89,349	6,701	5,156	178	14,772	347
22	Nai	Barbers	119,315	17,843	72,892	140,213	90,809	12,334	9,399	275	16,966	501
23	Pathan	Agriculturists and military servants	108,789	8,557	57,228	117,195	59,464	2,791	1,739	42	7,611	144
24	Qassab	Butchers	35,932	4,122	26,385	52,312	12,308	458	787	64	1,516	24
25	Rajput	Agriculturists and military servants	545,251	40,416	323,894	671,611	446,994	27,298	7,470	398	42,059	997
26	Saiyid	Priests and agriculturists	80,341	7,089	51,399	108,118	52,440	3,817	2,182	104	7,789	265
27	Sheikh	Traders	118,253	11,460	66,960	138,089	34,799	1,034	795	53	1,988	113
28	Tarkhan	Carpenters	215,964	13,449	138,722	274,863	133,684	1,330	19,601	173	27,160	97
29	Teli	Oil pressers	97,331	11,547	65,093	121,963	40,123	4,470	6,018	317	10,495	265
	UNITED PROVINCES											
1	Agarwal	Traders	99,296	8,682	59,384	117,216	74,142	4,654	3,293	84	9,666	752
2	Ahir	Herdsmen and milkmen	824,046	492,478	347,723	556,849	90,274	31,412	21,789	9,200	9,519	3,091
3	Barhai	Carpenters	207,055	50,456	104,855	222,446	102,989	3,954	48,037	771	30,325	652
4	Bhangi	Scavengers	127,599	93,063	62,110	77,737	84,388	84,860	3,773	966	11,311	3,634
5	Bhar	Agriculturists	128,258	119,424	62,647	76,483	84,748	68,955	1,297	977	2,961	1,806
6	Brahman	Priests	1,643,105	302,576	801,100	1,895,328	126,210	27,487	62,442	3,907	24,877	5,249
7	Chamar	Leather workers	2,089,295	1,378,112	1,010,116	1,590,949	108,348	21,885	33,804	4,401	22,758	3,354
8	Dhobi	Washermen	247,851	159,506	121,799	186,944	116,939	97,402	58,673	18,291	36,204	12,444
9	Dom	Scavengers	101,347	56,699	56,839	91,609	17,114	5,555	18,618	1,867	3,241	879
10	Gadariya	Shepherds and blanket weavers.	358,079	176,341	157,500	290,974	83,409	39,280	84,720	9,614	13,992	5,082
11	Gujar	Herdsmen and milkmen	121,631	12,127	65,196	129,775	14,702	2,358	1,397	116	652	121
12	Jat	Cultivators and landowners	271,491	20,307	141.146	297,108	232,582	15,008	1,954	80	16,861	622
13	Julaha	Weavers	321,200	174,359	182 923	302,031	160,785	89,254	12,974	1,895	21,492	2,906
14	Kahar	Palki-bearers	378,554	233,366	193,348	299,538	108,158	110,148	84,676	10,491	18,839	9,505
15	Kayastha	Writers	151,751	15,709	104,024	211,959	54,213	620	2,431	52	7,512	75
16	Kewat	Boatmen and fishermen	39,887	26,423	17,821	20,433	366	416	234	44	96	29
17	Kumhar	Potters	248,636	160,290	124,180	189,811	107,015	69,646	49,312	15,723	36,660	11,706
18	Kurmi	Cultivators	423,103	228,183	178,772	330,705	361,780	187,358	4,408	1,296	28,481	10,556
19	Lodha	Agriculturists	389,932	191,381	179,474	319,083	337,810	163,050	6,956	1,692	25,012	10,620
20	Lohar	Blacksmiths	201,591	78,391	102,125	198,652	82,655	6,576	46,397	1,162	29,420	1,355
21	Mallah	Boatmen and fishermen	68,779	64,407	39,046	58,784	10,549	4,572	6,342	2,191	4,725	1,024
22	Nai	Barbers	314,571	163,236	157,709	271,897	172,131	82,301	71,483	7,315	51,139	5,595
23	Pasi	Toddy makers	455,190	321,146	210,657	316,107	2,441	1,363	1,964	502	797	347
24	Pathan	Military servants and landholders	315,353	75,094	183,247	384,273	3,784	2,500	52	2	264	8
25	Rajput		1,291,876	240,211	645,680	1 451,731	588,817	149,328	30,156	1,850	91,060	9,408
26	Saiyid	Priests and agriculturists	74,670	14,357	52,894	104 061	229	863	13	4	83	8
27	Sheikh	Traders	436,986	103,287	252,959	514,401	7,430	2,952	49	4	327	14
28	Teli	Oil pressers	306,216	190,942	144,532	227,387	111,057	105,827	60,436	28,437	38,507	11,172

RECORDED PRINCIPAL OCCUPATION OF ACTUAL WORKERS.																				
I.—Exploitation of the surface of the soil.												II.—Extraction of minerals.				III.—Industries.				
Income from rent of land.		Cultivators of all kinds.		Agents and managers of landed estates, planters, forest officers and their clerks, rent collectors, etc.		Field labourers, wood cutters, etc.		Raisers of livestock, milkmen and herdsmen.		Fishing and hunting.		Owners, managers, etc.		Labourers.		Owners, managers, clerks, etc.		Artisans and other workmen.		
Males.	Females.	Males.	Females.	Males.	Females.	Males.	Females.	Males.	Females.	Males.	Females.	Males.	Females.	Males.	Females.	Males.	Females.	Males.	Females.	Serial Number.
13	14	15	16	17	18	19	20	21	22	23	24	25	26	27	28	29	30	31	32	
256	215	10,692	9,903	11	8	1,456	4,920	98	11	..	..	..	..	1	1	196	1	391	1,853	9
868	526	2,125	1,252	44	..	196	1,189	17	1	..	..	..	..	..	..	..	1	2,939	199	10
1,347	225	8,559	1,633	34	10	43,729	46,504	2,311	166	16	65	1	..	6	5	..	..	816	1,406	11
347	272	29,010	14,232	176	23	135	62	8,336	459	189	1	..	..	11	3	..	..	6,287	2,188	12
936	524	41,035	16,037	139	80	1,125	726	384	38	8	..	..	..	..	..	30	5	2,958	7,817	13
235	71	46,158	11,185	1,718	199	56,174	66,224	901	26	59	1	2	..	10	..	388	9	14,367	35,078	14
1,966	471	10,460	613	68	1	556	80	291	2	..	..	58	..	100	7	380	4	1,419	2,970	1
161	111	23,976	10,236	387	4	559	35	..	..	..	..	1	..	105	4	166	3	1,073	404	2
..	..	..	.	982	2	417	18	6,498	86	36	..	4	..	256	12	438	11	6,827	4,388	3
10,817	1,379	20,279	412	707	17	1,373	100	771	10	44	1	106	1	136	8	826	14	8,721	8,803	4
..	..	..	..	96	9	11	1	6,730	287	10	9	71	..	733	92	95	14	3,211	2,798	5
..	..	..	..	150	..	45	3	14,020	759	142	..	14	..	258	18	98	12	3,676	3,173	6
11,158	4,113	174,866	25,636	428	15	5,172	3,237	6,490	480	13	..	66	..	173	49	1,785	36	4,751	3,223	7
1,383	342	76,454	13,913	488	..	71,823	20,641	16,129	700	17	..	11	..	951	324	2,513	13	49,187	22,132	8
654	75	31,799	590	569	83	78,792	3,597	10,247	138	11	3	1	1	361	15	405	16	15,430	5,751	9
..	..	..	..	1,472	3	1,331	80	67,715	1,018	445	8	86	..	1,487	136	1,529	177	29,200	13,089	10
600	92	17,330	1,280	170	..	7,129	1,132	2,555	40	603	18	87	..	203	5	636	15	10,134	5,216	11
1,067	305	24,472	3,754	306	2	7,030	1,393	5,502	219	104	..	9	..	391	16	261	31	5,598	10,242	12
..	..	..	..	189	..	227	38	4,297	1,285	5	..	..	..	43	1	47	..	597	220	13
700	145	7,058	287	126	8	698	43	858	21	13	..	4	1	913	21	321	22	20,838	4,986	14
6,605	1,247	11,163	660	360	8	452	52	982	37	11	1	151	2	244	19	1,440	39	6,422	3,716	15
1,359	223	32,175	2,810	117	3	4,243	1,218	4,310	146	76	1	51	4	1,227	74	486	20	7,362	4,729	16
1,795	314	9,516	867	16	..	441	186	376	31	20	..	8	..	6	..	24	10	161	147	17
1,152	363	23,980	3,259	180	23	2,880	833	1,685	105	88	..	9	..	221	37	260	6	5,270	2,220	18
1,420	104	18,989	198	602	2	8,230	327	2,352	45	82	2	7	..	170	9	283	117	8,936	15,887	19
398	51	4,280	121	117	4	1,164	187	717	21	22	..	4	..	46	2	67	14	2,259	1,397	20
1,152	154	16,622	428	178	2	4,222	583	2,491	46	35	..	1	1	128	9	274	22	11,205	5,258	21
1,311	285	17,688	1,290	165	4	1,557	595	1,645	53	29	1	2	..	91	9	63	27	1,322	2,246	22
..	..	..	..	179	5	44	4	2,386	214	35	3	43	..	409	2	624	10	12,424	3,102	23
240	40	4,963	159	24	2	1,068	285	1,997	33	12	2	1	..	36	..	66	47	4,645	2,299	24
..	..	..	..	567	9	643	42	20,209	442	194	9	115	..	1,539	92	1,303	57	20,467	7,856	25
..	..	..	..	136	3	53	7	1,019	12	9	..	16	1	164	1	130	4	3,587	1,488	26
3,434	577	21,081	614	371	3	2,806	335	2,122	145	85	5	32	..	584	2	859	24	19,365	5,576	27
4,112	968	50,777	4,170	400	26	3,687	1,189	2,784	69	25	..	29	..	114	13	579	48	11,111	4,416	28
997	143	22,055	1,444	194	2	5,276	888	4,823	65	65	1	3	..	114	12	246	7	11,241	3,243	29
3,247	184	6,821	482	1,236	8	721	59	250	16	18	..	45	..	64	12	217	15	2,586	1,896	1
6,840	3,456	608,538	360,800	1,936	7	71,025	74,276	..	..	13	51	..	..	10	9	122	35	5,333	6,970	2
860	560	86,506	34,376	182	8	4,339	4,320	2,981	253	28	1	1	..	208	44	60	150	3,742	4,185	3
319	59	10,444	1,518	944	..	6,464	878	5,627	1,216	75	..	..	..	28	31	75	..	6,237	2,250	4
992	686	..	..	313	559	29,233	36,216	5,061	2,605	16	13	..	..	5	10	15	58	1,031	1,704	5
34,344	8,269	1,230,389	202,301	16,747	1,692	23,014	7,461	23,992	2,294	33	39	69	2	93	28	955	73	9,869	13,111	6
10,151	4,224	906,320	448,302	3,886	301	661,449	583,863	98,457	14,465	1,452	701	52	..	1,484	1,316	360	178	40,695	101,553	7
1,207	343	104,528	49,115	310	19	10,874	8,167	6,153	1,001	26	12	2	..	23	3	28	8	861	1,249	8
34	5	69,973	41,114	58	8	1,908	3,164	1,383	382	38	20	..	..	18	18	..	..	2,240	1,424	9
2,421	947	215,251	96,993	683	139	30,016	21,289	..	..	73	20	1	..	94	13	48	125	3,583	7,511	10
2,492	451	94,889	7,339	430	21	3,922	387	..	..	16	1	..	..	32	1	1	45	780	834	11
..	..	..	..	709	53	15,866	1,142	7,541	351	124	..	16	..	101	5	43	3	2,226	2,557	12
983	222	80,801	45,683	1,312	46	17,477	13,575	5,191	615	84	39	69	2	48	2	1,739	35	11,757	13,026	13
1,885	1,043	185,352	66,364	1,089	31	22,049	14,246	8,953	1,191	6,240	2,302	..	19	..	104	207	566	16,009	23,294	14
6,804	1,867	54,654	8,134	4,498	22	1,444	497	334	59	17	1	22	..	27	26	532	13	3,012	1,548	15
70	83	30,217	25,499	28	..	5,326	7,373	1,064	339	3	..	13	..	7	29	..	5	1,080	1,099	16
750	551	102,712	64,248	170	11	12,934	14,243	5,998	1,606	36	8	6	..	47	20	39	35	2,917	3,461	17
1,906	381	..	..	3,540	21	27,088	26,852	7,609	1,231	6	2	3	..	49	14	238	43	4,713	5,982	18
2,880	1,021	..	..	364	7	6,997	5,099	10,768	1,975	49	69	2	..	72	6	80	667	7,060	7,596	19
1,368	581	94,803	56,706	107	11	5,782	7,606	2,930	541	21	3	19	..	4	18	72	44	8,091	2,999	20
330	325	41,062	29,895	215	..	7,176	16,448	1,270	343	164	108	..	..	39	20	64	114	2,663	5,204	21
1,396	986	116,687	48,681	498	12	5,397	7,677	4,652	579	35	9	2	32	9	17	27	12	1,586	3,135	22
2,254	1,247	302,249	189,292	2,756	2,115	86,957	94,919	21,530	11,161	245	195	4	2	32	13	262	14	4,192	8,338	23
7,151	2,173	155,694	37,602	8,101	61	15,092	5,469	5,182	448	277	24	4	2	246	2	363	50	23,877	11,332	24
..	..	568,675	55,907	10,249	163	33,268	7,026	21,926	2,412	198	13	76	3	215	36	298	244	9,315	10,452	25
7,770	2,517	21,682	3,277	3,637	64	2,115	390	622	30	19	1	5	..	36	..	167	4	7,868	2,973	26
11,264	3,667	165,417	39,932	8,183	165	17,122	5,525	6,509	473	348	96	9	..	409	33	1,031	123	59,935	22,378	27
1,861	535	147,783	65,228	702	32	13,048	8,433	4,588	551	10	3	8	..	15	6	122	45	3,743	3,672	28

TABLE XVI.—Occupation by Selected Castes, Tribes

Serial Number.	Caste, Tribe or Race.	Traditional Occupation.	RECORDED PRINCIPAL OCCUPATION: IV.—Transport. Owners, managers, ships' officers, etc. Males.	IV.—Transport. Owners, managers, ships' officers, etc. Females.	IV.—Transport. Labourers, boatmen, carters, palki-bearers, etc. Males.	IV.—Transport. Labourers, boatmen, carters, palki-bearers, etc. Females.	V.—Trade. Males.	V.—Trade. Females.	VI.—Public Force. Commissioned and Gazetted Officers. Males.	VI.—Public Force. Commissioned and Gazetted Officers. Females.	VI.—Public Force. Others. Males.	VI.—Public Force. Others. Females.
	1	2	33	34	35	36	37	38	39	40	41	42
	MADRAS—*contd.*											
9	Kammalan	Metal and wood-workers	12	..	84	..	418	684	..	..	32	..
10	Kamsala		..	..	11	..	490	239	1	..	57	..
11	Madiga	Leather workers	1	..	221	62	558	852	..	..	911	..
12	Mala	Field labourers	1	..	883	87	1,460	1,361	..	..	845	..
13	Shanan	Toddy drawers	..	..	1,398	79	5,090	2,876	..	..	42	..
14	Tiyan	Toddy drawers	320	..	7,394	344	8,212	850	..	..	385	..
	PUNJAB.											
1	Agarwal	Traders	689	77	879	20	..	..	10	..	283	..
2	Ahir	Herdsmen and milkmen	102	3	1,816	52	585	113	34	..	434	..
3	Arain	Agriculturists	663	5	7,577	78	6,735	7,104	60	..	1,274	..
4	Arora	Traders	1,514	4	7,917	109	..	..	69	..	719	..
5	Awan	Agriculturists	195	6	2,897	24	649	90	56	..	2,844	..
6	Biloch	Agriculturists	738	16	13,218	107	1,078	207	87	..	1,741	..
7	Brahman	Priests	2,731	43	6,660	79	30,949	737	227	..	3,172	..
8	Chamar	Leather workers	311	45	3,917	2,524	1,305	308	11	..	590	..
9	Chuhra	Sweepers and scavengers	336	15	4,696	210	1,841	139	1	..	423	5
10	Jat	Agriculturists	1,945	28	26,959	328	8,460	594	1,025	..	16,215	5
11	Jhinwar	Village menials	138	36	3,111	156	2,996	262	..	..	556	1
12	Julaha	Weavers	345	39	5,531	880	2,447	131	3	..	965	..
13	Kanet	Agriculturists	17	9	630	69	486	81	18	..	170	..
14	Kashmiri	Traders	298	49	2,204	36	..	..	43	..	1,041	..
15	Khatri	Traders	4,050	17	4,830	65	..	..	256	..	2,029	1
16	Kumhar	Potters	920	18	18,542	748	5,482	243	8	..	293	..
17	Labana	Rope makers	52	2	652	4	332	24	13	..	702	..
18	Lohar	Ironsmiths	197	8	1,341	54	506	35	17	..	174	..
19	Machhi	Water carriers and fishermen	109	1	2,970	78	1,439	200	11	..	470	..
20	Mirasi	Minstrels and genealogists	58	1	793	12	480	10	..	..	468	..
21	Mochi	Shoemakers	82	5	1,560	117	1,312	50	14	..	364	..
22	Nai	Barbers	114	7	659	49	705	24	7	..	266	..
23	Pathan	Agriculturists and military servants	791	6	7,709	169	6,407	318	..	..	..	..
24	Qassab	Butchers	114	15	1,705	18	6,717	229	2	..	228	..
25	Rajput	Agriculturists and military servants	1,933	15	13,059	587	8,405	528	..	..	..	..
26	Saiyid	Priests and Agriculturists	693	3	2,628	13	1,679	40	187	..	2,149	3
27	Sheikh	Traders	1,519	26	5,580	45	..	..	213	..	2,627	..
28	Tarkhan	Carpenters	336	8	2,028	75	818	91	27	..	320	..
29	Teli	Oil pressers	312	34	3,486	112	3,401	125	18	..	448	..
	UNITED PROVINCES.											
1	Agarwal	Traders	350	8	1,587	69	..	..	58	..	293	..
2	Ahir	Herdsmen and milkmen	221	27	7,877	1,788	2,272	1,492	14	..	4,282	..
3	Barhai	Carpenters	60	12	822	184	555	277	2	..	121	..
4	Bhangi	Scavengers	23	2	1,080	193	1,146	216	..	..	1,356	..
5	Bhar	Agriculturists	14	140	607	312	531	564	22	..	546	..
6	Brahman	Priests	2,642	40	14,737	1,234	42,443	5,996	588	..	10,905	..
7	Chamar	Leather workers	479	606	18,621	15,253	13,502	23,720	..	..	8,519	..
8	Dhobi	Washermen	9	..	1,743	145	614	140	..	..	297	..
9	Dom	Scavengers	16	..	1,525	476	224	83	..	..	55	..
10	Gadariya	Shepherds and blanket weavers	63	14	3,445	1,164	2,377	1,892	14	..	1,174	..
11	Gujar	Herdsmen and milkmen	56	2	492	6	237	122	2	..	355	..
12	Jat	Cultivators and landowners	74	..	1,753	27	1,545	275	30	..	1,553	..
13	Julaha	Weavers	227	38	4,042	223	10,307	2,756	30	..	1,536	..
14	Kahar	Palki-bearers	200	105	4,445	1,713	6,490	5,513	..	..	1,320	..
15	Kayastha	Writers	1,211	11	1,993	66	3,985	643	123	..	1,199	..
16	Kewat	Boatmen and fishermen	..	97	103	17	289	206	..	..	62	..
17	Kumhar	Potters	161	8	5,722	878	3,290	1,224	1	..	225	..
18	Kurmi	Cultivators	341	5	2,362	351	2,157	966	74	..	461	..
19	Lodha	Agriculturists	106	32	4,431	1,659	4,064	2,034	23	..	520	..
20	Lohar	Blacksmiths	64	8	1,150	181	608	254	7	..	191	..
21	Mallah	Boatmen and fishermen	25	11	930	270	723	1,253	1	..	83	..
22	Nai	Barbers	108	21	992	1,330	1,251	409	..	..	490	..
23	Pasi	Toddy makers	232	18	2,165	296	1,439	1,144	..	..	7,515	..
24	Pathan	Military servants and landholders	818	10	13,042	986	17,345	2,156	163	..	11,770	..
25	Rajput		856	123	11,135	1,179	11,886	2,234	.	..	..	..
26	Saiyid	Priests and agriculturists	509	8	2,146	155	4,645	478	207	..	3,924	
27	Sheikh	Traders	1,377	4	22,002	1,704	42,600	5,273	212	..	9,798	..
28	Teli	Oil pressers	99	6	3,237	593	9,947	2,504	..	..	334	..

or Races. Part I.—Indigenous Castes, etc.—*continued*.

OF ACTUAL WORKERS—*contd.*

VII.—Public Administration.				VIII.—Arts and Professions.						IX.—Persons living on their income.		X.—Domestic service.		XI.—Contractors, clerks, cashiers, etc., otherwise unspecified.		XII.—Labourers unspecified.		XIII.—Beggars, prostitutes, criminals and inmates of jails and asylums.		
Gazetted Officers.		Others.		Religious.		Lawyers, doctors and teachers.		Others.												
Males.	Females.	Males.	Females.	Males.	Females.	Males.	Females.	Males.	Females.	Males.	Females.	Males.	Females.	Males.	Females.	Males.	Females.	Males.	Females.	Serial Number.
43	44	45	46	47	48	49	50	51	52	53	54	55	56	57	58	59	60	61	62	
..	..	39	..	56	9	141	10	30	6	11	8	5	43	56	1	244	1,545	73	47	9
..	..	41	..	9	..	79	12	18	1	69	31	9	33	15	..	35	56	54	73	10
..	..	509	..	1	..	24	8	24	31	7	7	88	32	23	1	968	309	725	559	11
..	..	716	..	58	3	140	39	231	2	14	21	755	269	93	24	3,628	298	1,978	1,617	12
..	..	66	..	57	14	108	15	43	10	4	6	19	67	280	26	5,518	6,582	138	91	13
1	..	972	..	145	4	1,798	83	181	..	123	9	1,420	1,245	1,124	511	1,457	429	508	170	14
57	..	1,541	..	55	2	838	45	331	21	3,488	553	2,113	191	239	6	129	55	219	75	1
8	..	240	1	24	..	41	10	28	13	65	9	1,343	90	51	..	599	87	175	36	2
150	..	1,774	2	1,006	10	654	46	186	151	306	100	3,861	262	256	2	3,274	358	2,279	440	3
205	..	3,216	3	1,534	75	1,714	114	512	19	657	247	4,651	365	882	2	3,446	825	1,328	335	4
30	..	650	4	1,180	58	331	38	91	30	136	13	1,806	213	44	3	609	184	2,424	539	5
41	..	905	4	436	17	260	25	151	38	208	14	1,490	191	69	23	3,208	383	3,205	447	6
..	..	..	..	..	..	1,105	51	1,293	107	1,568	361	12,649	1,362	814	14	1,299	216	9,690	2,415	7
2	..	577	1	174	9	108	40	2,205	255	144	62	2,486	542	156	5	7,700	2,487	2,945	957	8
..	..	1,790	99	210	4	65	40	727	194	149	22	5,642	1,493	108	3	4,721	811	4,447	1,512	9
353	..	4,615	14	5,117	119	1,687	99	1,462	362	3,182	461	10,797	1,082	807	16	9,843	1,191	14,949	2,133	10
4	..	834	1	101	12	99	29	277	160	187	55	3,713	424	159	26	1,119	178	682	270	11
4	..	1,100	17	1,579	97	368	64	330	303	150	25	3,002	417	142	7	2,937	807	3,054	1,040	12
14	..	380	2	68	1	25	2	35	5	118	64	841	299	60	1	631	182	457	187	13
158	..	1,096	6	605	78	217	53	311	246	322	75	1,652	300	263	10	1,192	334	1,168	445	14
339	..	6,543	14	925	57	3,491	112	457	22	1,822	519	6,277	354	1,074	26	1,137	215	1,065	175	15
13	..	300	4	709	50	96	23	202	102	429	77	1,278	198	157	5	2,369	447	1,469	463	16
7	..	21	..	51	2	9	..	4	3	81	50	92	5	10	..	261	47	75	22	17
11	..	285	4	324	7	90	16	91	47	92	32	583	77	99	1	436	184	677	191	18
8	..	333	1	231	16	62	54	274	670	194	233	1,416	786	64	2	1,057	306	886	232	19
14	..	370	2	238	251	145	14	436	118	131	14	1,626	288	30	1	362	150	27,274	5,989	20
7	..	399	8	491	47	111	18	208	259	154	13	1,209	165	81	1	1,101	321	1,637	529	21
19	..	308	1	228	24	228	19	114	72	161	51	739	313	39	..	352	207	694	282	22
228	..	2,392	3	810	28	648	39	545	101	751	169	4,372	466	426	12	4,346	229	3,756	866	23
9	..	189	1	112	8	31	6	51	92	21	9	446	88	49	4	572	174	326	153	24
270	..	4,443	13	2,314	73	1,374	95	838	228	1,350	227	9,021	677	838	6	4,048	759	5,327	1,403	25
336	..	2,376	9	..	..	1,287	79	216	37	464	100	1,718	127	183	15	659	102	8,217	1,228	26
289	..	3,613	9	1,860	87	1,567	142	1,337	234	982	318	7,057	962	527	14	1,540	185	4,004	1,123	27
15	..	575	1	527	13	155	26	328	56	336	92	685	156	289	6	1,146	278	1,097	388	28
10	..	577	8	311	18	83	30	208	169	138	33	1,083	126	79	29	1,204	280	841	308	29
63	..	1,575	..	68	5	930	12	119	5	594	626	2,778	310	485	..	627	236	422	85	1
99	..	751	..	85	4	101	..	67	..	461	185	6,016	2,947	720	..	14,825	8,045	2,160	974	2
4	..	48	..	14	..	50	4	42	16	69	74	604	499	172	..	2,109	1,320	487	219	3
..	..	328	..	50	5	91	..	531	..	35	78	4,079	814	190	..	3,369	696	720	247	4
..	..	93	..	22	..	5	..	9	..	33	1	848	905	62	..	3,377	6,392	675	304	5
465	..	9,495	..	..	..	11,147	291	1,788	270	4,444	1,624	32,687	7,406	4,704	..	16,789	7,254	24,556	15,704	6
..	..	591	..	70	15	113	..	988	1,786	1,031	301	23,027	6,828	1,800	..	185,602	145,642	7,208	5,173	7
..	..	49	..	25	2	7	..	29	8	24	11	612	285	56	..	3,032	1,377	403	219	8
..	..	14	..	7	3	14	..	121	168	81	49	2,362	889	78	..	2,283	1,586	1,801	1,755	9
13	..	263	..	38	3	45	..	72	31	139	124	2,516	1,389	202	..	11,275	5,058	864	349	10
4	..	59	..	44	..	24	..	14	5	64	21	617	86	53	..	1,875	399	471	49	11
248	..	242	..	54	1	170	5	50	56	297	28	1,608	258	96	..	4,028	413	535	125	12
17	..	812	..	296	10	814	..	534	151	229	81	6,780	3,923	888	..	12,447	3,370	1,995	1,308	13
..	..	737	..	40	6	127	..	215	128	273	80	..	..	1,185	..	18,427	6,003	1,153	510	14
242	..	7,887	..	196	14	3,158	102	302	45	1,190	529	2,399	734	807	..	767	416	645	362	15
..	..	9	..	..	..	5	..	1	..	62	..	181	171	14	..	872	1,015	115	74	16
..	..	51	..	4	1	31	..	38	11	45	12	1,123	939	78	..	4,142	3,056	503	302	17
35	..	177	..	52	5	137	..	86	20	849	98	2,748	1,655	620	..	4,703	2,727	1,367	472	18
7	..	131	..	14	..	39	..	72	10	167	173	2,468	1,220	832	..	10,611	6,425	863	338	19
5	..	56	..	12	1	41	..	105	3	85	53	541	703	117	..	2,372	1,849	385	254	20
..	..	43	..	12	..	9	..	92	91	32	109	467	646	63	..	2,498	4,828	269	175	21
..	..	256	..	90	32	556	..	227	327	165	77	5,191	13,852	182	..	1,927	3,233	717	514	22
..	..	721	..	103	2	49	..	123	101	956	223	2,755	705	1,113	..	13,305	9,315	1,792	686	23
135	..	6,915	..	669	80	2,576	132	1,613	517	2,132	611	20,368	6,633	1,728	..	12,836	2,446	3,473	1,860	24
..	..	..	..	326	30	1,622	81	489	344	1,721	643	13,462	3,264	1,582	..	15,148	4,525	5,613	2,204	25
258	..	3,757	..	977	92	2,726	166	580	94	1,300	587	4,754	1,530	763	..	2,082	433	1,898	696	26
380	..	8,637	..	1,637	216	6,142	201	5,833	1,337	2,385	729	29,847	10,277	2,735	..	17,198	3,619	8,546	4,581	27
..	..	134	..	47	1	76	..	35	17	164	75	1,782	528	217	..	6,553	2,533	654	354	28

TABLE-XVI.—Occupation by Selected Castes, Tribes

Serial Number.	Caste, Tribe or Race.	Traditional Occupation.	Population dealt with. Actual Workers. Males.	Actual Workers. Females.	Dependants. Males.	Dependants. Females.	Number of actual workers whose traditional caste occupation was returned as their Principal means of livelihood. Males.	Principal means of livelihood. Females.	Subsidiary means of livelihood. Males.	Subsidiary means of livelihood. Females.	Number of actual workers returning their traditional occupation as their principal means of livelihood who had some subsidiary occupation. Males.	Females.
	1	2	3	4	5	6	7	8	9	10	11	12
	CENTRAL INDIA AGENCY.											
1	Agarwal	Traders	16,675	6,899	11,035	23,679	11,784	3,767	1,493	2,032	207	67
2	Bhil (*Hindu*)	Agriculturists	7,526	5,061	6,167	7,077	3,785	1,725	336	10	122	1
3	Bhil (*Animist*)	Agriculturists	76,330	59,122	57,715	76,743	48,009	26,010	1,254	245	147	41
4	Bhilala (*Hindu*)	Agriculturists	9,374	9,396	6.977	8,017	7,157	7,844	62	..	81	3
5	Bhilala (*Animist*)	Agriculturists	26,156	24,583	18,665	20,208	22,876	22,122	268	48	601	21
6	Brahman	Priests	179,467	80,976	110,336	207,189	17,176	6,114	4,982	2,060	1,274	226
7	Gond (*Hindu*)	Agriculturists and hunters	49,036	47,267	27,717	39,265	38,009	32,830	1,410	606	132	23
8	Gond (*Animist*)		24,064	20,468	10,547	16,308	7,669	5,704	198	5	126	37
9	Oswal (*Hindu*)	Traders	3,305	2,205	2,767	6,032	2,105	1,302	320	324	20	3
10	Oswal (*Jain*)	Traders	9,902	2,821	6,772	13,371	7,918	1,406	890	103	165	25
11	Parwal (*Hindu*)	Traders	4,840	2,054	2,776	5,686	2,864	796	416	8	97	3
12	Parwal (*Jain*)	Traders	6,881	2,252	4,536	9,034	5,437	1,321	442	75	117	59
13	Pathan	Military servants	47,036	16,006	26,440	49,040	14,754	..	1,057	..	354	..
14	Rajput	Military servants	113,437	39,437	72,301	113,281	20,125	..	2,779	..	765	..
15	Saiyid	Military servants	10,628	3,373	6,831	11,365	3,708	..	181	..	94	..
16	Sheikh	Military servants and cotton cleaners	55,289	22,797	33,293	60,205	12,716	660	880	44	319	31
	HYDERABAD STATE.											
1	Bhoi	Fishermen	54,668	43,786	34,701	43,849	23,793	15,756	3,953	3,178	589	185
2	Brahman	Priests	83,159	14,210	50 033	113,839	29,564	..	5,272	..	284	..
3	Chakala	Washermen	60,227	49,136	29,564	36,699	47,212	40,293	9,652	5,069	696	276
4	Chambhar	Shoemakers	23,957	14,893	12,036	19,732	13,488	5,158	1,325	576	79	6
5	Devang	Weavers	22,062	12,682	14,195	22,461	14,711	6,224	1,241	446	86	1
6	Dhangar	Shepherds	159,069	99,653	86,318	143,569	84,041	31,679	10,481	3,820	180	22
7	Dhobi	Washermen	20,129	17,288	13,471	15,710	12,355	10,043	1,649	753	20	4
8	Golla	Cowherds	156,889	131,544	77,740	94,587	92,411	45,733	12,915	5,308	862	501
9	Gond (*Animist*)	Cultivators	38,780	32,022	23,803	29,736	25,923	14,765	40	18	..	..
10	Goundla	Toddy sellers	102,288	68,766	54,093	80,930	76,934	46,679	12,453	7,076	773	254
11	Kapu	Cultivators	214,989	161,036	115,913	156,316	164,713	103,267	11,852	10,402	1,927	914
12	Koli	Cultivators	84,084	49,798	56,348	82,616	54,760	20,247	9,902	2,163	20	12
13	Komati	Traders	73,528	34,829	40,593	74,430	62,490	27,145	8,748	2,825	488	272
14	Kombhar	Potters	47,375	34,629	30,605	39,377	33,719	20,694	4,926	2,332	263	150
15	Lambadi	Carriers	48,625	34,422	28,078	30,919	7,007	4,870	567	401	142	74
16	Lingayat	Traders and Shopkeepers	226,135	115,707	155,066	260,703	181,802	91,195	60,406	29,814	602	165
17	Madiga and Mang	Menial servants	363,911	307,673	217,608	256,160	192,380	89,314	24,109	12,114	3,118	641
18	Mahar and Mala	Menial servants	367,860	286,668	206,525	276,536	167,377	94,473	18,039	8,931	987	460
19	Maratha	Cultivators	506,638	320,451	266,240	445,545	308,002	163,190	25,564	11,335	385	81
20	Munnur	Cultivators	73,033	55,565	42,087	57,669	46,109	29,292	3,861	1,965	276	64
21	Mutrasi	Hunters	81,925	65,813	52,548	60,484	30,171	15,014	6,176	3,427	877	447
22	Panchal	Smiths	35,734	14,105	24,256	43,615	29,950	8,648	5,184	1,332	341	181
23	Rajput	Soldiers	17,935	8,011	13,361	22,330	8,860	3,505	846	407	15	8
24	Sale	Weavers	112,781	87,289	63,187	79,873	90,671	56,702	7,411	5,425	392	305
25	Sunar	Goldsmiths	28,484	10,763	16,794	31,996	28,324	5,047	2,634	447	66	67
26	Telaga	Cultivators	150,730	119,552	82,476	105,864	84,915	51,363	9,334	6,288	1,358	471
	MYSORE STATE.											
1	Agasa	Washermen	23,939	6,202	25,173	42,458	10,342	3,606	4,996	335	3,374	318
2	Banajiga	Traders	33,647	8,848	33,569	56,891	4,948	2,353	1,250	..	752	119
3	Beda	Hunters and fowlers.	61,647	19,019	73,950	113,838	31	19	33	13	20	..
4	Besta	Fishermen and boatmen	38,980	12,660	39,248	65,975	766	66	259	6	201	5
5	Brahman	Priests	49,101	5,861	49,496	90,112	3,261	144	1,372	12	1,140	21
6	Ganiga	Oil pressers	9,615	2,464	10,606	17,694	2,289	693	1,132	84	962	71
7	Golla	Cowherds	35,340	8,586	41,277	65,639	817	149	110	10	27	3
8	Holeya	Village watchmen and agriculturists	172,541	66,109	136,995	237,603	33,820	13,140	7,324	613	4,452	576
9	Kumbara	Potters	10,549	2,605	10,775	17,881	5,318	1,414	1,832	96	1,452	95
10	Kuruba	Shepherds and wool weavers	96,213	21,897	105,754	179,502	6,215	1,310	3,973	129	1,270	57
11	Madiga	Leather workers	80,135	27,856	75,450	124,642	5,245	262	1,539	37	1,479	53
12	Maratha	Military servants	13,412	3,064	10,497	18,925	648	15	10	..	123	..
13	Nayinda	Barbers	9,950	1,424	10,027	18,013	5,030	..	2,061	..	1,632	..
14	Neygi	Weavers and dyers	24,706	5,654	23,865	42,241	13,716	2,168	1,107	18	1,905	83
15	Panchala	Smiths	34,118	4,699	31,672	57,609	22,066	536	5,173	59	5,537	56
16	Tigala	Cultivators	17,187	3,801	18,239	30,066	13,054	1,005	139	7	1,107	55
17	Uppara	Salt workers	26,754	7,983	27,787	45,607	552	60	426	11	135	8
18	Vakkaliga	Agriculturists	308,135	59,757	357,572	605,565	263,483	30,254	2,228	96	14,712	683
19	Vodda	Earth workers and stone dressers	36,079	11,650	36,483	58,260	8,384	2,684	2,796	46	1,708	124

or Races. Part I.—Indigenous Castes, etc.—concluded.

RECORDED PRINCIPAL OCCUPATION OF ACTUAL WORKERS.

Income from rent of land.		I.—Exploitation of the surface of the soil.										II.—Extraction of minerals.				III.—Industries.				
		Cultivators of all kinds.		Agents and managers of landed estates, planters, forest officers and their clerks, rent collectors, etc.		Field labourers, wood cutters, etc		Raisers of live-stock, milkmen and herdsmen.		Fishing and hunting.		Owners, managers, clerks, etc.		Labourers.		Owners, managers, clerks, etc.		Artisans and other workmen.		
Males.	Females.	Males.	Females.	Males.	Females.	Males.	Females.	Males.	Females.	Males.	Females.	Males.	Females.	Males.	Females.	Males.	Females.	Males.	Females.	Serial Number.
13	14	15	16	17	18	19	20	21	22	23	24	25	26	27	28	29	30	31	32	
102	629	2,511	598	6	..	..	..	37	8	..	..	1	..	64	15	13	1	73	35	1
..	..	..	..	15	..	1,388	1,922	365	73	146	..	..	..	4	8	5	..	24	12	2
..	..	..	..	28	..	13,647	21,667	2,851	1,057	6	..	..	..	..	..	6	..	448	162	3
..	..	..	..	10	..	1,293	1,045	313	91	9	..	..	..	..	7	46	..	25	15	4
..	..	..	..	27	..	1,193	1,508	510	216	..	..	..	..	..	..	..	..	39	27	5
6,818	1,927	109,072	46,096	1,033	..	8,357	7,288	1,826	325	..	..	17	..	103	72	198	..	529	176	6
..	..	..	..	..	..	4,379	5,264	545	181	296	..	..	..	70	11	..	..	..	..	7
..	..	..	..	..	..	8,663	9,383	1,446	271	..	..	..	..	..	..	..	..	142	156	8
23	134	464	216	4	..	..	..	7	..	..	..	1	..	15	5	..	..	57	11	9
54	34	733	423	7	..	..	..	5	1	..	..	..	..	7	..	8	..	122	241	10
50	83	713	152	..	..	..	..	40	30	..	..	2	..	30	1	1	..	26	19	11
50	25	703	401	7	7	..	..	3	5	..	..	2	..	3	..	1	..	11	7	12
484	174	10,123	4,301	118	8	3,279	2,863	490	102	137	76	7	..	24	13	115	..	2,312	2,246	13
7,835	2,558	60,114	20,196	248	32	9,862	7,403	2,176	205	132	..	16	..	179	72	37	..	1,906	792	14
146	90	2,159	635	54	..	522	699	121	8	60	25	9	..	5	..	18	..	377	389	15
427	149	10,593	4,822	197	116	5,180	3,863	852	135	117	59	8	..	161	11	78	1	3,736	2,841	16
608	887	9,161	3,796	..	..	7,661	17,060	2,105	594	..	..	..	..	995	1,220	..	..	432	78	1
6,358	1,897	11,775	3,894	1,363	191	..	..	200	36	..	..	505	..	..	..	958	..	..	..	2
284	115	6,081	2,678	..	..	2,874	4,028	1,243	179	94	19	..	..	342	542	..	..	..	..	3
338	206	1,568	1,074	..	..	3,590	5,534	1,081	223	50	60	..	..	181	201	..	..	..	..	4
705	186	2,343	1,316	40	..	1,678	2,873	76	54	..	..	..	..	..	..	..	..	..	..	5
6,982	3,443	28,751	15,523	15	..	24,995	35,536	..	..	..	..	..	..	1,185	..	27	..	2,158	1,182	6
527	171	2,156	1,202	..	..	3,769	4,460	66	27	3	..	..	..	56	142	..	..	..	..	7
713	891	34,347	26,174	78	1	19,102	54,824	..	..	..	..	..	..	771	27	..	..	248	204	8
210	197	..	..	..	..	8,344	14,682	2,262	686	..	..	..	..	332	349	..	..	22	53	9
188	99	15,053	6,976	..	..	6,983	12,248	289	41	16	5	..	..	397	827	..	..	205	86	10
2,906	850	..	..	270	57	18,111	45,545	10,160	1,642	332	7	38	..	1,878	1,562	97	..	973	247	11
2,933	1,093	..	..	116	14	12,856	20,757	3,322	1,033	361	93	53	..	404	670	..	..	602	264	12
591	252	6,319	4,632	137	30	..	..	..	..	..	..	29	..	..	..	53	..	187	308	13
679	317	5,672	3,508	..	..	3,181	7,578	..	..	..	..	..	..	202	412	..	1	..	..	14
32	82	24,993	11,981	62	..	6,886	13,194	5,144	1,023	149	10	..	..	470	359	28	..	70	88	15
4,674	2,457	19,821	9,541	933	..	2,477	3,118	..	..	..	..	234	..	111	119	88	..	1,038	129	16
5,351	3,030	45,570	30,563	..	..	87,238	157,829	..	..	1,011	220	..	..	5,120	7,469	..	..	5,961	2,525	17
7,834	3,639	54,179	30,386	..	..	92,916	124,783	..	..	505	932	..	..	8,495	5,431	..	..	4,913	1,921	18
32,827	8,806	..	..	1,931	262	84,545	103,706	24,791	2,946	126	55	90	..	2,244	3,350	320	..	1,914	904	19
2,295	695	..	..	168	..	9,215	18,183	3,088	451	176	..	..	..	970	735	..	..	1,162	133	20
535	347	22,521	12,758	282	10	16,192	27,965	252	85	..	..	..	..	623	959	..	..	1,149	474	21
521	258	3,067	2,926	46	..	..	..	..	..	..	..	..	..	201	844	26	..	..	..	22
476	446	2,800	1,423	137	..	..	..	..	..	18	..	181	..	214	177	39	..	600	298	23
653	268	8,171	5,989	..	..	7,517	18,619	..	..	..	..	..	..	1,232	1,119	..	..	..	..	24
768	242	2,029	1,401	36	..	886	2,841	..	..	..	..	..	..	105	130	..	..	..	..	25
1,528	204	..	..	428	..	25,253	45,815	7,393	1,819	2,727	433	24	..	1,493	2,396	298	..	2,012	968	26
354	241	11,162	1,003	22	2	654	318	182	18	3	..	..	..	16	..	..	..	116	31	1
994	491	16,710	1,463	53	15	1,088	417	190	48	2	..	19	14	870	9	58	..	2,164	585	2
817	815	40,276	3,995	59	14	7,288	3,918	1,422	165	..	1	3	..	150	9	12	..	842	310	3
599	589	26,327	2,455	68	2	2,099	1,003	309	63	22	..	..	..	39	25	1	..	880	680	4
14,080	2,689	8,189	1,005	440	11	160	59	12	5	..	..	14	..	10	..	111	1	400	44	5
198	98	4,358	351	31	5	323	106	42	7	..	..	13	..	125	..	6	..	253	161	6
442	399	26,039	2,668	20	3	2,280	1,355	1,217	70	..	..	2	..	92	1	5	..	476	163	7
1,480	1,188	74,091	6,880	82	397	2,710	1,679	2,665	606	4	1	88	..	9,894	700	42	..	7,497	2,862	8
186	69	3,786	439	17	..	342	127	32	6	..	..	..	..	3	..	..	..	82	16	9
1,103	1,514	71,567	6,685	127	11	5,579	1,950	560	263	17	..	1	..	100	5	9	..	1,487	822	10
725	378	33,305	2,688	93	274	13,642	4,638	1,500	212	7	5	2	..	512	110	4	..	2,228	1,018	11
313	186	5,662	580	80	2	688	392	94	26	37	34	2	..	68	5	17	..	1,091	283	12
146	96	3,532	377	8	2	167	150	29	6	..	..	..	..	12	1	..	..	92	58	13
283	190	6,750	576	22	..	523	354	82	19	..	..	..	..	6	..	8	..	449	244	14
899	451	8,874	1,126	11	7	403	311	51	10	..	..	..	..	60	2	5	..	235	201	15
150	157	..	..	1	..	710	127	137	30	16	1	12	..	376	4	18	..	467	87	16
351	311	18,606	1,699	76	1	1,956	871	367	98	2	10	..	1	28	22	16	..	458	322	17
3,329	5,174	2,240	412	253	20	12,108	4,443	2,919	631	2	2	16	..	398	7	39	..	3,034	1,538	18
304	167	15,637	988	25	6	2,732	1,099	383	80	..	..	1	..	327	169	11	..	938	497	19

TABLE XVI.—Occupation by Selected Castes, Tribes

Serial Number.	Caste, Tribe or Race.	Traditional Occupation.	RECORDED PRINCIPAL OCCUPATION — IV.—Transport. Owners, managers, ships' officers, etc. Males.	IV.—Transport. Owners, managers, ships' officers, etc. Females.	IV.—Transport. Labourers, boatmen, carters, palki-bearers, etc. Males.	IV.—Transport. Labourers, boatmen, carters, palki-bearers, etc. Females.	V.—Trade. Males.	V.—Trade. Females.	VI.—Public Force. Commissioned and Gazetted Officers. Males.	VI.—Public Force. Commissioned and Gazetted Officers. Females.	VI.—Public Force. Others. Males.	VI.—Public Force. Others. Females.
	1	2	33	34	35	36	37	38	39	40	41	42
	CENTRAL INDIA AGENCY.											
1	Agarwal	Traders	9	..	30	2	..	..	8	..	10	..
2	Bhil (*Hindu*)	Agriculturists	7	..	75	4	80	122	..	..	195	1
3	Bhil (*Animist*)	Agriculturists	..	..	133	24	82	37	7	..	514	..
4	Bhilala (*Hindu*)	Agriculturists	..	..	26	..	11	7	..	..	43	2
5	Bhilala (*Animist*)	Agriculturists	..	..	7	2	17	4	1	..	16	..
6	Brahman	Priests	68	3	555	120	2,719	801	349	..	2,977	..
7	Gond (*Hindu*)	Agriculturists and hunters	..	..	48	..	275	100	..	..	61	..
8	Gond (*Animist*)	Agriculturists and hunters	..	..	8	76	133	152	..	..	26	..
9	Oswal (*Hindu*)	Traders	..	..	3	..	..	..	4	..	2	..
10	Oswal (*Jain*)	Traders	1	..	19	2	..	..	..	..	24	..
11	Parwal (*Hindu*)	Traders	..	..	6	..	..	..	2	..	4	..
12	Parwal (*Jain*)	Traders	2	..	31	..	..	..	..	..	8	..
13	Pathan	Military servants.	24	..	664	127	2,407	1,049	..	..	..	..
14	Rajput	Military servants.	30	..	226	80	992	378	..	..	..	..
15	Saiyid	Military servants.	6	1	96	7	540	189	..	..	..	..
16	Sheikh	Military servants and cotton cleaners	41	..	744	74	4,896	2,035	..	..	53	..
	HYDERABAD STATE.											
1	Bhoi	Fishermen	..	..	1,191	253	848	1,760	..	..	307	..
2	Brahman	Priests	170	..	..	..	4,724	656	87	..	1,458	..
3	Chakala	Washermen	..	..	391	177	41	16	..	..	47	..
4	Chambhar	Shoemakers	..	..	289	70	700	377	..	..	36	..
5	Devang	Weavers	..	..	..	..	1,148	232	..	..	45	..
6	Dhangar	Shepherds	..	..	680	744	..	..	..	..	228	..
7	Dhobi	Washermen	..	..	53	5	42	68	..	..	8	..
8	Golla	Cowherds	..	..	1,032	..	..	..	..	..	182	..
9	Gond (*Animist*)	Cultivators	..	..	234	34	133	200	..	..	7	..
10	Goundla	Toddy sellers	..	..	..	..	..	..	..	..	..	..
11	Kapu	Cultivators	106	..	1,461	457	3,102	1,525	12	..	293	..
12	Koli	Cultivators	32	..	421	207	1,425	692	..	..	181	27
13	Komati	Traders	128	..	466	..	..	..	..	..	35	..
14	Kumbhar	Potters	..	..	153	107	712	578	..	..	30	..
15	Lambadi	Carriers	7	..	85	162	740	489	..	..	40	..
16	Lingayat	Traders and shopkeepers	..	..	720	110	..	..	6	..	88	..
17	Madiga and Mang	Menial servants	..	..	2,877	2,530	..	..	..	..	504	24
18	Mahar and Mala	Menial servants	..	..	6,471	1,433	..	..	..	..	..	..
19	Maratha	Cultivators	123	..	3,492	793	7,830	2,530	..	..	1,428	..
20	Munnur	Cultivators	..	..	497	165	1,932	1,609	..	..	251	..
21	Mutrasi	Hunters	..	..	1,602	700	2,716	3,346	5	..	182	1
22	Panchal	Smiths	..	..	48	69	500	264	..	..	..	..
23	Rajput	Soldiers	160	..	205	15	1,158	587	..	..	..	..
24	Sale	Weavers	..	..	..	..	1,598	929	..	..	..	..
25	Sunar	Goldsmiths	..	..	53	17	679	278	..	..	..	..
26	Telaga	Cultivators	115	..	1,683	1,081	7,849	6,747	34	..	380	..
	MYSORE STATE.											
1	Agasa	Washermen	1	..	46	..	82	47	..	..	45	..
2	Banajiga	Traders	35	..	574	6	..	..	2	..	610	1
3	Beda	Hunters and fowlers.	13	..	231	29	532	743	..	..	2,098	125
4	Besta	Fishermen and boatmen	3	..	186	41	1,533	2,029	..	..	353	9
5	Brahman	Priests	410	1	462	2	1,771	319	9	..	1,095	1
6	Ganiga	Oil-pressers	2	..	65	13	983	415	..	..	54	..
7	Golla	Cowherds	5	..	121	2	452	374	2	..	106	1
8	Holeya	Village watchmen and agriculturists	7	1	1,208	54	941	2,508	6	..	774	12
9	Kumbara	Potters	1	..	28	1	137	52	..	..	12	..
10	Kuruba	Shepherds and wool weavers	9	1	371	9	1,060	900	..	..	322	9
11	Madiga	Leather workers.	6	..	249	9	553	572	..	..	1,749	183
12	Maratha	Military servants.	21	..	294	..	1,030	299	..	..	264	..
13	Nayinda	Barbers	..	..	6	..	61	73	..	..	9	..
14	Neygi	Weavers and dyers	2	..	69	14	1,211	424	..	..	46	2
15	Panchala	Smiths	2	..	39	3	139	235	..	..	22	..
16	Tigala	Cultivators	..	..	148	8	438	1,197	..	..	282	..
17	Uppara	Salt workers	2	..	75	3	324	681	..	..	32	..
18	Vakkaliga	Agriculturists	13	..	1,279	11	2,847	3,487	..	..	737	4
19	Vodda	Earth workers and stone dressers	17	1	154	12	413	273	..	..	29	5

or Races. Part I.—Indigenous Castes, etc.—*concluded.*

of actual workers—*contd.*

VII.—Public Administration. Gazetted Officers. Males.	VII.—Gazetted Officers. Females.	VII.—Others. Males.	VII.—Others. Females.	VIII.—Arts and Professions. Religious. Males.	VIII.—Religious. Females.	VIII.—Lawyers, doctors and teachers. Males.	VIII.—Lawyers, doctors and teachers. Females.	VIII.—Others. Males.	VIII.—Others. Females.	IX.—Persons living on their income. Males.	IX.—Females.	X.—Domestic service. Males.	X.—Females.	XI.—Contractors, clerks, cashiers, etc., otherwise unspecified. Males.	XI.—Females.	XII.—Labourers unspecified. Males.	XII.—Females.	XIII.—Beggars, prostitutes, criminals and inmates of jails and asylums. Males.	XIII.—Females.	Serial Number.
43	44	45	46	47	48	49	50	51	52	53	54	55	56	57	58	59	60	61	62	
1	..	395	..	12	..	32	1	34	12	212	374	814	153	..	..	671	1,257	46	46	1
..	..	83	..	..	1	..	..	28	6	..	4	364	44	..	..	913	997	64	142	2
..	..	447	..	7	..	1	..	44	34	..	..	428	314	..	..	9,384	9,810	280	7	3
..	..	13	..	..	..	..	..	1	2	2	2	165	65	..	..	258	312	2	4	4
11	..	90	..	..	..	1	..	..	..	4	..	181	75	..	..	1,165	570	18	59	5
81	..	3,873	..	..	..	341	11	446	57	1,207	630	4,986	1,180	..	..	7,584	9,911	9,050	6,265	6
..	..	31	..	15	..	..	..	18	30	25	3	348	42	..	..	4,595	8,368	321	443	7
..	..	22	..	..	..	..	..	9	..	8	5	79	84	..	..	5,672	4,620	187	17	8
..	..	14	..	1	..	15	..	100	7	84	101	282	28	..	..	110	353	14	48	9
..	..	119	..	15	5	19	..	16	13	93	65	666	116	..	..	150	465	16	50	10
3	..	24	..	..	..	11	2	62	29	241	90	311	85	..	..	434	737	16	30	11
1	..	19	..	10	1	7	..	30	2	105	24	244	77	..	..	191	323	16	59	12
29	..	1,645	..	99	5	187	5	741	275	906	420	3,763	903	..	..	2,612	2,720	1,916	719	13
103	..	505	..	34	..	48	3	262	66	539	546	2,697	1,379	..	..	4,678	5,381	693	344	14
28	..	327	..	78	1	75	2	116	29	333	149	668	224	..	..	334	245	848	680	15
21	..	1,719	..	90	10	193	6	1,208	337	849	371	6,047	945	..	..	3,397	5,249	1,971	1,113	16
..	..	1,266	..	..	..	5	3	85	34	..	..	4,387	1,211	..	..	1,393	1,139	521	495	1
192	..	10,712	..	..	..	2,390	45	327	22	1,504	2,698	6,334	2,526	648	..	..	..	3,885	2,245	2
..	..	10	..	..	..	..	..	..	..	213	61	663	282	..	..	462	496	270	250	3
..	..	70	..	..	..	..	..	33	..	229	124	509	253	..	..	1,384	1,302	321	311	4
..	..	..	..	14	..	1	..	3	..	166	692	533	283	38	..	410	655	156	167	5
..	..	220	..	2	..	5	1	4	..	862	578	3,671	3,626	..	..	3,208	6,108	2,035	1,233	6
..	..	51	..	..	..	..	..	12	..	196	182	224	400	..	..	438	480	162	108	7
..	..	871	..	8	..	99	..	18	..	969	423	3,802	1,381	226	..	799	834	1,513	1,052	8
..	..	17	..	..	..	..	..	..	14	261	46	429	370	..	..	334	359	372	267	9
..	..	..	..	4	..	..	..	..	..	685	259	820	717	29	..	165	395	525	328	10
47	..	3,261	..	48	..	172	5	268	136	1,435	1,306	2,540	2,153	151	..	511	1,450	1,104	825	11
..	..	292	..	28	..	46	..	146	91	230	167	2,968	1,342	141	..	2,049	2,491	718	610	12
..	..	336	..	71	..	135	..	40	..	421	1,021	1,372	1,168	207	..	56	21	455	252	13
..	..	88	..	..	..	..	..	..	..	1,611	214	684	297	12	..	441	577	241	346	14
..	..	98	..	..	..	..	..	2	8	272	281	355	255	8	..	427	605	1,741	1,515	15
..	..	547	..	86	..	370	9	165	49	5,405	4,012	1,259	1,851	273	..	1,105	570	4,933	2,547	16
..	..	2,966	473	..	..	..	..	..	..	3,149	1,309	..	..	401	..	6,728	6,838	4,658	5,549	17
..	..	..	..	..	..	..	..	..	..	3,360	1,105	..	..	..	..	14,183	17,032	7,627	5,563	18
21	..	3,878	..	468	348	839	330	235	189	1,549	984	10,067	8,226	297	..	15,985	21,280	3,686	2,552	19
..	..	973	..	..	..	51	..	116	215	623	426	2,943	1,167	158	..	1,319	1,821	992	673	20
..	..	1,206	69	..	..	..	..	58	145	902	525	2,646	1,728	353	..	720	997	710	690	21
..	..	..	..	..	..	18	..	216	16	154	365	474	338	38	..	174	188	301	189	22
19	..	741	..	..	..	57	..	124	30	250	197	1,444	752	95	..	178	435	220	145	23
..	..	..	..	..	..	..	..	..	..	358	553	1,543	1,180	23	..	499	1,354	516	576	24
..	..	..	..	36	1	1	..	37	30	154	230	20	90	65	..	131	301	170	155	25
40	..	2,861	..	254	..	227	97	256	111	2,340	1,223	5,558	3,394	276	..	1,457	2,000	1,236	1,901	26
..	..	79	1	10	4	23	2	14	2	9	7	48	47	5	11	660	788	66	74	1
4	..	607	12	125	21	246	27	328	160	204	80	216	145	210	2	2,407	2,200	961	849	2
..	..	1,044	61	138	35	106	13	40	60	61	24	256	131	38	2	5,638	7,309	552	1,241	3
..	..	699	20	231	35	50	10	85	25	31	18	233	94	66	1	4,106	5,073	294	422	4
118	..	9,708	91	282	24	4,290	104	681	20	909	332	794	305	606	2	434	217	765	485	5
..	..	64	..	14	2	28	..	13	3	18	6	60	36	17	3	588	575	71	50	6
..	..	390	10	90	18	43	..	11	5	43	18	124	69	58	3	1,895	2,726	610	552	7
..	..	2,038	188	143	42	94	10	409	19	308	60	4,590	1,366	149	26	28,390	32,814	1,121	1,566	8
..	..	10	..	9	..	7	..	1	..	4	1	15	9	2	..	526	428	31	43	9
..	..	910	38	116	24	111	11	68	23	67	40	336	262	69	7	5,470	7,529	539	484	10
..	..	5,850	670	103	24	13	5	55	20	35	7	312	123	89	5	13,267	15,337	591	1,326	11
1	..	392	4	40	14	79	6	112	16	134	19	284	48	76	1	1,218	854	767	370	12
..	..	37	1	22	5	21	9	475	13	6	7	6	20	1	..	259	535	31	71	13
..	..	92	4	61	6	108	8	22	10	29	16	42	27	20	4	906	1,406	259	182	14
..	..	34	3	61	9	72	3	20	8	15	36	46	70	28	11	896	1,470	140	213	15
..	..	121	..	23	4	22	2	19	1	19	7	76	45	13	3	985	984	100	139	16
..	..	137	2	41	3	29	1	17	5	7	12	184	57	66	21	3,393	3,705	85	96	17
4	..	2,680	24	240	27	330	29	171	76	166	296	863	818	303	86	9,682	11,318	909	1,093	18
..	..	70	21	7	5	8	3	8	5	9	4	113	56	78	7	6,228	5,343	303	231	19

TABLE XVI.—OCCUPATION BY SELECTED CASTES, TRIBES OR RACES.

Serial Number.	Province, State or Agency.	Population dealt with. Actual Workers. Males.	Actual Workers. Females.	Dependants. Males.	Dependants. Females.	Recorded principal occupation. I.—Exploitation of the surface of the soil. Income from rent of land. Males.	Income from rent of land. Females.	Cultivators of all kinds. Males.	Cultivators of all kinds. Females.	Agents and managers of landed estates, planters, forest officers and their clerks, rent collectors, etc. Males.	Agents and managers … Females.	Field labourers, wood-cutters, etc. Males.	Field labourers, wood-cutters, etc. Females.	Raisers of livestock, milkmen and herdsmen. Males.	Raisers of livestock … Females.	Fishing and hunting. Males.	Fishing and hunting. Females.
	1	2	3	4	5	6	7	8	9	10	11	12	13	14	15	16	17
	EUROPEANS.	99,681	5,853	18,538	39,904	111	76	124	10	2,207	54	36	9	13	8	30	1
1	Ajmer-Merwara	1,285	49	117	304	..	..	..	1	..	..	..	..	..	..	..	..
2	Assam	1,460	89	134	564	2	..	4	..	914	7	..	..	..	..	..	..
3	Baluchistan	3,098	70	284	758	..	..	..	..	1	..	..	..	..	..	..	..
4	Bengal	11,887	1,307	3,855	7,039	29	14	19	2	407	11	34	9	4	..	..	..
5	Bihar and Orissa	3,125	513	734	1,852	22	17	60	..	224	5	..	..	1	5	..	..
6	Burma	8,764	611	1,114	2,681	36	15	20	3	99	..	..	..	1	1	27	..
7	C. P. and Berar	4,893	375	554	1,511	..	..	3	1	26	1	..	..	..	..	..	..
8	Coorg	105	15	20	67	..	..	..	..	77	3	..	..	..	..	..	..
9	Madras	6,961	1,123	2,164	4,623	2	12	5	2	256	16	..	..	2	..	2	..
10	N.-W. F. Province	4,643	92	270	722	..	..	..	..	1	..	..	..	..	..	..	..
11	Punjab	21,651	873	2,737	6,978	3	7	4	..	29	5	1	..	3	1	1	1
12	United Provinces	21,139	59	3,322	8,291	11	1	7	..	53	4	1	..	..	..	..	..
13	Baroda State*	85	12	39	105	..	..	..	..	..	..	..	..	..	..	..	..
14	Central India Agency	3,327	61	389	805	..	..	..	..	5	..	..	..	2	..	..	..
15	Hyderabad State	2,756	90	1,555	981	..	..	..	..	13	..	..	..	..	..	..	..
16	Kashmir State	117	34	17	82	..	..	..	..	5	..	..	..	..	..	..	..
17	Mysore State	3,920	406	981	2,155	2	9	1	1	94	2	..	..	..	1	..	..
18	Rajputana Agency	465	74	252	386	4	1	1	..	3	..	..	..	..	..	..	..
	ANGLO-INDIANS.	21,028	5,436	18,164	33,397	74	115	81	32	221	6	5	..	2	6	12	..
1	Ajmer-Merwara	227	19	152	312	..	..	..	..	..	..	..	..	..	..	..	..
2	Assam	175	17	97	186	..	..	1	2	7	..	.	..	..	..	..	..
3	Baluchistan	49	15	15	44	..	..	..	..	..	..	..	..	..	..	..	..
4	Bengal	5,434	1,747	4,514	8,138	27	34	9	5	7	1	1	..	1	1	..	..
5	Bihar and Orissa	954	271	812	1,368	12	8	26	4	51	..	4	..	..	..	5	..
6	Bombay (Sind)	353	67	223	549	..	1	..	..	1	..	..	..	..	..	..	..
7	Burma	3,606	563	2,433	4,504	8	26	21	8	39	1	..	..	1	..	5	..
8	C. P. and Berar	950	194	933	1,411	1	2	1	3	9	.	..	..	..	..	..	..
9	Madras	3,749	1,160	3,830	7,340	12	22	15	10	61	1	..	..	..	..	2	..
10	N.-W. F. Province	36	3	14	47	.	..	..	..	..	..	..	..	..	..	..	..
11	Punjab	976	180	827	1,496	3	3	2	..	3	..	..	..	..	..	..	..
12	United Provinces	1,990	528	2,054	3,522	11	13	3	..	13	1	..	..	..	..	..	..
13	Central India Agency	174	39	122	230	..	..	..	..	..	..	..	..	..	..	..	..
14	Hyderabad State	1,004	231	544	1,225	..	..	..	..	9	..	..	..	..	..	..	..
15	Kashmir State	8	4	1	3	..	.	..	..	..	..	..	..	..	..	..	..
16	Mysore State	1,211	376	1,462	2,778	..	6	2	..	21	2	..	..	..	5	..	..
17	Rajputana Agency	132	22	131	244	..	..	1	..	..	..	..	..	..	..	..	..
	ARMENIANS.	561	122	403	551	8	6	..	1	4	..	..	..	..	..	..	..
1	Assam	4	.	..	1	.	.	..	..	..	..	..	..	..	..	..	..
2	Bengal	337	78	292	356	8	3	..	1	1	..	..	..	..	..	..	..
3	Bihar and Orissa	51	6	20	15	..	1	..	..	1	..	..	..	..	..	..	..
4	Burma	104	13	42	114	..	2	..	..	2	..	..	..	..	..	..	..
5	Madras	11	1	15	7	..	..	..	..	..	..	..	..	..	..	..	..
6	N.-W. F. Province	9	..	..	5	..	..	..	..	..	..	..	..	..	..	..	..
7	Punjab	13	7	5	14	..	..	..	..	..	..	..	..	..	..	..	..
8	United Provinces	31	15	28	38	..	..	..	..	..	..	..	..	..	..	..	..
9	Hyderabad State	1	..	..	1	..	..	..	..	..	..	..	..	..	..	..	..
10	Mysore State		..	1	..	..	..	..	..	..	..	..	..	..	..	..	..
11	Rajputana Agency		2	..	..	..	..	..	..	..	..	..	..	..	..	..	..

NOTE.—The figures for Provinces are inclusive of those for the States attached to
* The figures for Baroda State relate to

PART II.—EUROPEANS, ANGLO-INDIANS AND ARMENIANS.

OF ACTUAL WORKERS.

II.—Extraction of minerals.				III.—Industries.				IV.—Transport.				V.—Trade.		VI.—Public force.				VII.—Public administration.				
Owners, managers, clerks, etc.		Labourers.		Owners, managers, clerks, etc.		Artisans and other workmen.		Owners, managers, ships' officers, etc.		Labourers, boatmen, carters, palki-bearers, etc.				Commissioned and Gazetted Officers.		Others.		Gazetted Officers.		Others.		
Males.	Females.	Males.	Females.	Males.	Females.	Males.	Females.	Males.	Females.	Males.	Females.	Males.	Females.	Males.	Females.	Males.	Females.	Males.	Females.	Males.	Females.	Serial Number.
18	19	20	21	22	23	24	25	26	27	28	29	30	31	32	33	34	35	36	37	38	39	
945	**6**	**414**	..	**1,258**	**79**	**883**	**135**	**9,362**	**159**	**1,184**	**11**	**3,541**	**331**	**4,378**	**1**	**61,593**	**27**	**1,947**	**18**	**1,988**	**73**	
..	..	..	..	6	..	..	2	193	..	..	..	3	..	61	..	945	..	8	..	2	..	1
8	..	10	..	4	..	2	2	94	..	11	..	26	1	60	..	10	..	36	..	13	...	2
2	..	..	..	13	3	..	..	95	..	..	..	9	5	312	..	2,593	1	17	.	5	..	3
145	2	1	..	579	34	309	53	2,393	37	53	..	1,670	122	368	..	3,242	6	391	4	418	14	4
147	2	2	..	78	3	42	6	613	51	76	2	73	29	148	..	1,091	1	145	6	45	..	5
403	..	22	..	130	10	90	7	1,709	14	118	2	743	45	270	1	3,197	18	285	.	266	13	6
22	..	..	..	82	..	..	..	378	6	..	..	40	1	211	..	3,602	..	129	..	136	3	7
..	..	..	..	..	..	4	..	..	..	..	1	..	..	..	..	4	..	3	..	..	..	8
27	..	6	..	108	1	99	23	708	13	335	6	326	71	147	..	2,769	..	233	1	102	3	9
5	1	..	..	6	..	1	..	37	..	..	..	15	2	554	..	3,869	..	33	..	16	..	10
11	..	..	..	59	7	97	15	638	15	492	..	240	25	930	..	17,645	1	242	1	463	32	11
..	..	1	..	103	16	..	..	1,899	18	..	..	196	12	825	..	15,957	..	197	1	306	7	12
..	..	..	..	5	..	..	..	28	..	..	..	2	..	13	..	..	..	12	..	..	..	13
3	..	..	..	11	..	..	..	140	1	..	..	1	2	129	..	2,904	..	29	..	3	..	14
12	..	..	..	7	..	193	4	199	..	..	..	116	..	177	..	1,339	..	116	5	175	1	15
..	..	..	..	14	..	2	..	..	..	..	..	3	2	20	..	1	..	29	..	11	..	16
150	1	372	..	53	5	39	23	52	4	69	..	67	14	124	..	2,338	..	29	..	26	..	17
10	..	..	..	..	..	5	..	191	..	..	..	11	..	29	..	87	.	13	..	11	..	18
214	**2**	**339**	**3**	**859**	**93**	**861**	**333**	**5,892**	**226**	**1,524**	**7**	**1,254**	**284**	**135**	..	**503**	**2**	**431**	**5**	**2,251**	**108**	
..	..	..	..	..	..	..	..	215	..	..	..	1	..	..	..	3	..	.	..	1	..	1
1	..	2	..	2	..	7	3	88	..	4	..	2	..	1	..	12	.	2	..	15	..	2
..	..	..	..	..	..	..	..	21	..	..	..	..	..	1	..	5	..	1	.	3	..	3
25	..	..	..	274	59	134	49	1,818	91	82	..	461	104	25	..	51	1	135	..	475	23	4
59	2	1	..	6	..	19	1	423	3	89	..	71	4	7	..	20	1	41	2	15	3	5
..	..	..	..	3	2	11	..	127	3	69	..	27	..	2	..	3	..	9	..	26	..	6
26	..	5	..	95	14	45	20	930	31	159	1	381	94	38	..	94	..	83	..	550	34	7
8	..	..	..	56	4	..	..	217	3	..	..	8	..	6	..	38	..	35	..	360	21	8
1	..	2	..	88	4	435	203	508	42	635	6	124	40	..	..	76	..	14	..	198	11	9
1	..	..	..	..	..	1	..	12	..	..	..	1	..	..	..	1	..	..	..	6	..	10
1	..	..	..	9	..	13	6	292	12	247	..	23	16	9	..	44	..	15	..	141	12	11
..	..	..	3	222	9	4	2	945	38	1	..	45	6	11	..	70	..	18	..	124	2	12
..	..	..	..	8	..	..	..	95	..	..	..	..	..	12	..	..	..	..	..	4	..	13
8	..	48	..	77	..	46	..	22	..	94	..	30	..	20	..	51	..	66	3	285	2	14
..	..	..	..	..	..	..	..	..	..	..	..	..	..	..	..	.	..	2	..	4	..	15
80	..	281	..	16	1	144	49	81	3	144	..	79	20	1	..	33	..	9	..	40	.	16
4	..	..	..	3	..	2	..	98	..	..	..	1	..	2	..	2	..	1	..	4	..	17
13	..	**2**	..	**31**	**3**	**12**	**5**	**79**	**3**	**42**	..	**136**	**10**	..	..	**4**	..	**10**	.	**35**	**2**	
..	..	..	..	..	..	..	..	4	..	..	..	..	..	..	..	..	..	..	..	..	..	1
10	..	2	..	13	1	12	5	42	3	35	..	75	8	..	..	1	..	7	..	12	2	2
3	..	..	..	4	..	..	..	19	..	..	..	17	..	..	..	...	.	1	.	..	..	3
..	..	..	..	6	2	..	..	2	..	3	..	35	2	..	..	..	..	1	..	17	..	4
..	..	..	..	..	..	..	..	..	..	3	..	2	..	..	..	..	..	..	..	.	..	5
..	..	..	..	..	..	..	..	..	..	..	..	5	..	..	..	..	..	..	..	1	..	6
..	..	..	..	..	..	..	..	4	..	1	..	1	..	..	..	2	..		..	2	..	7
..	..	..	..	8	..	..	..	8	..	..	..	1	..	..	..	1	..	1	..	3	..	8
..	..	..	..	..	..	..	..	..	..	..	..	.	..	..	..	..	..	..	..	..	..	9
..	..	..	..	..	..	..	..	..	..	..	..	..	..	..	..	.	..	..	..	..	..	10
..	..	..	..	..	..	..	..	..	..	..	..	..	..	..	..	..	..	..	..	..	..	11

them, except in the case of Madras where they exclude Cochin and Travancore.
both Europeans and Anglo-Indians.

TABLE XVI.—Occupation by Selected Castes, Tribes or Races. Part II.—Europeans, Anglo-Indians and Armenians—*concluded.*

Serial Number.	Province, State or Agency.	RECORDED PRINCIPAL OCCUPATION OF ACTUAL WORKERS—*contd.* VIII.—Arts and Professions. Religious. Males.	Religious. Females.	Lawyers, doctors and teachers. Males.	Lawyers, doctors and teachers. Females.	Others. Males.	Others. Females.	IX.—Persons living on their income. Males.	IX. Females.	X.—Domestic service. Males.	X. Females.	XI.—Contractors, clerks, cashiers, etc., otherwise unspecified. Males.	XI. Females.	XII.—Labourers unspecified. Males.	XII. Females.	XIII.—Beggars, prostitutes, criminals and inmates of jails and asylums. Males.	XIII. Females.
	1	40	41	42	43	44	45	46	47	48	49	50	51	52	53	54	55
	EUROPEANS.	**1,943**	**1,236**	**2,340**	**1,565**	**1,716**	**512**	**1,585**	**716**	**427**	**476**	**1,557**	**139**	**42**	**116**	**77**	**95**
1	Ajmer-Merwara	28	23	22	4	2	11	13	8	2	..	..	..	..	..	..	..
2	Assam	70	39	63	13	123	16	5	5	..	5	5	1	..	..	..	..
3	Baluchistan	7	2	29	11	3	14	9	7	3	27	..	..	..	..	..	..
4	Bengal	176	148	326	282	528	249	149	140	36	62	584	85	2	..	24	33
5	Bihar and Orissa	109	66	113	66	12	46	65	37	7	36	38	5	12	109	2	21
6	Burma	133	79	431	296	304	17	102	25	50	44	318	5	..	..	10	16
7	C. P. and Berar	145	188	45	96	11	1	53	38	2	36	7	..	..	..	1	4
8	Coorg	6	1	5	5	4	..	1	..	..	5	1	..	..	..	..	..
9	Madras	658	360	256	353	302	15	261	163	14	40	318	37	15	7	15	..
10	N.-W. F. Province	14	4	61	11	18	10	7	17	..	47	2	..	4	..	..	..
11	Punjab	181	207	246	200	75	93	136	117	23	126	112	1	4	..	16	19
12	United Provinces	196	..	444	..	27	..	502	..	275	..	126	..	5	..	8	..
13	Baroda State*	5	2	18	10	..	..	2	..	..	..	..	..	..	..	..	..
14	Central India Agency	25	21	43	13	23	6	9	2	..	16	..	..	..	..	..	..
15	Hyderabad State	78	6	118	64	199	5	12	4	..	1	2	..	..	..	..	..
16	Kashmir State	10	9	9	10	..	2	10	11	1	..	2	..	..	..	..	..
17	Mysore State	87	73	90	111	60	21	213	112	12	22	41	5	..	..	1	2
18	Rajputana Agency	15	8	21	20	25	6	36	30	2	9	1	..	..	..	..	..
	ANGLO-INDIANS.	**229**	**215**	**1,168**	**1,401**	**694**	**517**	**1,189**	**909**	**462**	**352**	**2,014**	**266**	**162**	**15**	**452**	**630**
1	Ajmer-Merwara	..	4	1	7	1	2	5	6	..	..	..	..	..	..	..	..
2	Assam	1	..	3	3	22	8	3	..	1	..	1	..	..	..	..	1
3	Baluchistan	..	..	4	6	14	7	..	..	..	2	..	..	..	..	..	..
4	Bengal	27	43	239	257	234	267	311	234	50	54	758	139	10	5	280	380
5	Bihar and Orissa	22	15	18	30	3	8	33	26	15	25	11	2	1	..	2	137
6	Bombay (Sind)	4	3	28	24	1	14	15	10	1	10	28	..	..	..	..	..
7	Burma	18	5	263	225	143	17	91	38	133	8	463	41	..	..	15	..
8	C. P. and Berar	16	22	116	44	6	12	53	55	15	26	4	1	..	..	1	1
9	Madras	21	21	141	325	191	9	333	235	16	54	614	77	145	6	117	94
10	N.-W. F. Province	..	..	11	..	1	..	2	1	..	2	..	..	..	..	..	..
11	Punjab	16	7	70	38	19	36	20	18	12	29	24	..	1	..	12	3
12	United Provinces	25	36	136	243	5	31	169	106	110	25	66	4	..	1	12	8
13	Central India Agency	25	12	17	7	1	5	5	2	7	13	..	..	..	..	..	..
14	Hyderabad State	38	23	72	103	20	45	20	9	95	48	3	..	..	..	..	..
15	Kashmir State	2	2	..	2	..	..	..	..	..	..	..	..	..	..	..	..
16	Mysore State	13	20	43	76	28	57	127	65	7	52	44	2	5	3	13	16
17	Rajputana Agency	1	2	6	11	5	1	2	4	..	4	..	..	..	..	..	..
	ARMENIANS.	**11**	**11**	**37**	**20**	**23**	**8**	**32**	**36**	**5**	**5**	**73**	**9**	..	..	**4**	**3**
1	Assam	..	..	..	..	..	..	..	..	..	..	..	..	..	..	..	..
2	Bengal	7	7	28	9	12	7	14	19	1	2	54	8	..	..	3	3
3	Bihar and Orissa	..	1	2	..	..	..	2	3	..	1	2	..	..	..	..	..
4	Burma	1	..	4	2	10	..	11	4	..	..	11	1	..	..	1	..
5	Madras	3	..	1	..	..	..	1	1	1	..	..	..	..	..	..	..
6	N.-W. F. Province	..	..	..	..	..	..	..	..	1	..	2	..	..	..	..	..
7	Punjab	..	..	1	4	1	1	1	1	..	1	..	..	..	..	..	..
8	United Provinces	..	2	1	5	..	..	3	7	2	1	3	..	..	..	..	..
9	Hyderabad State	..	..	..	..	..	..	..	..	..	..	1	..	..	..	..	..
10	Mysore State	..	..	..	..	..	..	..	..	..	..	..	..	..	..	..	..
11	Rajputana Agency	..	1	..	..	..	..	..	1	..	..	..	..	..	..	..	..

Note.—The figures for Provinces are inclusive of those for the States attached to them, except in the case of Madras where they exclude Cochin and Travancore.

* The figures for Baroda State relate to both Europeans and Anglo-Indians.

TABLE XVII.

Christians by Race and Denomination.

1. This Table is divided into three parts:—Part I shows, by race, the total number of Christians in India distributed (*a*) according to their sect or denomination and (*b*) by locality. Part II shows the denominations returned by the Christian community of each Province, State or Agency and Part III gives the territorial distribution of each denomination. The term Anglo-Indian is used under the orders of the Government of India to designate the persons hitherto known as Eurasians. It includes all persons of mixed European and Asiatic descent. Goanese, when shown as such in the schedules, have been treated as Indian Christians; but some, no doubt, returned themselves as Portuguese or Eurasians. The Feringis of East Bengal (males 593, females 609) and of Assam (males 4, female 1) have been classed as Anglo-Indians for the purpose of this Table, but not so in Table XVIII. Armenians have here been grouped with "European and Allied Races;" their number will be found in Table XVIII.

2. Many denominational names were entered in the schedules other than those shown in this Table. The headings under which they have been tabulated are noted at the end of the Table.

3. The Christians of the following five missions are now organized as one body under the name of the "South India United Church," *viz.*, the United Free Church of Scotland Mission in and about Madras, the Arcot Mission of the Reformed Church of America in the Arcot and Cuddapah districts, the American Madura Mission and the two great branches of the London Missionary Society—the Travancore Mission and the South India District Committee Mission. In order to permit of comparison with the returns of previous censuses, the adherents of each Mission have been shown according to its original denomination but it should be understood that the sectarian differences connoted by these names are now a thing of the past. For further information on this subject the Report Volume should be referred to.

4. The figures for Madras States include those for Cochin and Travancore.

TABLE XVII.—Christians by Race and Denomination.

Part I-A.—General Distribution by Denomination.

Denomination.	Total Returned.			Distribution by Race.					
				European and Allied Races.		Anglo-Indian.*		Indian.	
	Persons.	Males.	Females.	Males.	Females.	Males.	Females.	Males.	Females.
1	2	3	4	5	6	7	8	9	10
All Denominations.	**3,876.203**	**2,010,729**	**1,865,474**	**143,974**	**55,802**	**51,232**	**50,425**	**1,815,523**	**1,759,247**
Abyssinian	25	7	18	...	...	...	...	7	18
Anglican Communion	492,752	278,014	214,738	91,728	33,664	17,591	16,962	168,695	164,112
Armenian	1,200	778	422	737	400	25	5	16	17
Baptist	337,226	170,426	166,800	1,671	1,145	1,156	1,083	167,599	164,572
Congregationalist	135,265	68,776	66,489	443	298	173	116	68,160	66,080
Greek	594	447	147	408	113	8	9	31	25
Lutheran	218,500	108,280	110,220	974	495	124	65	107,182	109,660
Methodist	171,844	91,595	80,249	5,099	1,805	1,122	1,451	85,374	76,993
Minor Protestant Denominations	12,469	6,414	6,055	295	286	80	106	6,039	5,663
Presbyterian	181,130	99,914	81,216	11,991	3,159	1,164	747	86,759	77,310
Protestant (Unsectarian or sect not specified)	32,180	17,467	14,713	1,849	1,048	924	775	14,694	12,890
Quaker	1,245	647	598	21	24	3	3	623	571
Roman Catholic	1,490,863	758,314	732,549	27.338	12,781	28,542	28,482	702,434	691,286
Salvationist	52,407	27,803	24,604	93	96	11	8	27,699	24,500
Syrian, Chaldæan	13,780	7,247	6,533	3	...	...	...	7,244	6,533
Syrian, Jacobite	225,190	114,233	110,957	1	1	...	...	114,232	110,956
Syrian, Reformed	75,848	39,801	36,047	...	...	...	...	39,801	36,047
Syrian, Romo-Syrian	413,142	209,413	203,729	1	1	3	3	209,409	203,725
Syrian, Unspecified	344	194	150	...	...	...	...	194	150
Sect not returned	17,954	9,644	8,310	857	376	271	601	8,516	7,333
Indefinite Beliefs	2,245	1,315	930	465	115	35	9	815	806

* And other persons of mixed

TABLE XVII.—Christians by Race and Denomination.

Part I-B.—General Distribution by Locality.

Province, State or Agency.	Total Returned.			Distribution by Race.					
				European and Allied Races.		Anglo-Indian.		Indian.	
	Persons.	Males.	Females.	Males.	Females.	Males.	Females.	Males.	Females.
1	2	3	4	5	6	7	8	9	10
INDIA.	**3,876,203**	**2,010,729**	**1,865,474**	**143,974**	**55,802**	**51,232**	**50,425**	**1,815,523**	**1,759,247**
Provinces.	2,492,284	1,301,555	1,190,729	128,935	49,973	43,818	42,794	1,128,802	1,097,962
1. Ajmer-Merwara	5,432	3,258	2,174	1,402	353	379	331	1,477	1,490
2. Andamans and Nicobars	566	384	182	199	52	35	43	150	87
3. Assam	66,430	33,545	32,882	1,583	647	254	183	31,711	32,052
4. Baluchistan	5,030	3,892	1,138	3,366	824	59	59	467	255
5. Bengal	129,518	70,127	59,391	16,657	8,772	10,529	10,479	42,941	40,140
6. Bihar and Orissa	229,825	114,009	115,816	3,895	2,354	1,728	1,613	108,386	111,849
Bihar	*22,076*	*11,360*	*10,716*	*2,638*	*1,549*	*1,004*	*928*	*7,718*	*8,239*
Orissa	*8,007*	*3,804*	*4,203*	*192*	*224*	*218*	*263*	*3,394*	*3,716*
Chota Nagpur	*199,742*	*98,845*	*100,897*	*1,065*	*581*	*506*	*422*	*97,274*	*99,894*
7. Bombay (*Presidency*)	233,246	134,480	98,766	23,541	8,799	4,517	4,416	106,422	85,551
Bombay	*219,621*	*124,455*	*95,166*	*17,245*	*7,339*	*3,922*	*3,788*	*103,288*	*84,039*
Sind	*10,911*	*7,658*	*3,253*	*4,359*	*1,249*	*576*	*616*	*2,723*	*1,388*
Aden	*2,714*	*2,367*	*347*	*1,937*	*211*	*19*	*12*	*411*	*124*
8. Burma	210,081	111,033	99,048	10,014	3,419	6,039	5,067	94,980	90,562
9. Central Provinces and Berar	34,697	19,731	14,966	5,395	1,853	1,812	1,531	12,524	11,582
Central Provinces	*31,874*	*18,210*	*13,664*	*5,299*	*1,755*	*1,656*	*1,382*	*11,255*	*10,527*
Berar	*2,823*	*1,521*	*1,302*	*96*	*98*	*156*	*149*	*1,269*	*1,055*
10. Coorg	3,558	1,986	1,567	125	82	74	64	1,787	1,421
11. Madras	1,191,266	586,836	604,430	9,138	3,746	12,642	13,361	565,056	585,323
12. North-West Frontier Province (*Districts and Administered Territories*)	6,585	5,414	1,171	4,825	799	49	50	540	322
13. Punjab	198,106	116,039	82,067	24,060	7,620	1,657	1,549	90,322	72,898
14. United Provinces of Agra and Oudh	177,949	100,818	77,131	24,735	8,653	4,044	4,048	72,039	64,430
Agra	*163,069*	*91,311*	*71,758*	*19,112*	*7,097*	*3,283*	*3,246*	*68,916*	*61,415*
Oudh	*14,880*	*9,507*	*5,373*	*5,623*	*1,556*	*761*	*802*	*3,123*	*3,015*
States and Agencies.	1,383,919	709,174	674,745	15,039	5,829	7,414	7,631	686,721	661,285
15. Assam State (Manipur)	132	84	48	15	5	22	21	47	22
16. Baluchistan States	55	49	6	16	4	5	...	28	2
17. Baroda State	7,203	3,855	3,348	90	69	34	48	3,731	3,231
18. Bengal States	228	133	95	14	8	12	15	107	72
19. Bihar and Orissa States	38,440	19,177	19,263	35	32	38	26	19,104	19,205
20. Bombay States	12,411	6,307	6,104	247	140	131	111	5,929	5,853
21. Central India Agency	9,358	6,170	3,188	3,716	866	296	269	2,158	2,053
22. Central Provinces States	38,704	19,477	19,227	52	33	71	74	19,354	19,120
23. Hyderabad State	54,296	29,495	24,801	4,312	1,072	1,548	1,456	23,635	22,273
24. Kashmir State	975	618	357	134	116	9	7	475	234
25. Madras States	1,154,209	587,412	566,797	321	177	2,161	2,055	584,930	564,565
26. Mysore State	59,844	31,853	27,991	4,902	2,561	2,673	3,154	24,278	22,276
27. North-West Frontier Province (*Agencies and Tribal areas*)	133	110	23	97	20	1	...	12	3
28. Punjab States	1,645	946	699	346	252	146	127	454	320
29. Rajputana Agency	4,256	2,409	1,847	717	462	263	266	1,429	1,119
30. Sikkim State	285	155	130	13	1	4	...	138	129
31. United Provinces States	1,745	924	821	12	11	...	2	912	808

European and Asiatic descent.

TABLE XVII.—Christians by

Part II.—Distribution by

Province and Denomination.	Total returned.	Distribution by Race. European and Allied Races.	Anglo-Indian.*	Indian.
1	2	3	4	5
AJMER-MERWARA	**5,432**	**1,755**	**710**	**2,967**
Anglican Communion	1,689	1,200	333	156
Baptist	20	15	......	5
Congregationalist	2	2	......	......
Greek	2	2	......	......
Methodist	565	60	18	487
Presbyterian	1,943	108	15	1,820
Protestant (Unsectarian or sect not specified)	1	1	......	......
Quaker	2	1	1	......
Roman Catholic	1,199	362	342	495
Salvationist	1	1	......	...
Sect not returned	4	......	......	4
Indefinite Beliefs	4	3	1	......
ANDAMANS AND NICOBARS	**566**	**251**	**78**	**237**
Anglican Communion	383	202	54	126
Baptist	1	1	......	......
Lutheran	1	......	......	1
Methodist	7	4	......	3
Minor Protestant Denominations	1	......	1	......
Presbyterian	2	2	......	......
Protestant (Unsectarian or sect not specified)	1	1	......	......
Roman Catholic	138	41	20	77
Sect not returned	30	......	......	30
Indefinite Beliefs	3	......	3	......
ASSAM	**66,436**	**2,236**	**437**	**63,763**
Anglican Communion	4,985	1,388	189	3,408
Armenian	2	2	......	......
Baptist	21,408	81	24	21,303
Congregationalist	29	21	......	8
Greek	3	3	...	......
Lutheran	3,752	13	......	3,739
Methodist	30	11	2	17
Minor Protestant Denominations	162	1	1	160
Presbyterian	31,184	473	44	30,668
Protestant (Unsectarian or sect not specified)	1,701	14	4	1,683
Roman Catholic	2,756	187	172	2,397
Sect not returned	16	15	1	......
Indefinite Beliefs	403	23	......	380
BALUCHISTAN	**5,030**	**4,190**	**118**	**722**
Anglican Communion	3,322	2,857	53	412
Baptist	10	10	......	......
Congregationalist	2	2	......	......
Methodist	191	158	4	29
Minor Protestant Denominations	7	1	......	6
Presbyterian	157	136	2	19
Roman Catholic	1,334	1,020	59	255
Sect not returned	5	5	......	......
Indefinite Beliefs	2	1	......	1
BENGAL	**129,518**	**25,429**	**21,008**	**83,081**
Anglican Communion	38,976	14,299	6,703	17,974
Armenian	798	768	17	13
Baptist	23,893	589	459	22,845
Congregationalist	2,534	148	50	2,336
Greek	192	184	4	4
Lutheran	1,212	230	7	975
Methodist	3,971	565	369	3,037
Minor Protestant Denominations	217	55	24	138
Presbyterian	7,722	2,661	946	4,115
Protestant (Unsectarian or sect not specified)	1,482	422	196	864
Quaker	4	3	1	...
Roman Catholic	46,258	5,290	12,172	28,796
Salvationist	1	1	......	......
Syrian, Romo-Syrian	4	...	2	2
Sect not returned	2,114	105	49	1,960
Indefinite Beliefs	140	109	9	22
BIHAR AND ORISSA	**229,825**	**6,249**	**3,341**	**220,235**
Anglican Communion	37,307	4,023	1,244	32,040
Armenian	12	12	......	......
Baptist	7,374	136	136	7,102
Congregationalist	29	16	1	12
Greek	6	5	1	......
Lutheran	88,051	120	9	87,922
Methodist	1,311	91	51	1,169
Minor Protestant Denominations	122	10	5	107
Presbyterian	1,536	418	44	1,074
Protestant (Unsectarian or sect not specified)	268	38	11	219
Quaker	1	1	......	......
Roman Catholic	93,511	1,334	1,833	90,344
BIHAR AND ORISSA—*contd.*				
Sect not returned	273	30	6	246
Indefinite Beliefs	25	25	......	......
BOMBAY	**233,246**	**32,340**	**8,933**	**191,973**
Abyssinian	25	......	......	25
Anglican Communion	34,339	20,908	1,882	11,549
Armenian	58	48	......	10
Baptist	327	234	25	68
Congregationalist	11,678	152	7	11,519
Greek	215	211	......	4
Lutheran	1,304	208	......	1,096
Methodist	13,007	1,173	225	11,609
Minor Protestant Denominations	1,660	108	15	1,537
Presbyterian	6,760	1,373	80	5,307
Protestant (Unsectarian or sect not specified)	6,588	624	262	5,702
Quaker	3	3	......	......
Roman Catholic	147,121	7,144	6,432	133,545
Salvationist	9,986	58	4	9,924
Syrian, Romo-Syrian	12	2	......	10
Sect not returned	68	3	......	65
Indefinite Beliefs	95	91	1	3
BURMA	**210,081**	**13,433**	**11,106**	**185,542**
Anglican Communion	20,734	7,023	3,713	9,999
Armenian	256	241	13	2
Baptist	122,265	759	957	120,549
Congregationalist	5	1	......	4
Greek	49	47	......	2
Lutheran	329	69	3	257
Methodist	1,675	281	215	1,179
Minor Protestant Denominations	49	18	24	7
Presbyterian	1,009	875	67	67
Protestant (Unsectarian or sect not specified)	2,782	311	113	2,358
Roman Catholic	60,283	3,594	5,918	50,770
Sect not returned	581	163	70	348
Indefinite Beliefs	66	52	14	......
CENTRAL PROVINCES AND BERAR	**34,697**	**7,248**	**3,343**	**24,106**
Anglican Communion	8,119	4,941	1,365	1,813
Armenian	10	5	......	5
Baptist	1,068	30	16	1,022
Congregationalist	10	8	2	......
Greek	13	12	......	1
Lutheran	1,598	71	3	1,524
Methodist	3,479	351	53	3,075
Minor Protestant Denominations	2,655	123	9	2,523
Presbyterian	4,144	139	48	3,957
Quaker	1,160	18	2	1,140
Roman Catholic	11,630	1,497	1,807	8,326
Sect not returned	789	33	37	719
Indefinite Beliefs	22	20	1	1
COORG	**3,553**	**207**	**138**	**3,208**
Anglican Communion	200	145	45	10
Baptist	4	......	......	4
Lutheran	363	10	6	347
Methodist	14	3	1	10
Presbyterian	14	14	......	......
Protestant (Unsectarian or sect not specified)	2	2	......	......
Roman Catholic	2,947	33	84	2,830
Sect not returned	9	......	2	7
MADRAS	**1,191,266**	**14,884**	**26,003**	**1,150,379**
Anglican Communion	168,702	8,837	8,661	151,204
Armenian	19	19	......	......
Baptist	141,804	301	303	141,200
Congregationalist	36,885	177	143	36,565
Greek	6	5	......	1
Lutheran	104,827	620	133	104,074
Methodist	8,027	575	555	6,897
Minor Protestant Denominations	3,242	140	38	3,064
Presbyterian	9,554	630	201	8,723
Protestant (Unsectarian or sect not specified)	11,039	591	571	9,877
Quaker	2	2	......	......
Roman Catholic	678,194	2,815	15,364	660,015
Salvationist	4,902	20	6	4,876
Syrian, Chaldæan	2	......	......	2
Syrian, Jacobite	3,101	......	......	3,101
Syrian, Reformed	398	......	......	398
Syrian, Romo-Syrian	19,548	......	......	19,548
Syrian, Unspecified	344	......	......	344

* And other persons of mixed

Race and Denomination.

Denomination in each Province, State or Agency.

Province and Denomination.	Total returned.	Distribution by Race. European and Allied Races.	Anglo-Indian.*	Indian.
1	2	3	4	5
MADRAS—*contd.*				
Sect not returned	514	51	22	441
Indefinite Beliefs	168	101	6	61
NORTH-WEST FRONTIER PROVINCE.	**6,585**	**5,624**	**99**	**862**
Anglican Communion	4,357	3,839	63	455
Baptist	31	31	......	......
Congregationalist	12	12	......	......
Greek	14	2	......	12
Lutheran	7	7	......	......
Methodist	248	229	3	12
Minor Protestant Denominations	8	......	......	8
Presbyterian	182	169	8	5
Roman Catholic	1,439	1,275	18	146
Syrian, Jacobite	1	1	......	......
Sect not returned	286	54	8	224
Indefinite Beliefs	5	5	......	...
PUNJAB	**198,196**	**31,680**	**3,286**	**163,229**
Anglican Communion	52,661	21,840	1,964	28,857
Armenian	11	11	......	......
Baptist	1,268	183	35	1,050
Congregationalist	25	25	......	......
Greek	18	18	......	......
Lutheran	114	33	......	81
Methodist	12,685	1,024	79	11,582
Minor Protestant Denominations	1,462	22	......	1,440
Presbyterian	94,728	2,106	148	92,474
Protestant (Unsectarian or sect not specified)	930	64	9	857
Quaker	3	......	......	3
Roman Catholic	15,581	6,182	956	8,443
Salvationist	18,029	59	......	17,970
Syrian, Jacobite	1	1	......	......
Sect not returned	538	69	13	456
Indefinite Beliefs	52	43	2	7
UNITED PROVINCES OF AGRA AND OUDH	**177,949**	**33,388**	**8,092**	**136,469**
Anglican Communion	30,902	20,329	4,264	6,309
Armenian	27	24	......	3
Baptist	2,594	257	121	2,216
Congregationalist	987	108	21	858
Greek	36	22	10	4
Lutheran	189	41	3	145
Methodist	104,148	1,348	421	102,379
Minor Protestant Denominations	574	51	25	498
Presbyterian	14,442	4,440	212	9,790
Protestant (Unsectarian or sect not specified)	2,218	446	258	1,514
Quaker	19	11	2	6
Roman Catholic	10,698	5,699	2,223	2,776
Salvationist	991	14	......	977
Syrian, Chaldæan	1	1	......	......
Syrian, Jacobite	1	......	......	1
Sect not returned	10,041	539	526	8,976
Indefinite Beliefs	81	58	6	17
ASSAM STATE (MANIPUR)	**132**	**20**	**43**	**69**
Anglican Communion	34	17	17	......
Baptist	71	2	......	69
Roman Catholic	27	1	26	......
BALUCHISTAN STATES	**55**	**20**	**5**	**30**
Anglican Communion	24	13	5	6
Lutheran	2	1	......	1
Presbyterian	3	3	......	......
Roman Catholic	26	3	......	23
BARODA STATE	**7,203**	**159**	**82**	**6,962**
Anglican Communion	139	97	42	......
Baptist	4	4	......	......
Lutheran	7	3	4	......
Methodist	4,850	15	2	4,833
Presbyterian	193	4	......	189
Roman Catholic	468	34	34	400
Salvationist	1,540	......	......	1,540
Indefinite Beliefs	2	2	......	......
BENGAL STATES	**228**	**22**	**27**	**179**
Anglican Communion	45	12	2	31
Armenian	1	1	......	......
Baptist	67	1	8	58
Greek	7	7	......	......
Lutheran	2	1	......	1
Roman Catholic	106	......	17	89
BIHAR AND ORISSA STATES	**38,440**	**67**	**64**	**38,309**
Anglican Communion	252	26	24	202
Baptist	3,759	3	5	3,751
Lutheran	11,365	8	3	11,354
Methodist	1	......	1	......
Presbyterian	3	3	......	......
Protestant (Unsectarian or sect not specified)	92	3	......	89
Roman Catholic	22,969	25	31	22,913
BOMBAY STATES	**12,411**	**387**	**242**	**11,782**
Anglican Communion	477	216	95	166
Baptist	12	2	6	4
Greek	1	1	......	...
Methodist	976	8	2	966
Minor Protestant Denominations	43	5	......	38
Presbyterian	1,633	57	......	1,576
Protestant (Unsectarian or sect not specified)	475	26	2	447
Roman Catholic	8,204	53	136	8,015
Salvationist	115	......	......	115
Sect not returned	465	9	1	455
Indefinite Beliefs	10	10	...	...
CENTRAL INDIA AGENCY	**9,358**	**4,582**	**565**	**4,211**
Anglican Communion	3,663	3,196	147	320
Armenian	2	2	......	......
Baptist	75	33	......	42
Greek	2	1	1	......
Lutheran	2	1	1	......
Methodist	124	100	......	24
Presbyterian	1,470	181	12	1,277
Protestant (Unsectarian or sect not specified)	473	29	8	436
Quaker	48	3	......	45
Roman Catholic	3,241	926	352	1,963
Salvationist	2	2	......	......
Sect not returned	249	101	44	104
Indefinite Beliefs	7	7	......	......
CENTRAL PROVINCES STATES	**38,704**	**85**	**145**	**38,474**
Anglican Communion	121	43	69	9
Baptist	102	1	3	98
Lutheran	4,201	......	......	4,201
Methodist	1,234	14	3	1,217
Minor Protestant Denominations	97	6	......	91
Presbyterian	8	2	......	6
Roman Catholic	32,922	16	65	32,841
Sect not returned	19	3	5	11
HYDERABAD STATE	**54,296**	**5,384**	**3,004**	**45,908**
Anglican Communion	14,261	4,305	1,100	8,856
Baptist	9,630	39	34	9,557
Congregationalist	355	5	2	348
Greek	3	1	1	......
Lutheran	24	......	1	23
Methodist	8,614	311	182	8,121
Minor Protestant Denominations	427	8	3	416
Presbyterian	1,148	132	17	999
Protestant (Unsectarian or sect not specified)	1,346	18	67	1,261
Roman Catholic	18,473	559	1,592	16,322
Syrian, Romo-Syrian	5	......	4	1
Indefinite Beliefs	11	6	1	4
KASHMIR STATE	**975**	**250**	**16**	**709**
Anglican Communion	194	171	6	17
Baptist	3	1	2	......
Congregationalist	9	8	......	1
Lutheran	62	11	......	51
Minor Protestant Denominations	8	......	......	8
Presbyterian	617	24	......	593
Protestant (Unsectarian or sect not specified)	6	4	1	1
Roman Catholic	51	24	4	23
Sect not returned	24	6	3	15
Indefinite Beliefs	1	1	......	......
MADRAS STATES (*including Cochin and Travancore*)	**1,154,209**	**498**	**4,216**	**1,149,495**
Anglican Communion	58,045	229	163	57,653
Baptist	55	......	9	46
Congregationalist	82,321	28	47	82,246
Greek	24	......	......	24
Lutheran	914	9	13	892

* European and Asiatic descent.

TABLE XVII.—Christians by Race and Denomination.

Part II.—Distribution by Denomination in each Province, etc.—*concluded.*

Province and Denomination.	Total returned.	Distribution by Race. European and Allied Races.	Anglo-Indian.*	Indian.
1	2	3	4	5
MADRAS STATES *(including Cochin and Travancore)—contd.*				
Methodist	7	1	6	......
Minor Protestant Denominations	1,573	17	34	1,522
Presbyterian	35	25	......	10
Protestant (Unsectarian or sect not specified)	466	1	......	465
Roman Catholic	287,611	153	3,923	283,535
Salvationist	16,794	27	8	16,759
Syrian, Chaldæan	13,769	2	......	13,767
Syrian, Jacobite	222,084	......	......	222,084
Syrian, Reformed	75,462	......	......	75,462
Syrian, Romo-Syrian	393,573	......	......	393,573
Sect not returned	355	6	13	336
Indefinite Beliefs	1,121	......	......	1,121
Cochin State	*233,092*	*78*	*2,446*	*230,568*
Anglican Communion	1,623	36	66	1,521
Baptist	44	......	9	35
Congregationalist	167	......	......	167
Lutheran	135	1	13	121
Methodist	6	......	6	......
Minor Protestant Denominations	36	......	......	36
Presbyterian	1	1	......	......
Protestant (Unsectarian or sect not specified)	349	......	......	349
Roman Catholic	97,787	38	2,352	95,397
Syrian, Chaldæan	12,157	2	......	12,155
Syrian, Jacobite	20,025	......	......	20,025
Syrian, Reformed	596	......	......	596
Syrian, Romo-Syrian	100,166	......	......	100,166
Travancore State	*903,868*	*399*	*1,750*	*901,719*
Anglican Communion	56,251	183	93	55,975
Baptist	3	......	......	3
Congregationalist	81,573	27	47	81,499
Greek	24	......	......	24
Lutheran	391	6	......	385
Methodist	1	1	......	......
Minor Protestant Denominations	1,537	17	34	1,486
Presbyterian	34	24	......	10
Protestant (Unsectarian or sect not specified)	116	1	......	115
Roman Catholic	173,734	107	1,565	172,062
Salvationist	16,794	27	8	16,759
Syrian, Chaldæan	1,612	......	......	1,612
Syrian, Jacobite	202,059	......	......	202,059
Syrian, Reformed	74,866	......	......	74,866
Syrian, Romo-Syrian	293,407	......	......	293,407
Sect not returned	355	6	13	336
Indefinite Beliefs	1,121	......	......	1,121
MYSORE STATE	**59,844**	**7,463**	**5,827**	**46,554**
Anglican Communion	6,656	3,955	1,910	791
Armenian	1	1	......	......
Baptist	1,269	86	90	1,093
Congregationalist	374	15	16	343
Greek	4	......	......	4
Lutheran	160	7	3	150
Methodist	3,825	543	363	2,919
Minor Protestant Denominations	139	15	6	118
MYSORE STATE—*contd.*				
Presbyterian	1,141	1,030	34	77
Protestant (Unsectarian or sect not specified)	2,138	274	193	1,671
Roman Catholic	42,543	1,489	3,140	37,914
Syrian, Chaldæan	8	......	......	8
Syrian, Jacobite	2	......	......	2
Sect not returned	1,560	48	72	1,440
Indefinite Beliefs	24	20	...	4
NORTH-WEST FRONTIER PROVINCE *(Agencies and Tribal areas)*	**133**	**117**	**1**	**15**
Anglican Communion	105	97	1	7
Baptist	1	1	......	......
Presbyterian	11	11	......	......
Quaker	2	2	......	......
Roman Catholic	5	5	......	......
Sect not returned	9	1	......	8
PUNJAB STATES	**1,645**	**598**	**273**	**774**
Anglican Communion	766	409	163	194
Armenian	1	1	......	......
Baptist	72	3	2	67
Lutheran	1	1	......	......
Methodist	165	13	11	141
Minor Protestant Denominations	17	1	......	16
Presbyterian	311	34	12	265
Roman Catholic	266	138	84	54
Salvationist	44	6	1	37
Indefinite Beliefs	2	2	...	......
RAJPUTANA AGENCY	**4,256**	**1,179**	**529**	**2,548**
Anglican Communion	1,186	760	273	153
Armenian	2	2	...	...
Baptist	31	13	4	14
Congregationalist	8	8	......	......
Lutheran	14	5	1	8
Methodist	988	26	8	954
Minor Protestant Denominations	6	......	1	5
Presbyterian	1,007	98	19	890
Protestant (Unsectarian or sect not specified)	170	26	4	140
Quaker	1	1	......	......
Roman Catholic	836	235	219	382
Salvationist	2	1	......	1
Sect not returned	3	2	......	1
Indefinite Beliefs	2	2	......	......
SIKKIM STATE	**285**	**14**	**4**	**267**
Anglican Communion	99	7	3	89
Presbyterian	170	2	...	168
Roman Catholic	16	5	1	10
UNITED PROVINCES STATES	**1,745**	**23**	**2**	**1,720**
Anglican Communion	10	9	......	1
Baptist	8	......	......	8
Methodist	1,707	......	......	1,707
Presbyterian	4	2	2	......
Protestant (Unsectarian or sect not specified)	2	2	......	......
Roman Catholic	11	10	......	1
Sect not returned	3	......	......	3

* And other persons of mixed European and Asiatic descent.

TABLE XVII.—Christians by Race and Denomination.

Part III.—Territorial Distribution of each Denomination.

Denomination and Province.	Total returned.	Distribution by Race. European and Allied Races.	Anglo-Indian.*	Indian.
1	2	3	4	5
ABYSSINIAN	**25**	......	......	**25**
Bombay	25	......	......	25
ANGLICAN COMMUNION	**492,752**	**125,392**	**34,553**	**332,807**
Ajmer-Merwara	1,689	1,200	333	156
Andamans and Nicobars	382	202	54	126
Assam	4,985	1,388	189	3,408
Baluchistan	3,322	2,857	53	412
Bengal	38,976	14,299	6,703	17,974
Bihar and Orissa	37,307	4,023	1,244	32,040
Bombay	34,339	20,908	1,882	11,549
Burma	20,734	7,022	3,713	9,999
Central Provinces and Berar	8,119	4,941	1,365	1,813
Coorg	200	145	45	10
Madras	168,702	8,837	8,661	151,204
North-West Frontier Province	4,357	3,839	63	455
Punjab	52,661	21,840	1,964	28,857
United Provinces	30,902	20,329	4,264	6,309
Assam State	34	17	17	......
Baluchistan States	24	13	5	6
Baroda State	139	97	42	......
Bengal States	45	12	2	31
Bihar and Orissa States	252	26	24	202
Bombay States	477	216	95	166
Central India Agency	3,663	3,196	147	320
Central Provinces States	121	43	69	9
Hyderabad State	14,261	4,305	1,100	8,856
Kashmir State	194	171	6	17
Madras States	58,045	229	163	57,653
Cochin	*1,623*	*36*	*66*	*1,591*
Travancore	*56,251*	*183*	*93*	*55,975*
Mysore State	6,656	3,955	1,910	791
North-West Frontier Province (*Agencies and Tribal areas*)	105	97	1	7
Punjab States	766	409	163	194
Rajputana Agency	1,186	760	273	153
Sikkim State	99	7	3	89
United Provinces States	10	9	......	1
ARMENIAN	**1,200**	**1,137**	**30**	**33**
Assam	2	2	......	......
Bengal	798	768	17	13
Bihar and Orissa	12	12	......	......
Bombay	58	48	......	10
Burma	256	241	13	2
Central Provinces and Berar	10	5	......	5
Madras	19	19	......	......
Punjab	11	11	......	......
United Provinces	27	24	......	3
Bengal States	1	1	......	......
Central India Agency	3	3	......	......
Mysore State	1	1	......	......
Punjab States	1	1	......	......
Rajputana Agency	2	2	...	...
BAPTIST	**337,226**	**2,816**	**2,239**	**332,171**
Ajmer-Merwara	20	15	......	5
Andamans and Nicobars	1	1	......	......
Assam	21,408	81	24	21,303
Baluchistan	10	10	......	...
Bengal	23,593	589	459	22,845
Bihar and Orissa	7,374	136	136	7,102
Bombay	327	234	25	68
Burma	122,265	759	957	120,549
Central Provinces and Berar	1,068	30	16	1,022
Coorg	4	......	......	4
Madras	141,804	301	303	141,200
North-West Frontier Province	31	31	......	......
Punjab	1,268	183	35	1,050
United Provinces	2,594	257	121	2,216
Assam State	71	2	......	69
Baroda State	4	4	......	......
Bengal States	67	1	8	58
Bihar and Orissa States	3,759	3	5	3,751
Bombay States	12	2	6	4
Central India Agency	75	33	......	42
Central Provinces States	102	1	3	98
Hyderabad State	9,630	39	34	9,557
Kashmir State	3	1	2	......
Madras States	55	......	9	46
Mysore State	1,269	86	90	1,093
North-West Frontier Province (*Agencies and Tribal areas*)	1	1	......	......
Punjab States	72	3	2	67
Rajputana Agency	31	13	4	14
United Provinces States	8	......	......	8

Denomination and Province.	Total returned.	Distribution by Race. European and Allied Races.	Anglo-Indian.*	Indian.
1	2	3	4	5
CONGREGATIONALIST	**135,265**	**736**	**289**	**134,240**
Ajmer-Merwara	2	2	......	......
Assam	29	21	......	8
Baluchistan	2	2	......	......
Bengal	2,534	146	50	2,338
Bihar and Orissa	29	16	1	12
Bombay	11,678	152	7	11,519
Burma	5	1	......	4
Central Provinces and Berar	10	8	2	......
Madras	36,885	177	143	36,565
North-West Frontier Province	12	12	......	......
Punjab	25	25	......	......
United Provinces	987	108	21	858
Hyderabad State	355	5	2	348
Kashmir State	9	8	......	1
Madras States	82,321	28	47	82,246
Cochin	*167*	......	......	*167*
Travancore	*81,573*	*27*	*47*	*81,499*
Mysore State	374	15	16	343
Rajputana Agency	8	8	......	......
GREEK	**594**	**521**	**17**	**56**
Ajmer-Merwara	2	2	......	......
Assam	3	3	......	......
Bengal	192	184	4	4
Bihar and Orissa	6	5	1	......
Bombay	215	211	......	4
Burma	49	47	......	2
Central Provinces and Berar	13	12	......	1
Madras	6	5	......	1
North-West Frontier Province	14	2	......	12
Punjab	18	18	......	......
United Provinces	36	22	10	4
Bengal States	7	7	......	......
Bombay States	1	1	......	......
Central India Agency	2	1	1	......
Hyderabad State	2	1	1	......
Madras States	24	......	......	24
Mysore State	4	......	......	4
LUTHERAN	**218,500**	**1,469**	**189**	**216,842**
Andamans and Nicobars	1	......	......	1
Assam	3,752	13	......	3,739
Bengal	1,212	230	7	975
Bihar and Orissa	88,051	120	9	87,922
Bombay	1,304	208	......	1,096
Burma	328	69	2	257
Central Provinces and Berar	1,598	71	3	1,524
Coorg	363	10	6	347
Madras	104,827	620	133	104,074
North-West Frontier Province	7	7	......	......
Punjab	114	33	......	81
United Provinces	189	41	3	145
Baluchistan States	2	1	......	1
Baroda State	7	3	4	......
Bengal States	2	1	......	1
Bihar and Orissa States	11,365	8	3	11,354
Central India Agency	2	1	1	......
Central Provinces States	4,201	......	......	4,201
Hyderabad State	24	......	1	23
Kashmir State	62	11	......	51
Madras States	914	9	13	892
Mysore State	160	7	3	150
Punjab States	1	1	......	......
Rajputana Agency	14	5	1	8
METHODIST	**171,844**	**6,904**	**2,573**	**162,367**
Ajmer-Merwara	565	60	18	487
Andamans and Nicobars	7	4	......	3
Assam	30	11	2	17
Baluchistan	191	158	4	29
Bengal	3,971	565	369	3,037
Bihar and Orissa	1,311	91	51	1,169
Bombay	13,007	1,173	225	11,609
Burma	1,675	281	215	1,179
Central Provinces and Berar	3,479	351	53	3,075
Coorg	14	3	1	10
Madras	8,027	575	555	6,897
North-West Frontier Province	243	229	2	12
Punjab	12,685	1,024	79	11,582
United Provinces	104,148	1,348	421	102,379
Baroda State	4,850	15	2	4,833
Bihar and Orissa States	1	......	1	......
Bombay States	976	8	2	966
Central India Agency	124	100	......	24
Central Provinces States	1,234	14	3	1,217
Hyderabad State	9,614	311	182	9,121

* And other persons of mixed European and Asiatic descent.

TABLE XVII.—Christians by

Part III.—Territorial Distribution

Denomination and Province.	Total returned.	Distribution by Race. European and Allied Races.	Anglo-Indian.*	Indian.
1	2	3	4	5
METHODIST—*contd.*				
Madras States	7	1	6	......
Mysore State	3,825	543	363	2,919
Punjab States	165	13	11	141
Rajputana Agency	988	26	8	954
United Provinces States	1,707	......	......	1,707
MINOR PROTESTANT DENOMINATIONS	**12,469**	**581**	**186**	**11,702**
Andamans and Nicobars	1	......	1	......
Assam	162	1	1	160
Baluchistan	7	1	......	6
Bengal	217	55	24	138
Bihar and Orissa	122	10	5	107
Bombay	1,660	108	15	1,537
Burma	49	18	24	7
Central Provinces and Berar	2,655	123	9	2,523
Madras	3,243	140	38	3,064
North-West Frontier Province	8	......	......	8
Punjab	1,462	22	......	1,440
United Provinces	574	51	25	498
Bombay States	43	5	......	38
Central Provinces States	97	6	......	91
Hyderabad State	427	8	3	416
Kashmir State	8	......	......	8
Madras States	1,573	17	34	1,522
Mysore State	139	15	6	118
Punjab States	17	1	......	16
Rajputana Agency	6	......	1	5
PRESBYTERIAN	**181,130**	**15,150**	**1,911**	**164,069**
Ajmer-Merwara	1,943	108	15	1,820
Andamans and Nicobars	2	2	......	......
Assam	31,184	472	44	30,668
Baluchistan	157	136	2	19
Bengal	7,722	2,661	946	4,115
Bihar and Orissa	1,536	418	44	1,074
Bombay	6,760	1,373	80	5,307
Burma	1,009	875	67	67
Central Provinces and Berar	4,144	139	48	3,957
Coorg	14	14	......	......
Madras	9,554	630	201	8,723
North-West Frontier Province	182	169	8	5
Punjab	94,728	2,106	148	92,474
United Provinces	14,442	4,440	212	9,790
Baluchistan States	3	3	......	......
Baroda State	193	4	......	189
Bihar and Orissa States	2	2	......	......
Bombay States	1,633	57	......	1,576
Central India Agency	1,470	181	12	1,277
Central Provinces States	8	2	......	6
Hyderabad State	1,148	132	17	999
Kashmir State	617	24	......	593
Madras States	35	25	......	10
Mysore State	1,141	1,030	34	77
North-West Frontier Province (*Agencies and Tribal areas*).	11	11	......	......
Punjab States	311	34	12	265
Rajputana Agency	1,007	98	19	890
Sikkim State	170	2	......	168
United Provinces States	4	2	2	......
PROTESTANT (*Unsectarian or sect not specified*)	**32,180**	**2,897**	**1,699**	**27,584**
Ajmer-Merwara	1	1	......	......
Andamans and Nicobars	1	1	......	......
Assam	1,701	14	4	1,683
Bengal	1,483	423	196	864
Bihar and Orissa	268	38	11	219
Bombay	6,588	624	262	5,702
Burma	2,782	311	113	2,358
Coorg	2	2	......	......
Madras	11,039	591	571	9,877
Punjab	930	64	9	857
United Provinces	2,218	446	258	1,514
Bihar and Orissa States	92	3	......	89
Bombay States	475	26	2	447
Central India Agency	473	29	8	436
Hyderabad State	1,346	18	67	1,261
Kashmir State	6	4	1	1
Madras States	466	1	......	465
Mysore State	2,138	274	193	1,671
Rajputana Agency	170	26	4	140
United Provinces States	2	2	......	......
QUAKER	**1,245**	**45**	**6**	**1,194**
Ajmer-Merwara	2	1	1	......
Bengal	4	3	1	......
Bihar and Orissa	1	1	......	......
QUAKER—*contd.*				
Bombay	3	3	......	......
Central Provinces and Berar	1,160	18	2	1,140
Madras	2	2	......	......
Punjab	3	......	......	3
United Provinces	19	11	2	6
Central India Agency	48	3	......	45
North-West Frontier Province (*Agencies and Tribal areas*)	2	2	...	......
Rajputana Agency	1	1	......	......
ROMAN CATHOLIC	**1,490,863**	**40,119**	**57,024**	**1,393,720**
Ajmer-Merwara	1,199	362	342	495
Andamans and Nicobars	138	41	20	77
Assam	2,756	187	172	2,397
Baluchistan	1,334	1,020	59	255
Bengal	46,258	5,290	12,172	28,796
Bihar and Orissa	93,511	1,334	1,833	90,344
Bombay	147,121	7,144	6,432	133,545
Burma	60,282	3,594	5,918	50,770
Central Provinces and Berar	11,630	1,497	1,807	8,326
Coorg	2,947	33	84	2,830
Madras	678,194	2,815	15,364	660,015
North-West Frontier Province	1,439	1,275	18	146
Punjab	15,581	6,182	956	8,443
United Provinces	10,698	5,699	2,223	2,776
Assam State	27	1	26	......
Baluchistan States	26	3	......	23
Baroda State	468	34	34	400
Bengal States	106	......	17	89
Bihar and Orissa States	22,969	25	31	22,913
Bombay States	8,204	53	136	8,015
Central India Agency	3,241	926	352	1,963
Central Provinces States	32,922	16	65	32,841
Hyderabad State	18,473	559	1,592	16,323
Kashmir State	51	24	4	23
Madras States	287,611	153	3,923	283,535
Cochin	*97,787*	*38*	*2,352*	*95,397*
Travancore	*173,724*	*107*	*1,555*	*172,062*
Mysore State	42,543	1,469	3,140	37,934
North-West Frontier Province (*Agencies and Tribal areas*)	5	5	......	......
Punjab States	266	128	84	54
Rajputana Agency	836	235	219	382
Sikkim State	16	5	1	10
United Provinces States	11	10	...	1
SALVATIONIST	**52,407**	**189**	**19**	**52,199**
Ajmer-Merwara	1	1	......	......
Bengal	1	1	......	......
Bombay	9,986	58	4	9,924
Madras	4,902	20	6	4,876
Punjab	18,029	59	......	17,970
United Provinces	991	14	......	977
Baroda State	1,540	......	......	1,540
Bombay States	115	...	......	115
Central India Agency	2	2	......	......
Madras States	16,794†	27	8	16,759
Punjab States	44	6	1	37
Rajputana Agency	2	1	......	1
SYRIAN, CHALDÆAN	**13,780**	**3**	......	**13,777**
Madras	2	......		2
United Provinces	1	1	......	......
Madras States	13,769	2	......	13,767
Cochin	*12,157*	*2*	......	*12,155*
Travancore	*1,612*	......	......	*1,612*
Mysore State	8	......	......	8
SYRIAN, JACOBITE	**225,190**	**2**	......	**225,188**
Madras	3,101	......	......	3,101
North-West Frontier Province	1	1	......	......
Punjab	1	1	......	......
United Provinces	1	......	......	1
Madras States	222,084	......	......	222,084
Cochin	*90,025*	......	......	*90,025*
Travancore	*202,059*	......	......	*202,059*
Mysore State	2	......	......	2
SYRIAN, REFORMED	**75,848**	......	......	**75,848**
Madras	386	......	......	386
Madras States	75,462	......	......	75,462
Cochin	*596*	......	......	*596*
Travancore	*74,866*	......	......	*74,866*

* And other persons of mixed European and Asiatic descent.

† All in Travancore.

Race and Denomination.

of each Denomination—*concluded.*

Denomination and Province.	Total returned.	Distribution by Race. European and Allied Races.	Anglo-Indian.*	Indian.
1	2	3	4	5
SYRIAN, ROMO-SYRIAN	**413,142**	**2**	**6**	**413,134**
Bengal	4	......	2	2
Bombay	12	2	......	10
Madras	19,548	......	......	19,548
Hyderabad State	5	......	4	1
Madras States	393,573	......	......	393,573
Cochin	*100,166*	......	......	*100,166*
Travancore	*293,407*	......	......	*293,407*
SYRIAN, UNSPECIFIED	**344**	......	......	**344**
Madras	344	......	......	344
SECT NOT RETURNED	**17,954**	**1,233**	**872**	**15,849**
Ajmer-Merwara	4	......	......	4
Andamans and Nicobars	30	......	......	30
Assam	16	15	1	......
Baluchistan	5	5	......	......
Bengal	2,114	105	49	1,960
Bihar and Orissa	272	20	6	246
Bombay	68	3	......	65
Burma	581	163	70	348
Central Provinces and Berar	789	33	37	719
Coorg	9	......	2	7
Madras	514	51	22	441
North-West Frontier Province	286	54	8	224
Punjab	538	69	13	456
United Provinces	10,041	539	526	8,976
Bombay States	465	9	1	455
Central India Agency	249	101	44	104
Central Provinces States	19	3	5	11
SECT NOT RETURNED—*contd.*				
Kashmir State	24	6	3	15
Madras States	355†	6	13	336
Mysore State	1,560	48	72	1,440
North-West Frontier Province (*Agencies and Tribal areas*)	9	1	......	8
Rajputana Agency	3	2	......	1
United Provinces States	3	......	......	3
INDEFINITE BELIEFS	**2,245**	**580**	**44**	**1,621**
Ajmer-Merwara	4	3	1	......
Andamans and Nicobars	3	......	3	......
Assam	402	22	......	380
Baluchistan	2	1	......	1
Bengal	140	109	9	22
Bihar and Orissa	25	25	......	......
Bombay	96	91	1	3
Burma	66	52	14	......
Central Provinces and Berar	22	20	1	1
Madras	168	101	6	61
North-West Frontier Province	5	5	......	......
Punjab	52	43	2	7
United Provinces	81	58	6	17
Baroda State	2	2	......	......
Bombay States	10	10	......	......
Central India Agency	7	7	......	......
Hyderabad State	11	6	1	4
Kashmir State	1	1	......	......
Madras States	1,121†	......	......	1,121
Mysore State	24	20	......	4
Punjab States	3	3	......	......
Rajputana Agency	2	2	......	......

* And other persons of mixed European and Asiatic descent.
† All in Travancore.

Heads under which the entries actually found in the Schedules (other than those shown in this table) have been classified.

ANGLICAN COMMUNION.—Anglican Church, Cambridge Brotherhood, Catholic Anglican, Christian Anglican, Church Missionary Society, Church of England, Church of Ireland, Dublin Mission, Episcopal Church of America, Episcopalian, Established Church, High Church, Oxford Mission, Scotch Episcopal Mission, Society for the Propagation of the Gospel, St. James' Church, St. Paul's Church.

BAPTIST.—American Baptist, Anabaptist, Canadian Baptist.

CONGREGATIONALIST.—American Congregationalist, Independent, London Mission.

LUTHERAN.—American Evangelic Lutheran, American Lutheran, Basel Mission, Bohemian Brethren, Danish Lutheran, Evangelical Lutheran, German Church, German Mission, German Protestant, Moravian, National Missionary Society of Stockholm, Scandinavian Church, Swedish Church.

METHODIST.—American Episcopal Methodist, American Himalayan Mission Colony, American Methodist, Bible Christian, Methodist Episcopalian, Primitive Methodist, Wesleyan, Wesleyan Methodist.

MINOR PROTESTANT DENOMINATIONS.—Adventist, American Brethren Mission, American Church of God Mission, American Mennonite Mission, Assumption Church, Australian Christian Mission, Boys' Christian Home Mission, Catholic Apostolic, Ceylon and India General Mission, Christian and Missionary Alliance, Christian Women's Board of Missions, Church of Christ Mission, Church of India, Church of God, Church of God Faith Mission, Disciple of Christ, Evangelical, Evangelic Union, Evangelist Church, Hephzibah Faith Mission, Household of Faith, Indian Christian Realm, Industrial Evangelistic Mission of India, Irvingite, Mennonite Mission, Mormon, Nepal Mission, New Jerusalem, Open Brethren, Pentecostal Band, Pentecostal Mission Nazarene, Pentecostal Nazarene, Plymouth Brethren, Puritan, Regions beyond Mission, Seventh Day Adventist, Swedenborgian, Universal Church of God.

PRESBYTERIAN.—American Presbyterian, Arcot Mission, Calvinist, Canadian Presbyterian, Church of Scotland, Dutch Reformed Church, Free Church, Free Church of Scotland, Gwalior (Canadian) Presbyterian, Irish Presbyterian, Reformed Church, Reformed Presbyterian, Scottish Zenana Mission, United Free Church, United Presbyterian, Welsh Calvinist, Zwinglian.

PROTESTANT UNSECTARIAN OR SECT NOT SPECIFIED.—Bigthan Mission, Church of America, Dissenter, Foreign Christian Missionary Society, Korku and Central India Hill Mission, Lohaghat Tanakpur Medical Mission, Metropolitan Church Association, Non-Conformist, Non-Sectarian, Poona and India Village Mission, Protestant, South India United Church, Tibetan Mission, Undenominational, Unsectarian, Vanguard Mission, Zenana Bible Mission.

QUAKER.—Friend, Society of Friends.

ROMAN CATHOLIC.—Catholic, Church of Rome, Franciscan Friars, Italian, Latin Catholic, Latin Christian, Spanish Mission.

SALVATIONIST.—Salvation Army.

SYRIAN, CHALDÆAN.—Chaldæan Christian.

SYRIAN, JACOBITE.—Gregorian Church, Jacobite Christian, Nestorian.

SYRIAN, REFORMED.—St. Thomas' Christian.

SYRIAN, ROMO-SYRIAN.—Syrian Catholic, Syro-Roman.

SECT NOT RETURNED.—Christian, Heathen (Convert).

INDEFINITE BELIEFS.—Agnostic, Atheist, Deist, Free Thinker, Positivist, Rationalist, Sceptic, Theist, Theosophist, Unitarian, Yuyomayam.

Strictly speaking persons of Indefinite Beliefs should not be shown at all in Table XVII. Persons returned under the above heads, however, are usually Europeans, or Natives of India who have derived their religious views from Europeans, and it is convenient to show them here. All the persons classed under this head in Travancore are adherents of the Yuyomayam sect, a curious offshoot from Christianity of which an account will be found in the Report Volume.

TABLE XVIII.

Europeans, Armenians and Anglo-Indians by Race and Age.

1. The number of European and allied races given in this Table exceeds that shown in Table XVII owing to the inclusion of ten European males in Burma and one American female in Kashmir who were not returned as Christians. In Table VI the former were entered as Buddhists and the latter as Brahmo.

2. The difference of 1,206 in the number of Anglo-Indians is due to the exclusion from this Table of the marginally noted * Feringis who were classed as Anglo-Indians in Table XVII, and to the inclusion of one Anglo-Indian male in Kashmir who was entered as Musalman in Table VI.

	Males.	Females.
* Assam . .	4	1
Bengal . .	590	601
Bengal States	3	8
	597	610

3. The figures for Madras States include those for Cochin (males 1,299, females 1,225) and Travancore (males 1,161, females 988), the details of which are noted below :—

AGE.	STATE.	EUROPEAN AND ALLIED RACES.				ARMENIANS.		ANGLO-INDIANS.*	
		BRITISH SUBJECTS.		OTHERS.					
		Males.	Females.	Males.	Females.	Males.	Females.	Males.	Females.
All Ages	Cochin	30	17	26	3	2	...	1,241	1,205
	Travancore	216	104	34	45	...	...	911	839
0—12	Cochin	3	2	...	1	...	...	454	375
	Travancore	20	18	1	...	...	...	256	256
12—15	Cochin	...	...	...	...	...	...	95	95
	Travancore	1	1	...	...	...	...	115	61
15—30	Cochin	13	5	10	1	...	...	330	385
	Travancore	63	25	10	20	...	...	256	238
30—50	Cochin	12	6	12	1	1	...	243	229
	Travancore	113	52	19	24	...	...	182	181
50 and over	Cochin	3	4	4	...	1	...	119	121
	Travancore	19	8	4	1	...	...	102	84

* Include other persons of mixed European and Asiatic descent.

TABLE XVIII.—Europeans, Armenians

Province, State or Agency.	Total.			European and Allied Races.										
				British Subjects.										
				All Ages.			0—12.		12—15.		15—20.			
	Persons.	Males.	Females.	Persons.	Males.	Females.	Males.	Females.	Males.	Females.	Males.	Females.		
1	2	3	4	5	6	7	8	9	10	11	12	13		
INDIA	**300,238**	**194,620**	**105,618**	**185,434**	**134,950**	**50,484**	**13,254**	**12,431**	**1,964**	**2,073**	**80,243**	**15,055**		
Provinces	**264,334**	**172,169**	**92,165**	**166,011**	**120,672**	**45,339**	**11,899**	**11,174**	**1,717**	**1,879**	**71,236**	**13,543**		
1. Ajmer-Merwara	2,465	1,781	684	1,702	1,369	333	99	104	11	5	995	96		
2. Andamans and Nicobars	329	234	95	243	193	50	12	12	...	1	146	18		
3. Assam	2,662	1,833	829	2,153	1,542	611	122	130	2	12	482	167		
4. Baluchistan	4,308	3,425	883	4,150	3,345	805	249	256	20	20	2,294	248		
5. Bengal	45,246	26,596	18,650	22,315	14,652	7,663	1,929	1,669	310	274	5,863	2,321		
6. Bihar and Orissa	9,590	5,633	3,967	5,598	3,462	2,136	553	507	42	61	1,354	632		
Bihar	*6,119*	*3,642*	*2,477*	*3,957*	*2,504*	*1,453*	*391*	*350*	*23*	*33*	*1,066*	*491*		
Orissa	*897*	*410*	*487*	*373*	*169*	*204*	*31*	*39*	*2*	*12*	*35*	*55*		
Chota Nagpur	*2,574*	*1,571*	*1,003*	*1,268*	*789*	*479*	*131*	*118*	*17*	*16*	*253*	*156*		
7. Bombay (*Presidency*)	41,273	28,058	13,215	28,639	20,937	7,702	1,966	1,967	280	283	12,170	2,339		
Bombay	*32,294*	*21,167*	*11,127*	*21,517*	*15,176*	*6,341*	*1,600*	*1,585*	*247*	*242*	*8,287*	*1,912*		
Sind	*6,800*	*4,935*	*1,865*	*5,420*	*4,220*	*1,200*	*330*	*327*	*31*	*40*	*2,845*	*384*		
Aden	*2,179*	*1,956*	*223*	*1,702*	*1,541*	*161*	*36*	*55*	*2*	*1*	*1,038*	*43*		
8. Burma	24,549	16,063	8,486	11,828	8,904	2,924	726	756	102	122	4,706	941		
9. Central Provinces and Berar	10,591	7,207	3,384	6,957	5,274	1,683	440	481	60	65	3,565	470		
Central Provinces	*10,092*	*6,955*	*3,137*	*6,808*	*5,191*	*1,617*	*423*	*468*	*60*	*64*	*3,553*	*450*		
Berar	*499*	*252*	*247*	*149*	*83*	*66*	*17*	*13*	...	*1*	*12*	*20*		
10. Coorg	345	199	146	174	109	65	14	6	...	1	17	18		
11. Madras	40,887	21,780	19,107	12,726	7,886	4,840	1,258	1,107	177	213	3,446	1,400		
12. N.-W. F. Province (*Districts and Administered Territories*).	5,723	4,874	849	5,581	4,801	780	253	224	5	9	3,531	243		
13. Punjab	34,886	25,717	9,169	31,154	23,748	7,406	2,004	1,836	265	431	16,444	2,177		
14. United Provinces of Agra and Oudh	41,480	28,779	12,701	32,791	24,450	8,341	2,274	2,129	443	383	16,223	2,473		
Agra	*32,738*	*22,395*	*10,343*	*25,777*	*18,924*	*6,853*	*1,883*	*1,749*	*392*	*326*	*12,161*	*2,025*		
Oudh	*8,742*	*6,384*	*2,358*	*7,014*	*5,526*	*1,488*	*391*	*380*	*51*	*56*	*4,062*	*448*		
States and Agencies	**35,904**	**22,451**	**13,453**	**19,423**	**14,278**	**5,145**	**1,355**	**1,257**	**247**	**194**	**9,007**	**1,512**		
15. Assam State (Manipur)	63	37	26	19	14	5	...	1	...	...	4			
16. Baluchistan States	25	21	4	19	15	4	...	1	...	...	6	1		
17. Baroda State	241	124	117	123	72	51	14	10	3	1	16	20		
18. Bengal States	38	23	15	12	7	5	...	1	...	...	1	3		
19. Bihar and Orissa States	131	73	58	48	27	21	4	5	...	1	5	3		
20. Bombay States	629	378	251	344	220	124	30	15	2	3	72	31		
21. Central India Agency	5,147	4,012	1,135	3,968	3,414	554	129	113	39	31	2,673	188		
22. Central Provinces States	230	123	107	76	49	27	8	8	...	1	14	9		
23. Hyderabad State	8,388	5,860	2,528	5,230	4,251	979	238	305	20	22	3,339	270		
24. Kashmir State	268	144	124	226	124	102	23	16	...	3	25	24		
25. Madras States	4,714	2,482	2,232	382	257	125	23	21	1	1	79	33		
26. Mysore State	13,290	7,575	5,715	7,123	4,697	2,426	640	565	138	108	2,520	720		
27. North-West Frontier Province (*Agencies and Tribal areas*).	116	96	20	117	97	20	5	5	...	...	44	6		
28. Punjab States	871	492	379	578	331	247	39	60	6	3	119	69		
29. Rajputana Agency	1,708	980	728	1,127	682	445	197	181	37	20	167	124		
30. Sikkim State	18	17	1	11	10	1	...	...	...	...	2	...		
31. United Provinces States	25	12	13	20	11	9	5	...	1	...	1	3		

AND ANGLO-INDIANS BY RACE AND AGE.

				European and Allied Races.													
				Others.													
30—50.		50 and over.		All Ages.			0—12.		12—15.		15—20.		20—50.		50 and over.		Serial Number.
Males.	Females.	Males.	Females.	Persons.	Males.	Females.	Males.	Females.	Males.	Females.	Males.	Females.	Males.	Females.	Males.	Females.	
14	15	16	17	18	19	20	21	22	23	24	25	26	27	28	29	30	
22,272	**16,466**	**6,117**	**4,437**	**12,648**	**8,026**	**4,622**	**721**	**756**	**185**	**154**	**2,967**	**1,369**	**3,254**	**1,341**	**899**	**562**	
20,286	**14,886**	**5,424**	**3,915**	**11,215**	**7,275**	**3,940**	**617**	**607**	**168**	**139**	**2,750**	**1,153**	**2,947**	**1,611**	**793**	**490**	
226	106	38	22	53	33	20	3	2	...	...	4	3	25	14	1	1	1
24	17	1	2	8	6	2	...	1	...	...	1	1	5	...	...	...	2
780	277	147	25	73	38	35	2	6	...	1	3	5	28	16	5	7	3
745	262	37	19	40	21	19	4	1	...	...	6	7	6	10	5	1	4
5,450	2,678	1,120	724	2,052	1,377	675	124	110	40	21	490	203	525	262	196	79	5
1,211	706	302	230	560	363	197	53	46	15	5	95	51	160	79	40	16	6
306	*496*	*218*	*153*	*204*	*116*	*88*	*12*	*20*		*1*	*35*	*17*	*54*	*88*	*15*	*12*	
82	*78*	*19*	*20*	*37*	*18*	*19*	*6*	*4*	...	*1*	*5*	*4*	*5*	*9*	*2*	*1*	
325	*132*	*65*	*57*	*319*	*229*	*90*	*35*	*22*	*15*	*3*	*55*	*30*	*101*	*32*	*93*	*3*	
5,536	2,425	987	688	3,637	2,564	1,073	168	198	50	41	1,196	337	946	411	189	91	7
4,268	*1,997*	*834*	*605*	*3,007*	*2,031*	*976*	*167*	*169*	*50*	*39*	*864*	*305*	*788*	*378*	*162*	*85*	
887	*368*	*127*	*81*	*185*	*138*	*47*	*10*	*17*	...	*1*	*55*	*16*	*61*	*11*	*12*	*2*	
389	*60*	*26*	*2*	*445*	*395*	*50*	*6*	*7*	...	*1*	*277*	*16*	*97*	*22*	*15*	*4*	
2,939	940	441	165	1,342	974	368	65	60	18	22	382	118	419	127	90	41	8
1,073	546	136	121	291	121	170	11	10	1	...	27	39	67	94	15	29	9
1,026	*519*	*130*	*116*	*246*	*108*	*138*	*8*	*10*	*1*	...	*25*	*29*	*60*	*78*	*14*	*21*	
48	*27*	*6*	*5*	*45*	*13*	*32*	*3*	...	...	...	*2*	*10*	*7*	*16*	*1*	*6*	
46	28	32	12	33	16	17	4	3	...	...	2	6	7	7	3	1	10
2,320	1,546	685	574	2,124	1,226	898	112	135	39	40	385	239	517	391	173	93	11
978	274	34	30	29	15	14	2	1	...	...	4	10	4	2	5	1	12
4,480	2,471	546	501	488	295	193	36	14	5	6	84	68	131	85	39	20	13
4,592	2,555	918	802	485	226	259	18	25	...	3	71	66	107	112	30	52	14
3,685	*2,069*	*803*	*684*	*332*	*138*	*194*	*14*	*33*	...	*2*	*37*	*46*	*67*	*81*	*20*	*49*	
907	*486*	*115*	*118*	*153*	*88*	*65*	*4*	*2*	...	*1*	*34*	*20*	*40*	*32*	*10*	*10*	
2,976	**1,660**	**683**	**522**	**1,433**	**751**	**682**	**104**	**149**	**17**	**15**	**217**	**216**	**307**	**230**	**166**	**72**	
7	3	3	1	...	...	...	...	...	...	...	...	...	...	...	...	...	15
9	2	...	...	1	1	...	...	...	...	...	...	...	1	...	...	...	16
35	17	4	3	36	18	18	2	3	...	...	3	3	9	10	4	2	17
4	2	2	...	9	6	3	1	1	...	...	1	...	2	2	2	...	18
13	6	5	6	18	7	11	2	2	...	...	1	1	2	8	2	...	19
99	61	17	14	43	27	16	3	4	...	...	4	5	15	3	5	4	20
529	198	44	29	612	300	312	67	121	10	10	119	107	87	66	17	8	21
21	9	6	...	9	3	6	...	1	...	...	2	3	...	1	1	1	22
652	328	102	59	152	60	92	7	5	2	3	17	25	27	42	7	17	23
52	41	18	18	25	10	15	1	3	...	1	...	5	7	5	2	1	24
132	56	22	12	114	62	52	1	1	...	...	20	28	32	25	9	3	25
1,011	693	388	381	339	204	135	17	7	4	1	40	41	103	57	40	29	26
42	8	6	1	...	...	...	...	...	...	...	...	...	...	...	...	...	27
134	86	33	29	19	14	5	2	1	...	...	3	1	7	2	2	1	28
220	182	41	18	50	35	15	1	...	1	...	6	2	13	7	14	6	29
6	1	...	...	3	3	...	...	...	...	...	1	...	1	...	1	...	30
2	5	2	1	3	1	2	...	...	...	...	...	...	1	2	...	...	31

TABLE XVIII.—Europeans, Armenians and

Province, State or Agency.	Armenians.										
	All Ages.			0—12.		12—15.		15—20.		20—50.	
	Persons.	Males.	Females.	Males.	Females.	Males.	Females.	Males.	Females.	Males.	Females.
1	31	32	33	34	35	36	37	38	39	40	41
INDIA	1,705	1,008	697	123	160	70	35	366	172	302	205
Provinces	1,692	998	694	122	159	70	35	366	172	297	204
1. Ajmer-Merwara	...	...	...	...	...	...	...	...	...	...	...
2. Andamans and Nicobars	...	...	...	...	...	...	...	...	...	...	...
3. Assam	4	3	1	...	...	...	...	...	...	2	1
4. Baluchistan	...	...	...	...	...	...	...	...	...	...	...
5. Bengal	1,062	628	434	77	90	56	24	230	107	172	128
6. Bihar and Orissa	91	70	21	5	3	2	1	29	5	29	8
Bihar	*26*	*18*	*8*	*1*	...	*2*	...	*6*	*2*	*6*	*4*
Orissa	*6*	*5*	*1*	...	...	...	.	*1*	...	*3*	*2*
Chota Nagpur	*59*	*47*	*12*	*4*	*3*	...	*1*	*22*	*3*	*20*	*2*
7. Bombay (*Presidency*)	64	40	24	4	5	1	...	17	1	15	13
Bombay	*60*	*38*	*22*	*4*	*5*	*1*	...	*16*	*1*	*15*	*12*
Sind	*3*	*1*	*2*	...	...	...	...	*1*	...	...	*1*
Aden	*1*	*1*	...	...	...	...	...	...	...	...	...
8. Burma	273	146	127	23	39	5	7	56	36	45	26
9. Central Provinces and Berar	...	...	...	...	...	...	...	...	...	...	...
Central Provinces	...	...	...	...	...	...	...	...	...	...	...
Berar	...	...	...	...	...	...	...	...	...	...	...
10. Coorg	...	...	...	...	...	...	...	...	...	...	...
11. Madras	34	26	8	...	...	4	...	9	3	9	2
12. N.-W. F. Province (*Districts and Administered Territories*).	14	9	5	...	1	...	...	3	...	3	3
13. Punjab	38	17	21	3	4	...	1	7	8	4	5
14. United Provinces of Agra and Oudh	112	59	53	10	11	2	2	15	12	18	19
Agra	*100*	*50*	*50*	*10*	*11*	*2*	*2*	*10*	*10*	*16*	*19*
Oudh	*12*	*9*	*3*	...	...	...	.	*5*	*2*	*2*	...
States and Agencies	13	10	3	1	1	...	...	...	...	5	1
15. Assam State (Manipur)	1	1	...	...	...	...	...	...	...	1	...
16. Baluchistan States	...	...	...	...	...	...	...	...	...	...	...
17. Baroda State	...	...	...	...	...	...	...	...	...	...	...
18. Bengal States	1	1	...	...	...	...	...	...	...	1	...
19. Bihar and Orissa States	1	1	...	...	...	...	...	...	...	1	...
20. Bombay States	...	...	...	...	...	...	...	...	...	...	...
21. Central India Agency	2	2	...	...	...	...	...	...	...	...	...
22. Central Provinces States	...	...	...	...	...	...	...	...	...	...	...
23. Hyderabad State	2	1	1	...	1	...	...	...	...	1	...
24. Kashmir State	...	...	...	...	...	...	...	...	...	...	...
25. Madras States	2	2	...	...	...	...	...	...	...	1	...
26. Mysore State	1	1	...	1	...	...	...	...	...	...	...
27. North-West Frontier Province (*Agencies and Tribal areas*).	...	...	...	...	...	...	...	...	...	...	...
28. Punjab States	1	1	...	...	...	...	...	...	...	...	...
29. Rajputana Agency	2	...	2	...	...	...	...	...	...	...	1
30. Sikkim State	...	...	...	...	...	...	...	...	...	...	...
31. United Provinces States	...	...	...	...	...	...	...	...	...	...	...

Anglo-Indians by Race and Age—*concluded.*

50 and over.		Anglo-Indians and other persons of mixed European and Asiatic descent.													Serial Number.
50 and over.		All Ages.			0—12.		12—15.		15—30.		30—50.		50 and over.		
Males.	Females.	Persons.	Males.	Females.	Males.	Females.	Males.	Females.	Males.	Females.	Males.	Females.	Males.	Females.	
42	43	44	45	46	47	48	49	50	51	52	53	54	55	56	
147	**125**	**100,451**	**50,636**	**49,815**	**15,134**	**14,856**	**3,857**	**3,738**	**14,956**	**15,948**	**12,038**	**10,596**	**4,651**	**4,683**	
143	**124**	**85,416**	**43,224**	**42,192**	**12,703**	**12,478**	**3,227**	**3,132**	**13,062**	**13,592**	**10,371**	**8,994**	**3,861**	**3,996**	
...	...	710	379	331	104	94	23	23	135	115	95	71	22	28	1
...	...	78	35	43	13	16	1	3	8	12	12	10	1	2	2
1	...	432	250	182	67	51	5	8	84	77	78	39	16	7	3
...	...	118	59	59	14	11	2	3	22	30	19	12	2	3	4
93	79	19,817	9,939	9,878	2,902	2,906	805	675	2,986	3,155	2,364	2,108	882	1,032	5
5	4	3,341	1,728	1,613	521	487	158	126	466	459	429	365	154	176	6
3	*2*	*1,939*	*1,004*	*928*	*309*	*267*	*100*	*74*	*265*	*254*	*242*	*219*	*88*	*114*	
1	...	*481*	*218*	*263*	*64*	*83*	*17*	*24*	*53*	*80*	*58*	*48*	*26*	*38*	
1	*2*	*928*	*506*	*422*	*148*	*137*	*41*	*28*	*148*	*126*	*129*	*98*	*40*	*34*	
3	5	8,933	4,517	4,416	1,173	1,298	253	361	1,596	1,558	1,161	910	335	290	7
2	*4*	*7,710*	*3,922*	*3,788*	*1,004*	*1,085*	*228*	*308*	*1,427*	*1,367*	*983*	*771*	*280*	*257*	
...	*1*	*1,192*	*576*	*616*	*165*	*199*	*25*	*53*	*161*	*184*	*171*	*138*	*54*	*42*	
1	...	*31*	*19*	*12*	*4*	*4*	...	...	*7*	*7*	*7*	*1*	*1*	...	
17	19	11,106	6,099	5,007	1,765	1,688	444	407	1,860	1,688	1,600	960	370	304	8
...	...	3,343	1,812	1,531	494	504	136	95	570	487	470	316	142	129	9
...	...	*3,038*	*1,656*	*1,382*	*456*	*456*	*134*	*86*	*532*	*442*	*412*	*280*	*122*	*118*	
...	...	*305*	*156*	*149*	*38*	*48*	*2*	*9*	*38*	*45*	*58*	*36*	*20*	*11*	
...	...	138	74	64	20	16	...	4	24	24	15	11	15	9	10
4	3	26,003	12,642	13,361	3,914	3,741	972	1,019	3,548	4,205	2,806	2,900	1,402	1,496	11
3	2	99	49	50	12	12	...	5	18	16	18	14	1	3	12
3	3	3,206	1,657	1,549	498	490	119	119	519	486	408	332	123	122	13
14	9	8,092	4,044	4,048	1,216	1,172	309	284	1,227	1,280	896	926	396	386	14
12	*8*	*6,529*	*3,283*	*3,246*	*1,005*	*964*	*261*	*230*	*991*	*991*	*706*	*743*	*320*	*318*	
2	*1*	*1,563*	*761*	*802*	*211*	*208*	*48*	*54*	*236*	*289*	*190*	*183*	*76*	*68*	
4	**1**	**15,035**	**7,412**	**7,623**	**2,431**	**2,372**	**630**	**606**	**1,894**	**2,356**	**1,667**	**1,602**	**790**	**687**	
...	...	43	22	21	8	12	1	...	3	4	7	4	3	1	15
...	...	5	5	...	...	...	...	...	1	...	4	...	...	...	16
...	...	83	34	48	7	15	...	2	15	10	7	17	5	4	17
...	...	16	9	7	3	2	...	...	...	4	4	1	2	...	18
...	...	64	38	26	7	10	3	...	8	7	16	8	4	1	19
...	...	242	131	111	34	36	3	5	40	40	43	26	11	4	20
2	...	565	296	269	101	72	11	23	76	91	85	73	23	10	21
...	...	145	71	74	31	29	1	2	17	20	20	16	2	8	22
...	...	3,004	1,548	1,456	469	435	106	101	306	467	382	315	173	138	23
...	...	17	10	7	1	1	...	...	6	2	3	4	...	...	24
1	...	4,216	2,161	2,055	715	634	210	176	567	625	426	412	223	[illegible]	25
...	...	5,827	2,673	3,154	900	1,007	274	277	630	965	556	628	313	[illegible]	26
...	...	1	1	...	...	...	...	...	1	...	...	...	...	...	27
1	...	273	146	127	45	27	3	5	46	49	39	35	13	11	28
...	1	529	263	266	90	92	16	15	67	72	73	64	17	23	29
...	...	4	4	...	...	...	...	...	1	...	2	...	1	...	30
...	...	2	...	2	...	...	...	...	...	...	...	...	...	2	31

TABLE XIX.

Summary Figures for Districts.

1. This Table contains for easy reference a few of the salient figures for the individual Districts or States in each Province, State or Agency. For further particulars regarding these minor units the Provincial Census Reports should be referred to.

2. The figures for States in political relation with Local Governments are given below those for the British territory administered by the same Local Government.

3. The figures for the Central India Agency in this Table include those for the Gangapur pargana of Gwalior and Nandwai pargana of Indore, which are situated in the Mewar State of the Rajputana Agency. This is why there is a discrepancy between the area and population of the Central India and Rajputana Agencies as here shown and the corresponding figures in Imperial Table I.

TABLE XIX.—Summary

Serial Number.	District or State.	Area in square miles.	Population, 1911. Persons.	Males.	Females.	Population, 1901.	Percentage of Variation. 1901-11.	1891-01.	Number of persons per square mile in 1911.
1	2	3	4	5	6	7	8	9	10
	INDIA.	**1,802,657**	**315,156,396**	**161,338,935**	**153,817,461**	**294,361,056**	+ 7·1	+ 2·5	**175**
	AJMER-MERWARA.	**2,711**	**501,395**	**266,198**	**235,197**	**476,912**	+ 5·1	− 12·1	**185**
1	Ajmer	2,070	380,384	201,911	178,473	367,453	+ 3·5	− 13·0	184
2	Merwara	641	121,011	64,287	56,724	109,459	+ 10·6	− 8·8	189
	ANDAMANS AND NICOBARS.	**3,143**	**26,459**	**19,570**	**6,889**	**24,649**	+ 7·3	+ 57·9	**8**
1	Port Blair }	635	16,324	14,109	2,215	16,256	+ ·4	+ 4·1	28
2	Rest of Andamans }		1,317	628	689	1,882	− 30·0	..	
3	Nicobar Islands	2,508	8,818	4,833	3,985	6,511	+ 35·4	..	4
	ASSAM.	**61,471**	**7,059,857**	**3,638,287**	**3,421,570**	**6,126,343**	+ 15·2	+ 11·8	**115**
	British Territory.	**53,015**	**6,713,635**	**3,467,621**	**3,246,014**	**5,841,878**	+ 14·9	+ 6·7	**127**
	Surma Valley and Hill Districts Division.	*25,277*	*3,446,030*	*1,761,134*	*1,684,896*	*3,084,527*	+ *11·7*	+ *7·1*	*136*
1	Cachar	3,565	497,463	260,444	237,019	455,593	+ 9·2	+ 17·9	140
2	Sylhet	5,388	2,472,671	1,268,469	1,204,202	2,241,848	+ 10·3	+ 4·0	459
3	Khasi and Jaintia Hills	6,027	235,069	114,442	120,627	202,250	+ 16·2	+ 2·2	39
4	Naga Hills	3,070	149,623	74,751	74,872	102,402	+ 46·1	+ 6·0	49
5	Lushai Hills	7,227	91,204	43,028	48,176	82,434	+ 10·6	+ 88·9	18
	Assam Valley Division.	*27,738*	*3,267,605*	*1,706,487*	*1,561,118*	*2,757,351*	+ *18·5*	+ *6·1*	*118*
6	Goalpara	3,954	600,643	318,475	282,168	462,052	+ 30·0	+ 2·0	152
7	Kamrup	3,858	667,828	339,398	328,430	589,187	+ 13·3	− 7·1	173
8	Darrang	3,418	377,314	198,581	178,733	337,313	+ 11·9	+ 9·7	110
9	Nowgong	3,843	303,596	154,938	148,658	261,160	+ 16·2	− 24·8	79
10	Sibsagar	4,996	690,299	364,810	325,489	597,969	+ 15·4	+ 24·4	138
11	Lakhimpur	4,529	468,989	249,021	219,968	371,396	+ 26·3	+ 46·2	104
12	Garo Hills	3,140	158,936	81,264	77,672	138,274	+ 14·9	+ 13·7	51
	Assam State (Manipur).	**8,456**	**346,222**	**170,666**	**175,556**	**284,465**	+ 21·7	*	**41**
	BALUCHISTAN.	**134,638**	**834,703**	**466,419**	**368,284**	**810,746**	+ 3·0		**6**
	British Territory.	**54,228**	**414,412**	**239,181**	**175,231**	**382,106**	+ 8·5		**8**
1	Quetta—Pishin	5,220	127,648	76,467	51,181	114,087	+ 11·9		24
2	Loralai	7,525	80,769	44,923	35,846	68,332	+ 18·2		11
3	Zhob	10,315	70,366	40,346	30,020	69,718	+ ·9		7
4	Bolan	353	2,096	1,492	604	1,936	+ 8·3		6
5	Chagai	19,622	16,344	9,107	7,237	15,689	+ 4·2		1
6	Sibi (Administered Area)	3,925	82,423	47,558	34,865	77,987	+ 5·7		21
7	Mari-Bugti Country	7,268	34,766	19,288	15,478	34,357	+ 1·2		5
	Baluchistan States.	**80,410**	**420,291**	**227,238**	**193,053**	**428,640**	− 1·9	No Census was taken in 1891.	**5**
1	Kalat	73,278	359,086	194,598	164,488	372,531	− 3·6		5
	Sarawan	*5,230*	*63,781*	*35,082*	*28,699*	*65,549*	− *2·7*		*12*
	Jhalawan	*20,795*	*84,398*	*46,880*	*37,518*	*224,073*	− *62·3*		*4*
	Kachhi	*4,060*	*92,759*	*50,191*	*42,568*	*63,367*	+ *46·4*		*23*
	Makran	*23,269*	*71,942*	*37,698*	*34,244*	..	..		*3*
	Dombki Kaheri Country	*1,359*	*23,543*	*12,624*	*10,919*	*19,542*	+ *20·5*		*17*
	Kharan	*18,565*	*22,663*	*12,123*	*10,540*	..	..		*1*
2	Las Bela	7,132	61,205	32,640	28,565	56,109	+ 9·1		9
	BENGAL.	**84,092**	**46,305,642**	**23,803,593**	**22,502,049**	**42,881,776**	+ 8·0	+ 7·7	**551**
	British Territory.	**78,699**	**45,483,077**	**23,365,225**	**22,117,852**	**42,141,477**	+ 7·9	+ 7·8	**578**
	Burdwan Division.	*13,948*	*8,467,314*	*4,261,925*	*4,205,389*	*8,240,076*	+ *2·8*	+ *7·2*	*607*
1	Burdwan	2,691	1,538,371	770,324	768,047	1,532,716	+ ·4	+ 10·1	572
2	Birbhum	1,752	935,473	463,838	471,635	902,280	+ 3·7	+ 13·0	534
3	Bankura	2,621	1,138,670	562,585	576,085	1,116,411	+ 2·0	+ 4·4	434
4	Midnapore	5,186	2,821,201	1,410,714	1,410,487	2,789,114	+ 1·2	+ 6·0	544
5	Hooghly	1,188	1,090,097	555,823	534,274	1,049,041	+ 3·9	+ 1·4	918
6	Howrah	510	943,502	498,641	444,861	850,514	+ 10·9	+ 11·4	1,850
	Presidency Division.	*17,499*	*9,445,321*	*5,014,917*	*4,430,404*	*8,983,818*	+ *5·1*	+ *5·4*	*540*
7	24-Parganas	4,844	2,434,104	1,305,700	1,128,404	2,078,359	+ 17·1	+ 9·9	502
8	Calcutta	32	896,067	607,674	288,393	847,796	+ 5·7	+ 24·3	28,002
9	Nadia	2,790	1,617,846	812,580	805,266	1,658,281	− 2·4	+ 1·5	580
10	Murshidabad	2,143	1,372,274	678,292	693,982	1,333,184	+ 2·9	+ 6·6	640
11	Jessore	2,925	1,758,264	901,092	857,172	1,813,155	− 3·0	− 4·0	601
12	Khulna	4,765	1,366,766	709,579	657,187	1,253,043	+ 9·1	+ 6·4	287
	Rajshahi Division.	*19,235*	*10,138,308*	*5,256,785*	*4,881,517*	*9,373,620*	+ *8·2*	+ *6·1*	*527*
13	Rajshahi	2,618	1,480,587	755,206	725,381	1,460,584	+ 1·4	+ 1·6	566
14	Dinajpur	3,946	1,687,863	889,876	797,987	1,566,845	+ 7·7	+ 5·7	428
15	Jalpaiguri	2,919	902,660	490,228	412,432	786,326	+ 14·8	+ 15·7	309
16	Darjeeling	1,164	265,550	142,094	123,456	249,117	+ 6·6	+ 11·6	228
17	Rangpur	3,479	2,385,330	1,254,717	1,130,613	2,154,115	+ 10·7	+ 4·3	686
18	Bogra	1,359	983,567	502,526	481,041	858,504	+ 15·2	+ 11·8	724
19	Pabna	1,851	1,428,586	723,591	704,995	1,421,395	+ ·5	+ 4·3	772
20	Malda	1,899	1,004,159	498,547	505,612	881,734	+ 13·9	+ 8·5	529

* The census schedules were destroyed in the disturbances which took place in March 1891 before the results of the Census taken on the 1st of that month had been tabulated.

Figures for Districts.

Distribution by Religion.										Serial Number.
Hindu.		Musalman.		Christian.		Animistic.		Others.		
Males.	Females.	Males.	Females.	Males.	Females.	Males.	Females.	Males.	Females.	
11	12	13	14	15	16	17	18	19	20	21
110,725,612	**106,612,331**	**34,738,342**	**31,908,957**	**2,010,729**	**1,865,474**	**5,126,932**	**5,168,236**	**7,885,885**	**7,506,142**	
204,856	**183,696**	**43,833**	**37,202**	**3,258**	**2,174**	**1,987**	**1,992**	**12,264**	**10,133**	
155,993	140,083	32,585	27,880	2,996	1,914	1,308	1,870	9.029	7,226	1
48,863	43,613	11,248	9,322	262	260	679	622	3,235	2,907	2
7,927	**1,540**	**4,080**	**500**	**384**	**182**	**5,101**	**4,610**	**2,078**	**57**	
7,896	1,537	3,904	495	328	129	5	..	1,976	54	1
..	..	..	..	..	2	628	687	..	..	2
31	3	176	5	56	51	4,468	3,923	102	3	3
1,997,724	**1,841,845**	**984,968**	**916,064**	**33,632**	**32,930**	**612,899**	**626,381**	**9,064**	**5,150**	
1,898,460	**1,738,940**	**977,463**	**909,065**	**33,548**	**32,882**	**549,200**	**559,987**	**8,950**	**5,140**	
743,597	*692,637*	*783,772*	*739,216*	*19,184*	*20,535*	*213,843*	*232,206*	*738*	*302*	
167,424	152,680	82,560	73,536	649	532	9,743	10,253	68	18	1
564,266	534,684	699,470	665,289	863	649	3,701	3,574	169	26	2
6,738	2,716	1,172	356	14,855	16,402	91,447	101,006	230	147	3
2,737	1,476	281	37	1,554	1,754	70,136	71,604	43	1	4
2,432	1,081	289	18	1,263	1,198	38,816	45,769	228	110	5
1,154,863	*1,046,303*	*193,691*	*169,849*	*14,364*	*12,347*	*335,357*	*327,781*	*8,212*	*4,838*	
178,673	156,047	111,917	99,645	2,731	2,521	28,870	23,469	1,284	486	6
235,014	224,213	33,723	30,904	1,873	1,162	68,649	71,927	639	224	7
129,631	115,710	11,073	9,232	1,028	885	56,043	52,688	806	218	8
91,213	86,582	8,163	7,526	707	666	54,403	53,664	452	220	9
313,748	281,518	16,373	13,345	2,933	2,477	30,862	27,218	1,394	931	10
195,291	172,699	7,986	5,433	2,647	2,142	39,622	37,079	3,475	2,615	11
11,293	9,534	4,456	3,764	2,945	2,494	62,408	61,736	162	144	12
99,264	**102,105**	**7,505**	**6,999**	**84**	**48**	**63,699**	**66,394**	**114**	**10**	
25,008	**12,594**	**430,850**	**351,798**	**3,941**	**1,144**	..	..	**6,620**	**2 748**	
18,470	**7,294**	**211,828**	**165,528**	**3,892**	**1,138**	..	..	**4,991**	**1,271**	
9,600	3,644	60,950	45,752	3,549	1,015	..	..	2,368	770	1
2,038	920	41,955	34,800	58	13	..	..	872	113	2
1,150	198	38,363	29,725	154	14	..	..	679	83	3
416	107	972	450	14	12	..	..	90	35	4
264	112	8,800	7,116	6	3	..	..	37	6	5
4,796	2,146	41,704	32,374	111	81	..	..	945	264	6
204	167	19,084	15,311	..	..	..	..	..	..	7
6,538	**5,300**	**219,022**	**186,270**	**49**	**6**	..	..	**1,629**	**1,477**	
5,550	4,552	187,435	158,471	45	6	..	..	1,568	1,459	1
600	*403*	*34,411*	*28,249*	*3*	*2*	..	..	*68*	*45*	
380	*92*	*46,491*	*37,423*	..	..	..	..	*9*	*3*	
3,748	*3,428*	*45,823*	*38,566*	*4*	*2*	..	..	*616*	*572*	
126	*11*	*37,528*	*34,230*	*38*	*2*	..	..	*6*	*1*	
664	*598*	*11,091*	*9,483*	..	..	..	..	*869*	*838*	
32	*20*	*12,091*	*10,520*	..	..	..	..	..	..	
988	748	31,587	27,799	4	..	..	..	61	18	2
10,848,217	**10,097,162**	**12,377,215**	**11,860,013**	**70,260**	**59,486**	**371,581**	**359,199**	**136;320**	**126,189**	
10,545,714	**9,832,079**	**12,245,542**	**11,744,177**	**70,127**	**59,391**	**371,248**	**358,934**	**132,594**	**123,271**	
3,510,259	*3,460,901*	*571,234*	*566,818*	*7,545*	*6,237*	*171,709*	*170,895*	*1,178*	*538*	
609,485	611,066	146,574	143,807	2,055	1,765	12,069	11,314	141	95	1
325,364	331,689	110,336	112,451	419	394	27,550	27,042	169	59	2
488,848	501,313	25,845	25,862	530	482	47,356	48,421	6	7	3
1,240,620	1,236,652	96,209	97,360	2,229	1,937	71,131	74,306	525	232	4
451,784	432,056	91,670	92,339	501	350	11,783	9.505	85	24	5
394,158	348,125	100,600	94,999	1,811	1,309	1,820	307	252	121	6
2,557,229	*2,204,535*	*2,391,768*	*2,176,632*	*37,907*	*30,131*	*16,847*	*15,237*	*8,166*	*3,819*	
822,858	703,028	466,490	413,057	8,914	7,113	6,761	5,050	677	156	7
404,528	200,325	173.785	67,802	22,472	17,079	39	17	6,850	3,170	8
322,018	320,633	484,355	478,764	4,717	4,415	1,428	1,433	62	21	9
320,270	323,021	350,132	363,020	202	211	7,141	7,278	547	452	10
336,433	331,503	563,257	524,297	652	620	788	737	12	15	11
351,122	326,025	356,749	329,692	950	743	740	722	18	5	12
1,913,486	*1,688,662*	*3,157,160*	*3,020,321*	*9,422*	*7,745*	*145,708*	*137,062*	*31,009*	*27,727*	
164,998	150,642	581,669	566,645	163	160	8,296	7,899	80	35	13
406,872	352,437	429,946	394,399	1,019	945	51,866	50,165	173	41	14
300,227	247,100	128,193	109,263	2,928	2,573	54,421	49,584	4,459	3,912	15
101.840	87,777	5,775	3,675	4,377	3,312	5,622	5,156	24,480	23,536	16
435,136	368,848	812,402	756,628	336	263	5,532	4,889	1,311	125	17
89,834	76,862	409,319	401.033	91	70	3,124	3,030	158	46	18
180,732	173,522	542,016	531,062	296	204	224	182	323	25	19
233,847	231,674	247,840	257,556	212	218	16,623	16,157	25	7	20

Note.—The details in columns 11 to 20 against India do not work up to the total in columns 5 and 6, as they are exclusive of 1,608,556 persons who were not enumerated by religion.

TABLE XIX.—SUMMARY

Serial Number.	District or State.	Area in square miles.	Population, 1911. Persons.	Males.	Females.	Population, 1901.	Percentage of Variation. 1901-11.	1891-01.	Number of persons per square mile in 1911.
1	2	3	4	5	6	7	8	9	10
	BENGAL—contd.								
	Dacca Division.	*16,244*	*12,037,649*	*6,137,087*	*5,900,562*	*10,806,232*	+ *11·4*	+ *9·6*	*741*
21	Dacca	2,777	2,960,402	1,477,690	1,482,712	2,644,435	+ 11·9	+ 10·6	1,066
22	Mymensingh	6,249	4,526,422	2,339,603	2,186,819	3,918,102	+ 15·5	+ 12·7	724
23	Faridpur	2,576	2,121,914	1,074,959	1,046,955	1,961,943	+ 8·7	+ 6·2	824
24	Backergunge	4,642	2,428,911	1,244,835	1,184,076	2,291,752	+ 6·0	+ 6·4	523
	Chittagong Division.	*11,773*	*5,394,491*	*2,694,511*	*2,699,980*	*4,737,731*	+ *13·9*	+ *13·1*	*458*
25	Tippera	2,499	2,430,138	1,243,081	1,187,057	2,117,991	+ 14·7	+ 18·8	972
26	Noakhali	1,644	1,302,090	645,898	656,192	1,141,728	+ 14·0	+ 13·1	792
27	Chittagong	2,492	1,508,433	722,837	785,596	1,353,250	+ 11·5	+ 4·9	605
28	Chittagong Hill Tracts	5,138	153,830	82,695	71,135	124,762	+ 23·3	+ 16·2	30
	Bengal States.	**5,393**	**822,565**	**438,368**	**384,197**	**740,299**	+ **11·1**	+ **3·3**	**153**
1	Cooch Behar	1,307	592,952	316,548	276,404	566,974	+ 4·6	— 2·1	454
2	Hill Tippera	4,086	229,613	121,820	107,793	173,325	+ 32·5	+ 26·1	56
	BIHAR AND ORISSA	**111,829**	**38,435,293**	**18,815,054**	**19,620,239**	**36,557,257**	+ **5·1**	+ **1·6**	**344**
	British Territory	**83,181**	**34,490,084**	**16,859,929**	**17,630,155**	**33,242,783**	+ **3·8**	+ **1·1**	**415**
	Patna Division.	*11,154*	*5,634,789*	*2,776,019*	*2,858,770*	*5,647,371*	— *·2*	— *5·4*	*505*
1	Patna	2,069	1,609,631	809,778	799,853	1,624,742	— ·9	— 8·4	778
2	Gaya	4,712	2,159,498	1,061,291	1,098,207	2,059,983	+ 4·8	— 3·7	458
3	Shahabad	4,373	1,865,660	904,950	960,710	1,962,696	— 4·9	— 4·8	427
	Tirhut Division.	*12,598*	*9,973,359*	*4,779,214*	*5,194,145*	*9,868,018*	+ *1·1*	+ *·3*	*792*
4	Saran	2,683	2,289,778	1,064,333	1,225,445	2,408,814	— 4·9	— 2·3	853
5	Champaran	3,531	1,908,385	942,012	966,373	1,790,463	+ 6·6	— 3·7	540
6	Muzaffarpur	3,036	2,845,514	1,360,200	1,485,314	2,756,180	+ 3·2	+ 1·5	937
7	Darbhanga	3,348	2,929,682	1,412,669	1,517,013	2,912,611	+ ·6	+ 3·9	875
	Bhagalpur Division.	*18,609*	*8,144,821*	*4,051,199*	*4,093,622*	*7,844,823*	+ *3·8*	+ *1·0*	*438*
8	Monghyr	3,922	2,132,893	1,043,477	1,089,416	2,068,804	+ 3·1	+ 1·6	544
9	Bhagalpur	4,226	2,139,318	1,057,876	1,081,442	2,088,953	+ 2·4	+ 2·8	506
10	Purnea	4,998	1,989,637	1,016,421	973,216	1,877,329	+ 6·0	— 3·6	398
11	Sonthal Parganas	5,463	1,882,973	933,425	949,548	1,809,737	+ 4·0	+ 3·2	345
	Orissa Division.	*13,743*	*5,131,753*	*2,476,284*	*2,655,469*	*4,982,142*	+ *3·0*	+ *6·8*	*373*
12	Cuttack	3,654	2,109,139	1,001,175	1,107,964	2,060,313	+ 2·4	+ 6·5	577
13	Balasore	2,085	1,055,568	504,615	550,953	1,073,642	— 1·7	+ 7·7	506
14	Angul	1,681	199,451	98,372	101,079	191,911	+ 3·9	+ 12·8	119
15	Puri	2,499	1,023,402	506,570	516,832	1,017,284	+ ·6	+ 7·6	410
16	Sambalpur	3,824	744,193	365,552	378,641	638,992	+ 16·5	+ 3·8	195
	Chota Nagpur Division.	*27,077*	*5,605,362*	*2,777,213*	*2,828,149*	*4,900,429*	+ *14·4*	+ *5·9*	*207*
17	Hazaribagh	7,021	1,288,609	629,103	659,506	1,177,961	+ 9·4	+ 1·2	184
18	Ranchi	7,104	1,387,516	676,753	710,763	1,187,925	+ 16·8	+ 5·2	195
19	Palamau	4,914	687,267	341,613	345,654	619,600	+ 10·9	+ 3·6	140
20	Manbhum	4,147	1,547,576	788,537	759,039	1,301,364	+ 18·9	+ 9·1	373
21	Singhbhum	3,891	694,394	341,207	353,187	613,579	+ 13·2	+ 12·5	178
	Bihar and Orissa States	**28,648**	**3,945,209**	**1,955,125**	**1,990,084**	**3,314,474**	+ **19·0**	+ **9·5**	**138**
	Orissa Feudatory States.	*28,046*	*3,796,563*	*1,882,588*	*1,913,975*	*3,173,395*	+ *19·6*	+ *9·6*	*135*
1	Athgarh	168	46,813	23,319	23,494	43,784	+ 6·9	+ 19·6	279
2	Talcher	399	66,201	32,885	33,316	60,432	+ 9·6	+ 14·7	166
3	Mayurbhanj	4,243	729,218	362,570	366,648	610,383	+ 19·5	+ 14·7	172
4	Nilgiri	278	68,714	33,982	34,732	66,460	+ 3·4	+ 18·3	247
5	Keonjhar	3,096	364,702	182,020	182,682	285,758	+ 27·6	+ 15·2	118
6	Pal Lahara	452	25,680	12,762	12,918	22,351	+ 14·9	+ 13·5	57
7	Dhenkanal	1,463	270,175	131,477	138,698	273,662	— 1·3	+ 14·8	185
8	Athmallik	730	53,766	27,673	26,093	40,753	+ 31·9	+ 28·9	74
9	Hindol	312	49,840	23,944	25,896	47,180	+ 5·6	+ 24·2	160
10	Narsinghpur	199	39,964	19,502	20,462	39,613	+ ·9	+ 17·0	201
11	Baramba	134	41,429	20,344	21,085	38,260	+ 8·3	+ 17·6	309
12	Tigiria	46	23,240	11,454	11,786	22,625	+ 2·7	+ 10·1	505
13	Khandpara	244	73,821	36,700	37,121	69,450	+ 6·3	+ 9·7	303
14	Nayagarh	588	151,293	74,320	76,973	140,779	+ 7·5	+ 19·4	257
15	Ranpur	203	45,956	22,696	23,260	46,075	— ·3	+ 14·9	226
16	Daspalla	568	57,053	27,982	29,071	51,987	+ 9·7	+ 14·0	100
17	Baud	1,264	113,441	56,612	56,829	88,250	+ 28·5	— 1·4	90
18	Bamra	1,988	138,016	69,003	69,013	123,378	+ 11·9	+ 18·2	69
19	Bairakhol	833	31,729	15,938	15,791	26,888	+ 18·0	+ 32·3	38
20	Sonpur	906	215,701	105,739	109,962	169,877	+ 27·0	— 13·0	238
21	Patna	2,399	408,716	201,887	206,829	277,748	+ 47·2	— 16·4	170
22	Kalahandi	3,745	418,957	207,630	211,327	350,529	+ 19·5	+ 7·4	112
23	Gangpur	2,492	303,829	152,640	151,189	238,896	+ 27·2	+ 24·8	122
24	Bonai	1,296	58,309	29,509	28,800	38,277	+ 52·3	+ 19·2	45
	Chota Nagpur States.	*602*	*148,646*	*72,537*	*76,109*	*141,079*	+ *5·4*	+ *9·1*	*247*
25	Saraikela	449	109,794	53,780	56,014	104,539	+ 5·0	+ 11·4	245
26	Kharsawan	153	38,852	18,757	20,095	36,540	+ 6·3	+ 3·0	254

FIGURES FOR DISTRICTS—*contd.*

DISTRIBUTION BY RELIGION.										Serial Number.
HINDU.		MUSALMAN.		CHRISTIAN.		ANIMISTIC.		OTHERS.		
Males.	Females.	Males.	Females.	Males.	Females.	Males.	Females.	Males.	Females.	
11	12	13	14	15	16	17	18	19	20	21
1,891,484	*1,816,893*	*4,206,703*	*4,045,908*	*13,773*	*13,953*	*19,733*	*19,270*	*5,394*	*4,538*	
523,069	529,187	947,437	946,033	6,320	6,874	615	424	249	194	21
613,770	547,815	1,705,129	1,619,017	1,143	1,038	19,116	18,846	445	103	22
386,442	388,537	685,478	655,612	3,015	2,795	..	..	24	11	23
368,203	351,354	868,659	825,246	3,295	3,246	2	..	4,676	4,230	24
673,256	*661,088*	*1,915,677*	*1,934,498*	*1,480*	*1,275*	*17,251*	*16,470*	*86,847*	*86,649*	
348,521	329,149	898,503	856,897	236	174	..	..	821	887	25
151,571	148,675	493,701	506,952	370	373	..	..	256	192	26
166,772	177,417	519,413	569,611	784	646	302	275	32,566	37,847	27
8,392	5,847	4,060	1,038	90	82	16,949	16,195	53,204	47,973	28
302,508	**265,083**	**131,673**	**115,836**	**133**	**95**	**333**	**265**	**3,726**	**2,418**	
219,468	190,022	96,378	86,178	58	32	105	85	544	87	1
83,040	75,061	35,295	29,658	75	63	228	180	3,182	2,331	2
15,504,749	**16,184,269**	**1,775,656**	**1,907,782**	**133,186**	**135,079**	**1,333,660**	**1,386,628**	**7,803**	**6,461**	
13,998,520	**14,474,869**	**1,766,496**	**1,900,365**	**114,009**	**115,816**	**1,086,231**	**1,134,295**	**6,673**	**5,610**	
2,530,684	*2,569,443*	*239,380*	*284,135*	*2,183*	*1,451*	*835*	*827*	*2,937*	*2,914*	
726,192	706,538	79,942	90,441	1,630	955	..	..	2,014	1,919	1
962,047	974,787	98,832	123,111	199	150	21	23	192	136	2
842,445	888,118	60,606	70,583	354	346	814	804	731	859	3
4,183,356	*4,615,318*	*593,107*	*676,163*	*2,423*	*2,448*	..	..	*298*	*216*	
943,265	1,082,179	120,746	142,995	231	206	..	..	61	65	4
801,746	817,702	138,907	147,191	1,327	1,448	..	..	32	32	5
1,198,887	1,294,848	160,796	190,024	483	410	..	..	34	32	6
1,239,458	1,420,589	172,658	195,953	382	384	..	..	171	87	7
2,940,683	*2,972,746*	*709,083*	*714,802*	*6,754*	*6,817*	*392,929*	*398,095*	*1,750*	*1,162*	
945,299	977,212	93,143	107,196	955	851	3,712	3,798	368	359	8
940,251	959,359	105,564	110,141	603	499	11,024	11,191	434	252	9
577,527	549,292	422,624	408,608	270	230	15,247	14,724	753	367	10
477,606	486,883	87,752	88,862	4,926	5,237	362,946	368,382	195	184	11
2,366,369	*2,537,010*	*55,762*	*61,827*	*3,804*	*4,203*	*49,618*	*51,866*	*731*	*564*	
970,921	1,072,060	29,026	34,360	1,044	1,362	1	1	183	181	12
484,440	529,849	15,147	15,827	673	785	4,310	4,458	45	84	13
69,815	71,360	220	115	48	21	28,241	29,547	48	36	14
496,217	506,257	9,523	9,825	663	618	..	..	167	182	15
344,976	357,484	1,846	1,700	1,376	1,417	17,066	17,859	288	181	16
1,865,398	*1,879,552*	*169,164*	*163,438*	*98,845*	*100,897*	*642,849*	*683,508*	*957*	*754*	
519,367	546,700	65,246	68,082	1,024	762	48,072	43,684	394	328	17
273,485	277,067	25,622	25,536	87,418	90,055	289,961	317,859	267	246	18
291,508	295,415	28,754	28,915	3,912	3,871	17,439	17,444	5	9	19
635,688	614,270	45,080	37,696	2,364	2,136	105,177	104,779	233	156	20
145,360	146,100	4,462	3,209	4,127	4,078	187,200	199,792	58	15	21
1,678,226	**1,710,200**	**9,160**	**7,417**	**19,177**	**19,263**	**247,429**	**252,333**	**1,130**	**871**	
1,636,325	*1,667,140*	*8,279*	*6,691*	*19,169*	*19,253*	*217,682*	*220,020*	*1,130*	*871*	
22,925	23,147	138	143	174	185	..	..	82	19	1
32,644	33,070	66	59	2	1	173	186	..	..	2
332,605	336,826	2,591	2,065	380	387	26,986	27,365	8	5	3
31,630	32,378	100	37	48	47	2,201	2,270	3	..	4
151,306	152,811	553	390	18	16	30,120	29,450	21	15	5
12,753	12,914	9	4	..	..	..	..	..	..	6
126,024	133,283	461	339	12	8	4,759	4,888	221	180	7
25,801	24,288	68	66	..	..	1,804	1,794	..	..	8
23,324	25,283	100	61	3	1	517	551	..	..	9
19,427	20,399	73	60	2	3	..	..	..	..	10
19,858	20,617	90	85	3	3	..	..	393	380	11
11,006	11,381	216	220	..	..	..	..	233	185	12
34,644	37,078	56	43	..	..	..	..	..	..	13
68,616	71,207	414	304	2	4	5,288	5,458	..	..	14
22,517	23,107	178	150	1	3	..	..	..	..	15
27,931	29,047	49	21	2	3	..	..	..	..	16
56,447	56,688	115	94	5	5	38	39	7	8	17
48,566	48,315	168	127	3	2	20,240	20,557	26	12	18
14,361	14,314	34	27	9	6	1,532	1,440	2	2	19
104,872	109,061	320	304	8	8	535	587	4	2	20
199,356	204,527	396	369	1,530	1,504	504	390	101	39	21
126,870	128,335	371	360	24	14	80,352	82,611	13	7	22
102,869	101,396	1,639	1,315	16,791	16,901	31,325	31,561	16	17	23
17,975	17,729	74	48	152	150	11,308	10,878	..	..	24
41,901	*43,060*	*881*	*786*	*8*	*10*	*29,747*	*32,313*	..	..	
32,068	32,790	627	507	8	10	21,077	22,707	..	..	25
9,833	10,270	254	219	..	..	8,670	9,606	..	..	26

TABLE XIX.—SUMMARY

Serial Number.	District or State.	Area in square miles.	Population, 1911. Persons.	Males.	Females.	Population, 1901.	Percentage of Variation. 1901-11.	1891-01.	Number of persons per square mile in 1911.
1	2	3	4	5	6	7	8	9	10
	BOMBAY.	**186,923**	**27,084,317**	**14,011,248**	**13,073,069**	**25,468,209**	**+ 6·3**	**− 5·5**	**145**
	British Territory (excluding Aden).	**122,979**	**19,626,477**	**10,214,557**	**9,411,920**	**18,515,676**	**+ 6·0**	**− 1·7**	**160**
	Bombay City	23	979,445	640,288	339,157	776,006	+ 26·2	− 5·6	42,585
	Northern Division.	*13,721*	*3,683,383*	*1,910,908*	*1,774,475*	*3,513,532*	*+ 4·9*	*− 10·3*	*269*
2	Ahmadabad	3,824	827,809	432,386	395,423	795,967	+ 4·0	− 13·6	216
3	Broach	1,468	306,717	158,246	148,471	291,763	+ 5·1	− 14·6	209
4	Kaira	1,596	691,744	370,219	321,525	716,332	− 3·4	− 17·8	433
5	Panch Mahals	1,606	322,695	165,929	156,766	261,020	+ 23·6	− 16·7	201
6	Surat	1,651	654,109	326,908	327,201	637,017	+ 2·7	− 2·0	396
7	Thana	3,576	882,309	457,220	425,089	811,433	+ 8·7	− 1·0	247
	Central Division.	*37,221*	*6,387,064*	*3,221,042*	*3,166,022*	*5,944,536*	*+ 7·4*	*− 4·3*	*172*
8	Ahmadnagar	6,613	945,305	476,306	468,999	837,695	+ 12·8	− 5·7	143
9	Khandesh East	4,550	1,034,886	521,919	512,967	959,454	+ 7·9	+ 4·0	227
10	Khandesh West	5,439	580,723	293,320	287,403	469,743	+ 23·6	− 8·7	107
11	Nasik	5,879	905,030	455,946	449,084	814,778	+ 11·1	− 3·2	154
12	Poona	5,366	1,071,512	543,008	528,504	995,330	+ 7·7	− 6·8	200
13	Satara	4,818	1,081,278	539,070	542,208	1,145,495	− 5·6	− 6·5	224
14	Sholapur	4,556	768,330	391,473	376,857	722,041	+ 6·4	− 4·0	169
	Southern Division.	*25,028*	*5,061,150*	*2,502,995*	*2,558,155*	*5,070,692*	*− ·2*	*+ 1·3*	*202*
15	Belgaum	4,613	948,820	479,919	468,901	992,607	− 4·9	− 1·9	205
16	Bijapur	5,707	862,973	433,896	429,077	736,804	+ 17·1	− 7·6	151
17	Dharwar	4,604	1,026,005	520,515	505,490	1,113,298	− 7·8	+ 5·9	223
18	Kanara	3,946	430,548	220,139	210,409	454,490	− 5·3	+ 1·8	109
19	Kolaba	2,169	594,166	295,144	299,022	605,566	− 1·9	+ 1·8	274
20	Ratnagiri	3,989	1,203,638	553,382	650,256	1,167,927	+ 3·1	+ 5·6	302
	Sind.	*46,986*	*3,513,435*	*1,939,324*	*1,574,111*	*3,210,910*	*+ 9·4*	*+ 11·7*	*75*
21	Hyderabad	8,034	1,037,144	571,947	465,197	965,940	+ 7·4	+ 14·7	129
22	Karachi	11,782	521,721	294,291	227,430	446,513	+ 16·8	+ 3·6	44
23	Larkana	5,053	660,879	359,232	301,647	656,083	+ ·7	+ 10·3	131
24	Sukkur	5,585	573,913	312,931	260,982	523,345	+ 9·7	+ 10·3	103
25	Thar and Parkar	13,888	456,771	255,364	201,407	386,964	+ 18·0	+ 2·3	33
26	Upper Sind Frontier	2,644	263,007	145,559	117,448	232,045	+ 13·3	+ 32·9	99
	Aden.	**80**	**46,165**	**31,290**	**14,875**	**43,974**	**+ 5·0**	**− ·2**	**577**
	Bombay States.	**63,864**	**7,411,675**	**3,765,401**	**3,646,274**	**6,908,559**	**+ 7·3**	**− 14·5**	**116**
1	Cambay	350	72,656	37,675	34,981	75,225	− 3·4	− 16·2	208
2	Cutch	7,616	513,429	252,453	260,976	488,022	+ 5·2	− 12·6	67
3	Kathiawar	20,911	2,496,057	1,271,497	1,224,560	2,329,196	+ 7·2	− 15·4	119
4	Mahi Kantha Agency	3,124	412,631	208,922	203,709	361,545	+ 14·1	− 37·8	132
5	Palanpur Agency	6,393	515,092	267,999	247,093	467,271	+ 10·2	− 27·6	81
6	Rewa Kantha Agency	4,956	665,099	340,376	324,723	479,065	+ 38·8	− 34·7	134
7	Surat Agency	1,957	207,837	105,715	102,122	179,886	+ 15·5	− 15·9	106
8	Janjira	324	88,747	42,373	46,374	85,414	+ 3·9	+ 4·4	274
9	Jawhar	310	53,489	27,757	25,732	47,538	+ 12·5	− 10·0	173
10	Savantvadi	926	217,240	103,001	114,239	217,732	− ·2	+ 12·8	235
11	Akalkot	498	89,082	45,415	43,667	82,047	+ 8·6	+ 8·3	179
12	Bhor	925	144,601	71,936	72,665	137,268	+ 5·3	− 11·8	156
13	Khandesh Agency	963	23,624	12,170	11,454	14,639	+ 61·4	− 44·0	25
14	Satara Agency	898	124,991	62,555	62,436	109,660	+ 14·0	− 16·6	139
15	Surgana	360	15,180	7,884	7,296	11,532	+ 31·6	− 7·0	42
16	Bijapur Agency	980	78,643	40,134	38,509	68,665	+ 14·5	− 13·9	80
17	Kolhapur	3,217	833,441	424,435	409,006	910,011	− 8·4	− ·8	259
18½	Southern Marhatta Jagirs	3,036	618,139	312,500	305,639	626,084	− 1·3	− 2·1	204
19	Savanur	70	17,909	8,987	8,922	18,446	− 2·9	+ 8·7	256
20	Khairpur	6,050	223,788	121,617	102,171	199,313	+ 12·3	+ 55·0	37
	BURMA.	**230,839**	**12,115,217**	**6,183,494**	**5,931,723**	**10,490,624**	**+ 15·5**	**+ 35·9**	**52**
	Arakan Division	*14,307*	*839,896*	*441,925*	*397,971*	*762,102*	*+ 10·2*	*+ 13·2*	*57*
1	Akyab	5,136	529,943	289,474	240,469	481,666	+ 10·0	+ 15·7	103
2	Northern Arakan	1,500	22,234	11,405	10,829	20,682	+ 7·5	+ 41·4	15
3	Kyaukpyu	4,387	184,916	89,571	95,345	168,827	+ 9·5	+ 3·0	42
4	Sandoway	3,784	102,803	51,475	51,328	90,927	+ 13·1	+ 15·8	27
	Pegu Division.	*13,258*	*2,073,737*	*1,136,192*	*937,545*	*1,820,638*	*+ 13·9*	*+ 19·5*	*156*
5	Rangoon City	28	293,316	208,111	85,205	245,430	+ 19·5	+ 34·8	10,476
6	Hanthawaddy	3,048	539,109	295,886	243,223	474,262	+ 13·7	+ 20·0	177
7	Tharrawaddy	2,863	433,320	216,442	216,878	395,570	+ 9·5	+ 16·6	151
8	Pegu	4,404	429,121	229,540	199,581	339,572	+ 26·4	+ 42·9	97
9	Prome	2,915	378,871	186,213	192,658	365,804	+ 3·6	− ·9	130
	Irrawaddy Division.	*13,408*	*1,869,485*	*962,913*	*906,572*	*1,663,669*	*+ 12·4*	*+ 28·0*	*139*
10	Bassein	4,127	440,988	226,773	214,215	391,427	+ 12·7	+ 21·9	107
11	Henzada	2,843	532,357	264,319	268,038	484,558	+ 9·9	+ 10·7	187
12	Myaungmya	2,642	334,852	176,465	158,387	282,982	+ 18·4	+ 55·6	127
13	Ma-ubin	1,648	305,073	155,715	149,358	278,309	+ 9·6	+ 30·2	185
14	Pyapôn	2,148	256,215	139,641	116,574	226,443	+ 13·1	+ 55·1	119

Figures for Districts—*contd.*

DISTRIBUTION BY RELIGION.										
Hindu.		Musalman.		Christian.		Animistic.		Others.		Serial Number.
Males.	Females.	Males.	Females.	Males.	Females.	Males.	Females.	Males.	Females.	
11	12	13	14	15	16	17	18	19	20	21
10,741,836	**10,235,467**	**2,635,835**	**2,266,081**	**140,787**	**104,870**	**161,805**	**158,429**	**330,985**	**[illegible]**	
7,658,589	**7,261,678**	**2,165,278**	**1,822,199**	**132,113**	**98,419**	**85,863**	**84,490**	**172,714**	**145,194**	
436,521	227,521	118,984	60,362	38,583	18,772	4	2	46,196	32,500	1
1,617,268	*1,499,995*	*178,199*	*164,497*	*40,017*	*36,512*	*33,440*	*32,675*	*41,984*	*40,796*	
362,727	330,428	47,843	44,170	2,262	1,794	381	306	19,168	18,795	2
100,031	92,904	34,869	32,883	725	377	19,623	19,237	2,998	3,070	3
320,955	277,209	33,388	29,892	12,508	11,084	4	3	3,364	3,287	4
141,060	133,279	11,679	10,594	910	942	11,366	11,109	914	842	5
286,333	285,412	27,170	28,224	674	511	2,045	2,006	10,686	11,048	6
406,162	380,763	23,245	18,734	22,938	21,804	21	14	4,854	3,774	7
2,914,916	*2,883,912*	*190,475*	*177,034*	*26,264*	*21,930*	*47,553*	*47,768*	*41,834*	*35,378*	
429,535	426,141	24,746	23,213	13,228	11,708	643	557	8,154	7,280	8
454,035	448,096	50,613	48,908	800	620	11,105	10,888	5,366	4,455	9
239,190	235,010	16,517	14,806	315	314	34,993	35,549	2,305	1,724	10
423,799	419,906	24,708	22,997	1,839	1,414	755	731	4,845	4,086	11
498,908	492,817	26,589	22,847	8,516	6,420	43	32	8,952	6,888	12
511,674	516,502	18,729	17,959	684	611	1	..	7,982	7,186	13
357,775	345,440	28,573	26,804	882	843	13	11	4,230	3,759	14
2,225,810	*2,276,898*	*224,269*	*233,728*	*19,591*	*17,952*	*20*	*22*	*33,305*	*39,855*	
414,733	403,064	39,232	37,843	4,086	3,099	..	..	21,868	19,896	15
380,778	376,764	50,799	50,270	546	552	..	..	1,773	1,491	16
442,038	430,847	69,887	67,056	2,929	2,516	3	..	5,658	5,071	17
196,785	186,839	14,058	14,673	8,521	8,822	..	..	775	575	18
278,123	282,143	14,127	14,749	682	576	1	1	2,211	1,558	19
513,353	597,241	36,166	49,137	2,827	2,887	16	21	1,020	970	20
464,074	*373,352*	*1,453,351*	*1,186,578*	*7,658*	*3,253*	*4,846*	*4,023*	*9,396*	*6,905*	
133,820	112,121	432,291	348,928	891	289	3,031	2,401	1,914	1,568	21
66,329	45,192	218,951	177,383	6,304	2,709	23	7	2,684	2,189	22
54,971	46,680	308,805	254,212	41	31	8	7	907	717	23
83,652	71,379	226,817	187,854	333	252	13	17	2,116	1,480	24
110,006	86,781	142,117	112,101	62	18	1,771	1,591	1,408	916	25
15,296	11,199	129,870	106,100	27	4	..	..	366	145	26
1,559	**485**	**24,917**	**12,091**	**2,367**	**347**	**1**	**1**	**2,446**	**1,951**	
3,081,688	**2,973,304**	**445,640**	**431,791**	**6,307**	**6,104**	**75,941**	**73,938**	**155,825**	**161,137**	
31,245	28,323	4,827	4,888	113	82	1	..	1,489	1,688	1
147,933	147,503	63,014	63,119	56	7	..	..	41,450	50,847	2
1,052,467	998,568	159,424	167,145	631	360	..	..	58,975	58,487	3
191,837	187,416	9,859	8,920	436	343	2,124	2,087	4,666	4,943	4
230,949	211,989	23,362	21,795	149	62	820	769	12,719	12,478	5
251,743	239,707	14,234	12,678	578	503	72,712	70,941	1,109	894	6
102,835	99,273	2,345	2,416	36	22	34	36	465	375	7
85,568	87,688	6,415	8,354	5	..	..	..	385	332	8
27,430	25,515	258	187	23	..	..	..	46	30	9
97,377	107,974	2,669	2,964	2,715	3,100	..	..	240	301	10
38,807	37,305	6,329	6,105	2	..	..	..	277	257	11
70,624	71,589	901	747	24	13	..	..	387	316	12
11,723	11,018	444	436	..	..	..	..	3	5	13
59,968	59,860	2,135	2,172	10	5	..	..	442	399	14
7,730	7,136	121	135	..	..	..	..	33	25	15
37,557	36,060	2,431	2,311	7	5	..	..	139	133	16
385,725	373,166	17,272	16,058	1,117	1,288	..	..	20,321	18,494	17
273,435	268,095	26,637	26,049	399	308	..	..	12,023	11,187	18
6,280	6,153	2,687	2,761	4	2	..	..	16	6	19
20,455	18,971	100,276	82,551	2	4	250	105	624	340	20
		BUDDHIST.								
312,650	**77,029**	**5,113,459**	**5,271,120**	**111,033**	**99,048**	**368,143**	**333,330**	**278,209**	**151,196**	
14,755	*1,242*	*280,251*	*280,997*	*718*	*449*	*38,626*	*36,449*	*107,575*	*78,834*	
13,418	1,036	154,935	147,592	433	172	17,501	16,395	103,187	75,274	1
391	176	997	798	4	3	9,977	9,844	36	8	2
572	18	79,099	86,765	52	43	7,718	7,008	2,130	1,511	3
374	12	45,220	45,842	229	231	3,430	3,202	2,222	2,041	4
169,747	*42,648*	*844,606*	*843,575*	*30,568*	*24,462*	*21,131*	*7,832*	*70,140*	*19,028*	
89,028	19,822	52,137	45,330	13,977	9,067	5,936	1,281	47,033	10,205	5
44,951	12,186	227,611	220,027	6,733	5,914	4,024	651	12,567	4,445	6
6,125	1,281	202,639	210,945	3,011	3,041	1,965	411	2,702	1,200	7
25,357	8,993	188,279	181,338	6,341	5,975	4,110	1,281	5,453	1,999	8
4,286	866	173,940	185,940	506	465	5,096	4,208	2,385	1,179	9
36,513	*5,593*	*856,877*	*856,062*	*37,662*	*36,472*	*10,449*	*1,219*	*21,412*	*7,226*	
10,471	1,351	194,614	196,413	14,111	13,816	1,864	185	5,713	2,450	10
5,912	688	248,922	260,388	5,070	5,215	1,309	157	3,106	1,580	11
5,486	642	153,362	147,153	9,218	8,939	2,683	239	5,716	1,414	12
4,775	617	140,611	142,058	5,217	5,257	1,475	176	3,637	1,250	13
9,869	2,295	119,368	110,050	4,046	3,245	3,118	462	3,240	522	14

TABLE XIX.—SUMMARY

Serial Number.	District or State.	Area in square miles.	Population, 1911. Persons.	Males.	Females.	Population, 1901.	Percentage of Variation. 1901-11.	1891-01.	Number of persons per square mile in 1911.
1	2	3	4	5	6	7	8	9	10
	BURMA—*contd.*								
	Tenasserim Division	*35,886*	*1,429,294*	*750,626*	*678,668*	*1,159,558*	+ *23·3*	+ *27·1*	*40*
15	Toungoo	6,172	351,076	181,488	169,588	279,315	+ 25·7	+ 31·9	57
16	Salween	2,666	46,608	24,741	21,867	37,837	+ 23·2	+ 20·3	17
17	Thatôn	4,892	416,975	217,770	199,205	343,510	+ 21·4	+ 28·8	85
18	Amherst	7,059	367,918	198,430	169,488	300,173	+ 22·6	+ 28·5	52
19	Tavoy	5,308	135,293	68,667	66,626	109,979	+ 23·0	+ 15·9	25
20	Mergui	9,789	111,424	59,530	51,894	88,744	+ 25·6	+ 20·3	11
	Magwe Division.	*17,575*	*1,239,032*	*603,614*	*635,418*	*1,078,317*	+ *14·9*	+ *7·9*	*70*
21	Thayetmyo	4,750	248,275	122,231	126,044	239,706	+ 3·6	— 4·2	52
22	Pakôkku	6,210	409,909	196,159	213,750	357,632	+ 14·6	+ 14·3	66
23	Minbu	3,302	263,939	128,837	135,102	234,271	+ 12·7	+ 8·1	80
24	Magwe	3,318	316,909	156,387	160,522	246,708	+ 28·5	+ 12·6	96
	Mandalay Division.	*32,476*	*832,969*	*426,776*	*406,193*	*778,466*	+ *7·0*	+ *31·2*	*26*
25	Mandalay	2,117	340,770	170,750	170,020	366,507	— 7·0	— 2·8	161
26	Bhamo	6,903	107,811	55,528	52,283	79,515	+ 35·6	+ 89·6	16
27	Myitkyina	10,977	85,577	47,863	37,714	68,527	+ 24·9	+ 32·2	8
28	Katha	7,001	198,193	98,148	100,045	176,223	+ 12·5	+ 94·6	28
29	Ruby Mines	5,478	100,618	54,487	46,131	87,694	+ 14·7	+ 157·5	18
	Sagaing Division.	*26,182*	*1,155,271*	*543,289*	*611,982*	*994,466*	+ *16·2*	+ *21·8*	*44*
30	Shwebo	5,714	356,363	168,070	188,293	286,891	+ 24·2	+ 24·3	62
31	Sagaing	1,825	312,111	147,816	164,295	277,769	+ 12·4	+ 14·9	171
32	Lower Chindwin	3,480	316,175	141,262	174,913	276,383	+ 14·4	+ 18·5	91
33	Upper Chindwin	15,163	170,622	86,141	84,481	153,428	+ 11·2	+ 88·6	11
	Meiktila Division.	*10,819*	*1,170,572*	*567,380*	*603,192*	*995,659*	+ *17·6*	+ *10·1*	*108*
34	Kyaukse	1,274	141,426	68,868	72,558	141,253	+ ·1	+ 11·6	111
35	Meiktila	2,183	279,822	134,170	145,652	252,305	+ 10·9	+ 16·1	128
36	Yamethin	4,255	307,419	153,223	154,196	243,197	+ 26·4	+ 17·7	72
37	Myingyan	3,107	441,905	211,119	230,786	358,904	+ 23·1	+ 1·3	142
	Specially Administered Territories.	*66,428*	*1,504,961*	*750,779*	*754,182*	*1,237,749*	+ *21·6*	No Census was taken in 1891.	*23*
38	Northern Shan States	14,294	458,952	230,545	228,407	321,090	+ 42·9		32
39	Southern Shan States	40,434	900,202	448,705	451,497	816,354	+ 10·3		22
40	Pakôkku Hill Tracts	3,700	26,251	12,967	13,284	13,116	+ 100·1		7
41	Chin Hills	8,000	119,556	58,562	60,994	87,189	+ 37·1		15
	CENTRAL PROVINCES AND BERAR	**130,997**	**16,033,310**	**7,984,022**	**8,049,288**	**13,602,592**	+ **17·9**	— **7·9**	**122**
	British Territory	**99,823**	**13,916,308**	**6,930,392**	**6,985,916**	**11,971,452**	+ **16·2**	— **8·3**	**139**
	Jubbulpore Division.	*18,953*	*2,421,064*	*1,210,980*	*1,210,084*	*2,081,480*	+ *16·3*	— *12·4*	*128*
1	Saugor	3,962	541,410	276,233	265,177	469,479	+ 15·3	— 20·4	137
2	Damoh	2,816	333,047	168,060	164,987	285,326	+ 16·7	— 12·4	118
3	Jubbulpore	3,912	745,892	373,173	372,719	680,585	+ 9·6	— 9·0	191
4	Mandla	5,057	405,234	200,872	204,362	318,381	+ 27·3	— 6·5	80
5	Seoni	3,206	395,481	192,642	202,839	327,709	+ 20·7	— 11·6	123
	Nerbudda Division.	*18,388*	*2,081,477*	*1,043,239*	*1,038,238*	*1,785,008*	+ *16·6*	— *5·2*	*113*
6	Narsinghpur	1,976	325,677	161,795	163,882	315,518	+ 3·2	— 14·5	165
7	Hoshangabad	3,682	457,395	230,632	226,763	446,645	+ 2·4	— 9·6	124
8	Nimar	4,227	391,071	200,765	190,306	327,173	+ 19·5	+ 14·3	93
9	Betul	3,872	390,386	194,163	196,223	287,807	+ 35·6	— 11·9	101
10	Chhindwara	4,631	516,948	255,884	261,064	407,865	+ 26·7	+ ·1	112
	Nagpur Division.	*22,677*	*3,109,838*	*1,548,737*	*1,561,101*	*2,659,286*	+ *16·9*	— *8·6*	*137*
11	Wardha	[2,428	459,796	231,871	227,925	385,103	+ 19·4	— 3·9	180
12	Nagpur	3,840	809,901	408,843	401,058	751,844	+ 7·7	— ·8	211
13	Chanda	9,312	677,544	337,540	340,004	533,887	+ 26·9	— 14·6	73
14	Bhandara	3,965	773,677	380,014	393,663	663,062	+ 16·7	— 10·7	195
15	Balaghat	3,132	388,920	190,469	198,451	325,390	+ 19·5	— 14·9	124
	Chhattisgarh Division.	*23,039*	*3,246,767*	*1,576,822*	*1,669,945*	*2,691,662*	+ *20·6*	— *9·8*	*147*
16	Raipur	9,776	1,324,856	645,186	679,670	1,096,858	+ 20·8	— 2·5	136
17	Bilaspur	7,618	1,146,223	558,477	587,746	918,401	+ 24·8	— 12·2	150
18	Drug	4,645	775,688	373,159	402,529	676,318	+ 14·7	— 16·8	167
	Berar Division.	*17,766*	*3,057,162*	*1,550,614*	*1,506,548*	*2,754,016*	+ *11·0*	— *5·0*	*172*
19	Amraoti	4,733	875,904	447,216	428,688	809,499	+ 8·2	— 4·7	185
20	Akola	4,097	788,863	400,893	387,970	754,187	+ 4·6	— ·5	193
21	Buldana	3,731	669,182	337,179	332,003	614,373	+ 8·9	— 9·5	179
22	Yeotmal	5,205	723,213	365,326	357,887	575,957	+ 25·6	— 5·6	139
	Central Provinces States	**31,174**	**2,117,002**	**1,053,630**	**1,063,372**	**1,631,140**	+ **29·8**	— **4·8**	**68**
1	Makrai	155	15,021	7,530	7,491	13,035	+ 15·2	— 29·7	97
2	Bastar	13,062	433,310	218,015	215,295	306,501	+ 41·4	— 1·4	33
3	Kanker	1,429	127,014	63,010	64,004	103,536	+ 22·7	+ 25·7	89
4	Nandgaon	871	167,362	80,293	87,069	126,365	+ 32·4	— 31·3	192
5	Khairagarh	931	155,471	74,742	80,729	137,55a	+ 13·0	— 24·1	167

FIGURES FOR DISTRICTS—*contd.*

DISTRIBUTION BY RELIGION.										
HINDU.		BUDDHIST.		CHRISTIAN.		ANIMISTIC.		OTHERS.		Serial Number.
Males.	Females.	Males.	Females.	Males.	Females.	Males.	Females.	Males.	Females.	
11	12	13	14	15	16	17	18	19	20	21
44,807	*14,555*	*611,494*	*593,105*	*25,883*	*21,739*	*35,970*	*27,217*	*32,472*	*19,042*	
10,070	4,150	138,220	136,650	16,712	16,426	12,215	10,140	4,271	2,222	15
231	43	11,213	9,261	223	161	12,725	12,843	849	59	16
12,131	4,674	192,749	187,495	1,987	1,751	3,840	2,118	7,063	3,167	17
18,402	5,462	158,436	151,468	3,581	3,293	3,441	897	14,620	8,368	18
781	61	64,008	64,597	1,070	929	997	383	911	656	19
3,192	175	45,968	43,634	2,360	2,179	2,752	1,336	5,258	4,570	20
7,420	*1,219*	*577,817*	*619,779*	*952*	*556*	*12,819*	*12,004*	*4,606*	*1,860*	
1,605	581	111,290	116,768	357	235	7,594	7,638	1,385	822	21
1,016	154	192,432	211,605	166	118	1,831	1,641	714	232	22
2,449	202	122,133	181,794	98	52	3,056	2,702	1,101	852	23
2,350	282	151,962	159,612	331	151	338	23	1,406	454	24
20,539	*7,310*	*320,444*	*327,099*	*5,658*	*3,845*	*60,471*	*57,661*	*19,664*	*10,278*	
11,192	4,879	141,480	153,424	3,870	2,701	1,278	219	12,930	8,797	25
1,404	248	27,182	26,308	1,030	755	23,244	24,478	2,868	494	26
4,617	1,575	16,518	13,653	349	217	24,098	21,952	2,281	317	27
1,268	161	92,871	96,263	269	114	2,984	3,105	756	402	28
2,058	447	42,393	37,451	140	58	8,867	7,907	1,029	268	29
5,107	*1,524*	*526,593*	*602,348*	*2,436*	*1,793*	*2,240*	*1,767*	*6,913*	*4,550*	
1,841	464	161,070	183,782	1,617	1,129	101	10	3,441	2,908	30
1,228	544	144,311	162,105	492	521	75	20	1,710	1,105	31
629	155	139,518	174,321	179	118	74	8	862	311	32
1,409	361	81,694	82,140	148	25	1,990	1,729	900	226	33
7,812	*1,487*	*543,167*	*589,651*	*1,938*	*1,549*	*1,697*	*1,961*	*12,766*	*9,444*	
682	133	65,293	69,635	345	334	24	1	2,524	2,455	34
2,474	457	128,307	143,467	451	227	80	15	2,858	1,486	35
3,068	698	141,650	146,397	928	885	1,433	1,019	6,144	5,197	36
1,588	199	207,917	230,152	214	103	160	26	1,240	306	37
5,950	*1,441*	*552,210*	*558,504*	*5,218*	*5,153*	*184,740*	*188,120*	*2,661*	*934*	
2,250	357	167,904	167,532	222	126	59,217	60,103	952	289	38
2,638	644	384,220	390,936	4,866	4,952	55,696	54,435	1,285	530	39
115	36	22	13	4	..	12,817	13,234	9	1	40
947	404	64	23	126	105	57,010	60,848	415	114	41
		MUSALMAN.								
6,382,743	**6,425,131**	**302,227**	**282,802**	**39,208**	**34,193**	**1,219,551**	**1,270,804**	**40,293**	**36,358**	
5,731,936	**5,764,550**	**292,047**	**272,862**	**19,731**	**14,966**	**847,167**	**897,754**	**39,511**	**35,784**	
875,450	*868,312*	*53,341*	*48,611*	*6,259*	*3,585*	*257,700*	*273,220*	*18,230*	*16,356*	
240,356	231,294	13,632	12,203	777	7	12,154	12,770	9,314	8,233	1
152,873	150,316	5,680	5,322	337	100	5,461	5,654	3,709	3,595	2
298,484	300,476	22,117	19,222	4,554	2,826	44,113	47,430	3,905	3,265	3
77,986	77,020	3,329	3,013	491	380	118,656	123,605	410	344	4
105,751	109,206	8,583	8,851	100	102	77,316	83,761	892	919	5
790,633	*777,858*	*49,450*	*45,928*	*4,025*	*3,438*	*193,920*	*206,214*	*5,211*	*4,800*	
138,622	139,426	5,888	5,819	315	156	15,714	17,278	1,256	1,203	6
193,785	188,990	10,640	10,159	1,044	853	24,157	25,758	1,006	1,003	7
174,111	165,919	20,109	18,319	1,994	1,799	3,434	3,369	1,117	900	8
129,817	129,501	4,354	3,495	274	273	58,947	62,228	771	726	9
154,298	154,022	8,459	8,136	398	357	91,668	97,581	1,061	968	10
1,315,027	*1,322,886*	*46,883*	*44,570*	*4,631*	*3,201*	*177,747*	*186,428*	*4,449*	*4,016*	
197,583	193,480	9,331	8,843	117	61	23,549	24,282	1,291	1,259	11
365,125	360,274	20,047	18,387	3,764	2,481	17,870	18,133	2,037	1,783	12
269,465	270,248	6,205	5,967	304	237	61,161	63,195	405	357	13
337,335	348,007	7,434	7,273	250	288	34,669	87,755	326	340	14
145,519	150,577	3,866	4,100	196	134	40,498	43,063	390	277	15
1,393,430	*1,479,781*	*18,920*	*18,541*	*3,295*	*3,440*	*154,705*	*167,126*	*1,472*	*1,057*	
549,378	577,119	8,393	8,122	1,637	1,728	85,106	92,194	672	507	16
524,724	552,614	7,049	6,915	971	1,040	25,455	26,970	278	207	17
324,328	350,048	3,478	3,504	687	672	44,144	47,962	522	343	18
1,352,396	*1,315,713*	*123,453*	*115,212*	*1,521*	*1,302*	*63,095*	*64,766*	*10,149*	*9,555*	
377,352	360,942	37,896	35,415	827	662	28,198	28,993	2,943	2,676	19
360,644	350,381	36,342	33,806	365	301	491	443	3,051	3,039	20
305,993	302,616	28,435	26,822	183	195	204	178	2,364	2,192	21
308,407	301,774	20,780	19,169	146	144	34,202	35,152	1,791	1,548	22
650,807	**660,581**	**10,180**	**9,940**	**19,477**	**19,227**	**372,384**	**373,050**	**782**	**574**	
5,006	5,080	418	411	..	..	2,077	2,012	29	38	1
71,965	70,022	826	820	644	633	144,541	143,782	39	38	2
28,275	28,790	306	330	5	5	34,389	34,843	35	36	3
66,851	71,887	1,055	1,094	65	89	11,082	13,781	340	218	4
69,477	74,772	1,074	1,175	132	120	3,919	4,568	140	94	5

TABLE XIX.—SUMMARY

Serial Number.	District or State.	Area in square miles.	Population, 1911. Persons.	Males.	Females.	Population, 1901.	Percentage of Variation. 1901-11.	1891-01.	Number of persons per square mile in 1911.
1	2	3	4	5	6	7	8	9	10
	CENTRAL PROVINCES AND BERAR—*contd.*								
	Central Provinces States—*contd.*								
6	Chhuikhadan	154	31,150	15,117	16,033	26,368	+ 18·1	— 27·3	202
7	Kawardha	798	77,654	37,488	40,166	57,474	+ 35·1	— 37·4	97
8	Sakti	138	34,547	16,871	17,676	22,301	+ 54·9	— 12·1	250
9	Raigarh	1,486	218,860	107,850	111,010	174,929	+ 25·1	+ 3·8	147
10	Sarangarh	540	102,071	49,851	52,220	79,900	+ 27·7	— 4·0	189
11	Chang Bhakar	906	24,421	12,462	11,959	19,548	+ 24·9	+ 5·5	27
12	Korea	1,631	62,107	31,856	30,251	35,113	+ 76·9	— 3·1	38
13	Surguja	6,055	428,703	217,749	210,954	351,011	+ 22·1	+ 8·2	71
14	Udaipur	1,055	64,853	32,790	32,063	45,391	+ 42·9	+ 20·9	61
15	Jashpur	1,963	174,458	88,006	86,452	132,114	+ 32·1	+ 16·3	89
	COORG.	**1,582**	**174,976**	**97,279**	**77,697**	**180,607**	**— 3·1**	**+ 4·4**	**111**
	MADRAS	**152,879**	**46,217,245**	**22,794,713**	**23,422,532**	**42,417,740**	**+ 9·0**	**+ 7·3**	**302**
	British Territory	**142,330**	**41,405,404**	**20,382,955**	**21,022,449**	**38,229,654**	**+ 8·3**	**+ 7·3**	**291**
1	Ganjam	4,896	1,870,826	868,928	1,001,898	1,689,754	+ 10·7	+ 6·3	382
2	Agency, Ganjam	3,484	350,466	175,783	174,683	321,114	+ 9·1	+ 4·5	101
3	Vizagapatam	4,600	2,169,670	1,050,609	1,119,061	2,082,662	+ 4·2	+ 7·2	472
4	Agency, Vizagapatam	12,621	1,020,151	511,221	508,930	850,376	+ 20·0	— 1·0	81
5	Godavari	2,545	1,445,957	707,702	738,255	1,286,119	+ 12·4	+ 9·2	568
6	Agency, Godavari	3,676	206,902	104,496	102,406	180,060	+ 14·9	+ 17·4	56
7	Kistna	5,907	1,997,535	994,961	1,002,574	1,744,138	+ 14·5	+ 14·3	338
8	Guntur	5,735	1,697,551	856,665	840,886	1,490,685	+ 13·9	+ 15·3	296
9	Nellore	7,973	1,328,152	665,305	662,847	1,274,831	+ 4·2	+ 2·8	167
10	Cuddapah	5,892	893,998	454,061	439,937	880,060	+ 1·6	— ·3	152
11	Kurnool	7,580	935,199	471,426	463,773	872,070	+ 7·2	+ 6·6	123
12	Bellary	5,714	969,436	490,843	478,593	947,214	+ 2·3	+ 7·5	170
13	Anantapur	6,718	963,223	494,232	468,991	933,757	+ 3·2	+ 8·2	143
14	Madras	27	518,660	266,465	252,195	509,346	+ 1·8	+ 12·6	19,210
15	Chingleput	3,072	1,406,008	705,641	700,367	1,310,106	+ 7·3	+ 9·1	458
16	Chittoor	5,676	1,238,742	629,379	609,363	1,172,886	+ 5·6	+ 4·7	218
17	North Arcot	4,920	1,960,960	970,073	990,887	1,750,566	+ 12·0	+ 6·5	399
18	Salem	6,300	1,766,680	876,950	889,730	1,699,482	+ 4·0	+ 14·3	280
19	Coimbatore	7,196	2,116,564	1,044,429	1,072,135	1,979,464	+ 6·9	+ 10·5	294
20	South Arcot	4,208	2,362,566	1,172,807	1,189,759	2,105,809	+ 12·2	+ 7·6	561
21	Tanjore	3,727	2,362,689	1,123,084	1,239,605	2,245,029	+ 5·2	+ ·8	634
22	Trichinopoly	4,935	2,107,029	1,022,866	1,084,163	1,965,119	+ 7·2	+ 5·0	427
23	Madura	4,916	1,932,832	946,306	986,526	1,713,188	+ 12·8	+ 11·1	393
24	Ramnad	4,834	1,658,453	786,187	872,266	1,519,204	+ 9·2	+ 4·7	343
25	Tinnevelly	4,353	1,790,619	865,633	924,986	1,658,495	+ 8·0	+ 8·3	411
26	Nilgiris	1,009	118,618	63,509	55,109	112,882	+ 5·1	+ 11·6	118
27	Malabar (with Laccadives)	5,794	3,015,119	1,482,616	1,532,503	2,795,738	+ 7·8	+ 5·6	520
28	Anjengo	1	5,572	2,690	2,882	4,817	+ 15·7	+ 9·7	5,572
29	South Canara	4,021	1,195,227	578,088	617,139	1,134,713	+ 5·3	+ 7·4	297
	Madras States	**10,549**	**4,811,841**	**2,411,758**	**2,400,083**	**4,188,086**	**+ 14·9**	**+ 13·2**	**456**
1	Cochin	1,361	918,110	457,342	460,768	812,025	+ 13·1	+ 12·3	675
2	Travancore	7,594	3,428,975	1,731,363	1,697,612	2,952,157	+ 16·2	+ 15·4	452
3	Pudukkottai	1,178	411,886	196,566	215,320	380,440	+ 8·3	+ 2·0	350
4	Banganapalle	255	39,344	19,776	19,568	32,264	+ 21·9	— 9·1	154
5	Sandur	161	13,526	6,711	6,815	11,200	+ 20·8	— 1·7	84
	N.-W. F. PROVINCE.	**38,918**	**3,819,027***	**2,046,978**	**1,772,049**	**2,125,496**	**+ 79·7**	**+ 14·4**	**98**
	Districts and Administered Territories.	**13,418**	**2,196,933**	**1,182,102**	**1,014,831**	**2,041,534**	**+ 7·6**	**+ 9·9**	**164**
1	Hazara	2,984	603,028	320,465	282,563	560,288	+ 7·6	+ 8·5	202
2	Peshawar	2,605	865,009	470,421	394,588	788,707	+ 9·7	+ 10·8	332
3	Kohat	2,695	222,690	119,081	103,609	217,865	+ 2·2	+ 11·6	83
4	Bannu	1,674	250,086	133,707	116,379	226,801	+ 10·3	+ 10·9	149
5	Dera Ismail Khan	3,460	256,120	138,428	117,692	247,873	+ 3·3	+ 7·8	74
	Agencies	**25,500**	**1,102,054**	**585,885**	**516,169**	**71,591**	**+1,439·4**	..	**43**
1	Malakand (Dir, Swat and Chitral).		576,433	300,710	275,723	8,128	..	..	..
2	Khyber		181,134	97.077	84,057	..	..	..	..
3	Kurrum		98,692	54,271	44,421	54,257	..	..	..
4	Tochi		144,379	78,477	65,902	4,684	..	..	..
5	Wano		101,416	55,350	46,066	4,522	..	..	..
	Tribal Areas	Details not available.	**520,040**	**278,991**	**241,049**	**12,371**	..	..	..
	Trans-border Tribes under the political control of the Deputy Commissioner of—								
	Hazara		98,302	52,351	45,951	..	..	..	..
	Peshawar		240,250	127,838	112,412	..	..	..	..
	Kohat		144,000	78,423	65,577	..	..	..	..
	Bannu		17,884	9,631	8,253	..	..	..	..
	Dera Ismail Khan		19,604	10,748	8,856	12,371	..	..	..

* Statistics by religion of 2,210,471 persons only are available; the rest (1,608,556) were not enumerated by religion.

FIGURES FOR DISTRICTS—*contd.*

DISTRIBUTION BY RELIGION.										
HINDU.		MUSALMAN.		CHRISTIAN.		ANIMISTIC.		OTHERS.		Serial Number.
Males.	Females.	Males.	Females.	Males.	Females.	Males.	Females.	Males.	Females.	
11	12	13	14	15	16	17	18	19	20	21
12,457	13,107	452	451	4	6	2,133	2,425	71	44	6
28,998	31,042	734	783	12	16	7,702	8,298	42	27	7
14,330	14,963	176	176	7	7	2,353	2,529	5	1	8
98,116	100,969	701	675	27	24	8,939	9,271	67	71	9
48,630	50,864	168	188	9	7	1,039	1,158	5	3	10
5,948	5,498	37	23	..	..	6,477	6,438	..	..	11
11,269	10,118	300	240	3	1	20,284	19,892	..	..	12
135,879	131,314	2,911	2,665	..	..	78,950	76,971	9	4	13
8,303	8,094	156	129	6	2	24,325	23,888	..	..	14
45,303	44,111	866	780	18,563	18,317	23,274	23,244	..	..	15
76,822	**62,100**	**8,397**	**4,746**	**1,986**	**1,567**	**10,013**	**9,214**	**61**	**70**	
19,761,598	**20,366,761**	**1,511,811**	**1,543,095**	**1,174,248**	**1,171,227**	**331,186**	**327,230**	**15,870**	**14,219**	
18,108,939	**18,697,665**	**1,351,119**	**1,389,289**	**586,836**	**604,430**	**320 924**	**317,529**	**15,127**	**13,536**	
838,692	971,440	2,768	2,657	1,184	1,183	26,284	26,618	..	..	1
64,017	68,478	46	15	976	920	110,744	110,270	..	..	2
1,036,742	1,104,507	10,607	11,174	2,453	2,530	788	839	19	11	3
382,368	381,608	1,049	1,045	4,929	4,824	122,875	121,453	..	..	4
691,267	721,594	12,058	12,389	4,157	4,083	147	161	73	28	5
92,255	90,196	1,314	1,266	800	816	10,127	10,128	..	..	6
933,429	942,029	85,707	35,026	25,070	24,793	735	714	20	12	7
729,222	718,188	59,523	57,749	63,250	60,457	4,582	4,487	88	5	8
568,060	568,203	41,592	40,207	22,126	22,172	33,519	32,261	8	4	9
390,226	378,835	50,731	48,385	11,350	11,058	1,728	1,657	26	2	10
387,477	382,695	61,602	59,168	21,237	20,831	1,058	1,066	52	13	11
439,315	430,440	48,105	45,576	2,494	1,987	192	162	737	428	12
449,555	426,916	41,137	38,911	1,935	1,701	1,323	1,276	282	187	13
213,731	202,179	30,984	28,185	20,584	21,230	..	..	1,166	601	14
673,290	669,068	16,314	15,290	15,174	15,208	637	586	226	200	15
591,896	574,551	30,839	28,344	2,280	2,278	4,857	4,190	7	..	16
892,971	908,384	56,534	61,375	16,156	16,666	..	..	4,412	4,462	17
847,405	860,836	22,218	21,206	7,320	7,683	..	..	7	5	18
1,011,929	1,089,849	21,790	21,310	9,608	9,942	1,079	1,020	28	14	19
1,103,167	1,120,004	33,588	33,398	33,578	33,858	..	..	2,474	2,499	20
1,022,680	1,118,566	57,061	73,991	43,071	46,743	..	..	332	305	21
949,057	1,004,795	31,546	34,207	42,209	45,144	..	..	54	17	22
879,315	916,438	37,164	39,394	29,816	30,694	..	..	11	..	23
699,937	761,594	50,035	70,185	36,205	40,472	..	..	10	15	24
734,447	774,777	46,853	58,621	84,306	91,583	..	..	27	5	25
50,084	43,830	3,729	2,148	8,907	8,436	759	641	30	54	26
979,399	1,028,683	476,037	477,344	26,837	26,178	..	..	343	298	27
794	797	118	103	1,778	1,982	..	..	..	..	28
456,262	493,165	70,080	70,620	47,046	48,988	..	..	4,700	4,371	29
1,652,659	**1,669,096**	**160,692**	**153,806**	**587,412**	**566,797**	**10,252**	**9,701**	**743**	**683**	
304,002	311,706	32,707	31,115	117,848	115,244	2,127	2,050	658	653	1
1,145,511	1,137,106	116,488	110,129	461,165	442,703	8,123	7,650	76	24	2
182,387	199,657	6,240	7,205	7,939	8,454	..	..	..	4	3
15,379	15,122	3,972	4,062	422	363	2	1	1	..	4
5,380	5,505	1,285	1,275	38	38	..	..	8	2	5
73,732	**48,896**	**1,094,422**	**955,177**	**5,524**	**1,194**	..	..	**21,065**	**10,461**	
71,397	**48,545**	**1,085,276**	**954,718**	**5,414**	**1,171**	..	..	**20,015**	**10,397**	
14,882	9,507	302,124	270,848	120	58	..	..	3,339	2,150	1
22,599	12,768	432,422	375,366	4,727	877	..	..	10,673	5,577	2
6,758	4,090	110,101	98,767	148	74	..	..	2,074	678	3
11,648	9,073	119,518	105,861	184	61	..	..	2,362	1,384	4
15,510	13,107	121,116	103,876	235	101	..	..	1,567	608	5
2,294	**350**	**8,684**	**453**	**110**	**23**	..	..	**961**	**64**	
1,656	107	1,784	65	73	18	..	..	715	17	1
48	8	1,489	71	7	2	..	..	41	6	2
328	226	1,985	303	8	3	..	..	76	38	3
210	9	1,503	13	12	..	..	..	129	3	4
52	..	1,923	1	10	..	..	..	..	..	5
41	**1**	**462**	**6**	..	..	..	..	**89**	..	
..	..	52	..	..	..	..	..	..	..	
..	..	..	..	..	..	..	..	..	..	
..	..	..	..	..	..	..	..	..	..	
..	..	38	6	..	..	..	..	..	..	
41	18	372	..	..	..	..	..	89	..	

Hence the details in columns 11 to 20 against Agencies and Tribal areas do not work up to the totals in columns 5 and 6.

TABLE XIX.—SUMMARY

Serial Number.	District or State.	Area in square miles.	Population, 1911. Persons.	Males.	Females.	Population, 1901.	Percentage of Variation. 1901-11.	1891-01.	Number of persons per square mile in 1911.
1	2	3	4	5	6	7	8	9	10
	PUNJAB	**136,330**	**24,187,750**	**13,314,975**	**10,872,775**	**24,754,735**	**— 2·3**	**+ 6·4**	**177**
	British Territory	**99,779**	**19,974,956**	**10,992,067**	**8,982,889**	**20,330,337**	**— 1·7**	**+ 6·9**	**200**
	Delhi Division.	*15,389*	*4,176,236*	*2,292,018*	*1,884,218*	*4,587,150*	*— 8·9*	*+ 3·4*	*271*
1	Hissar	5,213	804,889	438,458	366,431	781,589	+ 3·0	+ ·7	154
2	Rohtak	1,797	541,489	291,257	250,232	630,672	— 14·1	+ 6·8	301
3	Gurgaon	1,984	643,177	342,484	300,693	746,208	— 13·8	+ 11·6	324
4	Delhi	1,290	657,604	363,238	294,366	689,039	— 4·6	+ 7·9	510
5	Karnal	3,153	799,787	437,698	362,089	883,367	— 9·5	+ 2·6	254
6	Ambala	1,851	689,970	394,165	295,805	815,924	— 15·4	— 5·5	373
7	Simla	101	39,320	24,718	14,602	40,351	— 2·6	+ 9·1	389
	Jullundur Division.	*19,391*	*3,967,724*	*2,184,423*	*1,783,301*	*4,305,724*	*— 7·8*	*+ 2·1*	*205*
8	Kangra	9,978	770,386	401,109	369,277	768,124	+ ·3	+ ·7	77
9	Hoshiarpur	2,247	918,569	501,510	417,059	989,738	— 7·2	— 2·1	409
10	Jullundur	1,431	801,920	449,876	352,044	917,587	— 12·6	+ 1·1	560
11	Ludhiana	1,452	517,192	293,531	223,661	673,097	— 23·2	+ 2·8	356
12	Ferozepore	4,286	959,657	538,397	421,260	957,178	+ ·3	+ 8·1	224
	Lahore Division.	*12,387*	*4,656,629*	*2,621,510*	*2,035,083*	*5,101,882*	*— 8·7*	*+ 6·8*	*376*
13	Lahore	2,824	1,036,158	595,234	440,924	1,044,277	— ·8	+ 10·7	367
14	Amritsar	1,601	880,728	496,584	384,144	1,023,828	— 14·0	+ 3·1	550
15	Gurdaspur	1,889	836,771	469,243	367,528	940,334	— 11·0	— ·4	443
16	Sialkot	1,991	979,553	542,234	437,319	1,083,909	— 9·6	— 3·2	492
17	Gujranwala	4,082	923,419	518,251	405,168	1,009,534	— 8·5	+ 22·6	226
	Rawalpindi Division.	*21,391*	*3,353,052*	*1,795,555*	*1,557,497*	*3,106,771*	*+ 7·9*	*+ 1·3*	*157*
18	Gujrat	2,051	745,634	400,596	345,038	750,548	— ·7	— 1·4	364
19	Shahpur	5,097	687,366	376,886	310,480	529,760	+ 29·8	+ 1·1	135
20	Jhelum	2,813	511,575	268,621	242,954	501,424	+ 2·0	— 2·6	182
21	Rawalpindi	2,010	547,827	296,518	251,309	558,699	— 1·9	+ 4·7	273
22	Attock	4,025	519,273	273,037	246,236	464,430	+ 11·8	+ 3·6	129
23	Mianwali	5,395	341,377	179,897	161,480	301,910	+ 13·1	+ 5·2	63
	Multan Division.	*31,218*	*3,821,315*	*2,098,525*	*1,722,790*	*3,228,810*	*+ 18·3*	*+ 31·0*	*122*
24	Montgomery	4,652	535,299	292,836	242,463	479,563	+ 11·6	+ ·5	115
25	Lyallpur	3,153	857,711	486,927	370,784	589,533	+ 45·5	+ 2,559·6	272
26	Jhang	3,363	515,526	277,128	238,398	425,534	+ 21·1	+ 3·6	153
27	Multan	6,107	814,871	444,703	370,168	710,626	+ 14·7	+ 11·8	133
28	Muzaffargarh	6,052	569,461	308,350	261,111	527,681	+ 7·9	+ 6·6	94
29	Dera Ghazi Khan	5,325	499,860	272,409	227,451	471,736	+ 5·9	+ 10·1	94
30	Biloch Trans-Frontier	2,566	28,587	16,172	12,415	24,087	+ 18·7	+ 305·9	11
	Punjab States.	**36,551**	**4,212,794**	**2,322,908**	**1,889,886**	**4,424,398**	**— 4·8**	**+ 3·3**	**115**
1	Loharu	222	18,597	9,980	8,617	15,229	+ 22·1	— 24·4	84
2	Dujana	100	25,485	13,388	12,097	24,174	+ 5·4	— 8·6	255
3	Pataudi	52	19,543	10,150	9,393	21,933	— 10·9	+ 15·4	376
4	Kalsia	168	55,909	31,297	24,612	67,181	— 16·8	— 2·1	333
5	Nahan	1,198	138,520	76,044	62,476	135,687	+ 2·1	+ 9·3	116
6	Simla Hill States	5,937	404,343	212,027	192,316	389,349	+ 3·9	+ 5·2	68
7	Mandi	1,200	181,110	93,678	87,432	174,045	+ 4·1	+ 4·3	151
8	Suket	420	54,928	29,014	25,914	54,676	+ ·5	+ 4·3	131
9	Kapurthala	630	268,133	150,220	117,913	314,351	— 14·7	+ 4·9	426
10	Maler Kotla	167	71,144	40,602	30,542	77,506	— 8·2	+ 2·3	426
11	Faridkot	642	130,294	73,836	56,458	124,912	+ 4·3	+ 8·6	203
12	Chamba	3,216	135,873	70,612	65,261	127,834	+ 6·3	+ 3·1	42
13	Patiala	5,412	1,407,659	792,540	615,119	1,596,692	— 11·8	+ ·8	260
14	Jind	1,259	271,728	149,947	121,781	282,003	— 3·6	— ·9	216
15	Nabha	928	248,887	139,319	109,568	297,949	— 16·5	+ 5·4	268
16	Bahawalpur	15,000	780,641	430,254	350,387	720,877	+ 8·3	+ 10·9	52
	UNITED PROVINCES OF AGRA AND OUDH.	**112,346**	**48,014,080**	**25,073,271**	**22,940,809**	**48,494,374**	**— 1·0**	**+ 1·7**	**427**
	British Territory.	**107,267**	**47,182,044**	**24,641,831**	**22,540,213**	**47,692,277**	**— 1·1**	**+ 1·7**	**440**
	Agra.	**83,109**	**34,624,040**	**18,157,131**	**16,466,909**	**34,859,109**	**— ·7**	**+ 1·3**	**417**
	Meerut Division.	*11,194*	*5,808,630*	*3,150,957*	*2,657,673*	*5,979,334*	*— 2·9*	*+ 13·2*	*519*
1	Dehra Dun	1,190	205,075	120,908	84,167	177,934	+ 15·3	+ 6·0	172
2	Saharanpur	2,135	986,359	541,091	445,268	1,045,330	— 5·6	+ 4·4	462
3	Muzaffarnagar	1,673	808,360	444,862	363,498	876,972	— 7·8	+ 13·5	483
4	Meerut	2,344	1,519,364	822,305	697,059	1,540,175	— 1·4	+ 10·7	648
5	Bulandshahr	1,906	1,123,792	592,267	531,525	1,138,101	— 1·3	+ 19·8	590
6	Aligarh	1,946	1,165,680	629,524	536,156	1,200,822	— 2·9	+ 15·1	599
	Agra Division.	*10,082*	*5,007,921*	*2,742,988*	*2,264,933*	*5,249,970*	*— 4·6*	*+ 10·1*	*497*
7	Muttra	1,450	656,310	361,507	294,803	763,099	— 14·0	+ 7·0	453
8	Agra	1,855	1,021,847	557,320	464,527	1,060,528	— 3·6	+ 5·7	551
9	Farrukhabad	1,683	900,022	494,017	406,005	925,721	— 2·8	+ 7·8	535
10	Mainpuri	1,674	797,624	438,920	358,704	829,357	— 3·8	+ 8·9	476
11	Etawah	1,691	760,121	416,648	343,473	806,798	— 5·8	+ 10·9	450
12	Etah	1,729	871,997	474,576	397,421	864,467	+ ·9	+ 23·1	504
	Rohilkhand Division.	*10,829*	*5,650,518*	*3,050,265*	*2,600,253*	*5,479,404*	*+ 3·1*	*+ 2·5*	*522*
13	Bareilly	1,579	1,094,663	593,836	500,827	1,090,117	+ ·4	+ 4·7	693
14	Bijnor	1,879	806,202	427,153	379,049	780,186	+ 3·3	— 1·8	429
15	Budaun	2,010	1,053,328	577,561	475,767	1,025,234	+ 2·7	+ 10·8	524
16	Moradabad	2,285	1,262,933	676,151	586,782	1,191,993	+ 6·0	+ 1·1	553
17	Shahjahanpur	1,726	945,775	513,562	432,213	921,535	+ 2·6	+ ·3	548
18	Pilibhit	1,350	487,617	262,002	225,615	470,339	+ 3·7	— 3·0	361

FIGURES FOR DISTRICTS—*contd.*

DISTRIBUTION BY RELIGION.										
HINDU.		MUSALMAN.		CHRISTIAN.		SIKH.		OTHERS.		Serial Number.
Males.	Females.	Males.	Females.	Males.	Females.	Males.	Females.	Males.	Females.	
11	12	13	14	15	16	17	18	19	20	21
4,762,767	**3,969,431**	**6,695,943**	**5,579,534**	**116,985**	**82,766**	**1,651,595**	**1,232,134**	**87,745**	[illegible]	
3,681,166	**2,954,585**	**5,967,466**	**4,988,313**	**116,039**	**82,067**	**1,197,922**	**895,882**	**79,590**	[illegible]	
1,558,563	*1,274,227*	*609,199*	*520,402*	*12,031*	*7,120*	*88,079*	*62,612*	*24,146*	*19,857*	
294,389	243,813	117,477	101,123	148	125	21,466	17,042	4,978	4,329	1
243,363	205,050	44,038	42,038	169	165	115	46	3,552	2,985	2
225,792	195,316	114,209	103,028	371	411	202	140	1,910	1,731	3
256,681	208,066	94,173	77,572	3,151	2,542	2,374	611	6,859	5,555	4
304,605	248,128	120,683	104,237	509	411	7,706	5,825	4,195	3,488	5
215,726	163,080	114,524	90,679	5,940	1,543	55,640	38,831	2,335	1,672	6
17,967	10,677	4,095	1,725	1,743	1,923	576	117	317	160	7
1,020,070	*863,077*	*699,911*	*572,400*	*6,719*	*3,279*	*446,487*	*335,349*	*11,236*	*9,196*	
375,317	347,564	21,339	17,520	207	179	1,055	855	3,191	3,150	8
269,678	286,138	152,891	128,914	1,693	1,285	74,955	59,191	2,293	1,581	9
147,610	114,887	196,436	160,615	1,789	615	101,913	74,314	2,128	1,613	10
73,705	55,987	98,058	77,985	479	409	119,319	87,723	1,970	1,577	11
153,760	118,521	231,187	187,366	2,551	791	149,245	113,266	1,654	1,316	12
616,598	*468,188*	*1,483,447*	*1,187,153*	*64,599*	*50,145*	*426,454*	*307,082*	*30,448*	*22,515*	
124,840	84,002	351,483	274,838	12,728	9,053	99,518	69,490	6,715	3,541	13
118,118	90,750	226,555	182,327	2,685	2,078	146,795	107,146	2,431	1,848	14
156,756	123,369	226,888	181,328	12,871	10,494	70,447	50,631	2,281	1,706	15
119,322	96,088	332,197	272,604	27,306	21,314	47,038	34,723	16,371	13,595	16
97,562	74,984	346,374	276,056	9,009	7,206	62,656	45,092	2,650	1,830	17
140,062	*113,338*	*1,548,563*	*1,357,117*	*12,652*	*6,179*	*89,132*	*77,087*	*5,146*	*3,876*	
25,515	21,285	350,088	300,805	341	229	23,197	21,496	1,455	1,222	18
39,067	31,350	312,988	259,577	4,865	3,751	18,639	14,817	1,327	985	19
18,193	15,241	236,359	215,901	280	170	13,225	11,211	564	431	20
28,127	19,055	242,775	215,326	6,470	1,850	17,736	14,103	1,410	978	21
10,484	9,036	248,020	223,870	593	114	13,793	13,121	147	95	22
18,676	17,271	158,333	141,638	103	65	2,542	2,339	243	167	23
295,815	*235,795*	*1,626,288*	*1,351,241*	*20,038*	*15,344*	*147,770*	*113,752*	*8,614*	*6,658*	
36,791	29,197	218,409	181,314	346	235	36,781	31,394	509	323	24
89,864	61,950	291,986	232,302	17,713	14,310	85,623	61,047	1,741	1,175	25
37,730	34,626	228,529	193,939	117	84	10,126	9,301	626	448	26
66,589	53,467	361,264	304,224	1,783	658	11,256	8,625	3,811	3,194	27
35,410	30,641	268,381	226,534	41	19	3,371	2,951	1,147	966	28
29,331	25,849	241,654	200,580	38	38	610	432	776	552	29
100	65	16,065	12,348	..	..	3	2	4	..	30
1,131,590	**964,966**	**728,535**	**591,221**	**946**	**699**	**453,873**	**336,252**	**8,155**	**6,366**	
8,802	7,276	1,171	1,230	..	..	..	..	7	11	1
10,840	9,321	2,548	2,776	..	..	..	..	..	..	2
8,447	7,666	1,655	1,683	7	2	..	..	41	42	3
17,239	13,366	10,258	8,562	23	8	3,671	2,587	116	89	4
71,365	58,843	3,386	2,630	18	19	1,196	946	79	38	5
202,224	184,644	6,655	4,719	126	98	1,636	1,275	1,386	1,580	6
92,010	86,105	1,547	1,252	3	1	23	3	95	71	7
28,658	25,610	311	276	1	1	44	27	..	..	8
34,338	26,413	84,436	67,681	59	48	30,876	23,399	511	372	9
13,159	9,574	14,510	11,432	3	11	12,058	8,960	872	565	10
21,219	16,104	20,642	16,463	5	1	31,699	23,698	271	192	11
65,521	60,701	4,614	4,136	43	38	83	58	351	328	12
312,588	249,974	171,508	135,876	445	294	305,371	226,921	2,633	2,054	13
114,809	94,210	20,244	17,276	94	93	13,428	9,138	1,372	1,064	14
69,587	56,795	25,315	20,717	3	2	44,269	31,929	145	125	15
60,808	45,204	359,785	294,512	116	83	9,319	7,311	279	277	16
21,969,572	**19,455,781**	**3,596,419**	**3,308,312**	**101,742**	**77,952**	**9,909**	**5,187**	**115,539**	**93,577**	
20,949,041	**19,172,597**	**3,466,267**	**3,192,086**	**100,818**	**77,131**	**9,988**	**5,172**	**115,097**	**93,227**	
15,349,789	**13,909,965**	**2,596,956**	**2,360,728**	**91,311**	**71,758**	**8,267**	**4,351**	**110,806**	**90,167**	
2,371,188	*1,998,293*	*693,995*	*591,335*	*29,792*	*23,575*	*4,273*	*2,793*	*51,709*	*41,677*	
99,241	70,373	17,108	10,686	2,844	2,192	833	325	882	591	1
350,151	288,203	179,846	149,248	3,333	2,215	1,316	739	6,445	4,863	2
308,607	250,186	126,338	105,535	1,485	1,098	410	310	8,022	6,369	3
609,606	515,261	184,472	160,416	10,724	7,418	1,472	1,234	16,031	12,730	4
467,987	418,282	108,724	99,643	5,213	4,898	197	171	10,196	8,531	5
535,646	455,968	77,507	65,807	6,193	5,754	45	14	10,133	8,593	6
2,452,456	*2,015,325*	*247,231*	*214,880*	*16,625*	*13,309*	*501*	*392*	*26,175*	*21,027*	
322,049	262,598	33,917	27,842	3,387	2,605	66	51	2,088	1,707	7
483,777	402,064	61,360	53,195	4,319	2,910	89	49	7,775	6,309	8
435,300	353,328	54,804	49,489	1,371	1,177	17	18	2,525	1,994	9
408,225	332,808	23,977	20,500	1,271	1,124	98	73	5,349	4,204	10
388,388	318,966	24,227	21,401	383	310	17	12	3,633	2,784	11
414,717	345,571	48,946	42,453	5,894	5,183	214	189	4,805	4,025	12
2,260,282	*1,893,311*	*742,773*	*669,036*	*27,866*	*22,400*	*762*	*481*	*18,582*	*15,025*	
437,200	364,302	146,503	129,727	7,731	4,860	276	200	2,126	1,738	13
272,619	236,186	145,339	135,162	1,712	1,603	121	140	7,362	5,958	14
473,457	386,231	94,727	81,649	6,034	5,264	76	62	3,267	2,561	15
424,397	360,153	238,140	215,129	9,084	7,989	248	48	4,282	3,513	16
437,842	363,432	72,768	166,391	2,154	1,800	30	26	768	564	17
214,767	183,007	45,296	40,978	1,151	984	11	5	777	691	18

TABLE XIX.—SUMMARY

Serial Number.	District or State.	Area in square miles.	Population, 1911. Persons.	Males.	Females.	Population, 1901.	Percentage of Variation. 1901-11.	1891-01.	Number of persons per square mile in 1911.
1	2	3	4	5	6	7	8	9	10
	UNITED PROVINCES OF AGRA AND OUDH—*contd.*								
	Allahabad Division.	*17,312*	*5,494,284*	*2,844,746*	*2,649,538*	*5,541,741*	*— ·9*	*— 3·8*	*317*
19	Cawnpore	2,372	1,142,286	623,437	518,849	1,258,868	— 9·3	+ 4·1	482
20	Fatehpur	1,642	676,939	350,207	326,732	686,391	— 1·4	— 1·9	412
21	Banda	2,965	657,237	332,161	325,076	631,058	+ 4·1	— 10·6	222
22	Hamirpur	2,292	465,223	234,842	230,381	458,542	+ 1·5	— 10·7	203
23	Allahabad	2,858	1,467,136	744,382	722,754	1,490,897	— 1·6	— 3·8	513
24	Jhansi	3,634	680,688	350,192	330,496	616,759	+ 10·4	— 9·8	187
25	Jalaun	1,549	404,775	209,525	195,250	399,726	+ 1·3	+ ·8	261
	Benares Division.	*10,427*	*4,809,478*	*2,402,245*	*2,407,233*	*5,068,618*	*— 5·1*	*— 5·6*	*461*
26	Benares	1,008	897,035	452,067	444,968	882,084	+ 1·7	— 4·3	890
27	Mirzapur	5,233	1,071,046	530,214	540,832	1,082,430	— 1·1	— 6·8	205
28	Jaunpur	1,550	1,156,254	576,070	580,184	1,202,920	— 3·9	— 4·9	746
29	Ghazipur	1,392	839,725	420,200	419,525	913,818	— 8·1	— 10·8	603
30	Ballia	1,244	845,418	423,694	421,724	987,366	— 14·4	— ·8	680
	Gorakhpur Division.	*9,543*	*6,524,419*	*3,280,721*	*3,243,698*	*6,333,012*	*+ 3·0*	*— 2·7*	*684*
31	Gorakhpur	4,528	3,201,180	1,604,635	1,596,545	2,938,685	+ 8·9	— 1·2	707
32	Basti	2,802	1,830,421	926,286	904,135	1,846,153	— ·9	+ 3·4	653
33	Azamgarh	2,213	1,492,818	749,800	743,018	1,548,174	— 3·6	— 11·4	675
	Kumaun Division.	*13,722*	*1,328,790*	*685,209*	*643,581*	*1,207,030*	*+ 10·1*	*+ 2·2*	*97*
34	Naini Tal	2,721	323,519	182,875	140,644	324,019	— ·2	— 12·0	119
35	Almora	5,372	525,104	266,516	258,588	453,111	+ 15·9	+ 11·8	98
36	Garhwal	5,629	480,167	235,818	244,349	429,900	+ 11·7	+ 5·4	85
	Oudh.	**24,158**	**12,558,004**	**6,484,700**	**6,073,304**	**12,833,168**	**— 2·1**	**+ 1·4**	**520**
	Lucknow Division.	*12,057*	*5,911,642*	*3,128,767*	*2,782,875*	*5,977,177*	*— 1·1*	*+ 2·1*	*490*
37	Lucknow	967	764,411	411,799	352,612	793,241	— 3·6	+ 2·5	790
38	Unao	1,787	910,915	478,585	432,330	976,639	— 6·7	+ 2·4	510
39	Rae Bareli	1,745	1,016,864	510,665	506,199	1,033,761	— 1·6	— ·3	583
40	Sitapur	2,250	1,138,996	606,339	532,657	1,175,473	— 3·1	+ 9·3	506
41	Hardoi	2,332	1,121,248	609,867	511,381	1,092,925	+ 2·6	— 1·8	481
42	Kheri	2,976	959,208	511,512	447,696	905,138	+ 6·0	+ ·2	322
	Fyzabad Division.	*12,101*	*6,646,362*	*3,355,933*	*3,290,429*	*6,855,991*	*— 3·0*	*+ ·9*	*549*
43	Fyzabad	1,732	1,154,109	575,621	578,488	1,225,374	— 5·8	+ ·7	666
44	Gonda	2,809	1,412,212	718,418	693,794	1,403,195	+ ·6	— 3·8	503
45	Bahraich	2,645	1,047,677	544,594	503,083	1,051,347	— ·3	+ 5·1	396
46	Sultanpur	1,713	1,048,524	515,980	532,544	1,083,904	— 3·3	+ ·7	612
47	Partabgarh	1,443	899,973	437,183	462,790	912,848	— 1·4	+ ·2	624
48	Bara Banki	1,759	1,0[illegible]2,867	564,137	519,730	1,179,323	— 8·1	+ 4·3	616
	United Provinces States.	**5,079**	**832,036**	**431,440**	**400,596**	**802,097**	**+ 3·7**	**+ 1·2**	**164**
1	Rampur	899	531,217	282,978	248,239	533,212	— ·4	— 3·3	591
2	Tehri-Garhwal	4,180	300,819	148,462	152,357	268,885	+ 11·9	+ 11·5	72
	BARODA STATE.	**8,182**	**2,032,798**	**1,055,935**	**976,863**	**1,952,692**	**+ 4·1**	**— 19·2**	**248**
	CENTRAL INDIA AGENCY.	**77,430**	**9,369,472**	**4,807,922**	**4,561,550**	**8,509,212**	**+ 10·1**	**— 16·2**	**121**
1	Gwalior	25,133	3,102,279	1,630,327	1,471,952	2,949,596	+ 5·2	— 13·1	123
2	Indore	9,506	1,007,856	517,501	490,355	853,012	+ 18·2	— 22·5	106
3	Bhopal	6,902	730,383	370,560	359,823	667,350	+ 9·4	— 29·9	106
4	Rewah	13,000	1,514,843	752,297	762,546	1,326,802	+ 14·2	— 12·0	117
5	Orchha	2,079	330,032	168,633	161,399	321,678	+ 2·6	— 3·4	159
6	Datia	911	154,603	80,175	74,428	173,905	— 11·1	— 6·7	170
7	Dhar	1,783	154,070	77,257	76,813	142,115	+ 8·4	— 16·1	86
8	Dewas S. B.	441	74,290	38,100	36,190	62,730	+ 18·4	— 23·9	168
9	Dewas J. B.	417	63,015	32,222	30,793	55,097	+ 14·4	— 20·9	151
10	Samthar	180	31,908	16,291	15,617	33,472	— 4·7	— 17·4	177
11	Jaora	568	75,951	39,054	36,897	77,040	— 1·4	— 34·5	134
12	Ratlam	643	75,291	38,277	37,014	79,336	— 5·1	— 4·5	117
13	Panna	2,596	228,880	114,936	113,944	192,986	+ 18·6	— 16·4	88
14	Charkhari	880	132,530	67,516	65,014	123,954	+ 6·9	— 13·4	151
15	Ajaigarh	802	87,093	44,286	42,807	78,236	+ 11·3	— 15·9	109
16	Bijawar	973	125,202	64,233	60,969	110,500	+ 13·3	— 10·5	129
17	Baoni	121	20,121	10,342	9,779	19,780	+ 1·7	+ 7·3	166
18	Chhatarpur	1,118	166,985	85,967	81,018	156,139	+ 6·9	— 10·3	149
19	Sitamau	185	26,484	13,646	12,838	23,863	+ 11·0	— 28·4	143
20	Sailana	279	26,885	13,678	13,207	24,266	+ 10·7	— 22·9	96
21	Rajgarh	962	127,293	66,070	61,223	94,924	+ 34·1	— 23·8	132
22	Narsinghgarh	734	109,854	56,706	53,148	92,093	+ 19·3	— 20·8	150
23	Jhabua	1,336	111,292	55,458	55,834	81,145	+ 37·2	— 32·3	83
24	Baraundha	218	16,982	8,666	8,316	15,724	+ 8·0	— 15·4	78
25	Nagod	501	74,592	36,382	38,210	62,806	+ 18·8	— 25·3	149
26	Maihar	407	73,155	35,565	37,590	63,908	+ 14·5	— 17·6	180
27	Barwani	1,178	108,583	54,488	54,095	76,136	+ 42·6	— 5·1	92
28	Ali Rajpur	836	72,454	36,326	36,128	50,185	+ 44·4	— 28·4	87
29	Khilchipur	273	40,075	20,990	19,085	31,143	+ 28·7	— 14·2	147
30	Other States	2,468	506,491	261,973	244,518	469,271	+ 7·9	— 12·0	205

FIGURES FOR DISTRICTS—*contd.*

DISTRIBUTION BY RELIGION.										
HINDU.		MUSALMAN.		CHRISTIAN.		SIKH.		OTHERS.		Serial Number.
Males.	Females.	Males.	Females.	Males.	Females.	Males.	Females.	Males.	Females.	
11	12	13	14	15	16	17	18	19	20	21
2,561,208	*2,386,158*	*261,380*	*247,650*	*10,343*	*6,804*	*2,157*	*418*	*9,658*	*8,808*	
361,249	468,314	56,828	47,173	3,251	1,973	372	76	1,737	1,813	19
310,830	287,136	39,052	39,256	53	89	..	..	272	251	20
313,268	306,032	18,435	18,633	116	82	6	3	336	326	21
219,756	214,268	14,777	15,678	97	266	20	10	192	159	22
688,541	621,551	100,082	97,539	4,134	2,921	865	168	760	575	23
322,428	307,248	18,166	16,003	2,584	1,386	871	142	6,148	5,717	24
195,141	181,609	14,040	13,368	108	87	23	19	213	167	25
2,301,760	*2,203,170*	*195,982*	*199,916*	*2,084*	*2,274*	*409*	*162*	*2,020*	*1,711*	
400,772	396,152	49,516	47,341	927	1,003	300	73	551	399	26
494,981	506,091	34,541	33,966	334	401	69	52	339	222	27
524,876	528,127	50,195	51,101	33	84	13	10	953	662	28
383,720	378,705	36,090	40,471	284	284	3	2	93	63	29
397,440	394,095	25,640	27,037	506	502	24	25	84	65	30
2,868,612	*2,836,757*	*409,617*	*404,848*	*973*	*847*	*101*	*77*	*1,418*	*1,169*	
1,440,546	1,434,856	162,535	160,411	854	754	39	22	661	502	31
771,991	753,394	154,063	150,613	46	23	3	..	183	105	32
656,075	648,507	93,019	93,824	73	70	59	55	574	562	33
634,293	*606,951*	*45,980*	*33,063*	*3,628*	*2,549*	*64*	*28*	*1,244*	*990*	
139,356	108,189	41,238	30,645	1,325	1,088	55	23	901	699	34
262,267	255,899	2,142	1,404	1,854	1,065	1	..	252	220	35
232,670	242,863	2,600	1,014	449	396	8	5	91	71	36
5,599,852	**5,232,632**	**869,329**	**831,358**	**9,507**	**5,373**	**1,721**	**821**	**4,291**	**3,120**	
2,722,618	*2,416,612*	*394,446*	*359,450*	*7,475*	*4,218*	*1,028*	*339*	*3,200*	*2,256*	
319,465	272,795	84,572	76,125	5,911	2,749	826	205	1,025	738	37
438,163	395,904	39,959	36,074	76	47	12	4	375	301	38
467,038	461,749	43,326	44,240	124	95	49	42	128	73	39
515,600	450,152	89,904	81,875	254	315	31	16	550	299	40
545,238	453,998	63,306	56,234	563	548	45	36	715	565	41
437,114	382,014	73,379	64,902	547	464	65	36	407	280	42
2,877,234	*2,816,020*	*474,883*	*471,908*	*2,032*	*1,155*	*693*	*482*	*1,091*	*864*	
510,594	512,962	63,137	64,817	1,450	461	212	67	228	181	43
603,433	581,174	114,652	112,255	222	279	29	28	82	58	44
439,357	405,458	104,477	96,983	172	176	442	371	146	95	45
460,104	471,746	55,724	60,596	36	98	4	..	112	104	46
392,062	414,067	44,985	48,628	42	30	3	1	91	64	47
471,684	430,613	91,908	88,629	110	111	3	15	432	362	48
299,931	**283,184**	**130,132**	**116,226**	**924**	**821**	**11**	**15**	**442**	**350**	
152,417	131,715	129,228	115,376	921	818	1	1	411	329	1
147,514	151,469	904	850	3	3	10	14	31	21	2
						ANIMISTIC.				
864,474	**812,672**	**82,986**	**77,901**	**3,855**	**3,348**	**58,858**	**56,553**	**25,762**	**26,299**	
4,947,410	**4,926,290**	**266,774**	**244,949**	**6,170**	**3,188**	**239,772**	**243,928**	**47,796**	**43,195**	
1,491,773	1,845,479	87,889	78,021	326	284	29,966	29,933	20,373	18,235	1
452,169	428,065	36,847	34,300	341	154	22,187	22,414	5,957	5,402	2
297,218	286,884	42,388	39,608	139	94	28,039	30,572	2,776	2,665	3
734,892	745,409	17,010	16,754	76	69	9	1	310	313	4
156,016	149,091	4,253	4,076	1	1	5,235	5,273	3,128	2,958	5
76,815	71,457	3,016	2,637	3	2	..	..	341	332	6
58,459	58,384	6,186	5,944	74	117	11,155	11,148	1,383	1,220	7
33,216	31,599	4,399	4,151	8	5	84	80	393	355	8
28,667	27,550	2,994	2,788	8	6	135	116	418	333	9
15,176	14,475	1,099	1,125	2	1	..	..	14	16	10
30,111	28,389	6,956	6,730	8	11	857	810	1,122	957	11
23,186	22,556	4,942	4,570	197	187	7,483	7,447	2,469	2,234	12
103,007	101,788	2,562	2,458	16	10	8,133	8,493	1,218	1,195	13
64,608	62,053	2,729	2,771	2	4	..	..	177	186	14
42,371	41,006	1,314	1,239	..	..	323	306	278	256	15
61,856	58,713	1,328	1,254	4	2	..	..	1,050	1,000	16
9,148	8,579	1,175	1,174	..	..	..	..	19	26	17
82,800	78,035	2,837	2,714	10	4	..	..	320	285	18
12,350	11,626	872	845	4	4	16	14	404	349	19
9,365	9,054	716	640	..	..	3,186	3,154	411	359	20
62,548	58,004	3,370	3,070	..	..	..	..	152	149	21
58,967	50,703	2,512	2,238	..	..	34	35	193	172	22
13,812	13,617	1,066	1,031	114	95	39,545	40,254	921	837	23
8,361	8,024	110	89	..	..	195	203	..	..	24
34,250	36,074	1,289	1,228	..	..	860	884	33	29	25
34,448	36,486	1,102	1,087	1	1	..	..	14	16	26
21,822	21,150	2,764	2,725	13	2	29,603	30,020	286	198	27
9,922	9,575	1,159	1,142	195	203	24,974	25,139	76	69	28
20,297	18,459	680	596	..	..	4	5	9	25	29
204,780	193,986	21,265	17,949	4,628	1,932	27,749	27,627	3,551	3,024	30

TABLE XIX.—Summary

Serial Number.	District or State.	Area in square miles.	Population, 1911. Persons.	Males.	Females.	Population, 1901.	Percentage of Variation. 1901-11.	1891-01.	Number of persons per square mile in 1911.
1	2	3	4	5	6	7	8	9	10
	HYDERABAD STATE.	**82,698**	**13,374,676**	**6,797,118**	**6,577,558**	**11,141,142**	**+20·0**	**—3·4**	**162**
1	Hyderabad City	50	500,623	258,454	242,169	462,321	+8·3	+8·1	10,012
2	Atraf-i-balda	2,561	520,159	265,184	254,975	431,502	+20·5	+5·3	203
3	Warangal	7,943	905,414	467,413	438,001	716,171	+26·4	+11·9	114
4	Karimnagar	5,733	1,131,637	586,260	545,377	835,324	+35·5	—4·3	197
5	Adilabad	7,294	620,426	314,428	305,998	484,281	+28·1	+7·6	85
6	Medak	3,215	687,137	348,410	338,727	531,359	+29·3	—·6	214
7	Nizamabad	3,273	568,009	283,621	284,388	497,569	+14·2	—·8	174
8	Mahbubnagar	5,147	747,178	379,712	367,466	601,749	+24·2	+4·6	145
9	Nalgonda	6,104	1,044,381	537,139	507,242	870,073	+20·0	+12·0	171
10	Aurangabad	6,212	869,787	437,495	432,292	725,556	+19·9	—13·0	140
11	Bhir	4,132	622,531	314,738	307,793	492,258	+26·5	—23·4	151
12	Nander	3,797	704,549	352,638	351,911	580,245	+21·4	—17·6	186
13	Parbhani	5,127	779,674	391,231	388,443	647,046	+20·5	+19·7	152
14	Gulbarga	6,719	1,150,983	582,447	568,536	1,054,145	+ 9·2	+12·0	171
15	Osmanabad	3,517	635,977	324,969	311,008	530,577	+19·9	—17·6	181
16	Raichur	6,791	996,684	503,541	493,143	933,015	+ 6·8	+4·0	147
17	Bidar	5,083	889,527	449,438	440,089	747,951	+18·9	—15·1	175
	KASHMIR STATE.	**84,432**	**3,158,126**	**1,674,367**	**1,483,759**	**2,905,578**	**+ 8·7**	**+ 14·2**	**37**
	Jammu Province.	*12,439*	*1,597,865*	*846,790*	*751,075*	*1,516,450*	*+ 5·4*	*+ 5·7*	*128*
1	Jammu	1,167	326,691	180,691	146,000	344,018	— 5·0	..	280
2	Jasrota	989	151,802	81,375	70,427	154,213	— 1·6	+ 1·8	153
3	Udhampur	4,399	215,725	113,877	101,848	} Not available			49
4	Riasi	1,875	206,809	109,026	97,783				110
5	Mirpur	1,754	324,933	169,276	155,657				185
6	Bhadarwah Jagir	607	37,512	18,975	18,537	34,311	+ 9·3	+ 5·8	62
7	Punch Ilaqa	1,648	334,393	173,570	160,823	304,488	+ 9·8	+ 13·4	203
	Kashmir Province.	*8,433*	*1,295,201*	*691,780*	*603,421*	*1,157,394*	*+ 11·9*	*+ 22·0*	*154*
8	Kashmir North	3,553	460,786	244,637	216,149	} 989,196	+ 11·2	..	{ 130
9	Kashmir South	2,806	639,210	342,835	296,375				{ 228
10	Muzaffarabad	2,074	195,205	104,308	90,897	168,198	+ 16·1	+ 24·8	94
	Frontier Districts.	*63,560*	*265,060*	*135,797*	*129,263*	*231,734*	*+ 14·4*	*+ 8·0*	*4*
11	Laddakh	45,762	186,656	93,220	93,436	Not available			4
12	Gilgit	3,118	23,969	13,299	10,670				8
13	Frontier Ilaqas	14,680	54,435	29,278	25,157	60,885	+ 28·8	..	4
	MYSORE STATE.	**29,475**	**5,806,193**	**2,934,621**	**2,871,572**	**5,539,399**	**+ 4·8**	**+ 12·1**	**197**
1	Bangalore City	10	88,651	45,997	42,654	69,447	+ 27·7	— 18·5	9,063
2	Bangalore District	3,068	759,522	382,726	376,796	720,217	+ 5·5	+ 15·7	248
3	Kolar Gold Fields City	15	48,635	27,960	20,675	38,204	+ 27·3	+ 439·2	3,242
4	Kolar District	3,164	731,518	368,386	363,132	685,396	+ 6·7	+ 17·4	231
5	Tumkur District	4,062	735,346	372,030	363,316	670,377	+ 9·7	+ 17·0	181
6	Mysore City	9	71,306	36,112	35,194	68,111	+ 4·7	— 8·0	7,506
7	Mysore District	5,488	1,270,765	629,516	641,249	1,227,061	+ 3·6	+ 10·8	232
8	Chitaldrug District	4,160	564,243	287,030	277,213	511,062	+ 10·4	+ 20·3	136
9	Hassan District	2,666	580,200	287,360	292,840	568,919	+ 2·0	+ 11·1	218
10	Kadur District	2,789	338,457	177,074	161,383	359,270	— 5·8	+ 9·2	121
11	Shimoga District	4,030	516,716	268,678	248,038	531,736	— 2·8	+ ·5	128
12	Civil and Military Station, Bangalore.	14	100,834	51,752	49,082	89,599	+ 12·5	— 10·5	7,447
	RAJPUTANA AGENCY.	**128,924**	**10,517,946**	**5,508,818**	**5,009,128**	**9,841,959**	**+ 6·9**	**— 19·0**	**82**
1	Bikaner	23,315	700,983	371,489	329,494	584,755	+ 19·9	— 29·7	30
2	Jaisalmer	16,062	88,311	48,500	39,811	73,370	+ 20·4	— 36·6	5
3	Marwar	34,963	2,057,553	1,075,269	982,284	1,935,565	+ 6·3	— 23·4	59
4	Mewar	12,693	1,281,234	664,237	616,997	1,018,805	+ 25·8	— 40·4	101
5	Banswara	1,606	165,463	81,620	83,843	149,128	+ 11·0	— 17·3	103
6	Kushalgarh	340	22,005	10,956	11,049	16,222	+ 35·6	+ 180·9	65
7	Partabgarh	886	62,704	31,735	30,969	52,025	+ 20·5	— 40·9	71
8	Dungarpur	1,447	159,192	79,105	80,087	100,103	+ 59·0	+ 1·7	110
9	Sirohi	1,964	189,127	98,289	90,838	154,544	+ 22·4	— 17·8	96
10	Jaipur	15,579	2,636,647	1,385,750	1,250,897	2,658,666	— ·8	— 5·9	169
11	Kishangarh	858	87,191	45,718	41,473	90,970	— 4·2	— 27·5	102
12	Lawa	19	2,564	1,302	1,262	2,671	— 4·0	— 20·5	135
13	Alwar	3,141	791,688	413,659	378,029	828,487	— 4·4	+ 7·9	252
14	Bharatpur	1,982	558,785	302,254	256,531	626,665	— 10·8	— 2·1	282
15	Dholpur	1,155	263,188	144,244	118,944	270,973	— 2·9	— 3·2	228
16	Karauli	1,242	146,587	80,081	66,506	156,786	— 6·5	+ ·1	118
17	Jhalawar	810	96,271	50,034	46,237	90,175	+ 6·8	— 40·3	119
18	Tonk	2,553	303,181	156,390	146,791	273,267	+ 10·9	— 28·1	119
19	Bundi	2,220	218,730	113,211	105,519	171,227	+ 27·7	— 42·1	99
20	Kotah	5,684	639,089	330,324	308,765	544,879	+ 17·3	— 24·2	112
21	Shahpura	405	47,397	24,595	22,802	42,676	+ 11·1	— 32·9	117
	SIKKIM STATE	**2,818**	**87,920**	**45,059**	**42,861**	**59,014**	**+ 49·0**	**+ 93·8**	**31**

FIGURES FOR DISTRICTS—*concld.*

DISTRIBUTION BY RELIGION.										
HINDU.		MUSALMAN.		CHRISTIAN.		ANIMISTIC.		OTHERS.		Serial Number.
Males.	Females.	Males.	Females.	Males.	Females.	Males.	Females.	Males.	Females.	
11	12	13	14	15	16	17	18	19	20	21
5,897,158	**5,722,968**	**706,821**	**674,169**	**29,495**	**24,801**	**149,023**	**136,699**	**14,621**	**12,901**	
135,638	126,493	111,770	108,126	9,623	6,617	38	3	1,385	930	1
231,505	223,698	30,602	28,740	686	605	2,255	1,812	136	120	2
372,793	351,091	26,709	23,370	6,202	5,777	61,473	57,548	236	215	3
556,441	518,213	24,345	22,178	286	300	5,041	4,557	147	129	4
264,837	259,663	15,843	13,825	19	9	38,601	32,363	128	138	5
312,690	302,862	32,269	32,815	1,124	1,079	2,179	1,837	148	134	6
261,053	262,106	21,036	20,915	375	845	972	848	185	174	7
341,109	331,641	30,853	29,168	221	230	7,991	6,401	38	26	8
483,032	458,662	27,721	26,151	5,565	5,001	20,760	17,877	61	51	9
367,581	366,671	57,629	53,820	3,222	3,147	5,956	5,888	3,107	2,816	10
285,573	280,481	25,749	25,151	1	1	407	428	2,008	1,732	11
313,495	314,157	36,708	35,481	40	29	1,194	1,142	1,201	1,102	12
350,575	349,100	36,789	35,685	250	159	1,627	1,516	1,990	1,963	13
490,220	480,185	86,152	83,174	633	411	4,469	3,973	973	793	14
292,192	280,241	30,602	28,846	130	122	163	143	1,882	1,656	15
453,629	446,788	48,402	45,076	920	791	188	130	452	358	16
384,795	376,936	63,142	61,648	198	178	759	783	544	544	17
372,089	**317,253**	**1,265,535**	**1,132,785**	**618**	**357**	..	..	**36,125**	**33,364**	
335,621	*289,835*	*500,690*	*452,603*	*450*	*222*	..	..	*10,029*	*8,415*	
106,196	87,274	69,976	56,683	304	159	..	..	2,215	1,884	1
61,994	54,273	19,146	16,028	128	42	..	..	107	84	2
68,786	61,962	44,811	39,579	..	..	..	..	280	307	3
42,629	38,257	66,121	59,308	1	..	..	..	275	228	4
30,956	26,231	136,886	127,961	7	3	..	..	1,927	1,462	5
11,375	11,556	7,599	6,981	..	..	..	..	1	..	6
11,685	10,282	156,651	146,068	10	18	..	..	5,224	4,455	7
35,056	*27,312*	*648,685*	*569,083*	*118*	*100*	..	..	*7,921*	*6,926*	
5,935	3,982	236,289	209,959	25	14	..	..	2,388	2,194	8
26,298	21,456	314,965	273,676	80	82	..	..	1,492	1,161	9
2,823	1,874	97,431	85,448	13	4	..	..	4,041	3,571	10
1,412	*106*	*116,160*	*111,099*	*50*	*35*	..	..	*18,175*	*18,023*	
358	49	74,719	75,351	32	31	..	..	18,111	18,005	11
770	46	12,471	10,604	17	4	..	..	41	16	12
284	11	28,970	25,144	1	..	..	..	23	2	13
2,689,851	**2,651,057**	**165,824**	**148,670**	**31,853**	**27,991**	**36,969**	**35,197**	**10,094**	**8,657**	
37,472	35,160	5,826	4,761	2,048	2,196	389	316	267	222	1
347,159	343,989	25,207	23,184	3,130	2,677	5,910	5,657	1,320	1,289	2
20,209	15,186	2,282	821	5,194	4,466	4	2	271	200	3
337,237	333,930	24,875	23,097	1,637	1,616	3,646	3,635	991	854	4
345,499	338,472	17,981	17,237	1,119	512	5,702	5,497	1,729	1,598	5
28,183	27,743	6,696	6,129	1,006	1,146	6	11	221	165	6
606,856	619,541	19,861	17,935	809	784	2,076	2,108	914	981	7
266,161	258,006	14,156	13,059	131	114	6,076	5,660	506	372	8
272,438	279,231	9,425	8,348	1,971	1,857	2,607	2,521	919	883	9
160,441	149,186	9,457	7,123	3,042	1,500	3,360	3,017	774	557	10
240,536	222,725	17,899	16,349	1,514	1,001	7,051	6,596	1,678	1,365	11
28,660	27,886	12,159	10,627	10,257	10,173	172	175	504	221	12
4,594,454	**4,146,529**	**517,280**	**468,022**	**2,469**	**1,847**	**226,354**	**218,042**	**168,315**	**174,688**	
306,659	269,040	49,347	42,582	97	54	..	..	15,386	17,818	1
33,198	27,753	12,506	9,593	..	..	2,246	1,912	550	558	2
899,634	810,864	87,489	78,056	235	205	26,254	22,703	61,657	70,956	3
524,220	486,624	23,900	21,329	152	85	81,640	77,148	34,375	31,811	4
29,611	30,728	2,483	2,408	..	..	47,323	48,511	2,208	2,201	5
1,848	1,846	349	348	..	..	8,488	8,612	271	248	6
17,077	16,771	1,856	1,725	..	..	10,530	10,390	2,272	2,074	7
35,549	37,132	3,320	3,383	1	1	37,523	36,758	2,712	2,813	8
83,887	75,519	4,124	3,116	522	282	2,308	2,123	7,448	9,798	9
1,262,280	1,136,600	101,225	94,535	689	637	955	824	20,601	18,301	10
40,171	36,471	3,577	3,208	8	15	263	272	1,699	1,607	11
1,143	1,139	83	56	..	..	..	..	76	67	12
307,425	280,805	108,972	95,177	50	42	17	14	2,195	1,991	13
245,735	206,995	54,550	47,899	315	251	..	..	1,654	1,386	14
133,416	109,318	9,560	8,702	26	15	..	..	1,242	909	15
75,485	62,504	4,345	3,815	15	13	6	2	230	172	16
44,137	40,448	4,265	4,360	18	8	228	192	1,386	1,229	17
127,901	119,245	20,516	19,916	6	6	3,751	3,835	4,216	3,789	18
102,040	94,879	5,414	5,242	..	..	2,275	2,257	3,482	3,141	19
301,657	282,480	23,163	21,406	274	233	1,558	1,517	3,672	3,129	20
21,381	19,868	1,236	1,171	1	..	989	963	988	800	21
30,035	**28,640**	**38**	**6**	**155**	**130**	..	..	**14,831**	**14,065**	

SPECIAL TABLES FOR CITIES.

A series of tables in the form of Imperial Tables VII, VIII, XI, XV and XVIII have been prepared for all cities. The term city is here used in its ordinary statistical acceptation, and includes only those places which contain a population of not less than 100,000 persons. In the Provincial Volumes smaller towns of local importance have sometimes been treated as cities.

In these Tables the population of Calcutta is exclusive of that of its suburbs—Cossipore-Chitpur, Manicktola and Garden Reach, and that of Bareilly excludes its cantonment.

TABLE VII.

Age, Sex and Civil Condition.

TABLE VII.—Age, Sex

City and Age.	Population.			Unmarried.		Married.		Widowed.	
	Persons.	Males.	Females.	Males.	Females.	Males.	Females.	Males.	Females.
1	2	3	4	5	6	7	8	9	10
CALCUTTA	**896,067**	**607,674**	**288,393**	**206,146**	**81,896**	**379,924**	**133,784**	**21,604**	**72,713**
0—5	62,528	32,275	30,253	32,125	30,092	146	137	4	24
5—10	67,309	35,400	31,909	34,603	30,297	784	1,531	13	81
10—15	67,743	43,478	24,265	38,675	11,715	4,721	12,086	82	464
15—20	82,641	56,316	26,325	38,609	2,652	17,347	21,706	360	1,965
20—40	413,683	308,615	105,068	57,353	5,374	242,947	76,332	8,315	23,362
40—60	160,842	108,988	51,854	4,072	1,425	96,500	19,494	8,416	30,935
60 and over	41,321	22,602	18,719	709	341	17,479	2,496	4,414	15,882
BOMBAY	**979,445**	**640,288**	**339,157**	**241,489**	**96,656**	**377,514**	**183,754**	**21,285**	**58,747**
0—5	65,677	33,007	32,670	32,551	32,254	449	402	7	14
5—10	65,854	34,393	31,461	33,381	29,665	996	1,730	16	66
10—15	76,285	48,224	28,061	42,963	17,293	5,185	10,395	76	373
15—20	106,150	68,339	37,811	49,259	7,431	18,795	29,210	285	1,170
20—40	498,941	349,248	149,693	78,179	8,800	262,260	120,428	8,809	20,465
40—60	140,487	92,879	47,608	4,518	1,037	79,699	19,581	8,662	26,990
60 and over	26,051	14,198	11,853	638	176	10,180	2,008	3,480	9,669
MADRAS	**518,660**	**266,465**	**252,195**	**135,285**	**89,721**	**120,117**	**114,240**	**11,063**	**48,234**
0—5	57,021	28,236	28,785	28,173	28,701	59	68	4	16
5—10	57,640	28,650	28,990	28,542	28,582	101	387	7	21
10—15	52,816	27,709	25,107	27,384	20,568	319	4,444	6	95
15—20	50,867	24,935	25,932	22,438	6,579	2,471	18,722	26	631
20—40	182,426	95,127	87,299	26,850	4,368	65,776	70,780	2,501	12,156
40—60	91,920	48,631	43,289	1,583	781	42,026	18,453	5,022	24,055
60 and over	25,970	13,177	12,793	315	147	9,365	1,386	3,497	11,260
HYDERABAD	**500,623**	**258,454**	**242,169**	**120,212**	**76,674**	**125,377**	**115,747**	**12,865**	**49,748**
0—5	50,219	24,481	25,738	24,369	25,566	109	157	3	15
5—10	53,711	26,492	27,219	26,229	24,876	255	2,274	8	69
10—15	50,101	26,715	23,386	25,484	15,688	1,216	7,518	15	180
15—20	44,170	21,417	22,753	16,420	5,251	4,913	16,916	84	586
20—40	175,869	92,745	83,124	25,079	4,222	64,384	68,458	3,282	10,444
40—60	92,079	49,447	42,632	2,118	820	42,065	18,416	5,264	23,396
60 and over	34,474	17,157	17,317	513	251	12,435	2,008	4,209	15,058
RANGOON	**293,316**	**208,111**	**85,205**	**86,830**	**39,077**	**115,843**	**36,631**	**5,438**	**9,497**
0—5	18,681	9,450	9,231	9,426	9,210	23	20	1	1
5—10	19,259	10,034	9,225	9,984	9,159	49	64	1	2
10—15	20,426	12,370	8,056	11,997	7,683	371	364	2	9
15—20	28,967	19,940	9,027	16,323	5,467	3,587	3,469	30	91
20—40	151,793	118,607	33,186	35,770	6,354	80,847	24,661	1,990	2,171
40—60	45,089	32,528	12,561	2,890	1,025	27,460	7,121	2,178	4,415
60 and over	9,101	5,182	3,919	440	179	3,506	932	1,236	2,808
LUCKNOW	**259,798**	**144,785**	**115,013**	**61,643**	**36,024**	**70,332**	**57,790**	**12,810**	**21,199**
0—5	27,080	13,491	13,589	13,485	13,589	6			...
5—10	25,948	13,362	12,586	13,136	11,901	196	640	30	45
10—15	22,546	13,130	9,416	11,996	6,245	1,080	3,078	54	93
15—20	21,104	12,221	8,883	8,251	1,929	3,744	6,666	226	288
20—40	96,220	55,784	40,436	13,107	1,612	38,636	34,732	4,041	4,092
40—60	49,659	27,766	21,893	1,347	435	21,504	11,264	4,915	10,194
60 and over	17,241	9,031	8,210	321	313	5,166	1,410	3,544	6,487
DELHI	**232,837**	**133,864**	**98,973**	**57,318**	**30,977**	**64,591**	**51,165**	**11,955**	**16,831**
0—5	23,532	11,768	11,764	11,763	11,734	3	24	2	6
5—10	23,402	12,299	11,103	12,084	10,501	185	571	30	31
10—15	25,290	14,530	10,760	12,806	6,639	1,632	4,031	92	90
15—20	23,519	13,506	10,013	8,305	1,026	4,803	8,660	296	327
20—40	86,911	52,903	34,008	10,811	774	37,617	29,245	4,475	3,989
40—60	39,497	23,104	16,393	1,217	216	17,087	7,899	4,800	8,278
60 and over	10,686	5,754	4,932	232	87	3,264	735	2,258	4,110
LAHORE	**228,687**	**143,249**	**85,438**	**70,284**	**31,540**	**61,356**	**40,333**	**11,609**	**13,565**
0—5	23,718	11,820	11,898	11,820	11,898	...	...	...	...
5—10	21,490	11,992	9,498	11,885	9,342	89	108	18	48
10—15	21,033	12,857	8,176	12,317	6,296	498	1,815	42	65
15—20	24,456	16,433	8,023	12,499	1,656	3,714	6,131	220	236
20—40	89,603	61,906	27,697	19,651	1,514	37,385	23,317	4,870	2,866
40—60	37,671	22,452	15,219	1,761	499	16,450	7,772	4,241	6,948
60 and over	10,716	5,789	4,927	351	335	3,220	1,190	2,218	3,402
AHMADABAD	**216,777**	**117,302**	**99,475**	**46,298**	**24,033**	**62,746**	**55,809**	**8,258**	**19,633**
0—5	26,324	13,501	12,823	12,876	12,024	573	776	52	23
5—10	19,390	10,364	9,026	8,950	7,405	1,338	1,564	76	57
10—15	19,032	11,727	7,305	8,856	3,326	2,717	3,835	154	144
15—20	21,443	12,286	9,157	6,724	591	5,228	8,291	334	275
20—40	83,205	45,685	37,520	7,857	526	34,896	32,454	2,932	4,540
40—60	36,850	18,852	17,998	859	137	14,995	8,027	2,996	9,834
60 and over	10,533	4,887	5,646	176	24	2,999	862	1,712	4,760
BENARES	**203,804**	**105,815**	**97,989**	**43,446**	**27,450**	**53,082**	**45,707**	**9,287**	**24,832**
0—5	23,421	11,441	11,980	11,268	11,724	163	223	10	33
5—10	22,326	11,142	11,184	10,751	10,270	365	804	26	110
10—15	19,245	10,987	8,258	9,453	3,888	1,468	4,249	66	171
15—20	15,857	8,700	7,157	4,933	509	3,614	6,325	153	323
20—40	64,582	34,684	29,898	5,465	701	26,764	24,452	2,455	4,745
40—60	40,407	20,714	19,693	1,138	299	15,993	8,546	3,583	10,848
60 and over	17,966	8,147	9,819	438	109	4,715	1,108	2,994	8,602

AND CIVIL CONDITION.

CITY AND AGE.	POPULATION.			UNMARRIED.		MARRIED.		WIDOWED.	
	Persons.	Males.	Females.	Males.	Females.	Males.	Females.	Males.	Females.
1	2	3	4	5	6	7	8	9	10
AGRA	**185,449**	**101,335**	**84,114**	**43,540**	**26,063**	**48,589**	**43,466**	**9,206**	**14,585**
0—5	20,744	10,542	10,202	10,470	10,172	65	23	7	7
5—10	21,403	11,141	10,262	10,891	9,640	224	571	26	51
10—15	19,817	11,452	8,365	9,701	4,340	1,668	3,923	83	102
15—20	17,918	9,791	8,127	5,140	688	4,404	7,125	247	314
20—40	60,506	33,800	26,706	5,941	786	25,085	23,022	2,774	2,898
40—60	34,246	18,832	15,414	1,119	336	13,866	7,988	3,847	7,090
60 and over	10,815	5,777	5,038	278	101	3,277	814	2,222	4,128
HOWRAH	**179,006**	**114,566**	**64,440**	**40,155**	**15,961**	**69,083**	**32,378**	**5,328**	**16,101**
0—5	14,685	7,672	7,013	7,655	6,978	17	35	...	...
5—10	14,629	7,790	6,839	7,686	6,239	146	556	8	44
10—15	14,307	9,123	5,184	7,821	1,955	1,266	3,111	36	118
15—20	16,209	10,266	5,943	6,622	306	3,533	5,233	111	404
20—40	79,305	55,139	24,166	9,528	375	43,390	18,803	2,221	4,988
40—60	32,159	20,584	11,575	788	90	17,765	4,231	2,031	7,254
60 and over	7,712	3,992	3,720	105	18	2,966	409	921	3,293
CAWNPORE	**178,557**	**103,316**	**75,241**	**39,454**	**21,947**	**51,931**	**38,590**	**11,931**	**14,704**
0—5	17,562	8,818	8,744	8,818	8,744	...	...	...	...
5—10	16,359	8,211	8,148	7,981	7,765	218	369	12	14
10—15	14,194	8,455	5,739	7,486	3,437	930	2,239	39	63
15—20	13,763	7,923	5,840	5,019	619	2,689	4,962	265	259
20—40	72,718	44,075	28,643	8,921	1,034	30,416	24,057	4,738	3,552
40—60	34,278	20,653	13,625	991	249	15,033	6,342	4,629	7,034
60 and over	9,683	5,181	4,502	238	99	2,695	621	2,248	3,782
ALLAHABAD	**171,697**	**96,208**	**75,489**	**38,126**	**23,443**	**50,317**	**38,540**	**7,765**	**13,506**
0—5	19,876	10,057	9,819	0,923	9,650	127	150	7	19
5—10	18,870	9,682	9,188	9,182	8,275	463	843	37	70
10—15	15,881	9,139	6,742	7,431	3,317	1,648	3,339	60	86
15—20	14,477	8,826	6,151	4,411	757	3,742	5,230	173	164
20—40	62,581	36,797	25,784	6,237	1,101	27,979	21,771	2,581	2,912
40—60	30,152	17,113	13,039	755	250	13,392	6,391	2,966	6,398
60 and over	9,860	5,094	4,766	187	92	2,966	816	1,941	3,857
POONA	**158,856**	**85,319**	**73,537**	**41,392**	**22,491**	**39,219**	**34,391**	**4,708**	**16,655**
0—5	18,657	9,191	9,466	9,112	9,337	74	116	5	13
5—10	16,586	8,484	8,102	8,324	7,411	149	667	11	24
10—15	15,891	8,983	6,908	8,273	3,598	678	3,188	32	122
15—20	15,532	8,673	6,859	6,405	833	2,209	5,683	59	343
20—40	59,118	33,108	26,010	8,552	1,050	23,170	19,950	1,386	5,010
40—60	25,672	13,398	12,274	598	218	10,779	4,340	2,021	7,716
60 and over	7,400	3,482	3,918	128	44	2,190	447	1,194	3,427
AMRITSAR	**152,756**	**88,879**	**63,877**	**44,315**	**21,633**	**36,496**	**31.073**	**8,066**	**11,171**
0—5	15,660	8,102	7,558	8,102	7,558	...	...	...	...
5—10	16,144	8,691	7,453	8,667	7,390	24	53	...	10
10—15	17,403	10,543	6,860	10,020	5,341	498	1,485	25	34
15—20	14,414	9,114	5.300	6,606	839	2,371	4,322	137	139
20—40	53,783	32,450	21,333	9,316	375	20,322	18,548	2,812	2,410
40—60	27,478	15,687	11,791	1,320	95	11,093	6,013	3,274	5,683
60 and over	7,874	4,292	3,582	284	35	2,190	652	1,818	2,895
KARACHI	**151,903**	**90,233**	**61,670**	**44,546**	**23,492**	**40,847**	**29,365**	**4.838**	**8,813**
0—5	19,375	9,636	9,739	9,615	9,725	18	13	3	1
5—10	16,435	8,497	7,938	8,464	7,830	30	103	3	5
10—15	11,897	7,133	4,764	6,767	3,468	345	1,267	21	29
15—20	13,322	8,126	5,196	6,136	1,147	1,922	3,918	68	131
20—40	64,468	41,230	23,238	12,587	1,133	26,664	19,655	1,979	2,450
40—60	21.204	12,949	8,255	843	148	10,213	3,989	1,893	4,118
60 and over	5,202	2,662	2,540	136	41	1,655	420	371	2,079
MANDALAY	**136,299**	**69,718**	**68,581**	**37,110**	**31,410**	**28,207**	**25,188**	**4,401**	**11,983**
0—5	14,211	6,891	7,320	6,891	7,320	...	...	...	...
5—10	13,804	6,805	6,999	6,805	6,999	...	...	...	...
10—15	13,514	6,737	6,777	6,737	6,773	...	4	...	...
15—20	12,648	6,242	6,406	5,638	4,607	569	1,684	35	115
20—40	48,338	26,437	21,901	9,126	4,310	16,039	15,251	1,272	2,340
40—60	25,352	12,410	12,942	1,498	1,071	9,227	7,004	1,685	4,867
60 and over	10,432	4,196	6,236	415	830	2,872	1,245	1,409	4,661
JAIPUR	**137,098**	**70,846**	**66,252**	**26,686**	**14,784**	**36,769**	**35,179**	**7,391**	**16,289**
0—5	12,740	6,300	6,440	6,292	6,421	8	19	...	...
5—10	12,253	6,323	5,930	6,220	5,516	99	398	4	16
10—15	10,923	6,235	4,688	5,347	2,075	885	2,533	52	80
15—20	11,938	6,284	5,654	3,448	278	2,661	5,097	175	279
20—40	48,563	25,013	23,550	4,170	330	18,715	19,602	2,128	3,618
40—60	30,456	15,836	14,620	987	121	11,789	6,834	3,060	7,665
60 and over	10,225	4,855	5,370	222	43	2,662	696	1,971	4,631
PATNA	**136.153**	**70,841**	**65,312**	**28,944**	**18,453**	**35,527**	**30,831**	**6.370**	**16.028**
0—5	15,620	7,734	7,886	7,689	7,782	40	83	5	21
5—10	15,524	8,003	7,521	7,774	6,790	218	679	11	52
10—15	13,980	8,012	5,968	6,757	2,908	1,188	2,911	67	149
15—20	10,313	5,768	4,545	3,242	357	2,351	3,937	175	251
20—40	45,060	23,353	21,707	3,063	446	18,236	17,420	2,054	3,841
40—60	25,484	13,250	12,234	277	132	10,617	5,116	2,356	6,986
60 and over	10,172	4,721	5,451	142	38	2,877	685	1,702	4,728

TABLE VII.—Age, Sex and Civil Condition—*concluded*.

City and Age.	Population.			Unmarried.		Married.		Widowed.	
	Persons.	Males.	Females.	Males.	Females.	Males.	Females.	Males.	Females.
1	2	3	4	5	6	7	8	9	10
MADURA	**134,130**	**67,091**	**67,039**	**33,489**	**22,695**	**31,333**	**31,119**	**2,269**	**13,225**
0—5	15,561	7,586	7,975	7,583	7,960	3	15	...	...
5—10	14,987	7,395	7,592	7,378	7,515	17	71	...	6
10—15	14,789	7,762	7,027	7,619	5,388	141	1,615	2	24
15—20	13,896	7,239	6,657	6,232	1,197	997	5,285	10	175
20—40	44,008	22,138	21,870	4,351	499	17,258	18,060	529	3,311
40—60	23,398	11,566	11,832	270	111	10,355	5,530	941	6,191
60 and over	7,491	3,405	4,086	56	25	2,562	543	787	3,518
BAREILLY*	**117,521**	**62,127**	**55,394**	**29,675**	**20,202**	**27,310**	**25,674**	**5,142**	**9,518**
0—5	14,955	7,422	7,533	7,422	7,530	...	3	...	...
5—10	15,446	7,952	7,494	7,862	7,289	82	184	8	21
10—15	12,435	6,917	5,518	6,457	3,959	420	1,510	40	49
15—20	10,097	5,435	4,662	3,729	770	1,594	3,755	112	137
20—40	35,428	19,017	16,411	3,607	457	13,901	14,291	1,509	1,663
40—60	21,130	11,333	9,797	482	143	8,850	5,346	2,001	4,308
60 and over	8,030	4,051	3,979	116	54	2,463	585	1,472	3,340
SRINAGAR	**126,344**	**68,378**	**57,966**	**35,922**	**21,469**	**28,405**	**28,660**	**4,051**	**7,837**
0—5	16,407	8,162	8,245	8,162	8,245	...	...	...	...
5—10	16,752	8,384	8,368	8,370	8,320	14	45	...	3
10—15	13,825	8,061	5,764	7,753	4,325	304	1,421	4	13
15—20	11,149	6,421	4,728	5,029	400	1,334	4,173	58	155
20—40	40,911	22,027	18,884	5,721	140	15,241	17,246	1,065	1,498
40—60	21,253	11,968	9,285	738	28	9,484	5,362	1,746	3,895
60 and over	6,047	3,355	2,692	149	11	2,028	413	1,178	2,268
TRICHINOPOLY	**123,512**	**61,560**	**61,952**	**33,705**	**23,528**	**25,761**	**26,814**	**2,094**	**12,410**
0—5	15,596	7,613	7,983	7,613	7,982	...	1	...	...
5—10	15,410	7,658	7,752	7,643	7,698	15	50	...	4
10—15	13,992	7,533	6,459	7,460	5,531	73	924	...	4
15—20	12,161	6,294	5,867	5,634	1,605	660	4,186	...	76
20—40	38,026	18,992	19,034	4,912	608	13,627	15,788	453	2,643
40—60	20,738	10,126	10,612	374	90	8,944	4,565	808	5,957
60 and over	7,589	3,344	4,245	69	14	2,442	505	833	3,726
MEERUT	**116,227**	**66,286**	**49,941**	**29,647**	**16,374**	**29,965**	**25,946**	**6,674**	**7,621**
0—5	13,156	6,673	6,483	6,670	6,481	3	2	...	...
5—10	12,418	6,577	5,841	6,472	5,534	105	293	...	14
10—15	12,386	7,337	5,049	5,864	3,053	1,435	1,944	38	52
15—20	10,739	5,969	4,770	3,440	528	2,365	4,114	164	128
20—40	38,375	22,643	15,732	5,332	583	15,255	13,684	2,056	1,515
40—60	21,850	13,029	8,821	1,661	202	8,708	5,286	2,660	3,333
60 and over	7,303	4,058	3,245	208	43	2,094	623	1,756	2,579
SURAT	**114,868**	**59,634**	**55,234**	**24,500**	**15,621**	**30,166**	**29,066**	**4,968**	**10,527**
0—5	14,229	7,101	7,128	6,924	6,917	170	206	7	5
5—10	13,554	6,971	6,583	6,045	4,994	908	1,570	18	19
10—15	12,996	7,363	5,633	4,888	2,453	2,390	3,085	85	95
15—20	10,985	5,880	5,105	2,955	618	2,787	4,327	138	160
20—40	38,649	19,971	18,678	3,075	554	15,357	15,446	1,539	2,678
40—60	18,380	9,409	8,971	486	78	6,948	4,011	1,975	4,882
60 and over	6,075	2,939	3,136	127	7	1,606	441	1,206	2,688
DACCA	**108,551**	**63,091**	**45,460**	**29,246**	**15,181**	**31,848**	**20,550**	**1,997**	**9,729**
0—5	12,591	6,313	6,278	6,291	6,244	20	24	2	10
5—10	12,816	6,521	6,295	6,463	6,019	56	249	2	27
10—15	10,587	6,174	4,413	5,866	2,146	299	2,197	9	70
15—20	11,093	6,447	4,646	4,973	260	1,444	4,128	30	268
20—40	39,090	24,864	14,226	5,242	409	18,962	11,004	660	2,813
40—60	16,939	10,063	6,876	327	87	8,977	2,675	759	4,114
60 and over	5,435	2,709	2,726	84	16	2,090	278	535	2,432
NAGPUR	**101,415**	**53,696**	**47,719**	**22,659**	**14,064**	**27,430**	**23,926**	**3,607**	**9,739**
0—5	12,706	6,320	6,386	6,245	6,303	69	79	6	4
5—10	11,107	5,599	5,508	5,471	4,965	116	527	12	26
10—15	8,701	4,858	3,843	4,257	1,909	565	1,841	36	93
15—20	7,410	3,935	3,475	2,621	320	1,251	3,030	63	125
20—40	36,777	20,123	16,654	3,654	425	15,275	13,972	1,194	2,257
40—60	17,552	9,408	8,144	323	102	7,827	3,892	1,258	4,150
60 and over	7,162	3,453	3,709	88	40	2,327	585	1,038	3,084
BANGALORE CIVIL AND MILITARY STATION.	**100,834**	**51,752**	**49,082**	**29,229**	**20,449**	**20,310**	**19,843**	**2,213**	**8,790**
0—5	13,125	6,359	6,766	6,359	6,766	...	...	...	...
5—10	13,043	6,577	6,466	6,576	6,436	1	30	...	...
10—15	10,716	5,486	5,230	5,465	4,398	21	813	...	19
15—20	9,569	4,546	5,023	4,198	1,397	341	3,500	7	126
20—40	34,139	18,375	15,764	6,245	1,189	11,616	12,230	514	2,345
40—60	15,139	7,840	7,299	300	226	6,633	2,955	907	4,118
60 and over	5,103	2,569	2,534	86	37	1,698	315	785	2,182
JUBBULPORE	**100,651**	**56,035**	**44,616**	**26,156**	**14,111**	**26,539**	**22,387**	**3,340**	**8,118**
0—5	12,890	6,341	6,549	6,316	6,515	25	30	...	4
5—10	10,991	5,564	5,427	5,488	5,053	74	358	2	16
10—15	8,973	5,371	3,602	4,803	1,790	542	1,771	26	41
15—20	7,997	4,578	3,419	2,994	353	1,490	2,972	94	94
20—40	39,943	23,728	16,215	6,215	344	16,176	13,899	1,337	1,972
40—60	15,385	8,422	6,963	291	47	6,862	3,066	1,269	3,850
60 and over	4,472	2,031	2,441	49	9	1,370	291	612	2,141

* The figures for Bareilly do not include those for the cantonment, as its statistics by age periods are not available.

TABLE VIII.

Education.

TABLE VIII.—

City and Age.	Population. Total. Persons.	Population. Total. Males.	Population. Total. Females.	Population. Literate. Persons.	Population. Literate. Males.	Population. Literate. Females.	Population. Illiterate. Persons.	Population. Illiterate. Males.	Population. Illiterate. Females.	Literate in English. Persons.	Literate in English. Males.	Literate in English. Females.
1	2	3	4	5	6	7	8	9	10	11	12	13
CALCUTTA	**896,067**	**607,674**	**288,393**	**287,867**	**240,432**	**47,435**	**608,200**	**367,242**	**240,958**	**127,234**	**111,131**	**16,103**
0—10	129,837	67,675	62,162	15,204	10,330	4,874	114,633	57,345	57,288	5,202	3,819	1,383
10—15	67,743	43,478	24,265	25,937	19,301	6,636	41,806	24,177	17,629	12,568	10,497	2,071
15—20	82,641	56,316	26,325	33,322	26,470	6,852	49,319	29,846	19,473	15,983	13,941	2,042
20 and over	615,846	440,205	175,641	213,404	184,331	29,073	402,442	255,874	146,568	93,481	82,874	10,607
BOMBAY	**979,445**	**640,288**	**339,157**	**222,513**	**180,760**	**41,753**	**756,932**	**459,528**	**297,404**	**80,947**	**67,376**	**13,571**
0—10	131,531	67,400	64,131	9,157	5,792	3,365	122,374	61,608	60,766	1,982	1,161	821
10—15	76,285	48,224	28,061	19,439	14,292	5,147	56,846	33,932	22,914	6,247	4,645	1,602
15—20	106,150	68,339	37,811	27,627	21,489	6,138	78,523	46,850	31,673	10,617	8,514	2,103
20 and over	665,479	456,325	209,154	166,290	139,187	27,103	499,189	317,138	182,051	62,101	53,056	9,045
MADRAS	**518,660**	**266,465**	**252,195**	**144,758**	**112,258**	**32,500**	**373,902**	**154,207**	**219,695**	**56,695**	**48,043**	**8,652**
0—10	114,661	56,886	57,775	5,460	3,400	2,060	109,201	53,486	55,715	1,234	798	436
10—15	52,816	27,709	25,107	15,925	10,625	5,300	36,891	17,084	19,807	5,511	4,225	1,286
15—20	50,867	24,935	25,932	19,759	13,752	6,007	31,108	11,183	19,925	8,528	7,035	1,493
20 and over	300,316	156,935	143,381	103,614	84,481	19,133	196,702	72,454	124,248	41,422	35,985	5,437
HYDERABAD	**500,623**	**258,454**	**242,169**	**72,380**	**61,830**	**10,550**	**428,243**	**196,624**	**231,619**	**18,997**	**16,334**	**2,663**
0—10	103,930	50,973	52,957	2,207	1,504	703	101,723	49,469	52,254	567	337	230
10—15	50,101	26,715	23,386	6,545	4,974	1,571	43,556	21,741	21,815	1,753	1,376	377
15—20	44,170	21,417	22,753	8,299	6,606	1,693	35,871	14,811	21,060	2,448	2,061	387
20 and over	302,422	159,349	143,073	55,329	48,746	6,583	247,093	110,603	136,490	14,229	12,560	1,669
RANGOON	**293,316**	**208,111**	**85,205**	**121,978**	**91,348**	**30,630**	**171,338**	**116,763**	**54,575**	**31,472**	**25,204**	**6,268**
0—10	37,940	19,484	18,456	4,424	2,698	1,726	33,516	16,786	16,730	1,188	685	503
10—15	20,426	12,370	8,056	10,303	6,876	3,427	10,123	5,494	4,629	3,050	2,180	870
15—20	28,967	19,940	9,027	14,354	9,821	4,533	14,613	10,119	4,494	4,412	3,447	965
20 and over	205,983	156,317	49,666	92,897	71,953	20,944	113,086	84,364	28,722	22,822	18,892	3,930
LUCKNOW.	**259,798**	**144,785**	**115,013**	**33,179**	**28,256**	**4,923**	**226,619**	**116,529**	**110,090**	**14,177**	**12,323**	**1,854**
0—10	53,028	26,853	26,175	1,115	731	384	51,913	26,122	25,791	456	278	178
10—15	22,546	13,130	9,416	2,603	2,039	564	19,943	11,091	8,852	1,044	799	245
15—20	21,104	12,221	8,883	3,818	3,096	722	17,286	9,125	8,161	1,837	1,594	243
20 and over	163,120	92,581	70,539	25,643	22,390	3,253	137,477	70,191	67,286	10,840	9,652	1,188
DELHI	**232,837**	**133,864**	**98,973**	**27,354**	**23,893**	**3,461**	**205,483**	**109,971**	**95,512**	**7,151**	**6,633**	**518**
0—10	46,934	24,067	22,867	600	378	222	46,334	23,680	22,645	85	58	27
10—15	25,290	14,530	10,760	2,278	1,800	478	23,012	12,730	10,282	365	330	35
15—20	23.519	13,506	10,013	3,265	2,712	553	20,254	10,794	9,460	888	820	68
20 and over	137,094	81,761	55,333	21,211	19,003	2,208	115,883	62,758	53,125	5,813	5,425	388
LAHORE	**228,687**	**143,249**	**85,438**	**47,836**	**37,947**	**9,889**	**180,851**	**105,302**	**75,549**	**20,820**	**17,856**	**2,964**
0—10	45.208	23,812	21,396	1,809	1,070	739	43,399	22,742	20,657	450	267	183
10—15	21,033	12,857	8,176	5,482	3,516	1,966	15,551	9.341	6,210	1,785	1,302	483
15—20	24,456	16,433	8,023	8,186	5,653	2,533	16,270	10,780	5,490	3,464	2,772	692
20 and over	137,990	90,147	47,843	32,359	27,708	4,651	105,631	62,439	43,192	15,121	13,515	1,606
AHMADABAD	**216,777**	**117.302**	**99.475**	**17,218**	**14,148**	**3,070**	**199,559**	**103,154**	**96.405**	**2,444**	**2,141**	**303**
0—10	45,714	23,865	21,849	1,005	662	343	44,709	23,203	21,506	50	27	23
10—15	19,032	11,727	7,305	2,037	1,577	460	16,995	10,150	6,845	322	283	39
15—20	21,443	12,286	19,157	2,035	1,577	458	19,408	10,709	8,699	418	371	47
20 and over	130,588	69,424	61,164	12,141	10,332	1,809	118,447	59,092	59,355	1,654	1,460	194
BENARES.	**203,804**	**105,815**	**97,989**	**31,202**	**25,699**	**5,503**	**172,602**	**80,116**	**92,486**	**6,735**	**6,257**	**478**
0—10	45,747	22,583	23,164	1,443	1,021	422	44,304	21,562	22,742	201	161	40
10—15	19,245	10,987	8,258	2,895	2,284	611	16,350	8,703	7,647	795	742	53
15—20	15,857	8,700	7,157	3,462	2,786	676	12,395	5,914	6,481	1,048	988	60
20 and over	122,955	63,545	59,410	23,402	19,608	3,794	99,553	43,937	55,616	4,691	4,366	325

EDUCATION.

CITY AND AGE.	POPULATION.									LITERATE IN ENGLISH.		
	TOTAL.			LITERATE.			ILLITERATE.					
	Persons.	Males.	Females.	Persons.	Males.	Females.	Persons.	Males.	Females.	Persons.	Males.	Females.
1	2	3	4	5	6	7	8	9	10	11	12	13
AGRA	**185,449**	**101,335**	**84,114**	**21,088**	**18,085**	**3,003**	**164,361**	**83,250**	**81,111**	**7,398**	**6,575**	**823**
0—10 . .	42,147	21,683	20,464	991	713	278	41,156	20,970	20,186	272	205	67
10—15 . .	19,817	11,452	8,365	2,148	1,743	405	17,669	9,709	7,960	658	574	84
15—20 . .	17,918	9,791	8,127	2,995	2,508	487	14,923	7,283	7,640	865	757	108
20 and over .	105,567	58,409	47,158	14,954	13,121	1,833	90,613	45,288	45,325	5,603	5,039	564
HOWRAH .	**179,006**	**114,566**	**64,440**	**46,705**	**40,532**	**6,173**	**132,301**	**74,034**	**58,267**	**21,583**	**19,580**	**2,013**
0—10 . .	29,314	15,462	13,852	3,626	2,809	817	25,688	12,653	13,035	1,549	1,202	347
10—15 . .	14,307	9,123	5,184	4,676	3,524	1,152	9,631	5,599	4,032	2,214	1,797	417
15—20 . .	16,209	10,266	5,943	5,358	4,171	1,187	10,851	6,095	4,756	2,541	2,191	350
20 and over .	119,176	79,715	39,461	33,045	30,028	3,017	86,131	49,687	36,444	15,289	14,390	899
CAWNPORE	**178,557**	**103,316**	**75,241**	**23,504**	**20,714**	**2,790**	**155,053**	**82,602**	**72,451**	**6,576**	**5,426**	**1,150**
0—10 . .	33,921	17,029	16,892	733	442	291	33,188	16,587	16,601	256	131	125
10—15 . .	14,194	8,455	5,739	1,784	1,425	359	12,410	7,030	5,380	438	302	136
15—20 . .	13,763	7,923	5,840	2,283	1 943	340	11,480	5,980	5,500	667	535	132
20 and over .	116,679	69,909	46,770	18,704	16,904	1,800	97,975	53,005	44,970	5,215	4,458	757
ALLAHABAD	**171,697**	**96,208**	**75,489**	**22,219**	**18,396**	**3,823**	**149,478**	**77,812**	**71,666**	**9,657**	**7,868**	**1,789**
0—10 . .	38,746	19,739	19,007	1,339	960	379	37,407	18,779	18,628	415	270	145
10—15 . .	15,881	9,139	6,742	2,735	2,160	575	13,146	6,979	6,167	1,113	858	255
15—20 . .	14,477	8,326	6,151	2,850	2,825	525	11,627	6,001	5,626	1,473	1,226	247
20 and over .	102,593	59,004	43,589	15,295	12,951	2,344	87,298	46,053	41,245	6,656	5,514	1,142
POONA . .	**158,856**	**85,319**	**73,537**	**39,668**	**31,705**	**7,963**	**119,188**	**53,614**	**65,574**	**15,352**	**12,923**	**2,429**
0—10 . .	35,243	17,675	17,568	2,123	1,495	628	33,120	16,180	16,940	396	199	197
10—15 . .	15,891	8,983	6,908	5,150	3,829	1,321	10,741	5,154	5,587	1,487	1,141	346
15—20 . .	15,532	8,673	6,859	5,797	4,556	1,241	9,735	4,117	5,618	2,754	2,348	406
20 and over .	92,190	49,988	42,202	26,598	21,825	4,773	65,592	28,163	37,429	10,715	9,235	1,480
AMRITSAR .	**152,756**	**8,879**	**63,877**	**18,479**	**16,533**	**1,946**	**134,277**	**72,346**	**61,931**	**3,668**	**3,333**	**335**
0—10 . .	31,804	16,703	15,011	418	339	79	31,386	16,454	14,932	23	9	14
10—15 . .	17,403	10,543	6,860	1,636	1,367	269	15,767	9,176	6,591	274	215	59
15—20 . .	14,414	9,114	5,300	2,371	2,098	273	12,043	7,016	5,027	643	584	59
20 and over .	89,135	52,429	36,706	14,054	12,729	1,325	75,081	39,700	35,381	2,728	2,525	203
KARACHI .	**151,903**	**90,233**	**61,670**	**32,502**	**28,595**	**3,907**	**119,401**	**61,638**	**57,763**	**11,494**	**9,522**	**1,972**
0—10 . .	35,810	18,133	17,677	1,201	797	404	34,609	17,336	17,273	400	202	198
10—15 . .	11,897	7,133	4,764	2,744	2,242	502	9,153	4,891	4,262	811	579	232
15—20 . .	13,322	8,126	5,196	3,976	3,488	488	9,346	4,638	4,708	1,455	1,191	264
20 and over .	90,874	56,841	34,033	24,581	22,068	2,513	66,293	34,773	31,520	8,828	7,550	1,278
MANDALAY	**138,299**	**69,718**	**68,581**	**54,166**	**41,760**	**12,406**	**84,133**	**27,958**	**56,175**	**3,151**	**2,477**	**674**
0—10 . .	28,015	13,696	14,319	1,247	822	425	26,768	12,874	13,894	199	122	77
10—15 . .	13,514	6,737	6,777	4,783	3,447	1,336	8,731	3,290	5,441	387	259	128
15—20 . .	12,648	6,242	6,406	6,482	4,637	1,845	6,166	1,605	4,561	533	411	122
20 and over .	84,122	43,043	41,079	41,654	32,854	8,800	42,468	10,189	32,279	2,032	1,685	347
JAIPUR .	**137,098**	**70,847**	**66,251**	**14,351**	**13,469**	**882**	**122,747**	**57,378**	**65,369**	**1,646**	**1,569**	**77**
0—10 . .	24,993	12,623	12,370	256	210	46	24,737	12,413	12,324	32	27	5
10—15 . .	10,923	6,235	4,688	917	834	83	10,006	5,401	4,605	155	150	5
15—20 . .	11,938	6,284	5,654	1,547	1,423	124	10,391	4,861	5,530	328	322	6
20 and over .	89,244	45,705	43,539	11,631	11,002	629	77,613	34,703	42,910	1,131	1,070	61
PATNA .	**136,153**	**70,841**	**65,312**	**20,049**	**17,838**	**2,211**	**116,104**	**53,003**	**63,101**	**4,770**	**4,293**	**477**
0—10 . .	31,144	15,737	15,407	655	496	159	30,489	15,241	15,248	162	114	48
10—15 . .	13,980	8,012	5,968	2,282	1,921	361	11,698	6,091	5,607	504	383	121
15—20 . .	10,313	5,768	4,545	2,631	2,289	342	7,682	3,479	4,203	904	825	79
20 and over .	80,716	41,324	39,392	14,481	13,132	1,349	66,235	28,192	38,043	3,200	2,971	229

TABLE VIII.—Education—*concluded.*

City and Age.	Population.									Literate in English.		
	Total.			Literate.			Illiterate.					
	Persons.	Males.	Females.	Persons.	Males.	Females.	Persons.	Males.	Females.	Persons.	Males.	Females.
	2	3	4	5	6	7	8	9	10	11	12	13
MADURA	**134,136**	**67,091**	**67,039**	**30,991**	**27,656**	**3,335**	**103,139**	**39,435**	**63,704**	**5,675**	**5,136**	**539**
0—10	30,548	14,981	15,567	902	709	193	29,646	14,272	15,374	67	50	17
10—15	14,789	7,762	7,027	3,987	3,260	727	10,802	4,502	6,300	777	676	101
15—20	13,896	7,239	6,657	4,458	3,876	582	9,438	3,363	6,075	1,118	986	132
20 and over	74,897	37,109	37,788	21,644	19,811	1,833	53,253	17,298	35,955	3,713	3,424	289
BAREILLY*	**117,521**	**62,127**	**55,394**	**10,012**	**8,661**	**1,351**	**107,509**	**53,466**	**54,043**	**2,248**	**2,041**	**207**
0—10	30,401	15,374	15,027	545	411	134	29,856	14,963	14,893	46	35	11
10—15	12,435	6,917	5,518	1,091	892	199	11,344	6,025	5,319	176	169	7
15—20	10,097	5,435	4,662	1,262	1,046	216	8,835	4,389	4,446	389	345	44
20 and over	64,588	34,401	30,187	7,114	6,312	802	57,474	28,089	29,385	1,637	1,492	145
SRINAGAR	**126,344**	**68,378**	**57,966**	**10,609**	**10,493**	**116**	**115,735**	**57,885**	**57,850**	**2,975**	**2,910**	**65**
0—10	33,159	16,546	16,613	237	230	7	32,922	16,316	16,606	72	70	2
10—15	13,825	8,061	5,764	1,169	1,155	14	12,656	6,906	5,750	481	479	2
15—20	11,149	6,421	4,728	1,208	1,199	9	9,941	5,222	4,719	733	728	5
20 and over	68,211	37,350	30,861	7,995	7,909	86	60,216	29,441	30,775	1,689	1,633	56
TRICHINOPOLY	**123,512**	**61,560**	**61,952**	**31,983**	**26,650**	**5,333**	**91,529**	**34,910**	**56,619**	**8,937**	**8,126**	**811**
0—10	31,006	15,271	15,735	1,181	842	339	29,825	14,429	15,396	150	95	55
10—15	13,992	7,533	6,459	3,931	2,963	968	10,061	4,570	5,491	964	810	154
15—20	12,161	6,294	5,867	4,843	3,818	1,025	7,318	2,476	4,842	1,838	1,662	176
20 and over	66,353	32,462	33,891	22,028	19,027	3,001	44,325	13,435	30,890	5,985	5,559	426
MEERUT	**116,227**	**66,286**	**49,941**	**16,015**	**14,543**	**1,472**	**100,212**	**51,743**	**48,469**	**4,707**	**4,513**	**194**
0—10	25,574	13,250	12,324	734	613	121	24,840	12,637	12,203	77	73	4
10—15	12,386	7,337	5,049	1,676	1,301	375	10,710	6,036	4,674	354	314	40
15—20	10,739	5,969	4,770	1,576	1,397	179	9,163	4,572	4,591	407	401	6
20 and over	67,528	39,730	27,798	12,029	11,232	797	55,499	28,498	27,001	3,869	3,725	144
SURAT	**114,868**	**59,634**	**55,234**	**31,278**	**25,405**	**5,873**	**83,590**	**34,229**	**49,361**	**4,347**	**4,045**	**302**
0—10	27,783	14,072	13,711	1,621	1,202	419	26,162	12,870	13,292	11	5	6
10—15	12,996	7,363	5,633	4,694	3,690	1,004	8,302	3,673	4,629	485	437	48
15—20	10,985	5,880	5,105	4,078	3,152	926	6,907	2,728	4,179	842	775	67
20 and over	63,104	32,319	30,785	20,885	17,361	3,524	42,219	14,958	27,261	3,009	2,828	181
DACCA	**108,551**	**63,091**	**5,460**	**28,937**	**24,479**	**4,518**	**79,554**	**38,612**	**40,942**	**11,408**	**10,714**	**694**
0—10	25,407	12,834	12,573	1,497	1,070	427	23,910	11,764	12,146	391	342	49
10—15	10,587	6,174	4,413	3,018	2,261	757	7,569	3,913	3,656	1,245	1,089	156
15—20	11,093	6,447	4,646	4,310	3,578	732	6,783	2,869	3,914	2,210	2,092	118
20 and over	61,464	37,636	23,828	20,172	17,570	2,602	41,292	20,066	21,226	7,562	7,191	371
NAGPUR	**101,415**	**53,696**	**47,719**	**13,854**	**11,686**	**2,168**	**87,561**	**42,010**	**45,551**	**5,591**	**4,732**	**859**
0—10	23,813	11,919	11,894	632	407	225	23,181	11,512	11,669	185	111	74
10—15	8,701	4,858	3,843	1,243	954	289	7,458	3,904	3,554	467	381	86
15—20	7,410	3,935	3,475	1,573	1,257	316	5,837	2,678	3,159	761	628	133
20 and over	61,491	32,984	28,507	10,406	9,068	1,338	51,085	23,916	27,169	4,178	3,612	566
BANGALORE CIVIL AND MILITARY STATION	**100,834**	**51,752**	**49,082**	**24,094**	**18,303**	**5,791**	**76,740**	**33,449**	**43,291**	**11,451**	**8,105**	**3,346**
0—10	26,168	12,936	13,232	1,004	581	423	25,164	12,355	12,809	556	303	253
10—15	10,716	5,486	5,230	2,374	1,513	861	8,342	3,973	4,369	1,187	742	445
15—20	9,569	4,546	5,023	2,807	1,889	918	6,762	2,657	4,105	1,339	867	472
20 and over	54,381	28,784	25,597	17,909	14,320	3,589	36,472	14,464	22,008	8,369	6,193	2,176
JUBBULPORE	**100,651**	**56,035**	**44,616**	**19,298**	**16,815**	**2,483**	**81,353**	**39,220**	**42,133**	**7,519**	**6,468**	**1,051**
0—10	23,881	11,905	11,976	773	563	210	23,108	11,342	11,766	228	131	97
10—15	8,973	5,371	3,602	1,873	1,546	327	7,100	3,825	3,275	507	393	114
15—20	7,997	4,578	3,419	2,231	1,824	407	5,766	2,754	3,012	802	664	138
20 and over	59,800	34,181	25,619	14,421	12,882	1,539	45,379	21,299	24,080	5,982	5,280	702

* The figures for Bareilly do not include those for the cantonment, as its statistics by age periods are not available.

TABLE XI.

Birthplace.

In this Table figures for Assam, Bengal and Bihar and Orissa as now constituted could not be given in all cases, as, in many Provinces the Table was compiled long before the new arrangement of Provinces had been announced. Bengal (Old) and Eastern Bengal and Assam therefore appear in this- Tablo in some cases.

The figures for Madras in this Table are exclusive of those for Cochin and Travancore.

TABLE XI.—Distribution of

Birthplace.	Population.		
	Persons.	Males.	Females.
1	2	3	4
1. CALCUTTA	**896,067**	**607,674**	**288,393**
A.—Born in India	**883,063**	**597,567**	**285,496**
Bengal	539,374	319,573	219,801
Calcutta	*256,719*	*136,549*	*120,170*
24-Parganas	*88,372*	*47,793*	*40,579*
Hooghly	*48,032*	*33,413*	*14,619*
Midnapore	*28,713*	*18,513*	*10,200*
Burdwan	*21,368*	*12,904*	*8,464*
Dacca	*16,574*	*13,240*	*3,334*
Elsewhere	*79,596*	*57,161*	*22,435*
Bihar and Orissa	204,484	172,649	31,835
United Provinces	89,695	69,921	19,774
Rajputana Agency	20,888	13,976	6,912
Punjab	8,635	6,736	1,899
Bombay	5,130	3,650	1,480
Assam	5,013	4,310	703
Madras	2,944	1,891	1,053
C. P. and Berar	2,666	1,630	1,036
Central India Agency	1,234	1,060	174
Burma	650	359	291
N.-W. F. Province	482	421	61
Kashmir State	203	171	32
Mysore State	194	113	81
Ajmer-Merwara	153	105	48
Elsewhere	228	134	94
French and Portuguese Settlements	1,090	868	222
B.—Born in Countries beyond India	**12,973**	**10,090**	**2,883**
China	2,349	2,026	323
Nepal	758	632	126
Afghanistan	542	484	58
Arabia	357	238	119
Persia	303	245	58
Turkey in Asia	118	54	64
Japan	116	29	87
Ceylon	81	51	30
England and Wales	5,111	4,007	1,104
Scotland	1,034	824	210
Ireland	424	289	135
Germany	256	214	42
Austria-Hungary	142	96	46
France	114	70	44
Russia	112	34	78
Italy	95	57	38
Greece	60	51	9
Belgium	53	44	9
Turkey in Europe	51	35	16
Australia	150	87	63
Elsewhere	747	523	224
C.—Born at Sea	**31**	**17**	**14**
2. BOMBAY	**979,445**	**640,288**	**339,157**
A.—Born in India	**964,626**	**628,829**	**335,797**
Bombay	814,896	514,356	300,540
Ratnagiri	*216,060*	*143,498*	*72,562*
Bombay	*191,581*	*103,367*	*88,214*
Poona	*71,185*	*42,114*	*29,071*
Kathiawar	*58,775*	*38,586*	*20,189*
Satara	*56,754*	*39,818*	*16,936*
Kolaba	*37,119*	*23,580*	*13,539*
Cutch	*36,470*	*25,000*	*11,470*
Surat	*35,072*	*24,331*	*10,741*
Ahmadabad	*16,298*	*11,925*	*4,373*
Thana	*15,705*	*10,112*	*5,593*
Ahmadnagar	*14,611*	*8,979*	*5,632*
Elsewhere	*65,266*	*43,046*	*22,220*
United Provinces	50,682	40,279	10,403
Rajputana Agency	12,453	10,852	1,601
Hyderabad State	9,302	5,681	3,621
Punjab	8,616	7,240	1,376
Madras	8,278	5,981	2,297
Ajmer-Merwara	6,937	5,853	1,084
Baroda State	4,501	3,255	1,246
Central India Agency	4,055	3,010	1,045
Elsewhere	12,800	9,090	3,710
French and Portuguese Settlements	32,106	23,232	8,874
B.—Born in Countries beyond India	**14,803**	**11,457**	**3,346**
Persia	2,442	1,690	752
Arabia	2,322	1,901	421
Afghanistan	1,167	1,039	128
China	476	416	60
Turkey in Asia	291	226	65
Japan	270	141	129
England and Wales	4,878	3,896	982
Scotland	539	426	113
Ireland	342	249	93
Germany	257	202	55
Austria-Hungary	206	136	70
Italy	175	148	27
France	135	55	80
Elsewhere	1,303	932	371
Birthplace not returned	**16**	**2**	**14**
3. MADRAS	**518,660**	**266,465**	**252,195**
A.—Born in India	**515,641**	**264,347**	**251,294**
Madras	496,788	253,010	243,778
Madras	*345,317*	*172,729*	*172,588*
Chingleput	*69,576*	*34,447*	*35,129*
North Arcot	*23,667*	*12,526*	*11,141*
South Arcot	*9,859*	*5,049*	*4,310*
Tanjore	*9,496*	*5,352*	*4,144*
Elsewhere	*38,873*	*22,907*	*15,966*
Mysore State	5,341	2,924	2,417
Bombay	2,732	1,713	1,019
Hyderabad State	2,318	1,448	870
C. P. and Berar	995	579	416
Burma	794	391	403
United Provinces	678	491	187
Travancore State	634	461	173
Bengal	633	435	198
Elsewhere	2,539	1,811	728
French and Portuguese Settlements	2,189	1,084	1,105
B.—Born in Countries beyond India	**3,017**	**2,117**	**900**
England and Wales	1,603	1,250	353
Ireland	208	80	128
Scotland	186	137	49
Germany	98	88	15
Elsewhere	922	567	355
C.—Born at Sea	**2**	**1**	**1**
4. HYDERABAD	**500,623**	**258,454**	**242,169**
A.—Born in India	**494,788**	**253,375**	**241,413**
Hyderabad State	449,623	226,017	223,606
Hyderabad	*387,451*	*190,292*	*197,159*
Atraf-i-balda	*16,563*	*8,632*	*7,931*
Medak	*10,595*	*6,158*	*4,437*
Mahbubnagar	*4,662*	*2,913*	*1,749*
Nizamabad	*4,610*	*3,006*	*1,604*
Gulbarga	*4,047*	*2,363*	*1,684*
Aurangabad	*4,017*	*2,363*	*1,654*
Elsewhere	*17,678*	*10,290*	*7,388*
Madras	15,118	8,165	6,953
United Provinces	6,824	4,647	2,177
Rajputana Agency	6,417	4,200	2,217
Punjab	3,935	2,976	959
Bombay	3,634	2,122	1,512
C. P. and Berar	3,112	1,440	1,672
Mysore State	2,347	1,343	1,004
Ajmer-Merwara	1,096	670	426
Elsewhere	2,463	1,654	809
French and Portuguese Settlements	219	141	78
B.—Born in Countries beyond India	**5,832**	**5,077**	**755**
Arabia	1,684	1,425	259
Afghanistan	180	163	17
Persia	67	42	25
England and Wales	3,437	3,120	317
Ireland	95	66	29
Italy	61	40	21
Scotland	49	39	10
Elsewhere	259	182	77
C.—Born at Sea	**3**	**2**	**1-**

Population by Birthplace.

Birthplace.	Population.		
	Persons.	Males.	Females.
1	2	3	4
5. RANGOON	**293,316**	**208,111**	**85,205**
A.—Born in India	**275,885**	**193,630**	**82,255**
Burma	122,407	62,914	59,493
Rangoon	*91,446*	*44,332*	*47,114*
Mandalay	*6,189*	*3,561*	*2,628*
Hanthawaddy	*4,266*	*2,559*	*1,707*
Amherst	*4,146*	*2,107*	*2,039*
Prome	*1,882*	*1,093*	*789*
Pegu	*1,669*	*1,119*	*550*
Elsewhere	*12,809*	*8,143*	*4,666*
Madras	90,828	74,377	16,451
United Provinces	22,348	20,600	1,748
E. B. and Assam	17,397	17,045	352
Bengal (Old)	9,266	7,655	1,611
Bombay	5,463	4,161	1,302
Punjab	3,978	3,507	471
Elsewhere	3,465	2,732	733
French and Portuguese Settlements	733	639	94
B.—Born in Countries beyond India	**17,431**	**14,481**	**2,950**
China	11,759	9,991	1,768
Japan	341	129	212
Straits Settlements and Malaya	334	242	92
Ceylon	219	162	57
Nepal	122	114	8
Persia	122	105	17
England and Wales	2,543	2,183	360
Scotland	580	494	86
Ireland	213	137	76
Germany	153	135	18
Austria-Hungary	112	111	1
Elsewhere	933	678	255
6. LUCKNOW	**259,798**	**144,785**	**115,013**
A.—Born in India	**255,423**	**141,097**	**114,326**
United Provinces	243,789	133,548	110,241
Lucknow	*144,275*	*74,957*	*69,318*
Bara Banki	*12,758*	*8,303*	*4,455*
Gonda	*4,834*	*3,331*	*1,503*
Unao	*4,766*	*2,570*	*2,196*
Rae Bareli	*4,499*	*2,736*	*1,763*
Sitapur	*3,807*	*2,394*	*1,413*
Hardoi	*2,775*	*1,650*	*1,125*
Elsewhere	*66,075*	*37,607*	*28,468*
Punjab	4,575	3,311	1,264
Bengal (Old)	3,323	1,907	1,416
Rajputana Agency	549	325	224
Central India Agency	524	279	245
Elsewhere	2,663	1,727	936
B.—Born in Countries beyond India	**4,372**	**3,687**	**685**
United Kingdom	3,534	3,100	434
Elsewhere	838	587	251
C.—Born at Sea	**3**	**1**	**2**
7. DELHI	**232,837**	**133,864**	**98,973**
A.—Born in India	**231,845**	**133,032**	**98,813**
Punjab	172,590	96,666	75,924
Delhi	*148,677*	*80,842*	*67,835*
Gurgaon	*7,632*	*4,382*	*3,250*
Rohtak	*4,279*	*2,724*	*1,555*
Hissar	*1,755*	*1,063*	*692*
Patiala	*1,639*	*1,112*	*527*
Karnal	*1,058*	*646*	*412*
Elsewhere	*7,550*	*5,897*	*1,653*
United Provinces	34,817	21,005	13,812
Rajputana Agency	19,510	11,886	7,624
Central India Agency	1,103	639	464
N.-W. F. Province	1,044	960	84
Bengal (Old)	1,004	650	354
Elsewhere	1,774	1,226	548
French and Portuguese Settlements	3	..	3
B.—Born in Countries beyond India	**992**	**832**	**160**
Afghanistan	258	251	7
England and Wales	496	392	104
Elsewhere	238	189	49
8. LAHORE	**228,687**	**143,249**	**85,438**
A.—Born in India	**224,661**	**140,168**	**84,493**
Punjab	205,235	126,097	79,138
Lahore	*128,970*	*72,142*	*56,828*
Amritsar	*18,348*	*12,977*	*5,371*
Sialkot	*9,936*	*6,771*	*3,165*
Gujranwala	*7,029*	*4,306*	*2,723*
Hoshiarpur	*6,047*	*5,305*	*742*
Ferozepore	*4,620*	*3,567*	*1,053*
Elsewhere	*30,285*	*21,029*	*9,256*
United Provinces	9,304	6,966	2,338
N.-W. F. Province	3,106	2,418	688
Kashmir State	2,720	2,120	600
Rajputana Agency	1,105	701	404
Bombay	760	432	328
Bengal (Old)	650	319	331
Madras	252	152	100
Baluchistan	233	146	87
Burma	233	186	47
Central India Agency	226	145	81
Ajmer-Merwara	216	165	51
Elsewhere	621	321	300
B.—Born in Countries beyond India	**4,626**	**3,681**	**945**
Afghanistan	909	660	249
Persia	118	65	53
Arabia	65	46	19
England and Wales	2,254	1,871	383
Ireland	219	127	92
Scotland	139	86	53
Portugal	78	73	5
Elsewhere	244	153	91
9. AHMADABAD	**216,777**	**117,302**	**99,475**
A.—Born in India	**216,313**	**116,980**	**99,333**
Bombay	170,205	89,919	80,286
Ahmadabad	*138,790*	*72,208*	*66,582*
Kathiawar	*8,335*	*4,662*	*3,673*
Kaira	*7,020*	*3,965*	*3,055*
Mahi Kantha	*4,780*	*2,773*	*2,007*
Palanpur	*4,452*	*2,527*	*1,925*
Surat	*2,059*	*1,184*	*875*
Elsewhere	*4,769*	*2,600*	*2,169*
Baroda State	28,001	15,830	12,171
Rajputana Agency	9,226	4,936	4,290
Ajmer-Merwara	2,648	1,971	677
United Provinces	2,581	1,892	689
Elsewhere	3,652	2,432	1,220
B.—Born in Countries beyond India	**464**	**322**	**142**
Afghanistan	107	84	23
England and Wales	83	56	27
Elsewhere	274	182	92
10. BENARES	**203,804**	**105,815**	**97,989**
A.—Born in India	**203,026**	**105,394**	**97,632**
United Provinces	181,794	94,553	87,241
Benares	*158,032*	*81,272*	*76,760*
Jaunpur	*4,251*	*2,346*	*1,905*
Azamgarh	*3,918*	*2,325*	*1,593*
Mirzapur	*3,872*	*1,808*	*2,064*
Ghazipur	*3,224*	*1,739*	*1,485*
Allahabad	*1,077*	*500*	*577*
Elsewhere	*7,420*	*4,563*	*2,857*
Bengal (Old)	13,258	5,933	7,325
Punjab	2,449	1,850	599
Rajputana Agency	1,282	780	502
Central India Agency	780	436	344
Elsewhere	3,463	1,842	1,621
B.—Born in Countries beyond India	**778**	**421**	**357**
United Kingdom	329	254	75
Elsewhere	449	167	282

TABLE XI.—DISTRIBUTION

BIRTHPLACE.	POPULATION.		
	Persons.	Males.	Females.
1	2	3	4
11. AGRA	**185,449**	**101,335**	**84,114**
A.—Born in India	**182,715**	**98,916**	**83,799**
United Provinces	169,958	92,307	77,651
Agra	*150,999*	*81,149*	*69,850*
Muttra	*4,179*	*2,249*	*1,930*
Aligarh	*2,234*	*1,215*	*1,019*
Etah	*1,152*	*607*	*545*
Mainpuri	*1,142*	*601*	*541*
Elsewhere	*10,252*	*6,486*	*3,766*
Rajputana Agency	6,674	3,571	3,103
Central India Agency	1,987	1,056	931
Punjab	1,761	999	762
Bengal (Old)	711	369	342
Elsewhere	1,624	614	1,010
B.—Born in Countries beyond India	**2,734**	**2,419**	**315**
United Kingdom	1,435	1,319	116
Elsewhere	1,299	1,100	199
12 HOWRAH	**179,006**	**114,566**	**64,440**
A.—Born in India	**178,419**	**114,094**	**64,325**
Bengal	99,244	59,424	39,820
Howrah	*43,639*	*25,607*	*18,032*
Hooghly	*29,010*	*18,113*	*10,897*
Calcutta	*9,847*	*5,401*	*4,446*
Midnapore	*6,047*	*3,890*	*2,157*
24-Parganas	*4,031*	*2,171*	*1,860*
Burdwan	*2,247*	*1,488*	*759*
Dacca	*1,365*	*964*	*401*
Elsewhere	*3,058*	*1,790*	*1,268*
Bihar and Orissa	38,831	27,783	11,048
United Provinces	37,946	25,198	12,748
Rajputana Agency	513	316	197
Punjab	458	327	131
Assam	408	387	21
Madras	283	151	132
Bombay	258	189	69
C. P. and Berar	252	137	115
Elsewhere	208	168	40
French and Portuguese Settlements	18	14	4
B.—Born in Countries beyond India	**587**	**472**	**115**
Afghanistan	116	115	1
England and Wales	164	117	47
Scotland	133	112	21
Elsewhere	174	128	46
13. CAWNPORE	**178,557**	**103,316**	**75,241**
A.—Born in India	**176,447**	**101,566**	**74,881**
United Provinces	167,379	95,677	71,702
Cawnpore	*102,090*	*57,846*	*44,244*
Unao	*13,497*	*7,464*	*6,033*
Lucknow	*5,422*	*3,088*	*2,334*
Rae Bareli	*3,368*	*1,970*	*1,398*
Furrukhabad	*3,276*	*1,999*	*1,277*
Allahabad	*3,004*	*1,736*	*1,268*
Fatehpur	*2,914*	*1,698*	*1,216*
Jalaun	*2,389*	*1,196*	*1,193*
Sultanpur	*2,277*	*1,633*	*644*
Hamirpur	*2,035*	*1,146*	*889*
Elsewhere	*27,107*	*15,901*	*11,206*
Punjab	3,157	2,381	776
Central India Agency	1,820	1,067	753
Bengal (Old)	1,344	885	459
Rajputana Agency	1,333	794	539
Elsewhere	1,414	762	652
B.—Born in Countries beyond India	**2,110**	**1,750**	**360**
United Kingdom	862	682	180
Elsewhere	1,248	1,068	180
14. ALLAHABAD	**171,697**	**96,208**	**75,48**
A.—Born in India	**169,449**	**94,639**	**74,810**
United Provinces	161,127	88,969	72,158
Allahabad	*142,509*	*77,409*	*65,100*
Partabgarh	*2,951*	*2,064*	*887*
Jaunpur	*2,087*	*1,141*	*946*
Mirzapur	*1,681*	*1,014*	*667*
Elsewhere	*11,899*	*7,341*	*4,558*
Bengal (Old)	2,928	1,826	1,102
Punjab	1,241	813	428
Central India Agency	811	511	300
Rajputana Agency	279	179	100
Elsewhere	3,063	2,341	722
B.—Born in Countries beyond India	**2,248**	**1,569**	**679**
United Kingdom	1,765	1,314	451
Elsewhere	483	255	228
15. POONA	**158,856**	**85,319**	**73,537**
A.—Born in India	**155,294**	**82,293**	**73,001**
Bombay	141,646	73,789	67,857
Poona	*105,150*	*53,162*	*51,988*
Satara	*7,595*	*4,578*	*3,017*
Ahmadnagar	*4,434*	*2,386*	*2,048*
Ratnagiri	*3,883*	*2,253*	*1,630*
Sholapur	*3,807*	*1,866*	*1,941*
Bombay	*2,546*	*1,241*	*1,305*
Elsewhere	*14,231*	*8,303*	*5,928*
Hyderabad State	3,627	1,991	1,636
Punjab	1,580	968	612
Rajputana Agency	1,490	1,124	366
C. P. and Berar	1,300	753	547
Madras	1,272	570	702
United Provinces	1,134	830	304
Elsewhere	2,431	1,533	898
French and Portuguese Settlements	814	735	79
B.—Born in Countries beyond India	**3,562**	**3,026**	**536**
Persia	222	120	102
England and Wales	2,836	2,584	252
Ireland	180	136	44
Scotland	122	77	45
Elsewhere	202	109	93
16. AMRITSAR	**152,756**	**88,879**	**63,877**
A.—Born in India	**152,296**	**88,494**	**63,802**
Punjab	145,875	83,769	62,106
Amritsar	*121,938*	*67,420*	*54,518*
Gurdaspur	*5,793*	*3,789*	*2,004*
Sialkot	*3,249*	*2,156*	*1,093*
Hoshiarpur	*2,878*	*2,328*	*550*
Lahore	*2,541*	*1,468*	*1,073*
Elsewhere	*9,476*	*6,603*	*2,868*
United Provinces	2,651	1,834	817
Kashmir State	1,795	1,597	198
Rajputana Agency	1,075	726	349
Elsewhere	897	567	330
French and Portuguese Settlements	3	1	2
B.—Born in Countries beyond India	**460**	**385**	**75**
Afghanistan	103	92	11
Ireland	147	147	..
England and Wales	134	85	49
Elsewhere	76	61	15
17. KARACHI	**151,903**	**90,233**	**61,670**
A.—Born in India	**146,551**	**85,812**	**60,739**
Bombay	114,884	64,981	49,853
Karachi	*62,007*	*32,274*	*29,733*
Cutch	*20,080*	*11,311*	*8,769*
Kathiawar	*14,728*	*8,990*	*5,738*
Hyderabad	*5,316*	*3,956*	*1,360*
Ratnagiri	*3,911*	*2,770*	*1,141*
Elsewhere	*8,798*	*5,680*	*3,118*
Baluchistan	12,849	6,461	6,388
Punjab	7,097	5,366	1,731
United Provinces	3,176	2,592	584
Rajputana Agency	2,971	2,137	834
N.-W. F. Province	1,822	1,551	271
Elsewhere	2,191	1,535	656
French and Portuguese Settlements	1,611	1,189	422

Population by Birthplace—*continued*.

Birthplace.	Population. Persons.	Males.	Females.
1	2	3	4
—Born in Countries beyond India	**5,352**	**4,421**	**931**
Afghanistan	1,336	1,209	127
Persia	472	272	200
Arabia	249	147	102
England and Wales	2,844	2,476	368
Ireland	107	79	28
Scotland	75	60	15
Elsewhere	269	178	91
18. MANDALAY	**138,299**	**69,718**	**68,581**
A.—Born in India	**136,584**	**68,227**	**68,357**
Burma	125,436	58,973	66,463
Mandalay	*110,364*	*50,402*	*59,962*
Sagaing	*3,936*	*2,059*	*1,877*
Lower Chindwin	*3,768*	*1,839*	*1,929*
Shwebo	*1,964*	*1,088*	*876*
Elsewhere	*5,404*	*3,585*	*1,819*
Madras	3,416	2,645	771
Punjab	2,802	2,419	383
Bengal (Old)	2,028	1,617	411
United Provinces	1,130	1,004	126
Bombay	969	856	113
Elsewhere	801	711	90
French and Portuguese Settlements	2	2	..
B.—Born in Countries beyond India	**1,715**	**1,491**	**224**
China	1,140	1,024	116
England and Wales	147	112	35
Ireland	256	233	23
Scotland	86	78	8
Elsewhere	86	44	42
19. JAIPUR	**137,898**	**70,846**	**66,252**
A.—Born in India	**137,833**	**70,805**	**66,228**
Rajputana Agency	132,951	68,513	64,438
Jaipur	*130,083*	*67,109*	*62,974*
Alwar	*816*	*432*	*384*
Marwar	*614*	*269*	*345*
Tonk	*560*	*266*	*294*
Mewar	*168*	*87*	*81*
Elsewhere	*710*	*350*	*360*
United Provinces	1,998	1,152	846
Punjab	954	527	427
Ajmer-Merwara	292	114	178
Bombay	246	171	75
Central India Agency	243	123	120
Bengal	171	88	83
Elsewhere	164	105	59
French and Portuguese Settlements	14	12	2
B.—Born in Countries beyond India	**65**	**41**	**24**
England and Wales	19	9	10
Elsewhere	46	32	14
20. PATNA	**136,153**	**70,841**	**65,312**
A.—Born in India	**135,981**	**70,742**	**65,239**
Bihar and Orissa	132,059	68,534	63,525
Patna	*122,858*	*62,962*	*59,896*
Gaya	*2,654*	*1,598*	*1,056*
Muzaffarpur	*2,194*	*1,222*	*972*
Saran	*1,584*	*1,045*	*539*
Shahabad	*1,298*	*854*	*444*
Elsewhere	*1,471*	*853*	*618*
United Provinces	1,867	1,149	718
Bengal	1,287	741	546
Punjab	376	156	220
Rajputana Agency	199	47	152
Elsewhere	182	110	72
French and Portuguese Settlements	11	5	6
B.—Born in Countries beyond India	**172**	**99**	**73**
Nepal	38	28	10
England and Wales	51	26	25
Elsewhere	83	45	38
21. MADURA	**134,130**	**67,091**	**67,039**
A.—Born in India	**133,973**	**67,030**	**66,943**
Madras	133,059	66,379	66,680
Madura	*114,023*	*56,429*	*57,594*
Ramnad	*6,627*	*3,439*	*3,188*
Tinnevelly	*5,091*	*2,631*	*2,460*
Trichinopoly	*2,376*	*1,240*	*1,136*
Tanjore	*2,004*	*1,022*	*982*
Elsewhere	*2,938*	*1,618*	*1,320*
Bombay	407	342	65
Mysore State	124	68	56
Hyderabad State	98	76	22
Elsewhere	166	93	73
French and Portuguese Settlements	119	72	47
B.—Born in Countries beyond India	**157**	**61**	**96**
Ceylon	61	20	41
England and Wales	27	17	10
Elsewhere	69	24	45
22. BAREILLY*	**117,521**	**62,127**	**55,394**
A.—Born in India	**117,353**	**61,999**	**55,354**
United Provinces	116,123	61,166	54,957
Bareilly	*104,654*	*54,781*	*49,873*
Moradabad	*1,423*	*749*	*674*
Budaun	*1,392*	*783*	*609*
Shahjahanpur	*1,264*	*687*	*577*
Pilibhit	*1,167*	*574*	*593*
Elsewhere	*6,223*	*3,592*	*2,631*
Punjab	504	339	165
Rajputana Agency	259	169	90
Bengal (Old)	238	174	64
Elsewhere	229	151	78
B.—Born in Countries beyond India	**168**	**128**	**40**
United Kingdom	56	34	22
Elsewhere	112	94	18
23. SRINAGAR	**126,344**	**68,378**	**57,966**
A.—Born in India	**126,237**	**68,313**	**57,924**
Kashmir State	125,127	67,540	57,587
Kashmir Valley	*123,912*	*66,594*	*57,318*
Jammu	*419*	*308*	*111*
Elsewhere	*796*	*638*	*158*
Punjab	632	441	191
N.-W. F. Province	294	201	93
United Provinces	119	88	31
Elsewhere	65	43	22
B.—Born in Countries beyond India	**66**	**37**	**29**
England and Wales	35	15	20
Elsewhere	31	22	9
Birthplace not returned	**41**	**28**	**13**
24. TRICHINOPOLY	**123,512**	**61,560**	**61,952**
A.—Born in India	**123,166**	**61,339**	**61,827**
Madras	121,309	60,202	61,107
Trichinopoly	*100,125*	*48,877*	*51,248*
Tanjore	*6,674*	*3,336*	*3,338*
Madura	*2,730*	*1,465*	*1,265*
Salem	*2,082*	*1,175*	*907*
Madras	*1,703*	*991*	*712*
Elsewhere	*7,995*	*4,358*	*3,637*
Mysore State	729	380	349
Bombay	228	175	53
Hyderabad State	220	120	100
Elsewhere	484	375	109
French and Portuguese Settlements	196	87	109
B.—Born in Countries beyond India	**346**	**221**	**125**
Ceylon	117	70	47
England and Wales	98	60	38
Elsewhere	131	91	40

* This is exclusive of the cantonment area, as its statistics by birthplace are not available.

TABLE XI.—Distribution of Population by Birthplace—*concluded.*

Birthplace	Population. Persons.	Males.	Females.
1	2	3	4
25. MEERUT	**116,227**	**66,286**	**49,941**
A.—Born in India	**114,065**	**64,264**	**49,801**
United Provinces	105,551	58,318	47,233
Meerut	*87,730*	*47,202*	*40,528*
Bulandshahr	*2,375*	*991*	*1,384*
Muzaffarnagar	*1,533*	*851*	*682*
Moradabad	*1,067*	*551*	*516*
Bijnor	*724*	*472*	*252*
Elsewhere	*12,122*	*8,251*	*3,871*
Punjab	4,918	3,479	1,439
Rajputana Agency	1,268	757	511
Bengal (Old)	370	297	73
Central India Agency	352	184	168
Elsewhere	1,606	1,229	377
B.—Born in Countries beyond India	**2,162**	**2,022**	**140**
United Kingdom	1,976	1,890	86
Elsewhere	186	132	54
26. SURAT	**114,868**	**59,634**	**55,234**
A.—Born in India	**114,728**	**59,547**	**55,181**
Bombay	107,796	55,242	52,554
Surat	*97,042*	*49,164*	*47,878*
Kathiawar	*3,394*	*1,870*	*1,524*
Ahmadabad	*1,469*	*844*	*625*
Kaira	*1,190*	*742*	*448*
Broach	*1,074*	*557*	*517*
Elsewhere	*3,627*	*2,065*	*1,562*
Baroda State	3,775	2,221	1,554
United Provinces	1,372	938	434
Elsewhere	1,637	1,056	581
French and Portuguese Settlements	148	90	58
B.—Born in Countries beyond India	**140**	**87**	**53**
Afghanistan	26	24	2
England and Wales	11	2	9
Elsewhere	103	61	42
27. DACCA	**108,551**	**63,091**	**45,460**
A.—Born in India	**108,192**	**62,837**	**45,355**
Bengal	96,803	53,298	43,505
Dacca	*87,046*	*45,875*	*41,171*
Mymensingh	*2,043*	*1,710*	*333*
Tippera	*1,950*	*1,676*	*274*
Faridpur	*1,440*	*1,067*	*373*
Backergunge	*1,007*	*779*	*228*
Elsewhere	*3,317*	*2,191*	*1,126*
Bihar and Orissa	7,079	6,206	873
United Provinces	2,528	1,942	586
Assam	1,362	1,087	275
Punjab	176	123	53
Elsewhere	230	171	59
French and Portuguese Settlements	14	10	4
B.—Born in Countries beyond India	**359**	**254**	**105**
Nepal	114	98	16
England and Wales	93	62	31
Elsewhere	152	94	58
28. NAGPUR	**101,415**	**53,696**	**47,719**
A.—Born in India	**101,062**	**53,474**	**47,588**
C. P. and Berar	88,221	45,172	43,049
Nagpur	*72,903*	*36,995*	*35,908*
Bhandara	*5,944*	*2,992*	*2,952*
Balaghat	*1,323*	*694*	*629*
Wardha	*1,061*	*500*	*561*
Chanda	*1,049*	*587*	*462*
Amraoti	*1,017*	*605*	*412*
Elsewhere	*4,924*	*2,799*	*2,125*
United Provinces	5,007	3,404	1,603
Bombay	2,942	1,827	1,115
Central India Agency	1,029	715	314
Madras	980	533	447
Hyderabad State	764	423	341
Elsewhere	1,923	1,251	672
French and Portuguese Settlements	196	149	47
B.—Born in Countries beyond India	**353**	**222**	**131**
England and Wales	214	152	62
Elsewhere	139	70	69
29. BANGALORE CIVIL AND MILITARY STATION	**100,834**	**51,752**	**49,082**
A.—Born in India	**97,985**	**49,543**	**48,442**
Mysore State	70,776	34,898	35,878
Bangalore	*66,257*	*32,665*	*33,592*
Mysore	*2,684*	*1,295*	*1,389*
Kolar	*1,071*	*505*	*566*
Elsewhere	*764*	*433*	*331*
Madras	19,509	9,897	9,612
Hyderabad State	2,532	1,351	1,181
Punjab	1,071	935	136
Bombay	897	452	445
C. P. and Berar	777	424	353
United Provinces	568	473	95
Rajputana Agency	526	385	141
N.-W. F. Province	272	263	9
Bengal (Old)	227	102	125
Burma	192	88	104
Coorg	171	87	84
Elsewhere	279	100	179
French and Portuguese Settlements	188	88	100
B.—Born in Countries beyond India	**2,846**	**2,206**	**640**
Ceylon	67	30	37
England and Wales	1,615	1,265	350
Scotland	696	655	41
Ireland	161	106	55
France	57	32	25
Elsewhere	250	118	132
C.—Born at Sea	**3**	**3**	..
30. JUBBULPORE	**100,651**	**56,035**	**44,616**
A.—Born in India	**97,564**	**53,207**	**44,357**
C. P. and Berar	67,493	34,751	32,742
Jubbulpore	*57,556*	*29,397*	*28,159*
Saugor	*2,440*	*1,294*	*1,146*
Narsinghpur	*1,801*	*931*	*870*
Damoh	*1,176*	*616*	*560*
Elsewhere	*4,520*	*2,513*	*2,007*
United Provinces	13,914	8,528	5,386
Central India Agency	7,942	4,451	3,491
Punjab	2,236	1,832	404
Bombay	1,430	821	609
Rajputana Agency	1,415	1,061	354
Madras	793	453	340
Hyderabad State	645	309	336
Bihar and Orissa	639	347	292
Elsewhere	941	562	379
French and Portuguese Settlements	116	92	24
B.—Born in Countries beyond India	**3,087**	**2,828**	**259**
England and Wales	2,756	2,558	198
Ireland	121	98	23
Scotland	56	46	10
Elsewhere	154	126	28

TABLE XV.

Occupation or Means of Livelihood.

This Table contains occupation statistics for each Class, Sub-Class, Order and Group in the Classified Scheme for the aggregate population of all cities taken together, and also separate figures for each of ten important cities. For the corresponding figures for the remaining cities the Provincial Volumes should be referred to. Actual Workers have been distinguished from Dependants, but sex details have been given only in the summary for all cities.

TABLE XV—Occupation or

Group No	Occupation.	All Cities. Actual Workers. Males.	All Cities. Actual Workers. Females.	All Cities. Dependants.	Calcutta. Actual Workers.	Calcutta. Dependants.	Bombay. Actual Workers.	Bombay. Dependants.	Madras. Actual Workers.	Madras. Dependants.
	1	2	3	4	5	6	7	8	9	10
	TOTAL POPULATION	2,933,918	587,132	3,542,791	543,454	352,613	596,120	382,325	290,311	318,349
	A.—Production of raw materials	173,622	34,908	252,538	16,353	19,457	14,563	7,501	11,771	19,108
	I.—Exploitation of the surface of the earth	*170,591*	*34,698*	*249,952*	*16,121*	*19,394*	*13,559*	*6,907*	*11,734*	*18,982*
	1.—Pasture and agriculture	159,872	32,488	236,993	15,403	18,744	10,125	5,288	9,784	15,856
	(a) Ordinary Cultivation	*123,045*	*24,577*	*195,161*	*10,561*	*17,621*	*4,062*	*1,747*	*6,683*	*11,019*
1	Income from rent of agricultural land	27,238	5,690	65,374	6,807	15,158	172	286	1,910	3,950
2	Ordinary cultivators	59,032	9,889	83,341	2,303	1,225	2,792	1,331	3,638	5,560
3	Agents, managers of landed estates (not planters), clerks, rent collectors, etc.	16,572	54	23,170	1,169	1,132	..	..	157	300
4	Farm servants and field labourers	20,203	8,944	23,276	282	106	1,098	130	978	1,209
	(b) Growers of special products and market gardening	*17,574*	*2,460*	*18,326*	*2,564*	*280*	*2,942*	*2,636*	*2,216*	*3,961*
5	Tea, coffee, cinchona and indigo plantations	473	34	302	132	52	..	..	19	72
6	Fruit, flower, vegetable, betel, vine, areca nut, etc., growers	17,101	2,426	18,024	2,432	228	2,942	2,636	2,197	3,889
	(c) Forestry	*7,526*	*2,399*	*8,988*	*1,557*	*428*	*72*	*24*	*523*	*403*
7	Forest officers, rangers, guards, etc.	914	34	1,657	1	5	22	7	29	134
8	Wood-cutters; fire-wood, lac, catechu, rubber, etc., collectors, and charcoal burners	6,612	2,365	7,331	1,556	423	50	17	494	269
	(d) Raising of farm stock	*11,649*	*2,772*	*14,316*	*721*	*415*	*3,049*	*881*	*361*	*473*
9	Cattle and buffalo breeders and keepers	7,048	1,977	8,606	588	354	2,854	813	203	301
10	Sheep, goat and pig breeders	255	82	468	2	4	..	..	27	9
11	Breeders of other animals (horses, mules, camels, asses, etc.)	245	12	340	5	24	25	9	8	23
12	Herdsmen, shepherds, goatherds, etc.	4,101	701	4,902	126	33	170	59	123	140
13	*(e) Raising of small animals* (birds, bees, silkworms, etc.)	*78*	*280*	*202*	..	..	..	..	*1*	*2*
	2.—Fishing and hunting	10,719	2,140	12,959	718	650	3,434	1,619	1,950	3,124
14	Fishing	10,098	2,130	11,874	706	629	3,434	1,618	1,941	3,104
15	Hunting	621	10	1,085	12	21	..	1	9	20
	II.—Extraction of minerals	*3,031*	*280*	*2,586*	*239*	*63*	*1,004*	*594*	*37*	*106*
	3.—Mines	419	18	366	41	58	52	57	26	89
16	Coal mines and petroleum wells	384	14	219	40	54	52	57	12	25
17	Mines and metallic minerals (gold, iron, manganese, etc.)	35	4	147	1	4	..	..	14	64
18	**4.—Quarries of hard rocks.**—[Other minerals (jade, diamonds, limestone, etc.)]	1,304	205	1,137	1	1	339	473	7	23
	5.—Salt, etc.	1,308	57	1,083	196	4	113	64	4	4
19	Rock, sea and marsh salt	612	33	570	190	4	113	64	3	13
20	Extraction of saltpetre, alum and other substances soluble in water	695	24	513	..	..	..	..	1	1
	B.—Preparation and supply of material Substances	1,662,520	316,418	2,053,020	286,374	181,817	369,345	236,694	112,598	179,874
	III.—Industry	*859,639*	*207,600*	*1,056,145*	*119,629*	*75,974*	*206,450*	*116,690*	*56,553*	*83,618*
	6.—Textiles	253,948	90,183	271,606	11,848	4,825	120,499	53,339	11,936	15,653
21	Cotton ginning, cleaning and pressing	7,035	1,814	7,909	18	10	148	184	339	160
22	Cotton spinning, sizing and weaving	168,571	60,207	160,815	538	255	118,512	52,663	9,701	12,637
23	Jute spinning, pressing and weaving	23,237	5,211	14,280	10,750	4,090	22	13	24	39
24	Rope, twine and string	1,850	2,126	2,583	99	65	95	50	44	30
25	Other fibres (cocoanut, aloes, flax, hemp, straw, etc.)	1,118	231	1,289	71	9	..	..	8	16
26	Wool carders and spinners, weavers of woollen blankets, carpets, etc.	9,580	1,054	12,617	28	87	146	37	23	32
27	Silk spinners and weavers	20,823	10,629	30,113	11	18	51	26	491	508
28	Hair, camel and horse hair, bristles work, brush makers, etc.	280	16	419	34	45	8	6	14	44
29	Persons occupied with feathers	49	..	42	17	20	2	..	..	..
30	Dyeing, bleaching, printing, preparation and sponging of textiles	7,382	2,365	10,248	190	66	17	12	325	560
31	Other (lace, crape, embroideries, fringes, etc.), and insufficiently described textile industries	14,023	6,530	31,201	92	160	1,496	848	967	1,627
	7.—Hides, skins and hard materials from the animal kingdom	9,654	998	16,364	469	156	1,556	747	307	571
32	Tanners, curriers, leather dressers and dyers, etc.	7,575	888	12,512	400	110	1,552	703	293	533
33	Makers of leather articles, such as trunks, water-bags, etc.	1,198	65	1,948	62	37	1	13	5	22
34	Furriers	3	..	7	..	..	..	..	2	3
35	Bone, ivory, horn, shell, etc., workers	878	45	1,897	7	9	3	31	7	13
	8.—Wood	69,109	6,572	85,242	9,308	4,746	13,068	11,854	4,543	7,972
36	Sawyers, carpenters, turners and joiners, etc.	62,439	1,299	75,004	8,113	4,235	11,760	11,335	4,236	7,582
37	Basket makers and other industries of woody materials including leaves	6,670	5,273	10,238	1,195	511	1,308	519	307	390
	9.—Metals	46,878	1,514	68,375	5,998	4,966	7,567	6,553	3,849	6,168
38	Forging and rolling of iron and other metals	760	15	1,718	117	159	10	14	153	297
39	Plough and agricultural implement makers	134	..	112	..	..	120	5	..	1
40	Makers of arms, guns, etc.	1,056	18	1,869	57	54	1	3	207	435
41	Other workers in iron and makers of implements and tools, principally or exclusively of iron	26,277	814	35,258	2,587	1,443	4,889	4,085	1,672	2,878
42	Workers in brass, copper and bell-metal	10,742	458	18,733	1,424	1,537	1,179	1,126	408	999
43	Workers in other metals (tin, zinc, lead, quick-silver, etc.)	6,943	200	9,484	1,636	1,635	1,229	1,222	907	1,557
44	Workers in mints, die-sinkers, etc.	966	9	1,171	177	158	139	98	2	1
	10.—Ceramics	14,334	5,355	19,987	762	418	625	421	653	816
45	Makers of glass and crystal ware	581	104	966	84	89	15	22	67	126
46	Makers of porcelain and crockery	405	77	354	4	2	..	..	80	56
47	Potters and earthen pipe and bowl makers	9,048	4,195	13,708	464	271	492	317	292	395
48	Brick and tile makers	4,133	979	4,715	201	54	118	82	212	221
49	Others (mosaic, talc, mica, alabaster, etc., workers)	167	..	249	9	2	..	..	2	12

Means of Livelihood.

Rangoon Actual Workers.	Rangoon Dependants.	Delhi Actual Workers.	Delhi Dependants.	Ahmadabad Actual Workers.	Ahmadabad Dependants.	Agra Actual Workers.	Agra Dependants.	Howrah Actual Workers.	Howrah Dependants.	Cawnpore Actual Workers.	Cawnpore Dependants.	Karachi Actual Workers.	Karachi Dependants.	Group No.
11	12	13	14	15	16	17	18	19	20	21	22	23	24	
186,806	**106,510**	**104,431**	**128,406**	**96,693**	**118,084**	**80,961**	**104,546**	**101,911**	**77,085**	**84,644**	**93,913**	**70,458**	**81,445**	
5,122	**4,029**	**13,208**	**5,260**	**3,690**	**3,862**	**8,818**	**15,921**	**3,228**	**3,696**	**3,808**	**4,712**	**4,421**	**5,089**	
5,116	*4,093*	*13,519*	*4,805*	*3,656*	*3,848*	*8,818*	*15,878*	*3,917*	*3,678*	*3,808*	*4,703*	*3,878*	*4,388*	
4,511	**3,844**	**12,482**	**4,764**	**3,580**	**3,758**	**8,729**	**15,784**	**3,030**	**3,462**	**3,697**	**4,527**	**1,983**	**2,273**	
2,353	*3,009*	*11,427*	*3,587*	*2,575*	*2,438*	*8,137*	*15,148*	*2,359*	*2,615*	*2,661*	*3,155*	*820*	*1,000*	
711	1,223	1,288	211	385	492	2,050	3,119	800	1,477	509	890	211	381	1
1,329	1,403	7,612	2,143	1,573	1,439	3,456	8,963	859	720	1,438	1,483	431	248	2
17	39	11	14	21	58	122	272	56	108	227	287	1	20	3
296	344	2,516	1,219	596	449	2,509	2,794	644	310	487	495	177	351	4
1,823	*658*	*572*	*689*	*149*	*167*	*63*	*108*	*248*	*178*	*289*	*361*	*644*	*551*	5
..	..	..	..	..	..	1	5	..	1	..	..	..	..	6
1,823	658	572	689	149	167	62	103	248	177	289	361	644	551	
126	*98*	*351*	*334*	*563*	*883*	*98*	*119*	*25*	*2*	*37*	*9*	*149*	*170*	
50	51	..	..	1	9	4	2	..	..	1	3	19	6	7
76	47	351	334	562	874	94	117	25	2	36	6	130	164	8
195	*70*	*132*	*154*	*270*	*247*	*431*	*409*	*393*	*667*	*710*	*1,002*	*370*	*552*	
4	2	47	21	70	67	115	78	388	663	662	917	182	357	9
2	1	..	..	2	..	76	132	..	..	..	..	38	29	10
..	..	25	14	1	..	..	..	..	..	..	..	19	18	11
189	67	60	119	197	180	240	199	10	4	48	85	131	148	12
14	*9*	..	..	*23*	*23*	..	..	..	..	..	..	..	..	13
605	**179**	**37**	**41**	**76**	**90**	**89**	**94**	**187**	**216**	**111**	**176**	**1,895**	**2,115**	
603	179	..	14	74	86	47	23	181	208	96	145	1,865	2,063	14
2	..	37	27	2	4	42	71	6	8	15	31	30	52	15
6	*6*	*689*	*455*	*34*	*14*	..	*43*	*11*	*18*	..	*9*	*543*	*701*	
2	**6**	**3**	**1**	..	..	..	..	**11**	**18**	..	**9**	..	..	
..	4	3	1	..	..	..	..	11	18	..	3	..	..	16
2	2	..	..	..	..	..	..	..	..	..	6	..	..	17
4	..	..	..	33	12	..	..	..	..	..	..	225	262	18
..	..	**686**	**454**	**1**	**2**	..	**43**	..	..	..	..	**318**	**439**	
..	..	7	1	1	2	..	32	..	..	..	..	318	439	19
..	..	679	453	..	..	..	11	..	..	..	..	..	..	20
107,762	66,341	66,338	96,879	74,896	90,472	45,393	61,507	63,062	45,898	36,793	49,045	47,043	59,907	
50,953	*29,035*	*37,249*	*56,073*	*55,549*	*60,115*	*30,353*	*38,526*	*33,618*	*24,145*	*21,563*	*26,500*	*17,479*	*20,771*	
133	**81**	**7,261**	**16,534**	**35,419**	**36,497**	**5,633**	**5,976**	**20,390**	**11,303**	**3,937**	**5,783**	**1,513**	**1,750**	
..	..	76	306	408	415	1,679	1,543	..	..	244	594	146	188	21
15	8	1,388	2,306	28,006	29,034	3,187	3,516	2,393	944	3,296	4,654	381	690	22
..	..	..	2	..	40	1	4	17,590	10,014	..	..	..	..	23
38	17	91	65	5	6	338	224	402	345	39	59	170	158	24
10	..	..	..	110	69	..	..	..	..	29	44	29	3	25
24	22	17	5	65	81	23	143	..	..	20	37	427	343	26
..	..	319	531	3,565	3,313	7	80	..	..	..	..	25	35	27
..	..	86	129	5	4	77	23	..	..	30	94	3	3	28
..	..	..	..	..	..	..	..	..	..	..	..	7	7	29
32	30	42	50	2,840	2,927	24	74	5	..	235	220	151	237	30
14	4	5,242	13,140	415	608	297	369	..	..	44	81	174	86	31
29	**27**	**675**	**1,344**	**86**	**82**	**1,003**	**2,163**	**38**	**168**	**1,449**	**1,826**	**231**	**307**	
11	6	42	367	79	82	993	2,128	38	168	1,449	1,826	162	232	32
2	11	619	965	3	..	10	35	..	..	..	..	16	24	33
1	4	..	..	..	..	..	..	..	..	..	..	..	..	34
15	6	14	12	4	..	..	..	..	..	..	..	53	51	35
6,761	**7,445**	**2,167**	**1,615**	**2,811**	**4,048**	**1,614**	**2,355**	**1,911**	**1,925**	**1,215**	**1,351**	**2,868**	**2,567**	
6,659	7,279	1,509	1,040	1,891	3,006	868	1,332	1,800	1,837	975	1,115	2,393	2,353	36
102	166	658	575	920	1,042	746	723	111	88	240	236	475	214	37
1,927	**1,793**	**2,435**	**5,245**	**1,352**	**2,188**	**1,185**	**1,945**	**1,466**	**2,345**	**1,542**	**2,060**	**934**	**1,681**	
..	..	..	8	1	..	..	..	371	924	..	2	55	81	38
3	..	..	..	..	..	..	..	..	..	..	..	..	..	39
5	34	..	..	..	..	3	5	..	..	10	19	..	..	40
1,376	1,157	637	846	879	1,372	765	1,279	869	1,097	1,236	1,690	650	1,116	41
104	126	1,454	3,802	358	589	396	612	82	129	226	276	48	104	42
439	476	158	348	112	244	21	49	140	194	70	73	171	380	43
..	..	186	241	2	3	..	..	4	1	..	..	..	..	44
451	**169**	**1,258**	**1,037**	**934**	**1,068**	**1,836**	**1,763**	**139**	**106**	**597**	**526**	**495**	**559**	
..	..	42	46	13	8	31	14	..	..	16	53	..	..	45
1	..	..	..	..	..	175	205	..	..	70	..	3	1	46
121	26	1,040	636	654	754	1,456	1,172	84	67	452	436	442	454	47
329	143	176	355	267	326	154	260	55	39	59	37	50	104	48
..	..	..	..	..	..	20	103	..	..	..	..	..	..	49

TABLE XV—Occupation or

Group No.	OCCUPATION.	ALL CITIES. Actual Workers. Males.	ALL CITIES. Actual Workers. Females.	ALL CITIES. Dependants.	CALCUTTA. Actual Workers.	CALCUTTA. Dependants.	BOMBAY. Actual Workers.	BOMBAY. Dependants.	MADRAS. Actual Workers.	MADRAS. Dependants.
	1	2	3	4	5	6	7	8	9	10
	11.—Chemical products properly so called, and analogous	**10,931**	**1,708**	**15,233**	**2,043**	**2,382**	**290**	**232**	**478**	**822**
50	Manufacture of matches and explosive materials	373	89	690	11	29	49	31	26	52
51	Manufacture of aerated and mineral waters	275	12	501	11	38	34	48	74	116
52	Manufacture of dyes, paint and ink	689	25	865	292	130	27	11	100	251
53	Manufacture and refining of vegetable and mineral oils	8,132	1,166	11,248	2,103	2,075	156	119	250	348
54	Manufacture of paper, cardboard and papier maché	232	44	371	3	30	6	5	10	8
55	Others (soap, candles, lac, cutch, perfumes and miscellaneous drugs)	1,230	372	1,558	223	90	18	18	18	47
	12.—Food industries	**74,127**	**37,723**	**98,584**	**5,433**	**4,001**	**9,937**	**6,271**	**6,413**	**7,630**
56	Rice pounders and huskers and flour grinders	23,288	24,743	22,559	1,143	444	510	167	1,888	763
57	Bakers and biscuit makers	9,697	1,973	10,481	1,251	439	1,212	624	1,417	1,501
58	Grain parchers, etc.	3,226	1,657	5,566	190	186	56	10	4	10
59	Butchers	14,788	1,492	27,854	1,484	2,201	1,272	1,737	965	1,762
60	Fish curers	137	6	139	19	20	..	..	7	32
61	Butter, cheese and ghee makers	88	13	199	..	..	..	..	2	4
62	Makers of sugar, molasses and gur	461	16	803	131	118	76	7	29	29
63	Sweetmeat makers, preparers of jam and condiments, etc.	12,383	1,576	15,797	632	271	2,106	1,139	240	236
64	Brewers and distillers	345	34	492	3	19	2	4	7	7
65	Toddy drawers	3,067	48	4,637	61	45	893	829	1,282	2,560
66	Manufacturers of tobacco, opium and ganja	6,647	6,165	10,057	519	258	3,810	1,754	582	726
	13.—Industries of dress and the toilet	**157,230**	**29,589**	**191,616**	**28,900**	**19,276**	**25,198**	**15,811**	**9,061**	**13,966**
67	Hat, cap and turban makers	1,607	536	2,718	626	382	157	150	76	128
68	Tailors, milliners, dress makers and darners, embroiderers on linen	52,867	10,625	70,060	7,120	7,546	8,980	5,087	4,570	6,799
69	Shoe, boot and sandal makers	40,779	4,055	48,545	11,498	5,630	4,888	3,650	1,229	2,293
70	Other industries pertaining to dress-gloves, socks, gaiters, belts, buttons, umbrellas, canes, etc.	2,330	438	3,295	794	306	94	65	60	86
71	Washing, cleaning and dyeing	31,130	11,592	37,470	4,776	3,339	6,705	3,774	1,795	2,508
72	Barbers, hairdressers and wig makers	28,070	1,902	28,844	4,060	2,071	4,373	2,285	1,286	2,123
73	Other industries connected with the toilet (tattooers, shampooers, bath houses, etc.)	447	451	684	26	2	1	..	45	29
	14.—Furniture industries	**4,420**	**218**	**5,070**	**717**	**365**	**474**	**367**	**159**	**382**
74	Cabinet makers, carriage painters, etc.	4,287	215	4,979	709	356	471	367	159	382
75	Upholsterers, tent makers, etc.	133	3	91	8	9	3	..	..	..
	15.—Building industries	**79,106**	**7,919**	**94,566**	**16,970**	**10,557**	**7,653**	**4,632**	**5,067**	**7,970**
76	Lime burners, cement workers	860	356	1,609	1	2	46	13	483	609
77	Excavators, plinth builders and well-sinkers	2,435	615	2,986	290	216	53	38	112	78
78	Stone and marble workers, masons and bricklayers	60,648	5,650	74,551	12,806	8,425	6,682	3,431	4,086	6,581
79	Others (thatchers, building contractors, house painters, tilers, plumbers, locksmiths, etc.)	15,163	1,298	15,422	3,873	1,914	872	1,150	366	702
	16.—Construction of means of transport	**4,138**	**52**	**4,793**	**714**	**676**	**298**	**336**	**367**	**722**
80	Cart, carriage, palki, etc., makers and wheelwrights	2,637	24	2,710	349	444	105	184	208	415
81	Saddlers, harness makers, whip and lash makers	824	23	1,675	108	126	75	166	129	292
82	Ship and boat builders	677	5	408	257	106	28	36	30	15
83	**17.—Production and transmission of physical forces (heat, light electricity, motive power, etc.)** (Gas works, electric light and ice factories)	**4,414**	**35**	**4,096**	**2,449**	**1,168**	**860**	[illegible]	**382**	[illegible]
	18.—Industries of luxury and those pertaining to literature and the arts and sciences	**92,418**	**4,875**	**137,262**	**17,312**	**17,106**	**11,643**	**11,242**	**11,170**	**18,926**
84	Printers, lithographers, engravers, etc.	25,012	136	32,744	6,297	6,259	4,848	4,903	4,762	7,546
85	Newspaper and magazine managers and editors, journalists, etc.	563	13	900	157	210	50	98	157	273
86	Book-binders and stitchers, envelope makers, etc.	6,923	118	6,412	3,288	1,304	528	483	1,211	1,415
87	Makers of musical instruments	727	25	906	276	313	107	48	15	42
88	Makers of watches and clocks and optical, photographic and surgical instruments	2,609	21	4,296	628	958	331	469	227	517
89	Workers in precious stones and metals, enamellers, imitation jewellery makers, gilders, etc.	49,187	2,194	80,534	6,018	7,277	5,314	4,815	4,424	8,686
90	Makers of bangles, rosaries, bead and other necklaces, spangles, lingams and sacred threads	3,579	1,867	6,253	82	231	165	72	54	58
91	Toy, kite, cage, fishing tackle, etc., makers, taxidermists, etc.	1,821	223	2,425	109	112	51	61	67	126
92	Others, including managers, persons other than performers employed in theatres and other places of public entertainment, employés of public societies, race course service, huntsmen, etc.	1,997	278	2,792	457	442	249	343	253	366
93	**19.—Industries concerned with refuse matter.** (Sweepers, scavengers, dust and sweeping contractors)	**36,925**	**20,840**	**43,347**	**9,069**	**5,302**	**6,872**	**4,145**	**2,688**	**1,367**
	IV.—Transport	***349,528***	***17,005***	***316,684***	***79,190***	***31,189***	***78,570***	***43,660***	***93,477***	***38,130***
	20.—Transport by water	**102,569**	**4,732**	**39,966**	**46,257**	**9,396**	**38,230**	**9,571**	**4,129**	**6,636**
94	Harbour works, dockyards and pilots	23,024	3,073	14,239	6,002	2,920	16,557	6,752	1,840	2,820
95	Ship owners and their employés, ship brokers, ships' officers, engineers, mariners and firemen	43,633	154	11,138	14,344	6,255	18,961	2,470	362	300
96	Persons employed on the maintenance of streams, rivers and canals (including construction)	642	51	2,576	36	20	1	3	15	24
97	Boat owners, boat men and tow men	35,270	1,454	11,913	19,875	203	3,691	346	1,922	3,494

MEANS OF LIVELIHOOD—*continued.*

Rangoon.		Delhi.		Ahmadabad.		Agra.		Howrah.		Cawnpore.		Karachi.		Group No.
Actual Workers.	Dependants.	Actual Workers.	Depen-dants.	Actual Workers.	Depen-dants.	Actual Workers.	Depen-dants.	Actual Workers.	Depen-dants.	Actual Workers.	Depen-dants.	Actual Workers.	Depen-dants.	
11	12	13	14	15	16	17	18	19	20	21	22	23	24	
661	**110**	**522**	**889**	**480**	**619**	**761**	**1,379**	**638**	**480**	**565**	**881**	**375**	**437**	
1	..	..	..	38	53	7	25	..	..	12	33	9	2	50
9	4	..	80	1	..	12	15	..	..	..	..	2	..	51
..	1	..	..	4	7	19	25	..	..	..	6	7	..	52
442	67	279	402	280	408	689	1,296	637	429	500	676	356	434	53
..	..	..	..	146	131	..	..	..	..	..	..	1	1	54
149	33	243	198	21	25	34	18	1	..	58	118	..	..	55
22,847	**8,250**	**3,220**	**3,084**	**4,615**	**2,967**	**2,895**	**4,160**	**951**	**534**	**2,305**	**3,171**	**2,963**	**3,141**	
19,242	6,364	1,750	648	2,822	1,278	1,159	779	584	237	1,068	800	659	418	56
984	222	144	178	177	284	109	202	70	35	37	76	605	494	57
..	26	77	164	417	508	277	202	24	9	276	338	..	..	58
523	529	470	261	224	344	1,240	2,609	89	86	488	760	259	855	59
..	..	..	..	..	..	..	8	..	..	..	..	18	8	60
..	..	..	..	62	117	..	..	..	..	..	..	..	..	61
..	..	..	61	3	3	5	7	..	6	4	10	..	..	62
99	26	779	1,787	305	345	207	117	184	161	970	1,184	588	569	63
..	..	..	..	..	..	2	42	..	..	2	3	..	..	64
42	10	..	..	..	..	..	..	..	..	..	..	..	..	65
2,017	1,082	..	..	5	3	96	53	..	..	..	..	634	797	66
8,503	**4,167**	**7,162**	**9,152**	**2,771**	**2,557**	**7,572**	**11,146**	**2,707**	**2,504**	**4,250**	**5,236**	**3,323**	**4,317**	
43	9	209	711	104	127	71	147	..	..	4	..	40	25	67
4,150	1,518	2,084	1,653	1,467	881	1,346	2,590	593	839	1,818	1,777	1,182	1,464	68
1,336	944	2,407	4,541	740	957	2,569	5,671	370	245	1,467	2,001	793	1,220	69
180	136	50	297	4	1	27	52	11	200	82	61	20	29	70
2,427	1,265	1,196	1,058	774	700	1,592	1,378	1,251	1,075	941	901	1,175	1,343	71
1,253	193	1,196	862	682	891	952	1,302	479	235	947	1,195	683	736	72
104	104	..	..	..	..	15	6	3	..	..	1	..	..	73
228	**161**	**556**	**798**	**82**	**125**	**269**	**145**	**1**	**1**	**55**	**87**	**17**	**39**	
228	161	556	798	82	125	169	145	1	1	55	87	17	39	74
..	..	..	..	..	..	100	..	..	..	..	..	..	..	75
1,872	**1,119**	**3,992**	**5,227**	**3,132**	**3,796**	**597**	**1,001**	**2,686**	**1,993**	**582**	**1,067**	**1,997**	**2,785**	
9	..	18	128	152	151	75	33	..	..	1	9	26	41	76
107	16	..	..	3	4	38	7	151	..	..	..	..	3	77
842	286	3,035	4,231	2,856	3,503	373	795	1,655	1,475	558	1,086	1,962	2,723	78
914	817	939	868	121	138	111	116	880	518	23	12	9	18	79
394	**283**	**211**	**254**	**9**	**9**	**76**	**72**	**23**	**31**	**9**	**253**	**2**	**2**	
89	201	109	27	..	..	3	4	13	18	6	16	2	2	80
13	16	102	227	9	9	35	22	..	..	3	237	..	..	81
292	66	..	..	..	..	38	46	10	13	..	..	..	..	82
61	**180**	**30**	**118**	**19**	**28**	**30**	**186**	**97**	**114**	**13**	**31**	**11**	**14**	83
4,087	**4,462**	**5,080**	**9,468**	**2,381**	**4,380**	**1,730**	**2,612**	**1,212**	**1,703**	**1,218**	**1,716**	**1,048**	**1,285**	
1,168	1,410	53	173	817	479	98	184	591	867	107	141	201	181	84
37	61	2	5	..	24	..	..	26	22	..	..	5	4	85
516	241	57	107	238	495	35	86	21	48	55	25	29	27	86
8	5	68	80	6	47	4	2	..	..	19	18	..	..	87
122	186	324	180	28	81	46	69	35	86	39	76	82	148	88
2,026	2,383	4,508	7,941	1,529	2,880	1,023	1,015	538	676	872	1,087	722	859	89
8	23	451	692	3	1	72	136	..	3	52	181	7	6	90
27	7	230	205	44	133	435	151	..	..	56	100	..	..	91
179	167	6	19	216	249	27	69	1	..	18	88	2	..	92
2,069	**868**	**2,061**	**1,504**	**1,041**	**738**	**4,082**	**2,754**	**1,350**	**900**	**2,557**	**1,272**	**1,208**	**1,447**	93
23,650	***7,258***	***9,627***	***10,287***	***4,202***	***5,696***	***4,558***	***6,444***	***15,596***	***10,855***	***5,361***	***5,633***	***19,016***	***24,355***	
12,062	**2,926**	**66**	**320**	**50**	**96**	**15**	**68**	**2,079**	**1,702**	**9**	**92**	**1,212**	**2,822**	
56	58	..	..	..	..	..	..	1,271	1,052	..	..	315	510	94
8,979	782	..	..	1	11	..	20	456	269	..	..	324	694	95
3	4	55	312	45	63	15	48	..	..	4	64	119	385	96
4,623	3,100	11	8	13	12	..	..	352	381	5	28	554	1,233	97

TABLE XV—Occupation or

Group No.	OCCUPATION.	ALL CITIES.			CALCUTTA.		BOMBAY.		MADRAS.	
		Actual Workers.		Dependants.	Actual Workers.	Dependants.	Actual Workers.	Dependants.	Actual Workers.	Dependants.
		Males.	Females.							
	1	2	3	4	5	6	7	8	9	10
	21.—Transport by road	**145,153**	**10,521**	**140,565**	**28,555**	**12,073**	**20,658**	**15,893**	**10,757**	**15,104**
98	Persons employed on the construction and maintenance of roads and bridges	10,739	2,545	10,496	410	92	220	136	2,040	1,668
99	Cart owners and drivers, coachmen, stable boys, tramway, mail carriage, etc., managers and employés (excluding private servants)	89,785	1,537	86,809	23,791	11,023	15,316	13,359	7,201	11,580
100	Palki, etc., bearers and owners	5,462	19	4,889	839	143	3	..	365	450
101	Pack elephant, camel, mule, ass and bullock owners and drivers	1,902	74	2,825	..	..	..	..	3	2
102	Porters and messengers	37,265	6,346	35,546	3,545	815	5,119	2,398	1,148	1,404
	22.—Transport by rail	**87,074**	**1,517**	**112,100**	**7,851**	**7,362**	**15,951**	**15,367**	**5,568**	**11,877**
103	Railway employés of all kinds other than construction coolies	76,071	724	104,946	7,851	7,362	12,789	13,526	5,264	11,343
104	Labourers employed on railway construction	11,003	793	7,154	..	..	3,162	1,841	304	534
105	**23.—Post Office, Telegraph and Telephone services**	**14,732**	**235**	**24,153**	**2,457**	**2,356**	**2,731**	**2,829**	**2,013**	**4,511**
	V.—Trade	*453,360*	*91,813*	*680,191*	*94,639*	*74,654*	*84,395*	*76,414*	*33,568*	*58,196*
106	**24.—Banks, establishments of credit, exchange and insurance.** (Bank managers, money lenders, exchange and insurance agents, money changers and brokers and their employés)	**27,571**	**3,230**	**44,712**	**3,884**	**3,428**	**4,379**	**3,423**	**2,100**	**3,195**
107	**25.—Brokerage, commission and export.** (Brokers, commission agents, commercial travellers, warehouse owners and their employés)	**23,344**	**849**	**33,407**	**6,249**	**7,164**	**6,143**	**6,472**	**1,258**	**3,612**
108	**26.—Trade in textiles.** (Trade in piece goods, wool, cotton, silk, hair and other textiles)	**52,201**	**3,103**	**74,760**	**12,182**	**10,450**	**9,396**	**9,765**	**2,682**	**4,166**
109	**27.—Trade in skins, leather and furs.** (Trade in skins, leather, furs, feathers, horns, etc.)	**7,192**	**212**	**10,414**	**3,370**	**2,039**	**278**	**406**	**631**	**1,105**
110	**28.—Trade in wood.** [Trade in wood (not fire-wood), cork, bark, etc.]	**7,043**	**1,021**	**9,276**	**1,635**	**1,150**	**530**	**1,077**	**447**	**1,103**
111	**29.—Trade in metals.** (Trade in metals, machinery, knife, tools, etc., sellers)	**5,461**	**197**	**7,181**	**1,633**	**1,297**	**1,605**	**1,471**	**145**	**351**
112	**30.—Trade in pottery**	**352**	**474**	**909**	**190**	**284**	..	**1**	**27**	**48**
113	**31.—Trade in chemical products.** (Trade in chemical products, drugs, dyes, paints, petroleum, explosives, etc.)	**6,346**	**427**	**10,586**	**1,540**	**923**	**548**	**756**	**555**	**1,206**
	32.—Hotels, cafés, restaurants, etc.	**22,285**	**3,470**	**27,671**	**3,298**	**2,379**	**7,774**	**5,724**	**2,290**	**4,271**
114	Vendors of wine, liquors, ærated waters, etc.	11,913	1,608	18,082	1,964	1,601	1,940	2,681	1,395	2,929
115	Owners and managers of hotels, cookshops, sarais, etc., and their employés	10,372	1,862	9,589	1,334	778	5,834	3,043	895	1,342
	33.—Other trade in food stuffs	**175,609**	**59,406**	**273,255**	**35,712**	**24,475**	**25,176**	**18,623**	**16,371**	**24,789**
116	Fish dealers	3,955	5,517	8,827	1,484	1,480	1,403	698	1,721	1,271
117	Grocers and sellers of vegetable oil, salt and other condiments	33,127	5,279	48,414	8,101	7,053	5,291	4,577	3,642	6,956
118	Sellers of milk, butter, ghee, poultry, eggs, etc.	20,716	6,899	32,187	4,412	2,634	2,761	2,048	1,877	3,061
119	Sellers of sweetmeats, sugar, gur and molasses	14,876	5,368	20,076	4,972	3,262	324	319	2,412	2,388
120	Cardamom, betel-leaf, vegetables, fruit and areca nut sellers	36,478	20,580	63,422	7,368	4,105	6,279	4,718	3,107	4,051
121	Grain and pulse dealers	46,962	8,995	71,573	5,851	3,476	6,925	4,278	2,367	4,940
122	Tobacco, opium, ganja, etc., sellers	12,537	3,628	18,267	2,159	1,794	1,522	1,295	891	1,542
123	Dealers in sheep, goats and pigs	962	144	2,117	162	278	13	18	202	442
124	Dealers in hay, grass and fodder	5,986	2,996	8,422	1,203	393	658	672	152	138
125	**34.—Trade in clothing and toilet articles.** [Trade in ready-made clothing and other articles of dress and the toilet (hats, umbrellas, socks, ready made shoes, perfumes, etc.)]	**17,961**	**1,346**	**28,411**	**5,241**	**2,420**	**1,228**	**1,551**	**850**	**1,975**
	35.—Trade in furniture	**6,792**	**751**	**11,399**	**1,936**	**2,171**	**1,232**	**1,814**	**894**	**1,638**
126	Trade in furniture, carpets, curtains and bedding	1,748	277	3,144	371	213	413	465	104	228
127	Hardware, cooking utensils, porcelain, crockery, glassware, bottles, articles for gardening, the cellar, etc.	5,044	474	8,255	1,565	1,958	819	1,349	790	1,410
128	**36.—Trade in building materials** (Stones, bricks, plaster, cement, sand, tiles, thatch, etc)	**1,567**	**474**	**2,637**	**306**	**338**	**426**	**187**	**170**	**461**
129	**37.—Trade in means of transport** [Dealers and hirers of elephants, camels, horses, cattle, asses, mules, etc., sellers (not makers) of carriages, saddlery, etc.]	**2,692**	**211**	**4,721**	**278**	**355**	**324**	**157**	**114**	**234**
130	**38.—Trade in fuel.** (Dealers in firewood, charcoal, coal, cowdung, etc.)	**14,052**	**5,034**	**19,124**	**2,726**	**1,387**	**3,854**	**2,630**	**1,148**	**1,684**
	39.—Trade in articles of luxury and those pertaining to letters and the arts and sciences	**24,890**	**3,004**	**40,799**	**5,328**	**5,774**	**4,035**	**3,847**	**2,209**	**4,097**
131	Dealers in precious stones, jewellery (real and imitation), clocks, optical instruments, etc.	10,967	919	17,372	1,479	1,821	2,519	2,409	1,032	2,083
132	Dealers in common bangles, bead necklaces, fans, small articles, toys, hunting and fishing tackle, flowers, etc.	7,865	1,771	13,874	1,393	913	596	484	812	1,312
133	Publishers, booksellers, stationers, dealers in music, pictures, musical instruments and curiosities	6,058	314	9,558	2,456	3,040	920	954	365	702

Means of Livelihood—*continued.*

Rangoon.		Delhi.		Ahmadabad.		Agra.		Howrah.		Cawnpore.		Karachi.		Group No.
Actual Workers.	Dependants.	Actual Workers.	Dependants.	Actual Workers.	Dependants.	Actual Workers.	Dependants.	Actual Workers.	Dependants.	Actual Workers.	Dependants.	Actual Workers.	Dependants.	
11	12	13	14	15	16	17	18	19	20	21	22	23	24	
6,182	**1,842**	**6,929**	**5,743**	**2,976**	**2,554**	**2,925**	**3,405**	**4,796**	**2,347**	**3,150**	**2,595**	**14,191**	**16,253**	
1,180	180	2,564	2,098	194	157	138	119	174	23	35	82	..	..	98
4,825	1,652	828	1,414	347	743	2,512	2,966	3,702	2,066	2,594	2,201	2,335	2,851	99
137	3	875	818	1	..	56	71	159	14	79	73	..	..	100
29	7	220	180	23	23	142	103	..	..	..	..	211	208	101
11	..	2,442	1,233	2,411	1,631	77	146	761	244	442	239	11,645	13,194	102
3,489	**2,154**	**2,086**	**3,176**	**1,448**	**2,466**	**725**	**1,394**	**8,464**	**6,651**	**1,929**	**2,648**	**3,216**	**4,903**	
3,484	2,152	1,691	2,910	1,448	2,370	586	1,255	8,464	6,651	1,823	2,543	3,047	4,815	103
5	2	395	266	..	96	139	139	..	..	106	105	169	88	104
317	**338**	**556**	**1,048**	**319**	**590**	**893**	**1,577**	**187**	**155**	**173**	**298**	**297**	**377**	105
33,159	*30,048*	*19,459*	*30,519*	*14,559*	*24,661*	*10,489*	*16,537*	*13,918*	*10,898*	*9,969*	*16,919*	*10,548*	*14,781*	
994	**1,292**	**2,445**	**2,237**	**1,584**	**3,403**	**612**	**1,212**	**391**	**360**	**535**	**965**	**408**	**389**	106
2,841	**3,016**	**888**	**338**	**260**	**523**	**149**	**190**	**232**	**461**	**754**	**1,308**	**719**	**1,175**	107
2,874	**2,342**	**2,876**	**5,256**	**2,897**	**5,397**	**635**	**1,169**	**654**	**935**	**979**	**1,581**	**2,189**	**2,926**	108
87	**141**	**268**	**519**	**89**	**252**	**6**	**409**	**13**	**19**	**192**	**140**	**213**	**358**	109
2,107	**1,105**	**3**	**29**	**255**	**449**	**17**	**23**	**451**	**252**	**23**	**13**	**100**	**314**	110
146	**94**	**159**	**337**	**134**	**322**	**82**	**133**	**358**	**399**	**32**	**155**	**8**	**13**	111
38	**14**	**3**	..	..	..	**2**	**61**	**33**	**17**	..	..	**9**	**17**	112
220	**131**	**452**	**1,247**	**166**	**254**	**171**	**356**	**164**	**44**	**55**	**129**	**9**	**30**	113
1,989	**1,178**	**284**	**477**	**505**	**642**	**199**	**388**	**425**	**367**	**138**	**135**	**544**	**530**	
728	291	212	421	131	326	155	276	310	305	112	93	300	223	114
1,261	887	72	56	374	316	44	112	115	62	26	42	244	307	115
13,751	**13,734**	**4,017**	**6,428**	**5,755**	**8,122**	**6,829**	**9,662**	**7,268**	**5,094**	**5,585**	**7,642**	**5,562**	**8,274**	
1,212	1,113	..	..	..	..	8	4	662	397	1	11	183	193	116
1,790	1,039	241	636	1,514	2,330	198	336	2,999	2,200	154	494	1,450	3,150	117
1,254	451	475	824	810	1,238	911	1,495	320	311	85	200	377	661	118
1,202	624	296	160	388	603	1,098	1,632	583	491	205	290	20	17	119
2,894	1,949	1,451	2,452	1,099	1,460	1,680	2,303	1,180	849	1,644	2,173	585	810	120
3,809	7,532	1,051	1,263	697	1,213	1,740	2,519	975	493	4,930	3,556	2,676	2,888	121
1,165	899	61	240	1,029	974	1,063	1,239	317	118	273	475	40	64	122
25	17	2	250	37	8	2	49	5	6	1	3	69	89	123
400	110	440	603	181	296	134	85	227	159	292	440	212	402	124
209	**180**	**2,509**	**3,599**	**315**	**491**	**380**	**723**	**229**	**292**	**767**	**2,309**	**95**	**20**	125
390	**580**	**62**	**429**	**32**	**66**	**46**	**30**	**95**	**186**	**29**	**82**	**85**	**150**	
92	159	50	303	14	32	19	23	8	134	5	3	11	28	126
298	421	12	117	18	34	27	57	87	52	24	70	74	122	127
62	**50**	**26**	**51**	**67**	**112**	**42**	**67**	**35**	**89**	..	**1**	**7**	..	128
270	**209**	**68**	**38**	**190**	**283**	**108**	**436**	**13**	**1**	**20**	**51**	**14**	**27**	129
396	**306**	**142**	**346**	**460**	**746**	**668**	**677**	**1,611**	**379**	**515**	**1,018**	**52**	**63**	130
680	**590**	**1,831**	**2,343**	**1,122**	**2,849**	**287**	**496**	**552**	**846**	**202**	**589**	**235**	**246**	
319	323	1,128	1,560	527	1,112	5	113	42	100	19	29	59	58	131
201	165	54	587	348	687	246	263	187	207	146	186	112	88	132
160	102	149	196	247	550	36	122	323	339	37	374	64	105	133

TABLE XV—Occupation of

Group No.	OCCUPATION.	ALL CITIES. Actual Workers. Males.	ALL CITIES. Actual Workers. Females.	ALL CITIES. Dependants.	CALCUTTA. Actual Workers.	CALCUTTA. Dependants.	BOMBAY. Actual Workers.	BOMBAY. Dependants.	MADRAS. Actual Workers.	MADRAS. Dependants.
	1	2	3	4	5	6	7	8	9	10
134	**40.—Trade in refuse matter.** (Dealers in rags, stable refuse, etc.)	**365**	**100**	**517**	**75**	**39**	**48**	**8**	**3**	**6**
	41.—Trade of other sorts	**57,635**	**8,502**	**80,412**	**9,049**	**8,581**	**17,349**	**18,567**	**2,279**	**4,845**
135	Shopkeepers otherwise unspecified	48,364	7,882	69,225	6,655	7,072	15,205	16,220	1,825	3,878
136	Itinerant traders, pedlars, hawkers, etc.	6,333	423	7,233	2,102	1,312	1,808	1,983	349	638
137	Conjurors, acrobats, fortune tellers, recitors, exhibitors of curiosities and wild animals	1,843	124	2,691	183	95	213	158	52	219
138	Other trades (including farmers of pounds, tolls and markets).	1,096	73	1,263	109	102	123	146	53	110
	C—Public administration and liberal arts	**374,382**	**41,852**	**582,554**	**49,299**	**63,426**	**41,018**	**46,210**	**28,174**	**59,865**
	VI.—Public force	***191,411***	***287***	***105,626***	***8,568***	***1,860***	***6,883***	***4,172***	***2,990***	***5,640***
	42.—Army	**80,590**	**221**	**58,470**	**4,225**	**661**	**2,930**	**843**	**1,079**	**1,338**
139	Army (Imperial)	58,720	14	24,088	4,225	653	2,930	843	1,077	1,338
140	Army (Native States)	21,870	207	34,382	..	8	..	..	2	..
141	**43.—Navy**	**371**	..	**94**	..	..	**349**	**13**	..	..
	44.—Police	**40,450**	**66**	**47,072**	**4,343**	**1,199**	**3,604**	**3,316**	**1,911**	**4,302**
142	Police	36,456	23	43,680	4,343	1,197	3,510	3,307	1,905	4,285
143	Village watchmen	3,994	43	3,392	..	2	94	9	6	17
	VII.—(Order 45) Public administration	***85,951***	***3,016***	***150,750***	***13,109***	***18,183***	***9,599***	***10,442***	***7,083***	***17,011***
144	Service of the State	44,057	473	88,269	8,582	15,721	4,152	5,849	4,227	11,481
145	Service of native and foreign States	16,599	350	30,050	23	25	18	73	30	188
146	Municipal and other local (not village) service	23,487	2,148	29,089	4,497	2,436	5,394	4,517	2,769	5,194
147	Village officials and servants other than watchmen	1,808	45	3,342	..	1	28	3	57	148
	VIII.—Professions and liberal arts	***130,969***	***21,562***	***231,806***	***21,535***	***30,405***	***17,897***	***17,780***	***11,540***	***23,990***
	46.—Religion	**49,488**	**7,158**	**68,389**	**7,304**	**6,556**	**4,634**	**3,149**	**1,953**	**3,634**
148	Priests, ministers, etc.	30,527	3,075	40,627	4,829	5,445	2,769	2,360	819	1,577
149	Religious mendicants, inmates of monasteries etc.	8,966	2,690	10,042	1,942	436	1,015	181	164	122
150	Catechists, readers, church and mission service	1,652	654	5,672	220	445	39	84	254	824
151	Temple, burial or burning ground service, pilgrim conductors, circumcisers	8,343	739	12,048	313	230	811	524	716	1,111
	47.—Law	**12,971**	**56**	**34,856**	**2,865**	**7,368**	**1,039**	**2,031**	**799**	**2,725**
152	Lawyers of all kinds, including Kazis, law agents and mukhtiars	7,382	44	23,047	1,862	5,597	872	1,771	381	1,759
153	Lawyers' clerks, petition writers, etc.	5,589	12	11,809	1,003	1,771	167	260	418	966
	48.—Medicine	**17,491**	**5,491**	**40,761**	**3,906**	**6,942**	**3,202**	**3,434**	**2,286**	**4,733**
154	Medical practitioners of all kinds including dentists, oculists and veterinary surgeons	13,041	844	31,914	2,513	5,980	1,653	2,505	1,269	3,455
155	Midwives, vaccinators, compounders, nurses, masseurs, etc.	4,450	4,647	8,847	1,393	962	1,549	929	1,017	1,278
156	**49.—Instruction.** [Professors and teachers of all kinds (except law, medicine, music, dancing and drawing) and clerks and servants connected with education]	**19,879**	**4,426**	**39,891**	**3,100**	**4,231**	**2,687**	**2,763**	**2,247**	**5,436**
	50.—Letters and arts and sciences	**30,440**	**4,431**	**47,909**	**4,360**	**5,308**	**6,265**	**6,463**	**3,655**	**7,392**
157	Public scribes, stenographers, etc.	943	323	1,930	508	414	154	148	28	65
158	Architects, surveyors, engineers and their employés	9,386	137	19,466	1,658	2,811	1,604	2,942	1,474	3,620
159	Others (authors, photographers, artists, sculptors, astronomers, meteorologists, botanists, astrologers, etc.)	7,514	136	10,361	781	962	2,732	2,575	1,184	2,255
160	Music composers and masters, players on all kinds of musical instruments (not military), singers, actors and dancers	12,597	3,835	16,152	1,413	1,121	1,774	738	969	1,452
	IX.—(Order 51)—Persons living principally on their income	***36,751***	***16,987***	***94,372***	***6,094***	***12,978***	***6,716***	***13,816***	***6,561***	***13,294***
161	Proprietors (other than of agricultural land), fund and scholarship holders and pensioners	36,751	16,987	94,372	6,094	12,978	6,716	13,816	6,561	13,294
	D.—Miscellaneous	**723,394**	**193,954**	**654,679**	**191,428**	**87,913**	**171,194**	**92,920**	**47,768**	**59,502**
	X.—(Order 52)—Domestic service	***299,187***	***93,847***	***279,239***	***79,564***	***30,530***	***54,866***	***17,090***	***16,223***	***18,405***
162	Cooks, water carriers, door-keepers, watchmen and other indoor servants	256,182	93,150	235,892	73,889	28,927	48,490	13,950	13,407	13,242
163	Private grooms, coachmen, dog boys, etc.	43,005	697	43,347	5,675	1,603	6,376	3,140	2,816	5,163
	XI.—Insufficiently described occupations (Order 53). General terms which do not indicate a definite occupation	***361,736***	***57,298***	***337,414***	***89,834***	***53,830***	***106,554***	***73,644***	***26,538***	***38,773***
164	Manufacturers, business men and contractors otherwise unspecified	7,483	216	15,260	1,428	2,314	1,189	2,163	540	1,516
165	Cashiers, accountants, book-keepers, clerks and other employés in unspecified offices, warehouses and shops	116,731	2,728	152,246	34,014	36,617	36,083	38,403	12,166	21,495
166	Mechanics otherwise unspecified	15,390	195	19,439	2,592	2,770	5,783	7,090	998	2,025
167	Labourers and workmen otherwise unspecified	222,132	54,159	150,469	51,800	12,129	63,499	25,988	12,834	13,737
	XII.—Unproductive	***62,471***	***42,809***	***38,096***	***22,030***	***3,553***	***9,774***	***2,186***	***5,007***	***2,324***
168	**54.—Inmates of jails, asylums and hospitals**	**22,852**	**1,988**	**2,368**	**4,576**	..	**383**	**508**	**1,667**	**325**
169	**55.—Beggars, vagrants, prostitutes.** (Beggars, vagrants, procurers, prostitutes, receivers of stolen goods, cattle poisoners)	**39,619**	**40,821**	**35,663**	**17,454**	**3,553**	**9,391**	**1,678**	**3,340**	**1,999**

Means of Livelihood—*concluded.*

Rangoon. Actual Workers.	Rangoon. Dependants.	Delhi. Actual Workers.	Delhi. Dependants.	Ahmadabad. Actual Workers.	Ahmadabad. Dependants.	Agra. Actual Workers.	Agra. Dependants.	Howrah. Actual Workers.	Howrah. Dependants.	Cawnpore. Actual Workers.	Cawnpore. Dependants.	Karachi. Actual Workers.	Karachi. Dependants.	Group No.
11	12	13	14	15	16	17	18	19	20	21	22	23	24	
27	11	8	1	7	21	42	37	5	5	..	..	3	2	134
6,078	**5,073**	**3,911**	**6,864**	**772**	**1,229**	**211**	**417**	**1,389**	**1,431**	**143**	**794**	**296**	**247**	
5,683	4,727	3,385	6,632	706	1,154	120	280	1,229	1,334	110	736	63	87	135
279	158	23	81	42	56	..	..	154	94	1	..	191	127	136
101	141	111	114	8	5	73	88	4	2	8	17	42	30	137
15	47	392	37	16	14	18	49	2	1	24	41	..	3	138
17,205	16,174	11,550	12,815	8,599	13,368	7,619	9,122	5,154	6,721	8,749	9,401	10,624	8,651	
4,707	*1,892*	*3,775*	*2,234*	*1,301*	*1,919*	*3,135*	*1,959*	*548*	*983*	*3,898*	*2,009*	*4,831*	*2,068*	
3,525	**720**	**2,926**	**920**	**19**	**18**	**1,520**	**246**	**5**	..	**2,585**	**872**	**3,613**	**818**	
5,526	720	2,924	912	18	18	1,520	246	5	..	2,585	872	3,613	818	139
..	..	2	8	1	..	..	..	..	..	..	..	..	..	140
11	16	..	..	..	..	..	4	..	..	..	..	..	..	141
1,171	**1,086**	**849**	**1,314**	**1,282**	**1,201**	**1,615**	**1,009**	**543**	**283**	**1,313**	**1,137**	**1,218**	**1,250**	
1,171	1,074	827	1,295	1,282	1,201	1,012	671	541	283	1,056	843	1,218	1,250	142
..	12	22	19	..	..	603	338	2	..	257	294	..	..	143
5,715	*6,299*	*987*	*2,094*	*1,917*	*3,484*	*1,494*	*1,903*	*1,310*	*1,461*	*790*	*1,916*	*2,655*	*2,476*	
3,648	5,185	722	1,169	731	1,821	736	1,138	625	1,030	668	1,628	1,849	2,068	144
3	3	6	91	66	166	3	18	..	..	3	3	..	..	145
2,047	1,079	231	779	1,082	1,295	663	684	685	431	110	250	586	271	146
17	32	28	55	38	202	22	63	..	..	93	85	220	137	147
6,499	*7,196*	*4,417*	*6,991*	*3,797*	*6,317*	*2,726*	*5,981*	*2,478*	*3,834*	*3,019*	*4,013*	*2,804*	*3,555*	
2,672	**2,101**	**1,966**	**2,968**	**1,539**	**1,936**	**648**	**1,328**	**1,186**	**1,238**	**1,621**	**1,382**	**1,142**	**980**	
2,364	1,691	1,659	2,543	86	114	477	907	823	1,115	967	1,094	228	226	148
239	308	51	63	524	874	1	..	331	54	288	10	878	710	149
39	64	82	34	123	197	74	267	29	44	32	68	..	..	150
30	38	174	328	806	751	96	154	3	20	384	210	36	44	151
363	**851**	**359**	**726**	**270**	**756**	**432**	**1,007**	**309**	**888**	**227**	**794**	**13 5**	**271**	
139	432	126	292	117	438	217	555	214	695	79	282	78	187	152
224	419	233	434	153	320	215	452	95	193	148	442	57	84	153
1,331	**1,601**	**577**	**813**	**511**	**969**	**445**	**972**	**347**	**350**	**284**	**877**	**428**	**468**	
834	1,377	255	643	388	875	256	676	221	780	186	699	164	247	154
497	224	322	170	123	124	189	296	126	70	98	178	264	221	155
781	**1,155**	**494**	**639**	**696**	**1,244**	**647**	**956**	**360**	**533**	**355**	**412**	**687**	**1,090**	156
1,282	**1,418**	**1,691**	**1,084**	**781**	**,380**	**554**	**1,018**	**276**	**330**	**532**	**618**	**412**	**746**	
74	45	82	113	1	1	..	..	7	1	81	61	1	4	157
295	473	131	247	178	432	49	299	157	272	39	80	120	317	158
167	225	42	61	117	263	235	333	19	30	22	50	85	258	159
746	675	836	663	485	684	270	336	93	27	440	427	206	167	160
354	*927*	*2,371*	*2,266*	*1,584*	*2,348*	*334*	*679*	*818*	*1,143*	*1,042*	*1,463*	*334*	*552*	
354	927	2,371	2,266	1,584	2,348	334	679	818	1,143	1,042	1,463	334	552	161
56,717	19,966	13,335	13,452	11,508	10,382	19,071	17,998	30,467	20,780	35,294	30,755	8,370	7,798	
17,959	*5,063*	*7,840*	*6,448*	*4,949*	*3,594*	*6,789*	*8,737*	*5,926*	*2,037*	*11,399*	*9,983*	*5,700*	*5,139*	
16,401	4,788	7,080	5,045	3,130	2,168	6,381	7,858	5,640	1,974	10,130	8,456	5,314	4,849	162
1,551	275	760	1,408	1,112	1,426	408	879	286	63	1,269	1,527	386	290	163
34,611	*14,509*	*3,103*	*5,694*	*4,349*	*4,764*	*7,458*	*7,863*	*21,797*	*18,935*	*21,941*	*19,368*	*1,936*	*2,069*	
689	1,342	386	207	84	252	45	135	186	326	254	459	220	388	164
7,727	8,842	536	2,697	1,918	2,816	20	34	7,096	9,019	1,073	1,675	1,002	1,663	165
1,721	1,381	1	1	..	4	15	33	3,137	4,214	45	125	13	16	166
24,474	2,944	2,180	2,719	2,340	1,692	7,378	7,661	11,378	4,676	20,569	17,109	1	2	167
4,154	*394*	*2,399*	*1,380*	*2,224*	*2,094*	*4,894*	*1,398*	*2,744*	*508*	*1,954*	*1,404*	*1,434*	*590*	
2,721	**38**	**651**	..	**46**	**312**	**2,863**	**56**	**47**	..	**340**	**5**	**318**	**12**	168
1,433	**356**	**1,741**	**1,386**	**2,878**	**1,712**	**1,961**	**1,342**	**2,697**	**506**	**1,614**	**1,399**	**1,116**	**578**	169

TABLE XVIII.

Europeans, Armenians and Anglo-Indians by Race and Age.

TABLE XVIII.—EUROPEANS, ARMENIANS

City.	Total.			European and Allied Races. British Subjects. All ages.			—12.		12—15.		15—30.	
	Persons.	Males.	Females.	Persons.	Males.	Females.	Males.	Females.	Males.	Females.	Males.	Females.
1	2	3	4	5	6	7	8	9	10	11	12	13
1. Calcutta	28,474	16,234	12,240	12,080	7,890	4,190	873	748	123	129	3,023	1,307
2. Bombay	16,082	10,434	5,648	10,131	6,821	3,310	793	712	156	107	2,903	1,083
3. Madras	14,522	7,463	7,059	3,687	2,281	1,406	308	280	45	56	987	449
4. Hyderabad	7,020	5,081	1,939	4,803	4,012	791	207	250	17	18	3,177	214
5. Rangoon	11,782	7,569	4,213	5,162	3,866	1,296	286	296	37	34	1,852	429
6. Lucknow	6,400	4,672	1,728	5,067	4,013	1,054	277	266	43	44	3,024	308
7. Delhi	1,144	774	370	841	604	237	46	44	4	5	349	67
8. Lahore	5,736	3,758	1,978	4,595	3,106	1,489	351	368	46	50	1,769	434
9. Ahmadabad	303	172	131	180	111	69	26	15	...	1	29	27
10. Benares	555	378	177	434	325	109	32	28	4	6	221	25
11. Agra	2,264	2,118	146	1,735	1,682	53	177	6	20	...	1,112	26
12. Howrah	1,631	923	708	755	468	287	66	75	9	5	141	89
13. Cawnpur	2,048	1,530	518	1,767	1,411	356	73	90	4	8	1,099	101
14. Allahabad	4,510	2,773	1,737	3,194	2,145	1,049	296	273	57	51	1,160	322
15. Poona	3,889	2,834	1,055	3,201	2,527	674	172	148	11	29	1,987	300
16. Amritsar	514	343	171	442	303	139	16	25	...	8	218	48
17. Karachi	4,504	3,202	1,302	3,764	2,915	849	219	227	16	30	2,066	270
18. Mandalay	1,591	988	603	892	577	315	72	85	7	29	330	180
19. Jaipur	116	68	48	76	44	32	14	4	...	1	8	6
20. Patna	502	169	333	172	70	102	13	19	1	5	14	24
21. Madura	524	261	263	111	55	56	14	19	1	...	14	18
22. Bareilly*	323	166	157	238	133	105	25	24	2	2	36	34
23. Srinagar	94	38	56	85	35	50	6	5	...	1	8	10
24. Trichinopoly	1,162	573	589	348	181	167	49	46	5	7	40	48
25. Meerut	1,797	1,387	410	1,590	1,280	310	50	95	5	6	1,101	91
26. Surat	63	25	38	40	20	20	4	5	...	...	5	6
27. Dacca	653	397	256	350	229	121	23	26	1	4	69	36
28. Nagpur	1,691	1,043	648	261	165	96	13	13	2	...	95	24
29. Bangalore Civil and Military Station	8,077	4,441	3,636	4,865	3,049	1,816	460	411	127		1,745	550
30. Jubbalpore	4,378	3,336	1,042	3,822	3,094	728	208	237	41	31	2,323	211

* The figures for Bareilly do not include those for the cantonment, as its statistics by age pe iods are not available

AND ANGLO-INDIANS BY RACE AND AGE.

EUROPEAN AND ALLIED RACES.																		
				Others.														Serial Number.
30—50.		50 and over.		All ages.			0—12.		12—15.		15—20.		20—50.		50 and over.			
Males.	Females.	Males.	Females.	Persons.	Males.	Females.	Males.	Females.	Males.	Females.	Males.	Females.	Males.	Females.	Males.	Females.		
14	15	16	17	18	19	20	21	22	23	24	25	26	27	28	29	30		
3,185	1,539	736	467	1,402	944	458	65	77	27	11	387	144	344	173	121	58	1
2,523	1,079	548	379	1,724	1,263	463	80	77	31	17	560	176	505	155	86	37	2
746	498	195	123	485	248	237	37	31	5	4	85	79	99	108	33	20	3
525	264	85	45	112	38	74	7	5	2	3	8	20	15	31	6	15	4
1,468	467	223	70	570	431	139	24	24	9	7	194	44	169	54	35	10	5
595	354	75	83	112	68	44	3	2	...	...	27	13	31	27	7	2	6
175	96	30	25	64	40	24	3	2	...	...	10	8	25	13	2	2	7
789	522	160	115	136	79	57	9	8	1	2	26	17	32	27	11	3	8
42	19	14	7	21	12	9	1	1	...	...	5	2	4	6	2	...	9
61	43	7	8	12	4	8	...	...	...	...	1	4	2	2	1	2	10
321	16	52	5	18	18	...	2	...	...	...	4	...	11	...	1	...	11
315	87	37	31	53	31	22	2	3	...	...	6	5	15	13	8	2	12
189	123	46	34	12	5	7	1	2	...	...	2	1	2	3	...	1	13
526	310	106	94	1	...	1	...	...	...	...	...	1	...	...	...	...	14
394	221	63	76	212	102	110	10	10	2	5	26	28	30	40	25	18	15
56	53	14	11	18	13	5	2	...	...	...	1	3	8	2	2	...	16
548	260	71	63	95	53	42	9	15	...	1	21	14	14	10	9	2	17
152	86	26	16	47	28	19	1	...	...	...	9	7	14	9	4	2	18
15	12	7	8	15	11	4	...	...	...	...	3	...	3	2	5	2	19
32	36	10	8	19	2	17	...	...	...	...	...	...	2	11	...	6	20
20	12	6	6	33	14	19	...	...	...	...	5	3	6	12	3	3	21
51	35	19	10	2	2	...	...	...	...	...	...	...	1	...	1	...	22
14	28	7	11	5	1	4	...	...	...	...	...	4	...	...	1	...	23
70	50	17	16	54	35	19	...	...	1	10	10	9	16	...	8	...	24
105	108	19	15	31	19	12	...	...	...	...	10	4	6	7	3	1	25
6	7	3	2	...	...	...	...	...	...	...	...	...	...	...	...	...	26
107	47	20	8	34	17	17	...	...	...	...	4	7	8	9	5	1	27
40	53	6	7	35	...	35	...	3	...	...	...	4	...	22	...	7	28
440	485	257	277	176	76	100	12	6	4	1	13	26	25	44	21	23	29
463	196	59	52	25	10	15	1	1	...	...	1	3	7	9	1	2	30

TABLE XVIII.—Europeans, Armenians and

City.	ARMENIANS.										
	All ages.			0—12.		12—15.		15—20.		20—30.	
	Persons.	Males.	Females.	Males.	Females.	Males.	Females.	Males.	Females.	Males.	Females.
1	31	32	33	34	35	36	37	38	39	40	41
1. Calcutta	815	480	335	60	65	52	18	176	80	116	103
2. Bombay	39	28	11	1	4	1	...	14	1	11	4
. Madras	24	20	4	...	...	4	...	8	1	6	...
4. Hyderabad	2	1	1	...	1	...	...	...	...	1	...
5. Rangoon	219	120	99	19	29	8	4	46	27	37	22
6. Lucknow	5	2	3	...	...	...	...	2	2	...	...
7. Delhi	3	3	...	...	...	...	...	2	...	...	...
8. Lahore	10	5	5	...	...	...	...	3	1	...	3
9. Ahmadabad	1	...	1	...	...	...	...	...	...	...	1
10. Benares	...	...	...	...	...	...	...	...	...	...	...
11. Agra	2	2	...	...	...	...	...	...	...	2	...
12. Howrah	34	20	14	4	4	...	1	5	3	8	3
13. Cawnpur	7	4	3	2	...	...	...	...	...	1	3
14. Allahabad	71	36	35	7	8	2	2	7	6	12	14
15. Poona	...	...	...	...	...	...	...	...	...	...	...
16. Amritsar	3	...	3	...	...	...	...	...	3	...	...
17. Karachi	1	1	...	...	...	...	...	1	...	...	...
18. Mandalay	13	4	9	...	2	...	1	4	2	...	2
19. Jaipur	...	...	...	...	...	...	...	...	...	...	...
20. Patna	3	1	2	...	...	...	...	...	1	1	...
21. Madura	...	...	...	...	...	...	...	...	...	...	...
22. Bareilly*	...	...	...	...	...	...	...	...	...	...	...
23. Srinagar	...	...	...	...	...	...	...	...	...	...	...
24. Trichinopoly	1	1	...	...	...	...	...	1	...	...	...
25. Meerut	...	...	...	...	...	...	...	...	...	...	...
26. Surat	...	...	...	...	...	...	...	...	...	...	...
27. Dacca	67	36	31	6	10	1	1	12	9	11	10
28. Nagpur	...	...	...	...	...	...	...	...	...	...	...
29. Bangalore Civil and Military Station	1	1	...	1	...	...	...	...	...	...	...
30. Jubbalpore	...	...	...	...	...	...	...	...	...	...	...

* The figures for Bareilly do not include those for the cantonment, as its statistics by age periods are not available.

ANGLO-INDIANS BY RACE AND AGE—*concluded.*

50 and over.		Anglo-Indians and other persons of mixed European and Asiatic descent.														Serial Number.
		All ages.			0—12.		12—15.		15—30.		30—50.		50 and over.			
Males.	Females.	Persons.	Males.	Females.	Males.	Females.	Males.	Females.	Males.	Females.	Males.	Females.	Males.	Females.	
42	43	44	45	46	47	48	49	50	51	52	53	54	55	56	
76	87	14,177	6,920	7,257	1,962	2,027	510	495	3,073	2,318	1,681	1,570	694	947	1
1	2	4,188	2,323	1,865	512	435	146	101	953	747	569	425	144	157	2
3	8	10,326	4,914	5,412	1,421	1,399	394	396	1,399	1,724	1,065	1,222	635	671	3
...	...	2,103	1,030	1,073	326	304	84	33	272	384	210	234	138	118	4
15	17	5,831	3,152	2,679	856	856	263	205	1,095	945	765	520	173	153	5
...	1	1,216	589	627	164	156	43	47	186	229	140	141	57	54	6
1	...	236	127	109	31	38	4	4	44	34	35	23	13	10	7
3	1	995	568	427	148	104	29	26	210	148	140	100	41	49	8
...	...	101	49	52	24	20	2	3	7	11	13	15	3	3	9
...	...	109	49	60	16	19	3	2	10	16	17	16	3	7	10
...	...	509	416	93	162	20	11	9	111	45	117	11	15	8	11
2	3	789	404	385	113	111	19	17	117	125	126	95	29	37	12
1	...	262	110	152	40	29	4	5	29	55	25	33	12	30	13
8	5	1,244	592	652	181	178	65	63	169	216	120	139	57	56	14
...	...	476	205	271	55	72	11	26	54	104	66	46	19	23	15
...	...	51	27	24	5	4	1	1	9	8	9	7	3	4	16
...	...	734	323	411	96	123	17	43	91	124	86	90	33	31	17
...	2	639	379	260	120	82	52	25	92	90	89	58	26	15	18
...	...	25	13	12	2	1	...	...	6	3	3	3	2	5	19
...	1	308	96	212	30	74	3	46	25	51	26	26	12	15	20
...	...	380	192	188	66	70	8	13	51	60	57	34	10	13	21
...	...	83	31	52	6	13	2	3	8	8	14	20	1	8	22
...	...	4	2	2	...	...	...	...	...	2	2	...	...	...	23
...	...	759	356	403	115	131	34	41	87	123	78	77	42	31	24
...	...	176	88	88	15	18	11	...	20	10	27	39	15	21	25
...	...	23	5	18	2	10	...	...	3	3	...	3	...	2	26
5	1	202	115	87	40	31	25	13	33	21	14	18	3	4	27
...	...	1,305	878	517	208	151	98	30	310	165	197	108	65	63	28
...	...	3,035	1,315	1,720	443	484	190	165	300	522	194	357	189	192	29
...	...	531	232	299	84	107	18	26	64	86	49	63	17	17	30